This
special edition of

Encyclopaedia Britannica

entitled the

Heritage Edition

is limited to
49,999 Sets
numbered from
1 to 49,999.
This is set number

1498

The New
Encyclopædia
Britannica

in 32 Volumes

FOUNDED 1768
15 TH EDITION

Encyclopædia Britannica, Inc.
Robert P. Gwinn, Chairman, Board of Directors
Peter B. Norton, President
Robert McHenry, General Editor

Chicago
Auckland/Geneva/London/Madrid/Manila/Paris
Rome/Seoul/Sydney/Tokyo/Toronto

THE UNIVERSITY OF CHICAGO

"Let knowledge grow from more to more
and thus be human life enriched."

The *Encyclopædia Britannica* is published with the editorial advice
of the faculties of the University of Chicago.

Additional advice is given by committees of members drawn from
the faculties of the Australian National University, the universities
of Adelaide (Australia), British Columbia (Can.), Cambridge (Eng.),
Copenhagen (Den.), Edinburgh (Scot.), Florence (Italy), London
(Eng.), Marburg (Ger.), Melbourne (Australia), Oxford (Eng.),
Queensland (Australia), the Ruhr (Ger.), Sussex (Eng.), Sydney
(Australia), Toronto (Can.), Victoria (Can.), Waterloo (Can.), and
Western Australia; the Complutensian University of Madrid (Spain);
the Institute of Public Affairs (Australia); the Max Planck Institute
for Biophysical Chemistry (Ger.); the New University of Lisbon
(Port.); the School of Higher Studies in Social Sciences (Fr.); Simon
Fraser University (Can.); and the State University of Leiden (Neth.).

First Edition	1768–1771
Second Edition	1777–1784
Third Edition	1788–1797
Supplement	1801
Fourth Edition	1801–1809
Fifth Edition	1815
Sixth Edition	1820–1823
Supplement	1815–1824
Seventh Edition	1830–1842
Eighth Edition	1852–1860
Ninth Edition	1875–1889
Tenth Edition	1902–1903

Eleventh Edition
© 1911
By Encyclopædia Britannica, Inc.

Twelfth Edition
© 1922
By Encyclopædia Britannica, Inc.

Thirteenth Edition
© 1926
By Encyclopædia Britannica, Inc.

Fourteenth Edition
© 1929, 1930, 1932, 1933, 1936, 1937, 1938, 1939, 1940, 1941, 1942, 1943,
    1944, 1945, 1946, 1947, 1948, 1949, 1950, 1951, 1952, 1953, 1954,
    1955, 1956, 1957, 1958, 1959, 1960, 1961, 1962, 1963, 1964,
    1965, 1966, 1967, 1968, 1969, 1970, 1971, 1972, 1973
By Encyclopædia Britannica, Inc.

Fifteenth Edition
© 1974, 1975, 1976, 1977, 1978, 1979, 1980, 1981, 1982, 1983, 1984, 1985,
    1986, 1987, 1988, 1989, 1990, 1991, 1992
By Encyclopædia Britannica, Inc.

© 1992
By Encyclopædia Britannica, Inc.

Printed in U.S.A.

Library of Congress Catalog Card Number: 90-84190
International Standard Book Number: 0-85229-553-7

ENCYCLOPÆDIA BRITANNICA

PHILIP W. GOETZ
Editor in Chief

ROBERT McHENRY
Managing Editor

ENCYCLOPÆDIA BRITANNICA, INC.

ROBERT P. GWINN, *Chairman, Board of Directors*
PETER B. NORTON, *President*

ENCYCLOPÆDIA BRITANNICA

The New Encyclopædia Britannica

PROPÆDIA

Outline of Knowledge
and
Guide to the Britannica

How to use the PROPAEDIA

As its title indicates, the PROPAEDIA, or Outline of Knowledge, is intended to serve as a topical guide to the contents of the *Encyclopædia Britannica,* enabling the reader to carry out an orderly plan of reading in any field of knowledge or learning chosen for study in some depth. The PROPAEDIA's table of contents gives the reader an overview of the Outline of Knowledge as a whole; the introductory essays for each of the ten parts illuminate the major concerns of that part of human knowledge; the headnotes that are affixed to parts and divisions prepare the reader for examination of the subjects being covered there; and the outlined presentations of these subjects, with their lists of related article titles, enable the reader to carry on a course of study that may be more or less extensive and detailed in accordance with individual interests and desires.

Structure. Each of the 10 parts, 40 divisions, and 176 sections that make up the PROPAEDIA is marked in the table of contents by a heading, which is followed by the number of the page on which that unit of the PROPAEDIA begins. This structure provides three ways to utilize the outline: (1) one may turn to any of the parts as a whole and examine the contents of that part; (2) one may select a particular division of a part and examine the contents of that division; or (3) one may focus on a single section or several sections of such a division and examine the contents of that section or those sections.

Sectional outlines. The sectional outlines present, in an orderly arrangement of topics, subjects that are treated in articles in the MACROPAEDIA and MICROPAEDIA. Each section number incorporates the numbers of the part and division to which it belongs. For example, Section 725 is the fifth section in Part Seven, Division II; Section 96/10 is the tenth section in Part Nine, Division VI. In each sectional outline the major subjects are indicated by

capital letters ("A," "B," etc.). There are always at least two major subjects, but there may be many more in a given section. When it is necessary to subdivide a major subject, up to three additional levels may appear in the outline; the first is indicated by Arabic numerals, the second by lowercase letters, and the third by Roman numerals, as shown below:

B. Metallurgy

    1. Mineral dressing: crushing and grinding, concentration or mineral preparation

    2. Process metallurgy

        a. Pyrometallurgy: metallurgical processes that involve the use of heat

            i. Gas–solid reactions; *e.g.,* roasting

            ii. Distillation: processes for refining metals by condensing metal vapours

The INDEX, with its alphabetically arranged subject headings, is indispensable in finding where a given subject appears in the Outline of Knowledge. These headings, where appropriate, carry specific citations pointing to the part, division, or section of the PROPAEDIA that covers the subject in question. A subject referred to in a sectional outline is, in many cases, treated fully in an article of the same title in the MACROPAEDIA or MICROPAEDIA, each such title being included in the list of suggested reading at the end of the section. These titles, as well as significant references to the subjects in other contexts, are cited in the INDEX. It may be helpful to compare the functions of the PROPAEDIA and the INDEX: Both are guides to the contents of the *Encyclopædia Britannica,* but the PROPAEDIA's primary purpose is to indicate *what* subjects are covered, while the INDEX's primary purpose is to indicate *where* they are covered.

THE CIRCLE OF LEARNING

"The alphabetical system of arrangement," observed the Editors of the Eleventh Edition of the *Encyclopædia Britannica* (1910–11), "with its obvious advantages, necessarily results in the separation from one another of articles dealing with any particular subject." Consequently, "the student who desires to make a complete study of a given topic must exercise his imagination if he seeks to exhaust the articles in which that topic is treated." This result is certainly a serious defect in the system for anyone who feels—as did the Editors of the Eleventh Edition—that an encyclopaedia should not be merely a "storehouse of facts," but should also be "a systematic survey of all departments of knowledge." To remedy this defect, the Editors constructed a "Classified Table of Contents," which they believed to be "the first attempt in any general work of reference at a systematic subject catalogue or analysis of the material contained in it."

Remarkable as it was at the time, that Table of Contents did not fully succeed in achieving its objective of overcoming the defects of an alphabetical organization of encyclopaedic articles by means of a topical presentation of their content. A quick glance at the 24 major categories into which the Table of Contents was divided will reveal that the alphabet was still the thread on which the parts were strung: I. Anthropology and Ethnology; II. Archaeology and Antiquities; III. Art; IV. Astronomy; V. Biology; VI. Chemistry; VII. Economics and Social Science; VIII. Education; IX. Engineering; X. Geography; XI. Geology; XII. History; XIII. Industries, Manufactures and Occupations; XIV. Language and Writing; XV. Law and Political Science; XVI. Literature; XVII. Mathematics; XVIII. Medical Science; XIX. Military and Naval; XX. Philosophy and Psychology; XXI. Physics; XXII. Religion and Theology; XXIII. Sports and Pastimes; XXIV. Miscellaneous. In each of these categories, the only further subdivisions involved the distinction of general from particular subjects, and the distinction of both of these from biographical entries. Under each of these headings, titles of the encyclopaedia's articles were listed in strictly alphabetical order.

In planning this Fifteenth Edition of *Encyclopædia Britannica,* the Editors, while deciding to retain the alphabetical ordering of the articles in the set, sought to improve upon the effort that their predecessors had made to overcome the defects of an alphabetical organization by giving the reader a truly topical, and totally nonalphabetical, Table of Contents. It would

serve the purpose that the Editors of the Eleventh Edition had in mind, which was to enable the reader to "make a complete study of a given topic"—that is, a department of knowledge or field of learning.

It may be asked why it was not thought better to abandon the alphabetical principle entirely and construct a purely topical encyclopaedia, in which all the articles would be assembled, volume after volume, according to some general schema for the organization of human knowledge. The answer is twofold. First, a purely topical organization of the articles themselves cannot avoid the appearance of a certain tendentiousness or arbitrariness in the editorial commitment to one rather than another organizing schema or set of principles. The reader is, therefore, provoked to ask: Does this order, volume by volume and article by article, reflect the only right or proper exposition of the whole of human knowledge?

Second, a purely topical encyclopaedia provides its readers with only one mode of access to its contents. This may be alleviated somewhat, perhaps, by the addition of an alphabetical index; but an index, by its very nature, serves the purpose of enabling the reader to look up *particular* items of information; it does not provide a general and systematic mode of access to the contents of the encyclopaedia.

The basic plan of the new *Britannica,* therefore, aims to give its readers access to its contents by both the topical and the alphabetical modes. General and systematic topical access is provided by the Outline of Knowledge contained in this volume, called the "Propædia" because it is a kind of preamble or antechamber to the world of learning that the rest of the encyclopaedia aims to encompass. Alphabetical access is provided not only by the two-volume Index but also by the alphabetical ordering of the short articles in the Micropædia.

Unlike the Classified Table of Contents in the Eleventh Edition, which was alphabetically organized by categories and subjects, the Outline of Knowledge in this Fifteenth Edition is a purely topical presentation of the subjects covered in the articles to be found in both the Macropædia and the Micropædia. It is, therefore, reasonable to ask how such a purely topical outline of encyclopaedic content avoids the tendentiousness or arbitrariness that is attributable to an encyclopaedia in which the articles themselves are topically rather than alphabetically arranged. Does not the Outline of Knowledge here presented reflect, perhaps even conceal, a commitment to one set of organizing principles rather than another? Does it not embody biases or preconceptions that are not universally acceptable?

It is hardly possible to say "No, not at all" to these questions. Two points, however, can be made affirmatively that tend to reduce or alleviate whatever degree of arbitrariness remains unavoidable in a topical outline of the whole of human knowledge. One is that the Outline of Knowledge, while conceived by the Editors, was constructed and corrected in the light of detailed recommendations, directions, and analytical contributions from scholars and experts in all the fields of knowledge represented. A list that includes the advisers who worked with the Editors in the construction of the Outline of Knowledge follows Part Ten of the Propædia.

The second point is that the Outline of Knowledge is conceived as a circle of learning. To say that the contents of an *en-cyclo-paedia* form a circle of learning is more than a literal transliteration from Greek to English. In Greek or English, reference to the circle introduces a powerful metaphor, the understanding of which should help the reader to overcome whatever arbitrariness still resides in the Outline of Knowledge in spite of determined efforts on the part of all concerned to minimize this defect. A circle is a figure in which no point on the circumference is a beginning, none is a middle, none is an end. It is also a figure in which one can go from any point, in either direction, around the circumference; in addition, one can go across the circle from any point to any other; or, by any number of transecting lines, starting from a given point, one can go to any number of other points on the circumference, near or far.

The 10 parts into which the Outline of Knowledge is divided are disposed not along a finite straight line beginning at this point and ending at that; they are disposed rather as segments of the circle. While it is true that, in this arrangement, one part may lie next to another and at some distance from still another, it is also true that, since the circle can rotate around its axis, any one of the 10 parts may be regarded as standing at the top of the circle, or at the left or right side of it, or at the bottom. In other words, with the circular arrangement of the parts, and with the rotation of the circle, the reader can begin anywhere in the circle of learning and go to adjacent parts around the circle; or, moving along interior transecting lines, the reader can go from any part across the circle to parts that are not adjacent on the circumference. This view of the Outline of Knowledge can be represented in a number of diagrams.

For a synopsis of the subject matter covered in each of the 10 parts of the outline, the reader is referred to the Table of Contents set forth on pages 9–15 of this volume. The titles of the individual parts are given in the following list:

Part One.   Matter and Energy
Part Two.   The Earth
Part Three.   Life on Earth
Part Four.   Human Life
Part Five.   Human Society
Part Six.   Art
Part Seven.   Technology
Part Eight.   Religion
Part Nine.   The History of Mankind
Part Ten.   The Branches of Knowledge

The pair of diagrams below shows the 10 parts as segments of a circle. Part One is placed at the top of the diagram to the left, and Part Nine is at the top of the diagram to the right, to illustrate the effect achieved by rotating the circle.

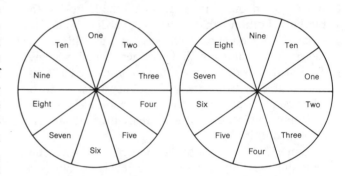

The second pair of diagrams, following, places one of the 10 parts at the centre of the circle with the remaining nine parts as segments of the circle formed by lines radiating from the centre. The point being made here is that any part can occupy the central position— the place in the circle of learning at which one begins, going thence in all directions to the remaining nine parts. To illustrate this, Part Five occupies the centre in the diagram to the left; Part Three, the centre in the diagram to the right.

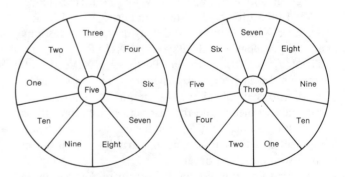

The final diagram offers still another approach to the circle of learning. In this diagram, Part Ten occupies the central position; and here there is only one diagram rather than a pair because the reason for placing Part Ten in the central position applies to it alone and to none of the other nine parts.

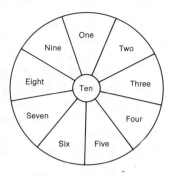

The reason for this special placement of Part Ten stems from the one organizing principle to which the Editors were explicitly committed in planning and producing this new *Britannica*. Briefly stated, that principle involves a distinction between (a) what we know about the world of nature, of man and society, and of human institutions *by means of* the various branches of learning or departments of scholarship; and (b) what we know about the branches of learning or departments of scholarship—the various academic disciplines themselves. For the most part—there are a few exceptions—Parts One through Nine represent the knowledge of nature, of human society, of human institutions, and their history. In clear contradistinction, Part Ten mainly covers the disciplines themselves— the branches of knowledge or fields of scholarship— by which one inquires into, thinks about, or comes to have knowledge of the world in which he lives. Part Ten examines the nature, methods, problems, and history of the various branches of knowledge or scholarly disciplines, the actual content of which is set forth in Parts One through Nine.

Thus, for example, Section 10/34 in Division III of Part Ten examines the nature, methods, problems, and history of the biological sciences; but the knowledge of life that the biological sciences afford is outlined in Part Three. Or, to take another example, Section 10/41 in Division IV of Part Ten examines historiography and the study of history; but the actual history of mankind is outlined in Part Nine.

There are, however, three departments of learning that are exclusively treated in Part Ten—both with regard to the nature and history of the disciplines themselves and also with regard to the knowledge or understanding afforded by these disciplines. They are logic (in Division I of Part Ten), mathematics (in Division II), and philosophy (in Division V). The reason for this exceptional treatment of these three disciplines is given in the Introductory Essay to Part Ten.

The special character of Part Ten thus explains the diagram in which it occupies the centre of the circle of learning, but that must not be interpreted as attributing prime importance to it. This diagram simply indicates the special function Part Ten performs in relation to the other parts. It alone stands in close relation to all the rest; there are varying degrees of relatedness among the other parts. For example, Parts Three and Four,

dealing with Life on Earth and with Human Life, are closely related; Parts Four and Five, dealing with Human Life and with Human Society, are also closely related; but Part Four has a different relatedness to Part Three, on the one hand, and to Part Five, on the other. In the presentation of the Outline of Knowledge, the headnotes and the cross-references give the reader an indication of these interrelationships.

Anyone who is in a position to compare the classified list of articles in the Eleventh or even the Fourteenth Edition with the Outline of Knowledge will be persuaded, the Editors think, that whereas the immediately preceding editions of *Britannica* represented a 19th- and early 20th-century view of the state of human knowledge, the new *Britannica,* in its Fifteenth Edition, is an encyclopaedia that reflects the many changes and innovations in man's knowledge and understanding that are emerging at the end of this century and will continue into the next.

The reader's attention should be called to the following features of the Propædia, or Outline of Knowledge:

1. It serves as a Table of Contents for the long articles in the Macropædia and also for the tens of thousands of shorter articles in the Micropædia.
2. Each of the 10 Parts of the Outline and the several Divisions of each of those Parts is prefaced by a brief summary of the topics covered.
3. The Divisions of each Part are followed by a number of Sections in which each of the topics covered is outlined.
4. At the end of each sectional outline, there is a list of Suggested Readings, first in the Macropædia, second in the Micropædia, which is followed by a list of the biographical articles that are relevant to the subjects covered in the outline of that Section.
5. In the topical outline of each Section, cross-references are made, when relevant, to other Sections in the Propædia on which related subjects are treated.

Because it is constructed in this manner, the Propædia provides the reader who wishes to pursue the study of a whole field of knowledge with an easily used guide. The Propædia thus offers readers a more comprehensive and detailed study guide for the use of the *Encyclopædia Britannica* than has ever been furnished before.

To facilitate their use of the Propædia as a study guide, readers should turn to pages 9–15, which follow. Here they will find a synoptic Table of Contents of the Propædia itself, set forth in the order of the 10 Parts, under each of which the component Divisions are listed, and under each Division, the component Sections.

This synoptic Table of Contents gives readers an overview of the Outline of Knowledge as a whole. The introductory essays for each of the 10 Parts, each written by an authority in that field, illuminate the major concerns of that area of human knowledge.

The Propædia, or Outline of Knowledge, helps readers answer for themselves the question that, in its most general form, is as follows: *What can I learn from the Britannica concerning one or another area of human knowledge?* More specifically, the question might be: *What can I learn about the Earth?* or *What can I learn about art?* The reader's interest may be even more specific. In the field of the Earth sciences, the question might be: *What can I learn about the Earth's constituent minerals and rocks?* or *What can I learn about weather and climate?* In the field of art, the question might be: *What can I learn about the theory and classification of the arts?* or *What can I learn about music?*

Another point should be mentioned because, in the view of the Editors, it distinguishes the Fifteenth Edition from all preceding editions.

The Outline of Knowledge presented in this Propædia volume was constructed *before* those articles themselves were named, outlined, commissioned, written, and edited. The outline served as the basis for determining what articles should be written, what their scope should be, how they should be related to other articles, and so on. It was, therefore, in origin a table of *intents* rather than a table of *contents*. It represented the intentions of the Editors in laying down a

comprehensive plan for producing a new encyclopaedia, appropriate to the state of human knowledge and learning at the end of the 20th century and looking forward to emergent developments in the century to follow. What was originally, or in the planning stage of the work, a Table of Intents, then subsequently became, after the writing and editing of the articles was completed, a Table of Contents that tries to reflect accurately and faithfully the actual content of the articles.

All preceding editions of *Britannica,* as most other encyclopaedias, have been constructed from classified lists of articles. Such classified lists may vary from one edition to another, as they have from the First Edition of *Britannica* through the Fourteenth, but the variations are relatively minor as compared with the fact that they are all the same in form—nothing but classified lists of articles, as exemplified by the one presented in the Eleventh Edition, already referred to. In sharp contrast to such editorial procedures, the Fifteenth Edition has the distinction of being planned not in accordance with a classified list of articles, but rather in the light of an orderly topical outline of the whole of human knowledge, in the form of the circle of learning that is an *en-cyclo-paedia.*

MORTIMER J. ADLER
Director of Planning

CONTENTS

Part Three. Life on Earth

Part Four. Human Life

Part Five. Human Society

Part Six. Art

Part Seven. Technology

Part Eight. Religion

Part Nine. The History of Mankind

Part Ten. The Branches of Knowledge

Introduction to Part One:

The Universe of the Physicist, the Chemist, and the Astronomer

by Nigel Calder

"Give me matter and I will build a world from it." For 200 years since the philosopher Immanuel Kant uttered it, physicists, chemists, and astronomers have striven to make good that boast. That they can now tell an almost unbroken story of events from the birth of the universe to the origin of life on Earth is the cumulative result of many lifetimes spent in careful observation and experiment. Yet even amid this success in updating the first verses of Genesis, new questions nag. Why does familiar matter adopt the forms it does? Are the laws of nature that are known to us enforced throughout the vast, tumultuous universe? What unimaginable worlds of fire or blackness can nature conjure up, quite different from our own?

When men presume to take the fire of the Sun and put it experimentally in a bottle, they forfeit all hope of certainty and repose. Yet the great quest for control over nature starts gently enough. A child at play with building blocks or sand or a rubber ball is a human mind engaged in discovering how matter behaves. Experiments with the rubber ball, for example, reveal laws of reflection. The child finds that the ball will come back to him only if he projects it accurately at a right angle to a flat surface (wall or floor); otherwise it bounces away from him and another child may grab it and interrupt the research program.

If all grown-up children had abandoned this kind of play, the human species would still believe that the Earth was at the centre of the universe, that the planets were propelled by angel-power, and that thunder was the voice of God. But some adults retained the boundless inquisitiveness of the young. Isaac Newton, not the most modest of discoverers, likened himself to a child playing on the seashore. Critics nowadays refer scathingly to the "expensive toys" of the physicists who want many millions of dollars to build a particle accelerator. Not unfairly—a particle accelerator, for all its awesome complexity and cost, is simply a modern way of continuing the experiments with the rubber ball, to see what happens when the ball is very small and travels almost at the speed of light.

By strange paths, play leads to far-reaching results. After the discovery that an electric current creates magnetism, Michael Faraday made a note to look for electricity from magnetism. He played repeatedly with magnets and wires until, ten years later, he discovered electromagnetic induction. Today, giant turbogenerators confirm his discovery 60 times a second, as they feed electric power to our factories and kitchens. In James Clerk Maxwell's hands, Faraday's ever-changing electric currents transformed themselves into mathematical equations predicting the existence of waves that traveled at the speed of light—indeed *were* light and invisible radiations of a similar kind, including radio waves. Other researchers who were unwittingly taking atoms to pieces came up with a beam of electrons, which inventors turned into a magic pencil;

today those waves and electrons enable lesser men to preen themselves on television screens in 260,000,000 homes.

In this latter part of the 20th century, a word-association test for *physicist* may very well evoke *bomb*. By coincidence, investigators of the nature of matter and energy stumbled upon a way of breaking open the storehouse of energy in the nucleus of the atom just at the time the human species was entering a period of unprecedented warfare. The swarms of nuclear-powered submarines that cruise with nuclear-tipped, city-killing missiles are a grim enough outcome of the "game." The fact remains that the heart of physics itself is not directed to any such purpose but is an open, cooperative effort by scientists of all nations to understand the material universe we live in.

We inhabit an electric world. It is true that gravity stops us from falling headfirst into the abyss of space; true also that the daylight that powers all life comes from the nuclear reactor that we call the Sun. But of the great set of natural forces known to the physicist—gravitational, nuclear, and electromagnetic—the last, electromagnetism, is the chief governor of events on Earth.

It operates so discreetly, though, that when men started rubbing amber on their sleeves and found it attracted dust, or considered the seeming magic of the north-pointing lodestone, nothing suggested that these were more than curiosities. There was laughter when Benjamin Franklin said that lightning was electric—until he proved it. Nothing suggested that the colour, quality, and chemical behaviour of all familiar matter would be explained by research in electricity and magnetism. But that is in the nature of physics: you ponder the falling of an apple and realize what holds the planets in their courses; you look to see what happens when you pass electric currents through a gas and, in due course, you find out what holds a stone together and why grass is green.

A series of discoveries in the late 19th and early 20th centuries illuminated the hidden mechanisms of our electric world like star shells on a dark night. Diligent work by chemists had shown that all matter was composed of vast numbers of atoms, different for each chemical element and capable of combining in predictable ways to make molecules and crystals. Indeed there was a remarkable pattern in the so-called "periodic table": when the chemical elements were listed by weight, it turned out that elements 3, 11, and 19 . . . all had similar properties; 4, 12, and 20 . . . were also very much alike, and so on.

This pattern made sense only when the physicists discovered the construction of atomic matter. An atom consists of a heavy nucleus surrounded by a number of lightweight electrons exactly neutralizing the electric charge on the nucleus. The electrons group themselves around the nucleus in "shells," like the layers of an onion, each shell being capable of accommodating a definite number of electrons. The outward face of the atom, its outermost shell of electrons, is crucial in determining its chemical behaviour. The number of electrons to be fitted in depends on the charge on the nucleus. In some elements, the metals, there are only one or two easily detachable electrons in the outermost shell. Other elements, the most reactive nonmetals, fall short by only one or two electrons in having a complete outermost shell. These "surplus" and "missing" electrons create a supply-and-demand situation in which atoms combine chemically by exchanging or sharing electrons. The repetition of chemical properties throughout the periodic table arises as one shell of electrons is completed and the next one begins to fill.

The mechanisms sketched in these last few sentences account for almost all the chemical behaviour of all the matter on Earth. The electrical and magnetic behaviour of materials also depends on the arrangements of electrons in their atoms and, in some cases, on the combined effects of many atoms packed together in a crystal. The strength of the chemical bonds formed by electrons, and the related forces between molecules, determine whether materials are solids, liquids, or gases; and they help to fix the strength and flexibility of solids, but in this case the explanations are complicated by the invisible flaws that exist in all materials. The colour of materials is explicable by the "jumps," from one position to another in the vicinity of an atom, which the rules allow an electron to make as the atom, molecule, or crystal absorbs or emits light of particular energy, or colour. Make the same electrons in vast numbers of atoms "jump" the same way simultaneously and you have a very intense laser beam.

Light and its invisible counterparts—radio waves, infrared, ultraviolet, and X-rays—are the purest form of energy. These "electromagnetic radiations" are created by the jerking of electrons, sometimes quite gently, as in a radio antenna, and sometimes very fiercely, as when a beam of fast-moving electrons is suddenly halted by the target in an X-ray tube. The normal "jumps" of electrons in atoms are of intermediate intensity. All these radiant forms of energy can travel through empty space, for example from the Sun to the Earth.

But energy can readily change from one form to another. Sunlight captured by green leaves is converted into the chemical energy of plant-stuff. Coal is plant-stuff buried millions of years ago when continents collided, and a boiler can convert the chemical energy of coal into a scalding jet of steam that turns the blades of a turbine—these are forms of kinetic energy, the energy of directed movement. Using Faraday's trick, the turbine can generate electrical energy. At the end of this chain of transformations, you can switch on the electrical energy and reconvert it to light energy, thereby enjoying the benefits of sunlight after the Sun has set.

The vibrations of sound and the gravitational energy of water about to cascade down a mountainside are other forms of energy. Sooner or later, though, a shout dies away, water comes to rest, the light from your electric bulb is absorbed in the wallpaper. Where has the energy gone? It has been taken up in those random motions of atoms and molecules that we call heat. All energy degrades to meaningless heat eventually.

Unless there were continuous supplies of new energy,

life and indeed all interesting activity in the universe would quickly cease. For example, your brain is kept functioning by food—chemical energy produced by sunlight just in the past few months. Those new supplies of energy come from the transformation of matter into energy.

The Sun is a very ordinary star, lying in the suburbs of a galaxy consisting of about 100,000,000,000 stars; we see the rather flat cross section of the galaxy as the Milky Way, a brushstroke of light across the night sky. There is nothing special, even, about our Galaxy; it is just one of vast numbers of galaxies scattered like ships in a great ocean of space.

The universe is a battleground between gravity and nuclear forces. To make a star, gravity sweeps together a mass of hydrogen gas; it becomes hot and nuclear reactions begin. The nuclei of hydrogen atoms combine together to make heavier elements almost, but not quite, as heavy as the sum of the hydrogen nuclei that went into them. The little bit of matter that is lost is converted into a relatively immense amount of energy. It would blow the star apart but for the strenuous restraint of gravity. A balance is struck, and the size and brightness of a star depends on its mass and on how much of its nuclear fuel has been burned. Fortunately, our star, the Sun, is a slow-burner; nevertheless, inexorable physical changes billions of years from now will make the Sun grow to fill the whole of our sky and swallow the Earth.

In a star more massive than the Sun, this "burning" of nuclear fuel proceeds faster and culminates in a vast explosion called a supernova. In the explosion, nuclear reactions proceed apace and make all the different chemical elements. The diverse atoms, heavier than hydrogen, of which our own bodies are constructed, were made in stars that exploded before the Sun was formed. Some of the heavy material was left swirling around the newborn Sun and made the Earth. Radioactive energy stored in some of the elements provided an internal source of heat for the Earth that accounts for volcanoes, earthquakes, and the slow movements of continents. Sunlight stirred the materials on the surface of the Earth into chemical activity. Eventually this activity became organized in peculiar ways, and life began.

So far, so good. But there are new mysteries that are "out of this world," in the sense that matter and energy are involved in events far more violent than anything normally encountered on the Earth or even in the Sun. The paramount questions with which physicists are now wrestling can be paraphrased as follows: Why is hydrogen the raw material of the universe? Experiments with the nucleus of the hydrogen atom—the proton—are undertaken in the big accelerators that transform the stuff of the atomic nucleus into bizarre, short-lived particles. These particles have properties, similar to electric charge, called the hypercharge and the baryon number. For example, the proton itself has, besides an electric charge of +1, a hypercharge of +1 and a baryon number of 1. However the particles may transform themselves in violent interactions, the totals of charge, hypercharge, and baryon number do not change.

Attempting to find out why this partial order remains amid the confused varieties of nuclear matter, theorists are led to the idea that the particles we see consist of combinations of other, quite different particles that they have named quarks. An early success of this theory was the prediction of the existence of a new combination, a particle called the omega minus that eventually turned up in 1964 during an experiment with the big machine at the Brookhaven National Laboratory, Long Island, N.Y. The quarks themselves have not been discovered at the time of writing.

The next big leap in understanding may well come when the theory of how small pieces of matter behave is blended with the theory of gravity, which at present concerns the huge pieces of matter that make up our universe of galaxies, stars, and planets. With such a "unified" theory physicists may at last be able to answer that question about the raw material of the universe—why hydrogen? At the same time, we shall perhaps come to understand why matter was formed in the "big bang," with which (as many astronomers now suppose) the universe came into existence some 10,000,000,000 years ago, or why the "big bang" was not merely a "big flash."

Even so fundamental an advance would not exhaust the opportunity for fresh discovery in the physical sciences. Another set of pregnant problems results from very strange objects recently discovered in the sky, namely "hot" galaxies, quasars and pulsars. The quasars, in particular, are compact objects of such extraordinary energy that existing laws of physics seem scarcely able to account for them. The pulsars, which flash many times a minute, are also very odd, but less baffling. They are evidently remnants of exploded stars that have collapsed to the enormous density of the material of the atomic nucleus. If an ocean liner were compressed to the density of a pulsar, it would be no bigger than a grain of sand.

The evidence of the pulsars encourages a further idea—one of the strangest in the whole history of man's study of matter and energy. In a pulsar, nuclear forces prevent collapse to even greater densities. But if the collapsed star were even more massive, gravity would be stronger and it would overwhelm even the nuclear forces. Then there would be nothing to stop the process until the whole star had collapsed to smaller than a peanut. Through the intense gravitational field thus set up, no light could escape, and the star would in effect disappear from the universe. Only its gravity would remain, like the grin of the Cheshire Cat in *Alice in Wonderland,* and, if a space traveler ran into one of these "black holes," he too would be drawn to the same invisible kernel, there to disappear forever—or at least until the laws of physics change.

The possibility that such black holes exist holds out a hope of explaining the quasars as objects of this kind from which material somehow "bounces" out. But that is only a little comfort when scientists have now to reexamine the theory of gravity, which they thought Einstein had cleared up 60 years ago, and to work out the implications of a universe peppered with black holes where the familiar laws of nature are unlikely to apply. There is even the uncomfortable suggestion that our whole universe may be just a big black hole in someone else's universe! Physics, the master science, cannot evade these new battles of the mind.

Part One. Matter and Energy

Three points should be noted about the scope of Part One and its relations to other parts.

The sciences of physics, chemistry, and astronomy have themselves been the object of historical and analytical studies regarding their nature, scope, methods, and interrelations. Part Ten, on the branches of knowledge, is concerned with such studies. The outline in Section 10/32 of Part Ten deals with the sciences of physics, chemistry, and astronomy and treats their history, their nature and scope, and their principal problems and interrelations.

The design and operation of observational and experimental instruments are important in the development of the physical sciences. The treatment of scientific instrumentation is placed in Section 723 of Part Seven, on technology.

Accounts of the several kinds of mathematics used in observation and experiments, and in the derivation and application of physical theories, are set forth in Division II of Part Ten.

The three increasingly complementary physical sciences of physics, chemistry, and astronomy house the knowledge and the organizing theories about matter in all its dimensions, from subatomic particles to the cosmos, about all the states of matter, all the forms of energy, and all the interrelations of matter and energy.

Division I.   Atoms: Atomic Nuclei and Elementary Particles

The outlines in the two sections of Division I deal with subatomic and atomic physics.

Section 111.   The Structure and Properties of Atoms

A. The atomic nature of matter

   1. The atom as consisting of the nucleus surrounded by electrons, the arrangement and behaviour of which determine atomic interactions

   2. Early philosophical speculations on the possible atomic nature of matter

   3. The scientific evidence for the existence and the nature of atoms

     a. Developments in chemistry

     b. The development of spectroscopy and the discovery of atomic spectra

     c. The discovery of the electron as a particle and as a component of all matter

     d. The discovery of X-rays

     e. The discovery of the radioactive transformation of one element into another

     f. The Brownian movement of suspended particles

     g. The development of mass spectrometry

     h. The development of scattering and resonance studies with atomic and molecular beams

   4. Models of atomic structure

     a. The Rutherford model of the atom

     b. The Bohr–Sommerfeld model

     c. The wave-mechanical theory of the electronic structure of the atom

B. Atomic weights

   1. Variations in atomic weight as a result of variations in isotopic composition

   2. Significance of atomic weights in chemistry

   3. Atomic weight scales

   4. Methods used for determining atomic weights: chemical methods, physical methods

C. Atomic spectra and the electronic structures of the atom

   1. Atomic spectra: their significance and interpretation

      a. The spectrum of the hydrogen atom

      b. The emission spectra of singly and multiply ionized atoms

      c. Atomic absorption spectra

      d. The effects of magnetic fields and the effects of electric fields on atomic spectra

      e. Intensities, isotope shifts, and fine and hyperfine structures of atomic spectral lines as related to atomic structure

   2. Theories of the origin of atomic spectra in quantized electronic transitions: the classical Bohr theory, wave-mechanical interpretations

D. X rays and atomic structure

   1. General X-ray phenomena

   2. The theory of X rays and their spectra

      a. The structure of the atom as related to the emission of characteristic X rays, absorption edges, fluorescence yield, mesic atoms

      b. Continuous X rays and bremsstrahlung; *i.e.,* the radiation produced by the sudden retardation of a fast-moving charged particle in an intense electrical field

   3. Detection and measurement of X rays

   4. Applications of X rays in biological, medical, industrial, and scientific fields
[see 423.B. and 723.G.8.]

   5. Diffraction of X rays by crystals
[see 125.A.2.]

E. The concept of antimatter

   1. General properties of antimatter

   2. Production of antiparticles in high-energy collisions

   3. Invariance of the laws of physics under charge conjugation, an operation in relativistic mechanics that transforms every particle into its antiparticle

   4. Speculations about the possible existence and role of antimatter in the universe

F. The fundamental physical constants: dimensional and dimensionless constants

   1. Measurement of the physical constants

   2. Interrelationships among the constants

   3. Standards of measurement

Suggested reading in the *Encyclopædia Britannica:*

MACROPAEDIA: Major articles dealing with the structure and properties of atoms

    Analysis and Measurement, Physical and Chemical
    Atoms: Their Structure, Properties, and Component Particles
    Physical Science, Principles of
    Physical Sciences, The

MICROPAEDIA: Selected entries of reference information

General subjects

atom models:
Aufbau principle
Bohr atomic model
electronic
    configuration
octet
Rutherford atomic
    model
shell atomic model
*experimental effects
    results:*
Auger effect
Brownian motion
electron
    paramagnetic
    resonance

Franck–Hertz
    experiment
Fraunhofer lines
ionization
    potential
magnetic
    resonance
spectral line series
Stark effect
Stern–Gerlach
    experiment
Zeeman effect
*fundamental
    constants:*
molar gas constant
Planck's constant

laws and principles:
Bose–Einstein
    statistics
complementarity
    principle
Fermi–Dirac
    statistics
Pauli exclusion
    principle
quantum
    mechanics
Schrödinger
    equation
selection rule
uncertainty
    principle

wave–particle
    duality
other:
antimatter
atom
atomic mass
atomic radius
energy state
excitation
matter
orbital
positronium
quantum
quantum number
transition
X ray
zero-point energy

Biographies

See Section 10/32 of Part Ten

INDEX: See entries under all of the terms above

Section 112.   **The Atomic Nucleus and Elementary Particles**

A. The structure of the atomic nucleus and general nuclear phenomena

1. General properties of atomic nuclei

    a. Mass

    b. Charge: atomic number

    c. Radius

    d. Spin

    e. Magnetic moment: nuclear magnetic resonance phenomena

    f. Electric quadrupole moment

2. Components of atomic nuclei

    a. Neutrons
    [see D., below]

    b. Protons

    c. Other possible short- and long-lived components

3. Isotopes: atomic species with the same atomic number but with different atomic masses
[see B., below]

4. Systematic relationships between nuclear masses and nuclear binding energies

5. Nuclear models and the properties of nuclear states

6. Theories of nuclear structure and nuclear binding force

7. General nuclear phenomena and reactions
[see C. and E., below]

8. The formation and evolution of the atomic nuclei in the universe

B. Isotopes: atomic species with the same atomic number but with different atomic masses

1. Classification of isotopes or nuclides

2. Isotopic composition of the elements

3. Formation of isotopes by nuclear reactions
[see E., below]

    4. Effects of isotopic substitution on physical and chemical properties of substances

    5. Chemical and physical separation of isotopes

      a. Mass spectrometry

      b. Other methods of separation; *e.g.,* diffusion, centrifugal separation, thermal diffusion

    6. Applications of radioactive and stable isotopes
   [see 242.D.2 and 723.G.8.]

C. Radioactive nuclei: their properties and their radiations

    1. The phenomenon of radioactivity

    2. Types of radioactivity

    3. Sources of radioactivity: naturally occurring radioactive elements, particle bombardment

    4. Interaction of radiation with matter
   [see I., below]

    5. The energy release associated with radioactive decay

    6. Nuclear models used to explain nuclear binding: the liquid drop model, the shell model, the unified model

    7. Rates of radioactive transitions

      a. Exponential decay law

      b. Alpha decay

      c. Beta decay

      d. Gamma transition

    8. Applications of radioactivity
   [see 723.G.8.]

    9. Measurement and characterization of radioactivity
   [see I.4., below]

D. The neutron as a component of the nucleus and in nuclear reactions

    1. Properties of neutrons

    2. Sources of neutrons

    3. Manipulation and control of neutrons

    4. Nuclear reactions produced by neutrons

    5. Neutron detection based on the secondary effects of nuclear reactions

E. Reactions of atomic nuclei

    1. The classification of nuclear reactions

      a. The types of nuclear reactions classified according to the kind of bombarding radiation or particles

      b. The types of nuclear reactions classified according to the nuclear processes involved or according to their products

    2. The energy relationships of nuclear reactions

    3. Theories and models of nuclear reactions

F. The splitting of atomic nuclei by nuclear fission

    1. Phenomena of nuclear fission

      a. Spontaneous and induced fission reactions

      b. Products of nuclear fission

      c. The energy released in fission

    2. Fission chain reactions: the critical mass

      a. Nuclear explosions: nuclear, or atomic, bombs

      b. Controlled nuclear fission

    3. Nuclear models and theories of nuclear fission: liquid drop model, adiabatic models, statistical models

G. The fusion of atomic nuclei

   1. Phenomena of nuclear fusion

   2. Nuclear fusion reactions

      a. General types of fusion reactions

      b. The energy released in fusion reactions

      c. Requirements for intensive fusion reactions

   3. Occurrence of thermonuclear reactions

      a. Thermonuclear reactions in the Sun and the stars

      b. Thermonuclear explosions: the hydrogen, or thermonuclear, bomb

   4. Basic conditions required for a thermonuclear reactor

      a. The formation of a suitable plasma

      b. The confinement and control of high-temperature plasma

   5. The possible approaches to controlled fusion: prospects for the future

H. Subatomic, or elementary, particles

   1. Development of the concept of subatomic particles as the fundamental units of matter and energy

      a. The discovery of the various particles

      b. Yukawa mesons and the theory of nuclear forces

      c. Advances in quantum field theory: renormalization theory, dispersion theory

      d. The known elementary particles

   2. The basic forces associated with particle interactions

   3. Systems for classifying the elementary particles

      a. According to the forces that influence them

      b. According to the kind of statistics they follow

      c. According to their particle–antiparticle symmetries

      d. According to stability

      e. According to charge multiplets

      f. According to unitary symmetry, or the SU(3) classification

      g. According to charged-hypercharge multiplets

   4. Elementary particles and the laws of conservation and symmetry

      a. The theory of subatomic particles and the quantum mechanical symmetry operations

      b. Dynamic symmetries: space and time inversion

      c. Violation of conservation laws: charge conjugation, time reversal, parity

      d. Internal symmetries

   5. Sources of the unstable elementary particles

      a. Formation of resonances in high-energy accelerators

      b. Production by cosmic ray interactions

   6. Relations of the weak interactions to strong and electromagnetic interactions described by conserved current and algebra of current

   7. Other particles suggested by contemporary theoretical ideas

   8. Reactions of elementary particles with atoms

   9. Theories of nuclear structure and nuclear forces involving the elementary particles

I. Effects of the passage of nuclear, or elementary, particles, nuclear radiations, or ionizing radiation through matter

   1. The fundamental processes involved when energetic particles or radiations interact with or pass through matter

      a. The passage of electromagnetic waves and their interaction with atomic structure

b. The passage of particles or radiations through matter

2. Secondary and tertiary effects of radiation: physical effects, molecular activation and related phenomena, chemical effects, biological effects

3. Utilization of high-energy radiation in biological, medical, and technological fields

4. The use of fundamental processes of interaction between radiation and matter for the detection and characterization of nuclear and elementary processes

a. Mechanisms of detection systems: ionization and charge collection, conversion of the distributed energy of the primary ionizing particle into light

b. Properties of ionization media

c. Major types of radiation detectors: scintillation counters, ionization detectors, spark chambers, cloud chambers, bubble chambers
[see 723.F.7.]

d. Applications of radiation detectors in science, technology, and industry
[see 723.G.8.]

Suggested reading in the *Encyclopædia Britannica:*

MACROPAEDIA: Major articles dealing with the atomic nucleus and elementary particles

Analysis and Measurement, Physical and Chemical
Atoms: Their Structure, Properties, and Component Particles
Physical Sciences, The
Radiation
Subatomic Particles

MICROPAEDIA: Selected entries of reference information

General subjects

conservation laws and symmetry:
charge conjugation
charge conservation
CP violation
Eightfold Way
energy, conservation of
gauge theory
isospin
momentum, conservation of
parity
spin
time reversal
nuclear interactions:
excitation
fission product
neutron capture
nuclear energy
nuclear fission
nuclear fusion
nuclear reaction
nucleosynthesis
spallation
spontaneous fission
thermonuclear reaction
transmutation
nuclear structure:
binding energy

collective model
compound-nucleus model
isotope
liquid-drop model
magic number
magnetic resonance
nuclear magnetic resonance
nuclear model
nuclide
shell nuclear model
particle interactions:
cross section
fundamental interaction
pair production
proton-proton cycle
scattering
radiation detection:
cloud chamber
coincidence counting
ionization chamber
scintillation counter
solid-state detector
spark chamber

radioactivity:
activity
alpha decay
beta decay
decay constant
fallout
gamma decay
gamma ray
half-life
isomer
metastable state
radioactive isotope
radioactive series
radioactivity
subatomic particles:
alpha particle
antiparticle
antiproton
baryon
boson
electron
hadron
hyperon
J/psi particle
lepton
magnetic monopole
meson
muon
neutrino
neutron
photon

positron
proton
quark
quasiparticle
subatomic particle
thermal neutron
W particle
other:
bremsstrahlung
Cherenkov radiation
Compton effect
de Broglie wave
electron diffraction
electron optics
Millikan oil-drop experiment
neutron optics
quantum electrodynamics
radiation
Stern–Gerlach experiment
synchrotron radiation
unified field theory
wave function

Biographies
See Section 10/32 of Part Ten

INDEX: See entries under all of the terms above

Division II.   Energy, Radiation, and the States and Transformation of Matter
[For Part One headnote see page 21.]

Division I deals with modern advances in subatomic and atomic physics.

The outlines in the first three sections of Division II treat, respectively, chemical elements, chemical compounds, and chemical reactions. The last five sections of this division are concerned with heat, thermodynamics, and the nonsolid states of matter; with the solid state of matter; with the mechanics of particles, rigid bodies, and deformable bodies; with electricity and magnetism; and with waves and wave motion.

Section 121.   Chemical Elements: Periodic Variation in Their Properties

A. The systematic classification of the elements on the basis of their chemical and physical properties and atomic structures: the periodic law of the elements

B. The groups of the chemical elements in the long form of the periodic table: their occurrence, history, physical and chemical properties, principal compounds, production, and uses

1. Hydrogen, its forms, isotopes, and compounds: water, its structure, forms, and physical and chemical properties

2. The alkali metals, or the Group Ia elements of the periodic table: lithium, sodium, potassium, rubidium, cesium, francium

3. The alkaline-earth metals, or the Group IIa elements of the periodic table: beryllium, magnesium, calcium, strontium, barium, radium

4. The boron group of the elements, or the Group IIIa elements of the periodic table: boron, aluminum, gallium, indium, thallium

5. The carbon group of the elements, or the Group IVa elements of the periodic table: carbon, silicon, germanium, tin, lead

6. The nitrogen group of the elements, or the Group Va elements of the periodic table: nitrogen, phosphorus, arsenic, antimony, bismuth

7. The oxygen group of the elements, or the Group VIa elements of the periodic table: oxygen, sulfur, selenium, tellurium, polonium

8. The halogen elements, or the Group VIIa elements of the periodic table: fluorine, chlorine, bromine, iodine, astatine

9. The noble gases, or the Group 0 elements of the periodic table, formerly called the inert gases: helium, neon, argon, krypton, xenon, radon

10. The zinc group elements, or the Group IIb elements of the periodic table: zinc, cadmium, mercury

11. The transition elements: elements with partly filled d or f orbitals occupying the middle portion of the periodic table

    a. Individual elements of the first transition series: titanium, vanadium, chromium, manganese, iron, cobalt, nickel, copper

b. Individual elements of the second and third transition series: zirconium and hafnium, niobium and tantalum, molybdenum and tungsten, technetium and rhenium, ruthenium and osmium, rhodium and iridium, palladium and platinum, silver and gold

c. The lanthanide elements
[see B.12., below]

d. The actinide elements
[see B.13., below]

12. The rare-earth, or lanthanide, elements of the periodic table: scandium, yttrium, lanthanum, cerium, praseodymium, neodymium, promethium, samarium, europium, gadolinium, terbium, dysprosium, holmium, erbium, thulium, ytterbium, lutetium
[see 724.C.3.u.]

13. The actinide elements of the periodic table: actinium, thorium, protactinium, uranium, neptunium, plutonium, americium, curium, berkelium, californium, einsteinium, fermium, mendelevium, nobelium, lawrencium

14. The transactinide elements of the periodic table: rutherfordium (or kurchatovium), hahnium (or nielsbohrium), element 106, element 107

C. Other classifications of the elements or groups of them

1. Metals; semimetals, or metalloids; nonmetals

2. Stable and radioactive elements

3. Native and combined elements

4. Noble metals, including the platinum group of metals

5. Synthetic elements: transuranium elements

6. Biologically active or essential elements
[see 335.A.3.]

7. Technologically significant elements
[see 724.C.3.]

D. The origin of the elements and their relative abundances in nature

1. On Earth

a. In the crust
[see also 214.C.]

b. In the hydrosphere
[see also 222.B. and C.]

·c. In the atmosphere
[see also 221.A.1.]

d. In the biosphere

2. In the solar system
[see also 133.A.]

3. In the stars
[see also 132.D.7.b.]

4. In the rest of the universe
[see also 131.A.1.a.]

Suggested reading in the *Encyclopædia Britannica*:

MACROPAEDIA: Major articles dealing with chemical elements: periodic variation in their properties

Chemical Compounds
Chemical Elements

MICROPAEDIA: Selected entries of reference information

General subjects

actinide elements:	cerium	nobelium	cesium
actinide	einsteinium	plutonium	francium
actinium	fermium	protactinium	lithium
americium	lawrencium	thorium	potassium
berkelium	mendelevium	uranium	rubidium
californium	neptunium	*alkali metals:*	sodium
		alkali metal	

alkaline-earth metals:
  alkaline-earth
    metal
  barium
  beryllium
  calcium
  magnesium
  radium
  strontium
boron group:
  aluminum
  boron
  boron group
    element
  gallium
  indium
  thallium
carbon group:
  carbon
  carbon group
    element
  germanium
  lead
  silicon
  tin
halogen elements:
  astatine
  bromine
  chlorine
  fluorine
  halogen
  iodine
*hydrogen and its
  isotopes:*
  deuterium
  hydrogen
  tritium

nitrogen group:
  antimony
  arsenic
  bismuth
  nitrogen
  nitrogen group
    element
  phosphorus
noble gases:
  argon
  helium
  krypton
  neon
  noble gas
  radon
  xenon
oxygen group:
  oxygen
  oxygen group
    element
  polonium
  selenium
  sulfur
  tellurium
rare-earth elements:
  cerium
  dysprosium
  erbium
  europium
  gadolinium
  holmium
  lanthanum
  lutetium
  neodymium
  praseodymium
  promethium
  rare-earth metal

  samarium
  scandium
  terbium
  thulium
  ytterbium
  yttrium
*synthetic elements,
  including the
  transuranium
  elements:*
  americium
  berkelium
  californium
  curium
  einsteinium
  element 106
  element 107
  element 108
  element 109
  fermium
  hahnium
  lawrencium
  mendelevium
  neptunium
  nobelium
  plutonium
  promethium
  rutherfordium
  technetium
  transuranium
    element
transition eléments:
  chromium
  cobalt
  copper
  gold
  hafnium
  iridium

  iron
  manganese
  molybdenum
  nickel
  niobium
  osmium
  palladium
  platinum
  rhenium
  rhodium
  ruthenium
  silver
  tantalum
  technetium
  titanium
  transition element
  tungsten
  vanadium
  zirconium
zinc group:
  cadmium
  mercury
  zinc
  zinc group
    element
other:
  allotropy
  Aufbau principle
  chemical element
  chemical symbol
  group
  lanthanide
    contraction
  metal
  metalloid
  nonmetal
  nucleosynthesis
  periodic law

Biographies
  See Section 10/32 of Part Ten

INDEX: See entries under all of the terms above

Section 122.   Chemical Compounds: Molecular Structure and Chemical Bonding

A. The theory of molecular structure: its history and development

1. Early concepts of molecular structure

2. Quantum mechanical and electrostatic approaches to the theory of molecular structure

3. Molecular bonds and shapes

   a. Spatial arrangement of atoms: chains, rings, chelates, polymers

   b. Isomers: structural isomers, stereoisomers

4. Time-dependency properties of molecules

5. Molecular structure and its relation to the properties of bulk matter

   a. The physical properties of matter as affected by molecular size, shape, and interactions, and interactions of molecules with radiations and fields

   b. The chemical behaviour of matter as determined by the nature of molecular bonds

   c. The chemical, physical, and biochemical properties of a substance inferred from its known or postulated molecular structure

B. Experimental and theoretical procedures for the determination of molecular structures

1. The separation, isolation, and purification of chemical substances based on chemical equilibria and rate phenomena

   a. By volatility differences: distillation, sublimation, evaporization

   b. By chromatography: liquid phase, gas phase, thin layer

   c. By solubility differences: precipitation, crystallization, zone melting, solvent extraction

   d. By ion-exchange reactions

   e. By electrophoresis and electrolytic methods

   f. By mechanical methods: filtration, sedimentation, sieving, flotation, centrifugation

2. Classical methods of qualitative and quantitative analysis

3. Instrumental methods used to identify functional groups, molecular sub-units, and structural features

   a. Spectrochemical methods: microwave, infrared, ultraviolet, Raman spectroscopy, colorimetry, atomic absorption spectroscopy

   b. Mass spectrometry

   c. Magnetic resonance spectrometry

   d. Thermometric methods: thermogravimetry, calorimetry, cryoscopy

   e. Radiochemical methods: radiometric analysis, activation analysis, isotopic dilution

   f. Electrochemical methods: potentiometry, polarography, electrodeposition, oscillometry

4. Diffraction methods for determining molecular structures: electron, X-ray, and neutron beam diffraction

5. Physical methods used to determine optical activity, magnetic susceptibility, calorific values, heat of combustion, activation energy, and reaction rates

6. The synthesis and characterization of derivatives, or specifically modified molecules

7. The determination of molecular weight based on thermodynamic theory, on transport phenomena, and on known spatial arrangements of atoms in the solid state

8. The principles of conformational analysis as related to molecular structure

9. The scattering of molecular beams and its usefulness in the study of molecular interactions

C. Spectra of molecules

1. The theory of molecular spectra

2. Types of molecular spectra: microwave, infrared, Raman, visible, and ultraviolet spectra

3. The interpretation of molecular band spectra in determining molecular structure

D. The theory of chemical bonding: its development and experimental bases

1. Nonquantum treatments of chemical bonding

   a. Early ideas and concepts of chemical bonding: valence

   b. The early electronic theory of bonding

      i. The nature of ionic bond: shell theory, ion pairs

      ii. The nature of covalent and coordinate bond: the octet

   c. Application of the quantum theory to atomic structure

2. Quantum-mechanical treatment of chemical bonding

   a. Atomic and molecular orbital concepts

   b. Bonding in the hydrogen molecule

   c. Bonding in simple polyatomic molecules

   d. Quantum-mechanical calculations

3. Other bonding effects: hydrogen bonding; metallic bonds in metals, intermetallic compounds, and coordination compounds; bonds in crystals, in weak associations, and in electron-deficient compounds

4. Experimental observation of chemical bonding

5. Anomalous molecular structures, or molecular fragments with apparently anomalous valences: free radicals, carbenes, carbanions, carbonium ions

E. Systems of classification of chemical compounds or substances

   1. By their elemental composition or molecular structure: organic, inorganic, organometallic, and nonstoichiometric compounds

   2. By their bond type: ionic, covalent, and coordination compounds

   3. By their chemical reactivity: acids, bases, and salts; oxidizing and reducing agents

   4. By their physical state: gas, liquid, and solid

   5. By their origin: natural and synthetic

F. Inorganic compounds

   1. Nomenclature of binary, ternary, and coordination compounds

   2. Structural classification of inorganic compounds

      a. Salts

      b. Oxides, anhydrides, acids, and bases

      c. Coordination compounds

      d. Organometallic compounds
         [see G.1.c., below]

      e. Catenates

      f. Inorganic polymers

      g. Special nonmetallic derivatives

   3. Methods of preparation of inorganic compounds

   4. Reactions of inorganic compounds; *e.g.,* acid–base, substitution, isomerization, oxidation–reduction, addition

G. Organic compounds

   1. The major groups of organic compounds: their nomenclature, chemical and physical properties, synthesis, occurrence, reactions, and analysis

      a. Hydrocarbons: aliphatic and aromatic

      b. Organic halogen compounds: alkyl, alkenyl, and alkynyl halides; aryl halides

      c. Organometallic compounds

      d. Alcohols, phenols, and ethers

      e. Carboxylic acids and their derivatives

      f. Aldehydes, ketones, and their derivatives

      g. Organic nitrogen compounds

      h. Organic sulfur compounds

      i. Organic phosphorus compounds

      j. Organic silicon compounds

      k. Heterocyclic compounds

      l. Oils, fats, and waxes

      m. Carbohydrates

      n. Amino acids, proteins, and peptides

      o. Isoprenoids and terpenes

      p. Steroids and their derivatives

      q. Nucleotides and nucleosides

      r. Nucleic acids: DNA and RNA

      s. Alkaloids

      t. Dyestuffs and pigments

      u. Organic polymers

2. Preparation and purification of organic compounds

3. Physical properties of organic compounds

4. Reactions of organic compounds: addition, substitution, displacement, hydrolysis, pyrolysis, condensation, polymerization, molecular rearrangement

---

Suggested reading in the *Encyclopædia Britannica*:

MACROPAEDIA: Major articles dealing with chemical compounds: molecular structure and chemical bonding

Biochemical Components of Organisms
Chemical Compounds

MICROPAEDIA: Selected entries of reference information

General subjects

alcohols and phenols:
alcohol
amyl alcohol
butyl alcohol
cetyl alcohol
chlorophenol
cresol
ethyl alcohol
fusel oil
glycerol
glycol
methanol
naphthol
phenol
phytol
picric acid
propyl alcohol
pyrogallol
resorcinol
aldehydes and ketones:
acetone
aldehyde
benzaldehyde
ethyl acetoacetate
formaldehyde
ketone
alkaloids:
alkaloid
atropine
caffeine
cocaine
codeine
curare
ephedrine
heroin
ibogaine
mescaline
morphine
nicotine
piperine
quinidine
quinine
scopolamine
theophylline

amino acids, proteins, and peptides:
amino acid
collagen
glutamic acid
glutamine
gluten
histidine
histone
hydroxyproline
insulin
keratin
myoglobin
pepsin
peptide
prolamin
protein
proteolytic enzyme
renin
scleroprotein
serotonin
transaminase
carbides:
carbide
silicon carbide
tungsten carbide
carbohydrates:
carbohydrate
cellulose
disaccharide
glucose
glycoside
monosaccharide
pectin
polysaccharide
starch
sugar
carboxylic acids:
acetic acid
benzoic acid
butyric acid
carboxylic acid
citric acid
fatty acid
formic acid

gallic acid
lactic acid
maleic acid
malonic acid
oxalic acid
peroxy acid
salicylic acid
soap
stearic acid
succinic acid
tartaric acid
coordination compounds:
chelate
coordination compound
coordination number
effective atomic number
ligand
ligand field theory
metal carbonyl
dyes and pigments:
alizarin
anthraquinone
anthraquinone dye
auxochrome
azo dye
carmine
chlorophyll
chromophore
cochineal
dye
flavonoid
indigo
lake
melanin
porphyrin
Prussian blue
quercitron bark
triphenylmethane dye
ultramarine

esters:
ester
ethyl acetoacetate
lactone
polyester ethers:
ether
ethylether
polyether
heterocyclic compounds:
coumarin
furan
imidazole
indole
lactone
melamine
purine
pyran
pyrazine
pyrazole
pyridine
pyrimidine
pyrrole
quinoline
thiazine
thiazole
thiophene
hydrocarbons:
acetylene
benzene
biphenyl
butadiene
butane
butene
ethane
ethylene
hydrocarbon
methane
naphthalene
olefin
paraffin hydrocarbon
propane
styrene

toluene
xylene
*inorganic acids and
 oxides:*
  acid
  carbon dioxide
  carbon monoxide
  Dry Ice
  hydrogen chloride
  hydrogen cyanide
  hydrogen ion
  nitric acid
  nitric oxide
  nitrous acid
  nitrous oxide
  oxide
  phosphoric acid
  phosphorous acid
  rare-earth metal
  silica gel
  silicic acid
  sulfur oxide
  sulfuric acid
  water glass
*inorganic nitrogen
 compounds:*
  ammonia
  ammonium
   hydroxide
  azide
  hydrazine
  hydroxylamine
*isoprenoids and
 terpenes:*
  abietic acid
  camphor
  carotene
  isoprene
  limonene
  menthol
  pinene
  terpene
*methods of chemical
 analysis:*
  assaying
  chemical
   precipitation
  chromatography
  colorimetry
  countercurrent
   distribution
  differential thermal
   analysis
  electrophoresis
  gas
   chromatography
  gel
   chromatography
  gravimetric
   analysis
  iodine value

nephelometry and
 turbidimetry
paper
 chromatography
polarimetry
polarography
qualitative
 chemical analysis
quantitative
 chemical analysis
spectrochemical
 analysis
thin-layer
 chromatography
titration
volumetric
 analysis
*molecular bonds and
 shapes:*
  configuration
  conformation
  diastereoisomer
  enantiomorph
  isomerism
  optical activity
  racemate
  resolution
  strain theory
  tautomerism
*nucleic acids and
 their components:*
  adenine
  adenosine
   triphosphate
  cytosine
  deoxyribonucleic
   acid
  guanine
  nuclease
  nucleic acid
  nucleoside
  nucleotide
  ribonucleic acid
  thymine
  uracil
oils, fats, and waxes:
  babassu palm
  castor oil
  Chinese wax
  cod-liver oil
  cohune oil
  copra
  cottonseed
  essential oil
  fat
  fish oil
  grease
  lard
  linseed
  lipid
  oil
  phospholipid

pine oil
sperm oil
spermaceti
tallow
triglyceride
wax
whale oil
*organic halogen
 compounds:*
  acid halide
  aldrin
  benzene
   hexachloride
  carbon
   tetrachloride
  chloral
  chloral hydrate
  chlordane
  chlorobenzene
  chloroform
  chlorotrifluoro-
   ethylene
  cyanogen halide
  DDT
  dichlorobenzene
  ethyl chloride
  ethylene bromide
  ethylene chloride
  Freon
  halocarbon
  halon
  iodoform
  methyl bromide
  methyl chloride
  methylene chloride
  phosgene
  polychlorinated
   biphenyl
  tear gas
  tetrachloroethane
  tetrachloroethylene
  tetrafluoroethylene
  toxaphene
  trichloroethane
  trichloroethylene
  vinyl chloride
  vinylidene chloride
*organic nitrogen,
 sulfur, or
 phosphorus
 compounds:*
  amide
  amine
  aniline
  azo compound
  benzidine
  biotin
  choline
  diazonium salt
  dimethoate
  ethanolamine

isocyanide
nitrile
nitro compound
nitrobenzene
nitroglycerin
nitroso compound
oxime
parathion
PETN
phorate
picric acid
polysulfide
sulfide
sulfonamide
sulfonic acid
sulfoxide
thiol
thiourea
urea
xanthate
*organometallic
 compounds:*
  carborane
  ferrocene
  Grignard reagent
  metal carbonyl
  tetraethyllead
peroxy compounds:
  hydrogen peroxide
  peroxide
  peroxy acid
*petroleum, gasoline,
 oil, and coal:*
  gasoline
  kerosine
  microcrystalline
   wax
  napalm
  naphtha
  paraffin wax
  petrochemical
  petroleum
polymers and resins:
  balsam
  copal
  copolymer
  dammar
  dragon's blood
  elastomer
  frankincense
  gamboge
  initiator
  latex
  Lucite
  macromolecule
  mastic
  monomer
  neoprene
  polyacrylonitrile
  polychlorotri-
   fluoroethylene

polyester
polyether
polyolefin
polystyrene
polysulfide
polysulfone
polytetrafluoro-
  ethylene
polyurethane
polyvinyl alcohol
polyvinyl chloride
resin
rubber
silicone
turpentine
urea–formaldehyde
  resin
vinyl compound
polysulfide
quinone
radical

salts:
  alum
  ammonium
    chloride
  ammonium nitrate
  lithium carbonate
  Rochelle salt

saltpetre
silver nitrate
soap
silane
steroids and their
  derivatives:
  aldosterone
  cholesterol
  corticoid
  cortisol
  cortisone
  ergosterol
  sapogenin
  saponin
  steroid
  steroid hormone
  testosterone
theory of chemical
  bonding:
  chemical
    association
  chemical bonding
  covalent bond
  electronegativity
  ion
  ion pair
  ionic bond

metallic bond
orbital
resonance,
  theory of
valence
van der Waals
  forces
water:
  anomalous water
  deliquescence
  efflorescence
  hard water
  heavy water
  hydrate
  ice
  steam
  water
other:
  alicyclic
  alkali compound
  anhydride
  base
  carbanion
  carbene
  carbon disulfide
  carbonate
  carbonium ion
  carbonyl group

chemical
  compound
chemical formula
chemical indicator
definite
  proportions,
  law of
excitation
functional group
homologous series
ion-exchange resin
ketene
lecithin
litmus
macromolecule
molecular sieve
molecule
multiple
  proportions,
  law of
nonstoichiometric
  compound
phenolphthalein
phosphine
polysulfide
quinone
radical
sulfide

Biographies

See Section 10/32 of Part Ten

INDEX: See entries under all of the terms above

Section 123.   Chemical Reactions

A. General considerations of chemical reactions

   1. Basic concepts involved in the study of chemical reactions: transformation, conservation of mass and energy, law of simple multiple proportions in compounds

   2. Growth of major theories concerning chemical reactions

   3. Classification and nomenclature of the principal kinds of chemical reactions

       a. According to the relationship involved between the starting materials and the final products

           i. Decomposition reactions

          ii. Polymerization reactions

         iii. Chain reactions

          iv. Substitution reactions

           v. Addition and elimination reactions

          vi. Oxidation–reduction reactions
              [see F., below]

         vii. Acid–base reactions
              [see E., below]

       b. According to the energy changes involved
          [see B.1., below]

       c. According to the reaction rates or chemical kinetics involved
          [see C.6., below]

       d. According to the reaction mechanism involved
          [see D.4., below]

B. Energy changes in chemical reactions

    1. The classification of chemical reactions according to energy changes involved: exothermic and endothermic

    2. The significance of activation energy in chemical reactions

    3. Thermodynamic relations in chemical reactions: chemical equilibrium, free energy and entropy changes

C. Rates of chemical reactions

    1. Factors that affect the rate or direction of chemical reactions

        a. Solvents

        b. Temperature

        c. Pressure

        d. Catalysts

        e. Collisions

        f. Light

        g. Isotopic substitution

        h. Molecular structure

    2. Factors that affect the kinetic order of chemical reactions: concentration of reactants, mechanism of reaction, conditions of the reaction

    3. Factors that affect the extent of chemical reactions: equilibrium constant

    4. Complex reactions: reactions governed by more than one reaction rate

    5. Experimental methods for studying chemical kinetics

        a. Measurement of reaction rates

        b. Determination of the order of reactions

        c. Relaxation methods

    6. Kinetic studies as a means of elucidating reaction mechanisms

D. Mechanisms of chemical reactions

    1. Factors influencing the course of a reaction: reactants, transition state, solvent, catalysts, products, reaction conditions

    2. Energy changes through single-stage and multi-stage processes

    3. Factors that reveal the mechanisms of a reaction: chemical and stereochemical nature of the reactants, intermediates, and products; kinetics of the reaction

    4. Classification of reaction mechanisms based on the nature of electron pairing in the transition state, on the nature of the attacking species, on the nature of catalysis, on the number of components of the transition state

    5. Mechanisms of the principal types of reactions: nucleophilic and electrophilic substitution, addition and elimination reactions

E. Acid–base reactions and equilibria

    1. General properties of acids and bases

    2. Theoretical approaches to acid–base concepts

        a. The definition of an acid as a substance that gives rise to hydrogen ions and of a base as a substance that gives rise to hydroxyl ions in aqueous solutions

        b. The Brønsted–Lowry concept defining an acid as a proton donor and a base as a proton acceptor

        c. The Lewis electronic theory defining an acid as an electron acceptor and a base as an electron donor

    3. Acid–base reactions

        a. Proton-transfer reactions

        b. Lewis acid reactions

        c. Acid–base catalysis

4. Quantitative aspects of acid–base equilibria

   a. Equilibria in aqueous solutions

   b. Equilibria in nonaqueous solvents

   c. Equilibria involving Lewis acids

   d. The effect of molecular structure on acid–base equilibria

5. The experimental study of acid–base reactions and equilibria

F. Oxidation–reduction reactions

   1. Major classes of oxidation–reduction reactions: oxygen atom transfer, hydrogen atom transfer, electron transfer

   2. Definitions of oxidation and reduction based on the reaction's stoichiometry

   3. Theoretical aspects of oxidation–reduction processes

      a. The concept of oxidation state

      b. Half reactions and the determination of redox potentials

      c. Oxidation–reduction equilibria and reaction rates

      d. Mechanisms of redox reactions

   4. Electrochemical reactions: chemical changes associated with the passage of an electrical current

      a. The electrochemical process: types of reactions

      b. Complex electrochemical reactions

      c. The Nernst and Butler–Volmer equations

   5. Oxidation–reduction reactions in biological systems

   6. Oxidation–reduction reactions in combustion and flames

G. Photochemical reactions

   1. The photochemical process

   2. Experimental methods used in the study of the photochemical process and photochemical reactions

   3. The application of photochemical processes

H. Chemical reactions and chemical theory in the synthesis of chemical compounds

   1. Factors that affect the choice of a specific synthetic path

   2. Factors that affect the choice of reaction conditions

   3. The separation and purification of reaction products
      [see 122.B.1.]

   4. The identification, characterization, and analysis of reaction products
      [see 122.B.2. through 9.]

Suggested reading in the *Encyclopædia Britannica:*

MACROPAEDIA: Major articles dealing with chemical reactions

   Chemical Reactions
   Physical Sciences, The

MICROPAEDIA: Selected entries of reference information

General subjects

acid–base reactions and equilibria:	Lewis theory	*electrochemistry:*	electromotive series
acid–base reaction	pH	anodizing	Faraday's laws of
Brønsted–Lowry	*catalysis of reactions:*	electrical double	electrolysis
theory	acid–base catalysis	layer	*kinetics and*
buffer	catalysis	electrochemical	*mechanism:*
hydrogen ion	catalyst	reaction	activation energy
hydroxide	catalyst poison	electrochemistry	Arrhenius equation
	Ziegler–Natta	electrolysis	chain reaction
	catalyst	electrolytic cell	

chemical
  equilibrium
chemical
  intermediate
collision theory
initiator
inversion
isotopic
  fractionation
Markovnikov rule
mass action, law of
microscopic
  reversibility,
  principle of
reaction rate
relaxation
  phenomenon
transition state
  theory

*oxidation and
  reduction:*
  anti-oxidant
  combustion
  oxidation–
    reduction
    reaction
  spontaneous
    combustion
photochemistry:
  actinometer
  photochemical
    equivalence law
  photochemical
    reaction
  photolysis
  photosensitization

*preparative
  procedures:*
  alkylation
  asymmetric
    synthesis
  chemical synthesis
  condensation
    reaction
  cracking
  hydrogenation
  hydrolysis
  ion-exchange
    reaction
  isomerization
  polymerization
  sulfation

others:
  chemical reaction
  equivalent weight
  Hess's law of heat
    summation
  heterogeneous
    reaction
  homogeneous
    reaction
  reaction, heat of

Biographies
  See Section 10/32 of Part Ten

INDEX: See entries under all of the terms above

Section 124.   Heat, Thermodynamics, and the Nonsolid States of Matter

A. The principles of thermodynamics

1. The description of physical phenomena based on the concepts of system, state of a system, and changes of state

2. The first law of thermodynamics

3. The second law of thermodynamics

4. Stable equilibrium

   a. Equations relating properties of systems that are in, or are passing through, stable equilibrium states

   b. Temperature considered as the potential governing the flow of energy between systems

   c. Heat

      i. The definition of heat as a form of energy transferred from one body to another under the influence of a difference in temperature

      ii. Theories of heat: the phlogiston theory, the caloric theory, the kinetic molecular theory

      iii. Heat transfer in matter: heat conductivity in solids, convection in liquids and gases, heat transfer in boiling liquids, evaporation and condensation

      iv. Technical applications of heat energy
          [see 721.B.7. and 725.A.5.a.]

      v. Heat and its relation to entropy, work, and change of energy

5. Thermodynamic relations in simple systems

   a. The Carnot cycle

   b. Maxwell's equations relating entropy to pressure, volume, and temperature for closed systems that assume only stable equilibrium states

   c. Phase changes and equilibria

   d. Simple one-component systems: processes at constant volume and at constant pressure; the equation of state, which relates pressure, volume, and temperature for stable equilibrium states

   e. Simple multicomponent systems: Gibbs equation for entropy change, the Gibbs–Dalton rule for mixture of gases, Raoult's law and Henry's law for ideal solutions

f. Bulk flow

g. Equilibrium in chemical reactions
[see 123.B.3.]

6. The third law of thermodynamics

7. The effects of applied force fields on simple systems

8. Steady rate processes; *e.g.,* systems approaching stable equilibrium, flow of a substance through a barrier

9. Statistical thermodynamics

a. The laws of thermodynamics that consider the detailed microscopic structure of physical systems and the states of such systems

b. Statistics of grand systems

B. The gaseous state of matter

1. The nature and properties of a gas

2. The thermodynamic approach to gases: the macroscopic view that deals with bulk measurable properties

a. The simple gas laws

b. The thermal equation of state for perfect gases

c. Empirical equations of state for real gases

3. The particle-description approach to gases

a. The distribution function

b. The Boltzmann transport equation, the single-particle distribution function

c. The N-particle distribution function and the thermodynamic-equilibrium properties and transport properties of dense gases

d. The behaviour of a gas at the hydrodynamic and thermal relaxation stages

C. The liquid state of matter

1. The behaviour and properties of liquids at equilibrium

2. The molecular structure of liquids based on distribution functions, which measure the probable distribution of some property of molecules through the liquid

3. Properties of liquids

a. Transport properties

b. Acoustical properties: propagation of sound waves

c. Electrical and magnetic properties

d. Thermodynamic properties

e. Optical properties

f. Surface tension

D. Solutions and solubility

1. General classes of solutions: electrolytes and nonelectrolytes, solutions of weak electrolytes, endothermic and exothermic solutions

2. Properties of solutions

a. Composition ratios: molarity, molality, mole fraction

b. Equilibrium properties: correlation of the vapour pressure of a solution to its composition

c. Colligative properties: rise in boiling point, decrease in freezing point, osmotic pressure

d. Transport properties: viscosity, thermal conductivity, diffusivity

3. Thermodynamic and molecular aspects of solvent and solute interactions

a. Energy considerations: entropy, enthalpy, Gibbs free energy

b. Effects of molecular structure and weak intermolecular forces

c. Effects of chemical interactions; *e.g.,* hydrogen bonding, chemical combinations

4. General theories of solution: the prediction of solubility and solution properties

        a. Solutions of nonelectrolytes: Raoult's law and Henry's law for ideal solutions; theoretical expressions for the excess properties of regular athermal, associated, and solvated solutions

        b. Solutions of electrolytes: Debye–Hückel theory and modifications, Arrhenius dissociation theory

    5. Effects of temperature and pressure on the solubility of solids and gases

E. Physical effects at surfaces

    1. Surface tension and surface energy: cohesion and adhesion

    2. Adsorption on liquid and solid surfaces

    3. Tribological phenomena, the mechanical and physical effects at interfaces: friction, wear, lubrication

    4. Colloids: the kinds of dispersions and their properties and preparation

        a. Irreversible colloidal systems: lyophobic sols, emulsions, foams, pastes, gels

        b. Reversible colloidal systems: solutions of polymers and proteins, solutions of soaps and dyes

F. The plasma state of matter: completely ionized gases interacting with magnetic and electric fields

    1. Basic plasma properties and parameters: electrical quasineutrality, electron density, kinetic temperature, particle velocities, magnetic and electric field strengths

    2. Elastic and inelastic collisions of plasma particles

    3. Radiation from plasmas; *e.g.,* X-rays, synchrotron radiation, excitation radiation

    4. The formation of plasmas

    5. The behaviour of plasmas in magnetic and electric fields

    6. The determination of plasma variables

    7. Fluidlike behaviour in plasmas

    8. Applications of plasmas; *e.g.,* power production, jet propulsion
[see 112.G.4., 721.B.8.a., and 721.C.3.]

    9. The existence of plasmas in nature: in the extraterrestrial medium, in the Sun and stars, on Earth

G. The properties of matter at extreme conditions

    1. Properties of matter at low temperatures

        a. Effects of low temperature on entropy, heat capacity, magnetic properties, and conductivity

        b. Special physical phenomena at very low temperatures: superconductivity, superfluidity

        c. Special methods for obtaining and characterizing low temperatures: adiabatic cooling, adiabatic dilution

    2. Special properties of matter at high temperatures

    3. Effects of high pressure on the physical, chemical, electronic, and magnetic properties of matter

H. Transport phenomena

    1. The kinetic molecular theory of the transport properties of gases, liquids, suspensions, and polymers

    2. Phenomenological expressions of transport

    3. Hydrodynamic aspects of transport phenomena

    4. Transport phenomena in macrosystems

Suggested reading in the *Encyclopædia Britannica:*

MACROPAEDIA: Major articles dealing with heat, thermodynamics, and the nonsolid states of matter

    Matter: Its Properties, States, Varieties, and Behaviour
    Physical Sciences, The
    Thermodynamics, Principles of

MICROPAEDIA: Selected entries of reference information

General subjects

colloids:
  aerosol
  colloid
  dialysis
  emulsion
  foam
  gel
gaseous state of matter:
  Avogadro's law
  Boyle's law
  Dalton's law
  degenerate gas
  diffusion
  fluid
  gas
  kinetic theory of gases
  Maxwell–Boltzmann distribution law
  mean free path
  perfect gas
  van der Waals forces
heat transfer in matter:
  adiabatic demagnetization

caloric theory
convection
heat transfer
thermal conduction
liquid state of matter:
  capillarity
  detergent
  diffusion
  fluid
  glass
  liquid
  osmosis
  superfluidity
  surface-active agent
  surface tension
phase changes and equilibria:
  boiling point
  condensation
  critical point
  distillation
  eutectic
  freezing point
  latent heat
  melting point
  phase
  phase diagram

phase rule
thermal fusion
vaporization
solutions and solubility:
  amalgam
  Arrhenius theory
  exsolution
  Henry's law
  ideal solution
  saturation
  solid solution
  solution
thermodynamics and statistical mechanics:
  absolute zero
  canonical ensemble
  carnot cycle
  energy, equipartition of
  enthalpy
  entropy
  free energy
  freedom, degree of
  Hamiltonian function
  heat

heat capacity
internal energy
Lagrangian function
Maxwell's demon
Rankine cycle
reversibility
specific heat
temperature
thermodynamics
other:
  adsorption
  cohesion
  friction
  liquid crystal
  plasma
  Stefan–Boltzmann law
  thermal expansion
  transport phenomenon
  tribology
  wear

Biographies

See Section 10/32 of Part Ten

INDEX: See entries under all of the terms above

Section 125.   **The Solid State of Matter**

A. Crystals and crystallography

  1. Patterns of atoms in crystals

    a. The three-dimensional periodic arrangement of atoms in crystals: crystal planes and their notation

    b. Symmetry considerations in the classification of crystal systems

  2. Diffraction of X-rays, electrons, and neutrons by crystal structures

  3. Processes of crystal growth

    a. Theoretical aspects of crystal growth: energy considerations, growth of eutectics, constitutional supercooling, nucleation

    b. Preparation of crystals: monocomponent and polycomponent crystal growth

  4. Imperfections and dislocations in crystalline materials and their effects on the properties of the crystals

  5. Effects of temperature, pressure, and alloying on the strength and hardness of crystals

B. The theory of the crystalline solid state

  1. The classification of solids according to their electronic structure and bonding: ionic solids, covalent solids, metallic solids, molecular solids, hydrogen-bonded solids

2. The arrangement of atoms in crystalline solids
   [see A.1.a., above]

3. The elastic and plastic properties of solids

4. The thermal and thermodynamic properties of solids: specific heat, thermal conductivity

5. The electronic structure of solids

   a. The nature and mobility of electrons in conductors, insulators, and semiconductors

   b. Electron emission: thermionic emission, photoelectric emission, field emission

   c. The nearly free electron approximation

   d. The energy-band theory of the solid state

6. The principal types of magnetic behaviour exhibited by solids: paramagnetism, diamagnetism, ferromagnetism

7. The interaction of light with solids

   a. The behaviour of solids illuminated with radiation: reflection, absorption, or transmission of photons

   b. The generation of electromagnetic radiation from the energy supplied to the solid

   c. The photoelectric effect

C. Ionic crystals

1. Bonding in ionic crystals

2. The structure of ionic crystals

   a. Perfect ionic crystals

   b. Defects in ionic crystals: Frenkel defect, Schottky defect, colour centres

3. Properties of ionic crystals

   a. Vibrational and electronic properties

   b. Thermal properties

   c. Polarizing and diffusion properties and the nature of ionic conduction

   d. Optical properties

D. Metals

1. Structural aspects of metals and alloys

2. Elementary description of metals: the use of the free electron model to explain thermal and electrical conductivity of metals

3. The electronic structure of metals and related effects

   a. The interaction between the periodic lattice and the conduction electrons: the weak pseudopotential

   b. Electron motion in a magnetic field and conduction-related effects

4. Band structure and properties of metal groups: alkali metals, semimetals, noble metals, transition metals

5. Lattice vibrations: interaction between ions; interaction between electrons, phonons, and dispersion

6. Metal surface phenomena: thermionic and field emission of electrons, electron tunnelling, photoemission, free carrier absorption and interband transitions

7. Many-body effects: plasma oscillations, spin waves, Fermi liquid theory, dynamic effects and shake-off electrons

8. Superconductivity in metals

   a. Thermal properties of superconductors: transition temperature, specific heat and thermal conductivity, energy gaps

   b. Magnetic and electromagnetic properties of superconductors: critical field, Meissner effect, phase coherence effects

9. Magnetic phenomena in metals: diamagnetism, paramagnetism, ferromagnetism, antiferromagnetism, nuclear magnetic resonance

E. Semiconductors and insulators

   1. General properties of semiconductors and insulators

   2. Mechanisms of conduction: mobility of charged particles and electrons in solids

   3. Electrical conduction in semiconductors

      a. Chemical approach: impurity conduction, hopping process

      b. Physical approach: energy band and gaps, lattice vibrations, statistical properties

      c. Extrinsic and intrinsic semiconductors

      d. Measurement of conductivity and of energy gaps

   4. Principles involved in semiconductor applications

      a. Optical effects: photoelectric effect, photovoltaic effect, luminescence

      b. Electrical and related effects: hot electron effects, thermoelectric effects

      c. Junction effects

      d. Pressure and stress effects

F. The glassy or amorphous state of matter

   1. Effects of temperature and composition on glass properties

   2. The structure of glass

   3. General properties of glasses: mechanical, chemical, optical, and electrical properties

---

Suggested reading in the *Encyclopædia Britannica:*

MACROPAEDIA: Major articles dealing with the solid state of matter

    Matter: Its Properties, States, Varieties, and Behaviour
    Minerals and Rocks

MICROPAEDIA: Selected entries of reference information

<u>General subjects</u>

crystal systems:	polycrystal	photovoltaic effect	Bragg law
hexagonal system	single crystal	semiconductor	electronic work
isometric system	*electrical currents and*	superconductor	function
monoclinic system	*related effects:*	*structural features of*	exciton
orthorhombic	avalanche effect	*crystals:*	Fermi level
system	band theory	axis	Fermi surface
point group	BCS theory	Bravais lattice	free-electron model
space group	dopant	colour centre	of metals
tetragonal system	Gunn effect	Miller indices	Laue diffraction
triclinic system	Hall effect	polymorphism	pattern
trigonal system	hole	slip	magnon
crystals:	insulator	Steno's law	metal
crystal	Josephson effect	symmetry	metallography
crystalline rock	Meissner effect	trap	phonon
crystallite	minority carrier	twinning	polaron
epitaxy	injection	vacancy	quasicrystal
nucleation	mobility	*other:*	reststrahlen
optical	photoconductivity	allotropy	
crystallography	photoelectric effect	anisotropy	

<u>Biographies</u>

    See Section 10/32 of Part Ten

INDEX: See entries under all of the terms above

Section 126.   **Mechanics of Particles, Rigid Bodies, and Deformable Bodies: Elasticity, Vibrations, and Flow**

A. The principles of classical mechanics

   1. The fundamental parameters and concepts of classical mechanics: matter, space, motion, time

   2. Statics, the equilibrium of systems at rest: force, friction

   3. Dynamics: motion of systems

      a. Kinematics: motion of particles and rigid bodies without consideration of the forces producing the motion

         i. Velocity and acceleration

         ii. Rotation about a fixed axis

         iii. Motion in a circular path

         iv. Simple harmonic motion

         v. Relative motion

      b. Kinetics: motion of bodies under the action of forces upon them

         i. Newton's laws of motion: the law of inertia, the law of force, the law of action and reaction

         ii. Motion under a constant force

         iii. Ballistics: phenomena and laws of projectiles and their propulsion, flight, and impact

         iv. The motion of the pendulum

         v. Newton's law of universal gravitation

         vi. Kepler's laws of planetary motion

      c. Impulse and momentum

      d. Work and power

      e. Energy

         i. The concepts of energy and energy conservation

         ii. Forms of energy and examples of energy transformations associated with each energy form

         iii. The equivalence of mass and energy

      f. The conservation of momentum

   4. Mechanics of nonrigid bodies

      a. The collision of bodies or particles: centre of mass system, elastic collisions, inelastic collisions

      b. Stiffness in mechanical vibrations

   5. Motion in a rotating frame of reference: inertia forces and Coriolis forces

   6. Mechanics of complex systems

      a. The principle of virtual work

      b. The rotation of spinning tops and gyroscopes

      c. The precession and nutation of rotating bodies

      d. Lagrange's and Hamilton's equations of motion

B. Relativistic mechanics in inertial systems of reference

   1. Mechanical foundations of special relativity

   2. Relativistic kinematics

   3. The relationship between gravitational mass and inertial mass

C. The stress dynamics of elastic materials

   1. The phenomenon of elasticity: stress-strain relationships

   2. Elasticity in viscous and crystalline bodies

3. Elastic constants

4. The theory of elasticity: mathematical expressions defining elastic properties

D. Vibrations of elastic bodies

1. The nature of vibrations: natural or free vibrations, damped and forced vibrations

2. Vibrators and their sources of energy

3. Types of vibrational waves: their properties and modes of propagation

4. The behaviour of materials undergoing vibration

5. Detection and utilization of vibrations
   [see 723.F.6. and 735.K.2.]

E. Fluid mechanics, including gas dynamics

1. General properties of fluids, ideal and actual: mechanical and thermodynamic properties

2. Fluid statics and equilibrium

   a. The basic equation of fluid statics

   b. Fluid forces on plane and curved surfaces: analysis of forces, buoyancy, stability of floating and submerged bodies

3. Fluids in motion: hydrodynamics and aerodynamics

   a. Frictionless one-dimensional fluid flow

   b. Flow in pipes and channels: laminar flow, turbulent flow, special types of flow

   c. General two- and three-dimensional flow: mathematical conditions, vorticity, boundary layers, drag

   d. Compressible fluid flow: isentropic flow, shock waves

F. Rheological phenomena: deformation and flow

1. Continuum mechanics

   a. Kinematics of deformation and flow: strain, shear, compression, elongation

   b. Dynamics: balance of forces and torques

2. Constitutive equations: stress-deformation relations in different media

3. Yield strength of materials: fracture and fatigue

4. The application of molecular theories to explain rheological phenomena

---

Suggested reading in the *Encyclopædia Britannica*:

MACROPAEDIA: Major articles dealing with the mechanics of particles, rigid bodies, and deformable bodies: elasticity, vibrations, and flow

> Energy Conversion
> Matter: Its Properties, States, Varieties, and Behaviour
> Mechanics: Energy, Forces, and Their Effects

MICROPAEDIA: Selected entries of reference information

General subjects

deformation and	yield point	kinetics	statics
elasticity:	Young's modulus	mass	velocity
bulk modulus	*elementary classical*	mechanics	*energy:*
deformation and	*mechanics:*	momentum	energy
flow	acceleration	motion	kinetic energy
elasticity	collision	motion,	mechanical energy
Hooke's law	d'Alembert's	equation of	potential energy
plasticity	principle	Newton's law of	power
shear modulus	dynamics	gravitation	work
slip	force	Newton's laws of	*fluid mechanics:*
strain	gravity, centre of	motion	Archimedes'
stress	inertia	position vector	principle
tensile strength	kinematics		

austausch coefficient	Magnus effect	precession	ballistics
Bernoulli's theorem	Pascal's principle	reduced mass	celestial mechanics
boundary layer	Reynolds number	torque	chaos
capillarity	terminal velocity	uniform circular motion	density
cavitation	Torricelli's theorem	*vibrations:*	equilibrium
convergence and divergence	turbulent flow	damping	equivalence principle
eddy	viscosity	pendulum	escape velocity
fluid	*rotary motion:*	periodic motion	Kepler's laws of planetary motion
fluid mechanics	angular momentum	reduced mass	pressure
Froude number	angular velocity	resonance	reference frame
hydraulics	centrifugal force	simple harmonic motion	specific gravity
laminar flow	Coriolis force	vibration	statistical mechanics
Mach number	couple	*others:*	
	inertia, moment of	action	

Biographies

See Section 10/32 of Part Ten

Section 127.   Electricity and Magnetism

A. The static electric charge

   1. General phenomena of static electricity

     a. The basic laws of electrostatics that relate the interaction of charged bodies at rest

     b. The electrostatic field

     c. The electric dipole

     d. Electrostatic energy and force

     e. Electricity in the atmosphere
       [see also 212.C., 221.A.3.b., and 223.B.2.]

   2. Electrostatics of dielectrics and capacitors: polarization

   3. Electrostatic potential

     a. High-voltage phenomena

     b. Electric fields and potential distributions in two and three dimensions

   4. Measurement of electrostatic forces and fields
      [see 723.D.1.e.]

B. Moving charges and electric currents

   1. Direct electric current: current that flows in one direction

     a. General phenomena of moving electric charges: definitions of electric quantities and their units

     b. Electromotive force

     c. Behaviour of direct currents in electric circuits: Ohm's law; Kirchhoff's laws; the principles of devices that measure or indicate the presence of current, potential difference, and resistance

   2. The conduction of electricity

     a. The motion of charged particles in an electric field

     b. The mechanisms of the conduction of electricity: in a vacuum, in gases, in liquids and solids, in metals and semiconductors

     c. Thermoelectric effects: phenomena in which electric energy is transformed into thermal energy or vice versa

     d. Electron emission: thermionic emission, secondary emission, photoelectric emission

   3. Alternating electric currents: current that reverses itself with uniform frequency

    a. Faraday's law of electromagnetic induction

    b. The mathematical and graphical representation of alternating currents

    c. Basic laws of alternating current circuits

    d. The detection and measurement of alternating currents and voltages
       [see 723.D.1.e.]

    e. Parallel resonant circuits

    f. Alternating current bridges for determining impedance

    g. Propagation of electric waves in cables

    h. Filters that select signals

    i. Transient phenomena of alternating circuits

    j. Eddy currents and skin, or surface, effects

    k. Principles of generation and transmission of ac single- and multiphase power

4. Primary effects and properties of electric fields and currents

    a. Magnetic effects of steady electric currents
       [see C.2., below]

    b. Magnetic effects of changing currents
       [see C.4., below]

    c. Force, energy, and power associated with electromagnetic fields

    d. The generation of electromagnetic radiation by the changing of currents in circuits

5. Effects of electricity on matter

    a. Piezoelectricity and applications of the phenomenon

    b. Optical effects: electroluminescence, Kerr effect, Stark effect

    c. Thermal effect: resistance heating

    d. Chemical effects: electrolysis, electro-osmosis, electrophoresis

    e. Bioelectric effects: effects associated with nerve, brain, and muscle action in which potential differences occur and can be influenced by applied potential

C. Magnetism

  1. General phenomena of magnetic systems

  2. Magnetic effects of steady electrical currents

    a. The magnetic field of steady currents: Ampère's law, the law of Biot and Savart

    b. The magnetic moment of a current loop

    c. The magnetic field of a solenoid

  3. Motion of charged particles in magnetic and electric fields

    a. The force on a moving charge

    b. Motion of charges in uniform flux density

    c. Motion of charges in combined electric and magnetic fields

    d. Magnetic dipole moments: atomic moments, nuclear moments, magnetic resonance

  4. Magnetic effects of varying currents

    a. The laws of electromagnetic induction

    b. Inductance and magnetic energy

  5. Properties of magnetic materials

    a. The classification of magnetic substances

    b. Induced and permanent atomic magnetic dipoles

    c. Magnetism of matter

       i. Diamagnetism

       ii. Paramagnetism

       iii. Ferromagnetism

       iv. Antiferromagnetism

      v. Ferrimagnetism

     vi. Terrestrial magnetism
        [see also 212.B.]

   d. Atomic structure and magnetism

D. The theory of fields in physics

   1. The definition of a field in physics: the scope of field theory

   2. Mathematical treatment of fields

   3. Classification of fields: material and nonmaterial fields; scalar, vector, and tensor fields

   4. Examples of scalar, vector, and tensor fields in ordinary space

   5. Fields with distributions in more than three dimensions

E. The electromagnetic field and the theory of electromagnetic radiation

   1. The classical theory of radiation

     a. The development of concepts and theories concerning the nature of light

     b. Semiquantitative treatment of electromagnetic radiation: Maxwell's equations for the electromagnetic nature of light

     c. The electromagnetic spectrum

   2. The quantum theory of radiation

     a. Evidences of the particle nature of electromagnetic radiation: Compton effect, photoelectric effect, Raman effect

     b. The wave–particle duality of the photon

     c. The interaction of electromagnetic radiation with atomic and molecular structures: absorption, emission, and scattering processes

     d. The relation of electromagnetic radiation to quantum theory and relativity

   3. The mathematical formulation of electromagnetic theory

     a. Maxwell's equations for electromagnetic fields and radiation

     b. Transmission of radiation in free space

     c. Wave equations in space bounded by conductors

     d. Scattering of electromagnetic waves

     e. Electromagnetic waves in material media

     f. The functions of antennas

F. Relativistic electrodynamics

   1. Electrodynamics in four-dimensional notation

   2. Applications of relativistic principles in the treatment of electromagnetic and nuclear force fields of relativistic particles

---

Suggested reading in the *Encyclopædia Britannica:*

MACROPAEDIA: Major articles dealing with electricity and magnetism

   Electricity and Magnetism
   Electromagnetic Radiation
   Energy Conversion

MICROPAEDIA: Selected entries of reference information

General subjects

stationary electric charges and related phenomena:	dielectric constant	electric field	electrostatic
	electret	electric	induction
	electric charge	polarization	Stark effect
capacitance	electric dipole	electric potential	*electric currents and*
Coulomb force	electric	electric	*related phenomena:*
dielectric	displacement	susceptibility	alternating current

Biography
  Maxwell, James Clerk
  See also Section 10/32 of Part Ten

Section 128.   Waves and Wave Motion

A. General wave phenomena and the theory of wave motion

  1. General properties of waves: frequency, amplitude, wavelength, phase

  2. Classification of waves

      a. Waves classified by the medium supporting the transmission of wave motion: water waves, sound waves, electromagnetic waves

      b. Waves classified by the motion of particles in a wave: transverse, longitudinal, torsional, and cylindrical waves

      c. Other classifications: bow waves and shock waves

  3. The theory of waves

      a. General characteristics of vibratory motion: periodicity, group velocity, energy content

      b. The velocity of waves

      c. The wave equation: the space–time description of wave motion

      d. Transport of energy and momentum

  4. The principle of superposition of waves

      a. Standing waves: waves with stationary nodes

      b. Modulation of waves

      c. Pulse and wave trains

  5. The behaviour of waves at boundaries or interfaces: reflection, transmission, refraction

  6. The diffraction and interference of waves

  7. The interaction of waves with matter: absorption, dispersion

B. Electromagnetic waves

1. Properties and behaviour of electromagnetic waves

2. Waves of the electromagnetic spectrum and their properties

   a. Radio waves

   b. Microwaves

   c. Infrared radiation

   d. Visible light
   [see C., below]

   e. Ultraviolet waves

   f. X rays
   [see 111.D.]

   g. Gamma rays

3. Sources of incoherent electromagnetic waves

   a. Sources of radio waves: oscillators, antennas, cosmic objects

   b. Sources of microwaves: klystrons, magnetrons, Gunn diodes, tunnel diodes, cosmic sources

   c. Sources of infrared, visible, and ultraviolet waves

      i. Blackbody radiation

      ii. Luminescence, fluorescence, phosphorescence

      iii. The passage of electrical current through a resisting medium

   d. Sources of X rays: X-ray tubes (bremsstrahlung), synchrotron radiation

   e. Sources of gamma rays: radioactive nuclei

4. Sources of coherent electromagnetic waves: lasers and masers
   [see 725.B.5.g. and 735.G.3.]

5. The transmission of electromagnetic waves: through matter, through space, by wave guides and transmission lines

C. Light waves

1. Light as a wave motion: the wave theory of light

   a. The properties of light consistent with the wave theory: diffraction, interference, polarization, dispersion

   b. The spectrum of light: the description of colour in terms of wavelengths

2. The velocity of light and its measurement

3. Interference of light

4. Diffraction phenomena

5. Polarization

   a. Superposition of polarized beams: plane, circularly, or elliptically polarized light

   b. Double refraction: waves in anisotropic media

   c. Characterization of polarized light by Stokes's parameters and Poincaré sphere

6. Properties and behaviour of light waves based on Maxwell's equations of electromagnetic theory

7. The interaction of light with matter

   a. Reflection and refraction

   b. Dispersion and scattering

   c. Absorption: mechanical and chemical effects of light

8. The quantum theory of light: the photon

   a. Observed photon phenomena: photoelectric effect, Compton scattering, Rayleigh scattering

   b. The uncertainty principle in relation to the study of the phenomena of light

   c. The detection and counting of photons

9. The separation of light into its constituent wavelengths, the analysis of light spectra

10. Sources of light

11. The biological effects of light, including photosynthesis
[see 322.A. and 335.B.]

D. The focusing and imaging of light waves

1. Geometrical optics: the geometry of light rays and their image-forming properties through optical systems

a. Theoretical considerations: law of reflection, law of refraction, Lagrange theorem, Gauss theory of lenses

b. Optical systems: components, applications, lens aberrations, brightness of image formed

2. Optics and information theory

a. Optical data processing

b. Holography: a two-step image-forming process using coherent light

E. Sound waves

1. The nature and properties of sound waves

2. Shock waves and their characteristics

3. Sources of sound waves

4. The reception of sound

5. Applications of acoustics

a. Recording and reproduction
[see 735.F.]

b. Architectural and acoustical design
[see 733.A.8.]

c. Speech and music
[see 514.D.1. and 624.B.]

d. Military acoustical detectors
[see 735.J.2.]

e. Noise control
[see 733.A.8.]

6. Physical aspects of musical sound
[see 624.B.1.]

a. The special properties of musical sound: pitch, timbre, loudness; fundamentals and overtones

b. The production of sound waves by musical instruments

Suggested reading in the *Encyclopædia Britannica:*

MACROPAEDIA: Major articles dealing with waves and wave motion

Colour
Electromagnetic Radiation
Light
Optics, Principles of
Sound

MICROPAEDIA: Selected entries of reference information

General subjects

behaviour and	Doppler effect	longitudinal wave	Snell's law
properties of waves:	double refraction	moiré pattern	standing wave
absorption	Faraday effect	Newton's rings	transverse wave
amplitude	Fermat's principle	phase	wave front
beat	frequency	Rayleigh scattering	wave motion
Brewster's law	Huygens' principle	reflection	wave number
diffraction	interference	refraction	
dispersion	line broadening		

wave velocity	ultraviolet	magnification	sound barrier
wavelength	radiation	mirror	sound intensity
Young's	X ray	optical image	timbre
experiment	*lasers and masers:*	optics	tone
electromagnetic	laser	periscope	whistler
waves:	maser	prism	white noise
chemiluminescence	optical pumping	projection screen	*other:*
colour	stimulated	projector	aureole
electroluminescence	emission	pupil	Cellini's halo
electromagnetic	*manipulation of light*	relative aperture	halo
radiation	*waves:*	spectroscopy	Michelson–Morley
ether	aberration	stereoscopy	experiment
gamma ray	aperture	*sound waves:*	mirage
infrared radiation	collimator	combination tone	Mössbauer effect
light	critical angle	loudness	Munsell colour
luminescence	diffraction grating	overtone	system
phosphor	diopter	pitch	photoelasticity
phosphorescence	fibre optics	resonance	pleochroism
radiation	Fresnel lens	resonator	Poynting vector
rainbow	holography	shock wave	Stokes lines
spectrum	lens	siren	wave–particle
thermoluminescence	light modulator	sound	duality

Biographies

See Section 10/32 of Part Ten

INDEX: See entries under all of the terms above

Division III.   **The Universe: Galaxies, Stars, the Solar System**
[For Part One headnote see page 21.]

The outlines in the three sections of Division III deal with the subject matter of cosmology and cosmogony, of astronomy, and of astrophysics.

Accounts of the complex instrumentation involved in these disciplines are set forth in Section 723 of Part Seven. Historical and analytical studies of the nature and scope of astronomy and astrophysics are set forth in Section 10/32 of Part Ten.

Section 131.   **The Cosmos**

A. The structure and properties of the universe

   1. Basic data for the universe

      a. The estimated chemical composition of the universe
        [see also 121.D.]

      b. The large-scale structure and behaviour of the universe: evidence that the universe is expanding, Hubble's law and the theory of the red shift

      c. The age of the universe

      d. The clustering of galaxies

      e. Cosmic microwave background radiation

      f. The missing mass problem

      g. Space–time: a four-dimensional continuum used to describe the universe

   2. Cosmological models: theoretical representations of the original behaviour of the universe
     [see E.1., below]

3. The known and postulated components of the universe

    a. Distant galaxies
       [see 132.A.]

    b. The Local Group of galaxies
       [see 132.A.1.c.]

    c. Quasars and related objects, including such hypothetical phenomena as supermassive black holes at the centres of galaxies

    d. Nebulae

    e. Stars and stellar groups
       [see 132.C. and 132.D.]

    f. Planetary systems: solar and extrasolar systems
       [see 133.A.]

B. Gravitation: a universal force of mutual attraction that is postulated as acting between all matter

1. Development of gravitational theory

    a. Early concepts: the Aristotelian viewpoint, contributions of Kepler and Galileo

    b. Newton's law of gravity
       [see also 126.A.3.b.v.]

2. Interpretation of gravity measurements

    a. Potential theory: mathematical representation of the gravitational fields of irregular mass distributions
       [see also 10/22.D.2.c.]

    b. Effects of local mass differences: measurement of small gravity anomalies

3. Modern gravitational theory and its relation to other aspects of physical theory

    a. Field theories of gravity and their general properties and predictions

    b. Gravitational fields and the general theory of relativity: principles and consequences
       [see D.2., below]

4. Acceleration of gravity on the Earth's surface
    [see 212.A.]

5. The gravitational constant, G: methods of measurement, possible variation in time and space

C. Celestial mechanics
    [see also 126.A.]

1. The scope and history of celestial mechanics

2. The two-body problem and perturbations that cause the orbits of planets and satellites to deviate from ellipses

3. The unsolved three-body problem

4. The general n-body problem

D. Properties of the space–time continuum: the astronomical implications of relativity theory

1. The special theory of relativity

    a. Historical background: the search for the ether

    b. Relativity of space and time

    c. Consequences of the special theory

2. The general theory of relativity

    a. Use of relativity to interpret gravitational phenomena

    b. Experimental confirmation of the theory

    c. Implications of general relativity

E. The origin and development of the universe

1. The development of the universe as a whole

    a. Big-bang versus steady-state models of the universe

b. Primordial nucleosynthesis

c. The early universe: extrapolations backward in time to the beginning of the universe

2. The formation and development of components of the universe: galaxies, stars, the solar system
[see also 132.B., 132.D., and 133.A.]

a. The origin and development of galaxies: protogalaxies

b. The formation and development of stars

c. The origin of the solar system

3. Time scale of the universe: dating of significant events in the history of the universe

4. Theories of the possible fate of the universe

Suggested reading in the *Encyclopædia Britannica:*

MACROPAEDIA: Major articles dealing with the cosmos

Analysis and Measurement, Physical and Chemical
Cosmos, The
Gravitation
Physical Sciences, The
Relativity

MICROPAEDIA: Selected entries of reference information

General subjects

cosmology:	*element synthesis:*	free-fall	Lorentz–Fitzgerald
big-bang model	carbon cycle	gravitation	contraction
cosmology	nucleosynthesis	gravitational radius	relativistic mass
cosmos	proton-proton	Newton's law of	relativity
expanding universe	reaction	gravitation	time dilation
Hubble's constant	*extraterrestrial life:*	weight	*other:*
Mach's principle	Green Bank	weightlessness	cosmic ray
Olbers' paradox	equation	*relativity:*	ephemeris
quasar	Ozma, Project	Einstein's mass–	Scorpius X-1
steady-state	*gravitation:*	energy relation	supernova
theory	Cavendish	equivalence	
	experiment	principle	

Biographies

See Section 10/32 of Part Ten

INDEX: See entries under all of the terms above

Section 132.   Galaxies and Stars

A. Galaxies in general

1. Statistical properties

a. Classification of galaxies

b. Observational methods of determining the distances to galaxies

c. Distribution of galaxies

2. Physical properties: size, mass, luminosity, age, composition

3. Structural features

4. Clusters of galaxies

a. Types and distribution

b. Interactions between cluster members

5. Extragalactic radio and X-ray sources

   a. Radio galaxies

   b. X-ray galaxies

   c. Quasars

6. The origin and evolution of the galaxies
   [see also 131.E.2.]

B. The Galaxy: the Milky Way system

   1. Distance determinations in the Galaxy

   2. Stellar velocities: the motions of stars with respect to the Sun, the motion of the Sun with respect to the Local Standard of Rest (LSR)

   3. The stars and star clusters nearest the Sun

   4. The classification of stars according to the Hertzsprung–Russell diagram

   5. The galactic composition

      a. The stellar populations

      b. Emission nebulae: composition and physical characteristics of H II regions

      c. Planetary nebulae

      d. Supernova remnants

      e. Dust clouds

      f. The general interstellar medium: principal components and their distribution throughout the various galactic regions

         i. Grains of interstellar dust

         ii. Interstellar regions of neutral hydrogen (H I regions)

         iii. Interstellar molecules and radicals

      g. Primary cosmic rays

      h. Interstellar magnetic field

   6. Structure and dynamics of the Galaxy

      a. The spatial structure of the Galaxy: the dimensions of the Galaxy

      b. Regions of the Galaxy: the nucleus, the central bulge, the dish, the spiral arms, the spherical component, the massive halo

      c. The magnetic field of the Galaxy: its origin and its effects on cosmic rays, radio waves, and light

      d. The rotation of the Galaxy: the differential rotation of stars, gas about the galactic centre

   7. The evolution of the Galaxy
      [see also 131.E.2.]

      a. Hydromagnetic and gravitational theories of the formation of spiral structure

      b. Chemical evolution: the problem of the distribution of heavy elements

      c. Star formation: theories concerning the gravitational condensation of galactic dust and gas clouds

C. Star clusters and stellar associations

   1. Globular clusters: systems containing many thousands to a million old stars in a symmetrical, roughly spherical form

   2. Open clusters: systems containing about a dozen to hundreds of stars, usually in an unsymmetrical arrangement

   3. Stellar associations: loose groupings containing dozens to a few hundred stars of similar spectoal type and common origin

   4. Relationship of clusters to the Galaxy: the formation and dispersion of clusters and their locations in the Galaxy

   5. Clusters in external galaxies

D. Stars

  1. The identification and nomenclature of the stars

    a. The celestial sphere and celestial coordinate systems

    b. The constellations and other sky divisions

    c. Star names and designations

    d. Modern star maps and catalogs

  2. Observable stellar characteristics

    a. Stellar positions and motions

    b. The apparent brightness or apparent luminosity of the stars: the UBV and other systems

    c. Stellar spectra
      [see also 111.C.]

  3. Derived, or calculated, stellar characteristics

    a. Intrinsic stellar brightness: absolute magnitudes, total luminosities

    b. Stellar masses

    c. Stellar diameters

    d. Stellar temperatures

    e. The average characteristics of main-sequence, or dwarf, stars

  4. Stellar variability

    a. Geometric variables; *e.g.,* eclipsing binaries

    b. Intrinsic variables

        i. Pulsating stars; *e.g.,* Cepheid, RR Lyrae, and Beta Canis Majoris variables

        ii. Explosive variables; *e.g.,* novae, supernovae, and novalike variables

  5. Statistics of stars

    a. Correlations between luminosity, spectrum, mass, and radius: the Hertzsprung–Russell diagram and other relations

    b. Statistics of binary star systems

    c. Statistics of special types of stars

  6. Stellar structure

    a. Stellar atmospheres

    b. Internal structure of stars

  7. Stellar evolution
    [see also 131.E.2.]

    a. The life history of a typical star

        i. Formation of a protostar by gravitational contraction

        ii. Attainment of the main sequence

        iii. Evolution away from the main sequence

        iv. Estimates of stellar ages

    b. Formation of chemical elements in stars

    c. Probable fates of stars: white dwarfs, neutron stars, black holes

---

Suggested reading in the *Encyclopædia Britannica:*

MACROPAEDIA: Major articles dealing with galaxies and stars

  Cosmos, The
  Galaxies
  Nebula
  Physical Sciences, The
  Stars and Star Clusters

MICROPAEDIA: Selected entries of reference information

General subjects

astronomical catalogs and instruments:
AG catalog
Almagest
armillary sphere
astronomical map
Carte du ciel
celestial globe
Henry Draper Catalogue
Hertzsprung–Russell diagram
Messier catalog
New General Catalogue of Nebulae and Clusters of Stars
star catalog

constellations:
Aquarius
Aries
Cancer
Capricornus
constellation
Crux
Gemini
Leo
Orion
Pisces
Sagittarius
Scorpius
Taurus
Ursa Major
Virgo

galaxies:
Andromeda Galaxy
Cygnus A
galaxy
Maffei I and II
Magellanic Cloud
Milky Way Galaxy
Seyfert galaxy
Virgo A

nebulae:
Crab Nebula
Cygnus Loop
Horsehead Nebula
Lagoon Nebula
nebula
North American Nebula
Orion Nebula
Ring Nebula
30 Doradus
Trifid Nebula

radio and X-ray emission:
cosmic ray
forbidden lines
pulsar
radio source
red shift
Sagittarius A
Scorpius X-1
synchrotron radiation
21-centimetre radiation

star pairs and groups:
binary star
eclipsing variable star
Pleiades
star cluster
stellar association

stars:
Algol
Alpha Centauri
Barnard's star
Betelgeuse
Bethlehem, Star of
colour index
Eta Carinae
Fomalhaut
Harvard classification system
Kepler's Nova
magnitude
Mira Ceti
Sirius
star
Sun
Tycho's Nova

stellar evolution:
black hole
carbon cycle
Chandrasekhar limit
giant star
neutron star
nucleosynthesis
Population I and II

proton–proton cycle
white dwarf star

variable stars:
Cepheid variable
eclipsing variable star
flare star
light curve
long-period variable star
nova
supernova
T Tauri star
U Geminorum star
variable star

other:
degenerate gas
galactic coordinate
H I region
H II region
infrared source
interstellar medium
light-year
limb darkening
parallax
parsec

Biographies

See Section 10/32 of Part Ten

INDEX: See entries under all of the terms above

Section 133. **The Solar System**

A. A survey of the solar system

1. The Sun
[see B., below]

2. The major planets of the solar system, their surfaces and atmospheres, their satellites
[see also C., D., and E., below]

3. Other constituents of the solar system

a. Minor planets, or asteroids

b. Comets

c. Meteoroids, meteors, and meteorites

d. The interplanetary medium

4. Regularities of the solar system: the distances of the planets from the Sun, the distribution of natural satellites

5. Interactions among various bodies in the solar system: gravitational perturbations, actual physical encounters

6. Theories of the origin of the solar system: origin by an orderly process, origin by catastrophe
[see also 131.E.2.c.]

B. The Sun

1. The Sun's surface layers and their features: the quiet Sun

a. Solar data derived from observations of the photosphere, the visible luminous surface of the Sun

b. The chromosphere, the relatively transparent layer that forms a transition zone between the Sun's photosphere and corona: the flash spectrum, spicules, supergranulation

c. The corona, the luminous, high-temperature, rarefied gas envelope of the Sun: form, structure, physical properties; the solar wind

2. Solar features that occur with increased frequency during the active phase of the solar cycle: the active Sun

a. Centres of activity: areas of localized strong magnetic fields at the Sun's surface

b. Sunspots: their physical nature, the sunspot cycle of about 11 years

c. Other features; *e.g.,* faculae, prominences, flares, coronal condensations

3. The solar interior: energy generation, the evolution of the Sun
[see also 132.D.7.]

4. Solar radiation, including light, radio waves, and particles

5. Solar-terrestrial relationships and interactions

C. The planets and their satellites

1. The terrestrial planets

a. Mercury

b. Venus

c. Earth
[see D., below]

d. Mars

2. The minor planets, or asteroids
[see A.3.a., above]

3. The giant planets and Pluto

a. Jupiter

b. Saturn

c. Uranus

d. Neptune

e. Pluto

D. The Earth as a planet

1. The distance of the Earth from the Sun: the astronomical unit and solar parallax

2. The orbital motion of the Earth around the Sun and the rotation of the Earth on its axis: the year, the day, the precession of the equinoxes
[see also E.7.a., below]

3. Effects of the Earth's orbital position and speed on astronomical observations

a. Astronomical parallax

b. Aberration of light

4. The Earth's magnetism, temperature, and other physical properties
[see 212]

5. The structure and composition of the Earth's interior
[see 213]

6. The origin of the Earth, its atmosphere, hydrosphere, and surface features
[see 232 and 241]

E. The Moon

1. The shape, radius, mean density, and varying brightness of the Moon

2. The motion of the Moon

    a. The apparent motion: the month, or sidereal and synodic periods of the Moon; optical and physical librations
    [see 7.a.ii., below]

    b. The actual motion

3. The mass and gravitational field of the Moon

    a. Underlying theory: basic gravitational properties of the Moon

    b. Discovery of lunar mascons: gravity anomalies on the Moon

4. The physical nature of the Moon

    a. Observations from Earth and from space vehicles: results of remote lunar photography, manned lunar landings, and close-up photography
    [see also 738.C.]

    b. The lunar surface features: craters, lineaments (*e.g.,* mare ridges, the lunar grid system, rilles), temporary or transient features

    c. Theories of origin of the Moon's surface features: the volcanic and impact theories

5. The origin and evolution of the Moon

    a. Probable development of the Moon's orbit

    b. Evidence from the composition and physical properties of the Moon

6. The chemical nature of the Moon

    a. Surface composition: findings of the chemical analysis of lunar rock samples

    b. Possible zonal variations of the interior

7. The Sun–Earth–Moon system

    a. Relative motions of the Sun, Earth, and Moon

        i. The geometry of the Sun–Earth–Moon system: the celestial equator, the apparent motion of the Sun along the ecliptic, the inclination of the Earth's axis to its orbit

        ii. Motions of the Sun–Earth–Moon system as the astronomical basis of chronology: the day, month, and year; the Sothic cycle, Metonic cycle, and other complex cycles

    b. Eclipses of the Sun and Moon

    c. Tides in the Earth and in the Moon
    [see also 222.G.3.]

Suggested reading in the *Encyclopædia Britannica:*

MACROPAEDIA: Major articles dealing with the solar system. See also Section 211 of Part Two

Calendar
Earth, The: Its Properties, Composition, and Structure
Eclipse, Occultation, and Transit
Physical Sciences, The
Solar System, The

MICROPAEDIA: Selected entries of reference information

General subjects

calendars:	Dionysian period	Gregorian calendar	Julian calendar
Aztec calendar	Egyptian calendar	intercalation	Julian period
calendar	French republican	international date	leap year
Chinese calendar	calendar	line	lunar calendar
day	Greek calendar	Jewish calendar	Mayan calendar

Biographies

See Section 10/32 of Part Ten

INDEX: See entries under all of the terms above

Introduction to Part Two:
The Great Globe Itself

by Peter J. Wyllie

We all have a sense of awareness and appreciation of the Earth; we all admire the scenery. One of the rewards of studying and understanding the Earth is the development of this sense to a greater extent. This development brings us closer to nature, closer to an awareness of some transcendental power, closer to God if we choose to define God in these terms. To "commune with nature" is to seek peace, but of course the Earth is not always peaceful and benevolent; sometimes it is powerful and savage. Even cities, the culmination of man's domination of the landscape, are not immune to the ravages of nature. They have been devastated by floods, wracked and ripped by tornadoes and hurricanes, ruined by ash or lava from volcanoes, and demolished by earthquakes. These events, too, we wish to understand.

Man's appreciation of the Earth begins with physical contact. This immediate experience of the senses is followed by the spiritual desire and need to understand where the Earth and its human observers came from, and why. The third stage of appreciation comes from scientific analysis and interpretation. Before we examine the relationship between man and the Earth in more detail, we should consider our position in the solar system and the universe.

Human civilization has developed and flourished in a small niche in space. Our home is perched on the surface of a sphere, enormous to us but tiny compared to the universe, that spins around its axis once each day while moving at a fantastic speed around the Sun, completing an orbit once each year. Although normally unaware of it, we too are spinning and moving at the same speed as the Earth, but we are held securely on the surface by the gravitational attraction of the mass of rocks beneath us.

The Sun, a huge globe of burning gas, provides the energy that fuels the activities and processes of our immediate environment, the boundary layer between the rocky surface of the Earth and the fluid envelope of air and water that separates the Earth from the starkness of space. The air and water nurture life and simultaneously protect it from the potentially damaging radiation and particles that approach the Earth from other parts of the solar system and beyond.

A view of the Earth from space differs markedly from what we see from within our own restricted environment at the Earth's surface. From where we stand, it appears that the Sun, the Moon, and the stars are moving in great arcs around the Earth, and it was once believed that this was the way of the universe. Man on his world was surely the centre of all things. But we know now that this is only a relative picture; although the Moon does orbit the Earth, the Earth–Moon system moves around the Sun, which is itself speeding through the universe.

We exist because the Earth exists, and we claim the Earth as our own by referring to it as Mother Earth, the universal provider. The Earth provides all of our material needs and satisfies some of our spiritual needs: "I will lift up mine eyes unto the hills, from whence cometh my help." A day in the mountains, at the seashore, or in the countryside sharpens that sense of awareness of the Earth which was compared above with an awareness of God.

Since he first appeared on Earth, man has wondered at nature's awesome beauty and trembled at its indomitable power. The dread engendered by the physical experience of nature on the rampage, in storms, floods, or earthquakes, has shaped the development of primitive religions. Mystical or sacred attributes were assigned to natural objects and phenomena, and ceremonies were devised to honour and placate the unknown powers. Modern man has become increasingly insulated from his natural surroundings, partly because he is separated from them by masses of concrete, partly because scientific investigation tends to dispel the mystery of nature. This is not to imply that no problems remain to be solved, but we have learned enough to be reasonably sure that all are ultimately explicable in terms of rational science. Therefore, we no longer feel the need to populate the sky, mountains, trees, and winds with gods, spirits, and souls. But we can still enjoy the sensuous and spiritual appreciation of the Earth and retain or rediscover the intimacy with our natural surroundings that was experienced by primitive man.

One of the appealing aspects of Earth study is that wherever we go, our favourite subject is right there with us. There is always something new to be seen, to be admired, or to be examined in detail. While traveling in a commercial airliner, a meteorologist can examine the upper portions of the clouds as a change from his normal ground-based view and can track the flight right through the fronts and the high- and low-pressure regions charted on the newspaper weather map in his lap. An oceanographer flying over the coastline can see at a glance the large-scale patterns in the waves rolling shoreward and the effect of coastal prominences on these patterns. A geologist peering through the plane window can examine the distribution of hills and valleys laid out below him, gaining a bird's-eye view to supplement the pattern of features that he had previously seen only on maps. These pleasures are not reserved for the professional Earth scientist. Anyone can observe the Earth and Earth processes in action, almost anywhere.

Man is a curious species; he needs to know how and why things happen. The simple, visual pictures of nature are beautiful, awe-inspiring, and on occasion terrifying, but they can be more satisfying if they invoke a series of additional images. Just as one's appreciation of any work of art is enhanced by knowing something of the artist and his position in art history, so one's appreciation of nature's pictures is enhanced by knowing something about natural history. For a full appreciation of the splendour of mountain peaks rising abruptly from the plains, reaching for the puffs of cloud that ride above them, we need to know something of the processes that raise mountains— or were they always there? We need to know something of the winds that carry moisture from the oceans to the skies, because we see that the clouds come, change their shapes, and then disappear. We can gain a great deal by learning a little about the scientific approach to appreciation of the Earth. And it is not at all difficult for the nonprofessional to read about and to understand many of the necessary concepts.

Two of the most troublesome concepts are time and size—dimensions that distinguish the Earth sciences from any other Earth-bound subject. It is very difficult for us to grasp the meaning of the statement that the Earth formed 4,600,000,000 years ago. Similarly, the enormous volume of water in the oceans or the volume of rocks in a mountain range almost defy comprehension. We have been considering the Earth and scenery as it is exposed to us at the present. But when we study the Earth, we realize that the present scenery is merely a transient feature in the immense span of geological time. Early students of the Earth were hampered by the belief that the Earth was only a few thousand years old. Many of them were seeking answers to two recurrent questions that we find throughout human history. How and when was the Earth formed? How and when was man formed? Attempts to answer these questions are responsible for many myths and religions in various cultures, both ancient and modern.

In the early part of the 19th century the study and interpretation of rocks led geologists to conclude that the Earth must be of far greater antiquity than the age implied by a literal interpretation of the Bible. They realized that the layers of rock now exposed at the surface contain records of the history of the Earth during the times that each layer was formed. One major branch of the Earth sciences is devoted to the discovery, translation, and interpretation of the "record of the rocks." Many rock layers enclose fossils, and these remnants of animals and plants serve as illustrations in the historical book of nature, making it possible to trace the development and changes of species through time.

Fossil hunting has been a popular pastime for many generations. With a little experience and a little knowledge, an amateur fossil hunter can add interpretation to his discoveries. From a few fossil shells and corals in a limestone, he can reconstruct in his mind's eye the whole flourishing community of life that once existed on a coral reef, now frozen into the rock record. A piece of coal, with fossil imprints of leaves, ferns, and other plant remains from which the coal was formed, can conjure up a picture of a luxuriant swamp of 300,000,000 years ago, populated by strange beasts long since vanished from the Earth. The history of the Earth, the evolution of life, and the origin of man, at least in part, are preserved in the rocks. It is here that fundamentalists still supporting "creationism" will find much evidence for the evolution of life forms, if they care to examine it. This aspect of Earth study has almost universal appeal. Earth history and human history overlap in archaeology, and the records of early civilizations exposed in excavation sites always excite public curiosity.

The scientific approach to the appreciation of nature informs us that the key to interpretation of the past history of the Earth from the record of the rocks lies in processes occurring at the present time. These processes have been grouped into great cycles. Two of the most important are the hydrologic cycle, concerned with the circulation of water, and the mountain-building cycle.

The oceans constitute a vast reservoir for the hydrologic cycle. The atmosphere and the oceans are in constant motion, driven by the energy from the Sun and the rotation of the Earth. Masses of humid air, carrying water that has evaporated from sun-drenched tropical oceans, migrate to cooler latitudes, where the water is precipitated as rain or snow and thus returned to the ocean reservoir either directly or indirectly, over or through the ground. The moving air masses and ocean currents bring to the continental masses rain or drought, heat or cold, making them hospitable, habitable, or uninhabitable for human colonies. Minor changes in atmospheric circulation have converted fertile plains to barren deserts and caused major changes in the development of ancient civilizations.

The hydrologic cycle shapes our local environment. The features that we know collectively as scenery are produced mainly by flowing water, although ice, wind, and solar energy also contribute. The force of gravity and the rivers together carry the products of weathering downhill to the ocean reservoir. The average rate at which the surface of the land is being worn down and the land dispersed into the oceans is a trivial 1.5 inches per 1,000 years, but the dimensions of geological time gives significance to small numbers. At this rate, all of the continents would be worn down to sea level within 20,000,000 years. This means that during the 4,600,000,000 years since the Earth was formed, the continents could have been worn down to sea level at least 200 times. By now there should be no land rising above sea level, but we still see high mountains.

The mountains exist and persist because the effects of the hydrologic cycle are offset by the mountain-building cycle. Forces within the Earth cause large regions of the surface to rise very slowly, imperceptibly in human terms. Imperceptible, that is, until an earthquake signals an abrupt movement in the continuing process of mountain building. While some parts of the Earth rise, other regions sink. This slow rhythm has been termed "the pulse of the Earth." Although we do not understand the details of what is happening within the Earth, we are now confident that internal forces are responsible for shaping the major features of the Earth's surface, such as the distinction between continents and ocean basins and the persistence of mountain ranges on the land and beneath the ocean. The detailed sculpture of the surface results from the conflict between the mountain-building cycle and the hydrologic cycle.

The internal forces do more than cause the land surface to rise and fall; they cause the land to move sideways as well. It is now generally believed by most scientists that the continents drift. There is persuasive evidence that the surface of the Earth is covered by a small number of very large shell-like plates, about 60 miles thick, across which the continents are scattered rather like logs frozen into the ice on a lake. The rigid shells of rock slide over the Earth's interior, carrying the continents with them and grinding against each other along their edges like ice floes. The plate boundaries are sites of geological activity: earthquakes and volcanoes are concentrated along them. Because of these movements, supercontinents have been rifted apart, and ocean basins have opened, expanded, and closed again as continents collided. Collisions of continents have thrust up great mountain ranges such as the Himalayas. The continents are still drifting at rates of an inch or two per year: the Atlantic Ocean is increasing in size, and the Pacific Ocean is becoming smaller. Most people are fascinated by the theory of continental drift. The theory is not only aesthetically pleasing but also has practical applications.

What stokes the subterranean fires that drive the Earth's engine, causing continental drift, mountain building, volcanic eruptions, and earthquakes? We have no satisfactory answer to this question, but we do know that an enormous amount of energy is involved in the activity along the plate margins. One major earthquake releases more energy than a hydrogen bomb. Modern man is a powerful animal, thanks largely to his exploitation of the Earth for material and energy, and he dominates the landscape like no species before him. He feels reasonably secure in his command of the environment while contemplating the urban scene, because the landscape is largely a product of his industry, and it is clearly subservient to his wishes and his computer-operated control panels. But when the Earth releases a minute fraction of its internal energy in a major earthquake, man becomes helpless. All control is lost while the surface of the Earth rises and falls in solid waves.

Man cannot live in harmony with his environment during an earthquake. It has become clear, however, that he must learn to do so at other times if he is to avoid the dire predictions of those who evaluate such factors as projected world populations, the material and energy resources of the Earth, projected rates of consumption of these resources, and the volume and toxicity of waste materials discarded. We live in a restricted environment with finite space and resources, and we have become a force producing major modifications in the environment at rates very rapid compared with normal rates of Earth evolution. Social decisions about the continued exploitation of the Earth should be made with full information about the problems, and social decisions are based on votes, in theory at least. This alone is sufficient reason for any intelligent person to inform himself about the Earth, quite apart from the fascination of the subject, because his future depends upon it.

Part Two. The Earth

Several points about the relations of this part to other parts should be noted. The consideration here of the Earth's physicochemical properties presupposes the physical and chemical knowledge and theories set forth in Part One. Knowledge of the Earth is in turn presupposed by Parts Three, Four, and Five, which are Life on Earth, Human Life, and Human Society, respectively. The several Earth sciences have themselves been the objects of historical and analytical studies concerned with their nature, scope, methods, and interrelations. These studies are set forth in Section 10/33 of Part Ten. The instrumentation used in the Earth sciences is dealt with in Section 723 of Part Seven.

Division I. **The Earth's Properties, Structure, and Composition**

The outlines in the four sections of Division I treat the Earth as a planet; the Earth's physical properties; the structure and composition of the Earth's interior; and the Earth's constituent minerals and rocks.

Section 211. **The Planet Earth**

A. The orbital motions of the Earth

  1. The revolution of the Earth about the Sun, the rotation of the Earth on its axis

  2. Forces and dynamic effects related to the rotation of the Earth

    a. The Coriolis force

    b. The effects of centrifugal force

    c. Tidal friction

B. The figure of the Earth

  1. The conventional definition of the figure of the Earth: the geoid

  2. The development of improved approximations to the Earth's size and shape

  3. The world geodetic system: the measurement of geodetic parameters

    a. The astrogravimetric method

    b. Satellite measurements

    c. Correlation of data from different methods

  4. International reference systems: standard reference figures, precision measurements and their implications concerning global structure and processes

Section 212.   The Earth's Physical Properties

A. The Earth's gravitational field
[see also 131.B.]

  1. Characteristics of the terrestrial field

  2. Measurement of gravitational acceleration
  [see also 723.D.2.d.]

  3. Interpretation of gravity data: inferences about the Earth's interior

   a. Isostasy: the approximate balance between the elevation of the Earth's surface and the density of the rocks below

   b. Gravity anomalies

B. The Earth's magnetic field

  1. Measurement and representation of magnetic fields

  2. Sources and characteristics of the Earth's main magnetic field

  3. Variations in the main magnetic field, including polarity reversals, magnetic storms, magnetospheric substorms, and magnetic pulsations

C. The Earth's electrical properties
[see also 127.B.]

  1. Currents produced by the motion of charged particles in the Earth's ionosphere
  [see also 221.A.3.b]

  2. Electrical conductivity and dielectric behaviour of the Earth's rocks and minerals

  3. Currents induced by magnetic field variations, currents generated by the Earth's core

D. The Earth's thermal properties
[see also 124.A.4.c.]

  1. Sources of the Earth's heat
  [see also 112.C.5.]

  2. Transmission of heat from the Earth's interior to its surface: thermal conductivity and gradients, heat flow data

  3. Geological aspects of heat flow: convection currents in the Earth, rock metamorphism, and mountain building

  4. Surface manifestations of heat flow: volcanoes, hot springs, geysers, and related phenomena

E. The mechanical properties of the Earth

   1. The fundamental mechanical properties of the Earth's body and the indirect evidence used to determine them

   2. Nature of deformable media: stress and strain, models of the stress-strain behaviour of materials, seismic waves
     [see also 126.C. and F.]

   3. The basic internal mechanical properties of the Earth

   4. The Earth's departures from spherical symmetry: oblateness, lateral variations associated with crustal structure, isostasy and its effects
     [see also 211.A.2.b.]

   5. Anelasticity in the Earth

   6. Response of the Earth to stresses of long duration

F. Physical properties of Earth materials

   1. Volumetric properties: rock density and porosity

   2. Mechanical properties
     [see also 126.C.,D., and F.]

   3. Thermal properties: specific heat and thermal conductivity, thermal expansion and rock melting

   4. Magnetic and electrical properties
     [see also C.2., above]

   5. Hydraulic properties: porosity and permeability, the capacity to store and transmit fluids

   6. Optical properties: colour, lustre

G. The deformation of materials in the Earth's crust

   1. Stress and strain of rocks

     a. Response to stress

     b. Elastic and plastic deformation

   2. Folding of rocks

     a. Tectonic folding

     b. Foliation, lineation

     c. Nappes (large rock sheets thrust over other rock formations)

     d. Salt domes and other diapiric structures
       [see also 724.B.1.b.]

     e. Nontectonic folding; *e.g.,* slumping of recently deposited sediments

   3. Fracture in rocks: joints, faults

   4. Structural interference: the superposition of strains produced by the tectonic events of different ages

   5. The deformation of ice in sheets and glaciers
     [see also 222.A.3.a.]

Suggested reading in the *Encyclopædia Britannica:*

MACROPAEDIA: Major articles dealing with the Earth's physical properties

   Earth, The: Its Properties, Composition, and Structure
   Minerals and Rocks
   Volcanism

MICROPAEDIA: Selected entries of reference information

General subjects

continental drift	dynamo theory	Earth tide	fault
dipolar hypothesis	Earth	earthquake	fold

geosyncline	plate tectonics	seafloor spreading
gravitation	polar wandering	hypothesis
isostasy	remanent	telluric current
orogeny	magnetism	volcanism

Biographies

See Section 10/33 of Part Ten

INDEX: See entries under all of the terms above

Section 213.   The Structure and Composition of the Earth's Interior

A. The Earth's concentric layers

   1. Physical properties and zonal structure of the Earth
[see also 212]

   2. The basic divisions of the solid Earth

     a. The crust: the Earth's outer layer, which may be differentiated into continental and oceanic crust

     b. The Mohorovičić discontinuity: the zone that separates crust from mantle

     c. The mantle: the layer between crust and core that comprises the bulk of the Earth's volume

     d. The core: the Earth's innermost region, thought to be molten liquid except for a solid inner portion

   3. The development of the Earth's structure and composition
[see 241.A.]

B. Earthquakes: sources of seismic waves within the Earth

   1. Causes of earthquakes

   2. Distribution of earthquakes

   3. Magnitude, motion, and energy of earthquakes
[see also 126.C. and 128.A.]

   4. Seismic measurements and their interpretation
[see also 723.F.6.]

C. Distribution of elements in the Earth's core, mantle, and crust
[see 214.C.]

D. The indirect geophysical and geochemical evidence used to infer the structure and composition of the Earth's interior
[see also 212.E.]

   1. Geophysical evidence, mainly from earthquake analyses
[see also 212.E.]

     a. Seismic wave velocities

     b. Density distribution

   2. Geochemical evidence

     a. Investigations of geochemical equilibria at high temperatures and pressures: phase transitions in the Earth's interior

     b. The composition and mineralogy of meteorites that may correspond to rocks forming the Earth's interior
[see also 133.D.5.]

     c. Evidence from crustal igneous rocks that are derived from the upper mantle; *e.g.*, andesite lava flows, peridotite and eclogite inclusions in lava flows and some igneous rocks

---

Suggested reading in the *Encyclopædia Britannica*:

MACROPAEDIA: Major articles dealing with the structure and composition of the Earth's interior

   Earth, The: Its Properties, Composition, and Structure
   Earthquakes

Section 214.   **The Earth's Constituent Minerals and Rocks**

A. The mineral constituents of the Earth

    1. The chemical composition, internal structure, and morphology of minerals

    2. The physical properties of minerals: cleavage; hardness; tenacity; specific gravity; magnetic, optical, and radioactive properties

    3. Classification of minerals in terms of crystal structure and chemical composition

        a. The principal nonsilicate minerals

            i. Native elements

            ii. Sulfides and sulfarsenides

            iii. Sulfosalts

            iv. Oxides and hydroxides

            v. Halides

            vi. Carbonates

            vii. Nitrates

            viii. Borates

            ix. Sulfates

            x. Phosphates

        b. The silicate minerals

            i. Silicate structure and composition: the basic structural unit, the silicon-oxygen tetrahedron

            ii. Isolated and double tetrahedral group silicates

            iii. Ring silicates

            iv. Chain silicates

            v. Sheet silicates

            vi. Framework silicates

    4. The occurrence of minerals in nature

        a. The major rock-forming mineral groups

            i. The olivines; *e.g.,* forsterite, fayalite

            ii. The pyroxenes; *e.g.,* augite, jadeite

            iii. The amphiboles; *e.g.,* hornblende, tremolite

            iv. The micas; *e.g.,* muscovite, biotite

            v. The feldspars; *e.g.,* orthoclase, albite

            vi. The feldspathoids; *e.g.,* nepheline, leucite

            vii. The silica minerals; *e.g.,* quartz, tridymite

            viii. The clay minerals; *e.g.,* kaolinite, illite

      ix. The carbonates; *e.g.,* calcite, dolomite
         [see A.3.a.vi., above]

      x. The garnets; *e.g.,* almandine, pyrope

      xi. Other major rock-forming minerals; *e.g.,* magnetite, pyrite

  b. The occurrence of mineral associations and phase equilibrium

    i. In igneous and metamorphic rocks

    ii. In sedimentary rocks and precipitates

    iii. In the Moon, planets, and meteorites
      [see also 133.C., 133.E.6.]

  c. Ore deposits: concentrations of metals and metalliferous minerals
    [see also 724.C.3.]

  d. Minerals of gem quality

B. Rocks and other constituents of the Earth's crust

  1. Igneous rocks

    a. Properties of igneous rocks: composition, texture, and structure

    b. Classification of igneous rocks

    c. Formation of igneous rocks: magmas
      [see also 212.D.4.]

    d. Distribution and abundance of igneous rocks

    e. Principal families of igneous rocks

      i. The intrusive igneous rocks that result when magma cools and solidifies below the surface of the Earth; *e.g.,* granite, gabbro, diorite

      ii. The extrusive igneous rocks that form from magma that erupts at the surface of the Earth; *e.g.,* basalt, rhyolite, andesite

      iii. The pyroclastic igneous rocks that form from deposits of explosive volcanic eruptions; *e.g.,* pumice, tuff, scoria

  2. Sedimentary rocks

    a. Properties of sedimentary rocks: texture and mineralogical and geochemical composition

    b. Classification systems: clastic, nonclastic

    c. Sedimentary structures

    d. Sedimentary environments: marine, nonmarine

    e. Principal types of sedimentary rocks

      i. Conglomerates, breccias, tillites, and other heterogeneous clastic rocks

      ii. Sandstones: arenites and wackes

      iii. Mudrocks, including shales

      iv. Limestones and dolomites

      v. Siliceous rocks

      vi. Phosphorites

      vii. Evaporites
        [see also 724.B.1.b.]

      viii. Iron-rich sedimentary rocks

      ix. Organic-rich sedimentary rocks
        [see 5., below]

    f. Distribution of sedimentary rocks through time

  3. Metamorphic rocks

    a. Metamorphic variables: temperature, pressure, and rock composition

    b. Textural and structural features

    c. Origin of metamorphic rocks

    d. Rocks of the principal facies

    e. Distribution of metamorphic rocks

  4. The rock associations formed in different environments of the Earth's crust

    a. In the oceanic regions: basaltic lavas, reef limestones, abyssal sediments of the deep oceans

    b. In the stable continental regions: conglomerates, sandstones, evaporites, coal measures

    c. In the continental borderlands: sandstones, shales, limestones

    d. In the island arcs: andesite and spilite lavas, ultrabasic intrusive rocks, graywackes, shales

    e. In the major mountain ranges: regionally metamorphosed rocks, granitic batholiths, early-stage basalts and peridotites, late-stage andesite lavas

    f. In the piedmont regions that are adjacent to mountain ranges: gabbros, basalts, arkoses

  5. Fossil fuels

    a. Coals
      [see also 724.B.1.b. and C.2.]

    b. Petroleum
      [see also 122.G.1.a. and 724.B.2. and C.1.]

    c. Tar sands and oil shales
      [see also 724.B.2. and C.1.]

    d. Natural gas
      [see also 122.G.1.a. and 724.B.2.]

C. Occurrence of the elements in the Earth and its envelope
  [see also 121.D.1.]

  1. Core

  2. Mantle (depleted and undepleted)

  3. Crust: igneous, sedimentary, and metamorphic rocks; soils

  4. Hydrosphere
    [see 222.B. and C.]

  5. Atmosphere
    [see 221.A.]

  6. Biosphere: selective concentration of elements by plants and animals

  7. The geochemical cycle: the primary geochemical differentiation of the Earth; the migration of elements throughout the atmosphere, hydrosphere, and solid Earth

---

Suggested reading in the *Encyclopædia Britannica:*

MACROPAEDIA: Major articles dealing with the Earth's constituent minerals and rocks

    Chemical Elements
    Earth, The: Its Properties, Composition, and Structure
    Fuels, Fossil
    Minerals and Rocks
    Volcanism

MICROPAEDIA: Selected entries of reference information

General subjects

borate minerals:	malachite	analcime	nepheline
borate mineral	nahcolite	anorthite	orthoclase
borax	rhodochrosite	aventurine	peristerite
ulexite	siderite	celsian	perthite
carbonate minerals:	*feldspar and*	feldspar	plagioclase
aragonite	*feldspathoid*	feldspathoid	sanidine
bastnaesite	*minerals:*	labradorite	scapolite
calcite	adularia	leucite	sodalite
carbonate mineral	albite	microcline	wairakite
magnesite	alkali feldspar	micropegmatite	

halide minerals:
  calomel
  cerargyrite
  fluorite
  halide mineral
  halite
igneous rocks and
  formations:
    acid and basic
      rocks
    amygdule
    andesite
    anorthosite
    aplite
    basalt
    basanite
    batholith
    dacite
    diabase
    dike
    diorite
    dunite
    felsic rock
    gabbro
    granite
    granodiorite
    greisen
    igneous rock
    kimberlite
    laccolith
    lamprophyre
    latite
    leucitite
    mafic rock
    magma
    monzonite
    myrmekite
    nephelinesyenite
    nephelinite
    obsidian
    pegmatite
    peridotite
    perlite
    phonolite
    picrite
    pitchstone
    pumice
    pyroxenite
    rhyolite
    roof pendant
    sill
    spilite
    syenite
    tachylyte
    teschenite
    trachyte
    tuff
    volcanic glass
    xenolith
metamorphic rocks
  and their formation:
    amphibolite facies
    anatexis
    cataclastite

charnockite
eclogite
epidote-amphibolite
  facies
glaucophane schist
  facies
gneiss
granitization
granulite facies
greenschist facies
hornfels facies
induration
marble
metamorphic rock
metamorphism
metatexis
migmatite
phyllite
sanidinite facies
schist
skarn
slate
zeolitic facies
mineral fuels and
  deposits:
    anthracite
    asphalt
    asphaltite
    bitumen
    bituminous coal
    brown coal
    cannel coal
    coal
    crude oil
    gas reservoir
    Gilsonite
    lignite
    maceral
    natural gas
    oil shale
    ozokerite
    peat
    petroleum
    petroleum trap
    pitch lake
    pyrobitumen
    shale oil
    subbituminous
      coal
    tar sand
    wet gas
molybdate and
  tungstate minerals:
    molybdate
      and tungstate
      minerals
    scheelite
    wolframite
    wulfenite
native elements:
  diamond
  electrum
  graphite

industrial
  diamond
native element
oxide and hydroxide
  minerals:
    anatase
    bauxite
    boehmite
    cassiterite
    chromite
    chrysoberyl
    columbite
    corundum
    cuprite
    emery
    gibbsite
    goethite
    gossan
    hematite
    ilmenite
    limonite
    magnetite
    oxide mineral
    pitchblende
    pyrochlore
    pyrolusite
    ruby
    ruby spinel
    rutile
    sapphire
    spinel
    thorianite
    uraninite
phosphate minerals:
  amblygonite
  apatite
  arsenate mineral
  carnotite
  descloizite
  erythrite
  fluorapatite
  lazulite
  mimetite
  phosphate mineral
  pyromorphite
  scorodite
  triphylite
  turquoise
  vanadate mineral
  variscite
sedimentary rocks
  and their formation:
    arkose
    banded-iron
      formation
    black shale
    breccia
    cementation
    conglomerate
    diagenesis
    diatomaceous earth
    dolomite
    evaporite
    flysch

geode
gravel
graywacke
hälleflinta
limestone
lithification
loess
lutite
marl
molasse
nodule
oölite
phosphorite
porcellanite
quartzite
sand
sandstone
sedimentary facies
sedimentary rock
shale
siliceous rock
silt
siltstone
stratification
stylolite
subgraywacke
tillite
silica minerals:
  agate
  amethyst
  aventurine
  carnelian
  chalcedony
  chert and flint
  chrysotile
  citrine
  coesite
  cristobalite
  fulgurite
  jasper
  lechatelierite
  moss agate
  onyx
  opal
  phillipsite
  quartz
  rock crystal
  rose quartz
  sard and sardonyx
  sepiolite
  serpentine
  silica
  silica mineral
  smoky quartz
  tridymite
silicate minerals:
  actinolite
  aegirine
  almandine
  amphibole
  andalusite
  andradite
  augite
  beryl

biotite
chlorite
chrysotile
clay mineral
cordierite
diopside
emerald
enstatite
epidote
forsterite-fayalite
    series
garnet
glauconite
glaucophane
grossular
hornblende
humite
jadeite
kaolinite
kyanite
lepidolite
melilite
mica
monticellite
montmorillonite
muscovite
nephrite
olivine
orthopyroxene
peridot
phenakite
phlogopite
pyrophyllite
pyroxene

rhodonite
riebeckite
serpentine
silicate mineral
staurolite
talc
topaz
tourmaline
vermiculite
vesuvianite
wollastonite
zircon
zoisite
sulfate minerals:
    alunite
    anhydrite
    barite
    celestite
    gypsum
    halotrichite
    sulfate mineral
sulfide minerals:
    antimonide
    argentite
    arsenide
    arsenopyrite
    galena
    marcasite
    orpiment
    pyrite
    pyrrhotite
    sphalerite
    stibnite
    sulfide mineral

sulfosalt
tetrahedrite
zeolite minerals:
    apophyllite
    chabazite
    clinoptilolite
    epistilbite
    erionite
    faujasite
    heulandite
    laumontite
    mordenite
    natrolite
    zeolite
other:
    accessory mineral
    amphibolite
    bentonite
    chromate mineral
    clay mineralogy
    cleavage
    colour index
    crocoite
    devitrification
    Eh-pH diagram
    filter-pressing
    foliation
    fracture
    fuller's earth
    gemstone
    geochemical facies
    grade scale
    hydraulic
        equivalence

hydrothermal ore
    deposit
iridescence
kaolin
lapis lazuli
lustre
metallogenic
    province
metasomatic
    replacement
mineral
Mohs hardness
nitrate and iodate
    minerals
nuée ardente
ore
paragenesis
phase diagram
phase rule
placer deposit
pleochroic halo
polymorphism
primary mineral
pseudomorph
pyroelectricity
Riecke's principle
rock
saussuritization
sinter
streak
vein

Division II.   The Earth's Envelope: Its Atmosphere and Hydrosphere
[For Part Two headnote see page 65.]

The outlines in the three sections of Division II treat the Earth's atmosphere, its hydrosphere, and weather and climate.

Section 221.   The Atmosphere

A. The composition, structure, and features of the atmosphere
   [see also 241.B. and 723.G.5.]

   1. Division of the atmosphere by composition

     a. The homosphere

        i. Water cycle
           [222.D.3 and 223.A.1.]

        ii. Carbon budget

        iii. Nitrogen budget

        iv. Sulfur budget

     b. The heterosphere

        i. Oxygen dissociation

        ii. Escape of helium and hydrogen from the upper atmosphere

  2. Thermal structure

    a. The troposphere

    b. The stratosphere

    c. The mesophere

    d. The thermosphere

  3. Regions and phenomena of the upper atmosphere

    a. The ozonesphere

        i. Absorption of ultraviolet radiation of wavelengths harmful to plant and animal life

        ii. Heating of the upper atmosphere

    b. The ionosphere

        i. Ionospheric variations and disturbances of atmospheric origin

        ii. Ionospheric variations and disturbances of solar origin: auroras and magnetic storms
           [see also 133.B. and 212.B.]

        iii. The effects of the ionosphere on radio waves
            [see also 735.I.5.]

    c. The exosphere

        i. Effects of low particle density on the properties of the exosphere

        ii. Determination of the critical zone, the layer above which the number of particle collisions is negligible

        iii. The Van Allen radiation belts
            [see also 133.B. and 212.B.]

B. The large-scale motions of the atmosphere
[see also 223, 232.A.5., and 723.G.5.]

  1. The general nature and relative scales of atmospheric motions: the resolution of winds into zonal (east–west), meridional (north–south), and vertical components

  2. The relation of wind to pressure and temperature: the cause of winds, the effect of Coriolis force, idealized winds derived from simplified models—the geostrophic and thermal winds
    [see also 211.A.2.a.]

  3. Jet streams

  4. The westerlies of the mid-latitudes

    a. Standing waves of the mid-latitude westerlies and related systems

    b. Mid-latitude traveling disturbances: cyclones, anticyclones
      [see also 223.B.1.]

  5. Tropical wind systems

    a. Trade winds

    b. Tropical disturbances: noncyclonic storms, hurricanes and typhoons
      [see 223.B.4.]

    c. Monsoons

  6. Stratospheric and mesospheric wind systems

    a. Polar-night westerlies

    b. Summer easterlies of the mesosphere and stratosphere

  7. The mean meridional circulations of the atmosphere

  8. The driving mechanism of the atmosphere: the energy balance and the transport of heat and momentum

---

Suggested reading in the *Encyclopædia Britannica:*

MACROPAEDIA: Major article dealing with the atmosphere

  Atmosphere

MICROPAEDIA: Selected entries of reference information

<u>General subjects</u>

atmospheric motion and disturbances:
anticyclone
atmospheric circulation
atmospheric turbulence
cyclone
cyclostrophic wind
doldrums
eddy
extratropical cyclone
Ferrel cell
geostrophic motion
gradient wind
Hadley cell
hurricane
jet stream

monsoon
polar anticyclone
Rossby wave
Siberian anticyclone
thunderstorm
tricellular theory
tropical cyclone
updraft and downdraft
wind

atmospheric optical phenomena:
airglow
atmospheric corona
aureole
aurora
halo

regions and zones of the atmosphere:
D region
E region
exosphere
F region
ionosphere
magnetosphere
mesosphere
ozonosphere
protonosphere
stratosphere
thermosphere
troposphere
Van Allen radiation belt
other:
air
air mass

atmosphere
atmospheric pressure
greenhouse effect
lapse rate
magnetic storm
solar wind
temperature inversion
whistler

<u>Biographies</u>

See Section 10/33 of Part Ten

INDEX: See entries under all of the terms above

Section 222. The Hydrosphere: the Oceans, Freshwater Bodies, and Ice Masses

A. The distribution of water in the hydrosphere

   1. Saltwater bodies

      a. Oceans and marginal seas

      b. Gulfs and bays

   2. Freshwater bodies

      a. Rivers, lakes, and marginal bodies such as estuaries and swamps
[see 232.C.1., 2., and 3.]

      b. Groundwater contained within the pores of rocks

   3. Ice

      a. Ice sheets and glaciers
[see also 212.G.5. and 232.C.6.]

      b. Icebergs and pack ice

      c. River ice and lake ice

   4. Water in the biosphere
[see 351]

B. The physical and chemical properties of seawater
[see also 241.C.]

C. The physical and chemical properties of freshwater

D. The hydrologic cycle

   1. The general nature of the hydrologic cycle: the types of processes involved and their complex interaction, scales of magnitude of the interrelated components of the global hydrologic system, influences of climate and other factors

2. The roles of evaporation and transpiration in the hydrologic cycle
[see also 336.B.4.]

3. The role of water vapour in the hydrologic cycle: condensation, precipitation
[see also 223.A. and E.1.e.]

4. Runoff and subsurface water in the hydrologic cycle
[see also 232.A.4.]

5. The role of ice in the hydrologic cycle
[see also A.3., above]

6. Water resources and supply
[see also 737.A.1.]

E. Ocean-atmosphere interactions

1. Radiation, heat, and water budgets

2. Oceanic waters as an important sink for carbon dioxide

3. Impact of ocean-atmosphere interactions on climate and weather

   a. Link between ocean surface temperature and climate anomalies

   b. El Niño/Southern Oscillation (ENSO)

   c. Moderating effects of the Gulf Stream system on climate

F. Effects of human activities on the hydrosphere; *e.g.,* cultural eutrophication; acidification
of precipitation resulting from the emission of sulfur dioxide and nitrogen oxides; potential
disruption of the water balance due to greenhouse warming induced by carbon dioxide buildup

G. Waves in the hydrosphere
[see also 126.E., 128.A., and 232]

1. Surface waves: simple waves, ocean waves, tsunamis

2. Internal waves

3. Tides
[see also 133.E.7.c.]

H. Ocean currents

1. The distribution of ocean currents

2. The forces that cause and affect ocean currents: pressure gradients, Coriolis force, frictional
forces
[see also 211.A.2.a.]

3. The general surface circulation

4. Subsurface ocean currents

   a. The general deep-sea circulation

   b. Tidal currents: periodic currents associated with tides in the sea

   c. Density currents down continental slopes, produced by differences in temperature, salinity,
   or sediment concentration
   [see also 231.C.3.]

Suggested reading in the *Encyclopædia Britannica:*

MACROPAEDIA: Major articles dealing with the hydrosphere: the oceans, freshwater bodies, and ice
masses

Earth, The: Its Properties,	Lakes
Composition, and Structure	Oceans
Hydrosphere, The	Rivers
Ice and Ice Formations	

MICROPAEDIA: Selected entries of reference information

General subjects

freshwater resources:	groundwater	lake	river
aquifer	ice	reservoir	spring

water resource	*motions of the sea:*	*ocean zones:*	*other:*
well	density current	bottom water	acid rain
ice masses:	ocean current	halocline	air–sea interface
firn	rip current	thermocline	bore
glacier	seiche	*saltwater bodies:*	eutrophication
ice formation	tide	bay	fetch
ice shelf	tsunami	estuary	greenhouse effect
iceberg	undertow	gulf	hydrologic cycle
pack ice	wave	lagoon	hydrosphere
permafrost	whirlpool	ocean	sea level
polynya			water mass

Biographies

See Section 10/33 of Part Ten

INDEX: See entries under all of the terms above

Section 223.   **Weather and Climate**

A. Condensation of water in the atmosphere producing clouds, fogs, and precipitation

   1. Moisture in the atmosphere
     [see also 221.A.1.a. and 723.G.5.]

     a. Humidity indices: absolute, specific, and relative humidity; dew-point temperature

     b. Climatic aspects of atmospheric humidity
       [see E.1.e., below]

     c. Effects of atmospheric humidity on the life and health of humans and other life-forms
       [see E.4., below]

   2. Condensation of atmospheric water vapour

     a. Convection, air-mass convergence, and other processes that lead to condensation
       [see also 221.B.]

     b. Condensation nuclei: atmospheric ions, salt and dust particles

     c. Dew

     d. Frost

   3. Clouds and fogs

     a. Formation and growth of clouds

     b. Description and classification of clouds

     c. Clouds and weather

     d. Fog

     e. Artificial modification of clouds and fogs

   4. Precipitation
     [see also 222.D. and 723.G.5.]

     a. Origin of precipitation in clouds, mechanisms of precipitation release
       [see A.3.a., above]

     b. Types of precipitation: drizzle, rain, freezing rain; snow; sleet, hail

     c. The world distribution of rainfall

     d. Effects of precipitation

B. Winds and storms
   [see also 221.B.]

   1. Development and distribution of cyclones and anticyclones

   2. Lightning and thunderstorms
     [see also 127.A. and B.]

   3. Tornadoes, hail, and other severe phenomena associated with organized storms or squall lines

   4. Tropical cyclones: hurricanes and typhoons

C. Weather forecasting

    1. Synoptic weather data: the collection and correlation of meteorological observations

    2. Numerical weather prediction and numerical climate modeling

    3. Short-range forecasting

        a. Nowcasting: predictions based on computer analyses of radar and satellite observations of local atmospheric conditions

        b. Model Output Statistics: extrapolation of weather conditions, using statistical relations between numerical model forecasts and past weather phenomena

    4. Long-range forecasting

        a. Enhancing the reliability of extended-range prediction through systematic studies of atmosphere-ocean interactions; *e.g.,* El Niño/Southern Oscillation (ENSO)

        b. Limits to predictability

D. Weather lore

E. Climate: the aggregate of weather
[see also 133.B.5., 221, and 723.G.5.]

    1. Factors that generate climate

        a. Solar radiation

            i. Variability of incident radiation; the solar constant

            ii. Effects of the atmosphere: absorption by dust and gases, including the trapping of solar radiation of infrared wavelength (the so-called greenhouse effect)

            iii. Variations in the Earth's albedo due to clouds and ice

        b. Temperature

        c. Atmospheric pressure

        d. The world's oceans

        e. The moisture cycle

    2. Climatic variation

        a. Seasonal changes resulting from the north–south migration of belts of cyclonic activity and other cyclic processes

        b. Local effects: modification of climate by local terrain and surface conditions

        c. Effects of human activities on global climate; *e.g.,* greenhouse warming induced by high concentrations of carbon dioxide (from the burning of fossil fuels) and other trace gases in the atmosphere
[see also 241.B.5. and 737.C.1.]

    3. Climatic types: the Köppen classification system, world climates and their distribution

    4. Influences of climate on terrestrial life

    5. Microclimates
[see also 351.B.]

    6. Climatic change

        a. Evidence: *e.g.,* landscape features associated with glaciations; fluctuations of lake and sea levels; pollen stratigraphy; archaeological and historical data

        b. Identified causes of certain forms of climatic variation: variations in the tilt of the Earth's axis and orbital motion; variations in atmospheric composition; volcanic dust loading of the atmosphere; and changes in the distribution of land and sea due to plate-tectonic activity

---

Suggested reading in the *Encyclopædia Britannica:*

MACROPAEDIA: Major article dealing with weather and climate

    Climate and Weather

MICROPAEDIA: Selected entries of reference information

General subjects

atmospheric humidity
and precipitation:
　aerosol
　cloud
　condensation
　　nucleus
　dew
　fog
　frost
　hail
　hoarfrost
　humidity
　precipitation
　rain
　rime
　snow
atmospheric pressure
and wind:
　anticyclone
　atmospheric
　　circulation
　atmospheric
　　pressure
　bora
　breeze
　Buys Ballot's law
　convergence and
　　divergence
　cyclone
　cyclostrophic wind
　etesian wind
　foehn

geostrophic motion
gradient wind
gregale
haboob
Hadley cell
harmattan
horse latitude
jet stream
katabatic wind
khamsin
lee wave
levanter
lightning
microburst
mistral
monsoon
polar anticyclone
　Siberian
　　anticyclone
sirocco
subtropical high
surge
tricellular theory
updraft and
　downdraft
wind
climate and climatic
variation:
　autumn
　climate
　drought

Indian summer
Köppen climatic
　classification
microclimate
pluvial regime
season
snow line
spring
summer
timberline
urban climate
winter
meteorological
measurement and
weather forecasting:
　Beaufort scale
　hygrometer
　isentropic chart
　isobar
　isotherm
　psychrometric
　　chart
　temperature–
　　humidity index
　weather bureau
　weather forecasting
　weather map
　weather station
　windchill
　World Weather
　　Watch

weather disturbances
and related
phenomena:
　atmospheric
　　turbulence
　blizzard
　extratropical
　　cyclone
　hurricane
　lightning
　storm
　thunder
　thunderstorm
　tornado
　tropical cyclone
weather lore:
　Groundhog Day
　Saint Swithin's
　　Day
other:
　almanac
　atmospheric
　　electricity
　El Niño
　front
　greenhouse effect
　smog
　sunshine
　urban dust
　weather
　weather
　　modification

Biographies

　See Section 10/33 of Part Ten

INDEX: See entries under all of the terms above

Division III.　**The Earth's Surface Features**
[For Part Two headnote see page 65.]

The outlines in the two sections of Division III deal with the basic physical features of the Earth's surface and with the features produced by geomorphic processes acting on the Earth's surface.

Section 231.　**Physical Features of the Earth's Surface**

A. Vertical relief of the Earth's surface

　1. Hypsography of the Earth's surface: distribution of land and sea, elevation of the continents, coastlines

　2. Physiography of the continents: Europe, Asia, Africa, Australia, North America, South America, Antarctica

　3. The oceanic regions

　　a. Principal oceanic features: continental margins, oceanic ridges, deep-sea trenches, and abyssal hills and plains
　　　[see also 723.G.3. and 735.J.2.]

      b. Oceanic physiography

B. The stable platform regions of the continents

   1. The continental shield areas and their age, structure, and constituent rocks
[see also 214.B.4.]

   2. Uplift, downwarp, and fracture of continental platforms

      a. Plateaus and basins

      b. Rift valleys

      c. Water bodies occupying fault-bounded structural depressions: lakes and landlocked seas; inland seas with outlets to the oceans; elongated seas formed by crustal separation

C. The continental shelf, slope, and rise

   1. Composition: evidence from bottom samples, geophysical techniques

   2. Structure and origin

   3. Submarine canyons incising the continental terrace

D. The oceanic deeps

   1. Components of ocean basins

      a. The oceanic crust

      b. Major features of the deep-ocean floor: oceanic ridges, aseismic ridges, trenches, fracture zones, and transform faults; seamounts and guyots; abyssal hills and plains; sediments of the ocean floor
[see G., below, and 241.F.3.]

   2. The origin of ocean basins

E. Coral islands, coral reefs, and atolls
[see also 354.B.]

F. The major mountain ranges and fracture zones of the Earth's crust on the continents and beneath the oceans

   1. Types of mountains; *e.g.,* volcanic, block-fault, folded

   2. The worldwide system of mountain ranges, fracture zones, and volcanic island arcs

      a. The Circum-Pacific System

      b. The Tethyan System

      c. Subsidiary mountain ranges

      d. The volcanic island arc systems

      e. The rock types constituting the folded mountain ranges and island arcs
[see also 212.G. and 214.B.4.]

G. Oceanic ridges

   1. Classification of ridges

      a. The global oceanic ridge system; spreading-centre zones and associated phenomena

      b. Aseismic ridges

   2. Origin and growth of ridges

      a. General geophysical properties

      b. Oceanic ridges as manifestations of divergent lithospheric plate boundaries
[see also 241.F.]

   3. Occurrence and distribution of ridges in the Atlantic, Pacific, and Indian oceans
[see also A.3., above]

Suggested reading in the *Encyclopædia Britannica:*

MACROPAEDIA: Major articles dealing with the physical features of the Earth's surface

Continental Landforms	Oceans
Earth, The: Its Properties,	Plate Tectonics
Composition, and Structure	Volcanism

MICROPAEDIA: Selected entries of reference information

General subjects

continental shelf and slope:	continental shield	volcanic dome	oceanic ridge
	cuesta	volcano	oceanic trough
continental shelf	dome	*oceanic structures and features:*	seamount
continental slope	drumlin		submarine gap
submarine canyon	esker	abyssal hill	*other:*
submarine fan	meteorite crater	abyssal plain	continent
submarine slump	mountain	archipelagic apron	density current
landforms and surface features:	pediment	atoll	landform
	plain	cay	lake
alluvial fan	plateau	coral reef	marine sediment
basin	playa	deep-sea trench	ocean
beach	rift valley	guyot	ooze
canyon	saline flat	island	
cave	salt dome	island arc	
cinder cone	sand dune	oceanic plateau	

Biographies

See Section 10/33 of Part Ten

INDEX: See entries under all of the terms above

Section 232. **Features Produced by Geomorphic Processes Acting on the Earth's Surface**

A. The action of the hydrosphere and atmosphere on the Earth's surface features

  1. The process of weathering: the disintegration and alteration of rocks at or near the Earth's surface

  2. Soil formation as a result of weathering

    a. Processes and factors in soil formation
    [see also 354.A.2.b.]

    b. Classification and distribution of soils

    c. Soil crusts

    d. Soil erosion and deterioration

  3. Gravitational processes: earth movements on slopes

  4. Fluvial processes
  [see also 126.E.3.]

    a. Entrainment and transport of materials

    b. Erosion, deposition

    c. The sediment yield of drainage systems

    d. The formation of hillslopes

  5. Eolian processes

    a. Transportation of rock debris by wind

    b. Effects of wind transport

    c. Deposition by wind: formation and migration of dunes, the role of vegetation

    d. Wind action and the works of humankind

  6. Marine processes

    a. Erosion and deposition of coastal materials by waves and currents

    b. Transport of sediment by density flows

  7. Glacial processes: erosion, transport, deposition, glacial loading and unloading, periglacial processes
  [see also C.6., below]

  8. Lacustrine processes

    a. Erosion and deposition by waves and currents

    b. Sedimentation in lakes

    c. Effects of flora and fauna on lakes and lake systems
      [see 354.B.3.a.]

B. The actions of the biosphere, exosphere, and lithosphere upon the Earth's surface features

    1. Biological processes
      [see 351]

      a. Effects of plants and organisms on rock weathering and soil formation
        [see A.1., above]

      b. Effects of vegetation type and density on sediment yield
        [see A.4.c., above]

      c. Effects of humankind on the Earth's surface features; *e.g.,* land cultivation, mining; construction of artificial channels and dams
        [see also 355, 731, 733.B., 734, 736, and 737]

    2. Extraterrestrial processes: the occurrence of meteorite craters
      [see also 133.A.3.c.]

    3. Volcanic-tectonic processes
      [see also 212.D.4., 212.G., 231.F., and 241.E.]

C. The characteristic features of the Earth's major environments

    1. The fluvial environment
      [see also 354.B.3.b.]

      a. Distribution of rivers in nature

      b. Drainage patterns

      c. The geometry of river systems

      d. Streamflow and fluvial landforms: peak discharge and flooding, river floodplains and terraces, river deltas, ephemeral streams, waterfalls

      e. The evolution of river systems through geological time

    2. The lacustrine environment
      [see also 354.B.3.a.]

      a. Lake basins

      b. Lake hydraulics: lake currents, surface waves, seiches, effects of wave and current action
        [see also 222.G.1.]

      c. Lakes in arid regions
        [see C.5.c., below]

      d. Glacial lakes
        [see C.6.c., below]

      e. Swamps, marshes, and bogs

    3. The estuarine environment

      a. The formation and destruction of estuaries

      b. Hydrologic features of estuaries

    4. The marine environment
      [see also 354.B.4.]

      a. Coastal features resulting from depositional processes

        i. Beaches: materials, morphological features, physical processes

        ii. Sand dunes and sandbars

        iii. River deltas
          [see C.1.d., above]

        iv. Coral reefs
          [see 231.E.]

        v. Lagoons

        vi. Marshes
          [see C.2.e., above]

      b. Coastal features resulting from erosional processes: sea cliffs and related landforms

    c. Coastal features dependent on bedrock type, bedrock structure, or local topography: grottoes, spouting holes, fjords, peninsulas, islands

    d. Submerged coastal features: the continental shelf and slope, submarine canyons
[see 231.C.]

5. The desert environment
[see also 354.A.1.c.]

    a. Geomorphic processes that shape desert landforms

    b. Surficial features of deserts

        i. Mountains, plateaus, pinnacles, and similar features

        ii. Alluvial fans: fan-shaped sedimentary deposits bordering highlands from which the sediment was derived

        iii. Pediments: bedrock surfaces fringing desert highlands

        iv. Desert plains, basins, depressions

        v. Playas, pans, saline flats

        vi. Sand sheets and sand dunes

    c. Desert boundaries: expansion and contraction of desert areas
[see also 223.E.6.]

6. The glacial environment
[see also 354.A.1.d.]

    a. Processes of glaciation
[see A.7., above]

    b. Landforms produced by glacial erosion

        i. Rock polish, striations, grooves, and other small-scale features

        ii. Glaciated valleys, cirques, arêtes, horns, fjords

        iii. Glacially eroded rock basins in non-mountainous regions

    c. Landforms produced by glacial deposition

        i. Glacial till, moraines, drumlins, and other landforms of nonstratified drift

        ii. Ice-contact deposits, kames, eskers, and other landforms of stratified drift

        iii. Glaciolacustrine sediments and associated landforms

    d. Landforms produced by periglacial processes

        i. Permafrost

        ii. Talus, rock glaciers, block fields

        iii. Patterned ground, including stone nets, stripes, and polygons, and features related to the melting of buried ice masses

7. The polar environment
[see C.6., above, and 354.A.1.d.]

8. The tropical environment: jungles, rain forests
[see also 354.A.1.c.]

9. The temperate environment: woodlands and grasslands
[see also 354.A.1.c.]

10. The subterranean environment: *e.g.,* caves and cave systems
[see also 354.A.1.d.]

11. Karst topography

D. Basic concepts in the theory of landform evolution

1. The concept of uniformitarianism
[see also 242.A.2.a.]

2. The concept of the cycle of erosion

3. The concept of morphogenetic regions

4. The concept of dynamic equilibrium

5. The concept of entropy
[see also 124.A.]

Suggested reading in the *Encyclopædia Britannica*:

MACROPAEDIA: Major articles dealing with the features produced by geomorphic processes acting on the Earth's surface

Continental Landforms
Earth, The: Its Properties,
  Composition, and Structure
Geomorphic Processes
Ice and Ice Formations

Lakes
Oceans
Rivers
Soils
Volcanism

MICROPAEDIA: Selected entries of reference information

General subjects

effects of fluvial
processes:
  alluvial fan
  arroyo
  badland
  bajada
  delta
  desert pavement
  drainage basin
  floodplain
  fluvial process
  inselberg
  meander
  oxbow lake
  river
  river terrace
  streambed
  valley
  waterfall
effects of
weathering:
  calcrete
  cave
  duricrust
  exfoliation
  ferricrete
  pediment
  pepino hill
  sinkhole
  weathering
glacial features and
landforms:
  chatter mark
  cirque

drumlin
esker
estuary
fjord
glacial stage
glacial valley
ice cave
kettle
moraine
moulin
outwash
roche
  moutonnée
till
gravitational
processes on
hillslopes:
  avalanche
  creep
  landslide
  mass movement
  mudflow
  rock glacier
marine features
produced by wave
action:
  beach
  beach cusp
  chenier
  lagoon
  sandbar
  sea cave
  wave-cut
    platform

physiographic effects
of eolian processes:
  barchan
  desert varnish
  playa
  saline flat
  sand dune
  seif
soil formation and
major soil types:
  alfisol
  aridisol
  chernozem
  clay
  entisol
  histosol
  humus
  inceptisol
  kaolisol
  laterite
  mollisol
  oxisol
  podzol
  podzolic soil
  soil
  spodosol
  ultisol
  vertisol
volcanic structures
and related
phenomena:
  cinder cone
  fumarole

geyser
hot spring
lava cave
mud volcano
volcanic dome
volcano
other:
  astrobleme
  meteorite crater
  morphogenetic
   region
  peneplain
  permafrost
  pingo
  polder
  residual landform
  thermokarst

Biographies

See Section 10/33 of Part Ten

INDEX: See entries under all of the terms above

Division IV. **The Earth's History**
[For Part Two headnote see page 65.]

The outlines in the three sections of Division IV deal with the origin and development of the Earth and its envelopes; the interpretation of the geological record; and the eras and periods of geological time.

Section 241. **Origin and Development of the Earth and Its Envelopes**

A. The origin and evolution of the lithosphere
[see also 213.A.]

   1. Theories of the origin of the Earth
   [see also 133.D.6.]

   2. The development of crust from mantle: processes involved in the geochemical differentiation of the Earth's outer layers

B. The origin and evolution of the atmosphere
[see also 133.D.6. and 221.A.]

   1. The relation of the development of the Earth's atmosphere to the origin of the solar system, the development of other planetary atmospheres

   2. The original atmosphere of the Earth

   3. Development of the present terrestrial atmosphere
   [see also 335.B.]

   4. The present atmosphere
   [see 221.A.]

   5. Effects of human activities and their ramifications; *e.g.,* acid rain resulting from the emission of sulfur dioxide; ozone depletion caused by the release of chlorofluorocarbons; greenhouse warming induced by the buildup of carbon dioxide
   [see also 223.E.2.c.]

C. The origin and evolution of the hydrosphere

   1. The early oceans

   2. The chemical view of the modern oceans

   3. The present hydrosphere
   [see 222]

D. The formation and growth of the continents

   1. The Earth's crust and upper mantle
   [see also 212.D.2., 213.A., 214.B.1.c., and 232]

   2. Endogenic regimes of the continents: geosynclines, platforms, rifts, continental margins
   [see also 231]

   3. The relation between endogenic regimes and deep-seated Earth processes

E. The formation and growth of mountain ranges and belts

   1. The distribution of mountain belts in relation to global tectonics

   2. The tectonic mountain belts
   [see also 212.G., 214.B., and 231.F.]

   3. The geosynclinal hypothesis of mountain building

   4. The development of mountain systems

F. The theory of plate tectonics

   1. Early speculations about the existence of a single supercontinent and its fragmentation into the present-day landmasses

2. Wegener's concept of continental drift

3. Hess' seafloor spreading model

4. Plate tectonics as a unifying theory

    a. A Lithospheric plate boundaries as sites of volcanism, seismicity, and orogeny

    b. The impact of continental drift on the evolution of life forms

---

Suggested reading in the *Encyclopædia Britannica:*

MACROPAEDIA: Major articles dealing with the origin and development of the Earth and its envelopes

    Atmosphere
    Earth, The: Its Properties, Composition, and Structure
    Plate Tectonics
    Volcanism

MICROPAEDIA: Selected entries of reference information

General subjects

atmosphere and hydrosphere:	*landmasses and ocean basins:*	plate tectonics	orogeny
atmosphere	continental drift	seafloor spreading hypothesis	sedimentation
Earth	Gondwanaland	*evolution of the*	subsidence
hydrosphere	Laurasia	*Earth's crust:*	uplift
ocean	Pangaea	epeirogeny	volcanism
		erosion	weathering

Biographies

    See Section 10/33 of Part Ten

INDEX: See entries under all of the terms above

Section 242.   **The Interpretation of the Geological Record**

A. The stratigraphic interpretation of the geological record

1. The layered rocks of the Earth's crust and their depositional environments: the nature of the rock record
[see also 214.B.2.]

    a. Clastic sedimentary rocks

    b. Carbonate rocks

    c. Volcanic rocks

    d. Cyclic deposits: cyclothems, varved deposits

2. Stratigraphic classifications and their historical development: criteria for the correlation of layered deposits

    a. The principle of uniformitarianism

    b. The principle of superposition of strata

    c. The idea of a fossil succession

    d. The facies concept

    e. The stage concept

    f. The recognition of zones

    g. Radiometric dating
    [see D.2., below]

3. Stratigraphic nomenclature in theory and practice

a. Stratigraphic terminology and its standardization

b. Stratigraphic boundary problems

c. Special stratigraphic terminologies and divisions

B. The interpretation of the geological record

1. The nature of fossils and fossilization processes

2. The fossil record

a. Precambrian life: the Proterozoic fossil record

i. The origin of life
[see also 241 and 312.A.]

ii. Precambrian protists, plants, and animals: the Gunflint Chert deposits, Ediacara fauna, and other remains

b. Post-Precambrian life: the Phanerozoic fossil record
[see also 313]

i. Plants

ii. Protista

iii. Porifera

iv. Cnidaria (Coelenterata)

v. Mollusca

vi. Conodonta

vii. Bryozoa

viii. Brachiopoda

ix. Arthropoda

x. Echinodermata

xi. Graptolithina

xii. Fishes

xiii. Amphibia

xiv. Reptilia

xv. Birds

xvi. Mammals

3. The appearance and disappearance (mass extinctions and background extinctions) of species revealed in the fossil record
[see also 312.C.]

4. The paleontological criteria for the correlation of layered rocks

a. Index fossils

b. Faunal and floral assemblages

c. Organic microfossils: pollen, spores, tests

C. Relative age dating

1. Application to geological problems: the relative geological time scale

2. Application to archaeological problems
[see 10/41.B.2.b.]

D. Absolute dating

1. General considerations: the meaning of absolute age, requirements for absolute dating, the rate of record accumulation

2. Radiometric dating
[see also 723.G.8.]

a. Radioactivity and radioactive decay
[see 112.C.]

b. Principles of radiometric dating

c. Definition of time zero, sources of error in radiometric dating

d. Dating methods

3. Non-radiometric dating: biological and geological processes as absolute chronometers

4. Applications of absolute dating

a. The absolute geological time scale

b. Determination of the age of the Earth and the ages of rocks and meteorites

c. Determination of the rates of seafloor spreading

E. The paleogeographical interpretation of the geological record

F. The reconstruction of the geological history of the Earth based on the global correlation of the accumulated evidence from the rock record
[see 241 and 243]

Suggested reading in the *Encyclopædia Britannica:*

MACROPAEDIA: Major articles dealing with the interpretation of the geological record

Earth, The: Its Properties, Composition, and Structure
Geochronology: The Interpretation and Dating of the Geological Record

MICROPAEDIA: Selected entries of reference information

General subjects

carbon-14 dating	fossil	polychaete	sedimentary facies
common-lead dating	geochronology	hypothesis	tephrochronology
dating	helium dating	potassium–argon dating	uniformitarianism
dendrochronology	horizon		varved deposit
Earth	index fossil	protactinium-231– thorium-230 dating	
faunal succession, law of	ionium–thorium dating	radiation-damage dating	
fission-track dating	lead-210 dating paleogeography		

Biographies

See Section 10/33 of Part Ten

INDEX: See entries under all of the terms above

Section 243.   The Eras and Periods of Geological Time

A. Precambrian time: from the time of formation of the oldest rocks to 570 million years ago

B. The Paleozoic Era: from 570 to 245 million years ago

1. The Cambrian Period
2. The Ordovician Period
3. The Silurian Period
4. The Devonian Period
5. The Carboniferous Period
6. The Permian Period

C. The Mesozoic Era: from 245 to 66.4 million years ago

1. The Triassic Period
2. The Jurassic Period
3. The Cretaceous Period

D. The Cenozoic Era: from 64.4 million years ago to the present

    1. The Tertiary Period

    2. The Quaternary Period
       [see also 411.B. and 412]

        a. The Pleistocene Epoch
           [see also 232.A.7. and C.6.]

        b. The Holocene, or Recent, Epoch
           [see also 412]

Suggested reading in the *Encyclopædia Britannica*:

MACROPAEDIA: Major articles dealing with the eras and periods of geological time

    Earth, The: Its Properties, Composition, and Structure
    Geochronology: The Interpretation and Dating of the Geological Record
    Volcanism

MICROPAEDIA: Selected entries of reference information

General subjects

Cenozoic:
- Allerød
- Blytt-Sernander system
- Boreal Climatic Interval
- Bracheux Sands
- Bronze Age
- Cenozoic Era
- Eocene Epoch
- Florissant Formation
- Great Drought
- Holocene Epoch
- Hypsithermal Climatic Interval
- ice age
- Iron Age
- Laurentide Ice Sheet
- London Clay
- Mauer
- Mesolithic Period
- Miocene Epoch
- Neogene Period
- Neolithic Period
- Oligocene Epoch
- Paleocene Epoch
- Paleogene Period
- Paleolithic Period
- Pleistocene Epoch
- Pliocene Epoch
- Quaternary Period
- Salpausselkä Ridges
- Scandinavian Ice Sheet
- Sub-Atlantic Climatic Interval
- Sub-Boreal Climatic Interval
- Tertiary Period
- Trinil faunal zone

Mesozoic:
- Clarence Series
- Coniacian Stage
- Cretaceous Period
- Gulf Series
- Hell Creek Formation
- Jurassic Period
- Lance Formation
- Mesozoic Era
- Niobrara Limestone
- Pierre Shale
- Purbeck Beds
- Solnhofen Limestone
- Stormberg Series
- Taitai Series
- Triassic Period
- Wealden Series

Paleozoic:
- Alberta Basin
- Arenig Series
- Ashgill Series
- Beaufort Series
- Cambrian Period
- Caradoc Series
- Carboniferous Period
- Catskill Delta
- Cayugan Series
- Chesterian Series
- Cincinnati Arch
- Cincinnatian Series
- Coal Measures
- Conemaugh Series
- Dalradian Series
- Devonian Period
- Lipalian Interval
- Llandeilo Series
- Llandoverian Series
- Llanvirn Series
- Ludlow Series
- Mississippian Period
- Monongahela Series
- Nashville Dome
- Niagaran Series
- Old Red Sandstone
- Ordovician Period
- Osagian Series
- Paleozoic Era
- Paradoxides Series
- Pennsylvanian Period
- Permian Basin
- Permian Period
- Pottsville Series
- Queenston Delta
- Salado Formation
- Silurian Period
- Stephanian Series
- Virgilian Series
- Wenlock Series
- Williston Basin

Precambrian:
- Animikie Series
- Belt Series
- Bitter Springs microfossils
- Bruce Series
- Coutchiching Series
- Grand Canyon Series
- Gunflint microfossils
- Katangan Complex
- Lewisian Complex
- Longmyndian
- Onverwacht Series
- Phanerozoic Eon
- Precambrian Time
- Proterozoic Eon
- Seine Series
- Sturtian Series

Biographies

  See Section 10/33 of Part Ten

INDEX: See entries under all of the terms above

Introduction to Part Three:
The Mysteries of Life

By René Dubos

We take for granted the existence of life on Earth. Yet, as far as we now know, life exists nowhere else in the solar system, its origin is still a mystery, and its effects on our planet have been little short of miraculous. Without life the surface of the Earth and its atmosphere would be very different from what they are now. We are both spectators and actors in a continuing performance where life is both author and producer, and for which the Earth serves as an ever-changing stage.

Cataclysms give us now and then a glimpse of what our planet would look like without life. In 1883, a series of stupendous volcanic eruptions destroyed two-thirds of Krakatoa Island in the Malay archipelago and covered what was left of it with a thick layer of lava. All living things were killed, not only on Krakatoa itself, but also on the neighbouring islands that were in the path of the tidal wave generated by the explosion and of the volcanic fallout. What had once been a luscious tropical forest suddenly became a gray and lifeless landscape, as desolate as the surface of the Moon.

Pictures taken of Krakatoa in the months following the disaster help us to realize that what we regard as the surface of the Earth is less a geological structure than a living mantle. Our planet would be drab and dusty, an insignificant object in space, if it were not for the myriad of living forms that have generated its atmosphere and its soil out of gases and rocks. In fact, the phrase "life on Earth" is somewhat misleading because the surface of the Earth as we experience it, with its entrancing diversity and colourful warmth, is literally a product of biological activities—a creation of life.

Krakatoa remained a desolate landscape for a long time after the 1883 volcanic explosion. But progressively the wind and the sea brought back to its sterilized surface a multiplicity of living things, some of which managed to establish a permanent foothold on the lava. Today, the island harbours once more a rich flora and fauna, not very different from that of the native forest of the Malay archipelago.

There is a paradox in the marvelous resiliency of nature. On the one hand, all individual forms of life are extremely delicate. And yet life itself has been capable of prevailing over brute physical forces for several billion years, and has generated immensely diversified ecosystems that have remained viable even under the most inhospitable conditions. Life probably emerged from inanimate matter, but it is now more powerful than inanimate matter.

All biological phenomena are of practical importance because they determine the characteristics of the Earth's surface and therefore affect the quality of human life. Men have always been concerned with the contributions that living things make to their immediate environment and to the global economy; they have wondered how the flora and fauna become more or less stabilized under normal conditions, and manage to reestablish stable ecosystems after cataclysms; in our times they worry to what extent living things can be disturbed or eliminated by urbanization and industrialization without thereby threatening human welfare.

But the phrase "life on Earth" also raises other questions of a more philosophical character, questions that have been in the minds of humble, uneducated people even before they became the preoccupation of scholars. In the universe at large, lifelessness is the rule, life the puzzling exception. How do living things differ from inanimate matter? How did they originate? And can life be created *de novo*? Is man qualitatively different from the rest of the living world or merely a higher, or the highest, specimen in its evolution, the paragon of animals?

It is clear from the geological record that life has been at home on the Earth for immense periods of time. The types of fossils found in rock formations indicate that all major groups of animals and plants were already represented by recognizable ancestors some 400,000,000 years ago. Furthermore, microscopic structures closely related to the present forms of blue-green algae have been found in geologic formations that are even very much older—some 3,000,000,000 years old. Since these fossils of algae-like organisms have a complex cellular organization, it can be assumed that they had been preceded by simpler forms, and that the origin of life is more ancient than the oldest traces of it which have been detected. In fact, there is no way to know when life first appeared on Earth, because its earliest manifestations were certainly so minute, fragile, and undifferentiated that none of them have survived as fossils.

There is a peculiar fascination to the phrase "the origin of life" because it means different things to different men, and reaches into the deepest layers of their beliefs. For the religious man, it implies the mysteries of divine creation—whether expressed as biological species in their final forms, or as the potentialities posited by Aristotelian philosophers and medieval theologians. For the student of myths, it evokes Aphrodite emerging fully developed from the foam of the sea. The myth may have a factual basis if it is true, as it is commonly believed, that the cradle of life was to be found in the primitive oceans. For the modern scientist the phrase "origin of life" refers to the kind of chemical reactions that first generated complex organic molecules and assembled them in such a manner that they could duplicate themselves—thus converting inanimate matter into living substance.

Whatever the mystical or rational basis of a person's beliefs, there is a universal poetic quality in the thought that life once arose from matter, and has been perpetuating itself ever since. But the only real clue to the origin of life is

91

that all its forms—at least all the living things we know—have many physicochemical characteristics in common. In particular, they all transfer their hereditary endowment from one generation to the next through the agency of a peculiar kind of molecule known as nucleic acid, the now famous DNA. This uniformity of fundamental structure holds true irrespective of the size, shape, and complexity of the organism—whether it be microbe, plant, animal, or man. Indeed, the similarity in structure of the genetic apparatus throughout the living world is so perfect that it cannot possibly be a matter of chance. The conclusion seems inescapable that all the living forms that now exist have had a common origin.

The simplest hypothesis to account for the origin and evolution of life is that all biological phenomena are caused by the physicochemical forces that govern the inanimate world. Some scientists believe, indeed, that there is nothing very unusual in the emergence of a living molecule from matter. According to them, it is probable that life repeatedly emerged *de novo* on Earth and that it is still emerging today somewhere in the cosmos. By making the reasonable assumption that one of the living forms that appeared on Earth proved more vigorous than the others, it is easy to account for the single origin of all surviving species. If an entirely new genetic form of life were to appear today on Earth, it would have no chance of success, because it could not compete with the established form and all its variations.

The hypothesis that life is nothing more than a special manifestation of ordinary physicochemical forces has the merit of being economical of thought; in addition, it is supported by the fact that all biological phenomena go hand in hand with the kind of reactions observed in the inanimate world. But even if we grant that living phenomena always obey physicochemical laws, this does not constitute decisive evidence that life is merely an expression of these laws. Other theories are conceivable. One of them, rarely voiced because it is not scientifically fashionable, is that some unknown principle runs like a continuous thread through all living forms and governs the organizations of their physicochemical processes. The illustrious Danish physicist Niels Bohr, for example, suggested that "the very existence of life must be considered an elementary fact, just as in atomic physics the existence of a quantum of action has to be taken as a basic fact that cannot be derived from ordinary mechanical physics."

Uncertainties concerning the fundamental nature of life and its origin would disappear if it were possible to generate at will self-reproducing molecules from inert material. Some experimental findings have recently been quoted as evidence of this possibility.

A fully developed virus, which had been naturally produced by a living organism, was separated into its component parts by chemical procedures. When these separate parts were tested for biological activity, they were found to be inert, that is, they were unable to multiply in a susceptible organism. This biological activity was restored, however, when the parts of the virus were chemically reassembled in the test tube under the proper conditions. Spectacular as this achievement is from the chemical point of view, it does not constitute—as has been claimed—the production of life *de novo.* Since the virus first had to be produced by a living organism, and since its reassembled parts showed activity only when introduced into a living susceptible organism, all the biological machinery essential for its reproduction had to be provided by preexisting life.

In a completely unrelated kind of experiment, several complex molecules similar to those found in living things have been produced in the laboratory by exposing simple chemicals to the kind of radiation that probably existed in the primitive atmosphere. But this chemical feat does not constitute production of life *de novo* because the molecules so produced have not been assembled—*organized*—in a way enabling them to duplicate themselves and to develop. An organic molecule, however complex and similar to the kind found in living things, still belongs to the realm of inanimate matter if it cannot reproduce and evolve.

To become "living," an assembly of biogenic molecules must contain the information needed for its further development and must be able to transmit this information to its progeny. Even in its simplest manifestations, life is historical; it embodies the past and carries instructions for the future.

More than a century ago, the French physiologist Claude Bernard gave a clear formulation of the now classical view that the earmark of a living thing is not the chemical composition of its parts but their organization. He wrote: "Admitting that vital phenomena rest upon physicochemical activities, which is the truth, the essence of the problem is not thereby cleared up; for it is no chance encounter of physico-chemical phenomena which constructs each being according to a preexisting plan, and produces the admirable subordination and the harmonious concert of organic activity.

"There is an arrangement in the living being, a kind of regulated activity, which must never be neglected, because it is in truth the most striking characteristic of living beings. . . ."

In this celebrated passage, Bernard used the word "arrangement" to denote the interdependence and integration of the structures and properties of any given living organism. But biological organization applies also to the ecological system of which the organism is a part. All living things, without exception, depend on other living things for their survival and development. Furthermore, the higher the organism is on the evolutionary scale, the more exacting is its dependence on a complex web of life.

One of the major trends of evolution has thus been the emergence of more and more complex ecosystems, exhibiting high degrees of integration. But, paradoxically, an opposite trend can also be detected as one ascends the evolutionary scale—namely, a trend toward freedom or at least toward increasing independence of the individual organism within the constraints of the ecosystem. Freedom becomes more and more apparent as one proceeds from the protoplasmic jelly of biological beginnings to warm-blooded animals roaming in the wild, and finally to man who modifies his environment according to his views of the future. In a real way, evolutionary development is associated with the gradual insertion of more and more freedom into matter and into individual lives.

In the *Outline of Knowledge,* Part Three, concerned with life on Earth, is placed between Parts Two and Four, concerned, respectively, with the Earth itself and with human life. This positioning is reasonable enough, but one could read into it an assumption that reaches far deeper than the logical ordering of concepts and facts. The tacit assumption is that human life has emerged from the inanimate matter of the Earth through the same kind of evolutionary continuum that links all the other living forms in a great chain of being. In reality, however, the theory of evolution does not provide decisive evidence for this assumption. What is *known* of biological evolution applies only to the anatomical structures and physiological functions of organisms that have lived in the past or are living now. The successive steps from matter to life, and from life to consciousness, have not yet been shown to have taken place through the kind of mechanisms that account for the evolutionary changes of anatomical structures of physiological functions. There exists a continuum from one form of life to another, but extending this continuum to inanimate matter on the one hand, and to human consciousness on the other, is a matter of faith rather than of scientific knowledge.

Even the most cursory observation of nature reveals that all living forms are conditioned by environmental forces, and that reciprocally they shape the environment, thereby contributing to the triumph of life. But it must be realized that the word "life" encompasses different kinds of relations to nature. At its lowest level, "life" implies, as mentioned above, the deterministic and blind chemical reactions through which an organism—simple or complex as it may be—transmits its distinctive characteristics to its descendants and reacts adaptively to its environment. At its highest, "life" involves man's consciousness and free will and refers to the deep reality of the world within and the affirmation of the individual self, irrespective of the external world.

There is no way at present to link these two extreme and apparently incompatible manifestations of life—biological determinism and human freedom. Yet both are real, and both have been immensely influential in giving the present characteristics to our planet.

The surface of the Earth reflects the activities of countless living things. Even though these operate chiefly through blind, deterministic mechanisms, life introduces on Earth a degree of order, organization, and diversity not found anywhere else in the cosmos, not even in the movement of the celestial bodies. Man emerged, not on the bare planet, but in this orderly and diversified biological world. As soon as he achieved his identity as *Homo sapiens,* he began to insert his free will into ecological determinism. For good or evil, he has now become the most powerful influence in changing the face of the globe. His conscious choices will determine not only his own fate, but also the fate of life on Earth.

Part Three. Life on Earth

Several points about the relations of Part Three to other parts should be noted. The separation of Part Three from Part One, on matter and energy, and from Part Two, on the Earth, reflects a traditional division of labour among the natural sciences. However, the separation is not rigid. The borderline disciplines of biophysics and biochemistry appear throughout Part Three, especially in Division II, concerned with the molecular basis of vital processes. The effects of the Earth's atmosphere and hydrosphere on living things are reflected throughout Part Three, especially in Division V, which is concerned with the biosphere and with ecosystems.

Some fundamental biological knowledge of humans is involved in the treatment throughout Part Three of what is common to all life and to all animals. And Section 355, the last section of Part Three, deals with mankind's place and activities in the biosphere. However, what is specific to human life, human health, and human behaviour is separately dealt with in Part Four, on human life.

The biological sciences have themselves been the object of historical and analytical studies. Such studies are dealt with in Section 10/34 in Part Ten, which treats the historical development of the biological sciences; the methodology, scope, and conceptual structure of biology as a whole; and the several component disciplines at the different levels of biological research.

The design and operation of observational and experimental instruments are important in the development of the biological sciences. Such scientific instrumentation is dealt with in Section 723 of Part Seven.

Division I. The Nature and Diversity of Living Things

The outlines in the three sections of Division I deal with the nature, the origin and evolution, and the classification of living things.

Section 311. Characteristics of Living Things

A. The concept of life on Earth

1. Properties of life

   a. Order and form

   b. Metabolism: catabolism and anabolism

   c. Sensory reception

   d. Reproduction, growth, and development

   e. Interaction with the environment

2. Levels of biotic organization

   a. Molecular: polymers, carbohydrates, lipids, proteins, and nucleic acids

   b. Cellular: procaryotic cells and eucaryotic cells

   c. Organ: tissues, tissue systems, and the whole organism

   d. Population: species and communities

B. Life beyond the Earth

    1. The concept of extraterrestrial life and its chemistry

    2. The significance of the search for life beyond Earth

    3. Exobiological survey of the solar system: physical environments and biological prospects

---

Suggested reading in the *Encyclopædia Britannica:*

MACROPAEDIA: Major articles dealing with the characteristics of living things

Animals	Growth and Development, Biological
Bacteria and Other Monerans	Life
Behaviour, Animal	Metabolism
Biological Sciences, The	Mimicry
Biosphere, The	Photosynthesis
Cells: Their Structures and Functions	Plants
Coloration, Biological	Protists
Evolution, The Theory of	Reproduction and Reproductive Systems
Fungi	Sensory Reception
Genetics and Heredity, The Principles of	

MICROPAEDIA: Selected entries of reference information

General subjects

cell	homeostasis	life cycle
evolution	life	metabolism

Biographies

    See Section 10/34 of Part Ten

INDEX: See entries under all of the terms above

Section 312.   **The Origin of Life and the Evolution of Living Things**

A. Stages in the emergence of life

    1. Hypotheses about the origin of life

    2. Steps in the production of chemical precursors of life

        a. Formation of the Earth's primitive reducing atmosphere

        b. Production of simple organic molecules

        c. Production of long-chain molecules consisting of repeating units

        d. Origin of the genetic code

    3. The earliest living systems

        a. Evolution of enzymatic reaction chains

        b. Origin of procaryotic and eucaryotic cells

        c. Evolution of photosynthesis

    4. The antiquity of life: evidence of biological activity in the geological record
       [see also 242 and 243]

B. The theory of evolution

    1. The history of evolutionary theory

        a. Lamarck's contribution

        b. Darwin's theory of natural selection

        c. Mendel's theory of heredity

        d. The synthetic theory of evolution

        e. Molecular and genetic studies

2. The evidence for evolution

   a. The fossil record of gradual change

   b. Structural similarities (homologies) of different species

   c. Vestiges of ancestral forms in embryonic development

   d. Molecular clues to evolutionary history

C. The process of evolution

  1. Genetic variation through gene or chromosomal mutation

  2. Changes in gene frequencies within a population through gene mutation, gene migration, and genetic drift

  3. Natural selection

   a. Adaptation and fitness

   b. Aspects of the process of natural selection; coloration; mimicry; polymorphism

   c. Natural selection in the process of genetic change

   d. Types of selection: stabilizing, directional, diversifying, sexual, and kin

D. The origin of species and the process of speciation

  1. The distinctiveness of species

  2. The criterion of reproductive isolation

  3. The properties of species

  4. Modes of speciation (*e.g.,* geographic speciation, adaptive radiation, quantum speciation)

  5. Genetic differentiation during speciation

  6. Patterns and rates of species evolution

   a. The topology (or configuration) of phylogenies

   b. The rate of morphological change: gradual or punctuational evolution

   c. Molecular evolution

  7. The relationship between species and other taxonomic categories: family, order, class, phylum

---

Suggested reading in the *Encyclopædia Britannica*:

MACROPAEDIA: Major articles and a biography dealing with the origin of life and the evolution of living things

   Coloration, Biological
   Darwin
   Evolution, Human
   Evolution, The Theory of
   Mimicry

MICROPAEDIA: Selected entries of reference information

<u>General subjects</u>

adaptation	coloration	genetic drift	orthogenesis
aggressive mimicry	concealing	homology	phylogeny
analogy	coloration	Lamarckism	polymorphism
auxochrome	Darwinism	mimicry	selection
biopoiesis	dialectic	mosaic evolution	species
carotene	eobiont	Müllerian mimicry	spontaneous
chromophore	evolution	mutation	generation
clone	founder principle	Origin of Species	

<u>Biographies</u>
  See Section 10/34 of Part Ten

INDEX: See entries under all of the terms above

Section 313.   **The Classification of Living Things**

A. Viruses

B. Monerans: bacteria and other prokaryotes

C. Protists

   1. Algae

   2. Protozoans

   3. Slime molds

D. Fungi

E. Plants

   1. Bryophytes

      a. Mosses

      b. Liverworts

      c. Hornworts

   2. Psilotophytes, or whisk ferns

   3. Lycophytes (club mosses and allies)

   4. Sphenophytes, or horsetails

   5. Filicophytes, or ferns

      a. Ophioglossopsids

      b. Marattiopsids

      c. Filicopsids

   6. Conifers

   7. Ginkgos

   8. Cycads

   9. Gnetophytes

   10. Angiosperms (magnoliophytes), or flowering plants

      a. Magnoliopsids, or dicots

      b. Liliopsids, or monocots

F. Animals

   1. Placozoans

   2. Porifera, or sponges

      a. Calcispongiaens

      b. Hyalospongiaens

      c. Demospongiaens

   3. Mesozoans

      a. Dicyemids

      b. Orthonectids

   4. Cnidarians, or coelenterates

      a. Anthozoans (corals; sea anemones; sea fans and sea whips; sea pens and sea pansies)

      b. Scyphozoans (jellyfish)

      c. Hydrozoans (hydra)

      d. Cubozoans (box jellyfishes)

   5. Ctenophores, or comb jellies

   6. Platyhelminthes, or flatworms

      a. Turbellarians

      b. Monogeneans

      c. Aspidocotyleans

      d. Trematodes, or flukes

      e. Cestodes, or tapeworms

7. Nemerteans, or ribbon worms

8. Acanthocephalans, or spiny-headed worms

9. Aschelminthes

    a. Rotifers, or wheel animacules

    b. Gastrotrichs

    c. Kinorhynchates

    d. Nematodes, or roundworms

    e. Nematomorphs, or horsehair worms

10. Priapulids

11. Annelid worms

    a. Polychaetes, or marine worms

    b. Oligochaetes, or terrestrial worms

    c. Hirudineans, or leeches

12. Tardigrades, or water bears

13. Onychophorans, or velvet worms

14. Arthropods

    a. Crustaceans

    b. Uniramians (millipedes, centipedes, pauropods, symphylans, and insects)

    c. Chelicerates (sea spiders, horseshoe crabs, and arachnids)

15. Mollusks

    a. Tryblids, or neopilinids

    b. Solenogastres, or narrow-footed gliders

    c. Caudofoveatans, or mudmoles

    d. Placophorans, or chitons

    e. Pelecypods, or bivalves (clams, mussels, oysters, scallops, and cockles)

    f. Scaphopods, or tusk shells

    g. Gastropods (limpets, snails, and slugs)

    h. Cephalopods (nautiluses; cuttlefishes, squids, and octopuses)

16. Bryozoans, or moss animals

    a. Phylactolaemates

    b. Stenolaemates

    c. Gymnolaemates

17. Phoronids, or horseshoe worms

18. Brachiopods, or lamp shells

    a. Inarticulates

    b. Articulates

19. Sipunculid worms, or peanutworms

20. Chaetognaths, or arrowworms

21. Echiurids, or spoonworms

22. Echinoderms

    a. Crinozoans, or sea lilies

    b. Echinozoans (sea urchins, heart urchins, and sand dollars; sea cucumbers)

    c. Asterozoans (starfish, brittle stars, and sea daisies)

23. Hemichordates

    a. Enteropneusts, or acorn worms

    b. Pterobranchs

24. Pogonophors, or beardworms

25. Chordates

    a. Tunicates (sea squirts, appendicularians, and thaliaceans)

    b. Cephalochordates, or lancelets

    c. Vertebrates (hagfishes and lampreys; placoderms; sharks, skates, and rays; bony fishes; amphibians; reptiles; birds; mammals)

Suggested reading in the *Encyclopædia Britannica*:

angiosperms—caper order:
  Brassicaceae
  broccoli
  Brussels sprouts
  cabbage
  candytuft
  Capparales
  cauliflower
  charlock
  Chinese cabbage
  collard
  cress
  kale
  Kerguelen cabbage
  kohlrabi
  marsh cress
  mustard
  peppergrass
  radish
  rape
  rock cress
  rocket
  spiderflower
  stock
  toothwort
  turnip
  wallflower
  whitlow grass
angiosperms— composite order:
  artichoke
  Asteraceae
  basket-flower
  boneset
  chamomile
  Chrysanthemum
  cineraria
  coneflower
  dandelion
  endive
  fleabane
  goldenrod
  groundsel
  guayule
  Jerusalem
    artichoke
  lettuce
  marigold
  pussy-toes
  safflower
  sunflower
  thistle
  zinnia
angiosperms— dogwood order:
  angelica
  anise
  Apiaceae
  Araliaceae
  carrot
  Cornales
  cow parsnip

dogwood
fatsia
ivy
parsnip
poison hemlock
schefflera
tupelo
angiosperms—ebony and primrose orders:
  Bumelia
  Ebenales
  ebony
  persimmon
  pimpernel
  primrose
  Primulales
  sapodilla
  storax
angiosperms— euphorbia order:
  boxwood
  Buxaceae
  cassava
  castor-oil plant
  copperleaf
  croton
  crown of thorns
  Euphorbiaceae
  Euphorbiales
  jatropha
  jojoba
  manchineel
  mercury
  Omphalea
  Phyllanthus
  poinsettia
  redbird cactus
  sandbox tree
  spurge
  tung tree
angiosperms—figwort order:
  Acanthaceae
  belladonna
  Bignoniaceae
  bladderwort
  broomrape
  eggplant
  figwort
  foxglove
  Gesneriaceae
  henbane
  Indian paint brush
  jacaranda
  mullein
  nightshade
  petunia
  potato
  sausage tree
  Scrophulariales
  Solanaceae
  toadflax
  tobacco

tomato
witchweed
angiosperms— gentian order:
  Apocynaceae
  Asclepiadaceae
  bedstraw
  buckbean
  carrion flower
  coffee
  Gentianales
  Indian hemp
  Loganiaceae
  madder
  oleander
  partridgeberry
  periwinkle
  Rubiaceae
angiosperms— geranium order:
  Barbados cherry
  flax
  Geraniales
  geranium
  Impatiens
  lignum vitae
  nasturtium
  Oxalis
  shamrock
  wood sorrel
angiosperms—ginger order:
  abaca
  arrowroot
  banana
  bird-of-paradise
    flower
  Cannaceae
  ginger
  ginger lily
  Marantaceae
  Musaceae
  plantain
  prayer plant
  Strelitziaceae
  Zingiberaceae
  Zingiberales
angiosperms—grass order:
  agrostology
  Arundinaria
  bamboo
  barley
  beach grass
  bent grass
  bluegrass
  bluestem
  bromegrass
  cordgrass
  corn
  crabgrass
  esparto
  fescue

foxtail
grass
love grass
millet
muhly
needlegrass
oat grass
oats
panicum
Paspalum
Pennisetum
Poaceae
quack grass
reed
Restionales
rice
rye
ryegrass
sorghum
sugarcane
wheat
wild rice
angiosperms—heath order:
  Arbutus
  azalea
  bilberry
  blueberry
  Clethra
  cranberry
  crowberry
  Ericales
  Gaultheria
  heath
  heather
  huckleberry
  Indian pipe
  kalmia
  kiwi
  Labrador
    tea
  leatherleaf
  Lyonia
  Pieris
  pipsissewa
  rhododendron
  Vaccinium
  wintergreen
angiosperms—laurel order:
  avocado
  California laurel
  greenheart
  lambkill
  Laurales
  laurel
  sassafras
  sweet shrub
angiosperms—lily and iris orders:
  Agavaceae
  Alliaceae

Amaryllidaceae
Asparagus
asphodel
bear grass
blue-eyed grass
cantala
chive
Colchicum
Crocus
Dioscoreaceae
Dracaena
elephant's-foot
Erythronium
fritillary
garlic
Gladiolus
henequen
Iridales
Iris
leek
Liliaceae
Liliales
mariposa lily
Mauritius hemp
Narcissus
onion
phormium
pickerelweed
Sansevieria
Smilax
ti
tulip
water hyacinth
yam
angiosperms—
  magnolia order:
  Annonaceae
  champac
  cherimoya
  lancewood
  magnolia
  Magnoliaceae
  Magnoliales
  Myristicaceae
  pawpaw
  tulip tree
  Winteraceae
  ylang-ylang
angiosperms—
  mallow order:
  Abutilon
  balsa
  baobab
  Bombacaceae
  cacao
  cotton
  durian
  hibiscus
  jute
  kapok
  kenaf
  linden
  mallow
  Malvaceae

Malvales
okra
roselle
sisal
Sterculiaceae
Tiliaceae
urena
angiosperms—mint
  order:
  balm
  Coleus
  dittany
  dragonhead
  glory-bower
  Lamiaceae
  Lamiales
  Lantana
  lavender
  lemon verbena
  Mentha
  peppermint
  rosemary
  Salvia
  spearmint
  teak
  Verbenaceae
angiosperms—myrtle
  order:
  allspice
  cannonball tree
  Cuphea
  Epilobium
  Eucalyptus
  Eugenia
  feijoa
  fireweed
  Fuchsia
  guava
  jaboticaba
  Leptospermum
  loosestrife
  mangrove
  mare's-tail
  Myrtales
  myrtle
  Onagraceae
  paperbark tree
  pomegranate
  water chestnut
angiosperms—nettle
  order:
  Cannabis
  elm
  Ficus
  fig
  hackberry
  hemp
  India rubber plant
  jackfruit
  Moraceae
  mulberry
  Osage orange
  Pilea

ramie
Ulmaceae
Urticaceae
Urticales
angiosperms—orchid
  order:
  bucket orchid
  cattleya
  Dendrobium
  Epidendrum
  greenhood
  helleborine
  jewel orchid
  ladies' tresses
  lady's slipper
  Odontoglossum
  Oncidium
  Ophrys
  orchid
  Orchis
  Pogonia
  twayblade
  Vanda
  vanilla
angiosperms—palm
  and related orders:
  Anthurium
  Arales
  Arisaema
  Arum
  babassu palm
  calla
  coco de mer
  coconut palm
  Cyclanthales
  date palm
  dumb cane
  oil palm
  palm
  Pandanales
  Philodendron
  skunk cabbage
  Typhales
angiosperms—pea
  order:
  acacia
  Albizia
  bean
  bluebonnet
  broom
  chick-pea
  Clianthus
  clover
  cowpea
  crown vetch
  Fabales
  honey locust
  indigo
  kudzu vine
  laburnum
  lentil
  lespedeza
  locoweed

locust
logwood
lupine
mesquite
Mimosa
narra
pagoda tree
palo verde
pea
peanut
redbud
rosewood
senna
sensitive plant
smoke tree
soybean
sunn
vetch
Wisteria
angiosperms—pepper
  and birthwort
  orders:
  birthwort
  Peperomia
  Piperaceae
  Piperales
  wild ginger
angiosperms—phlox
  order:
  alkanet
  bindweed
  borage
  Boraginaceae
  bugloss
  Convolvulaceae
  dodder
  forget-me-not
  Hydrophyllaceae
  Ipomoea
  Lennoaceae
  Loasaceae
  Mertensia
  phlox
  Polemoniales
  Rivea
  sweet potato
  waterleaf
angiosperms—
  pineapple and
  related orders:
  Aechmea
  Bromeliaceae
  Commelinales
  Cryptanthus
  Cyperales
  Dyckia
  Eriocaulales
  Juncales
  papyrus
  pineapple
  Puya
  Spanish moss
  spiderwort
  Tillandsia

umbrella plant
Zebrina
angiosperms—pink order:
Amaranthaceae
baby's breath
beet
Bougainvillea
campion
carnation
Caryophyllaceae
Caryophyllales
Celosia
chard
chickweed
goosefoot
Halogeton
Lychnis
Nyctaginaceae
pigweed
pink
poke
Portulacaceae
purslane
spinach
sugar beet
angiosperms—poppy order:
bleeding heart
bloodroot
bush poppy
California poppy
celandine
Corydalis
Fumariaceae
fumitory
horned poppy
Hypecoaceae
Papaveraceae
Papaverales
poppy
prickly poppy
angiosperms—rose order:
almond
Amelanchier
apple
apricot
attar of roses
blackberry
boysenberry
cherry
chokecherry
cinquefoil
cotoneaster
crab apple
firethorn
hawthorn
loganberry
loquat
medlar
nectarine
peach
pear

plum
quince
raspberry
Rosales
rose
spirea
strawberry
sweetbrier
angiosperms—rue order:
Anacardiaceae
bel fruit
burning bush
Burseraceae
cashew
citron
grapefruit
kumquat
lemon
lime
mahogany
mango
Meliaceae
myrrh
orange
pili nut
Pistacia
poison ivy
Rhus
Rutaceae
Rutales
shaddock
Simaroubaceae
sumac
tree of heaven
angiosperms—sandalwood order:
Australian
  Christmas tree
Balanophoraceae
bastard toadflax
dwarf mistletoe
Loranthaceae
mistletoe
sandalwood
Santalaceae
Santalales
Viscaceae
angiosperms—saxifrage order:
Astilbe
currant
Echeveria
gooseberry
houseleek
hydrangea
kalanchoe
Philadelphus
Pittosporaceae
Ribes
Saxifragaceae
Saxifragales
saxifrage
sedum

angiosperms—soapberry order:
Aceraceae
akee
box elder
buckeye
guarana
horse chestnut
litchi
maple
red maple
Sapindales
silver maple
sugar maple
angiosperms—staff-tree, buckthorn, olive orders:
alder buckthorn
ash
bittersweet
buckthorn
Ceanothus
Celastraceae
Celastrales
Euonymus
Forsythia
holly
jasmine
jujube
lilac
Oleaceae
olive
privet
Rhamnales
tea olive
Vitaceae
angiosperms—tamarisk order:
boojum tree
ocotillo
Tamaricales
tamarisk
angiosperms—tea order:
Camellia
Clusiaceae
Dipterocarpaceae
Elatinaceae
franklinia
Gordonia
mammee apple
mangosteen
Ochnaceae
Saint-John's-wort
stewartia
Theaceae
Theales
angiosperms—teasel order:
bush honeysuckle
Caprifoliaceae
Dipsacaceae
Dipsacales
elder

feverwort
honeysuckle
scabious
snowberry
teasel
Valerianaceae
Viburnum
angiosperms—violet and related orders:
Begonia
Begoniales
bottle gourd
bryony
cucumber
Cucurbitales
Datiscaceae
dishcloth gourd
Flacourtiaceae
gourd
melon
pansy
papaya
Passiflorales
passion-flower
pumpkin
rock rose
squash
sun rose
Viola
Violales
watermelon
angiosperms—walnut order:
butternut
hickory
Juglandales
pecan
walnut
angiosperms—water lily order:
fanwort
hornwort
Nymphaeales
Rafflesiales
water lily
water shield
angiosperms—water-plantain and related orders:
Alismales
arrowhead
Elodea
Hydrocharitales
Najadales
pondweed
water plantain
angiosperms—witch-hazel and related orders:
Casuarinales
Didymelales
Eucommiales
Fothergilla
Hamamelidaceae

Hamamelidales
katsura tree
Myricales
plane tree
sweet gum
Trochodendrales
winter hazel
witch hazel
angiosperms—other:
aspen
barbeya
buckwheat
buffalo berry
carnivorous plant
cobra plant
Connarales
Daphne
Diapensiales
dicotyledon
Dilleniales
everlasting
Glossopteris
hardwood
Hippuridales
Illicales
Leitneriales
lotus
macadamia
monocotyledon
Nelumbonales
Nepenthales
Nepenthes
Paeoniales
peony
pitcher plant
Plumbaginales
Podostemales
Polygalales
Polygonales
poplar
Proteales
Rafflesiales
rhubarb
Salicales
Sarraceniales
sundew family
taro
Theligonales
Thymelaeales
Triuridales
Venus's-flytrap
wild flower
willow
arthropods—
  arachnids:
arachnid
black widow
brown spider
chigger
crab spider
daddy longlegs
false scorpion
funnel weaver

funnel-web spider
garden spider
giant water
  scorpion
jumping spider
mite
nursery-web spider
red spider
scorpion
silk spider
spider
sunspider
tarantula
tick
trap-door spider
whip scorpion
wolf spider
arthropods—
  crustaceans:
amphipod
barnacle
blue crab
branchiopod
brine shrimp
clam shrimp
copepod
crab
crayfish
crustacean
crustacean louse
decapod
Dungeness crab
fiddler crab
fish louse
gammarid
ghost crab
gribble
hermit crab
hooded shrimp
horseshoe shrimp
isopod
krill
land crab
lobster
malacostracan
mantis shrimp
mantle
mussel shrimp
mustache shrimp
opossum shrimp
pea crab
pill bug
robber crab
sand flea
scampi
shellfish
shrimp
skeleton shrimp
sow bug
spider crab
tadpole shrimp
tanaid
water flea

arthropods—
  other:
arthropod
centipede
eurypterid
horseshoe crab
insect
millipede
myriapod
Paradoxides
pauropod
sea spider
symphylan
trilobite
bacteria:
actinomycete
archaebacterium
Bacillus
bacterium
blue-green algae
Clostridium
denitrifying
  bacteria
episome
eubacterium
gliding bacterium
gram stain
Haemophilus
Lactobacillus
Micrococcus
mycoplasma
Pasteurella
pneumococcus
pseudomonad
rickettsia
Salmonella
sheathed bacteria
Spirillum
spirochete
Staphylococcus
streptococcus
Streptomyces
sulfur bacterium
Vibrio
birds—anseriform
  order:
Anatidae
anseriform
black duck
bufflehead
Canada goose
canvasback
dabbling duck
diving duck
duck
eider
gadwall
goldeneye
goose
magpie goose
mallard
merganser
néné

perching duck
pintail
pochard
redhead
ring-necked duck
scaup
scoter
screamer
sheldgoose
shelduck
shoveler
snow goose
stifftail
swan
teal
whistling duck
white-fronted
  goose
wigeon
wood duck
birds—
  caprimulgiform and
  apodiform orders:
apodiform
caprimulgiform
chuck-will's-widow
crested swift
frogmouth
hummingbird
nighthawk
nightjar
oilbird
owlet frogmouth
poorwill
potoo
swift
swiftlet
whippoorwill
birds—charadriiform
  order:
auk
auklet
avocet
charadriiform
courser
curlew
dotterel
dowitcher
godwit
great auk
greenshank
guillemot
gull
jacana
jaeger
killdeer
knot
lapwing
murre
murrelet
oystercatcher
painted snipe
phalarope

plover
pratincole
puffin
redshank
ruff
sandpiper
seedsnipe
sheathbill
skimmer
skua
snipe
stilt
surfbird
tattler
tern
thickknee
turnstone
willet
woodcock
yellowlegs
birds—columbiform
and psittaciform
orders:
  bristlehead
  cockatoo
  columbiform
  conure
  dodo
  domestic pigeon
  lovebird
  macaw
  parakeet
  parrot
  passenger pigeon
  pigeon
  psittaciform
  sandgrouse
  turtledove
  wood pigeon
birds—coraciiform
and piciform orders:
  barbet
  coraciiform
  flicker
  honey guide
  hornbill
  ivory-billed
    woodpecker
  jacamar
  kingfisher
  kookaburra
  motmot
  piciform
  piculet
  puffbird
  roller
  sapsucker
  toucan
  woodpecker
birds—cuculiform
and owl orders:
  ani
  barn owl
  coucal

cuckoo
cuculiform
eagle owl
fish owl
ground cuckoo
hawk owl
horned owl
owl
roadrunner
screech owl
short-eared owl
turaco
wood owl
birds—extinct:
  Aepyornis
  Archaeopteryx
  Diatryma
  Hesperornis
  Ichthyornis
birds—falconiform
order:
  accipiter
  bald eagle
  bateleur
  bird of prey
  buzzard
  caracara
  condor
  eagle
  falcon
  falconiform
  golden eagle
  goshawk
  gyrfalcon
  harrier
  hawk
  hobby
  kestrel
  kite
  lammergeier
  merlin
  osprey
  peregrine falcon
  secretary bird
  sparrowhawk
  turkey vulture
  vulture
birds—galliform and
gruiform orders:
  bustard
  button quail
  coot
  crake
  crane
  curassow
  finfoot
  galliform
  gallinule
  grouse
  gruiform
  guinea fowl
  hoatzin
  jungle fowl
  limpkin

megapode
mesite
partridge
peacock
pheasant
ptarmigan
quail
rail
seriema
trumpeter
turkey
whooping crane
birds—passeriform
order:
  accentor
  Aegithalidae
  antbird
  becard
  bell-magpie
  bellbird
  bird-of-paradise
  bishop
  blackbird
  Bombycillidae
  bowerbird
  broadbill
  buffalo weaver
  bulbul
  bunting
  butcherbird
  Callaeidae
  Campephagidae
  canary
  Carduelidae
  catbird
  Certhiidae
  chat
  chat-thrush
  chough
  cisticola
  cock-of-the-rock
  cordon bleu
  Corvidae
  Cotingidae
  creeper
  crow
  cuckoo-shrike
  currawong
  Dendrocolaptidae
  dipper
  drongo
  Emberizidae
  Estrildidae
  fairy bluebird
  false sunbird
  fantail
  flowerpecker
  flycatcher
  forktail
  Furnariidae
  Galápagos finch
  gnatcatcher
  goldfinch
  grackle

Grallinidae
grass finch
grosbeak
ground thrush
helmet-shrike
Hirundinidae
honeycreeper
honeyeater
house sparrow
hypocoly
Icteridae
Irenidae
jay
kingbird
kinglet
kiskadee
lark
laughing thrush
Leiothrix
lyrebird
magpie
magpie-robin
manakin
mannikin
martin
meadowlark
Mimidae
mockingbird
monarch
Muscicapidae
mynah
Nectariniidae
nightingale
nightingale thrush
nuthatch
oriole
oropendola
ovenbird
Panuridae
Paridae
Parulidae
passeriform
pewee
Philepittidae
phoebe
pipit
pitta
Ploceidae
prinia
quelea
raven
redstart
Remizidae
robin
rockfowl
rosefinch
scrub-bird
seedeater
sharpbill
shrike
shrike-vireo
silky flycatcher
song-babbler
songbird

sparrow
starling
Sturnidae
sunbird
swallow
Sylviidae
tailorbird
tanager
tapaculo
thickhead
thrush
tit
tit-babbler
tityra
towhee
treecreeper
Turdidae
tyrannulet
tyrant flycatcher
umbrellabird
vanga-shrike
vireo
wagtail
warbler
wattle-eye
waxbill
waxwing
weaver
white-eye
whydah
woodcreeper
woodswallow
woodwarbler
wren
Xenicidae

birds—others:
albatross
aviary
aviculture
bird
bittern
booby
cassowary
casuariiform
ciconiiform
coly
Colymbiformes
cormorant
diving petrel
egret
emu
flamingo
frigate bird
fulmar
gannet
grebe
hammerhead
heron
ibis
kiwi
loon
moa
ornithology
ostrich

pelecaniform
pelican
penguin
petrel
plumage
prion
procellariiform
rhea
shearwater
shoebill
snakebird
spoonbill
stork
storm petrel
syrinx
tinamou
trogon
tropic bird

bryophytes:
bryophyte
bug-on-a-stick
carpet moss
cord moss
cushion moss
granite moss
hair-cap moss
hornwort
leafy liverwort
liverwort
luminous moss
Marchantia
moss
peat moss
screw moss
tree moss
wind-blown moss

classification:
classification
nomenclature
taximetrics
taxon
taxonomy

enterocoelomates:
acornworm
amphioxus
arrowworm
beardworm
bêche-de-mer
blastoid
brittle star
cake urchin
carpoid
chordate
crinoid
crown-of-thorns
   starfish
cystoid
echinoderm
echinoid
graptolite
heart urchin
hemichordate
protochordate
pterobranch

sand dollar
sea cucumber
sea lily
sea squirt
sea urchin
shellfish
starfish
tunicate

fishes—atheriniform
and related orders:
atheriniform
dealfish
dory
flying fish
grunion
killifish
lantern-eye fish
live-bearer
molly
oarfish
silversides
spiny-finned fish

fishes—
batrachoidiform and
related orders:
anglerfish
batfish
brotula
cave fish
clingfish
cod
frogfish
goosefish
grenadier
hake
paracanthopterygian
pearlfish
pollock
toadfish
whiting

fishes—
cartilaginous:
basking shark
blue shark
carcharhinid
chimaera
chondrichthian
Cladoselache
devil ray
dogfish
electric ray
guitarfish
hammerhead shark
mackerel shark
mako shark
monkfish
ray
saw shark
sawfish
shark
skate
stingray
thresher shark

tiger shark
white shark

fishes—cypriniform
and siluriform
orders:
barb
bitterling
bullhead
carp
catfish
characin
chub
corydoras
dace
electric catfish
electric eel
goldfish
hatchetfish
knifefish
labeo
loach
madtom
minnow
ostariophysan
pencil fish
piranha
roach
sucker
tench
tetra
tigerfish
wels
zebra fish

fishes—
gasterosteiform
order:
cornetfish
gasterosteiform
pipefish
sea horse
shrimpfish
stickleback
swamp eel
trumpet fish

fishes—jawless fish
and placoderms:
Agnatha
antiarch
Arctolepis
arthrodire
Bothriolepis
Cephalaspis
hagfish
lamprey
ostracoderm
Palaeospondylus
placoderm
spiny shark
swim bladder

fishes—perciform
order:
angelfish
archer fish
barracuda

bass
bigeye
black bass
blenny
bluegill
bonito
butterfish
butterfly fish
carangid
cichlid
crappie
damselfish
darter
discus fish
dragonet
drum
fingerfish
glassfish
goatfish
goby
gourami
grouper
grunt
hind
hogfish
jack
jewfish
labyrinth fish
mackerel
marlin
mojarra
moonfish
mudskipper
mullet
Nile perch
parrot fish
perch
perciform
pikeperch
pomfret
pompano
porgy
prickleback
rabbitfish
ragfish
remora
sailfish
scad
scat
sea bass
sheepshead
Siamese fighting
  fish
sleeper
slipmouth
snapper
snook
soapfish
spadefish
spearfish
spiny eel
stargazer
sunfish
surfperch

surgeonfish
swordfish
threadfin
tilefish
tripletail
tuna
weakfish
weever
wolffish
wrasse
fishes—
  pleuronectiform
  and tetraodontiform
  orders:
  boxfish
  dab
  filefish
  flatfish
  flounder
  halibut
  mola
  plaice
  porcupine fish
  puffer
  sole
  tetraodontiform
  triggerfish
  turbot
fishes—salmoniform
  order:
  Atlantic salmon
  bristlemouth
  brook trout
  brown trout
  capelin
  char
  coho
  hatchetfish
  king salmon
  lake trout
  mudminnow
  pike
  rainbow trout
  salmon
  salmoniform
  sandfish
  scaleless dragonfish
  smelt
  spookfish
  trout
  viperfish
  whitefish
fishes—scorpaeniform
  and related orders:
  dragonfish
  flathead
  flying gurnard
  greenling
  lion-fish
  lumpsucker
  poacher
  redfish
  scorpaeniform
  scorpion fish

sculpin
sea robin
snailfish
stonefish
zebra fish
fishes—others:
  alewife
  anchovy
  bichir
  bony fish
  bowfin
  Cheirolepis
  chondrostean
  clupeiform
  coelacanth
  crossopterygian
  deep-sea fish
  Dipterus
  eel
  elopiform
  Eusthenopteron
  fish
  gar
  gulper
  herring
  holostean
  ladyfish
  lungfish
  menhaden
  moray
  mormyrid
  notopterid
  osteoglossomorph
  paddlefish
  Rhipidistia
  sardine
  shad
  sturgeon
  tarpon
  teleost
  wolf herring
gymnosperms:
  alerce
  American
    arborvitae
  Araucaria
  arborvitae
  bald cypress
  big tree
  California nutmeg
  cedar
  conifer
  Cordaitales
  Cupressaceae
  cycad
  Cycadeoidales
  Cycas
  cypress
  cypress pine
  dawn redwood
  Douglas fir
  eastern red cedar
  English yew
  Ephedra

false cypress
fir
giant arborvitae
ginkgo
Gnetaceae
Greek fir
hemlock
incense cedar
Japanese cedar
Japanese torreya
Japanese yew
juniper
larch
Lebachia
Pinaceae
pine
Podocarpaceae
redwood
seed fern
Sequoia
spruce
stinking yew
Taxaceae
Taxodiaceae
Torreya
umbrella pine
Welwitschiaceae
yellowwood
yew
insects—coleopteran
  order:
  alfalfa weevil
  bark beetle
  beetle
  bess beetle
  billbug
  blister beetle
  boll weevil
  branch and twig
    borer
  carrion beetle
  casebearing beetle
  chafer
  checkered beetle
  click beetle
  coleopteran
  Colorado potato
    beetle
  cucumber beetle
  darkling beetle
  dermestid beetle
  dung beetle
  elm bark beetle
  firefly
  flat bark beetle
  flea beetle
  flower chafer
  glowworm
  ground beetle
  Japanese beetle
  June beetle
  ladybird beetle
  leaf-rolling weevil
  long-horned beetle

metallic
 wood-boring
  beetle
net-winged beetle
plum curculio
potato beetle
predaceous
 diving beetle
primitive weevil
rhinoceros beetle
rove beetle
seed beetle
shining leaf chafer
soldier beetle
spider beetle
stag beetle
strepsipteran
tiger beetle
tortoise beetle
tumbling flower
 beetle
unicorn beetle
water scavenger
 beetle
weevil
whirligig beetle
insects—fly order:
 anthomyiid fly
 bee fly
 biting midge
 black fly
 blow fly
 bot fly
 crane fly
 dipteran
 flesh fly
 fly
 fruit fly
 fungus gnat
 gall midge
 Hessian fly
 horse fly
 housefly
 hover fly
 leaf miner
 louse fly
 midge
 mosquito
 robber fly
 tachinid fly
 tsetse fly
 vinegar fly
 warble fly
insects—
 hymenopteran order:
 ant
 Apocrita
 bee
 braconid
 bumblebee
 chalcid
 cuckoo wasp
 fig wasp
 gall wasp

honey ant
honeybee
horntail
hymenopteran
ichneumon
leaf-cutter bee
sand wasp
sawfly
spider wasp
Symphyta
thread-waisted
 wasp
velvet ant
wasp
wood wasp
insects—lepidopteran
 order:
bagworm moth
blue butterfly
bollworm
brush-footed
 butterfly
butterfly
carpenter moth
casebearer
clearwing moth
copper butterfly
diamondback
 moth
flour moth
forester moth
gelechiid moth
geometrid moth
gossamer-winged
 butterfly
gypsy moth
hairstreak
harvester
hawk moth
lappet
leaf roller moth
lepidopteran
measuring worm
milkweed butterfly
monarch butterfly
morpho
moth
olethreutid moth
owlet moth
painted lady
parnassian
 butterfly
peppered moth
pyralid moth
regal moth
saturniid moth
silkworm moth
skipper
slug caterpillar
 moth
sulfur butterfly
swallowtail
 butterfly

tent caterpillar
 moth
tiger moth
tineid moth
tussock moth
white butterfly
yucca moth
zebra swallowtail
 butterfly
insects—others:
 alderfly
 ambush bug
 antlion
 aphid
 apterygote
 assassin bug
 back swimmer
 bedbug
 bristletail
 bug
 burrower bug
 caddisfly
 chewing louse
 chinch bug
 cicada
 cockroach
 cone-headed
  grasshopper
 coreid bug
 cottony-cushion
  scale
 cricket
 dipluran
 dobsonfly
 dragonfly
 earwig
 ephemeropteran
 flea
 flower bug
 froghopper
 giant water bug
 grape phylloxera
 grasshopper
 harlequin
  cabbage bug
 heteropteran
 homopteran
 human louse
 jumping plant
  louse
 katydid
 lace bug
 lacewing
 leaf insect
 leafhopper
 locust
 long-horned
  grasshopper
 louse
 lygaeid bug
 mantid
 mantispid
 marsh treader
 mayfly

meadow
 grasshopper
mealybug
mole cricket
neuropteran
odonate
orthopteran
plant bug
proturan
psocid
pygmy grasshopper
red bug
San Jose scale
scale insect
scorpionfly
shield-backed
 grasshopper
short-horned
 grasshopper
smaller water
 strider
snakefly
springtail
stinkbug
stonefly
sucking louse
termite
thrips
treehopper
walkingstick
water boatman
water scorpion
water strider
webspinner
whitefly
lophophorates:
 Atrypa
 horseshoe worm
 lamp shell
 lingulid
 moss animal
 Tetractinella
lower invertebrates:
 archaeocyathid
 Ascaris
 aschelminth
 Aurelia
 bread-crumb
  sponge
 Cassiopea
 Chrysaora
 clionid
 cnidarian
 coral
 ctenophore
 eelworm
 entoproct
 eye worm
 filarial worm
 flatworm
 fluke
 freshwater jellyfish
 gastrotrich
 Gonionemus

guinea worm
hookworm
horny sponge
Hydra
Hydractinia
hydroid
jellyfish
Leucosolenia
Liriope
lungworm
medusa
mesozoan
millepore
nematocyst
nematode
Obelia
pinworm
planarian
polyp
Portuguese
  man-of-war
priapulid
ribbon worm
rotifer
Rugosa
sea anemone
sea fan
sea gooseberry
sea pen
sea walnut
siliceous sponge
spiny-headed
  worm
sponge
tapeworm
threadworm
trichina
Venus's flower
  basket
worm
zoanthid
mammals—
  artiodactyl order:
alpaca
antelope
aoudad
artiodactyl
aurochs
babirusa
bighorn
bison
boar
bongo
bovid
brocket
buffalo
bush pig
camel
cattle
chamois
chevrotain
deer
dibatag
duiker

eland
fallow deer
gaur
gazelle
gerenuk
giraffe
gnu
goat
guanaco
hartebeest
hippopotamus
ibex
impala
Kobus
kudu
llama
moose
mountain goat
mule deer
muntjac
musk deer
musk-ox
nyala
okapi
oryx
peccary
Père David's deer
pig
pronghorn
red deer
reedbuck
reindeer
roe deer
ruminant
saiga
sassaby
sheep
sika
springbok
tahr
vicuña
wapiti
warthog
water buffalo
white-tailed deer
yak
mammals—bat
  order:
bat
brown bat
bulldog bat
disk bat
false vampire bat
free-tailed bat
Hipposideridae
horseshoe bat
Jamaican fruit bat
New Zealand
  short-tailed bat
Phyllostomatidae
Pteropodidae
sheath-tailed bat
vampire bat
Vespertilionidae

mammals—carnivore
  order:
aardwolf
African
  hunting dog
Arctic fox
Asiatic black bear
badger
bat-eared fox
bear
bearded seal
binturong
black bear
bobcat
brown bear
bush dog
cacomistle
Caffre cat
canine
caracal
carnivore
cat
cheetah
civet
clouded leopard
coati
coyote
crabeater seal
dhole
dingo
dog
elephant seal
fennec
ferret
fisher
flat-headed cat
fossa
fox
fur seal
genet
golden cat
gray fox
grison
grizzly bear
harbour seal
harp seal
hooded seal
hyena
jackal
jaguar
jaguarundi
kinkajou
leopard
leopard cat
linsang
lion
lynx
margay
marten
mink
mongoose
monk seal
mustelid
ocelot

olingo
otter
ounce
Pallas's cat
panda
polar bear
polecat
procyonid
puma
raccoon
raccoon dog
ratel
sable
sea lion
seal
serval
skunk
sloth bear
South
  American fox
spectacled bear
stoat
sun bear
suricate
tayra
tiger
viverrid
walrus
weasel
Weddell seal
wildcat
wolf
wolverine
mammals—cetacean
  order:
ambergris
baleen whale
beaked whale
beluga
blue whale
bottlenose whale
cetacean
dolphin
fin whale
gray whale
humpback whale
killer whale
narwhal
pilot whale
porpoise
right whale
sei whale
sperm whale
whale
mammals—extinct:
baluchitherium
Barylambda
brontothere
Camelops
cave bear
Chalicotherium
Condylarthra
Coryphodon
Creodonta

dawn horse
Dinohyus
Dryopithecus
Elasmotherium
Glyptodon
Irish elk
litoptern
mammoth
mastodon
Merychippus
Miacis
Moeritherium
Moropus
multituberculate
Notoungulata
Oreopithecus
Phenacodus
sabre-toothed cat
Thylacosmilus
titanothere
Toxodon
Triconodon
Uintatherium
woolly rhinoceros
mammals—
insectivore and
edentate orders:
anteater
armadillo
edentate
elephant shrew
golden mole
hedgehog
insectivore
mole
otter shrew
short-tailed shrew
shrew
sloth
solenodon
tenrec
mammals—
monotremes and
marsupials:
bandicoot
cuscus
echidna
glider
kangaroo
koala
marsupial
marsupial mole
marsupial mouse
monotreme
native cat
numbat
opossum
phalanger
platypus
rat kangaroo
rat opossum
Tasmanian devil
Tasmanian wolf
wallaby

wombat
mammals—
perissodactyl
order:
ass
donkey
equine
horse
mule
perissodactyl
Przewalski's horse
rhinoceros
tapir
zebra
mammals—primate
order:
ape
avahi
aye-aye
baboon
capuchin monkey
Celebes black ape
chimpanzee
colobus
diana monkey
drill
durukuli
galago
gelada
gibbon
gorilla
guenon
hamadryas
howling monkey
indri
langur
lemur
loris
macaque
mandrill
mangabey
marmoset
monkey
orangutan
patas monkey
potto
primate
proboscis monkey
rhesus monkey
saki
siamang
sifaka
spider monkey
squirrel monkey
tarsier
titi
tree shrew
uakari
woolly monkey
woolly spider
monkey
mammals—rodent
order:
agouti

bamboo rat
bandicoot rat
beaver
cane rat
capybara
cavy
chinchilla
chipmunk
cloud rat
cotton rat
dormouse
field mouse
flying squirrel
gerbil
gopher
grasshopper
mouse
ground squirrel
guinea pig
gundi
hamster
harvest mouse
hutia
jerboa
jumping mouse
kangaroo rat
lemming
maned rat
marmot
mole rat
mouse
muskrat
nutria
paca
pocket mouse
porcupine
pouched rat
prairie dog
rat
rice rat
rock rat
rodent
sewellel
spiny rat
springhare
squirrel
tuco-tuco
viscacha
vole
water rat
white-footed
mouse
wood rat
woodchuck
mammals—others:
aardvark
colugo
dugong
elephant
hare
hyrax
lagomorph
mammal
manatee

pangolin
pika
proboscidean
rabbit
sea cow
sirenian
ungulate
protists—algae:
Acetabularia
agar
alga
algology
brown algae
Chlorella
desmid
diatom
dulse
Fucus
green algae
Irish moss
kelp
laver
Nostoc
Oedogonium
phytoplankton
Pleurococcus
red algae
Sargassum
sea lettuce
seaweed
spirogyra
stonewort
Ulothrix
Vaucheria
water bloom
water net
protists—fungi:
Agaricales
Amanita
Ascomycetes
Basidiomycetes
Boletaceae
cup fungus
Deuteromycetes
fungus
Lycoperdales
mushroom
mycorrhiza
Oomycetes
Polyporales
stinkhorn
truffle
water mold
yeast
Zygomycetes
protists—
protozoans:
actinomyxidian
amoeba
astome
Balantidium
Ceratium
Chlamydomonas
chloromonad

chrysomonad
ciliate
cilium
cnidosporidian
coccolith
cryptomonad
dinoflagellate
Entamoeba
entodiniomorph
Euglena
flagellate
flagellum
foraminiferan
fusulinid
gregarine
Gymnodinium
gymnostome
haplosporidian
helioflagellate
heliozoan
heterochlorid
heterotrich
Holomastigotoides
hymenostome
hypermastigote
hypotrich
leishmania
microsporidian
myxosporidian
Nosema
odontostome
oligotrich
opalinid
Paramecium
peritrich
Plasmodium
proteomyxid
protomonad
protozoan
pseudopodium
radiolarian
rhizomastigote
Sarcocystis
sarcodine
sporozoan
suctorian
testacean
tintinnid
trichocyst
trichomonad
trichostome
trypanosome
volvocid
Volvox
Vorticella
protists—others:
 beard lichen
 Iceland moss
 lichen
 manna
 Myxomycetes
 oak moss
 Parmelia

Plasmodio-
 phoromycetes
protist
slime mold
reptiles—
 crocodilians:
 alligator
 caiman
 crocodile
 gavial
reptiles—extinct:
 Albertosaurus
 Allosaurus
 Anatosaurus
 Ankylosaurus
 Apatosaurus
 Bradysaurus
 camptosaur
 Clidastes
 Coelophysis
 cynodont
 Cynognathus
 Dicynodon
 Dimetrodon
 Dimorphodon
 dinosaur
 Diplodocus
 Edaphosaurus
 Euparkeria
 ichthyosaur
 iguanodon
 Limnoscelis
 Mesosaurus
 mosasaur
 Moschops
 Nothosaurus
 Ornitholestes
 Ornithomimus
 Oviraptor
 Pachycephalo-
 saurus
 Pentaceratops
 phytosaur
 Plateosaurus
 Plesiosaurus
 Protoceratops
 Psittacosaurus
 Pteranodon
 pterodactyl
 pterosaur
 Rhamphorhyn-
 chus
 sauropterygian
 Stegosaurus
 Struthiomimus
 therapsid
 triceratops
 tritylodont
 tyrannosaur
reptiles—lizards:
 anole
 Calotes
 chameleon
 gecko

Gila monster
glass snake
horned toad
iguana
Komodo dragon
lizard
monitor lizard
racerunner
skink
reptiles—snakes:
 adder
 anaconda
 Aniliidae
 black snake
 blind snake
 boa
 boomslang
 brown snake
 bull snake
 bushmaster
 Cerastes
 coachwhip
 cobra
 colubrid
 copperhead
 coral snake
 egg-eating snake
 elapid
 fer-de-lance
 flying snake
 garter snake
 green snake
 hognose snake
 indigo snake
 king snake
 krait
 mamba
 mangrove snake
 moccasin
 python
 racer
 rat snake
 rattlesnake
 sea snake
 shieldtail snake
 sidewinder
 snake
 taipan
 tree snake
 vine snake
 viper
 wart snake
 water snake
reptiles—turtles:
 Blanding's turtle
 box turtle
 Emydidae
 mud turtle
 musk turtle
 painted turtle
 pond turtle
 sea turtle
 side-necked turtle

snake-necked
 turtle
snapping turtle
softshell turtle
terrapin
tortoise
turtle
wood turtle
reptiles—others:
 reptile
 tuatara
schizocoelomates—
 annelids:
 annelid
 earthworm
 fanworm
 feather-duster
 worm
 fireworm
 leech
 lugworm
 oligochaete
 palolo worm
 peacock worm
 polychaete
 rag worm
 sea mouse
schizocoelomates—
 mollusks:
 ammonoid
 ark shell
 belemnoid
 bivalve
 bubble shell
 cephalopod
 chiton
 clam
 cockle
 conch
 cone shell
 coquina clam
 cowrie
 cuttlefish
 ear shell
 gaper clam
 gastropod
 geoduck
 jingle shell
 land snail
 mantle
 mollusk
 monoplacophoran
 murex
 mussel
 nautilus
 nudibranch
 octopus
 olive shell
 opisthobranch
 oyster
 periwinkle
 piddock
 prosobranch
 pteropod

pulmonate	onychophoran	horsetail	staghorn fern
razor clam	peanutworm	Lepidodendron	tracheophyte
scallop	pentastomid	Lycophyta	whisk fern
seashell	schizocoelomate	Marattiaceae	*viruses:*
shellfish	spoonworm	Ophioglossaceae	adenovirus
shipworm	tardigrade	Osmundaceae	arbovirus
slug	trochophore	Pleuromeia	cytomegalovirus
squid	*tracheophytes:*	Polypodiaceae	lysogeny
top shell	Adiantaceae	prefern	myxovirus
triton shell	angiosperm	Psilotophyta	picornavirus
tusk shell	Aspleniaceae	quillwort	plant virus
whelk	bracken	Rhynie plants	polyoma virus
worm shell	cliffbrake	Salviniales	poxvirus
schizocoelomates—	club moss	Schizaeaceae	virion
others:	fern	Sphenophyta	virology
oncopod	gymnosperm	spike moss	virus

Biographies

See Section 10/34 of Part Ten

INDEX: See entries under all of the terms above

Division II. **The Molecular Basis of Vital Processes**
[For Part Three headnote see page 95.]

The outlines in the three sections of Division II deal with the molecular level of biotic organization and set forth theories of the chemical transformations and the exchanges of energy that occur in the distinctively vital processes treated in Section 311 of Division I.

Section 321. **Chemicals and the Vital Processes**

A. The inorganic milieu of living systems

B. Organic chemicals participating naturally in the life processes

  1. Carbohydrates

  2. Lipids

  3. Proteins and peptides

  4. The major carrier of chemical energy: ATP

  5. Nucleic acids

    a. General features

    b. Deoxyribonucleic acid (DNA)

    c. Ribonucleic acid (RNA)

  6. Biological pigments and coloration

  7. Enzymes

  8. Vitamins

  9. Hormones

    a. General features of hormones: relationship between endocrine regulation and neural regulation, the evolution of hormones

    b. The hormones of vertebrates

    c. The hormones and hormonelike substances of invertebrates: neurohormones, molting hormones, pheromones

    d. The hormones of plants

10. Other natural products: alkaloids, steroids and sterols, isoprenoids and terpenes

C. Drugs: chemicals administered to an organism to change its physiological state or to combat pathogens

1. Sources and development of drugs

2. General aspects of drug action

3. Absorption, distribution, metabolism, and excretion of drugs

4. Classification of drugs by organ or organ system of principal effect

  a. Drugs affecting the cardiovascular system

  b. Drugs affecting smooth and skeletal muscle systems

  c. Drugs affecting the central nervous system

  d. Drugs affecting the autonomic nervous system and the eyes

  e. Drugs affecting the excretory system

  f. Drugs affecting the digestive system

  g. Drugs affecting the reproductive systems

  h. Drugs affecting the immune response system

  i. Drugs affecting the histamine response system

5. Drugs directed against disease organisms

  a. Drugs derived from living microorganisms: antibiotics

  b. Chemical compounds used to treat infectious diseases: chemotherapeutic drugs

6. Drugs directed at the suppression of cancer

7. Drug use and abuse: the nature of drug addiction and dependence
   [see 522.C.9.]

D. Ethyl alcohol, alcohol consumption
   [see 522.C.9.]

E. Biocides and biorepellents

1. Antiseptics and disinfectants

2. Biocides directed by mankind against animal and plant pests

3. Biotoxins produced by microorganisms, plants, and animals: microbial toxins, phytotoxins, zootoxins

4. Biological and chemical warfare agents

F. The selective concentration of chemicals by organisms

Suggested reading in the *Encyclopædia Britannica*:

MACROPAEDIA: Major articles dealing with chemicals and the vital processes

Biochemical Components of Organisms   Drugs and Drug Action
Cells: Their Structures and Functions   Poisons and Poisoning
Chemical Compounds

MICROPAEDIA: Selected entries of reference information

General subjects

biocides:		*biotoxins:*	
Agent Orange	fungicide	lambkill	cellulose
aldrin	herbicide	mycotoxin	disaccharide
chemosterilant	insecticide	poison	glucose
chloral	Malathion	toxin	glycoside
chlordane	parathion	venom	monosaccharide
DDT	phorate	*carbohydrates:*	pectin
dichlorobenzene	rodenticide	carbohydrate	polysaccharide
dimethoate	Toxaphene		starch
fumigant			sugar

*drugs affecting the
autonomic nervous
system:*
  adrenergic drug
  anticholinesterase
  atropins
  beta blocker
  cholinergic drug
  ganglion blocking
    agent
  neuromuscular
    blocking agent
*drugs affecting the
cardiovascular
system:*
  digitalis
  heparin
  nitroglycerin
drugs—analgesics:
  acetaminophen
  acetanilide
  acetylsalicylic acid
  analgesic
  antipyrine
  salicylic acid
drugs—anesthetics:
  anesthetic
  chloroform
  cocaine
  curare
  cyclopropane
  procaine
    hydrochloride
drugs—antibiotics:
  allopurinol
  ampicillin
  antibiotic
  cephalosporin
  erythromycin
  penicillin
  streptomycin
  tetracycline
drugs—antiseptics:
  Dakin's solution
  iodoform
  melachite green
  merbromin
  silver nitrate
*drugs—
  chemotherapeutic:*
  allopurinol
  anthelmintic
  catechu
  chloroquine
  diethylcarbamazine
    citrate
  diethylstilbestrol
  isoniazid
  pamaquine
  Prontosil
  quinacrine
  quinine
  sulfa drug

sulfadiazine
sulfanilamide
sulfonamide
tryparsamide
drugs—hallucinogens:
  bufotenine
  Cannabis
  DMT
  hallucinogen
  hashish
  ibogaine
  LSD
  marijuana
  mescaline
  PCP
  peyote
  psilocin and
    psilocybin
drugs—narcotics:
  codeine
  fentanyl
  heroin
  methadone
  morphine
  narcotic
  opium
drugs—sedatives:
  barbiturate
  chloral hydrate
  paraldehyde
  sedative–hypnotic
    drug
  thalidomide
drugs—stimulants:
  amphetamine
  caffeine
  imipramine
  iproniazid
  isocarboxazid
  methamphetamine
  stimulant
  tranylcypromine
drugs—tranquilizers:
  chlordiazepoxide
  chlorpromazine
  diazepam
  lithium carbonate
  meprobamate
  reserpine
  tranquilizer
*drugs—other drugs
  and drug action:*
  adjuvant
  antacid
  antagonism
  antihistamine
  antimicrobial agent
  astringent
  cytotoxic drug
  diuretic
  drug
  ephedrine
  laxative
  phenol coefficient

promethazine
quinidine
scopolamine
synergism
theophylline
urethane
*enzymes and enzyme
  action:*
  allosteric control
  amylase
  cofactor
  cooperativity
  enzyme
  feedback inhibition
  hydrolase
  induction
  inhibition
  ligase
  lipase
  Michaelis–Menten
    hypothesis
  nuclease
  pepsin
  proteolytic enzyme
  renin
  serotonin
  transaminase
  zymogen
hormones:
  aldosterone
  androgen
  corticoid
  cortisol
  enterogastrone
  epinephrine and
    norepinephrine
  estrogen
  growth hormone
  hormone
  insulin
  luteinizing
    hormone (LH)
  melatonin
  neurohormone
  progesterone
  testosterone
*isoprenoids and
  terpenes:*
  abietic acid
  camphor
  isoprene
  limonene
  menthol
  pinene
  terpene
lipids:
  capsaicin
  fatty acid
  lecithin
  lipid
  phospholipid
  prostaglandin
  sphingolipid
  triglyceride

nucleic acids:
  adenine
  cytosine
  deoxyribonucleic
    acid
  guanine
  nucleic acid
  nucleoside
  nucleotide
  ribonucleic acid
  thymine
  uracil
*pigments and
  coloration:*
  auxochrome
  carotene
  chlorophyll
  chromophore
  flavonoid
  melanin
  phytol
  porphyrin
  quinone
*proteins and
  peptides:*
  actin
  amino acid
  collagen
  glutamic acid
  glutamine
  gluten
  histidine
  histone
  hydroxyproline
  keratin
  myoglobin
  peptide
  prolamin
  protein
  scleroprotein
*steroids and
  sterols:*
  cholesterol
  cortisone
  ergosterol
  saponin
  steroid hormone
vitamins:
  biotin
  carnitine
  choline
  folic acid
  lipoic acid
  niacin
  pantothenic acid
  para-aminobenzoic
    acid
  vitamin
  vitamin A
  vitamin B complex
  vitamin B_1
  vitamin B_2
  vitamin B_6
  vitamin B_{12}

vitamin C	*other:*	denaturation	sapogenin
vitamin D	adenosine	histamine	secretion
vitamin E	triphosphate	piperine	
vitamin K			

Biographies

    See Section 10/34 of Part Ten

INDEX: See entries under all of the terms above

Section 322.　**Metabolism: Bioenergetics and Biosynthesis**

A. Photosynthesis: the initiation of energy conversion in the biosphere
[see also 335.B.]

  1. The biological importance of photosynthesis

  2. Factors that influence the rate of photosynthesis and the energy efficiency of photosynthesis

  3. Determination of the mechanism of photosynthesis

  4. The site of the photosynthetic process in green plants: the chloroplast

  5. The photosynthetic pigments

  6. The energetics of photosynthesis: photoelectron transfer, photophosphorylation

  7. The metabolic path of carbon in photosynthesis: the carbon reduction cycle

B. Metabolism: the totality of all chemical processes in the living organism

  1. The fragmentation of complex molecules: catabolism

  2. The combustion of food materials and the conservation of part of the energy in them: cellular respiration, oxidation and transduction

  3. The biosynthesis of cell components: anabolism

  4. Regulation of metabolism

C. The nitrogen cycle: nitrogen fixation, nitrification and denitrification

---

Suggested reading in the *Encyclopædia Britannica:*

MACROPAEDIA: Major articles dealing with metabolism: bioenergetics and biosynthesis

    Cells: Their Structures and Functions
    Metabolism
    Photosynthesis

MICROPAEDIA: Selected entries of reference information

General subjects

adenosine	catabolism	feedback inhibition	metabolism
triphosphate	cellular respiration	gluconeogenesis	photosynthesis
anabolism	chloroplast	induction	tricarboxylic acid
antimetabolite	cytochrome	inhibition	cycle

Biographies

    See Section 10/34 of Part Ten

INDEX: See entries under all of the terms above

Section 323.   Vital Processes at the Molecular Level

A. The cell membrane

   1. The nature of membranes

   2. Compartmentalization of the cell

   3. Movement of water across cell membranes: osmosis

   4. Movement of solutes through membranes in response to a concentration gradient

   5. Movement of solutes through membranes independent of concentration gradients: active transport, pinocytosis

B. Bioelectricity

C. The nerve impulse

   1. The structure of the neuron

   2. Characteristics of artificially stimulated nerve fibres

   3. Nature of the nerve impulse

   4. Transmission of the nerve impulse: the synapse

D. Muscle contraction

   1. Contractile or motile activity of some type as a characteristic of all living things

   2. Striated, or skeletal, muscle in higher animals

   3. Cardiac muscle

   4. Smooth muscle

E. Bioluminescence

   1. The significance of bioluminescence in behaviour, metabolism, and research

   2. The range and variety of bioluminescent organisms

   3. The biochemical events of light emission: enzymic and nonenzymic systems

---

Suggested reading in the *Encyclopædia Britannica:*

MACROPAEDIA: Major articles dealing with vital processes at the molecular level

   Cells: Their Structures and Functions
   Electricity and Magnetism
   Muscles and Muscle Systems
   Nerves and Nervous Systems

MICROPAEDIA: Selected entries of reference information

General subjects

acetylcholine	bioluminescence	membrane	osmosis
actin	end-plate potential	muscle	pinocytosis
action potential	excitatory	nervous system	resting potential
adrenaline and	postsynaptic	neuromuscular	sodium pump
noradrenaline	potential	junction	synapse
all-or-none law	marine	neuron	
bioelectricity	phosphorescence	neurotransmitter	

<u>Biographies</u>

   See Section 10/34 of Part Ten

INDEX: See entries under all of the terms above

Division III.   **The Structures and Functions of Organisms**
[For Part Three headnote see page 95.]

Division I deals with the nature, origin, evolution, distinctive properties, and classification of living things. Division II deals with the molecular level of biotic organization. The outlines in the nine sections of Division III deal with life at the cellular level and at the organismic level.

Section 331.   **The Cellular Basis of Form and Function**

A. Cell theory and classification

  1. The cell theory

    a. Historical background

    b. Challenges to and revisions of the cell theory in the light of later knowledge

  2. Classification of cells

    a. General features: comparisons between cells and viruses and between procaryotic and eucaryotic cells, tissues as providing a functional classification of cells

    b. Cells and tissues of animals: absorptive cells, secretory cells, nerve cells, sensory cells, muscle cells, cells in supporting tissues, circulating cells, reproductive cells

    c. Cells and tissues of higher plants: outstanding features of the plant cell; meristematic, epidermal, and other types of plant cells

    d. Comparison between animal cells and plant cells

B. Cell design and cell organization

  1. The cell as a molecular system

    a. Macromolecules in cells: nucleic acids, proteins, polysaccharides

    b. Small molecules in cells: lipids, nucleotides, amino acids, fatty acids

  2. Form and structure of the cell

    a. Sizes and shapes of cells

    b. Morphological elements: parts of cells—cell membrane, extracellular matrix, mitochondria, ribosomes, cytoskeleton, nuclear envelope, chromosomes, nucleolus

    c. Procaryotic and eucaryotic cells
    [see 312.A.3.]

C. Functional aspects of cells

  1. The internal environment and the cell matrix: the concept of the cell as a "protoplasm," the concept of the cell as a "bag" containing a water solution of molecules

  2. Cell membranes

  3. Interplay of nucleus and cytoplasm

  4. Cell movement: ciliary, flagellar, and amoeboid

  5. Cells in combination: cohesion and communication to form tissues and multicellular organisms

D. The cell cycle

  1. Cell growth: doubling of size, genetic replication, preparation for division

2. Cell division

a. Mitosis: condensation of chromosomes and dissolution of nuclear envelope; splitting of chromosomes; formation of new nuclear envelopes

b. Cytokinesis: constriction of animal cell into halves by contractile ring of actin filaments; division of plant cell by formation of cell plate and new cell wall

c. Meiosis: division of germ cell into gametes, or reproductive cells, each with one-half of the genetic material of parent cell

E. Fertilization

1. Characteristics of the mature egg

2. Events of fertilization

3. Biochemical analysis of the events of fertilization

4. Mechanisms that aid in the union of gametes

Suggested reading in the *Encyclopædia Britannica:*

MACROPAEDIA: Major article dealing with the cellular basis of form and function

Cells: Their Structures and Functions

MICROPAEDIA: Selected entries of reference information

General subjects

cell	fission	nucleus
chromosome	gamete	ploidy
cytology	in vitro	protoplasm
cytoplasm	fertilization	receptor
cytoplasmic	meiosis	recombination
streaming	mitosis	ribosome
cytoskeleton	multicellular	
fertilization	organism	

Biographies

See Section 10/34 of Part Ten

INDEX: See entries under all of the terms above

Section 332.   **The Relation of Form and Function in Organisms**

A. Biological form and function

B. Plant tissues and fluids: classification, organization, main functions

1. Relatively undifferentiated tissues of nonvascular plants

2. Well-differentiated tissues in vascular plants

a. Meristematic (cell-producing) tissues: apical, lateral, intercalary

b. Mature tissues

i. Dermal (protective) tissues: the epidermis of the primary plant body, the periderm of the secondary plant body

ii. Vascular (conducting) tissues: the xylem, the phloem

iii. Fundamental (ground) tissues: the parenchyma, the supportive collenchyma and sclerenchyma, the endodermis

3. Cells of plant tissues
[see 331.A.2.c.]

C. Organs of plants: tissue organization, functions, and types

1. Development of organs in vascular plants: internal and external morphology, tissue organization, functions, types, and modifications; the stem; the leaf; the root

2. Physiology of organs in vascular plants

3. Diverse sizes and forms of organ systems in vascular plants: potential for unlimited growth

   a. Varieties of shoot systems

   b. Varieties of root systems

   c. Varieties of reproductive organs and organ systems

4. Organs of nonvascular plants: analogues of stem, leaf, and root

5. Evolution of plant organs and organ systems into the complex, multicellular state

D. Animal tissues and fluids: classification, organization, and main functions

   1. Classification of tissues: anatomical, embryological, functional

   2. Tissues for assimilation, storage, transport, and excretion: alimentary, liver, kidney, and lung tissues; blood and lymph

   3. Tissues for coordination: nervous and sensory tissues, endocrine tissues

   4. Tissues for support and movement: connective tissues, cartilage, bone, muscle

   5. Other tissues: reproductive tissues, hemopoietic tissues, tissue fluids

   6. Cells of animal tissues
   [see 331.A.2.b.]

E. Animal organs and organ systems

   1. Specialized organ systems

      a. Relating to the environment primarily: integumentary, skeletal, muscular, nervous, and endocrine systems
      [see also 333.C. and D.; 334.A., B., and C.]

      b. Serving cell metabolism primarily: digestive, respiratory, circulatory, and excretory systems
      [see also 335.C.; 336.A., B., and C.]

      c. Serving genetic continuity primarily: the reproductive system

   2. Interrelationships between organ systems: functional interdependence, feedback mechanisms

   3. Development of organ systems
   [see also 338.D.]

   4. Evolution of organ systems

Suggested reading in the *Encyclopædia Britannica:*

MACROPAEDIA: Major article dealing with the relation of form and function in organisms

   Tissues and Fluids

MICROPAEDIA: Selected entries of reference information

General subjects

bark	inflorescence	pistil	tissue
cambium	leaf	placenta	vascular bundle
connective tissue	lignin	root	vascular system
cortex	meristem	sclerenchyma	vessel
epithelium	mucus	sieve tube	wood
flower	organ	stomate	xylem
growth ring	parenchyma	symmetry	
	phloem		

Biographies
   See Section 10/34 of Part Ten

INDEX: See entries under all of the terms above

Section 333.   **Coordination of Vital Processes: Regulation and Integration**

A. Maintenance of steady states in biological systems: homeostasis

1. The nature of homeostatic systems

2. Homeostatic processes

3. Homeostatic control hierarchies: homeostatic subsystems that serve either organisms or natural communities

4. Origin and evolution of homeostasis

5. Individual adjustments to gradual changes in the physical environment: acclimatization

6. Inactive states accompanied by a lower than normal rate of metabolism: dormancy

B. Information reception and processing: sensory reception

1. Classification of sensory systems

a. According to location of receptors: exteroceptors, interoceptors

b. According to type of stimulus: photoreceptors, thermoreceptors, chemoreceptors, mechanoreceptors, electroreceptors, sound receptors

2. Evolution of sensory systems: specialized organs and information-processing structures

3. Sensory information: interactions between adjacent sense cells and sensory neurons

C. Endocrine systems in animals

1. General features of hormonal coordination: the relationships between endocrine and neural regulation

2. Vertebrate endocrine systems

a. Relationships of endocrine glands to each other and to the blood

b. Structure and function

3. Invertebrate endocrine systems: insects, crustaceans, annelid worms

4. Comparative, adaptive, and evolutionary aspects of endocrine systems: the neurosecretory cell, hypothalamus-pituitary control systems

5. The human endocrine system
    [see 421.E.]

D. Nervous systems in animals

1. Comparison of chemical and nervous regulation: control mechanisms located between the stimulus and the response

2. Nervous coordination

a. Intracellular coordination: general cytoplasmic responsiveness, or irritability, to a stimulus

b. Organelle systems: the channeling of responsiveness at the subcellular level within more complex protozoans

c. Nervous systems: the channeling of responsiveness at the cellular level within multicellular organisms

i. The neuron, or nerve cell

ii. The transmission of the nerve impulse and the synapse
    [see 323.C.]

3. Invertebrate nervous systems

a. Theories of the evolutionary origin of the nervous system

b. Diffuse nervous systems

c. Centralized nervous systems

4. Vertebrate nervous systems

a. The central nervous system: the brain and its components; the spinal cord; the brain coverings (meninges), cavities, cerebrospinal fluid, and neuroglia (nonnervous tissue)

b. The peripheral nervous system

c. Embryonic development of the vertebrate nervous system

d. Evolution of the vertebrate nervous system

e. Biodynamics of the vertebrate nervous system

5. The human nervous system
[see 421.J.]

E. The biological clock: periodicity

1. Rhythms without apparent external correlates: brain waves, breathing, heartbeat

2. Rhythms correlated with natural geophysical cycles: solar-day rhythms, lunar-tidal rhythms, monthly rhythms, annual or seasonal rhythms, epochal rhythms

3. The mechanism of the biological clock

4. Factors affecting biological periodicities

5. The amplification and superimposition of individual rhythms in communities
[see 352.C.1.b.]

Suggested reading in the *Encyclopædia Britannica*:

MACROPAEDIA: Major articles dealing with the coordination of vital processes: regulation and integration

Endocrine Systems
Nerves and Nervous Systems
Sensory Reception
Tissues and Fluids

MICROPAEDIA: Selected entries of reference information

General subjects

endocrine systems:	ganglion	rod	lateral line system
adrenal gland	meninges	visual pigment	mechanoreception
endocrine system	nervous system	*sensory reception—*	receptor
parathyroid gland	neuron	*sound reception:*	sense
pituitary gland	reflex	ear	smell
secretion	spinal cord	echolocation	taste
thyroid gland	synapse	external auditory	thermoreception
nervous systems:	vagus nerve	canal	touch reception
adrenergic nerve	*sensory reception—*	sound reception	*other:*
fibre	*photoreception:*	tympanic	acclimatization
autonomic nervous	cone	membrane	biological rhythm
system	eye	vestibulocochlear	diapause
brain	eyespot	nerve	hibernation
cerebral fissure	macula lutea	*sensory reception—*	homeostasis
cerebrospinal fluid	photoreception	*other:*	tropism
cranial nerve	rhodopsin	chemoreception	

Biographies

See Section 10/34 of Part Ten

INDEX: See entries under all of the terms above

Section 334.   **Covering and Support: Integumentary, Skeletal, and Musculatory Systems**

    A. The body covering

        1. General features of the body covering, of integument: comparisons among unicellular organisms, plants, and animals

        2. Invertebrate integuments: organization and function

            a. Cellular components and their derivatives

            b. Noncellular coatings of the integument

        3. Vertebrate integuments: cellular components and their derivatives

            a. Skin layers: the epidermis, the dermis

            b. Skin derivatives and appendages: skin glands and pigment; epidermal scales; claws, nails, and hoofs; horns and antlers; feathers and hair; dermal derivatives

        4. Skin variations among vertebrates

        5. Embryology and evolution of the vertebrate skin

        6. The biodynamics of vertebrate skin

        7. Human integument and derivatives: skin, hair, nails, sebaceous glands, sweat glands

    B. The body skeleton

        1. The roles of the body skeleton

        2. Description and composition of the skeletal elements

            a. Cuticular structures: bone, crystals, cuticle, ossicles, spicules

            b. Semirigid structures: flexible cuticular structures, calcareous spicules that are not tightly packed, keratin, notochord, cartilage

            c. Other elements: connective tissue, the hydrostatic skeleton, elastic structures, buoyancy devices

        3. The invertebrate skeleton: organization and function

        4. The vertebrate skeleton: structure and function

            a. General features

            b. Embryology of vertebrate skeletons

            c. Vertebral column and thoracic skeleton

            d. Appendicular skeleton: pectoral girdle, pelvic girdle, limbs

        5. Joints in vertebrates and invertebrates permitting various types of movement

        6. Properties of bone and its development

        7. The human skeletal system

    C. The body musculature

        1. General features of muscle tissue: its role in movement, support, colour changes, temperature regulation, and discharge of certain glands; arrangement and gross function

        2. Muscle contractile systems

            a. Simple contractile systems: simple contractile fibrils and epithelio-muscular cells

            b. Complex contractile tissues: striated muscle, smooth muscle

        3. Muscle contraction
           [see 323.D.]

        4. Invertebrate muscle systems

        5. Vertebrate muscle systems

            a. Embryonic development and divisions of the muscular system

            b. Evolution of the vertebrate musculatory system

c. Function and regulation of muscle action

d. Electric organs in certain fishes

6. The human musculatory system
[see 421.H.6. and 7.]

Suggested reading in the *Encyclopædia Britannica*:

MACROPAEDIA: Major articles dealing with covering and support: integumentary, skeletal, and musculatory systems

Integumentary Systems
Muscles and Muscle Systems
Supportive and Connective Tissues
Tissues and Fluids

MICROPAEDIA: Selected entries of reference information

General subjects

integument:	extensor muscle	fontanel	vertebral column
bark	flexor muscle	humerus	zygomatic arch
beak	gluteus muscle	joint	*other:*
claw	iliocostalis muscle	ligament	ankle
dermis	latissimus dorsi	mast cell	arm
epidermis	levator muscle	metacarpal	digit
exoskeleton	muscle	occipital	elbow
feather	pectoralis muscle	parietal bone	face
hair	sphincter muscle	pelvic girdle	foot
horn	trapezius muscle	radius	hand
integument	triceps muscle	rib	heel
nail	*supportive and*	sacrum	hip
scale	*connective tissues:*	scapula	jaw
test	bone	skeleton	knee
musculature:	carpal bone	skull	leg
abdominal muscle	cartilage	sternum	shoulder
abductor muscle	clavicle	tarsal	tail
adductor muscle	femur	tibia	thorax
biceps muscle	fibula	ulna	wrist

Biographies
See Section 10/34 of Part Ten

INDEX: See entries under all of the terms above

Section 335.   Nutrition: the Procurement and Processing of Nutrients

A. The basic features of nutrition

1. The various nutritional patterns; *e.g.,* autotrophism and heterotrophism, phototrophism and chemotrophism

2. Methods of ingestion or penetration
[see C., below]

3. The essential nutrients: compounds that cannot be synthesized by an organism and must be supplied in food; the nutritional needs of organisms

4. Syntrophism: nutritional interrelationships in which the immediate or end products of metabolism of one organism may provide essential nutrients for another

B. Photosynthesis: the production of food in green plants
[see also 322.A.]

C. Digestion and digestive systems

1. The contrast between autotrophs and heterotrophs

2. The alimentary system in animals other than man

   a. Invertebrate digestive systems: vacuolar systems, channel-network systems, saccular systems, tubular systems

   b. Vertebrate digestive systems: oral cavity, teeth, and pharynx; esophagus and stomach; small intestine, pancreas, and liver; the large intestine

   c. Embryology and evolutionary development of the vertebrate digestive system

   d. Biodynamics of the vertebrate digestive system: control of secretions and intestinal movements

3. The human alimentary system
   [see 421.D.]

Suggested reading in the *Encyclopædia Britannica:*

MACROPAEDIA: Major articles dealing with nutrition: the procurement and processing of nutrients

   Digestion and Digestive Systems
   Nutrition

MICROPAEDIA: Selected entries of reference information

General subjects

digestive system:	Paneth cell	*nutrients and*	periodontal
alimentary canal	pharynx	*nutrition:*	membrane
anal canal	plica circularis	carbohydrate	permanent tooth
anus	pylorus	fat	premolar
appendix	rectum	nutrition	primary tooth
argentaffin cell	small intestine	nutritional type	saliva
cecum	stomach	protein	salivary gland
colon	villus	vitamin	tongue
digestion	*ingestion and*	*oral cavity:*	tooth
digestive nerve	*digestion:*	canine tooth	*other:*
plexus	appetite	cementum	bile
esophagus	chewing	dentine	bilirubin
gallbladder	defecation	enamel	chyme
gastric gland	digestion	gum	feces
large intestine	peristalsis	ivory	intestinal gas
liver	satiety	palate	
pancreas	swallowing		

Biographies

   See Section 10/34 of Part Ten

INDEX: See entries under all of the terms above

Section 336.   Gas Exchange, Internal Transport, and Elimination

A. Respiration and respiratory systems

   1. The process of extracting oxygen and releasing carbon dioxide

   2. Gases in the environment: the range of respiratory problems faced by aquatic and terrestrial animals

   3. Basic types of respiratory structures

      a. Respiratory organs of invertebrates: tracheae and gills

      b. Respiratory organs of vertebrates: gills and lungs

   4. Dynamics of respiratory mechanisms

   5. The control of respiration: neural reflexes, muscular feedback, chemically sensitive controls

   6. Adaptation to special environmental conditions

7. The human respiratory system
[see 421.C.]

B. Circulation and circulatory systems

1. Circulation and transport patterns: general aspects common to all circulatory systems

a. Circulation in single cells: streaming movements within the protoplasm

b. Circulation in multicellular animals

2. The fluid media involved in circulation: blood and lymph

a. Evolutionary origins of circulating fluids

b. Plasma

c. Formed elements of the circulating fluid: red cells, white cells, platelets, thrombocytes

d. Lymphocytes and lymph in vertebrates

3. Transport systems in animals

a. Invertebrate circulatory systems

b. Vertebrate circulatory systems

c. Coronary circulation

d. Embryonic development of the circulatory system

e. Biodynamics of vertebrate circulation

f. The human cardiovascular system
[see 421.A.]

4. Plant internal transport

C. Elimination: the disposal of wastes

1. General features of elimination

2. Excretion and excretory systems

a. Excretory mechanisms

b. Invertebrate excretory systems

c. Vertebrate excretory systems

d. The evolution of the vertebrate excretory system

e. The human excretory system
[see 421.G.]

Suggested reading in the *Encyclopædia Britannica:*

MACROPAEDIA: Major articles dealing with gas exchange, internal transport, and elimination

Cells: Their Structures and Functions
Circulation and Circulatory Systems
Excretion and Excretory Systems
Respiration and Respiratory Systems
Tissues and Fluids

MICROPAEDIA: Selected entries of reference information

General subjects

blood and lymph:	serum albumin	cardiovascular	lung
agglutinin	thymus	system	lymph node
blood	*circulatory and*	circulation	lymph nodule
complement	*respiratory systems:*	coronary artery	portal vein
erythrocyte	aorta	diaphragm	pulmonary
hemoglobin	artery	diastole	circulation
hemolysis	asphyxia	gill	pulse
leukocyte	atrium	heart	renal vein
lymph	blood pressure	hepatic vein	respiration
lymphocyte	capillary		
platelet			

systemic	*excretory systems:*	perspiration	phloem
circulation	cloaca	renal capsule	root
systole	excretion	renal pelvis	sieve tube
trachea	kidney	renal pyramid	translocation
valve	loop of Henle	urinary bladder	transpiration
vein	malpighian tubule	urine	transport
vena cava	nasal gland	*plant internal*	vascular bundle
venous sinus	nephridium	*transport system:*	vessel
ventricle	nephron	mass flow	xylem

Biographies

See Section 10/34 of Part Ten

INDEX: See entries under all of the terms above

Section 337.   Reproduction and Sex

A. The forms of reproduction and their comparative adaptive significance

   1. Levels of reproduction

      a. Molecular replication and reproduction

      b. Cell reproduction: binary and multiple fission

      c. Reproduction of organisms
         [see A.2., below]

      d. Life cycles of plants and animals

   2. Reproduction of organisms: sexual and asexual reproduction

   3. Natural selection and reproduction: the evolution of reproduction and variation control
      [see also 312.C.]

B. Sex and sexuality

   1. The distinctions between sex, sexuality, and reproduction

   2. Transduction and transformation as sexlike recombination in viruses and bacteria

   3. The adaptive significance of sex: establishment of genetic diversity

   4. The origin of sex and sexuality

   5. Sex patterns

   6. Determination of the sex of individuals

      a. The sex chromosomes

      b. Abnormal chromosome effects

      c. The effect of parthenogenetic development

      d. Environmental and hormonal influences

C. The reproductive system in plants: its organization and function

   1. General features: asexual systems that create new plants identical to the parent plant, sexual systems that create new plants different from either of the two parents

   2. The sex organs of bryophytes

      a. In liverworts and hornworts

      b. In mosses

   3. The variations of sex organs in tracheophytes

      a. In spore plants

      b. In seed plants

   4. Variations in reproductive cycles: apogamy and apospory (apparent secondary loss of capacity for sexual reproduction)

5. The physiology of reproduction: the influence of internal and environmental factors on the maturation of sporophytes and gametophytes as manifested by their ability to produce spores and gametes

D. The reproductive system in animals: its organization and function

1. General features

2. Reproductive systems of invertebrates

   a. Gonads, associated structures, and products in monoecious and dioecious types

   b. Mechanisms that aid in the union of gametes

   c. Specializations associated with parthenogenesis

   d. Provisions for the developing embryo
      [see 338.D.2.b.]

3. Reproductive systems of vertebrates

   a. Gonads, associated structures, and products

   b. Adaptations for internal fertilization; *e.g.,* the cloaca, intromittent (copulatory) organs, accessory structures

   c. Role of gonads in hormone cycles

   d. Provision for the developing embryo
      [see 338.D.2.b.]

   e. The human reproductive system
      [see 421.F.]

Suggested reading in the *Encyclopædia Britannica*:

MACROPAEDIA: Major articles dealing with reproduction and sex

   Behaviour, Animal
   Reproduction and Reproductive Systems
   Sex and Sexuality

MICROPAEDIA: Selected entries of reference information

General subjects

plant reproduction:	cross-fertilization	menopause	sperm
gametophyte	fertilization	menstruation	spermatogenesis
ovary	fission	ovary	testis
ovule	gestation	ovulation	*other:*
pistil	incubation	ovum	alternation of
pollen	meiosis	placenta	generations
pollination	parturition	uterus	courtship
propagation	recombination	vagina	fertility and
pseudocopulation	reproduction	*reproductive*	infertility
spore	self-fertilization	*system—male:*	gamete
sporophyte	sexual intercourse	bulbourethral	gonad
reproductive	viviparity	gland	hermaphroditism
processes:	*reproductive*	ductus deferens	orgasm
artificial	*system—female:*	epididyme	sex
insemination	egg	penis	sex chromosome
budding	estrus	prostate gland	
conjugation	fallopian tube	seminal vesicle	

Biographies

   See Section 10/34 of Part Ten

INDEX: See entries under all of the terms above

Section 338.   Development: Growth, Differentiation, and Morphogenesis

A. The nature and scope of biological development

B. The constituent processes of development and their control

1. Growth

2. Morphogenesis

3. Differentiation

4. Control and integration of development

C. Development of plants

1. General features: types of life cycles, alternation of generations as independent phases of the life cycle

2. Preparatory events

a. Formation of sex cells

b. Pollination

c. Fertilization

3. Early development: from fertilized egg (zygote) to seedling

a. Embryo formation

b. Independent dormant stages and germination of the seeds and fruits of higher plants, dispersal

4. Later development: the sporophyte plant body

D. Development of animals

1. Preparatory events: the egg and its activation by normal fertilization or by parthenogenesis

2. Early development

a. Embryo formation: cleavage, gastrulation

b. Embryonic adaptations for the maintenance of the developing embryo: shell, yolk stores, membranous sacs, placenta

3. Organ formation

4. Postembryonic development: transformation of the newborn into the adult

E. Aging and decline in animals: life span, death
[for aging in man, see 422.A.]

1. Senescence in mammals

2. Causes of aging

3. The duration of life

F. Specialized patterns of development

1. Biological regeneration

2. The healing processes and scar tissue formation

3. Biological malformation

4. Twinning: multiple births

5. Development in vitro: cell and tissue cultures

6. Development of transplanted tissues and organs

Suggested reading in the *Encyclopædia Britannica*:

MACROPAEDIA: Major articles dealing with development: growth, differentiation, and morphogenesis

Death
Growth and Development, Biological
Tissue Culture

MICROPAEDIA: Selected entries of reference information

General subjects

animal development:	larva	*development*	parthenocarpy
amnion	metamorphosis	*processes:*	seed
blastocyst	neural crest	aging	*other:*
chorion	notochord	death	blastema
cleavage	nymph	development	dysplasia
ectoderm	paedomorphosis	histogenesis	monster
embryo	parturition	organogenesis	
endoderm	placenta	regeneration	
fetus	pupa	*plant development:*	
gastrula	segmentation	endosperm	
gestation	umbilical cord	germination	
incubation		fruit	

Biographies

See Section 10/34 of Part Ten

INDEX: See entries under all of the terms above

Section 339.   **Heredity: the Transmission of Traits**

A. Basic features of heredity

   1. Early speculations on the nature of heredity

   2. Mendelian genetics: Mendel's experiments and their significance, the universality of Mendel's laws, interactions among genes and their variant forms (alleles)

   3. The combined action of heredity and environment in producing an organism

B. The physical basis of heredity

   1. Chromosomes and genes: the cellular basis of heredity

   2. Molecular genetics: the chemical and molecular nature of genes, the genetic code and its mutations, the expression and regulation of genes, applications of molecular genetics

C. Heredity and evolution
   [see also 312.C.]

   1. Population genetics: the gene pool, the Hardy–Weinberg principle, changes in gene frequencies

   2. Natural selection as an agent of evolutionary change

   3. Artificial selection for genetic improvements of selected organisms: domesticated animals, cultivated plants, humankind
   [see also 355.B.3.]

   4. Outbreeding and inbreeding: the effects of consanguinity on the vigour of offspring

---

Suggested reading in the *Encyclopædia Britannica*:

MACROPAEDIA: Major article dealing with heredity: the transmission of traits

   Genetics and Heredity, The Principles of

MICROPAEDIA: Selected entries of reference information

General subjects

albinism	genetic drift	linkage group	recessiveness
allele	genotype	Mendelism	testcross
character	Hardy–Weinberg	mutation	transformation
chimera	law	operon	variation
chromosome	heredity	pedigree	
dominance	hybrid	phenotype	
gene	inbreeding	plasmid	
genetic code	Lamarckism	polyploidy	

Biographies
  See Section 10/34 of Part Ten

<small>INDEX:</small> See entries under all of the terms above

---

Division IV.   Behavioral Responses of Organisms
[For Part Three headnote see page 95.]

Several of the sections in Division III deal with the structure and internal functioning of organisms. The outlines in the two sections of Division IV deal with the external actions and reactions of living things in relation to changes in their environment.

Section 341.   Nature and Patterns of Behavioral Responses

A. Diverse conceptions of animal behaviour

  1. The variety of animal behaviour

  2. Classification of animal behaviour

  3. Components of animal behaviour

B. Patterns of stereotyped response: unlearned behavioral reactions of organisms to some environmental stimulus

  1. Plant movements: tropic and nastic movements, nutation, other autonomous movements

  2. Animal movements: reflex and reflexlike activities, taxes, fixed action patterns and instinct

  3. Photoperiodism

C. Hormonal and nervous control of behaviour

  1. Interaction of endocrine and nervous systems

  2. Hormonal influences on behaviour; *e.g.*, by sex hormones

  3. The nervous system and behaviour: the role of the nervous system in receiving information, processing it in the brain and spinal cord, and initiating the appropriate response

D. Evolution of behaviour

  1. Evidence of the genetic determination of behaviour

  2. The influence of experience on behaviour: phyletic patterns in the evolution of learning

  3. Evolutionary origins and evolutionary consequences of behaviour patterns

---

Suggested reading in the *Encyclopædia Britannica*:

<small>MACROPAEDIA:</small> Major article dealing with the nature and patterns of behavioral responses
  Behaviour, Animal

<small>MICROPAEDIA:</small> Selected entries of reference information
General subjects

animal behaviour	instinct	play	tropism
behaviour genetics	photoperiodism	reflex	

Biographies
  See Section 10/34 of Part Ten

<small>INDEX:</small> See entries under all of the terms above

Section 342.   Development and Range of Behavioral Capacities: Individual and Group Behaviour

A. Basic behavioral activities of individuals

    1. Food getting

    2. Locomotion

    3. Avoidance behaviour

    4. Aggressive behaviour: attack and defensive threats

    5. Behaviour related to habitat

    6. Behaviour related to reproduction

B. Higher behavioral characteristics of individual animals

    1. Simple nonassociative learning; *e.g.,* habituation, sensitization

    2. Associative learning; *e.g.,* classical and instrumental, or operant, conditioning

    3. Spatial learning; *e.g.,* maze learning, navigation

    4. Perceptual learning: imitation and observational learning; *e.g.,* song learning, imprinting

    5. Complex problem solving

        a. Discriminations of relational and abstract stimuli

        b. Generalized rule learning

        c. Insight and reasoning

        d. Language learning

C. The behaviour of animals in groups

    1. Distinctions between groups of social animals and groups of nonsocial ones

    2. Animal communication

    3. The range of social behaviour among social and nonsocial animals

    4. Dynamics of social behaviour

D. Evolution of behaviour
[see 341.D.]

Suggested reading in the *Encyclopædia Britannica*:

MACROPAEDIA: Major articles dealing with the development and range of behavioral capacities: individual and group behaviour

    Behaviour, Animal
    Learning, Animal

MICROPAEDIA: Selected entries of reference information

General subjects

aggressive	brooding	habituation	social learning
behaviour	cannibalism	homing	sound production
alarm signal	cleaning behaviour	imprinting	submissive
animal behaviour	colony	learning	behaviour
animal	conditioning	locomotion	suckling
communication	courtship	motivation	terrestrial
aquatic locomotion	display behaviour	nest	locomotion
associative learning	dominance	pheromone	territorial
avoidance	hierarchy	predation	behaviour
behaviour	feeding behaviour	reproductive	
bird song	flight	behaviour	
brachiation	habit	scavenger	

Biographies
See Section 10/34 of Part Ten

INDEX: See entries under all of the terms above

Division V.   **The Biosphere: the World of Living Things**
[For Part Three headnote see page 95.]

Division I of Part Three deals with the nature, origin, evolution, distinctive properties, and classification of living things. Divisions II, III, and IV deal with life at the molecular, cellular, organismal, and behavioral levels.

The outlines in the five sections of Division V deal with the world of living things taken as a single system of biotic and environmental interactions and interdependencies.

Section 351.   **Basic Features of the Biosphere**

A. The extent of the biosphere

1. Preconditions of the biosphere: the Earth as an ideal medium for life
   [see 312.A.2.]

2. The levels of organization within the biosphere: the biocycle, the ecosystem, the community, the population
   [see 352.A. and C.; 354]

3. Energy flow in the biosphere

4. Cycling of matter in the biosphere

   a. The general pattern of chemical cycles in nature
      [see also 214.C.]

   b. The carbon and oxygen cycles

   c. The nitrogen cycle

   d. The sulfur cycle

   e. The water cycle
      [see also 222.D.]

   f. The sedimentary cycles of essential minerals

5. The concept of the noosphere: mankind's place in the biosphere
   [see 355.B.]

B. The ecosystem: a collection of integrated communities and their environment

1. Definition of an ecosystem

2. The biotic components of the ecosystem

   a. Producers

   b. Consumers

   c. Decomposers

3. The abiotic components of the ecosystem

   a. Pressure and temperature
      [see 223.E.1.]

   b. Radiation

   c. Illumination

d. Water and soil characteristics, salts

e. Wave action: wind and water

f. Fire as a limiting factor

4. The conditioning of the abiotic environment by living organisms

5. The effect of microenvironments on the ecosystem

6. Processes that determine the nature and productivity of the ecosystem

7. Types of ecosystems
[see 354]

Suggested reading in the *Encyclopædia Britannica:*

MACROPAEDIA: Major article dealing with the basic features of the biosphere

Biosphere, The

MICROPAEDIA: Selected entries of reference information

General subjects

biochemical oxygen demand	carbon cycle	nitrogen cycle	sulfur cycle
biogeochemical cycle	ecosystem	oxygen cycle	vernalization
biosphere	eutrophication	phosphorus cycle	
body heat	food chain		
	microclimate		

Biographies
See Section 10/34 of Part Ten

INDEX: See entries under all of the terms above

Section 352.   Biological Populations and Communities

A. Biological populations

1. The study of populations
[see 10/34.B.4.]

2. The measurable characteristics of biological populations

a. Age, sex, and genetic differences and their distribution

b. Numbers and density: the effects of natality and mortality, the reproductive rate and death rate

3. Growth of populations: growth form and carrying capacity

4. Fluctuations in stable populations: variations in population size

5. Movements: migration; emigration; dispersion; dispersal; the influence of topographical, climatic, and biological barriers

6. Interactions of populations
[see B., below]

7. Factors affecting the structure of human populations
[see 524.A.]

B. Biotic interactions

1. Intraspecific interactions: positive and negative interactions of individuals within a species

2. Interspecific interactions: interactions among members of different species

a. The range of interspecies associations

b. Negative interactions, in which one or both populations are harmed: consumption, parasitic interactions, amensalism and antagonism

    c. Positive interactions, in which one or both populations are benefited: commensalism, mutualism

    d. Neutralistic interactions

  3. Interactions between populations of different species and the ecological, evolutionary, and biogeographical aspects of interaction on the population level

C. Biological communities

  1. Community structure

    a. Vertical and horizontal patterns: the influence of variations in environmental conditions on the stratification and zonation of organisms

    b. Time relations: periodicity and population changes in the community

    c. Interactions in the community: heterotrophic nutrition, predation, symbiosis

    d. Niches and species diversity

    e. Ecotones and the "edge effect"

  2. Community function: energy flow

  3. Community succession: growth toward a stable, mature condition

  4. Communities in space

    a. Landscape patterns: the habitats of a landscape as forming a pattern of environmental gradients

    b. Climax interpretation: monoclimax theory, polyclimax theory, and climax pattern hypothesis

    c. Community gradients: coenclines

  5. Community classification and its bases

    a. The association as the unit of classification

    b. The biome or formation as the unit of classification

    c. Other bases for classification: *e.g.,* ecological succession, habitat, community metabolism

  6. Community structure in past ages: biogeographical succession
[see 242.B. and 243]

Suggested reading in the *Encyclopædia Britannica:*

MACROPAEDIA: Major articles dealing with biological populations and communities

    Behaviour, Animal
    Biosphere, The

MICROPAEDIA: Selected entries of reference information

General subjects

amensalism	competition	herbivore	parasitology
biome	ecology	homing	predation
carnivore	ecosystem	migration	symbiosis
climax	ecotone	mutualism	trophic level
commensalism	epiphyte	niche	
community	flyway	parasitism	

Biographies

    See Section 10/34 of Part Ten

INDEX: See entries under all of the terms above

Section 353.   **Hazards of Life in the Biosphere: Disease and Death**

A. Disease as a departure from the "normal" state, or a disruption of homeostasis; death as the irreparable disruption of life processes

1. The nature of noncommunicable disease: metabolic defects, environmental hazards

2. The nature of communicable, or contagious, disease

   a. The multifactorial concept of contagious disease

   b. Endemic disease and epidemic disease

3. Immunity
   [see also 422.C.2.]

4. Control of disease: prevention, treatment

B. Plant diseases

C. Animal diseases

D. Human diseases
   [see 423]

Suggested reading in the *Encyclopædia Britannica*:

MACROPAEDIA: Major articles dealing with hazards of life in the biosphere: disease and death

   Death
   Disease
   Immunity

MICROPAEDIA: Selected entries of reference information

General subjects

animal diseases and	mastitis	drug allergy	ergot
zoonoses:	mycosis	immunity	fruit spot
actinomycosis	myopathy	immunization	leaf blister
African swine fever	nagana	interferon	mosaic
anthrax	pox disease	interleukin	Panama disease
ascariasis	Q fever	phagocytosis	powdery mildew
aspergillosis	rabies	toxoid	psorosis
bloat	Rift Valley fever	transfer factor	rot
brucellosis	rinderpest	vaccine	rust
canine distemper	salmonellosis	variolation	scab
cestodiasis	scrapie	*plant diseases:*	scorch
coccidiosis	strangles	aster yellows	smut
equine encephalitis	swine fever	black knot	snow mold
erysipelothrix	toxoplasmosis	black spot	sunscald
infection	trichomoniasis	blight	wilt
feline distemper	tularemia	bulb rot	*other:*
foot-and-mouth	yellow fever	bunt	bacteria
disease	zoonosis	canker	disease
glanders	*immunity and*	clubroot	drowning
histoplasmosis	*immunization:*	crown gall	epidemic
hookworm disease	antibody	curly top	germfree life
hyperkeratosis	antigen	damping-off	prion
leptospirosis	antitoxin	dieback	quarantine
listeriosis	autoantibody	downy mildew	veterinary science
lungworm	autoimmunity	Dutch elm disease	virus
malaria			

Biographies

   See Section 10/34 of Part Ten

INDEX: See entries under all of the terms above

Section 354.   **Biogeographic Distribution of Organisms: Ecosystems**

    A. Terrestrial ecosystems

        1. The land environment

           a. Land as a medium for life and the comparison of the terrestrial and aquatic ecosystems

           b. Limiting factors to living on land

           c. Major terrestrial biomes: the tundra, the coniferous forest, the middle-latitude forest, the tropical rain forest, the grassland and savanna, the scrublands, the desert

           d. Specialized biomes: polar biomes, subterranean biomes

        2. Major life-forms

           a. Growth habits and indicator organisms

           b. Classification by habitat: soil organisms, trees and other rooted plants, epiphytes and periphytes, permeants

           c. Classification by niche: producers, consumers, decomposers

        3. Productivity in terrestrial ecosystems

    B. Aquatic ecosystems

        1. The aquatic environment

        2. The ocean and its communities: communities of the open sea

           a. The sea as a biological environment

           b. Character of oceanic populations: benthos, plankton, nekton

           c. Adaptations to marine conditions

           d. Productivity of marine communities as judged by biological oxygen consumption or by nutrient concentration

        3. Inland waters and their communities: freshwater communities

           a. Lacustrine, or standing-water, communities: in lakes and ponds; in swamps, marshes, and bogs

           b. Riverine, or flowing-water, communities: in rivers and streams, in springs

        4. Boundary ecosystems: between waters or between water and land

           a. Estuarine communities: communities in brackish water

           b. Neritic communities: life along seacoasts

        5. Productivity in aquatic ecosystems: the problem of determining productivity, comparisons of productivity

    C. The distribution of organisms

    D. Biogeographic regions and their inhabitants: regional floras and faunas

        1. The Megagaean realm

           a. Holarctic region: the nontropical parts of Eurasia, northern Africa, and North America

           b. Ethiopian region: Africa south of the Sahara, southwestern Arabia, Madagascar

           c. Oriental region: tropical southern and southeastern Asia

        2. The Notogaean realm: Australia, New Guinea, New Zealand, tropical Pacific islands

        3. The Neogaean realm: Central and South America

        4. The Antarctic realm: Antarctica and most of the sub-Antarctic islands

Suggested reading in the *Encyclopædia Britannica:*

MACROPAEDIA: Major articles dealing with biogeographic distribution of organisms: ecosystems

Biosphere, The	Rivers
Lakes	Soil Organisms
Oceans	Trees

MICROPAEDIA: Selected entries of reference information

General subjects

biogeographic regions:	plain	*ocean layers:*	Mediterranean
Australian region	prairie	abyssal zone	vegetation
Ethiopian region	savanna	air–sea	scrubland
faunal region	turf	interface	thorn forest
floristic region	*ecosystems— other:*	bathyal zone	*other:*
Holarctic region	biome	bottom water	dispersion
Neotropical region	desert	halocline	land bridge
Oriental region	ecosystem	littoral zone	Marine
ecosystems—forests:	estuary	pelagic zone	Biological
cloud forest	lacustrine	photic zone	Laboratory
coniferous forest	ecosystem	*ocean populations:*	mesofauna
deciduous forest	polar	benthos	shrub
forest	biome	nekton	soil organism
rain forest	rangeland	plankton	tree
ecosystems— grasslands:	riverine ecosystem	zooplankton	Wallace's Line
grassland	tundra	*scrublands:* chaparral	

Biographies

See Section 10/34 of Part Ten

INDEX: See entries under all of the terms above

Section 355.   The Place of Humans in the Biosphere

A. The qualities that set human beings apart in the biosphere

  1. Structural characteristics and physical capabilities providing humans with a versatility unparalleled in the biosphere

  2. Physiological characteristics underlying the unique behaviour of humans: lack of a definite breeding season, long life span with slow development and lengthy dependency to maturity

  3. Behavioral capacity as the basis of the unique culture of humans: communication through propositional speech, intellect and conceptualization

B. The effects of human action upon the biosphere

  1. The influence of the human species on the modification of the environment

  2. The influence of the environment on the modification of the human species

  3. The attempts to change genetic endowments through deliberate selective measures: eugenics

C. The utilization of organisms by humans

  1. Domestication of plants and animals: distribution and development

  2. The cultivation of plants: plant breeding and growing

  3. The uses of plants

  4. The cultivation of animals: animal breeding and raising

  5. Major uses of animals
     [see also 724.C.8. and 731]

6. The maintenance of public and private collections of live and preserved animals and plants

   a. Museums of natural history

   b. Zoological gardens and aviaries

   c. Institutional and private aquariums

   d. Botanical gardens and arboretums

D. The conservation and management of natural resources

   1. The nature and scope of conservation management

   2. Types of natural resources

   3. Management of natural resources

   4. Management of the world's food supply

      a. The problem of food supply: special difficulties facing the developing countries

      b. Attempts to increase the production and utilization of food supplies: the quest for new sources of food and food additives

---

Suggested reading in the *Encyclopædia Britannica:*

MACROPAEDIA: Major articles dealing with the place of humans in the biosphere

Biosphere, The	Farming and Agricultural Technology
Cats, Domestic	Forestry and Wood Production
Conservation of Natural Resources	Gardening and Horticulture
Dogs	Horses and Horsemanship

MICROPAEDIA: Selected entries of reference information

General subjects

conservation and	nature reserve	dog	terrarium
management of	surface mining	domestic cat	vegetable
natural resources:	terrace cultivation	domestication	zoological garden
conservation	wildlife	fowl	*pollution and*
desalination	conservation	fruit	*pollution control:*
drainage	*domestication and*	gardening	acid rain
ecosystem	*raising of plants and*	genecentre	emission control
endangered species	*animals:*	horse	system
flood	animal breeding	horticulture	greenhouse effect
forestry	animals, cruelty to	hydroponics	pollution
Greenpeace	aquarium	livestock	refuse disposal
hunting	arboriculture	oceanarium	system
irrigation	botanical garden	pet	sewage system
national forest	breed association	plant breeding	smog
national park	cereal	studbook	water purification

Biographies

See Section 10/34 of Part Ten

INDEX: See entries under all of the terms above

Introduction to Part Four:
The Cosmic Orphan

by Loren Eiseley

When I was a young lad of that indefinite but important age when one begins to ask, Who am I? Why am I here? What is the nature of my kind? What is growing up? What is the world? How long shall I live in it? Where shall I go? I found myself walking with a small companion over a high railroad trestle that spanned a stream, a country bridge, and a road. One could look fearfully down, between the ties, at the shallows and ripples in the shining water some 50 feet below. One was also doing a forbidden thing, against which our parents constantly warned. One must not be caught on the black bridge by a train. Something terrible might happen, a thing called death.

From the abutment of the bridge we gazed down upon the water and saw among the pebbles the shape of an animal we knew only from picture books—a turtle, a very large, dark mahogany-coloured turtle. We scrambled down the embankment to observe him more closely. From the little bridge a few feet above the stream, I saw that the turtle, whose beautiful markings shone in the afternoon sun, was not alive and that his flippers waved aimlessly in the rushing water. The reason for his death was plain. Not too long before we had come upon the trestle, someone engaged in idle practice with a repeating rifle had stitched a row of bullet holes across the turtle's carapace and sauntered on.

My father had once explained to me that it took a long time to make a big turtle, years really, in the sunlight and the water and the mud. I turned the ancient creature over and fingered the etched shell with its forlorn flippers flopping grotesquely. The question rose up unbidden. Why did the man have to kill something living that could never be replaced? I laid the turtle down in the water and gave it a little shove. It entered the current and began to drift away. "Let's go home," I said to my companion. From that moment I think I began to grow up.

"Papa," I said in the evening by the oil lamp in our kitchen. "Tell me how men got here." Papa paused. Like many fathers of that time, he was worn from long hours, he was not highly educated, but he had a beautiful resonant voice and he had been born on a frontier homestead. He knew the ritual way the Plains Indians opened a story.

"Son," he said, taking the pattern of another people for our own, "once there was a poor orphan." He said it in such a way that I sat down at his feet. "Once there was a poor orphan with no one to teach him either his way, or his manners. Sometimes animals helped him, sometimes supernatural beings. But above all, one thing was evident. Unlike other occupants of Earth he had to be helped. He did not know his place, he had to find it. Sometimes he was arrogant and had to learn humility, sometimes he was a coward and had to be taught bravery. Sometimes he did not understand his Mother Earth and suffered for it. The old ones who starved and sought visions on hilltops had

known these things. They were all gone now and the magic had departed with them. The orphan was alone; he had to learn by himself; it was a hard school."

My father tousled my head; he gently touched my heart. "You will learn in time there is much pain here," he said. "Men will give it to you, time will give it to you, and you must learn to bear it all, not bear it alone, but be better for the wisdom that may come to you if you watch and listen and learn. Do not forget the turtle, nor the ways of men. They are all orphans and they go astray; they do wrong things. Try to see better."

"Yes, papa," I said, and that was how I believe I came to study men, not the men of written history but the ancestors beyond, beyond all writing, beyond time as we know it, beyond human form as it is known today. Papa was right when he told me men were orphans, eternal seekers. They had little in the way of instinct to instruct them, they had come a strange far road in the universe, passed more than one black, threatening bridge. There were even more to pass, and each one became more dangerous as our knowledge grew. Because man was truly an orphan and confined to no single way of life, he was, in essence, a prison breaker. But in ignorance his very knowledge sometimes led from one terrible prison to another. Was the final problem then, to escape himself, or, if not that, to reconcile his devastating intellect with his heart? All of the knowledge set down in great books directly or indirectly affects this problem. It is the problem of every man, for even the indifferent man is making, unknown to himself, his own callous judgment.

Long ago, however, in one of the Dead Sea Scrolls hidden in the Judaean Desert, an unknown scribe had written: "None there be, can rehearse the whole tale." That phrase, too, contains the warning that man is an orphan of uncertain beginnings and an indefinite ending. All that the archaeological and anthropological sciences can do is to place a somewhat flawed crystal before man and say: This is the way you came, these are your present dangers; somewhere, seen dimly beyond, lies your destiny. God help you, you are a cosmic orphan, a symbol-shifting magician, mostly immature and inattentive to your own dangers. Read, think, study, but do not expect this to save you without humility of heart. This the old ones knew long ago in the great deserts under the stars. This they sought to learn and pass on. It is the only hope of men.

What have we observed that might be buried as the Dead Sea Scrolls were buried for 2,000 years, and be broken out of a jar for human benefit, brief words that might be encompassed on a copper scroll or a ragged sheet of vellum? Only these thoughts, I think, we might reasonably set down as true, now and hereafter. For a long time, for many, many centuries, Western man believed in what we might call the existent world of nature; form as form was seen as constant in both animal and human guise. He believed in the instantaneous creation of his world by the Deity; he believed its duration to be very short, a stage upon which the short drama of a human fall from divine estate and a redemption was in progress.

Worldly time was a small parenthesis in eternity. Man lived with that belief, his cosmos small and man-centred. Then, beginning about 350 years ago, thoughts unventured upon since the time of the Greek philosophers began to enter the human consciousness. They may be summed up in Francis Bacon's dictum: "This is the foundation of all. We are not to imagine or suppose, but to *discover,* what nature does or may be made to do."

When in following years scientific experiment and observation became current, a vast change began to pass over Western thought. Man's conception of himself and his world began to alter beyond recall. "'Tis all in pieces, all coherence gone," exclaimed the poet John Donne, Bacon's contemporary. The existing world was crumbling at the edges. It was cracking apart like an ill-nailed raft in a torrent—a torrent of incredible time. It was, in effect, a new nature comprising a past embedded in the present and a future yet to be.

First, Bacon discerned a *mundus alter,* another separate world that could be drawn out of nature by human intervention—the world that surrounds and troubles us today. Then, by degrees, time depths of tremendous magnitude began, in the late 18th century, to replace the Christian calendar. Space, from a surrounding candelabrum of stars, began to widen to infinity. The Earth was recognized as a mere speck drifting in the wake of a minor star, itself rotating around an immense galaxy composed of innumerable suns. Beyond and beyond, into billions of light years, other galaxies glowed through clouds of wandering gas and interstellar dust. Finally, and perhaps the most shocking blow of all, the natural world of the moment proved to be an illusion, a phantom of man's short lifetime. Organic novelty lay revealed in the strata of the Earth. Man had not always been here. He had been preceded, in the 4,000,-000,000 years of the planet's history, by floating mollusks, strange fern forests, huge dinosaurs, flying lizards, giant mammals whose bones lay under the dropped boulders of vanished continental ice sheets.

The Orphan cried out in protest, as the cold of naked space entered his bones, "Who am I?" And once more science answered. "You are a changeling. You are linked by a genetic chain to all the vertebrates. The thing that is you bears the still aching wounds of evolution in body and in brain. Your hands are made-over fins, your lungs come from a creature gasping in a swamp, your femur has been twisted upright. Your foot is a reworked climbing pad. You are a rag doll resewn from the skins of extinct animals. Long ago, 2,000,000 years perhaps, you were smaller, your brain was not so large. We are not confident that you could speak. Seventy million years before that you were an even smaller climbing creature known as a tupaiid. You were the size of a rat. You ate insects. Now you fly to the Moon."

"This is a fairy tale," protested the Orphan. "I am here, I will look in the mirror."

"Of course it is a fairy tale," said the scientists, "but so is the world and so is life. That is what makes it true. Life is indefinite departure. That is why we are all orphans. That is why you must find your own way. Life is not stable. Everything alive is slipping through cracks and crevices in time, changing as it goes. Other creatures, however, have instincts that provide for them, holes in which to hide. They cannot ask questions. A fox is a fox, a wolf is a wolf, even if this, too, is illusion. You have learned to ask questions. That is why you are, an orphan. *You are the only creature in the universe who knows what it has been.* Now you must go on asking questions while all the time you are changing. You will ask what you are to become. The world will no longer satisfy you. You must find your way, your own true self."

"But how can I?" wept the Orphan, hiding his head. "This is magic. I do not know what I am. I have been too many things."

"You have indeed," said all the scientists together. "Your body and your nerves have been dragged about and twisted in the long effort of your ancestors to stay alive, but now, small orphan that you are, you must know a secret, a secret magic that nature has given to you. No other creature on the planet possesses it. You use language. You are a symbol-shifter. All this is hidden in your brain and transmitted from one generation to another. You are a time-binder, in your head the symbols that mean things in the world outside can fly about untrammeled. You can combine them differently into a new world of thought or you can also hold them tenaciously throughout a lifetime and pass them on to others."

Thus out of words, a puff of air, really, is made all that is uniquely human, all that is new from one human generation to another. But remember what was said of the wounds of evolution. The brain, parts of it at least, is very old, the parts laid down in sequence like geological strata. Buried deep beneath the brain with which we reason are ancient defense centres quick to anger, quick to aggression, quick to violence, over which the neocortex, the new brain, strives to exert control. Thus there are times when the Orphan is a divided being striving against himself. Evil men know this. Sometimes they can play upon it for their own political advantage. Men crowded together, subjected to the same stimuli, are quick to respond to emotion that in the quiet of their own homes they might analyze more cautiously.

Scientists have found that the very symbols which crowd our brains may possess their own dangers. It is convenient for the thinker to classify an idea with a word. This can sometimes lead to a process called hypostatization or reification. Take the word "Man," for example. There are times when it is useful to categorize the creature briefly, his history, his embracing characteristics. From this, if we are not careful of our meanings, it becomes easy to speak of all men as though they were one person. In reality men have been seeking this unreal man for thousands of years. They have found him bathed in blood, they have found him in the hermit's cell, he has been glimpsed among innumerable messiahs, or in meditation under the sacred bô tree; he has been found in the physician's study or lit by the satanic fires of the first atomic explosion.

In reality he has never been found at all. The reason is very simple: men have been seeking Man capitalized, an imaginary creature constructed out of disparate parts in the laboratory of the human imagination. Some men may thus perceive him and see him as either totally beneficent or wholly evil. They would be wrong. They are wrong so long as they have vitalized this creation and call it "Man." There is no Man; there are only men: good, evil, inconceivable mixtures marred by their genetic makeup, scarred or improved by their societal surroundings. So long as they live they are *men,* multitudinous and unspent potential for action. Men are great objects of study, but the moment we say "Man" we are in danger of wandering into a swamp of abstraction.

Surveying our fossil history perhaps we are not even justified as yet in calling ourselves true men. The word carries subtle implications that extend beyond us into the time stream. If a remote half-human ancestor, barely able to speak, had had a word for his kind, as very likely he did, and just supposing it had been "man," would we approve the usage, the shape-freezing quality of it, now? I think not. Perhaps no true orphan would wish to call himself anything but a traveler. Man in a cosmic timeless sense may not be here.

The point is particularly apparent in the light of a recent and portentous discovery. In 1953 James D. Watson and Francis H.C. Crick discovered the structure of the chemical alphabet out of which all that lives is constituted. It was a strange spiral ladder within the cell, far more organized and complicated than 19th-century biologists had imagined; the tiny building blocks constantly reshuffled in every mating had both an amazing stability and paradoxically, over long time periods, a power to alter the living structure of a species beyond recall. The thing called man had once been a tree shrew on a forest branch; now it manipulates abstract symbols in its brain from which skyscrapers rise, bridges span the horizon, disease is conquered, the Moon is visited.

Molecular biologists have begun to consider whether the marvelous living alphabet which lies at the roof of evolution can be manipulated for human benefit. Already some varieties of domesticated plants and animals have been improved. Now at last man has begun to eye his own possible road into the future. By delicate excisions and intrusions could the mysterious alphabet we carry in our bodies be made to hasten our advancement into the future? Already our urban concentrations, with all their aberrations and faults, are future-oriented. Why not ourselves? It is in our power to perpetuate great minds *ad infinitum?* But who is to judge? Who is to select this future man? There is the problem. Which of us poor orphans by the roadside, even

those peering learnedly through the electron microscope, can be confident of the way into the future? Could the fish unaided by nature have found the road to the reptile, the reptile to the mammal, the mammal to man? And how was man endowed with speech? *Could* men choose their way? Suddenly before us towers the blackest, most formidable bridge of our experience. Across what chasm does it run?

Biologists tell us that in the fullness of time more than ninety percent of the world's past species have perished. The mammalian ones in particular are not noted for longevity. If the scalpel, the excising laser ray in the laboratory, were placed in the hands of some one person, some one poor orphan, what would he do? If assured, would he reproduce himself alone? If cruel, would he by indirection succeed in abolishing the living world? If doubtful of the road, would he reproduce the doubt? "Nothing is more shameful than assertion without knowledge," the great Roman statesman and orator Cicero once pronounced as though he had foreseen this final bridge of human pride—the pride of a god without foresight.

After the disasters of the second World War when the dream of perpetual progress died from men's minds, an orphan of this violent century wrote a poem about the great extinctions revealed in the rocks of the planet. It concludes as follows:

> I am not sure I love
>   the cruelties found in our blood
>   from some lost evil tree in our beginnings.
> May the powers forgive and seal us deep
>   when we lie down,
> May harmless dormice creep and red leaves fall
>   over the prisons where we wreaked our will.
> Dachau, Auschwitz, those places everywhere.
> If I could pray, I would pray long for this.

One may conclude that the poet was a man of doubt. He did not regret man; he was confident that leaves, rabbits, and songbirds would continue life, as, long ago, a tree shrew had happily forgotten the ruling reptiles. The poet was an orphan in shabby circumstances pausing by the roadside to pray, for he did pray despite his denial; God forgive us all. He was a man in doubt upon the way. He was the eternal orphan of my father's story. Let us then, as similar orphans who have come this long way through time, be willing to assume the risks of the uncompleted journey. We must know, as that forlorn band of men in Judaea knew when they buried the jar, that man's road is to be sought beyond himself. *No man there is who can tell the whole tale.* After the small passage of 2,000 years who would deny this truth?

Part Four. Human Life

The outlines in the three divisions and fifteen sections of Part Four treat stages in the development of human life on Earth; human health and diseases; and human behaviour and experience.

Several points should be noted about the relations of Part Four to preceding and subsequent parts.

The fundamental physical and chemical properties of matter are dealt with in Part One. The treatment of the Earth in Part Two encompasses those properties of the Earth that are supportive of human life. Much fundamental biological knowledge concerning human life is involved in the treatment—in Part Three, Life on Earth—of what is common to all animal life; the last section of Part Three deals with mankind's place in the biosphere.

Knowledge of the biomedical and psychological aspects of human life is not wholly separable from, and is germane to, the subjects covered in Parts Five through Ten, which treat human society, the fine arts, technology, religion, the history of peoples and civilizations, and man as logician, mathematician, scientist, historian, and philosopher.

The biological, medical, and psychological sciences have been themselves the object of historical and analytical studies concerned with their nature, methods, and interrelations. These studies are set forth in Sections 10/34, 10/35, and 10/36 of Part Ten. The instrumentation involved in these sciences is dealt with in Section 723 of Part Seven.

Division I.   Stages in the Development of Human Life on Earth

The outlines in the two sections of Division I present studies in historical comparative anatomy that place *Homo sapiens* within a general taxonomy; the theory of human evolution; and studies, in genetics and physical anthropology, of human heredity and the races of mankind.

Section 411.   Human Evolution

A. The evolutionary process

B. Human evolutionary relationships with living and fossil primates

  1. The primates

    a. Distinguishing characteristics of the primates

    b. The natural history of primate life

    c. Evolution and paleontology

    d. Classification of the primates: the two main groups or suborders, the prosimians (principally lemurs, lorises, and tarsiers) and the anthropoids (monkeys, apes, and man)
[see also 313.F.25.c.]

  2. Distinguishing characteristics of the Hominidae

    a. Morphological characteristics

    b. Inferred behavioral characteristics

    c. Contrasting adaptations of Hominidae and Pongidae

C. The fossil record of the Hominidae

  1. The discovery and recognition of the hominid fossil record

2. Classification of the Hominidae

   a. *Australopithecus*

   b. *Homo habilis*

   c. *Homo erectus*

   d. *Homo sapiens*

      i. Fossil remains of early *Homo sapiens; e.g.,* Vértesszőllős man, Ngaloba man, Border Cave man, Swanscombe man, Omo hominids

      ii. The Neanderthals

      iii. The Cro-Magnons

      iv. *Homo sapiens* of Africa

      v. *Homo sapiens* of Asia and Australasia

Suggested reading in the *Encyclopædia Britannica*:

MACROPAEDIA: Major articles dealing with human evolution

   Evolution, Human
   Life

MICROPAEDIA: Selected entries of reference information

General subjects

cultural stages:
   Mesolithic Period
   Neolithic Period
   Paleolithic Period
hominid fossils:
   Amud remains
   Chad australopithecine
   Chancelade skeleton
   Ferassie skeletons, La
   Hadar remains
   Heidelberg jaw
   Java man
   Kabwe man
   Kafzeh
   Kanapoi fossil
   Koobi Fora remains
   Krapina remains
   Laetolil remains
   Lantian man

   Makapansgat
   Olduvai Gorge
   Omo remains
   Peking man
   Petralona skull
   Piltdown man
   Ramapithecus
   Saccopastore skulls
   Solo man
   Sterkfontein
   Swanscombe skull
   Telanthropus capensis
hominids:
   Australopithecus
   Cro-Magnon
   Homo erectus
   Homo habilis
   Homo sapiens
   Homo transvaalensis
   hominid
   Neanderthal

tools and tool industries:
   Abbevillian industry
   Acheulian industry
   Aterian industry
   Aurignacian culture
   Azilian industry
   Chopper chopping-tool industry
   Clactonian industry
   Ertebølle industry
   Fauresmith industry
   flake tool
   Ibero-Maurusian industry
   Levalloisian stone-flaking techniques

   Magdalenian culture
   Maglemosian industry
   Mousterian industry
   Oldowan industry
   Osteodontokeratic tool industry
   Perigordian industry
   Solutrean industry
   Stillbay industry
   stone-tool industry
other:
   evolution
   Gigantopithecus
   missing link

Biographies
   See Section 10/36 of Part Ten

INDEX: See entries under all of the terms above

Section 412. **Human Heredity: the Races of Mankind**

A. Heredity in humans

    1. The biological basis of human heredity: genetic reproduction

    2. Inheritance of behavioral traits

       a. Fraternal and identical twins and the inferences that can be made from twin studies

       b. Genetic explanations for abnormalities: chromosome variations, mutation

    3. Applications of human genetics

    4. Specific behavioral traits affected by inheritance

    5. Consanguinity and its effects

B. The nature and origin of human races

    1. Aspects of racial diversity

    2. Measures of race

       a. Old measures; *e.g.,* colour, hair form, body measurements, features such as eyes and nose

       b. Modern measures; *e.g.,* blood groups and genetic evidence

    3. The races of mankind

       a. Geographic races

       b. Local races

       c. Microraces

Suggested reading in the *Encyclopædia Britannica:*

MACROPAEDIA: Major articles dealing with human heredity: the races of mankind

    Evolution, Human
    Genetics and Heredity, The Principles of
    Life

MICROPAEDIA: Selected entries of reference information

General subjects

human heredity:
  assortative mating
  character
  climatic adaptation
  consanguinity
  dominance
  eugenics
  founder principle
  genetic drift
  heterospecific
    mating
  pedigree
  recessiveness
race—aspects of
racial diversity:
  anthropometry
  beta aminoisobutyric
    acid excretion
  geographic race
  local race

microrace
phenylthiocarbamide
  tasting
race
race—races of man:
  African Pygmy
    local race
  Alpine local race
  American
    Coloured local
    race
  American Indian
    geographic race
  Aryan
  Australoid
    geographic race
  Capoid local race
  Caucasoid
    geographic race

Central American
  Indian local race
East African local
  race
Forest Negro local
  race
Indic geographic
  race
Mediterranean
  local race
Melanesian
  geographic race
Micronesian
  geographic race
Mongoloid
  geographic race
Negrito local race
Negroid geographic
  race

Neo-Hawaiian
  local race
North American
  Indian local race
northeast
  European local
  race
northern
  Mongoloid local
  race
northwest
  European local
  race
Polynesian
  geographic race
South American
  Indian local race
Southeast Asian
  local race

Biographies

    See Sections 10/34 and 10/36 of Part Ten

INDEX: See entries under all of the terms above

Division II. **The Human Organism: Health and Disease**
[For Part Four headnote see page 143.]

The outlines in the four sections of Division II treat the structures and functions of the human body; human health; the manifestation, recognition, and treatment of human disease; and the practice of medicine.

The outline referred to in Section 421 deals with the structures and the functions of the several organ systems, the proper coordination and regulation of which constitute the health of the human body.

The outline in Section 422 begins with an enumeration of the stages in human life and the definitions of normality in human health. It then treats of the various ways that the body maintains itself and recovers from injury. The Section concludes with a listing of other significant influences on human health.

The outline in Section 423 first treats the general characteristics, causes, and classifications of human disease. It then treats the concepts, principles, and methods of the medical art, in the two stages of diagnosis and therapy. The outline encompasses the symptoms, diagnosis, and treatment of diseases that affect the body as a whole, and of diseases that affect each of the organ systems dealt with in their healthy state in Section 421.

The outline in Section 424 deals with issues relating to the professionalization of the practice of medicine—not only those internal to the profession but also those arising from the educational, economic, social, political, and legal dimensions of institutionalized medicine.

Section 421. **The Structures and Functions of the Human Body**

A. The structures and functions of the cardiovascular system

　1. The heart

　2. The blood vessels: arteries, veins, and capillaries

　3. Human blood

　　a. Components of blood: plasma, red blood cells (erythrocytes), white blood cells (leukocytes), platelets (thrombocytes)

　　b. Blood groups

　　c. Bleeding and blood clotting

　4. Blood circulation: the central pump, the systemic circulation, the pulmonary circulation

B. The structures and functions of the lymphatic system: lymphocytes, lymphatic vessels, lymph nodes, and the lymph

C. The structures and functions of the respiratory system

　1. The upper portion of the respiratory tract: nasal cavity, pharynx, larynx, and trachea

　2. The lungs and bronchi

　3. The regulation, control, and dynamics of breathing

D. The structures and functions of the digestive system

　1. Structure of the components of the digestive tract

　　a. Mouth and related structures

　　b. Pharynx and esophagus

　　c. Stomach

　　d. The small intestine and the small bowel mucosa

　　e. Large intestine, rectum, and anus

　　f. Associated glands and structures: pancreas, liver, gallbladder, and bile ducts

　2. The digestive process

E. The structures and functions of the endocrine system

Principal Parts of
THE HUMAN BODY

This Plate on gross anatomy comprises 14 Views, 12 of which are transparent, showing all principal parts of the human anatomy. Below is a list in English (insofar as this is possible) of the names of the parts illustrated. The number immediately following the name is the code number for that part; the other number or numbers indicate the View or Views on which it is shown. A key to the Plate, with Latin names, is given on the last page.

Abdominal oblique muscle, external, 87: 1, 8
Abdominal oblique muscle, internal, 88: 1
Adductor longus muscle, 68: 6, 7, 14
Adductor brevis muscle, 67: 7
Adrenal gland: see Suprarenal gland
Aorta, 3: 5, 6, 10, 11, 14
Aponeurosis of external abdominal oblique muscle, 4: 1
Appendix, vermiform, 5: 4, 12, 13
Atrium, left, 19: 11
Axillary artery, 6: 5, 6, 14
Axillary vein, 178: 3, 10, 11
Biceps brachii muscle, 69: 5, 6, 10, 11
Bile duct, common, 35: 4, 5, 10, 11, 13
Brachial artery, 7: 5, 6, 14
Brachial muscle, 70: 14
Brachial plexus, 140: 5, 6, 7, 14
Brachial vein, 179: 3, 8, 10, 11
Brachiocephalic trunk, 164: 5, 14
Brachiocephalic vein, 180: 3, 4, 10, 11
Brachioradialis muscle, 71: 12, 13, 14
Breastbone, 160: 1, 2, 8, 9
Bronchus, left, 20: 5, 14
Buccinator muscle, 72: 1
Carotid artery, common, 8: 5, 14
Celiac trunk, 165: 5, 10, 12, 14
Cephalic vein, 183: 3, 4, 8, 9, 11, 12, 13, 14
Cerebellum, 22: 11, 14
Cerebrum, 23: 11, 14
Cheekbone, 134: 1
Collarbone, 24: 1, 2, 7, 8, 9, 14
Colon, ascending, 25: 3, 4, 12, 13
Colon, descending, 26: 3, 4, 12, 13
Colon, sigmoid, 27: 3, 4, 12, 13
Colon, transverse, 28: 3, 4, 11
Coracobrachialis muscle, 73: 5, 14
Corpus callosum, 32: 11, 14
Deltoid muscle, 74: 5, 6, 8, 9, 14
Depressor anguli oris muscle, 75: 1, 10
Diaphragm, 34: 2, 3, 4, 5, 6, 9, 10, 11, 14
Digastric muscle, 76: 3
Ductus deferens, 36: 5, 6
Duodenum, 37: 5, 12, 13
Epigastric vessels, deep, 169: 5, 8, 9
Esophagus, 122: 5, 6, 12, 13, 14
Extensor carpi radialis longus muscle, 77: 14
Falx cerebri, 38: 12, 13
Femoral artery, 9: 5, 6, 14
Femoral nerve, 114: 7, 14
Femoral vein, 184: 5, 6, 14
Femur, 39: 7
Flexor carpi radialis muscle, 78: 14
Fossa ovalis, 40: 8
Frontal bone, 126: 3, 7
Gall bladder, 200: 3, 4, 10, 11
Gastric vessels, 170: 11
Gastro-omental vessels, 171: 10
Glans penis, 46: 1
Gluteus medius muscle, 79: 1, 5, 6, 7, 14
Gluteus minimus muscle, 80: 7
Gracilis muscle, 81: 6, 7, 14
Heart: see Atrium; Pericardium; Ventricle
Humerus, 48: 7
Ileum, 49: 12
Iliac artery, common, 10: 5, 6, 14
Iliac artery, external, 11: 5, 6, 14
Iliac artery, internal, 12: 5, 6, 14
Iliac spine, anterior superior, 159: 1, 2, 7, 8, 14
Iliacus muscle, 82: 7, 14

Iliac vein, common, 185: 5, 6, 14
Iliac vein, external, 186: 5, 6, 14
Iliac vein, internal, 187: 5, 6, 14
Iliohypogastric nerve, 115: 7
Ilioinguinal nerve, 116: 7
Inguinal ligament, 55: 1, 2, 3, 5, 6, 8, 13, 14
Inguinal ring, deep, 1: 1, 2
Inguinal ring, superficial, 2: 1
Innominate artery: see Brachiocephalic trunk
Innominate vein: see Brachiocephalic vein
Intercostal muscle, external, 83: 1
Intercostal muscle, internal, 84: 2, 9
Intestine, large: see Colon
Intestine, small, 50: 3, 4, 10, 11
Ischium, 127: 7
Jaw, lower, 61: 1, 2, 3, 4, 5, 6, 7, 11, 14
Jaw, upper, 62: 2, 3, 4, 5, 6, 7, 11, 12, 13, 14
Jugular vein, internal, 188: 3, 4, 5, 10
Kidney, 149: 5, 6, 14
Lacrimal gland, 41: 2
Larynx, 51: 4, 7, 11, 14
Ligament of the liver, falciform, 53: 3, 9
Ligament of the liver, round, 56: 2, 9
Ligament of the penis, fundiform, 54: 1
Line, arcuate, 58: 2
Line, semilunar, 59: 1, 2, 8, 9
Linea alba, 57: 1, 2, 8
Liver, 47: 3, 4, 9, 10, 11
Lumbosacral plexus, 141: 7
Lung, 146: 3, 4, 5, 6, 10, 11, 14
Mammary vessels, internal: see Thoracic vessels, internal
Masseter muscle, 85: 1
Median nerve, 117: 5, 6, 14
Medulla oblongata, 63: 11, 14
Mesenteric artery, inferior, 14: 5, 6, 14
Mesenteric artery, superior, 15: 14
Mesenteric vein, inferior, 189: 3
Mesenteric vein, superior, 190: 5
Mesenteric vessels, inferior, 173: 12, 13
Mesenteric vessels, superior, 174: 5, 12, 13
Mesentery, 65: 4, 11, 12
Mesocolon, transverse, 66: 11, 12
Mylohyoid muscle, 86: 2, 3
Nasal concha, inferior, 29: 4, 7, 11, 14
Nasal concha, middle, 30: 4, 7, 11, 14
Nasal concha, superior, 31: 4, 7, 11, 14
Nasal septum, 152: 5, 6, 12, 13
Obturator nerve, 118: 7
Occipital bone, 128: 4, 5, 7
Omentum, greater, 123: 10
Omentum, lesser, 124: 3, 4, 9, 10, 11
Omohyoid muscle, 89: 1, 2, 9
Orbicularis oris muscle, 90: 1
Ovarian vessels, 175: 14
Ovary, 135: 14
Pancreas, 136: 5, 12, 13
Parietal bone, 129: 3, 7
Parotid gland, 42: 1, 2
Pectoralis major muscle, 91: 1, 2, 5, 8, 9, 14
Pectoralis minor muscle, 92: 2, 5, 9, 10, 11
Penis, 137: 2, 3, 5
Pericardium, 138: 10
Phrenic nerve, 119: 10
Platysma muscle, 139: 8, 9
Pons, 144: 11, 14
Portal vein, 191: 5, 11, 12, 13
Pronator teres muscle, 93: 14
Prostate, 145: 6

Psoas major muscle, 94: 7, 14
Pterygoid muscle, internal, 95: 2
Pubis, 130: 3, 6, 7, 13, 14
Pulmonary artery, 16: 5, 10, 11, 14
Pulmonary vein, 192: 11, 14
Pylorus, 147: 12, 13
Quadratus lumborum muscle, 96: 14
Quadriceps femoris muscle, 97: 3, 4, 5, 6, 14
Rectum, 148: 7, 14
Rectus abdominis muscle, 98: 1, 2
Renal artery, 17: 6, 14
Renal vein, 193: 6, 14
Rib, 125: 1, 2, 7, 9
Sacrum, 131: 7
Saphenous hiatus: see Fossa ovalis
Saphenous vein, greater, 194: 8, 9
Sartorius muscle, 99: 1, 2, 9
Scalene muscle, anterior, 100: 14
Scrotum, 151: 1, 2, 5
Seminal duct: see Ductus deferens
Seminal vesicle, 202: 6
Serratus muscle, anterior, 101: 1
Shoulder blade, 150: 7
Sinus, frontal, 153: 2, 3, 4, 5, 6, 7, 11, 12, 13, 14
Sinus, inferior sagittal, 156: 12, 13
Sinus, maxillary, 154: 2, 3
Sinus, sphenoidal, 158: 4, 5, 6, 7, 11, 12, 13, 14
Sinus, straight, 155: 12, 13
Sinus, superior sagittal, 157: 12, 13
Skull, 33: 2
Sphenoid bone, 132: 7
Spinal cord, 64: 7, 14
Spleen, 52: 5, 12, 13
Splenic artery, 13: 5
Splenic vessels, 172: 12, 13
Sternohyoid muscle, 103: 1, 2, 9
Sternomastoid muscle, 102: 1, 2, 8, 9, 10
Sternothyroid muscle, 104: 2, 9
Stomach, 196: 3, 4, 10, 11
Styloglossus muscle, 105: 3
Subclavian artery, 18: 5, 6, 14
Subclavian vein, 195: 3, 4, 10, 11
Submandibular gland, 43: 1, 2
Suprarenal gland, 44: 5, 6, 14
Temporal bone, 133: 3, 7
Temporal muscle, 106: 1
Tensor fasciae latae muscle, 107: 1, 5, 6, 14
Tentorium cerebelli, 161: 11, 14
Testicle, 162: 5
Testicular vessels, 176: 5, 6
Thoracic vessels, internal, 177: 9, 10
Thyrohyoid muscle, 108: 2
Thyroid cartilage, 21: 3
Thyroid gland, 45: 3, 4, 10, 11
Tongue, 60: 3, 4, 5, 6, 7, 11, 14
Transversus abdominis muscle, 109: 1, 2
Transversus thoracis muscle, 110: 2, 9
Trapezius muscle, 111: 5, 6, 10, 14
Triceps brachii muscle, 112: 5, 6, 14
Turbinate bones: see Nasal concha
Ulnar nerve, 120: 5, 6, 14
Umbilical fold, medial, 142: 9
Umbilical fold, median, 143: 9
Ureter, 166: 5, 6, 13, 14
Urinary bladder, 201: 3, 4, 5, 6, 12, 13
Uterus, 167: 14
Vagina, 168: 14
Vagus nerve, 121: 14
Vena cava, inferior, 181: 5, 6, 11, 14
Vena cava, superior, 182: 4, 5, 10, 11
Ventricle, left, 198: 5, 10, 11
Ventricle, right, 197: 5, 10, 11
Vertebra, 199: 6, 7, 11, 14
Windpipe, 163: 5, 6, 14
Womb: see Uterus
Zygomaticus major muscle, 113: 1, 10

Abbreviations: A. (Arteria); L. (Ligamentum);
M. (Musculus); N. (Nervus); and V. (Vena).

24. Clavicula
29. Concha nasalis inferior
30. Concha nasalis media
31. Concha nasalis superior
39. Femur
48. Humerus
51. Larynx
60. Lingua (tongue)
61. Mandibula
62. Maxilla
64. Medulla spinalis
67. M. adductor brevis
68. M. adductor longus
79. M. gluteus medius
80. M. gluteus minimus
81. M. gracilis
82. M. iliacus
94. M. psoas major
114. N. femoralis
115. N. iliohypogastricus
116. N. ilio-inguinalis
118. N. obturatorius
125. Os costate
126. Os frontale
127. Os ischii
128. Os occipitale
129. Os parietale
130. Os pubis
131. Os sacrum
132. Os sphenoidale
133. Os temporale
140. Plexus brachialis
141. Plexus lumbosacralis
148. Rectum
150. Scapula
153. Sinus frontalis
158. Sinus sphenoidalis
159. Spina iliaca anterior superior
199. Vertebra

3. Aorta
6. A. axillaris
7. A. brachialis
8. A. carotis communis
9. A. femoralis
10. A. iliaca communis
11. A. iliaca externa
12. A. iliaca interna
14. A. mesenterica inferior
15. A. mesenterica superior
16. A. pulmonalis
17. A. renalis
18. A. subclavia
20. Bronchus principalis
22. Cerebellum
23. Cerebrum
24. Clavicula
29. Concha nasalis inferior
30. Concha nasalis media
31. Concha nasalis superior
32. Corpus callosum
34. Diaphragma
44. Glandula suprarenalis
51. Larynx
55. L. inguinale
60. Lingua (tongue)
61. Mandibula
62. Maxilla
63. Medulla oblongata
64. Medulla spinalis
68. M. adductor longus
70. M. brachialis
71. M. brachioradialis
73. M. coracobrachialis
74. M. deltoideus
77. M. extensor carpi
    radialis longus
78. M. flexor carpi radialis
79. M. gluteus medius
81. M. gracilis
82. M. iliacus
91. M. pectoralis major
93. M. pronator teres
94. M. psoas major
96. M. quadratus lumborum
97. M. quadriceps femoris
    (rectus)
100. M. scalenus anterior
107. M. tensor fasciae latae
111. M. trapezius
112. M. triceps brachii
114. N. femoralis
117. N. medianus
120. N. ulnaris
121. N. vagus
122. Oesophagus (esophagus)
130. Os pubis
135. Ovarium (ovary)
140. Plexus brachialis
144. Pons
146. Pulmo (lung)
148. Rectum
149. Ren (kidney)
153. Sinus frontalis
158. Sinus sphenoidalis
159. Spina iliaca anterior superior
161. Tentorium cerebelli
163. Trachea
164. Truncus brachiocephalicus
165. Truncus coeliacus
166. Ureter
167. Uterus
168. Vagina
175. Vasa ovarica
181. V. cava inferior
183. V. cephalica
184. V. femoralis
185. V. iliaca communis
186. V. iliaca externa
187. V. iliaca interna   193. V. renalis
192. V. pulmonalis   199. Vertebra

14

Principal Parts of
THE HUMAN BODY
KEY TO PLATE, VIEWS 1-14

On the list below, the number at left is a code number for the part of the body named.
The number or numbers at right indicate the View or Views on which that part of the body is shown.

Abbreviations: A. (Arteria); L. (Ligamentum); M. (Musculus); N. (Nervus); and V. (Vena).

1. Annulus inguinalis profundus, 1,2
2. Annulus inguinalis superficialis, 1
3. Aorta, 5,6,10,11,14
4. Aponeurosis m. obliquus externus abdominis, 1
5. Appendix vermiformis, 4,12,13
6. A. axillaris, 5,6,14
7. A. brachialis, 5,6,14
8. A. carotis communis, 5,14
9. A. femoralis, 5,6,14
10. A. iliaca communis, 5,6,14
11. A. iliaca externa, 5,6,14
12. A. iliaca interna, 5,6,14
13. A. lienalis (a. splenica), 5
14. A. mesenterica inferior, 5,6,14
15. A. mesenterica superior, 14
16. A. pulmonalis, 5,10,11,14
17. A. renalis, 6,14
  A. splenica: see 13
18. A. subclavia, 5,6,14
19. Atrium sinistrum, 11
20. Bronchus principalis, 5,14
21. Cartilago thyroidea, 3
22. Cerebellum, 11,14
23. Cerebrum, 11,14
24. Clavicula, 1,2,7,8,9,14
25. Colon ascendens, 3,4,12,13
26. Colon descendens, 3,4,12,13
27. Colon sigmoideum, 3,4,12,13
28. Colon transversum, 3,4,11
29. Concha nasalis inferior, 4,7,11,14
30. Concha nasalis media, 4,7,11,14
31. Concha nasalis superior, 4,7,11,14
  Cor (heart): see 19,138,197,198
32. Corpus callosum, 11,14
33. Cranium, 2
34. Diaphragma, 2,3,4,5,6,9,10,11,14
35. Ductus choledochus, 4,5,10,11,13
36. Ductus deferens, 5,6
37. Duodenum, 5,12,13
  Esophagus: see 122
38. Falx cerebri, 12,13
39. Femur, 7
40. Fossa ovalis (hiatus saphenus), 8
  Gall Bladder: see 200
  Gaster: see 196
41. Glandula lacrimalis, 2
42. Glandula parotidea, 1,2
43. Glandula submandibularis, 1,2
44. Glandula suprarenalis, 5,6,14
45. Glandula thyreoidea, 3,4,10,11
46. Glans penis, 1
  Heart: see 19,138,197,198
47. Hepar (liver), 3,4,9,10,11
  Hiatus saphenus: see 40
48. Humerus, 7
49. Ileum, 12
50. Intestinum tenue, 3,4,10,11
  Kidney: see 149
51. Larynx, 4,7,11,14
52. Lien (splen; spleen), 5,12,13
53. L. falciforme hepatis, 3,9
54. L. fundiforme penis, 10
55. L. inguinale, 1,2,3,5,6,8,13,14
56. L. teres hepatis, 2,9
57. Linea alba, 1,2,8
58. Linea arcuata, 2
59. Linea semilunaris, 1,2,8,9
60. Lingua (tongue), 3,4,5,6,7,11,14
  Liver: see 47
  Lung: see 146

61. Mandibula, 1,2,3,4,5,6,7,11,14
62. Maxilla, 2,3,4,5,6,7,11,12,13,14
63. Medulla oblongata, 11,14
64. Medulla spinalis, 7,14
65. Mesenterium, 4, 11, 12
66. Mesocolon transversum, 11,12
67. M. adductor brevis, 7
68. M. adductor longus, 6,7,14
69. M. biceps brachii, 5,6,10,11
70. M. brachialis, 14
71. M. brachioradialis, 12,13,14
72. M. buccinator, 1
73. M. coracobrachialis, 5,14
74. M. deltoideus, 5,6,8,9,14
75. M. depressor anguli oris, 1,10
76. M. digastricus, 3
77. M. extensor carpi radialis longus, 14
78. M. flexor carpi radialis, 14
79. M. gluteus medius, 1,5,6,7,14
80. M. gluteus minimus, 7
81. M. gracilis, 6,7,14
82. M. iliacus, 7,14
83. M. intercostalis externus, 1
84. M. intercostalis internus, 2,9
85. M. masseter, 1
86. M. mylohyoideus, 2,3
87. M. obliquus externus abdominis, 1,8
88. M. obliquus internus abdominis, 1
89. M. omohyoideus, 1,2,9
90. M. orbicularis oris, 1
91. M. pectoralis major, 1,2,5,8,9,14
92. M. pectoralis minor, 2,5,9,10,11
93. M. pronator teres, 14
94. M. psoas major, 7,14
95. M. pterygoideus medialis, 2
96. M. quadratus lumborum, 14
97. M. quadriceps femoris, 3,4,5,6,14
98. M. rectus abdominis, 1,2
99. M. sartorius, 1,2,9
100. M. scalenus anterior, 14
101. M. serratus anterior, 1
102. M. sternocleidomastoideus, 1,2,8,9,10
103. M. sternohyoideus, 1,2,9
104. M. sternothyroideus, 2,9
105. M. styloglossus, 3
106. M. temporalis, 1
107. M. tensor fasciae latae, 1,5,6,14
108. M. thyrohyoideus, 2
109. M. transversus abdominis, 1,2
110. M. transversus thoracis, 2,9
111. M. trapezius, 5,6,10,14
112. M. triceps brachii, 5,6,14
113. M. zygomaticus major, 1,10
114. N. femoralis, 7,14
115. N. iliohypogastricus, 7
116. N. ilio-inguinalis, 7
117. N. medianus, 5,6,14
118. N. obturatorius, 7
119. N. phrenicus, 10
120. N. ulnaris, 5,6,14
121. N. vagus, 14
122. Oesophagus (esophagus), 5,6,12,13,14
123. Omentum majus, 1
124. Omentum minus, 3,4,9,10,11
125. Os costate, 1,2,7,9
126. Os frontale, 3,7
127. Os ischii, 7
128. Os occipitale, 4,5,7
129. Os parietale, 3,7
130. Os pubis, 3,6,7,13,14
131. Os sacrum, 7

132. Os sphenoidale, 7
133. Os temporale, 3,7
134. Os zygomaticum, 1
135. Ovarium (ovary), 14
136. Pancreas, 5,12,13
137. Penis, 2,3,5
138. Pericardium, 10
139. Platysma, 8,9
140. Plexus brachialis, 5,6,7,14
141. Plexus lumbosacralis, 7
142. Plica umbilicalis medialis, 9
143. Plica umbilicalis mediana, 9
144. Pons, 11,14
145. Prostata, 6
146. Pulmo (lung), 3,4,5,6,10,11,14
147. Pylorus, 12,13
148. Rectum, 7, 14
149. Ren (kidney), 5,6,14
150. Scapula, 7
151. Scrotum, 1,2,5
152. Septum nasi, 5,6,12,13
153. Sinus frontalis, 2,3,4,5,6,7,11,12,13,14
154. Sinus maxillaris, 2,3
155. Sinus rectus, 12,13
156. Sinus sagittalis inferior, 12,13
157. Sinus sagittalis superior, 12,13
158. Sinus sphenoidalis, 4,5,6,7,11,12,13,14
159. Spina iliaca anterior superior, 1,2,7,8,14
  Spleen: see 52
  Splen: see 52
160. Sternum, 1,2,8,9
  Stomach: see 196
161. Tentorium cerebelli, 11,14
  Tongue: see 60
162. Testis, 5
163. Trachea, 5,6,14
164. Truncus brachiocephalicus, 5,14
165. Truncus coeliacus, 5,10,12,14
166. Ureter, 5,6,13,14
167. Uterus, 14
168. Vagina, 14
169. Vasa epigastrica inferior, 5,8,9
170. Vasa gastrica, 11
171. Vasa gastro-omentalis, 10
172. Vasa lienalis (vasa splenica), 12,13
173. Vasa mesenterica inferior, 12,13
174. Vasa mesenterica superior, 5,12,13
175. Vasa ovarica, 14
  Vasa splenica: see 172
176. Vasa testicularis, 5,6
177. Vasa thoracicae internae, 9,10
178. V. axillaris, 3,10,11
179. V. comitans a. brachialis, 3,8,10,11
180. V. brachiocephalica, 3,4,10,11
181. V. cava inferior, 5,6,11,14
182. V. cava superior, 4,5,10,11
183. V. cephalica, 3,4,8,9,11,12,13,14
184. V. femoralis, 5,6,14
185. V. iliaca communis, 5,6,14
186. V. iliaca externa, 5,6,14
187. V. iliaca interna, 5,6,14
188. V. jugularis interna, 3,4,5,10
189. V. mesenterica inferior, 13
190. V. mesenterica superior, 5
191. V. portae hepatis, 5,11,12,13
192. V. pulmonalis, 11,14
193. V. renalis, 6,14
194. V. saphena magna, 8,9
195. V. subclavia, 3,4,10,11
196. Ventriculus (gaster; stomach), 3,4,10,11
197. Ventriculus dexter, 5,10,11
198. Ventriculus sinister, 5,10,11
199. Vertebra, 6,7,11,14
200. Vesica biliaris (vesica fellea; gall bladder), 3,4,10,11
201. Vesica urinaria, 3,4,5,6,12,13
202. Vesicula seminalis, 6

1. The glands and tissues making up the system and their secretions

    a. The thyroid

    b. The adrenal glands

    c. The pituitary

    d. Hypothalamus

    e. Pancreatic islets

    f. Parathyroid glands

    g. Gastrointestinal mucosa

    h. Thymus, pineal gland, kidneys, and other possible endocrine organs or hormones

2. The effects of the endocrine system upon sex-oriented processes

    a. Glands affected by endocrine secretions: the testes, the ovaries, the placenta

    b. Female processes under endocrine control: the menstrual cycle, gestation, parturition, the secretion of milk, and the termination of menstrual life

F. The structures and functions of the reproductive system

    1. The male reproductive system

    2. The female reproductive system

G. The structures and functions of the excretory system

    1. The structures: kidneys, ureters, urinary bladder, urethra

    2. The excretory process

H. The structures and functions of the supportive-protective system

    1. The composition and properties of bone

    2. The connective tissues

    3. The joints

    4. The bursae

    5. The sinuses

    6. The muscular system

    7. The structure and properties of muscle

        a. Striated, skeletal, or voluntary muscle

        b. Nonstriated, smooth, or involuntary muscle

        c. Cardiac muscle

        d. The contraction of muscle fibres
        [see 323.D.]

    8. The integument and derivatives: skin, hair, and nails

I. The body cavities and their membranes: the thoracic cavity, the abdominal cavity

J. The structure and functions of the nervous system

    1. The central nervous system: the brain and spinal cord, the cerebrospinal fluid

    2. The peripheral nervous system: cranial nerves, spinal nerves, and that part of the autonomic system that is outside the brain and spinal cord

    3. The autonomic nervous system: the sympathetic and parasympathetic systems

    4. The eye and the process of vision

    5. The ear and the process of audition

    6. Other sensory receptors

        a. Cutaneous (skin) senses: touch, heat, cold, and pain

        b. Kinesthetic (motion) sense

        c. Vestibular sense (equilibrium): acceleration, rotation, orientation, and balance

d. Taste (gustatory) sense

e. Smell (olfactory) sense

K. The composition and properties of body fluids and tissues
[see 332.D.]

Suggested reading in the *Encyclopædia Britannica*:

MACROPAEDIA: Major articles dealing with the structures and functions of the human body

Biochemical Components of Organisms	Digestion and Digestive Systems	Muscles and Muscle Systems	Respiration and Respiratory Systems
Blood	Endocrine Systems	Nerves and Nervous Systems	Sensory Reception
Circulation and Circulatory Systems	Excretion and Excretory Systems	Nutrition	Supportive and Connective Tissues
	Integumentary Systems	Reproduction and Reproductive Systems	Tissues and Fluids

MICROPAEDIA: Selected entries of reference information

General subjects

bones and skeletal system:
bone
bone marrow
cartilage
joint
osteoblast
osteoclast
osteocyte
osteon
periosteum
skeleton

cardiovascular system—blood:
ABO blood group system
agglutinin
blood
blood cell formation
blood typing
coagulation
complement
erythrocyte
hemoglobin
hemolysis
leukocyte
lymphocyte
plasma
platelet
Rh blood group system
serum albumin

cardiovascular system—blood vessels:
aorta
artery
capillary
vein
vena cava

cardiovascular system—heart:
atrium
coronary circulation
diastole
heart
systole
ventricle

cardiovascular system—other:
blood pressure
cardiovascular system
pulmonary circulation
pulse
systemic circulation

cavities and membranes:
abdominal cavity
peritoneum
pleura
sinus
thoracic cavity

connective tissues:
collagen
connective tissue
elastic fibre
ligament
mast cell
reticular fibre
tendon

digestive system:
anal canal
anus
appetite
argentaffin cell
bile

bilirubin
cecum
chewing
chyme
colon
defecation
digestion
digestive nerve plexus
duodenum
esophagus
feces
flatulence
gallbladder
gastric gland
ileum
intestinal gas
large intestine
liver
pancreas
Paneth cell
peristalsis
pharynx
plica circularis
pylorus
rectum
satiety
small intestine
stomach
swallowing
villus

endocrine system:
adrenal gland
adrenaline and noradrenaline
adrenocorticotropic hormone
androgen
calcitonin
corticoid
endocrine system
enterogastrone

estrogen
follicle-stimulating hormones
gastrin
glucagon
growth hormone
hormone
insulin
Langerhans, islets of
luteinizing hormone
neurohormone
ovary
oxytocin
parathyroid gland
pineal gland
pituitary gland
progesterone
prolactin
relaxin
renin
steroid hormone
testis
testosterone
thymus
thyroid gland

excretory system:
excretion
kidney
loop of Henle
renal artery
renal capsule
renal collecting tubule
renal pelvis
renal pyramid
ureter
urethra
urinary bladder

urination
urine
*integument and its
  derivatives:*
  dermis
  epidermis
  hair
  mammary gland
  nail
  perspiration
  sebaceous gland
  sweat gland
lymphatic system:
  adenoids
  lymph
  lymph node
  lymph nodule
  lymphoid tissue
  Peyer's patch
  spleen
  thymus
  tonsil
*mouth, teeth, and
  gums:*
  canine tooth
  cementum
  dentine
  enamel
  gum
  mouth
  palate
  periodontal
    membrane
  permanent tooth
  premolar
  primary tooth
  saliva
  salivary gland
  tongue
  tooth
muscles:
  abdominal muscle
  abductor muscle
  adductor muscle

biceps muscle
extensor muscle
flexor muscle
gluteus muscle
iliocostalis muscle
latissimus dorsi
levator muscle
muscle
pectoralis muscle
sphincter muscle
*nervous system—
  autonomic:*
  adrenergic nerve
    fibre
  autonomic nervous
    system
  cranial nerve
  facial nerve
  ganglion
  spinal nerve
  vagus nerve
*nervous system—
  central:*
  brain
  cerebellum
  cerebral cortex
  cerebral fissure
  cerebrospinal fluid
  cerebrum
  hypothalamus
  laterality
  medulla oblongata
  meninges
  pons
  spinal cord
  thalamus
*nervous system—ear
  and hearing:*
  auricle
  bone conduction
  ear
  eustachean tube

external auditory
  canal
inner ear
sound reception
tympanic
  membrane
vestibulocochlear
  nerve
*nervous system—eye
  and vision:*
  aqueous humour
  cone
  eye
  eyelid
  focusing
  iris
  lens
  macula lutea
  optic nerve
  retina
  rhodopsin
  rod
  tear duct and
    gland
*nervous system—
  other:*
  nervous system
  neuron
  neurotransmitter
  proprioception
  smell
  taste
*reproductive
  system—female:*
  clitoris
  fallopian tube
  menopause
  menstruation
  oogenesis
  ovary
  ovulation
  ovum
  puerperium
  uterine cervix

uterus
vagina
vulva
*reproductive
  system—male:*
  bulbourethral
    gland
  ductus deferens
  ejaculation
  epididyme
  erection
  penis
  prostate gland
  scrotum
  semen
  seminal vesicle
  sperm
  spermatic cord
  spermatogenesis
  testis
*reproductive
  system—other:*
  artificial
    insemination
  orgasm
  placenta
  sexual intercourse
  umbilical cord
respiratory system:
  diaphragm
  larynx
  lung
  nose
  pulmonary
    alveolus
  respiration
  trachea
other:
  bursa
  human body
  mucus
  reticuloendothelial
    system

Biographies

See Section 10/34 of Part Ten

INDEX: See entries under all of the terms above

Section 422.   **Human Health**

A. Stages in the human life cycle

  1. Fertilization: the beginning of life
[see also 331.E.]

  2. Prenatal development
[see also 338.B.]

  3. Birth

  4. Postnatal development
[see also 338.B.]

  5. Reproduction
[see also 337]

  6. Aging

  7. Dying and death

B. Definitions and ranges of normality in human health

C. Bodily mechanisms for the maintenance of human health during stress

  1. The maintenance of the internal environment and the adaptation of cells to severe stress

  2. Defenses against disease

    a. Maintenance of integrity of skin and mucosal linings

    b. Role of the phagocytic cells of the body

    c. Inflammation: the response to biological insult

    d. The immune response

  3. Role of the blood in the prevention of hemorrhage

  4. Healing: the processes of regeneration and organization in the repair of tissues

  5. The alarm reaction: preparation through the effects of certain hormones for either flight or resistance
[see 421.E.1.b.]

D. Other regimes affecting standard values in human health

  1. Nutrition and diet

    a. Functions of food

    b. Classes of food

    c. Recommended intakes of nutrients to meet standards of physiological and metabolic requirements

    d. Feeding behaviour

    e. Therapeutic diets

  2. Exercise and physical conditioning

    a. Exercise needs: maintenance of health, avoidance of exercise injuries, and assessment of exercise adequacy

    b. Physiological responses to exercise and the effects of physical conditioning

  3. The state of sleep and its effects

    a. The nature of sleep: criteria for and problems in defining sleep

    b. Psychophysiological variations in sleep; *e.g.,* REM, NREM, light and deep sleep, dreaming

    c. Effects of general and selective sleep deprivation

Suggested reading in the *Encyclopædia Britannica*:

MACROPAEDIA: Major articles dealing with human health

Death
Exercise and Physical Conditioning
Immunity
Nutrition

MICROPAEDIA: Selected entries of reference information

General subjects

baths and spas:
bath
furo
sauna
spa
Turkish bath
exercise:
aerobics
exercise
jogging
physical
education
life cycle—birth:
natural childbirth
parturition
presentation

life cycle—prenatal:
embryo
fertilization
fetus
implantation
in vitro
fertilization
pregnancy
life cycle—other:
adolescence
aging
death
middle age
old age

protective
mechanisms of the
body:
antibody
antigen
coagulation
homeostasis
human leukocyte
antigen
immunity
inflammation
interferon
interleukin
phagocytosis

reticuloendothelial
system
tumour necrosis
factor
other:
dieting
health
immunization
nutrition
preventive
medicine
sleep
vegetarianism

Biographies

See Section 10/35 of Part Ten

INDEX: See entries under all of the terms above

Section 423.   Human Diseases

A. Characteristics, causes, and classifications of human disease

B. The detection and diagnosis of disease

C. The treatment of disease: therapeutics

1. Aspects of medical treatment: factors for consideration in the formulation of a therapeutic regimen

2. Major therapeutic techniques

a. Surgical treatment

b. Biological therapy

c. Pharmacodynamic therapy

d. Chemotherapy

e. Substitution therapy

f. Radiation therapy

g. Physical therapy

h. Occupational therapy

i. Shock therapy

j. Burn treatment

k. Organ and tissue transplants

l. Psychological therapy
[see 436.D.4.]

D. The symptoms, diagnosis, and treatment of diseases of the body as a whole

   1. Physiological shock

   2. Metabolic diseases and disorders

   3. Nutritional diseases: disorders related to nutritional deficiencies and excesses

   4. Diseases and disorders of fluid and electrolyte balance

   5. Infectious or contagious diseases: the impairment of health by living invaders of the body

   6. Diseases and disorders present at the time of birth

   7. Childhood diseases

   8. Disorders and injuries caused by physical agents: electrical shock; exposure to extremes of temperature, radiation, and pressure; motion sickness; wounds

   9. Dehydration and associated disorders

  10. Poisoning

  11. Allergenic diseases and anaphylactic shock

E. The symptoms, diagnosis, and treatment of diseases affecting any organ or tissue of the body: tumours, hyperplasia, atrophy

F. Diseases of particular bodily systems

   1. The cardiovascular system

     a. The heart and the great vessels

     b. The blood vessels

     c. Blood circulation

     d. The blood and blood-forming tissues

   2. The lymphatic system

     a. Disorders of lymphatic vessels and their drainage

     b. Disorders of lymphoid tissue

   3. The respiratory system

     a. Infectious diseases of the respiratory system

     b. Allergic lung diseases

     c. Bronchopulmonary diseases

     d. Diseases of the nonpulmonary structures

     e. Disorders in the dynamics of respiration

   4. The digestive system

     a. The mouth, pharynx, and associated structures

     b. The esophagus

     c. The stomach and duodenum

     d. The small intestine and appendix

     e. The large intestine

     f. The digestive glands

     g. Disorders in the digestion and absorption of foods

   5. The endocrine system

     a. The pituitary

     b. The thyroid

     c. The parathyroids

     d. The adrenals

     e. The gonads and placenta

     f. Female sex-oriented process under endocrine control: menstrual disorders, abnormal changes in pregnancy

g. The pancreas

h. Other endocrine glands: pineal gland, thymus

6. The reproductive system

    a. Genetic and congenital abnormalities

    b. Functional genital disorders

    c. Infections

    d. Structural changes of unknown causes: tumours and injuries

    e. Diseases of the mammary glands

7. The excretory system
   [see also 10/35.B.1.d.]

    a. Functional aspects: disorders of urine production and micturition

    b. The kidneys and tubules

    c. The urinary tract: ureters, bladder, and urethra

8. The supportive-protective system

    a. The skeletal system and bone

    b. Connective tissue: bone and periosteum, cartilage, tendon, and ligament

    c. The joints

    d. The bursae

    e. The sinuses and the body cavities and their membranes

    f. Muscle

    g. The skin

9. The nervous system
   [see also 10/35.B.1.f.]

    a. Neurological manifestations secondary to other diseases, neurochemical disorders, and development defects

    b. Disorders of the peripheral nerves

    c. Disorders of the spinal cord and autonomic nervous system

    d. Disorders of the central nervous system

    e. Other disorders of the general nervous system

    f. Disorders of the eye and vision

    g. Disorders of the ear and hearing

    h. Disorders of other sensory receptors

    i. Disorders of speech

    j. Headache

Suggested reading in the *Encyclopædia Britannica:*

MACROPAEDIA: Major articles dealing with human diseases

Blood	Digestion and	Integumentary	Respiration and
Cancer	Digestive Systems	Systems	Respiratory
Childhood	Disease	Metabolism	Systems
Diseases and	Endocrine Systems	Muscles and	Sensory Reception
Disorders	Excretion and	Muscle Systems	Supportive and
Circulation and	Excretory	Nerves and	Connective
Circulatory	Systems	Nervous Systems	Tissues
Systems	Immunity	Nutrition	Transplants, Organ
Diagnosis and	Infectious Diseases	Poisons and	and Tissue
Therapeutics		Poisoning	

MICROPAEDIA: Selected entries of reference information

<u>General subjects</u>

angioma
atresia and stenosis
cerebral palsy
chromosomal
  disorder
cleft palate
cleidocranial
  dysostosis
congenital disorder
craniosynostosis
cretinism
cryptorchidism
cutis laxa
D1-trisomy
digit malformation
Down syndrome
Dupuytren's
  contracture
dwarfism
dysplasia
E-trisomy
erythroblastosis
  fetalis
Fallot, tetralogy of
harelip
heart
  malformation
hemophilia
hereditary
  spherocytosis
hermaphroditism
intussusception
Klinefelter's
  syndrome
mandibulofacial
  dysostosis
Marfan's syndrome
microcephaly
Morquio's
  syndrome
muscular
  dystrophy
neural tube defect
neurofibromatosis
osteochondroma
osteogenesis
  imperfecta
patent ductus
  arteriosus
pectus excavatum
peromelia
pseudohermaphroditism
respiratory distress
  syndrome
Rett syndrome
Siamese twin
sickle cell anemia
teratology
thalassemia
Turner's syndrome
urogenital
  malformation
vitiligo

von Willebrand's
  disease
*disorders—connective
tissue:*
  amyloidosis
  Dupuytren's
    contracture
  herniated disk
  lupus
    erythematosus
  tendinitis
*disorders—ear and
hearing:*
  deafness
  ear squeeze
  earwax impaction
  labyrinthitis
  Menière's disease
  otitis media
  presbycusis
  stirrup fixation
disorders—endocrine:
  acromegaly
  Addison's disease
  adrenogenital
    syndrome
  Albright's
    syndrome
  chromophobe
    adenoma
  cretinism
  cryptorchidism
  Cushing's
    syndrome
  diabetes insipidus
  diabetes mellitus
  dwarfism
  endemic goitre
  Fröhlich's
    syndrome
  gigantism
  granulomatous
    thyroiditis
  Graves' disease
  Hashimoto's
    disease
  hyperglycemia
  hyperparathyroidism
  hypoglycemia
  hypothyroidism
  myxedema
  parathyroid
    adenoma
  pheochromocytoma
  Plummer's disease
  Riedel thyroiditis
  Sheehan's
    syndrome
  Stein–Leventhal
    syndrome
  thyroid tumour
  thyroiditis

*disorders—excretory
system:*
  Bright's disease
  cystitis
  enuresis
  hematuria
  kidney failure
  kidney stone
  nephroblastoma
  nephrosclerosis
  nephrotic
    syndrome
  pyelonephritis
  renal carcinoma
  renal cyst
  renal
    osteodystrophy
  uremia
  urethritis
  urinary tract
    obstruction
*disorders—eye and
vision:*
  amblyopia
  astigmatism
  blepharitis
  blindness
  cataract
  colour blindness
  conjunctivitis
  detached retina
  double vision
  exophthalmos
  glaucoma
  hyperopia
  iris
  keratitis
  lens dislocation
  myopia
  night blindness
  nystagmus
  ophthalmoplegia
  optic atrophy
  optic neuritis
  presbyopia
  ptosis
  retinitis
    pigmentosa
  retrolental
    fibroplasia
  scleritis
  strabismus
  sty
  trachoma
  uveitis
  visual-field defect
*disorders—
gastrointestinal:*
  appendicitis
  cestodiasis
  cholera
  coccidiosis
  colic
  colitis

constipation
diarrhea
dysentery
enteritis
fasciolopsiasis
gastritis
gastroenteritis
hookworm disease
ileitis
indigestion
intestinal
  diverticulum
intestinal
  obstruction
intestinal squeeze
intussusception
megacolon
myiasis
nausea
pancreatitis
peptic ulcer
proctitis
salmonellosis
trichinosis
trichomoniasis
vomiting
*disorders—hepatic
and biliary:*
  cholecystitis
  cirrhosis
  clonorchiasis
  fatty liver
  gallstone
  hepatitis
  jaundice
*disorders—infectious
diseases caused
by bacteria
and related
organisms:*
  anthrax
  bacteremia
  bartonellosis
  bejel
  boutonneuse fever
  brucellosis
  chancroid
  chlamydia
  cholera
  diphtheria
  dysentery
  glanders
  gonorrhea
  granuloma
    inguinale
  impetigo
  Legionnaires'
    disease
  leprosy
  leptospirosis
  listeriosis
  Lyme disease
  lymphogranuloma
    venereum

mastitis
melioidosis
osteomyelitis
paresis
plague
psittacosis
puerperal fever
pyelonephritis
Q fever
rat-bite fever
rheumatic fever
Rocky Mountain
  spotted fever
salmonellosis
scarlet fever
scrub typhus
septicemia
streptobacillary
  fever
sty
syphilis
tetanus
toxic shock
  syndrome
trachoma
trench fever
tuberculosis
tularemia
typhoid
typhus
whooping cough
yaws
disorders—infectious
diseases caused by
fungi:
  actinomycosis
  aspergillosis
  blastomycosis
  candidiasis
  cryptococcosis
  histoplasmosis
  Madura foot
  mycosis
  nocardiosis
  ringworm
  sporotrichosis
  thrush
disorders—infectious
diseases caused by
parasites:
  ascariasis
  cestodiasis
  Chagas' disease
  clonorchiasis
  coccidiosis
  dysentery
  echinococcosis
  fasciolopsiasis
  filariasis
  hookworm
  kala-azar
  malaria
  onchocerciasis
  paragonimiasis

schistosomiasis
sleeping sickness
toxoplasmosis
trichinosis
trichomoniasis
disorders—infectious
diseases caused by
various agents:
  conjunctivitis
  endocarditis
  infection
  meningitis
  otitis media
  pharyngitis
  pneumonia
  scrub typhus
  septic arthritis
  sexually
    transmitted
    disease
  splenitis
  tonsillitis
  zoonosis
disorders—infectious
diseases caused by
viruses:
  AIDS
  chicken pox
  Colorado tick fever
  common cold
  dengue
  encephalitis
  herpes simplex
  herpes zoster
  infectious
    mononucleosis
  influenza
  kuru
  measles
  mumps
  pappataci fever
  poliomyelitis
  pox disease
  rabies
  Rift Valley fever
  roseola infantum
  rubella
  smallpox
  wart
  yellow fever
disorders—lymphatic
system:
  Hodgkin's disease
  lymphedema
  lymphogranuloma
    venereum
  sporotrichosis
  tonsillitis
disorders—muscle:
  cramp
  dermatomyositis
  lumbago

muscle tumour
muscular
  dystrophy
myasthenia gravis
myositis
myotonia
tetanus
tetany
trichinosis
disorders—nervous
system:
  Alzheimer's disease
  amyotrophic
    lateral
    sclerosis
  analgesia
  aphasia
  apraxia
  ataxia
  cerebral palsy
  chorea
  coma
  convulsion
  dementia
  dyslexia
  encephalitis
  epilepsy
  focal seizure
  grand mal
  herpes zoster
  hydrocephalus
  hyperactivity
  kernicterus
  kuru
  listeriosis
  meningitis
  microcephaly
  multiple sclerosis
  neural tube defect
  neuralgia
  neuritis
  paralysis
  paresis
  Parkinson's disease
  petit mal
  Pick's disease
  poliomyelitis
  psychomotor
    seizure
  rabies
  Rett syndrome
  sciatica
  senile dementia
  sleeping sickness
  spinal curvature
  syringomyelia
  tic
  Tourette syndrome
  vertigo
disorders—nutritional
diseases:
  anorexia
  anorexia nervosa

beriberi
bulimia
calcium deficiency
celiac disease
chlorine deficiency
cobalt deficiency
copper deficiency
fluorine deficiency
iodine deficiency
kwashiorkor
magnesium
  deficiency
malnutrition
manganese
  deficiency
obesity
osteomalacia
pellagra
phosphorus
  deficiency
rickets
scurvy
tropical sprue
vitamin A
  deficiency
vitamin A excess
vitamin B₂
  deficiency
vitamin B₁₂
  deficiency
vitamin D excess
vitamin E
  deficiency
vitamin K
  deficiency
disorders—oral:
  canker sore
  caries
  gingivitis
  glossitis
  periodontitis
  thrush
  tooth squeeze
disorders—poisoning:
  antimony
    poisoning
  arsenic poisoning
  botulism
  cadmium
    poisoning
  fish poisoning
  food poisoning
  lead poisoning
  medicinal
    poisoning
  mercury poisoning
  mushroom
    poisoning
  poison
  shellfish poisoning
  venom

disorders—pregnancy
  related:
    abortion
    ectopic pregnancy
    hydatidiform mole
    miscarriage
    placenta accreta
    placenta praevia
    placentae abruptio
    placental infarction
    preeclampsia and
      eclampsia
    premature birth
      and postmature
      birth
disorders—pressure
  injuries and other
  disorders caused by
  physical agents:
    acceleration stress
    acoustic trauma
    air embolism
    altitude sickness
    barotrauma
    bends
    blast injury
    burn
    crush injury
    deceleration injury
    decompression
      sickness
    ear squeeze
    ebullism
    electrical shock
    frostbite
    heatstroke
    hypothermia
    intestinal squeeze
    mediastinal
      emphysema
    motion sickness
    nitrogen narcosis
    radiation injury
    rotational stress
    snakebite
    spatial
      disorientation
    sunburn
    taravana syndrome
    thoracic squeeze
    tooth squeeze
    wound
disorders—
  reproductive:
    amenorrhea
    cervical erosion
    cervicitis
    chlamydia
    cryptorchidism
    dysmenorrhea
    dyspareunia
    endometriosis

galactorrhea
gynecomastia
hermaphroditism
hydrocele
impotence
leukorrhea
oligomenorrhea
orchitis
premenstrual
  syndrome
priapism
prostatic disorder
pseudohermaphroditism
puerperal fever
Stein–Leventhal
  syndrome
uterine bleeding
vaginitis
vesiculitis
vulvitis
disorders—
  respiratory system:
    adenovirus
      infection
    alveolar proteinosis
    anthracosis
    asbestosis
    atelectasis
    berylliosis
    bronchiectasis
    bronchitis
    byssinosis
    common cold
    cough
    emphysema
    hyperventilation
    hypoxia
    influenza
    laryngeal cancer
    laryngitis
    Legionnaires'
      disease
    lung congestion
    lung infarction
    nasal polyp
    nasal tumour
    paragonimiasis
    pharyngitis
    pickwickian
      syndrome
    pneumoconiosis
    pneumonia
    psittacosis
    respiratory distress
      syndrome
    silicosis
    tracheitis
    tuberculosis
    whooping cough
disorders—sexually
  transmitted
  diseases:
    AIDS

chancre
chancroid
chlamydia
gonorrhea
granuloma
  inguinale
herpes simplex
lymphogranuloma
  venereum
proctitis
syphilis
disorders—skeletal:
  achondroplasia
  acromegaly
  bone lesion
  callus
  cervical
    spondylosis
  cleidocranial
    dysostosis
  craniosynostosis
  dislocation
  dysplasia
  dwarfism
  Ewing's tumour of
    bone
  flatfoot
  fluorosis
  fracture
  gigantism
  hamartoma
  listeriosis
  mastoiditis
  metatarsalgia
  Morquio's
    syndrome
  multiple myeloma
  neurogenic
    anthropathy
  osteoarthritis
  osteochondroma
  osteogenesis
    imperfecta
  osteomyelitis
  osteoporosis
  osteosarcoma
  Paget's disease of
    bone
  parathyroid
    adenoma
  rheumatoid
    arthritis
  septic arthritis
  spondylolisthesis
  spondylosis
disorders—skin:
  acne
  baldness
  bedsore
  blister
  boil
  carbuncle
  corn
  cutis laxa

erythema
exfoliative
  dermatitis
hemangioma
herpes simplex
herpes zoster
hives
hyperhidrosis
ichthyosis
impetigo
insect bite and
  sting
itching
keratosis
mole
nevus
pemphigus
pinta
pseudoxanthoma
  elasticum
psoriasis
ringworm
scleroderma
seborrheic
  dermatitis
ulcer
vitiligo
wart
disorders—other:
  asthenia
  atrophy
  childhood diseases
    and disorders
  cyst
  dehydration
  disease
  diverticulum
  edema
  empyema
  fetal alcohol
    syndrome
  fever
  gangrene
  hamartoma
  headache
  hernia
  hiccup
  hypophosphatemia
  Kawasaki
    syndrome
  lesion
  potassium
    deficiency
  progeria
  prolapse
  Reye's syndrome
  sarcoidosis
  Sjögren's syndrome
  sodium deficiency
  splenitis
  splenomegaly
  sudden infant
    death syndrome
  tumour

infectious agents:	treatments—surgery:	transplant	hydropathy
bacteria	abortion	vasectomy	hydrotherapy
prion	amputation	treatments—	hyperbaric
virus	cesarean section	therapeutics:	chamber
treatments—	coronary bypass	acupuncture	massage
prosthetic devices:	cryosurgery	adjuvant	moxa treatment
artificial heart	gastrectomy	antidepressant	occupational
contact lens	heart transplant	artificial	therapy
denture	hysterectomy	respiration	physical therapy
eyeglasses	kidney transplant	blood transfusion	pseudolaryngeal
hearing aid	microsurgery	chemotherapy	speech
pacemaker	radial keratotomy	desensitization	radiation therapy
prosthesis	skin graft	dialysis	respiratory therapy
	surgery	diathermy	therapeutics

Biographies

See Section 10/35 of Part Ten

Section 424. **The Practice of Medicine and the Care of Health**

A. Medical education

B. Fields of specialized medical research; the related disciplines of osteopathy, dentistry, and nursing [see 10/35.C.]

C. The practice of medicine

  1. The kinds of medical practice in various countries

    a. General practice and first-contact care: the general practitioner versus the specialist, clinic and health centre practice

    b. Hospital and specialist practice: general surgery, pediatrics, anesthetics, pathology, teaching practice

    c. Governmental practice: public health service, military practice, space medicine

    d. Research

  2. Maintenance of professional standards

    a. The ethical basis of medical practice; *e.g.,* the Hippocratic oath, problems relating to euthanasia and abortion

    b. Licensure requirements for practice: the wide variation among countries

    c. Legal restrictions on practice

    d. Professional organizations and the maintenance of standards

D. Public health services and administration

E. Hospital services and facilities

F. Environmental sanitation and health: the control of air, water, and soil pollution [see 737.C.1.]

G. Efforts directed toward the prevention of malnutrition: the recognition and attempted solution of problems relating to nutrient requirements, world food supply, and world population

H. The prevention and control of infection

  1. Vaccination and immunization

  2. The quarantine and isolation of infected victims

  3. Destruction of infectious agent or carrier; *e.g.,* aseptic and antiseptic precautions, control of disease carriers, disinfection

  4. The use of therapeutic agents and prophylactic medication

  5. The prevention and control of epidemics

I. Industrial and social medicine

1. The scope of industrial and occupational medicine

2. Health and safety laws: the regulation of working hours; restrictions on female and child labour; the elimination of health, safety, and fire hazards; the control of foods and drugs; pollution control
[see 552.D.]

J. The economics of health and disease

Suggested reading in the *Encyclopædia Britannica:*

MACROPAEDIA: Major articles dealing with the practice of medicine and the care of health

Birth Control
Medicine
Occupational Diseases and Disorders

MICROPAEDIA: Selected entries of reference information

General subjects

agencies and programs:	*health-care fields:*	psychiatry	birth control
Food and Drug Administration	aerospace medicine	surgery	blood bank
	chiropractic	*medical ethics:*	contraception
	dental auxiliary	abortion	flying doctor
International Fund for Agricultural Development	dentistry	euthanasia	service
	epidemiology	Hippocratic oath	health maintenance
	hematology	medical	organization
Medicare	industrial medicine	jurisprudence	hospice
National Health Service	midwifery	*preventive medicine:*	hospital
	nursing	immunization	medical association
National Institutes of Health	optometry	preventive	planned
	osteopathy	medicine	parenthood
World Food Programme	paramedical personnel	quarantine	public health
		other:	social security
World Health Organization	pharmacy	American Medical Association	
	plastic surgery		

Biographies
See Section 10/35 of Part Ten

INDEX: See entries under all of the terms above

Division III.   **Human Behaviour and Experience**
[For Part Four headnote see page 143.]

The outlines in the six sections of Division III set forth the discoveries and theories in the psychological sciences concerning human capacities, human behaviour, and human experience.

Section 431 is concerned with the questions of the definition and origins of human behaviour and experience. It also indicates the stages in the development of a person's behaviour and experience.

The outline in Section 432 deals with the capacities by which humans receive, organize, and interpret information about the current environment that influences behaviour. It treats the following subjects: attention; sensation; perception; the perception of time, of space, and of movement; perceptual illusions and hallucinations; and parapsychological phenomena.

Section 433 is concerned with current internal states that affect behaviour and conscious experience. It treats the determinants and manifestations of activation level; motivational states; emotional states; and transient states affecting behaviour and experience, such as sleep, dreams, hypnosis, fatigue, and intoxication.

Section 434 is concerned with persisting capacities that influence human behaviour and conscious experience. The outline treats the nature and assessment of human abilities and attitudes; sensorimotor abilities; intellectual abilities; and the distribution of intelligence.

Section 435 is concerned with the development of a person's potentials by learning and thinking. The outline treats diverse general theories of learning; deals separately with psychomotor, perceptual, and conceptual learning; and then treats memory and forgetting and the theories about and the types of the higher thought processes.

The outline in Section 436 sets forth those parts of psychology, psychopathology, and psychotherapy that consider the functioning, the integration, and the disintegration of the person as a whole. It treats diverse definitions and theories of personality and the self; theories of personality adjustment and maladjustment; and the kinds of mental disorders and their psychiatric treatment.

Section 431.   Human Nature and Experience: General Considerations

A. The relative contribution of opposing factors in human behaviour and conscious experience, the degree to which these factors interact to produce human behaviour and conscious experience

  1. Mankind as radically distinct from nature and mankind as homogeneous and continuous with the rest of nature

     a. Behavioral capacities and performances that humans have in common with other primates and higher mammals

     b. Behavioral capacities and performances held to be distinctive of humans; *e.g.*, propositional language, cumulative transmission of culture

     c. The explanation of allegedly distinctive human traits in accordance with the principle of phylogenetic continuity: the evolutionary development of mankind
     [see also 341 and 411]

  2. The relative weights of genetic and environmental factors: the nature–nurture controversy

     a. Elements of genetic endowment; *e.g.*, physiological and psychological characteristics, reflexes and instincts

     b. Environmental conditions; *e.g.,* ecological factors, cultural conditioning, personal socialization experiences

  3. Cognitive, conative, and affective dimensions of behaviour and experience

     a. The cognitive dimension: sensation and perception; memory and imagination; concept formation, ideation, and reasoning

     b. The conative dimension: desires, needs, cravings, drives; motivation and purpose; the voluntary and the involuntary

     c. The affective dimension: the emotions, the pleasant and the unpleasant; the sentiments

  4. The observed elements of behaviour and the inferred dispositional tendencies: actions and powers; habits, inclinations, and capacities

  5. Emergent problems in the study of human behaviour and experience: the data and hypotheses of parapsychology; the comparison of human and artificial, machine-created intelligence

B. Stages in the development of human behaviour

  1. General aspects of human development

  2. Prenatal growth and development

  3. Birth: effects of the birth experience on the person's subsequent history

  4. Infancy: the first 18 months

  5. Early childhood and childhood: one to 12 years

  6. Adolescence: puberty to adulthood

  7. Young adulthood and maturity

  8. Old age and death
     [see also 338.E.]

Suggested reading in the *Encyclopædia Britannica:*

MACROPAEDIA: Major article dealing with human nature and experience: general considerations

Behaviour, The Development of Human

MICROPAEDIA: Selected entries of reference information

General subjects

adolescence	emotion	instinct	puberty
attitude	etiquette	intelligence	reflex
behaviour genetics	habit	memory	sibling rivalry
child development	human behaviour	middle age	thanatology
culture	imitation	old age	thought
creativity	insight	psychological development	

Biographies

See Sections 10/35 and 10/36 of Part Ten

INDEX: See entries under all of the terms above

Section 432.   Influence of the Current Environment on a Person's Behaviour and Conscious Experience: Attention, Sensation, and Perception

A. Attention to the environment: awareness of internal and external events
   [see 341]

   1. The problem of defining attention

   2. Development of theories of attention: influence of stimulus–response and behaviourist studies

   3. Classification of attentive phenomena: influence of adaptive processes on modes and degrees of attention

   4. Determinants of attention: temperament, health, social suggestion, novelty, interests, and unconscious influences

   5. Physiological mechanisms of attention

   6. Analysis of attentive phenomena in terms of information theory

B. Sensation: the reception of information about the environment

   1. The senses in general
      [see 421.J. and 423.F.9.]

   2. Vision

      a. The work of the retina

      b. The transduction process: the conversion of the retinal image into a set of messages in the brain

      c. Perceptual processes of vision

      d. Responses of the cerebral cortex to visual stimuli

   3. Audition

      a. The mechanisms of the external, middle, and inner ear: functions and processes involved in the transmission of sound and its conversion into neural messages

      b. The work of the auditory nerve and the auditory pathways of the central nervous system: encoding, processing, and discrimination of pitch, loudness, localization, and duration of sound

      c. The measurement of auditory phenomena: diagnosis and correction of hearing disorders

      d. The function of the semicircular canals in maintaining equilibrium: the vestibular systems
         [see B.6., below]

   4. Cutaneous senses: the punctate nature and discriminatory capacity of skin to respond to pressure, pain, heat, and cold

      a. The variety of nerve terminals exhibiting a broad range of sensitivity to different stimuli

   b. Localization of skin sensations: the nature of dermatomes

   c. The concept of adequate stimulation and paradoxical cold: adaptation to pressure and thermal situations; itch, tickle, and vibration

   d. The sensory experience of pain: its cause and function; external signs and qualities, theories of pain, modes of treatment

  5. Kinesthesis: the function and types of sensory structures and the role of kinesthetic feedback in movement control and orientation

  6. Vestibular senses: the role of the vestibular receptors and the semicircular canals of the inner ear in maintaining equilibrium

  7. The taste sense: the form and location of taste buds, the neural pathways, types of taste receptors, factors affecting taste

  8. The olfactory sense: the form, location, and nerve supply of olfactory receptors; olfactory qualities; odour-inducing factors; factors affecting odour sensitivity; effects on behaviour

C. Perception: the process of translating sensory stimulation into organized experience

  1. Contemporary theories and new concerns: the influence of Gestalt and behaviourist theories

  2. Central problems of continuing concern

  3. Principles of perceptual organization

   a. The Gestalt principle of *Prägnanz,* or good form, and the laws of grouping under it: closure, good continuation, similarity, proximity, and common fate; the significance of the phi phenomenon

   b. Context effects: the influence of surrounding stimuli and of previously experienced stimuli on the observer

   c. Perceptual constancy: the tendency of objects to appear stable in size, shape, brightness, or colour despite changing conditions of stimulation

  4. Differences in perceptual functioning among individuals, among classes of individuals, and within individuals

D. The perception of time

  1. Sequential activities related to time perception

  2. Perception of sequence and duration

  3. Factors affecting time perception; *e.g.,* type of activity, level of motivation, personality traits, drugs, sensory deprivation, hypnosis

E. The perception of space

  1. The nature of space perception: orientation to the environment

  2. Perception of depth and distance: gross tactual-kinesthetic, eye muscle, visual, and auditory cues

  3. Interrelations among the senses

  4. Social and interpersonal aspects of space perception: territorial behaviour, reason in perception, and nativistic and empiricistic considerations

F. The perception of movement

  1. Visual cues for perceiving self-motion and motion of objects

  2. Nonvisual cues: auditory, kinesthetic, and vestibular cues

G. Perceptual illusions and hallucinations

  1. Types of illusory experience

  2. Hallucinations

   a. Neurological factors in hallucinations

   b. Types of hallucinatory experience

H. Theories of parapsychological phenomena

  1. Extrasensory perception: telepathy, clairvoyance, precognition, and prophecy

  2. Parapsychological phenomena of a nonperceptual nature: psychokinesis

3. Theories of perceptual and of nonperceptual parapsychological phenomena: physical theories, field theories, and theories of the collective unconscious; projection hypothesis

---

Suggested reading in the *Encyclopædia Britannica:*

MACROPAEDIA: Major articles dealing with the influence of the current environment on a person's behaviour and conscious experience: attention, sensation, and perception

Attention
Perception, Human

MICROPAEDIA: Selected entries of reference information

General subjects

parapsychological	consciousness	synesthesia	sensation
phenomena:	delirium	time perception	sense
extrasensory	eidetic image	*sensation:*	smell
perception	hallucination	chemoreception	sound reception
parapsychological	illusion	flavour	thermoreception
phenomenon	movement	mechanoreception	*other:*
precognition	perception	pain	attention
telepathy	pain	photoreception	circadian rhythm
perception:	perception	proprioception	stress
autokinetic effect	space perception	receptor	human behaviour

Biographies

See Sections 10/35 and 10/36 of Part Ten

INDEX: See entries under all of the terms above

Section 433.   **Current Internal States Affecting a Person's Behaviour and Conscious Experience**

A. Motivational states: needs and desires that channel a person's behaviour and experience

1. Diverse theories of motivation: psychoanalytic, drive, arousal, incentive, and hedonic theories

2. Specific human needs and motives, *with special attention to* achievement, anxiety, aggression, and sexual behaviour and deviations

3. Situational and interactional factors: stresses in stimulus field, cognitive evaluation, balance and congruity, and cognitive dissonance

4. Recent developments and practical applications of motivation theory: emphasis on reinforcement and instinct, the use of token systems

B. Emotional states: bodily conditions and feelings accompanying motivation and arousal conditions

1. The nature of emotion

2. Diverse conceptions of emotion: the roles of the nervous system

3. Expression of emotions: the startle response; facial, vocal, and postural manifestations

C. Transient states affecting behaviour and experience

1. Sleep

2. Dreams

3. Hypnosis and related states of altered consciousness

4. Fatigue

5. Transient states caused by altered body chemistry
[see also 321.C.4.c]

Suggested reading in the *Encyclopædia Britannica:*

Section 434.   **Persisting Capacities and Inclinations That Influence Human Behaviour and Conscious Experience**

A. The nature of human capacities
[see 435.A.]

B. The assessment of human abilities: psychological measurement

  1. Types of testing instruments and methods

  2. Development of standardized tests

  3. Assessment of test results

C. Sensorimotor abilities: bodily skills and mechanical abilities

D. Intellectual abilities: theories of intelligence

E. The distribution of intelligence

  1. Problems concerning the establishment of intelligence standards and intelligence distribution

  2. Retardation

  3. The gifted

  4. Group differences in intelligence: the measurement and interpretation of differences in age, socioeconomic class, race, sex, and other factors

F. Personal propensities and idiosyncrasies affecting behaviour and experience

G. Attitudes

  1. The nature of attitudes

2. The functions of attitudes

3. The development of attitudes

4. The measurement of attitudes: the use and validity of questionnaires, interviews, sampling techniques, opinionnaires, and content analysis

H. Persuasion and change of attitude

Suggested reading in the *Encyclopædia Britannica:*

MACROPAEDIA: Major articles dealing with the persisting capacities and inclinations that influence human behaviour and conscious experience

Intelligence, Human
Psychological Tests and Measurement

MICROPAEDIA: Selected entries of reference information

General subjects

aptitude test	genius	intelligence test	psychological
creativity	gifted child	mental age	testing
differential	human behaviour	mental retardation	sensorimotor skill
psychology	intelligence	prodigy	

Biographies

See Sections 10/35 and 10/36 of Part Ten

INDEX: See entries under all of the terms above

Section 435. **Development of a Person's Potentials: Learning and Thinking**

A. Diverse theories of human learning

1. Modern learning theories

2. Major issues in learning theories

3. Transfer of training

B. Psychomotor learning

C. Perceptual learning

D. Conceptual learning and concept formation

E. Memory: retention and forgetting of learned habits and content

F. Abnormalities of memory: amnesia, paramnesia and confabulation, hypermnesia—enhancement of memory

G. The higher thought processes

1. The psychology of higher thought processes

2. The role of language in the higher thought processes

3. Meaning

4. Types of thinking: realistic and autistic

Suggested reading in the *Encyclopædia Britannica:*

MACROPAEDIA: Major articles dealing with the development of a person's potentials: learning and thinking

Learning and Cognition, Human
Memory
Thought and Thought Processes

MICROPAEDIA: Selected entries of reference information

<u>General subjects</u>

amnesia	conditioning	memory	recognition
association	discrimination	mnemonic	social learning
attitude	generalization	perceptual learning	suggestion
brainwashing	imitation	persuasion	thought
cognition	insight	psychomotor	training, transfer of
concept formation	learning	learning	

<u>Biographies</u>

See Sections 10/35 and 10/36 of Part Ten

INDEX: See entries under all of the terms above

Section 436.   **Personality and the Self: Integration and Disintegration of the Person as a Whole**

A. Definitions of personality

    1. Physiological theories of personality: theories based on body humours, somatotypes, physiognomy, and phrenology

    2. Psychoanalytic theories of personality: the importance of id, ego, superego, life and death instincts, and the collective unconscious

    3. Social analytic theories of personality: the importance of drive to power, need achievement, and functional autonomy

    4. Eclectic theories of personality: role theories, factor analysis of personality traits

B. Measurement of personality

    1. Methods of assessment

    2. Evaluating assessment techniques

C. Personality functioning and adjustment

    1. The subjective aspect of personality: development of awareness of self

    2. Strains and challenges put on adequate personality functioning: physical, psychological, and social stresses; *e.g.,* frustration, conflict, personal inadequacy, deprivation of accustomed gratification

    3. Responses to environmental strains on personality functioning: reactions, defense mechanisms, and adjustment dynamisms for coping with environmental demands

D. Persisting disturbances of personality integration or functioning: mental disorders

    1. Major categories of mental disorders: organic mental disorders, schizophrenia, paranoid disorders, affective disorders, anxiety disorders, obsessive-compulsive disorders, posttraumatic stress disorders, somatoform disorders, dissociative disorders, personality disorders, psychosexual disorders, disorders of infancy or childhood

    2. Prevalence of mental disorders: epidemiology

    3. Causation of mental disorders

    4. Psychiatry, the treatment of mental disorders: pharmacotherapies, psychotherapies, other therapies

Suggested reading in the *Encyclopædia Britannica*:

MACROPAEDIA: Major articles and a biography dealing with personality and the self: integration and disintegration of the person as a whole

Freud
Mental Disorders and
  Their Treatment
Personality

MICROPAEDIA: Selected entries of reference information

General subjects

personality—tests:
  association test
  projective test
  Rorschach Test
personality—theories:
  anal stage
  analytic psychology
  defense mechanism
  ego
  extrovert
  humour
  id
  inferiority complex
  introvert
  Oedipus complex
  oral stage
  personality
  self
  superego

*psychiatric
disturbances:*
  affective disorder
  anxiety
  autism
  delusion
  depression
  fetishism
  hypochondriasis
  hysteria
  kleptomania
  lycanthropy
  manic-depressive
    psychosis
  mental disorder
  multiple
    personality

obsessive–
  compulsive
  disorder
paranoia
personality disorder
phobia
psychoneurosis
psychosis
psychosomatic
  disorder
pyromania
schizophrenia
therapies:
  aversion therapy
  behaviour therapy
  biofeedback
  child psychiatry
  group therapy

lobotomy
nondirective
  psychotherapy
psychoanalysis
psychodrama
psychopharma-
  cology
psychosurgery
psychotherapy
sensitivity training
shock therapy
other:
  Bedlam
  counselling
  human behaviour
  mental hygiene
  sibling rivalry
  stress

Biographies

See Sections 10/35 and 10/36 of Part Ten

INDEX: See entries under all of the terms above

Introduction to Part Five:
Man the Social Animal
by Harold D. Lasswell

We are part of society when we share in comprehensive arrangements for living with one another and for managing the environment. The simplest societies are the primitive bands who to this day live in jungles and deserts, and on isolated mountains and beaches around the globe. The most complex technological societies bind the world's cities together as part of an evolution that, barring catastrophe, is forming a planetary society of mankind.

Whether primitive or civilized, all societies must cope with the parallel problems that are generated by the urgencies of human nature and the necessities of a common life. Arrangements are made for kinship and procreation; for safety, health, and comfort; for producing and consuming commodities and services. Arrangements also develop latent talent into skills of communication, body movement, and environmental management. Institutions specialize in the gathering and dissemination of news and images of the natural and social environment. Some institutions give respect or disrespect to individuals and groups on a temporary or permanent basis, and distinguish between what is considered to be responsible or irresponsible conduct. Government, law, and politics seek to resolve the conflicting demands that arise within or among communities.

At first glance we are less likely to be impressed by the parallels than by the differences among societies. The differences are conspicuous, if we consider, say, a horde of big-city commuters as compared with a band of technologically handicapped people who are continually in search of the next meal. An anthropologist who lived with such a band a few years ago in the rain forests of eastern Bolivia reported that apart from the hammocks they slept in, three-foot digging sticks, and cumbersome long bows and arrows, these naked seminomads carried no material objects with them. Modern urban dwellers usually feel some contempt for these bearers of an Old Stone Age culture and speculate on a possible weakness of the brain to account for their lack of technological progress. Such speculations are dismissed by modern anthropologists as without foundation. As we get acquainted with primitive societies it dawns upon us that they have met some of the same problems that we have by adopting solutions whose ingenuity equals or even excels our own. This may apply, for instance, to arrangements for transmitting political authority from one generation to the next, or for preventing violently aggressive behaviour.

Societies do indeed differ from one another in the degree that they encourage specialization. In the simplest societies everybody does everything, with exceptions that are closely linked to differences of sex and age. On the other hand, many tribes use professional specialists, such as warriors, medicine men, blacksmiths, potters, weavers, musicians, and carvers. The world that we call civilized appeared with the invention of writing. Literacy provides a means of storing and retrieving information without relying exclusively on the memory of the old. Records and education multiply the number of learned professions. Urban civilization marks the emergence of such institutions as the territorial state, formal legislative codes of law, regular taxes, bureaucratized civil and military services, monumental public works, complex systems of taxation, and official records.

One way to bring out the degrees of likeness and difference among societies, whether primitive or civilized, is to compare the priorities that are given to institutions of the same kind. No one doubts that every society must concern itself to some extent with food. It is only in bands of the kind mentioned above that near-total preoccupation with hunger deemphasizes, although without abolishing, all other interests. Where existence is less hard the accumulation of wealth may become the principal value sought, as among some merchant cities and trading tribes. War and preparation for war may take top priority as it did for millennia among the shepherds of Inner Asia and the river-valley agriculturalists who were conquered by herdsmen-warriors. Some agricultural societies emphasize worship and encourage forms of knowledge, like astronomy, that enhance religion. In some societies, notably in East India, the accent is on ritual purity or impurity, and every kin group is assigned a position in the respect system of caste and class.

While priorities may remain stable for generations in a given society, this is not necessarily the case. At one time the peoples of Scandinavia were warriors and brigands. Today we perceive them as among those who are most involved with the values of civil society. In the United States, the early colonizers of New England were heavily oriented toward religion, morality, and political freedom. More recently, the most general trend has been toward secular activities, especially those connected with wealth. Throughout the contemporary world, "development" often carries the connotations of economic modernization, political independence, scientific education and research, personal freedom, and social justice.

Besides allocating priorities, every society strikes a temporary or durable balance between the accumulation and the immediate enjoyment of every value. The modes of accumulation depend on the value in question. Investment in wealth production, for instance, may involve adding fertilizers to the soil, or building an infrastructure of roads and bridges, or inculcating the values of saving and investment. Expanded educational opportunity implies that more per capita hours of teaching and learning, and more physical equipment, are made available, and that the importance of education is successfully communicated. If health opportunities are to be multiplied, it is necessary to add facilities and to spread the practice of personal hygiene. A society cultivates public enlightenment with installations for scientific and scholarly purposes, and for mass communication. Human relations improve as the roles of love, friendship, and loyalty expand in "an era of good feeling," and as social discrimination wanes. Levels of responsible conduct typically rise as opportunities become more available for worship and more people join in formulating and applying moral standards. During a given period the institutions of government, law, and politics sometimes accumulate more support.

The examples mentioned above refer to the "positive" accumulation of a valued outcome. Accumulations may be "negative," as when disasters destroy property, spread epidemics, or interfere with education.

All societies necessarily make arrangements for the sharing of wealth, power, and other values. Among individuals and groups these arrangements exhibit all degrees of equality and inequality. Wealth and income are sometimes widely distributed. By contrast, they may be monopolized in the hands of a few. Political participation may be dispersed or concentrated. Opportunities may be equalized or monopolized for health, education, and information; or for respect, affection, and responsible conduct.

Characteristic of every society is the attempt to maintain itself by controlling the minds of young and old. People not only hunt or plow, trade or fight. They are also likely to believe in what they do and how they do it. It is not necessarily true that in a system of inequality those who occupy any particular station, however exalted or lowly, entertain any doubts about the justification of the system. A stable society carries on within the framework of a common map of perception, belief, and identity. In such a setting the individual learns from earliest infancy to think, feel, and act in ways that bring positive rather than negative consequences from the social and natural environment. Socialization is the process by which private motivations are channeled into acceptable public acts.

In civilized societies reliance on the results of early education is heavily supplemented by government, law, and politics. The legal system is made up of several sets of authoritative and controlling prescriptions. One set is constitutive. It prescribes "who decides what and how." It centralizes or decentralizes formal and effective power, and it separates power among agencies and groups. Structures may be differentiated to plan, to promote, to legislate, to execute, or to review and appraise. Regulation defines the degree of protection given to the fundamental institutions of every sector of society. Tradition alleges that a legal order is blind to values and practices that lie outside the established beliefs, faiths, and loyalties ("ideologies") of the society with which it is involved. In consequence, legal systems may defend widely different balances between value accumulation and enjoyment, and sharply contrasting patterns of equality and inequality in the sharing of political power, wealth, respect, or any other value. The legal order may protect economic systems whose structures are capitalistic, socialistic, or cooperative; family systems that permit one or more members of the sexes to marry and raise children; religious faiths that exalt monotheism and polytheism; and so on through the infinite variety of human practices.

One set of prescriptive norms is supervisory. Individuals and groups may be given wide latitude to make private

contractual agreements or to seek redress of private wrongs. Nonetheless, the decision makers of the community are prepared to play a supervisory role by enforcing common norms if an unsettled private controversy is brought to their notice by the parties. Prescriptions also lay down the principles and procedures to be followed if the body politic organizes and administers a continuing enterprise, of which services of transportation, communication, banking, insurance, and housing are examples. A legal system includes correctional or sanctioning measures to obtain compliance with prescribed norms. Value deprivations are imposed on those who have failed or are expected to fail to comply. Deprivations range in severity from capital punishment, confiscation of property, or life imprisonment, to a light fine or reprimand.

A legal system is stabilized when the effective elements in society perceive themselves as relatively better off by continuing the system than by adopting alternative arrangements. To some extent a legal order may exhibit cyclical fluctuations, as when deviations are tolerated within limits which, if exceeded, generate reform activities that restore the former situation with little change. In a capitalist economy "creeping monopoly" may invade trade unions, employers' associations, or natural resource and industrial enterprises. In a socialist economy "black markets" may introduce "creeping competition." In either case, cyclical movements may restore the original relationship before they have quietly stabilized a structural innovation, or prepared the way for violent revolutionary change.

If the view is correct that worldwide interdependence is increasing, the traditional blindfold of legal systems must be put aside long enough to give explicit consideration to competing value goals and practices around the globe. Interdependence implies that whether they like it or not, the members of an emerging planetary society must take one another into account. Being taken into account implies that beliefs, faiths, and loyalties, as well as overt behaviours, are examined by public and private decision makers. The demand to be better informed about the social environment creates an enormous opportunity and responsibility for those who study society.

We expect anthropologists to provide us with knowledge of primitive societies and other specialists to focus on the processes and institutions of civilized society. Political scientists and legal scholars concentrate on government, law, and politics. Economists specialize in the production and distribution of wealth. The role of educators is relatively clear. So, too, is the role of sociologists who concern themselves with a sector of society, such as the family, social class and caste, professions and occupations, communication, public health, or comparative morals and religion.

Social scientists are continually under pressure to provide a map of the past and probable future impact of the forces that shape society. They are asked, for instance, to explain the causes of war and other forms of violence, and to suggest strategies that lead to "victory" in a specific conflict or to show how war itself may be eliminated as an instrument of public policy. Social scientists are asked for explanations of why an economy experiences inflation, or how it generates changing levels of employment and unemployment. Specialists are expected to discover the sources of alienation that separate young and old or threaten the unity of a family, a school, a church, a political party, or a national state. These examples suggest the wide-ranging demands that confirm the importance of adding to our knowledge of society.

We recognize the existence of a problem when we perceive that our goals are inconsistent with one another or when there are discrepancies between what we want and what we have or expect. In public policymaking, the first step is to answer the question, "Whose values are to be realized?" The social scientist who participates in tackling or solving a policy problem has an option: he may adopt the criteria of a "client" or he may rely on his own values.

The study of social institutions is sometimes affected by diverging norms of professional responsibility. No conflict need arise if a social scientist is personally committed to a line of research that happens to be popular with influential members of the body politic. No anxiety or guilt is felt if the findings are applied by current decision makers. A frequent example is the study of administrative agencies according to their "dollar efficiency" or according to the accuracy and speed of communication between central offices and field stations.

In contrast to this harmonious relationship is the inner and perhaps visible turmoil of social scientists whose research interests are unacceptable to many members of the current establishment. The researchers may want to study the effect of military expenditures on society. The problem may be to find how a given level of military outlay modifies the structure of the civilian economy and influences both the production and delivery of services specialized for health, education, public information, family welfare, and other social outcomes. If the information gathered in the course of a given project is classified as secret, no scientist can lawfully report his findings. Perhaps the investigator will violate the letter of the law in the hope of mobilizing an effective demand for change. But it may be that such a strategy will backfire. Instead of arousing community protest against authority, the revelations may result in established leaders successfully taking advantage of an alleged "breach of security" to suppress inquiry and discussion.

Another complication affecting the social investigator is the degree of genuine consent that he must obtain from those whom he proposes to study. Physicians, surgeons, and biologists confront similar questions when they plan to give a test, run an experiment, administer a drug, or perform an operation. Is it always necessary to explain to a prospective subject the risks he will run? Is the investigator professionally or legally bound to make sure that the language of explanation can be understood by the individual concerned? If a social scientist plans to study the facts of life in a prison or a mental hospital, should he reveal his purpose, even when it would be easier to gain confidence by posing as a fellow prisoner or a fellow patient? Similar issues rise in connection with field studies of primitive tribes, of peasant communities, of foreign societies, and of many other social settings.

In recent times, professional opinion has emphasized the importance of obtaining "shared participation" in the pursuit of knowledge. Many investigators willingly accept the challenge of cultivating group demand for a project and for a hand in data gathering and analysis. At every stage, arrangements are made for laymen to work side by side with professional sociologists, social psychologists, political scientists, and other investigators. As a result, some communities have learned to study themselves, assessing the degree to which they are involved in ethnic and other forms of discrimination. Unusual groups have joined in self-study. For instance, murderers and persons who have survived as targets of murderous assault have cooperated in scientific research on the causes and consequences of murder, and on possible strategies of prevention. Instead of resenting the role of "guinea pig" in science, it is typical for those who choose to participate in programs of self-observation to improve their individual insight while contributing to the enhancement of society's stock of knowledge.

Whether the client or the investigator is the source of the value criteria adopted for a policy problem, questions of value priority are bound to arise. The relative importance of political, economic, and other aims cannot be satisfactorily settled in programs of national or regional development unless the full range of possible goals is considered. It is essential to take timing into account. When a new nation-state first secedes from an empire, political power has top priority. The "ex-colony" tries to ensure its independence of external control, to obtain support from outside powers, and to unify its people. Economic development occupies a high priority position. Other targets, such as health, education, the expressive arts, and environmental protection, seem to be less urgent. The allocation of manpower and facilities to various institutions depends on the priority of the specific outcomes in which these institutions specialize.

Social scientists have an indirect influence on priorities by asking questions about them, and also by presenting a factual map of past trends, causes, and future contingencies. Scientists often devise small-scale pretests in order to try out solutions that may eventually be applied on a larger scale.

In adapting to the needs of this interdependent world, the scientists of society require of themselves that they measure the direction and intensity of the value demands of political, economic, ethnic, and all other identifiable groups anywhere on the globe. Acknowledging the perils of a divided and militant world, the most compelling task is to discern and make public the conditions under which a world public order of government and law could become a more perfect instrument of human dignity, security, and welfare. Many small-scale programs show how to reduce the human cost of transforming today's inadequate institutions into more effective systems of communication and organization.

For the first time in history it can be truly asserted that the scientists of society have been provided with technological instruments of sufficient sophistication to assist in meeting the demands that are made upon them. Retrieval and dissemination make it possible to map past, present, and future events. Social analysts know that the key question for the future is to resolve whether or not the spectacularly changing technology of knowledge, and especially knowledge of society, will be in the hands of a limited class or caste that seeks to serve its own advantage. The alternative is to share the control of information widely among all territorial and pluralistic groups. Unless individuals and groups are able to obtain access to comprehensive stocks of information, they will be blind judges of public policy. Without adequate access, their criticism will be dismissed as exercises in ignorance and bias. Critics will be in no position to develop realistic alternatives to the plans of governmental or private monopolists of knowledge. "Knowledge is power"; if there is to be self-control, there must be prompt and total access to information.

The chief novelty about the computer and other technically advanced means of processing and transmitting information is that, in principle, everyone can be given prompt access to a selective "map of the whole." An image of the total deployment of man in space or of the total activities of a corporate enterprise can be made available to everyone from the highest official to the humblest worker. The salient facts can be made vivid, concise, and substantially accurate in images that may be supplemented in whatever detail is desired. The range of possible expenditures for any political, economic, or social program can be summarized and related to its potential impact on society.

Human society has attained an unparalleled height of danger and opportunity. The study of society shares in both. The unprecedented accumulation of knowledge enables us to recognize that the scale of our problems is also without precedent.

Part Five. Human Society

All studies of mankind take account of the effect of the social nature of humans. This is true of the treatment in Part Four of human evolution, health, and general nature and behaviour. It is also true of the treatments, in subsequent parts, of art, technology, religion, history, and the sciences and philosophy.

A special set of interrelated sciences, however, takes society and social behaviour as its direct subject of inquiry. The outlines in the six divisions and the twenty-five sections of Part Five are concerned with the complementary work of these social sciences.

The social sciences have themselves been the object of historical and analytical study. These studies are presented in the articles referred to in Section 10/36 of Part Ten. The outline in that section covers the history of the social sciences generally, and the nature, scope, methods, and interrelations of anthropology, sociology, economics, and political science.

The social sciences have become increasingly interdependent and interpenetrating, and no regulative agreement exists about how their distinction should be understood. Nevertheless, the diverse domains are, in practice, distinguishable. The breakdown of Part Five into six divisions reflects the currently operative distinction between cultural and social anthropology, the several branches of sociology, economics, political science, jurisprudence and law, and educational philosophy and science.

Division I. Social Groups: Peoples and Cultures

The outlines in the four sections of Division I set forth anthropological accounts of the development and the variety of sociocultural forms.

Section 511. Peoples and Cultures of the World

A. In the Arctic

    1. In the eastern Arctic

    2. In the western Arctic

B. In North America

    1. In the sub-Arctic

    2. On the Northwest Coast

    3. In California

    4. On the Plateau

    5. In the Great Basin

    6. In the Southwest

    7. On the Plains

    8. In the eastern woodlands

    9. In the Southeast

C. In Middle America

   1. In northern Mexico

   2. In Meso-America

   3. In Central America and the northern Andes

   4. In the Caribbean

D. In South America

   1. In the central and southern Andes

   2. In the tropical forest

   3. Among the South American nomads

E. In Europe

   1. On the Atlantic fringe

   2. On the plain

   3. Along the Mediterranean

   4. On the Alpine climax

F. In the Middle East and North Africa

   1. In the Maghrib: northwestern Africa

   2. In the Mashriq: northeastern Africa and southwest Asia

   3. In Iran

   4. In Turkey

G. In Asia

   1. In Siberia

   2. In Central Asia

   3. In East Asia

   4. In South Asia

   5. In Southeast Asia

H. In sub-Saharan Africa

   1. In the western Sudan

   2. In the eastern Sudan

   3. On the Guinea coast

   4. In the Congo

   5. In central and lower East Africa

   6. In the East African Horn

   7. Among the Khoisan peoples: Hottentots and Bushmen

I. In Oceania

   1. In Australia

   2. In Melanesia

   3. In Polynesia

   4. In Micronesia

Suggested reading in the *Encyclopædia Britannica*:

MACROPAEDIA: Major articles dealing with the peoples and cultures of the world

Africa
American Indians
Arctic, The
Asia
Australia
Central Africa
Culture, The Concept and Components of
Eastern Africa
Europe
Iran

North Africa
Pacific Islands
Sudan
Turkey and Ancient Anatolia
Union of Soviet Socialist Republics
West Indies
Western Africa

MICROPAEDIA: Selected entries of reference information

General subjects

Africa—Congo:
Ambo
Azande
Bemba
Bulu
Chokwe
Duala
Fang
Ila
Kaonde
Kongo
Kuba
Lozi
Luba
Lunda
Mangbetu
Maravi
Mbundu
Mbuti
Mongo
Ovimbundu
Tabwa
Yaka
Yao
Yaunde
Africa—Ethiopian
and Somalian:
Afar
Amhara
Gurage
Konso
Oromo
Saho
Sidamo
Somali
Tigre
Africa—Guinea
Coast:
Adangme
Akan
Anyi
Ashanti
Baga

Baule
Dan
Edo
Efik
Ekoi
Ewe
Fanti
Fon
Ga
Guro
Ibibio
Idoma
Igbira
Igbo
Ijo
Isoko
Itsekiri
Kissi
Kpelle
Kru
Lamba
Mamprusi
Mbembe
Mende
Nupe
Temne
Tiv
Urhobo
Yako
Yoruba
Africa—Malagasy:
Antaimoro
Antandroy
Bara
Betsileo
Merina
Sakalava
Tanala
Tsimihety
Africa—southern and
lower eastern:
Acholi
Anuak
Bantu peoples

Baster
Bergdama
Chaga
Chewa
Ganda
Gogo
Gusii
Ha
Haya
Hehe
Herero
Hutu
Kamba
Karamojong
Khoikhoin
Kikuyu
Kipsikis
Lango
Lovedu
Luguru
Luhya
Luo
Luvale
Makonde
Manyika
Masai
Mfengu
Mpondo
Nandi
Ndebele
Ngoni
Nguni
Nkole
Nsenga
Nyakyusa
Nyamwezi
Nyika
Nyoro
Pedi
San
Sandawe
Shona
Soga

Sotho
Swazi
Tembu
Tonga
Toro
Tsonga
Tswana
Turkana
Tutsi
Venda
Xhosa
Zaramo
Zulu
Africa—Sudan:
Baga
Bagirmi
Bambara
Bamileke
Bamum
Banda
Baqqārah
Bari
Baya
Bobo
Bongo
Dagomba
Dinka
Dogon
Fali
Fulani
Fur
Grusi
Guang
Gurma
Hausa
Igala
Kabābīsh
Kanuri
Lala
Lotuko
Lugbara
Madi
Malinke
Mande

Quiché
Sumo
Taino
Tairona
Tarasco
Tepehuan
Tojolabal
Totonac
Tzeltal
Tzotzil
Tzutujil
Yaqui
Yucatec Maya
Zapotec
Middle East and
  North Africa:
  Arab
  Armenian
  Bakhtyārī
  Baluchi
  Baqqārah
  Bedouin
  Beja
  Berber
  Cuman
  Druze
  Ḥarāṭīn
  Kabābīsh
  Kabyle
  Kurd
  Lur
  Rif
  Shawia
  Teda
  Tuareg
  Turkmen
North America—
  Californian:
  Cahuilla
  Chumash
  Diegueño
  Juaneño
  Luiseño
  Maidu
  Mission Indians
  Miwok
  Pomo
  Serrano
  Shastan
  Wintun
  Yana
  Yokuts
  Yuki
North America—
  Eastern Woodland:
  Abnaki
  Cayuga
  Conoy
  Delaware
  Erie
  Fox
  Huron
  Illinois

Kickapoo
Mahican
Malecite
Massachuset
Menominee
Miami
Mohawk
Mohegan
Montauk
Nanticoke
Narraganset
Nauset
Neutral
Nipmuc
Ojibwa
Oneida
Ottawa
Pamlico
Passamaquoddy
Pennacook
Penobscot
Pequot
Potawatomi
Powhatan
Sauk
Seneca
Shawnee
Susquehanna
Tionontati
Tuscarora
Wampanoag
Wappinger
Wendat
Wenrohronon
Winnebago
North America—
  Great Basin:
  Bannock
  Mono
  Paiute
  Shoshoni
  Ute
  Washo
North America—
  Northwest
  Coast:
  Bella Coola
  Chinook
  Coast Salish
  Haida
  Hupa
  Kwakiutl
  Nootka
  Tlingit
  Tsimshian
  Wiyot
  Yurok
North America—
  Plains:
  Arapaho
  Arikara
  Assiniboin
  Atsina

Blackfoot
Cheyenne
Comanche
Crow
Hidatsa
Kansa
Kiowa
Mandan
Omaha
Osage
Oto
Ponca
Quapaw
Sarcee
Sioux
Tonkawa
Wichita
North America—
  Plateau:
  Flathead
  Kutenai
  Modoc and
    Klamath
  Nez Percé
  Sahaptin
  Salish
  Yakima
North America—
  Southeast:
  Apalachee
  Caddo
  Calusa
  Catawba
  Cherokee
  Chickasaw
  Chitimacha
  Choctaw
  Creek
  Natchez
  Seminole
  Timucua
North America—
  Southwest:
  Apache
  Chiricahua
  Hopi
  Jicarilla Apache
  Karankawa
  Mescalero
  Mojave
  Navajo
  Papago
  Pima
  Pueblo Indians
  Yuman
  Zuni
North America—
  Sub-Arctic:
  Algonquin
  Beaver
  Beothuk
  Carrier
  Chipewyan

Cree
Dogrib
Ingalik
Kutchin
Micmac
Montagnais and
  Naskapi
Sekani
Slave
Tahltan
Tanaina
Tanana
Yellowknife
Oceania:
  Aranda
  Australian
    aborigine
  Chamorro
  Hawaiian
  Kariera
  Maori
  Trobriander
South America—
  central and southern
  Andean:
  Andean
    civilization
  Araucanian
  Atacama
  Aymara
  Chavín
  Chimú
  Diaguita
  Huarpe
  Inca
  Mapuche
  Quechua
South America—
  nomadic:
  Abipón
  Charrúa
  Chono
  Guató
  Makú
  Mataco
  Mbayá
  Ona
  Puelche
  Purí and Coroado
  Querandí
  Sirionó
  Tehuelche
  Warrau
  Yámana
  Yaruro
South America—
  tropical forest:
  Apapocuva
  Bororo
  Botocudo
  Canelo
  Carajá
  Chiriguano

Ge	Maxakali	Sherente	Tupinambá
Guaraní	Mundurukú	Shipibo	Witoto
Jívaro	Mura	Tucuna	Yanomamö
Kawaíb	Shavante	Tupian	

Biographies

See Section 10/36 of Part Ten

INDEX: See entries under all of the terms above

Section 512. **The Development of Human Culture**

A. Diverse theories of culture: conceptions involved in the analysis of culture

1. Definitions of culture

2. Culture and personality

3. Cultural comparisons: ethnocentrism, cultural relativism

4. Cultural adaptation and change

5. Cultural patterns

6. Cultural institutions
[see 513]

B. Types of cultures

1. Cultures of primitive and nonurban societies

a. Cultures of nomadic and settled hunters and gatherers

b. Horticultural societies: societies in which primitive agriculture is supplemental to hunting and gathering

c. Cultures of pastoralists and herdsmen: distribution and characteristics

d. Cultures of peasants and settled agriculturists

2. Cultures of civilized societies: theories of their origin and evolution

3. The development of modern industrial civilization: mass society

C. Processes of cultural change
[see Division II, below]

Suggested reading in the *Encyclopædia Britannica:*

MACROPAEDIA: Major articles dealing with the development of human culture

Culture, The Concept and Components of
Modernization and Industrialization
Social Differentiation

Social Sciences, The
Social Structure and Change

MICROPAEDIA: Selected entries of reference information

General subjects

acculturation	culture area	Kulturkreis	region
age–area hypothesis	environmentalism	Mesolithic Period	social Darwinism
	folk society	modernization	survival
cultural evolution	Gemeinschaft and Gesellschaft	Neolithic Period	transhumance
culture		nomadism	urban revolution
culture-and-personality studies	hydraulic civilization	Paleolithic Period	
	industrialization	peasant	
		primitive culture	

Biographies

See Section 10/36 of Part Ten

INDEX: See entries under all of the terms above

Section 513. **Major Cultural Components and Institutions of Human Societies**

    A. Systems of relationship based upon marriage and descent: kinship

        1. General aspects of kinship

        2. Laws and customs regarding mate selection, sexual behaviour, marriage and divorce, legitimacy
        [see also 553.B.]

        3. Rules of residence; *e.g.,* virilocal, uxorilocal, neolocal

        4. Descent systems: unilineal, cognatic, and variant forms

        5. Control of resources, inheritance, and succession: the family as a centre for transmission of economic, religious, political, and other powers and goods

        6. Kinship and social change: kinship as an evolving social institution

    B. Other social structures

        1. The varieties of groups and other associations within societies

        2. Organization by status: class systems, caste systems, systems characterized by slavery or serfdom

    C. Types of economic systems

        1. The economic systems of primitive or nonurban peoples

            a. Production, division of labour, role differentiation

            b. Exchange of goods, distribution of wealth

            c. Property and property rights

        2. The economic systems of developed nations
        [see Division III, below]

    D. Other elements common to all cultures but differing in expression or practice between cultures

        1. Education and socialization: formal and informal enculturation

        2. Religious belief, folklore
        [for religious belief, see 811]

        3. Legal systems
        [see 551.B.]

        4. Artistic expression: literature, visual arts, performing arts; crafts
        [see 611, 612, and 613]

        5. Linguistic systems
        [see 514, below]

        6. Recreation, sports and games

Suggested reading in the *Encyclopædia Britannica:*

MACROPAEDIA: Major articles dealing with major cultural components and institutions of human societies

    Culture, The Concept and Components of
    Family and Kinship
    Inheritance and Succession
    Social Differentiation
    Social Sciences, The
    Sports, Major Team and Individual

MICROPAEDIA: Selected entries of reference information

General subjects

kinship:	clan	joint family	nuclear family
avoidance	cross-cousin	kin	patriarchy
relationship	descent	kinship	phratry
avunculate	extended family	kinship terminology	tribe
band	family	lineage	
blood brotherhood	gens	matriarchy	

marital and sexual	exchange marriage	*primitive economic*	number game
relationships:	exogamy and	*systems:*	serfdom
betrothal	endogamy	barter	slavery
bridewealth	group marriage	gift exchange	social class
circumcision	henogamy	kula	social group
clitoridectomy	incest	potlatch	social status
concubinage	levirate	silent trade	*Sporting Record*
couvade	residence	*other:*	sports and games
divorce	seigneur, droit du	card game	See also Sections
dowry	sororate	caste	522 and 523
dual organization	tree marriage	children's game	

Biographies

See Section 10/36 of Part Ten

INDEX: See entries under all of the terms above

Section 514.   Language and Communication

A. Communication as a foundation of human culture and as the essential element in social and cultural interaction, the role of communication in the modification of human behaviour

B. Nonverbal communication

   1. Communication by means of bodily gestures and posture, by facial expression

   2. Laughter and nonword sounds as communication

   3. The use of signals, signs, symbols, icons, and cultural artifacts

   4. Cybernetic communication: computer languages, human language–computer interfaces, and artificial intelligence and expert systems

   5. Parapsychological forms of communication: telepathy
   [see 432.H.]

C. The nature of language

   1. Definitions of language

   2. Ways of studying language: phonetics, grammar, semantics

   3. Language variants: dialects, slang, and specialized variants (*e.g.,* jargon, pidgins, creoles)

   4. Speech: the psychological and physiological bases

   5. Meaning and style in language: structural and lexical meanings; semantic flexibility; language and conceptualization; style

   6. Language and culture: transmission of language; language and social differentiation; control of language for cultural ends; language learning and literacy; written language and spoken language

   7. Linguistic change and language typology

   8. Cryptology: codes, ciphers, and other means of encrypting language

D. The structure of speech and language

   1. The phonetics of speech (articulatory, acoustic, linguistic); phonetic transcription; experimental phonetics

   2. The physiology of speech: regulators (respiratory and brain functions); the larynx; voice production (including synthetic voice production)

   3. Speech disorders

E. Written language: systems of notation

   1. The nature, origin, and evolution of writing: from pictures to the alphabet

    2. Types of writing systems: logographic, syllabic, consonantal, alphabetic, featural

    3. Systems of writing: hieroglyphic, cuneiform, alphabetic, ideographic

    4. Adjuncts to writing: punctuation, shorthand

    5. Calligraphy and the art of handwriting: early Semitic, Arabic, Greek, Latin, Indic, East Asian

F. Linguistics: the scientific study of language and language development
[see also 10/36 H.]

    1. The development of linguistic theory

    2. Synchronic linguistics: structural, transformational-generative grammar, tagmemics, stratificational grammar, the Prague school

    3. Diachronic linguistics: linguistic change, comparative method, language classification

    4. Dialectology and the study of linguistic geography

    5. Semantics: the study of language and meaning

    6. The study of writing

G. Language and society

    1. Attitudes toward language: taboos in language use, myths about the origin of language, the relation of language and thought

    2. The connection of language with history, the role of language in the transmission of culture

    3. The role of language in cross-cultural relations

    4. The use of language as a political instrument

    5. The role of language in unifying social and occupational groups

H. Languages of the world

    1. The classification of language

    2. Languages spoken in Europe and areas of European colonization

        a. Indo-European languages

            i. Indo-Iranian languages
[see H.3.a.i., below]

            ii. Celtic languages

            iii. Italic languages
[see H.6.c., below]

            iv. Romance languages

            v. Greek language

            vi. Baltic languages

            vii. Slavic languages

            viii. Germanic languages

            ix. English language

            x. Albanian language

            xi. Armenian language

            xii. Tocharian language
[see H.6.e., below]

        b. Non-Indo-European languages

            i. Uralic languages

            ii. Basque language

    3. Languages of Asia and Oceania

        a. Languages of Asia

            i. Indo-Iranian languages

      ii. Dravidian languages

     iii. Austro-Asiatic languages

     iv. Sino-Tibetan languages

      v. Tai languages

     vi. Japanese language

    vii. Korean language

   viii. Altaic languages

     ix. Uralic languages
         [see H.2.b.i., above]

      x. Paleosiberian languages

     xi. Caucasian languages

  b. Languages of Oceania

      i. Austronesian languages

     ii. Australian Aboriginal languages

    iii. Papuan languages

4. Languages of Africa and the Middle East

  a. African languages

      i. Niger-Congo languages

     ii. Chari-Nile and Nilo-Saharan languages

    iii. Khoisan languages

  b. Hamito-Semitic languages

      i. Semitic languages

     ii. Egyptian language

    iii. Berber languages

    iv. Cushitic languages

     v. Chadic languages

5. Indian languages of the Americas

  a. Eskimo-Aleut languages

  b. North American Indian languages

  c. Mexican and Central American Indian languages

  d. South American and Caribbean Indian languages

6. Extinct languages of the world

  a. Anatolian languages

  b. Etruscan language

  c. Italic (non-Romance) languages

  d. Sumerian language

  e. Tocharian language

  f. Sources of other ancient languages: ancient epigraphic remains

7. Constructed languages

  a. Special international or universal languages, including Esperanto and Interlingua; Basic English

  b. Machine languages: *e.g.,* Fortran, Algol
    [see 735.D.3.]

Suggested reading in the *Encyclopædia Britannica*:

MACROPAEDIA: Major articles dealing with language and communication

Communication	Linguistics
Cryptology	Names
Humour and Wit	Speech
Language	Writing
Languages of the World	

MICROPAEDIA: Selected entries of reference information

General subjects

alphabets and other writing systems:
alphabet
Arabic alphabet
Aramaic alphabet
Armenian alphabet
Brāhmī
Braille
Canaanite inscriptions
Chinese writing system
cuneiform writing
Cypriot syllabary
Cyrillic alphabet
demotic script
Devanāgarī
Eggjum Stone
Ethiopic alphabet
Etruscan alphabet
Glagolitic alphabet
Gothic alphabet
Grantha alphabet
Greek alphabet
Gregg shorthand
Gupta script
Gurmukhi alphabet
Hankul
Hebrew alphabet
hieroglyph
Hittite hieroglyphic writing
Iguvine Tables
Indic writing systems
kana
Kensington Stone
Kharoṣṭī
Kök Turki alphabet
Latin alphabet
Linear B

Mayan hieroglyphic writing
Myazedi inscription
Nabataean alphabet
North Semitic alphabet
ogham writing
Pahlavi alphabet
Palmyrenian alphabet
Phoenician alphabet
pictography
Pitman shorthand
Rosetta Stone
runic alphabet
Sarada script
shorthand
Sinaitic inscriptions
South Semitic alphabet
Speedwriting
stenotypy
syllabary
Syriac alphabet
Ugaritic alphabet
writing

grammar, syntax, and vocabulary:
abbreviation
agglutination
auxiliary
gender
grammar
honorific
mood
morpheme
name
patronymic

punctuation
slang
speculative grammar
surname
syntax
tense
voice

languages—African:
African languages
Bantu languages
Central Sudanic languages
Eastern Sudanic languages
Khoikhoin language
Khoisan language
Kwa languages
Meroitic language
Niger-Congo languages
Nilotic languages
Nubian languages
San languages
Swahili language
West Atlantic languages
Xhosa language
Zulu language

languages—Altaic:
Altaic languages
Chuvash language
Kazakh language
Kirgiz language
Mongol language
Mongolian languages
Tatar language
Turkic languages
Turkish language
Turkmen language
Uighur language

Ural-Altaic languages
Uzbek language

languages—Austro-Asiatic:
Austro-Asiatic languages
Khmer language
Mon-Khmer languages
Munda languages
Nicobarese languages
Vietnamese language

languages—Austronesian:
Austronesian languages
Cebuano
Javanese language
Malay language
Melanesian languages
Micronesian languages
Oceanic languages
Polynesian languages
Tagalog language

languages—Caucasian:
Avar-Ando-Dido languages
Caucasian languages
Georgian language
Kartvelian languages
Laz language
Mingrelian language
Nakh languages

languages—
  Dravidian:
  Dravidian
    languages
  Kannada language
  Malayalam
    language
  Tamil language
  Telugu language
languages—
  Hamito-Semitic:
  Akkadian language
  Amharic language
  Arabic language
  Aramaic language
  Berber languages
  Chadic languages
  Coptic language
  Cushitic languages
  Eblaite language
  Egyptian language
  Ge'ez language
  Hamito-Semitic
    languages
  Hausa language
  Hebrew language
  Phoenician
    language
  Semitic languages
  South Arabic
    language
  Syriac language
languages—Indo-
  European (Baltic):
  Baltic languages
  Latvian language
  Lithuanian
    language
  Old Prussian
    language
languages—
  Indo-European
  (Celtic):
  Breton language
  Brythonic
    languages
  Celtic languages
  Cornish language
  Goidelic languages
  Irish language
  Pictish language
  Scottish Gaelic
    language
  Welsh language
languages—
  Indo-European
  (Germanic):
  Afrikaans language
  Danish language

English language
Faeroese language
Frisian language
German language
Germanic
  languages
Gothic language
Icelandic language
Luxemburgian
  language
Middle English
  language
Netherlandic
  language
Norwegian
  language
Old English
  language
Old Norse
  language
Old Saxon
  language
Scandinavian
  languages
Swedish language
Swiss German
  language
Yiddish
languages—
  Indo-European
  (Greek):
  Demotic Greek
    language
  Greek language
  Katharevusa Greek
    language
  Koine
languages—
  Indo-European
  (Indo-Iranian):
  Apabhraṃsa
    language
  Assamese language
  Avestan language
  Balochi language
  Bengali language
  Bihari languages
  Burushaski
    language
  Dardic languages
  Dari language
  Gujarati language
  Hindi language
  Hindustani
    language
  Indian languages
  Indo-Aryan
    languages
  Indo-Iranian
    languages

Iranian languages
Kashmiri language
Marathi language
Oriya language
Ossetic language
Pahari languages
Pahlavi language
Pāli language
Parthian language
Pashto language
Persian language
Prākrit languages
Punjabi language
Romany language
Sanskrit language
Sindhi language
Sinhalese language
Urdu language
languages—
  Indo-European
  (Romance and
  Italic):
  Catalan language
  Franco-Provençal
    dialect
  French language
  Italian language
  Italic language
  Ladino language
  Latin language
  Mozarabic
    language
  Occitan language
  Oscan language
  Osco-Umbrian
    language
  Portuguese
    language
  Rhaetian dialects
  Romance
    languages
  Romanian
    language
  Sabellic dialects
  Sardinian language
  Spanish language
  Umbrian language
  Vulgar Latin
languages—
  Indo-European
  (Slavic):
  Belorussian
    language
  Bulgarian language
  Czech language
  Lekhitic languages
  Macedonian
    language

Old Church
  Slavonic language
Polish language
Russian language
Serbo-Croatian
  language
Slavic languages
Slovak language
Slovene language
Sorbian languages
Ukrainian
  language
languages—
  Indo-European
  (other):
  Albanian language
  Anatolian
    languages
  Armenian
    language
  Hittite language
  Indo-European
    languages
  Indo-Hittite
    languages
  Luwian language
  Lydian language
  Raetian language
  Tocharian
    language
languages—
  international and
  artificial:
  Basic English
  Esperanto
  Ido
  Interlingua
  Novial
  Volapük
languages—
  Meso-American
  Indian:
  American Indian
    languages
  Cakchiquel
    language
  Maya languages
  Mixe-Zoque
    languages
  Nahua language
  Oto-Manguean
    languages
  Quiché language
  Uto-Aztecan
    languages
  Yucatec language

INDEX: See entries under all of the terms above

Division II. **Social Organization and Social Change**
[For Part Five headnote see page 173.]

The outlines in the four sections of Division II present general sociological theories of social order and social change, and sociological studies of basic social institutions, social processes, and social problems.

Section 521. **Social Structure and Change**

A. The structure of society: diverse theories of social structure and organization, various types of social structure

B. The social effects of bureaucratic and industrial specialization

   1. The social effects of industrialization and modernization

   2. The social effects of organizational specialization: bureaucracy

   3. The social effects of industrial specialization and automation
    [see also 712.C.]

C. Social control

   1. The process of socialization: the transmission of patterns of normative behaviour by family, peer groups, and education

   2. Theories of alienation: definitions, causes, manifestations, and proposed solutions

   3. The regulation of behaviour that departs from social norms

      a. By punishment, rehabilitation, and reform of criminals

      b. By psychological therapy

      c. By persuasion

D. Factors operative in social change

   1. The role of ideology in social change

   2. Contact with other cultures as a factor in social change

   3. The influence of environment as a factor in social change

   4. The role of demographic factors in social change

   5. The role of art in social change: art as an ideological instrument

   6. Religion as a factor for and against social change

   7. The role of intellectual factors in social change

   8. The relationship of economic factors to social stability

   9. Technological factors in social change

   10. The role of collective behaviour in social change

   11. The role of public opinion in social behaviour

E. Social movements and social change

   1. Characteristics of social movements

   2. Selected types of social movements

      a. Movements centred on religious concepts or personalities

      b. Humanitarian and reform movements

      c. Interest group movements

      d. Revolutionary movements

      e. Nationalist movements
        [see also 541.C.3.b.vii.]

Suggested reading in the *Encyclopædia Britannica:*

MACROPAEDIA: Major articles dealing with social structure and change

> Collective Behaviour
> Crime and Punishment
> Modernization and Industrialization
> Propaganda
> Public Opinion
> Social Sciences, The
> Social Structure and Change
> Work and Employment

MICROPAEDIA: Selected entries of reference information

General subjects

punishment and	Irish system	torture	*social norms*
rehabilitation:	mark system	workhouse	*and associated*
amnesty	ostracism	*social change:*	*phenomena:*
Auburn system	panopticon	civil disobedience	assimilation
Baumes Laws	parole	sanction	collective
Borstal system	penal colony	satyāgraha	behaviour
commutation	Pennsylvania	sit-in	folkway
deportation	system	social change	norm
Elmira system	prison	social Darwinism	public opinion
exile and	probation	social movement	role
banishment	recidivism	temperance	social structure
indeterminate	reformatory	movement	
sentence			

Biographies

> See Section 10/36 of Part Ten

INDEX: See entries under all of the terms above

Section 522.   **The Group Structure of Society**

A. The various types of groups: patterns of group relations

   1. Classifications of groups

   2. The modern family: its organization and functions

   3. Special-interest groups
   [see also 541.B.3.]

   4. Minorities and ethnic groups

B. The social effects of racial and ethnic prejudice

C. Special social concerns

   1. The adolescent

   2. The aged

   3. Women

   4. Cultural minorities
   [see A.4., above]

   5. The poor

   6. Criminals and delinquents

   7. Sexual deviants

   8. Prostitutes

   9. Drug and alcohol users

   10. Suicidal persons

D. Social service: organized public and private activities to alleviate human wants and needs

    1. The background of social and welfare services: modern and historical influences

    2. Fields of service

       a. Family welfare

       b. Child welfare

       c. Youth welfare

       d. Group welfare

       e. Disaster relief

       f. Community development

       g. Medical and psychiatric social services

       h. School social services
          [see also 561.C.4.]

       i. Correctional services: probation, parole, and delinquency control

---

Suggested reading in the *Encyclopædia Britannica*:

MACROPAEDIA: Major articles dealing with the group structure of society

Alcohol and Drug Consumption	Social Differentiation
Crime and Punishment	Social Sciences, The
Family and Kinship	Social Welfare
Sex and Sexuality	

MICROPAEDIA: Selected entries of reference information

General subjects

family and marriage:
adoption
betrothal
bridewealth
divorce
dowry
exchange marriage
exogamy and
  endogamy
family
group marriage
henogamy
joint family
levirate
marriage
nuclear family
parent
polyandry
polygamy

surrogate
  motherhood
interest groups and
  social movements:
  black nationalism
  Civil Rights
    Movement
  ethnic group
  interest group
  lobbying
  minority
  social group
  temperance
    movement
  women's liberation
    movement
social legislation and
  social services:
  affirmative action
  almoner

almshouse
child welfare
philanthropic
  foundation
prohibition
service club
social service
social settlement
social welfare
  program
woman suffrage
social problems:
alcoholism
child abuse
crime
delinquency
drug abuse
habitual offender
incest
old age

organized crime
poverty
prostitution
racial segregation
racism
rape
suicide
white-collar crime
other:
assimilation
charisma
Gemeinschaft and
  Gesellschaft

Biographies
  See Section 10/36 of Part Ten

Section 523.   **Social Status**

A. Social differentiation and stratification

1. The concepts of differentiation and stratification: distinctions and interrelationships

2. Factors producing social, economic, and cultural differences: sex differentiation, age differentiation, racial differentiation, intellectual differentiation, social and cultural factors [see 521.D.]

3. The process of stratification: its relationship to differentiation

   a. Economic differentiation: the basis of stratification

   b. Class, status, and power as forms of stratification

   c. The relation of the individual to society: the effects of differentiation and stratification

B. Varieties of social stratification and social mobility

1. The relation of social class to caste, status, elites, and other concepts

2. Theories of social class: divergent conceptions of the importance of classes in social structures and of the nature of class relationships

3. Types and characteristics of and comparisons among modern social classes: upper class, working class, and middle class; the special case of the peasant class

4. Social mobility

5. The idea of a classless society: approximations to an equality of conditions

6. Social immobility: slavery, serfdom, and forced labour

Suggested reading in the *Encyclopædia Britannica*:

MACROPAEDIA: Major articles dealing with social status

Slavery
Social Differentiation
Social Sciences, The

MICROPAEDIA: Selected entries of reference information

General subjects

labour and servitude:	serfdom	caste	racial segregation
abolitionism	slavery	clan	social class
contract labour	statute labour	ethnic group	social mobility
forced labour	*social differentiation,*	family	social status
freedman	*stratification, and*	ghetto	
labour, division of	*segregation:*	kinship	
migrant labour	age set	minority	
peonage	apartheid		

Biographies

See Section 10/36 of Part Ten

INDEX: See entries under all of the terms above

Section 524.   **Human Populations: Urban and Rural Communities**

A. The composition and change of human populations

    1. Determinants of population

        a. Human fertility and its control

        b. Mortality: death rates and longevity

        c. Migration and refugee movements

    2. Historical changes in population

    3. Theories of population

        a. Premodern beliefs: pronatalism versus birth control

        b. Mercantilist theory

        c. Laissez-faire theory

        d. Malthusian theory

        e. Marxist theory

        f. Modern theories of population; *e.g.,* optimum population size, optimum rate of population growth, relationship between population and demographic movements

        g. Ecological theories concerning the relationship between human population growth and the conservation of natural resources

    4. Governmental policies influencing population growth and composition

    5. The future of the world's population: population projections and problems of the population explosion

B. Development of modern cities

    1. Characteristics of urbanization

    2. History of urbanization

    3. Patterns of urban planning

        a. Methods and materials of urban planning and redevelopment

        b. Social aspects of urban planning and redevelopment

    4. Trends in urbanization

        a. Megalopolis: the coalescence of several metropolitan areas into a contiguous agglomeration of people and activity

        b. Suburbanization: the growth of politically separate but economically dependent residential communities surrounding large cities

        c. Regional integration: levels of economic and cultural interaction between the city and its hinterland

        d. The role of technology in extending the dominance and influence of urban concentrations

        e. Problems of urban growth and population control

        f. Problems of environmental change: pollution, climatic change

C. Development of modern rural societies

Suggested reading in the *Encyclopædia Britannica:*

MACROPAEDIA: Major articles dealing with human populations: urban and rural communities

Birth Control

Cities

Climate and Weather

Modernization and Industrialization

Population

Social Sciences, The

MICROPAEDIA: Selected entries of reference information

General subjects

age distribution	human migration	pollution	urban renewal
birth control	metropolitan area	population	urbanization
census	mortality	refugee	vital rates
city	new town	rural society	zoning
contraception	planned	urban climate	
demography	parenthood	urban planning	

Biographies

See Section 10/36 of Part Ten

INDEX: See entries under all of the terms above

Division III.   **The Production, Distribution, and Utilization of Wealth**
[For Part Five headnote see page 173.]

The outlines in the seven sections of Division III deal with the economic order in human society.

Section 531.   **Economic Concepts, Issues, and Systems**

A. Some basic concepts of economics

1. The concept of economic activity as a process of choosing among scarce resources

2. The concept of division of labour

3. The concepts of diminishing returns and optimization

4. The concept of marginality

5. The concept of capital

6. The concept of competition

7. The concept of comparative advantage

8. The concepts of growth and development

B. Levels of economic analysis

1. Microeconomics: the economic decisions of individuals, households, and firms

2. Sectoral economics: the economic arrangements of industries, groups, and regions

3. Macroeconomics: the economy as a whole

C. The comparison of different economic systems

1. Archetypal economic systems

a. The pure private enterprise economy: a theoretical model

b. The centrally planned economy: the pure socialist model

c. The mixed economy with various degrees of economic planning

2. Western-type market economies

3. Soviet- and socialist-type economic systems

4. Mixed economies in developing countries

5. Other economic systems

a. Primitive economic systems

b. Feudal economic systems

Suggested reading in the *Encyclopædia Britannica:*

MACROPAEDIA: Major articles dealing with economic concepts, issues, and systems

Economic Systems
Economic Theory
Government Finance
International Trade

MICROPAEDIA: Selected entries of reference information

General subjects

economic concepts:	marginal utility	communism	potlatch
capital	microeconomics	economic system	silent trade
diminishing	supply and	socialism	*other:*
returns, law of	demand	*primitive economic*	bourgeoisie
distribution theory	*economic systems:*	*activities:*	Gosplan
labour, division of	capitalism	barter	labour, hours of
laissez-faire	command	gift exchange	mercantilism
macroeconomics	economy	kula	proletariat
margin			

Biographies

See Section 10/36 of Part Ten

INDEX: See entries under all of the terms above

Section 532.   The Consumer and the Market: Pricing and the Mechanisms for Distributing Goods

A. Scarcity, utility, and value: their roles in pricing, their relationship to the consumer

B. The satisfaction of material wants: the behaviour of consumers

1. National consumption levels in the private sector: trends in expenditures for goods and services

2. Factors influencing consumers' tastes and spending

3. The protection of consumer interests

C. Markets as an economic institution in a mixed economy

1. Markets classified by reference to competition and monopoly

a. Purely competitive markets as distinguished from markets of imperfect competition: monopoly, oligopoly, and monopolistic competition

b. Influences affecting the behaviour of sellers under various competitive conditions

c. The concept of workable competition

d. Government regulation of monopolistic practices

2. Major types of markets

a. Markets for primary commodities

b. Markets for manufactured goods

c. Markets for money and capital: the market for short-term loans, the securities market

d. The market for labour and services
[see 533.C.1.]

3. The counterpart of the market under full-scale economic planning: markets under socialism

4. The historical development of markets: the market in economic theory, the relationship of the market to social welfare and politics

5. Markets in international trade
[see 533.F.]

6. The function of the market in the establishment of equilibrium between supply and effective demand

D. The price system in capitalist economies

1. The price system as a means of organizing economic activity: the determination of what is to be produced, how goods are to be produced, and who gets the product

2. Limitations on and failures of the price system: areas in which the price system does not function

   a. Control of prices by business: price-fixing
   [see C.1.a., above]

   b. Government-established price controls and subsidies: regulations concerning public utilities and bank interest rates
   [see 534.B.4.b., and 534.B.6.b.]

   c. Economic relationships not susceptible to control by prices: "externalities," such as air pollution and highway congestion
   [see 737.C.1.]

   d. Imperfect knowledge on the part of buyers as to alternative uses of their buying power
   [see B.2., above]

3. The role of the public sector in the distribution of goods and services: government budgets
   [see 534.B.1.]

Suggested reading in the *Encyclopædia Britannica*:

MACROPAEDIA: Major articles dealing with the consumer and the market: pricing and the mechanisms for distributing goods

Economic Theory
Government Finance
International Trade
Markets
Social Sciences, The

MICROPAEDIA: Selected entries of reference information

General subjects

consumer protection:
antitrust law
Better Business Bureau
consumerism
fair-trade law
consumption:
consumer's surplus
consumption
consumption function
credit card

demand curve
indifference curve
marginal utility
propensity to consume
supply and demand
market organization and pricing:
auction
bazaar
black market

cartel
cobweb cycle
commodity exchange
commodity trade
futures
hedging
marginal-cost pricing
market
marketing board

monopolistic competition
monopoly
price
price discrimination
price maintenance
rebate

Biographies

See Section 10/36 of Part Ten

INDEX: See entries under all of the terms above

Section 533.   **The Organization of Production and Distribution**

A. The organization of the production of goods

1. Analysis of costs and output in the short run: the production function, substitution, the relationship of marginal cost to market price, marginal product

2. Analysis of costs and output in the long run for profit maximization and cost minimization

B. The organization of the distribution of goods

1. The relation between the productive process and the incomes derived from it
   [see also 534.A.2. and A.3.b.]

2. The earnings of land, labour, and capital employed in the productive process

C. The inputs of the productive process

1. Labour as an input in the productive process

   a. The labour force: size, quality, and deployment of work force

   b. Methods of fixing rates of pay

   c. The structure of pay: differences in the earnings of various occupations

   d. Changes in the general level of pay

   e. Employment and unemployment

   f. The inferior economic and social status of temporary, seasonal migrant labourers

   g. The organization of unions

   h. The influence of the union on the supply of labour, wages, and output

   i. Capital elements in labour: education and training

   j. The economic role of managers and entrepreneurs

2. Land and raw materials as inputs
   [see also 724]

3. Energy as an input

4. Capital as an input in the productive process

D. Institutional arrangements that facilitate production and output

1. The nature and characteristics of money

   a. The basic functions of money

   b. The various forms of money

   c. The quantity theory of money: views of classical and neoclassical monetary theorists, views of Keynesian income theorists

2. The monetary functions of commercial banks and central banks

   a. Historical development of banking systems

   b. The structure of modern national banking systems

   c. Principles and functions of commercial banking systems

   d. Principles and functions of central banking systems

   e. The money market: various national and international markets for short-term funds

   f. International monetary institutions: proposals for future monetary cooperation and an international currency unit

   g. The market for long-term funds: savings institutions, the stock and bond market, credit unions, mortgage institutions, farm cooperative banks, insurance institutions, mutual funds, pension funds

   h. The nature and functions of government credit agencies

3. The use of economic statistics in the determination of production and output

   a. National income statistics

      b. Price statistics: the use and construction of indexes of retail and wholesale prices

      c. Economic forecasting

    4. The business corporation

E. Agricultural economics

    1. The relationship between agricultural and economic development

    2. Efforts to control prices and production in agriculture: government price supports, subsidies, and acreage limitations

    3. The behaviour of farm prices and the consequences for the incomes of farmers

    4. The effect of technology on world agriculture: the increase in acreage and in crop yields

    5. The organization of farming: types of farms

F. The geographical distribution of resources and markets: international trade

    1. Classical and contemporary theories of international and interregional trade

    2. National and regional factors influencing trade

      a. Tariffs, embargoes, and quotas imposed to obtain revenue, protect domestic industry, and secure a favourable balance of payments

      b. Changes in the conditions of production: costs, labour, and technology

      c. Price movements

      d. National domestic taxes and subsidies
        [see also 534.B.4.]

    3. International trade arrangements

G. The role of government in production and distribution

    1. The theory of public expenditures: the role of taxation in the budgetary process and problems of effective tax administration

    2. The justification of the government's claim to share in resource use: problems of balancing resource consumption between the public and private sectors

    3. The growth in government spending in the 19th and 20th centuries: the rise in military and social welfare expenditures

    4. Government operation of basic industries

H. Methods of business organization

    1. The keeping of accounts

      a. Accounting as an information system

      b. Various types of company financial statements; *e.g.,* the balance sheet, the income statement

      c. Principles of accounting measurement: asset and cost measurement

      d. Cost accounting: formulation of budgetary plans, performance reports, profit analyses

    2. The management of business funds

      a. Short-term and intermediate-term financial operations: planning and control, the cash budget, accounts receivable, inventories

      b. Long-term financial operations: the design of capital structure and the issuance of securities

      c. Consolidations and mergers

    3. The management of human resources: personnel administration

      a. Personnel departments: their functions and services

      b. Manpower planning, recruitment, and placement

      c. Employee training and development

      d. Methods of maintaining employee incentive and commitment

    4. The administration and control of production

      a. The flow channels of information and materials

      b. The control function: maintaining conformity between operations and the plan

  c. Production scheduling

  d. Inventory adjustment

 5. The distribution of goods

  a. The functions of a marketing department in a large firm

  b. Retailing

  c. Wholesaling

  d. Marketing goods to industry, marketing farm products

  e. The application of market research techniques to merchandising

I. Advertising

J. The distribution of risk

 1. The nature of insurance

 2. Fire and marine insurance

 3. Casualty and surety insurance: liability insurance, theft insurance, aviation insurance, workmen's compensation or industrial injury insurance, credit insurance, title insurance, suretyship

 4. Private life and health insurance

 5. Government-sponsored and/or government-administered health insurance
[see 534.B.4.c.]

 6. Underwriting of risks: rate making

 7. Legal aspects of insurance

K. Consumer credit

 1. Types of consumer credit: installment loans and noninstallment, or single-payment, loans

 2. Historical development of consumer credit in industrialized countries

  a. Lending institutions and the question of interest rates

  b. Costs and hazards of consumer credit

 3. Efforts to protect the consumer: the dimensions of consumer credit

---

Suggested reading in the *Encyclopædia Britannica:*

MACROPAEDIA: Major articles dealing with the organization of production and distribution

Accounting	Economic Growth	International Trade	Social Sciences, The
Banks and	and Planning	Marketing and	Work and
Banking	Economic Theory	Merchandising	Employment
Business	Government	Markets	
Organization	Finance	Money	
Coins and Coinage	Insurance	Public Enterprises	

MICROPAEDIA: Selected entries of reference information

General subjects

agricultural	central bank	Federal Deposit	money order
economics:	commercial bank	Insurance	mutual fund
agricultural	consumer credit	Corporation	national bank
economics	credit	Federal Reserve	over-the-counter
kolkhoz	credit, letter of	System	market
tenant farming	credit card	finance company	promissory note
banking and	credit union	interest	revolving credit
financing:	deposit,	investment	risk
acceptance	certificate of	investment bank	saving
arbitrage	development bank	investment trust	savings and loan
bank	discount rate	liquidity preference	association
bond	dividend	marginal efficiency	savings bank
business finance	exchange, bill of	of investment	security
capital		money market	sinking fund

Biographies

Section 534.   The Distribution of Income and Wealth

A. The distribution of wealth and income by categories of the population

  1. The nature and measurement of wealth and income

  2. Methods of classifying the distribution of wealth and income

    a. Distribution by factor shares: wages, profits, interest, and rent

    b. Distribution according to the number of persons in various classes of wealth and income

  3. Patterns of wealth and income distribution among various countries and among persons within a country

    a. Frequency distributions: the Lorenz diagram, the Gini and Pareto coefficients

    b. Comparisons among wealth and income groups

B. The routes by which government affects the distribution of wealth and income

  1. The national budget as the program of the government's revenues and expenditures

  2. The nature and purposes of taxation

    a. Principles of taxation; *e.g.,* adequacy, adaptability, universality, ability to pay

    b. The effect of taxes on the distribution of income: progressive and regressive taxes

    c. The burden of taxation: the problem of shifting and incidence

    d. Characteristics of national tax systems: comparisons of tax burdens

  3. Kinds of taxes

    a. Taxes on real and personal property

    b. Sales and excise taxes

    c. Tariffs and export taxes

    d. Taxes on personal income and capital gains

    e. Taxes on corporation income and excess profits

    f. Death and gift taxes

    g. Social security and payroll taxes

  4. Transfers and subsidies

    a. Interest payments on the public debt
      [see B.5., below]

    b. Subsidies and tax concessions

    c. Government-sponsored and government-administered welfare programs

  5. The financing of budgetary deficits and surpluses

  6. Direct controls over the private sector

    a. Price, wage, and profit control

    b. Control of restrictive practices: antitrust legislation, regulations imposed upon public utilities, labour legislation imposed on unions
      [see also 532.C.1.d.]

    c. Economic mobilization for war

  7. Land reform: the redistribution of land tenure

Suggested reading in the *Encyclopædia Britannica:*

MACROPAEDIA: Major articles dealing with the distribution of income and wealth

Economic Theory
Government Finance
International Trade
Land Reform and Tenure

Social Sciences, The
Social Welfare
Taxation

MICROPAEDIA: Selected entries of reference information

General subjects

*government revenue
and spending:*
  ad valorem tax
  aid
  assessment
  capital gains tax
  capital levy
  death tax
  depletion
   allowance
  estate tax
  excess-profits tax
  gift tax
  government budget
  guaranteed
   minimum income
  income tax
  indexation

inheritance tax
likin
luxury tax
poll tax
progressive tax
property tax
public debt
regressive tax
relief
revenue bond
sales tax
single tax
social insurance
social security
social welfare
   program
subsidy
tariff

taxation
toll
treasury bill
unemployment
 insurance
use tax
value-added tax
war finance
welfare state
worker's
 compensation
*regulation of
 economic activity:*
  antitrust law
  fair-trade law
  laissez-faire
  land reform
  nationalization

protectionism
rationing
wealth and income:
  absentee
   ownership
  allodium
  disposable income
  ejido
  enclosure
  equal-field system
  investment credit
  living, standard of
  métayage
  profit
  wealth
   and income,
    distribution of

Biographies

See Section 10/36 of Part Ten

INDEX: See entries under all of the terms above

Section 535.   Macroeconomics

A. National income and employment theory

  1. The concern of income and employment theory with changes in aggregate output, employment, and prices

     a. The classical law of markets contrasted with the Keynesian theory of effective demand

     b. The classical and Keynesian theories of unemployment

  2. The circular flow of income and expenditure: national product as goods and as earnings

  3. Analyses of fluctuations in national income

B. International economic and financial equilibrium and disequilibrium

  1. Foreign exchange markets: problems of alternative monetary standards and fixed and fluctuating exchange rates

     a. Equilibrating movements in the balance of payments and the mechanisms of adjustment: arbitrage, short-term movements, interest rates, and forward exchange

     b. Disequilibrating movements as a response to currency devaluation: covering, hedging, and speculation

     c. Balance of payments accounting

     d. Methods for adjusting to fundamental disequilibrium: fiscal and monetary policy, incomes policy, devaluation and revaluation, and restrictions on capital movements

  2. International monetary and financial institutions: the International Monetary Fund, the Group of Ten, and other attempts at international cooperation

   a. Problems of maintaining adequate gold and currency reserves: gold crises, special drawing rights

   b. The aftermath of major wars: economic and financial crises, economic nationalism

C. Business cycles

   1. The statistical study of cycles: the identification and measurement of business cycles, various cyclical theories

   2. Theories of the business cycle and business cycle models

   3. Countercyclical monetary and fiscal policy

D. Inflation and deflation

Suggested reading in the *Encyclopædia Britannica*:

MACROPAEDIA: Major articles dealing with macroeconomics

   Economic Theory
   Government Finance
   International Trade
   Social Sciences, The

MICROPAEDIA: Selected entries of reference information

General subjects

economic cycles:
   business cycle
   depression
   inflation
   Keynesian
      economics
   panic
   Phillips curve
   recession
fiscal and monetary policy:
   bimetallism
   bullionism
   deficit financing
   economic stabilizer
   fiscal policy
   fractional reserve
      system
   gold-exchange
      standard
   gold standard
   Gresham's law
   incomes policy
   interest

monetarism
monetary policy
national income
   accounting
nationalization
open-market
   operation
parity
regional
   development
   program
silver standard
sterling area
two-tier gold
   system
international monetary and financial institutions:
   International
   Bank for
   Reconstruction
   and Development

International
   Development
   Association
International
   Finance
   Corporation
International
   Monetary Fund
United Nations
   Capital
   Development
   Fund
trade:
   comparative
      advantage
   customs union
   embargo
   exchange rate
   free port
   free trade
   General
      Agreement on
      Tariffs and Trade
   imperial preference

international
   exchange
international
   payment
international trade
most-favoured-
   nation treatment
payments,
   balance of
protectionism
quota
reciprocity
tariff
trade, balance of
trade, terms of
trade agreement

Biographies
   See Section 10/36 of Part Ten

INDEX: See entries under all of the terms above

Section 536.   **Economic Growth and Planning**

A. The nature and causes of economic growth

1. Various factors influencing economic growth; *e.g.,* technology, markets, the supply of capital, the labour force, governmental fiscal policies

2. The theory of economic growth and models of growth

   a. Various models of economic growth: supply-determined models, demand-determined models, and target-instrument models

   b. The practical functions of growth theory and mathematical growth models

3. Social costs and benefits of economic growth

4. Economic growth in developing countries

   a. The relationship between economic underdevelopment and low per capita income: the rate of increase of gross domestic product (GDP) as compared to population growth

   b. Various theories of national economic development and economic retardation

5. Changes in economic efficiency as measured by changes in output per unit of input: economic productivity

B. Planning for economic growth and stability

1. The nature of economic planning

2. Economic planning in Communist countries

3. Economic planning in developed non-Communist countries

4. Economic planning in developing countries

Suggested reading in the *Encyclopædia Britannica*:

MACROPAEDIA: Major articles dealing with economic growth and planning

   Economic Growth and Planning
   Economic Theory
   Government Finance
   International Trade
   Social Sciences, The

MICROPAEDIA: Selected entries of reference information

General subjects

economic development	economic growth	Gosplan	international trade
	economic planning	government budget	productivity

Biographies

   See Section 10/36 of Part Ten

INDEX: See entries under all of the terms above

Division IV.   Politics and Government
[For Part Five headnote see page 173.]

The outlines in the four sections of Division IV treat general theories of the state and of government; the structure, branches, and offices of government; the functioning of government; and international relations in peace and war.

Section 541.   Political Theory

A. The national state as viewed in political theory

1. Properties of statehood: sovereignty

2. The state and the individual

3. The national state in the international community
   [see also 552.B.]

4. Various conceptions of the bases of legitimacy and authority of government

   a. Continuing consent of the governed: popular sovereignty

   b. The social contract

   c. Venerable sanction: hereditary monarchy, constitutional succession

   d. Divine right: God as the source of political authority

5. Theories of constitutionalism, modern constitutional governments
   [see also 551.B.4.]

   a. Origins and theories of constitutional government

   b. Features of constitutional government

   c. Methods of constitutional growth: evolution and substantive replacement

B. Patterns of political action as viewed in political theory

1. Political action within small groups, villages, or communities

2. Political action by organized parties

3. Political action by special-interest groups

4. The political influence of public opinion

C. Political concepts, ideologies, and problems

1. The concept of political power

2. The concept of human rights

3. Modern ideologies

   a. The importance of ideology to a political system or movement: the relationship between ideological and civil politics

   b. Current political ideologies and tendencies

      i. Anarchism

      ii. Communism

      iii. Conservatism

      iv. Fascism

      v. Liberalism

      vi. Marxism

      vii. Nationalism

      viii. Socialism

4. Contemporary political issues and problems

   a. The problem of church and state: its background and contemporary form

   b. The urban problem: the administration of cities and metropolitan areas
      [see also 524.B. and 542.A.1.c.]

   c. The problem of international cooperation and integration
      [see also 544.A.]

   d. The issue of centralization of power versus decentralization

   e. The problem of adapting traditional political forms to changing conditions

   f. Bureaucracy: the issue of responsive government
      [see 542.C.]

Suggested reading in the *Encyclopædia Britannica*:

MACROPAEDIA: Major articles dealing with political theory

Constitution and Constitutional Government	Political Parties and Interest Groups
Human Rights	Social Sciences, The
Ideology	Socio-Economic Doctrines
Marxism, Marx and	and Reform Movements, Modern

MICROPAEDIA: Selected entries of reference information

General subjects

charters and documents:
  Constitution of the United States of America
  Kapital, Das
  Magna Carta
  Rights, Bill of
  Rights of Man and of the Citizen, Declaration of the
  Universal Declaration of Human Rights
concepts of sovereignty:
  church and state
  divine right of kings
  established church
  powers, separation of

representation
self-determination
social contract
sovereignty
political ideologies:
  anarchism
  Christian Socialism
  collectivism
  communism
  conservatism
  corporatism
  democracy
  dialectical materialism
  Eurocommunism
  fascism
  Fourierism
  Guild Socialism
  Idéologie
  ideology

individualism
jingoism
Leninism
liberalism
Maoism
Marxism
National Socialism
nationalism
nihilism
pluralism
radical
revisionism
social democracy
socialism
Stalinism
Syndicalism
totalitarianism
Trotskyism
utopia

political organizations:
  commonwealth
  interest group
  political machine
  political party
  popular front
  soviet
status of the individual:
  alien
  bourgeoisie
  citizenship
  freedman
  nationality
  naturalization
  proletariat
  refugee

Biographies

Bakunin, Mikhail Aleksandrovich
Bebel, August
Bentley, Arthur F.
Bernstein, Eduard
Blanc, Louis
Brecht, Arnold
Burke, Edmund
Engels, Friedrich

Herzen, Aleksandr
Jefferson, Thomas
Kropotkin, Peter
Laski, Harold J.
Lasswell, Harold D.
Lenin, Vladimir Ilich
Lippman, Walter

Mao Zedong
Marx, Karl
Plekhanov, Georgy Valentinovich
Proudhon, Pierre-Joseph
Rousscau, Jean-Jacques

Tocqueville, Alexis de
Trotsky, Leon
Webb, Sidney and Beatrice
See also Section 10/36 of Part Ten

INDEX: See entries under all of the terms above

Section 542.   Political Institutions: the Structure, Branches, and Offices of Government

A. Political systems

    1. Levels and structures of various systems of government

        a. Supranational political systems: empires; leagues, confederations, and commonwealths; regional federations; world congresses
        [see 544.A.]

        b. National political systems: the unitary nation-state system, the federal state system

        c. Urban governments

        d. Other subnational political systems: tribal community governments, rural community governments, regional community governments
        [see 521.A.]

    2. Types and models of political systems

B. The branches of government

    1. The concentration of legislative and executive functions: parliamentary rule

    2. The legislature

    3. The executive

    4. The judiciary
        [see also 552.F.1.]

C. Public administration: the planning, organization, and coordination of governmental bureaucratic operations; civil service

---

Suggested reading in the *Encyclopædia Britannica*:

MACROPAEDIA: Major articles dealing with political institutions: the structure, branches and offices of government

    Cities
    Government, The Forms of
    Political Systems
    Public Administration
    Social Sciences, The

MICROPAEDIA: Selected entries of reference information

General subjects

administrative units:
  borough
  canton
  city
  city-state
  commonwealth
  commune
  county
  hsien
  municipality
  shire
  township
courts and judiciary:
  See Section 552
governmental forms and systems:
  absolutism
  aristocracy
  bicameral system
  democracy

federalism
government
military
  government
monarchy
oligarchy
two-party system
legislative bodies:
  Commons, House of
  Congress of the United States
  Diet
  Knesset
  Lords, House of
  Parliament
  Representatives, House of
  Senate

municipal government:
  alderman
  burgomaster
  city manager
  mayor
  pao chia
  town meeting
public administration:
  administrative law
  bureaucracy
  cabinet
  civil service
  commission
  ombudsman
  public administration
  regulatory agency
  spoils system

titles and offices:
  chancellor
  count
  duke
  emperor
  grand duke
  king
  landgrave
  lord
  president
  prime minister
  prince
  tsar
other:
  assembly
  local option
  states' rights
  tenure

Biographies
    See Section 541

INDEX: See entries under all of the terms above

Section 543.   The Functioning of Government: the Dynamics of the Political Process

A. The ways in which political power is exercised

1. Internal and external security functions of government

2. The conduct of foreign relations: the function of government in relation to other sovereign states, its own dependencies, and international organizations
[see 544.A. and 544.E.]

3. Supervisory functions of government: the resolution of conflicts through mediation and the adjudication of suits
[see also 552.F.1. and 3.]

4. Regulatory functions of government: the establishment and active enforcement of standards

5. Law enforcement and the corrective functions of government: sanctions, inducements, and penalties
[see also 522.C.6. and D.2.i.]

6. Enterprising functions of government
[see 355.D., 424.D., 522.D., 533.G.4., 534.B.4.c. and 6.b., 561, 724.A.2.a., and 732.I.]

B. Government's role in production and consumption

C. Methods of changing the form of government

1. Peaceful changes: by electoral process (plebiscite), by constitutional mandate

2. Violent changes: revolution, civil war, conquest by a foreign power

---

Suggested reading in the *Encyclopædia Britannica*:

MACROPAEDIA: Major articles dealing with the functioning of government: the dynamics of the political process

Censorship
Crime and Punishment
Police
Political Parties and Interest Groups
Political Systems
Social Sciences, The

MICROPAEDIA: Selected entries of reference information

General subjects

censorship:
    banning
    censor
    censorship
    obscenity
    pornography
electoral constituencies:
    gerrymandering
    legislative apportionment
    pocket borough
    proportional representation

electoral process:
    absentee voting
    Australian ballot
    election
    electoral college
    plebiscite
    plurality system
    political convention
    political party
    primary election
    referendum and initiative
    suffrage

law enforcement:
    capital punishment
    constable
    criminal investigation
    Federal Bureau of Investigation
    Interpol
    KGB
    police
    posse comitatus
    punishment
    ranger
    Royal Canadian Mounted Police

    sheriff
    torture
legislative procedure:
    cloture
    filibuster
    legislative investigative powers
    parliamentary procedure
other:
    revolution
    sabotage
    terrorism

Biographies

See Section 541

INDEX: See entries under all of the terms above

Section 544.   **International Relations: Peace and War**

A. The politics of international relations

B. International treaties and agreements
[see also 533.F.3.]

C. Foreign policy and diplomacy

D. The use of intelligence and counterintelligence activities in the preservation of national security and the conduct of international affairs

E. War among states

    1. Degrees and kinds of war: limited war; total war; ethnic or tribal wars; religious wars; national, regional, and worldwide wars; civil wars and insurrections

    2. The conduct of war

        a. Military strategy

        b. Military tactics

        c. Military logistics

        d. Effects of psychological warfare on troops and civilians during wartime

        e. International law relating to the treatment of persons during wartime
[see also 552.B.4.]

Suggested reading in the *Encyclopædia Britannica:*

MACROPAEDIA: Major articles dealing with international relations: peace and war

Diplomacy
Intelligence and Counterintelligence
Social Sciences, The
United Nations
War, The Theory and Conduct of

MICROPAEDIA: Selected entries of reference information

General subjects

aggression and	terrorism	geopolitics	MI-5
warfare:	total war	international	MI-6
aggression	trench warfare	agreement	Mossad
air warfare	visit and search	international	National Security
amphibious	war	organization	Agency
warfare	*diplomacy and*	legate	Ultra
annexation	*international*	mediation	*military organization*
belligerency	*agreements:*	neutralism	*and personnel:*
blitzkrieg	alliance	power, balance of	admiral
blockade	ambassador	treaty	air force
civil defense	armistice	United Nations	army
conquest	arms control	*intelligence gathering:*	battalion
convoy	collective security	BND	brevet
economic warfare	consul	Central Intelligence	captain
embargo	diplomacy	Agency	cavalry
infiltration	executive	counterespionage	centurion
mobilization	agreement	espionage	chasseur
sabotage	foreign service	intelligence	coast guard
safe-conduct	Geneva	KGB	
	Convention		

commandant	mercenary	strategy	*other:*
company	military police	tactics	American Legion
division	militia	*sovereignty:*	concentration
dragoon	navy	colonialism	camp
frogman	phalanx	dominion	conscientious
general	platoon	exterritoriality	objector
general staff	privateer	home rule	conscription
grenadier	ranger	imperialism	fifth column
guerrilla	regiment	influence,	impressment
hussar	streltsy	sphere of	martial law
infantry	*military science:*	protectorate	military, naval,
legion	deterrence	sovereignty	and air academies
lieutenant	just war	territorial waters	
marine	logistics		
marshal	sea power		

Biographies

diplomats and statesmen:
Adenauer, Konrad
Ben-Gurion, David
Bismarck,
 Otto von
Bunche, Ralph
Chamberlain,
 Neville
Chou En-lai
Churchill, Winston
Clemenceau,
 Georges
Curzon, George
 Nathaniel
Curzon,
 Marquesse
Disraeli, Benjamin
Dulles, John
 Foster
Eisenhower,
 Dwight D.
Gandhi, Mohandas
 Karamchand
Gaulle, Charles de

Gladstone,
 William Ewart
Goebbels, Joseph
Gromyko, Andrey
 Andreyevich
Hammarskjöld,
 Dag
Hitler, Adolf
Ho Chi Minh
Kennedy, John F.
Khrushchev,
 Nikita S.
Kissinger,
 Henry A.
Lie, Trygve
Marshall,
 George C.
Metternich,
 Klemens,
 Fürst von
Mussolini, Benito
Nasser, Gamal
 Abdel
Nehru, Jawaharlal

Roosevelt,
 Franklin D.
Stalin, Joseph
Stevenson,
 Adlai E.
Sun Yat-sen
Thant, U
Weizmann, Chaim
Wilson, Woodrow
intelligence agents and officers:
Baker, Lafayette
 Curry
Bancroft, Edward
Boyd, Belle
Burgess, Guy; and
 Maclean, Donald
Donovan,
 William J.
Hiss, Alger
Mata Hari
Redl, Alfred
Schulmeister, Karl
Van Deman,
 Ralph H.

Winterbotham,
 Fredrick William
Yardley, Herbert
 Osborne
military theorists:
Clausewitz,
 Carl von
Douhet, Giulio
Jomini, Henri,
 baron de
Liddell Hart, Sir
 Basil
Mahan, Alfred
 Thayer
Montalembert,
 Marc-René,
 marquis de
Montecuccoli,
 Raimonde
Scharnhorst,
 Gerhard Johann
 David von
Vauban, Sébastien
 le Prestre de

INDEX: See entries under all of the terms above

Division V.   Law
[For Part Five headnote see page 173.]

The outlines in the three sections of Division V treat philosophies and systems of law; the profession and practice of law; the branches of public law; and the branches of private law.

Section 551.   Philosophies and Systems of Law; the Practice of Law

A. Western and non-Western philosophies of law

  1. Western philosophy of law

      a. The scope of the Western philosophy of law and its relationship to other branches of philosophy

      b. Problems of the philosophy of law, various approaches to a theory of law or jurisprudence

      c. The relationship between law and morality: the influence of the principles of natural law

      d. Historical survey of legal theories from the ancient world to the 20th century

  2. Non-Western philosophies of law: Islāmic, Chinese, and other non-Western philosophies of law

B. Ancient and modern legal systems

  1. Primitive law: the legal systems of nonliterate peoples

  2. Ancient systems of law

      a. Egyptian law

      b. Cuneiform law

      c. Chinese law

      d. Greek law

      e. Hellenistic law

      f. Roman law

      g. Germanic law

  3. Medieval European law

      a. Origins and development of medieval European law

      b. Sources and institutions of medieval constitutional law

      c. Institutions of private law in medieval Europe

      d. Development of canon law

  4. Modern systems of law

      a. Anglo-American common law

      b. Continental civil law

      c. Soviet and socialist law

C. The study of the distinctions and parallels among diverse legal systems

D. The profession and practice of law

  1. The profession of law

  2. Legal ethics

  3. Educational requirements for the legal profession

Suggested reading in the *Encyclopædia Britannica*:

MACROPAEDIA: Major articles dealing with the philosophies and systems of law; the practice of law

Law, The Profession and Practice of
Legal Systems, The Evolution of Modern Western

MICROPAEDIA: Selected entries of reference information

General subjects

ancient legal codes, principles and institutions:
aedile
archon
Basilica
censor
civitas
clientship
comitia
concubinage
cuneiform law
decemviri
delator
delict
dharmashastra
dicastery
Egyptian law
emphyteusis and superficies
Greek law
Hammurabi, Code of
hypothec
interdict
jus gentium
jus Latii
Justinian, Code of
manus
nomos
Pandects
patria potestas
proscription
Roman law
Roman legal procedure
talion
Twelve Tables, Law of the
ecclesiastical law:
canon law
Codex Juris Canonici
Corpus Juris Canonici

decretal
dispensation
ecclesiastical court
excommunication
False Decretals
Gratian's Decretum
Ḥadīth
Halakha
Mishna
penitential book
Sharīʿah
Talmud
Torah
legal practitioners:
advocate
assessor
attorney general
barrister
lawyer
notary
solicitor
medieval European law—codes and systems:
Anglo-Saxon law
Brehon law
capitulary
Germanic law
Jerusalem, Assizes of
Sachsenspiegel
Salic Law
Salic Law of Succession
Scandinavian law
Welsh law
Westminster, Statutes of
medieval European law—institutions and officers:
audiencia
Augmentations, Court of

Chambre des Comptes
Chambre des Enquêts
Chambre des Requêts
Clarendon, Assize of
court baron
Court Leet
curia
fehmic court
High Commission, Court of
High Court of Admirality
law merchant
legal glossator
manorial court
Parlement
piepoudre court
prerogative court
Privy Council
Reichskammergericht
Requests, Court of
Star Chamber, Court of
medieval European law—principles:
blood money
clergy, benefit of
composition
compurgation
copyhold
demesne
entail
feudal land tenure
feudalism
fief
frankpledge
freehold
heriot
homage and fealty
liege
peine forte et dure

right, petition of
seisin
sergeanty
socage
tallage
usury
wardship and marriage
wergild
modern legal codes and systems:
adat
Chinese law
German Civil Code
Indian law
Israeli law
Japanese Civil Code
Japanese law
Napoleonic Code
Prussian Civil Code
Roman-Dutch law
Scottish law
Soviet law
Swiss Civil Code
other:
assize
bar association
civil law
common law
custom
disbarment
duel
equity
feud
law
law code
movable and immovable
natural law
sumptuary law

Biographies

Austin, John
Blackstone, Sir William
Brandeis, Louis
Brennan, William J., Jr.

Brougham and Vaux, Henry Peter Brougham, 1st Baron
Burger, Warren E.

Cardozo, Benjamin Nathan
Cockburn, Sir Alexander James Edmund
Coke, Sir Edward

Darrow, Clarence
Draco
Erskine, Thomas Erskine, 1st Baron

INDEX: See entries under all of the terms above

Section 552.   Branches of Public Law, Substantive and Procedural

   A. Laws defining and implementing the authority and power of the state

     1. Basic laws governing the organization and functions of the state: constitutional law

     2. Laws governing public administration: regulation of the organization, powers, duties, and functions of public administrative authorities

   B. Laws governing relations among sovereign states

     1. Sources and concepts of international law

     2. The attempt to create a supranational legislative and executive authority: the United Nations

     3. The attempt to create a supranational judicial authority

     4. The attempt to impose rules of warfare

     5. The attempt to limit and punish war crimes and crimes against peace and humanity

     6. The attempt to preserve the peaceful uses and exploration of outer space

   C. Laws governing acts viewed as crimes

     1. Principles and doctrines of criminal law: comparisons between common law and civil law systems
[see also 543.A.5.]

     2. Laws governing offenses committed by military forces and other persons subject to military discipline

   D. Laws promoting the public welfare

     1. Laws providing for general social security and welfare

     2. Laws promoting public health and safety

     3. Laws regulating the health, safety, and welfare of workers

   E. Laws governing taxation
[see also 534.B.2. and 3.]

   F. Laws of judicial procedure

     1. The organization and administration of the legal system: the courts and the judiciary

     2. Methods and procedures of the law

       a. Criminal procedure

       b. Civil procedure
[see 553.E.]

       c. Administrative procedure

     3. Methods of adjudicating litigious disputes: the jury system, systems of arbitration

Suggested reading in the *Encyclopædia Britannica:*

MACROPAEDIA: Major articles dealing with branches of public law, substantive and procedural

Constitutional Law
Criminal Law
International Law
Judicial and Arbitrational Systems

Public Administration
Taxation
United Nations
War, The Theory and Conduct of

MICROPAEDIA: Selected entries of reference information

General subjects

constitutional law:
advisory opinion
attainder
commerce clause
constitution
due process
equal protection
ex post facto law
interstate
  commerce
judicial review
police power
powers,
  delegation of
privacy, rights of
standing to sue
states' rights
courts, court officials,
  and juries:
amicus curiae
Appeal, Court of
assigned counsel
attorney general
bailiff
Chancery, Court of
Common Pleas,
  Court of
comrades' court
coroner
Conseil d'État
Cour de Cassation
court
court-martial
Crown Court
family court
Federal
  Constitutional
  Court
grand jury
High Court of
  Justice
juge d'instruction
jury
justice of the peace
juvenile court
lord chancellor
lord chief justice
lord high steward
lord steward
magistrates' court
ministère public

petit jury
prosecutor
public defender
Queen's Bench,
  Court of
rapporteur
Supreme Court of
  Japan
Supreme Court of
  the United States
Tax Court
United States
  Claims Court
United States
  Court of Appeals
United States
  Court of Military
  Appeals
United States
  District Court
criminal law:
accomplice
arson
assault and battery
bribery
child abuse
confidence game
conspiracy
contempt
counterfeiting
crime, délit, and
  contravention
criminal law
delinquency
diminished
  responsibility
disorderly conduct
disturbing the
  peace
embezzlement
entrapment
extortion
felony and
  misdemeanour
forgery
fraud
hijacking
homicide
infamy
insanity

kidnapping
lynching
mayhem
mens rea
mutiny
obscenity
pardon
perjury
poaching
rape
riot
sedition
seduction
self-defense
smuggling
solicitation
theft
treason
unlawful assembly
usury
vagrancy
criminal procedure:
accused, rights of
acquittal
arraignment
arrest
bail
clergy, benefit of
commutation
confession
double jeopardy
exclusionary rule
extenuating
  circumstances
extradition
habeas corpus
impeachment
indictment
inquest
interrogation
outlawry
preventive
  detention
probation
recognizance
search and seizure
self-incrimination
sentence
warrant

general procedural
  law:
adversary
  procedure
appeal
assize
brief
certiorari
circumstantial
  evidence
competence and
  jurisdiction
complaint
demurrer
domicile
equity
evidence
examination
interlocutory
  decree
judgment
law report
legal fiction
legal maxim
limitation,
  statute of
mistrial
nolle prosequi
pleading
privileged
  communication
procedural law
stare decisis
summary
  jurisdiction
venue
international law:
aggression
air law
armistice
asylum
Berne Convention
Calvo Doctrine
continuous voyage
contraband
genocide
Hague Convention
high seas
international law
laws, conflict of
mutiny

neutrality	sequestration	war, law of	legislative
Nürnberg trials	space law	war crime	investigative
piracy	territorial waters	*other:*	powers
prisoner of war	Universal	administrative law	military law
prize court	Copyright		United Nations
safe-conduct	Convention		

Biographies

See Section 551

INDEX: See entries under all of the terms above

Section 553.   **Branches of Private Law, Substantive and Procedural**

A. Law of property

1. Historical development of property rights

2. Methods of acquiring property rights

3. Types of property rights classified by types of ownership

4. Laws concerning tangible property: the distinctions between real and personal property

5. Laws protecting intangible or incorporeal property rights

    a. Easements and servitudes: profits and mineral rights

    b. Rights to the exclusive exploitation of literary, dramatic, musical, and other artistic works

    c. Rights to the exclusive exploitation of inventions and other discoveries of useful processes and materials

    d. Rights to the exclusive exploitation of symbols and other devices used to identify the origin or ownership of business products

6. Laws concerning the temporal division of property rights

    a. Common law land ownership: freehold and leasehold estates

    b. Civil law land ownership: dominium (absolute ownership) and usufruct (life estate)

7. Laws concerning trusts: ownership for the benefit of others

    a. The elements of a trust: settlor, trust property, trustee, beneficiary, trust instrument

    b. Types of trusts: express, implied, constructive, statutory, and public and private trusts

    c. Trusts established for the benefit of families, social and philanthropic organizations, and business corporations

    d. The status of the trust in civil law systems: a comparison of the trust and the fidei commissum

8. Law of mortgages

9. Laws concerning bankruptcy

B. Family law

1. Laws governing the institution of the family and the relationships among its members
[see also 513.A.2.]

    a. Laws concerning the marriage contract: civil effects of marriage, the legal status of married women

    b. Laws concerning children: legitimacy, adoption, and guardianship; parental obligations and rights

    c. Laws concerning the termination of marriage: divorce and other forms of marital dissolution

2. Laws concerning the devolution of property by means of inheritance

C. Law of torts

1. The doctrine of strict liability as compared with negligence liability: recent changes in tort liability burden

2. Intentional personal injuries: battery and assault, false imprisonment, mental anguish

3. Intentional injuries to property: trespass to land and chattels, nuisance, unlawful appropriation and conversion of property

4. Injuries resulting from negligent acts

   a. Injuries resulting from failure to comply with required standards of care: the proximate cause doctrine, effects of contributory negligence and third-party intervention

   b. The employer's liability and the master–servant relationship

   c. The manufacturer's liability to the consumer

5. Injuries to personality and personal relationships: physical, mental, and economic injuries

   a. Defamation: libel and slander, other invasions of privacy and interference with familial relationships

   b. Interference with economic relationships: deceptive practices, unfair competition, infringement

D. Laws governing economic transactions

1. Law of contracts

2. Law of commercial transactions

   a. Principal elements of commercial law: commercial transactions as contracts

      i. Sales of goods and requirements for delivery

      ii. Transfer of negotiable instruments; *e.g.,* promissory notes, checks, drafts or bills of exchange

      iii. Issuance of documents of title; *e.g.,* bills of lading, warehouse receipts

      iv. Issuance of letters of credit

      v. The use of security interests (liens and pledges) as collateral for loans of money

   b. Laws governing the relationship between agent and principal in the transaction of commercial and other legal affairs

3. Law of business associations

   a. Principal forms of business associations

      i. Partnerships

      ii. Corporate companies or corporations

      iii. Cooperative and mutual organizations

      iv. State and municipal corporations, quasi-public enterprises and utilities
         [see also 533.G.4. and 534.B.6.b.]

   b. Laws governing the management and control of business entities

   c. The structure of corporate finance

      i. Common and preferred shares of stock: rights and interests of owners of equity capital

      ii. Borrowed capital: rights acquired by holders of bonds and debentures

      iii. Reinvestment of company earnings

   d. Trends in laws governing mergers and consolidations: employee participation
      [see also 533.H.2.c.]

   e. Laws governing the liquidation of insolvent business and nonbusiness estates: the law of bankruptcy

4. Labour law

5. Laws governing commercial transportation

   a. Laws regulating the carriage of goods

   b. Maritime law

   c. Air law

E. Civil procedural law

1. Elements of civil procedure

   a. National or territorial jurisdiction and venue of courts: the competence of a court to handle a case

    b. Jurisdiction or venue in private international law: the source and nature of the conflict of laws, foreign judgments and choice of law

    c. Definitions and limitations of parties to a suit: class actions and amicus curiae

    d. Provisional remedies sought prior to trial; *e.g.,* writs of attachment, injunctions, and other restraining orders

    e. The commencement of civil action: summons, pleadings, appearance, pretrial motions, discovery procedures, and pretrial conference

2. The conduct of civil trials: the law of evidence

3. The rendering of judgment in civil cases: assessment of damages, res judicata, collateral estoppel

4. Post-trial appeals and other methods of review

Suggested reading in the *Encyclopædia Britannica*:

MACROPAEDIA: Major articles dealing with branches of private law, substantive and procedural

Business Law	Property Law
Family Law	Torts
Inheritance and Succession	Transportation Law
Procedural Law	

MICROPAEDIA: Selected entries of reference information

General subjects

business law:	attorney,	concubinage	preemption
affreightment	power of	consensual union	prescription
agency	damages	divorce	property
air law	declaratory	guardian	real and personal
antitrust law	judgment	illegitimacy	property
average	escrow	marriage law	remainder
bankruptcy	foreclosure	minor	restrictive covenant
business law	garnishment	morganatic	reversion
caveat emptor	injunction	marriage	riparian right
cessio bonorum	joinder and	separation	servitude
composition	impleader	*property law:*	treasure trove
consideration	liability	abandonment	trust
contract	lien	adverse possession	use
copyright	mandamus, writ of	ancient lights	usufruct
debtor and creditor	replevin	bailment	*tort law:*
guaranty and	settlement	beneficiary	assault and battery
suretyship	writ	condominium	contributory
hypothec	*estate law:*	deforcement	negligence
insolvency	executor	domain	conversion
labour law	gift	easement	damages
lading, bill of	heir	ejectment	defamation
liquidation	inheritance	eminent domain	delict
maritime law	intestate succession	emphyteusis and	fraud
patent	legacy	superficies	manufacturer's
performance	probate	entail	liability
receivership	will	escheat	misrepresentation
right-to-work law	*family law:*	landlord and	negligence
salvage	adoption	tenant	nuisance
trademark	alimony	mortgage	tort
civil procedure:	annulment	mortmain	trespass
abatement	common-law	movable and	trover
arbitration	marriage	immovable	
attachment	community	ownership	
	property	possession	

Biographies

    See Section 551

INDEX: See entries under all of the terms above

Division VI.   **Education**
[For Part Five headnote see page 173.]

The outlines in the two sections of Division VI treat the subjects of education and the world's educational systems.

Section 561.   **The Aims and Organization of Education**

A. Philosophies of education
[see also 435.A.]

B. The learning process and the teaching art

   1. Processes of learning and thinking: experimental findings and theories
[see 435]

   2. Pedagogy: the art and science of teaching

     a. Components of the teaching situation

     b. General theories concerning the role of the teacher in the learning process

     c. The organization of instruction: contemporary practices and techniques

     d. Instructional media: speaking–listening facilities, visual and observational aids, computer-based instruction

C. The organization of education

   1. Phases or levels of education

     a. Preschool education

     b. Elementary and secondary education

     c. Higher education: colleges, universities, and professional schools

     d. Special education: education of exceptional children

     e. Education of the adult population

     f. Vocational training: apprenticeship and employee training

   2. The preparation and performance of teachers

     a. The education of teachers

     b. The teaching profession

   3. The economics of education

   4. Social aspects of education

Suggested reading in the *Encyclopædia Britannica:*

MACROPAEDIA: Major articles dealing with the aims and organization of education

   Philosophies of the Branches of Knowledge
   Teaching

MICROPAEDIA: Selected entries of reference information

General subjects

adult education:	*elementary and*	eleven-plus	Hauptschule
adult education	*secondary education:*	graded school	high school
chautauqua	comprehensive	grammar school	informal school
movement	school	Grundschule	
folk high school	elementary	Gymnasium	
lyceum movement	education		

Section 562.   **Education Around the World**

A. Systems of education

  1. The formation of educational policy

  2. Administrative functions and procedures

  3. Types of educational systems and their characteristics

    a. Centralized systems: systems in which control is exercised through a national administrative agency

    b. Decentralized systems: systems in which control is exercised at the regional or local level

    c. Joint national and local systems

    d. Systems controlled by political parties

    e. Sectarian systems: national and regional sectarian systems, sectarian education as an alternative system to public education

B. History of education: philosophies, practices, and institutions

  1. Education in ancient cultures

    a. Ancient Indian education

    b. Ancient Chinese education

    c. Ancient Hebrew education

    d. Ancient Greek education

    e. Ancient Roman education

  2. Education in the Persian, Byzantine, early Russian, and Islāmic civilizations

    a. Ancient Persian education: influences of Zoroastrian and Sāsānid cultures

    b. Byzantine education: influences of Greek Christian and humanistic culture; development of primary, secondary, and higher educational institutions

    c. Kiev and Muscovy: Russian education to the period of the early Romanovs

    d. Islāmic education

  3. Education in the European Middle Ages

a. Christian education to the 8th century: early schools; development of monastic schools in England, Ireland, Italy, and Spain

b. The cultural revival under Charlemagne and his successors

c. The 12th-century renaissance: reform of monastic schools and the rise of secular urban schools, development of universities and grammar schools, courtly education

4. Education in Asian civilizations from *c.* 700 to the eve of Western influence

a. Indian education from *c.* 700 to 1707

b. Chinese education from 618 to 1911

c. Japanese education from ancient times to 1867

5. European education during the Renaissance and Reformation

a. Development of Renaissance education: Arabic and secular influences on Humanism

b. The humanistic tradition in Italy

c. The humanistic tradition in northern and western Europe

d. Education during the Reformation and Counter-Reformation

6. European education in the 17th and 18th centuries

a. The social and historical setting

b. Educational theories and practices

c. European influences in New World educational development

7. Western education in the 19th century

a. The social and historical setting: nationalism, industrialism, urbanization, political revolution and reform

b. The early reform movements: the new pedagogy and psychology

c. Development of national systems of education

d. Spread of Western educational practices to Asian countries

8. Education in the 20th century

a. Political, social, economic, and intellectual trends

b. Traditional and experimental educational movements in the West

c. The modernization of education in Asia and Africa

d. Education in colonies and newly emerging nations in Africa, Asia, and Latin America

C. International educational activities

Suggested reading in the *Encyclopædia Britannica:*

MACROPAEDIA: Major articles dealing with education around the world

Education, History of
Teaching

MICROPAEDIA: Selected entries of reference information

General subjects

educational systems:	*history of education:*	juku	*other:*
coeducation	American	land-grant college	academy
correspondence	Missionary	lyceum movement	Nobel Prize
education	Association	mechanics'	Pugwash
educational system	cathedral school	institute	Conference
liberal arts	charity school	nation	
minority education	chautauqua	normal school	
monitorial system	movement	philanthropinum	
parochial education	Dalton Plan	Quincy Plan	
progressive	hornbook		
education			

Biographies

Adler, Mortimer J.	Cygnaeus, Uno	Hutchins,	Richards, Ellen
Alcuin	Dewey, John	Robert M.	Swallow
Ascham, Roger	Eaton, John	Lancaster, Joseph	Sadler, Sir Michael
Bagley, William	Froebel, Friedrich	Mann, Horace	Ernest
Chandler	Griswold, Alfred	Melanchthon,	Stowe, Calvin E.
Basedow, Johann	Whitney	Philipp	Vittorino da Feltre
Bernhard	Herbart, Johann	Montessori, Maria	Vives, Juan Luis
Comenius, John	Friedrich	Pestalozzi, Johann	
Amos	Hopkins, Johns	Heinrich	

INDEX: See entries under all of the terms above

Introduction to Part Six:
The World of Art

by Mark Van Doren

Let us imagine if we can a world entirely without art: without story, image, edifice, or significant sound. If we can, for perhaps it is impossible. Such a world might well be invisible, inaudible, ineffable, and intangible. Even if we could see it, hear it, feel it, we would not know we did, at least as men know things. Without the earliest of all arts, language, we would scarcely know of what we were deprived: the privilege, namely, of expressing our satisfaction or dissatisfaction with what had taken place before our eyes. Without the arts of speaking, listening, thinking, counting, and measuring—without the intellectual arts—we could not assess or repossess the experience we had undergone. Without the useful arts we could make nothing, build nothing worthy to contain and shelter our bodies, to be a home wherein our thought might rest. And then without the fine arts—the arts that serve only themselves, that are ends, not means, that justify themselves when they give us nothing but pleasure—we would be shallow and poor of mind, with little or no sense of the world's depth and colour, or of ourselves as creatures for whom the present moment is also past and future. We call these arts fine not because they are better than the others but because they are different, as beauty is different from use—beauty that is its own excuse for being.

None of them is more intimately ours than story. The art of literature is the art of story; there are songs and there are essays long and short, there are histories, there are biographies, there are treatises, sermons, and discussions of everything under the sun, but story is our first and last entertainment—when we are children and when we are too old to care any more what truth is unless it comes in the past tense, with persons reflecting in their lives the peculiar radiance that attends the accidents of time and character. Stories may vary in length from the anecdote to the epic, from the fairy tale to the novel, the imaginary biography, the romance. And they may reach us in many forms: in the theatre, for instance, where they may employ flesh-and-blood actors to convey their meaning or where they may be only flickers of light and shade upon a screen that has no depth save what we give it in our imaginations; where, in other words, they call themselves plays or motion pictures or where, if music also sounds and dancers whirl and pose, they call themselves ballets.

Nature does not tell stories; only artists do, and in the process they work transformations that measure the distance between matter and mind. In nature, so far as we can know it, there are no beginnings and no ends in the sense familiar to both writers and readers of fiction and drama, or for that matter history, which likewise imposes form upon a welter of events. No matter how simple a tale is, or how complex, how few the words in it or how many, it is a human construction that no animal or plant, and of course no stone, would find in the least degree interesting;

whereas human beings hold their breaths until an end is reached. Ends are intelligible as the raw materials of life seem not to be; if life itself does not become intelligible through story, it becomes in some mysterious way both beautiful and clear, and for the time being that suffices.

Each of the fine arts flourishes both in large and in little forms. Just as story has a choice between the brevity of folk tales and the elaboration of epics and romances, so statements about life may be as compendious as a proverb—the wisdom of many and the wit of one—or as bulky as the longest book in numberless volumes. So music—the sound of other worlds—reaches our ears either as simple song or as opera and symphony and other complex forms. There are those who say that the song, like the anonymous fable or tale, is more lasting and important than compositions of great complexity can ever be; and they also say that the lyric poem, at least when it is perfect, as in truth it seldom is, has more to tell us, or at least deeper ways of touching us, than the most tremendous tragedy in five acts or the subtlest comic novel in a thousand pages. When a memorable melody attaches itself to a lyric or a ballad, something indeed does come into existence and hang there as if for perpetuity. Music is the most ineffable of all the arts. It has its own language and it listens to itself; we do not so much hear it as overhear it, nor can we speak very sensibly about what we have overheard. Successful music, powerful music, has an effect upon us that many have tried in vain to describe; it takes us out of ourselves, they say, and perhaps they need to say no more than that. Even then they may be speaking only of the music that is native to them; Eastern music sounds like mere noise to untrained Western ears, and Western music has a monotony, say the Chinese, that Europeans of course deny is there. The same thing is true, though in lesser measure, of all the arts. East and West have different eyes as well as ears, and different thoughts.

The arts of drawing and painting, of etching and lithography, of engraving and decorative design, have covered many surfaces—canvas, plaster, parchment, paper—which no longer show where the artist's hand once worked; for the materials of these arts are perishable, as the marble of sculptors has been, as the bronze, as the wood. Much remains, but more does not. Even the cave paintings of prehistoric France and Africa, hailed by modern man when he discovered them as miracles of survival, may not survive the visits that living people rushed to pay them. Ancient Greek music has failed to survive for a further reason: we do not know how it was written or how it sounded; we are told that it had almost magical powers over those who heard it in its time, but that time is gone, along with the time when paintings adorned the walls and columns of Greek temples and houses. Painting has been for centuries the queen of the arts in Europe. Belgium,

219

The Netherlands, France, Germany, Spain, Italy, and England—each of them in its turn, and sometimes in more than one turn, has enriched the world with shapes and colours that only genius could have foretold, only passion could have brought into being. And that is but half the story; in China long before, in India, in Persia, in Japan, in Russia, the brushes of painters, sometimes tipped with gold, beautified and glorified the palaces of emperors, the tombs of princes, and the dwelling places of great gods. In Egypt for millennia the order of the world was registered in stone and gold, and the written word itself was pictures.

Sculpture, that once was solid and now is full of spaces—or may be—left open by the ingenuity of workers in metal, has changed as architecture has changed. Both arts now cultivate openness: buildings are closed, but the exterior is glass, so that space plays games with itself inside, and the effect is of a lightness that winds might blow away, except of course that the buildings look lean and strong enough to remain just where they are. It has always been true that architects desired the effect of lightness, as all art does, heaviness being a quality that no mind admires; any building weighs tons, but we are not supposed to think of that; rather indeed we are expected to imagine that brick and stone for once have learned to lie lightly on the earth, which they do not seem to press at all. So with Classical sculpture, from Greek days on; the charm of it was its poise, its grace, its management of idea in marble. So too with Classical architecture; the Parthenon is both massive and weightless, like a ship that might sail yet does not. And always in China and Japan there have been those curled and tapered roofs that still look as if at this very instant in time they are taking wing. The open revolution, then, was only a restatement of what had long been understood though some of its secrets were forgotten.

Abstraction in all the arts, for there is no art from which it is absent, is again a restatement of what has always been true, however feebly it was recognized by schools of artists who had lost contact with reality. Great painting, great music, great poetry, great architecture—great landscape architecture too—have never been strangers to abstraction, just as they have never been slaves to an incomplete understanding of what is meant when we say that art is imitation. It *is* imitation, but of what? Of essences, not accidents; of the truth that is hard to see; of beauty that is basic; of shapes that will not change; of colours that will not fade. And if, say, the great painters of the past, comprehending this, still "copied nature," they did not do so inanely. They did so, on the contrary, with huge effort aimed at the verities that underlie verisimilitude, so that in one sense they were not copying at all; they were extracting essences, they were reducing appearances to the ideas that informed them; they were, in a word, abstracting truth from vessels that contained it. But they did not say they were doing this. They said they were copying nature. And when later on they were taken at their word by painters with inadequate aspiration, the result was woeful insipidity, was mediocrity and flatness. The heroic remedy was warfare against representation as such, was a shortcut to abstraction that could have its weakness too, was a loss, in all but the great revolutionaries, of the contact with Earth

which no art ever can be without. Abstract painting at its best—and the worst does not matter—imitates nature at nature's best; is "like" nature after all, for nature is brilliant and strong, and abstract painting convinces us of this even though it dispenses with the particulars with which we used to be fascinated and of which we were quite properly fond.

A world entirely without art would be worse than invisible, inaudible, ineffable, and intangible. It would be a world without temporal dimension, it would be a world that human minds could not remember. Human memory is unique in its capacity not only to recall but also to utilize the past, and to apply it; and better still, to re-create it so that it becomes a part of the present moment, which is more like eternity than anything else we shall ever experience. Human memory is nothing less than the origin of human art.

"The Greeks fabled not unwisely," said Sir Thomas Browne, "in making Memory the mother of the Muses." The memory of man is indeed a wonderful thing, and his richest possession. Not only is it the source of all our arts, it is their record too, stored in the mind of the beholder, the listener. Plato even asked us to conceive "in the mind of man a block of wax, the gift of Memory, and when we wish to remember anything which we have seen, or heard, or thought in our own minds, we hold the wax to the perceptions and thoughts, and in that material receive the impression of them as from the seal of a ring; and we remember and know what is imprinted as long as the image lasts." An artist whose poems or pictures or musical ideas have great power is certainly, we feel, the possessor of a memory that is always at his command, bringing to him at any moment whatever detail he needs, and reminding him too of the knowledge he has, and never forgets, of the way the world is put together, so that he does not misrepresent things as they are. The human race itself can be said to be such an artist, for it has its myths which it keeps alive, its stories that are "so true," someone has said, "that they couldn't have happened." There is such a thing as folk memory, the mother perhaps of all our thoughts and feelings, and the guardian of such wisdom as we have.

A story that cannot be remembered, a song that fades out of the mind, a hero whose name escapes us, a sentence we thought we would never forget but somehow do—such works of art must be defective at the core. But there are others that we could not forget if we tried, and it is those we live with in the company of friends who remember them too. Perhaps the final justification of art is the two-fold pleasure it gives: the pleasure of remembering great and beautiful things that we cannot lose, and the pleasure of sharing them with others who possess them in the same fashion.

There is a limited number of such things, of these greatest of human works of art; by definition there can be no superfluous masterpieces. The ones we have are numerous after all, and no single person can claim to have done justice to every one of them, or can claim to know what further ones are still unborn, Mnemosyne, goddess of Memory and Mother of the Muses, will have the deciding vote as to which ones, now or in the future, will survive the ravages of time.

Part Six. Art

The outlines in the twelve sections of Part Six are concerned with mankind's creation, experience, and evaluation of works made primarily for aesthetic enjoyment and contemplation. The arts of making things primarily for practical use are treated in Part Seven, on technology.

Division I.	Art in General

The outlines in the three sections of Division I treat the theory and classification of the arts; the experience and criticism of works of art; and the nonaesthetic contexts of art.

Section 611.	Theory and Classification of the Arts

A. The philosophy of art

  1. Diverse conceptions of the scope of art

  2. Diverse theories concerning the nature, functions, and effects of art: mimetic theories, expressive theories, formalist theories, pragmatic theories

  3. The making of works of art: the creative process

B. Classification of the arts

  1. Major distinctions among the kinds of art

    a. By reference to the intention of the maker or the recipient of the work of art: useful art, fine art, arts that are both useful and fine

    b. By reference to the manipulation of physical matter: the production of artistic works that are physical objects

    c. By reference to performers as interpreters or creators of works of art

    d. By reference to the use of notational devices; *e.g.,* literature, music, dance

  2. Other distinctions among the kinds of art; *e.g.,* space and time arts, primary and auxiliary arts

  3. The characterization of works of art by reference to the cultural or social circumstances of their production or the extent and character of their audience: the primitive, folk, and popular arts

  4. Style in the arts

    a. The nature of style

    b. The varieties of style; *e.g.,* personal, school, ethnic, regional, and period styles

    c. The dynamics of style: the historical development, diffusion, change, and duration of style in the arts

Suggested reading in the *Encyclopædia Britannica*:

MACROPAEDIA: Major articles dealing with the theory and classification of the arts

Philosophies of the Branches of Knowledge

MICROPAEDIA: Selected entries of reference information

art	folk art	mimesis	race, milieu, and
fine art	inspiration	popular art	moment

INDEX: See entries under all of the terms above

Section 612.   **Experience and Criticism of Works of Art; the Nonaesthetic Context of Art**

A. The aesthetic experience: the apprehension, interpretation, and appreciation of works of art

1. Influences affecting the apprehension of works of art: individual temperament, social and cultural conditioning, acquired attitudes and values

2. The interpretation of works of art

a. Meaning in art

b. Symbol and myth in the arts
[see Division II, below]

3. The appreciation of works of art

4. Special problems of appreciation and apprehension

a. In the sphere of literature
[see 621]

b. In the sphere of the theatrical arts
[see 622, 623, and 625]

c. In the sphere of music
[see 624]

d. In the sphere of the visual arts
[see 626, 627, 628, and 629]

B. The criticism of works of art

1. Diverse criteria of evaluation: aesthetic criteria; criteria related to the union of form and content; criteria related to meaning; criteria related to social, moral, or religious significance; criteria related to technique; criteria related to the intention of the artist

2. The practice of criticism

a. The functions of the critic in relation to the artist, to his work, and to its public reception

b. Critical methods: analytical, interpretative, and descriptive types of criticism

c. Critical styles: journalistic criticism, scholarly criticism, annotative and referential criticism

d. Critical approaches to the arts

e. Factors affecting the excellence of criticism

C. Scholarship in the arts

1. Resources and methods of scholarship in the field of the arts

2. The relation of scholarship in the arts to other humanistic disciplines; *e.g.*, to linguistic studies, to history, to archaeology

D. The interaction of the arts with social, economic, and cultural institutions

1. Social uses of art
[see 521.D.5.]

2. Social control of art: censorship and related forms of regulation

3. The arts and religion
[see 811.E.1.]

4. Technology, science, and the arts
[see 711.B.4.]

5. The arts in education: aesthetic education

E. The economics of art

1. Factors affecting the economic value of a work of art

2. Systems of financing artistic activities

3. The art market

4. Remuneration of artists and protection of their rights

5. Fraudulence in the arts: forgery, piracy, plagiarism

F. The training and work of the artist

1. The preparation of the artist: methods of training

2. Art as a vocation: conditions of work in the arts

3. Professionalism and amateurism in the arts

G. The preservation and dissemination of works of art

1. The role of institutions: libraries and archives; museums and galleries; producing associations—the preservation of works of art by performance

2. The role of writing and notation

3. The role of industry and commerce

4. The role of mechanical and electronic media

5. The role of oral tradition

6. The role of imitative tradition

7. The role of fairs, festivals, exhibitions, expositions, and related phenomena

---

Suggested reading in the *Encyclopædia Britannica*:

MACROPAEDIA: Major articles dealing with the experience and criticism of works of art; the nonaesthetic contexts of art

Arts, Practice and Profession of the
Libraries
Museums

MICROPAEDIA: Selected entries of reference information

General subjects

Actors Studio, The	forgery	Stanislavsky	WPA Federal Art
antique	library	method	Project
Armory Show	little magazine	Treasury Relief Art	
art collection	maniera	Project	
art conservation	Mbari Mbayo Club	Treasury Section	
art criticism	museum	of Painting and	
art history	PEN, International	Sculpture	
Beaux-Arts,	pinacotheca	Universal	
École des	Royal Academy of	Copyright	
Berne Convention	Dramatic Art	Convention	
censorship	Salon	World Intellectual	
copyright	Salon des	Property	
Degenerate Art	Indépendants	Organization	

Biographies

Baumgarten, Alexander Gottlieb	Fenollosa, Ernest F.	Ruskin, John	Vasari, Giorgio
Cotton, Sir Robert Bruce, 1st Baronet	Fry, Roger	Santayana, George	Winckelmann, Johann
	Read, Sir Herbert	Thou, Jacques- Auguste de	
	Rossetti, William		

INDEX: See entries under all of the terms above

Section 613. **Characteristics of the Arts in Particular Cultures**

A. Arts of the Stone Age peoples

B. Arts of the Western tradition

 1. In antiquity: the arts of ancient Egypt and the ancient Middle East, ancient Greek and Hellenistic arts, ancient Roman and Early Christian arts

 2. Arts of the Middle Ages

 3. Arts from the Renaissance to the present in Europe and America

C. Arts of Asian peoples

 1. In East Asia: China, Japan, Korea

 2. In Central Asia: Turkey, Afghanistan, Turkistan, Mongolia, and Siberia; Tibet and other Himalayan countries; the arts of the nomadic peoples

 3. In South Asia: India, Sri Lanka, Kashmir, Pakistan, Bangladesh

 4. In Southeast Asia: Burma, Cambodia, Indonesia, Malaysia, Thailand, Vietnam, the Philippines

D. Arts of the Middle East and of the Islāmic peoples

 1. Arts of the Jewish peoples

 2. Arts of North Africa and of the Arab world

E. Arts of the African peoples

 1. Arts of Sudanic cultures

 2. Arts of Central African cultures

 3. Arts of East African cultures

 4. Arts of Southern African cultures

 5. Arts of West African cultures

F. Arts of the Oceanian peoples

 1. Arts of Melanesia

 2. Arts of Micronesia

 3. Arts of Polynesia

 4. Arts of the Australian Aboriginal peoples

G. Arts of the American Indian peoples

 1. Arts of the Eskimo and North American Indian peoples

 2. Arts of Meso-American peoples

 3. Arts of South American peoples

H. Primitive, folk, and popular arts
 [see also 611.B.3.]

Suggested reading in the *Encyclopædia Britannica:*

MACROPAEDIA: Major articles dealing with the characteristics of the arts in particular cultures; historical development of the arts

African Arts	Egyptian Arts	Middle Eastern	South Asian Arts
American	and Architecture,	Arts and	Southeast
Indians	Ancient	Architecture,	Asian Arts
Central Asian	Folk Arts	Ancient	
Arts	Islāmic Arts	Prehistoric Peoples	
East Asian Arts	Oceanic Arts	and Cultures	

MICROPAEDIA: Selected entries of reference information

arts in particular	Art Deco	Futurism	Ottonian art
cultures:	Art Nouveau	Georgian style	Pop art
African arts	Baroque period	Gothic art	Queen Anne style
Central Asian arts	Bohemian school	Henry IV style	realism
East Asian arts	Byzantine art	Impressionism	Régence style
Egyptian art	Carolingian art	Jacobean age	Regency style
Islāmic arts	Classicism and	Louis XIII style	Renaissance
Korean art	Neoclassicism	Louis XIV style	Rococo style
Oceanic arts	Constructivism	Louis XV style	Romanesque art
Paleolithic Period	Coptic art	Louis XVI style	Romanticism
South Asian arts	Cubism	Mannerism	Stijl, de
Southeast Asian	Dada	minimalism	Stuart style
arts	Early Christian art	modern art	Surrealism
historical periods,	Early	Mozarabic art	Symbolist
styles, schools, and	Netherlandish art	naïve art	movement
movements:	Empire style	Naturalism	Visigothic art
Aestheticism	Expressionism	Novembergruppe	
Anglo-Saxon art	formalism	Op art	

INDEX: See entries under all of the terms above

Division II.   **The Particular Arts**
[For Part Six headnote see page 221.]

Division I deals generally with the theory and classification of the arts, the experience and criticism of works of art, and the interaction of the arts with social, cultural, and economic institutions.

The outlines in the nine sections of Division II treat the particular arts: literature; theatre; motion pictures; music; dance; architecture, garden and landscape design, and urban design; sculpture; drawing, painting, printmaking, and photography; and the arts of decoration and functional design.

Section 621.   **Literature**

A. The art of literature

   1. The nature and scope of literature: the distinction between literature and other forms of writing

   2. Literary composition

   3. The contents of literature: its subject matter

    4. Literature and its audience

    5. The integration of literature with other arts

    6. Literary genres: diverse systems of classifying literary works

    7. Writings on literature: theoretical treatises, scholarly research and writing, critical writing

B. Techniques of literature

    1. Rhetoric: the art of discourse

        a. Elements of rhetoric: figures of speech; *e.g.*, metaphor, simile, personification, hyperbole, allegory, parallelism

        b. The relation of rhetoric to grammar and syntax, to literary diction and style, and to prosody

    2. Prosody: the manipulation of the elements of language that contribute to acoustic and rhythmic effects in literature

        a. Elements of prosody

            i. Rhythmic elements; *e.g.*, accent, beat, cadence, the foot, the stanza, metre

           ii. Acoustic elements; *e.g.*, rhyme, assonance, alliteration

        b. Prosodic style: the uses of prosody in verse, prose, drama, and oratory

C. Kinds of literary composition

    1. Poetry: distinctions between verse and prose

    2. Narrative imaginative literature

        a. Epic; *e.g.*, the "literary" epic, the beast epic, the mock epic, the romantic epic

        b. Saga: the king's sagas, legendary sagas, the sagas of Icelanders, and related forms

        c. Romance: the romance of love, chivalry, and adventure; *e.g.*, Arthurian romance, the pastoral romance, the Gothic romance, the historical romance

        d. The novel and the tale

        e. The short story and its antecedents

        f. Fable, parable, allegory, and related forms

        g. Ballad, lay, idyll

    3. Dramatic or theatrical literature

        a. Tragedy

        b. Comedy

        c. Tragicomedy

        d. Farce and related forms

        e. Melodrama

        f. Religious drama and ritual

        g. Radio, motion-picture, and television scripts

    4. Lyric literature

        a. Music-based lyrics; *e.g.*, ballad, hymn, madrigal

        b. Language-based lyrics; *e.g.*, sonnet, ode, elegy, pastoral

    5. Satiric literature: satire, parody, lampoon

    6. Nonfictional prose literature

        a. The essay

        b. History as literature

        c. Criticism as literature

        d. Doctrinal and religious literature

        e. Philosophical literature

        f. Political literature

        g. Polemical literature

    h. Scientific literature

    i. Reportage: journalism

    j. Aphorism, epigram, adage, maxim, and related short forms

    k. The dialogue: philosophical and literary dialogues

    l. Travel literature

    m. Epistolary literature: the letter as literature

    n. The oration, the speech, and related forms

    o. Biographical and autobiographical literature; *e.g.*, character sketch, critical biography, popular biography, interpretive biography, letter, diary, journal, memoir

  7. Children's literature

  8. Primitive, folk, and popular literature
[see 613]

D. The history of literature

  1. Literature of Western peoples

  2. Literatures of non-Western peoples
[see also 613]

Suggested reading in the *Encyclopædia Britannica*:

MACROPAEDIA: Major articles and biographies dealing with literature

General subjects

African Arts	Dutch Literature	Latin-American	Scandinavian
American Indians	English Literature	Literature	Literature
American	French Literature	Latin Literature	South Asian Arts
Literature	German Literature	Literature, The	Southeast Asian
Australia and	Greek Literature	Art of	Arts
New Zealand,	Hebrew Literature	Literature, The	Spanish Literature
Literatures of	Homeric	History of	Yiddish Literature
Belgian Literature	Epics, The	Western	Yugoslav
Canadian	Hungarian	Oceanic Arts	Literature
Literature	Literature	Polish Literature	
Celtic Literature	Islāmic Arts	Portuguese	
Central Asian Arts	Italian Literature	Literature	
Chinese Literature	Japanese Literature	Rhetoric	
Czechoslovak	Korean Literature	Russian Literature	
Literature			

Biographies

Cervantes	Dostoyevsky	Johnson, Samuel	Shakespeare
Chaucer	Goethe	Milton	Tolstoy
Dante	Greek Dramatists,	Molière	Virgil
Dickens	The Classical	Montaigne	Voltaire

MICROPAEDIA: Selected entries of reference information

General subjects

dramatic literature:	comedy	humours,	revenge tragedy
Absurd, Theatre	dialogue	comedy of	Senecan tragedy
of the	domestic tragedy	intrigue,	sentimental
anagnorisis	dramatic literature	comedy of	comedy
catharsis	fabula Atellana	manners,	slapstick
chronicle play	fabula palliata	comedy of	sotie
climax	farce	melodrama	tragedy
cloak and sword	hamartia	New Comedy	tragicomedy
drama	Hocktide play	Old Comedy	unities
comédie	hubris	prologue and	Wakefield plays
larmoyante		epilogue	

well-made play
York plays
elements of prosody:
  accent
  alliteration
  anapest
  assonance
  caesura
  cynghanedd
  dactyl
  euphony and
    cacophony
  foot
  hexameter
  iamb
  metre
  pentameter
  prosody
  refrain
  rhyme
  rhythm
  spondee
  sprung rhythm
  stanza
  trochee
elements of rhetoric:
  conceit
  hyperbole
  metaphor
  metonymy
  parallelism
  personification
  rhetoric
  simile
epics:
  beast epic
  bylina
  chanson de geste
  cycle
  epic
  epyllion
  Heike monogatari
  Heldenlieder
  heroic poetry
  mock-epic
  skaldic poetry
fable, parable,
  allegory, and
  related forms:
  allegory
  bestiary
  dream allegory
  fable
  parable
  proverb
  riddle
folk literature and
  folklore:
  ballad revival
  dilemma tale

fairy tale
folklore
gaucho literature
good-night
legend
praise song
Raven cycle
romancero
tall tale
trickster tale
literary criticism:
  affective fallacy
  Cambridge critics
  Chicago critic
  Formalism
  Freudian criticism
  literary criticism
  New Criticism
  New Humanism
  organic unity
  race, milieu, and
    moment
  sublime
literary devices:
  anachronism
  anaphora
  consciousness,
    stream of
  flashback
  in medias res
  interior monologue
  irony
  malapropism
  palindrome
  paradox
  pathetic fallacy
  plot
literary groups and
  schools:
  Acmeist
  arcádia
  Arzamas society
  Black Mountain
    poet
  Bloomsbury group
  Cavalier poet
  cénacle
  Confederation
    group
  crepuscolarismo
  Decadent
  fleshly school of
    poetry
  Göttinger Hain
  graveyard school
  Gruppe 47
  Hartford wit
  Heidelberg
    Romantics

Imagist
Kailyard school
Knickerbocker
  school
Lost Generation
makar
Metaphysical poet
Montreal group
neōteros
1927,
  Generation of
'98, Generation of
Northeastern
  school
Parnassian
philosophe
rhetoriqueur
Sicilian school
University wit
lyric poetry:
  alcaic
  alexandrine
  alliterative verse
  alphabet rhyme
  blank verse
  bouts-rimés
  Breton lay
  broadside ballad
  clerihew
  couplet
  cywydd
  dithyramb
  doggerel
  dramatic
    monologue
  eclogue
  elegy
  epigram
  epinicion
  epithalamium
  fabliau
  Fescennine verse
  flyting
  free verse
  fu
  ghazal
  gnomic poetry
  haiku
  Horatian ode
  idyll
  jōruri
  Klephtic ballad
  lauda
  light verse
  limerick
  lyric
  macaronic
  muwashshah
  nonsense verse

nursery rhyme
ode
ottava rima
pattern poetry
Pindaric ode
poetry
praise song
qasida
rhyme royal
sestina
sonnet
Spenserian stanza
terza rima
triolet
vers de société
vers libre
villanelle
waka
yüeh-fu
movements and
  periods:
  American
    Renaissance
  Arabic literary
    renaissance
  Augustan Age
  Beat movement
  Ciceronian period
  Creacionismo
  Decadentism
  Elizabethan
    literature
  Gaelic revival
  Gilded Age
  Golden Age
  Harlem
    Renaissance
  Hermeticism
  Imaginism
  Irish literary
    renaissance
  Midwestern
    Regionalism
  moderne
  gennembrud, det
  Modernismo
  Negritude
  Restoration
    literature
  scapigliatura
  Socialist Realism
  Sturm und Drang
  Transcendentalism
  Ultraísmo
  Unanimism
  verismo
  Young Germany
  Young Poland
    movement

national literatures:
African arts
Albanian literature
American
  literature
Anglo-Norman
  literature
Arabic literature
Armenian
  literature
Australian
  literature
Belgian literature
Breton literature
Bulgarian literature
Burmese literature
Canadian literature
Caribbean
  literature
Celtic literature
Central Asian arts
Chinese literature
Coptic literature
Czechoslovak
  literature
Danish literature
Dutch literature
English literature
Estonian literature
Ethiopian
  literature
Finnish literature
French literature
Frisian literature
Georgian literature
German literature
Greek literature
Hebrew literature
Hungarian
  literature
Icelandic literature
Indian literature
Indonesian
  literatures
Irish literature
Italian literature
Japanese literature
Korean literature
Latin literature
Latin-American
  literature
Latvian literature
Lithuanian
  literature
New Zealand
  literature
Norwegian
  literature
Oceanic arts
Polish literature

Portuguese
  literature
Provençal
  literature
Romanian
  literature
Russian literature
Sanskrit literature
Scandinavian
  literature
Scottish literature
South African
  literature
Southeast Asian
  arts
Spanish literature
Swahili literature
Swedish literature
Swiss literature
Syriac literature
Thai literature
Tibetan literature
Turkish literature
Ukrainian
  literature
Urdu literature
Walloon literature
Welsh literature
Yiddish literature
Yugoslav literature
popular literature:
best-seller
detective story
hard-boiled fiction
mystery story
Onitsha market
  literature
science fiction
work song
prose forms:
antinovel
apology
Bildungsroman
biography
confession
diary
epistolary novel
essay
frame story
Gothic novel
historical novel
I novel
Indianista novel
Künstlerroman
literary sketch
manners, novel of
maqāmah
memoir
nonfiction novel
novel

novella
picaresque novel
psychological novel
roman à clef
roman-fleuve
sentimental novel
short story
romances:
Alexander
  romance
Arthurian legend
Hellenistic
  romance
rímur
romance
*sagas and related
  heroic prose:*
Edda
Fenian cycle
fornaldar saga
heroic prose
Icelanders' sagas
Ossianic ballads
saga
scél
Ulster cycle
satire:
burlesque
fool's literature
Juvenalian satire
parody
pasquinade
satire
travesty
themes and types:
ancients and
  moderns
archetype
Beatrice
Bluebeard
courtly love
Deirdre
Dietrich von Bern
Don Juan
Excalibur
Faust
Galahad
Grail
Griselda
Guinevere
Hagan
hero
Isengrim
Lancelot
Lear
Lohengrin
Mephistopheles
Merlin
Morgan le Fay

noble savage
Perceval
poèt maudit
Round Table
superfluous man
Tristram and
  Isolde
type name
other:
anthology
bard
black humour
Bluestocking
cancioneiro
cànkam literature
chapbook
character writer
children's
  literature
classical literature
conceptismo
costumbrismo
culteranismo
dolce stil nuovo
emblem book
fellow traveller
fili
frontier humour
goliard
Hindi literature
jongleur
journalism
literature
local colour
Marinism
pastoral literature
poet laureate
preciosity
rāwī
saudade
Spielmann
troubadour
trouvère
Utopian literature
Weltschmerz
yellow journalism
Zhdanovshchina

Biographies

African writers:
Achebe, Chinua
Beti, Mongo
Bosman, Herman
  Charles
Boudjedra, Rachid
Clark, John Pepper
Cordeiro da Matta,
  Joaquim Dias
Dib, Mohammed
Ekwensi, Cyprian
Ferreira, Manuel
Kateb Yacine
Kezilahabi,
  Euphrase
Khatibi,
  Abdelkebir
Laye, Camara
Mutswairo,
  Solomon M.
Ngugi, James
Okara, Gabriel
Ousmane
  Sembene
Oyono, Ferdinand
  Léopold
Rabéarivelo,
  Jean-Joseph
Soromenho,
  Fernando
  Monteiro de
  Castro
Soyinka, Wole
Tutuola, Amos

American writers:
Adams, Henry
Alger, Horatio
Anderson,
  Sherwood
Baldwin, James
Bellow, Saul
Berryman, John
Bradstreet, Anne
Bryant, William
  Cullen
Burroughs,
  William
Caldwell, Erskine
Capote, Truman
Cather, Willa
Chapman,
  John Jay
Cooper, James
  Fenimore
Crane, Hart
Crane, Stephen
Dennie, Joseph
Dickinson, Emily
Donnelly, Ignatius

Dos Passos, John
Dreiser, Theodore
Emerson, Ralph
  Waldo
Faulkner, William
Fitzgerald, F. Scott
Frost, Robert
Green, Julien
Harte, Bret
Hawthorne,
  Nathaniel
Hearn, Lafcadio
Hecht, Ben
Hemingway,
  Ernest
Henry, O.
Hughes, Langston
Inge, William
Irving, Washington
James, Henry
Lanier, Sidney
Lewis, Sinclair
Locke, Alain
London, Jack
Longfellow, Henry
  Wadsworth
Lowell, Robert, Jr.
Mailer, Norman
Melville, Herman
Miller, Arthur
Miller, Henry
Nabokov, Vladimir
Nevins, Allan
O'Neill, Eugene
Parker, Dorothy
Poe, Edgar Allan
Pound, Ezra
Salinger, J.D.
Sandburg, Carl
Saroyan, William
Shepard, Sam
Sherwood,
  Robert E.
Simms, William
  Gilmore
Sinclair, Upton
Stein, Gertrude
Steinbeck, John
Stevens, Wallace
Stowe, Harriet
  Beecher
Thoreau, Henry
  David
Thurber, James
Twain, Mark
Van Doren, Mark
Vidal, Gore
Warren, Robert
  Penn

Whitman, Walt
Whittier, John
  Greenleaf
Wiesel, Elie
Williams,
  Tennessee
Wolfe, Thomas
Wright, Richard

Australian writers:
Boldrewood, Rolf
Clarke, Marcus
FitzGerald, Robert
  David
Lawson, Henry
McAuley, James
  Phillip
Paterson, A.B.
Richardson, Henry
  Handel
Stewart, Douglas
White, Patrick

*British and Irish
  writers:*
Addison, Joseph
Akenside, Mark
Arden, John
Auden, W.H.
Austen, Jane
Beaumont, Francis
Behan, Brendan
Belloc, Hilaire
Bennett, Arnold
Blake, William
Boswell, James
Brontë, Charlotte
Brontë, Emily
Browne, Sir
  Thomas
Browning,
  Elizabeth Barrett
Browning, Robert
Bunyan, John
Burns, Robert
Butler, Samuel
Byron, George
  Gordon Byron,
  6th Baron
Carlyle, Thomas
Carroll, Lewis
Cary, Joyce
Chatterton,
  Thomas
Chaucer, Geoffrey
Chesterton, G.K.
Coleridge, Samuel
  Taylor
Collins, William
Congreve, William
Conrad, Joseph

Cowper, William
Crabbe, George
Crichton, James
De Quincey,
  Thomas
Defoe, Daniel
Dickens, Charles
Donne, John
Douglas, Gawin
Dowson, Ernest
Dryden, John
Dunbar, William
Durrell, Lawrence
Edgeworth, Maria
Eliot, George
Eliot, T.S.
Evelyn, John
Farquhar, George
Fielding, Henry
Fletcher, John
Forster, E.M.
Foxe, John
Galsworthy, John
Gascoigne, George
Gaskell, Elizabeth
  Cleghorn
Gay, John
Glyn, Elinor
Graves, Robert
Greene, Graham
Greene, Robert
Hardy, Thomas
Hazlitt, William
Herrick, Robert
Heywood, John
Hopkins, Gerard
  Manley
Housman, A.E.
Hudson, W.H.
Hunt, Leigh
Isherwood,
  Christopher
Johnson, Samuel
Jonson, Ben
Joyce, James
Keats, John
Kipling, Rudyard
Kyd, Thomas
Lawrence, D.H.
Lewis, Wyndham
Lyndsay,
  Sir David
Lytton, Edward
  George Earle
  Bulwer-Lytton,
  1st Baron
Mandeville, Sir
  John

Marlowe,
  Christopher
Meredith, George
Middleton,
  Thomas
Milton, John
Moore, George
O'Casey, Sean
Orwell, George
Otway, Thomas
Pinter, Harold
Pope, Alexander
Ramsay, Allan
Richardson,
  Samuel
Rossetti, Dante
  Gabriel
Ruskin, John
Scott, Sir Walter,
  1st Baronet
Shakespeare,
  William
Shaw, George
  Bernard
Shelley, Percy
  Bysshe
Sheridan, Richard
  Brinsley
Sidney, Sir Philip
Skelton, John
Smollett, Tobias
Southey, Robert
Spenser, Edmund
Steele, Sir Richard
Sterne, Laurence
Stevenson, Robert
  Louis
Swift, Jonathan
Swinburne,
  Algernon Charles
Synge, John
  Millington
Tennyson, Alfred
  Tennyson,
  1st Baron
Thackeray,
  William
  Makepeace
Thomas, Dylan
Trollope, Anthony
Udall, Nicholas
Walpole, Horace,
  4th earl of
  Orford
Waugh, Evelyn
Wells, H.G.
Wilde, Oscar
Wither, George
Woolf, Virginia

Wordsworth,
  William
Yeats, William
  Butler
Canadian writers:
  Callaghan, Morley
  Crémazie, Octave
  Davies, Robertson
  de la Roche, Mazo
  Grove, Frederick
  Philip
  Hémon, Louis
  Johnson, Pauline
  Lampman,
  Archibald
  Layton, Irving
  Leacock, Stephen
  MacLennan, Hugh
  Moodie, Susanna
  Strickland
  Pratt, E.J.
  Richardson, John
  Richler, Mordecai
  Roberts, Sir
  Charles George
  Douglas
  Scott, Duncan
  Campbell
  Scott, F.R.
  Service, Robert W.
  Smith, A.J.M.
*Early Greek and
  Roman writers:*
  Aeschylus
  Aristophanes
  Bacchylides
  Catullus, Gaius
  Valerius
  Cicero, Marcus
  Tullius
  Ennius, Quintus
  Euripides
  Hesiod
  Homer
  Horace
  Juvenal
  Lucan
  Lucian
  Lucretius
  Martial
  Menander
  Ovid
  Petronius Arbiter,
  Gaius
  Pindar
  Plautus
  Pliny the Elder
  Pliny the Younger
  Pollio, Gaius
  Asinius

Propertius, Sextus
Sappho
Seneca, Lucius
  Annaeus
Sophocles
Statius
Suetonius
Tacitus
Terence
Theocritus
Tibullus, Albius
Varro, Marcus
  Terentius
Virgil
Xenophon
East Asian writers:
  Akutagawa
  Ryūnosuke
  Bashō
  Buson
  Cheng Chen-to
  Chikamatsu
  Monzaemon
  Chou Tso-jen
  Ding Ling
  Fujiwara Sadaie
  Futabatei Shimei
  Ihara Saikaku
  Kakinomoto
  Hitomaro
  Kawabata
  Yasunari
  Kuo Mo-jo
  Lao She
  Li Po
  Lu Hsün
  Mao Dun
  Mori Ōgai
  Mishima Yukio
  Murasaki Shikibu
  Natsume Sōseki
  Ōe Kenzaburō
  Ou-yang Hsiu
  Shiga Naoya
  Tu Fu
  Wang An-shih
  Zeami
French writers:
  Adamov, Arthur
  Anouilh, Jean
  Apollinaire,
  Guillaume
  Artaud, Antonin
  Balzac, Honoré de
  Baudelaire, Charles
  Beauvoir,
  Simone de
  Beckett, Samuel
  Camus, Albert

Chateaubriand,
  François-Auguste-
  René, vicomte de
Chenier, André de
Chrétien de Troyes
Claudel, Paul
Cocteau, Jean
Colette
Constant,
  Benjamin
Corneille, Pierre
Diderot, Denis
Dumas, Alexandre
Duras, Marguerite
Flaubert, Gustave
France, Anatole
Gautier, Théophile
Genet, Jean
Gide, André
Giraudoux, Jean
Hugo, Victor
Huysmans,
  Joris-Karl
Ionesco, Eugène
Jarry, Alfred
La Fontaine,
  Jean de
Laforgue, Jules
Lamartine,
  Alphonse de
Machaut,
  Guillaume de
Mallarmé,
  Stéphane
Marivaux, Pierre
Marot, Clément
Maupassant,
  Guy de
Mauriac, François
Mérimée, Prosper
Mistral, Frederic
Molière
Nerval, Gérard de
Proust, Marcel
Rabelais, François
Racine, Jean
Rimbaud, Arthur
Sade, Marquis de
Sand, George
Sartre, Jean-Paul
Scarron, Paul
Staël,
  Germaine de
Stendhal
Valéry, Paul
Verlaine, Paul
Vigny,
  Alfred-Victor,
  comte de
Villon, François

Voltaire
Zola, Émile
German writers:
Alexis, Willibald
Arndt, Ernst
Moritz
Arnim,
Bettina von
Böll, Heinrich
Brecht, Bertolt
Broch, Hermann
Büchner, Georg
Chamisso,
Adelbert von
Dürrenmatt,
Friedrich
Fontane, Theodor
Freiligrath,
Ferdinand
Freytag, Gustav
Frisch, Max
George, Stefan
Goethe, Johann
Wolfgang von
Görres, Joseph von
Gottfried von
Strassburg
Grass, Günter
Grillparzer, Franz
Grimm, Jacob
Ludwig Carl and
Wilhelm Carl
Grimmelshausen,
Hans Jacob
Christoph von
Haller,
Albrecht von
Hartmann
von Aue
Hauptmann,
Gerhart
Hebbel, Friedrich
Heine, Heinrich
Herder, Johann
Gottfried von
Hesse, Hermann
Hoffmann, E.T.A.
Hoffmannsthal,
Hugo von
Hölderlin,
Friedrich
Immermann, Karl
Leberecht
Jean Paul
Johnson, Uwe
Kafka, Franz
Kaiser, Georg
Kaschnitz, Marie
Luise
Keller, Gottfried

Kleist,
Heinrich von
Mann, Thomas
Meyer, Conrad
Ferdinand
Morgenstern,
Christian
Mörike, Eduard
Friedrich
Novalis
Opitz, Martin
Rilke, Rainer
Maria
Schiller,
Friedrich von
Schnitzler, Arthur
Sternheim, Carl
Stifter, Adalbert
Storm, Theodor
Woldsen
Sudermann,
Hermann
Tieck, Ludwig
Trakl, George
Walafrid Strabo
Walther von der
Vogelweide
Wedekind, Frank
Werfel, Franz
Wieland,
Christoph Martin
Wolfram von
Eschenbach
Zuckmayer, Carl
Zweig, Stefan
Hebrew writers:
Agnon, Shmuel
Yosef
Berdichevsky,
Micah Joseph
Bialik, Ḥayyim
Naḥman
Ḥisdai ibn Shaprut
ibn Ezra, Moses
Ibn Gabirol
Judah ha-Levi
Zunz, Leopold
Hungarian writers:
Ady, Endre
Arany, János
Eötvös, József
Báró
Kazinczy, Ferenc
Petöfi, Sándor
Indian writers:
Chatterjee, Bankim
Chandra
Harishchandra
Iqbāl, Sir
Muḥammad

Kālidāsa
Tagore,
Rabindranath
Tulsīdās
Italian writers:
Alfieri, Vittorio,
Conte
Amicis,
Edmondo De
Angiolieri, Cecco
Aretino, Pietro
Ariosto, Ludovico
Bacchelli, Riccardo
Bandello, Matteo
Basile,
Giambattista
Belli, Giuseppe
Gioacchino
Betti, Ugo
Boccaccio,
Giovanni
Boiardo, Matteo
María
Buzzati, Dino
Calvino, Italo
Campanella,
Tommaso
Carducci, Giosuè
Casa, Giovanni
Della
Castiglione,
Baldassare
Cavalcanti, Guido
Chiabrera, Grazia
D'Annunzio,
Gabriele
Dante
Eco, Umberto
Folengo, Teofilo
Foscolo, Ugo
Gadda, Carlo
Emilio
Giraldi,
Giambattista
Goldoni, Carlo
Gozzi, Carlo,
Conte
Leopardi,
Giacomo
Levi, Carlo
Machiavelli,
Niccolò
Maffei, Francesco
Scipione
Malaparte, Curzio
Manzoni,
Alessandro
Marinetti, Filippo
Tommaso

Marino,
Giambattista
Metastasio, Pietro
Montale, Eugenio
Moravia, Alberto
Parini, Giuseppe
Pascoli, Giovanni
Pavese, Cesare
Petrarch
Pirandello, Luigi
Politian
Pratolini, Vasco
Pulci, Luigi
Quasimodo,
Salvatore
Sannazzaro,
Jacopo
Silone, Ignazio
Svevo, Italo
Tasso, Torquato
Tassoni,
Alessandro
Ungaretti,
Giuseppe
Verga, Giovanni
Vittorini, Elio
*Latin-American
writers:*
Agustini, Delmira
Alegría, Ciro
Alencar, José de
Amado, Jorge
Asturias, Miguel
Angel
Azuela, Mariano
Bandeira, Manuel
Bello, Andrés
Benedetti, Mario
Bioy Casares,
Adolfo
Blest Gana,
Alberto
Borges, Jorge Luis
Cardenal, Ernesto
Carpentier, Alejo
Cruz, Sor Juana
Inés de la
Cunha, Euclides de
Darío, Rubén
Durão, José de
Santa Rita
Echeverría,
Esteban
Ercilla y Zúñiga,
Alonso de
Fernández de
Lizardi, José
Joaquín
Freyre, Gilberto de
Mello

Fuentes, Carlos
Gallegos, Rómulo
Gama, José
 Basílio da
García Márquez,
 Gabriel
Gonçalves Dias,
 Antônio
Gonzaga, Thomaz
 Antônio
Graça Aranha,
 Jośe Pereira da
Guillén, Nicolás
Guimarães Rosa,
 João
Güiraldes, Ricardo
Hernández, José
Herrera y Reissig,
 Julio
Huidobro, Vicente
 García
Ibarbourou,
 Juana de
Icaza, Jorge
Isaacs, Jorge
Lins do Rego, José
López y Fuentes,
 Gregorio
Lugones, Leopoldo
Lynch, Benito
Machado de Assis,
 Joaquim María
Mallea, Eduardo
Mármol, José
Martí, José Julián
Matto de Turner,
 Clorinda
Mera, Juan León
Mistral, Gabriela
Neruda, Pablo
Nervo, Amado
Olmedo, José
 Joaquín
Onetti, Juan
 Carlos
Palma, Ricardo
Paz, Octavio
Quiroga, Horacio
Ramos, Graciliano
Reyes, Alfonso
Riviera, José
 Eustacio
Roa Bastos,
 Augusto
Sabato, Ernesto
Sarmiento,
 Domingo
 Faustino
Silva, José
 Asunción
Storni, Alfonsina

Torres Bodet,
 Jaime
Vallejo, César
Vargas Llosa,
 Mario
Vega, Garcilaso de
 la: el Inca
Veríssimo, Enrico
 Lopes
Zorrilla de San
 Martín, Juan
*Middle Eastern
 writers:*
 Cevdet Paşa,
 Ahmed
 Edib Adıvar,
 Halide
 Ferdowsī
 Gökalp, Ziya
 Ḥāfeẓ
 Ḥakīm, Tawfīq al-
 Ibn Baṭṭūṭah
 Ibn Ḥazm
 Jāḥiẓ, al-
 Jamalzadeh,
 Mohammad Ali
 Kemal, Namık
 Ma'arrī, al-
 Mutanabbī, al-
 Omar Khayyam
 Sa'dī
 Taha Hussein
New Zealand writers:
 Baxter, James K.
 Mansfield,
 Katherine
 Sargeson, Frank
 Sinclair, Sir Keith
Portuguese writers:
 Camões, Luís de
 Castelo Branco,
 Camilo
 Deus, João de
 Eça de Queirós,
 José Maria de
 Herculano
 de Carvalho
 e Araújo,
 Alexandre
 Quental, Antero
 Tarquínio de
 Sá de Miranda,
 Francisco de
 Vicente, Gil
 Vieira, António
Scandinavian writers:
 Almqvist, Carl
 Jonas Love
 Andersen, Hans
 Christian
 Asbjørnsen, Peter
 Christen; and

Moe, Jørgen
 Engebretsen
Bergman, Hjalmar
 Fredrik Elgérus
Bjørnson,
 Bjørnst-jerne
 Martinius
Dinesen, Isak
Ewald, Johannes
Fröding, Gustaf
Hamsun, Knut
Holberg, Ludvig,
 Friherre Holberg
Ibsen, Henrik
Jensen,
 Johannes V.
Lagerkvist, Pär
Lagerlöf, Selma
Laxness, Halldór
Pontoppidan,
 Henrik
Rydberg, Viktor
Snorri Sturluson
Strindberg, August
Undset, Sigrid
Wergeland, Henrik
 Arnold
Slavic writers:
 Akhmatova, Anna
 Aksakov, Sergey
 Timofeyevich
 Andrić, Ivo
 Babel, Isaak
 Emmanuilovich
 Bely, Andrey
 Bezruč, Petr
 Blok, Aleksandr
 Aleksandrovich
 Březina, Otakar
 Bulgakov, Mikhail
 Afanasyevich
 Čapek, Karel
 Chekhov, Anton
 Dostoyevsky,
 Fyodor
 Ehrenburg, Ilya
 Grigoryevich
 Fredro, Aleksander
 Gogol, Nikolay
 Gorky, Maksim
 Havel, Václav
 Ilf, Ilya; and
 Petrov, Yevgeny
 Ivanov, Vsevolod
 Vyacheslavovich
 Jirásek, Alois
 Katayev, Valentin
 Khomyakov,
 Aleksey
 Stepanovich
 Krleža, Miroslav
 Kundera, Milan

Lermontov,
 Mikhail
 Lomonosov,
 Mikhail
 Vasilyevich
Mandelstam, Osip
 Emilyevich
Mayakovsky,
 Vladimir
 Vladimirovich
Modrzewki,
 Andrzej
Pasternak, Boris
Pilnyak, Boris
Potocki, Wacław
Pushkin,
 Aleksandr
Rozanov, Vasily
 Vasilyevich
Saltykov, Mikhail
 Yevgrafovich,
 Graf
Seifert, Jaroslav
Sienkiewicz,
 Henryle
Sinyavsky, Andrey
 Donatovich
Slowacki, Juliusz
Solzhenitsyn,
 Aleksandr
Tikhonov, Nikolay
 Semyonovich
Tolstoy, Leo
Tsvetayeva,
 Marina Ivanovna
Turgenev, Ivan
Voznesensky,
 Andrey
 Andreyevich
Yesenin, Sergey
 Aleksandrovich
Yevtushenko,
 Yevgeny
Zamyatin,
 Yevgeny
 Ivanovich
Spanish writers:
 Alarcón y Ariza,
 Pedro Antonio de
 Aleixandre,
 Vicente
 Azorín
 Baroja, Pío
 Bécquer, Gustavo
 Adolfo
 Benavente y
 Martínez, Jacinto
 Blasco Ibáñez,
 Vicente
 Buero Vallejo,
 Antonio

Calderón de la
Barca, Pedro
Cervantes
Saavedra,
Miguel de
Echegaray y
Eizaguirre, José
Encina, Juan del
Espronceda y
Delgado, José de
García Lorca,
Federico
Góngora y Argote,
Luis de
Herrera,
Fernando de
Jiménez, Juan
Ramón
León, Luis de
Palacio Valdés,
Armando
Pardo Bazán,
Emilia
Pérez Galdós,
Benito
Quevedo y
Villegas,
Francisco
Gómez de
Rojas,
Fernando de

Rueda, Lope
Ruiz, Juan
Sender, Ramón
José
Tamayo y Baus,
Manuel
Tirso de Molina
Torres Naharro,
Bartolomé de
Unamuno,
Miguel de
Valera y Alcalá
Galiano, Juan
Valle-Inclán,
Ramón María del
Vega, Garcilaso
de la
Vega, Lope de
Zorrilla y Moral,
José
theorists and critics:
Arnold, Matthew
Barbey d'Aurevilly,
Jules-Amédée
Boileau, Nicolas
Brandes, Georg
Breton, André
Burke, Kenneth
Empson, Sir
William
Frye, Northrop

Fuller, Margaret
Gottsched, Johann
Christoph
Henley, William
Ernest
Howells, William
Dean
Lamb, Charles
Leavis, F.R.
Lessing, Gotthold
Ephraim
Lowell, James
Russell
Menéndez Pidal,
Ramón
Menéndez y
Pelayo, Marcelino
Merezhkovsky,
Dmitry
Sergeyevich
Mochnacki,
Maurycy
Ortega y Gasset,
José
Papini, Giovanni
Pater, Walter
Roy, Camille
Rymer, Thomas
Sainte-Beuve,
Charles-Augustin
Saintsbury, George

Schlegel, August
Wilhelm von
Schlegel,
Friedrich von
Stephen, Sir Leslie
Wilson, Edmund
Yiddish writers:
Ansky, S.
Asch, Sholem
Goldfaden,
Abraham
Mendele Moykher
Sforim
Peretz, Isaac Leib
Singer, Isaac
Bashevis
other:
Conscience,
Hendrik
Ghelderode,
Michel de
Kazantzákis,
Níkos
Koraïs,
Adamántios
Verhaeren, Émile
Vondel, Joost
van den

Section 622. **Theatre**

A. The art of theatre

   1. The nature and origins of theatre as an art

   2. Functions of theatre and theatrical production; *e.g.*, theatre as social, moral, or religious expression; theatre as entertainment

   3. Problems of theatre and theatrical production

   4. Interrelation of theatrical performance and audience

   5. The arts of design in the theatre: staging and the design of stages, sets, lights, costumes, and makeup
     [see C.2., below]

   6. Directing

   7. Acting

   8. The roles of other arts in the theatre: literature, music, dance, painting, and architecture
     [see C., below]

B. Kinds and methods of theatrical production

   1. Diverse kinds of theatrical production

     a. Kinds defined by the nature of the production itself

       i. The traditional dramatic forms or genres; *e.g.*, tragedy, comedy
        [for these forms as literature, see 621.C.3.]

       ii. Dramatic improvisation: commedia dell'arte and related forms

       iii. Mime and pantomime

        iv. Puppet, marionette, and shadow plays and related forms

        v. Nondramatic theatrical production
        [see B.1.f., below]

    b. Kinds defined by their special purpose or audience; *e.g.*, religious theatre, civic theatre, educational theatre, court theatre

    c. Kinds defined by their system of production; *e.g.*, single-performance productions, repertory systems, stock companies, touring companies

    d. Kinds defined by the controlling artist; *e.g.*, actor-dominated productions, dramatist-controlled productions, productions controlled by a nonperforming director

    e. Kinds defined by their style: general aesthetic style; styles of particular countries, historical periods, and playwrights

    f. Kinds defined by the lack of a unified dramatic structure

        i. Circuses and carnivals

        ii. Pageants, parades, and related forms

        iii. Popular entertainments: music hall, variety, and burlesque productions; nightclub shows; cabaret; musical comedy and revue

    g. Kinds defined by the cultural character of their audience: primitive, folk, and popular theatre
    [see 611.B.3.]

  2. Methods of theatrical production

C. Elements of theatrical production

  1. The production area: theatre buildings, stages, auditoriums

    a. Theatre as place: kinds and uses of theatre buildings, stages, and auditoriums

    b. The historical development of theatres in Western and non-Western cultures

  2. Staging and stage design: the arrangement of words, dance, music, costumes, makeup, lighting, sound, and properties for theatrical effect

D. The history of theatre

  1. Western theatre

  2. Non-Western theatre
  [see also 613]

Suggested reading in the *Encyclopædia Britannica*:

MACROPAEDIA: Major articles dealing with the theatre

African Arts	Oceanic Arts	Theatre, The Art	Theatrical
American Indians	Puppetry	of the	Production
Central Asian Arts	South Asian Arts	Theatre, The	
Circus	Southeast Asian	History of	
East Asian Arts	Arts	Western	
Folk Arts			

MICROPAEDIA: Selected entries of reference information

General subjects

dramatic conventions and techniques:	courtyard theatre	stock company	environmental theatre
agon	directing	summer theatre	Fact, Theatre of
lazzo	hanamichi	theatre	little theatre
soliloquy	open stage	theatre-in-the-round	Living Newspaper
elements of theatrical production:	proscenium	*movements and tendencies:*	Open Theatre
acting	régisseur	Absurd, Theatre	theatricalism
actor-manager	repertory theatre	of the	
system	skene	biomechanics	
chorus	Stanislavsky	Cruelty, Theatre of	
	method		

popular dramatic
entertainment:
burlesque show
cabaret
carnival
circus
conjuring
Fasching
ice show
masque
mime and
pantomime
minstrel show
music hall and
variety
pageant
revue
shell game
son et lumière
vaudeville
Wild West show
staging and stage
design:
cyclorama
deus ex machina
eccyclema
limelight
Linnebach lantern

mansion
multiple setting
pageant wagon
perspective scenery
scene shifting
sound effects
spotlight
stage design
stage machinery
trap
stock characters:
Brighella
Capitano
Columbine
Dottore
Guignol
Harlequin
Kasperle
Miles Gloriosus
Pantaloon
Pedrolino
Punch
Scaramouche
soubrette
zanni
types of theatrical
production:
afterpiece
auto sacramental

black theatre
bunraku
ching-hsi
Comédie-Française
Comédie-Italienne
commedia dell'arte
commedia erudita
drame bourgeois
droll
epic theatre
farce
Fastnachtsspiel
interlude
Jesuit drama
kabuki
Karagög
liturgical drama
ludi scaenici
melodrama
miracle play
morality play
mumming play
mystery play
nō theatre
ombres chinoises
Passion play
sacra
rappresentazione
Satyr play

wayang
Yiddish drama
other:
benefit
performance
children's
company
choragus
civic theatre
claque
clown
East Asian arts
Enfants san Souci
Englische
Komödianten
improvisation
Islāmic arts
juggler
Misrule, Lord of
Oceanic arts
peep show
South Asian arts
Southeast Asian
arts
toy theatre
ventriloquism

Biographies

actors and actresses:
Ashcroft, Dame
Peggy
Barrymore, Lionel
Bernhardt, Sarah
Booth, Edwin
Cooper, Dame
Gladys
Duse, Eleonora
Gwyn, Nell
Irving, Sir Henry
Kean, Edmund
Kemble, John
Philip
Kendal, Dame
Margaret; and
William Hunter
Kortner, Fritz

Lenya, Lotte
Lunt, Alfred; and
Fontanne, Lynn
Mathews, Charles
Murdoch, James
Edward
Nakamura
Utaemon
Neuber, Caroline
Olivier, Laurence
Paxinou, Katina
Siddons, Sarah
Taylor, Laurette
Terry, Ellen
Worth, Irene
directors:
Barrault,
Jean-Louis
Burian, Emil

Craig, Edward
Gordon
Guthrie,
Sir Tyrone
Littlewood,
Joan
Popov, Alexey
Dmitriyevich
Reinhardt, Max
Stanislavsky,
Konstantin
Zavadsky, Yury
Alexandrovich
producers:
Belasco, David
Meyerhold,
Vsevolod
Yemilyevich

Richardson, Tony
Shubert brothers
other:
Barnum, P.T.
Henslowe, Philip
Lupino family
Macready, William
Charles
Ringling Brothers

INDEX: See entries under all of the terms above

Section 623.   Motion Pictures

A. The art of motion pictures

   1. The nature of motion-picture art: the classification of motion pictures

2. The component arts of motion pictures

   a. The role of the writer of the script or screenplay
      [see 621.C.3.g.]

   b. Motion-picture acting: characteristics that distinguish it from acting in the theatre

   c. The role of the director

   d. The role of the film editor

   e. The use of technology in the creative process: the camera, sound, animation, and other special effects

3. Motion-picture production: scenic design, costumes and make-up, lighting, shooting, editing, film processing

B. The interrelation of other arts in motion pictures: literature, music, dance, painting and drawing, architecture

C. The nonaesthetic contexts of motion pictures

   1. The motion-picture industry

   2. Functions of motion pictures: their use as media of education and propaganda

   3. The study and appreciation of motion pictures

D. The history of motion pictures

Suggested reading in the *Encyclopædia Britannica*:

MACROPAEDIA: Major article dealing with motion pictures

   Motion Pictures

MICROPAEDIA: Selected entries of reference information

General subjects

animation	dubbing	musical film	3-D
auteur theory	horror film	New Wave	underground film
cinéma vérité	Metro-Goldwyn-Mayer,	newsreel	Warner Brothers
CinemaScope	Inc.	reel	
cinematography	montage	script	
documentary film	motion picture	Technicolor	

Biographies

actors and actresses:	Muni, Paul	Fellini, Federico	Sternberg,
Astaire, Fred	Newman, Paul	Ford, John	Josef von
Bergman, Ingrid	Olivier, Laurence	Godard, Jean-Luc	Stroheim,
Bogart, Humphrey	Pickford, Mary	Griffith, D.W.	Erich von
Brando, Marlon	Stewart, James	Hawks, Howard	Truffaut, François
Chaplin, Charlie	Sydow, Max von	Hitchcock, Sir	Vertov, Dziga
Crawford, Joan	Tracy, Spencer	Alfred	*producers:*
Davis, Bette	Wayne, John	Huston, John	Disney, Walt
De Niro, Robert	Welles, Orson	Kurosawa Akira	Goldwyn, Samuel
Garbo, Greta	*directors:*	Lean, Sir David	Korda, Sir
Gish, Lillian	Antonioni,	Lubitsch, Ernst	Alexander
Grant, Cary	Michelangelo	Malle, Louis	Mayer, Louis B.
Guinness, Sir Alec	Bergman, Ingmar	Ousmane	Selznick, David O.
Hepburn,	Buñuel, Luis	Sembene	*other:*
Katharine	Capra, Frank	Pabst, G.W.	Lumière, Auguste
Hoffman, Dustin	Cavalcanti, Alberto	Pagnol, Marcel	and Louis
Lloyd, Harold	Clair, René	Paul	Mankiewicz,
March, Fredric	deMille, Cecil B.	Ray, Satyajit	Herman
Mastroianni,	Dreyer, Carl	Renoir, Jean	Muybridge,
Marcello	Theodor	Rossellini, Roberto	Eadweard
Mifune Toshiro	Eisenstein, Sergey	Sennett, Mack	Westmore family
Monroe, Marilyn			

Section 624.   Music

A. The art of music

   1. Diverse conceptions of music as an art

   2. Problems of musical meaning

   3. Problems of musical interpretation

   4. The relation of music to other human activities

   5. Writings about music

B. The sources of musical sound

   1. The physical aspects of musical sound: tone, movement, pitch, timbre
      [see 128.E.6.]

   2. The human voice: techniques, styles, and historical developments of the art of singing in Western and non-Western cultures
      [see also 421.C.1. and 3.]

   3. Musical instruments: the history, technology, and technique of classes and specific types of instruments

      a. Idiophonic and membranophonic instruments: instruments that produce sound by means of percussion

      b. Aerophonic instruments: instruments that produce sound by the vibration of a column of air

      c. Chordophonic instruments: instruments that produce sound by the vibration of struck, plucked, or bowed strings

      d. Electrophonic instruments: instruments that produce sound by electrical, electromechanical, or electronic means; *e.g.*, electronic organs, tape recorders, synthesizers, computers

C. The elements of music: their patterning and modes of organization in composition

   1. Pitch

      a. Interval: the difference in pitch between two tones

      b. Scale: a pattern of pitch relationships expressed as a series of intervals dividing an octave

      c. Tuning and temperament: the organization and modification of systems of pitch relationships

      d. Motive and theme

      e. Mode, melody type, tune family

   2. Duration (time)

      a. Pulse and metre

      b. Rhythm

      c. Tempo

   3. Timbre

   4. Harmony

   5. Counterpoint

   6. Texture: monophonic, homophonic, heterophonic, polyphonic

   7. Orchestration and instrumentation

   8. Musical forms and variations

D. Musical notation

E. Forms of musical composition

   1. Instrumental forms

      a. Sonata

      b. Symphony

       c. Concerto

       d. Variation forms; *e.g.*, chaconne, passacaglia, variation set

       e. Fugue

       f. Forms for electrophonic instruments: *e.g.*, tape music, computer music

   2. Vocal forms

       a. Solo vocal forms

          i. Liturgical chant

         ii. Secular song; *e.g.*, chanson, canzone

        iii. "Art song"; *e.g.*, lied, concert aria

       b. Choral forms

          i. Sacred choral forms; *e.g.*, mass, motet, anthem, cantata, oratorio

         ii. Secular choral forms; *e.g.*, secular cantata, symphonic choral music

        iii. Occasional choral music: choral forms composed to commemorate an occasion of state; *e.g.*, a royal marriage

       c. Vocal forms for solo or choral performance

          i. Madrigal

         ii. Lied, chanson, glee

F. Musical performance

G. Chamber music

H. Music for the theatre
[see also 622.A.8.]

   1. General considerations about theatrical music; *e.g.*, its nature and elements, its role as distinct from the role of concert music, its relation to other elements of theatre

   2. Types of theatrical music

       a. Opera

       b. Music for theatrical dance; *e.g.*, ballet, modern dance
[see 625]

       c. Music theatre; *e.g.*, musical, operetta, zarzuela, Nō theatre
[see 622.B.1.]

       d. Incidental and background music; *e.g.*, for the theatre, for motion pictures and television

I. Jazz

   1. General considerations about jazz: its differentiation from and relation to folk music, popular music, and "art" music; its emphasis on the performer as creator; the importance of improvisation; its reflection of social and cultural forces

   2. Development of jazz styles

J. Primitive, folk, and popular music
[see 613]

K. Recording and reproduction of music

   1. Types of music reproduction: mechanical, acoustical, electrical
[see 735.F.]

   2. Techniques of music recording: the role of the producer

   3. Effects of music recording: on composition, on teaching, on criticism, on performance, on musicology

   4. Development of music recording

L. The history of music

   1. Western music

   2. The music of non-Western peoples
[see also 613]

Suggested reading in the *Encyclopædia Britannica:*

MACROPAEDIA: Major articles and biographies dealing with music

African Arts	Folk Arts	Musical Forms and	Southeast Asian
American Indians	Mozart	Genres	Arts
Bach	Music, The Art of	Musical	
Beethoven	Music, The	Instruments	
Central Asian Arts	History of	Oceanic Arts	
East Asian Arts	Western	South Asian Arts	

MICROPAEDIA: Selected entries of reference information

General subjects

aerophones—brass	saxophone	lute	arrangement
instruments:	shakuhachi	mandolin	cadenza
alphorn	shawm	mandora	canon
bugle	sheng	p'i-p'a	cantus firmus
cornet	whistle	rabāb	coda
euphonium	*chordophones—harp*	rebec	counterpoint
French horn	*family:*	samisen	fauxbourdon
horn	Aeolian harp	san-hsien	fugue
ophicleide	angular harp	sārangī	ground bass
saxhorn	arched harp	sitar	hocket
serpent	frame harp	tar	instrumentation
trombone	harp	theorbo	leitmotiv
trumpet	Irish harp	'umd	melody
tuba	konghou	viol	musical variation
aerophones—	musical bow	viola	ornamentation
keyboard	pedal harp	violin	ostinato
instruments:	*chordophones—*	yüeh-ch'in	paraphrase
accordion	*keyboard*	*chordophones—lyre*	parody
barrel organ	*instruments:*	*family:*	period
concertina	clavichord	crwth	ritornello
harmonium	clavicytherium	kinnor	*elements of pitch:*
organ	dulce melos	kithara	church mode
positive organ	harpsichord	lyre	combination tone
regal	piano	pluriarc	comma
aerophones—	player piano	*chordophones—zither*	consonance and
woodwind	spinet	*family:*	dissonance
instruments:	square piano	Autoharp	diatonic
aulos	upright piano	ch'in	ēchos
bagpipe	virginal	cimbalom	equal temperament
basset horn	*chordophones—lute*	dulcimer	gamut
bassoon	*and fiddle families:*	koto	hexachord
clarinet	balalaika	monochord	meantone
curtal	banjo	psaltery	temperament
English horn	cello	trumpet marine	microtonal music
fife	chitarrone	vina	mode
flageolet	cittern	wagon	musica ficta
flute	double bass	yang-ch'in	octave species
harmonica	erh-hu	zither	overtone
heckelphone	fiddle	*electrophones:*	pentatonic scale
hichiriki	gittern	electronic carillon	pitch
hornpipe	guitar	electronic organ	scale
musette	gusla	music synthesizer	solmization
oboe	hu-ch'in	ondes martenot	tessitura
ocarina	hurdy-gurdy	theremin	tetrachord
panpipe	kamanjā	trautonium	timbre
pipe and	koboz	*elements of*	tone
tabor	lira	*composition:*	tonos
recorder		accompaniment	

tune family
tuning and
  temperament
white noise
whole-tone scale
ensembles—
  instrumental:
  band
  orchestra
  quartet
  quintet
  trio
ensembles—vocal:
  choir
  quartet
  responsorial
   singing
  trio
forms—general:
  aleatory music
  aria
  Bar form
  barcarole
  berceuse
  binary form
  caccia
  cantilena
  capriccio
  carol
  character piece
  clausula
  conductus
  cyclic form
  finale
  fuging tune
  lai
  minuet
  nocturne
  quodlibet
  recitative
  serenade
  ternary form
harmonic elements:
  appoggiatura
  atonality
  cadence
  chord
  chromaticism
  drone
  enharmonic
  harmony
  interval
  inversion
  key
  modulation
  monody
  organum
  pedal point
  polytonality
  thorough bass
  tonality
  tritone

idiophones:
  bell
  bell chime
  carillon
  castanets
  celesta
  clapper
  claves
  crotal
  cymbal
  glass harmonica
  glockenspiel
  gong
  handbell
  Jew's harp
  jingling Johnny
  lamellaphone
  marimba
  music box
  rattle
  scraper
  sistrum
  slit drum
  steel drum
  stone chimes
  triangle
  tubular bells
  vibraphone
  wind-bell
  xylophone
instrumental forms:
  canzona
  chaconne
  chamber music
  chorale prelude
  concerto
  concerto grosso
  courante
  divertimento
  estampie
  étude
  fanfare
  fantasia
  gigue
  impromptu
  invention
  Konzertstück
  march
  musique concrète
  overture
  passacaglia
  prelude
  quartet
  quintet
  ricercare
  rondo
  scherzo
  sinfonia
  sonata
  sonatina
  suite

symphonic poem
symphony
toccata
trio
trio sonata
vocal-instrumental
  concerto
instruments—
  classifications:
  aerophone
  brass instrument
  chordophone
  electronic
   instrument
  electrophone
  idiophone
  keyboard
   instrument
  membranophone
  percussion
   instrument
  reed instrument
  stringed
   instrument
  transposing
   musical
   instrument
  wind instrument
  woodwind
instruments—
  components:
  crook
  pipe
  tracker action
  valve
jazz styles:
  bebop
  Chicago style
  cool jazz
  Dixieland
  free jazz
  jazz
  jazz-rock
  Kansas City style
  New Orleans style
  scat
  swing
medieval musicians:
  meistersinger
  minnesinger
  minstrel
  troubadour
  trouvère
  wait
membranophones:
  bass drum
  drum
  dùndún pressure
   drum
  friction drum

kettledrum
snare drum
tablā
tambourine
timpani
tsuzumi
music history, theory,
  and training:
  affections, doctrine
   of the
  Ars Antiqua
  Ars Nova
  colour music
  conservatory
  ethnomusicology
  musical societies
   and institutions
  musicology
  program music
  Roman de Fauvel
  schola cantorum
  solfeggio
musical schools and
  styles:
  Burgundian school
  concertato style
  empfindsamer Stil
  Franco-Netherlandish
   school
  Gebrauchsmusik
  gymel
  Mannheim school
  Notre-Dame
   school
  Postromantic
   music
  serialism
  Tin Pan Alley
musical textures:
  heterophony
  homophony
  monophony
  polyphony
non-Western music:
  ālāpa
  Carnatic music
  Chinese music
  dastgah
  gagaku
  gamelan
  Hindustani music
  Indian music
  Japanese music
  Korean music
  maqām
  nagauta
  raga
  tāla
  taqsīm
  Vedic chant

notation:
accidental
clef
mensural notation
musical notation
neume
note
score
shape-note hymnal
staff
tablature
time signature
performance
technique:
bel canto
conductor
improvisation
musical expression
singing
popular forms:
bluegrass
blues
boogie-woogie
bossa nova
calypso
country and
western
gospel music
kivela
ragtime
reggae
rhythm and blues
rock
shanty
spiritual
rhythmic elements:
accent
aksak
beat
eurhythmics

īqāʿāt
isorhythm
metre
polyrhythm
rhythm
rhythmic mode
rubato
syncopation
theatre music:
ballad opera
cabaletta
Camerata
cavatina
drinking song
incidental music
intermezzo
libretto
music drama
musical
Nigerian theatre
opera
opera buffa
opéra-comique
opera seria
operetta
Singspiel
verismo
zarzuela
vocal forms—sacred:
Ambrosian chant
Anglican chant
anthem
antiphon
Armenian chant
Byzantine chant
canonical hours
cantata
canticle
chorale
Coptic chant

Ethiopian chant
Gallican chant
Gregorian chant
hymn
kontakion
liturgical music
mass
Mi-Sinai tune
motet
Mozarabic chant
Old Roman chant
oratorio
Passion music
plainsong
psalm tone
psalmody
requiem mass
responsory
Russian chant
Sarum chant
sequence
Syrian chant
Te Deum
Laudamus
troparion
trope
vocal forms—secular:
air de cour
ayre
ballade
balletto
cantiga
cantillation
canzonetta
carnival song
catch
chanson
frottola
glee
goliard

lied
madrigal
madrigal comedy
mélodie
musique mesurée
nigun
rondeau
serenata
song
villancico
villanella
villota
virelai
yodel
vocal registers:
alto
baritone
bass
castrato
countertenor
falsetto
soprano
tenor
other:
bull-roarer
cantor
change ringing
computer music
Greek music
metronome
music
musical
composition
national anthem

Biographies

composers—Ars Nova
period:
Adam de la Halle
Landini, Francesco
Machaut,
Guillaume de
Sachs, Hans
composers—Baroque:
Bach, Johann
Sebastian
Buxtehude,
Dietrich
Corelli, Arcangelo
Couperin, François
Couperin, Louis
Dittersdorf, Karl
Ditters von
Frescobaldi,
Girolamo
Handel, George
Frideric
Purcell, Henry

Rameau,
Jean-Philipp
Scarlatti,
Domenico
Schein, Johann
Hermann
Schütz, Heinrich
Telemann, Georg
Philipp
Vivaldi, Antonio
composers—Classical
period:
Arne, Thomas
Bach, Carl Philipp
Emanuel
Beethoven,
Ludwig van
Boccherini, Luigi
Boyce, William
Cherubini, Luigi
Clementi, Muzio

Gluck, Christoph
Willibald
Haydn, Joseph
Mozart, Wolfgang
Amadeus
Pleyel, Ignace
Joseph
composers—modern:
Barber, Samuel
Bartók, Béla
Berg, Alban
Bernstein, Leonard
Boulez, Pierre
Cage, John
Carter, Elliott, Jr.
Copland, Aaron
Cowell, Henry
Debussy, Claude
Hindemith, Paul
Honegger, Arthur
Ives, Charles

Janáček, Leoš
Krenek, Ernst
Messiaen, Olivier
Milhaud, Darius
Penderecki,
Krzysztof
Poulenc, Francis
Prokofiev, Sergey
Ravel, Maurice
Roussel, Albert
Satie, Erik
Schoenberg,
Arnold
Scriabin,
Aleksandr
Shostakovich,
Dmitry
Stockhausen,
Karlheinz
Strauss, Richard
Stravinsky, Igor

Villa-Lobos, Heitor
Webern,
  Anton von
Weill, Kurt
Xenakis, Iannis
composers—opera:
  Bellini, Vincenzo
  Bizet, Georges
  Britten, Benjamin,
    Baron Britten of
    Aldeburgh
  Cimarosa,
    Domenico
  Donizetti, Gaetano
  Gounod, Charles
  Henze, Hans
    Werner
  Lully,
    Jean-Baptiste
  Massenet, Jules
  Menotti, Gian
    Carlo
  Meyerbeer,
    Giacomo
  Offenbach, Jacques
  Paisiello, Giovanni
  Puccini, Giacomo
  Rossini,
    Gioacchino
  Scarlatti,
    Alessandro
  Sullivan, Sir
    Arthur
  Verdi, Giuseppe
  Wagner, Richard
composers—popular:
  Arlen, Harold
  Billings, William
  Comden, Betty;
    and Green, Adolf
  Duke, Vernon
  Foster, Stephen
  Gershwin, George
  Lerner, Alan Jay
  Lloyd Webber,
    Andrew
  Loewe, Frederick
  Mercer, Johnny
  Porter, Cole
  Rodgers, Richard
  Sondheim, Stephen
  Warren, Harry
composers—
  Renaissance:
  Blow, John
  Byrd, William
  Cabezón,
    Antonio de
  Dowland, John
  Dufay, Guillaume
  Gabrieli, Andrea
  Gabrieli, Giovanni
  Gibbons, Orlando
  Isaac, Heinrich

Josquin des Prez
Lasso, Orlando di
Monteverdi,
  Claudio
Morley, Thomas
Ockeghem, Jean d'
Palestrina,
  Giovanni
  Pierluigi da
Tallis, Thomas
Weelkes, Thomas
Wilbye, John
Zarlino, Gioseffo
composers—
  Romantic period:
  Balakirev, Mily
  Berlioz, Hector
  Borodin,
    Aleksandr
  Brahms, Johannes
  Bruckner, Anton
  Chabrier,
    Emmanuel
  Chopin, Frédéric
  Delius, Frederick
  Dukas, Paul
  Dvořák, Antonín
  Elgar, Sir Edward
  Fauré, Gabriel
  Franck, César
  Glière, Reinhold
  Glinka, Mikhail
  Grieg, Edvard
  Holst, Gustav
  Indy, Vincent d'
  Liszt, Franz
  MacDowell,
    Edward
  Mahler, Gustav
  Mendelssohn, Felix
  Mussorgsky,
    Modest
  Paderewski, Ignacy
  Paganini, Niccolò
  Rachmaninoff,
    Sergey
  Respighi, Ottorino
  Rimsky-Korsakov,
    Nikolay
  Rubinstein, Anton
    Grigoryevich
  Saint-Saëns,
    Camille
  Schubert, Franz
  Schumann, Robert
  Sibelius, Jean
  Smetana, Bedřich
  Strauss, Johann
  Tchaikovsky, Peter
    Ilich
  Vaughan Williams,
    Ralph
  Weber, Carl
    Maria von

Wolf, Hugo
conductors:
  Ansermet, Ernest
  Beecham, Sir
    Thomas
  Beinum,
    Eduard van
  Bernstein, Leonard
  Damrosch, Walter
    Johannes
  Furtwängler,
    Wilhelm
  Goossens, Sir
    Eugene
  Karajan,
    Herbert von
  Klemperer, Otto
  Koussevitzky,
    Serge
  Mengelberg,
    Willem
  Monteux, Pierre
  Munch, Charles
  Nikisch, Arthur
  Ormandy, Eugene
  Reiner, Fritz
  Solti, Sir George
  Stokowski,
    Leopold
  Szell, George
  Thomas, Theodore
  Toscanini, Arturo
  Walter, Bruno
  Weingartner, Felix
instrument makers:
  Amati family
  Bohn, Theodor
  Cavaille-Coll,
    Aristide
  Cristofori,
    Bartolomeo
  Guarneri family
  Hammond,
    Laurens
  Stein, Johann
    Andreas
  Steinway, Henry
    Engelhard
  Stradivari, Antonio
  Willis, Henry
  Wurlitzer family
musicians—blues,
  country, gospel, pop,
  rock:
  Acuff, Roy
  Baez, Joan
  Beatles, the
  Carter family
  Charles, Ray
  Crosby, Bing
  Franklin, Aretha
  Guthrie, Woody
  Hendrix, Jimi
  Jackson, Mahalia

Jolson, Al
Lauder, Sir Harry
Monroe, Bill
Presley, Elvis
Rainey, Ma
Rolling Stones
Seeger, Pete
Sinatra, Frank
Smith, Bessie
musicians—ragtime,
  jazz, swing, bebop:
  Armstrong, Louis
  Basie, Count
  Coltrane, John
  Davis, Miles
  Dorsey, Jimmy
    and Tommy
  Ellington, Duke
  Gillespie, Dizzy
  Goodman, Benny
  Hines, Earl
  Holiday, Billie
  Joplin, Scott
  Kenton, Stan
  Miller, Glenn
  Parker, Charlie
  Shaw, Artie
  Silver, Horace
  Whiteman, Paul
musicologists:
  Adler, Guido
  Burney, Charles
  Chrysander, Karl
    Franz Friedrich
  Guido of Arezzo
  Hornbostel, Erich
    Moritz von
  Sachs, Curt
  Sharp, Cecil
pianists:
  Bülow, Hans,
    Freiherr von
  Busoni, Ferruccio
  Cortot,
    Alfred-Denis
  Gieseking, Walter
  Godowsky,
    Leopold
  Hess, Dame Myra
  Horowitz,
    Vladimir
  Paderewski,
    Ignacy Jan
  Rubinstein, Anton
    Grigoryevich
  Schnabel, Artur
singers—baritones
  and basses:
  Chaliapin, Feodor
  Fischer, Johann
    Ignaz Ludwig
  Fischer-Dieskau,
    Dietrich

Lablache, Luigi
Maurel, Victor
Pinza, Ezio
  Fortunato
Robeson, Paul
Warren, Leonard
singers—contraltos:
Alboni, Marietta
Anderson, Marian
Butt, Dame Clara
  Ellen
Ferrier, Kathleen
Homer, Louise
Schumann-Heink,
  Ernestine
singers—
  mezzo-sopranos:
Artot, Désirée
Baker, Dame Janet
  Abbott
Berganza, Teresa
Gerhardt, Elena

Horne, Marilyn
Malibran, Maria
Viardot, Michelle
  Ferdinande
singers—sopranos:
Callas, Maria
Destinn, Emma
Farrar, Geraldine
Flagstad, Kirsten
Galli-Curci,
  Amelita
Garden, Mary
Grisi, Giulia
Lehmann, Lotte
Lind, Jenny
Melba, Dame
  Nellie
Nilsson, Marta
  Birgit
Pons, Lily
Ponselle, Rosa
Price, Leontyne

Schumann,
  Elisabeth
Sills, Beverly
Sutherland, Dame
  Joan
singers—tenors:
Björling, Jussi
Caruso, Enrico
Domingo, Plácido
Duprez,
  Gilbert-Louis
García, Manuel del
  Popolo
Garciá, Manuel
  Patricio
  Rodriguez
Gigli, Beniamino
McCormack, John
Mario, Giovanni
  Matteo
Nourrit, Adolphe
Pavarotti, Luciano

Pears, Sir Peter
Raaff, Anton
Reszke, Jean de
Rubini, Giovanni
  Battista
Slezak, Leo
Tucker, Richard
violinists:
Auer, Leopold
Elman, Mischa
Heifetz, Jascha
Joachim, Joseph
Menuhin, Sir
  Yehudi
Oistrakh, David
  Fyodorovich
Paganini, Niccolò
Perlman, Itzhak
Ysaÿe, Eugène

INDEX: See entries under all of the terms above

Section 625.   Dance

A. The art of dance

  1. The nature of dance as art: its origins and functions

  2. Choreography and dance notation

  3. Diverse classifications of kinds of dance

  4. Theoretical, critical, and descriptive writing about dance

  5. The integration of dance with other arts: dance in the theatre, in motion pictures
     [see 622.A.8. and 623.B.]

B. Ballet

  1. The nature of ballet as an art

  2. The integration of ballet with other arts; *e.g.*, with opera, drama, motion pictures, television

  3. Major kinds of ballet: traditional, classical, modern, abstract, expressive

  4. The history of ballet

C. Modern dance

  1. Principles underlying modern dance: expression and communication of feeling

  2. The relation of modern dance to other arts; *e.g.*, with musical theatre, drama, motion pictures, television

  3. Development of modern dance: kinds, theories, techniques, and methods of modern dance

D. Primitive, folk, and popular dance
   [see 613]

E. The history of dance

  1. The dance of Western peoples

  2. The dance of non-Western peoples
     [see also 613]

Suggested reading in the *Encyclopædia Britannica*:

MACROPAEDIA: Major articles dealing with dance

African Arts
American Indians
Central Asian Arts
Dance, The Art of
Dance, The
 History of
 Western

East Asian Arts
Folk Arts
Oceanic Arts
South Asian Arts
Southeast Asian
 Arts

MICROPAEDIA: Selected entries of reference information

General subjects

ballet:
 assemblé
 ballet
 Ballet comique de
  la reine
 ballet movement
 ballet position
 battement
 brisé
 classical ballet
 entrechat
 fouetté en tournant
 International Ballet
  Competitions
 pirouette
folk dance:
 bourrée
 capoeira
 carole
 clog dance
 conchero
 country dance
 fandango
 farandole
 flamenco

hora
hornpipe
huayño
hula
jarabe
jig
jota
juba
kolo
ländler
maypole dance
mazurka
Morris dance
polka
polska
reel
rigaudon
sarabande
seguidilla
square dance
sword dance
syrtos
Virginia reel
voladores, juego
 de los

*Indian classical
dance:*
 bharata natya
 garabā
 kathak
 kathākali
 manipuri
 oṛissī
popular dance:
 allemande
 basse danse
 bergamasca
 branle
 cakewalk
 cha-cha
 chaconne
 Charleston
 contredanse
 courante
 estampie
 fox-trot
 galliard
 gavotte
 gigue
 jazz dance

jitterbug
mambo
minuet
passacaglia
passepied
pavane
quadrille
rumba
samba
tango
twist
volta, la
waltz
other:
 bugaku
 choreography
 dance
 dance notation
 eurythmics
 Labanotation
 modern dance
 tap dance

Biographies

Balanchine,
 George
Baryshnikov,
 Mikhail
Bournonville,
 August
Cunningham,
 Merce
deMille, Agnes

Diaghilev, Sergey
Dolin, Anton
Duncan, Isadora
Fokine, Michel
Fonteyn, Dame
 Margot
Graham, Martha
Helpmann, Sir
 Robert

Humphrey, Doris
Jooss, Kurt
Laban, Rudolf
Lifar, Serge
Massine, Léonide
Nijinsky, Vaslav
Nikolais, Alwin
Nureyev, Rudolf
Pavlova, Anna

Petit, Roland
Rambert, Dame
 Marie
Saint Denis, Ruth
Tamiris, Helen
Taylor, Paul
Weidman, Charles

INDEX: See entries under all of the terms above

Section 626. **Architecture, Garden and Landscape Design, and Urban Design**

A. The art of architecture

  1. Elements of design and principles of composition

  2. Aesthetic aspects of building materials and constructional systems used in architecture
[for technological aspects, see 733]

    a. Building materials; *e.g.*, stone, brick, wood, iron and steel, concrete

    b. Constructional systems; *e.g.*, load-bearing wall and nonload-bearing wall, post and lintel, arch, vault, dome, truss, framed structures

  3. Diverse structural elements and details of buildings; *e.g.*, floors, walls, ceilings, roofs, windows, doors, stairways

  4. Architectural ornamentation: mimetic ornament, applied ornament, organic ornament

  5. Diverse kinds of architecture and building types determined by their functions

    a. Domestic, or residential, architecture; *e.g.*, houses, apartments, castles, hotels

    b. Religious and commemorative architecture; *e.g.*, temples, churches, synagogues, mosques, tombs, shrines, memorials, monuments

    c. Governmental architecture; *e.g.*, town halls, capitols, courthouses, post offices

    d. Recreational architecture; *e.g.*, theatres, auditoriums, athletic facilities, museums, libraries

    e. Educational and public welfare architecture; *e.g.*, schools and universities, hospitals, prisons, aqueducts

    f. Commercial and industrial architecture; *e.g.*, office buildings, banks, stores, factories, refineries

    g. Agricultural architecture; *e.g.*, barns, stables, silos

    h. Military architecture; *e.g.*, forts, castles, armouries
[see also 736]

  6. Primitive and folk architecture
[see 613]

  7. The history of architecture

    a. Western architecture

    b. The architecture of non-Western peoples
[see also 613]

B. Garden and landscape design

C. Urban design: the artistic aspects of city planning
[for the sociological, political, economic, and psychological aspects of urban design, see 524.B.; for the technological aspects, see 737.C.2.]

Suggested reading in the *Encyclopædia Britannica*:

MACROPAEDIA: Major articles dealing with architecture, garden and landscape design, and urban design

African Arts	Folk Arts
American Indians	Garden and Landscape Design
Architecture, The Art of	Middle Eastern Arts and
Architecture, The History of Western	Architecture, Ancient
Central Asian Arts	Oceanic Arts
East Asian Arts	South Asian Arts
Egyptian Arts and Architecture, Ancient	Southeast Asian Arts

MICROPAEDIA: Selected entries of reference information

<u>General subjects</u>

architecture—	*architecture—*	fortification	acroterion
building materials	*military:*	kremlin	anthemion
and techniques:	alcázar	*architecture—*	brattishing
See Section 733 of	castle	*ornamentation:*	bucranium
Part Seven		acanthus	

candelabrum
coffer
diaper
finial
fluting and reeding
fret
frieze
hoodmold
ornament
pinnacle
pulvinated frieze
reticulated work
rinceau
running-dog
  pattern
rustication
scrollwork
stalactite work
strapwork
stringcourse
stuccowork
swag
architecture—
  recreational:
  amphitheatre
  auditorium
  furo
  Islāmic bath
  odeum
  stadium
  thermae
  Turkish bath
architecture—
  religious:
  abbey
  aisle
  ambo
  ambulatory
  apse
  baldachin
  baptistery
  basilica
  campanile
  chancel
  chantry
  chapel
  chapter house
  chevet
  choir
  choragic
    monument
  church
  cloister
  confessional
  crypt
  gopura
  hagioscope
  hall church
  iconostasis
  jinja
  Lady chapel
  lantern of the dead
  lych-gate

minaret
mosque
narthex
nave
obelisk
pagoda
presbytery
pulpit
rood screen
sacristy
sedilia
śikhara
slype
stave church
stūpa
temple
torii
transept
triforium
ziggurat
architecture—
  residential:
  apartment house
  bungalow
  chalet
  château
  cliff dwelling
  desert palace
  domus
  hogan
  igloo
  inn
  insula
  lodge
  log cabin
  longhouse
  manor house
  palace
  pueblo
  ranch house
  saltbox
  tent
  tepee
  villa
  yurt
architecture—
  structural elements
  and building details:
  alcove
  anta
  arcade
  arch
  atlas
  atrium
  balcony
  balustrade
  bay window
  beam
  belvedere
  bema
  bond
  bracket
  brise-soleil

buttress
canopy
cantilever
capital
carrel
caryatid
casement window
chigai-dana
chimneypiece
clerestory
colonnade
column
console
corbel
corbel table
cornerstone
cupola
cusp
dome
door
dormer
entablature
exedra
fenestration
foyer
framed building
gable
gallery
gargoyle
geodesic dome
hip roof
hypocaust
intercolumniation
lantern
loft
loggia
louver
lunette
megaron
moucharaby
newel
oriel
Palladian window
patio
pedestal
pediment
pendant
pendentive
penthouse
piano nobile
pilaster
podium
porch
porte cochere
portico
quoin
retaining wall
roof
rose window
rotunda
salomónica
setback
spandrel

spire
squinch
staircase
term
thermal window
tracery
truss
tympanum
vault
wall
window
architecture—
  styles, schools, and
  movements:
  African arts
  Akbar period
    architecture
  Art Deco
  Art Nouveau
  Baroque period
  Bauhaus
  Burgundian
    Romanesque style
  Byzantine art
  Carolingian arts
  Carpenter Gothic
  Central Asian arts
  Chicago School
  Churrigueresque
  Cistercian style
  Classicism and
    Neoclassicism
  Composite order
  Constructivism
  Corinthian order
  Doric order
  Early Christian art
  Egyptian Art
  Empire style
  Federal style
  Functionalism
  Futurism
  Gothic art
  Gothic Revival
  Greek Revival
  Henry IV style
  International Style
  Ionic order
  Isabelline
  Islāmic arts
  Kara-yo
  Karnatic temple
    architecture
  Manueline
  Mozarabic art
  New Brutalism
  Norman style
  North Indian
    temple
    architecture
  Oceanic arts
  order
  Palladianism

Picturesque style
Plateresque
Prairie style
rocaille
Rococo style
Romanesque art
Second Empire
  style
Shāh Jahān period
  architecture
shinden-zukuri
Shingle style
shoin-zukuri
South Asian arts
South Indian
  temple
  architecture
Southeast
  Asian arts
Steamboat Gothic
Stijl, de
superposed order
tap'o style
Tenjiku
Tudor style

türbe
Tuscan order
architecture—
  other:
architecture
belfry
caravansary
cenotaph
cha-shitsu
columbarium
cortile
court
crannog
entasis
folly
Gujarāt woodwork
high-rise building
hôtel-Dieu
hypostyle hall
kiosk
kiva
mausoleum
megalith
module
orientation

quadrangle
skyscraper
stela
tholos
tower
triumphal arch
landscape design:
allée
arbor
broderie
cascade
conservatory
espalier
fountain
gazebo
green theatre
greenhouse
grotto
jardin anglais
labyrinth
landscape
  architecture
nymphaeum
orangery
park

parterre
pavilion
pergola
topiary
urban design:
acropolis
bastide
boulevard
Cité Industrielle
civic centre
forum
garden city
green belt
new town
promenade
urban planning

Biographies

architects:
Aalto, Alvar
Adam, Robert
Adler, Dankmar
Alberti, Leon
  Battista
Behrens, Peter
Bernini, Gian
  Lorenzo
Blondel,
  Jacques-François
Borromini,
  Francesco
Boullée,
  Étienne-Louis
Bramante, Donato
Breuer, Marcel
Brunelleschi,
  Filippo
Bulfinch, Charles
Butterfield,
  William
Cerceau, du,
  family
Chambers, Sir
  William
Churriguera family
Corbusier, Le
Delorme, Philibert
Fischer von Erlach,
  Johann Bernhard
Fuller, R.
  Buckminster

Garnier, Charles
Gaudí, Antoni
Gropius, Walter
Guarini, Guarino
Hoffman, Josef
Hunt, Richard
  Morris
Jenney, William
  LeBaron
Johnson, Philip C.
Jones, Inigo
Kahn, Albert
Kahn, Louis I.
Kent, William
Klint, Kaare
Latrobe, Benjamin
Ledoux,
  Claude-Nicolas
Loos, Adolf
Lutyens, Sir Edwin
Mansart, François
Mansart, Jules
  Hardouin-
Meigs,
  Montgomery C.
Mendelsohn, Erich
Michelozzo
Mies van der
  Rohe, Ludwig
Nervi, Pier Luigi
Neutra, Richard
  Joseph
Niemeyer, Oscar

Olbrich, Josef
Palladio, Andrea
Pei, I.M.
Phidias
Pietro da Cortona
Pugin, Augustus
  Welby
  Northmore
Richardson, Henry
  Hobson
Root, John
  Wellborn
Rudolph, Paul
Saarinen, Eero
Sangallo family
Sansovino, Jacopo
Schinkel, Karl
  Friedrich
Serlio, Sebastiano
Sinan
Soufflot,
  Jacques-Germain
Stone, Edward
  Durell
Street, George
  Edmund
Strickland,
  William
Sullivan, Louis
Tange Kenzō
Upjohn, Richard
Vanbrugh, Sir
  John

Venturi, Robert
Vignola,
  Giacomo da
Viollet-le-Duc,
  Eugène-
  Emmanuel
Wagner, Otto
Walter, Thomas
White, Stanford
Wren, Sir
  Christopher
Wright, Frank
  Lloyd
urban planners:
Brown, Lancelot
Burnham,
  Daniel H.
Fry, E. Maxwell
  and Jane Drew
Le Nôtre, André
L'Enfant,
  Pierre-Charles
Loudon, John
  Claudius
Nash, John
Olmsted,
  Frederick Law
Repton, Humphry
Soleri, Paolo

Section 627.   **Sculpture**

 A. The art of sculpture

  1. Elements of design and principles of composition

  2. The iconography of sculpture

  3. Materials of sculpture; *e.g.*, stone, wood, metal, clay, ivory, plaster, concrete, glass fibre, wax, paper

  4. Tools, methods, and techniques of sculpture; *e.g.*, carving, modeling, casting and molding, surface finishing

 B. The diverse kinds of sculpture

  1. Kinds of sculpture distinguished by their spatial context; *e.g.*, sculpture in the round, relief sculpture, kinetic sculpture, environmental sculpture

  2. Kinds of sculpture distinguished by subject matter

   a. Representational sculpture; *e.g.*, human figures, devotional images and objects, portraits, still lifes, animal figures

   b. Nonrepresentational sculpture

   c. Decorative sculpture

  3. Kinds of sculpture distinguished by their special uses or functions

   a. Ceremonial and ritualistic objects

   b. Coins and medals

   c. Commemorative sculpture; *e.g.*, monuments, tombs, tombstones, stelae
    [see 626.A.5.b.]

   d. Masks

  4. Primitive and folk sculpture
   [see 613]

 C. The history of sculpture

  1. Western sculpture

  2. The sculpture of non-Western peoples
   [see also 613]

Suggested reading in the *Encyclopædia Britannica*:

MACROPAEDIA: Major articles dealing with sculpture

African Arts	Middle Eastern Arts and Architecture,
American Indians	Ancient
Central Asian Arts	Oceanic Arts
East Asian Arts	Sculpture, The Art of
Egyptian Arts and Architecture, Ancient	Sculpture, The History of Western
Folk Arts	South Asian Arts
Islāmic Arts	Southeast Asian Arts
Masks	

MICROPAEDIA: Selected entries of reference information

General subjects

styles:	Eastern Indian	Massim style	Sukhothai style
Amarāvati	bronze	Mathurā art	Tami style
sculpture	Fujiwara style	Northern Wei	Tempyō style
Baroque art	Futurism	sculpture	Tori style
beak style	Gandhāra art	Renaissance	U Thong style
Bhārhut sculpture	Jōgan style	Rococo style	Western Indian
Classicism and	korwar style	Romanesque art	bronze
Neoclassicism	Kushān art	Sānchi sculpture	*types:*
Cubism	malanggan style	South Indian	Airport art
	Mannerism	bronze	bieri

bird stone	kachina	stabile	lost-wax process
colossus	kinetic sculpture	Tanagra figurine	modeling
cylinder seal	kore	telum figure	Oceanic arts
Daedalic sculpture	kouros	terra-cotta	sculpture
death mask	mbulu-ngulu	*other:*	South Asian arts
environmental	minimalism	African arts	Southeast
sculpture	moai figure	armature	Asian arts
figurehead	mobile	Central Asian arts	
gigaku mask	relief	contrapposto	
gisant	segoni-kun	Gothic art	

Biographies

Ammannati,	Donatello	Houdon,	Pisano, Nicola
Bartolommeo	Epstein, Sir Jacob	Jean-Antoine	Praxiteles
Bernini, Gian	Flaxman, John	Lehmbruck,	Puget, Pierre
Lorenzo	Gabo, Naum	Wilhelm	Rodin, Auguste
Berruguete, Alonso	Ghiberti, Lorenzo	Lipchitz, Jacques	Saint-Gaudens,
Brancusi,	Giacometti,	Lysippus	Augustus
Constantin	Alberto	Maillol, Aristide	Sluter, Claus
Brunelleschi,	Giambologna	Michelangelo	Smith, David
Filippo	Gill, Eric	Milles, Carl	Thorvaldsen,
Calder, Alexander	Girardon, François	Moore, Henry	Bertel
Canova, Antonio	Hepworth, Dame	Myron	Tinguely, Jean
Cellini, Benvenuto	Barbara	Oldenburg, Claes	Verrocchio,
Della Robbia,	Hildebrand,	Phidias	Andrea del
Luca	Adolf von	Pisano, Giovanni	

INDEX: See entries under all of the terms above

Section 628.   Drawing, Painting, Printmaking, and Photography

A. Drawing

1. Elements of design and principles of composition

2. Drawing media; *e.g.*, chalk, charcoal, crayon, ink, pastel, pencil, scratchboard, silverpoint, wash

3. Diverse kinds of drawing

   a. Kinds of drawing determined by subject matter; *e.g.*, portraits, landscapes, figure compositions, still lifes

   b. Kinds of drawing determined by special uses
   [for aspects of drawing related to writing, see 629.C.4.]

      i. Animation

      ii. Caricature, cartoon, comic strip

      iii. Cartography and mapping

      iv. Drafting

4. The history of drawing

B. The art of painting

1. Elements of design and principles of composition

2. The iconography of painting

3. Painting media; *e.g.*, acrylic, casein, encaustic, fresco, gouache, ink, oil, tempera, watercolour

4. Related media and techniques

   a. Calligraphy
   [see 629.C.4.a.]

   b. Drawing
   [see A., above]

   c. Mosaic

d. Photography
[see D., below]

e. Printmaking
[see C., below]

f. Stained glass

g. Tapestry

5. The kinds of painting

  a. Kinds of painting determined by the type of form of the physical object on which the picture is painted

   i. Fixed objects; *e.g.*, cave painting, mural painting

   ii. Movable objects: easel painting, fan painting, manuscript illumination, miniature painting, screen painting, scroll painting

  b. Kinds of painting determined by subject matter

   i. Representational painting; *e.g.*, devotional painting, genre painting, landscape painting, narrative painting, portrait painting

   ii. Nonrepresentational painting

  c. Kinds of painting determined by the maker or by the audience: primitive and folk painting
  [see 613]

6. The history of painting

  a. Western painting

  b. The paintings of non-Western peoples
  [see also 613]

C. Printmaking

1. Printmaking as an art: its characteristics and problems; *e.g.*, the problem of originality versus reproduction

2. Printmaking media

  a. Relief or cameo media; *e.g.*, woodcuts and linoleum cuts, wood engraving

  b. Intaglio media; *e.g.*, aquatint, drypoint, etching, lift-ground prints, line engraving, mezzotint, soft-ground prints, stipple, engraving

  c. Surface media: lithography, monoprint, serigraphy

3. Printmaking tools and techniques
  [see 735.E.4.]

D. Photography as an art

1. The nature and problems of photography as an art

2. Photographic equipment and techniques: lenses; cameras; exposure, processing, and printing
  [for technological aspects, see 735.G.]

3. The kinds of photography

  a. Major kinds of photography determined by subject matter; *e.g.*, portraits, landscapes

  b. Kinds of functional photography; *e.g.*, photojournalism and photo reportage, holography, astronomical photography, aerial photography, radiography

---

Suggested reading in the *Encyclopædia Britannica*:

MACROPAEDIA: Major articles and biographies dealing with drawing, painting, printmaking, and photography

General subjects

Caricature, Cartoon,
  and Comic Strip
Drafting
Drawing
Folk Arts

Painting, The Art of
Painting, The
  History of Western
Photography
Printmaking

Biographies

Leonardo da Vinci	Picasso	Titian
Michelangelo	Rembrandt	Velázquez

MICROPAEDIA: Selected entries of reference information

General subjects

drawing:
aerial perspective
anamorphosis
animation
blot drawing
brush drawing
caricature
cartoon
chalk drawing
charcoal drawing
chiaroscuro
comic strip
crayon
drapery
drawing
écorché
foreshortening
isometric drawing
line-and-wash
  drawing
metal point
pastel
pen drawing
pencil drawing
perspective
sanguine
scratchboard
sgraffito
silhouette
sketch
squaring
wash drawing
*mosaics and stained
glass:*
  commesso
  Cosmati work
  emblema
  gemmail
  mosaic
  opus sectile
  opus tassellatum
  opus vermiculatum
  pebble mosaic
  pietra dura
  stained glass
  tessara
  tessellated
    pavement
painting:
  aerial perspective
  anamorphosis
  bark painting
  casein painting
  drapery
  encaustic painting

gesso
gouache
grisaille
oil painting
painting
panel painting
perspective
sand painting
sizing
tempera painting
watercolour
photography:
  albumen paper
  carte-de-visite
  Fotoform
  gelatin process
  Group f.64
  Linked Ring
  Photo-Secession
    Group
  photomontage
  tintype
  vortograph
prehistoric painting:
  Altamira
  Font-de-Gaume
  Franco-Cantabrian
    school
  Gargas
  Lascaux Grotto
  macaroni
  Tassili-n-Ajjer
  Trois Frères, Les
  X-ray style
printing:
  aquatint
  bookplate
  cliché-verre
  decal
  drypoint
  embossing
  engraving
  etching
  ink
  intaglio
  linocut
  lithography
  mezzotint
  monotype
  printmaking
  relief printing
  rubbing
  stencilling
  wood engraving
  woodcut

*styles of painting—
Chinese:*
  Ch'an painting
  Che school
  Eight Eccentrics of
    Yang-chou
  Eight Masters of
    Nanking
  Four Masters of
    Anhwei
  Four Masters
    of the Yüan
    Dynasty
  kung-pi
  Ma-hsia school
  p'o-mo
  scroll painting
  Six Masters of
    the early Ch'ing
    period
  ts'un
  wen-jen-hua
  Wu school
*styles of painting—
Indian:*
  Basohli painting
  Būndi painting
  Company school
  Deccani painting
  Eastern Indian
    painting
  Kālīghāṭ painting
  Kishangarh
    painting
  Mālwa painting
  Mewār painting
  Mughal painting
  Pahari painting
  Rājasthānī
    painting
  South Asian arts
  Western Indian
    painting
*styles of painting—
Islāmic:*
  Baghdad school
  Eṣfahān school
  Herāt school
  Islāmic arts
  Jalāyirid school
  Mosul school
  Shīrāz school
  Tabriz school

*styles of painting—
Japanese:*
  chinsō
  Kanō school
  Nan-ga
  nise-e
  scroll painting
  Shijō school
  suiboku-ga
  Tosa school
  Ukiyo-e
  Yamato-e
*styles of painting—
Western:*
  Abstract
    Expressionism
  Abstraction-Création
  Action painting
  Ada group
  Antwerp
    Mannerists
  art brut
  Automatism
  Avignon school
  Bambocciati
  Barbizon school
  Biedermeier style
  Blaue Reiter, Der
  Bolognese school
  Brücke, Die
  Camden Town
    group
  Cobra
  Cubism
  Dada
  Danube school
  Düsseldorf school
  Eight, The
  English school
  Fauvism
  fête champêtre
  Flemish art
  Fontainebleau,
    school of
  fore-edge painting
  Futurism
  genre painting
  Geometric style
  Ghent-Bruges
    school
  Hiberno-Saxon
    style
  Hudson River
    school
  Impressionism

Intimism
Italianate painters
Jack of Diamonds
Japanism
London group
Luminism
Macchiaioli
Metaphysical
 painting
minimalism
Moscow school
Nabis
Nazarene
Neo-Expressionism
Neo-Impressionism
Neue
 Künstlervereinigung
Neue Sachlichkeit
New York school
Norwich school

Novgorod school
Op art
Orphism
Peredvizhniki
plein air painting
Pont-Aven school
Pop art
Postimpressionism
Pre-Raphaelite
 Brotherhood
Precisionism
Pskov school
Purism
Rayonism
Romanticism
singerie
Social Realism
still-life painting
Stroganov school
Suprematism

Surrealism
Symbolist
 movement
Synchromism
Synthetism
Tachism
tondo
trompe l'oeil
Utrecht school
vanitas
veduta
Venetian school
Vingt, Les
Vladimir-Suzdal
 school
Winchester school
Worpswede school
styles of painting—
other:
 African arts

Amarna style
Central Asian arts
Egyptian art
Sogdian art
Southeast
 Asian arts
wandjina style
other:
 collage
 design
 diorama
 folk art
 limner
 mural
 panorama
 popular art
 Poussinist
 Rubenist
 tapestry

Biographies

illustrators:
Beardsley, Aubrey
Beerbohm,
 Sir Max
Crane, Walter
Daumier, Honoré
Gibson, Charles
 Dana
Leech, John
Nast, Thomas
Pyle, Howard
Rockwell, Norman
Thurber, James
painters—British:
Burne-Jones, Sir
 Edward Coley
Constable, John
Gainsborough,
 Thomas
Hogarth, William
Lawrence, Sir
 Thomas
Lewis, Wyndham
Millais, Sir John
 Everett, 1st
 Baronet
Palmer, Samuel
Reynolds, Sir
 Joshua
Rossetti, Dante
 Gabriel
Stubbs, George
Turner, J.M.W.
Wilson, Richard
painters—Dutch:
Bosch,
 Hiëronymus
Bouts, Dirck
Cuyp, Aelbert
 Jacobsz

Gogh, Vincent van
Hals, Frans
Mondrian, Piet
Rembrandt
 Harmenszoon
 van Rijn
Ruisdael,
 Jacob van
Scorel, Jan van
Steen, Jan
Terborch, Gerard
Vermeer, Jan
painters—East Asian:
Hasegawa, Tōhaku
Hiroshige
Hokusai
Hsia Kuei
Ma Yüan
Ogata Kōrin
Sesshū
Shiba Kōkan
Tomioka Tessai
Tung Ch'i-ch'ang
painters—Flemish:
Bruegel, Pieter, the
 Elder
Campin, Robert
David, Gerard
Eyck, Jan van
Goes, Hugo
 van der
Mabuse, Jan
Massys, Quentin
Memling, Hans
Rubens, Peter Paul
Van Dyck, Sir
 Anthony
Weyden, Rogier
 van der

painters—French:
Bonnard, Pierre
Bourdon, Sébastien
Braque, Georges
Cézanne, Paul
Chardin,
 Jean-Baptiste-Siméon
Claude Lorrain
Corot, Camille
Courbet, Gustave
David,
 Jacques-Louis
Degas, Edgar
Delacroix, Eugène
Duchamp, Marcel
Fouquet, Jean
Fragonard,
 Jean-Honoré
Gauguin, Paul
Géricault,
 Théodore
Gros,
 Antoine-Jean,
 Baron
Ingres,
 Jean-Auguste-
 Dominique
Le Brun, Charles
Léger, Fernand
Manet, Édouard
Matisse, Henri
Monet, Claude
Pissarro, Camille
Poussin, Nicolas
Renoir,
 Pierre-Auguste
Rouault, Georges
Rousseau, Henri
Seurat, Georges

Toulouse-Lautrec,
 Henri de
Vuillard, Édouard
Watteau, Antoine
painters—German:
Cranach, Lucas,
 the Elder
Dürer, Albrecht
Ernst, Max
Grünewald,
 Matthias
Holbein, Hans, the
 Elder
Holbein, Hans, the
 Younger
Kirchner, Ernst
 Ludwig
Lochner, Stefan
Marc, Franz
Nolde, Emil
Pacher, Michael
painters—Italian:
Andrea del Sarto
Angelico, Fra
Antonello da
 Messina
Bassano, Jacopo
Bellini, Gentile
Bellini, Giovanni
Bellini, Jacopo
Boccioni, Umberto
Botticelli, Sandro
Bramantino
Canaletto
Caravaggio
Carracci family
Castagno,
 Andrea del
Cavallini, Pietro
Cimabue

INDEX: See entries under all of the terms above

Section 629.   Arts of Decoration and Functional Design

A. The nature and scope of the arts of decoration and functional design

B. The kinds of decorative arts and types of decorative objects classified by the materials and methods used to produce or decorate them, or both

1. Clay; *e.g.,* earthenware, stoneware, porcelain

2. Fabrics

3. Gems

4. Glass

5. Metals

6. Paper; *e.g.,* papier-mâché, wallpaper

7. Stone

8. Wood

9. Other kinds of inorganic materials
   with special attention to

   a. Plaster, cement, and concrete

   b. Plastics and other synthetic materials

10. Other kinds of organic materials
    with special attention to

    a. Flowers, foliage, and related botanical materials; *e.g.*, bouquets, garlands, wreaths
       [for garden and landscape design, see 626.B.]

    b. Plant fibres, reeds, branches, and related materials; *e.g.*, baskets, mats

    c. Skins, furs, and related materials

    d. Shell, horn, bone, ivory, and related materials

    e. Wax

11. Special decorative finishing materials, processes, and techniques

    a. Enamelwork; *e.g.*, cloisonné, champlevé, painted enamels

    b. Lacquerwork; *e.g.*, carved lacquer, inlaid lacquer, laque burgauté

    c. Inlay work; *e.g.*, veneering, intarsia, marquetry

C. The arts of functional design: kinds and types of artistic object classified by their function

   1. Dress design and body decoration

      a. Dress and dress accessories
         [for the technological aspects of garment making, see 732.B.3.]

      b. Jewelry

      c. Body decoration: cosmetics; hairdressing and hair adornment; physical modification; perfumes, scents, and fragrances

   2. Industrial design

      a. Industrial design as an art

      b. Diverse kinds of industrial design classified by function; *e.g.*, design of commercial equipment, design of communications equipment, design of household appliances, design of transportation equipment

   3. Interior design

      a. Interior design as an art

      b. The integration of interior design and decoration with architecture: the design and decoration of interior architectural elements

         i. Ceilings

         ii. Floors

         iii. Floor coverings; *e.g.*, rugs, carpets, mats

         iv. Walls; *e.g.*, molding, paneling, wallpaper

         v. Windows and doors

         vi. Other interior architectural elements; *e.g.*, heating units, stairs and staircases

      c. Objects used for interior decoration: furniture and accessory furnishings
         [for technological aspects, see 732.B.4.]

   4. The design of materials and objects for communication and identification

      a. Handwriting systems and styles: calligraphy, lettering, illuminating
         [for forms of writing, see 514.E.]

      b. Printing arts: typography and printing design, illustration, bookbinding
         [for printmaking, see 628.C.]

      c. Advertising art and design

      d. The design of signs and symbols used primarily for identification; *e.g.*, heraldic design

      e. The design of exhibitions and displays; *e.g.*, museum and gallery display

5. The design and decoration of diverse kinds of specialized functional objects

    a. The design of coins and currency and of medals

    b. The design and decoration of play materials

    c. Automata: the design of decorative mechanical objects

    d. The design and decoration of arms
       [for the technological aspects of arms, see 736]

Suggested reading in the *Encyclopædia Britannica:*

MACROPAEDIA: Major articles dealing with the arts of decoration and functional design

African Arts	East Asian Arts	Printing,	Southeast Asian
Central Asian Arts	Folk Arts	Typography, and	Arts
Decorative Arts	Heraldry	Photoengraving	Writing
and Furnishings	Marketing and	South Asian Arts	
Dress and	Merchandising		
Adornment	Oceanic Arts		

MICROPAEDIA: Selected entries of reference information

General subjects

body decoration:	Art Deco	*dress and adornment:*	stomacher
barber	Art Nouveau	aigrette	suit
body modifications	Arts and Crafts	buckle	surcoat
and mutilations	Movement	bustle	sweater
hairdressing	auricular style	button	swimsuit
mustache	Biedermeier style	Chilkat weaving	tippet
tattoo	Central Asian arts	chiton	toga
toupee	chinoiserie	cockade	trousers
wig	curvilinear style	codpiece	tunic
calligraphy:	Directoire style	commode	turban
black letter	Empire style	corset	yashmak
bokuseki	Gates of Paradise	crinoline	*enameling and*
calligraphy	ghaṭa-pallava	dhoti	*enamelware:*
cancellaresca	Islāmic arts	doublet	Battersea
corsiva	istoriato style	dress	enamelware
Carolingian	Koguryŏ style	fan	Canton enamel
minuscule	Louis XIII style	farthingale	champlevé
chia-ku-wen	Louis XIV style	glove	cloisonné
chrysography	Louis XV style	hat	en résille
hsiao-chuan	Louis XVI style	hoopskirt	enamel miniature
Insular script	Mosan school	hosiery	enamelwork
italic script	Mosul school	inrō	Limoges painted
ku-wen	Oceanic arts	kashmir shawl	enamel
Kūfic script	patralata	kimono	*floral and foliage*
li-shu	Proto-Geometric	loincloth	*decorations:*
majuscule	style	moccasin	corsage
Merovingian script	Queen Anne style	pajamas	floral decoration
minuscule	Régence style	p'ao	garland
naskhī script	Regency style	paṭolā	ikebana
palimpsest	rocaille	peplos	Ikenobō
rubrication	Scythian art	petticoat	Ko
ta-chuan	South Asian arts	Phrygian cap	lei
ta'liq script	Southeast	poke bonnet	moribana
testegiatta	Asian arts	redingote	nageire
ts'ao-shu	streamlining	ruff	nosegay
uncial	Turkish style	sandal	Ohara
decorative art styles	William and Mary	sari	rikka
and motifs:	style	shawl	shōka
African arts	vyāla	shoe	wreath
arabesque	Yi style	skirt	zen'ei ikebana
		sokutai	

*furniture and
accessories:*
  Act of Parliament
    clock
  armoire
  banjo clock
  bath chair
  bed
  bedspread
  bench
  bentwood furniture
  bonheur du jour
  bookcase
  bureau
  cabinet
  cabriole leg
  cane furniture
  Carlton House
    table
  cassone
  cellarette
  chair
  chest
  chest of drawers
  cheval glass
  Chippendale
  coffer
  commode
  console
  corner furniture
  cottage furniture
  couch
  country furniture
  court cupboard
  cupboard
  davenport
  desk
  dresser
  dressing table
  drop-leaf table
  drum table
  Early American
    furniture
  escutcheon
  furniture
  gateleg table
  highboy
  klismos
  ladder-back chair
  love seat
  marquetry
  ming ch'i
  ogee clock
  ottoman
  Parsons table
  Pembroke table
  pew
  pillar and scroll
    shelf clock
  prie-dieu

  scissors chair
  secretary
  settee
  settle
  Shaker furniture
  sideboard
  stool
  table
  taboret
  throne
  tilt-top table
  tripod
  trundle bed
  upholstery
  vargueno
  veneer
  wainscot chair
  wardrobe
  whatnot
  wickerwork
  Windsor chair
glassware:
  Altare glass
  amberina glass
  Amelung glass
  Baccarat glass
  Blaschka glass
  Bohemian glass
  cameo glass
  crown glass
  crystallo ceramie
  cut glass
  engraved glass
  etched glass
  façon de Venise
  flint glass
  Hedwig glass
  Humpen glass
  lustred glass
  Mary Gregory
    glass
  millefiori glass
  mosaic glass
  Mughal glass
  opaline glass
  perfume bottle
  Portland Vase
  pressed glass
  Römer
  ruby glass
  Sandwich glass
  satin glass
  Venetian glass
  verre églomisé
  Waterford glass
  witch ball
  Zwischengoldgläser
*heraldry, arms, and
  insignia:*
  armorial ensign
  arms, coat of

  chevron
  ecclesiastical
    heraldry
  fasces
  flag
  fleur-de-lis
  herald
  heraldic memorial
  heraldry
  labarum
  monogram
  orb
  sceptre
  tartan
*interior design
  accessories:*
  chandelier
  Coromandel
    screen
  curtain
  doorstop
  mirror
  molding
  niche
  paneling
  sconce
  toko-no-ma
  wainscot
  wallpaper
*jewelry and
  gemstones:*
  agate
  almandine
  amethyst
  andradite
  armlet
  aventurine
  baroque pearl
  bead
  beryl
  birthstone
  brooch
  cameo
  carat
  carnelian
  cat's-eye
  chatelaine
  Chinese jade
  choker
  chrysoberyl
  citrine
  coronet
  crown
  crown jewels
  cultured pearl
  diamond
  diamond cutting
  earring
  emerald
  fibula

  filigree
  Florentine
    diamond
  garnet
  gemstone
  granulation
  hei tiki
  jadeite
  jewelry
  lapis lazuli
  lip ring, lip plug,
    and lip plate
  magatama
  nephrite
  netsuke
  nose ring
  onyx
  opal
  parure
  pearl
  pendant
  peristerite
  phenakite
  ring
  ruby
  ruby spinel
  sapphire
  sard and sardonyx
  topaz
  torque
  ts'ung
  turquoise
  variscite
  watch fob
  zircon
*lacquerwork and
  related techniques:*
  chinkin-bori
  decoupage
  fundamiji
  gilding
  hiramaki-e
  hirameji
  japanning
  Kamakura-bori
  kanshitsu
  lacquerwork
  laque burgauté
  maki-e
  nashiji
  raden
  rō-iro
  togidashi maki-e
*metalwork and
  metalware:*
  Bīdrī ware
  britannia metal
  bronze work
  caudle cup
  chasing

textile arts—lace:
Alençon lace
blonde lace
bobbin lace
Brussels lace
Buckinghamshire
  lace
Genoese lace
lace
lace pattern book
needle lace
Spanish lace
Valenciennes lace
Venetian needle
  lace

textile arts—needlework:
bargello work
beadwork
Berlin woolwork
broderie anglaise
chikan work
crewel work
embroidery
needlepoint
opus anglicanum
petit point
quillwork
raised work
sampler
Turkey work
whitework

textile arts—rugs and carpets:
Admiral carpet
Afghan carpet
Alcaraz carpet
Ardabīl Carpet
Arraiolos rug
Aubusson carpet
Axminster carpet
Baku rug

Balochi rug
Bergama carpet
Bījār carpet
bird rug
Bokhara rug
Cairene rug
Chichi rug
Chodor carpet
Cuenca carpet
Dagestan rug
Damascus rug
Dragon rug
Ersari carpet
Ferahan carpet
Garden carpet
Gendje carpet
Ghiordes carpet
Hamadan rug
Hatchlu rug
Herāt carpet
Hereke carpet
Heriz carpet
Indo-Isfahan carpet
Joshagan rug
Karabagh rug
Kāshān carpet
Kazakh rug
Kermān carpet
Khorāsān carpet
Khotan rug
kilim
Kirshehr rug
Konya carpet
Kuba carpet
Kula carpet
Kurdish rug
Lâdik carpet
Lotto carpet
medallion carpet
Mekri carpet
Melas carpet
Mughal carpet

Mujur rug
Ottoman carpet
palas
prayer rug
Qashqā'ī rug
rug and carpet
rya rug
Salor rug
Sarūk carpet
Savonnerie carpet
Senna rug
Seraband rug
Shīrāz rug
Shirvan rug
Smyrna carpet
Soumak
Spring of Khosrow
  Carpet
Tabrīz carpet
Tekke carpet
Transylvanian rug
Ushak carpet
Vase carpet
Verné rug
Yomut carpet
Yürük rug

textile arts—other:
bāndhanī work
crochet
jāmdānī
kimkhwāb
knitting
Navajo weaving
paisley
qalamkārī textile
quilting
tapestry
tatting
textile
toile de Jouy
verdure tapestry
weaving

other:
altarpiece
ampulla
aryballos
automaton
azulejo
basketry
Bauhaus
billboard
cha-shitsu
Christmas tree
decorative art
Deutscher
  Werkbund
effigy mound
featherwork
frame design
interior design
ivory carving
kirikane
krater
mazer
paper folding
papier-mâché
parfleche
patch box
pichhwāi
pilgrim bottle
piqué work
poster
retable
sandwich board
sign
snuffbox
t'ao-t'ieh
tatami
tea ceremony
tester
tortoiseshell
totem pole
trencher
umbrella
yurt

Biographies

Aalto, Alvar
Asam, Cosmas
  Damian and Egid
  Quirin
Astbury, John
Boulle,
  André-Charles
Breuer, Marcel
Chippendale,
  Thomas
Cressent, Charles
Deskey, Donald

Didot family
Eames, Charles;
  and Eames, Ray
Exekias
Gallé, Émile
Germain, Thomas
Gill, Eric
Goddard family
Hepplewhite,
  George
Klint, Kaare
Majorelle, Louis

Mardersteig,
  Giovanni
Mi Fei
Morison, Stanley
Morris, William
Northwood, John
Palissy, Bernard
Phyfe, Duncan
Pisanello, Il
Poggio Bracciolini,
  Gian Francesco

Roentgen, David
Saarinen, Eero
Sheraton, Thomas
Sōtatsu
Tassie, James
Thonet, Michael
Tiffany, Louis
  Comfort
Townsend family
Wedgwood, Josiah
Wood family

INDEX: See entries under all of the terms above

Introduction to Part Seven:
Knowing How and Knowing Why
by Lord Ritchie-Calder

Benjamin Franklin defined man as "the tool-making animal." If he had added the phrase "with foresight," he would have adequately described *Homo faber,* man the technologist.

Inventiveness was the indispensable condition for the survival of the human species. Without fur or feather, carapace or scale, ancestral man stood naked to the elements; and without fang or claw or tusk to fight his predators, without speed to elude them, without camouflage to deceive them or the ability to take to the trees like his cousin, the ape, he was physically at a hopeless disadvantage. What he developed to deal with his deficiencies was the capacity to invent. He possessed not only sensory perceptions (though these were less acute than those of many of his fellow creatures), he also possessed imagination and finger-skills. He did not just improvise to meet an emergency as an ape might in using a broken branch as a weapon; he also saw the need for keeping a club handy—he planned ahead. Other creatures had their inherited instincts, their built-in experience. Some, like the beaver or the weaverbird, with their biological tools, could contrive quite elaborate structures; others, like the bees or the ants, could evolve efficient organizations; others, like the squirrel, were provident in the sense of laying in stores. With nimbleness of brain and hand, a combination of gray matter and motor-cells, man could scheme to outreach, with club, or spear or sling, his natural enemies; he could manage nature and escape from the restraints of his environment. He clothed himself in pelts and moved to inhospitable climes, he mastered fire and dared to bring it into his dwelling for heating and cooking, he learned to cultivate and plant the soil, he domesticated animals, and he devised specialized tools like the hoe and the ax to improve the efficiency of his labour.

From earliest time and beginning with the simplest contrivances, every discovery and invention has depended on the fact that the human being is not only a perceptual but also a conceptual creature capable of observing, memorizing, and juxtaposing images. He can make a mental design, a techno-poetic fantasy, even when the means of actually producing it are not available. Seven hundred years ago Roger Bacon could imagine a power-driven ship, a horseless carriage, an airplane, the miniaturized servo-motor, "but one finger in length and one in width," and the bathysphere. The vision cannot materialize, however, unless man has the method. This is the process by which he makes an observation (perceptual); forms a hypothesis (conceptual); experiments to test this "hunch"; formulates a theory to justify his insights; and by further proofs produces "laws" according to which anyone can go on repeating the results. With spoken language, he can transfer experience, father to son, master to apprentice, generation to generation. With written language, he can produce the textbooks that are the ready-reckoners for other innovators who thereby do not have to rediscover Newton's laws or the laws of thermodynamics every few years. This systematic treatment of the arts and crafts is the simplest expression of the meaning of "technology," from the Greek roots *techne,* arts, and *logia,* words. The ancient Greeks had no such combined term because their philosophers divorced manual skills from intellectual pursuits. Plato berated Eudoxus and Archytas when by experiments and recourse to instruments they solved problems that the theorists considered insoluble. He accused them of "making use of matter which requires manual labour and is the object of servile trades."

This intellectual condescension still persists, although individual technologists have won recognition from scientific societies and learned academies. The prejudice is suggested by the acceptance of the term "science *and* technology." Yet both science and technology use the scientific method. Was Leonardo da Vinci, apart from being an artist, a scientist or a technologist? In terms of discovering and testing new knowledge he was a man of science, but his designs for practical innovations outnumbered those of Thomas Alva Edison. Edison, 400 years later, patented over 1,000 inventions. They included major ones, for which he is remembered, but also hundreds of bits of useful hardware, important in their way. He made only one scientific discovery, the Edison effect, which he patented but did not pursue. The rest were derived from scientific knowledge and developments. He saw the profitable relevancies that lesser men missed; he fitted the mental nut to the mental bolt and created things.

Customarily, science, or the scientific hierarchy, is divided into four categories:

Pure, or academic, research is the pursuit of knowledge for its own sake. It is mainly the work of an individual, or the group he leads. The pure scientist has to justify himself only before a jury of his peers. He is judged not by the usefulness but by the integrity of his work. He is the Maker Possible.

Oriented fundamental research is still basic science; that is to say, the scientist is still questioning nature, seeking to extend knowledge and understanding, but he is not a free agent indulging his curiosity. He is restrained within a frame of reference. For instance, in studying chemical reactions at high pressures he is not assuming that he is going to discover polyethylene, or if he is studying gases at high temperatures he is not necessarily thinking of jet engines or rockets; but he is compiling data that will be important in a general field and likely to have some foreseen applications. In the big corporations, this is called "speculative research." Such a scientist is likely to have adequate research facilities, endowments, or contracts. He is the Maker Probable.

Applied research is programmed research. The target is specified, and results are expected. The predicted yield is

261

the measure of the support. The scientist is held accountable in the annual report. He is the Maker to Happen.

Development is really technology, but coupling it with research (R and D) keeps it in the scientific hierarchy and away from the "rude mechanicals." It is the transfer of laboratory results, through the pilot plant, to the production line. R and D is far and away the most expensive scientific bracket because large-scale trial and error ("back to the drawing board") involves multimillions of dollars. The R and D scientist is the Maker to Work.

Through the craft guilds and their "mysteries" and their conversion to factory methods, technology had an evolutionary history in many cultures and many lands. Alfred North Whitehead claimed that "the greatest invention of the nineteenth century was the invention of the method of invention." Nowhere was this better demonstrated than at Edison's "invention factory" at Menlo Park, New Jersey, where, starting in 1876, Edison organized the first industrial research laboratory. In folklore, he is regarded as a "loner," who invented by intuition. In fact, he systematized the process of invention, coordinating and applying relevant knowledge through a hard-worked team that included mathematicians, physicists, chemists, and skilled mechanics. Invention was no longer the private indulgence of the gifted amateur or the rare professional; a techno-methodology had been created to guarantee commercial success. In Edison's case the result was often a "package deal"—not just the incandescent lamp, but the generating plant and the transmission system. In the case of Henry Ford, it was not just the Model T, but the assembly line, which he enlarged to a factory that was one-fifth of a mile long, with a conveyor-belt system that synchronized each stage of construction with the delivery of each part to the operator. He embodied scientific management, with its time-and-motion studies and production engineering.

The feedback system between the know-why (academic science) and the know-how (technology) is recalibrating the time-function of change. A new scientific discovery (explanation of a phenomenon) is seized by the technologists and put to work. In turn the technologists provide the instruments that, with greater refinements and speed, enable the scientists to make further discoveries. An outstanding example is cybernetics. The pencil-and-paper mathematicians had long known the principles of the computer, but they had to wait for the post-World War II electronic engineers to produce the "hardware." Now with instant responses, or nearly so, and vast computer capacities and prodigious "memories," with means not only for numerical calculation but for logical simulation, with feedback (like a burned finger signaling to the brain and the brain withdrawing the finger from the hot plate), scientists are not only able to do calculations so complex that they would not previously have attempted them, but they are also learning, from the engineers, about the nature of systems, including the systems of nature itself. Cybernetics deals with the information-processing aspects, as distinguished from the energy-transforming aspects, of all systems regardless of their physical nature. This has facilitated the development of automatic control, telecommunications, and computing; it is applicable also to systems engineering, economics, and neurophysiology.

Though we acknowledge the truth of Whitehead's apho-

rism, his essentially engineering approach to technology is too restrictive. Every advance in the practical arts from hunting to food-gathering to cultivation, to animal husbandry, to irrigation, to mining, and on through construction, transportation, food-processing, heating, power generation, lighting, communications, military engineering, and clinical medicine has produced social and cultural changes. The Neolithic Revolution was as climacteric as the Industrial Revolution. Moreover, the preoccupation with Western technology ignores the cultural origins of many major innovations and forgets that, historically, the European Dark Ages (not so dark as is often supposed) coincided with Golden Ages of material advances in China, India, and pre-Columbian America. Only in recent years have historians (Singer, Crombie, Lynn White, Hall, Needham, Forbes, and others) given serious attention to these facts. The anthropologists, looking at cultural influences, have been similarly remiss. Economists have been preoccupied with the "production function" and sociologists with the social effects of innovation (from television to freeways) and with work-force redundancy. The present distortions, produced by rapid technological change, obscure the fact that civilization itself derived from excess production and redundancy. When agriculture surpassed subsistence, fewer tillers were required to support the cities, with their artisans (specializing in other forms of production), their priesthoods, their scholars, their soldiery and warrior-kings, their tithe-gatherers, their merchants, and their money-changers. Technological displacement today, whether it is called unemployment, underemployment, leisure, or nonwork, similarly calls for social readjustments to find nonmanufacturing expressions of human capacities.

No explanation of the intrinsic or historic attributes of technology can convey the love-hate overtones that the term has acquired. In the ogre sense of the word, it has become a threat to lives and livelihoods and to the total environment. In the efficiency sense, it is hailed as the methodological solution of all our problems from government administration to the production of miracle grains to abolish hunger. Some, like Jacques Ellul and B.F. Skinner, claim that we are already the hostages of our man-made environment: the first maintaining that technology has taken over all of man's activities and not just his productive activities; the second, that autonomous man, with free will and freedom and dignity, is now an anachronism and has to be intentionally controlled by the "technology of behaviour."

Obviously this usage is stretching the meaning of "technology" beyond the foregoing derivations and descriptions—the etymology; the cultural origins; the scientific precedents; the nuts-and-bolts and something popularly promoted to capital letters as "The Machine." This usage expands even Harold Lasswell's accommodating version: "The ensemble of practices by which one uses available resources to achieve values." It is more consistent with the French *la technique,* which refers to any complex of standardized means for attaining predetermined ends. Thus it would apply to organization, government institutions, systems of politics or religions, or anything which reduces spontaneous or impulsive behaviour to a rationale. As was said of *la technique* of wartime operational research, "it ran the war by numerical thinking instead of gusts of emotion."

In adventurously exploring the three divisions and fifteen sections of the encyclopaedia's treatment of technology of which this introduction is, hopefully, the appetizer, the reader will find other interpretations and probably produce his own. In common usage, however, the preoccupation is with "The Machine" and the effects of its products on our lives.

Resentment against the replacement of men by machines goes back beyond Ned Ludd and the machine-wreckers of the Industrial Revolution, but present-day attitudes are of a different order of magnitude. They derive from the speed and scale of change. Hahn and Strassmann's laboratory discovery of uranium fission in 1938 was transformed into a nuclear bomb in 1945. If there is no nuclear war, history will consider the Manhattan Project, which produced the bomb, as important as the bomb it produced. It is the archetype of the crash program in which men, materials, and methods are mobilized to attain an objective in a given time. Man on the Moon by 1970 was another example, with the time-target beaten by six months. The time-lapse between a fundamental scientific discovery and its practical application has been reduced from centuries to decades to years to months. Since World War II, we have had the Atomic Age, the Cybernetic Age, the Space Age, and now the Bioengineering Age, in which not only by organ transplants but also by the deliberate manipulation of genes it may be possible to engineer the nature of man himself. Thus in the growing up of the postwar generation there have been four major epochs nearly as significant as the Stone Age, the Iron Age, the Renaissance, and the Industrial Revolution. At the same time there has come the shocked awareness of the effects on the environment of the wastes of technology. Again this is a matter of scale and lack of prescience. (The ore miners and metal workers of Cyprus and Asia Minor were polluting the Mediterranean with heavy metals 5,000 years ago, but the effects were insignificant compared with volcanic debris.) When people complain, however, of "interference with the environment" they should be mindful that such interference has been the *sine qua non* of the survival of *Homo sapiens*. Moreover, when we try to get rid of our guilt-sense about the effects of misused technology and reject the gadgeting we ashamedly enjoy, we should not go too far and "throw out the baby with the bathwater." We cannot go back to the apes nor even to Arcadia.

The great problem is how to force ebullient technology and its transnational expansion to produce human well-being, not just in the quantity of artifacts but in improving the quality of life, including redressing of the mischief in the environment. This requires an enlightened and informed society that knows what it wants and is not cult-ridden or crash-programmed into accepting what it does not want or need. This cannot be achieved through programmed learning nor the technology of behaviour nor systems engineering. We are back with the know-why as the initiator and the monitor of the know-how.

Part Seven. Technology

Several points should be noted about the relations of this part to other parts. Technology involves applications of the knowledge of nature dealt with in Parts One, Two, and Three and in turn has an influence on the development of that knowledge. It has a major role in relation to human communication and an influence on the cultural, social, economic, political, legal, and educational life of mankind, dealt with in Part Five; and a conditioning effect on the development of the fine arts, dealt with in Part Six. To a degree, technological developments affect developments in the religious life of humans, dealt with in Part Eight. Technology is a major dimension in the history of mankind, the subject of Part Nine.

The branches of technology and of engineering have themselves become the subject of historical and analytical studies. Those studies are presented in Section 10/37 of Part Ten.

Division I.   The Nature and Development of Technology

The outlines in the two sections of Division I treat the scope and history of technology, and the organization of human work.

Section 711.   Technology: Its Scope and History

A. General conceptions or definitions of technology

B. Relations between technology and other spheres of contemporary life

1. Technology and wealth

2. Technology and war

3. Technology and education

4. Technology and art
   [see also 612.D.4.]

5. Technology and social institutions
   [see also 512.B.3.]

6. Technology and the underdeveloped regions: the export of Western technology
   [see also 512.B.3.]

7. Effects of technology on the environment

C. History of technology: sociocultural consequences of technological changes
   [see also 512.B.]

1. Technology in the ancient world

   a. The beginnings of technology (to *c.* 3000 BC): emergence of the earliest communities, use of stone tools and weapons, beginnings of mining and agriculture

   b. The urban revolution (*c.* 3000–500 BC): early civilization in the valleys of the Nile and Tigris–Euphrates, waterworks for irrigation, urban manufacturing

   c. Technological achievements of Greece and Rome (500 BC–AD 500): mastery of iron, invention of mechanical contrivances, architectural and constructional works

2. Technology from the Middle Ages to 1750

a. Medieval advances (AD 500–1500): harnessing of wind power and waterpower; construction of canals, tunnels, and bridges; construction of full-rigged ships; invention of printing

b. The emergence of Western technology (1500–1750): invention of early scientific instruments and tools, birth of steam power, development of agricultural and constructional techniques

3. The Industrial Revolution (1750–1900)

a. Advances in power technology: development of steam power, internal-combustion engine, and electric power; exploitation of mineral and fossil fuels

b. Development of industries: iron and steel, textiles, chemicals, transportation, communications

4. Technology in the 20th century

a. Early developments: exploitation of hydroelectric power; synthesizing of fibres, plastics, rubber, dyes, and drugs; rationalization of production

b. Space Age technology: atomic power, automation and the computer, rocketry and space exploration, advances in agricultural technology, advances in transportation and communication

c. Effects of technology on the environment

Suggested reading in the *Encyclopædia Britannica*:

MACROPAEDIA: Major articles and a biography dealing with technology: its scope and history

Edison
Technology, The History of

MICROPAEDIA: Selected entries of reference information

General subjects

industrial engineering	industrialization manufacturing	safety safety engineering	service industries technology
Industrial Revolution	research and development	security and protection system	

Biographies

See Section 10/37 of Part Ten

INDEX: See entries under all of the terms above

Section 712.   The Organization of Human Work

A. The organization of work

1. The organization of work in the prehistoric world
[see also 512.B.1.]

a. Origin of division of labour based on age and sex differences, initial absence of class divisions

b. Communal organization: specialization required by the development of pottery, textiles, agriculture, and metallurgy

2. The organization of work in the ancient world

a. Theories of civilization's development: explanations of the origin of hierarchical organization

b. Effect of social classes on the organization of labour

c. Organization of agricultural labour

d. Organization of industrial labour by craft

e. Organization of labour for large-scale construction

3. The organization of work in the medieval world: the manor system, the craft guilds, organization of free labour for large-scale construction

4. Changes in production techniques from the 16th to the 18th century: foundations of modern industrial production

5. Mass production: the organization of labour by product rather than by process

6. The use of machines as replacements for labour

B. The application of scientific methods to managerial functions

1. Operations research: the application of scientific method to the management of organized systems

2. Systems engineering: the utilization of scientific and technological knowledge in planning and designing complex systems

3. Systems-design techniques, tools, and procedures

a. Techniques: use of flow charts and other symbolic models, precise formulation of suitable objectives

b. Tools: optimization theory, communication theory, queuing theory, game theory
[see also 10/23.E. and F.]

c. Procedures: exploratory planning, development planning

C. The relation between man and machine in industrial production

1. The effects on mankind of the rationalization of work: psychological and social aspects of mass production and automation

2. The human-factors approach: the design of machines, tools, and work environments with consideration for the capabilities and limitations of humans

---

Suggested reading in the *Encyclopædia Britannica*:

MACROPAEDIA: Major articles dealing with the organization of human work

Automation
Industrial Engineering and Production Management
Modernization and Industrialization
Work and Employment

MICROPAEDIA: Selected entries of reference information

General subjects

assembly line	game theory	mathematical	systems engineering
automation	Hawthorne	programming	time-and-motion
critical path	research	operations research	study
analysis	human-factors	queuing theory	trade organization
domestic service	engineering	robot	work
domestic system	mass production	standardization	

Biographies

See Section 10/37 of Part Ten

INDEX: See entries under all of the terms above

Division II. **Elements of Technology**
[For Part Seven headnote see page 265.]

Division I is concerned with the nature and effects of technology as a whole. The outlines in the five sections of Division II deal with technical processes not specific to any of the major fields of technology. The technologies of the major fields are dealt with in Division III.

Section 721. **Technology of Energy Conversion and Utilization**

A. Major types of energy useful to mankind

　1. Primary energy sources: thermonuclear reaction, nuclear fission, radioactivity

　2. Recurring energy sources: solar energy, natural thermal energy, wind and water energy

　3. Nonrenewable energy sources: coal, gas, petroleum

B. Devices and techniques for the utilization of energy

　1. Devices for utilizing muscle energy: pulley, lever, block and tackle, treadmill
　　[see 722.B.2.]

　2. Devices for utilizing wind and water energy: sails and sailboats, windmills, waterwheels, turbines

　3. Devices for utilizing gravitational energy: pendulums, counterweight mechanisms

　4. Devices for utilizing strain and compression energy

　　a. Steam engines and steam power plants

　　b. Steam turbines
　　　[see B.2., above]

　　c. Compressed-air and compressed-gas tools and machines

　　d. Hydraulic devices

　5. Devices for utilizing magnetic and electrical energy

　　a. Magnets, electromagnets

　　b. Electric motors: induction motors, synchronous motors, commutator motors utilizing ac and dc

　6. Devices for utilizing rotational energy: centrifuges, gyroscopes

　7. Devices for utilizing heat energy: heat exchangers, refrigeration equipment

　8. Devices for utilizing chemical energy

　　a. Internal-combustion engines: gasoline and gas turbine engines; diesel engines; jet, turbojet, fan-jet, and turboprop engines; rocket engines

　　b. Chemical explosives: black powder, nitroglycerin, dynamites, nitrocellulosic explosives, military explosives, other modern high explosives

　9. Devices and materials for utilizing nuclear energy: nuclear reactors, radioactive isotopes
　　[see also 112.B.]

C. Devices for energy conversion

　1. Thermoelectric devices

　2. Thermionic devices

　3. Magnetohydrodynamic and electrogasdynamic devices

　4. Batteries and fuel cells

　5. Lamps and other lighting devices

6. X-ray tubes
[see also 111.D.1.]

7. Devices for electric power generation: turbine-driven generators, engine-driven generators, nuclear-powered generators, hydraulic-turbine-driven generators, thermoelectric generators, dynamos

D. Devices for energy concentration and control

1. Electron tubes

2. Solid-state devices; *e.g.,* transistors, semiconductor diodes, integrated circuits

3. Optoelectronic devices; *e.g.,* liquid-crystal displays, optical fibres, semiconductor lasers

E. Devices for unlimited production of free energy: attempts to design perpetual motion machines

---

Suggested reading in the *Encyclopædia Britannica:*

MACROPAEDIA: Major articles dealing with the technology of energy conversion and utilization

Electronics	Industries, Chemical Process
Energy Conversion	Industries, Extraction and Processing

MICROPAEDIA: Selected entries of reference information

General subjects

chemical explosives:
blasting
blasting cap
dynamite
explosive
firework
gunpowder
nitrocellulose
RDX
compression energy and its devices:
bellows
cogeneration
compressor
piston and cylinder
pneumatic device
propellant
steam engine
electrical devices:
battery
cell
electric generator
electric motor
electrolytic cell
electromagnet
fuel cell
fuse
linear motor
magneto
motor generator
voltage regulator

electronic devices:
amplifier
antenna
antenna array
band-pass filter
diode
electric circuit
electric switch
electron tube
electronics
ferrite
grid
ignitron
integrated circuit
klystron
laser
magnetron
microprocessor
photoelectric cell
photomultiplier
tube
printed circuit
semiconductor
device
transistor
heat exchange and related devices:
boiler
cogeneration
condenser
cooling system
evaporator

heat exchanger
heat pipe
refrigeration
internal-combustion engines:
carburetor
choke
diesel engine
fuel injection
gasoline engine
ignition system
internal-combustion
engine
jet engine
ramjet
rotary engine
spark plug
supercharger
turbojet
turboprop
major types of energy:
electric power
energy
fire
fossil fuel
geothermal energy
hydraulic power
hydroelectric power
solar energy
tidal power
waterpower

moving-fluid devices:
centrifugal pump
hydraulic
transmission
pump
turbine
waterwheel
windmill
nuclear reactors:
breeder reactor
fusion reactor
nuclear reactor
rockets:
Atlas rocket
Delta
launch vehicle
rocket
Saturn
Thor rocket
V-2 rocket
other:
blowpipe
magnetohydro-
dynamic power
generator
perpetual motion
thermionic power
converter
thermoelectric
device
transducer

<u>Biographies</u>

Braun, Wernher von	Goddard, Robert	Sperry, Elmer	Watt, James
De Forest, Lee	Hutchings	Ambrose	Westinghouse,
Diesel, Rudolf	Nobel, Alfred	Stevens, John	George
Evans, Oliver	Bernhard	Tesla, Nikola	

See also Section 10/37 of Part Ten

INDEX: See entries under all of the terms above

Section 722. **Technology of Tools and Machines**

A. Hand tools

    1. Early history of hand tools: Paleolithic and Neolithic stone tools, development of metal tools

    2. Basic types of hand tools

        a. Percussive tools: hammers, axes

        b. Cutting, drilling, and abrading tools: knives, saws, files

        c. Screw-based tools: screwdrivers, wrenches

        d. Measuring and defining tools: levels, dividers, rules

        e. Tool auxiliaries: workbench, vise

    3. Power-driven hand tools: electric drills and circular saws, pneumatic hammers and riveters

B. Machines and machine components

    1. Simple machines: lever, wedge, wheel and axle, pulley, and screw

    2. Machine mechanisms: devices that transmit motion by means of flexible connectors, rigid connecting links, or direct contact

    3. Machine components

        a. Gears

        b. Cams

        c. Linkages

        d. Flywheels

        e. Belt and chain drives

        f. Couplings

        g. Clutches

        h. Brakes

        i. Bearings

        j. Shafts and shaft accessories

        k. Screws

        l. Springs

    4. Friction accommodation and reduction

        a. Bearings
          [see B.3.i., above]

        b. Lubricants and their functions, types, and properties

C. Machine tools: stationary power-driven machines for shaping and forming parts made of metal or other materials

    1. History and characteristics of machine tools

    2. Operation of metal-cutting tools

    3. Basic machine tools: turning machines, shapers and planers, drilling machines, milling machines, grinding machines, power saws, and presses

    4. Modifications of basic machines; *e.g.,* turret lathes, production millers

    5. Special-purpose machines; *e.g.,* gear-cutting machines, broaching machines

D. Computer-aided machining

1. Computer numerical control

2. Computer-aided design and computer-aided manufacturing (CADCAM)

3. Robots

4. Computer-integrated manufacturing

E. Nonconventional methods of machining

1. Electrical methods: electron-beam machining, electrical-discharge machining, electrochemical machining, ion beam machining, laser machining, plasma arc machining

2. Other methods: ultrasonic machining, chemical machining, photochemical machining, water-jet machining

---

Suggested reading in the *Encyclopædia Britannica*:

MACROPAEDIA: Major article dealing with the technology of tools and machines

Tools

MICROPAEDIA: Selected entries of reference information

General subjects

basic machine tools:	saw	gear	transmission
auger	screwdriver	Geneva	washer
boring machine	vise	mechanism	*simple machines:*
drill press	wrench	governor	capstan
grinding machine	*machine components:*	Harmonic Drive	crank
lathe	air brake	linkage	inclined plane
milling machine	air spring	machine	lever
planer	automatic	mandrel	pulley
punch press	transmission	mechanism	wheel
reamer	ball bearing	nut	wheel and axle
router	bearing	pin fastener	*other:*
shaper	belt drive	rack and pinion	block and tackle
hand tools:	bolt	ratchet	divider
adz	brake	Rolamite	jack
ax	cam	roller bearing	level
brace and bit	clutch	screw	lubrication
chisel	differential gear	shaft coupling	pantograph
drill	eccentric-and-rod	shaft seal	square
file	mechanism	slider-crank	tool
hammer	escapement	mechanism	tool and die
pliers	flexible shaft	spring	making
router	flywheel	toggle mechanism	

Biographies

See Section 10/37 of Part Ten

INDEX: See entries under all of the terms above

Section 723. **Technology of Measurement, Observation, and Control**

A. Theory of measurement
[see 10/31.B.3.b.]

B. Units and standards of measurement

1. Systems of weights and measures: standards for the measurement of mass and length

2. Standards and techniques for measurement of time

C. Principles and processes by which instruments of measurement operate

D. Common types of measuring instruments

    1. Instruments for measuring basic dimensions

       a. Devices for measuring length: rules, calipers, micrometers

       b. Devices for measuring mass and weight: scales, balances

       c. Devices for measuring time: mechanical, electric, and atomic clocks

       d. Devices for measuring temperature: gas, liquid, and electrical resistance thermometers

       e. Devices for measuring electric current and other electrical properties: galvanometers, ammeters, voltmeters

       f. Devices for measuring light intensity: photometers, light meters, exposure meters

    2. Instruments for measuring physical properties and relationships derived from basic dimensions

       a. Instruments for measuring pressure: barometers, manometers

       b. Instruments for measuring rate of flow: flowmeters, water meters, gas meters

       c. Instruments for measuring position by angulation and direction finding

           i. Compasses: magnetic compasses, gyrocompasses
            [see also 212.B.]

          ii. Surveying instruments: levels, transits, sextants

       d. Instruments for measuring gravity: gravimeters

       e. Instruments for making optical measurements: polarimeters, refractometers

       f. Instruments for measuring ionizing radiation: Geiger counters, scintillation counters

       g. Instruments for measuring volumetric and mechanical properties of materials, including density, viscosity, and mechanical strength

E. Instruments used for observing and recording

    1. Instruments for observing phenomena

       a. Microscopes: optical, electron, acoustic, and scanning tunneling microscopes

       b. Telescopes: optical, radio, and other types (*e.g.,* infrared, ultraviolet, X-ray, and gamma-ray systems)

       c. Spectroscopes and spectrographs

       d. Interferometers

    2. Instruments for recording phenomena: cameras
       [see 735 G.]

F. Special instruments and apparatus used in scientific research

    1. General laboratory equipment: filters, mixers, centrifuges

    2. Research reactors

    3. Particle accelerators: betatrons, cyclotrons, linear resonance accelerators, synchrotrons

    4. Mass spectrometers

    5. Chromatographs

    6. Seismographs
      [see also 213.B.]

    7. Particle detectors: bubble chambers, scintillation counters

G. Major systems of measurement and observation

    1. Surveying
      [see D.2.c.ii., above, and 733.A.2.]

    2. Mapping and cartography

    3. Hydrographic charting

    4. Oceanographic measurement
      [see also 222.B., E., F., and G. and 738.B.]

    5. Meteorological measurement
      [see also 221 and 223]

    6. Astronomical observations

7. Navigational techniques and devices

8. Radiological techniques and devices

H. Instrumentation and control systems

1. Instrumentation systems: systems that operate or actuate control devices or record measurements automatically

2. Control systems

3. Telemetry systems: remote monitoring and control

Suggested reading in the *Encyclopædia Britannica*:

MACROPAEDIA: Major articles dealing with technology of measurement, observation, and control

Analysis and Measurement, Physical and Chemical
Calendar
Climate and Weather
Mapping and Surveying
Measurement Systems
Microscopes
Navigation
Particle Accelerators
Radar
Telescopes
Time

MICROPAEDIA: Selected entries of reference information

General subjects

astronomical devices:
  astrolabe
  astronomical observatory
  Cassegrain reflector
  coronagraph
  Keplerian telescope
  Mills cross
  radio interferometer
  radio telescope
  Schmidt telescope
  telescope
  X-ray telescope
calendars:
  Aztec calendar
  Chinese calendar
  Dionysian period
  Egyptian calendar
  French republican calendar
  Greek calendar
  Gregorian calendar
  international date line
  Jewish calendar
  Julian calendar
  leap year
  lunar calendar
  Mayan calendar
  Muslim calendar
  perpetual calendar
  Roman republican calendar
  solar calendar
  Tibetan calendar
instruments for measuring distance:
  altimeter
  caliper

depth finder
gauge
range finder
strain gauge
vernier caliper
instruments for measuring force:
  balance
  gravimeter
  Roberval balance
  spring balance
  torsion balance
instruments for measuring electrical and magnetic quantities:
  ammeter
  bridge
  cathode-ray oscilloscope
  electrometer
  electroscope
  galvanometer
  magnetometer
  ohmmeter
  oscillograph
  signal generator
  voltmeter
  watt-hour meter
instruments for measuring motion and fluid flow:
  accelerometer
  airspeed indicator
  anemometer
  gas meter
  speedometer
  tachometer
  venturi tube

instruments and techniques for measuring properties of liquids:
  hydrometer
  Jolly balance
  pH meter
  polarimetry
  viscometer
instruments and techniques for measuring radiation:
  actinometer
  bolometer
  cloud chamber
  coincidence counting
  densitometer
  dosimeter
  frequency meter
  ionization chamber
  photometer
  radiometer
  scintillation counter
  solid-state detector
  spark chamber
  wavemeter
mapping and surveying:
  aerial photography
  cartography
  contour mapping
  hydrography
  isobar
  isotherm
  itinerarium
  map
  metes and bounds

photogrammetry
projection
surveying
theodolite
topographic map
triangulation
trilateration
weather map
meteorology:
  anemometer
  barometer
  ceilometer
  hygrometer
  isentropic chart
  isobar
  isotherm
  radiosonde
  temperature-humidity index
  weather bureau
  wind rose
  World Weather Watch
navigational techniques and devices:
  celestial navigation
  compass
  consol
  dead reckoning
  direction finder
  great circle route
  inertial guidance system
  loran
  loxodrome
  navigation
  navigation chart
  portolan chart

See also Section 10/37 of Part Ten

Section 724. Extraction and Conversion of Industrial Raw Materials

A. The world's physical and biological resources

  1. The identification and distribution of natural resources

  2. The management of resources

   a. Conservation of natural resources

   b. Salvage operations

B. Technology of the extraction industries

  1. Mining and quarrying
    [see also 214.A.4.c.]

   a. Processes: underground mining, surface mining and quarrying

   b. Products: coal, salt, stone, metal ores, sulfur, phosphates

  2. Techniques of extracting petroleum and gas
    [see also 214.B.5]

C. Primary conversion of raw materials

   1. Petroleum refining
      [see also 214.B.5.b.]

   2. Coal processing: production of coke, coal tar, light oil, gas, and chemicals
      [see also 214.B.5.a.]

   3. Production and processing of metal ores and metals
      [see also 214.A.4.c.]

      a. Aluminum

      b. Calcium

      c. Chromium

      d. Cobalt

      e. Copper

      f. Gold

      g. Iron

      h. Lead

      i. Magnesium

      j. Mercury

      k. Nickel

      l. Platinum

      m. Silver

      n. Sodium and potassium

      o. Steel and steel alloys

      p. Tin

      q. Titanium

      r. Tungsten

      s. Uranium

      t. Zinc

      u. Rare-earth metals
         [see 121.B.12.]

      v. Metal alloys

   4. Production of synthetic gemstones and industrial crystals

   5. Processing of stone, sand, clay, and gravel

      a. Manufacture of conventional and special types of glass and glass products

      b. Manufacture of cement, gypsum plasters, and plastic cements

      c. Manufacture of industrial ceramics

      d. Manufacture of bricks and tiles

   6. Processing of water to obtain salt, magnesium, oxygen, hydrogen, and other elements

   7. Processing of air to obtain oxygen, nitrogen, noble gases, and other gases

   8. Processing of plant and animal products

      a. To obtain paper and pulp

      b. To obtain roundwood, sawn wood, veneer, plywood and laminated constructions, particleboard, and fibreboard

      c. To obtain tobacco and other nonfood products

      d. To obtain leather and hides

      e. To obtain furs

      f. To obtain natural fibres

      g. To obtain pharmaceuticals

      h. To obtain oils, fats, and waxes

      i. To obtain resins and other products

Suggested reading in the *Encyclopædia Britannica*:

MACROPAEDIA: Major articles dealing with the extraction and conversion of industrial raw materials

Conservation of Natural Resources
Forestry and Wood Production
Industrial Glass and Ceramics
Industries, Extraction and Processing

MICROPAEDIA: Selected entries of reference information

General subjects

alloys:
alloy
aluminum bronze
amalgam
brass
bronze
calamine brass
cupronickel
Duralumin
electrum
ferroalloy
misch metal
pewter
solder
stainless steel
steel
animal fibres, furs,
and hides:
alpaca
camel hair
cashmere
fur
horsehair
leather
mohair
rabbit hair
silk
wool
ceramics:
adobe
brick
cement
firebrick
kiln
mullite
porcelain
enamelling
Portland cement
pottery
refractory
tile
coal and its
processing:
coal
coal tar
coke
lignite
forest products—
lumber:
balsa
ebony
fir

greenheart
hardwood
lancewood
logging
mahogany
narra
oak
pine
rosewood
seasoning
spruce
teak
wood
forest products—oils
and resins:
balsam
copal
dammar
dragon's blood
drying oil
gamboge
gum
lac
mastic
myrrh
naval stores
pine oil
resin
rosin
tall oil
turpentine
wood tar
forest products—
rubber:
balata
chicle
guttapercha
latex
rubber
forest products—
other:
cork
lignin
paper pulp
tannin
glassmaking:
Bakewell glass
blow molding
fibreglass
flint glass
glassblowing

Jena glass
mirror
Orrefors glass
Pitkin glass
Pittsburgh glass
plate glass
Pyrex
safety glass
silvering
soda-lime glass
South Jersey glass
metals of major
economic
importance:
aluminum
calcium
cast iron
chromium
cobalt
copper
gold
iron
lead
magnesium
mercury
nickel
platinum
potassium
silver
sodium
tin
titanium
tungsten
uranium
wrought iron
zinc
mineral sources of
nonmetals:
asbestos
barite
chrysotile
feldspar
fluorite
gilsonite
graphite
gypsum
kaolin
kimberlite
limestone
mica
phosphorite
pumice

quartz
shale
soapstone
spodumene
sulfur
tremolite
mining and
quarrying:
Frasch process
mining
placer mining
quarry
stoping
surface mining
oils, fats, and
waxes—edible:
See Section 731
oils, fats, and
waxes—inedible:
castor oil
Chinese wax
drying oil
essential oil
fat
fish oil
grease
lanolin
lavender
linseed
oil
oil cake
oil extraction
oil palm
oil plant
perilla oil
pine oil
sperm oil
spermaceti
tall oil
wax
whale oil
ore processing:
basic oxygen
process
Bessemer process
blast furnace
Cowper stove
crucible process
cupola furnace

Biographies
  See Section 732

INDEX: See entries under all of the terms above

Section 725.   **Technology of Industrial Production Processes**

A. Materials processing: the operations that are used to transform industrial materials from a raw-material state into finished parts or products

  1. Preliminary processing of raw materials

    a. Mechanical processing; *e.g.,* crushing, mixing, blending, separating, grading

    b. Chemical processing; *e.g.,* leaching, smelting, coagulation, polymerization

  2. Forming: processes in which parts are produced by casting or molding liquid materials or by applying pressure to solid materials

    a. Processing liquid materials

      i. Casting metals; *e.g.,* sand casting, die casting

      ii. Casting and molding nonmetals; *e.g.,* slip casting, injection molding

    b. Processing solid materials; *e.g.,* rolling, forging, stamping, pressing

  3. Material removal: processes for shaping parts by removing portions of a solid piece of material

  4. Joining: processes for bonding materials to each other

    a. Thermal joining: welding, brazing, and soldering
      [see B.5., below]

    b. Adhesive bonding: natural and synthetic adhesives and their uses

  5. Property modification: alteration or improvement of the properties of materials

    a. Thermal processing

      i. Basic heat-treating operations: annealing, stress relieving, and hardening

      ii. Radio-frequency heating: induction and dielectric heating

      iii. Zone melting: zone refining and other techniques

      iv. Exposure to cryogenic temperatures

    b. Processing of materials by exposure to physical conditions other than heat or cold

      i. Processing of materials in a vacuum

      ii. Use of ultrasonic and infrasonic waves

      iii. Other processes; *e.g.,* exposure to radiation

    c. Mechanical and chemical processing

  6. Finishing processes: modification of the surfaces of materials

    a. Mechanical and chemical processes; *e.g.,* cleaning, polishing, embossing, coating

    b. Electrochemical processes: electroplating

B. Metallurgy

  1. Mineral dressing: crushing and grinding, concentration or mineral preparation

  2. Process metallurgy

    a. Pyrometallurgy: metallurgical processes that involve the use of heat

      i. Gas–solid reactions; *e.g.,* roasting

      ii. Distillation: processes for refining metals by condensing metal vapours

      iii. Ferrous metallurgical processes: techniques for making iron and steel

      iv. Nonferrous metallurgical processes: techniques for producing copper, lead, zinc, and other metals

      v. Melting, alloying, casting, and ingot solidification

    b. Electrometallurgy: metallurgical processes that involve electrochemical reactions

      i. Electrowinning, electrorefining

      ii. Electroplating
       [see A.6.b., above]

    c. Hydrometallurgy

  3. Metal processing

    a. Cold and hot working; *e.g.,* forging, rolling, drawing

    b. Foundry processes; *e.g.,* sand casting, die casting

    c. Surface treatments; *e.g.,* hot dipping, metal cladding

    d. Powder metallurgy: powder manufacture, processes, and products

    e. Nuclear engineering metallurgy: production, fabrication, and application of uranium and other metals of importance in nuclear engineering

    f. Heat treatment: precipitation, allotropic transformation, and decomposition reactions

    g. Special products; *e.g.,* coins, medals, tokens

  4. Physical metallurgy

    a. Metallography
      [see also 125.D.1.]

    b. Corrosion

    c. Inspection and testing: mechanical and nondestructive testing

  5. Welding, brazing, and soldering

    a. Basic principles: the metallurgy of metal joining

    b. Welding processes; *e.g.,* forge welding, arc welding, resistance welding, brazing, soldering

      c. Types of joints; *e.g.,* fillet welds, brazed joints

      d. Weldability of metals

      e. Testing and inspection of welds: nondestructive and destructive methods

      f. Applications; *e.g.,* construction of bridges, storage tanks, and ships

      g. Recent developments; *e.g.,* plasma welding, laser welding, ultrasonic welding

C. Materials handling in the production process

    1. Types of materials-handling systems by process

    2. Materials-handling equipment; *e.g.,* wheeled carts, power trucks, trailer trains, racks, bins, conveyors

    3. Transportation of materials
       [see also 734]

    4. Technology of storage and warehousing

D. Technology of packaging

Suggested reading in the *Encyclopædia Britannica:*

MACROPAEDIA: Major articles dealing with the technology of the industrial production processes

    Industries, Extraction and Processing

MICROPAEDIA: Selected entries of reference information

General subjects

adhesives, fasteners,	hose	sintering	*packaging:*
and joining	industrial truck	wire	aerosol container
processes:	materials handling	*metal treating and*	barrel
adhesive	pipeline	*finishing:*	bottle
bolt	stoker	annealing	containerization
brazing	storage	anodizing	drum
cement	*metal forming:*	electroless plating	packaging
joint	anvil	electroplating	*thermal processing:*
mortar	die-casting	galvanizing	cryogenics
rivet	forging	plating	dielectric heating
screw	founding	porcelain	induction heating
soldering	goldbeating	enamelling	radio-frequency
water glass	grinding machine	surface hardening	heating
welding	investment casting	tempering	zone melting
materials handling:	mint	terneplate	
Archimedes screw	rolling	tinplate	
conveyor			

Biographies

    See Section 732

INDEX: See entries under all of the terms above

Division III. Major Fields of Technology
[For Part Seven headnote see page 265.]

Division I of Part Seven is concerned with the nature and effects of technology as a whole. Division II deals with technical processes not specific to any of the major fields of technology. The outlines in the eight sections of Division III deal with the major fields of technology, differentiated by the various needs, purposes, products, and services that have elicited technological development.

Section 731. Agriculture and Food Production

A. The history of agriculture

B. Farm management

1. Basic management problems and practices

2. Farm labour, draft animals, and farm machinery

3. Farm buildings

4. Farming in relation to other disciplines; *e.g.,* weather, pollution control

C. Crop farming

1. Soil preparation and care

2. Plant propagation, seeding and cultivation

3. Harvesting and crop processing

4. Specialized crop farming techniques: dryland farming, tropical farming, hydroponic farming, greenhouse farming

5. Control of pests and disease organisms

6. Major crops

   a. Horticultural crops: vegetables and legumes, fruits and nuts, flowers

   b. Cereals

   c. Forest crops: trees, rubber

   d. Production of other major field crops; *e.g.,* coffee, tea, cocoa, sugar, tobacco

D. Livestock farming

1. Animal breeding

2. Major flock and stock animals

   a. Cattle

   b. Swine

   c. Sheep and goats

   d. Horses

   e. Poultry

   f. Bees

   g. Other livestock; *e.g.,* buffalo, asses and mules, camels

3. Disease and pest control

E. Technology of hunting and fishing, whaling

F. Food processing

    1. Fruit and vegetable processing

    2. Cereals, cereal products, and other starch products

    3. Bakery products: basic ingredients, types of products and production methods, market preparation, quality maintenance and testing

    4. Confectionery and candy production

    5. Meat and meat products

    6. Fish and marine products

    7. Dairying and dairy products

        a. Milk production and handling techniques

        b. Dairy products: fluid and concentrated milk, dried milk, ice cream, butter, and cheese

    8. Beverage production

        a. Technology of brewing

        b. Technology of wine making

        c. Technology of producing distilled liquor

        d. Technology of producing nonalcoholic beverages: soft drinks, coffee, tea

    9. Spices, herbs, and flavourings

    10. Cane sugar, beet sugar, and other sweeteners

    11. Oils, fats, and waxes

    12. Eggs and egg products

    13. Cocoa and chocolate products

G. Food preservation

    1. Methods of preservation

        a. Low-temperature preservation: refrigeration and freezing

        b. Preservation by drying and by smoking

        c. High-temperature preservation: canning and pasteurization

        d. Fermentation and pickling

        e. Chemical preservation

        f. Preservation by heat radiation and by ionizing radiation

    2. Food storage and packaging

H. Techniques for controlling the quality of food

    1. Evaluation of food quality: sensory evaluation; objective evaluation by chemical, instrumental, and microbiological methods

    2. Control of food quality

    3. Regulation of food quality by legislation, grading, and inspection

I. Food sources and new product development

    1. History and development of new foods and new food products

    2. Utilization of new food sources; *e.g.,* oilseeds, leaves, grasses, single-cell protein

    3. Development of new market forms

    4. Development of special foods; *e.g.,* for space exploration

Suggested reading in the *Encyclopædia Britannica:*

MACROPAEDIA: Major articles dealing with agriculture and food production

Agricultural Sciences
Agriculture, The History of
Beverage Production
Farming and Agricultural Technology
Fishing, Commercial
Food Processing

Forestry and Wood Production
Gardening and Horticulture
Gastronomy
Industries, Extraction and Processing
Public Works

MICROPAEDIA: Selected entries of reference information

General subjects

beekeeping:
  beekeeping
  beeswax
  honey
  nectar
beverages:
  absinthe
  alcoholic beverage
  aquavit
  beer
  brandy
  champagne
  cider
  coffee
  cognac
  distilled liquor
  gin
  liqueur
  maté
  proof
  pulque
  rum
  sake
  soft drink
  tea
  tequila
  vodka
  whiskey
  wine
cereal crops:
  barley
  buckwheat
  cereal
  corn
  millet
  oats
  popcorn
  rice
  rye
  sorghum
  wheat
cereal grain products:
  bran
  breakfast cereal
  couscous
  dumpling
  hominy
  noodle

paella
pasta
tamale
cooking:
  baking
  boiling
  braising
  broiling
  cookbook
  frying
  leavening agent
  pressure cooker
  sauce
  shortening
  tandoori cookery
  wok
egg and dairy products:
  butter
  butterfat
  buttermilk
  candling
  cheese
  churn
  cream
  dairying
  egg
  ice cream
  milk
  yogurt
farm equipment and buildings:
  barbed wire
  barn
  binder
  cellar
  combine
  corn harvester
  cotton gin
  cotton harvester
  cream separator
  crib
  crop duster
  cultivator
  farm machinery
  fence
  grain drill
  grain elevator

harrow
hog house
millstone
plow
reaper
sakia
scarecrow
silo
thresher
tractor
windrower
farming techniques:
  chinampa
  contour farming
  crop rotation
  drainage
  dry farming
  fertilizer
  hacienda
  hydroponics
  irrigation
  Norfolk four-course system
  open-field system
  organic farming
  paddy
  plantation
  ranch
  spraying and dusting
  tenant farming
  terrace cultivation
  three-field system
  till-less agriculture
fishing and sea products:
  agar
  ambergris
  aquaculture
  baleen whale
  bêche-de-mer
  caviar
  commercial fishing
  factory ship
  fishery
  lobster pot
  net

roe
seafood
sponge
tuna
whaling
food preservation:
  dehydration
  fermentation
  food preservation
  freezing
  pasteurization
  preservative
  refrigeration
  smoking
horticulture:
  graft
  horticulture
  pruning
  transplant
livestock and feeds:
  cattle
  feed
  goat
  hay
  livestock
  pig
  sheep
  silage
meat products:
  aspic
  bacon
  beef
  frankfurter
  game
  gelatin
  ham
  hamburger
  lamb
  meat
  pork
  sausage
  veal
  venison
oils, fats, and waxes—edible:
  babassu palm
  beeswax
  butter

butterfat	oil plant	sugarcane	food processing
cocoa butter	perilla oil	sweetener	food processor
cod-liver oil	sperm oil	*tobacco:*	forestry
cohune oil	spermaceti	chewing tobacco	fowl
copra	wax	cigar	fruit
corn oil	whale oil	cigarette	pectin
cottonseed	*oils, fats, and*	pipe	sago
fat	*waxes—inedible:*	smoking	spice and herb
fish oil	See Section 724	snuff	straw
linseed	*sugars:*	tobacco	tapioca
margarine	honey	*other:*	tree ear
oil	maple syrup	additive	vegetable
oil cake	molasses	arrowroot	vinegar
oil extraction	sugar	emulsifier	
oil palm	sugar beet	food colouring	

Biographies

Burbank, Luther   McCormick, Cyrus Hall
Carver, George Washington

See also Section 10/34 of Part Ten

INDEX: See entries under all of the terms above

Section 732.   Technology of the Major Industries

A. Principles of organization of work and production
[see 712]

B. Major manufacturing industries

1. The aerospace industry

2. The automotive industry

3. The clothing and footwear industry

4. The furniture industry

C. The major fabrication industries

1. The textile industry

2. The steel industry
[see also 725.B.]

3. The leather and hide industry

4. The fur industry

5. The floor-covering industry

6. The electronics industry

7. The tool and die industry

8. The lumber industry

9. The cutlery industry

10. The abrasives industry

D. The major processing industries

1. The chemical industry

2. The petroleum industry
[see also 724.B.2.]

3. The paper industry

4. The pharmaceuticals industry
[see also 10/35.C.4.]

5. The plastics industry

6. The rubber industry

7. The surface-coating industry

8. The dye and pigment industry
   [see also 122.G.1.t.]

9. The man-made fibre industry

10. Production of industrial and residential gases

11. The cosmetics and personal care industry

E. The construction industries
   [see 733]

F. The service industries

   1. Hotels and motels

   2. Restaurants

   3. Food service systems

   4. The transportation industry
      [see 734]

   5. Security and protection systems

G. The utilities industries: the power, gas, telephone, and telegraph industries

H. The merchandising and marketing of consumer goods
   [see 533.H.5.]

I. Industrial research and development

J. Technology of industrial safety

Suggested reading in the *Encyclopædia Britannica*:

MACROPAEDIA: Major articles and a biography dealing with the technology of the major industries

Dress and Adornment
Ford, Henry
Forestry and Wood Production
Industrial Glass and Ceramics
Industries, Chemical Process

Industries, Extraction and Processing
Industries, Manufacturing
Industries, Textile

MICROPAEDIA: Selected entries of reference information

General subjects

abrasives:
   abrasive
   corundum
   emery
   silicon carbide
   synthetic diamond
aerospace:
   air-cushion
      machine
   airframe
   airplane
   airport
   airship
   Atlas rocket
   autogiro
   automatic pilot
   balloon
   biplane

blimp
Delta
flight simulator
fuselage
glider
helicopter
instrument landing
   system
jet engine
launch vehicle
monoplane
ramjet
rocket
Saturn
seaplane
STOL airplane
supersonic flight
Thor rocket

turbojet
turboprop
V-1 missile
V-2 rocket
wind tunnel
Zeppelin
automotive:
   automobile
   bus
   diesel engine
   electric automobile
   gasoline engine
   motorcycle
   tire
   tractor
   truck
   vehicular safety
      devices

chemical processing:
   ammonia-soda
      process
   autoclave
   contact process
   detergent
   drug
   dye
   fertilizer
   Haber–Bosch
      process
   Leblanc process
   man-made fibre
   paper
   pigment
   pitch
   retort

Section 733.   **Construction Technology**

A. General building construction

1. Preconstruction planning: design programming, drafting

2. Surveying procedures: techniques for laying out building foundations
[see also 723.D.2.c.ii.]

3. Building materials

   a. Earth, clay, and sod

   b. Vegetable matter: thatch, reeds, and other materials

   c. Lumber

   d. Bricks and tiles: other fired clay and ceramics
   [see 724.C.5.d.]

   e. Stone

   f. Mortar, cement, portland cement, and plaster
   [see 724.C.5.b.]

   g. Metals; *e.g.,* iron, steel, aluminum, copper
   [see 724.C.3.]

   h. Glass
   [see 724.C.5.a.]

   i. Concrete, reinforced concrete, and prestressed concrete

   j. Composition materials, plastics

   k. Structural fabrics

4. Testing of building materials

5. Construction machinery

   a. Transport machinery

   b. Lifting machinery; *e.g.,* cranes, cables, ropes

6. Construction techniques

   a. Wood and timber construction

   b. Masonry construction

   c. Concrete construction

   d. Steel construction

7. Building components

   a. Foundations and footings

   b. Structural systems

   c. Floor systems

d. Roof systems

e. Space-enclosure systems

f. Interior finishes: *e.g.,* carpeting, hardware, ceiling systems

g. Auxiliary systems

    i. Plumbing systems

    ii. Heating, ventilating, and air-conditioning systems

    iii. Electrical wiring

    iv. Systems for illumination: interior and exterior lighting

    v. Vertical transport systems; *e.g.,* elevators, moving stairways

    vi. Life-safety systems

8. Acoustics and sound-control techniques

B. Construction of civil engineering works

1. Dams

2. Aqueducts

3. Bridges

4. Underground construction

5. Harbour and hydraulic works

6. Lighthouses and lightships

C. Prefabrication and shop fabrication

Suggested reading in the *Encyclopædia Britannica:*

MACROPAEDIA: Major articles dealing with construction technology

Analysis and Measurement, Physical and Chemical
Building Construction
Drafting
Public Works

MICROPAEDIA: Selected entries of reference information

General subjects

bridges:	scaffold	putty	fan
bridge	skyscraper	rammed earth	fireplace
covered bridge	truss	shingle	furnace
military bridge	wall	shotcrete	heat pump
movable bridge	wattle and daub	tile	heating
pontoon bridge	*building foundations:*	wallboard	hypocaust
suspension	cofferdam	*construction*	stove
bridge	pier	*machinery:*	ventilating
viaduct	retaining wall	bulldozer	*lighting devices:*
building construction:	settling	crane	arc lamp
beam	shoring	dredge	Argand burner
box frame	soil mechanics	drilling machinery	candle
construction	*building materials:*	power shovel	electric discharge
cantilever	aggregate	*engineering graphics:*	lamp
carpentry	brick	blueprinting	flare
Chicago School	cement	drafting	flash lamp
drywall	clapboard	isometric drawing	fluorescent lamp
construction	concrete	*heating, ventilating,*	incandescent lamp
framed building	lath	*and air-conditioning*	kerosine lamp
half-timber work	mortar	*systems:*	lamp
hypostyle hall	nail	air-conditioning	lantern
log cabin	paris, plaster of	chimney	rushlight
post-and-lintel	portland cement	chimneypiece	safety lamp
system	pozzolana	electric heater	

	roof types:	tunnel	escalator
searchlight	dome	tunneling shield	gate
spotlight	geodesic dome	other:	hippodrome
masonry construction:	hip roof	acoustics	jetty
arch	roof	aqueduct	levee
cyclopean masonry	vault	construction	plumbing
masonry	tunneling:	dam	porch
mortar	air lock	dock	prefabrication
pointing	caisson	drydock	stadium
reticulated work		elevator	
rubble masonry			

Biographies

Brunel, Sir Marc Isambard   Nervi, Pier Luigi
Eads, James Buchanan   Roebling, John Augustus
Fuller, R. Buckminster   Roebling, Washington Augustus

See also Section 10/37 of Part Ten

INDEX: See entries under all of the terms above

Section 734.   Transportation Technology

A. History of transportation

1. Primitive transportation; *e.g.,* travois, slide car, sledge, pack animal, dugout

2. The wheel and the road: development of the vehicle wheel, roads of the ancient world, beginnings of the modern road

3. Sails and oars: beginnings of shipping and shipbuilding, growth of inland waterways

4. Steam transportation

   a. The railroad: the first locomotives, the spread of railways, the construction of railroad bridges and tunnels

   b. Steam navigation: the first steamships, introduction of iron ships, decline of sailing fleets

5. Development of modern transportation

   a. Construction of road vehicles, roads, bridges, and tunnels

   b. Development of mass urban transport and traffic networks

   c. Development of the air transport industry

B. Roads and highways and their construction

C. Vehicles and devices for transportation across country and on roads and highways

1. Nonwheeled transportation devices; *e.g.,* bridles, saddles, harnesses, stirrups

2. Animal-drawn wheeled vehicles: wagons, coaches, and carriages

3. Bicycles

4. Automobiles

5. Trucks and buses

D. Rail transportation

E. Stationary conveyance systems; *e.g.,* pipelines, conveyor belts
   [see 725.C.2.]

F. Water transportation

1. Types of ships and other waterborne vessels

2. Ship design and construction

   a. Ship design: hydrodynamic and hydrostatic factors that influence ship stability and maneuverability, structural strength and safety considerations

   b. Shipbuilding, shipyard layout and construction; planning, fabrication, and assembly; launching, outfitting, and trials

c. Power units for propulsion: steam generators, internal-combustion engines, gas turbines, and nuclear reactors

3. Canals and inland waterways

4. Harbour works: docks and quays, bulk terminals
   [see 733.B.5.]

G. Air transportation

1. Aircraft: configurations, flight characteristics, missions, and special uses

   a. Lighter-than-air craft: balloons, airships

   b. Heavier-than-air craft: fixed-wing aircraft, rotary-wing aircraft, experimental and research aircraft

   c. Air-cushion machines

2. Airports

3. Air transport industry

4. Space travel
   [see 738.C.]

5. Aeronautical and space research

H. Traffic control: history, problems associated with traffic, government regulations, conventional and computerized techniques of control

---

Suggested reading in the *Encyclopædia Britannica*:

MACROPAEDIA: Major article dealing with transportation technology

Transportation

MICROPAEDIA: Selected entries of reference information

General subjects

air transport:	Conestoga wagon	rail transport:	raft
air-cushion machine	curricle	coach	rigging
	gig	freight car	road at sea, rules of the
airframe	hansom cab	locomotive	
airplane	harness	marshalling yard	rowboat
airport	horsecar	railroad	rudder
airship	landau	sleeping car	sail
autogiro	one-horse shay	turbo train	ship
automatic pilot	phaeton	unit train	shipyard
balloon	post chaise	water transport:	square sail
biplane	ricksha	anchor	steamboat
blimp	rockaway	buoy	tanker
glider	saddle	canal	trawler
helicopter	sedan	canoe	tugboat
instrument landing system	stage wagon	castle	umiak
	stagecoach	clipper ship	other:
monoplane	sulky	fog signal	aqueduct
seaplane	troika	gondola	bicycle
STOL airplane	wagon	harbour	containerization
supersonic flight	highway transport:	hydrofoil	elevator
Zeppelin	automobile	jib	escalator
animal-powered transport:	boulevard	kayak	litter
	bus	keel	livery company
brougham	electric automobile	lateen sail	pipeline
buggy	expressway	lifeboat	Roman road system
carriage	motorcycle	lighthouse	
cart	road	lightship	shipping route
chaise	tire	lock	Silk Road
chariot	tractor	longship	tonnage
coach	truck	motorboat	traffic control
Concord coach		ocean liner	transportation
		paddle wheel	velocipede

Biographies

Cooper, Peter	MacCready, Paul	Piccard, Auguste	Tupolev, Andrey
Ford, Henry	Beattie	Sage, Russell	Nikolayevich
Fulton, Robert	Montgolfier,	Sikorsky, Igor Ivan	Wright, Orville
Gibbs, William	Joseph-Michel	Stephenson,	and Wilbur
Francis	and	George	
Langley, Samuel P.	Jacques-Étienne	Trevithick,	
Lear, William P.	Oberth, Hermann	Richard	
Lindbergh,	Julius		
Charles A.			

INDEX: See entries under all of the terms above

Section 735. **Technology of Information Processing and of Communications Systems**

A. Communication and information theory
[see 10/23.F.]

B. Calculating devices: the abacus, tally sticks, mechanical and electromechanical calculators
[see C.2., below]

C. Office machines

1. Writing and reproducing machines: typewriters, dictating and transcribing machines, word processors, duplicating machines and processes, copying machines and processes

2. Calculating and accounting machines

3. Miscellaneous office machines

D. Computers
[see also 10/23.A.6. and 7.]

1. Types of computers: analogue and digital computers, hybrid computer systems

2. Programming systems: the encoding and entering of instructions into computer memory, the concept of software, the systems approach to writing computer programs

3. Computer languages

4. Applications of microcomputers, minicomputers, and supercomputers

5. Developments in artificial intelligence: devising expert systems; natural-language processing; computer vision; robotics

E. General information-recording devices

1. Simple recording implements and devices; *e.g.,* writing implements, slates, chalkboards

2. Typewriters and word processors

3. Printing machines and processes

4. Production of printing plates: engraving and other techniques

   a. Mechanical techniques: woodcut, mechanical engraving, etching, lithography

   b. Photomechanical techniques: photoengraving

F. Sound and video recording and reproducing devices
[see also 128.E.]

1. Mechanical systems: phonographs

2. Magnetic systems: audio tape recorders, video tape recorders and players

3. Optical systems: audio and video disk players

4. Auxiliary equipment

5. High-fidelity concepts and systems

G. The technology of photography

1. Still photography
[see also 628.D.]

2. Motion-picture and television photography
   [see also 623]

3. Holography: laser photography
   [see also 128.B.4.]

H. Information processing and systems

1. Elements of information processing

   a. Recording and storage: image scanning and optical character recognition; mass storage via electromagnetic and electro-optical media (*e.g.,* magnetic tape and disk and optical disk, respectively); microform recording

   b. Organization and retrieval: indexes and indexing; bibliographic and numeric data bases; computerized catalogs in libraries and library networks

   c. Display and dissemination: television monitors and interactive computer terminals; electronic mail, bulletins, and teleconferencing; electronic printing and photocomposition; speech synthesis

2. Types of information systems

   a. Organizational systems

      i. Management-oriented systems (executive, command and control, and decision support)

      ii. Administration-oriented systems (financial, personnel, and project management)

      iii. Service-oriented systems (manufacturing, transaction processing, and expert)

   b. Public information utilities (on-line data base search systems)

   c. Educational and reference systems

      i. Dictionaries and lexicons

      ii. Encyclopaedias

      iii. Atlases and map collections

I. Major systems of communication

1. Book, newspaper, and magazine publishing

2. Postal systems and equipment

3. Telegraph systems and equipment

4. Telephone and telecommunications systems and equipment

5. Radio communications systems and equipment

6. Television communications systems and equipment

7. Communications satellite systems and equipment

8. Electronic networks

9. Encryption and decryption techniques and devices: signal security and message authentication, history of cryptology

J. Major systems of detection and remote sensing

1. Radar systems and equipment

2. Sonar systems and equipment

K. Electronic components and techniques used in communications

1. Components

   a. Active components: vacuum and gas-filled tubes, semiconductor devices

   b. Passive components: resistors, capacitors, and inductors; ferrites; other solid-state devices; antennas and waveguides

   c. Integrated circuits: miniature arrays of interconnected active or passive circuit elements

2. Sensing devices and transducers: piezoelectric devices, microphones and other pickups for sound and vibration, sensors

3. Circuitry

Suggested reading in the *Encyclopædia Britannica*:

MACROPAEDIA: Major articles dealing with the technology of information processing and of communications systems

Broadcasting	Encyclopaedias	Motion Pictures	Publishing
Computer Science	and Dictionaries	Photography	Telecommunications
Computers	Information	Postal Systems	Systems
Cryptology	Processing	Printing, Typography,	
Electronics	Libraries	and Photoengraving	

MICROPAEDIA: Selected entries of reference information
General subjects

computers:
  abacus
  analogue computer
  artificial
    intelligence
  computer
  computer-aided
    engineering
  computer-assisted
    instruction
  computer program
  computer
    programming
    languages
  computer science
  differential
    analyzer
  differentiator
  digital computer
  harmonic analyzer
  input/output
    device
  integrator
  microcomputer
  microprocessor
  supercomputer
  time-sharing
  word processing
electronic
  communication
  systems and devices:
  amateur radio
  broadcasting
  cable television
  citizen's band
    radio
  Comsat
  Echo
  facsimile
    transmission
  Intelsat
  loading
  minicam
  modem
  modulation
  Morse Code
  multiplexing
  radio
  satellite
    communication

shortwave radio
superheterodyne
  reception
telecommunications
  system
telegraph
telephone
teleprinter
television
Telex
Telstar
UHF
undersea cable
VHF
video tape recorder
videocassette
  recorder
videodisc
videophone
waveguide
libraries and their
  organization:
  archives
  Bliss Classification
  bookmobile
  Colon
    Classification
  Dewey Decimal
    Classification
  library
    classification
  Library of
    Congress
    Classification
  library science
  Universal Decimal
    Classification
office machines:
  accounting
    machine
  calculator
  cash register
  dictating machine
  duplicating
    machine
  hectograph
  mimeograph
  photocopying
    machine
  typewriter

photography and
  cameras:
  animation
  camera
  camera lucida
  camera obscura
  CinemaScope
  Cinématographe
  Cinerama
  collotype
  dye-transfer
    process
  electrophotography
  enlarger
  exposure meter
  filter
  fluorescence
    photography
  holography
  Kinetoscope
  microform
  minicam
  motion picture
  negative
  photography
  shutter
  speed
  Technicolor
  viewfinder
  wet collodion
    process
postal systems:
  airmail
  Penny Post
  postal system
  Thurn and Taxis
    postal system
  ZIP Code
printing and printing
  materials:
  colour printing
  computerized
    typesetting
  embossing
  engraving
  etching
  flatbed press
  gravure printing
  incunabula
  ink

intaglio
letterpress printing
Linotype
lithography
mezzotint
Monotype
offset printing
photocomposition
photoengraving
printing
proofreading
rotary press
rotogravure
  printing
typesetting
  machine
publishing:
  book
  codex
  colophon
  gazette
  journalism
  little magazine
  news agency
  newsletter
  newspaper
  newspaper syndicate
  pamphlet
  publishing
  royalty
  yellow journalism
sound recording and
  sound devices:
  cassette
  compact disc
  digital sound
    recording
  flutter and wow
  high-fidelity sound
    system
  loudspeaker
  magnetic recording
  microphone
  phonograph
  sound recording
  sound track
  stereophonic sound
    system
other:
  data base

dictionary	information	pen	qalam
encyclopaedia	processing	pencil	quill
eraser	information	public-address	stylus
	science	system	

Biographies

Alembert, Jean Le Rond d'	Fessenden, Reginald Aubrey	Macmillan, Daniel and Alexander	Pearson, Drew
Armstrong, Edwin H.	Girardin, Émile de	Manutius, Aldus, the Elder	Popov, Aleksandr Stepanovich
Beaverbrook, Sir Maxwell Aitken, 1st Baron	Gollancz, Sir Victor	Marconi, Guglielmo	Pulitzer, Joseph
Bell, Alexander Graham	Greeley, Horace	Morse, Samuel F.B.	Sarnoff, David
Benton, William	Gutenberg, Johannes	Murdoch, Rupert	Siemens, Werner von
Burnham, Edward Levy-Lawson, 1st Baron	Haley, Sir William	Muybridge, Eadweard	Siemens, Sir William
Caxton, William	Harper brothers	Nelson, William Rockhill	Stone, I.F.
Cotta family	Hearst, William Randolph	Niepce, Nicéphore	Thomas, Lowell
Cowles family	Josephson, Brian D.	Northcliffe, Alfred Charles William Harmsworth, Viscount	Vincent of Beauvais
Dana, Charles A.	Knopf, Alfred A.	Ochs, Adolph Simon	Wallace, DeWitt and Lila Bell Acheson
Diderot, Denis	Land, Edwin Herbert	Page, Walter Hines	Webster, Noah
Dimbleby, Richard	Lippmann, Walter	Paley, William S.	Winchell, Walter
Disney, Walt	Luce, Henry R.		Zworykin, Vladimir Kosma
Ferrié, Gustave-Auguste	Lumière, Auguste and Louis		

INDEX: See entries under all of the terms above

Section 736.   Military Technology

A. Offensive weaponry

    1. Early hand-powered weapons

        a. Construction materials: wood, stone, precious metals, copper, bronze, iron

        b. Shock weapons: *e.g.,* mace, axe, sword, halberd

        c. Missile weapons: *e.g.,* spear, javelin, sling, arrow

        d. Mechanical weapons: *e.g.,* ballista, catapult, ram, crossbow

    2. Gunpowder weapons

        a. Construction materials: cast bronze, cast or wrought iron, forged or stamped steel

        b. Loading: muzzle-, breech-, automatic

        c. Artillery: *e.g.,* cannon, howitzer, mortar

        d. Small arms: *e.g.,* musket, rifle, pistol, machine gun

        e. Ammunition

            i. Propellant: black powder, smokeless powder

            ii. Projectiles: *e.g.,* cannonball, shrapnel, shell, bullet

    3. Explosives: *e.g.,* grenades, mines, depth charges, bombs, missile warheads

    4. Self-propelled missiles

        a. Basing

            i. Land: *e.g.,* barrage rocket, ballistic missile, surface-to-air missile

            ii. Sea: *e.g.,* torpedo, submarine-launched ballistic missile, antiship missile

            iii. Air: *e.g.,* air-to-air missile, cruise missile

        b. Propulsion: rocket, jet, propeller

        c. Guidance: free-flight, energy-sensing, command, inertial

       d. Payloads: *e.g.,* single-warhead, cluster bomblet, multiple reentry vehicle

       e. Warheads: *e.g.,* high-explosive, antipersonnel, nuclear

    5. Nuclear weapons

       a. Energy sources: fission, fusion

       b. Effects: blast, heat, radioactive fallout

    6. Chemical and biological weapons

B. Defensive weaponry

    1. Personal protection

       a. Armour against early hand-powered weapons

           i. Materials: *e.g.,* leather, bronze, iron

           ii. Construction: *e.g.,* mail, scale, brigandine, plate

           iii. Protection: *e.g.,* shield, helmet, cuirrass, greave

       b. Armour against gunpowder and explosive weapons

           i. Materials: steel, plastic, Kevlar

           ii. Protection: *e.g.,* helmet, flak jacket, bullet-proof vest

       c. Protection against nuclear and chemical weapons: *e.g.,* gas mask, overgarments

    2. Fortification

       a. Field fortification: *e.g.,* log breastwork, wooden pallisade, trench, foxhole

       b. Permanent fortification before gunpowder: masonry citadel, motte-and-bailey castle

       c. Permanent fortification in the early gunpowder era: sunken profile, bastioned trace

       d. Permanent fortification in the modern gunpowder era: *e.g.,* concrete bunkers, pillboxes, reinforced aircraft hangars

       e. Antinuclear fortification: *e.g.,* hardened missile silos, bomb shelters

    3. Missile defense: surface-to-air missiles, rapid-fire guns

C. Weapon platforms

    1. Land vehicles

       a. Animal mounts: *e.g.,* horses, elephants, camels

       b. Man- and animal-powered vehicles: *e.g.,* chariots, siege towers

       c. Steam power: *e.g.,* railroad cars, early tanks

       d. Internal combustion: *e.g.,* tanks, armoured personnel carriers

    2. Surface ships and craft

       a. Oar-powered: *e.g.,* galleys, longboats

       b. Sail-powered: *e.g.,* galleons, ships of the line, frigates

       c. Steam-powered: *e.g.,* battleships, cruisers, aircraft carriers

       d. Internal combustion: *e.g.,* gunboats, landing craft

       e. Nuclear-powered: *e.g.,* aircraft carriers, cruisers

    3. Submarines

       a. Propulsion: steam turbine, diesel-electric, nuclear

       b. Vessels: attack, strategic missile launching

    4. Aircraft

       a. Fixed-wing airplanes

           i. Propulsion: internal combustion/propeller, jet

           ii. Configuration: *e.g.,* biplane, monowing, variable-geometry wing

           iii. Types: *e.g.,* fighter, bomber, early warning

       b. Helicopters

           i. Propulsion: internal combustion, gas turbine

           ii. Types: *e.g.,* attack, naval antisubmarine, transport

D. Engineering

    1. Tactical support: *e.g.,* fortification

    2. Strategic support: *e.g.,* roads, bridges, ports, airfields

    3. Ancillary support: *e.g.,* maps, bomb disposal

E. Logistics: supply, transport, lodging, services

F. Electronics

    1. Electromagnetic sensors and transmitters: radio, radar, infrared, ultraviolet, optical, laser

       a. Applications: communication, navigation, warning and detection, weapon guidance

    2. Electronic countermeasures: radar jammers, infrared flares, chaff

---

Suggested reading in the *Encyclopædia Britannica:*

MACROPAEDIA: Major articles dealing with military technology

    War, The Technology of   War, The Theory and Conduct of

MICROPAEDIA: Selected entries of reference information

General subjects

explosives and incendiaries:	B-17	minesweeper	Mauser rifle
atomic bomb	B-24	monitor	MG42
bomb	B-29	ship of the line	musket
depth charge	B-52	submarine	pistol
grenade	bomber	U-boat	repeating rifle
missile	F-4	*weapons:*	revolver
napalm	F-16	AK-47	rifle
neutron bomb	F-86	antiaircraft gun	sling
nitroglycerin	F-100	antitank weapon	spear
nuclear weapon	F-104	Armalite rifle	Spencer carbine
PETN	fighter aircraft	artillery	Springfield rifle
shell	Harrier	assault rifle	Sten gun
smart bomb	Hurricane	automatic pistol	submachine gun
thermonuclear bomb	Ilyushin IL-76	automatic rifle	sword
	ME-109	bayonet	Thompson submachine gun
torpedo	MiG	bazooka	
launch vehicles and rockets:	Mirage	Big Bertha	Uzi submachine gun
	Mosquito	bow and arrow	
Atlas rocket	P-38	Bren machine gun	weapon
cruise missile	P-47	Browning automatic rifle	*other:*
missile	P-51		Agent Orange
Nike missile	Spitfire	cannon	alcázar
Peacekeeper missile	Stuka	carbine	ammunition
	torpedo plane	catapult	biological warfare
Polaris missile	trainer	coastal artillery	camouflage
Poseidon missile	Zero	crossbow	chemical warfare
rocket	*personal protective equipment:*	dagger	fortification
Thor rocket	armour	field artillery	military bridge
Trident missile	chain mail	flame thrower	military engineering
V-1 missile	gas mask	flintlock	
V-2 rocket	helmet	Garand rifle	ram
mechanized ground warfare:	*warships:*	Gatling gun	sapper
	aircraft carrier	Greek fire	shrapnel
armoured vehicle	battleship	gun	snorkel
panzer division	cruiser	lance	stealth
tank	destroyer	Lee-Enfield rifle	Strategic Defense Initiative
military aircraft:	frigate	Luger pistol	strategic weapons system
attack aircraft	galleon	machine gun	
AWACS	galley	MAG machine gun	tactical weapons system
B-1	ironclad	matchlock	

Biographies

Abelson, Philip Hauge	Fokker, Anthony Herman Gerard	Krupp von Bohlen und Halbach, Gustav	Robins, Benjamin Rodman, Thomas Jackson
Braun, Wernher von	Forsyth, Alexander John	Lake, Simon	Sopwith, Sir Thomas Octave Murdoch
Brialmont, Henri-Alexis	Fulton, Robert Gatling, Richard	Lewis, Isaac Newton	Teller, Edward
Browning, John Moses	Jordan Goddard, Robert	Mannlicher, Ferdinand, Ritter von	Tupolev, Andrey Nikolayevich
Bushnell, David	Hutchings		Vauban, Sébastien
Chappe, Claude	Heinkel, Ernst Heinrich	Maxim, Sir Hiram Stevens	Le Prestre de
Colt, Samuel	Holland, John Philip	Maxim, Hudson	Whitehead, Robert
Congreve, Sir William	Ilyushin, Sergey Vladimirovich	Messerschmitt, Willy	Whittle, Sir Frank
Curtiss, Glenn (Hammond)	Krupp, Alfred	Oppenheimer, J. Robert	Zeppelin, Ferdinand (Adolf August
Dornier, Claudius	Krupp von Bohlen und Halbach, Alfried	Remington, Eliphalet	Heinrich), Graf von
Drebbel, Cornelis (Jacobszoon)		Rickover, Hyman G(eorge)	
Fermi, Enrico			

See also Section 544 of Part Five

INDEX: See entries under all of the terms above

Section 737. **Technology of the Urban Community**

A. Basic engineering services of the city

   1. Water-supply systems

   2. Sanitation systems

     a. Development and operation of sewage disposal systems

     b. Construction and operation of street clearance and refuse disposal systems

   3. Urban transportation systems

   4. Interurban transportation systems
     [see 734]

   5. Technology of electric power
     [see 721.C.7.]

   6. Fire prevention and control

B. Technology of the basic social services of the city

   1. Police technology

     a. Traffic control technology
       [see 734.H.]

     b. Crime control technology

   2. Design, construction, and maintenance of recreational facilities; *e.g.,* parks, stadiums, racetracks, planetariums, aquariums

C. Technological responses to new urban problems

   1. Control of air, water, land, and other pollution

   2. The planning of cities and urban environments: the systems approach to urban design and construction, the development of new towns

---

Suggested reading in the *Encyclopædia Britannica*:

MACROPAEDIA: Major articles dealing with technology of the urban community

Conservation of Natural Resources	Public Works
Police	

MICROPAEDIA: Selected entries of reference information

General subjects

fire prevention and control:	*police technology:*	pollution	refuse disposal
fire alarm	criminal	smog	system
fire engine	investigation	*urban transport:*	sedimentation tank
fire escape	electronic	elevated transit	sewage system
fire extinguisher	eavesdropping	line	sludge
fire fighting	fingerprint	monorail	*water-supply systems:*
fire prevention and	handcuffs	streetcar	conduit
control	lie detector	subway	desalination
fireboat	*pollution control:*	taxicab	qanat
halon	acid rain	trolleybus	reservoir
smoke detector	electrostatic	*waste disposal:*	water purification
sprinkler	precipitation	activated-sludge	water softener
system	emission-control	method	water-supply
	system	incinerator	system
	muffler		

Biographies

See Section 10/37 of Part Ten

INDEX: See entries under all of the terms above

Section 738.   Technology of Earth and Space Exploration

A. Techniques and equipment of surface and underground exploration

1. Types and purposes of exploration

   a. Scientific exploration: the determination of the properties of the Earth's interior

   b. Resource exploration: the discovery of sources of ores, building materials, fuels, water, and geothermal reserves

   c. Exploration for construction: the planning of tunnels, foundations, and other works

2. Methods of exploration

   a. Indirect methods: geophysical and geochemical methods

   b. Direct methods: on-site testing by means of excavation, boring, and sampling of soil and rock

B. Techniques and equipment of undersea exploration

1. Platforms for exploratory work

   a. Surface vessels; *e.g.,* deep-sea drilling ships and twin-hull vessels

   b. Submersibles

   c. Aircraft and satellites: application of remote sensing and satellite telemetry

   d. Buoys and other unmanned units; *e.g.,* the Self-Propelled Underwater Research Vehicle (SPURV)

2. Navigational methods and systems for establishing the precise location of discoveries

3. Developments in oceanographic sampling and measurement techniques; *e.g.,* acoustic methods and solid-state microelectronic ocean-current measuring devices

C. Techniques and equipment of space exploration

1. History of space flight prior to Sputnik I: early speculations and fictional accounts, development of space flight theory and technology during the 20th century

2. Space programs since 1957

   a. Space launch vehicles: rockets designed to provide orbital or escape velocity for manned or unmanned spacecraft

   b. Unmanned space probes

      i. The use of sounding rockets to explore the upper atmosphere of Earth

    ii. The use of orbiting satellites for scientific purposes; *e.g.*, to measure the natural phenomena of space; to study the relationship between Sun, Earth, and space; to test instrumentation and communication techniques

    iii. The use of unmanned spacecraft to probe the Moon and planets

  c. Manned space programs: the Mercury, Gemini, Apollo, and Space Shuttle programs of the U.S.; the Vostok, Voskhod, and Soyuz/Salyut programs of the U.S.S.R.

  d. The use of Earth-oriented satellites: communications, Earth survey, and navigation satellites

3. Elements of space flight

  a. The environment of space: the definition of space, characteristics affecting space flight

  b. Technology of spacecraft subsystems

  c. Launch principles and techniques: gravitational forces, staging techniques, and acceleration rates

  d. Mechanics and techniques of space flight

    i. Types of trajectories: suborbital, Earth orbital, Earth escape, and interplanetary

    ii. Navigation in space

    iii. Rendezvous and docking

    iv. Re-entry and recovery

4. Contributions of space exploration to advances in the physical sciences

D. Techniques of life-support systems for exploration

1. Systems used in undersea exploration

2. Systems used in space exploration

Suggested reading in the *Encyclopædia Britannica*:

MACROPAEDIA: Major articles dealing with the technology of earth and space exploration

  Exploration
  Public Works

MICROPAEDIA: Selected entries of reference information

Biographies

  Armstrong, Neil
  Oberth, Hermann Julius
See also Section 721

INDEX: See entries under all of the terms above

General subjects

launch vehicles:	Moon exploration	Voyager	Sputnik
Delta	Surveyor	Zond	TIROS
launch vehicle	Zond	*unmanned Earth*	Transit
Saturn	*ocean and seafloor*	*satellites:*	Vanguard
man in space:	*exploration:*	Aryabhata	Vela
Apollo program	bathymetry	Biosatellite	*other:*
astronaut	bathyscaphe	Cosmos	Hohmann orbit
Gemini	bathysphere	Discoverer	interplanetary
life-support system	Challenger	Earth satellite	exploration
Mercury	Expedition	Landsat	National
Mir	diving bell	Orbiting	Aeronautics
Skylab Program	Glomar Challenger	Astronomical	and Space
Soyuz	mesoscaphe	Observatory	Administration
space shuttle	*translunar probes:*	Orbiting	prospecting
space station	Galileo	Geophysical	seismic survey
Voskhod	Helios	Observatory	sounding rocket
Vostok	Mariner	Pegasus	space exploration
moon probes:	Pioneer	satellite	spacecraft
Apollo program	Venera	observatory	unidentified flying
Luna	Viking	Seasat	object

Introduction to Part Eight:
Religion as Symbolism

by Wilfred Cantwell Smith

There is more to human life than meets the eye. More to oneself; more to one's neighbour; more to the world that surrounds us. There is more to the past out of which we come; and especially, it would seem, more to the present moment, maybe even infinitely more. There is more to the interrelationships that bind us together as persons. And the further we probe, we have always found, the deeper the mystery, or the reward, or the involvement. It is this "more," perhaps, that provides at least one of the bases for human religion. We have seldom been content to be "superficial," to remain on the surface, to imagine that reality does not transcend our finite grasp; and throughout most of our history on this planet we have ordered our lives, both personal and cultural, in terms of that transcendence.

Yet how is one to point to what one does not visually see? How to resort to a milieu beyond all space? How to talk or to think about what transcends not only words but the reach of the mind? How even to feel about what one does not touch? Man's inherent and characteristic capacity to do these things finds expression through his special relation to symbols. These have proven over the centuries sometimes more, sometimes less, adequate to such a task, but in any case indispensable, and ubiquitous. Such symbols, it turns out, have the power not merely to express man's otherwise inchoate awareness of the richness of what lies under the surface, but also to nurture and to communicate and to elicit it. They have an activating as well as a representational quality, and an ability to organize the emotions and the unconscious as well as the conscious mind, so that into them we may pour the deepest range of our humanity and from them derive an enhancement of the personality. Without the use of symbols, including religious symbols, man would be radically less than human.

Quite diverse types of things have served the purpose: a beaver, the sky, a ceremonial procedure, silence; erotic love, or austere asceticism; the Qur'ān; a historical figure; reason. The variety has been immense, different groups having chosen different things to serve them as symbols, not all equally successful. Virtually universal, however, is that peoples have found it possible to designate some item from within the visible world and to sacralize it in such a way that it becomes then for them the symbol or locus of the invisible, the transcendent. In Japan, a simple open gateway (*torii*) marks off the shrine precincts: one passes through it, leaving behind psychologically, symbolically, the humdrum ordinary world to enter the sacred space of the temple; and after worship, one again moves through the gate in the other direction, to reenter now the realm of everyday life, but as a renewed person. Virtually all peoples have set aside some portion of what outsiders would regard as ordinary terrain to serve for them as sacred space, erecting in it temple, church, or shrine whereby is then

represented for them, often with great force, quite another dimension of reality.

Similarly with time: the Jew, for instance, sets apart one day in seven, whereby the other six days symbolize the mundane world with its bitter imperfections, perhaps its devastating pain, and at best its transient successes, while the Sabbath creatively represents the inviolate splendour of transcendence—with which therefore the other six days, however bleak, cannot keep him out of touch. Every people has its festivals, weekly or seasonal or occasional, its sacred times when life in its empirical and work-a-day aspects is transcended and life in its timeless dimension is reaffirmed, reactivated: moments when truth, significance, worth are recognized and cultivated—and carried back then into the ordinary world.

We are somehow aware, if only through imaginative vision or sensibility or our special capacity for hope, not only of what is but also of what ought to be. We have sensed that the *status quo* (nowadays, the *fluxus quo*) is not the final truth about man or the world. We have felt, to take one example, that social justice and concord, personal righteousness, health, joy stand over against the current observable condition of strife, loneliness, wickedness, poverty, and sorrow not as fancy against truth, wishful and irrational dreaming against reality, but in some fashion *vice versa*—as a norm by which the present imperfect world is judged, in some sense a truth in relation to which empirical actuality is in some sense an error. This too has been affirmed symbolically. One rather common way of doing so has been by representing a more perfect world elsewhere. Some have located their utopias chronologically in the past ("Once upon a time"; or Golden Age theories, as in Greece and India); or in the future (millennialisms, a coming just ruler, secular ideas of progress, a life after death); or geographically, somewhere else (the medieval Irish "Isle of the Blessed" in the then inaccessible Western Sea); or high above the sky (heaven, the heaven of heavens); or in a domain beyond time (Paradise); or in another realm than this universe (a metaphysical order, idealist realities).

However it be symbolized and articulated, a moral dimension to human life has been perceived and affirmed. Man has been aware not only of the profitable and the disadvantageous but also of the better and the worse, and has been inspired by some power to pursue the better; he has known that some actions are right, some wrong, and that it matters. At most times and most places, morality has been an integral part of the religious complex (although situations have on occasion arisen when the two have become historically dislocated—when a given form of religion has seemed not good; or to put it another way, when man's sense of what is worthwhile, and the inherited symbols by which worth used to be formulated, have no longer converged).

If the panorama of man's religious life is, in its outward form, selected mundane data symbolizing the more than mundane, then the task of the student of religion is to know those data but to consider them not in themselves but in their role in our lives. Our concern is not primarily the doctrines and scriptures and prayers and rites and institutions; but rather, what these do to us. Not the tribal dance, so much as what happens to the African dancing; not the caste system, so much as what kind of person the Hindu becomes within it, or without it; not the events at Sinai, so much as what role the recounting of these events has played in both Jewish and Christian life over the centuries since; not the Qur'ān, so much as what the Qur'ān means to a Muslim.

In illustration, let us consider as an example a statue of the Buddha, and take note specifically of one small part of it, the pose of the right hand. Among several such stylized poses used throughout the Buddhist world, we may choose just one, the *abhaya mudra* ("fearlessness pose"), in which the right arm is somewhat raised, that hand held straight up, palm facing out. Over and above the more universal significance of such a gesture (power, authority, benediction), in the Buddhist case this represents also an incident from the life of the Buddha, in which reputedly a wild elephant charging him and his group was stopped in its tracks when the Teacher raised his hand so, and became tame. The gesture gives artistic expression, then, to the Buddha's fearlessness in the face of the threat, and also to his conferring of fearlessness, and of grounds for fearlessness, on his disciples: his serene triumph over danger.

To say that this particular feature of sculpture symbolizes for Buddhists the overcoming of fear is to indicate not merely that it depicts an event in someone else's life, but also that it effects a change in one's own—since, to repeat, symbols not only represent but activate. The animal in its fury in the remembered anecdote may itself be taken as symbolic, representative of the pressures and assaults of life, which faith in the Buddha gives one the inner resources to withstand: the passions, for instance, to which such faith bestows on one the power quietly to say "no." To understand this particular item in the religious life of Buddhists, accordingly, is to know the history of how a Japanese emperor or a Thai merchant or a Chinese peasant through contemplating it in some nearby temple has had his life transformed, his fear removed, his personality healed. A parallel may be observed of the role in the lives of Christians, over the centuries, of the story of Christ's stilling of the tempest. His words, "Peace, be still!" read in the Lesson, and the portrayal of the scene in stained-glass windows, have served to symbolize, for people of faith, on the one hand Christ's power over the elements in his own life, and on the other hand the power that their faith in Him has in their lives, they have then found, to confer peace, to quell storms.

A special sort of symbolization, developed characteristically in, for instance, the Western world but by no means only there, has been the conceptual. A few recent philosophers have itched to legislate that concepts must be used to refer only to the sensible or phenomenal world; that it is illegitimate to use them symbolically to refer to a transcendent order. It would be manifestly stultifying to apply so austere a restriction to art or to most other human pursuits, apart from the natural sciences (from which these persons have learned it). Such an orientation has seemed to work rather well with the "objective" world—better, with the objective facets of the world (at least, until one raises moral questions about atomic bombs or ecology); but it appears stubbornly to misunderstand life in its distinctively human form.

One of the most powerful symbols in human history has, without question, been the *concept* "God." This concept, like other religious and other human symbols, has demonstrably meant different things to different persons and groups and ages; yet it is hardly too drastic an oversimplification to suggest that the concept has on the whole at least subsumed, integrated, deepened, and made operationally effective in the lives of many hundreds of millions of persons and in the life and social cohesion of many thousands of communities their awareness and their potential awareness of the entire range of transcendence with which they are surrounded or endued—of grandeur, order, meaning, aspiration, awe, hope, virtue, responsibility, rapport, integrity, worth, renewal. The highest, deepest, most comprehensive that they were capable of attaining, individually and socially, was organized, focused, and nurtured in and through this concept. (Given the distinction, observed by all believing theorists, between God and people's ideas of God, such theorists may themselves make this same point by saying that God has used the idea of God to enter people's lives; that the concept has served as a sacrament. More recent developments, with the concept "God" no longer serving so effectively, as a symbol, for many, will be touched on below.)

Although correlative conceptualizations are virtually worldwide and history-long, this particular concept was developed in its most powerful and characteristic form in the Near East and has permeated, at times dominated, the civilizations that have emerged from there to cover almost half the planet, especially the Islāmic and the Judeo-Christian. The Indian counterpart has been in many respects closely similar; in many, subtly different. China and Japan, although also employing symbolic concepts richly, have tended toward other religious and cultural patterns than this particular one.

Even so major a symbol, however, as the concept "God," however all-embracing it may seem, is in the end significant not in isolation but within a whole system of ideas, practices, values, and the like, forming a pattern of which it is no doubt the keystone but not the totality. Certainly minor symbols like the pose of the right hand in a piece of sculpture or medium ones like the ceremonial holiness of the Sabbath, however significant they have been in the lives of many millions of persons, derive their meaning and their power from each being one item within a large pattern of symbolic structures, such as the Buddhist complex or the Christian.

And even these great complexes, each of which has an elaborate and ever-changing history, constitute systems to be understood not in themselves, as structures to be looked at, but rather in terms of the ambience that they make available for men and women to live within. "In order to understand Buddhists, one must look not at something called Buddhism, but at the universe, so far as possible through Buddhist eyes." It is not the symbols themselves that one must grasp, so much as the orientation that they induce: how the whole complex of symbols enables those who live in terms of it to see a sunset, a broken marriage, prosperity, the onset of cancer, one's election to public office.

The religious history of the Hindu community is a history, in part, of traditional ceremonial and ideological and sociological patterns. Yet in more significant part it is a history, however difficult this may be to discern, of fortitude and of quiet humaneness, of a conviction that life is worth living and death worth dying, that goals are worth striving for, that the immediate is caught up in the eternal. The Buddhist metaphors have served to kindle in the mind and heart of the Buddhist the perhaps unconscious awareness that one's own fortune is not a reason for gloating, or one's neighbour's fortune, for envy; that knowledge is more important than wealth, and wisdom than knowledge; that the world is to be appreciated and not merely exploited; that one's fellow is to be treated as an end, not merely as a means; that sorrow is not a reason for despair. Islāmic law, theology, architecture, and the rest have been symbols that at their best have crystallized and nurtured, for Muslims, the courage and serenity, the sense of order and the aspiration to justice, the forbearance, the humility, the participation in community, that the Islāmic system traditionally inspired. Christian symbols have given both form and actuality, among Christians, to many things, including for instance the ability of human suffering to become redemptive.

Of course, religious symbols and sets of symbols have been used also for mean and destructive purposes. Man's wickedness, and not only his capacity for virtue, has been expressed and even encouraged by his symbol systems, at times. Through them he has found his freedom, his transcendence of the immediately given, his ability to move beyond being merely an organism reacting to its environment; but sometimes he has used these destructively, or has become a victim of their inherent ambiguities. Nothing has turned a society into a community so effectively as religious faith: to share common symbols is about the most powerful of social cohesions. And yet few gulfs have been greater than those that separate differing religious communities, few hostilities so fierce as those between groups whose symbols differ.

Religious symbols do not raise man above the human level; only to it.

A final word about history. The history of religion has at times been mistaken for the history of its symbols; but this is superficial. The same symbols have discernibly changed their meanings over time, and indeed from person to person, and even within one person's life; also,

persisting or widespread orientations and perceptions have been expressed in strikingly different symbolizations. The true history of religion is more deeply personalist—not in the sense of individualist: the personal is also the social, and especially so in the religious realm. The true history of religion, not yet written, is the history of the depth or shallowness, richness or poverty, genuineness or insincerity, splendid wisdom or inane folly, with which men and women and their societies have responded to such symbols as were around them. It is also, however, the tale, and to some degree this can be told, of when and in what fashion they have forged new symbols, or neglected or found themselves unable to respond to old. And nowadays it is also the story of how they deal or fail to deal with a plurality of symbolisms.

One's faith is in some sense the meaning that religious symbols have for one; but more profoundly, it is the meaning that life has, and that the universe has, in the light of those symbols. For religious symbols do not "have" meanings of their own; they crystallize in various ways the meaning of the world, of human life. There is a history of their varying ability to do this, at various times and places (or of people's varying ability to have them do it). How new symbols or patterns of symbols emerge is too complex or controversial a question to be summarized here; but how they develop once launched, how they are reinterpreted (sometimes radically) over the centuries, how their success in pointing beyond themselves often gives way to a rigidity and narrowness in which they or their institutions are prized or defended simply in themselves; how iconoclastic movements arise, to shatter the symbols (literally, smashing idols; or figuratively, attacking concepts and mores), whether in the name of something higher or out of misunderstanding, and often both; saddest of all, how a time may arrive when the symbols no longer serve a community, no longer communicate a transcendent vision, and then a profound malaise settles on the society and life comes to seem without meaning, and people become alienated from each other and even from themselves and from the world in which they live—all this the historian can trace.

In recent Western history an aberrational tendency has arisen to imagine that human life is fundamentally or naturally "secular," and that religion has been an added extra, tacked on here and there to the standardly human. This view now appears to be false. Rather, the various religious systems have expressed varying ways of being human. The unbiased historian cannot but report that it has been characteristic of man to find that life has meaning and to formulate that meaning in symbolic ways, whether grostesque or sublime.

Part Eight. Religion

The outlines in the eleven sections of Part Eight set forth studies of religion in general and studies of the particular religions. The ways in which religion is related to studies of human society, the fine arts, the history of civilizations, and science and philosophy are dealt with in Parts Five, Six, Nine, and Ten.

Division I.   **Religion in General**

The outlines in the two sections of Division I deal with diverse views of the nature, purpose, validity, and value of religion, and with the problems, methods, and results of the empirical, comparative, and phenomenological study of religions and of religious experience.

Section 811.   **Knowledge and Understanding of Religion**

A. The philosophy of religion: diverse views of the nature and characteristics of religion

  1. Basic questions and problems

    a. The existence of the divine or sacred (God)

    b. The attributes of the divine or sacred

    c. The extent to which mankind can have knowledge of the divine or sacred

    d. The special problems of free will, evil and suffering, and immortality

  2. Questions about the nature and character of the divine or sacred

    a. Whether the divine or sacred is personal or impersonal

    b. Whether the divine or sacred is one or more unique beings or powers

B. Religious experience: its nature, elements, and varieties

C. Religious phenomenology: the basic patterns of religious thought, action, and association

D. Theology as an attempt to understand and state the rationale of religious belief

  1. Theology in relation to divine revelation

    a. The role of Sacred Scriptures

    b. Doctrine and dogma

    c. Articles of faith: religious creeds

  2. Mystical theology: immediate experience of the divine or sacred

  3. Doctrines concerning God or the gods

    a. Polytheism

    b. Religious dualism

    c. Monotheism

      i. Theism

        ii. Deism

        iii. Pantheism and panentheism

    d. Atheism and agnosticism

  4. Doctrines of creation

  5. Angelology

  6. Doctrines of divine government and providence

  7. Eschatological theories

  8. Doctrines of grace and salvation

  9. Sacramental doctrines

  10. The doctrine of the Covenant

  11. Miracles

E. The study and classification of religions

F. Other systems of belief

  1. Myth and mythology

  2. Magic

  3. Witchcraft

  4. Shamanism

  5. Astrology and alchemy

  6. Ancestor worship

  7. Hero worship

  8. Nature worship

G. Religion in relation to other aspects of human experience

  1. Religion and art
    [see also Part Six]

  2. Religion and science

  3. Religion and society
    [see also 521.D.6.]

  4. Religion and morality
    [see also 10/52.B.6.]

  5. Religion and philosophy
    [see also Part Ten, Division V]

Suggested reading in the *Encyclopædia Britannica:*

MACROPAEDIA: Major articles dealing with the knowledge and understanding of religion

Doctrines and Dogmas, Religious	Religions, The Study and Classification of
Myth and Mythology	Religious and Spiritual Belief, Systems of
Occultism	Sacred Offices and Orders
Philosophies of the Branches of Knowledge	Theology

MICROPAEDIA: Selected entries of reference information

General subjects

basic concerns and phenomena of religion:			*conceptions of the divine or sacred:*
covenant	heaven	sacrament	agnosticism
creation myth	hell	sacrifice	animism
creed	immortality	salvation	anthropomorphism
eschatology	miracle	scripture	atheism
evil, problem of	moral theology	sin	Deism
faith	mysticism	soul	deus otiosus
first cause	myth	superstition	dualism
free will	paradise	theodicy	extrinsicism
	prayer	theology	
	prophet	theophany	
	revelation		

fideism	Neo-Paganism	religious	supernaturalism
High God	pantheism	syncretism	theism
monotheism	polytheism	secularism	

Biographies

Campbell, Joseph	Frazer, Sir James	Malinowski,	Tiele, Cornelius
Durkheim, Émile	George	Bronisław	Petrus
Eliade, Mircea	James, William	Müller,	Tylor, Sir Edward
Evans-Pritchard, Sir	Jung, Carl (Gustav)	(Friedrich) Max	Burnett
Edward (Evan)	Lang, Andrew	Otto, Rudolf	Wach, Joachim
Frankfort, Henri	Lévi-Strauss, Claude	Söderblom, Nathan	Weber, Max

INDEX: See entries under all of the terms above

Section 812.   The Religious Life: Institutions and Practices

A. Religious rites and customs

   1. Rituals of worship

      a. Prayer

      b. Confession

      c. Pilgrimage

      d. Sacrifice

   2. Passage and purification rites: birth, puberty, marriage, death

   3. Religious regulation of personal and social behaviour

      a. Religious law
         [see 551.B.3.d. and 827.F.6.a.]

      b. Dietary customs

      c. Monasticism

      d. Celibacy

      e. Asceticism

      f. Prophecy and divination

   4. Religious feasts and festivals

B. Religious leaders and institutions

   1. The religious state: theocracies, sacred kingships

   2. Forms of religious organization: church, temple, congregation, sect, council; the priesthood

   3. Sainthood

   4. Institutions of religious education

C. Material manifestations of religious beliefs

   1. Sacred writings

   2. Art and architecture, religious symbolism and iconography

   3. Ceremonial and religious objects, the sacraments

   4. Religious dress and vestments

Suggested reading in the *Encyclopædia Britannica*:

MACROPAEDIA: Major articles dealing with the religious life: institutions and practices

   Doctrines and Dogmas, Religious
   Religious Experience
   Religious Symbolism and Iconography
   Rites and Ceremonies, Sacred
   Sacred Offices and Orders

MICROPAEDIA: Selected entries of reference information

General subjects

disciplines and practices:	*places of worship:*	monasticism	cremation
asceticism	altar	priesthood	embalming
celibacy	church	prophet	marriage
fasting	high place	sacred kingship	passage rite
feast	mosque	saint	purification
human sacrifice	synagogue	shaman	*other:*
meditation	*religious offices, orders, and personages:*	*rites of passage and associated practices:*	amen
pilgrimage		anointment	aniconism
prayer	abbot	Baptism	confession of faith
sacrament	canonization	burial	creed
sacrifice	hagiology	circumcision	idolatry
tonsure	hermit	clitoridectomy	relic
	martyr		scripture

Biographies

See Section 811

INDEX: See entries under all of the terms above

Division II.   **The Particular Religions**
[For Part Eight headnote see page 303.]

The outlines in the nine sections of Division II treat the particular religions of mankind, in different historical eras and world areas.

Section 821.   **Prehistoric Religion and Primitive Religion**

A. Prehistoric religion

1. The study of prehistoric religion: nature, scope, methods of interpretation, problems special to the subject
   [see also 10/41.B.]

2. Inferred prehistoric religious beliefs and practices

   a. Burial customs and cults of the dead

   b. Cannibalism

   c. Sacrifices: human, animal, and other offerings

   d. Hunting rites and animal cults

   e. Female fertility deities

   f. Shamanism, sorcery, and magic

3. Religions attributed to various prehistoric cultural stages and regions

B. Primitive religion

1. The nature and significance of primitive religion

2. Primitive views of reality

  a. The distinction between the sacred and the profane

  b. Dynamistic, daemonistic, and theistic views of the sacred: the concept of mana

  c. Animism: external reality viewed as living presence

  d. Sacred time and times, sacred space and places, and man's nature, origin, and destiny: primitive cosmogonies, cosmologies, eschatologies

3. The nature and function of myth and symbol in primitive religion: their role in ritual, the iconographic character of primitive art

4. Primitive religious practices and institutions

  a. Sacrifice, purification, passage rites

  b. Worship or veneration centred on natural objects or forces

  c. Totemism: the socioreligious system in which men are intimately related to plants, animals, or other natural phenomena

  d. Worship of ancestors, kings, and heroes

  e. The roles of asceticism, shamanism, divination, and spiritualistic practices

5. The primitive religions of the major world areas

  a. Africa: traditional religions of the indigenous African peoples

  b. Australia and Oceania: religions of the Pacific Island peoples

  c. The Americas: religions of Indians of North, Central, and South America

  d. Asia: aboriginal religions of Asian peoples

  e. The Arctic: religions of the Eskimo, Aleuts, Saami (Lapps), Chukchi, Yakuts, Nganasan, Nenets, and other Arctic peoples

---

Suggested reading in the *Encyclopædia Britannica*:

MACROPAEDIA: Major articles dealing with prehistoric religion and primitive religion

Doctrines and Dogmas, Religious
Prehistoric Peoples and Cultures
Sacred Offices and Orders

MICROPAEDIA: Selected entries of reference information

General subjects

amulet	Dreaming, the	mother goddess	sun dance
animal worship	Earth Mother	phallicism	sun worship
animals, master	fire walking	rain dance	taboo
of the	headhunting	reindeer sacrifice	thunder cult
animism	hieros gamos	Rice Mother	tjurunga
Blessing Way	High God	sacred clown	totemism
bull cult	mana	sacred pipe	vision quest
cannibalism	medicine society	shaman	world tree
Corn Mother	megalith	skull cult	
devarāja	moon worship	Stonehenge	

Biographies

See Section 811

INDEX: See entries under all of the terms above

Section 822. **Religions of Ancient Peoples**

    A. Religions of the ancient Near Eastern peoples

        1. Characteristics of the ancient Near Eastern religions

        2. Mesopotamian religions

        3. Egyptian religion

           a. Historical developments from the late Neolithic Period to the Hellenistic Age

           b. Religious literature and mythology

           c. Beliefs and doctrines: the Egyptian pantheon

           d. Major forms of Egyptian religion

           e. Religious symbolism and iconography

        4. Religions of the ancient peoples of Asia Minor

        5. Syrian and Palestinian religions

        6. Religions in the Arabian Peninsula

    B. Religions of the Iranian peoples

        1. General characteristics of the Iranian religions

        2. Early Indo-Iranian religion: nature-polytheism
           [see also 823.A.1.]

        3. Religion of the Scythians, Sarmatians, and Alani
           [see F., below]

        4. The cult of Ahura Mazdā (Ormazd): its influence on the preaching of Zoroaster and the priestly institutions of the Magi

        5. Mithraism

        6. Zurvanism

        7. Manichaeism
           [see E.3., below]

    C. Greek religion

        1. Historical development

        2. Greek mythology and other religious literature

        3. Religious beliefs and speculation: the Greek pantheon

        4. Worship, practices, institutions

        5. Religious art and iconography

    D. Roman religion

        1. Historical development

        2. Roman gods, goddesses, numina, and genii and their place in family and civic religion

        3. Worship, practices, institutions

        4. Religious art: sculpture, metalwork, painting, mosaic

    E. Religions of the Hellenistic world

        1. Mystery religions

        2. Gnosticism

        3. Manichaeism

        4. Hellenistic religious philosophies: neoplatonism, stoicism, epicureanism
           [see also 10/51.A.1.c.]

        5. Quasi-scientific and magical cults; *e.g.*, numerology, astrology

        6. Judaism
           [see 826]

7. Christianity
[see 827]

F. Religions of the early peoples of eastern and central Europe

1. Scythian religion

2. Religions of the Sarmatians and associated peoples

3. Religion of the pre-Christian Slavic peoples

G. Religions of the ancient Celtic and Germanic peoples

1. Religion of the Celts

2. Religion of the Germanic peoples

H. Religions of the early peoples of northeastern Europe

1. Religion of the Baltic peoples

2. Religion of the Finno-Ugric peoples

I. Religions of pre-Columbian American civilizations

1. Inca religion

2. Mayan religion

3. Aztec religion

Suggested reading in the *Encyclopædia Britannica*:

MACROPAEDIA: Major articles dealing with religions of ancient peoples

Doctrines and Dogmas, Religious	Mystery Religions
European Religions, Ancient	Pre-Columbian Civilizations
Middle Eastern Religions, Ancient	Zoroastrianism and Parsiism

MICROPAEDIA: Selected entries of reference information

General subjects

Anatolian and Asia	Kalvis	Apepi	*Egyptian worship,*
Minor religions:	Laima	Apis	*practices, and*
Hebat	Iauma	Aton	*institutions:*
Kubaba	Mēness	Atum	Book of the Dead
Tarhun	Pērkons	Bast	Canopic jar
Teshub	Saule	Bes	Egyptian religion
Arabian religion	*Celtic religion:*	Buto	Heb-Sed festival
(*pre-Islāmic*):	Belenus	Geb	Hermetic writings
hanif	Brân	Hathor	mortuary temple
Ilumquh	Brigit	Horus	reanimation rite
Lāt, al-	Celtic religion	Hu, Sia, and Heh	scarab
Aztec religion:	Cernunnos	Isis	*Finno-Ugric religion:*
Chicomecóatl	Dôn	Ma'at	Finno-Ugric
Coatlicue	Druid	Mut	religion
Huitzilopochtli	Esus	Nekhbet	haltia
nagual	Goibniu	Nu	Kekri
Ometecuhtli	Llyr	Nut	kobdas
Quetzalcóatl	Lugus	Opet	lud
Tezcatlipoca	Medb	Osiris	maa-alused
Tlaloc	Ogmios	Ptah	Madderakka
Tlazoltéotl	Pwyll	Re	Manala
Tonatiuh	Sucellus	Sarapis	noiade
Xipe Totec	Teutates	Sebek	Peko
Xiuhtecuhtli	Tuatha Dé Danann	Seth	saivo
Baltic religion:	*Egyptian pantheon:*	Shu	
Dievs	Amon	Taurt	
gabija	Anubis	Thoth	

sampo
Tapio
tietäjä
väki
Ved-ava
Veralden-radien
voršud
Germanic mythology:
  Aurgelmir
  Balder
  Fenrir
  Freyja
  Germanic religion
    and mythology
  Heimdall
  Hel
  Idun
  Kvasir
  Loki
  Midgard
  Mimir
  Norn
  Odin
  Ragnarök
  Skadi
  Svadilfari
  Thor
  Tyr
  Ull
  Valhalla
  Valkyrie
  Yggdrasill
Gnosticism,
  Manichaeism, and
  related movements:
  aeon
  Archon
  Cainite
  Carpocratian
  Cathari
  Docetism
  Encratite
  Gnosticism
  Hellenistic
    religion
  Mandaeanism
  Manichaeism
  Marcionite
  Mazdakism
  Ophite
  Paulician
Greek mythology
  and legend:
  Acestes
  Achilles
  Actaeon
  Admetus
  Adonis
  aegis
  Agamemnon
  Aglauros

Ajax
Alcmaeon
Amazon
Amphitrite
Amphitryon
Ananke
Ancaeus
Andromache
Andromeda
Antigone
Antiope
Arethusa
Argonaut
Ariadne
Arion
Asclepius
Atalanta
Athamas
Atlas
Atreus
Autolycus
Bellerophon
Briareus
Britomartis
Busiris
Cadmus
Caeneus
Calchas
Calliope
centaur
Cephalus
Cyclops
Daedalus
Danaus
Daphne
Daphnis
demon
Dido
Echo
Endymion
Eos
Erechtheus
Erigone
Fama
Fate
Fury
Galinthias
Gorgon
Greek mythology
Hector
Hecuba
Helen
Helenus
Heracles
Hesperides
Hyacinthus
Hyperborean
Hypnos
Idomeneus
Ilos
Io
Iphigeneia

Ixion
Jason
Laocoön
Laomedon
Leto
Leucothea
Linus
Lotus-Eater
Lycaon
Marsyas
Medea
Medusa
Meleager
Memnon
Menelaus
Midas
Minos
Minotaur
Myrmidon
Narcissus
Neoptolemus
Niobe
Nisus
nymph
Odysseus
Oedipus
Orestes
Orion
Palamedes
Pandora
Paris
Pegasus
Peleus
Pelias
Pelops
Penelope
Perseus
Phaethon
Philoctetes
phoenix
Pirithous
Pleiades
Polyphemus
Priam
Protesilaus
Proteus
Pyramus and
  Thisbe
Sarpedon
Satyr and Silenus
Scylla and
  Charybdis
Semele
Seven Against
  Thebes
Sibyl
Siren
Sisyphus
Tantalus
Theseus
Thetis
Tiresias

Titan
Trojan horse
Typhon
Uranus
Greek pantheon:
  Aphrodite
  Apollo
  Ares
  Aristaeus
  Artemis
  Asclepius
  Athena
  Chaos
  Cronus
  Demeter
  Dionysus
  Eros
  Fury
  Grace
  Hades
  Hebe
  Hecate
  Helios
  Hephaestus
  Hera
  Hermes
  Hestia
  Hippolytus
  Hora
  Hygieia
  Muse
  Nemesis
  Nereus
  Nike
  Pan
  Persephone
  Poseidon
  Priapus
  Prometheus
  Rhea
  Selene
  Themis
  Tyche
  Zeus
Greek worship,
  practices, and
  institutions:
  Anthesteria
  Bacchanalia
  baetylus
  Carneia
  Daphnephoria
  Delphi
  Didyma
  Dodona
  Eleusinia
  Greek religion
  Heraeum
  herm
  lectisternium
  oracle
  Palladium

Section 823. **Hinduism and Other Religions of India**

  A. History of Hinduism

   1. The origins of Hinduism: Indo-European roots and other influences

   2. The prehistoric and protohistoric periods, through the 2nd millennium BC: the religions of the indigenous prehistoric peoples and of the Indus Valley civilization

   3. The Vedic period (2nd millennium–7th century BC)

     a. The religion of the Ṛgveda

     b. The religion of the later Vedas and *Brāhmaṇa*s

     c. The religion of the *Upaniṣad*s

   4. The heterodox period (7th–2nd century BC): challenges to Brahmanism by reformers and ascetic groups
     [see also D.l., below, and 824]

   5. The early Hindu period (2nd century BC–4th century AD): the rise of the major sects and other developments

   6. The Purāṇic period (4th–8th century)

   7. The rise of devotional Hinduism (8th–11th century): the Tamil hymnists, the *Bhāgavata-Purāṇa* after Hinduism

   8. The age of *bhakti* (11th–19th century)

   9. The modern period (19th–20th century)

   10. Hinduism today

  B. Intellectual, spiritual, and imaginative expressions of Hinduism
    [see also C.4., below]

   1. Hindu sacred literature

     a. Primary scriptures regarded as eternal revelations: the Veda

     b. Post-Vedic Sanskrit literature; *e.g.,* epics, *Purāṇa*s, *Tantra*s

     c. Sacred literature in Indian regional languages

   2. Hindu mythology: varieties of myths, modes of representation and themes

   3. Hindu philosophy: the integral relation of philosophy and religion in Hinduism

   4. Hindu mysticism: its general characteristics, varieties, goals, and methods

  C. Beliefs, practices, and institutions of Hinduism

   1. Common characteristics of Hindu belief

     a. Views about God or the sacred

     b. Views about the universe

     c. Views about mankind

        i. *Ahiṃsā,* the obligation to respect all living beings

        ii. The doctrines of *karman, saṃsāra,* and transmigration

        iii. The three *mārga*s: the paths of duties, of knowledge, and of devotion

   2. The forms of Hinduism

     a. Vedism and Brahmanism

     b. Vaiṣṇavism

     c. Śaivism

     d. Tantrism and Shaktism

     e. Folk Hinduism

     f. Ethical, social, and nationalist movements in modern Hinduism

3. Rituals, social practices, and institutions

   a. Sacrifice and worship

   b. Sacred times and places

   c. The class hierarchy: the caste system

   d. Religious orders, holy men, the four stages of life

4. Cultural expressions of Hindu values and ideas

   a. The traditional religious functions of Indian art: symbols and images

      i. Types of symbols: *yantra*s, *maṇḍala*s, *liṅga*s, *yoni*s

      ii. Icons: their role in expressing theological elements of Hinduism

   b. The religious expression of particular arts

D. Other religions of India

1. Jainism

   a. History of Jainism

      i. Early background: traditional accounts of Mahāvīra's predecessors

      ii. The life, work, and teachings of Vardhamāna Mahāvīra

      iii. Later developments (6th century BC–20th century AD)

   b. Myths about Jaina "great souls": Tirthaṅkaras, ascetic and monastic figures, and lesser deities

   c. Beliefs, practices, and institutions of Jainism

2. Sikhism

   a. History of Sikhism

      i. Islāmic and Hindu background (11th–15th century)
        [see also A., above, and 828.A.]

      ii. The origin of Sikhism in the life and work of Nānak, first of the ten Gurūs (15th–16th century)

      iii. The establishment and growth of Sikhism under the nine succeeding Gurūs, the establishment of Sikh militarism (16th–18th century)

      iv. The condition of Sikhism during the Sikh empire (18th–19th century)

      v. The condition of Sikhism under British rule (19th–20th century)

      vi. Sikhism in independent India and Pakistan

   b. Sikh religious literature

   c. Beliefs, practices, and institutions of Sikhism

3. Parsiism: Zoroastrianism in India
   [see 822.B.4.]

   a. History of Parsiism

   b. Sources of beliefs and doctrines in Zoroastrian literature

   c. Beliefs, practices, and institutions of the Parsis

Suggested reading in the *Encyclopædia Britannica*:

MACROPAEDIA: Major articles dealing with Hinduism and other religions of India

   Hinduism
   Indian Philosophy
   Jainism
   Sikhism

MICROPAEDIA: Selected entries of reference information

General subjects

Hinduism—
caste system:
Agarwālā
Bania
bhāīband
Brahman
Camār
caste
Christian caste
Dāsa
Devadāsī
Ḍom
dvija
gotra
Islāmic caste
jajmānī system
jāti
Kshatriya
kul
Mahar
Marāthā
Nambūdiri
Nāyar
outcaste
pañcāyat
pollution and
  purification
sabhā
Śūdra
untouchable
Vaisya
varna
Hinduism—deities
and mythology:
Aditi
Agni
Ardhanārīśvara
Balarāma
bhut
Brahmā
Caṇḍī
churning of the
  milky ocean
Dharma-Ṭhakur
Durgā
Gaṇeśa
Garuḍa
grāmadevatā
Hanumān
Harihara
Indra
Jagannātha
Kālī
Kalkin
Kāma
Krishna
Kubera
Kūrma
Lakṣmī

Manasā
Manu
Matsya
Meru, Mount
Murugaṉ
naga
Nandi
Narasiṃha
Naṭarāja
Paraśurāma
Pārvatī
Prajāpati
Rādhā
rakshasa
Rāma
Rāvaṇa
Saptamātṛkā
Sarasvati
Sītā
Śiva
Skanda
Sūrya
vāhana
Vāmana
Varāha
Varuṇa
Vāsudeva
Vishnu
yaksha
Yama
yuga
Hinduism—forms,
sects, movements,
and orders:
Ajīvika
Arya Samaj
Bhāgavata
bhakti
Brahmo Samaj
Caitanya
  movement
daśnāmī sannyāsin
Gāṇapatya
Kānphaṭa Yogi
Kāpālika and
  Kālāmukha
Kashmir Śaivism
Liṅgāyat
Nātha
Pāñcarātra
Pāśupata
Prarthana Samaj
Rādhā Soāmi
  Satsang
sādhu and swāmī
Śaiva-siddhānta
Śaivism
sampradāya
sannyasi

Satnāmī sect
Saura sect
Shaktism
Smārta sect
Śrīvaiṣṇava
Swāmī-Nārāyāṇī
Tantric Hinduism
Teṉkalai
Vaḍakalai
vairāgin
Vaishnavism
Vaiṣṇava-
  Sahajiyā
Vallabhācārya
Hinduism—
philosophy and
doctrine:
Advaita
ahaṃkāra
ānanda
anumāna
artha
āsana
ashrama
āstika
atman
avatar
bhedābheda
brahma
cakra
Cārvāka
cow, sanctity
  of the
deva
dharma
Dvaita
Haṭha Yoga
indriya
jnana
karman
kuṇḍālinī
mārga
māyā
Mīmāṃsā
nirguṇa
Nyāya
prakṛti
pramāṇa
prāṇa
prāṇāyāma
pratyakṣa
purusha
śabda
samadhi
Sāṃkhya
saṃsāra
tat tvam asi
upādhi

Vaisheshika
Vedānta
Viśiṣṭādvaita
yama
Yoga
Hinduism—ritual
and practice:
antyeṣti
ārtī
aśvamedha
darshan
dikṣā
Dīwālī
guru
Holī
Janmāṣṭamī
kīrtana
Kumbh Mela
liṅga
Mahā-śivarātrī
mudra
navaratra
Om
Poṅgal
pradakṣiṇa
puja
Rathayātrā
saṃskāra
soma
śrāddha
Śrī-Nāthajī
suttee
tapas
tilak
tīrtha
upanayana
Vedic sacrifice
yajña
Hinduism—
sacred and secular
literature:
Āgama
Araṇyakas
Artha-śāstra
Aṣṭchāp
Bhagavadgītā
Bhāgavata-Purāṇa
Brāhmaṇa
dharmashastra
dharmasutra
Gītagovinda
Gṛhya-sūtra
Kalpa-sūtra
Mahābhārata
maṅgal-kāvya
Manu-smṛti
Nāyaṉar

Purāṇa	aṣṭamaṅgala	nirjarā	Dasam Granth
Rāmāyaṇa	Bāhubali	Pārśvanātha	gurdwārā
Smṛti	Digambara	Paryuṣaṇa	Gurū
Śrauta-sūtra	dravya	Ṛṣabhanātha	Harimandir
Śruti	gaccha	Siddha	Khālsā
sūtra	guṇasthāna	Sthānakavāsī	Nāmdhārī
Tantra	Jaina canon	Śvetāmbara	Niraṅkārī
Upanishad	Jaina vrata	syādvāda	Rām Rāiyā
Veda	Jainism	Tīrthaṅkara	Sikhism
Jainism:	jiva	*Sikhism:*	Singh Sabhā
ahimsa	Kālakācāryakathā	Ādi Granth	Udāsī
ajiva	Kalpa-sūtra	Akāl Takht	*other:*
Ariṣṭanemi	leśyā	Akālī	Parsi

Biographies

Aurobindo, Śrī	Gobind Singh	Mīrā Bāī	Rāmānuja
Caitanya	Keshab	Nānak	Roy, Ram Mohun
Dādū	Chunder Sen	Ram Singh	Śaṅkara
Dayananda	Madhva	Ramakrishna	Tara Singh
Sarasvati	Mahāvīra	Ramana Maharshi	Vivekananda
Fateh Singh, Sant	Meher Baba		

INDEX: See entries under all of the terms above

Section 824.   Buddhism

A. History of Buddhism

  1. The cultural context: its background in Hinduism; its geographical, ethnic, and cultural base
[see also 823]

  2. The founding of Buddhism: the life, work, and teachings of Siddhārtha Gautama (6th–5th century BC)

  3. Developments in India (6th century BC–12th century AD)

  4. Buddhism in Central Asia and China
[see also 825.A.]

  5. Buddhism in Korea and Japan
[see also 825.D. and E.]

  6. Buddhism in Tibet and the Himalayan kingdoms

  7. Buddhism in Ceylon (Sri Lanka) and Southeast Asia to the mid-19th century

  8. Buddhism in the late 19th and 20th centuries

B. Intellectual, spiritual, and imaginative expressions of Buddhism
[see also C.4., below]

  1. Buddhist sacred literature

  2. Buddhist mythology: basic types, contents, and functions of myths

  3. Buddhist philosophy: the role and contribution of systematic reflective thought

  4. Buddhist mysticism: universal characteristics; regional and historical variations; goals, techniques, and approaches

C. Beliefs, practices, and institutions of Buddhism

  1. Traditional beliefs and doctrines

    a. Views of the nature of reality; *e.g.*, the impermanence of all existence, the absence of self, the underlying state of suffering and its causes

    b. The Eightfold Path to salvation or release

    c. The goal of the Eightfold Path: Nirvāṇa

    d. The Threefold Refuge—in the Buddha, the doctrine, and the community

e. Views of the gods, spirits, and demons: the role of miraculous powers

2. The main forms of Buddhism

a. The Theravāda school and other ancient schools

i. Views of the nature of things: cosmology, the classification of *dharma*s

ii. The emphasis on self-cultivation and self-salvation: the stages leading to *arhat*ship, the levels of meditation

iii. Doctrines concerning Buddha and Buddhahood

iv. Characteristics of the individual ancient and transitional schools

b. The Mahāyāna version

i. Views of the nature of absolute reality: the ultimate realization of the meditative quest

ii. Views of the transcendence of the Buddha: the three aspects of the Buddha, the *bodhisattva* ideal

iii. Characteristics of the individual Mahāyāna schools; *e.g.,* Mādhyamika, Yogācāra, Avataṃsaka, Zen, devotional schools

c. Esoteric Buddhism: Tantrism, Tibetan Buddhism, Shingon

3. Practices and institutions

a. Universal or prevalent ethical and religious practices

b. Monastic institutions: the characteristics and role of the *saṅgha*

c. Ceremonies and festivals: the religious year, popular traditions, passage rites

d. Regional variations in practices

4. The religious and cultural role of Buddhist art

a. Symbolism and iconography

b. Religious expression in the arts

5. The relationship of Buddhism to nationalist movements: its contemporary situation, its prospects

---

Suggested reading in the *Encyclopædia Britannica*:

MACROPAEDIA: Major article dealing with Buddhism

Buddhism, The Buddha and

MICROPAEDIA: Selected entries of reference information

General subjects

deities and mythology:	Ni-ō	Nichiren	*offices and personages:*
Amitābha	Saṃvara	Buddhism	bhikku
Avalokiteśvara	Shih Wang	Pure Land	bodhisattva
Bhaiṣajya-guru	Tārā	Buddhism	cakravartin
brahma-loka	Vairocana	Reiyū-kai	Dalai Lama
dharmapāla	Vajrapāṇi	Rinzai	lama
Dhyāni-Buddha	Vajrayoginī	Risshō-Kōsei-kai	mahāsiddha
Five Great Kings	yi-dam	Ritsu	Nechung oracle
Hārītī	*forms, sects, schools,*	Rnying-ma-pa	Panchen Lama
Hevajra	*and orders:*	Sammatīya	pratyeka-buddha
Kṣitigarbha	Bka'-brgyud-pa	Sarvāstivāda	upāsaka
lokapāla	Dge-lugs-pa	Sautrāntika	*philosophy and*
Lumbinī	eighteen schools	Shingon	*doctrine:*
Mahā Māyā	Hīnayāna	Sōka-gakkai	Abhidharmakośa
mahāpuruṣa	Jōjitsu	Sōtō	abhijñā
Maitreya	Kegon	Theravāda	akriyāvāda
Mañjuśrī	Kusha	Tibetan Buddhism	ālaya-vijñāna
Māra	Mādhyamika	T'ien-t'ai	anattā
Myō-ō	Mahāsaṅghika	Vajrayāna	arhat
nāman	Mahāyāna	Yogācāra	ariya-puggala
		Zen	

arūpa-loka	Buddhist	Bhadracaryā-	butsudan
āsrāva	meditation	praṇidhāna	caitya
bhava-cakra	dhāraṇī	bhāṇavāra	Gandhāra art
bhūmi	gcod	Bka'-'gyur	Jōgan style
bodhi	gtor-ma	Bstan-'gyur	kapāla
brahma-loka	koan	Buddhacarita	Kara-yo
brahmacarya	kyūdō	Dhammapada	Mai-chi-shan
brahmavihāra	mandala	Diamond Sūtra	mandala
dharma	mantra	gsung-'bum	Mathurā art
dukkha	mudra	Guhyasamāja	mudra
Eightfold Path	nang-mchod	Tantra	Northern Wei
Four Noble Truths	pabbajjā	Heart Sūtra	sculpture
kammaṭṭhāna	pāramitā	Jātaka	pagoda
karman	pātimokkha	Khuddaka Nikāya	prayer wheel
Kegon	phyi-mchod	Lalitavistara	Sānchi sculpture
Kusha	sādhana	Laṅkāvatāra-sūtra	stūpa
Mādhyamika	sangha	Lotus Sūtra	Sukhothai style
mahāmudrā	Smon-lam	Mahāvairocana-	Tempyō style
Nirvāṇa	chen-mo	sūtra	Tenjiku
pāramitā	upasaṃpadā	Mahāvastu	thang-ka
prajñapti	uposatha	Mahāyāna-śrad-	thread cross
Pramāṇa-vārttika	vassa	dhotpāda-śāstra	T'ien-lung Shan
pratītya-samutpāda	vihāra	Milinda-pañha	Tōdai Temple
pratyaya	zazen	Mūlamadhyama-	U Thong style
puñña	*sacred and secular*	kakārikā	vajra
saddhā	*literature:*	Prajñāpāramitā	yab-yum
samadhi	Abhidhamma	Pramāṇa-vārttika	Yün-kang caves
saṃsāra	Piṭaka	Pure Land Sūtra	*other:*
saṃvṛti-satya	Abhidhammattha-	Satyasiddhi-śāstra	Abhayagiri
Sarvāstivāda	saṅgaha	sūtra	Bon
Satori	Abhidhammāvatāra	Sutta Piṭaka	Buddhist council
sīla	Abhidharmakośa	Suttanipāta	Mahāvihāra
skandha	Abhisamayālaṅ-	Ta-ts'ang Ching	mappō
smṛtyupasthāna	kārāloka	Tipiṭaka	rock edicts
Triratna	Amitāyur-dhyāna-sūtra	Vinaya Piṭaka	
trisvabhāva	aṅgā	*symbolism,*	
practices and	aṭṭhakathā	*iconography, and*	
institutions:	Avadāna	*ritual objects:*	
abhiṣeka	Avataṃsaka-sūtra	Borobuḍur	

Biographies

Asaṅga	Fa-hsien	Hui-neng	Padmasambhava
Aśoka	Hasegawa Tōhaku	Kūkai	Shinran
Bodhidharma	Hōnen	Nāgārjuna	
Dōgen	Hsüan-tsang	Nichiren	

INDEX: See entries under all of the terms above

Section 825.   Indigenous Religions of East Asia: Religions of China, Korea, and Japan

A. Characteristics and development of Chinese religion

  1. The distinction and relationship between the folk religions and the literate religions in China

  2. History of religion in China

    a. The emergence of Chinese religion: ancestor worship, early cosmological beliefs

    b. The formulation of the Great Tradition: the development of the Confucian and Taoist ways (6th–lst century BC)

    c. The dominance of the Buddhist Way and the rise of Taoist-inspired cults (lst–16th century)

    d. The modern period: the effects of Western religions and of nationalism and secularism on familial and social systems

3. Traditional concepts in Chinese religious thought: the relation of the individual to the cosmos and to society

4. Ritual practices and institutions

5. Chinese religious symbolism

6. Chinese mythology

B. Confucianism

1. History of Confucianism

   a. Background in the institutions of the predynastic sage-emperors and the founders of the first three dynasties

   b. Origin in the life and teachings of Confucius (551–479 BC), the first Sage

   c. The Confucian school and its various forms: the teachings of Mencius, the second Sage, and of Hsün-tzu (c. 5th–3rd century BC)

   d. Establishment of Confucianism as the state orthodoxy of the Han Empire: eclectic tendencies, skeptical and rationalistic reactions (2nd century BC–3rd century AD)

   e. Introduction of Confucianism into Korea and Japan (1st and 4th centuries AD)
   [see D. and E., below]

   f. Confucianism during the time of Buddhist ascendancy: its continued role in the family system, the government bureaucracy, and the examination system; textual studies

   g. The emergence and development of Neo-Confucianism (11th–20th century): metaphysical and humanistic emphases, the teaching of Chu Hsi, the development of Neo-Confucian schools

   h. Varied responses to intellectual and material challenges of the West and to other developments: reformist and conservative movements, the effect of political developments on Confucian ideology and scholarship

   i. Confucianism today: its current demographic and social aspects

2. Confucian literature

3. Confucianism as a religion and as a philosophy

C. Taoism

1. History of Taoism

   a. Origin and early developments: the first evidence of the teachings of Lao-tzu and Chuang-tzu (c. 4th–3rd century BC)

   b. Developments during the Ch'in and Han periods (3rd century BC–3rd century AD): esoteric traditions, the Huang–Lao tradition, revolutionary messianism, developments in philosophy

   c. Developments from the 2nd to the 6th century: brief recognition of Taoism as the state religion; interaction with Buddhism; ceremonial, alchemical, and scriptural traditions

   d. Developments under the T'ang, Sung, and later dynasties: internal developments, the role of alchemy, syncretistic tendencies

   e. The later development of philosophical and religious Taoism from the 14th century to the present time

2. Taoist literature

3. Taoism as a religion and as a philosophy

D. The religions of Korea

1. History of Korean religion from prehistoric times to the present: the influence of Chinese, Japanese, and Western religions

2. Religious literature and mythology

3. Beliefs and doctrines

4. Practices and institutions

E. The religions of Japan

1. History of Japanese religion

   a. Early clan religion before the 6th century AD

b. Early historic and medieval periods (6th–16th century): the introduction of Buddhism, the impact of Chinese influences on Shintō, other developments

c. The Tokugawa era (1603–1867): Neo-Confucian Shintō, Sect Shintō, other developments

d. The Meiji era and after (1868 to the present): new religious movements

2. Shintō: the Way of the Gods

    a. History of Shintō
    [see E.1., above]

    b. Characteristics of primitive Shintō: the role of guardian shrines and shamans

    c. Shintō literature and mythology: the form and content of the *Koji-ki, Nihon-gi,* and other writings

    d. Basic beliefs and doctrines: concepts of mankind, the sacred and related precepts and principles

    e. Ritual practices and institutions

3. Japanese religious art and symbolism

4. Japanese mythology

Suggested reading in the *Encyclopædia Britannica:*

MACROPAEDIA: Major articles dealing with indigenous religions of East Asia: religions of China, Korea, and Japan

Chinese Literature   Shintō
Confucianism, Confucius and   Taoism
Japanese Literature

MICROPAEDIA: Selected entries of reference information

General subjects

Chinese deities and mythology:	shen	Shu Ching	tengu
Chang Kuo-lao	Shen Nung	Ssu shu	uji-gami
Ch'ang O	Shou Hsing	Ta hsüeh	Ukemochi no
Ch'eng Huang	Shun	Tso chuan	kami
ch'i-lin	Ta Yü	Wu ching	Yama-no-kami
Chih Nü	T'ien	*Japanese deities and*	Yorimitsu
Chung-li Ch'üan	Ts'ai Shen	*mythology:*	*Japanese religious*
feng-huang	Tsao Chün	Amaterasu	*movements:*
Fu Hsi	Ts'ao Kuo-chiu	Amenouzume	Hito-no-michi
Fu Shen	Tsao Shen	Benten	Hōtoku
Han Hsiang	T'u-ti	Daikoku	Kirishitan
Ho Hsien-ku	Wen Ti	Ebisu	Kokugaku
Hou Chi	Wu hsing	Fukurokuju	Konkō-kyō
Hou I	Yao	goryō	Kurozumi-kyō
Hou T'u	Yü Ti	Hachiman	Neo-Confucianism
Hsi Wang Mu	*Confucianism—*	hitogami	Ōmoto
Huang-ti	*philosophy:*	Ho-musubi	PL Kyōdan
Kuan Ti	Confucianism	Inari	Shinbutsu shūgō
K'uei Hsing	hsiao	Izanagi and	Tenshō Kōtai
Lei Kung	jen	Izanami	Jingū-kyō
Li T'ieh-kuai	li	Jimmu	*Korean religion:*
Lu Hsing	T'ien Ming	kami	changsŭng
Lü Tung-pin	*Confucianism—*	kappa	Ch'ŏndogyo
lung	*sacred literature:*	Kusanagi	mudang
Men Shen	Chou li	Ninigi	P'alkwanhoe
Nü Kua	Ch'un-ch'iu	Ōkuninushi	Poch'ŏngyo
Pa Hsien	Chung yung	Sarudahiko	p'ungsuchirisol
P'an Ku	I Ching	Shichi-fuku-jin	Sansin
p'an-t'ao	Li chi	Sugawara	*Shintō—precept and*
San Kuan	Lun yü	Michizane	*practice:*
She Chi	Mencius	Sukunahikona	harai
	Shih ching	Susanoo	jinja

kami	shōzoku	Shrine Shintō	hsü
kamidana	tamaya	Shugen-dō	Huai-nan-tzu
Kojiki	torii	State Shintō	Lieh-tzu
matsuri	ujigami	Tajong-gyo	p'o
musubi	*Shintō—sects and*	Tangun	p'u
Nihon shoki	*schools:*	Tenrikyō	tao
norito	Fukkom Shintō	*Taoism:*	Tao-te Ching
Shichi-go-san	Ise Shintō	Dōkyō	te
shinsen	Kyōha Shintō	Five Pecks of Rice	tzu-jan
shinshoku	Ryōbu Shintō	hsien	wu-wei
shintai	Sannō Ichijitsu	hsin-shu	
shinten	Shintō		

Biographies

Ch'eng Hao and	Hayashi Razan	Lieh-tzu	Tung Chung-shu
Ch'eng I	Hsün-tzu	Mencius	Wang Ch'ung
Chu Hsi	Lao-tzu	Motoori Norinaga	Wang Yang-ming
Chuang-tzu	Liang Shu-ming	Shao Yung	Yen Yüan

INDEX: See entries under all of the terms above

Section 826.   **Judaism**

A. History of Judaism

1. The biblical era

2. The Hellenistic era
[see also 822.E.]

3. The Talmudic era in Palestine and Babylonia: the foundations of rabbinic Judaism
[see also B.3., below]

4. The medieval era: the European and Islāmic phases of rabbinic Judaism (7th–18th century)

5. The modern era from *c.* mid-18th century: developments in modern Judaism

6. Judaism today: its current demographic and social aspects

B. Intellectual, spiritual, and imaginative expressions of Judaism
[see also C.4., below]

1. Biblical literature

   a. Canons, texts, and vernacular versions of the Bible; *e.g.,* Septuagint, Targum

   b. TaNaKh, the Hebrew Bible: Torah, Nevi'im, Ketuvim

   c. Noncanonical literature: Apocrypha, pseudepigrapha

2. Qumrān literature (Dead Sea Scrolls)

3. Talmud and Midrash

4. Judaic exegesis and hermeneutics

5. Mystical and devotional writings

6. Jewish philosophical writings

7. Jewish myth and legend

C. Beliefs, practices, and institutions of Judaism

1. Basic beliefs and doctrines

   a. Doctrines concerning God

   b. Doctrines concerning the Jewish people: the concept of Covenant
   [see also 811.B.10.]

   c. Doctrines concerning mankind

   d. Doctrines concerning the universe

e. Eschatology: views about the future age of mankind and the world, the King-Messiah and his reign
   [see also 811.B.7., 827.F.1.d., and 829.A.]

2. Basic practices and institutions

   a. Individual and familial practices

   b. Synagogue practices and other public institutions: the role of the rabbi, chief rabbinates, and general councils and conferences

   c. Sacred times: the sabbath, the Jewish holidays

   d. Sacred places: the land of Israel and Jerusalem

   e. The sacred language: Hebrew

3. Present-day forms of Judaism

   a. Orthodox Judaism

   b. Reform, or Liberal, Judaism

   c. Conservative Judaism

   d. Other variations in belief and practices: Reconstructionism, Ḥasidism, regional or ethnic groups

4. Art and iconography

   a. The anti-iconic principle: the influence of the biblical prohibition against idolatry

   b. Uses of the visual arts in ceremony and ritual: ceremonial objects, synagogue architecture, paintings, manuscript illumination

   c. Music: Jewish liturgical modes, the influence of folk traditions, vocal and instrumental music

   d. Literature: traditional legends and poetic exegesis, later religious poetry and tales

---

Suggested reading in the *Encyclopædia Britannica*:

MACROPAEDIA: Major articles and a biography dealing with Judaism

Doctrines and Dogmas, Religious
Judaism
Moses

MICROPAEDIA: Selected entries of reference information

General subjects

beliefs and doctrines:
  agunah
  'avera
  chosen people
  Derekh Eretz
  eschatology
  Gehenna
  gemilut ḥesed
  Halakha
  Hebraic law
  Israeli law
  messiah
  minhag
  mitzvah
  'olam ha-ba
  Shekhina
Bible:
  Amos, Book of
  Babel, Tower of
  Chronicles, books of the
  Daniel, Book of

Dead Sea Scrolls
Deuteronomy
Ecclesiastes
Eden, Garden of
Esther, Book of
Exodus
Ezekiel, Book of
Ezra and
  Nehemiah,
  books of
Genesis
Habakkuk,
  Book of
Haggai, Book of
Hexapla
Holiness, Code of
Hosea, Book of
Isaiah, Book of
Israel, Kingdom of
Jeremiah, Book of
Job, Book of
Joel, Book of

Jonah, Book of
Joshua, Book of
Judges, Book of
Ketuvim
Kings, books of
Lamentations of
  Jeremiah
Leviticus
Malachi, Book of
Masoretic text
Micah, Book of
Nahum, Book of
Nevi'im
Noahide laws
Numbers
Obadiah, Book of
Old Testament
Proverbs
Psalms
Ruth, Book of
Samuel, books of
Septuagint

Solomon, Song of
Ten
  Commandments
Torah
Zechariah, Book of
Zephaniah,
  Book of
*forms, sects, and
  movements:*
  Ashkenazi
  Bene-Israel
  Conservative
    Judaism
  Falasha
  Ḥasidism
  Oriental Jew
  Orthodox Judaism
  Reconstructionism
  Reform Judaism
  Samaritan
  Sephardi
  Zionism

history:
- Ammonite
- amora
- Ark of the
  Covenant
- Asher
- Babylonian Exile
- Benjamin
- Bethel
- Boethusian
- Canaan
- Dan
- Diaspora
- Elohim
- ephod
- Ephraim
- Essene
- Gad
- gaon
- golden calf
- Ḥasidean
- Haskala
- high priest
- Holocaust
- Holy of Holies
- Issachar
- Jerusalem,
  Temple of
- Judah
- Judaism
- K'ai-feng Jew
- Karaism
- Kenite
- Kneset ha-Gedola
- Levite
- ma'amadot
- Manasseh
- manna
- Midianite
- Mitnagged
- Moabite
- Musar
- Naphtali
- Nazirite
- Pharisee
- Qumrān
- Rechabite
- red heifer
- Reuben
- Sadducee
- Samaritan

- Sambation
- sanhedrin
- savora
- scapegoat
- shewbread
- Simeon
- Sinai, Mount
- Sodom and
  Gomorrah
- sofer
- Tabernacle
- tanna
- Ten
  Commandments
- Ten Lost Tribes of
  Israel
- Therapeutae
- Twelve Tribes of
  Israel
- Western Wall
- Yahweh
- Zealot
- Zebulun
- Zion

mysticism:
- ba'al shem
- devequt
- Ḥabad
- Kabbala
- kavvanah
- maggid
- Merkava
- Sefer ha-bahir
- Sefer ha-temuna
- Sefer ha-zohar
- Sefer Yetzira
- sefira
- Shabbetaianism
- tzaddiq

*rites, practices, and
  institutions:*
- 'alenu
- aliyah
- amidah
- anno mundi
- arba' kanfot
- ark
- Avinu Malkenu
- Bar Mitzvah
- berakha
- bet din

- bimah
- cantor
- chief rabbinate
- cohen
- David, Star of
- derasha
- Elijah's cup
- etrog
- exegesis
- gabbai
- gematria
- genizah
- get
- Hafṭarah
- ḥalitza
- Hallel
- hands,
  imposition of
- Ḥanukka
- Ḥavdala
- Hebraic law
- hermeneutics
- ḥol ha-mo'ed
- Kaddish
- kashruth
- ketubba
- Kiddush
- Kol Nidre
- kosher
- Lag ba-'Omer
- maarib
- mahzor
- matzeva
- menorah
- mezuzah
- middot
- mikvah
- minhah
- minyan
- musaf
- neilah
- Paschal lamb
- Passover
- peshaṭ
- phylactery
- pidyon ha-ben
- piyyut
- prosbul
- Purim
- rabbi
- Rosh Hashana

- Sabbath
- seder
- seliḥot
- Shabuoth
- shadkhan
- shaharith
- Shema
- shivah
- siddur
- sidra
- Simhath Torah
- siyyum
- Sukkot
- synagogue
- takkanah
- ṭallit
- Tammuz, Fast of
- tashlikh
- ṭerefa
- Three Weeks
- Tisha be-Av
- yahrzeit
- yeshiva
- yizkor
- Yom Kippur

*Talmud and
  Midrash:*
- Baraita
- Gemara
- Midrash
- Mishna
- Mishne Torah
- Mo'ed
- Nashim
- Neziqin
- Qodashim
- responsa
- Shulḥan 'arukh
- Talmud
- Thirteen Articles
  of Faith
- Ṭohorot
- tosafot
- Tosefta
- Zera'im

other:
- anti-Semitism
- Gentile
- I-Thou
- Jew

Biographies

Biblical figures:
- Abraham
- Amos
- David
- Deborah
- Ezekiel
- Isaiah
- Jacob

- Jeremiah
- Jezebel
- Jonah
- Jonathan
- Joseph
- Melchizedek
- Moses
- Noah

- Samson
- Samuel
- Saul
- Solomon

*commentators,
  scholars, teachers:*
- Akiba ben Joseph
- Ba'al Shem Ṭov

- Eleazar ben Judah
  of Worms
- Elijah ben
  Solomon
- Heller, Yom Ṭov
  Lipmann ben
  Nathan ha-Levi
- Hillel

	Jewish philosophers:	Baeck, Leo	Josephus, Flavius
Hirsch, Samson Raphael	Buber, Martin	Dubnow, Simon M.	Kohler, Kaufmann
Ishmael ben Elisha	Israeli, Isaac ben Solomon	Ezra	Maccabees
Johanan ben Zakkai	Maimon, Salomon	Frank, Jacob	Magnes, Judah Leon
Judah ben Samuel	Maimonides, Moses	Günzburg, Horace, Baron	Manasseh ben Israel
Judah ha-Nasi	Mendelssohn, Moses	Günzburg, Joseph (Yozel)	Shabbetai Tzevi
Karo, Joseph ben Ephraim	Philo Judaeus	Hertz, Joseph Herman	Wise, Isaac Mayer
Luria, Isaac ben Solomon	Rosenzweig, Franz	Herzl, Theodor	Zuckerman, Itzhak
Moses de León	*other:*	ibn Tibbon, Judah ben Saul	
Rashi	Anielewicz, Mordecai		
Sa'adia ben Joseph			

INDEX: See entries under all of the terms above

Section 827. Christianity

A. History of Christianity before the schism of 1054

  1. The development of the Christian Church from the time of Jesus to the reign of Constantine

    a. The origins and growth of the primitive church (*c.* AD 30–70)

    b. Post-apostolic developments in the early Christian Church (*c.* AD 70–325)

  2. The early Christian Church from the reign of Constantine to the pontificate of Gregory I the Great (*c.* 4th–6th century)

    a. The establishment of Christianity as the state religion of the Roman Empire: the problem of the alliance between church and empire, the increasingly important role played by the bishop of Rome as pope

    b. Doctrinal controversies that occasioned the further development of Christian theology

    c. The relation of the Christian religion to the culture of the late empire

  3. The growing division between Eastern and Western Christianity

    a. The political and religious bases of increasing tensions between Rome and Constantinople

    b. The relation of Christianity to the Western and Byzantine cultures (7th–11th century)

    c. Developments affecting institutions and practices in the East and the West: the expansion of Christianity in the West, the rise of the independent churches in the East

    d. The Photian schism and the beginnings of the great East–West schism

B. History of Eastern Orthodoxy from the schism of 1054 to the present

  1. The church of imperial Byzantium

  2. Developments from the fall of Constantinople (1453) to the early 19th century

  3. The Orthodox churches in the 19th century: developments in various areas

  4. The Orthodox Church since World War I

  5. The Eastern Church today

C. History of the Roman Catholic Church from the schism of 1054 to the present

  1. The medieval and Renaissance eras (*c.* 11th–16th century)
  [see 923.A.1.d. and A.2.a.i.]

    a. Development of the papacy as the chief spiritual and temporal power in the West

    b. Religious and cultural characteristics of Latin Christianity
    [see also F.6.a., below, 10/51.A.2., and 10/53.A.1.j.]

  2. The era of the Reformations and the wars of religion: from Luther's reform to the Peace of Westphalia (16th–17th century)

    a. Background of the Protestant Reformation in late medieval and Renaissance Catholicism
    [see D.1.a., below]

   b. The Protestant Reformation
      [see D.1., below]

   c. The Catholic Reformation and Counter-Reformation

   d. The wars of religion
      [see D.1.h., below]

   e. Missionary endeavours in other areas: the role of the church in the explorations and colonial policies of the European powers

3. The transition era: from the Peace of Westphalia to the French Revolution (17th–18th century)

4. The modern age: from the French Revolution to World War I (18th–20th century)

5. Developments in the 20th century
   [see also I., below]

6. Roman Catholicism today: its current demographic and social aspects

D. History of Protestantism

1. The Protestant Reformation and its aftermath, to the Peace of Westphalia (16th–17th century)
   [see also 961.A.]

   a. Its background in European Roman Catholic Christendom

   b. Luther and the German Reformation

   c. The Reformation in Switzerland, France, and the Low Countries
      [see 961.A.5.e., g., and h.]

   d. The English, Scottish, and Irish reformations
      [see 961.A.5.d.]

   e. Expansion of the Reformation to Scandinavia, the Baltic states, and eastern, central, and southern Europe

   f. Radical reform movements

   g. The Catholic Reformation and Counter-Reformation
      [see C.2., above]

   h. The wars of religion: church–state relations and the gradual development of the concept of religious liberty during the 16th and 17th centuries

2. The transition era: from the Peace of Westphalia to the French Revolution (17th–18th century)

   a. Political developments affecting the continental Protestant churches

   b. Developments in German Protestantism

   c. The challenge of Rationalism, Deism, and the Enlightenment: the Protestant response

   d. Developments in English Protestantism

   e. Developments in American Protestantism during the Colonial period

   f. Developments in the Dutch Reformed churches

   g. Developments in other continental European churches

3. The modern age: from the American and French revolutions to World War I (18th–20th century)

4. Developments in Protestantism after World War I
   [see also I., below]

5. Protestantism today: its current demographic and social aspects

E. Intellectual, spiritual, and imaginative expressions of Christianity
   [see also F.7., below)

1. Biblical literature: the Old Testament, the New Testament, the Apocrypha

2. Biblical exegesis and hermeneutics

3. Patristic literature

4. Formal, official statements of beliefs and doctrines: creeds, dogmas, confessions of faith

5. Writings of the post-patristic theologians, reformers, and church leaders

6. Writings of the great mystics

7. The relation of philosophy to Christian thought and statement: Christian philosophy

8. Myth and legend: biblical folk and nonbiblical literature, the role of myth in Christianity

F. Beliefs, practices, and institutions of Christianity

1. Doctrines concerning the nature and activity of God

   a. The nature of God: the oneness of God, the transcendence of God, God as Father

   b. The self-revelation of God: the understanding of God as Creator, Sustainer, and Judge

   c. Christology: teachings concerning the person of Jesus Christ

   d. Eschatology: political and apocalyptic messianic concepts, expectation of the Kingdom of God
   [see also 826.C.1.e.]

   e. The role of the Holy Spirit in the church: the tensions between continuity and revolution, institutional authority and charismatic activity, and order and freedom

   f. The doctrine of the Holy Trinity

2. Doctrines concerning intermediary beings, powers, or principles; *e.g.,* the angels, Satan
   [see also 811.B.5.]

3. Doctrines concerning the physical world

4. Doctrines concerning mankind

5. Doctrines concerning the church: Scripture, tradition, creeds, and confessions as normative expressions of Christian belief; the nature and role of doctrine and dogma

6. Practices and institutions common or predominant among the various traditional forms of Christianity

   a. The structure of church institutions: canon law and church polity

   b. The role and characteristics of the liturgy: the church as a worshiping community, the church year

   c. Forms of Christian life: monasticism, the saintly life

7. Art and iconography

   a. Major eras, regions, and schools of Christian art

   b. The expression of Christian faith and themes in the arts

G. The major traditional forms of Christianity

1. Eastern Orthodoxy
   [see also J.1., below]

2. Roman Catholicism: Latin and Eastern rite churches

3. Protestantism

H. Major forms of Protestantism

1. Lutheran churches

2. Reformed and Presbyterian churches: Calvinism

3. The Anglican Communion

4. The Free churches

   a. Baptists

   b. Disciples of Christ

   c. Congregationalists

   d. Methodists

   e. Friends

   f. Unitarians and Universalists

I. Ecumenical, interdenominational, and intradenominational associations

J. Variations of the traditional forms of Christianity and special new forms

1. In Eastern Christianity
   a. Syrian Orthodox Church of Antioch
   b. East Syrian Church
   c. Armenian Church
   d. Coptic Orthodox Church
   e. Ethiopian Church

2. In Roman Catholicism
   a. Ritual and other variations within the jurisdiction of the Roman Catholic Church
   [see G.2., above]
   b. Old Catholic churches

3. In Protestantism
   a. Holiness churches
   b. Pentecostal churches
   c. Millenarian churches
      i. Adventists
      ii. Jehovah's Witnesses
   d. Old-line Protestant sects and their derivations
      i. Mennonites, including Amish and Hutterites
      ii. The Moravian Church
      iii. Brethren
   e. Other independent churches: various Fundamentalist, evangelical, and other sectarian groups
   f. The Negro churches

4. Special forms tangentially related to traditional Christianity
   a. New Thought: Unity and other groups
   b. Christian Science
   c. Mormonism

Suggested reading in the *Encyclopædia Britannica*:

MACROPAEDIA: Major articles and biographies dealing with Christianity

Biblical Literature and Its Critical Interpretation	Jesus: The Christ and Christology
Calvinism, Calvin and Christianity	Luther
Doctrines and Dogmas, Religious	Paul, The Apostle
Eastern Orthodoxy	Protestantism
	Roman Catholicism
	Sacred Offices and Orders

MICROPAEDIA: Selected entries of reference information

General subjects

belief, doctrine, and dogma:	Ascension	concordat	Holy Spirit
absolution	Assumption	confession	hope
adiaphorism	atonement	consubstantiation	Immaculate
agape	benefice	deadly sin	Conception
Alpha and Omega	blasphemy	Erastianism	imprimatur
anathema	bull	eschatology	Incarnation
angel	catechism	evangelical church	indulgence
Annunciation	catechumen	faith	Inner light
Antichrist	catholic	God, Kingdom of	justification
apostasy	charity	grace	kerygma and
apostolic	cherub	heaven	catechesis
succession	Christ, two	hell	Last Judgment
	natures of	heresy	limbo

logos
Mariology
martyr
millennium
miracle
Monophysite
moral theology
mystical body of
  Christ
nomocanon
original sin
orthodox
predestination
purgatory
resurrection
Sacred Heart
saint
saints, communion
  of the
Satan
Second Coming
seraph
sin
soul
stigmata
Theotokos
tongues, gift of
transubstantiation
Trinity
Turin, Shroud of
Virgin Birth
Visitation
canon law:
  annates
  benefice
  canon law
  Codex Juris
    Canonici
  conclave
  concordat
  consistory
  Corpus Juris
    Canonici
  decretals
  dispensation
  ecclesiastical court
  encyclical
  excommunication
  False Decretals
  Gratian's
    Decretum
  legate
  nomocanon
  nuncio
  ordination
  papal infallibility
  penitential book
  simony
church polity and
  ecclesiastical
  hierarchy:
  almoner
  archbishop

archdeacon
autocephalous
  church
bishop
Bishops, Synod of
cardinal
cathedral
chaplain
church
churchwarden
clergy
collegiality
conciliarism
congé d'élire
congregation
council
deacon
diocese
elder
episcopacy
episcopus vagans
free church
holy order
metropolitan
ministry
papacy
parish
patriarch
pope
prelate
presbyter
presbyterian
presbytery
priest
primate
Roman Curia
schism
secular institute
synod
vicar
churches—Eastern
  Independent:
  Armenian
    Apostolic Church
  Christians of Saint
    Thomas
  Coptic Orthodox
    Church
  Ethiopian
    Orthodox Church
  Nestorian
  Syrian Orthodox
    Patriarchate
    of Antioch
churches—Eastern
  Orthodox:
  Bulgarian
    Orthodox Church
  Cyprus, Church of
  Ecumenical
    Patriarchate of
    Constantinople

Georgian
  Orthodox Church
Greece, Church of
Greek Orthodox
  Patriarchate of
  Alexandria
Greek Orthodox
  Patriarchate of
  Antioch and All
  the East
Greek Orthodox
  Patriarchate of
  Jerusalem
Japanese Orthodox
  Church
Jerusalem,
  Synod of
Old Believer
Orthodox Church
  in America
Orthodox Church
  of Czechoslovakia
Orthodox Church
  of Finland
Orthodox Church
  of Poland
Renovated Church
Romanian
  Orthodox Church
Russian Orthodox
  Church
Serbian Orthodox
  Church
churches—
  Protestant (Anglican
  Communion):
  Anglican Church
    of Australia
  Anglican
    Communion
  Anglican
    Evangelical
  Anglican
    religious
    community
  Anglo-Catholicism
  Broad Church
  Canada, Anglican
    Church of
  Canterbury,
    archbishop of
  Canterbury
    and York,
    Convocations of
  Church Army
  Church
    Commissioners
  Church Missionary
    Society
  England,
    Church of
  Episcopal Church
    in Scotland

Ireland, Church of
Lambeth
  Conference
New Zealand,
  Church of the
  Province of
Nonjuror
Oxford Movement
Protestant
  Episcopal Church
South Africa,
  Church of the
  Province of
Wales, Church in
churches—Protestant
  (Baptist):
  All-Union Council
    of Evangelical
    Christians and
    Baptists
  American Baptist
    Association
  American Baptist
    Churches in the
    U.S.A.
  Baptist Federation
    of Canada
  Baptist General
    Conference
  Baptist Missionary
    Association of
    America
  Baptist Union of
    Great Britain and
    Ireland
  National
    Association of
    Free Will Baptists
  Southern Baptist
    Convention
churches—Protestant
  (Congregationalist):
  Congregational
    Church of
    England and
    Wales
  Congregational
    Council for
    World Mission
  Congregationalism
churches—Protestant
  (Disciples of Christ):
  Disciples of Christ
  World Convention
    of Churches of
    Christ
churches—Protestant
  (Friends):
  Friends, Society of

Friends World
Committee for
Consultation
churches—Protestant
(*Holiness*):
Christian and
Missionary
Alliance
Free Methodist
Church of North
America
God (Anderson,
Ind.), Church of
Holiness
movement
Nazarene, Church
of the
Pillar of Fire
United House of
Prayer for All
People
Wesleyan Church
churches—Protestant
(*Lutheran*):
American
Evangelical
Lutheran Church
Augustana
Evangelical
Lutheran Church
Batak Protestant
Christian Church
Evangelical Church
in Germany, The
Evangelical Church
of Czech Brethren
Evangelical
Lutheran Church
in America
Evangelical
Lutheran People's
Church of
Denmark
Finland, Church of
Lutheran Church
in Württemberg
Lutheran
Church—
Missouri Synod
Lutheran Church
of Oldenburg
Lutheran Council
in the United
States of America
Lutheran
Synodical
Conference
Lutheran World
Federation

Lutheranism
National Church
of Iceland
Norway, Church of
Sweden, Church of
United Evangelical
Lutheran Church
United Evangelical
Lutheran Church
of Germany
Wisconsin
Evangelical
Lutheran Synod
churches—Protestant
(*Methodist*):
Evangelical United
Brethren Church
Methodism
United Methodist
Church
World Methodist
Council
churches—Protestant
(*millenarian*):
Adventist
Christadelphian
Christian Catholic
Church
Jehovah's Witness
Plymouth
Brethren
Shaker
churches—Protestant
(*Negro*):
African Methodist
Episcopal Church
African Methodist
Episcopal Zion
Church
Christian
Methodist
Episcopal Church
National Baptist
Convention,
U.S.A., Inc.
National Baptist
Convention of
America
National
Primitive Baptist
Convention, Inc.
churches—Protestant
(*old-line*):
Amish
Bohemian
Confession
Brethren
ecclesiola in
ecclesia

Ephrata
Community
Hussite
Hutterite
Mennonite
Moravian Church
Taborite
Ultraquist
Unitas Fratrum
churches—Protestant
(*Pentecostal*):
Assemblies of God
God, Church of
God in Christ,
Church of
International
Church of the
Foursquare
Gospel
Jesus Only
Latter Rain revival
Pentecostal
Assemblies of the
World, Inc.
Pentecostal
Church of God of
America, Inc.
Pentecostal
Holiness Church,
Inc.
Pentecostalism
churches—Protestant
(*Reformed and
Presbyterian*):
Christian
Reformed Church
in North America
Cumberland
Presbyterian
Church
Dutch Reformed
Church
Dutch Reformed
Church in Africa
Dutch Reformed
Mission Church
in South Africa
Evangelical Church
in Germany, The
Evangelical Church
of Czech Brethren
Free Church of
Scotland
Iona Community
Netherlands
Reformed
Church, The

Presbyterian
Church (U.S.A.)
Presbyterian
Church in
Ireland
Presbyterian
Church of
England
Presbyterian
Church of
Wales
Presbyterian
churches
Reformed church
Reformed Church
in America
Reformed Church
of France
Reformed Church
of Hungary
Reformed
Churches in The
Netherlands
Scotland,
Church of
United Church of
Canada
United Free
Church of
Scotland
United
Presbyterian
Church
churches—Protestant
(*Unitarian and
Universalists*):
Unitarian
Universalist
Association
Unitarianism
Universalism
churches—Protestant
(*United Church of
Christ*):
American Board of
Commissioners
for Foreign
Missions
Evangelical and
Reformed Church
General Council
of Congregational
Christian
Churches
United Church of
Christ

Judith, Book of
Maccabees, The
  Books of the
Manual of
  Discipline
Moses,
  Assumption of
Prophets, The
  Lives of the
Solomon,
  Psalms of
Solomon,
  Wisdom of
Tobit
Twelve Patriarchs,
  Testaments of the
War of the Sons
  of Light Against
  the Sons of
  Darkness, The
literature—patristic:
Ambrosiaster
Apologist
Apostolic
  Constitutions
Apostolic Father
Barnabas, Letter of
Clement, First
  Letter of
Clementine
  literature
Didachē
Diognetus,
  Letter to
Hippolytus,
  Canons of Saint
Martyrdom of
  Polycarp
patristic literature
Peregrinatio
  Etheriae
Shepherd of
  Hermas
Testamentum
  Domini
literature—other:
apocalyptic
  literature
apocrypha
biblical criticism
Douai-Reims Bible
exegesis
Geneva Bible
hermeneutics
Imitation of Christ
logia
Mormon, Book of
Peshitta
Philokalia
polyglot Bible
Targum
Vulgate

liturgical year:
Advent
All Saints' Day
All Souls' Day
Ascension of the
  Lord, Feast of the
Ash Wednesday
Candlemas
Christmas
church year
Corpus Christi,
  Feast of
Easter
Ember Days and
  Ember Weeks
Epiphany
Good Friday
holy days of
  obligation
Holy Family, Feast
  of the
Holy Innocents,
  Feast of the
Holy Saturday
Holy Week
Jubilee, Year of
Lent
Maundy Thursday
Michaelmas
Palm Sunday
Pentecost
Reformation Day
Rogation Days
Shrove Tuesday
Sunday
Transfiguration,
  Feast of the
*religious communities
and orders:*
Anglican religious
  community
Augustinian
Basilian
Benedictine
Bridgettine
Camaldolese
Capuchin
Carmelite
Carthusian
Charity of Saint
  Vincent de Paul,
  Daughters of
Christian Brother
Cistercian
Common Life,
  Brethren of the
Divine Word
  Missionary
Dominican
Franciscan
Good Shepherd
  Sister

Grandchamp
  and Taizé
  communities
Hesychasm
Holy Ghost Father
Jesuit
Knights of Malta
Little Brothers of
  Jesus and Little
  Sisters of Jesus
Marianist
Marist Brother
Marist Father
Mary Immaculate,
  Oblates of
Maurist
Mechitarist
mendicant
Mercedarian
Mercy, Sisters of
Minim
monasticism
Oratorian
Passionist
Poor Clare
Premonstratensian
Redemptorist
Sacred Heart,
  Society of the
Salesian
Servite
Spiritual
Templar
Teutonic Order
Trappist
Trinitarian
Ursuline
Vincentian
Visitandine
White Father
Zoe
*worship, liturgy,
ritual, and
iconography:*
acolyte
Agnus Dei
Alexandrian rite
anointment
Antiochene rite
Apostles' Creed
Armenian rite
Athanasian Creed
Baptism
Basil, Liturgy of
  Saint
bell, book, and
  candle
benediction
breviary
Byzantine rite
cantor
Chaldean rite
chalice

chrismation
Common Order,
  Book of
Common Prayer,
  The Book of
Concord, The
  Book of
confession
confessional
Confessions,
  Book of
confirmation
creed
cross
cross, sign of the
Cross, Stations
  of the
crucifixion
Dies Irae
divine office
doxology
Ecce Homo
epiclesis
Eucharist
exorcism
feet, washing of
godparent
Hail Mary
hands,
  imposition of
Heidelberg
  Catechism
Holy Family
Holy Sepulchre
holy water
icon
iconostasis
James, Liturgy of
  Saint
Jesus prayer
kanōn
Last Supper
Lord's Prayer
lector
Liturgical
  Movement
Madonna
Magnificat
mass
missal
monstrance
Nativity
Nicene Creed
orant
Pietà
prayer
Preconsecrated
  Offerings, Liturgy
  of the
procession
pyx
rosary
Sabbatarianism

sacrament	True Cross	See Section 624 of	liberation theology
shepherds,	vespers	Part Six for	Protestantism
adoration of the	Westminster	sacred music	Roman
thurible	Catechism	*other:*	Catholicism
tithe	Westminster	Christianity	World Council of
troparion	Confession	Eastern	Churches
		Orthodoxy	

Biographies

early Christian figures—to 1054:	Eusebius of Caesarea	Macarius the Egyptian	Theophilus of Alexandria, Saint
Ambrose, Saint	Eusebius of Nicomedia	Mark the Hermit	Ulfilas
Anastasius Sinaita, Saint	Euthymius I	Martin of Tours, Saint	Vigilius
Anastasius the Librarian	Euthymius the Great, Saint	Nemesius of Emesa	Vincent of Lérins, Saint
Ansgar, Saint	Evagrius Ponticus	Nestorius	Wilfrid, Saint
Anthony of Egypt, Saint	Fursey, Saint	Nicephorus I, Saint	Willibrord, Saint
Aphraates	Gennadius of Marseilles	Nicetas of Remesiana	Zosimus, Saint
Aristedes	Germanus I, Saint	Nicholas, Saint	*Christian figures— medieval and Renaissance:*
Arsenius the Great	Germanus of Auxerre, Saint	Nicholas I	
Athanasius, Saint	Gregory I, Saint	Nicholas I, Saint	Aelred of Rievaulx, Saint
Athenagoras	Gregory VII, Saint	Nilus of Ancyra, Saint	Ailly, Pierre d'
Augustine, Saint	Gregory of Nazianzus, Saint	Ninian, Saint	Alexander III
Augustine of Canterbury, Saint	Gregory of Nyssa, Saint	Novatian	Alexander VI
Basil the Great, Saint	Gregory of Tours, Saint	Origen	Arnold of Brescia
Bede the Venerable, Saint	Gregory Thaumaturgus, Saint	Oswald of York, Saint	Benedict (XIII)
Benedict Biscop, Saint	Hesychius of Jerusalem	Palladius	Bernard of Clairvaux, Saint
Benedict of Nursia, Saint	Hilarion, Saint	Paschal I, Saint	Bonaventure, Saint
Berengar of Tours	Hincmar of Reims	Paschasius Radbertus, Saint	Boniface VIII
Chad, Saint	Hippolytus of Rome, Saint	Patrick, Saint	Borgia, Cesare, duc de Valentinois
Chrysostom, Saint John	Honorius I	Pelagius I	Catherine of Siena, Saint
Clement I, Saint	Humbert of Silva Candida	Pelagius II	Celestine V, Saint
Clement of Alexandria, Saint	Ignatius of Antioch, Saint	Philoponus, John	Clare of Assisi, Saint
Colman of Lindisfarne, Saint	Irenaeus, Saint	Philostorgius	Clement V
Cuthbert, Saint	Isaac the Great, Saint	Philoxenus of Mabbug	Clement VI
Cyprian, Saint	Isidore of Seville, Saint	Photius, Saint	Dominic, Saint
Cyril and Methodius, Saints	Jerome, Saint	Polycarp, Saint	Duns Scotus, John
Cyril of Alexandria, Saint	Joan, Pope	Priscillian	Eckhart, Meister
Damasus I, Saint	John of Damascus, Saint	Rabanus Marus	Edmund of Abington, Saint
Diadochus of Photice	John of Jerusalem	Sergius I, Saint	Francis of Assisi, Saint
Dionysius of Alexandria, Saint	Justin Martyr, Saint	Severian of Gabala	Gerson, Jean de
Dustan of Canterbury, Saint	Kenneth, Saint	Severus of Antioch	Gilbert of Sempringham, Saint
Ennodius, Magnus Felix	Leo I, Saint	Simplicius, Saint	Gregory VII, Saint
Ephraem Syrus, Saint	Leo III, Saint	Sophronius	Gregory IX
Erigena, John Scotus	Leo IX, Saint	Stephen VI	Gregory of Rimini
	Liberius	Sulpicius Severus	Honorius III
	Lucifer	Symmachus, Saint	Hus, John
		Tertullian	Innocent II
		Theodore Ascidas	Innocent III
		Theodore of Canterbury, Saint	Innocent IV
		Theodore of Cyrrhus	Isaac of Stella
		Theodosius of Alexandria	Jerome of Prague
		Theōdūrus Abū Qurrah	

Joachim of Fiore
John XXII
John (XXIII)
John of Avila,
  Saint
John of Matha,
  Saint
John of Mirecourt
John of Salisbury
Julius II
Malachy, Saint
Martin V
Milíč of Kroměříž
Nicholas III
Nicholas IV
Nicholas V
Nicholas of
  Clémanges
Nicholas of Cusa
Nicholas of
  Hereford
Paschal II
Paul II
Peter Lombard
Petrus Aureoli
Pius II
Prester John
Rokycana, Jan
Savonarola,
  Girolamo
Seven Holy
  Founders
Sixtus IV
Suso, Heinrich
Thomas Aquinas
Urban II
Urban VI
William de la
  Mare
William of
  Auvergne
William of
  Auxerre
William of
  Champeaux
William of Hirsau
William of
  Saint-Amour
William of
  Saint-Thierry
Wycliffe, John
*Eastern Orthodox
figures—from 1054:*
  Akindynos,
    Gregorios
  Anthony of Kiev
  Antony
    Khrapovitshy
  Bulgakov,
    Macarius
  Cydones,
    Demetrius

Eugenikos,
  Markos
Euthymius of
  Tŭrnovo
Gemistus Plethon,
  George
Gennadios II
  Scholarios
Gregory of Sinai
Isidore of Kiev
Jeremias II
John XI Becchus
Joseph of
  Volokolamsk
Maximus the
  Greek
Mogila, Peter
Nicephorus
  Callistus
  Xanthopoulos
Nikon
Palamas, Saint
  Gregory
Planudes,
  Maximus
Prokopovich,
  Feofan
Sergius
Theophylactus of
  Orchida
Tikhon
*New Testament
figures:*
  Anne and
    Joachim, Saints
  James, Saint
  John the Apostle,
    Saint
  John the Baptist,
    Saint
  Joseph, Saint
  Judas Iscariot
  Luke, Saint
  Mark, Saint
  Mary
  Mary Magdalene,
    Saint
  Peter the Apostle,
    Saint
  Pilate, Pontius
  Stephen, Saint
  Thomas, Saint
*Old Testament
figures:*
  Abraham
  Amos
  David
  Deborah
  Ezekiel
  Isaiah
  Jacob
  Jeremiah

Jezebel
Jonah
Jonathan
Joseph
Melchizedek
Moses
Noah
Samson
Samuel
Saul
Solomon
Protestant figures:
  Agricola, Johann
  Arminius, Jacobus
  Ballou, Hosea
  Baxter, Richard
  Beecher, Henry
    Ward
  Beza, Theodore
  Biddle, John
  Bonhoeffer,
    Dietrich
  Bucer, Martin
  Bultmann, Rudolf
  Bunyan, John
  Bushnell, Horace
  Carey, William
  Chalmers, Thomas
  Channing, William
    Ellery
  Clauberg, Johann
  Cranmer, Thomas
  Dávid, Ferenc
  Eddy, Mary Baker
  Edwards, Jonathan
  Erastus, Thomas
  Farel, Guillaume
  Flacius Illyricus,
    Matthias
  Fox, George
  Franck, Sebastian
  Harnack,
    Adolf von
  Hembyze, Jan van
  Henderson,
    Alexander
  Hooker, Richard
  Huntingdon,
    Selina Hastings,
    countess of
  Jewel, John
  Joris, David
  Judson, Adoniram
  Karlstadt,
    Andreas Rudolf
    Bodenstein von
  Keble, John
  Knox, John
  Kuyper, Abraham
  Labadie, Jean de
  Lefèvre d'Étaples,
    Jacques

Leighton, Robert
McPherson, Aimee
  Semple
Mather, Cotton
Mather, Increase
Mather, Richard
Maurice, Frederick
  Denison
Melanchthon,
  Philipp
Melville, Andrew
Menno Simonsz
Müntzer, Thomas
Niebuhr, Reinhold
Ochino,
  Bernardino
Oecolampadius,
  John
Penn, William
Ritschl, Albrecht
Robinson, John
Rogers, John
Schaff, Philip
Schleiermacher,
  Friedrich
Schwenckfeld,
  Kaspar
Servetus, Michael
Smith, Joseph
Socinus, Faustus
Spalatin, Georg
Spener, Philipp
  Jakob
Strauss, David
  Friedrich
Swedenborg,
  Emanuel
Tait, Archibald
  Campbell
Tillich, Paul
Ussher, James
Vermigli, Peter
  Martyr
Wesley, Charles
Wesley, John
Whitman, Marcus
Williams, Roger
Young, Brigham
Zinzendorf,
  Nikolaus Ludwig,
  Graf von
Zwingli, Huldrych
*Roman Catholic
figures—
post-Reformation:*
  Arnauld, Antoine
  Arnauld family
  Bellarmine, Saint
    Robert
  Benson, Edward
    White

Section 828.   **Islām**

A. History of Islām

1. The pre-Islāmic setting in Arabia
[see also 822.A.6.]

2. The origin of Islām in the life and teachings of the Prophet Muḥammad, the Messenger of Allāh (6th–7th century AD)

3. The foundations of the Islāmic community and the early expansion of Islām beyond Arabia (7th and 8th centuries)

4. The development of Islāmic religion, culture, and society during the first centuries of the caliphate of the ʿAbbāsids (8th–11th century)

5. The Middle Ages of Islām: developments in theology, law, and culture (11th–18th century)

6. Islām in the modern world (18th–20th century)

7. Islām today

B. Intellectual, spiritual, and imaginative expressions of Islām
[see also C.4., below]

1. The Qurʾān: its form and contents, views about its origin, interpretations or translations

2. The Ḥadīth: the oral tradition

3. Islāmic law: Sharīʿah, *fiqh*

4. Islāmic theology and philosophy: philosophic and antiphilosophic trends in Islām, the major schools of Islāmic philosophy

5. The mystical path: Ṣūfism

6. Mythical elements and elaborations of Islāmic beliefs and doctrines

C. Beliefs, practices, and institutions of Islām

1. Beliefs and doctrines

a. Doctrines concerning God

b. Doctrines concerning the universe

c. Doctrines concerning mankind

d. Doctrines concerning Satan and other intermediate beings, powers, or principles
[see also 811.B.5.]

e. Doctrines concerning Muḥammad and the nature of prophecy

f. Eschatological doctrines

g. Social and ethical doctrines

2. The forms of Islām: the orthodox community and its variations

a. Khārijism: the doctrines of the Khārijīs and Ibāḍīs

b. Muʿtazilism

c. Sunnism

d. Shīʿism and its subsects: the Ismāʿīlīs and other Ismāʿīlī sects

e. Religious groups of Islāmic origin, now considered non-Islāmic; *e.g.*, Druzes, Bahāʾī faith
[see 829.E.]

f. Variations among the urban and rustic Ṣūfī orders

3. Practices and institutions

a. The Five Pillars of Islām: the profession of faith, the five daily prayers, the obligatory tax (zakat), fasting, the pilgrimage to Mecca

b. Sacred places and days: the mosque and festivals in public worship

c. The family: Islāmic teaching regarding marriage, divorce, chastity, and inheritance

d. The Sharīʿah: law and jurisprudence, the schools of law

4. Art and iconography

a. Major eras, regions, and schools of Islāmic art

b. The expression of Islāmic faith and themes in the arts

c. The religious and cultural context of Islāmic art and iconography: the effect of the anti-iconic principle on representational art

5. Modern reform movements

Suggested reading in the *Encyclopædia Britannica*:

MACROPAEDIA: Major articles dealing with Islām

Islām, Muḥammad and the Religion of
Islāmic World, The

MICROPAEDIA: Selected entries of reference information

General subjects

belief, law, and philosophy:	isnād	tawhid	miḥnah
ʿādah	istiḥsān	uṣūl al-fiqh	Murjiʾah
Ahl al-Kitāb	istiṣlāḥ	*history:*	Qarāmiṭah
Allāh	jihād	Almohads	rāshidūn, ar-
ʿaqil	kalām	Almoravids	Sālimīyah
ʿārīyah	kasb	Badr, Battle of	*myth, legend,*
bidʿah	kiswah	Bāṭinīyah	*eschatology:*
Dahrīyah	Mālikīyah	caliph	Barṣīṣā
diyah	mufti	Caliphate	Burāq
fayḍ	Muʿtazilah	Companions of the	Dajjāl, ad-
ghaybah	Qadarīyah	Prophet	Dhū al-faqār
Ḥadīth	qāḍī	Dīn-i Ilāhī	ghūl
Ḥanābilah	qiyas	Ditch, Battle of the	Hārūt and Mārūt
Ḥanafīyah	radāʿ	Hāshimīyah	hātif
ʿiddah	rahbānīyah	Hegira	houri
ijmāʿ	Shāfiʿīyah	Ḥudaybiyah, Pact	Iblīs
ijtihād	Sharīʿah	of Al-	Idrīs
ikhtilāf	shirk	Ikhwān aṣ-Ṣafāʾ	ifrit
ʿilm al-ḥadīth	taqlid	imam	Isrāʾ
imam	tashbīh	jizya	Isrāfīl
		kharāj	ʿIzrāʾīl

jahannam
Jibrīl
jinnī
Khiḍr, al-
mahdī
Mīkāl
mi'rāj
shaitan
Sheba, Queen of
Yājūj and Mājūj
offices and orders:
caliph
imam
marabout
qurrā'
Shādhilīyah
Qur'ānic literature:
basmalah
fātiḥah
fawātiḥ
Qur'ān
surah
ritual, practice,
observance:
adhān
'Āshūrā'
Black Stone of
Mecca
crescent
ghusl
hajj

Hegira
'īd
ihram
jihād
jum'ah
Ka'bah
khitān
khuṭbah
mawlid
minaret
minbar
mosque
muezzin
mullah
mut'ah
purdah
qibla
rajm
Ramaḍān
salat
ṣawm
sayyid
sharif
subḥah
sunna
tafsīr
tahajjud
talbīyah
taqiya
tazia
'umrah

zakat
zāwiyah
ziyārah
zuhd
sects, schools,
branches:
'Alawite
Bohrā
Deoband school
Dönme
Druze
Ismā'īlīte
Ithnā 'Asharīyah
Khārijite
Mahdist
Māturīdīyah
Mu'tazilah
Rāfiḍah
Shī'ite
Ṣūfism
Sunnite
Wahhābī
Yazīdī
Ṣūfism:
Aḥmadīyah
Bektashi
Chishtīyah
dervish
dhikr
fakir
fana

ḥāl
ḥaqīqah
kashf
khirqah
Malāmatīyah
maqām
Mawlawīyah
mujāhadah
mushāhadah
Naqshbandīyah
Qādirīyah
Qalandarīyah
Rifā'īyah
samā'
shaṭḥ
Shaṭṭārīyah
Subud
Ṣūfism
Suhrawardīyah
tariqa
other:
Ahl-e Ḥaqq
American Muslim
Mission
Islām
Muhammadiyah
M'zabite
sheikh
'ulamā'

Biographies

leaders and teachers:
'Abd Allāh
Abū Bakr
Ahmad Khan, Sir
Sayyid
Aḥsā'ī, al-
'Alī
Ghaznavid
Dynasty
Ḥallāj, al-
Ja'far ibn
Muḥammad

Jalāl ad-Dīn
ar-Rūmī
Jamāl ad-Dīn
al-Afghānī
Junayd, Shaykh
Mahdī, al-
Muḥammad
Rashīd Riḍā
Sha'rānī, ash-
'Umar I
'Umar II
'Umar Tal

theologians and
philosophers:
'Abduh,
Muḥammad
Abū Ḥanīfah
Aḥmad ibn
Ḥanbal
Ash'arī, Abū
al-Ḥasan al-
Averroës
Avicenna
Fakhr ad-Dīn
ar-Rāzī

Ghazālī, al-
Ḥasan
al-Baṣrī, al-
Ibn al-'Arabī
Ibn 'Aqīl
Ibn Ḥazm
Ibn Taymīyah
Muḥāsibī, al-
Sirhindī, Shaykh
Aḥmad
Suhrawardī, as-
Ṭabarī, aṭ-

Section 829. Other Religions and Religious Movements in the Modern World

A. New religious movements reflecting the impact of dominant cultures and religions

B. Negro cults in Western cultures

  1. The Nation of Islām, or Black Muslims
  [see E.3., below]

  2. Black Jewish cults: the Church of God; the Commandment Keepers, or Black Jews; the Church of God and Saints of Christ

C. Theosophical groups

D. Spiritualist groups

E. Religions and religious movements of Islāmic origin or influenced by Islām

  1. The Bahā'ī faith

  2. The Druze religion

  3. The Nation of Islām, or Black Muslims

F. Residues or revivals of ancient and primitive religious beliefs and practices in modern civilizations

  1. Witchcraft, black magic, Satanism
  [see also 811.D.3.]

  2. Prophecy, divination, astrology

  3. Healing cults or practices

  4. Pharmacological cults or practices

Suggested reading in the *Encyclopædia Britannica*:

MACROPAEDIA: Major article dealing with other religions and religious movements in the modern world

  Doctrines and Dogmas, Religious
  Occultism

MICROPAEDIA: Selected entries of reference information
General subjects

African Greek Orthodox Church	Ghost Dance	Kuga Sorta	Ringatu
Aiyetoro	Handsome Lake cult	Macumba	Rizalist cult
Aladura	Hare Krishna	magic	Rosicrucian
alchemy	Harris movement	Maria Legio	Santería
anthroposophy	Hauhau	mashriq al-adhkār	Scientology
astrology	healing cult	Moorish Science Temple of America	spiritual assembly
Azalī	ḥudūd		Telakhon
Bahā'ī faith	I Am movement	Native American Church	theosophy
Braid movement	Iglesia ni Kristo	New Thought	Unification Church
Cao Dai	Indian Shaker Church	Peace Mission	'uqqāl
cargo cult		Psychiana	voodoo
divination	Islam, Nation of	Rastafarian	witchcraft
Druze	Kimbanguist Church of Zaire	Ratana church	Zionist church
Ethiopianism		Religious Science	
faith healing			

Biographies

Bāb, the	Blavatsky, Helena Petrovna	Gurdjieff, Georges Ivanovitch	Muhammad, Elijah
Bhaktivedanta, A(bhay) C(haranaravinda)	Divine, Father	Mahesh Yogi, Maharishi	Smohalla
	Fard, Wallace D.	Moon, Sun Myung	Steiner, Rudolf

INDEX: See entries under all of the terms above

Introduction to Part Nine:
The Point and Pleasure of Reading History
by Jacques Barzun

Everything that we call the arts and the humanities comes out of some natural desire and acquires value by satisfying it. Painting and music and literature are important not because there are museums and concert halls and libraries to be kept supplied but because human beings want to draw and sing and tell stories as well as enjoy seeing others fulfill these native and universal impulses.

Among the humanities, history holds a special place in that its origin within each of us is not even dependent on impulse. A person may lack altogether the wish to sing or the knack of telling a story, but everybody without exception finds occasion to say: "I was there; I saw it; I remember it very well." In saying (or even thinking) these words, every man is a historian. History is inescapably a part of consciousness. The Greeks expressed this truth by describing Clio, the muse of history, as the daughter of memory.

Without going into the subtleties of how we are able to remember and what the contents of memory actually are, it is clear that as soon as we take thought about our experiences, whether the farthest back or the nearest and most immediate, we are dealing with what is past. The so-called present vanishes in the very act of reflecting upon it, and the future is all surmise and imagination. Hence the greater our interest in the facts and truths of human existence— our own existence included—the greater, necessarily, is our concern with the past. "To live in the past" ought not, therefore, to be the phrase of reproach that it commonly is. The larger part of the thoughtful life that one leads during the intervals of action cannot be anything but some form of living in the past. If this part of our lives is to be criticized, it should be in words different from the cliché. One should ask, *How* does he or she live in the past? *What past* does he or she recall, prefer, imagine?

It is at this point that history as the organized story of the whole human past comes in to contribute its pleasures and its illumination to the thoughtful life. A person who remembered only his own past would be pretty poor indeed—living on a starvation diet. Actually, it is a question whether such a life is not an impossible supposition. Everybody remembers pieces of other people's pasts; everybody, whether he means to or not, finds that he has learned about his country, his town, his street, his business office, or his factory many things that came to pass well before his time. To possess that information, if it is accurate, is in essence a knowledge of history. It differs in extent but not in kind from a knowledge of how Rome rose and fell. And this relation tells us what reading history affords in the first instance. Just as knowing about our neighbours' and friends' histories adds to our sense of reality, so does reading history: it gives us vicarious experience.

If we add to the habitual, unconscious intake of personal and local history the daily filling of the mind by news reports—which is contemporary history and which usually brings with it fragments of a remoter past—we begin to see that every man who lives in a modern, communicative society is forced to become in some sense a conscious historian. His interest begins with himself and his environment, but it is soon stretched out, haphazardly, into such domains of history as chance or special interests have developed. And special interests need not mean explicitly intellectual ones; baseball and chess, model trains and furniture, pottery and boat-building have their heroes and revolutions too, and whoever cares about these activities or artifacts for themselves inevitably becomes engrossed in their histories.

It is of course true that when we ordinarily speak of someone having an interest in history we mean the political, social, or cultural history of great civilizations; and for a long time history was arbitrarily taken to mean the sequence that leads from the ancient civilizations of the eastern Mediterranean to the modern ones of the West. It is a tremendous spectacle, even though concentrated on a relatively small territory. But now that certain dynamic elements of Western civilization have aroused the rest of the world to both imitation and resistance, it has become imperative to widen the panorama and see behind the vast and confused modern scene the several histories of the great Eastern civilizations as well as the traditions and vicissitudes of the African societies.

Two questions readily occur at the mere thought of so much to know. Can a reader who is not a professional historian find his way in this huge maze of names, dates, and facts? And if he can, why should he? The answer to the first question is the old reply of the mathematician to the nervous student: "What one fool can do, another can." A real compliment is concealed in this gruff retort, for what it implies is that given an interest, a motive, any man can inform himself about any part of world history through secondary accounts such as are digested in an encyclopaedia. There is no obligation to master every detail, to dispute or criticize sources—in a word, to ape the professional, who, for the best of reasons, limits himself to a small segment of the whole. A *reader* of history is one who follows with his mind the steps another took on his voyage of discovery; and this is easier in history than in mathematics, for history is told in plain words and deals with ordinary human relationships.

So the main difficulty lies in the second question: Why embark on the journey? The answers are numerous and varied, for temperaments differ, as do "special interests" in the sense referred to above. But there is one answer that covers the rest; it is the answer suggested by what was said earlier about every man's unconscious absorption of haphazard fragments of history. The best motive for reading history deliberately is curiosity about the portions missing from one's own picture of the past. Curiosity: How did things come to be as they are? How was it when they were different? Is it true that once upon a time men did thus and so? History deals with particulars, and most recorded particulars contain puzzles, contradictions, enormities, all of them spurs to curiosity: the Hudson River in the state of New York was named after the navigator often called Hendrik Hudson, who first sailed up the stream. But why Hendrik and not Henry? Well, Henry was his baptismal name; how did he acquire the other and why? The full answer leads really to a comprehensive view of exploration and colonization by the national states at the dawn of the modern age—the aims, drives, desires, errors, follies, cruelties, and incalculable consequences of a great movement that occupies two and a half centuries and that has continued in different forms down to the landings on the Moon.

The most striking feature of history is its fusion of purposeful direction and unexpected drift. For example, read about Plato, Aristotle, and the ancient mathematicians, and you will discover how their speculations and discoveries have been transformed and amplified into the methods and systems that we still work with. But you will also be told how at various times these same streams of thought or belief generated entirely new and remote, strange and absurd consequences. Again, ancient astrology led to the science of astronomy, and science (as we think) replaces superstition. Yet astrology fills columns in 20th-century newspapers and the minds of their millions of readers. What is the explanation? We lack the pythoness of Delphi, in whom Socrates believed or affected to believe, and we have no official college of augurs to scan the entrails of birds as a guide to future political action, but fortune-tellers are never out of business and we do have Gallup polls. Truly, the wonders of cultural history are infinite.

To conjure up these beliefs and institutions in this comparative fashion is not to equate them with one another or across the centuries; it is rather to stress the identity in diversity that is the principle of human affairs and that makes human history accessible to any willing reader. In different times and places, men are the same and also different. The differences are due to the varying emphases given by one people at one time to some element of life and feeling or to some form of its expression. This is most easily seen in the plastic arts. Think of the representations of the human body in Egypt, Greece, medieval Europe, the west coast of Africa, pre-Columbian America, and the art galleries of world capitals in the second half of the 20th century: is it the same human body or different? The question is really idle, for it is both and neither. In paint or marble there is strictly no human body, only a view of it, a feeling about it. Similarly, what we see in history is not so much Man distorted in one way or another as *men* who existed *only as we see them;* that is, in their society and culture, under their skies and gods, never staying put for more than a short time, never to be reduplicated elsewhere or at a later time, even when the effort to imitate is strong and shrewd—as in the Italian Renaissance, which tried to restore the ancient culture of Greece and Rome.

Despite this irreducible plasticity, diversity, and restlessness, we draw historical parallels, we make comparisons. That we can do so is what persuades us of the unity and continuity of history. When we find the Celtic druids and the Aztecs making human sacrifices to their gods we say we recognize a human tendency, though we profess to abhor it. Yet some future reader of history might be tempted to compare with those ancient peoples our contemporary revolutionists, who sacrifice 400,000 kulaks (or some other hapless group) for the good of the tribe and its eternal prosperity. But we also notice a strange difference: we know that fanatical faith presides over each type of human sacrifice, ancient and modern, but even as we condemn we think we understand the modern more readily: we know its background, have heard its advocates. It is one of the illuminations of history, not merely to know abstractly, but, by learning the local shape of things, to feel how the reality of each time and place differs; how the faiths diverge in contents and origins and thus in persuasiveness. We may now lump together the Celts and the Aztecs, but they were far apart in thought and character: in short, nothing is truly comparable; in history everything is *sui generis.*

The wise reader of history keeps his equilibrium between these two extremes of likeness and difference. He tries to see the unfamiliar in the familiar, and vice versa. He stands away from his own prejudices and satisfies his curiosity by trying to sympathize with what is farthest away or most alien. This is very hard to do when what is before us is a bloody sacrifice, a massacre, a piece of treachery or cynical greed that violates our sensibilities as well as our moral principles. But to sympathize is not to condone or approve, it is only to acknowledge in oneself the ever-present possibility of the same feeling or action. Certainly the enlightened 20th century has no warrant for looking down on times and places where treachery and massacre were commonplace. And it is a sobering observation to find in both past and present the evidence that inhumanities have been and are being committed by the brutish and civilized alike, the ignorant and the educated, the cynical and the devout, the selfish and the heroic.

A principal good derived from history is thus an increase in self-knowledge, through a fellow-feeling with men singly and in groups as history tells about them. That self-knowledge in turn makes the reader of history less ready to find "monsters of error" in his own time and place. Let it be said again, he need not condone or accept with indifference, but he is spared one of the very errors that perpetuates man's inhumanity to man—fanatical self-righteousness.

On the constructive side, what history tells is the long series of efforts to overcome the constraints of nature and the difficulties of living in society. Those efforts we call civilizations. They start small. In the West they first take the form of city-states. They clash, with one another or with the barbarians "outside." Trade and war, war and trade expand the scope of power, government, and law. Great men introduce broader conceptions of citizenship, morals, and religions. Others invent practical devices of administration, manufacture, and—again—war. Still others discover the workings of nature, create mathematics or art or systems of philosophy. A concentration of such activities over a given territory is what is meant by a high civilization—Egypt, Greece, the Hellenistic Age, Rome, the Saracens, the High Middle Ages, the Renaissance. And also China, Japan, the Khmers, India, the Mayas, the Incas, and so on.

Along this hazardous and always violent course, innumerable characters rise and play their parts. Their fates provide stories within the story. Visibly, biographies are the bricks of which history is made, for the story of mankind can only be the stories of men. But by a paradox of man's social existence, the life of communities is not a simple sum of individual lives. The reader of history must therefore imagine from the printed page characteristic acts, moods, errors, disasters, achievements that are nobody's doing and everybody's doing. This imagining is another important good bestowed by historical reading, for it dispels the illusion that H.G. Wells called the "governess view" of history: They (the bad people) are doing this terrible thing to Us (the good people). The fallacy in it is to suppose that any large group acts as with one mind, clear in purpose and aware of consequences. Such a projection of the single ego upon whole masses is a form of provincialism that is encountered in most political discussions and certainly in all social prejudices: "If the President would only act . . . if those people would only see reason. . . ." A reader of history is cured of this simple-mindedness by developing a new sense—the historical sense—of how mankind in the mass behaves, neither free nor fatally pushed, and in its clearest actions mysterious even to itself.

It is this peculiarity that, while marking the difference between history and biography (where acts can be deemed individual and responsible), has led many minds to postulate a meaning in history, a meaning discoverable but obscured by the multiplicity and confusion of facts. A famous passage in Cardinal Newman's *Apologia* records in admirable prose the feelings that lead to the elaboration of philosophies of history; for Newman it is of course the traditional Christian interpretation that unifies the multiplicity and resolves the confusion:

> To consider the world in its length and breadth, its various history, the many races of man, their starts, their fortunes, their mutual alienation, their conflicts; and then their ways, habits, governments, forms of worship; their enterprises, their aimless courses, their random achievements and acquirements, the impotent conclusion of long-standing facts, the tokens so faint and broken, of a superintending design, the blind evolution of what turn out to be great powers or truths, the progress of things, as if from unreasoning elements, not towards final causes, the greatness and littleness of man, his far-reaching aims, his short duration, the curtain hung over his futurity, the disappointments of life, the defeat of good, the success of evil, physical pain, mental anguish, the prevalence and intensity of sin, the pervading idolatries, the corruptions, the dreary hopeless irreligion, that condition of the whole race, so fearfully yet exactly described in the Apostle's words, "having no hope and without God in the world,"—all this is a vision to dizzy and appal; and inflicts upon the mind the sense of a profound mystery, which is absolutely beyond human solution.

Other famous philosophies, from Vico's and Hegel's to Marx's and Spengler's, discover a direction in history, or a principle of action, and often a goal or terminus (as in Marx), after which history as we know it shall cease and a kind of second Eden be restored.

To the practical writer or reader of history these philosophies appeal mainly by their suggestiveness; they are valued for their scattered insights and analogies. As systems they negate the very spirit of history, which seeks the concrete and particular, the opposite of system and abstraction. True, there have been historians who took a middle course and attempted to find empirical regularities in history— again with occasionally suggestive results—but very soon their methods begin to do violence to the facts in order to group them and count them and treat them like identities in physical science. When the physical world itself has not yet been fully systematized, to assume or "find" a system in history without the means and the liberties that science uses is to think like neither a scientist nor a historian. It is in fact an attempt to remove the difficulty of history at the cost of destroying its unique merit and interest.

By the "liberties" that science takes is meant the experimenter's elimination of all but a very few components in a given trial, so as to ascertain precisely the nature and amount of a given effect. When this is done, the result is usually stated in causal terms—so much of this, under such and such conditions, will produce so much of that. Hardly anyone needs to be told that history defies a similar treatment. Its elements cannot be exactly measured, and although each historical situation presents to the discerning eye a variety of clear conditions or factors, the isolating of *a* cause for what happens is beyond reach.

That is but another way of saying that history is and must remain a story. And a story, if properly told, is a whole, to be understood as a whole—synthetically, not analytically. History in this regard resembles the arts. We say we "analyze" a work of art, but that is to speak metaphorically. We can enjoy and understand the products of art only as wholes. In history, the artful story is offered as a true story, and great pains are taken to see that it is true. But except in the broadest sense, the historical wholes are not given as such in the record; they are devised by the historian, to make the welter of facts intelligible and hence able to be remembered. Clio was not only the muse of history but also of eloquence, by which the Greeks meant good, intelligible prose, to be spoken before an audience unused to books. The same requirements still hold; written history must be readable with pleasure, or Clio is defeated.

But, it will be said, from many diverse writers will come divergent stories, rival interpretations. That is true, for only a divine mind could know "how it actually happened." But this limitation of history is also a merit, for it can thereby be written and read over and over again in as many versions as are plausible or accessible. There is and will be no final statement; the perspective forever changes, and with it the interest of history renews itself into infinity. As the philosopher William James once remarked, "What has been concluded that we should conclude about it?"

Part Nine. The History of Mankind

The outlines in the thirty-nine sections, in seven divisions, of Part Nine deal with the history of the peoples and civilizations of the world.

Certain points should be noted about Part Nine.

History, like philosophy, has developed methods applicable to the subject matter of other disciplines. The results of these applications are set forth in other parts. Each of the nine sections of Division II of Part Six includes a historical treatment of each of the arts. Similarly, each of the nine sections of Division II of Part Eight includes a historical treatment of each of the particular religions dealt with. Certain sections of the five divisions of Part Ten set forth the history of logic and mathematics; the history of science generally; the history of each of the natural and social sciences; the history of medicine; the history of technology; the history of philosophy; the history of humanistic scholarship; and the history of historiography and of the study of history itself.

It should also be noted that here and in the other portions of the Outline of Knowledge that treat historical matters, the level of detail is greater than that elsewhere. This reflects the editors' belief that an outline of history imposed upon a geographical or chronological base requires a high degree of particularization.

The topical breakdown of the history of mankind into seven divisions and thirty-nine sections reflects more or less traditional judgments—judgments regarding the regional divisions of world history; the identification of peoples and civilizations; the temporal periodization in historical accounts of particular civilizations; and the periods of relative isolation and of relative confluence of different civilizations.

The titles of the seven divisions in this part indicate the regional and temporal divisions used. Introductory headnotes for each of the seven divisions indicate the temporal periodizations used in the accounts of particular civilizations.

Division I. **Peoples and Civilizations of Ancient Southwest Asia, North Africa, and Europe**

The outline in Section 911 first treats of the geography of the regions covered in the section, the sources for the history of the peoples in these regions, and the character and achievements of ancient Near Eastern, Aegean, and North African civilizations. It then deals separately with the history of each of the peoples in these regions in ancient times.

The outline in Section 912 begins with the history of the peoples of non-Classical ancient Europe. It then deals with the whole course of the Classical Greco-Roman civilization, extending from the emergence of Classical Greece from Archaic Greece, through the Hellenistic Age and the history of republican Rome, to the history of the Roman Empire up to AD 395.

Section 911.   **Early Peoples and Civilizations of Southwest Asia and Egypt, the Aegean, and North Africa**

A. The character and achievements of ancient Near Eastern, Aegean, and North African civilizations; the geography of these regions; archaeological and documentary historical sources; historiographic problems

B. Mesopotamia and Iran to *c.* 1600 BC

  1. Development of river valley civilization in Mesopotamia

    a. The Late Neolithic, Chalcolithic, and protohistoric (pre-urban) periods

    b. The Sumerians from their origins to the end of the Early Dynastic Period (*c.* 2350 BC)

      i. Their conjectured origins: literary and other historical sources (king lists and invention of cuneiform writing), early kings and legendary figures (Gilgamesh)

      ii. Foundation of city-states (*e.g.,* Kish, Ur, Uruk, Lagash, Mari, Umma): rivalry among the cities, the temple city and theocracy, social and economic organization, contacts with Egyptian and Indus Valley civilizations, Sumerian culture

    c. Sumer and Akkad from *c.* 2350 to 2000 BC

      i. The ascendancy of the Semitic Akkadians under Sargon I of Akkad and his successors, invasions and the fall of the dynasty

      ii. The unification of Sumer, Akkad, and Elam under the 3rd dynasty of Ur (*c.* 2112–2004 BC): administration and composition of the empire, Ur in decline

    d. The Old Babylonian Period and the early history of Assyria

      i. Isin and Larsa: rivalry and political fragmentation, literary texts, decentralization

      ii. Early Assyria: Ashur, Nineveh, and Urbilum; Akkadian inscriptions and language; the economy; the reign of Shamshi-Adad I (*c.* 1813–1781 BC)

      iii. Establishment of the Old Babylonian Empire under the dynasty of Hammurabi (*c.* 1792–1750 BC): law, society, and literature

    e. Hurrian expansion to *c.* 1600 BC and the decline of the Old Babylonian Empire after *c.* 1750 BC

  2. Early Elam (Iran): cultural ties and political and military interaction with Mesopotamia

C. Emergence of river valley civilization in Egypt (to *c.* 1600 BC)

  1. The Predynastic Period (to *c.* 2925 BC) and the Early Dynastic Period (1st through 3rd dynasties, *c.* 2925–*c.* 2575 BC): unification of Upper and Lower Egypt under King Menes (Narmer), capital at Memphis

  2. The Old Kingdom (*c.* 2575–2130 BC) and the First Intermediate Period (*c.* 2130–1939 BC)

    a. The Old Kingdom (4th–8th dynasties, *c.* 2575–*c.* 2130 BC): divine kingship; the building of the great pyramids near Memphis; centralized government; class structure; foreign trade; increased provincialization; instability of the throne

    b. The First Intermediate Period (9th–11th dynasties, *c.* 2130–1939 BC): governmental decentralization; collapse of the Old Kingdom and ensuing disunity and foreign raids; reunification by Mentuhotep I under the 11th dynasty, ruling from Thebes

  3. The Middle Kingdom (1938–*c.* 1600 BC) and the Second Intermediate Period (*c.* 1630–1540 BC)

    a. The Middle Kingdom (12th–14th dynasties, 1938–*c.* 1600 BC): the cult of Amon; developments in the monarchical institutions; the conquest of Lower Nubia; trade; immigration

    b. The Second Intermediate Period (15th–17th dynasties, *c.* 1630–1540 BC): internal decentralization and the Asiatic Hyksos occupation

D. Early civilizations in Syria and Palestine, Anatolia, and the Aegean to *c.* 1600 BC

  1. Emergence of civilization in Syria and Palestine

    a. The Stone Age cultures and their transition from the Neolithic to the Early Bronze Age until *c.* 2300 BC, agricultural and technological developments, Proto-Urban settlements, Jericho

      i. Paleolithic and Mesolithic periods: development of horticulture and the domestication of animals

      ii. Pre-Pottery Neolithic areas, grouped houses and town walls, arrival of new peoples and their rectangular architecture, Pottery Neolithic areas, molded plaster vessels, dark-faced burnished ware and the spread of its associated culture

      iii. The Chalcolithic Period and the Early Bronze Age: migrations and spread of Halafian culture, development of trade, beginnings of urbanization, Early Bronze Age cities

  b. The Intermediate Period (*c.* 2300–*c.* 1900 BC) and the Middle Bronze Age (*c.* 1900–*c.* 1525 BC): revival of trade and connecting link between the greater states; *e.g.,* Aleppo, Byblos, Alalakh in Syria

      i. The Amorite invasion: breakup of settled areas by nomadic peoples, bronze weapons and votive objects

      ii. Reappearance of urban civilization in the Middle Bronze Age: hieroglyphics, clay tablets, development of new pottery in Canaan

2. Emergence of civilizations in Anatolia, Cyprus, and the Aegean

  a. Anatolia: the Neolithic, Chalcolithic, and Bronze ages; settlement by the Hittites

      i. Neolithic farming communities: house styles, tools and weapons, pottery, foodstuffs

      ii. Appearance of painted pottery in the Chalcolithic Period, uses of metal

      iii. Bronze Age culture; *e.g.,* Troy, Alaca Hüyük: jewelry, pottery, burial customs, metalworking, weaponry, migrations

      iv. The Hittite occupation of Anatolia and establishment of the Old Hittite Kingdom (*c.* 1700–*c.* 1500 BC): expansion into northern Mesopotamia and Syria under Hattusilis and Mursilis, the Hurrian invasions, the Middle Kingdom

  b. The Late Neolithic, Chalcolithic, and Bronze ages in Cyprus

  c. The early Aegean civilizations (to *c.* 1450 BC)

      i. The Paleolithic, Neolithic, and Chalcolithic ages in Greece, Crete, and the Aegean islands; the pre-Greek (Early Bronze or Helladic) population of Greece from *c.* 3000 BC; the Early Bronze or Cycladic Age in the Aegean islands; the shaft grave period on the mainland

      ii. The Minoan civilization on Crete: the period of the Early Palaces (*c.* 2200–1700 BC), cultural efflorescence, Kamáres ware, commerce, Knossos, Middle Cycladic culture, period of the Later Palaces (*c.* 1700–*c.* 1450 BC) on Crete, the arts, Linear A tablets

E. The era of the Egyptian and Hittite empires (*c.* 1600–1050 BC): the expansion of the Indo-Europeans

1. The New Kingdom of Egypt (18th–20th dynasties, 1539–1075 BC)

  a. The 18th dynasty (1539–1292 BC): the emergence of strong centralized administration, territorial expansion, religious and cultural developments

      i. Expulsion of the Hyksos from Egypt under Ahmose (1539–1514 BC): cult of Amon-Re, expansion into Syria and Palestine, contacts with the Aegean and its arts

      ii. Egyptian culture and prosperity in the reigns of Amenhotep III (1390–1353 BC) and Akhenaton (Amenhotep IV; 1353–1336 BC): domination over Nubia, erection of new temples at Thebes, cult of the god Aton, subsequent eclipse of the dynasty

  b. The 19th and 20th dynasties (1292–1075 BC): political shift to the north, new construction, foreign policies

      i. Reassertion of Egyptian power: campaigns against the Hittites and Libyans, succession disputes

      ii. The reign of Ramses III (1187–1156 BC) and subsequent decline of the 20th dynasty, campaigns against the Sea Peoples, growth of influence of the priests of Amon-Re

  c. Society and culture in the New Kingdom: the king as the embodiment of the state; the civil service; the military; the priesthood; the artisans, common people, and slaves; trade and commerce

2. The Hittite Empire and its conflict with Egypt; Syria and Palestine under Egyptian and Hittite domination; the period of the migrations of new peoples

  a. The Hittite Empire (*c.* 1525–1190 BC)

      i. Expansion of the Hittite Empire under Suppiluliumas I into Syria (*c.* 1365 BC): reduction of the Mitannian state, ensuing conflicts and treaties with Egypt, relations with neighbouring states

    ii. The capital of the Hittite Empire at Hattusa (Boğazköy): geographical position, architecture, invasions from the West, fall of the empire and destruction of the capital (*c.* 1190 BC), emergence of the Indo-European Phrygians as the chief Anatolian power

  b. Syria and Palestine under Egyptian, Mitannian, and Hittite domination, and the period of the migrations of new peoples (*c.* 1550–1200 BC)

    i. The development of Levantine seafaring trade: the Levantine city-states (*e.g.,* Ugarit), political organization, economy, culture, development of the linear alphabet by the Canaanites and the spread of its use

    ii. The origins of the Hebrews in the patriarchal age and their sojourn in and Exodus from Egypt in the 13th century BC, their conquest of Palestine, the Sea Peoples and the Philistine conquest of the Palestinian littoral

    iii. The Syro-Hittite states and the migration of the Semitic Aramaeans into Syria and Palestine *c.* 1100 BC and their foundation of states in Syria: spread of the Aramaic language, trends in religion and the arts

3. Mesopotamia from *c.* 1600 to *c.* 900 BC

  a. The Kassites in Babylonia (*c.* 1595–*c.* 1155 BC): their conjectured origins, their adoption of Mesopotamian culture, Elamite and Assyrian invasions after *c.* 1250, the fall of the Kassites

  b. The kingdom of the Hurrians and the Mitanni (*c.* 1500–1360 BC) in northern Mesopotamia, its displacement by Assyria

  c. The rise of Assyria (*c.* 1360–1076 BC): expansion under Ashur-uballit I (*c.* 1365–*c.* 1330 BC), conquest of Babylon, continued expansion to Tiglath-pileser I (*c.* 1115–*c.* 1077 BC), temporary eclipse of Assyria (to *c.* 900 BC)

4. The Elamite kingdom and its struggle with Babylonia in the 13th and 12th centuries BC

5. Mycenaean (Achaean, Late Helladic) civilization in Greece (*c.* 1450–1100 BC): the eruption of Thera (*c.* 1500 BC), the conquest of Minoan Crete (*c.* 1450 BC), and the arrival of the Greeks

  a. The overthrow of the existing social order, introduction of new artistic styles, conquest of the Cyclades, the evidence of the Linear B tablets, destruction of the palace at Knossos and period of the Mycenaean Empire

  b. The end of the Bronze Age in the Aegean: destruction of Mycenaean centres, invasion from the north and the coming of the Greeks

  c. The people of the Bronze Age Aegean: physical types, dress, society, economy, warfare, religion, and arts

F. The era of the new states of Southwest Asia: the beginning of the Iron Age (*c.* 1050–700 BC)

1. Egypt and Babylonia in decline, further Assyrian expansion

  a. Egypt under the 21st–25th dynasties (*c.* 1075–656 BC): loss of influence in Syria, disunity and the diminution of royal power, Libyan domination, civil war and Kushite (Ethiopian) rule, the Assyrian conquest (671–664 BC)

  b. Babylonia (*c.* 1050–750 BC): the brief resurgence of Babylonian power under Nebuchadrezzar I (1124–1103 BC); the cult of Marduk; Aramaean, Assyrian, and Chaldean invasions from the 11th to the 9th century BC

  c. Emergence of Assyria as the dominant Mesopotamian state after *c.* 900 BC: internal dissension and the challenge of Urartu in the 8th century BC

2. Palestine, Syria, Anatolia, and Iran

  a. Development of Canaanite–Phoenician commercial city-states from *c.* 1100 to *c.* 700 BC (*e.g.,* Tyre, Sidon): trade and colonization, Phoenician civilization

  b. The Hebrew kingdom (*c.* 1020–*c.* 700 BC): subjection of the Philistines, territorial expansion in Syria and Palestine

    i. The reigns of David and Solomon in the 10th century, growth of separate kingdoms of Judah (south) and Israel (north, conquered by Assyria in 722 BC)

    ii. The cult of Yahweh and biblical literature, social and political structure, arts

  c. The neo-Hittite states of southeastern Anatolia: Carchemish, Milid (Malatya), Tabal, and Que (*c.* 1180–700 BC); conquest by the Aramaeans and Assyrians

  d. Foundation of Urartu in about the 13th century BC, rise of the Urartian kingdom (*c.* 840–*c.* 744 BC), Assyrian influences, the Cimmerian invasion (*c.* 714 BC) and destruction of the kingdom (*c.* 609 BC), influence of the Urartian state, the Armenian Empire under the Artaxiads

e. Phrygia in central and western Anatolia (*c.* 1180–*c.* 700 BC): capital at Gordium, relations with Assyrians and Luwians, the Cimmerian invasions in the beginning of the 7th century, the cult of Cybele

f. The Aramaean kingdoms (*e.g.,* Damascus) and their cultural and commercial role: conquest by Assyria

g. The Neo-Elamite period: the occupation of Iran by the Indo-European Medes and Persians by the 9th century BC

G. The era of the Assyrian and Neo-Babylonian empires and the Achaemenid Persian Empire (746–250 BC)

1. The first imperial unification of the ancient Near East under the Assyrian Empire (746–609 BC)

a. Assyrian culture in the context of the Mesopotamian tradition: the great cities; *e.g.,* Nineveh

b. Expansion of the empire under Tiglath-pileser III (744–727 BC), Sargon II (721–705 BC), and Sennacherib (704–681 BC); decline from the reign of Ashurbanipal (668–627 BC); conquest by the Medes (625–609 BC)

2. The interval between Assyrian and Achaemenid hegemony (610–539 BC)

a. The Neo-Babylonian Empire (636–539 BC): conquests, treatment of Jews, decline of the empire

i. The reign of Nebuchadrezzar II (604–562 BC): subjection of Syria and Palestine, the Babylonian Exile of the Jews and the post-Exile period, building activities

ii. The last kings of Babylonia: internal dissension and early relations with Persia, surrender to Cyrus II the Great (539 BC)

b. The Anatolian kingdom of Lydia (*c.* 700–*c.* 547 BC): early relations with Assyria, the Cimmerian invasions, suzerainty over the Greeks in Anatolia, Greco-Lydian culture, growth of independent Cilicia in the late 7th century, conquest by Persia

c. Saite Egypt (26th dynasty, 664–525 BC) and its reassertion of independence after Assyrian rule; revival of traditional Egyptian culture, subjection to Persia

d. The Kingdom of the Medes in Iran (*c.* 700–550 BC) and the establishment of the Achaemenid Persian Empire

i. Conjectured origins of the Median state, expulsion of the Scythians, extension of control over the other Iranian peoples and into Armenia and eastern Anatolia after the downfall of Assyria

ii. Cyrus II the Great's (550–529 BC) establishment of his rule from Anatolia to east of Iran, relative generosity toward subject peoples

3. The Achaemenid Persian Empire (529–330 BC) under the successors of Cyrus II the Great, Greek rule to *c.* 250 BC

a. The empire under Cambyses II, Darius I, and Xerxes I (529–465 BC): the subjugation of Egypt, establishment of peace in the empire, penetration of the Balkan Peninsula and the unsuccessful attempts to conquer mainland Greece

b. Xerxes' weak successors: continued involvement in Greek affairs; internal disunity in the 4th century, resulting in conquest by Alexander III the Great (330 BC)

c. Achaemenid society and culture: Zoroastrianism, Persepolis and other capitals, social structure and economy

d. Seleucid rule to *c.* 250 BC, movement of Iranian peoples, revolt of the high satrapies

H. The Parthian and Sāsānian empires (*c.* 250 BC–AD 651), Armenia

1. The revival of Iranian power with the establishment of the Parthian Empire by Arsaces, formation of the Arsacid Parthian state

a. The "Philhellenistic Period" (*c.* 171 BC–*c.* AD 10): eastern and western expansion until the mid-1st century BC, wars with Rome until the settlement of 20 BC

b. The "Anti-Hellenistic Period" (AD 2–162): Parthian government under Artabanus III (AD 12–38), dissolution of the Parthian state

c. Roman invasions and the end of the Parthian Empire (AD 162–226)

2. Extension of Iranian power under the Sāsānian Empire

a. Foundation of the empire: the rise of Ardashīr I in the early 3rd century BC, the wars of Shāpūr I (AD 241–272), organization of the empire

      b. Religious developments: Zoroastrianism, Christianity, Manichaeism; art and literature

      c. Foreign policy: conflicts with the Romans, Byzantines, and Turks under Khosrow I (AD 531–579) and Khosrow II (AD 590/591–628); subsequent decline and extinction of the empire with the Arab conquest (AD 636/637–651)

   3. Armenia: client status under the Iranian empires of Rome in the period dominated by the Arsacids

I. The Nilotic Sudan, South Arabia, and Ethiopia until *c.* AD 600; North Africa until the Roman conquest (from 146 BC)

   1. Emergence of civilization in the Nilotic Sudan (Nubia): the origins of Nubian culture

   2. Egyptianization and the Kingdom of Kush (*c.* 1786–751 BC), conquest of Egypt (*c.* 730 BC) and later expulsion by the Assyrians (by 654 BC), conquest by Aksum (AD 350)

   3. Pre-Islāmic South Arabia: the kingdoms of Maʿīn, Sabaʾ, Qatabān, Ḥaḍramawt, and the tribes of central and northern Arabia; economic activities; religion; foreign relations

   4. Ethiopia to *c.* AD 650

      a. Remotest antiquity: the land of Punt, the Sabaean period

      b. The Aksumite Empire (2nd century AD): the Abyssinian peoples, maritime trade, Ezana's rule (4th century AD), reign of Ella-Asbeha (6th century AD) and relations with Persia

   5. North Africa until the Roman conquest

      a. Emergence of civilization in North Africa: the Early Neolithic culture in the Maghrib and Libya, the Berbers, the influence of Egypt, the advent of the mercantile Phoenicians and their foundation of Carthage *c.* 814 BC (Utica, 1101 BC?), the Greeks in Cyrenaica from *c.* 630 BC

      b. Emergence of Carthage as the leading western Mediterranean power: conflicts with the Greeks in the western Mediterranean, extension of Carthaginian power into Spain and the clash with Rome in the Punic Wars resulting in the destruction of Carthage (146 BC)

      c. Roman penetration into North Africa: the native kingdoms of Numidia and Mauretania and their eventual incorporation into the Roman Empire

---

Suggested reading in the *Encyclopædia Britannica*:

MACROPAEDIA: Major articles dealing with early peoples and civilizations of Southwest Asia and Egypt, the Aegean, and North Africa

Afghanistan	Israel	North Africa	Turkey and
Arabia	Jordan	Palestine	Ancient Anatolia
Egypt	Lebanon	Prehistoric Peoples	
Greek and Roman	Mesopotamia,	and Cultures	
Civilizations,	The History of	Syria	
Ancient	Ancient		
Iran			

MICROPAEDIA: Selected entries of reference information

General subjects

Anatolia, Crete, and	Hittite	Perga	Kindah
Cyprus:	Karatepe	Phocaea	Nabataean
Ahhiyawa	Kaska	Phrygia	Sabaʾ
Alaca Hüyük	Kizzuwadna	Pisidia	Ṣāliḥ
Alişar Hüyük	Knossos	Sakcagöz	Tanūkh
Amathus	Kültepe	Salamis	Thamūd
Anatolia	Luwian	Sardis	*Egypt:*
Arzawa	Lycaonia	Soli	Abū Jirāb
Aspendus	Lycia	Tarsus	Abū Ruwaysh
Bithynia	Lydia	Troas	Abu Simbel
Boğazköy	Milid	Troy	Amarna, Tell el-
Çatalhüyük	Minoan	Xanthus	Amratian culture
Chalcedon	civilization	Yazılıkaya	Badarian culture
Cilicia	Muṣaṣir	Zincirli Höyük	Beni Hasan
Citium	Mysia	*Arabia:*	Canopus
Gordium	Pamphylia	Arabia Felix	
Harran	Paphlagonia	Ḥimyar	

Section 912.   Peoples of Ancient Europe and the Classical Civilizations of the Ancient Mediterranean World to AD 395

A. Non-Classical ancient Europe

  1. The geography and ethnography of Europe, archaeological and documentary historical sources, historiographic problems

  2. Europe before the Iron Age

    a. Spread of Neolithic farming communities throughout all of Europe by *c.* 2000 BC

    b. Spread of Bronze Age industry throughout Europe by *c.* 1500 BC: population movements into southeastern Europe and southwestern Asia in the 2nd millennium BC, the Indo-Europeans

  3. Non-Classical Europe in the Iron Age (*c.* 650 BC–*c.* AD 100)

    a. The Etruscans and other Italic peoples, the non-Greek peoples of the Balkan Peninsula

      i. Conjectured Etruscan origins; Etruscan language and writing; cities; government and society; art and religion; maritime expansion; foreign relations with the Greeks, Carthaginians, and other Italic peoples; decline after *c.* 500 BC and eventual Roman conquest in the mid-3rd century

      ii. Other Italic peoples: the Umbro-Sabellians, Oscans, Apulians, Latins, Siculi, Ligurians, Veneti, and Piceni; their cultures; their relations with the Greeks, Etruscans, and Carthaginians; eventual absorption by Rome

      iii. Non-Greek peoples of the Balkan Peninsula; *e.g.,* Illyrians, Thracians: their culture and relationship to Classical civilizations

    b. Trans-Alpine Europe and the Iberian Peninsula

      i. The Celts: the Hallstatt Period (7th–6th centuries BC); Celtic occupation of Europe from the Danube to the Iberian Peninsula and the British Isles by *c.* 500 BC; Celtic penetration of Italy, the Balkan Peninsula, and Anatolia during the La Tène period (after *c.* 500 BC); subjugation in Gaul by Rome by 50 BC and later by the Germans by the 5th century AD; Celtic art, religion, and social and political organization

      ii. The Germans: their acquisition of Iron Age culture, migration into the Elbe–Rhine region by *c.* 500 BC, pressure on the Celts and Rome, inundation of the western half of the Roman Empire by the 5th century AD, Germanic social and political organization, religion and mythology

    c. Ancient peoples of the European steppe

      i. The Cimmerians: conjectured origins; southward migration, under Scythian pressure, from north of the Caucasus into Southwest Asia in the 8th and 7th centuries BC

      ii. The Scythians (Sakas): westward migration from the 8th century BC and eventual establishment in India and southern Russia after *c.* 600 BC; the Kingdom of the Royal Scyths in southern Russia from *c.* 600 BC to *c.* AD 100; relations with the Greeks and with Achaemenid Persia; government, society, and military tactics; art and religion

      iii. The Sarmatian migration into southern Russia in the 4th century BC and gradual displacement of the Scythians by *c.* AD 100; conflict with Rome; conquest by the Goths and Huns in the 3rd and 4th centuries AD; society, art, and religion

B. Archaic Greece and the development of Classical Greek civilization (*c.* 1200–323 BC)

  1. The Early Archaic and Archaic periods (*c.* 1200–*c.* 500 BC)

    a. The Dorian invasions, the Greek migrations to Anatolia, and their results (Proto-Geometric Period, *c.* 1100–*c.* 900 BC)

    b. The Geometric Period (*c.* 900–*c.* 750 BC): the world of Homer and Hesiod, the beginning of writing and of the *polis,* mythology and religious developments, the panhellenic centres (*e.g.,* Olympia, Delphi), social and political organization

    c. The Archaic Period (*c.* 750–*c.* 500 BC)

      i. General trends in the *poleis:* displacement of monarchy by aristocracy, development of a money economy, socioeconomic crises and the rise and fall of tyranny, the colonization movement, relations among the *poleis* (*e.g.,* leagues, wars)

      ii. The *poleis* of mainland Greece: the emergence of Spartan dominance over the Peloponnese and of a military-oriented polity and repression; aristocracy and tyranny at Athens, the reforms of Solon, and the institution of democracy under Cleisthenes; tyranny, aristocracy, and economic expansion at Corinth; the other *poleis* of the Peloponnese, the Isthmus, Euboea, and Boeotia

      iii. The Greeks in Asia Minor (Anatolia): Dorian and Aeolian cities; Miletus, Ephesus, and other Ionian cities; their commercial and cultural efflorescence

      iv. The Greek islands: the Cyclades, Sporades, Crete, Cyprus, and the Ionian Islands

      v. The Greek colonies and emporia in the West and Africa: southern Italy and Sicily (*e.g.,* Cumae, Syracuse), Gaul and the Iberian Peninsula (*e.g.,* Massilia), Cyrene and Naukratis

      vi. The Greeks in the North: Chalcidice, Thrace, Propontis (*e.g.,* Byzantium, Abydos, Lampsacus), and Pontus (*e.g.,* Black Sea region, Sinope, and Trapezus)

      vii. The arts in the Archaic Period; rationalism and irrationalism and the beginnings of philosophy and science, Orphism and the cult of Dionysus

      viii. The Greco-Persian Wars: the Persian (Achaemenid) conquest of Asia Minor and Thrace and the Ionian revolt (499 BC), Darius' (490 BC) and Xerxes' (480 BC) invasions of Greece and eventual Greek victory, the Greek offensive (479 BC), results of the wars, Herodotus' account of the conflict

2. The Classical period (*c.* 500–323 BC)

    a. Athens in the age of Pericles

      i. The Delian League and the Athenian Empire

      ii. Temporary retardation and final development of the democracy, society and economy

      iii. Cultural efflorescence; *e.g.,* the rebuilding of the Acropolis, drama, the pre-Socratic philosophers

    b. The Peloponnesian League and the other Greek states in the 5th century BC: relations among the Greek states from 479 to 431 BC

    c. The Peloponnesian War (431–404 BC): the war to the Peace of Nicias (421), renewal of the war and the defeat of Athens, intellectual and political changes at Athens (*e.g.,* oligarchic revolution, the Sophists and Socrates), Thucydides' account of the war

    d. The era of the Spartan and Theban hegemonies in Greece: Spartan policies toward the Greek states, relations with Persia, Athens and Thebes against Sparta, the Second Athenian League and the restoration of democracy, Theban expansion and containment, peace and the balance of power in Greece

    e. The northern kingdoms: Epirus, the rise of Macedonia and the conquest of Greece under Philip II

    f. The western Greeks: conflict with Carthage, the rise of Syracuse under Dionysius the Elder

    g. Greek culture in the 4th century BC: developments in philosophy and the arts

    h. The empire of Alexander III the Great: relations with the Greeks; the conquest of the Persian Empire (334–330 BC), Bactria, and the Indus Valley (330–323 BC); the ideals and governing practices of Alexander and the diversity of his empire

C. The Hellenistic Age (323–27 BC)

1. Establishment of the Hellenistic kingdoms and monarchies

    a. The regency and warfare among rival generals after Alexander's death (323–276 BC)

    b. Macedonian and Ptolemaic Egypt (323–30 BC)

      i. The Ptolemaic dynasty: dynastic strife and the end of the dynasty with the death of Cleopatra (30 BC)

      ii. Government and civilization of Hellenistic Egypt

    c. The Seleucid Kingdom in Asia: the dynasty, government, society, culture, and economy in its diverse regions; Jewish resistance; territorial losses in the 3rd century

    d. Greek rule in Bactria and India

    e. The Attalid kingdom of Pergamum and the native states in Asia Minor: Bithynia, Pontus, Cappadocia, Galatia, and Rhodes

    f. The Antigonid kingdom of Macedonia: government and foreign policy

g. Greece: social and political changes in the *polis,* the Achaean and Aetolian leagues, Athens and the other Greek states

h. The western Greeks, Epirus, Sicily under Agathocles (317–289 BC) and Hieron II (*c.* 270–216/215 BC) until its absorption by Rome

2. Relations among the Hellenistic states and other peoples from *c.* 275 to 27 BC

a. Expansionist policies of the Ptolemies in the Aegean and Asia Minor and Syria and their conflicts with the Seleucids

b. Conflicts between the Greek leagues and the Antigonids in the 3rd century BC

c. The Celtic migrations: expansion into the Iberian Peninsula, the British Isles, and Rome and southern Italy; later expansion into central Europe, the Carpathians, and the Balkans

d. The vigorous policies of Antiochus III and Philip V; the breakup of the Seleucid Empire; the entrance of Rome into the affairs of the Hellenistic states, resulting in their eventual incorporation into the Roman Empire

3. Hellenistic political, social, economic, and cultural institutions

a. Hellenistic monarchy and royal administration

b. Cultural developments: developments in philosophy, science, the arts, education, and religion

D. The rise of Rome

1. The character and achievements of the Romans, the archaeological and documentary historical sources (*e.g.,* Pompeii and Herculaneum), historiographic problems

2. Early (regal) Rome to the 6th century BC

a. Myths of origins and the early monarchy

b. The Etruscan hegemony and formative influence over Rome

c. Development of Roman social, religious, political, and military institutions; Roman virtues

3. The early Roman Republic (6th century–264 BC)

a. Overthrow of the monarchy and establishment of the republic and its institutions: the magistracies, judicial institutions, the Senate, plebeian institutions

b. Expansion of Rome in Italy: Rome and its Latin neighbours, the Gallic invasion and further conquests, Roman mastery of Italy

4. The middle republic: the emergence of Rome as the leading Mediterranean power (264–133 BC)

a. The First and Second Punic Wars

i. The First Punic War (264–241 BC) and its aftermath: the emergence of Roman naval power and acquisition of Sicily (241 BC), later annexation of Corsica and Sardinia (238 BC)

ii. Roman expansion into Cisalpine Gaul and entry into Greek affairs

iii. The Second Punic War (218–201 BC): Hannibal's invasion of Italy, his initial victories, and the war of attrition in Italy; Roman defeat of the Carthaginians at the Battle of the Metaurus (207 BC); the First Macedonian War (214–205 BC) and the conflict in Spain; Roman counteroffensive and victory in Africa (202 BC); Roman pacification of conquered territories

b. Establishment of Roman hegemony in the Hellenistic world

i. Establishment of a Roman protectorate over Greece after the Second Macedonian War (200–196 BC), the conquest of Macedonia and Illyricum (168 BC), the reduction of Rhodes, Roman exclusion of Seleucid power from the Aegean

ii. The Third Punic War (149–146 BC): the destruction of Carthage, subjugation of Macedonia and Greece

iii. Beginning of Roman provincial administration, abuses, Romanization of the empire

c. Roman government and economy in the middle republic: consuls, the Senate, and popular assemblies; development of large business interests, grazing estates, and urban immigration

d. Roman culture in the middle republic: Hellenizing influences

5. The late Roman Republic (133–31 BC)

a. Social and economic ills in Italy and the reform movement of the Gracchi (133–121 BC) and its results: the rise of middle-class equites

b. Roman wars against the Celts and the conquest of Gallia Narbonensis (121 BC), wars against Jugurtha of Numidia (112–105 BC) and the Germans (105–101 BC), Marius' career and military reforms

c. Events in Asia and the first war with Mithradates VI Eupator (88–84 BC): Italian allies (*socii*) against Rome in the Social War (90–89 BC) and their subsequent enfranchisement, the dictatorship and constitution of Sulla (82–80 BC)

d. The Roman state in the two decades after Sulla

    i. Pompey's early career, revolts against Roman rule, Pompey's alliance with Crassus and repeal of the Sullan system, his extraordinary commands

    ii. Growing political suspicion and the outbreak of violence in the mid-1st century BC: the conspiracies of Catiline, Cicero's decline, the rise of Caesar and Pompey

e. The alliance of Caesar, Pompey, and Crassus (59–44 BC): Caesar's conquest of Gaul; political maneuvers and the outbreak of the Civil War; Caesar's triumph, dictatorship, and assassination

f. The initial cooperation of Octavian and Mark Antony in the Triumvirate and Octavian's achievement of sole power (43–31 BC): the annexation of Egypt and its administration

g. Roman law during the late republic: the development of new procedures, the role of magistrates, the law of succession

h. Culture in the late republic: oratory and philosophy, the arts

E. The Roman Empire (31 BC–AD 395)

1. Consolidation of the empire under the Julio-Claudians (31 BC–AD 68)

a. Augustus' establishment of the principate (27 BC–AD 14): the role of the *princeps;* the imperial administration, fiscal and military reforms, and the founding of new colonies; social and religious legislation; economic growth

b. The Roman Empire at the time of Augustus: provincial administration, the imperial frontiers, the western provinces, the eastern provinces, the economic unification of the Mediterranean

c. Foreign policy: Roman relations with Parthia and the other states in the East; the southern, western, and northern frontiers

d. The culture of the Augustan Age: contributions of Livy, Virgil, and Horace; religion; the visual arts

e. The empire under Tiberius (AD 14–37), Gaius (AD 37–41), Claudius I (AD 41–54), and Nero (AD 54–68): internal and frontier policies, the annexation of Britain, Tacitus' accounts, civil war and revolt in "the year of the four Emperors" (AD 69)

2. Growth of the empire under the Flavians and Antonines (AD 69–192)

a. The Flavian emperors (AD 69–96): Vespasian's fiscal and provincial reorganization, military and frontier policies, Titus and the suppression of the Jewish revolt, Domitian's despotism, military development and frontiers

b. The Antonine emperors (AD 96–192): the reigns of Nerva, Trajan, Hadrian, Antoninus Pius, Marcus Aurelius, and Commodus; the beginning of imperial decline after AD 180

3. The zenith of the Roman Empire in the late 1st and 2nd centuries AD

a. The city of Rome and the empire: methods of Roman imperialism; the cities, culture, society, politics, and economy of the western and eastern provinces; the legions and frontier defenses

b. Greco-Roman culture of the late 1st and 2nd centuries AD: developments in philosophy, religion, technology, and the arts

4. Changes and crises in the Roman Empire in the 3rd and 4th centuries AD

a. Civil wars, conflict with Parthia, the growth of bureaucracy, and militarization of government under the Severan dynasty (AD 193–235)

b. Religious and cultural life: the public religions under the empire, the rise and spread of Christianity and other Eastern religions, official persecution of Christianity

c. The transformation of Greco-Roman culture in late antiquity (3rd and 4th centuries AD), Greek revival and growth of Christian theology

d. Military anarchy and disintegration of the Roman Empire (AD 235–270): the Gordians, the beginning of Germanic invasions, loss of eastern provinces, economic and social crisis

e. The recovery of the Roman Empire and the establishment of the dominate (AD 270–337): the recovery measures of Aurelian and his immediate successors

    i. Diocletian's (284–305) fundamental political and economic measures: persecution of Christians, struggle for power

    ii. Constantine the Great (307–337) and his conversion to Christianity, administration, and founding of Constantinople

f. The Roman Empire under the 4th-century successors of Constantine to Theodosius I (AD 379–395)

    i. The rule of Constantine's sons (337–361): renewed wars with Sāsānid Persia and increased penetration of the empire by the Germans

    ii. Julian's reign (361–363): the attempt to restore the old empire

    iii. Establishment of Christianity as the sole state religion; social, economic, and urban decline; remnants of pagan culture

g. The provinces under the later empire and the eclipse of the empire in the West: Germanic hegemony and the invasions by other peoples

---

Suggested reading in the *Encyclopædia Britannica*:

MACROPAEDIA: Major articles and biographies dealing with peoples of ancient Europe and the Classical civilizations of the ancient Mediterranean world to AD 395

Alexander the Great	Constantine the Great	Germany	Greece
Athens	European History	Greek and Roman Civilizations, Ancient	Italy
Augustus	and Culture		Rome
Caesar	France		

MICROPAEDIA: Selected entries of reference information

General subjects

ancient Europe—	Boii	Lavinium	Isauria
Balkans:	Carnuntum	Ligurian	Pontus
Dacia	Chatti	Lucania	Sarmatian
Getae	Cimbri	Mamertini	Scythian
Illyria	Gepidae	Marsi	Side
Paeonia	Hallstatt	Paeligni	Soli
Triballi	Heuneburg	Piceni	Steppe, The
ancient Europe—	Lingones	Populonia	*Greece—Archaic*
Britain:	Marcomanni	Praeneste	*period:*
Caledonia	Reinheim	Sabine	Acarnania
Creswell Crags	*ancient Europe—*	Samnite	Achaean
Kent's Cavern	*Iberia:*	Segesta	Aetolia
Pict	Arevaci	Siculi	agora
Silures	Celtiberia	Stabiae	amphictyony
Skara Brae	Iberian	Umbri	Amphipolis
ancient Europe—	Lusitani	Veii	Apamea Cibotus
Gaul:	Numantia	Veneti	apella
Aedui	*ancient Europe—*	Villanovan culture	Archaic period
Arausio, Battle of	*Italy:*	Volsci	archon
Belgae	Alba Fucens	Volsinii	Areopagus
Gaul	Ardea	Vulci	Assus
Helvetii	Ateste	*ancient western Asia:*	Boeotian League
La Tène	Aurunci	Alani	Bosporus, kingdom of the
Morini	Boii	Anazarbus	boule
Senones	Caere	Antioch	Calydon
Sequani	Este	Bactria	Caulonia
Veneti	Etruscan	Cappadocia	Chersonese, Tauric
ancient Europe—	Felsina	Caria	Chersonese, Thracian
Germany:	Golasecca	Cimmerian	Clazomenae
Agri Decumates	Hernici	Commagene	
Alemanni	Hirpini	Doura-Europus	
Arevaci	Latium	Galatia	
		Hierapolis	

Cnidus
Colchis
Colophon
Corinth
Cumae
Cyrene
Cyzicus
deme
Dorian
Ecclesia
Eleusis
Elis
ephebus
Ephesus
ephor
Eretria
Erythrae
eupatrid
geōmoroi
Gortyn
Greco-Persian
 Wars
Halicarnassus
helot
Himera
hoplite
Ionia
Lampsacus
Lelantine War
Leontini
Magna Graecia
Magnesia ad
 Maeandrum
Mantineia
Marathon,
 Battle of
metic
Miletus
Olynthus
Orchomenus
Paestum
Parian Chronicle
Parthenon
Pella
Pergamum
Phaestus
phyle
Plataea
polis
Priene
prytaneum
Selinus
Sicyon
sortition
strategus
Tegea
Thermopylae

Theseum
Thespiae
Tiryns
Trojan War
trophy
tyrant
Greece—Classical
 period:
Anabasis
Aornos, Siege of
Artemis,
 Temple of
Chalcidian League
cleruchy
Corinth, League of
Delian League
Gaugamela,
 Battle of
Granicus, Battle
 of the
Hydaspes, Battle
 of the
Leuctra, Battle of
Macedonia
paideia
Peloponnesian War
Philippi
tetrarch
Hellenistic Age:
Achaean League
Aetolian League
Antioch
Bastarnae
Cynoscephalae
Hellenistic Age
Ipsus, Battle of
Issus, Battle of
Lamian War
Petra
Seleucia on the
 Tigris
Seleucid kingdom
Syrian Wars
Roman Empire:
Adrianople,
 Battle of
Aelia Capitolina
Althiburos
Antinoöpolis
Antonine Wall
Capernaum
Carrhae, Battle of
dominus
emperor
fasces
fiscus

Five Good
 Emperors
foedus
Hadrian's Wall
Herculaneum
indiction
itinerarium
labarum
Monumentum
 Ancyranum
Mursa, Battle of
Notitia Dignitatum
Ostia
Pompeii
princeps
procurator
Thugga
tribune
Tusculum
Roman provinces:
Africa
Alps
Arabia
Asia
Belgica
Dacia
Gallia Comata
Illyria
Lugdunensis
Mauretania
Moesia
Narbonensis
Numidia
Pannonia
Paphlagonia
Raetia
Transalpine Gaul
Roman Republic:
Acta
Actium, Battle of
aedile
aerarium
angaria
Cagliari
Cannae, Battle of
Capua
censor
civitas
clientship
colony
comitia
consul
curia
Decapolis
decemviri
decurio
delator

dictator
eques
fasti
gladiator
imperium
interrex
Italy
latifundium
Latin League
legate
lictor
limes
Macedonian
 Wars
Munda, Battle of
municipium
Optimates and
 Populares
pater patriae
patrician
Pharsalus, Battle of
plebeian
Pollentia
praetor
Praetorian Guard
prefect
proconsul
proscription
province
publican
Punic War, First
Punic War, Second
Punic War, Third
Pydna, Battle of
quaestor
Roman Republic
 and Empire
Rubicon
Secular Games
Senate
Social War
Thapsus, Battle of
tribe
triumph
triumvirate
other:
Beaker folk
Celt
Lake Dwellings
shell mound
Urnfield culture

Biographies

Greece and
 Macedonia:
Agesilaus II
Alcibiades
Argead dynasty

Cimon
Cleisthenes of
 Athens
Demosthenes
Dionysius the Elder

Epaminondas
Lycurgus
Miltiades the
 Younger
Peisistratus

Pericles
Philip II
Philip V
Pyrrhus
Solon

Themistocles

Theramenes

Hellenistic states:

  Antigonus I

    Monophthalmus

  Antigonus II

    Gonatas

  Antiochus I Soter

  Antiochus III

  Antiochus IV

    Epiphanes

  Arsinoe II

  Cleopatra VII

    Thea Philopator

  Mithradates VI

    Eupator

  Ptolemy I Soter

  Ptolemy II

    Philadelphus

  Ptolemy III

    Euergetes

Ptolemy IV

  Philopator

Ptolemy V

  Epiphanes

Ptolemy VI

  Philometor

Ptolemy IX

  Soter II

Ptolemy XII

  Auletes

Ptolemy XIII

  Theos Philopator

Seleucus I Nicator

Rome:

Agrippa, Marcus

  Vipsanius

Antony, Mark

Aurelian

Caesar, Julius

Caligula

Caracalla

Cato, Marcus

  Porcius

Cicero, Marcus

  Tullius

Claudius

Claudius Caecus,

  Appius

Constantine I

Diocletian

Domitian

Gallienus, Publius

  Licinius Egnatius

Germanicus Caesar

Gracchus, Gaius

  Sempronius

Gracchus, Tiberius

  Sempronius

Hadrian

Herod

Herod Agrippa I

Herod Antipas

Julian

Maecenas, Gaius

Marcus Aurelius

Marius, Gaius

Nero

Pilate, Pontius

Pompey the Great

Romulus and

  Remus

Seneca, Lucius

  Annaeus

Severus, Septimius

Severus Alexander

Scipio Africanus

  the Elder

Scipio Africanus

  the Younger

Sulla, Lucius

  Cornelius

Theodosius I

Tiberius

Trajan

Valentinian I

Vespasian

INDEX: See entries under all of the terms above

Division II.

Peoples and Civilizations of Medieval Europe, North Africa, and Southwest Asia
[For Part Nine headnote see page 343.]

The outlines in the four sections of Division II deal with the civilizations directly descendant from those of the ancient Near East and of Classical antiquity, which are treated in the two sections of Division I. The general period covered in Division II is the Middle Ages, beginning with the death of Theodosius I in AD 395, conventionally taken as marking the permanent division of the Roman Empire into East and West, and extending to *c.* 1500, conventionally taken as the starting point of modern history.

    The sectional organization of this division and the outlines in its four sections reflect significant cultural and political interaction between the Eastern Christian, Western Christian, and Islāmic spheres, and also involve some breaking points in the history of each sphere.

Section 921.

Western Europe, the Byzantine (Eastern Roman) Empire, and Eastern Europe from AD 395 to *c.* 1050

A. The study of medieval and Byzantine history: the historical sources, historiographic problems, chronological outline

B. The eclipse of the Roman Empire in the West and the development and Christianization of Germanic successor states (AD 395–*c.* 750)

    1. The end of the Western Roman Empire and the Germanic Völkerwanderung (AD 395–*c.* 500)

        a. The general decline of government, economy, society, and culture

        b. Establishment of the Germanic hegemony: the invasions of Vandals; the invasions of Angles, Saxons, and Jutes (Britain); the Visigothic invasions in the 5th century and settlement in Provence and Spain; the Frankish conquest of Gaul (*c.* 481/482–511) and the Burgundian flight to the south; the Huns; abolition of the Western Empire and Ostrogothic rule in Italy (493–553); other Germanic tribes—the issue of Arianism versus Catholic Christianity; Germanic law and society

2. The Germanic successor states and the remnants of the Roman Empire in the West from *c.* 500 to 750; the origins of early feudalism

   a. Byzantine conquests and later diminution of Byzantium's western possessions (540–751), the Exarchate of Ravenna, Lombard conquests in Italy, beginning of the political role of the Roman papacy

   b. Early development of the Germanic kingdoms

      i. The Visigothic kingdom to 711

      ii. The Anglo-Saxon kingdoms in England and the Celtic kingdoms in Ireland

      iii. The Franks under the Merovingians and early Carolingians: the successors of Clovis, rise and establishment of the Carolingians under Charles Martel and Pepin III the Short (714–768), Carolingian relations with the papacy and entry into Italian affairs; origins of the Papal States

   c. Effects of the rise of Islām on western Europe

3. Religion, the arts, and society in the early Middle Ages: the amalgamation of late Classical and Germanic cultures and Christianity

   a. Conversion of the Celts and the Germans to Catholic Christianity: religious and cultural functions of monasticism and the Western Church

   b. The arts, intellectual life, and education in the early Middle Ages

   c. Social and economic life in the early Middle Ages

C. The early Byzantine Empire (AD 395–717)

1. Origins of Byzantium in the late Roman Empire: the reforms of Diocletian and Constantine

2. Persistence of Greco-Roman society in the East in the 5th century: the empire from the death of Theodosius I to the accession of Heraclius (610)

   a. Economic and social policies: agriculture, coinage, relations with the barbarians (*e.g.,* Huns, Goths, Isaurians, Avars, Slavs)

   b. Ecclesiastical controversies, Syrian and Egyptian disaffection, and the beginning of conflict with the Western Church

   c. The empire at the end of the 5th century: internal tensions, political and economic policies under Anastasius I

   d. The reign of Justinian I (527–565): realignment with the Roman Church, Code of Justinian, military campaigns in the West, effects of the plague, later campaigns

   e. Early Byzantine culture: Christianity, the arts, and intellectual life

   f. Justinian's successors (565–610): relations with the barbarians and with the Persians, revolt of the army

3. Rehabilitation of the empire under the dynasty of Heraclius (610–685)

   a. Heraclius' reorganization of the empire along military lines: wars with Persia; the loss of Syria, Palestine, Armenia, and Egypt to the Arabs and continued Arab pressures; recognition of Byzantine overlordship in the Balkans

   b. Decline of the dynasty (685–711): renewed wars with the Slavs; settlement with the Arabs; fiscal, agricultural, and defensive policies; military anarchy (711–717)

D. Western Christendom and Scandinavia from the Carolingian era to the general European revival (*c.* 750–*c.* 1050)

1. The Carolingian Empire and its later dissolution (*c.* 750–887), France in the 10th century

   a. The reign of Charlemagne (king, 768–814; emperor from 800): further military expansion of the Frankish kingdom; legislation, administration, and defense; ecclesiastical policies; patronage of arts and learning

   b. Decline and dissolution of the Carolingian Empire under the successors of Charlemagne: the society, government, and culture of the Frankish world

      i. Louis the Pious; partitioning of the empire by the Treaty of Verdun (843) between Louis's sons (Lothair, Charles the Bald, and Louis the German); Muslim, Norman, and Magyar invasions and the debilitation of central authority

      ii. The Frankish world: society, institutions, economic life, the church (triumph and reform of Benedictine monasticism, birth of the Cluniac order), literature (Carolingian renaissance) and the arts

      c. The East Frankish kingdom (Germany): the last Carolingians (to 911), the emergence of the four stem duchies (Saxony, Franconia, Swabia, and Bavaria)

      d. The West Frankish kingdom (France): dynastic rivalry between Carolingians and Robertians (to 987) and the ascendancy of the feudal magnates

      e. The Middle Frankish kingdom (Lotharingia): Burgundy, Provence, and Italy

  2. The British Isles and Scandinavia (*c.* 800–1066)

      a. England: the decline of Mercia and the rise of Wessex; the 9th-century Danish invasions; King Alfred's legal, administrative, and ecclesiastical policies and patronage of the arts; Anglo-Saxon political unification and monastic revival in the 10th century; the conquest of the Danes and their rule over the Anglo-Danish state; the reign of Edward the Confessor and the Norman Conquest

      b. Development of the Kingdom of Scotland, the Welsh, Ireland during the Norse invasions

          i. Roman penetration in Scotland: Christianity, Norse influence

          ii. Early Christianity in Wales: relations with the Anglo-Saxons, Welsh society

          iii. Ireland: conversion to Christianity, monasticism, the Norse invasions

      c. The Viking Age in Scandinavia: the Vikings and Varangians, widespread raids and conquests (*c.* 800–*c.* 1050), social and political organization, arts, paganism and conversion to Christianity from *c.* 850

  3. Germany, Burgundy, and Italy: development of the Holy Roman (German) Empire (911–1056)

      a. Revival of central authority in Germany and intervention in Italy by the Saxon dynasty: Conrad (911–918), rise of the nobility, early opposition from Arnulf of Bavaria, drive against Magyars and Slavs, Germanic kingship

      b. Promotion of the German church under Otto I (936–973): his conquest of Italy and establishment of the Holy Roman Empire (962), early Salian kings (1024–56)

      c. Development of medieval Italy: political, economic, and social developments on the peninsula and in Sicily

          i. Growth in power of the papacy; early years of the commercial cities of Venice in the north and Gaeta, Naples, Sorrento, and Amalfi in Campania; the Arabs in Sicily

          ii. Cities and countryside: persistence of an urban tradition despite the exodus to rural areas, the role of bishops in urban life, economy and society

  4. The Kingdom of France under the early Capetians (987–1180): the relative weakness of the monarchy vis-à-vis the great feudatories, establishment of an Anglo-French domination in western France under the Plantagenets (Normandy, Anjou, Aquitaine), Capetian attempts to expand the royal domain

  5. Growth of the Christian states in northern Spain (Asturias–Leon–Castile, Navarre, Aragon–Catalonia): their relations with one another and with the Muslims in Spain, the first phase of the Reconquista to the fall of Toledo (1085)

  6. The sociopolitical and economic structure of early medieval Europe: origins, development, and spread of feudalism; its elements and structure; the manorial economy and mainly localized commerce to *c.* 1050

E. Peoples and states of eastern Europe to *c.* 1050: early empires and later development of Christianized states

  1. The Slavic peoples: origins, early society and culture, movement into Pannonia and south Russia, plundering expeditions and eventual settlement in the Balkans

  2. The eastern European states and peoples within the Byzantine orbit

      a. The Bulgarian domains to 1018: origins, migration into the Balkans (*c.* AD 650) and mixture with the local Slavic populations, early contacts and wars with Byzantium, adoption of Christianity (870), the First Bulgarian Empire (893–1014) and subsequent conquest by Byzantium

      b. The Balkans: the migration of the Croats and Serbs into the Balkans and their subsequent relations with the Bulgars and Byzantium to *c.* 1050

      c. Exploration and the rise of the Rus raids on Constantinople, development of trade routes, Khazar state north of the Black Sea

      d. The princes of Novgorod (end of the 9th century)

      c. The state of Kievan Rus (*c.* 980–1054): Slavic-Varangian (Scandinavian) origins, economic decline, social and political institutions

  3. Eastern European states within the orbit of Western Christendom

a. Developments in Moravia and Bohemia to 1055: the Celtic and Germanic tribes supplanted by Slavic peoples in the 6th century, Czech dominance in the 8th century, unification under the Přemysl rulers

    i. Unification of Greater Moravia under Mojmír (814): religious conflicts with Frankish clergy and temporary adherence to the Eastern rite, political expansion

    ii. The early Přemysl rulers of Bohemia: capital at Prague, ties with Bavaria and the Saxon dynasty, Boleslav I (929–967), Boleslav II (967–999), annexation of Moravia under Břetislav (1034–55)

b. The Avar Empire and the early Magyar (Hungarian) kingdom to *c.* 1050: alliance with the Carolingian ruler Arnulf, establishment of the Árpád dynasty, settlement of the central plain, conversion to Christianity, reign of Stephen I (997–1038)

c. Development of the Kingdom of Poland in the 10th century and Polish conversion to Western Christianity under the dynasty of the Piasts, civil strife and later restoration under Casimir I (1039–58)

F. The zenith and incipient decline of the Byzantine Empire (717–1081), the growth of Venice

1. The age of Iconoclasm (717–867): the reforms of Leo III the Isaurian, repulse of the Arabs, Bulgar incursions and continued religious dissension under Leo's successors

2. The Macedonian era (867–1025): territorial expansion, foreign relations, continued strength and prosperity under its rulers until 1025

    a. Military revival, relations with Slavs and Bulgars, estrangement from the West

    b. Culture and administration: legal reforms under Basil I and Leo VI

    c. Social and economic change: reforms of Basil II

3. Byzantine decline and subjection to Western influences: 11th-century weakness, arrival of new enemies, the schism with Rome (1054)

4. Venice: the development of its institutions, commerce, and naval power in the early Middle Ages

---

Suggested reading in the *Encyclopædia Britannica*:

MACROPAEDIA: Major articles and a biography dealing with Western Europe, the Byzantine (Eastern Roman) Empire, and the states of eastern Europe from AD 395 to *c.* 1050

Bulgaria	Greek and Roman	Istanbul	Steppe, The
Byzantine Empire,	Civilizations,	Italy	History of the
The History	Ancient	Kiev	Eurasian
of the	Holy Roman	Poland	Union of Soviet
Charlemagne	Empire, The	Rome	Socialist
European History	History of the	Spain	Republics
and Culture	Hungary		United Kingdom
France	Ireland		Venice
Germany			Yugoslavia

MICROPAEDIA: Selected entries of reference information

General subjects

barbarian invaders	Suebi	Justinian, Code of	*early medieval society*
and successor	Vandal	logothete	*and culture:*
kingdoms:	Visigoth	Manzikert,	feudal land tenure
Alani	*Byzantine and*	Battle of	feudalism
Alemanni	*Western Roman*	Mardaïte	fief
Angle	*empires:*	Mons Lactarius,	Germanic law
Antae	Byzantine Empire	Battle of	homage and fealty
Avar	Carthage,	Myra	knight
Frank	Exarchate of	Nicaea, empire of	knight service
Goth	Ecloga	pronoia system	liege
Hun	Epanagoge	Ravenna	manorialism
Jute	eparch	Rhodian Sea Law	Middle Ages
Lombard	Farmer's Law	Taginae, Battle of	serfdom
Ostrogoth	Ghassān	theme	serjeanty
Pecheneg	Iconoclastic		vassal
Saxon	Controversy		

wardship and
marriage
*Merovingian and
Carolingian era:*
Aquitaine
Austrasia
Frank
Gévaudan
Lorraine
missi dominici
Neustria
Pepin, Donation of
Poitiers, Battle of
Septimania
Toulouse
Valois
Verdun, Treaty of
*national
development—
British Isles:*
Alba
Angle
Anglo-Saxon
Anglo-Saxon
Chronicle
Anglo-Saxon law
Bernicia
ceorl

Connaught
Cornwall
Dalriada
Danegeld
Danelaw
Deira
East Anglia
Essex
frankpledge
Hadrian's Wall
Kent
Leinster
Lindsey
Lothian
Mercia
Middle Anglia
Munster
Northumbria
Ossory
Pict
Scot
Strathclyde
Sussex
Wessex
Whitby, Synod of
witan
*national
development—*

*eastern European
states:*
boyar
druzhina
Khazar
Lusatia
Mazovia
Moravia
Piast dynasty
Pomerania
Rus
Ukraine
*national
development—
France:*
Anjou
Aquitaine
Brittany
Gascony
Normandy
*national
development—
Germany,
Burgundy, and
Italy:*
Bavaria
Burgundy
Franconia

Holy Roman
Empire
Papal States
Provence
Saxony
Swabia
Thuringia
*national
development—
Iberia:*
Aragon
Asturias
Castile
Catalonia
Covandonga
Leon
Liber Judiciorum
Mozarab
Navarre
Reconquista
*national
development—
Scandinavia:*
Birka
Danewirk
Hedeby
housecarl
Norman

Biographies

*barbarian invaders
and successor
kingdoms:*
Aistulf
Alaric
Alaric II
Alboin
Amalasuntha
Árpád
Ataulphus
Athanaric
Attila
Ermanaric
Gaiseric
Krum
Leovigild
Liutprand
Odoacer
Ricimer
Rothari
Simeon I
Theodoric (Italy)
Totila
Ulfilas
Witigis
*Byzantine and
Western Roman
empires:*
Aetius, Flavius
Alexius I
Comnenus
Anastasius I
Andronicus I
Comnenus

Baldwin I
(Constantinople)
Baldwin II
(Constantinople)
Basil I
Basil II
Belisarius
Constans II
Constantine VII
Porphyrogenitus
Constantine IX
Monomachus
Eudocia
Macrembolitissa
Henry
(Constantinople)
Heraclius
Honorius
Irene (d. 803)
Irene (d. 1120)
John I Comnenus
John III Ducas
Vatatzes
John V
Palaeologus
Justin I
Justin II
Justinian I
Justinian II
Leo I
Leo III
Leo VI
Manuel I
Comnenus

Marcian
Maurice
Michael IV
Michael VIII
Palaeologus
Nepos, Julius
Nicephorus I
Nicephorus II
Phocas
Orestes
Phocas
Romanus III
Romulus
Augustulus
Stilicho
Theodora (d. 548)
Theodora (d. 1056)
Theodore I
(Nicaea)
Theodosius I
Theodosius II
Tiberius II
Valentinian III
Zeno
Zoe
*Merovingian and
Carolingian era:*
Alcuin
Arnulf of Metz,
Saint
Brunhild
Carolingian
dynasty
Charlemagne

Charles Martel
Childerich I
Chilperic I
Chlotar I
Chlotar II
Clovis I
Dagobert I
Eboin
Fredegund
Germanus of Paris,
Saint
Louis I (France)
Merovech
Merovingian
dynasty
Pepin I
(Aquitaine)
Pepin II
(Aquitaine)
Pepin I
(Carolingian
dynasty)
Pepin II
(Carolingian
dynasty)
Pepin III
(Carolingian
dynasty)
Pepin (Italy)
Sigebert I
Theodoric I
(Merovingian
dynasty)
Wala, Saint

Section 922. The Formative Period in Islāmic History, from AD 622 to *c.* 1055

A. The study of Islāmic history: the historical sources, historiographic problems

B. The rise and spread of Islām and the Arab Empire to the end of the Umayyad dynasty (AD 622–750)

   1. Islām and Arab expansion in the 7th century

      a. Arabia before Muḥammad

      b. The life and career of Muḥammad and the rise of Islām, the doctrine of the *jihād* (holy war)

    c. Muslim expansion outside Arabia under the four Patriarchal Caliphs (632–661)

        i. Abū Bakr (632–634) and ʿUmar I (634–644): the tribe of Quraysh; divisions among the followers of Muḥammad; the conquest of Iraq and the Sāsānid (Persian) Empire and the Byzantine territories of Jordan, Palestine, Syria, and Egypt

        ii. ʿUthmān (644–656) and ʿAlī (656–661): expeditions into North Africa, Armenia, and Persia; social and religious grievances; civil unrest; the origins of Shīʿism

2. The Umayyad caliphate (661–750)

    a. The consolidation of the caliphate (661–684) under Muʿāwiyah I and his successors: westward orientation of the caliphate and its capital at Damascus, growing opposition to the Umayyads

    b. The zenith of Umayyad power with the advent of the Marwānids: ʿAbd al-Malik (685–705) and al-Walīd (705–715), suppression of revolts, new conquests

    c. The later Umayyads (715–750): conciliation of state policies with religion, peace and prosperity under Hishām (724–743), disintegration of the empire under his successors and the ʿAbbāsid revolt

    d. Umayyad government and society

        i. Administration of the Arab lands: utilization of local officials, the position and functions of the caliph, Islāmization and Arabization, social classes

        ii. Cultural life under the Umayyads: spread of the Arabic language, literary revival, fragmentation into religious sects, accomplishment in the arts

C. The ʿAbbāsid Empire and its successor states (750–c. 1055)

    1. The ʿAbbāsid caliphate from 750 to 945

    a. Establishment of the new dynasty and its advance under Abū al-ʿAbbās as-Saffāḥ (749–754), al-Manṣūr (754–775), and al-Mahdī (775–785); the ʿAbbāsids at their zenith (786–861)

    b. Decline of the caliphate after the death of al-Mutawakkil (861): growth of provincial autonomy

    c. Economic and social life under the ʿAbbāsids: manufactures and trade

    d. Cultural life under the ʿAbbāsid caliphate

        i. Religion: theology and philosophy, Islāmic mysticism

        ii. The arts and sciences: Greek and Persian influences, the aniconic principle in the arts

    2. Eclipse of the ʿAbbāsids and the growth of provincial dynasties from c. 755 to 1055

    a. The Umayyad emirate and caliphate in Spain (756–1031) and its capital at Córdoba

        i. Conquest of southern and central Spain by Ṭāriq ibn Ziyād (711); defeat of the Muslims near Poitiers by the Frank Charles Martel (732); foundation of the independent emirate by ʿAbd ar-Raḥmān I (756–788); political and cultural splendour in the reign of ʿAbd ar-Raḥmān II, defeat of the *muwallad*s

        ii. The Umayyad caliphate under ʿAbd ar-Raḥmān an-Nāṣir III: relations with Arabs, Berbers, and the Christian states in Spain; conquest of Morocco by his successors; the *ṭāʾifa*s and internal disorders

        iii. Social and economic life in Muslim Spain: the culture of Muslim Spain, developments in literature and the sciences

    b. The Fāṭimid state of North Africa and Syria from 909 to c. 1055: the foundation of the Fāṭimid caliphate in Tunisia and Algeria, its conquest of Morocco (926) and Egypt (969), and expansion into Syria

    c. Other dynasties in North Africa and Syria: the Shīʿite Idrīsids of Morocco (789–926); the Rustamid kingdom in the central Maghrib (787–911); the Aghlabid state in Tunisia, Algeria, and Sicily (800–909); minor dynasties

    d. The Sāmānid dynasty of Khorāsān (875–999) and its role in the Islāmization of the Turkic peoples: patronage of art and learning

    e. The Būyid dynasty in Iran and Iraq (932–1055): Shīʿism and the Iranian revival, Isfahan

    f. Other eastern states: the Qarmaṭians in eastern Arabia (c. 900–1078), the Turkish Qarakhanid dynasty of Mā Warā ʿan-Nahr (Transoxania) and eastern Turkistan (922–c. 1050), the Turkish Ghaznavids of Afghanistan and northwestern India (998–1050), minor states and dynasties

Suggested reading in the *Encyclopædia Britannica*:

MACROPAEDIA: Major articles dealing with the Empire of the Caliphate and its successor states to *c.* AD 1055

Arabia	Egypt	Islāmic	North Africa
Baghdad	Iran	World, The	Spain
Damascus	Iraq	Mecca and Medina	Syria

MICROPAEDIA: Selected entries of reference information

General subjects

caliph	ḥājib	Mozarab	Ṣaqālibah
Caliphate	Hāshimīyah	Nahāvand,	Shī'ah
Córdoba	Hegira	Battle of	Ṣiffīn, Battle of
divan	iqṭāʻ	Poitiers, Battle of	Sunnite
emir	jizya	(732)	taifa
Fāṭimid	Karbalāʾ, Battle of	rāshidūn, ar-	Wāsiṭ
fitnah	kharāj	riddah	Zanj rebellion
Fusṭāṭ, al-	Khorram-dīnān	Rustamid	
ghanīmah	Kūfah	kingdom	

Biographies

'Abbāsid dynasty	Būyid dynasty	Ma'mūn, al-	Sāmānid dynasty
'Abd al-Malik	Fāṭimid dynasty	Manṣūr, al-	Sīmjūrid dynasty
'Abd	Ghaznavid dynasty	Mazyadid dynasty	'Umar I
ar-Raḥmān III	Ḥamdānid dynasty	Mosāferīd dynasty	'Umar II
Abū Bakr	Hārūn ar-Rashīd	Mu'āwiyah I	Umayyad dynasty
Abū Muslim	Hūdid dynasty	Mu'tamid, al-	'Uthmān ibn
'Alī	Kā'ūsīyeh dynasty	Najāḥid dynasty	'Affān
Barmakids	Mahmūd	Ṣaffārid dynasty	Zeyārid dynasty

INDEX: See entries under all of the terms above

Section 923.   Western Christendom in the High and Later Middle Ages (*c.* 1050–*c.* 1500)

A. The medieval western European revival and the economy, society, and culture of Western Christendom in the High Middle Ages

  1. Society, economy, and culture

    a. Western European society in the High Middle Ages: the three social orders (priests and monks; warriors; peasants and labourers); the feudal nobility; the bourgeoisie; the status of women

    b. Growth of agricultural productivity and population: revival of a money economy, manufacturing, and the commercial effects of the Crusades; revival of towns and population movements

    c. Technological inventions and improvements

    d. The church in medieval society: growth of papal hegemony, reform movements (eremitism, Cistercians, mendicant orders), ecumenical councils, emergence of the laity, struggle against heretics (Inquisition from 1233), role of religion in medieval society

    e. The culture of the High Middle Ages

      i. Establishment of schools and universities

      ii. The intellectual revival of the 11th and 12th centuries, Scholasticism, developments in philosophy and theology

      iii. The arts: Latin and vernacular literature, Romanesque and Gothic visual arts, music, theatre, the decorative arts

    f. The status of Jews in medieval society and their economic role, persecutions, and migrations

    g. Political institutions and ideas

      i. The two major powers, the Empire and the papacy; the relations between temporal and spiritual power

      ii. Kingship as the ideal Christian form of government: its relationship to sacrality and to the growing bureacracy; the three main forms of government inherited from antiquity: monarchy, oligarchy, tyranny

      iii. The city-state (Italy)

2. The Holy Roman Empire, the papacy, and Italy from *c.* 1050 to *c.* 1300

  a. The empire, the papacy, and Italy in the era of the Investiture Controversy

      i. Church reform in the 10th and 11th centuries and the clash between the papacy and the emperors over lay investiture (at its height between the emperor Henry IV and Pope Gregory VII): the resulting incipient decline of German monarchical authority under the Salian emperors

      ii. The Norman conquest of southern Italy and Sicily and establishment of a strong monarchy: relations with the papacy, Venice, and the Byzantine Empire

      iii. The growth of communes in northern Italy, the status of German imperial power, the political role of the papacy in Italy, the commercial expansion of Italian cities (*e.g.,* Genoa, Pisa), continued growth of Venetian maritime power

  b. The empire under the Hohenstaufen dynasty and after its extinction to *c.* 1300, the papacy and Italy

      i. Steady inroads of the German princes into German monarchical authority: colonization of Slavic territory, development of commercial centres (*e.g.,* Lübeck), the reign of Frederick I Barbarossa and Frederick II, extinction of the Hohenstaufen dynasty and the Great Interregnum (1250–73), the election and reign of Rudolf of Habsburg

      ii. The Kingdom of Sicily: centralized government, ethnic mixture, Palermo, control by the Hohenstaufens (1194–1266), the Angevin conquest and expulsion (1282), the advent of Aragonese control

      iii. The decline of German imperial control in northern Italy and the continued development of the communes (*e.g.,* Milan, Pisa, Florence, Siena): their internal and external conflicts

      iv. Continued commercial expansion of Italian cities: Venetian expansion in the Levant and aid to the Normans in the conquest of Byzantium (1204), commercial inroads into the Levantine trade by Genoa and Pisa

3. The growth of the Kingdom of France under the later Capetian dynasty (1180–1328), the Low Countries

  a. Growth of the power of the French kings and extension of the territory under their control

      i. Philip II Augustus (1180–1223): acquisition of territory and consolidation of the realm, royal administration, feudal policies

      ii. Louis VIII (1223–26) and Louis IX (1226–70): institution of the granting of appanages to younger sons of kings, the Albigensian Crusade, rise of bureaucracy, attitudes toward the clergy and the lay nobility; Louis's efforts for peace, justice, and morality; his canonization in 1297

      iii. The later Capetians: Philip IV the Fair (1285–1314), claims of the monarchy, beginnings of the States General, conflict with Boniface VIII, suppression of the Templars

      iv. Foreign relations: conflict with the Holy Roman Empire under Philip II, the religious crusades of Louis IX, the wars of Philip IV

      v. Economy, society, and culture in the 13th century: increase in population, growth of towns and urban prosperity, rural life, religion, culture and learning

  b. The Low Countries: development of the territorial principalities and the rise of towns; *e.g.,* Ghent, Bruges

      i. Secular and spiritual principalities

      ii. Struggle for independence, French and British influence

      iii. Social and economic structure

4. The Spanish Christian kingdoms of Castile and Leon, Aragon (including Barcelona and Catalonia), Portugal, and Navarre (1035–*c.* 1260): their expansion into Muslim territory, their mutual rivalries, their ethnic-cultural mixtures, and their internal political development; the role of the church

a. The medieval empire (1035–1157): the division of the kingdoms and the emergence of Portugal as an independent state

b. The rise of Castile and Aragon and the expulsion of the Muslims, led especially by the rulers of Aragon (James I, 1213–76) and Castile (Ferdinand III, 1217–52)

c. Society, economy, and culture: administration of the Spanish kingdoms; development of feudalism, growth of towns, and appearance of trade and industry; establishment of the Cortes; foundation of the universities of Valencia and Salamanca

5. The Kingdom of England and its continental dependencies from the Norman Conquest to the death of Edward I; Scotland, Wales, and Ireland (1066–1307)

a. The Norman Conquest: introduction of feudalism and the development of royal administration under William I the Conqueror (1066–87) and his immediate successors

    i. Church–state relations and the place of the clergy in the feudal structure, the Domesday survey

    ii. Strengthening of central government under William's successors: relations with the church in their reigns

    iii. The period of the Anarchy (1135–54): Matilda and Stephen, civil war

b. The early Plantagenets

    i. The reign of Henry II (1154–89): military and administrative reforms, Henry's conflict with the church and the struggle with Becket, the rebellions of Henry's sons

    ii. Richard I (1189–99): administration in Richard's absence, the Saladin Tithe, attempts to establish a standing army

    iii. The reign of John (1199–1216): loss of French possessions, John's conflict with Innocent III, the revolt of the barons and Magna Carta

    iv. Henry III (1216–72) and Edward I (1272–1307): Simon de Montfort and the Barons' War; Edward's restoration of royal power and his legal, administrative, and military policies; the growth of Parliament, development of Oxford and Cambridge universities

c. Scotland, Wales, and Ireland: relations between the Kingdom of Scotland and the English crown, the extent of English control in Wales and Ireland

    i. The unification of Scotland and the development of the monarchy

    ii. Norman infiltration in Wales, the three kingdoms, internal conflicts and the Edwardian settlement

    iii. Ireland: the Anglo-Norman invasion and its effects, establishment of the Irish Parliament

6. Scandinavia (c. 1050–c. 1300): establishment of the kingdoms of Denmark, Norway, and Sweden

a. The trend toward unity and strong monarchy: political developments in the three kingdoms

b. Expansion into Finland, Iceland, and Greenland: introduction of feudalism, economic developments and influence of the Hanseatic League, society

7. The Slavic and Magyar states of Western Christendom (c. 1050–c. 1300)

a. Poland: the reigns of Bolesław II (1058–79) and Bolesław III (1102–38), the division of Poland between Bolesław III's sons, the seniority system, territorial losses, the early role of the Teutonic Order in eastern Europe, internal developments

b. Bohemia under the later Přemysl rulers (1055–1306): struggles within the ruling family, privileges secured from the Holy Roman emperor, territorial expansion, losses to Rudolf of Habsburg

    i. German interference in Bohemia: attacks upon the position of the Prague princes by Frederick I Barbarossa, the Golden Bull of Sicily (1212)

    ii. Political and economic growth: German immigration, founding of urban communities, expansion under Otakar II (1253–78) into Austria, silver mining and coinage

c. Hungary: the early kings, expansion into Transylvania and Dalmatia, the nobility, Golden Bull (1222), Mongol invasion (1241), extinction of the Árpád dynasty in 1301

B. The decline of medieval European political institutions, economy, and culture and the incipient transition to the modern age (c. 1300–c. 1500)

1. The culture of the late Middle Ages in western Europe

    a. The early Renaissance in Italy: historiographic problems, the contribution of the city-states, developments in literature and the fine arts

        i. Revival of Greek studies and the formation of Classical libraries in Italy: Humanism, relationship of Humanism to Christianity

        ii. New concepts and techniques in painting, sculpture, and architecture: patronage of the arts by the papacy

    b. The late Gothic style in northern Europe

    c. Late medieval intellectual developments: political theory, law, and the decline of ideals of imperial unity and papal supremacy; the rising power of national monarchies; decline of Scholasticism; science; witchcraft

2. Late medieval society and economy

    a. The exaggeration of chivalry and declining importance of the feudal nobility in the face of changing military technology and organization: growing influence of the bourgeoisie, growth of royal government

    b. Gradual inflation and continued development of capitalism: peasant revolts; economic, social, and political effects of the Black Death (1347–50) and subsequent epidemics of the plague; development of a great maritime trade between the North Sea and the Mediterranean; progress of enclosures; recovery of the population and economy after the middle of the 15th century

3. The church in the later Middle Ages: papal monarchy and taxation, the Avignon papacy (1309–77) and the Great Schism (1378–1417), the conciliar movement and other reform movements with regard to the church, mysticism

4. Germany, Bohemia, and the Swiss Confederation (*c.* 1300–*c.* 1500)

    a. Limitations on the imperial office and the continued ascendancy of the princes in Germany: internal strife between the cities and the princes, the Habsburg and Luxemburg emperors, the division of the Habsburg lands and the enhancement of Habsburg power and influence in Europe by 1500

        i. Development of the individual states

        ii. Society, economy, and culture in the 14th and 15th centuries

    b. Bohemia in the later Middle Ages: political and religious developments

        i. The Luxemburg dynasty (1310–1437): territorial expansion under Charles I, growth of the city of Prague, Wenceslas IV

        ii. Beginning of the religious reform movement (*c.* 1360): the Chapel Bethlehem's preachers, the activities of Jan Hus and his execution at the Council of Constance (1415)

        iii. The struggle between Sigismund and the Hussites: the Four Articles of Prague, Žižka's leadership of the Hussites, the Hussite preponderance (1437–71), George of Poděbrady

        iv. The Jagiellon kings (1471–1526): the decline of royal authority, growth of power of the first two estates

    c. Early Swiss history, development of the Swiss Confederation after 1291, struggle against the Habsburgs, the French invasion and the Peace of Constance (1446)

5. Italy in the late Middle Ages and the Renaissance

    a. Social and political developments in the period 1300–1400: withdrawal of imperial and papal authority, Italian society, the crises of the 14th century (*e.g.,* the Black Death, economic decline, urban unrest)

    b. The Italian states in the 14th century: forms of rule, use of mercenaries, cultural developments

        i. Milan: the Visconti family, rule at home, expansion in northern Italy, Visconti attitudes toward the state

        ii. Florence: republicanism, the cloth industry, banking, movement into the city from the countryside, plots against the republic

        iii. Venice: republican institutions, economic prosperity and commercial empire

        iv. The Papal States: their locations and proprietors, breakdown of papal control during the Avignon papacy and the Great Schism (1378–1417)

        v. Naples, Sicily, and the other Italian states (*e.g.,* Angevin rule in Naples until its union with Sicily in 1442 under Alfonso V of Aragon); Savoy; Genoa; Verona

    c. The Italian states in the 15th century: expansion of the major Italian powers, Italy as a political system, cultural developments

        i. The crisis of Florentine republicanism: the threat from Gian Galeazzo Visconti of Milan and his successors, Florentine historiography, rule by the Medici

        ii. The Papal States: papal policy to strengthen its position, reliance of the popes on their relatives to control the domains

        iii. Despotisms: Alfonso I (Alfonso V of Aragon) in Naples and Sicily and division of the territory on his death in 1458, the Sforza in Milan

        iv. Venice: the stability of Venetian life, increased interests in activities on the Italian peninsula

6. France and the Low Countries (*c.* 1300–*c.* 1500)

    a. The period of the Hundred Years' War: the stages of the war, the role of the French kings in the conflict, the war's significance

        i. Remote and proximate causes of the war: the problem of English lands in France, the problem of the French succession, the Flemish revolt

        ii. From the outbreak of the war (1337) to the Treaty of Brétigny (1360): the reign of Philip VI (1328–50), the Crécy campaign and its aftermath (1346–54), negotiations during John II the Good's captivity (1356–60), burgeoning power of the estates and revolt of the peasants; the Parisian revolt and the bourgeois leader Etienne Marcel (1358)

        iii. From the Treaty of Brétigny (1360) to the accession of Henry V of England (1413): Charles V (1364–80), the dispute over Flanders, temporary peace, Charles VI (1380–1422), struggle between Burgundians and Armagnacs

        iv. From the accession of Henry V (1413) to the siege of Orléans (1428–29): Charles VII (1422–61); France divided between the dauphin Charles, Philip the Good of Burgundy, and Henry V of England

        v. Recovery and reunification (1429–83) and the expulsion of the English: Joan of Arc and the stirring of French national feeling, reconquest of Maine and Normandy, conquest of Guyenne (1453), final settlement at Picquigny (1475)

    b. Administrative and military reforms and the strengthening of royal power vis-à-vis the nobility and towns under Charles VII (1422–61) and Louis XI (1461–83): foreign, fiscal, and ecclesiastical policies; social and cultural developments; the States General (1484) and the failure of representative monarchy

    c. The Low Countries: continued growth of towns, industry, and commerce, with attendant class conflicts and interference by the French monarchy; unification under the House of Burgundy; Burgundian administration

7. England, Wales, Scotland, and Ireland (*c.* 1307–*c.* 1500)

    a. Royal decline under the later Plantagenets and the struggle for the crown between the Lancastrians and Yorkists

        i. Royal decline under Edward II (1307–27) and its restoration under Edward III (1327–77): the Hundred Years' War, domestic achievements, the crises of Edward III's later reign

        ii. Richard II (1377–99): the Peasants' Revolt (1381), the influence of John Wycliffe, later political struggles and Richard's deposition

        iii. Henry IV (1399–1413), Henry V (1413–22), and Henry VI (1422–61 and 1470–71): rebellions under Henry IV and his relations with Parliament, domestic rivalries and the loss of France under Henry VI, Cade's rebellion and the Wars of the Roses

        iv. The reigns of Edward IV (1461–70 and 1471–83) and Richard III (1483–85): England in the late Middle Ages

    b. Scotland: the wars of independence, relations with the English crown, Bruces and Stewarts, Scotland in the 15th century

    c. Establishment of English suzerainty over Wales, fluctuating English influence in Ireland and the rise to power of the earls of Kildare

8. Spain and Portugal (*c.* 1300–*c.* 1500)

    a. Castile and Leon: continued pressure on the Muslims under Alfonso XI (1312–50), increasing power of the Cortes, development of the woolen industry, literary achievements

b. The Aragon Confederation (Aragon, Catalonia, and Valencia): acquisition of Sicily (1282) and growth of Aragon as a Mediterranean power; the Cortes, law, and administration; acquisition of the Kingdom of Naples (1442) under Alfonso V (1416–58)

c. Creation of a united Spain and expansion of Spanish dominance in the early Age of Discovery

    i. The union of Aragon and Castile–Leon under Ferdinand and Isabella: strengthening of their positions vis-à-vis the nobility, the Inquisition and the treatment of Jews, conquest of Granada (1492) and acquisition of Naples (1503)

    ii. Spanish explorations and territorial acquisitions: colonial policy in the New World, the Atlantic trade

d. Portugal: development of the monarchy under the House of Avis (1383–1580); alliance with England; consolidation of the monarchy and establishment of its overseas empire under John I (1385–1433), Prince Henry the Navigator, and Manuel I (1495–1521)

9. The Scandinavian kingdoms (*c*. 1300–*c*. 1500)

a. Developments in the 14th century leading to the formation of the Kalmar Union (1397–1523), Scandinavia under the union

b. Developments in Denmark, Norway, and Sweden during the union: decline of Norway and rise of Sweden

10. Hungary, Poland–Lithuania, and the Teutonic Order

a. Hungary under foreign kings: foreign affairs, economy, and society under the Angevins and Sigismund; the reign of Matthias Corvinus (1458–90)

b. Poland–Lithuania, the Teutonic Order, and the Baltic peoples

    i. The Mongol invasions (1241–42) and reestablishment of the Kingdom of Poland (1253–1382): Władysław I and the struggle with the Teutonic Order; Casimir III and Louis I of Hungary; social classes, the church, and policies toward the Jews

    ii. The Jagiellon dynasty (1382–1492): the union of Poland and Lithuania (1385–86), extension of the empire, growth of parliamentarianism dominated by the nobility

---

Suggested reading in the *Encyclopædia Britannica*:

MACROPAEDIA: Major articles dealing with western Christendom in the High and later Middle Ages (*c*. 1050–*c*. 1500)

Amsterdam	France	Lisbon	Portugal
Antwerp	Germany	London	Prague
Austria	Habsburg, The	Luxembourg	Rome
Belgium	House of	Madrid	Spain
Crusades, The	Holy Roman	Milan	Sweden
Czechoslovakia	Empire, The	Naples	Switzerland
Denmark	History of the	Netherlands, The	United Kingdom
European History	Hungary	Norway	Venice
and Culture	Iceland	Paris	Vienna
Finland	Ireland	Poland	
Florence	Italy		

MICROPAEDIA: Selected entries of reference information

General subjects

European politics and polity:	Hundred Years' War	Teutonic Order	Barnet, Battle of
Agincourt, Battle of	Inquisition	Western Schism	Barons' War
Avignon papacy	Investiture	Worms, Concordat of	Bosworth Field, Battle of
Bouvines, Battle of	Controversy	*national affairs—*	Clarendon, Assize of
Castillon, Battle of	Norman	*Britain and Angevin Empire:*	Clarendon, Constitutions of
Crécy, Battle of	Orléans, Siege of	Angevin empire	Domesday Book
crusade	Poitiers, Battle of	Bannockburn, Battle of	
Holy Roman Empire	Templar		

Dupplin Moor,
 Battle of
Hastings, Battle of
Lollard
Magna Carta
Norman Conquest
Northampton,
 Assize of
Ordainer
Oxford,
 Provisions of
Paston Letters
Peasants Revolt
Roses, War of the
tanistry
Tewkesbury,
 Battle of
Towton, Battle of
Westminster,
 Statutes of
 (1275–90)
national affairs—east
central Europe:
 Cuman
 Golden Bull of
 1222
 Koszyce, Pact of
 Mazovia
 Moravia
national affairs—
France:
 Albigenses
 Aquitaine
 Brittany
 Burgundy
 Hundred
 Years' War
 Jacquerie
 Normandy

Praguerie
Provence
national affairs—
Germany and Low
Countries:
 Bayern
 Brabant
 Brandenburg
 Burgundy
 elector
 Flanders
 Golden Bull
 of Emperor
 Charles IV
 Hainaut
 Hanseatic League
 Holland
 Holy Roman
 Empire
 imperial city
 Limburg
 Namur
 Saxony
 Swabia
national affairs—
Iberian peninsula:
 Alarcos, Battle of
 Almohads
 Almoravids
 Andalusia
 Aragon
 Castile
 Catalonia
 converso
 Granada
 Leon
 Medina del
 Campo, Treaty of
 Morisco

Mudejar
Navarre
Navas de Tolosa,
 Battle of Las
Reconquista
Tordesillas,
 Treaty of
Valencia
Zamora, Treaty of
national affairs—
Italy:
 Ciompi, Revolt
 of the
 Eight Saints, War
 of the
 Guelf and
 Ghibelline
 Lodi, Peace of
 Lombard League
 Naples,
 kingdom of
 papacy
 Papal States
 Sicilian Vespers
 Two Sicilies,
 Kingdom of the
 Venetia
national affairs—
Scandinavia and
Baltic states:
 Birka
 Birkarlar
 Brothers of the
 Sword, Order
 of the
 Courland
 Danewirk

Heneby
Kalmar Union
Lithuania, Grand
 Duchy of
Livonia
Norman
national affairs—
Switzerland:
 Everlasting
 League
 Morat, Battle of
 Morgarten,
 Battle of
 Näfels, Battle of
 Sempach,
 Battle of
 Stans, Diet of
 Toggenburg
 Succession
society and
commerce:
 Black Death
 commune
 craft guild
 feudal land
 tenure
 feudalism
 Hanseatic League
 knight
 manorial court
 manorialism
 merchant guild
 Middle Ages
 Renaissance
 serfdom
 vassal

Biographies

British Isles and
Angevin Empire:
 Alexander I
 (Scotland)
 Alexander II
 (Scotland)
 Alexander III
 (Scotland)
 Beaufort, Henry
 Becket, Saint
 Thomas
 Bruce, House of
 Clarence, George
 Plantagenet,
 duke of
 David I (Scotland)
 David II (Scotland)
 David ap Llywelyn
 Despenser, Hugh
 Le and Hugh Le
 Edward (the
 Confessor;
 England)

Edward I
 (England)
Edward II
 (England)
Edward III
 (England)
Edward IV
 (England)
Edward V
 (England)
Edward the Black
 Prince
Eleanor of
 Aquitaine
Fortescue, Sir John
Gaveston, Piers
Glendower, Owen
Gloucester,
 Humphrey,
 duke of

Gloucester,
 Thomas of
 Woodstock,
 duke of
Henry I (England)
Henry II (England)
Henry III
 (England)
Henry IV
 (England)
Henry V (England)
Henry VI
 (England)
Henry VII
 (England)
Henry the Young
 King
Hubert Walter
James I (Scotland)
James II (Scotland)

James III
 (Scotland)
James IV
 (Scotland)
John (England)
John (Scotland)
John of Gaunt
Lancaster,
 House of
Lanfranc
Langton, Stephen
Llywelyn ap
 Gruffudd
Llywelyn ap
 Iowerth
Malcolm III
Margaret
 (Scotland)
Margaret
 of Anjou
Matilda

Iberian peninsula:
Afonso I
(Portugal)
Afonso II
(Portugal)
Afonso V
(Portugal)
Alfonso I
(Aragon)
Alfonso II
(Aragon)
Alfonso III
(Aragon)
Alfonso IV
(Aragon)
Alfonso V
(Aragon)
Alfonso VI
(Castile/Leon)
Alfonso VII
(Castile/Leon)
Alfonso IX
(Castile/Leon)
Alfonso X
(Castile/Leon)
Alfonso XI
(Castile/Leon)
Charles II
(Navarre)
Cid, the
Edward (Portugal)
Ferdinand II
(Aragon)
Ferdinand I
(Castile/Leon)
Ferdinand II
(Castile/Leon)
Ferdinand III
(Castile/Leon)
Ferdinand IV
(Castile/Leon)
García V (Navarre)
Henry II (Castile/
Leon)
Henry III (Castile/
Leon)
Henry IV (Castile/
Leon)
Isabella I
James I (Aragon)
James II (Aragon)
John I (Aragon)
John II (Aragon)
John II (Castile/
Leon)
John I (Portugal)
John II (Portugal)
Muḥammad XI
(Granada)
Peter II (Aragon)
Peter III (Aragon)
Peter IV (Aragon)

Peter I (Castile/
Leon)
Ramón
Berenguer I
Ramón
Berenguer II
Ramón
Berenguer III
Ramón
Berenguer IV
Sancho III Garcés
(Navarre)
Urraca
Italy and the papacy:
Adorno family
Alberti family
Alexander III
(pope)
Amadeus VI
(Savoy)
Amadeus VII
(Savoy)
Amadeus VIII
(Savoy)
Bardi family
Bentivoglio family
Boccanegra family
Bonacolsi family
Boniface VIII
(pope)
Borgia family
Carrara family
Castracani,
Castruccio
Charles I (Naples)
Charles II (Naples)
Charles III
(Naples)
Charles I (Sicily)
Cola di Rienzo
Colonna family
Contarini family
Corsini family
Dandolo, Enrico
Dandolo,
Vincenzo
Dandolo family
della Scala family
Drogo de
Hauteville
Este, House of
Ezzelino III da
Romano
Fieschi family
Gherardesca family
Gonzaga dynasty
Gregory VII (pope)
Gregory IX (pope)
Gregory X (pope)
Grimaldi family
Innocent III (pope)
Joan I (Naples)
Joan II (Naples)

Ladislas (Naples)
Lauria,
Ruggiero di
Leo IX (pope)
Louis (Naples)
Malaspina family
Malatesta family
Martin I (Sicily)
Medici,
Cosimo de'
Medici,
Lorenzo de'
Medici, Piero di
Cosimo de'
Medici, Piero di
Lorenzo de'
Medici family
Mocenigo family
Montefeltro family
Morosini family
Ordelaffi family
Orsini family
Paschal II (pope)
Pepoli family
Peruzzi family
Piccinino, Niccolò
Piccolomini family
Polenta family
Polo, Marco
Robert (Apulia)
Robert (Naples)
Roger (Apulia)
Roger I (Sicily)
Roger II (Sicily)
Sambuccio
d'Alando
Savonarola,
Girolamo
Sforza, Francesco
Sforza, Ludovico
Sforza family
Spinola family
Uguccione della
Fagginola
Urban II (pope)
Visconti family
Visconti, Gian
Galeazzo
Visconti, Matteo I
William I (Sicily)
William II (Sicily)
William de
Hauteville
Scandinavia and the
Baltic States:
Absalon
Algirdas
Canute IV
(Denmark)
Christian I
(Denmark)
Christopher I
(Denmark)

Christopher III
(Denmark)
Erik V
(Denmark)
Erik VI
(Denmark)
Erik VII
(Denmark)
Erik XIII
(Sweden)
Eskil
Gediminas
Haakon I
Haakon IV
Haakon V
Haakon VI
Inge I
John (Denmark)
Kestutis
Magnus I
(Norway)
Magnus III
(Norway)
Magnus IV
(Norway)
Magnus V
(Norway)
Magnus VI
(Norway)
Magnus I
(Sweden)
Magnus II
(Sweden)
Margaret I
(Denmark)
Mindaugas
Olaf II (Norway)
Olaf III (Norway)
Olaf (Sweden)
Sigurd I
Sverrir Sigurdsson
Sweyn II
(Denmark)
Valdemar II
(Denmark)
Valdemar IV
(Denmark)
Valdemar
(Sweden)
Vytautas
the Great
Władysław II
Jagiełło
Switzerland:
Brun, Rudolf
Bubenberg,
Adrian von
Nicholas of Flüe,
Saint
Stüssi, Rudolf
Waldman, Hans

INDEX: See entries under all of the terms above

Section 924. **The Crusading Movement, the Islāmic States of Southwest Asia, North Africa, and Europe, and the States of Eastern Christendom from *c.* 1050 to *c.* 1480**

A. The expansion of western Europe in the crusading movement and the Muslim response, the states of Eastern Christendom and the crusader states from *c.* 1050 to *c.* 1480

  1. The crusading era and the states of Eastern Christendom (*c.* 1050–*c.* 1480)

    a. The First Crusade (1096–99) and the establishment of the Latin states

      i. Background of the First Crusade: overcrowding in Christian Latin Europe and the wish of the church to divert the violence between Christians to an attack on the infidels, religious renewal in Europe, disruption of the pilgrimage routes by the Muslims, role of papal leadership at the Council of Clermont (1095), preparations for the Crusade and its participants

      ii. The sieges of Antioch (1097–98) and Jerusalem (1099): establishment of the crusader states

    b. The Second (1147–48) and Third (1188–92) crusades: Christian colonization in the East and export of feudalism, the crusader states to 1187, the institutions of the First Kingdom, the magnates of the Third Crusade

    c. The Byzantine Empire from 1081 to 1204, policies aimed at revival implemented by Comnenus dynasty

      i. Alexius I Comnenus and the First Crusade: pressures from the Seljuqs and Pechenegs

      ii. The later Comneni and fluctuating relations with the Venetians, Normans, and crusaders

      iii. The Fourth Crusade (1202–04) and the establishment of the Latin empire

    d. The later crusades: decline of the crusading movement and of the Latin enclaves, results of the crusades

      i. The Latin East after the Third Crusade: the Fifth (1218–21) and Sixth (1227–29) crusades; oriental politics of Emperor Frederick II

      ii. The crusades of Louis IX of France (1248–50, 1270), final loss of the crusader states, Kingdom of Cyprus; survival of the spirit of the crusades among Latin Christians

    e. Russia (1054–1300): the lands of Rus and the rise of new centres (*e.g.,* Novgorod, Vladimir, Galicia), the Mongol invasion (1223) and Tatar rule

    f. The Second Bulgarian Empire under the Asenid dynasty from *c.* 1185, decline after 1241

  2. The Slavic states of Eastern Christendom from *c.* 1300 to *c.* 1500

    a. Russia: the rise of the Muscovite state under the suzerainty of the Golden Horde and its later successful revolt (1380), expansion and establishment of Moscow as the leading Russian power under Tsar Ivan III (1462–1505), foreign policy

    b. The Balkans: growing strength of Serbia vis-à-vis the Byzantine and Bulgarian empires; subjugation of Albania, Macedonia, and Bulgaria under Stefan Dušan in the 14th century; Romania; subjection to the Ottoman Turks by 1453

  3. Restoration of the Byzantine Empire under the Palaeologus dynasty (1261), efforts to restore Byzantine power in the Balkans, foreign relations, cultural life

    a. Michael VIII (1261–82) and attempts to revive the empire, threats from the West, relations with the papacy

    b. The successors of Michael VIII: cultural revival, civil wars

    c. Turkish expansion, limited recovery by the Byzantine Empire before the final Turkish assault, the fall of Constantinople (1453)

B. The Islāmic states of Southwest Asia, North Africa, and Europe (*c.* 1050–*c.* 1480): Turkish and Kurdish dynasties, the Mongol invasions, and the rise of the Ottoman Empire

  1. Southwest Asia before the Mongol invasions

    a. The Great Seljuq Empire in Syria, Iraq, and Iran (*c.* 1050–*c.* 1190)

    i. Origins and conversion of the Seljuqs to Islām and their establishment in Khorāsān (*c.* 1000) under Maḥmūd of Ghazna, the foundation of the Seljuq state under Toghrïl Beg (1038–63), his conquest of Iran and Iraq and establishment of a protectorate over the 'Abbāsid caliphate

    ii. Extension of Seljuq hegemony into Syria and Palestine and victory over the Byzantines, partition and partial breakup of the empire after 1092, Seljuq restoration of Sunnī supremacy and patronage of the Iranian cultural revival

  b. Great Seljuq successor states (*c.* 1100–*c.* 1250): the Zangīd *atabeg*s in Syria and northern Iraq, the Ismā'īlī Assassins in Iran and Syria (*c.* 1090–*c.* 1250), the Khwārazm shahs of Iran and Central Asia (1097–1234), other dynasties

  c. The foundation of the independent sultanate of Rum from territory conquered from Byzantium in Anatolia (from 1071), commercial prosperity and territorial expansion in the 13th century, the Turkish Dānishmendid state in northern Anatolia (*c.* 1071–1177) and its absorption by the Seljuqs

2. The Mongolian invasions of eastern Europe and Southwest Asia in the 13th century

3. Southwest Asia and eastern Europe after the Mongolian invasions

  a. Mongol successor states (*c.* 1250–*c.* 1480)

    i. The Mongolian Il Khans in Iraq and Iran (*c.* 1250–1353): trade, administration, and eventual conversion to Islām; the Timurids and other Il Khan successor states

    ii. The khanate of the Golden Horde in eastern Europe (from 1240): adoption of Islām, gradual absorption of the Mongols into the Turkish *ulus* to form the Tatar people, the zenith of the empire in the early 14th century, Timur's invasion (1395) and its later partition

  b. Turkish Anatolia and the rise of the Ottoman Empire to 1481

    i. Origins and expansion of the Ottoman state (*c.* 1300–1402): its expansion in Anatolia and conquest of Serbia and Bulgaria in the 14th century, defeat by Timur (1402), restoration of the empire and beginning of the Ottoman challenge to the European states by the invasion of Hungary (1434), conquest of Constantinople (1453) and conquest of Anatolia

    ii. Development of Ottoman administrative and military institutions

4. North Africa and Muslim Spain (*c.* 1050–*c.* 1490)

  a. The decline of the Fāṭimids (*c.* 1050–1171) in the face of Seljuq and crusader invasions

  b. The Ayyūbids and Mamlūks in Egypt and Syria (1171–*c.* 1500)

    i. Establishment of the Ayyūbid dynasty in Egypt and expansion of its control over Muslim Syria under Saladin (1171–93): conflict with the crusader states, pacific policies of his successors

    ii. Displacement of the Ayyūbids by the Turkish Mamlūks in 1250, the Bahri Mamlūks' resistance to the Mongols and extension of European power in Syria under Quṭuz and Baybars I (1260–77), their displacement by the Burjī Mamlūks in 1382, Mamlūk administration and military institutions, the continued maintenance of Sunnī orthodoxy

  c. The Berber Almoravid and Almohad empires in northwest Africa and Spain (1056–1269)

    i. Almoravid origins as a religious reform federation in the western Sudan, conquest of Morocco and western Algeria under Abū Bakr and Yūsuf ibn Tāshufīn (1062–92), the latter's intervention in Spain against the expanding Christian states, Almoravid conquest of Muslim Spain (1090–91), weakness and decline in the face of the renewal of the Reconquista and the Almohad revolt in North Africa (*c.* 1123)

    ii. The Almohad religious reform movement under the Berber Muḥammad ibn Tūmart (d. 1130) and the extension of Almohad control over Muslim Spain (capital at Seville) and the Maghrib (1145–72), initial containment of the Reconquista and later disintegration of the empire in Spain after 1212, subsequent eclipse in the Maghrib, Almohad patronage of philosophy and the arts

  d. The east medieval dynasties of North Africa (13th–15th century): political and cultural developments

    i. The Ḥafṣids in Tunisia, the 'Abd al-Wādid kingdom of Tilimsān, the Marīnids in eastern Morocco and their problems with the Arabs, political life, the Naṣrid kingdom of Granada

    ii. Religious, intellectual, and artistic life: Ṣūfism, literary and artistic influences from Muslim Spain

Suggested reading in the *Encyclopædia Britannica:*

MACROPAEDIA: Major articles dealing with the crusading movement, the Islāmic states of Southwest Asia, North Africa, and Europe, and the states of Eastern Christendom from *c.* 1050 to *c.* 1480

Albania	Crusades, The	Jerusalem	Syria
Bulgaria	Egypt	North Africa	Turkey and
Byzantine Empire,	Islāmic	Romania	Ancient Anatolia
The History	World, The	Spain	Yugoslavia
of the			

MICROPAEDIA: Selected entries of reference information

General subjects

Balkans:	Barghawāṭah	Nicopolis, Battle of	Moscow, Grand
Bogomil	Granada	Saracen	Principality of
Croatia	Moor	*Middle East—other:*	Neva, Battle of the
Epirus,	Morisco	Ak Koyunlu	Novgorod,
Despotate of	Mozarab	Anatolia	Treaty of
Kosovo, Battle of	Navas de Tolosa,	Ankara, Battle of	Pechenegs
(1389)	Battle of Las	Assassin	Rus
Kosovo, Battle of	Reconquista	bashi-bazouk	Suzdal
(1448)	Valencia	Jalāyirid	Tver
Maritsa River,	*Middle East—*	Kara Koyunlu	Ugra, Battle of the
Battle of the	*Crusades:*	Little Armenia	veche
Moldavia	Antioch	Mamlūk	Vladimir
Morea,	Arsūf, Battle of	Myriocephalon,	Volhynia
Despotate of	Children's	Battle of	*other:*
Serbia	Crusade	Nicaea, empire of	Bari, Siege of
Thrace	crusade	Seljuq	pronoia system
Vlach	Haṭṭin, Battle of	*eastern Europe:*	
Walachia	Holy Lance	Crimea, Khanate	
Zara, Siege of	Jérusalem,	of the	
Iberia and	Assises de	Golden Horde	
northwestern Africa:	Jerusalem,	Kipchak	
Almohads	Kingdom of	Kulikovo, Battle of	
Almoravids			

Biographies

Christians—Balkans	Manuel I	*Muslims—Iberia and*	Mehmed II
and Russia:	Comnenus	*northwestern Africa:*	Murad I
Alexander Nevsky,	Manuel II	'Abd al-Mu'min	Murad II
Saint	Palaeologus	Aftasid dynasty	Niẓām al-Mulk
Ivan III	Metochites,	Ḥafṣid dynasty	Saladin
Ivan Asen I	Theodore	Ḥammūdid	Salghurid dynasty
Ivan Asen II	Michael VIII	dynasty	Sanjar
Kotromanić	Palaeologus	Hūdid dynasty	Toghrïl Beg
dynasty	*Christians—Crusader*	Zīrid dynasty	Zangid dynasty
Rurik dynasty	*states:*	*Muslims—Middle*	
Stefan Dušan	Bohemond I	*East:*	
Vasily I	John	Alp-Arslan	
Christians—	(Constantinople)	Artuqid dynasty	
Byzantine Empire:	Lusignan family	Baybars I	
Alexius I	Mézières,	Dānishmend	
Comnenus	Philippe de	dynasty	
Isaac II Angelus	Raymond	Eldegüzid dynasty	
John III Ducas	(Antioch)	Ghāzān, Maḥmūd	
Vatatzes	Reginald of	Khwārezm-Shāh	
	Châtillon	dynasty	

INDEX: See entries under all of the terms above

Division III. **Peoples and Traditional Civilizations of East, Central, South, and Southeast Asia**
[For Part Nine headnote see page 343.]

For each nation or group of peoples covered in this division, the outline treats first of the geography and ethnography and then moves into the chronology of the respective civilization: Sections 931 and 932 outline the Chinese dynasties from the Ch'in through the late Ch'ing (mid-19th century).

Section 933 deals with the peoples of inner Asia and the steppe and covers the early histories of Manchuria, Turkistan, and Afghanistan; of the Mongol Empire and its successor states; and of Tibet and Nepal.

Section 934 outlines the character and achievements of the Japanese and Korean civilizations from their beginnings until the Meiji Restoration of 1868 and the Japanese annexation of Korea in 1910.

Sections 935 and 936 treat of the civilizations of the Indian subcontinent, of the early political units of India and Ceylon, the period of Muslim hegemony, the Mughal and Marāthā empires, and, for Ceylon, the arrival of the Portuguese in 1505.

Section 937 deals with the peoples and civilizations of Southeast Asia, including the histories of Burma, Siam, Cambodia, Vietnam, and Malaya, as well as the islands of the Indonesian Archipelago, until *c.* 1600.

Section 931. **China to the Beginning of the Late T'ang (AD 755)**

A. The character and achievements of Chinese civilization, the geography and ethnography of China, archaeological and documentary historical sources, historiographic problems

B. The emergence of traditional Chinese civilization

　1. The prehistoric period

　　a. The Paleolithic and Mesolithic stages in North China: industries in the Ordos region, microlithic tools

　　b. The Neolithic stage: pebble tools and domesticated animals, "Mongolian Neolithic"

　　c. The Yang-shao Painted Pottery culture

　　　i. Stratigraphy: villages of Hsi-yin-ts'un and Yang-shao-ts'un, pottery styles

　　　ii. Painted pottery styles, sites in Kansu, ornamental designs, stone implements

　　d. The Lung-shan Black Pottery complex and western limits of Black Pottery culture, the Late Neolithic Period in South China and the Early Bronze Age in North China, bronze objects in the Ordos region

　2. The beginnings of the Chinese civilization: the early dynasties

　　a. Origins of the Chinese people and culture: legends and cultural centres, the Hsia dynasty (*c.* 2205–*c.* 1766 BC)

　　b. The Shang, or Yin, period (*c.* 1766–*c.* 1122 BC): Chengchow site as early capital and cultural centre at Anyang, social system, early calendar, warfare, industry and commerce, script

　　c. The Western (early) Chou (1122–771 BC): the conquest of Shang under Wen Wang and Wu Wang (1111 BC), Chou feudal system

　　d. The Eastern (later) Chou (771–481 BC), also called the Chun Ch'iu period; internal chaos; period of the Warring States (481–221 BC)

　　　i. Breakdown of the Chou feudal system: capital at Loyang, rivalry among Chou states, various Chou successor states in the Warring States period (481–221 BC)

　　　ii. Social, political, and cultural changes: decline of feudalism, urbanization and assimilation, rise of monarchy under Wen Kung, economic development

　　e. The Classical period of Chinese literature and philosophy: Chinese religion and cosmology, Confucianism and Taoism, the "hundred schools" (the Naturalists, the Dialecticians, Mo-tzu, Meng-tzu [Mencius], Chuang-tzu, the Legalists)

C. The unification of China under the Ch'in and Han dynasties (221 BC–AD 220)

    1. Establishment of the Ch'in empire (221–206 BC): development of central government, fall of the dynasty after death of Shih Huang Ti

        a. Early successes of the Ch'in under Mu Kung, reforms of Hsiao Kung and Shang Yang

        b. Ch'in strategy, unification of China by the Ch'in (221 BC), abolition of feudal system, highway building and construction of the Great Wall in the reign of Shih Huang Ti, the minister Li Ssu, political repression

    2. The Han dynasty

        a. Western (Former or Earlier) Han (206 BC–AD 8) and the Wang Mang usurpation (AD 9–23)

            i. Establishment of the dynasty by Liu Pang (Han Kao Tsu): the capital at Ch'ang-an, reign of Liu Heng (Han Wen Ti) from 179 to 157 BC, consolidation of Imperial power

            ii. Expansion under Han Wu Ti (140–87 BC) into southern China and Central Asia, dynastic crisis (91–87 BC), ascendancy of the Wang family and Wang Mang's usurpation of throne (AD 9–23)

        b. The Eastern (Later) Han: restoration of the dynasty by Liu Hsiu (Han Kuang Wu Ti) (AD 25–57), capital at Loyang, domestic and foreign policy, decline of government after AD 125

        c. Political developments, foreign relations, and cultural attainments in the Han period

            i. The Han political system: the structure and the practice of government

            ii. Relations with other peoples: the Hsiung-nu of Central Asia, Pan Ch'ao's campaigns in Central Asia

            iii. Han cultural life: educational developments, invention of paper, prose writing, developments in music and the visual arts, introduction of Buddhism

D. The breakdown and revival of the empire

    1. The Six Dynasties period (AD 220–589)

        a. The division of the empire into the Three Kingdoms of Wei (North China), Shu Han (Szechwan), and Wu (South China): era of barbarian invasions and rule, the period of the Sixteen Kingdoms (304–589)

        b. Intellectual and religious trends: decline in Confucianism, Taoist resurgence, spread of Buddhism

    2. The reunification of China under the Sui and early T'ang dynasties

        a. The Sui (581–618): Sui founder Yang Chien (Sui Wen Ti), institutional reforms

        b. The reign of Yang Ti (605–618): integration of the South, foreign affairs, military reverses and collapse of the dynasty

        c. The early T'ang (618–624) and the period of T'ang power (626–755)

            i. Li Yüan's (618–626) establishment of the dynasty: resistance to T'ang conquest, administration of the state, fiscal and legal system

            ii. The era of good government in the reign of T'ai Tsung (626–649): educational and administrative reforms, conquest of eastern Turks, Kao Tsung (649–683) and influence of Empress Wu, conquest of Oxus Valley and later military reverses

            iii. Prosperity and progress in the reign of Hsüan Tsung (712–756): internal reforms, military reorganization

---

Suggested reading in the *Encyclopædia Britannica*:

MACROPAEDIA: Major articles dealing with China to the beginning of the late T'ang (AD 755)

    Asia
    China
    Nanking

MICROPAEDIA: Selected entries of reference information

General subjects

ancient cultures and	Ch'in tomb	Hsiung-nu	Sha-ch'ing
historic sites:	Great Wall of	Lung-shan culture	*dynastic capitals:*
Ch'i-chia culture	China	Pan-p'o-ts'un	An-yang

Hsien-yang	Chou dynasty	T'ang dynasty	equal-field system
Lo-yang	Ch'u	Three Kingdoms	Five Pecks of Rice
Nanking	Han dynasty	Warring States	fu-ping
Sian	Hsia dynasty	Wei dynasty	Hanlin Academy
Ta-t'ung	Lu	*government and*	well-field system
Yang-chou	Nangnang	*society:*	
dynasties, periods,	Shang dynasty	Bamboo Annals	
and states:	Six Dynasties	censor	
Ch'i	Spring and	Chinese civil	
Chin dynasty	Autumn Period	service	
Ch'in dynasty	Sui dynasty		

Biographies

officials and military	Shang Yang	*rulers:*	T'ai-tsung (T'ang)
leaders:	Ts'ao Ts'ao	Hsiao-wen Ti	Wang Mang
Chao Kao	*philosophers:*	Hsüan-tsung	Wen-ti (Sui)
Hsiang Yü	Chuang-tzu	(T'ang)	Wu Hou
Li Ssu	Confucius	Kao-tsu (Han)	Wu-ti (Chin)
Lü Pu-wei	Lao-tzu	Kao-tsu (T'ang)	Wu-ti (Han)
Pan Ch'ao	Mencius	Kuang-wu Ti	Yang Ti
	Mo-tzu	Shih huang-ti	

INDEX: See entries under all of the terms above

Section 932. **China from the Late T'ang (AD 755) to the Late Ch'ing (c. 1839)**

A. The late T'ang dynasty, the Ten Kingdoms, the Five Dynasties, and the Sung dynasty

  1. The late T'ang and the Northern Sung

    a. The late T'ang (755–907): the rebellion of An Lu-shan (755–757) and its effects, provincial separatism, attempts to restore central authority, growth in power of provincial warlords

    b. T'ang cultural life: the growing influences of Buddhism, developments in music and the visual arts

    c. Social and economic developments: the decline of the aristocracy and social mobility, agricultural advances and expansion of trade

    d. The period of the Five Dynasties and the Ten Kingdoms (907–960)

      i. The short-lived Five Dynasties in North China: the Liang dynasty, advance of talented bureaucrats in government posts

      ii. The more permanent Ten Kingdoms: the Tanguts; the Khitan, or Liao, empire; the kingdoms of Wu, the Southern T'ang, the Southern P'ing, the Ch'u, the Earlier and Later Shu, the Min, the Southern Han, and the Wu-yüeh

    e. The Northern Sung (960–1126): foundation of the dynasty and its expansion under T'ai Tsu and T'ai Tsung and their successors

      i. Unification and centralization of the empire: development of the Imperial civil service in Chao K'uang-yin's (T'ai Tsu's) reign (960–976), further consolidation under Tseng Tsung (998–1022)

      ii. Reforms in the reign of Shen Tsung (1068–85): leadership of Wang An-Shih, criticism of the reforms leading to the decline and fall of the dynasty

  2. The Southern Sung (1126–1279): survival and consolidation, defeat by the Juchens and removal of the Sung to South China under Kao Tsung

  3. Sung cultural and economic developments; *e.g.,* resurgence of Neo-Confucianism, visual arts and music, scholarship, historiography, invention of printing, manufacturing advances

B. Mongol–Chinese rule under the Yüan dynasty (1279–1368)

  1. The Mongol conquest of China: imposition of Mongol government and policies

    a. Genghis Khan's conquest of the Chin (1211–34), invasion of the Sung and the establishment of the Yüan dynasty under Kublai Khan

    b. Mongol government and administration: transfer of the capital to Ta-tu (Peking), nonassimilation with the Chinese, expansion of trade

2. Religious and intellectual life, relations with the West, decline of Mongol rule

   a. Religious toleration and patronage of Buddhism, the status of the Confucian scholar, developments in the arts

   b. Yüan China and the West: commercial and cultural contacts, arrival of Catholic missionaries

C. The Ming and Ch'ing dynasties to *c.* 1839: the tribute system, relative stability, ethnocentrism, and emphasis on cultural unity

   1. The Ming dynasty (1368–1644)

      a. Foundation of the Ming and its political and social structure

         i. Peasant uprisings and the foundation of the dynasty (1368) by Chu Yüan-chang (Hung-wu): pattern of dynastic succession, gradual degeneration of Ming government

         ii. Government and administration: local and central government, later innovations to coordinate central government and regional administration

      b. Developments in foreign relations and economic policy

      c. Cultural life in the Ming period: philosophy and religion, developments in the visual arts, music, literature, and scholarship

   2. The Ch'ing (Manchu) dynasty to *c.* 1839

      a. The Manchu rise to power (1644): preservation of the Ming administration under joint Manchu–Chinese supervision

         i. Manchu entrance in Peking and territorial conquest ending with the seizure of Taiwan (1683): early Ch'ing institutions

         ii. Early foreign relations in Asia, contacts with the West

      b. Mid-Ch'ing social and economic developments: the role of religious associations, expansion of industry, social unrest, intellectual and cultural advances

         i. Advances in agriculture through increased rice cultivation and introduction of new crops, expansion of crafts and industries, commerce and finance

         ii. Population growth and immigration, religious associations, the White Lotus Rebellion (1796–1804)

         iii. Cultural developments; *e.g.,* government interference in scholarship; introduction of Western sciences; advances in music, literature, and the visual arts

      c. Dynastic degeneration and widespread governmental corruption beginning in the 1760s; economic decline, famine, and social unrest in the early 1800s

---

Suggested reading in the *Encyclopædia Britannica:*

MACROPAEDIA: Major articles and a biography dealing with China from the late T'ang (AD 755) to the late Ch'ing (*c.* 1839)

Asia	Genghis Khan
Canton	Nanking
China	Peking
Chungking	

MICROPAEDIA: Selected entries of reference information

General subjects

capital cities:	Yang-chou	Sung dynasty	kowtow
Canton	*dynasties, kingdoms,*	T'ang dynasty	pao-chia
Ch'ang-sha	*and states:*	Ten Kingdoms	Tung-lin
Ch'eng-tu	Chin dynasty	Yüan dynasty	*other:*
Chungking	(Juchen)	*government and*	Cathay
Hang-chou	Ch'ing dynasty	*society:*	Hakka
Lo-yang	Five Dynasties	Banner system	Nerchinsk,
Nanking	Hsi Hsia	Canton System	Treaty of
Peking	Liao dynasty	Chinese civil	White Lotus
Sian	Ming dynasty	service	Rebellion

Biographies

emperors:
Cheng-te	T'ai-tsu (Sung)	Cheng	Wu San-kuei
Chia-ch'ing	T'ai-tsung (Sung)	Ch'eng-kung	Yüeh Fei
Ch'ien-lung	Yung-cheng	Cheng Ho	*Westerners:*
(Ch'ing)	(Ch'ing)	Dorgon	Polo, Marco
Hung-wu	Yung-lo (Ming)	Hsü Kuang-ch'i	Ricci, Matteo
K'ang-hsi (Ch'ing)	*statesmen and*	Huang Tsung-hsi	
Kublai Khan	*military leaders:*	Nurhachi	
Shen Tsung (Sung)	An Lu-shan	Ou-yang Hsiu	
		Wang An-shih	

INDEX: See entries under all of the terms above

Section 933. **Inner (Central and Northeast) Asia to *c.* 1750**

A. The peoples of the steppes, their cultures, and their interactions with neighbouring civilizations; the geography and ethnography of Inner Asia; archaeological and documentary historical sources; historiographic problems

B. The peoples and states of Inner Asia to *c.* AD 1200

 1. The Hsiung-nu tribal confederation dominating Mongolia, southern Siberia, and eastern Turkistan from *c.* 400 BC to *c.* AD 50; pressure on it and its destruction by Han China

 2. The Manchurian tribes: attempts at unification, fluctuating relations with the Chinese until the advent of the Mongols

 a. The Tung-hu tribes and Chinese presence in Manchuria to the 3rd century BC, ascendancy of the Hsien-pei and establishment of the Yin kingdom by Mu-jung Hui (AD 352), the Parhae (P'o-hai) kingdom (AD 712)

 b. The Khitan and Juchen empires: penetration into China, Korea, and Mongolia; Juchen conquest of Chinese Sung territory; capital at Yen-ching (Peking); conquest by Mongols in 1234

 3. Development of West and East Turkistan to *c.* 1750

 a. West Turkistan: the early empires, Muslim rule, the Chagatai khans and Timurids, the Uzbek and Kazakh khanates

 b. East Turkistan (Kashgaria): Kirgiz, Uighur tribes, Qarakhanid rule in the 10th century, Mongol conquest and rule in the 13th century, conquest by Manchus (1758–59)

 4. The Mongolian and Tungusic states from the 10th to the 13th century: the Liao (Khitan) empire and the later Chin (Juchen) state in North China and Manchuria (947–1125), the Western Liao (Kara khitai) of Turkistan (1124–1211)

 5. The development of Afghanistan to *c.* 1700: rule by Achaemenians and Greeks to *c.* 1st century AD, various nomadic rulers, advent of Muslim control in the 7th century, Mongol conquest (1221), later rule by Timurids and Mughals

C. The Mongol Empire and its successor states

 1. The establishment of a united Mongol Empire in Central, eastern, and western Asia by Genghis Khan and his successors (1206–60)

 a. The rise of Genghis Khan and his military and political organization, tactics, and conquests

 b. The division of his empire among his sons: further expansion under Ögödei Khan, Mangu (Möngke) Khan's friendly relations with Western Christendom

 2. The Mongol successor states

 a. The completion of the conquest of China (1260–79) and the foundation of the Yüan dynasty by Kublai Khan

 b. The Chagatai khanate (*ulus*) of Turkistan in the 13th and 14th centuries

 c. Timur's (Tamerlane's) establishment of the Timurid dynasty (1370–1506): his capital at Samarkand; his conquests; Turkistan, Afghanistan, and Transoxania under his successors

 d. The Iranian Il Khans (1258–1335): the Golden Horde (later Kipchak empire) in eastern Europe and its successor states (1240–1783)

    e. Mongolia from the 13th to the 18th century: internecine strife, the revival of Buddhism, subjection to Yüan China and later autonomy and disunity until the ascendancy of the Manchus (Ch'ing China) in the 18th century

D. Tibet and Nepal to *c.* 1750

    1. Tibet to *c.* 1750

        a. The legendary origins of the Tibetan people, consolidation of Tibet under Gnam-ri srong-btsan (*c.* AD 570–619), later rulers to the 9th century, introduction of Buddhism, cultural developments

        b. Tibetan disunity from the 9th to the 14th century: eclipse and resurgence of Buddhism, conquest by Mongols, developments in literature and the visual arts

        c. Rule by the Dge-lugs-pa (Yellow Hat) monastic order, unification of Tibet (1642), Tibet under Chinese overlordship (1720)

    2. Nepal to *c.* 1750: rule by Indian princely families, influence of Hinduism, relations with China and Tibet

E. The waning of nomad power from the 16th to the 18th century: the Manchu conquest of China and parts of Inner Asia, the Afghans as the last nomad power in Inner Asia, Russian expansion into Siberia and western Turkistan

---

Suggested reading in the *Encyclopædia Britannica*:

MACROPAEDIA: Major articles and a biography dealing with inner (Central and Northeast) Asia to *c.* 1750

    Asia
    China
    Genghis Khan
    Mongolia
    Nepal

MICROPAEDIA: Selected entries of reference information

General subjects

dynasties and empires:	Uzbek dynasty	Oyrat	Samarkand
Chin dynasty	Yüan dynasty	Yüeh-chih	Sogdiana
(Juchen)	*peoples:*	*other:*	Turkistan
Golden Horde	Chahar	Karakorum	
Gtsang dynasty	Hsiung-nu	Parhae	
Liao dynasty	Juan-juan	Qarluq	
	Mongol	confederation	

Biographies

Abahai	Möngke	Phag-mo-gru	Timur
Batu	Mozaffarid dynasty	family	Timurid dynasty
Il-Khanid dynasty	Nurhachi	Qarakhanid	Willem van
Kublai Khan	Ögödei	dynasty	Ruysbroeck

INDEX: See entries under all of the terms above

Section 934.   **Japan to the Meiji Restoration (1868), and Korea to 1910**

   A. Introduction: the character and achievements of Japanese and Korean civilizations, the geography and ethnography of Japan and Korea, archaeological and documentary historical sources, historiographic problems

   B. Early Japan

     1. Prehistoric cultures: nonceramic cultures in the Paleolithic Period, Jōmon (5th or 4th millennium to *c.* 250 BC) and Yayoi (*c.* 250 BC–AD 250) Neolithic pottery cultures, agriculture and the influx of Chinese culture

     2. The ancient period: unification of Japan under the Yamato court and subsequent governments (*c.* 250–710)

       a. The rise and fall of the Yamato court: relations with Korea, internal power struggles, introduction of Buddhism

       b. The governmental reforms of Shōtoku Taishi of the Soga family: theories of ideal government, the 12 court rank and the "Seventeen Article Constitution," relations with China, spread of Buddhism

       c. The Taika reforms (645), elimination of the Soga family, land reform, intervention in Korea, the *ritsu-ryō* system of social and land reform

     3. The Imperial state from 710 to 1185

       a. Government-directed religious and cultural developments in the Nara period (710–784): flowering of Buddhism; Chinese and Indian influences on literature, music, and the visual arts

       b. The Heian period (794–1185): changes in the *ritsu-ryō* system, ascendancy of the Fujiwara family and growing importance of the aristocracy

         i. Failure of Taika land reforms, power struggles among the nobility, growth of Fujiwara control over government, rise of Japanese literature and rejection of Chinese culture

         ii. Government by "cloistered" emperors: decline of Fujiwara power and rise of the samurai class, the Hōgen (1156) and Heiji (1159) uprisings, introduction of feudalism

   C. Feudal Japan

     1. The Kamakura period (1192–1333)

       a. Minamoto Yoritomo and the founding of the *bakufu* (shogunate) at Kamakura (1192), the samurai *shugo* as feudal lords

       b. The rise of the Hōjō family from 1199: the Jōkyū Disturbance (1221), Hōjō Yasutoki's (1224–42) administrative reforms, the Jōei law code

       c. Resistance to the Mongol invasions of Japan (1274 and 1281), the Kamakura *bakufu* and feudal administration of farming regions

       d. Buddhist culture during the Kamakura period (*e.g.,* growth of Zen) and Neo-Confucianism; literature, philosophy, and the visual arts

       e. Decline of Kamakura society: economic problems leading to the rise of daimyo (domain lord) class and decline of *bakufu*

     2. The second feudal era: the Muromachi, or Ashikaga, period (1338–1573)

       a. The Kemmu Restoration (1333) and return to direct Imperial rule: the emperor Go-Daigo, the Kemmu legal code, Ashikaga Takauji and the dual dynasties (1336–92)

       b. Yoshimitsu's establishment of the Muromachi *bakufu* (1378) and unification of the dual dynasties (1392): taxation and strong military governors, feudal warfare after 1428

       c. Increased trade with China: piracy, the Ōnin War (1467–77), provincial self-government and growing influence of farmers

     3. The period of the "warring country" and the beginning of unification under the Oda regime

       a. Unification under *sengoku* (civil war) daimyo league leaders: development of commerce and guilds

       b. Arrival of the Portuguese (1543) and Spanish (1549): opening of trade, Catholic Jesuit missionary activity (1549)

    c. Cultural development in the 15th and 16th centuries: the influence of Zen Buddhism on philosophy, drama, literature, and the visual arts

    d. The Azuchi-Momoyama period (1574–1600): unification under Oda Nobunaga (1550–82) and Toyotomi Hideyoshi (1582–98)

  4. The Tokugawa period (1603–1867): military–bureaucratic rule

    a. Establishment (1603) and consolidation of the Tokugawa (Edo) *bakufu* by Tokugawa Ieyasu: Japanese policy of national seclusion (1630s) from Christian missionaries and most European traders

    b. The Tokugawa postfeudal military–bureaucratic system: class structure and *bakuhan* system

    c. Industrial and commercial developments, advances in literature and the visual arts

    d. The weakening of the *bakuhan* system and its eventual collapse

       i. Economic crises: impoverishment of small farmers and commercial problems, political reform, opening of Japan to Western influences (1840s)

       ii. Cultural developments in the 18th and 19th centuries: Confucianism and the Shintō revival, Buddhism, literature and the visual arts

       iii. The Tempō reform and downfall of the *bakuhan:* economic and administrative measures, pressure from Europe and the U.S.

D. Korea to 1910

  1. The prehistoric origins of the Korean people, the use of ironware and emergence of tribal states in the Bronze Age

  2. The Three Kingdoms of Korea (Koguryŏ, Paekche, and Silla) and their interactions (*c.* 57 BC–AD 668), introduction of Buddhism, literature and the visual arts

  3. The unification of Korea under Silla control (668–918): adoption of Chinese governmental organization and land tenure system, emergence of provincial magnates, cultural developments

  4. The Koryŏ dynasty (918–1392): social and cultural developments, military rule, land reform and social change after the Mongol invasions (1231–*c.* 1261)

  5. The Yi state of Chosen (1392–1910)

    a. The establishment of a Confucian state: royal bureaucratic government, decline of Buddhism and emergence of Confucian culture, introduction of printing

    b. Invasions by Japan (1592–98) and China (1619–27): Korea as a Ch'ing (Manchu) vassal, Silhak scholarship and cultural development, introduction of Roman Catholicism

    c. Relations with foreign countries: growth of Japanese influence, the Tonghak Revolt (1894) and government reform, Japanese supremacy in Korea (1910)

Suggested reading in the *Encyclopædia Britannica:*

MACROPAEDIA: Major articles dealing with Japan to the Meiji Restoration (1868), and Korea to 1910

  Asia
  Japan
  Korea
  Kyōto
  Ōsaka–Kōbe Metropolitan Area
  Tokyo–Yokohama Metropolitan Area

MICROPAEDIA: Selected entries of reference information

General subjects

Japan—government and society:	han	shugo	Hōgen Disturbance
be	kabane	tennō	Jinshin-no-ran
Bushidō	kampaku	uji	Ōnin War
chōnin	kebiishi	wakō	Sekigahara,
daimyo	rangaku	za	Battle of
Dajōkan	rōnin	*Japan—historic*	Shimabara
equal-field system	samurai	*events:*	Rebellion
	shogunate	Gempei War	

INDEX: See entries under all of the terms above

Section 935.   The Indian Subcontinent and Ceylon to *c.* AD 1200

A. The character and achievements of traditional Indian civilizations and their influence on Ceylonese and Southeast Asian civilizations, the geography and ethnography of the Indian subcontinent and Ceylon, archaeological and documentary historical sources, historiographic problems

B. India from the prehistoric period to AD 300: the emergence of civilization in the Indus River Valley, the growth of kingdoms and the great empires

  1. Late Stone Age hunters and Neolithic settlement in Baluchistan and the Indus Valley, first settlements east of the Indus

  2. Indus civilization (*c.* 2300–*c.* 1750 BC): social, economic, and cultural developments

    a. Development of urban centres; *e.g.,* Mohenjo-daro, Harappā, Kalibangan, Lothal

    b. Developments in agriculture, animal husbandry, metalwork and pottery, transportation, and trade

    c. Developments in languages, religion, and the visual arts

  3. The development of the Indo-Aryan states (*c.* 1500–600 BC): urbanization at Kāśī (Vārānasi) and elsewhere in the Ganges Valley, other cultures in the Indian subcontinent

    a. Early Ganges cultures to *c.* 1200 BC: social organization and religious development

    b. Later Ganges cultures to *c.* 600 BC: development of the caste system and emergence of Brahmin, Kṣatriya, Vaiśya, and Śūdra castes

4. Pre-Mauryan states (*c.* 600–150 BC): development of political and economic systems, Taxila as a cultural centre

   a. The early development of Buddhism and Jainism, growth of Magadhan ascendancy

   b. Invasion of Alexander the Great (327 BC) and establishment of Greek settlements

5. Development of the Mauryan Empire (*c.* 321–185 BC): the capital at Pāṭaliputra (Patna)

   a. Establishment of the empire by Candragupta Maurya (*c.* 321–*c.* 297 BC) and consolidation by Aśoka (*c.* 265–238 BC)

   b. Mauryan economic, social, and administrative developments, evolution of the concept of the state

6. The rise of small kingdoms in the north (150 BC–AD 300): Indo-Greek and Asian rulers, various local republics and kingdoms (Śuṅga, Kaliṅga, Andhra)

7. South Indian civilizations to AD 300

   a. Development of guilds, banking systems, and extensive maritime trade with the West

   b. Cultural and religious development; *e.g.,* patronage of religious art and literature, growth of sects in Hinduism and Jainism, assimilation of foreigners into caste society

C. North India, the Deccan, and South India (AD 300–750)

1. The Guptas of North India (AD 320–540): expansion and administration of territory, invasions by the Hūṇas (*c.* mid-5th century), successor states to the Guptas

2. Various kingdoms of the Deccan: the Vākāṭaka dynasty, the Viṣṇukuṇḍins, the Cālukyas, and the Rāṣṭrakūṭas

3. The Pallavas in South India: developments in religious art and architecture, literature, and science

D. North India (750–1200), the Deccan, and South India (750–*c.* 1330): new dynasties and centres of power

1. The tripartite struggle in North India, the Rājput kingdoms, Turkish control in Ghazna from 998

2. The decline of the Cālukyas in the Deccan and the rise of the Cōḻas in the 10th century, later Hoysaḷas and Pāṇḍyas control, relations with the south

3. Social, economic, and cultural developments; *e.g.,* feudalism and economic decentralization, partial social mobility, growth of Tantrism, literature and the visual arts

E. Ceylon from the prehistoric period to the end of the Classical Age (AD 1200)

1. Prehistoric settlements in Ceylon, colonization by Indo-Aryan tribes in the 5th century BC, conversion to Buddhism (*c.* 3rd century BC)

2. Ceylon in the Classical Age (*c.* 200 BC–AD 1200): the Polonnaruva dynasties, growth of Sinhalese political institutions, social and agricultural developments

---

Suggested reading in the *Encyclopædia Britannica*:

MACROPAEDIA: Major articles dealing with the Indian subcontinent and Ceylon to *c.* AD 1200

   Asia
   India
   Nepal
   Sri Lanka

MICROPAEDIA: Selected entries of reference information

General subjects

historic regions and sites:	Gedrosia	Patna	*kingdoms and states:*
Bhārhut	Halebīd	Śrāvastī	Anuradhapura,
Brahmarṣi-désa	Kalibangan	Taxila	kingdom of
Gandhara	Kaliṅga	Vaiśālī	Avanti
Gauḍa	Mālwa	Valabhī	Kosala
	Nālandā	Vārānasi	Magadha
			Mauryan empire

peoples and society:	Indus	Rājput	*other:*
Brahman	civilization	Sūdra	Dīpavaṃsa
Chandelā	Kulinism	Vaiśya	Rājataraṅgiṇī
Hephthalite	Licchavi	Varṇa	Serendib
	Mallas	Yavana	Tarāorī, Battles of

Biographies

Aśoka	Gaṅga dynasty	Mahendra	Śaiśunāga dynasty
Buddha	Gurjara-Pratihāra	Maitraka dynasty	Śaka satrap
Cālukya dynasty	dynasty	Menader	Samudra Gupta
Candra Gupta	Harṣa	Nanda dynasty	Sātavāhana
Candra Gupta I	Hoysaḷa dynasty	Pāla dynasty	dynasty
Candra Gupta II	Īśānavarman	Pallava dynasty	Sena dynasty
Cōla dynasty	Kalacuri dynasty	Pāṇḍya dynasty	Śuṅga dynasty
Duṭṭhagāmaṇī	Kaniṣka	Parākramabāhu I	Vākāṭaka dynasty
Gāhaḍavāla	Kauṭilya	Rāṣṭrakūṭa	Yādava dynasty
dynasty	Kushān	dynasty	

INDEX: See entries under all of the terms above

Section 936.   **The Indian Subcontinent from *c.* 1200 to 1761, and Ceylon from *c.* 1200 to 1505**

A. North India under Muslim hegemony (*c.* 1200–1526)

　1. The completion of the Ghurid conquest; the Delhi sultanate (1206–1526): the military and administrative policies of the five dynasties

　　a. The consolidation of the conquest of North India by the Slave dynasty (1206–90)

　　b. The revival of efficient administration by the Khaljī dynasty (1290–1320)

　　c. The Tughluq dynasty (1320–1413): administrative reforms by Muḥammad ibn Tughluq (1325–51), Mughal invasion (1398) and decline of Tughluq control

　　d. Tenuous control by the Sayyid dynasty (1414–51), expansion and decline of Lodī dynasty (1451–1526)

　　e. Cultural and religious developments during the Delhi sultanate; *e.g.,* Islāmic and Hindu movements and education

　2. The 14th-century rise of regional kingdoms in the north: Bengal, Mālwa, Gujarāt, Jaunpur, and Kashmir

B. The Deccan (*c.* 1320–1627) and South India (1336–1646)

　1. The Deccan (*c.* 1320–1627): the Bahmanī dynasty and the five Deccan sultanates

　　a. The Bahmanī dynasty (1347–*c.* 1527): introduction of Muslims into the Deccan and their relations with the Hindus

　　b. The rise (*c.* 1500) of the five sultanates of Ahmadnagar, Berār, Bīdar, Bijāpur, and Golconda; Muslim–Hindu relations; Mughal conquests in the Deccan in the 16th century

　2. The Hindu Vijayanagar Empire (1336–1646) in South India

　　a. Foundation of the state (1336) and its expansion in South India: conflicts with Muslim dynasties in the Deccan, decentralization and decline of state

　　b. Administrative and social organization of the empire, cultural and religious development

C. The beginning of the political and administrative unification of the subcontinent under the Mughal Empire (1526–1761)

　1. The origins of the Mughals: the conquest of North India under Bābur, the Mughals' use of firearms

　2. Extension and consolidation of empire by Akbar (1556–1605)

　　a. Subjection of neighbouring territories: the conquest and annexation of Bihār, Bengal, Afghanistan, and Kashmir

　　b. Akbar's administrative, fiscal, military, judicial, and religious policies

3. The empire under Jahāngīr (1605–27), Shāh Jahān (1628–58), and Aurangzeb (1659–1707): developments in the arts and agriculture

4. Mughal decline in the 18th century: dynastic disputes and weakness after 1707 culminating in foreign invasions (1731–61)

D. The emergence of the Marāthā Empire in Mahārāshtra: rise to power and decline after 1761

1. The foundation (1674–80) of the dynasty by Śivajī: his challenge to Mughal authority in the Deccan, the Marāthā war of independence

2. The Marāthās as the major power in India in the early 18th century: the contribution of the peshwas (prime ministers) to Marāthā success, struggle with the Portuguese, establishment of the Marāthā Confederacy

E. Ceylon from *c.* 1200 to the arrival of the Portuguese (1505)

1. Political and economic changes in the Sinhalese state: collapse of central authority, foreign invasions, growth of foreign trade

2. Developments in culture and the Buddhist religion

Suggested reading in the *Encyclopædia Britannica:*

MACROPAEDIA: Major articles dealing with the Indian subcontinent from *c.* 1200 to 1761, and Ceylon from *c.* 1200 to 1505

Asia
India
Nepal
Sri Lanka

MICROPAEDIA: Selected entries of reference information

General subjects

government and society:	*historic events:*	Bharatpur	*kingdoms and states:*
Ashta Pradhan	Barāri Ghāt, Battle of	Bijāpur	Bahmanī
Cūlavaṃsa	Gogūnda, Battle of	Chandragiri	sultanate
Faṣlīera	Jājau, Battle of	Gokonda	Bundelā
Ḥabshī	Karnāl, Battle of	Gulbarga	Delhi sultanate
jāgīrdār	Pānīpat, Battles of	Kāmarūpa	Hyderābad
Mahāvaṃsa	Tālikota, Battle of	Karnātaka	Jaffna
manṣabdār	*historic regions and sites:*	Mahāvihāra	Kotte
peshwa		Mālwa	Marāthā
Pindari	Asīrgarh	Serendib	confederacy
rājākariya	Bengal	Vijayanagar	
Rājāvaliya			

Biographies

Mughal emperors:	Gaṅga dynasty	Hyder Ali	Prithvi Nārāyaṇ
Akbar	Hoysaḷa dynasty	Iltutmish	Shah
Aurangzeb	Khaljī dynasty	Muḥammad ibn	Shēr Shāh of Sūr
Bābur	Lodī dynasty	Tughluq	Sirāj-ud-Dawlah
Humāyūn	Mughal dynasty	Mu'izz-ud-Dīn	Śivajī
Jahāngīr	Slave dynasty	Muḥammad ibn	
Shah Jahān	*others:*	Sām	
ruling families:	Gobind Singh	Quṭb-ud-Dīn	
'Adil Shāhī dynasty	Ḥusayan Shāh	Aybak	
Āravīdu dynasty	'Ala' ad-Dīn		

INDEX: See entries under all of the terms above

Section 937.   The Peoples and Civilizations of Southeast Asia to *c.* 1600

A. The character and achievements of traditional Southeast Asian civilizations, South and East Asian influences, the geography and ethnography of Southeast Asia, archaeological and documentary historical sources, historiographic problems

B. Mainland Southeast Asia to *c.* 1600

   1. Myanmar (Burma) from the Anyathian culture (5000 BC–AD 1600)

     a. Origins of civilization in Myanmar: the Anyathian Stone Age culture, the Mons of southern Myanmar (*c.* 3rd century BC–11th century AD), Indian trade and cultural influences

     b. The Tibeto-Burmese invasions of the Upper Irrawaddy Valley (*c.* 500 BC) and the establishment of the Pyu state of northern Myanmar (*c.* AD 50)

     c. The city kingdom of Pagan (849–1287): the influence of Theravāda Buddhism, Pagan as a cultural centre, destruction by the Mongols (1287)

     d. Myanmar from *c.* 1300 to *c.* 1600: reunification and expansion

   2. The Thai people and the kingdom of Siam to *c.* 1500

     a. The origins and settlement of the Thais: the kingdom of Nanchao in Yunnan (8th century AD)

     b. Establishment of Thai power at Sukhothai (*c.* 1220): social and cultural developments

     c. Establishment of the Thai state of Ayutthaya (1350): organization of administrative, social, and legal systems; wars with Cambodia during the reign of King Trailok (1448–88)

     d. Laos to *c.* 1600: the Lao as a branch of the Thai people, establishment of the Lan Xang kingdom by Fa Ngum (1353–71), later rulers to 1571, successful Burmese invasion (1574)

   3. Cambodia from the prehistoric period to *c.* 1500

     a. Prehistoric peoples in Cambodia, mythological origins of kingdom of Funan (*c.* AD 100) and the influence of Indian culture

     b. Emergence of the state of Chenla and its dominance (*c.* 598) over Funan

     c. Establishment of the state of Angkor (*c.* 800) by the Khmer dynasty, Javanese influences on religion and the concept of kingship, social and administrative structures, expansion (*c.* 1113) and decline (1177) of state

     d. Jayavarman VII (1181–*c.* 1218) and the reestablishment and extension of Khmer authority

     e. Decline of the Angkor kingdom after 1220, introduction of Theravāda Buddhism, Thai invasions (1369 and 1389) and fall of city of Angkor (1444)

   4. Vietnam from the prehistoric period to *c.* 1615

     a. The legendary and historical origins of the Vietnamese people, the influence of Chinese rule (from 111 BC) on Vietnamese society

     b. The states of Funan (*c.* 1st–6th century AD) and Champa (AD 192–1471) in southern Vietnam, annexation by Nam Viet in northern Vietnam (1471)

     c. Chinese political and cultural domination of Nam Viet from 111 BC to AD 939; independence under Ly, Tran, and Le dynasties (939–1600); political unification of Nam Viet and Champa (1471); government and society in precolonial Vietnam

   5. Malaya to the 16th century AD

     a. Rise of Indianized states and their role in the formation of Malaya: the advent of Islām and the rise of the sultanate of Malacca (*c.* 1400–1511)

     b. Early European intrusions: the Portuguese conquest of Malacca (1511), Chinese aggressions in the 16th century

C. Islands of the Indonesian Archipelago to *c.* 1600

   1. The settlement of the Indonesian Archipelago: the introduction of Hinduism by Indian Brahmins

   2. The Malay kingdom of Śrivijaya in southeast Java: the influence of Buddhism, the importance of the maritime trade with China from the 7th to the 12th century

   3. Central Java in the 8th and 9th centuries: cultural, religious, and economic development during the Shailendra dynasty; the concept of divine kingship

4. Eastern Java and the rest of the archipelago from 1019 to 1292: political and cultural developments, the Singhasāri empire of Kertanagara and the royal cult

5. The Majapahit empire in eastern Java (1319–89): religious and cultural developments

6. The spread of Islām in Indonesia: the rise of Muslim states in Sumatra and Java (c. late 13th century), conflicts between Islām and older Indonesian cultures

Suggested reading in the *Encyclopædia Britannica:*

MACROPAEDIA: Major articles dealing with the peoples and civilizations of Southeast Asia to c. 1600

Asia
Indonesia
Southeast Asia, Mainland

MICROPAEDIA: Selected entries of reference information

General subjects

Myanmar, Malaya, and Siam:	Ngasaunggyan, Battle of	Dong Son culture	Majapahit empire
Dvaravati	Nong Sa Rai,	Funan	priyayi
Hlutdaw	Battle of	Lovek	Singhasāri
Mon kingdom	Pagan	Nam Viet	Tarumanegara
Mrohaung,	Sadki Na grades	Vyadhapura	
Arakanese	Śrivijaya empire	*Indonesian*	
Kingdom of	*Indochina:*	*Archipelago:*	
Nanchao	Angkor	Buginese	
	Champa	Kaḍiri	

Biographies

Myanmar, Malaya, and Siam:	Ramkhamhaeng	Ly Bon	*Indonesian*
Anwarahta	Toungoo dynasty	Ngo Quyen	*Archipelago:*
Bayinnaung	Trailok	Nguyen dynasty	Erlangga
Mahmud Shah	*Indochina:*	Setthathirat I	Gajah Mada
Malacca,	Chan	Suryavarman I	Hayam Wuruk
sultanate of	Dinh Bo Lin	Suryavarman II	Kertanagara
Mangrai	Fa Ngum	Tran dynasty	Shailendra dynasty
Narameikhla	Jayavarman VII	Tran Hung Dao	
Naresuan	Later Ly dynasty	Trung Sisters	
Ramathibodi I	Le Loi		
	Le Thanh Tong		

INDEX: See entries under all of the terms above

Division IV. Peoples and Civilizations of Sub-Saharan Africa to 1885
[For Part Nine headnote see page 343.]

The history of North Africa, because of its early involvement with Europe and Islām, is dealt with up to c. 1480 in Sections 911 and 924; and it is carried to the 19th century in Section 962. The history of Nilotic Sudan to c. AD 550 and of Ethiopia to c. AD 650 is dealt with in Section 911.

With those exceptions, the five sections of Division IV deal first with the geography and ethnology and then with the histories of the peoples and civilizations of the African continent to c. 1885.

Section 941.   **West Africa to *c.* 1885**

A. The geography and ethnography of West Africa, definition of the region, the archaeological and documentary historical sources and historiographic problems, the character and achievements of civilizations in West Africa

B. West Africa until the advent of the Europeans (*c.* AD 1500)

   1. Development of the West African monarchies of Ghana and Kanem to *c.* AD 1000

   2. Development of the western Sudan empires

      a. Emergence of the Keita dynasty of the Mali empire (*c.* 1235): Timbuktu as the cultural and commercial centre of Mali, fall of the Mali empire (*c.* late 15th century) and rise of the Songhai empire of Gao

      b. The migrations of the Fulani people, migrations and military conquests of the Mande-speaking peoples, development of trade routes by the Dyula

C. The precolonial period of European activity (*c.* 1400–*c.* 1885): exploration, development of the slave trade, and eventual collapse of indigenous states

   1. Portuguese trade with the Guinea states from *c.* 1460

   2. The rise and expansion of the Atlantic slave trade (*c.* 1600–*c.* 1860): the pattern and development of European slave trade routes, the African slave merchant class

   3. The Islāmic revolutions in the western Sudan: spiritual and military leadership of Sīdī Mukhtār (d. 1811) and Usman dan Fodio (d. 1817), the Fulani and Hausa *jihād*s (holy wars) and conquests

   4. West Africa from 1800 to *c.* 1885

      a. The Guinea coastlands and the European antislavery movements

      b. British colonial settlements from *c.* 1800: the colonies of Sierra Leone, the Gold Coast, Lagos, and Ashanti

      c. 19th-century British and French exploration of the West African interior, establishment of colonies, and exploitation of trade

---

Suggested reading in the *Encyclopædia Britannica:*

MACROPAEDIA: Major articles dealing with West Africa to *c.* 1885

   Africa
   Western Africa

MICROPAEDIA: Selected entries of reference information

General subjects

Akan states	British West Africa	Hausa states	Songhai empire
Akwamu	Dahomey	Kanem-Bornu	Tukulor empire
Ashanti empire	Djénné	Kumbi	Wolof empire
Audaghost	Fanti confederacy	Mali	
Bambara states	French West Africa	Mossi states	
Benin	Fulani empire	Oyo empire	
Bono			

Biographies

Agaja	Mūsā	Sonni 'Alī
Beecroft, John	Osei Tutu	Sumanguru
Faidherbe, Louis	Park, Mungo	Sundiata
Muhammad I	Rābiḥ az-Zubayr	'Umar Tal
Askia	Samory	Usman dan Fodio

INDEX: See entries under all of the terms above

Section 942.   **The Nilotic Sudan and Ethiopia from *c.* AD 550 to 1885**

A. The Nilotic Sudan from *c.* 550 to 1885

1. The medieval Christian kingdoms of Nobatia, Maqurrah, and 'Alwah; the Beja people

2. The spread of Muslim domination from *c.* 639: Mamlūk attacks in the 13th and 14th centuries, invasion of nomadic Arabs in the 15th century and intermarriage with Nubians, Kingdom of 'Alwah as the last Christian barrier until its conquest (*c.* 1500)

3. The rise of the Funj (*c.* 1500), the spread of Islām

4. The Egyptian occupation from 1820 to 1885: the administration of Muḥammad 'Alī and his successors, Ismā'īl Pasha and the growth of British influence

B. Ethiopia and Eritrea from *c.* AD 650 to 1855

1. The decline of the Christian Aksum empire (*c.* 600–*c.* 976): cordial relations with Islāmic states to the 8th century, conflicts with neighbouring peoples in the 9th century

2. The Zagwe dynasty (*c.* 11th century), the Solomonid restoration (1270), the influence of the Coptic Church on culture and religion

3. Contacts with the Portuguese (1520–1632) and Turkish attacks on Ethiopia (1523–43, 1578, and 1589), brief conciliation with the Roman Catholic Church (1595–1610)

4. Gonder Ethiopia (1632–1855): alliance with Egyptian Coptic Church, friendly relations with Muslims, rivalry between the Gallas and Tigreans

---

Suggested reading in the *Encyclopædia Britannica*:

MACROPAEDIA: Major articles dealing with the Nilotic Sudan and Ethiopia from *c.* AD 550 to *c.* 1885

Africa
Eastern Africa
Sudan

MICROPAEDIA: Selected entries of reference information

General subjects

Adal	Ethiopia	Kordofan
Aksum,	Funj dynasty	Sudan, The
Kingdom of	Ifat	Zagwe dynasty
Darfur		

Biographies

Aḥmad Grāñ	Gordon, Charles	Menelik II	Sahle Selassie
Amda Tseyon	George	Mikael Sehul	Yohannes IV
Covilhã, Pêro da	Mahdī, al-		

INDEX: See entries under all of the terms above

Section 943. **East Africa and Madagascar to _c._ 1885**

A. The geography and ethnography of East Africa and Madagascar: definition of the region, the archaeological and documentary historical sources and historiographic problems, the character and achievements of civilizations in East Africa

B. East Africa to _c._ 1856 and Madagascar to _c._ 1810

   1. The development of the coastal regions and of Madagascar and other offshore islands

      a. Medieval commercial contacts of Azania with Arabia, India, and the Mediterranean: the development of coastal trading cities

      b. The Shirazi dynasty (_c._ late 12th–15th century): the spread of Islām and growth of towns

      c. The Portuguese invasions and occupation from 1502: gradual expulsion of the Portuguese (1631–98), the Omani influence (_c._ 1700–1856)

      d. Madagascar from _c._ AD 1000 to 1810: early Indonesian settlement, later Muslim and African influx, kingdoms of Sakalava and Merina (1500–1810)

   2. The peoples and states of the East African interior to _c._ 1800

      a. The Stone Age origins of the East African interior peoples in the Rift Valley (now Kenya, Tanzania, and Uganda)

      b. The Iron Age settlements in the Rift Valley, the Bantu migrations and the Chwezi peoples

      c. The Somali and Galla invasions (_c._ 10th–15th century), migrations of Nilotic and Kushitic peoples (_c._ 16th–18th century)

C. East Africa from 1856 to _c._ 1900 and Madagascar from 1810 to 1896

   1. Internal developments in East Africa

      a. Development of political institutions and military kingships as defenses against Ngoni raids and Masai raiders: expansion of Rwanda and Buganda

      b. The rise of Zanzibar as the leading East African coastal power: the slave trade

      c. European exploratory and missionary activities

   2. Formation of the Kingdom of Madagascar (1810–61), English and French influences in the late 19th century

---

Suggested reading in the _Encyclopædia Britannica:_

MACROPAEDIA: Major articles dealing with East Africa and Madagascar to _c._ 1885

   Africa
   Eastern Africa

MICROPAEDIA: Selected entries of reference information

General subjects

Boina	Bunyoro	Merina	Somaliland
Buganda	Menabé	Sakalava	Zanzibar

Biographies

Barghash	Livingstone, David	Mutesa I	Zwangendaba
Kirk, Sir John	Mirambo	Saʿīd ibn Sulṭān	

INDEX: See entries under all of the terms above

Section 944.   Central Africa to *c.* 1885

A. The geography and ethnography of Central Africa, definition of the region, the archaeological and documentary historical sources and historiographic problems, the character and achievements of civilizations in Central Africa

B. Central Africa to *c.* 1885

1. The origins of Central African cultures in the Stone Age, emergence and expansion of the Bantu-speaking peoples

2. The development of the Bantu states from *c.* AD 1400: the Luba and Lunda kingdoms, the Mongo people, the Kongo (Congo) kingdom

3. Development of Portuguese hegemony over Central Africa from 1491: trade and missionary activity, military support of the Kongo kingdom, control of the slave trade, influence on Central African unity

Suggested reading in the *Encyclopædia Britannica*:

MACROPAEDIA: Major articles dealing with Central Africa to *c.* 1885

    Africa
    Central Africa

MICROPAEDIA: Selected entries of reference information

General subjects

Anziku, Kingdom of	Berlin West Africa	Kongo kingdom	Lunda Empire
Association	Conference	Kuba, Kingdom of	Ngoy, Kingdom of
Internationale	Congo Free State	Loango,	Wadai,
Africaine	Kakongo,	Kingdom of	Kingdom of
Bagirmi,	Kingdom of	Luba-Lunda states	
Kingdom of	Kazembe		

Biographies

Afonso I	Livingstone, David
Brazza, Pierre-	Msiri
Paul-François-	Stanley, Sir Henry
Camille	Morton
Savorgnan de	Tippu Tib

INDEX: See entries under all of the terms above

Section 945.   Southern Africa to *c.* 1885

A. The geography and ethnography of southern Africa: definition of the region, the archaeological and documentary historical sources and historiographic problems, the character and achievements of civilizations in southern Africa

B. Southern Africa before *c.* 1500

1. Origins of mankind and development of culture in the Stone Age and Iron Age, the migrations of Bantu-speaking peoples in southern Africa from *c.* AD 200–400

2. The southeast coast trade in the Late Iron Age and interior trade routes to Great Zimbabwe (southwestern Rhodesia), Ingombe Ilede (Zambia), and Mapungubwe (northern Transvaal)

C. Southern Africa from *c.* 1500 to *c.* 1885

1. Portuguese expansion (1530s) into the Zambezi Valley and defeat of the Mwene Mutapa's empire in 1629: Portuguese defeats (1694) by the Rozwi empire

2. The Portuguese in west central Africa: conquests over the Kongo kingdom (1681) and Ndongo kingdom (early 17th century), control of the slave trade

3. The Dutch settlement at the Cape of Good Hope from 1652: expansion toward the Orange River and relations with the Khoisans

4. Early 19th-century African migrations and rise of the Zulu Empire (1816) under Shaka, later black migrations into Rhodesia

5. The slave and ivory trade north of the Zambezi in the 19th century: decline of the slave trade in some areas and increased commerce in ivory, Yao migration into present-day Malawi, influence of missionaries

6. The Cape eastern frontier: Boer and Xhosa resistance to the British, the Boer Great Trek (1835–54) into the interior, continued friction with the British

    a. Relations between Boers and the black population in the Transvaal

    b. Establishment of the Orange Free State, the British colonies of Natal and Cape Colony

7. The era of mineral discoveries and confederation: diamonds and gold, Transvaal–Pedi and Zulu wars

8. Portuguese loss of control in Angola and Mozambique in the mid-19th century, Portuguese reemergence of control in the early 20th century, German annexation of South West Africa (1884)

Suggested reading in the *Encyclopædia Britannica*:

MACROPAEDIA: Major articles dealing with Southern Africa to *c.* 1885

> Africa
> South Africa
> Southern Africa

MICROPAEDIA: Selected entries of reference information

General subjects

Afrikaner Bond	Gun War	Maravi	Rozwi
Blood River,	Imbangala	Confederacy	Sand River and
Battle of	Isandhlwana and	Matamba	Bloemfontein
Cape Frontier	Rorke's Drift,	Mfecane	conventions
Wars	Battles of	Mozambique	uitlanders
Gaza	Kaffraria	Conventions	Zimbabwe
Great Trek	Kasanje	Mwene Matapa	Zulu War
Griqua	Lunda Empire	Ndongo	Zululand

Biographies

Brand, Sir	Gungunhana	Mswati	Rhodes, Cecil
Johannes	Joubert, Petrus	Mzilikazi	Robinson, Sir
Henricus	Jacobus	Philip, John	Hercules
Burgers, Thomas	Kruger, Paul	Potgieter, Hendrik	Sebetwane
François	Livingstone, David	Pretorius, Andries	Shaka
Cetshwayo	Lobengula	Pretorius,	Shepstone, Sir
D'Urban, Sir	Mackenzie, John	Marthinus Wessel	Theophilus
Benjamin	Mshweshwe	Retief, Piet	Sobhuza I

INDEX: See entries under all of the terms above

Division V. **Peoples and Civilizations of Pre-Columbian America**
[For Part Nine headnote see page 343.]

The subject in Section 951 is Andean civilization to *c.* 1540. The outline begins with the character and achievements of Andean civilization, with the ethnography and geography of the Andean region, and with archaeological and documentary historical sources. It goes on to the history of the pre-Inca cultures and states in the Andean region. It then deals with the empire of the Incas to the time of the Spanish conquest (1532–40).

The subject in Section 952 is Meso-American civilization to *c.* 1540. The outline begins with the geography and ethnography of Meso-America and with the character and achievements of Meso-American civilization. It goes on to the history of Meso-American civilizations until their conquest and destruction by the Spanish.

Section 951. **Andean Civilization to *c.* AD 1540**

A. The character and achievements of Andean civilization, the geography and ethnography of the Andean region, archaeological and documentary historical sources, historiographic problems

B. Pre-Inca cultures and states

1. Late Preceramic (*c.* 3500–*c.* 1800 BC) cultures: development of agriculture

2. Initial (*c.* 1800–*c.* 1000 BC) and Early Horizon, or Chavín and Paracas (*c.* 1000–*c.* 200 BC), cultures in Peru: development of textiles, pottery, and ceremonial architecture

3. Early Intermediate (Florescent, or Classic) Period (*c.* 200 BC–*c.* AD 600): metallurgy, pottery, and textile production in the Nazca and Moche cultures

4. Middle Horizon Period (*c.* AD 600–*c.* 1000): the Huari and Tiahuanaco cultures, urban settlements, cultural decline after *c.* AD 800

5. Late Intermediate Period (*c.* AD 1000–*c.* 1400): pottery and the introduction of bronze, the Chimu Empire (*c.* 1300–*c.* 1460) located at Chan Chan, spread of urban settlements

C. The empire of the Incas (*c.* 1400–*c.* 1540)

1. The origins and development of the Inca Empire

   a. The autochthonic mythical origins of the Inca dynasty, establishment of the Cuzco Valley settlement (*c.* 1400)

   b. The reigns of Capac Yupanqui, Inca Roca, Yahuar Huacac, and Viracocha Inca: Inca expansion into the Urubamba Valley and Titicaca Basin, the Chancas invasion (1438)

   c. Inca victory over the Chancas (1438), Incan civil war between Cuzco and Calca factions, Cuzco victory and reign of Pachacuti Inca Yupanqui (1438–*c.* 1471), renewed battles with Chancas (*c.* 1445), further conquest of Titicaca Basin region, victory over Chimú Empire

   d. Inca conquests during the reign of Topa Inca Yupanqui (*c.* 1471–*c.* 1493): annexation of highland Bolivia, northern Chile, northwestern Argentina, and southern Peru

   e. Reign of Huayna Capac (*c.* 1493–*c.* 1525): conquest of northeastern Peru and northern Ecuador, Atahuallpa's victory (1532) over Huascar in civil war

   f. The Spanish conquest of the Incas (1532–40): Pizarro's execution of Atahuallpa and support of Topa Huallpa (1533), later support of Manco Inca (1533–35); Manco's rebellion and defeat (1536), Spanish consolidation of power

2. Incan government, society, and culture

   a. Divine monarchy and the royal corporations, administrative hierarchy, taxation, the census and the quipu system of numerical records

   b. The settlement of people loyal to the Incas in newly conquered territories, the spy system, religious practices, military policy and organization, technology, agriculture, transportation system, calendar, oral narratives

Suggested reading in the *Encyclopædia Britannica*:

MACROPAEDIA: Major articles dealing with Andean civilization to *c.* AD 1540

Argentina	Latin America, The History of
Bolivia	Lima
Chile	Peru
Colombia	Pre-Columbian Civilizations
Ecuador	

MICROPAEDIA: Selected entries of reference information

General subjects

Andean civilization	Chavín	Inca	Pachacamac
Araucanian	Chimú	Machu Picchu	Paracas
Atacama	El Paraíso	Moche	Quechua
Chan Chan	Huari	Nazca	Tiahuanaco

Biographies

Almagro, Diego de	Huascar	Pizarro, Gonzalo
Atahualpa	Pizarro, Francisco	

INDEX: See entries under all of the terms above

Section 952.   Meso-American Civilization to *c.* AD 1540

A. The character and achievements of Meso-American civilization, the geography and ethnography of Meso-America, archaeological and documentary historical sources, historiographic problems

B. Meso-America in the Pre-Classic and Classic periods

1. The development of Meso-American civilization in the Pre-Classic periods

a. Late Pleistocene and Early Hunter (*c.* 21,000–*c.* 6500 BC) peoples of Meso-America, development of agriculture (*c.* 6500–*c.* 1500 BC)

b. Early Formative Period (*c.* 1500–*c.* 900 BC): the Ocós and Caudros settlements, the Olmec civilization at San Lorenzo (*c.* 1150–*c.* 900 BC) and development of its stone monuments

c. Middle Formative Period (*c.* 900–*c.* 300 BC): the Olmecs at La Venta (*c.* 800–*c.* 400 BC); ceremonial architecture, pottery, and writing system; colonization and trade; pre-Maya villages in Guatemala

d. Late Formative Period (*c.* 300 BC–*c.* AD 100): regionalism and cultural integration, the Cuicuilco-Tilcomán cultures in the Valley of Mexico, the Zapotecs of Oaxaca, the Izapan civilization, Mayas of the Chicanel in northern Petén

2. Maya and non-Maya Meso-America in the Classic Period (*c.* AD 100–*c.* 900)

a. Early Classic Period (*c.* AD 100–*c.* 600)

i. Teotihuacán cultural and urban development, ceremonial architecture and pottery, the Zapotecs at Monte Albán

ii. The Cotzumalhuapo culture in the Maya highlands, Tzakol and Tepeu cultures in lowland Maya civilization (*c.* AD 300–*c.* 900)

b. Late Classic non-Maya Meso-America (*c.* AD 600–*c.* 900): decline of Teotihuacán political and cultural influence, rise of Xochicalco culture, the Mixtecs of northern Oaxaca

c. Late Classic lowland Maya culture (*c.* AD 600–*c.* 900)

i. Urban settlements, temple-pyramids and palaces, Maya art, the calendar and writing system

ii. Maya religion, social and political life, the collapse of the Maya civilization (*c.* AD 900)

C. Post-Classic Period in the Valley of Mexico and the Yucatán Peninsula (*c.* 900–*c.* 1519)

1. The rise and decline of the Toltec state in southern Mexico and the Yucatán Peninsula (*c.* 900–*c.* 1200): secular and religious institutions, art and architecture, the legend of Quetzalcóatl, Toltec–Maya culture of Tollan (Tula) and Chichén-Itzá

2. The development of the Aztec state and extension of Aztec rule over the Valley of Mexico (*c.* 1325–1519): military campaigns of Itzcoatl, Montezuma I, and Ahuitzotl; administrative techniques under Montezuma II (1502–20)

3. Aztec culture and society up to the time of the Spanish conquest; *e.g.,* agriculture and technology, political organization, governmental structure, militarism, economy, religion, art and architecture

D. The Spanish conquest of the Aztec state and the Yucatán Peninsula (1519–*c.* 1540): destruction of Aztec government and culture, imposition of Spanish colonial policies and religion

---

Suggested reading in the *Encyclopædia Britannica*:

MACROPAEDIA: Major articles dealing with Meso-American civilization to *c.* AD 1540

Latin America, The History of
Mexico
Mexico City
Pre-Columbian Civilizations

MICROPAEDIA: Selected entries of reference information

General subjects

cultural centres:		*peoples:*	Yucatec Maya
Chapultepec	Palenque	Chichimec	Zapotec
Chichén Itzá	Teotihuacán	Chol	*other:*
Kaminaljuyú	Texcoco	Lacandón	Aztec calendar
Mayapán	Tikal	Maya	Mayan calendar
Mitla	Tula	Olmec	Quetzalcóatl
Monte Albán	Uxmal	Toltec	
	Xochicalco		

Biographies

Alvarado, Pedro de   Cuauhtémoc
Cortés, Hernán,   Griljalba, Juan
   marqués del Valle   Marina
   de Oaxaca   Montezuma II

INDEX: See entries under all of the terms above

Division VI.   The Modern World to 1920
[For Part Nine headnote see page 343.]

The theme of western expansion, imperialism, and colonialism pervades Division VI. The separation of the history of the modern world (*c.* 1500–*c.* 1920) into eleven sections reflects conventional regional analyses of modern history, and, within each of those sections, conventional judgments regarding turning-point dates of the regional histories.

Section 961.   Western Europe from *c.* 1500 to *c.* 1789

    A. The effects of religious and cultural change: the emergence of the nation-state system, the predominance and decline of Habsburg power centred in Spain (*c.* 1500–1648)

        1. The later Renaissance in Italy and northern Europe

           a. The influence of Italian statecraft and political theory: Machiavelli and the principle of *raison d'état*

           b. Cultural and intellectual life in the later Renaissance

        2. The Scientific Revolution: the emergence of modern science and technology in the 16th and 17th centuries

        3. The emergence of a religiously divided Europe in the 16th century

           a. The Protestant Reformation and its political and social consequences

           b. The Catholic Reformation and Counter-Reformation

        4. International diplomacy and warfare (1494–1648)

           a. The Italian Wars (1494–1516) and the concept of balance of power: French and Austro-Spanish expansionism in Italy

           b. French and Austrian struggles for supremacy in Europe (1515–59): French anti-Habsburg alliances with England, German Lutheran princes, and the Turks

           c. Conflicts between Catholic and Protestant powers after *c.* 1555: religious wars in France and the Low Countries, conflict with the Ottoman Empire

           d. The Thirty Years' War (1618–48) and the Peace of Westphalia: the end of religious struggles and resecularization of international affairs

        5. National and dynastic states (*c.* 1500–1648)

           a. Italy in the 16th and 17th centuries: political, economic, social, and cultural developments

               i. The French invasion (1494) and conquests of Naples (1495) and Milan (1499), the influence of Savonarola, the anti-French League of Venice and the Spanish defeat of France (1525)

              ii. Italy under Spanish domination: Catholic religious reforms; Spanish Habsburg rule in Naples, Sicily, Sardinia, and Milan

             iii. Relations between Spain and the independent states of Italy: Savoy, Genoa, Tuscany, Venice, and the Papal States

           b. Spain from 1516 to 1665

               i. Establishment of the Habsburg dynasty (1516) by Charles I (Holy Roman Emperor Charles V), Spanish hegemony in Europe and the Americas, domestic and foreign policies of Philip II (1556–98), the Armada (1588), cultural developments in Spain's Golden Age

              ii. Political and economic decline during the reigns of Philip III (1598–1621) and Philip IV (1621–65): expulsion of the Moriscos (1609), Olivares' administration, loss of Portugal (1640)

           c. Portugal from *c.* 1500 to 1648: domination of East Indian trade, union with Spain (1580), independence under House of Bragança (1640)

           d. The British Isles (*c.* 1485–1649)

               i. Henry VII (1485–1509): dynastic unity in England after the Wars of the Roses; political, judicial, social, and economic developments

              ii. Henry VIII (1509–47): foreign and domestic policies; the divorce question, the English Reformation, and the establishment of the Church of England; Edward VI (1547–53) and Mary I (1553–58)

             iii. Elizabeth I (1558–1603): social and cultural developments; domestic policies; dynastic challenge of Mary, Queen of Scots; struggle with Spain

             iv. James I (1603–25) of England (James VI of Scotland) and establishment of the Stuart dynasty: developments in religious doctrine, foreign relations, economic policy, and the arts; conflicts between crown and Parliament

v. Charles I (1625–49) and the English Civil War (1642–51): economic and political disputes between crown and Parliament; royal personal rule (1629–40); persecution of Puritans; the Long Parliament, Oliver Cromwell, and the Civil War; execution of Charles I (1649)

vi. Scotland in the 16th and 17th centuries: reigns of James IV and James V; Mary, Queen of Scots (1542–67), and the Scottish Reformation; John Knox and Calvinism; James VI (1567–1625) of Scotland (James I of England, 1603–25) and personal union of the two crowns

vii. Ireland in the 16th and 17th centuries: subjugation of Ireland by Henry VIII and Elizabeth I, the Irish revolt of 1641, Cromwell's invasion and anti-Catholic policies during the Commonwealth

e. France from 1483 to 1643

i. Development of a standing army and a professional bureaucracy in the reigns of Charles VIII (1483–98), Louis XII (1498–1515), Francis I (1515–47), and Henry II (1547–59)

ii. The Protestant Reformation and the French Wars of Religion (1562–98): the reigns of Catherine de Médicis (1560–74) and Henry III (1574–89), religious compromise and restoration of strong monarchy under Henry IV of Bourbon (1589–1610)

iii. The reign of Louis XIII (1610–43) and Cardinal de Richelieu: suppression of the Huguenots and the nobles, French success in the Thirty Years' War

f. Germany and the Holy Roman Empire from *c.* 1500 to 1648: the Reformation, Counter-Reformation, and Thirty Years' War

i. Maximilian I (1493–1519), Martin Luther, and the origins of Lutheranism; Charles V and the Diet and Edict of Worms (1521); the Peasants' Revolt (1524–25); diets of Speyer (1526 and 1529) and Augsburg (1530); the Schmalkaldic League and ensuing wars; abdication of Charles V (1555) and Peace of Augsburg

ii. Ferdinand I (1556–64) and Maximilian II (1564–76), internal disunity under their successors, the Thirty Years' War (1618–48), political and religious settlements of the Peace of Westphalia (1648)

g. The Swiss Confederation from 1474 to 1648

i. Swiss victory over Charles the Bold in the Burgundian War (1474–77), military prestige of the confederation, victory over Maximilian I (1499), the Italian campaigns (1499–1516)

ii. The Swiss Reformation: Zwingli and Calvin, the Counter-Reformation and emergence of Catholic and Protestant cantons, neutrality in the Thirty Years' War (1618–48), European recognition by the Peace of Westphalia (1648)

h. The Low Countries from 1494 to 1648

i. Habsburg unification of the Low Countries (1494); further consolidation under the future emperor Charles V (1506–55); economic, cultural, and religious developments; revolt of the provinces (1567–79)

ii. Establishment of the United Provinces of the Netherlands (the Dutch Republic) in 1579: leadership of the House of Orange, continued war against Spanish Habsburg power

iii. Commercial supremacy of the Dutch Republic, intermittent wars with Spain (1621–48)

iv. Cultural, social, religious, and economic developments in the Dutch Republic

i. Scandinavia from 1523 to 1648: separation of Sweden from Denmark–Norway (1523) and Dano-Swedish conflicts; Christian III of Denmark (1534–59), Gustav I Vasa (1523–60), and Gustavus II Adolphus (1611–32) of Sweden; participation in Thirty Years' War (1618–48)

B. European overseas expansion and commercial development from *c.* 1400 to 1763

1. The beginning of European imperialism: rapid expansion of European trade with and control over the non-European world after *c.* 1450

a. Advances in geographical knowledge and technological improvements; *e.g.,* ship design, navigational instruments, cartography

b. Voyages of discovery and exploration: establishment of colonial empires

i. Discovery, exploration, and early settlement of the Americas

      ii. Discovery, exploration, and early settlement of the coastal regions of Africa, Australia, India, and the East Indies

2. The decline of the feudal system and growth of commercial activity

    a. The changing relationship between tenant and landlord, agricultural developments, evolving role of the guilds, decline of Hanseatic League, demographic movements

    b. The decline in Mediterranean trade and growth of Antwerp and Amsterdam as international trade centres, the growth of a landed merchant class

3. Technological advances and pre-Industrial Revolution manufacturing systems: development of "putting-out" system and decline of guild power

4. The impact of colonial expansion on Europe

    a. Economic effects

      i. Development of new business organizations to direct colonial exploitation: joint-stock and chartered companies

      ii. The "price revolution": the relationship between the influx of precious metals from the Americas to Europe and the price rise in the 16th century

      iii. Growth of mercantilism: theories and policies of economic nationalism developed by European powers, the concept of the balance of trade

      iv. Increase in volume of world trade: the growth of the luxury trade (silks, spices, precious metals), the agricultural trade (tobacco, sugar, and coffee), the raw materials trade

      v. Development and importance of the slave trade

    b. Political effects: the relationship between Spain's status as an international power and its colonial possessions in the 16th century, colonial rivalries among European powers in the 17th and 18th centuries

C. France and Great Britain as the dominant powers in Europe, the emergence of Prussia and Austria as European powers

1. International wars and diplomacy (*c.* 1649–*c.* 1790)

    a. The Age of Louis XIV (1661–1715): French successes in the War of Devolution (1667–68) and the Dutch War (1672–79), defeat in the War of the League of Augsburg (1689–97) and the War of the Spanish Succession (1701–14)

    b. Development of the alliance system: the balance of power

      i. The Quadruple Alliance: the emergence of Prussia and Austria as European powers, the War of the Austrian Succession (1740–48)

      ii. The Seven Years' War (1756–63) and France's defeat and loss of colonial territory in the Americas

      iii. French recovery and Franco-Spanish cooperation (1778–81) against Britain in the U.S. War of Independence, Russian-Prussian partition of Poland (1772)

2. The European states (*c.* 1648–*c.* 1790)

    a. Great Britain from 1649 to *c.* 1790

      i. Oliver Cromwell, the Commonwealth, and the Protectorate (1649–60); the Stuart Restoration (1660) under Charles II (1660–85) and James II (1685–88); the Glorious Revolution of 1688 and end of crown rule without Parliament

      ii. Limited monarchy under William III (1689–1702) and Mary II (1689–94) and Anne (1702–14); growth of Whig and Tory political parties (1689–1714); the Hanoverian succession and emergence of the cabinet system under George I and George II; Whig supremacy and political stability to 1760; ministries of Walpole, Pelham, and Pitt

      iii. Early years of George III's reign (1760–1820) to *c.* 1790: eclipse of Whig power and political instability (1760–70), failure of colonial policies and U.S. War of Independence, beginning of parliamentary and reform movements

      iv. Economic, cultural, and social developments: agricultural innovations, population growth, origins of the Industrial Revolution and factory system, influence of Methodism

      v. Formal union of England and Scotland (1707), Edinburgh's status as an intellectual centre, Protestant Ascendancy in Ireland and growth of Irish patriotism among the Anglo-Irish, Wales in the 18th century

    b. France from *c.* 1650 to *c.* 1790

ii. Social and economic conditions in the Scandinavian countries

iii. Denmark–Norway losses in the First Northern War with Sweden (1655–60); economic stagnation (1720–66), "Enlightened" reforms under Christian VII (1766–1808), Struensee, and Bernstorff; revival of settlement in Greenland (1714)

iv. Growth of parliamentary government in Sweden: Frederick I (1720–51) and Adolf Frederick (1751–71), the "Hats" and "Nightcaps" political parties, absolutism reestablished by Gustav III (1771–92)

i. The Swiss Confederation (*c.* 1650–1790): Villmergen wars (1656–1712), the influence of the Enlightenment

3. The age of the Enlightenment

a. Origins in the 17th century: Scientific achievements, developments in political and religious philosophies, developments in the arts

b. Expansion in the 18th century: the spread of religious, political, economic, and scientific theories in western Europe; cultural developments

---

Suggested reading in the *Encyclopædia Britannica*:

MACROPAEDIA: Major articles and biographies dealing with Western Europe from *c.* 1500 to *c.* 1789

Albania	Denmark	Greece	Manchester
Amsterdam	Dublin	Habsburg, The	Marseille
Antwerp	Edinburgh	House of	Milan
Arctic, The	Elizabeth I of	Hamburg	Naples
Athens	England	Holy Roman	Netherlands, The
Austria	European History	Empire, The	Norway
Bacon, Francis	and Culture	History of the	Paris
Barcelona	European Overseas	Hungary	Portugal
Belgium	Exploration and	Iceland	Rome
Berlin	Empires, The	Ireland	Spain
Bourbon, The	History of	Italy	Sweden
House of	Finland	Lisbon	Switzerland
Brussels	Florence	London	United Kingdom
Cologne	France	Luther	Venice
Columbus	Frederick the Great	Luxembourg	Vienna
Cromwell, Oliver	Geneva	Madrid	
Czechoslovakia	Germany	Malta	

MICROPAEDIA: Selected entries of reference information

General subjects

cultural and economic:	Bavarian Succession,	Medina del Campo, Treaty of	Russo-Turkish Wars
Baroque period	War of the	Mohács, Battle of	Seven Years' War
bullionism	Belgrade, Treaty of	Neva, Battle of the	Silesian Wars
Classicism and	Blenheim, Battle of	Nordlingen,	Spanish
Neoclassicism	Breda, Treaty of	Battle of	Succession, War
Enlightenment	Cambrai,	Northern War,	of the
mercantilism	League of	First	Stolbovo, Treaty of
philosophe	Carlowitz,	Northern War,	Thirty Years' War
physiocrat	Treaty of	Second	Utrecht, treaties of
Renaissance	Cateau-Cambresis,	Oudenaarde,	Vienna, Siege of
international relations:	Peace of	Battle of	Westphalia,
Åbo, Treaty of	Devolution,	Paris, Treaty of	Peace of
Aix-la-Chapelle,	War of	(1763)	Wittstock, Battle of
Treaty of	Dutch War	Pavia, Battle of	*national affairs—*
Altranstädt,	Fontenoy, Battle of	Poland,	*Britain:*
treaties of	Grand Alliance,	Partition of	Armada
Anglo-Dutch War	War of the	Pragmatic Sanction	Bishops' Wars
Austrian	Lepanto, Battle of	of Charles VI	Boyne, Battle
Succession, War	Lützen, Battle of	Pyrenees, Peace	of the
of the	Madrid, Treaty of	of the	cabal
	Marignano,	Ramillies, Battle of	Clarendon Code
	Battle of	Rocroi, Battle of	

Biographies

Cleveland, Barbara
Villiers, duchess of
Clive, Robert, 1st
baron Clive of
Plassey
Conway, Henry
Seymour
Cook, James
Cotton, Sir
Robert Bruce,
1st baronet
Cranmer, Thomas
Cromwell,
Oliver
Cromwell,
Richard
Cromwell,
Thomas, earl
of Essex
Darnley,
Henry Stewart,
Lord
Davison,
William
Digby,
Sir Kenelm
Drake,
Sir Francis
Edward VI
Eliot, Sir John
Elizabeth I
Essex, Robert
Devereux, 2nd
earl of
Fairfax of
Cameron,
Thomas Fairfax,
3rd Baron
Fawkes, Guy
Fisher, Saint John
Flood, Henry
Fox, Charles James
Gage, Thomas
Gardiner, Stephen
George I
George II
George III
Gilbert, Sir
Humphrey
Godolphin, Sidney
Godolphin,
earl of
Gowrie, John
Ruthven, 3rd
earl of
Grafton, Augustus
Henry Fitzroy,
3rd duke of
Grattan, Henry
Grenville, George
Grey, Lady Jane
Gwyn, Nell
Hakluyt, Richard

Hamilton, John
Hamilton, 1st
marquess of
Hampdon, John
Hastings, Warren
Hawkins, Sir John
Henderson,
Alexander
Henrietta Maria
Henry VII
Henry VIII
Howe, Richard
Howe, earl
Hudson, Henry
Huntly, George
Gordon, 1st
marquess and 6th
earl of
Hutchinson,
Thomas
James I (Britain)
James II (Britain)
James IV
(Scotland)
James V (Scotland)
Jane Seymour
Jeffreys (of Wem),
George Jeffreys,
1st baron
Knox, John
Lambert, John
Latimer, Hugh
Laud, William
Leeds, Thomas
Osborne, 1st
Duke of
Leicester, Robert
Dudley, earl of
Leven, Alexander
Leslie, 1st Earl of
Lilburne, John
Lovat, Simon
Fraser, 11th Lord
Maitland (of
Lethington),
William
Marlborough, John
Churchill, 1st
Duke of
Marlborough,
Sarah Jennings,
Duchess of
Mary (Queen of
Scots)
Mary I
Mary II
Masham, Abigail,
Lady Masham
Monck, George,
1st duke of
Albemarle
Monmouth, James
Scott, duke of

Montagu, Ralph
Montagu, 1st
duke of
Moray, James
Stewart, 1st
Earl of
More, Sir Thomas
Morton, James
Douglas, 4th
Earl of
Newcastle
(-upon-Tyne),
William
Cavendish, 1st
Duke of
Norfolk, Thomas
Howard, 3rd
Duke of
Norfolk, Thomas
Howard, 4th
Duke of
Northampton,
Henry Howard,
Earl of
Northumberland,
John Dudley,
Duke of
Oates, Titus
O'Donnell, Manus
O'Neill, Owen Roe
O'Neill, Shane
Ormonde, James
Butler, 12th earl
and 1st duke of
Oxford, Robert
Harley, 1st
Earl of
Pitt, William, the
Elder
Pole, Reginald
Pole, Richard de la
Portsmouth,
Louise-Renée
de Kéroualle,
Duchess of
Prynne, William
Pym, John
Raffles, Sir
Stamford
Raleigh, Sir Walter
Riccio, David
Rupert, Prince
Sackville (of
Drayton), George
Sackville-Germain,
1st Viscount
Saint John, Oliver
Salisbury, Robert
Cecil, 1st earl of
Sandwich, Edward
Montagu, 1st
Earl of

Saye and Sele,
William Fiennes,
1st viscount
Schomberg,
Frederick
Herman, duke of
Seymour (of
Sudley), Thomas
Seymour, Baron
Shaftesbury,
Anthony Ashley
Cooper, 1st
Earl of
Shrewsbury,
Charles Talbot,
duke and 12th
earl of
Somerset, Edward
Seymour, 1st
duke of
Stanhope, James
Stanhope, 1st earl
Stirling, William
Alexander, 1st
earl of
Strafford, Thomas
Wentworth, 1st
earl of
Stuart, House of
Sussex, Thomas
Radcliffe, 3rd
earl of
Tudor, House of
Tyrconnell, Rory
O'Donnell, 1st
Earl of
Tyrone, Conn
O'Neill,
1st earl of
Tyrone, Hugh
O'Neill, 2nd
earl of
Vane, Sir Henry,
the Younger
Walpole, Robert,
1st earl
of Orford
Walsingham, Sir
Francis
Wildman,
Sir John
Wilkes, John
William III
Winthrop,
John
Wolsey, Thomas,
Cardinal
Wyat, Sir
Thomas, the
Younger
France:
Anne of
Austria

Doria family
Este, House of
Farnese family
Ferdinand I
(Tuscany)
Ferdinand II
(Tuscany)
Fieschi family
Fieschi,
Gian Luigi
Francis (I)
(Tuscany)
Gonzaga dynasty
Guicciardini,
Francesco
Julius II (pope)
Leo X (pope)
Machiavelli,
Niccolò
Medici family
Medici,
Giovanni de'
Medici,
Lorenzino de'
Morosimi family
Savoy, House of
Sforza family
Sixtus V (pope)
Low Countries:
Coen, Jan
Pieterszoon
Diemen,
Anthony van
Egmond,
Lamoraal,
graaf van
Farnese,
Alessandro,
duca di Parma e
Piacenza
Frederick Henry,
prince of Orange
Hembyze, Jan van
Heyn, Piet
Hoorne, Filips van
Montmorency,
Graaf van

John Maurice of
Nassau
John William Friso
Louis of Nassau
Margaret of
Austria
Maurice
Oldenbarnevelt,
Johan van
Orange, House of
Ruyter, Michiel
Adriaanszoon de
Tasman, Abel
Janszoon
Tromp, Maarten
William I
William II
William III
William IV
William V
William Louis
Witt, Johan de
Portugal:
Albuquerque,
Afonso de, the
Great
Cabral, Pedro
Álvares
Covilhã, Pêro da
Dias, Bartolomeu
Gama, Vasco da,
1er conde da
Vidigueira
Henry the
Navigator
Magellan,
Ferdinand
Pombal, Sebastião
de Carvalho,
marquês de
Scandinavia:
Adolf Frederick
(Sweden)
Armfelt, Gustaf
Mauritz
Charles IX
(Sweden)

Charles X Gustav
(Sweden)
Charles XI
(Sweden)
Charles XII
(Sweden)
Christian II
(Denmark)
Christian III
(Denmark)
Christian IV
(Denmark)
Christina
De la Gardie,
Jacob Pontusson,
Greve
Frederick I
(Sweden)
Frederick I
(Denmark)
Frederick II
(Denmark)
Frederick III
(Denmark)
Gustav I Vasa
(Sweden)
Gustav II Adolf
(Sweden)
Gustav III
(Sweden)
John III (Sweden)
Oxenstierna (af
Södermöre), Axel,
Greve
Oxenstierna, Bengt
Gabrielsson,
Greve
Spain:
Alba, Fernando
Álvarez de
Toledo y
Pimentel, 3er
duque de
Alberoni, Giulio
Balboa, Vasco
Núñez de
Bonaparte, Joseph

Charles I
Charles II
Charles III
Farnese,
Alessandro,
duca di Parma e
Piacenza
Ferdinand V
Ferdinand VI
Floridablanca,
José Moñino
y Redondo,
conde de
Juan de Austria
Juan José de
Austria
Margaret of
Angoulême
Margaret
of Austria
Olivares, Gaspar
de Guzmán
y Pimental,
conde-duque de
Orry, Jean
Pérez, Antonio
Philip I
Philip II
Philip III
Philip IV
Philip V
Riperdá, Juan
Guillermo
Riperdá,
duque de
Santa Cruz,
Alvaro de
Bazán,
Marqués de
Soto,
Hernando de
Vespucci,
Amerigo

Section 962. **Eastern Europe, Southwest Asia, and North Africa from *c.* 1480 to *c.* 1800**

A. The Christian states of eastern Europe

  1. Poland–Lithuania (1492–1795): gradual weakening of the monarchy, decline and dismemberment of the state

    a. The Golden Age of the Polish–Lithuanian empire (1492–1572)

      i. Foreign relations: Ottoman invasions, Russian invasion of Lithuania, alliance with Turks (1533) and reestablishment of Polish security, renewed Russian aggression

      ii. Domestic developments: population movements, constitutional reform, prosperous foreign trade, exploitation of the peasantry and their reduction to serfdom, effects of the Renaissance and the Reformation

    b. Establishment of the royal republic (1572–1648)

      i. The Interregnum (1572–75) and reform of the monarchy: Stephen Bathory (1575–86) and Sigismund III Vasa (1587–1632), indecisive wars with Sweden for possession of the Baltic region

      ii. Władysław IV Vasa (1632–48): the Cossack revolt, economic prosperity, increased power of the nobility, effect of the Counter-Reformation

    c. The period of wars and disintegration (1648–97): the Cossack–Russian and Swedish invasions in the reign of John II Casimir (1648–68), loss of Ducal Prussia to Brandenburg (1657), Michael Wiśniowiecki (1669–73), John III Sobieski's (1674–96) victories over the Turks

    d. The Saxonian era, the Russian Protectorate, and the partitions of Poland among Russia, Prussia, and Austria

      i. The reigns of Augustus II (1697–1733) and Augustus III (1733–63): participation in the Great Northern War, relations with Prussia, the Seven Years' War (1756–63)

      ii. The reign of Stanisław II August Poniatowski (1764–95): the Confederation of Bar, reform, the partitions of Poland (1772, 1793, and 1795)

  2. Hungary: the Jagiellon kings (1490–1526) and the partition period (1526–1699)

    a. The peasant revolt (1514), defeat by the Ottoman Turks at Battle of Mohács (1526)

    b. Division into Ottoman and Habsburg sectors in the 16th century, the spread of Protestantism, the Fifteen Years' War, the rise of Transylvania, defeat of the Turks (1686) and subjection of all Hungary to the Habsburgs in 1699

  3. Emergence of the Russian Empire (*c.* 1500–1796)

    a. Extension of Muscovite control over Russia under Vasily III (1505–33), Ivan IV the Terrible (1533–84), and Boris Godunov (1598–1605); civil revolt in the Time of Troubles (1598–1613)

    b. The Romanov Muscovy: election of Michael Romanov as tsar (1613) and continued autocracy under his successors, expansion into the Ukraine, 17th-century cultural and religious life

    c. The beginning of westernization and further expansion under Peter I the Great (1689–1725): the Petrine state

      i. The Table of Ranks and the new nobility: reform of the clerical hierarchy, urban legislation, building of St. Petersburg, conquest of the Baltic provinces

      ii. Development of Russia's status as a European power in Peter's reign: westernization of its culture

      iii. Peter I's weak successors: Anna (1730–40) and Elizabeth (1741–62)

    d. Further westernization and expansion under Catherine II the Great (1762–96): partitions of Poland and successful wars against the Ottoman Empire

    e. Education and social change in the 18th century: the impact of the Enlightenment

B. The Islāmic states of eastern Europe, Southwest Asia, and North Africa

  1. The Ottoman Empire from 1481 to 1807, Morocco from 1459 to 1830

    a. The Ottoman Empire as the dominant power of Southwest Asia and southeastern Europe (1481–1566)

     i. Consolidation of the empire in the reign of Bayezid II (1481–1512), Selim I's (1512–20) successes against Iran and seizure of Syria and Egypt, Süleyman I's (1520–66) conflicts with the Habsburgs in Hungary and annexation of Iraq

     ii. Classical Ottoman society and administration: the class structure, the *mukata'a*, religious and civil law

  b. Decline of the Ottoman Empire (1566–1807): corruption and nepotism

     i. Foreign relations: conflicts with the Russians, Austrians, and Iranians

     ii. Attempts at reform in government administration; defeats by Poles, Habsburgs, and Russians

  c. Imperial disintegration in the 18th and early 19th centuries: westernization and rise of local rulers

  d. Morocco: disunity after the fall of the Marīnid dynasty, the anti-Portuguese policy of the Sa'dī of Marrakesh, increasing isolation under the 'Alawī dynasty (1659–1830)

2. Iran and Afghanistan

  a. Iran from *c.* 1500 to 1779

     i. The rise of the Shī'ite Ṣafavid dynasty: conflict with the Turks, possession of western Afghanistan, disintegration and later restoration of the state by 'Abbās I (1587–1629), relations with European powers, decline and foreign invasions in the later 17th century, the arts under the Ṣafavids

     ii. The expulsion (1730–32) of the Afghans, Russians, and Turks by Nādir Shāh; invasions of India and Turkistan (1738–39); attempts to unite Shī'ite and Sunnī Muslims; establishment of Zand and Qājār dynasties

  b. Afghanistan from *c.* 1500 to 1812: national awakening and rise of Afghan power in the early 18th century, subjection by Nādir Shāh (1732), establishment of the Durrānī dynasty (1747), intrusions in India and involvement in British affairs

---

Suggested reading in the *Encyclopædia Britannica*:

MACROPAEDIA: Major articles and biographies dealing with Eastern Europe, Southwest Asia, and North Africa from *c.* 1480 to *c.* 1800

Afghanistan	Cairo	Jerusalem	Saint Petersburg
Africa	Cyprus	Jordan	Steppe, The
Alexandria	Czechoslovakia	Lebanon	History of the
Arabia	Damascus	Moscow	Eurasian
Asia	Egypt	North Africa	Syria
Austria	European History	Palestine	Turkey
Baghdad	and Culture	Peter I the Great,	Union of Soviet
Baltic States	Hungary	of Russia	Socialist
Beirut	Iran	Poland	Republics
Budapest	Iraq	Prague	Warsaw
Bulgaria	Istanbul	Romania	Yugoslavia

MICROPAEDIA: Selected entries of reference information

General subjects

international:	Livonian War	Three Kings,	nizam-ı cedid
Åbo, Treaty of	Mohács, Battle of	Battle of the	Ottoman Empire
Altranstädt,	Northern War,	Transylvania	pasha
treaties of	First	Vienna, Siege of	Phanariote
Andrusovo,	Northern War,	Zenta, Battle of	Rumelia
Truce of	Second	*Ottoman Empire:*	Sublime Porte
Baltic states	Podolia	aga	vizier
Belgrade, Treaty of	Poland,	Aleppo	*Poland:*
Beresteczko,	Partitions of	'ayn	Bar,
Battle of	Polish Succession,	bey	Confederation of
capitulation	War of the	derebey	Galicia
Chāldirān,	Russo-Turkish wars	dey	Henrician Articles
Battle of	Silesia	Janissary	Warsaw,
Deulino, Truce of	Stolbovo, Treaty of	Jelālī Revolts	Compact of
Lepanto, Battle of		kanun	

Zebrzydowski Rebellion

Russian Empire:
Catherine the Great, Instruction of
Cossack

Gentry, Charter to the grand duke
oprichnina
pale
Pereyaslav Agreement

streltsy
Troubles, Time of
tsar
Ukraine
zemsky sobor
other:
'Abid al-Bukhārī

Barbary pirate
Dózsa Rebellion
dragoman
Peacock Throne
Wesselényi Conspiracy

Biographies

Hungary:
Bethlen, Gábor
Esterházy family
Ferdinand II
John

Iran:
'Abbās I
Ismā'īl I
Nādir Shāh
Şafavid dynasty
Zand dynasty

Ottoman Empire:
Bayezid II
Köprülü Fazıl Ahmed Paşa
Köprülü Mehmed Paşa
Mahmud I
Selim I
Selim II
Selim III
Süleyman I

Poland:
Augustus II
John III Sobieski
Kościuszko, Tadeusz
Sigismund I

Sigismund II Augustus
Sigismund III Vasa
Stanisław I
Stanisław II August Poniatowski
Stephen Báthory
Władysław IV Vasa
Zamoyski family

Russia:
Alexis
Anna
Bering, Vitus
Bestuzhev-Ryumin, Aleksey Petrovich, Graf
Biron, Ernst Johann, Reichsgraf von
Catherine II
Chirikov, Aleksey Ilich
Dmitry, false
Dolgoruky, Vasily Lukich, Knyaz
Dolgoruky, Vasily Vladimirovich, Knyaz
Dolgoruky family

Elizabeth
Godunov, Boris
Golitsyn, Vasily Vasilyevich, Knyaz
Golovkin, Gavriil Ivanovich, Graf
Gordon, Patrick
Ivan IV
Khmelnitsky, Bohdan
Križanić, Juraj
Michael
Münnich, Burkhard Christoph, Graf von
Ordyn-Nashchokin, Afanasy Lavrentyevich
Orlov, Grigory Grigoryevich, Graf
Osterman, Andrey Ivanovich, Graf
Panin, Nikita Ivanovich, Graf

Peter III
Potemkin, Grigory Aleksandrovich
Pugachov, Yemelyan Ivanovich
Razin, Stenka
Repnin, Nikolay Vasilyevich, Knyaz
Romanov dynasty
Shcherbatov, Mikhayl Mikhaylovich
Sophia
Stroganov family
Suvorov, Aleksandr Vasilyevich, Graf
Tolstoy, Pyotr Andreyevich, Graf
Vasily (IV) Shuysky
Vorontsov, Mikhail Illarionovich
other:
Aḥmad Shāh Durrānī
Āl Bū Sa'īd dynasty
Bashir Shihab II
Ismā'īl

INDEX: See entries under all of the terms above

Section 963.   Europe from 1789 to *c.* 1920

A. European political and economic revolution (1789–1850): the French Revolution and its effects, the development and effects of industrialization

1. The French Revolution and its reverberating effects on Europe (1789–1815)

   a. The climate of change: "patriotism" in America and the Netherlands (1770–90)

   b. France from 1789 to 1815: the Revolution, the First Republic, and the First Napoleonic Empire

      i. The revolt of the Third Estate: uprisings in Paris and the provinces, the reforms of the Constituent Assembly, abolition of the monarchy, Marat and the Jacobins, the Legislative Assembly

      ii. The First Republic to 1795: the Convention, Danton, Robespierre, the Committee of Public Safety and the Terror, the Thermidorian reaction

      iii. The directories (1795–99) and the rise of Napoleon Bonaparte: as first consul (1799–1804) and emperor (1804), the Code Napoléon and reconciliation with the church

      iv. France under the Napoleonic First Empire: social, economic, and religious reforms

   c. International war and diplomacy in the Age of the French Revolution

      i. The War of the First Coalition (1792–97): French support for revolution in neighbouring lands and annexation of Nice, Savoy, Austrian Netherlands, the Rhineland, and the Batavian Republic; Napoleon's Italian Campaign; the Treaty of Campo Formio (1797)

      ii. The French expedition to Egypt and Syria (1798–1802): Continental campaigns of the Second Coalition (1798–1802), French occupation of Rome and Naples, Marengo and Hohenlinden, Peace of Lunéville (1801) and Treaty of Amiens (1802), Napoleon's reorganization of the German states and the formal end of the Holy Roman Empire (1806)

      iii. The Third Coalition (1805–07) and the battles of Trafalgar, Austerlitz, Jena, and Friedland: the subjugation of Prussia, Treaty of Tilsit (1807) and the peak of Napoleon's power, the Continental System and its failure

      iv. The Franco-Austrian War (1809), the Spanish uprising and the Peninsular War (1808–14), Napoleon's defeat in the Russian campaign (1812) and the campaign of the Fourth Coalition, downfall (1814) and exile of Napoleon

      v. The Hundred Days and Napoleon's final defeat at Waterloo (1815), the Congress of Vienna and Metternich's attempt to restore the old order in Europe

d. Political, economic, and social effects of French occupation in Germany, Italy, Switzerland, and the Low Countries

e. Great Britain from 1789 to 1815

      i. The influence of the French Revolution on the growth of English radicalism: governmental hostility to reform, Pitt's ministries and the war with France, Canning and Castlereagh, British gains in the peace settlements

      ii. Suppression of the Irish Rebellion of 1798 and union of Great Britain and Ireland (1801): Irish social, economic, and cultural life in the 17th and 18th centuries

f. Russia in the reigns of Paul I (1796–1801) and Alexander I (1801–25): Russian participation in the Napoleonic Wars, the initial liberal reforms of Alexander I

g. Prussia (1786–1815)

      i. Military decline following the death of Frederick II the Great: participation in the French Revolutionary Wars, defeat by Napoleon in 1806

      ii. The Stein reforms: Prussian leadership of Germany in the wars of liberation (1813–14), territorial acquisitions in the Vienna peace settlement (1815)

h. Austria (1790–1815): the reigns of Leopold II (1790–92) and Francis II (1792–1806; as emperor of Austria, Francis I, 1804–35); participation in the coalitions against Napoleon, shift to compliance with him, and eventual intervention in the wars of liberation

i. The smaller German states under French influence: the Confederation of the Rhine

j. Spain and Portugal

      i. Spain in the reign of Charles IV (1788–1808), French occupation (1808) and British aid in the War of Independence (Peninsular War), restoration of the Bourbons

      ii. Portugal: alliance with Britain in the struggle against France

k. Scandinavia from 1789 to 1815

      i. Denmark: defeat by the British (1801), alliance with France after 1807, the loss of Norway to Sweden (1814)

      ii. Sweden: Gustav IV and Charles XIII, the loss of Finland to Russia (1809), installation of Bernadotte as crown prince (1810), his anti-Napoleonic policy and the acquisition of Norway

l. Italy during the French Revolution: support of revolutionary goals, French invasion and establishment of the republics, the French Consulate and the Napoleonic Empire

2. Pan-European developments in the first half of the 19th century: economic, intellectual, cultural, and social movements

a. The Industrial Revolution

      i. British commercial, agricultural, and military growth: the factory system and advances in textile and machine technology, development of railroads

      ii. Conditions on the Continent and the spread of the factory system to Belgium, France, and Germany

    iii. The social consequences of the Industrial Revolution: division between capitalist and worker, wages and living and working conditions, new abundance of manufactured goods

b. The legacy of the French Revolution: cultural nationalism, populism, influence of Napoleon

c. The Romantic movement: individualism and concern for nature and "folk" in contrast with the Enlightenment

d. New facilities for scientific study in France and other Continental countries: effects of technological developments and scientific thought on society, principle of evolution

e. Philosophy: the role of Immanuel Kant and his disciples (Fichte, Hegel, and Schopenhauer), German Idealism

f. Religion and its alternatives: Catholic and Protestant revivals, Jewish emancipation, scientific positivism and the cult of art

g. The beginning of "scientific history" and modern philology

h. International war and diplomacy in the age of Metternich

    i. Congress of Europe: the Quadruple and Holy alliances for maintenance of the Vienna settlement, French intervention in Spain (1823), Austrian intervention in Italy (1821 and 1830), changes in the Congress system with the Revolution of 1830 in France and Belgium

    ii. General European unrest: the revolutions of 1848 and their suppression, Austrian intervention in Italy, Russian intervention in Hungary

i. Great Britain and Ireland (1815–50)

    i. Economic depression and social unrest following the Napoleonic Wars: repression by the government

    ii. Political and social reform measures (1822–48); *e.g.,* penal reforms, Catholic Emancipation (1829), Peel's new police force (1829), First Reform Bill (1832), abolition of slavery in British colonies (1833), new Poor Law (1834), repeal of the Corn Laws (1846), Navigation Acts, the Chartist movement, the growth of trade unionism and the Factory Act (1847), Public Health Act (1848)

    iii. Developments in Ireland: the Great Famine of the 1840s, Roman Catholic unrest, O'Connell and the Young Ireland movement

j. France from 1814 to 1852

    i. The Restoration (1814, 1815–30): moderate constitutionalism under Louis XVIII, reaction and clericalism under Charles X

    ii. The Revolution of 1830, Louis-Philippe and the July monarchy, the preservation of the status quo under Guizot, growing dissatisfaction with the regime in the 1840s

    iii. The Revolution of 1848: Socialist thought and the establishment of the Second Republic, suppression of Socialist experiments, presidency of Louis-Napoléon

k. Germany from 1815 to *c.* 1850

    i. The German Confederation: Austrian domination under Metternich, the student national unity movement and its repression by the Carlsbad Decrees (1819), beginning of industrialization and the Zollverein

    ii. The revolutions of 1848–49: the Frankfurt National Assembly and its failure to unite Germany

    iii. Frederick William IV: restoration of the German Confederation, return to conservative policies, continued industrialization

l. The Austrian Empire from 1815 to 1850

    i. Development of national consciousness among the peoples of the empire: cultural revival among Magyars, Croats, Serbians, Poles, Romanians, Czechs, Slovaks, and Slovenes; German and Italian nationalism

    ii. Metternich's hostility to liberalism: Austria as a symbol of reaction in Italy

    iii. The revolutions of 1848 and 1849 in Vienna, Prague, and Budapest

m. The Italian states from 1815 to 1850

    i. The Vienna settlement: the Austrian Habsburgs in Lombardy–Venetia, the Bourbons in the Two Sicilies, Victor Emmanuel in Savoy, the Carbonari

ii. Abortive revolutions in Naples and Piedmont (1820); economic slump and revival; rebellions in Modena, Parma, the Romagna, the Marches, and Umbria (1831)

iii. The *Risorgimento:* Mazzini, Young Italy, and Young Europe; the early liberalism of Pope Pius IX

iv. The revolutions of 1848: the first phase of the Italian War of Independence, defeat of Piedmont by Austria (1848–49)

n. Switzerland from 1815 to 1860: conservative constitution of 1815, the Sonderbund War (1847), the new federal state established (1848–60), policy of neutrality

o. Russia from 1815 to *c.* 1850: later conservatism of Alexander I, the Decembrist revolt (1825), Nicholas I's (1825–55) conservative policies

i. Rule by bureaucracy, social classes, intellectual life, the empire and its various nationalities

ii. Foreign policy: conflict with Poland, relations with Turkey

p. The Low Countries from 1814 to 1848: union of The Netherlands, Luxembourg, and Belgium (1814); Belgian Revolution (1830) and establishment as a separate monarchy under Leopold I (1831–65); constitutional reform (1848) in The Netherlands

q. Spain and Portugal from 1815 to 1850

i. Spain under Ferdinand VII, revolution and abortive liberal government (1820–23), loss of South American empire (1820s), Isabella II and the succession dispute, First Carlist War (1833–39) and the "Spanish marriages" controversy

ii. Portuguese loss of Brazil (1822), civil war between constitutionalists and absolutists (1832–34), British intervention (1826–34), Maria II (1834–53) and civil strife between Septembrists and Saldanha

r. Scandinavia from 1815 to 1850

i. Denmark in the reigns of Frederick VI (1808–39) and Christian VIII (1839–48): beginning of economic problems, tendencies toward constitutional government culminating in the constitution of 1849, war over Schleswig-Holstein (1848–51)

ii. Developments in Sweden–Norway: conservative era under Charles XIV John (1818–44), liberal reforms after 1840 and under Oscar I (1844–59), Norway's struggle to assert independence from Sweden

iii. Finland and Iceland: Finnish political organization and Russian influence, the position of Iceland after the Treaty of Kiel (1814)

s. The Balkan states from *c.* 1804 to 1850

i. Serbian uprising (1804–13) and the rise of the principality, restoration of Ottoman power in Serbia (1813–15), Serbian autonomy (1830) under Ottoman Empire, Miloš Obrenović recognized as prince of Serbia (1833–39) and government of Alexander Karageorge (1842–58)

ii. Greek revolution (1821–30) and establishment of independence, internal strife under Otho I (1832–62), constitutional government introduced in 1843

B. Realism and materialism, nationalism, the reorganization of Europe, imperialist expansion (1850–*c.* 1920)

1. European cultural and economic life from 1850 to 1920

a. Philosophy and political and social thought: the prevalence of Determinism and Materialism

b. Developments in the arts, philosophy, and religion

c. Scientific theory and practice: Einsteinian relativity, the social effects of medical advances, development of the behavioral sciences, new views of the universe

d. Economic life: the course of industrialization (1870–1914)

i. Industrial proliferation: expansion into new areas such as the U.S., eastern Europe, and Japan

ii. Changing balance of economic power in Europe: emergence of Germany as the leading industrial power, decline of British industrial strength

iii. The revolution in transportation and communications: steam navigation and the beginning of air travel; the internal-combustion engine; the telegraph, telephone, and radio; industrialization on the eve of World War I

2. International war and diplomacy from 1850 to *c.* 1920: *Realpolitik* and European diplomatic realignments

   a. The era of Italian and German unification

      i. Final dissolution of the Congress of Vienna alliance system: the Crimean War (1853–56) and its aftermath

      ii. The Italian War of Independence: French intervention against Austria in Italy, the establishment of the Kingdom of Italy (1861)

      iii. Bismarck and the creation of the German Empire: victories over Denmark (1864), Austria (1866), and France (1870–71)

   b. The first period of German predominance

      i. Bismarck's system of alliances: the Dreikaiserbund and the isolation of France, the Russo-Turkish War (1877–78) and the Congress of Berlin (1878–79), the Triple Alliance (1882)

      ii. The Franco-Russian alliance (from 1893) and the Entente Cordiale (1904): Russia's defeat in the Far East (1904–05) and the formation of the Triple Entente (1907)

      iii. Prelude to World War I: the Moroccan and Bosnian crises, the Balkan Wars (1912–13), the outbreak of war between the great powers (1914)

   c. The resurgence of European imperialism (*c.* 1875–1914)

      i. Renewed interest in overseas expansion by the European powers in the late 19th century: new acquisitions and new colonial powers, development of new theories of imperialism

      ii. The European penetration of Asia and the partitioning of Africa: Russian expansion, economic penetration of China, rise of Japan, scramble for Africa

   d. World War I (1914–18) and the Treaty of Versailles (1919)

      i. The Serbian crisis and general mobilization: the opening German offensive in the east and west (August 1914), stabilization of the Western Front, trench warfare, new military technology (air power, tanks, and poison gas), the Battle of Verdun, renewed stalemate

      ii. The entrance of Italy, Turkey, Japan, and other nations into the war: campaigns in the Balkans and the Middle East

      iii. German submarine warfare and the U.S. entry into the war (1917); the Russian Revolution (1917), military collapse, and the Treaty of Brest-Litovsk (1918); the last Allied offensive and the armistice (1918)

      iv. Total war and the mobilization of whole populations; the dissolution of the Austro-Hungarian, Russian, and Ottoman empires

      v. The leadership, industrial strength, strategic plans and goals, and tactical and logistical procedures of the belligerents

      vi. The Paris Peace Conference (1919–20) and the peace treaty: Wilson's influence; German reparations, restrictions, and territorial losses; reorganization of central Europe and the Middle East by the Allies; the mandates and the League of Nations

3. The European states from 1850 to *c.* 1920

   a. Great Britain and Ireland and expansion of overseas empire (1850–1920)

      i. Mid-Victorian politics and economics: liberalism and free trade, the Great Exhibition (1851), Russell's and Palmerston's foreign policies regarding the Crimean War and the Indian Mutiny, Second Reform Bill (1867)

      ii. Mid-Victorian society and religion: Victorian social attitudes (duty, thrift, hard work, and character), liberalism and the High Church movement, revival of Scottish Calvinism

      iii. Gladstone's liberalism and "Tory Democracy" and imperialism under Disraeli; Third Reform Bill (1884); the Irish Question and the rise of Fenianism, Parnell, and the Home Rule movement; Chamberlain and the split in the Liberal Party; Fabian socialism and growth of the Labour movement; South African War (1899–1902)

      iv. The return of the Liberals (1905–14): Lloyd George's people's budget and National Insurance Act (1911), Parliament Act of 1911, continuing struggle over Ireland and Unionism in Ulster

v. British participation in World War I: Lloyd George's Coalition government, the Easter Rising of 1916 in Ireland

b. France from 1852 to 1920: the Second Empire and the Third Republic

   i. Napoleon III's authoritarian policies and reassertion of France's role in Europe (the Crimea and Italy): partnership with Britain (1852–60), the liberal years (1859–70), foreign policy failures and defeat by Germany (1871)

   ii. The siege of Paris, the Commune, and the establishment of the Third Republic (1870); attempts at restoration; the "Republican Republic"; opportunist control under Gambetta; the Boulangists; colonial expansion; the Dreyfus affair; separation of church and state (1905)

   iii. The prewar years: conflicts between French rightists and Socialists, alignment with Russia and Britain before World War I, nationalism and revanchism

   iv. World War I (1914–18): German occupation of northeastern France, the crisis of 1917, the Clemenceau government, French human and material losses in the war

c. The unification of Germany and Prussia (1850–1920)

   i. William I and tentative reform: clashes with the liberals, Bismarck and reform of the Prussian Army, parliamentary subservience to the crown

   ii. Prussian and Austrian differences over the subjugation of Schleswig-Holstein (1864–66), the exclusion of Austria and the union of north and south Germany in the German Empire after the defeat of France (1871)

   iii. Bismarck as imperial chancellor (1871–90): *Kulturkampf* and the breach with the National Liberals, anti-Socialist measures and social legislation, Bismarck's consolidation of German power and formation of the Triple Alliance (1882)

   iv. The accession of Emperor William II (1888) and the fall of Bismarck; chancellorships of Caprivi, Hohenlohe, and Bülow (1890–1909); estrangement from Russia and rivalry with Britain; colonial expansion; militarists and Social Democrats in the period before World War I

   v. World War I (1914–18) and increasing influence of the army: German military defeat (1918), establishment of the German Republic (1919)

d. The Austrian and Austro-Hungarian Empire from 1850 to 1920

   i. Constitutional experiments: the Kremsier and Stadion constitutions; the "Bach System," the October Diploma (1860), and the February Patent (1861); federalism and centralism (1850–67); the role of Emperor Francis Joseph (1848–1916); exclusion from Italy (1859) and Germany (1866); the *Ausgleich* (Compromise) and the establishment of the Dual Monarchy (1867)

   ii. Austria: the liberal ascendancy under the Auersperg ministry (1871–78) and the coalition of clericals, German aristocrats, and Slavs under Taaffe (1879–93); relations between Austrians and Slavic minorities in the empire; the introduction of universal male suffrage (1907); foreign policy (1878–1908); annexation of Bosnia and Hercegovina and the crises in the Balkans

   iii. Hungary: the Andrássy government, internal conflict between the opponents and advocates of the Compromise of 1867, social reforms and economic progress, Magyar supremacy maintained under Tisza (1875–90)

   iv. Adherence to the Triple Alliance, increasing governmental paralysis and subordination to Germany during World War I, the dissolution of the Habsburg monarchy (1918) and the dismemberment of the empire

e. The Russian Empire from *c.* 1850 to 1917

   i. Defeat in the Crimean War (1853–56), abolition of serfdom (1861) and local government reforms under Alexander II (1855–81), Polish rebellion of 1863 and the spread of revolutionary sentiment, the assassination of the Tsar (1881)

   ii. Reversal of the reform movement under Alexander III (1881–94), the *zemstvos,* government hostility to non-Russian minorities, Nicholas II (1894–1917), anti-reform policies, foundation of the Social Democrats and Social Revolutionaries

   iii. Economic, cultural, and social developments: Russification policies, foreign policies

   iv. Disorders following defeat in the Russo-Japanese War (1904–05), the Dumas, World War I and the abolition of the monarchy (1917)

f. Italy from 1850 to 1920

    i. Cavour and the unification of Italy under Victor Emmanuel of Piedmont: alliance with France and domestic liberalism, papal opposition, Austrian defeat and territorial cessions in northern Italy in the war of 1859, Garibaldi and the conquest of the south, the annexation of Venetia from Austria (1866) and acquisition of Rome (1870)

    ii. The Kingdom of Italy: Minghetti, Depretis, and Crispi; Italian adherence to the Triple Alliance; growth of Socialism, labour movements, and militant nationalism; the Giolitti era; participation in World War I

g. Switzerland from 1850 to 1920: domestic policies, neutrality in World War I

h. Spain and Portugal

    i. Continued civil strife in Spain: control by the military; Carlists, *moderados, progressistas,* and republicans; the First Republic (1873–74); constitutional monarchy in 1876; further colonial losses in the Spanish-American War (1898)

    ii. The reaction against liberalism following Spain's defeat, Spanish involvement in Morocco, civil tensions and neutrality in World War I

    iii. Alternating progressive and conservative governments in Portugal under Pedro V (1853–61) and Luís I (1861–89), dispute with Great Britain over colonial policies, financial difficulties, dictatorship in 1906, the Portuguese Republic (1910) and Portugal's adherence to the British alliance in World War I

i. Scandinavia from 1850 to 1920

    i. Denmark: the Schleswig-Holstein question, defeat by Prussia and Austria (1864) and loss of the duchies, social and economic change under the Conservative regime

    ii. Sweden–Norway: parliamentary reforms in Sweden under Charles XV (1859–72), foreign policy, attitudes in Sweden and in Norway toward the Swedish–Norwegian union

    iii. Finland and Iceland: the language problem and political reforms in Finland, its relations with Russia, Iceland's demands for self-government

j. The Low Countries from 1848 to 1920

    i. The Netherlands: liberalization after 1848, the establishment of the independence of Luxembourg (1890), Queen Wilhelmina and World War I

    ii. Belgian Liberal government (1857–84), rise of Catholic and Belgian Workers' (Socialist) parties, the education controversy and Catholic party rule (1884–1914), universal male suffrage and child labour laws, Leopold II's establishment of Congo Free State (1885) and annexation as Belgian Congo (1908), Flemish resistance to the French-speaking elite

    iii. World War I: Dutch neutrality and the German conquest of Belgium

k. The Balkan States from 1850 to 1920: power conflicts resulting in the Balkan Wars (1912–13) and World War I

    i. Greece: the overthrow of Otho I (1862), the constitution of 1864, acquisition of the Ionian Islands (1864) and Thessaly (1881), Cretan union with Greece (1908), Venizélos' policies, eventual adherence to the Triple Entente in World War I

    ii. Serbia: restoration of Miloš Obrenović in 1858, defeat by Turkey (1876), the Kingdom of Serbia (1882), the pro-Austrian policy of the Obrenović dynasty, restoration of the Karageorgević dynasty and pro-Russian orientation, conflict with Austria-Hungary, conquest by the Central Powers in World War I

    iii. Bulgaria: "great Bulgaria" established by the Treaty of San Stefano (1878), Prince Alexander I and Russian influence (1879–86), Ferdinand I (1887–1918) and Stambolov's formation of a government, revolt of the Macedonian minority (1903), separation from Turkey (1908), adherence to the Central Powers in World War I

    iv. Romania: union of Moldavia and Walachia under Alexandru Cuza (1861), Carol I (1866–1914; king after 1881), independence from Turkey (1878), alignment with the Triple Entente and conquest by the Central Powers in World War I

Suggested reading in the *Encyclopædia Britannica*:

Czechoslovakia	Iceland	Milan	Sweden
Denmark	International	Moscow	Switzerland
Dublin	Relations,	Naples	Union of Soviet
Edinburgh	20th-Century	Napoleon	Socialist
European History	Ireland	Netherlands, The	Republics
and Culture	Italy	Norway	United Kingdom
Finland	Lisbon	Paris	Venice
Florence	London	Poland	Victoria and the
France	Luxembourg	Portugal	Victorian Age
Geneva	Madrid	Prague	Vienna
Germany	Malta	Romania	Warsaw
Greece	Manchester	Rome	Wellington
Hamburg	Marseille	Spain	World Wars
Hungary			Yugoslavia

MICROPAEDIA: Selected entries of reference information

General subjects

culture:
  capitalism
  Classicism and
    Neoclassicism
  Industrial
    Revolution
  laissez-faire
  Marxism
  nationalism
  Romanticism
  Socialism
*international
relations—French
Revolutionary
period and
aftermath:*
  Aix-la-Chapelle,
    Congress of
  Amiens, Treaty of
  Batavian Republic
  Borodino, Battle of
  Campo Formio,
    Treaty of
  Çanak, Treaty of
  Dresden, Battle of
  Europe, Concert of
  Eylau, Battle of
  First of June,
    Battle of the
  Fleurus, Battle of
  French
    Revolutionary
    and Napoleonic
    wars
  Friedland, Battle of
  Holy Alliance
  Jassy, Treaty of
  Jena, Battle of
  Laibach,
    Congress of
  Leipzig, Battle of
  Lodi, Battle of
  Mantua, Siege of
  Marengo, Battle of
  Paris, Treaties of

Peninsular War
Pressburg,
  Treaty of
Pyramids, Battle
  of the
Quadruple Alliance
  (1813)
Schönbrunn,
  Treaty of
Tilsit, Treaties of
Toulon, Siege of
Trafalgar, Battle of
Troppau,
  Congress of
Ulm, Battle of
Verona,
  Congress of
Vienna,
  Congress of
Wagram, Battle of
Waterloo, Battle of
*international
relations—
nationalism and
balance of powers:*
  Algeciras
    Conference
  Alma, Battle of the
  Balaklava, Battle of
  Balkan League
  Balkan Wars
  Berlin, Congress of
  Bosnian Crisis of
    1908
  Bulgarian Horrors
  Crimean War
  Dreikaiserbund
  Dual Alliance
  Eastern Question
  Edirne, Treaty of
  1830,
    Revolutions of
  1848,
    Revolutions of
  Entente Cordiale

Europe, Concert of
Franco-German War
Greco-Turkish wars
Hague Convention
Italo-Turkish War
Königgrätz,
  Battle of
Moroccan crises
Neuchâtel crisis
Novara, Battle of
Pan-Slavism
Paris, Treaty of
power, balance of
Quadruple
  Alliance (1834)
Règlement
  Organique
Reinsurance
  Treaty
Russo-Japanese War
Russo-Turkish wars
San Stefano,
  Treaty of
Sedan, Battle of
Serbo-Bulgarian War
Serbo-Turkish War
Sevastopol,
  Siege of
Solferino, Battle of
Straits Question
Triple Alliance
Villafranca,
  Conference of
Vlorë
  proclamation
*international
relations—
World War I and
aftermath:*
  Allied Powers
  Brest-Litovsk,
    treaties of
  Constantinople
    Agreement
  Corfu Declaration

Dardanelles
  Campaign
Fourteen Points
Isonzo, Battles
  of the
June Offensive
Jutland, Battle of
Lusitania
Marne, First Battle
  of the
Marne, Second
  Battle of the
Meuse-Argonne,
  battles of the
Mudros,
  Armistice of
Paris Peace
  Conference
Saint-Germain,
  Treaty of
Saint-Jean-de-
  Maurienne,
  Agreement of
San Remo,
  Conference of
Somme, First
  Battle of the
Somme, Second
  Battle of the
Sykes-Picot
  Agreement
Trianon, Treaty of
Verdun, Battle of
Versailles,
  Treaty of
World War I
*national affairs—
Britain and Ireland:*
  Catholic
    Emancipation
  Chartism
  Clapham Sect
  Combination Acts
  Conservative Party
  Corn Laws

Don Pacifico
Affair
Easter Rising
Fabian Society
Fenian
Guild Socialism
Home Rule
Irish Rebellion
Labour Party
Land League
Liberal Party
London Dock
Strike
Luddite
Oxford Movement
Parliament Act of
1911
Peterloo Massacre
Phoenix Park
murders
pocket borough
Reform Bill
Taff Vale Case
test act
Tolpuddle Martyrs
Union, Act of
(Britain-Ireland)
United Irishmen,
Society of
national affairs—
France:
Action Française
Alsace-Lorraine
anticlericalism
assignat
Bastille
Batavian Republic
Bonapartist
Brumaire, Coup of
18–19
Chouan
Cisalpine Republic
Civil Constitution
of the Clergy
Continental
System
Corps Législatif
Directory
1801, Concordat of
émigré
Enragé
Entente Cordiale
Feuillants, Club
of the
Fourierism
French Revolution
Gauches,
Cartel des
Girondin
guillotine
Hébertist
Helvetic Republic

Hundred Days
Jacobin Club
July Revolution
Montagnard
Napoleonic Code
National Assembly
National
Convention
Orléanist
Paris,
Commune of
Peninsular War
Plain, The
Public Safety,
Committee of
Revolutionary
Tribunal
Rights of Man and
of the Citizen,
Declaration of the
Roman Republic
sansculotte
September
Massacres
Tennis Court Oath
Terror, Reign of
Thermidorian
Reaction
Vendée, Wars
of the
Ventôse Decrees
national affairs—
Germany and
Austria:
Agrarian League
Austria-Hungary
Burschenschaft
Carlsbad Decrees
Centre Party
Croato-Hungarian
Compromise of
1868
Deutschlandlied
1848,
Revolutions of
Ems telegram
Erfurt Union
Parliament
Frankfurt National
Assembly
Freikorps
German
Confederation
Heimwehr
Junker
Kulturkampf
March laws
Olmütz,
Punctation of
Pan-Germanism
Prussia

Rhine,
Confederation
of the
Seven Weeks' War
Social Democratic
Party of Germany
Spartacus League
Zollverein
national affairs—
Italy:
Carbonaro
Cisalpine Republic
Cispadine
Republic
Custoza, Battles of
fascio siciliano
Fiume question
Guarantees,
Law of
Irredentist
Italo-Turkish War
Ligurian Republic
Parthenopean
Republic
Popolare
Risorgimento
Roman Republic
Solferino, Battle of
Statuto Albertino
Thousand,
Expedition of the
Villafranca,
Conference of
Young Italy
national affairs—
Poland:
Congress Kingdom
of Poland
Cracow,
Republic of
January
Insurrection
liberum veto
November
Insurrection
Poland,
Partitions of
Warsaw, Duchy of
national affairs—
Russia:
Black Hundreds
Bloody Sunday
Bolshevik
Bund
Decembrist
Duma
Emancipation
Manifesto
January
Insurrection

Kadet
Labour,
Liberation of
Leninism
Liberation,
Union of
Menshevik
mir
Narodnaya Volya
Narodnik
November
Insurrection
October Manifesto
Octobrist
Orthodoxy,
Autocracy, and
Nationality
Pan-Slavism
Progressive Bloc
Russian
Revolution of
1905
Russian
Revolution of
1917
Russian
Social-Democratic
Workers' Party
Russo-Japanese War
Russo-Turkish
wars
Russification
Slavophile
Socialist
Revolutionary
Party
Stolypin land
reform
Third Department
Zemlya i Volya
zemstvo
national affairs—
Scandinavia:
Bodø Affair
Eider Program
Fennoman
movement
Kiel, Treaty of
Pan-Scandinavianism
Riksdag
national affairs—
Spain and Portugal:
Carlism
Oranges, War
of the
Peninsular War
Pragmatic
Sanction of King
Ferdinand VII
Spanish–
American War

Spanish Marriages,
Affair of the
Verona, Congress of
*national affairs—
other:*
Flemish Movement
Greek
Independence,
War of
Guarantees, Law of

Moldavia
Sonderbund
Wallachia
*overseas empires and
commerce:*
Algeciras
Conference
Berlin, Congress of
Bowring Treaty
British East Africa

British Empire
British South
Africa Company
British West Africa
Clayton-Bulwer
Treaty
East India
Company
Fashoda Incident

French Equatorial
Africa
French Morocco
French West Africa
German East Africa
German South West
Africa
influence, sphere of
Open Door policy
protectorate

Biographies

*Austrian Empire and
Austria-Hungary:*
Andrássy, Gyula,
Gróf
Berchtold,
Leopold,
Graf von
Beust, Friedrich
Ferdinand,
Graf von
Beneš, Edvard
Charles, Archduke
Cobenzl, Ludwig,
Graf von
Conrad von
Hötzendorf,
Franz, Graf
Deák, Ferenc
Francis II
(Germany/Holy
Roman Empire)
Francis Ferdinand,
Archduke of
Austria-Este
Francis Joseph
Gentz, Friedrich
Habsburg,
House of
Károlyi, Mihály,
Gróf
Kaunitz, Wenzel
Anton von
Kossuth, Lajos
Kun, Béla
Leopold II
(Germany/Holy
Roman Empire)
Mazaryk, Tomáš
Metternich,
Klemens,
Fürst von
Radetzky, Joseph,
Graf
Rudolf, Archduke
and Crown
Prince of Austria
Schwarzenberg,
Felix, Fürst zu
Schwarzenberg,
Karl Philipp,
Fürst zu

Stadion, Johann
Philipp, Graf von
Balkans:
Carol I
Dhiliyiánnis,
Theódoros
Ferdinand I
(Bulgaria)
Ferdinand I
(Romania)
Garašanin, Ilija
Kapodístrias,
Ioánnis Antónios,
Komis
Karageorge
Mavrokordátos,
Aléxandros
Milan IV (or II)
Miloš
Nicholas I
(Montenegro)
Otto (Greece)
Pašić, Nikola
Peter I
(Montenegro)
Peter I (Serbia)
Stamboliyski,
Aleksandŭr
Venizélos,
Eleuthérios
Britain and Ireland:
Aberdeen, George
Hamilton-Gordon,
4th earl of
Albert, Prince
Consort of Great
Britain and
Ireland
Asquith, H.H.
Balfour, Arthur
James Balfour,
1st earl of
Bentinck, Lord
William
Bright, John
Brougham and
Vaux, Henry
Peter Brougham,
1st Baron
Campbell-Bannerman,
Sir Henry

Canning, Charles
John Canning,
Earl
Canning, George
Cardigan,
James Thomas
Brudenell, 7th
Earl of
Carson, Edward
Henry Carson,
Baron
Casement, Sir
Roger
Castlereagh,
Robert Stewart,
Viscount
Chamberlain,
Joseph
Churchill, Lord
Randolph Henry
Spencer
Churchill, Sir
Winston
Clare, John
Fitzgibbon, 1st
earl of
Cobbett, William
Cobden, Richard
Cockburn, Sir
Alexander James
Edmund
Collingwood,
Cuthbert
Collingwood, 1st
Baron
Collins, Michael
Cornwallis, Charles
Cornwallis, 1st
Marquess and
2nd Earl
Cromer, Evelyn
Baring, 1st Earl of
Curzon, George
Nathaniel
Curzon,
Marquess
Dalhousie,
James Andrew
Broun Ramsay,
marquess and
10th earl of

Derby, Edward
Stanley, 14th
earl of
Devonshire,
Spencer Compton
Cavendish, 8th
Duke of
Dillon, John
Disraeli, Benjamin
Dundonald,
Thomas
Cochrane, 10th
earl of
Edward VII
Fisher, John
Arbuthnot Fisher,
1st Baron
Forster, William
Edward
Fox, Charles James
French, John
George III
George IV
George V
Gladstone,
William Ewart
Goldie, Sir George
Grenville, William
Wyndham
Grenville, Baron
Grey, Charles
Grey, 2nd Earl
Grey, Sir Edward
Griffith, Arthur
Haig, Douglas
Haig, 1st Earl
Haldane, Richard
Burdon
Hardie, J. Keir
Howe, Richard
Howe, Earl
Hyndman, Henry
Mayers
Jellicoe, John
Rushworth
Jellicoe, 1st Earl
Kitchener, Herbert
Lansdowne, Henry
Charles Keith
Petty-Fitzmaurice,
5th marquess of

Frederick
William II
Frederick
William III
Frederick
William IV
Gneisenau,
August, Graf
Neidhardt von
Hardenberg, Karl
August, Fürst von
Hindenburg,
Paul von
Hohenlohe-
Schillingsfürst,
Chlodwig Karl
Viktor, Fürst zu
Hohenzollern
dynasty
Holstein,
Friedrich von
Kiderlen-Wächter,
Alfred von
Louis I (Bavaria)
Louis II (Bavaria)
Ludendorff, Erich
Marx, Karl
Maximilian I
(Bavaria)
Maximilian II
(Bavaria)
Moltke,
Helmuth von
Radowitz, Joseph
Maria von
Roon, Albrecht
Theodor Emil,
Graf von
Scharnhorst,
Gerhard Johann
David von
Schlieffen, Alfred,
Graf von
Stein, Karl,
Reichsfreiherr
vom und zum
Tirpitz, Alfred von
William I (German
Empire)
William II
(German Empire)
Italy:
Bandiera, Attilio;
and Bandiera,
Emilio
Bonaparte, Joseph
Bourbon, House of
Cavour, Camillo
Benso, conte di
Charles Albert
Charles Felix
Consalvi, Ercole

Crispi, Francesco
D'Annunzio,
Gabriele
Depretis, Agostino
Farini, Luigi Carlo
Ferdinand I
(Naples)
Ferdinand II
(Naples)
Francis I (Naples)
Francis II (Naples)
Garibaldi,
Giuseppe
Gioberti, Vincenzo
Giolitti, Giovanni
Mazzini, Giuseppe
Murat, Joachim
Orlando, Vittorio
Emanuele
Pelloux, Luigi
Savoy, House of
Umberto I
Victor
Emmanuel I
Victor
Emmanuel II
Victor
Emmanuel III
Visconti-Venosta,
Emilio, Marchese
Low Countries:
Albert (Belgium)
Bonaparte, Louis
Leopold I
(Belgium)
Leopold II
(Belgium)
William I
(Netherlands:
king)
William II
(Netherlands:
king)
William III
(Netherlands:
king)
Portugal:
Beresford, William
Carr Beresford,
Viscount
Charles
John VI
Maria I
Maria II
Michael
Pedro I (Brazil)
Russia:
Alexander I
Alexander II
Alexander III
Alexandra

Arakcheyev,
Aleksey
Andreyevich,
Graf
Bennigsen, Leonty
Leontyevich,
Graf von
Catherine II
Chernyayev,
Mikhayl
Grigoryevich
Gorchakov,
Mikhail
Dmitriyevich,
Knyaz
Guchkov,
Aleksandr
Ivanovich
Ignatyev, Nikolay
Pavlovich, Graf
Kerensky,
Aleksandr
Fyodorovich
Kornilov, Lavr
Georgiyevich
Kutuzov, Mikhail
Illarionovich,
Knyaz
Lenin, Vladimir
Ilich
Lobanov-Rostovsky,
Aleksey
Borisovich,
Knyaz
Lvov, Georgy
Yevgenyevich,
Knyaz
Milyukov, Pavel
Nikolayevich
Milyutin, Dmitry
Alekseyevich,
Graf
Nesselrode, Karl
Vasilyevich, Graf
Nicholas I
Nicholas II
Orlov, Aleksey
Fyodorovich,
Knyaz
Paskevich, Ivan
Fyodorovich
Paul
Plekhanov,
Georgy,
Valentinovich
Pobedonostsev,
Konstantin
Petrovich
Pozzo di Borgo,
Charles-André,
comte

Rasputin, Grigory
Yefimovich
Rostopchin,
Fyodor
Vasilyevich, Graf
Savinkov, Boris
Viktorovich
Shāmil
Skobelev, Mikhail
Dmitriyevich
Speransky, Mikhail
Mikhaylovich,
Graf
Stolypin, Pyotr
Arkadyevich
Witte, Sergey
Yulyevich, Graf
Scandinavia:
Branting, Karl
Hjalmar
Charles XIII
(Sweden)
Charles XV
(Sweden)
Christian VIII
Christian IX
Christian X
Frederick VI
(Denmark)
Frederick VII
(Denmark)
Frederick VIII
(Denmark)
Gustav IV Adolf
Gustav V
Haakon VII
Oscar I
Oscar II
Spain:
Alfonso XII
Alfonso XIII
Bonaparte, Joseph
Cánovas del
Castillo, Antonio
Carlos Luís de
Borbón
Carlos María de
los Dolores de
Borbón
Carlos María
Isidro de Borbón
Castelar y Ripoll,
Emilio
Charles IV
Ferdinand VII
Godoy, Manuel de
Isabella II
María Cristina I
María Cristina II
Serrano y
Domínguez,
Francisco

INDEX: See entries under all of the terms above

Section 964.   **European Colonies in the Americas from 1492 to *c.* 1790**

A. The geography and ethnography of the Americas

B. Spanish and Portuguese colonies in the Americas, other European powers in South America and the Caribbean to *c.* 1790

   1. Spanish discovery, exploration, and conquest of the Caribbean islands, Mexico, Central America, Peru, Venezuela, Colombia, and Río de la Plata (1492–*c.* 1550)

   2. Spain's colonial empire

      a. Colonial administration: the Council of the Indies, viceroys and other provincial officials, *audiencias,* legal restrictions on public officials

      b. Indian policy: slavery and peonage under the *encomienda* and *repartimiento,* the missionary role of the Roman Catholic Church, decline of the Indian population, introduction of black slaves

      c. Colonial economy: expansion of agriculture; gold and silver mining; cattle industry; mercantilism, smuggling, and piracy

   3. The exploration and colonization of Brazil by the Portuguese (from 1500)

      a. Colonial economic policies: introduction of black slavery, gold and diamond mining, agricultural and commercial development

      b. Colonial administration: establishment of captaincies (1533), centralized royal control (1549), role of the Roman Catholic Church, the Brazilian racial mixture

   4. Administrative reforms of the Spanish Bourbon kings (1700–88): decentralization of the governments of Peru, Venezuela, and Chile; encouragement of trade and agriculture

   5. Spanish colonial expansion into North America (*c.* 1600–1790): settlements and religious missions

   6. English, French, and Dutch territorial and economic expansion (from *c.* 1600) into areas of Spanish and Portuguese colonization in Latin America and the Caribbean

C. Norse, English, Dutch, and Swedish discoveries, explorations, and settlements in North America (*c.* 1000–1763)

   1. Norse voyages to Greenland and North America (*c.* 1000)

   2. Early English exploration and attempted settlement (1497–*c.* 1600), Dutch and Swedish settlement and later expulsion by the English

   3. Development of the English colonies in North America

      a. The founding of the 13 Colonies: economic, political, and religious reasons for settlement

      b. Economic, political, and social development

         i. British economic policies: mercantilism and the Navigation Acts

         ii. Colonial administration: loose royal control prior to 1763, self-government and local political activity

         iii. Social mobility and the rise of economic classes: immigration and the introduction of slavery, agricultural and commercial development

      c. Colonial cultural and scientific achievements; *e.g.,* the American Philosophical Society, newspapers and almanacs, the beginning of public education, the "Great Awakening"

      d. Conflicts with the French and Indians and expulsion of French power from North America (1763)

D. French discoveries, explorations, and settlements in North America: New France and Louisiana (1524–1763)

   1. The settlement of New France: missionaries, Indian relations, and the fur trade; royal administration and joint-stock companies

   2. Expansion and eventual conflict with the English, resulting in the eclipse of French power in North America (1763)

Suggested reading in the *Encyclopædia Britannica:*

MACROPAEDIA: Major articles and a biography dealing with European colonies in the Americas from 1492 to *c.* 1790

Arctic, The	Latin America,	New Orleans	South America
Boston	The History of	New York City	United States of
Canada	Montreal	North America	America
Columbus		Philadelphia	

MICROPAEDIA: Selected entries of reference information

General subjects

English and French colonization of North America:	Molasses Act	Walking Purchase	New Granada,
	Monongahela,	Yamasee War	Viceroyalty of
	Battle of the	*Spanish and*	New Spain,
Acadia	New England,	*Portuguese*	Viceroyalty of
Albany Congress	Council for	*colonization of the*	Palmares,
Culpeper's	New England	*Americas:*	Republic of
Rebellion	Confederation	alcalde	Peru,
French and	New France	asiento de negros	Viceroyalty of
Indian War	New Hampshire	audiencia	Pueblo Rebellion
French Shore	Grants	bandeira	Real Cuerpo de
Hat Act	Nootka Sound	cabildo	Minería
Hudson's Bay	controversy	caciquism	reducción
Company	Paxton Boys	Cíbola, Seven	repartimiento
Iron Act	uprising	Golden Cities of	residencia
Iroquois League	Pilgrim Fathers	conquistador	Rió de la Plata,
Jamestown	Plymouth	Contratación,	Viceroyalty of the
King George's War	Company	Casa de	Santo Domingo
King Philip's War	Powhatan War	corregidor	Spanish treasure
King William's	proprietary colony	donatário	fleet
War	Quebec, Battle of	Eldorado	Strangford Treaty
London Company	Queen	encomienda	*other:*
Lost Colony	Anne's War	fazenda	Middle Passage
Massachusetts Bay	Salem witch trials	Indies,	New Sweden
Colony	1763,	Laws of the	Vinland
Mayflower	Proclamation of	mameluco	
Mayflower Compact	Sovereign Council		
Mississippi Bubble	Sugar Act		

Biographies

English explorers and colonizers:	*French explorers and colonizers:*	Laval, François de Montmorency	Narváez, Panfilo de
Cabot, John	Bienville,	*Spanish and*	Soto,
Cabot, Sebastian	Jean-Baptiste	*Portuguese explorers*	Hernando de
Cook, James	Le Moyne de	*and colonizers:*	Velázquez, Diego
Hudson, Henry	Cartier, Jacques	Balboa, Vasco	Vespucci,
Johnson, Sir	Champlain,	Núñez de	Amerigo
William, 1st	Samuel de	Cabral, Pedro	*other:*
Baronet	Frontenac, Louis	Álvares	Bering, Vitus
Mather, Cotton	de Buade, comte	Columbus,	Chirikov, Aleksey
Mather, Increase	de Palluau et de	Christopher	Ilich
Penn, William	Iberville, Pierre Le	Coronado,	John Maurice of
Pocahontas	Moyne d'	Francisco	Nassau
Smith, John	La Salle,	Vázquez de	
Stirling, William	René-Robert	Díaz de Solís,	
Alexander, 1st	Cavalier, sieur de	Juan	
earl of	La Vérendrye,	Las Casas,	
Williams, Roger	Pierre Gaultier de	Bartolomé de	
Winthrop, John	Varennes, sieur de		

INDEX: See entries under all of the terms above

Section 965.   Development of the United States and Canada from 1763 to 1920

A. The United States to 1865: national formation and territorial expansion, conflict between North and South

1. Establishment and consolidation of the United States (1763–1816)

   a. The American Revolutionary period (1763–87)

      i. Political and economic opposition to Britain's taxation policies culminating in the Declaration of Independence (1776)

      ii. The U.S. War of Independence (1775–83): land and sea campaigns, military leadership, French military support, peace treaty (1783)

      iii. The government of the Articles of Confederation (1781–87) and evolution of a western lands policy

   b. The strengthening of the national government (1787–1816)

      i. The Constitutional Convention, the federal Constitution, and the struggle for ratification (1787–89)

      ii. Development of national policies and formation of political parties: Hamilton's economic policies, foreign relations during the administrations of Washington and John Adams, Federalists and Democratic-Republicans

      iii. Jefferson's administration and the Louisiana Purchase (1803), Madison's administration and the War of 1812, role of the Supreme Court

2. The United States from 1816 to 1850: nationalism, expansionism, extension of the franchise, and industrialization

   a. Strengthening of national feelings: administrations of Monroe and John Quincy Adams, Supreme Court under Marshall

      i. "The Era of Good Feelings" (1816–24): nationalism and sectionalism, the Missouri Compromise (1820)

      ii. Developments in commerce and finance: industrialization and early labour movements, transportation and internal improvements, cotton and slavery

      iii. Social development: German and Irish immigration (1830–50), urbanization and social mobility

   b. Jacksonian democracy (1829–41): extension of the franchise; development of Democratic, Whig, and minor party politics; bank war; nullification; Indian removal policy

   c. The "Age of Reform" (1830–50): the Abolitionist movement and other reform activities, diverse religious attitudes

   d. Westward expansionism: annexation of Texas, acquisition of Oregon, the Mexican War (1846–48) and the annexation of California and New Mexico, the Compromise of 1850

   e. Cultural development to 1850: the growth of the novel, poetry, music, the visual arts, historical writings, the Transcendentalist movement

3. The United States from 1850 to 1865: sectionalism, secession, and Civil War

   a. Sectionalism and slavery: economic and psychological bases of slavery, the failure of popular sovereignty, the Abolitionist movement, literature of the period

   b. Political and geographical polarization: disruption of the Democratic and Whig parties, emergence of the Republican Party, and Lincoln's election (1860)

   c. Secession of the Southern states and the Civil War (1860–65)

      i. Relative military strengths: strategies and tactics of North and South

      ii. The land and sea war (1861–65): initial Confederate victories, Union success in the West and final victory over the South

      iii. Foreign affairs of the Union and the Confederacy, moves toward emancipation during the war

B. The United States from 1865 to 1920: Reconstruction, industrialization, increased immigration, development of the West, and emergence as a world power

1. Radical Reconstruction (1866–77) and the New South (1877–1900)

a. Lincoln's plan for Reconstruction and congressional opposition (1864–65), conflicts between the Radical Republican-controlled Congress and Andrew Johnson, state "Black Codes" and federal civil rights legislation

b. Reconstruction (1866–77): freedmen, sharecropping, and "Black Reconstruction"; Grant's administrations and the decline of Republican control in the South

c. The New South (1877–1900): conservative Democrats in control and erosion of black rights, Populist resurgence in the 1890s, white supremacy and Jim Crow legislation, the black response

2. The transformation of American society: the United States from 1865 to 1900

a. Urbanization and immigration: southern and eastern European immigrants and growth of slums, problems of prejudice, rise of city machine politics, development of public education

b. The development of the West (1865–1900)

    i. The quest for gold and silver: boom and bust in mining towns

    ii. Cattlemen and the open range: the cattle industry (1866–88), the cowboy and cattle drives, conflicts with settlers

    iii. Westward expansion of the railroads: early government subsidies, relationship of the transcontinental carriers to the national economy

    iv. Violation of the Indian treaties: settlers' encroachments on Indian lands, Indian wars, corruption among agents of the Bureau of Indian Affairs

c. The industrialization of the American economy: the manufacturing boom

    i. Technological advances in the iron and steel industry; exploitation of oil, ores, lumber, and other natural resources

    ii. Development of trusts and holding companies: development of a legal climate favourable to big business

d. U.S. foreign trade and commerce: growth of exports and imports

e. Emergence of national labour union organizations: strikes and boycotts, collective bargaining, antilabour stance of government, the Haymarket Riot (1886)

f. National politics (1877–1900): general ascendancy of Congress and decline of the presidency

    i. Aftermath of the disputed election of 1876: the Compromise of 1877, the end of Southern Reconstruction, and Hayes's administration (1877–81); inflation and the silver issue

    ii. The election of 1880 and the presidency of Garfield: Garfield's assassination (1881), Arthur's administration (1881–85), establishment of the Civil Service Commission (1883)

    iii. The election of 1884 and Cleveland's first administration (1885–89): the reemergence of presidential leadership, the Treasury surplus and tariff issues, the Interstate Commerce Act (1887) and federal regulation of railroads

    iv. The election of 1888 and Benjamin Harrison's administration (1889–93): congressional leadership, the Sherman Anti-Trust and Sherman Silver Purchase acts, and the McKinley Tariff Act (1890)

    v. Depressed agricultural conditions (1887–97): the Farmers' Alliances and the establishment of the Populist Party (1891), farmers' defection from Republican Party

    vi. The election of 1892 and Cleveland's second administration (1893–97): gold reserves and the Panic of 1893, repeal of the Sherman Silver Purchase Act (1893), lowering of the tariff

    vii. The election of 1896 and McKinley's administration (1897–1901): the raising of the tariff (1897) and the Gold Standard Act (1900), gradual economic recovery

3. Imperialism, the Progressive Era, and the rise to world power (1896–1920)

a. The emergence of the U.S. as an imperial power

    i. The Spanish–American War and U.S. suzerainty over Cuba; acquisition of the Philippines, the Hawaiian Islands, and Puerto Rico (1898)

    ii. The "Open Door" policy and armed intervention in China (1900)

    iii. Acquisition of the Panama Canal Zone (1903) and the Roosevelt Corollary to the Monroe Doctrine: intervention in Haiti, the Dominican Republic, Cuba, and Nicaragua

b. The Progressive Movement (*c.* 1896–1920)

   i. Scholars, social workers, and "muckrakers" as leaders of the Progressive Movement; social and political urban reforms by state government

   ii. Theodore Roosevelt's administrations (1901–09) and expansion of presidential power and regulatory legislation, Taft's administration (1909–13) and the defection of Progressive Republicans in the 1912 election

   iii. Wilson's first administration (1913–17): tariff, currency, credit, tax, and labour reforms; intervention in Mexican affairs

c. The role of the U.S. in World War I

   i. Initial U.S. neutrality: loans and supplies to the Allies, submarine warfare and the break with Germany

   ii. U.S. entry into the war: mobilization of manpower and the economy, decisive effect of U.S. military forces on the Western Front (1918)

   iii. Wilson's policies at the Paris Peace Conference (1919) and the U.S. Senate rejection of the Treaty of Versailles (1920), the election of 1920 and the return to isolationism

4. Cultural developments from 1865 to 1920

   a. Advances in fiction, poetry, drama, music, and the visual arts

   b. Developments in education and historical writings, growth of American philosophy

C. Canada under British colonial rule from 1763 to 1867, the Dominion of Canada from 1867 to 1920

1. British colonial administration: the Quebec Acts of 1763 and 1774, immigration of United Empire Loyalists after U.S. War of Independence, establishment of French- and English-speaking provinces

2. Social, political, and economic development from 1790 to 1850

   a. Immigration, westward expansion, and the fur trade; participation in the War of 1812

   b. Dissension between French and English settlers: the rebellions of 1837, the Union of Upper and Lower Canada (1841), self-government for domestic affairs (1848)

3. The Dominion of Canada from 1867 to 1920

   a. The Confederation movement and the establishment of the Dominion (1867)

   b. Westward expansion and internal disunity

      i. Louis Riel and the first Métis-Indian rebellion (1870), establishment of the provinces of Manitoba and British Columbia

      ii. The transcontinental railroad, suppression of the second Métis-Indian rebellion (1885), economic depression and downfall of the Conservative government (1896)

   c. Liberal governments under Laurier and economic prosperity (1896–1911)

      i. The Klondike gold rush (1897) and the settlement of the Northwest Territories, creation of the provinces of Alberta and Saskatchewan (1905)

      ii. Involvement in Britain's imperialist policies: participation in South African War (1899), border disputes with the United States

   d. Economic nationalism and the Conservative government (1911–17): participation in World War I, recognition of Canadian autonomy (1917)

Suggested reading in the *Encyclopædia Britannica*:

MACROPAEDIA: Major articles and biographies dealing with the development of the United States and Canada from 1763 to 1920

Boston	Lincoln	Philadelphia	Washington, D.C.
Canada	Montreal	San Francisco	Washington,
Chicago	New Orleans	Toronto	George
Franklin	New York City	United States of	
Jefferson	North America	America	

MICROPAEDIA: Selected entries of reference information

General subjects

Canada:
Aroostook War
Assiniboia
Bering Sea Dispute
British North
  America Act
Canada Company
Canada East
Canada West
Charlottetown
  Conference
Clear Grits
Clergy Reserves
Hunters' Lodges
Jesuit Estates
  controversy
Liberal Party of
  Canada
métis
North West
  Company
Pacific Scandal
Parti Rouge
Progressive
  Conservative
  Party of Canada
Quebec, Battle of
Quebec Act
Red River
  Settlement
Reform Party
Rush–Bagot
  Agreement
Seven Oaks
  Massacre
*United States—
Revolutionary
period:*
Bennington,
  Battle of
Bonhomme
  Richard
  and Serapis,
  engagement
  between
Boston, Siege of
Boston Tea Party
Brandywine, Battle
  of the
Bunker Hill,
  Battle of
Camden, Battle of
Carlisle
  Commission
Cherokee wars and
  treaties
Cherry Valley Raid

Continental
  Congress
Correspondence,
  Committees of
Cowpens, Battle of
Declaratory Act
Democratic Party
Embargo Act
Essex Junto
Fallen Timbers,
  Battle of
Franco-American
  Alliance
Germantown,
  Battle of
Gnadenhütten
  Massacre
Green Mountain
  Boys
Guilford Court
  House, Battle of
Independence,
  Declaration of
Intolerable Acts
Kings Mountain,
  Battle of
Lexington and
  Concord,
  Battles of
Long Island,
  Battle of
Loyalist
minuteman
Monmouth Court
  House, Battle of
Moore's Creek
  Bridge, Battle of
Nonimportation
  Agreements
Oriskany, Battle of
Paris, Peace of
Pinckney's Treaty
Purple Heart
Quartering Act
Quebec, Battle of
Regulators of
  North Carolina
Republican Party
Saintes, Battle
  of the
Saratoga,
  Battles of
Stamp Act
Stars and Stripes
Suffolk Resolves
Tea Act
Townshend Acts

Trenton and
  Princeton,
  battles of
Tripolitan War
United States War
  of Independence
Valley Forge
Virginia Capes,
  Battle of
Virginia
  Declaration of
  Rights
White Plains,
  Battle of
Wyoming
  Massacre
XYZ Affair
Yorktown,
  Siege of
*United States—early
years:*
Alien and Sedition
  Acts
American Fur
  Company
Annapolis
  Convention
Anti-Federalists
Châteauguay,
  Battle of
Chippewa,
  Battle of
Confederation,
  Articles of
Constitution of the
  United States
Constitutional
  Convention, U.S.
Creek War
Democratic Party
1812, War of
Embargo Act
Essex Decision
Fallen Timbers,
  Battle of
Federalist, The
Federalist Party
Fries's Rebellion
Ghent, Treaty of
Hartford
  Convention
Jay Treaty
Lake Erie,
  Battle of
Lewis and Clark
  Expedition
Locofoco Party
Louisiana Party

Lundy's Lane,
  Battle of
Marbury v.
  Madison
Monroe Doctrine
National
  Republican Party
New Orleans,
  Battle of
Northwest
  Ordinances
Northwest
  Territory
nullification
Pinckney's Treaty
Republican Party
Rights, Bill of
Saint Clair's Defeat
Shays's Rebellion
Star-Spangled
  Banner, The
Thames, Battle
  of the
Tippecanoe,
  Battle of
Uncle Sam
Virginia and
  Kentucky
  Resolutions
War Hawk
West Florida
  Controversy
Western Reserve
Whig Party
Whiskey
  Rebellion
Workingmen's
  Party
*United States—
nationalism and
westward
expansion:*
Alamo
Alaska Purchase
Bear Flag Revolt
Buena Vista,
  Battle of
Cerro Gordo,
  Battle of
Chisholm Trail
Clayton–Bulwer
  Treaty
Comstock Lode
Contreras,
  Battle of
cowboy
Gadsden
  Purchase

Guadalupe
Hidalgo,
Treaty of
Homestead
Movement
Indian
Removal Act
Indian Territory
Little Bighorn,
Battle of the
Manifest Destiny
Mexican War
Oregon Question
Oregon Trail
Ostend Manifesto
Palo Alto,
Battle of
Russian-
American
Company
San Jacinto,
Battle of
Sante Fe Trail
Seminole Wars
Southern Overland
Mail Company
Westward
Movement
Young America
Movement
*United States—
sectional crisis:*
Ableman v. Booth
abolitionism
Alabama claims
American
Anti-Slavery
Society
American
Colonization
Society
Antietam, Battle of
Appomattox Court
House
Atlanta Campaign
Big Black River,
Battle of
black code
Bleeding Kansas
Bull Run,
battles of
carpetbagger
Chancellorsville,
Battle of
Chattanooga,
Battle of
Chickamauga
Creek, Battle of
Civil War
Cold Harbor,
battles of

Confederate States
of America
Confiscation Acts
Constitutional
Union Party
Copperhead
Crittenden
Compromise
Dixie
Draft Riot of 1863
Dred Scott
decision
1850,
Compromise of
Electoral
Commission
Emancipation
Proclamation
Force Acts
Fredericksburg,
Battle of
Free-Soil Party
Freedmen's Bureau
Fugitive Slave Acts
Gettysburg,
Battle of
Gettysburg
Address
Hampton Roads
Conference
Harpers Ferry
Raid
Hunkers and
Barnburners
Jim Crow law
Kansas-
Nebraska Act
Kenner mission
Know-Nothing
party
Ku Klux Klan
Lecompton
Constitution
Liberal Republican
Party
Liberty Party
Lincoln-Douglas
Debates
McCardle, Ex
Parte
Memphis Race
Riot
Merryman, Ex
Parte
Milligan, Ex Parte
Missouri
Compromise
Mobile Bay,
Battle of

Monitor and
Merrimack,
Battle of
Nashville, Battle of
Nashville
Convention
Ohio Idea
Pea Ridge,
Battle of
Peninsular
Campaign
personal liberty
laws
Petersburg
Campaign
popular
sovereignty
Radical
Republican
Reconstruction
Red River
Campaign
Seven Days'
Battles
Shenandoah
Valley
Campaigns
Shiloh, Battle of
Stones River,
Battle of
Tenure of
Office Act
Topeka
Constitution
Underground
Railroad
Union League
Vicksburg
Campaign
Wade-Davis Bill
Wilderness, Battle
of the
Wilmot Proviso
Wilson's Creek,
Battle of
*United States—
urbanization,
industrialization,
and the agrarian
revolt:*
Coxey's Army
Free Silver
Movement
Granger
movement
Greenback
movement
Hammer v.
Dagenhart
Haymarket Riot

Industrial Workers
of the World
Knights of Labor
Molly Maguires
Mugwump
Populist
Movement
Pullman Strike
Slaughterhouse
Cases
*United States—
war with Spain,
Progressivism, and
the rise to world
power:*
Big Stick Policy
Bryan-Chamorro
Treaty
Bull Moose Party
Dollar Diplomacy
Fourteen Points
Gentlemen's
Agreement
Hay-Bunau-Varilla
Treaty
International
Boundary
Waters Treaty
King-Crane
Commission
Lansing-Ishii
Agreement
Maine,
destruction
of the
Manila Bay,
Battle of
New Nationalism
Open Door policy
Paris, Treaty of
(1898)
Platt Amendment
Preparedness
Movement
Root-Takahira
Agreement
Rough Rider
Santiago, Battle of
Spanish-
American War
Veracruz incident
other:
Anti-Saloon
League
Atlanta
Compromise
Bank War
Bering Sea
Dispute
Black Friday
Brook Farm

Brownsville Affair
Chicago Race
    Riot of 1919
Crédit Mobilier
    Scandal
Dawes General
    Allotment Act

East Saint Louis
    Race Riot
    of 1917
Niagara
    Movement
Nonpartisan
    League

Prohibition Party
Resumption Act
    of 1875
slave rebellions
Stalwart
Talented Tenth

Tammany Hall
Universal Negro
    Improvement
    Association
Wounded Knee

Biographies

American Indian
  leaders:
  Brant, Joseph
  Cochise
  Crazy Horse
  Dull Knife
  Geronimo
  Joseph, Chief
  McGillivry,
    Alexander
  Pontiac
  Red Jacket
  Sitting Bull
  Tecumseh
  Washakie
Canadians:
  Baldwin, Robert
  Borden, Sir Robert
  Brown, George
  Durham, John
    George Lambton,
    1st earl of
  Galt, Sir
    Alexander
    Tilloch
  Lansdowne, Henry
    Charles Keith
    Petty-Fitzmaurice,
    5th marquess of
  Laurier, Sir Wilfrid
  Macdonald, Sir
    John
  Mackenzie,
    William Lyon
  Papineau, Louis
    Joseph
  Riel, Louis
U.S. Abolitionists:
  Brown, John
  Delany, Martin R.
  Douglass,
    Frederick
  Garrison, William
    Lloyd
  Julian, George W.
  Tappan, Arthur
U.S. diplomats:
  Blaine, James
  Harris, Townsend
  House, Edward M.
  Page, Walter
    Hines
  Randolph, John

U.S. explorers and
  frontiersmen:
  Boone, Daniel
  Carson,
    Christopher
  Clark, George
    Rogers
  Cody, William F.
  Crockett, Davy
  Frémont, John C.
  Peary, Robert
    Edwin
  Whitman, Marcus
U.S. industrialists:
  Hanna, Mark
  Hewitt, Abram
  Martin, Luther
  Rockefeller,
    John D.
  Vanderbilt family
  See also Section
    732 of Part Seven
U.S. military
  leaders—Civil War:
  Beauregard, Pierre
    Gustave Toutant
  Bragg, Braxton
  Breckinridge,
    John C.
  Burnside, Ambrose
    Everett
  Butler,
    Benjamin F.
  Early, Jubal A.
  Farragut, David
  Forrest, Nathan
    Bedford
  Grant, Ulysses S.
  Hood, John B.
  Hooker, Joseph
  Jackson, Thomas
    Jonathan
  Johnston,
    Joseph E.
  Lee, Robert E.
  Longstreet, James
  McClellan,
    George B.
  Meade, George G.
  Pope, John
  Rosecrans,
    William S.

Sheridan, Philip H.
Sherman, William
  Tecumseh
Stuart, J.E.B.
Thomas,
  George H.
U.S. military
  leaders—Mexican
  War:
  Gorgas, Josiah
  Kearney, Stephen
    Watts
  Scott, Winfield
  Taylor, Zachary
U.S. military
  leaders—
  Revolutionary War:
  Arnold, Benedict
  Greene, Nathanael
  Hale, Nathan
  Hampton, Wade
  Jones, John Paul
  Kościuszko,
    Tadeusz
  Lafayette,
    Marie-Joseph-
    Paul-Yves-
    Roch-Gilbert
    du Motier,
    marquis de
  Washington,
    George
U.S. military
  leaders—other:
  Custer, George
    Armstrong
  Jackson, Andrew
  Mitchell, William
  Perry, Matthew C.
  Pershing, John J.
U.S. presidents:
  Adams, John
  Adams, John
    Quincy
  Arthur, Chester A.
  Buchanan, James
  Cleveland, Grover
  Fillmore, Millard
  Garfield, James A.
  Grant, Ulysses S.
  Harrison,
    Benjamin

Harrison, William
  Henry
Hayes,
  Rutherford B.
Jackson, Andrew
Jefferson, Thomas
Johnson, Andrew
Lincoln, Abraham
McKinley,
  William
Madison, James
Monroe, James
Pierce, Franklin
Polk, James K.
Roosevelt,
  Theodore
Taft, William
  Howard
Taylor, Zachary
Tyler, John
Van Buren,
  Martin
Washington,
  George
Wilson, Woodrow
U.S. social reformers
  and religious
  leaders:
  Garvey, Marcus
  Grimké, Sarah and
    Angelina
  La Follette,
    Robert M.
  Noyes, John
    Humphrey
  Truth, Sojourner
  Washington,
    Booker T.
  Woodhull,
    Victoria
  Wright, Frances
  Young, Brigham
U.S. statesmen and
  political figures—
  Civil War and
  Reconstruction:
  Bates, Edward
  Blair, Francis
    Preston, Jr.
  Boutwell, George
    Sewall
  Brownlow,
    William G.

Chase, Salmon P.
Clay, Henry
Crittenden,
　John J.
Davis, Henry
　Winter
Davis, Jefferson
Douglas,
　Stephen A.
Mason, James
　Murray
Owen,
　Robert Dale
Revels, Hiram R.
Seward,
　William H.
Sherman, John
Stanton, Edwin M.
Stevens, Thaddeus
Sumner, Charles
Vallandigham,
　Clement L.

Vance, Zebulon B.
Welles, Gideon
U.S. statesmen and
political figures—
Federalist period:
Burr, Aaron
Clinton, Dewitt
Dayton, Jonathan
Hamilton,
　Alexander
Pinckney, Charles
U.S. statesmen and
political figures—
Revolutionary War:
Adams, John
Adams, Samuel
Franklin,
　Benjamin
Henry, Patrick
Mason, George
Otis, James

Paine, Thomas
Pendleton,
　Edmund
Revere, Paul
Rush, Benjamin
Wilkinson, James
U.S. statesmen and
political figures—
other:
Altgeld, John Peter
Benton, Thomas
　Hart
Bryan, William
　Jennings
Hay, John
Houston, Sam
Lansing, Robert
Lodge, Henry
　Cabot
Root, Elihu
Webster, Daniel

U.S. Supreme Court
justices:
Brandeis, Louis
Field, Stephen J.
Harlan, John
　Marshall
Holmes, Oliver
　Wendell
Jay, John
Marshall, John
Matthews, Stanley
Miller, Samuel
　Freeman
Story, Joseph
Taney, Roger
　Brooke
Waite, Morrison
　Remick
White, Edward
　Douglas

INDEX: See entries under all of the terms above

Section 966.　Development of the Latin-American and Caribbean Nations to *c.* 1920

A. The Latin-American independence movement (1790–1825)

　1. Background of the Latin-American wars of independence

　　a. Discontent among Indians, Creoles, and mestizos: the influence of the Enlightenment, the U.S. War of Independence, and the French Revolution

　　b. Influence of Toussaint-Louverture's successful slave revolt (1791–94): war with the French (1802–03) and the establishment of Haiti (1804)

　　c. Spanish involvement in European wars: the Peninsular War in Spain (1808–14), Napoleon's seizure of the Spanish throne and Creole support of Ferdinand VII

　2. The Spanish South American War of Independence (1810–25), the establishment of the independent Empire of Brazil (1822)

　　a. The struggle for independence in New Granada

　　　i. Initial phases of the revolt under Miranda and Bolívar (1811–14), military setbacks (1815)

　　　ii. Final expulsion of the Spanish from Venezuela, Colombia, Ecuador, and Panama (1821); establishment of the Republic of Gran Colombia (1821–29)

　　b. Establishment of the United Provinces of the Río de la Plata (1813) at Buenos Aires; division of provinces into states of Paraguay, Buenos Aires, and Uruguay (1828)

　　c. San Martín's military support of the Chilean independence movement under O'Higgins (1817–18), the liberation of Peru (1821)

　　d. San Martín's withdrawal and assumption of control by Simón Bolívar, final defeat of Spanish troops (1824), Upper Peru's emergence as independent state of Bolivia (1825) under Sucre

　　e. The Portuguese government in exile in Brazil (1808–22): reforms of King John VI (1816–22), establishment of the independent Empire of Brazil under Pedro I (1822)

　3. The Mexican War of Independence (1810–21): Hidalgo's revolt (1810–11), social and economic reforms under Morelos (1811–15), Iturbide's leadership (1820–21)

B. Mexico from independence (1821) through the end of the Revolution (1917)

　1. Mexico from 1821 to 1855

a. The independent Mexican Empire under Iturbide (1821–23), Santa Anna and the establishment of the Mexican Republic (1824), the constitution of 1824, Centralist–Federalist struggles

b. Santa Anna's military career and intermittent terms as president (1833 to 1855): the Alamo (1836); war with U.S. (1846–48) over Texas, New Mexico, and California

2. Mexico from 1855 to 1876

a. Juárez and La Reforma: social and economic reforms of the 1857 constitution, anticlericalism, the civil war (1857–60)

b. French intervention (1862) and Emperor Maximilian's puppet rule (1864–67): attempted liberal reforms; loss of conservative support; French withdrawal, defeat of imperial forces, and Maximilian's execution (1867)

c. Restoration of the republic under Juárez' leadership (1867–72), educational and economic reforms, Lerdo's presidency (1872–76), further separation of church and state

3. The Porfirio Díaz dictatorship (1876–1911)

a. Díaz' economic and social policies: maintenance of public order and suppression of dissent, economic development through foreign investment, reconciliation with church, middle-class control of land

b. Emergence of radical and liberal political clubs (*c.* 1900): internal unrest; labour strikes; Madero's unsuccessful challenge to Díaz' reelection (1909); armed revolt, Díaz' resignation, and Madero's election (1911)

4. The Mexican Revolutionary period (1910–17): Huerta's coup and Madero's execution (1913); Carranza's loose alliance with Pancho Villa, Zapata, and Obregón; civil war; the constitution of 1917; Carranza's election (1917)

C. Central America and the Caribbean to *c.* 1920

1. The Central American republics to *c.* 1920

a. Independence from Spain (1821), participation in Mexican Empire (1822–23), federation of United Provinces of Central America (1823), armed conflict between Conservatives and Liberals, collapse of the federation (1838)

b. Guatemala from 1838 to 1920: Carrera's Conservative dictatorship (1838–65), social and economic reforms of Barrios (1873–85) and subsequent Liberal regimes to 1898, Estrada Cabrera's administration (1898–1920)

c. Honduras from 1838 to 1920: Conservative domination to the 1870s, Aurelio Soto's Liberal regime (1876), return of Conservative control (1885), U.S. investments and military intervention (1912)

d. El Salvador to 1930: establishment of the republic (1841), Liberal–Conservative conflicts to 1885, coffee economy, political stability (1899–1930)

e. Nicaragua from 1838 to 1920: Liberal–Conservative conflicts, foreign intervention in the 1850s, stable Conservative governments (1857–93), economic growth, Zelaya's Liberal regime (1893–1909), U.S. military intervention from 1910

f. Costa Rica from 1838 to 1920: the coffee economy and social stability, Guardia dictatorship (1870–82) and the 1871 constitution, orderly presidential succession after 1890, Río San Juan dispute with Nicaragua

g. Panama to 1920: union with Gran Colombia (1821–1903), civil war, U.S. intervention and establishment of Republic of Panama (1903), building of Panama Canal (1904–14), U.S. control of Canal Zone

h. British colonial and U.S. economic interests in, and conflicts over, the Central American region; *e.g.,* in British Honduras

2. The island states of the Caribbean (*c.* 1800–1930)

a. Haiti to 1934: independence in 1804, civil war between the blacks and mulattoes, black hegemony under Christophe (later Henri I, 1806–20), ascendancy of mulattoes under Boyer (1820–43), political instability (1843–1915), U.S. military occupation (1915–34)

b. The Dominican Republic to 1930: the struggle for independence (to 1844), despotic regimes (1844–1916), U.S. armed intervention (1916–30)

c. Cuba from 1790 to 1934

i. 19th-century social and economic developments: growth of the sugar industry, the abolition of slavery (1886)

ii. Spanish suppression of Cuban liberation movement in the Ten Years' War (1868–78), economic relations with United States, the Cuban War of Independence from Spain (1895–98)

iii. Cuba as a U.S. protectorate until 1934: military occupation (1899–1901), Republic of Cuba (1902), later U.S. occupation (1906–09), dictatorships and the sugar industry

d. The remaining European insular and mainland possessions in the Caribbean region from *c.* 1810 to *c.* 1920

D. The successor states of Gran Colombia to *c.* 1930

1. Venezuela from 1810 to 1935

a. Venezuelan independence movement (1810–30), national development under Páez (1830–48), Conservative Party rule

b. Monagas family regime (1848–58) and turmoil between Liberal and Conservative parties to 1870, regime of Guzmán Blanco (1870–88)

c. Political instability to 1892, Crespo's regime (1892–96), the Castro (1899–1908) and Gómez (1908–35) dictatorships

2. Colombia from 1819 to 1930

a. Independence (1819), participation in Gran Colombia to 1830, power struggle between Conservative and Liberal parties (1840–80), social reforms, anticlericalism

b. Political instability and civil wars (1880s and 1899–1903), loss of Panama (1903), development of coffee industry (1909–28)

E. The Indian nations of the Andes to *c.* 1930

1. Ecuador from 1822 to 1925

a. Participation in Gran Colombia (1822–30), independent republic (1830), dictatorial regimes to 1845, political instability (1845–60)

b. Clericalism in García Moreno's dictatorship (1860–75), Liberal ascendancy after 1875, Alfaro's administrations (1897–1911), social problems, depression in the 1920s

2. Peru from 1824 to 1930

a. Establishment of republic (1824), power struggle among caudillos (1824–41), temporary union with Bolivia (1836–39), orderly government under Castilla (1845–51 and 1855–62)

b. Spanish military invasion (1864–69), Pardo's civilian government (1872–76) and economic crises, War of the Pacific (1879–84) and loss of territory to Chile, establishment of Peruvian Corporation (1889)

c. Economic and social reforms of Piérola's administration (1895–1908), conflict between Democratic and Civilian parties, Leguía's administrations (1908–12 and 1919–30) and economic development, formation of the Aprista Movement

3. Bolivia from 1809 to 1930

a. Participation in Latin American wars of independence (1810–25), Bolivian independence (1825), Sucre's presidency (1826–28), economic decline

b. Dictatorship of Santa Cruz (1829–39), temporary union with Peru (1836–39), silver-mining boom, War of the Pacific (1879–84) and territorial loss to Chile

c. Conservative Party rule (1880–99), economic growth, the Federal Revolution (1899), Montes' leadership in Liberal Party rule (1899–1920), growth of tin-mining industry, Republican Party coup (1920), economic decline

F. Chile from 1810 to 1920

1. Chile from the 1810 establishment of the republic to 1860

a. The provisional government (1810–12), return of Spanish rule (1812), defeat of Spanish troops by combined Chilean–Argentinian army (1817)

b. Bernardo O'Higgins as head of state (1817–23): liberal reforms and conservative opposition, O'Higgins' abdication (1823), political instability (1823–30)

c. The conservative hegemony (1830–61): the 1833 constitution; political stability and conservative governments under Portales, Ovalle, Prieto, Bulnes, and Montt; economic prosperity; growth of liberal faction

2. The widening of liberal influence and the growth of political splinter groups (1861–91)

   a. The "Liberal Republic" under Pérez (1861–71) and the liberal–conservative alliance: cultural and economic ties with Great Britain, political conflict over church–state relations (1872)

   b. The War of the Pacific (1879–84) and threatened European intervention: annexation of saltpetre-mining provinces from Peru and Bolivia, civil war and Balmaceda's abdication (1891)

3. The parliamentary republic (1891–1920): era of legislative supremacy; growth of middle and lower classes; formation of Democratic (1887), Radical (1888), and Socialist (1901 and 1912) parties

G. The successor states of the Río de la Plata (excluding Bolivia) to *c.* 1920

1. Argentina to 1930

   a. Efforts toward reconstruction (1820–29), confederation under Rosas and ascendancy of Buenos Aires (1829–52)

      i. Dominance of Buenos Aires: interprovincial rivalries, presidency of Rivadavia (1826–27)

      ii. The Rosas government (1829–52): domestic politics and foreign policies

   b. Period of national consolidation (1852–80), conservative regimes (1880–1916)

      i. The constitution of 1853 and civil wars (1853–60), government under Mitre (1862–68) and his successors

      ii. Economic development during Roca's administration (1880–86), economic crisis of 1890

      iii. The rise of radicalism: growth of social unrest, electoral reform of 1912

   c. The Radical regimes (1916–30): Irigoyen's presidency (1916–22), continued Radical rule in the 1920s, growth of foreign influence in the economy, military coup (1930)

2. The Uruguayan struggle for independence and national unity (1811–1929)

   a. Independence from Spain (1811) and participation in United Provinces of the Río de la Plata (1813–28), establishment of independent Uruguay (1828)

   b. Civil war (1839–51) between Colorado and Blanco political parties, participation in war against Paraguay (1865–70), military rule (1875–90)

   c. Civilian rule and continued political crises and insurrections (1890–1904), Peace of Acequá (1904) and return to orderly government, social and economic reforms, economic boom during World War I

3. Paraguay from 1810 to 1924

   a. Independence from Spain (1811), struggle with Buenos Aires for autonomy, establishment of independent Paraguay (1813)

   b. Isolationism during Rodríguez Francia's dictatorship (1814–40), encouragement of foreign trade during Carlos Antonio López' dictatorship (1841–62)

   c. Francisco Solano López' regime (1862–70): loss of territory after war with Brazil and Argentina (1864–70), political instability after 1870

H. Brazil from the establishment of the empire to the fall of the First Republic (1822–1930)

1. The independent Empire of Brazil (1822–89)

   a. The empire under Pedro I (1822–31): the constitution of 1824, Pedro's abdication (1831), internal disunity during the regency (1831–40)

   b. The empire under Pedro II (1840–89): intervention in Uruguayan affairs and war with Paraguay (1864–70); cessation of slave trade (1853), gradual emancipation, and abolition of slavery (1888)

2. Brazil during the First Republic (1889–1930)

   a. The constitution of 1891 and social reforms, military dictatorships (1891–94), civilian governments (1894–1914)

   b. Brazilian participation in World War I, postwar prosperity to 1922, economic problems during the 1920s, increasing political role of the military, civil disorders leading to the revolution of 1930

Suggested reading in the *Encyclopædia Britannica:*

MACROPAEDIA: Major articles dealing with the development of the Latin-American and Caribbean nations to *c.* 1920

Argentina	Colombia	Mexico	South America
Bolivia	Ecuador	Mexico City	Suriname
Brazil	Guyana	North America	Uruguay
Buenos Aires	Havana	Paraguay	Venezuela
Caracas	Latin America,	Peru	West Indies
Central America	The History of	Rio de Janeiro	
Chile	Lima	São Paulo	

MICROPAEDIA: Selected entries of reference information

General subjects

Central America and	Chapultepec	*South America:*	Pacific, War of the
the Caribbean:	Chilpancingo,	Acto Adicional	Paraguayan War
Canal Zone	Congress of	of 1834	Pavón, Battle of
Cuban	científico	Ayacucho,	Peruvian-Bolivian
Independence	Contreras,	Battle of	Confederation
Movement	Battle of	Bidlack Treaty	Pipiolo and
Hay-Bunau-Varilla	Gadsden Purchase	Boyacá, Battle of	Pelucón
Treaty	Guadalupe	Bryan–Chamorro	Rio Branco Law
Maine, destruction	Hidalgo,	Treaty	Talambo affair
of the	Treaty of	Carabobo,	Tenentismo
Platt Amendment	Iguala Plan	Battle of	Thousand Days,
Santiago, Battle of	Indigenismo	Cepeda, battles of	The War of a
Spanish–	Mexican	Chacabuco,	Tucumán,
American War	Revolution	Battle of	Congress of
United Provinces	Mexican War	Civilista	Water Witch
of Central	Palo Alto, Battle of	estancia	incident
America	Pastry War	gaucho	
Mexico:	Puebla, Battle of	Gran Colombia	
Buena Vista,	Reforma, La	Guayaquil	
Battle of	Rurales	Conference	
Celaya, Battle of	San Jacinto,	Itata and	
Cerro Gordo,	Battle of	Baltimore	
Battle of		incidents	

Biographies

Central America and	Díaz, Porfirio	Artigas, José	O'Higgins,
the Caribbean:	Guerrero, Vicente	Gervasio	Bernardo
Barrios, Justo	Hidalgo y Costilla,	Batlle y Ordóñez,	Pedro I
Rufino	Miguel	José	Pedro II
Dessalines,	Huerta, Victoriano	Bolívar, Simón	Reyes, Rafael
Jean-Jacques	Iturbide,	Carrera, José	Rivadavia,
Estrada Cabrera,	Agustín de	Miguel	Bernardino
Manuel	Juárez, Benito	Fonseca, Manuel	Rosas, Juan
Estrada Palma,	Madero, Francisco	Deodoro da	Manuel de
Tomás	Maximilian	Guzmán Blanco,	San Martín,
Martí (y Pérez),	Morelos (y Pavón),	Antonio	José de
José Julián	José María	Haya de la Torre,	Silva Xavier,
Morazán,	Santa Anna,	Víctor Raúl	Joaquim José da
Francisco	Antonio López de	López, Francisco	Sucre, Antonio
Toussaint-Louverture	Villa, Pancho	Solano	José de
Zelaya, José Santos	Zapata, Emiliano	Miranda,	Uriburu,
Mexico:	*South America:*	Francisco de	José Félix
Carranza,	Andrada e Silva,	Mitre, Bartolomé	Urquiza, Justo
Venustiano	José Bonifácio de	Moreno, Mariano	José de

INDEX: See entries under all of the terms above

Section 967.   **Australia and Oceania to *c.* 1920**

A. The character and historical development of the diverse peoples of Oceania and the effects of colonization

   1. The historical sources and historiographic problems

   2. Geography, ethnography, and prehistory of Australia, Melanesia, Micronesia, and Polynesia (including New Zealand)

   3. European exploration and colonial settlement: missionaries, trading societies, and colonial government

B. Australia to 1920

   1. Early European exploration by sea and land

   2. British colonization of New South Wales in 1788, expansion and development of self-government (1830–60), economic growth and the federation movement (1860–1901), the establishment of the commonwealth in 1901, social tensions, cultural developments

   3. Early years of the commonwealth: establishment of a White Australia immigration policy, Labor Party reforms, industrial growth, cooperation with Britain in World War I

   4. Relations with the Aboriginal population

C. New Zealand to 1928

   1. The extension of British control over, and annexation of, North and South Islands (1838–41)

   2. Relations between the indigenous Maori people and the British: encroachments and ensuing conflicts

   3. Establishment of self-government (1852): economic development and immigration

   4. Politics and foreign relations (1890–1928): Liberal and Reform Party governments, radical politics, the Labour Party, cooperation with Britain in World War I

Suggested reading in the *Encyclopædia Britannica:*

MACROPAEDIA: Major articles dealing with Australia and Oceania to *c.* 1920

   Australia
   Melbourne
   New Zealand
   Pacific Islands
   Sydney
   United States of America: *Hawaii*

MICROPAEDIA: Selected entries of reference information

General subjects

Australia:	Immigration	United Australia	New Zealand
ANZAC	Restriction Act	Party	Political Reform
Australian	Kanaka	Van Diemen's	League
Colonies	Lambing Flat	Land	Waitangi,
Government Act	Riots	White Australia	Treaty of
Australian Labor	Liberal Party of	Policy	Young Maori
Party	Australia	*New Zealand:*	Party
Australian	National Party	ANZAC	*other:*
Patriotic	New South Wales	Hauhau	Lapita culture
Association	Corps	Maori	Melanesia
Black War	Port Phillip	Representation	Micronesia
blackbirding	Association	Act	Polynesia
bushranger	Port Phillip	New Zealand	
Castle Hill Rising	District	Company	
Emancipist	Rum Rebellion	New Zealand	
Eureka Stockade	squatter	Labour Party	
Exclusive			

Biographies

Australia:
Arthur, Sir George,
1st Baronet
Barton, Sir
Edmund
Bligh, William
Deakin, Alfred
Forrest, Sir John
Hughes, William
Morris
Macarthur, John
Macquarie,
Lachlan

Parkes, Sir Henry
Phillip, Arthur
Sturt, Charles
Torrens, Sir
Robert Richard
Wentworth, W.C.
New Zealand:
Kingi, Wiremu
Massey, William
Ferguson
Pomare, Sir Maui
Seddon, Richard
John

other:
Bougainville,
Louis-Antoine de
Clunies-Ross
family
Cook, James
Dumont d'Urville,
Jules-Sébastien-César
Flinders, Matthew
Kamehameha I
Kamehameha IV

Mitchell, Sir
Thomas
Livingstone
Oxley, John
Tasman, Abel
Janszoon
Wakefield,
Edward Gibbon
Weld, Sir
Frederick
Aloysius

INDEX: See entries under all of the terms above

Section 968. **South Asia Under the Influence of European Imperialism from *c.* 1500 to *c.* 1920**

A. European activity in India (1498–*c.* 1760)

1. Portuguese commercial relations with India from 1498: establishment of the colony of Goa, decline of Portuguese hegemony and rise of British and Dutch influence

2. Dutch trading posts and conflicts with the British

3. The British and French in India

   a. Establishment and growth of British settlements and trading posts (1600–1740): the East India Company, relations with indigenous peoples

   b. Development of French trading companies from 1674: Anglo-French rivalry (1740–63) and establishment of British hegemony

   c. The British seizure of Calcutta (1757) and Clive's establishment of British control over the local Bengal ruler (1757–60)

B. Extension of British power (1760–1858)

1. Growth of the political power of the British East India Company and attempts by the British crown to regulate its affairs

   a. Securing of British supremacy in Bengal

   b. Warren Hastings (1774–85) and the transition of the status of the company from revenue farmer to a ruling power in India

   c. Wars with the Marāthās and Mysore at the end of the 18th century

   d. Expansion and consolidation of British control over various Indian states during administrations of Lord Wellesley (1798–1805), Lord Minto (1807–13), and Lord Hastings (1813–23)

   e. The organization and determination of administrative policy: Cornwallis and the transition toward British administrative procedures

   f. Completion of British annexation of, or domination over, the Afghan, Sikh, and Lower Burmese kingdoms in the 1840s and 1850s

2. The political, legal, economic, social, and cultural effects of the first century of British influence

3. The cause, outbreak, suppression, and effects of the Indian Mutiny (1857): the British crown's assumption of total responsibility for the government of India

C. British imperial power (1858–1920)

1. Climax of the raj: social and economic policies, government organization, the influence of the viceroys

2. British foreign policy in India: conflicts with Russia over the northwest frontier, the incorporation of Burma (1886), the Second Afghan War (1878–80) and the creation of the North-West Frontier Province (1901), the Third Afghan War (1919)

3. Beginning of Indian nationalism in the late 19th century and the British response: formation of the Indian National Congress (1885), policies of Lord Curzon (1899–1905), partition of Bengal, founding of the nationalist Muslim League, the Indian Councils Act of 1909

4. World War I and its aftermath: India's contribution to the war effort, anti-British activity, the Amritsar massacre, the Government of India Act (1919), Hindu–Muslim relations, the emergence of Mahatma Gandhi and the adoption of his noncooperation policy

D. Ceylon under foreign rulers from *c.* 1505 to 1920

1. Portuguese political and commercial activities in Ceylon (1505–1658): conflict with the Kandyan kingdom

2. Dutch rule in Ceylon (1658–1796) and its influence on the political, economic, judicial, and administrative systems; commercial enterprises and missionary attempts

3. The British in Ceylon from 1796: unification and early administration, the reforms of 1833, the transition from a subsistence to a commercial economy, the beginnings of constitutional government, nationalist unrest during World War I

E. Tibet and Nepal from *c.* 1750 to *c.* 1920

1. Decline of Chinese influence in Tibet: administration and culture under the Manchus

2. Nepal's territorial expansion under the Shah rulers, decline of Shah family and rise of Thapa and Rana families, accommodation with the British to preserve Nepal's independence

---

Suggested reading in the *Encyclopædia Britannica*:

MACROPAEDIA: Major articles dealing with South Asia under the influence of European imperialism from *c.* 1500 to *c.* 1920

Asia
Calcutta
India
Nepal
Sri Lanka

MICROPAEDIA: Selected entries of reference information

General subjects

colonial administration and policy:
Afrīdī
Bengal, Partition of
Colebrook–Cameron Commission
Cornwallis Code
Defence of India Act
Durand Line
East India Company
forward policy
Government of India Act
lapse, doctrine of
McMahon Line
maḥalwārī system
Sadr Dīwānī 'Adlāt
Thesavalamai

tombo
zamindar
historic events:
Amritsar, Massacre of
Baksar, Battle of
Barrackpore Mutiny
Black Hole of Calcutta
Carnatic Wars
Fīroz Shāh, Battle of
Gujrat, Battle of
Indian Mutiny
Marāthā Wars
Miāni, Battle of
Mysore Wars
Sikh Wars
Sobraon, Battle of
Vellore Mutiny
historic states and sites:
Cis-Sutlej states

Kandy
Saint David, Fort
Saint George, Fort
William, Fort
nationalist groups and movements:
Ghadr
Indian Association
Indian National Congress
Muslim League
Noncooperation Movement
Servants of India Society
treaties:
Amritsar, Treaty of
Banaras, Treaties of
Bassein, Treaty of

Lucknow Pact
Malvana, Convention of
Purandhar, Treaty of
Surji-arjungaon, Treaty of
Wadgaon, Convention of

Biographies

Britons:

Auckland, George
Eden, earl of
Bentinck, Lord
William
Canning, Charles
John Canning,
Earl
Chelmsford,
Frederic John
Napier Thesiger,
1st Viscount and
3rd Baron
Clive, Robert, 1st
Baron Clive of
Plassey
Coote, Sir Eyre
Curzon (of
Kedleston),
George Nathaniel
Curzon,
Marquess
Dalhousie,
James Andrew
Broun Ramsay,
marquess and
10th earl of
Ellenborough,
Edward Law,
Earl of

Elphinstone,
Mountstuart
Fitch, Ralph
Frere, Sir Bartle
Hastings, Francis
Rawdon-Hastings,
1st marquess of
Hastings, Warren
Hume, Allan
Octavian
Lansdowne, Henry
Charles Keith
Petty-Fitzmaurice,
5th marquess of
Lawrence,
Sir Henry
Montgomery
Lawrence (of the
Punjab and of
Grately), John
Laird Mair
Lawrence, 1st
Baron
Lytton, Robert
Bulwer-Lytton,
1st Earl of
Mayo, Richard
Southwell
Bourke, 6th
earl of

Metcalfe (of Fern
Hill), Charles T.
Metcalfe, Baron
Minto, Gilbert
Elliot-Murray-
Kynynmound, 1st
earl of
Minto,
Gilbert John
Elliot-Murray-
Kynynmound,
4th earl of
Napier of Magdala,
Robert Napier,
1st Baron
Outram, Sir James
Ripon, George
Frederick Samuel
Robinson, 1st
Marquess of
Wellesley (of
Norragh),
Richard Colley
Wellesley,
Marquess
Younghusband, Sir
Francis Edward

Indians:

Banerjea, Sir
Surendranath

Dalip Singh
Das Chitta Ranjan
Dogra dynasty
Gandhi,
Mohandas
Karamchand
Holkar dynasty
Lajpat Rai, Lala
Mīr Ja'far
Ram Singh
Roy, Ram Mohun
Sankaran Nair,
Sir Chettur
Sapru, Sir Tej
Bahadur
Sastri, Srinivasa
Shāh 'Ālam II
Tilak, Bal
Gangadhar

other:

Albuquerque,
Afonso de, the
Great
Dupleix,
Joseph-François
Gama, Vasco da,
1er conde da
Vidigueira
Jung Bahadur

INDEX: See entries under all of the terms above

Section 969. **Southeast Asia Under the Influence of European Imperialism to *c.* 1920**

A. The states and European colonies of mainland Southeast Asia from *c.* 1600 to *c.* 1920

  1. Myanmar (Burma) and Malaya from *c.* 1600 to *c.* 1920: the advent of British rule

    a. Myanmar from *c.* 1600 to *c.* 1920

      i. Renewed expansionism and wars with the Mons, Thais, and Chinese under the Alaungpaya dynasty from 1752: the First and Second Anglo-Burmese Wars (1824–26, 1852), traditional administration in Myanmar

      ii. The Third Anglo-Burmese War (1885) and union with British India (1886): effects of British colonialism

    b. Malaya from *c.* 1630 to *c.* 1920: loss of autonomy through Dutch and British intrusions

      i. Dutch intervention in the Malay states (1633), immigration (*c.* 1650) of Minangkabau and Bugis people from Sumatra

      ii. British invasions in Malaya (1795), clashes between Malays and Chinese immigrants (1874), British intervention and assumption of power from sultanates of Malaya

  2. Indochina and the development of French rule from *c.* 1615

    a. Portuguese and French missionary involvement in Vietnam and Vietnamese reaction (1615–1858), French intervention in Indochina and territorial acquisition of Cochinchina and Cambodia (1858–63)

    b. Period of colonization (1873–93); establishment of French protectorates in Annam, Tongking, and Laos; French administration in Indochina

3. Siam from *c.* 1620 to *c.* 1910

   a. Trade relations with China and other Asian countries, influence of Theravāda Buddhism, Dutch and French intrusions and establishment of trade in the 1660s

   b. Invasion by Myanmar (1767) and end of Ayutthayan kingdom domination; political reunification and establishment of Chakkri dynasty (1782); social, cultural, and legal development in the early 19th century; Chinese immigration; expansion of trade with the U.S. and with European countries; reign of Mongkut (1851–68)

   c. Political, social, and economic reforms in the reign of Chulalongkorn (1868–1910): Anglo-French activity in Southeast Asia and acquisition of Siamese territory (1893–1909)

4. Laos from *c.* 1600: establishment of separate kingdoms of Luang Prabang and Vientiane in 1707, Siamese domination from 1778, establishment of French protectorate in 1893

B. The states and European colonies of the Indonesian Archipelago and the Philippines from *c.* 1500 to *c.* 1920

   1. The Portuguese and the Spanish in Southeast Asia

      a. Portuguese naval and commercial activities, domination of the Strait of Malacca, and rivalry with the Spanish in the Spice Islands; collapse of Portuguese commercial empire with the defeat by the Dutch (1641)

      b. The Philippines to *c.* 1920

         i. The people and culture of the Philippines prior to the arrival of the Spanish

         ii. Spanish control of the Philippines (1571–1898): government administration and influence of the Roman Catholic Church, land policy and overseas trade, rise of nationalism in the 19th century

         iii. The Philippine Revolution of 1896–98, U.S. support in ousting the Spanish, subsequent U.S. takeover and administration to *c.* 1920

   2. The Dutch and other European powers in Indonesia from *c.* 1600 to *c.* 1920

      a. The Dutch East India Company (1602–1799): Coen's establishment of Dutch commercial supremacy, company rule in Java, decline and abolition of the company

      b. The French and British in Java (1806–15), Dutch rule in the 19th century

         i. The Culture System (Cultuur-stelsel) and its deleterious effects on Java (1830–70): the Liberal Policy

         ii. The Ethical Policy and the rise of nationalism: social and economic benefits, formation of nationalist organizations

---

Suggested reading in the *Encyclopædia Britannica*:

MACROPAEDIA: Major articles dealing with Southeast Asia under the influence of European Imperialism to *c.* 1920

Asia	Manila
Indonesia	Philippines
Jakarta	Southeast Asia, Mainland

MICROPAEDIA: Selected entries of reference information

General subjects

Indonesian	Muhammadiyah	Annam	Perak War
Archipelago:	Padri War	Barrackpore	Saigon, Treaty of
Achinese War	Peranakan	Mutiny	Selangor Civil War
Amboina	Perhimpunan	Bowring Treaty	Sino-French War
Massacre	Indonesia	Cochinchina	Straits Settlements
Budi Utomo	priyayi	Hai San	Tonkin
Buginese	Sarekat Islām	Hlutdaw	*Philippine Islands:*
Culture System	Volksraad	Indochina	barangay
Dutch East Indies	*mainland Southeast*	Naning War	Cavite Mutiny
Ethical Policy	*Asia:*	Pangkor	Friar Lands
Gianti Agreement	Anglo-Burmese	Engagement	Question
Mataram	Wars		

INDEX: See entries under all of the terms above

Section 96/10. China from 1839 Until the Onset of Revolution (to *c.* 1911), and Japan from the Meiji Restoration to *c.* 1910

A. China under the late Ch'ing: the challenges of rebellion and Western penetration

   1. The Western challenge (1839–60) and the collapse of the tributary system: rebellion and the reestablishment of the Ch'ing government

      a. Problems created by the opium trade: British demands for trade advantages and diplomatic parity culminating in the Opium War (1839–42)

         i. The Opium War and its aftermath: granting of commercial privileges to Western powers

         ii. Reactions to foreign trade gains: anti-foreign movements concentrated at Canton

      b. Popular uprisings of the Taiping and Nien and rebellions in western China, the effects of the rebellions

   2. Contending forces of westernization and Chinese tradition from *c.* 1850

      a. The "self-strengthening" movement: its effect on foreign relations and on domestic life

         i. Western attempts at treaty revision and the chilling of Sino-Russian relations, hostility toward Christian missionaries

         ii. Industrialization for self-strengthening: mining and the weapons industry, malpractice and corruption in business

      b. Increasing foreign encroachments (1870–95): loss of Central Asian territories, problems resulting from Chinese hesitancy to engage in regular diplomatic relations, Korea and the Sino-Japanese War (1894–95)

c. The reform movement of K'ang Yu-wei, the conservative reaction, and the Boxer Rebellion (1900) as expressions of anti-foreign feelings: Western seizure of Peking (1900) and further Ch'ing concessions, U.S. Open Door Policy

d. Reformist and revolutionist movements at the end of the dynasty: Ch'ing reforms after 1901, the Republican movement and the 1911 Revolution

    i. Sun Yat-sen and the United League: constitutional movements after 1905

    ii. Peasant uprisings and the 1911 Revolution

B. The modernization of Japan and its emergence as a world power (1868–c. 1910)

1. The Meiji Restoration and the process of modernization

a. The fall of the Tokugawa, leadership and initial policies of the new government, samurai opposition and government countermeasures

b. Beginning of Japanese modernization: abolition of feudalism; fiscal and economic policies; growth of *zaibatsu* (cartels); development of national loyalties; religious, educational, and cultural policies

c. Politics in Meiji Japan: creation of political parties, oligarchic control and gradual development of representative institutions

2. Foreign relations in Imperial Japan: dispute with China over Korea, success in the Russo-Japanese War (1904–05), annexation of Korea (1910), economic expansion in China

---

Suggested reading in the *Encyclopædia Britannica*:

MACROPAEDIA: Major articles dealing with China from 1839 until the onset of revolution (to c. 1911), and Japan from the Meiji Restoration to c. 1910

Asia	Japan	Shanghai	Tokyo-Yokohama
Canton	Korea	Taiwan	Metropolitan
China	Nanking	Tientsin	Area
Hong Kong	Peking		

MICROPAEDIA: Selected entries of reference information

General subjects

China—domestic affairs:	T'ung-wen kuan	kazoku	Root–Takahira
Chinese Revolution	*China—international relations:*	Meiji Restoration	Agreement
Ch'ing dynasty	Boxer Rebellion	Paulownia Sun, Order of the	Russo-Japanese War
Ch'ing-liu tang	Chinese Eastern Railway	Rising Sun, Order of the	Tsushima, Battle of
cohong	Kuldja, Treaty of	zaibatsu	*other:*
Five-Power Constitution	Lay–Osborn flotilla	*Japan—international relations:*	capitulation
Hundred Days of Reform	Open Door policy	Anglo-Japanese Alliance	Sino-Japanese War (1894–95)
Kiangnan Arsenal	Opium Wars	Gentlemen's Agreement	Shimonoseki, Treaty of
likin	Sino-French War	Lansing–Ishii Agreement	South Manchurian Railway
Nien Rebellion	Tientsin Massacre	Portsmouth, Treaty of	treaty port
Taiping Rebellion	*Japan—domestic affairs:*		Unequal Treaty
Three Principles of the People	Charter Oath		
	genro		
	Kaishintō		

Biographies

China:	Li Hung-chang	Tso Tsung t'ang	Fukuzawa Yukichi
Chang Chih-tung	Liang Ch'i-ch'ao	Tuan ch'i-jui	Gotō Shōjirō,
Chang Ping-lin	Lin Tse-hsü	T'ung-chih	Hakushaku
Ch'i-ying	Sheng Hsüan-huai	Tz'u-hsi	Inoue Kaoru,
Huang Hsing	Soong family	Yang Hsiu-ch'ing	Kōshaku
Hung Hsiu-ch'üan	Sun Yat-sen	*Japan:*	Itagaki Taisuke,
K'ang Yu-wei	Sung Chiao-jen	Abe Isoo	Hakushaku
Kuang-hsü	Ts'ai Yüan-p'ei	Etō Shimpei	Itō Hirobumi,
Kung Ch'in-wang	Tseng Kuo-fan	Fujita Tōko	Kōshaku

Section 96/11.   Southwest Asia and North Africa (*c.* 1800–1920), and Sub-Saharan Africa (1885–*c.* 1920) Under the Influence of European Imperialism: the Early Colonial Period

A. The Ottoman Empire from 1807 to 1920: European intervention and the continuation of westernization

   1. The empire under Mahmud II: internal reforms and centralization, the Greek revolt (1821–32), the Egyptian revolt (1831–41), Russian intrusions in Turkey

   2. Reaction, revolt, and further disintegration until World War I

      a. The era of the Tanzimat reforms (1839–76)

      b. Crisis of 1875–78 and the loss of Romania, Serbia, Montenegro, and most of Bulgaria; the constitution of 1876

      c. The growth of Turkish nationalism in the reign of Abdülhamid II (1876–1909) and dissolution of the empire, domination by Germany in World War I

B. Egypt, the Maghrib, and the Arabian Peninsula: the development of Arab nationalism and Zionism

   1. The emergence of modern Egypt (1798–1922)

      a. Egypt under French (1798–1801) and British (1801–03) occupation, centralized administration of Muḥammad ʿAlī and his successors (1805–82), construction of Suez Canal (1858–69), European financial and military intervention

      b. Egypt under British rule (1882–1922): reforms by Baring's (later 1st Earl Cromer) administration (1883–1907), revival of nationalism, World War I and independence (1922)

   2. The Maghrib from 1830 to *c.* 1930: European penetration into Algeria, Tunisia, Libya, and Morocco

      a. Algeria from 1830 to 1920: the French conquest (1830–71) and colonial settlements, national resistance movement under Abdelkader, suppression of the Muslim population

      b. Tunisia from 1830 to *c.* 1930: French influence to 1881 and status as a French protectorate from 1881

      c. Morocco from 1830 to 1920: growth of French, Spanish, and British influence and decline of the traditional government; establishment of French and Spanish zones and protectorates (1912)

      d. Libya (Tripolitania and Cyrenaica) from *c.* 1834 to 1920: subjection to direct Turkish rule (1835), growth of Italian influence resulting in conquest (1911–12)

   3. Arab nationalism from *c.* 1850 to 1920, emergence of Zionism as a factor in Middle Eastern affairs

      a. Origins, growth, and early accomplishments of Arab nationalism; British encouragement in World War I; the postwar settlement

      b. Origins of the Zionist movement and Jewish immigration to Palestine after 1880, World War I developments and the beginning of conflict between Zionists and Arab nationalists

C. Iran under the Qājār dynasty from 1779 to 1925, Afghanistan from 1809 to 1921

    1. Iran: the reign of Āghā Moḥammad Khān and the subsequent European penetration of Iran by the British and Russians, overthrow of the Qājār dynasty (1925)

    2. Afghanistan: the Barakzai dynasty, conflicts with the British government of India, British recognition of Afghan independence (1921)

D. Sub-Saharan Africa from *c.* 1885 to *c.* 1920

    1. The decline in the slave trade; European commercial, missionary, and exploratory activities in the 19th century; the imperialistic scramble for African colonies; the Berlin West Africa Conference (1884–85) and the European partition of Africa

    2. The establishment of European colonies in West Africa in the late 19th century

        a. French, British, and German rivalry: takeover of the Gold Coast, Senegal, Togo, the Cameroons, Dahomey, and the Ivory Coast

        b. Problems in establishing effective colonial regimes: military problems, control of the territories, reliance on Africans and development of indirect rule

    3. Northeast Africa: foreign influences and national movements

        a. The Mahdist movement in the Sudan (1881–98) and the Anglo-Egyptian condominium from 1899

        b. The consolidation of central governmental power in Ethiopia: Tewodros II (1855–68), Yohannes IV (1872–89), and Menelek II (1889–1913); struggles against Egypt, the Sudan, and Italy

    4. East Africa and Madagascar: German, British, French, and Italian conquests and establishment of colonies; relations with indigenous peoples

    5. European penetration into Central Africa during the 19th century and establishment of permanent colonies

        a. British explorations under Livingstone and Stanley: attempts to explore the interior

        b. King Leopold II's colonial enterprise in the Congo: establishment of the Belgian Congo (Congo Free State) and Belgium's Congo policies until World War I

        c. The French colonies and colonial administration until World War II

    6. The scramble for southern Africa, the British–Boer conflict and the establishment of the Union of South Africa (1910), curtailment of economic and political rights of Africans and Asians, the Botha (1910–19) and Smuts (1919–24) governments and Nationalist Party opposition under Hertzog

---

Suggested reading in the *Encyclopædia Britannica:*

MACROPAEDIA: Major articles dealing with Southwest Asia and North Africa (*c.* 1800–1920), and sub-Saharan Africa (1885–*c.* 1920) under the influence of European Imperialism: the early colonial period

Afghanistan	Eastern Africa	North Africa	Syria
Africa	Egypt	Palestine	Turkey and
Arabia	Iran	South Africa	Ancient Anatolia
Asia	Israel	Southern Africa	Western Africa
Central Africa	Lebanon	Sudan	

MICROPAEDIA: Selected entries of reference information

General subjects

Arabian peninsula:	*Egypt and the Nilotic*	Wafd	*Ottoman Empire:*
'Abdali sultanate	*Sudan:*	*North Africa:*	Armenian
Āl Bū Sa'īd	Anglo-Egyptian	Algeciras	massacres
dynasty	Condominium	Conference	Bulgarian Horrors
Dir'iyah, Battle	Fashoda Incident	Ḥusaynid dynasty	Çanak, Treaty of
of ad-	Khartoum,	Italo-Turkish War	Capitulation
Mulaydah, Battle	Siege of	Moroccan Crises	Constantinople
of al-	Mahdist	Tripolitan War	Agreement
Qu'aiti sultanate	Omdurman,	Young Tunisians	
Wahhābīyah	Battle of		

Defense of Rights, Associations for the
Edirne, Treaty of
Greco-Turkish wars
Greek Independence, War of
Halepa, Pact of
Hünkâr İskelesi, Treaty of
Italo-Turkish War
Mudros, Armistice of
Navarino, Battle of
Ottoman Empire
Pan-Turanianism
Pan-Turkism
Pleven, Siege of
Rumelia
Saint-Jean-de-Maurienne, Agreement of
San Stefano, Treaty of
Serbo-Turkish War
Sèvres, Treaty of
Straits question
Tanzimat
Young Ottomans
Young Turks
sub-Saharan Africa:
Adowa, Battle of
Afrikaner Bond
Belgian Congo
Berlin West Africa Conference
British East Africa
British South Africa Company
British West Africa
Buganda
Congo Free State
German East Africa
Moyen-Congo
Mozambique Conventions
National Party of South Africa
Rwanda, Kingdom of
Somaliland
South Africa Act
South African War
Togoland
Tukulor Empire
Ucciali, Treaty of
uitlander
Vereeniging, Peace of
Wadai, Kingdom of
Zanzibar Treaty
other:
Durrand Line
King-Crane Commission
Mizraḥi
Zionism

Biographies

Afghanistan:
'Abdor Raḥmān Khān
Dōst Moḥammad Khān
Ḥabībollāh Khān
Shāh Shojāʿ
Shīr ʿAlī Khān

Egypt:
Cromer, Evelyn Baring, 1st Earl of
Ismāʿīl Pasha
Kāmil, Muṣṭafā
Muḥammad ʿAlī
Nubar Pasha
Saʿīd Pasha
ʿUrābī Pasha

Iran:
Khazʿal Khan
Nāṣer od-Dīn Shāh
Qājār dynasty
Taqī Khān

Ottoman Empire:
Abdulhamid II
Abdülmecid I
Enver Paşa
Mahmud II

Mehmed V
Mehmed VI
Midhat Paşa
Reşid Paşa, Mustafā
Selim III
Şevket Paşa, Mahmud

sub-Saharan Africa:
Botha, Louis
Brazza, Pierre-Paul-François-Camille Savorgnan de
Chilembwe, John
De la Rey, Jacobus Hercules
Goldie, Sir George
Gungunhana
Hofmeyr, Jan
Jameson, Sir Leander Starr, Baronet
Kagwa, Sir Apolo
Kruger, Paul

Loch of Drylaw, Hengy Brougham Loch, 1st Baron
Lugard (of Abinger), Frederick John Dealtry Lugard, Baron
Maxamed Cabdulle Xasan
Menelik II
Milner (of Saint James's and Cape Town), Alfred Milner, Viscount
Msiri
Rābiḥ as-Zubayr
Rhodes, Cecil
Roberts, Joseph Jenkins
Robinson, Sir Hercules
Samory
Smuts, Jan Christian

Stanley, Sir Henry Morton
Steyn, Marthinus Theunis
Tippu Tib
Wet, Christiaan Rudolf de
Yohannes IV

Sudan:
'Abd Allāh
Gordon, Charles George
Kitchener, Herbert Kitchener, 1st Earl
Mahdī, al-
Osman Dinga

other:
Abdelkader
Ibrahim Pasha
Jamāl ad-Dīn al-Afghānī
Lawrence, T.E.

INDEX: See entries under all of the terms above

Division VII. **The World Since 1920**
[For Part Nine headnote see page 343.]

The first of the eight sections in Division VII, reflecting the increasing internationalization since 1920, broadly treats major developments in contemporary world history. The remaining seven sections deal separately with the histories, since 1920, of the several regions of the world.

Section 971.   **International Movements, Diplomacy, and War Since 1920**

A. The period between the World Wars (1920–39)

   1. Immediate postwar problems (1920–24)

      a. Failure of attempts to establish Socialist and new democratic governments in Europe: dictatorships in the new nations of central and eastern Europe

      b. Diplomacy after the Paris Peace Conference (1919–20): establishment of the League of Nations; U.S., Soviet Russian, and German diplomatic isolation; crises concerning enforcement of the peace settlement

   2. The temporary amelioration of international relations by the Locarno (1925) and Kellogg–Briand (1928) agreements, European recovery and the rapprochement with Germany

   3. International affairs in the 1930s

      a. The upsurge of strife in Asia: civil conflict in China and the Japanese seizure of Manchuria (1931–32), rise of the militarists in Japan and the Greater East Asia Coprosperity Sphere

      b. The Popular Front and the Spanish Civil War (1936–39): unchecked Italian aggression against Ethiopia (1935–36), failure of the League of Nations and other diplomatic attempts (*e.g.,* the Munich Conference) to avert war

      c. The European colonial empires and client states: increased demands for self-determination among subject peoples, realignment of colonial powers

   4. Economic developments in the postwar period (1920–39)

      a. Increased government control (1920–29): reconstruction, social welfare, and inflation

      b. Economic and political impact of the Great Depression (1929): collapse of the world market and responses by various governments

      c. The establishment of Nazi Germany and economic recovery based on rearmament, Germany's alignment with Italy and Japan, the New Deal policy in the U.S., War Communism and the New Economic Policy in Soviet Russia

B. World War II (1939–45)

   1. German conquest of Poland (1939) and France (1940); the German–Soviet pact (1939) and subsequent German invasion of the Soviet Union (1941); the Battle of Britain (1940) and the war in North Africa (1940–42)

   2. The war in Asia and the Pacific (1937–45)

      a. Further Japanese aggression in China from 1937: the clash between U.S. and Japanese interests in the Pacific, the attack on Pearl Harbor (1941) and U.S. entry into the war

      b. Japanese conquests in the western Pacific and Southeast Asia (1941–42); the Allied counteroffensive from 1942, resulting in Japanese defeat (1945)

   3. The war in Europe and North Africa (1942–45)

a. Beginning of U.S. active participation (1942), Allied progress against the Axis Powers in North Africa and Europe

b. Collapse of the German Eastern Front (1944) and Soviet conquest of eastern Europe (1944–45), Allied invasions of Italy (1943) and France (1944) and the defeat of Germany (1945)

4. The leadership, industrial strength, strategic plans and goals, and tactical and logistical procedures of the Axis Powers

5. Allied wartime leadership and diplomacy: the Atlantic Charter; industrial strength, strategic plans and goals, and tactical and logistical procedures

6. The burgeoning of military technology; *e.g.,* developments in communications devices, naval ships and aircraft, ground weapons and missiles, atomic bombs

C. International relations

1. International relations before and during World War II

a. The Eurocentric world and its collapse

b. Ideologies in World War II

i. The Nazi–Soviet pact

ii. Roosevelt, Churchill, and the Atlantic Charter

iii. Soviet expansion, Stalin and the Nazis, annexations

2. The postwar years (1945–57)

a. The end of the war and the early United Nations (UN)

i. The atomic bombs

ii. Truman's fundamental principles

iii. The UN as a Western organization

b. Reconstruction and European political instability

c. The beginnings of the Cold War

i. Consolidation of Soviet power in eastern Europe: the "iron curtain"

ii. The Cold War as *Realpolitik* and as ideology

iii. The confrontation in Germany: the Berlin blockade

iv. The formation of the North Atlantic Treaty Organization (NATO)

d. East, South, and Southeast Asia, 1945–57

i. The colonial territories of Asia

ii. Civil war in China and Communist rule

iii. The Korean War: its meaning, course, and consequences

iv. The transformation of the American role in Southeast Asia

e. The Middle East (1945–57)

i. The U.S. in the Middle East

ii. The Iranian and Turkish cases

iii. Palestine: Israel and the Arabs

iv. Nasser and the Suez crisis

f. The continuing Cold War

i. The U.S. policy of containment

ii. The late Truman administration

iii. The Eisenhower years and McCarthyism

iv. De-Stalinization in the Soviet Union

v. Unrest among the satellites

vi. NATO and European economic recovery

vii. Soviet responses

viii. The problem of nuclear energy: the balance of terror, France as a nuclear power

ix. The Austrian treaty and the German problem

3. The period since 1957

    a. The Great Powers and the world

        i. Postwar economic growth: U.S. economic dominance

        ii. Decolonization

        iii. The Soviet Union and "national liberation"

        iv. The new states: nonalignment and domestic problems, aid programs

        v. The Third World as a zone of conflict in the Cold War

        vi. Latin America in the Cold War: Fidel Castro

        vii. The Berlin Wall and the Cuban Missile Crisis: consequences

        viii. Sino-Soviet relations: the consequences of their rift

        ix. Peaceful coexistence and détente

        x. Resolution of the German problem, the two Germanys

        xi. The Helsinki conference (1973)

        xii. Arms buildup and deterioration of superpower relations

    b. The lesser powers

        i. Peace in postwar Europe

        ii. Integration movements in western Europe, Gaullism

        iii. The new Europe: regional separatism

        iv. Eastern Europe: the Soviet variety of imperialism

    c. Areas of conflict

        i. Southeast Asia: the Indochina War

        ii. The Middle East: the Arab–Israeli wars, the new role of petroleum, the Iranian revolution

        iii. East–West involvement in Africa south of the Sahara

D. Economic developments from 1940

Suggested reading in the *Encyclopædia Britannica:*

MACROPAEDIA: Major articles dealing with international affairs since 1920

European History and Culture	United Nations
International Relations, 20th-Century	World Wars

MICROPAEDIA: Selected entries of reference information

General subjects

between the World Wars:	Kellogg–Briand Pact	Nations, League of	American States, Organization of
Anschluss	Lausanne, Treaty of	Polish Corridor	Antarctic Treaty
Anti-Comintern Pact	Lausanne Conference (1932)	Russo-Polish War	Arab–Israeli wars
Dawes Plan	Little Entente	San Remo, Conference of	Arab League
Fiume question	Locarno, Pact of	Spanish Civil War	Bandung Conference
Genoa, Conference of	London Naval Conference	Sudetenland	Berlin blockade and airlift
German-Soviet Nonaggression Pact	Maginot Line	Vilnius dispute	Central Treaty Organization
Great Depression	mandate	Washington Conference	CERN
Italo-Ethiopian War	Memel dispute	Young Plan	Cold War
	Mukden Incident	*since 1945:*	Colombo Plan
	Munich agreement	African Unity, Organization of	Cuban Missile Crisis
		Alliance for Progress	

Biographies

INDEX: See entries under all of the terms above

Section 972.   **Europe Since *c.* 1920**

A. The nations of western Europe since *c.* 1920

  1. Great Britain and Ireland

    a. Developments in Great Britain

      i. Economic depression and labour unrest in the interwar period: formation of the first Labour government under MacDonald (1923), Baldwin's government (1924–29) and the General Strike of 1926, the National Government (1931–39)

      ii. British colonial and Commonwealth relations (1920–39): division of Ireland (1922), the Indian problem

      iii. Interwar foreign policy (1931–39), Churchill's government (1940–45) and Britain's stand against the Axis Powers in World War II

      iv. The Labour government (1945–51) and the welfare state, role in NATO and relationship to the European Economic Community (Common Market), the Conservative government (1951–64), disintegration of the British Empire, Labour government (1964–70), Conservative government (1970–74), Labour government (1974–79), entrance into the Common Market (1973), Conservative government under Thatcher (1979–90) and denationalization of state-owned enterprises, Falklands war with Argentina (1982), European Communities issues, Conservative government of Major (elected 1990)

    b. Developments in Ireland since *c.* 1920

      i. Division of Ireland and establishment of the Irish Free State (from 1937, Eire) and Northern Ireland (1922), the Cosgrave and De Valera governments, entrance into the Common Market (1973), death of De Valera (1975), Jack Lynch as prime minister (1966–73 and 1977–79), the Haughey and FitzGerald governments

      ii. Northern Ireland since 1922: growing antagonism between Roman Catholics and Protestants, economic stagnation, continuing violence

  2. France since 1920

    a. From 1920 to the end of World War II

      i. Developments in the interwar period: internal financial crises and German reparations, collective security, the Great Depression, political instability and conflicts between right and left in the 1930s

      ii. Social, cultural, and economic developments under the Third Republic

      iii. World War II: defeat by Germany (1940) and the Vichy government; de Gaulle, the Free French, and Resistance movements; French participation in the Allied victory (1944–45)

    b. The postwar period

      i. The Fourth Republic (1946–58): constitution of the Fourth Republic; the realignment of parties; colonial independence movements; the French Indochina War, the Algerian War, and the crisis of 1958; de Gaulle's return to power

      ii. The Fifth Republic: settlement of the Algerian question, independence of the French African colonies, Common Market, the student revolt of 1968, de Gaulle's retirement and continued rule by the Gaullist coalition, government of Valéry Giscard d'Estaing, election of François Mitterrand and Socialist government in 1981, cohabitation government (1986–88), reelection of Mitterand in 1988

  3. Germany since 1920

    a. From 1920 to the end of World War II

      i. The German Republic (1919–33): the Weimar Constitution, reaction to the Treaty of Versailles and reparations payments, opposition from the left and the right, attempts to stabilize the republic and reestablish Germany's international position, the rise to power of National Socialists (Nazis) and the end of the republic

      ii. The Third Reich (1933–45): the Nazi revolution and establishment (1934–39) of the totalitarian police state by Hitler; persecution of the Jews; rearmament, expansion in eastern Europe, and formation of Axis alliance; World War II conquests throughout Europe; defeat by Allies (1945)

b. The postwar period

  i. Germany after World War II (1945–49): occupation by the Allies, partition between west and east zones

  ii. The formation of the Federal Republic of Germany and the leadership of Konrad Adenauer, role in NATO, economic recovery, continued Christian Democratic Union rule under Erhard and Kiesinger, Social Democratic chancellors Willy Brandt and Helmut Schmidt, success of *Ostpolitik*, Euromissiles controversy, return to power of Christian Democrats under Helmut Kohl (1982)

  iii. The German Democratic Republic: the Ulbricht government, the Berlin Wall, economic recovery and the beginning of rapprochement with the West, collective leadership under Erich Honecker (1971), formal relations between two Germanys (1972), admission to UN (1973), fall of the Communist regime

  iv. The reunification of Germany (1990) and all-German elections, reelection of Kohl (1991)

4. Italy since 1920

  a. The Fascist era

    i. The postwar cabinets, foreign relations and the Fiume affair, the Fascist Party's rise to power (1922), Mussolini and the Fascist dictatorship

    ii. Rapprochement with Germany, conquest of Ethiopia, effects of the Great Depression, Italian participation in World War II, the fall of Mussolini

  b. Postwar Italy: the politics of the republic, the De Gasperi era (1947–53), ministerial instability, economic recovery, struggle against terrorism in the late 1970s and early 1980s, parliamentary shift to the centre-left, declining strength of the Christian Democrats, first Socialist premier (1983)

5. Spain and Portugal

  a. Spain since 1920

    i. The military government of Primo de Rivera and establishment of the republic: the Civil War, German and Italian intervention, and Franco's victory; Spain's neutralism in World War II

    ii. Rapprochement with the NATO powers in the postwar era: the Franco regime

    iii. Last years of the Franco regime, government under King Juan Carlos, constitution of 1978, Basque separatism, moves toward regional self-government (1979)

  b. Portugal: military revolt (1926), the Salazar regime (1928–68), the constitution of 1933, neutralism in World War II, the effort to maintain the Portuguese colonial empire in the 1950s and 1960s, revolution of 1974, end of colonial involvement, constitution of 1976, minority and coalition governments

6. Scandinavia since *c.* 1900

  a. Denmark since *c.* 1900

    i. Foreign policy, World War I, and economic effects of the war; the Great Depression; German occupation

    ii. The postwar period: 1953 constitution; military, economic, and social policies; coalition governments

  b. Sweden since *c.* 1900

    i. Political reforms and defense policies prior to World War I, neutrality during the war

    ii. Politics in the interwar period: economic reforms and foreign policy, neutrality in World War II

    iii. Social and political reforms and establishment of the welfare state, neutralist foreign policy, new constitution (1975), defeat (1976) and return to power (1982) of the Social Democrats

  c. Norway since *c.* 1900

    i. Separation from Sweden (1905); World War I, the Great Depression, and gradual economic recovery; foreign policy and German occupation during World War II

    ii. Political and social developments in the postwar period, foreign policy, economic effects of North Sea petroleum discoveries

  d. Finland and Iceland since *c.* 1900

i. Finland: liberation from Russia (1918), parliamentary government, agrarian reform, growth of political parties, language problems, foreign policy and activities during World War II, domestic and foreign policies in the postwar period, presidency of Urho Kekkonen (1956–81), neutrality and relations with the Soviet Union

ii. Iceland: political developments (in union with Denmark) in the interwar period, aid to the Allies in World War II, establishment as an independent republic (1944), foreign relations, economic dependence on fishing, "cod wars" with Britain (1975–76)

7. The Low Countries since 1920: Belgium, The Netherlands, and Luxembourg in the interwar period; German occupation in World War II; postwar loss of colonial possessions and integration in the European Economic Community; Benelux membership in NATO; Dutch industrialization and development of North Sea gas; Walloon–Fleming division in Belgium; attempts to resolve communal disputes

8. Switzerland since 1920: Swiss neutrality in World War II, immigration and economic policies, dependence on alien workers and resulting tension, postwar neutrality policy

B. Eastern and central Europe

1. The Soviet Union from the establishment of the Communist state

a. From 1917 to the end of World War II

i. The governments of 1917; the October Revolution and establishment of the Soviet government; Civil War, War Communism, and the New Economic Policy; the struggle for succession after Lenin's death (1924) and the rise of Stalin

ii. Foreign policy, society, and culture under the New Economic Policy: purges and consolidation of Stalinism, Soviet foreign policy in the 1930s

iii. World War II: consolidation in eastern Europe, the German offensive (1941) and the Battle of Stalingrad, Soviet advance into Europe, resurgent nationalism and strengthening of the regime, Soviet military and political position in 1945

b. The postwar period

i. Soviet economic recovery after the war: Stalin's monopoly of power until his death (1953), Cold War relations with the U.S. and other countries, deterioration of relations with the People's Republic of China

ii. De-Stalinization and the Khrushchev era (1957–64): ideological disputes with China, economic problems

iii. The Brezhnev–Kosygin era (1964–82) and collective leadership: agricultural problems and achievements in industrial production, foreign policy and space exploration, continued censorship and discontent among intellectuals

iv. Short rule of Andropov (1982–84) and Chernenko (1984–85), efforts to alleviate economic stagnation, deterioration of relations with the U.S.

v. Succession of Gorbachev (1985), introduction of *glasnost* and *perestroika;* economic crisis and plans for a market economy; moves toward independence by Soviet republics and resurgence of ethnic tensions; failure of hard-line Communist coup (1991)

2. The states of central Europe

a. Austria since 1918

i. Establishment of the First Republic (1918), economic reconstruction and political strife, association with Italy, authoritarian rule of the Dollfuss and Schuschnigg governments, the *Anschluss* (annexation by Germany) and participation in World War II

ii. The Second Republic: independence in 1945, Allied occupation to 1955, restoration of sovereignty and establishment as a neutral state (1955), relative economic and political stability, controversy surrounding presidency of Waldheim (1986)

b. Hungary since 1918

i. Establishment of the republic (1918); Béla Kun's "soviet republic"; loss of Transylvania, Slovakia, and Croatia by the Treaty of Trianon (1920); the Horthy regency (1920–45); financial crisis and the rise of the radical right; reacquisition of Slovakian territory in partnership with Germany; restoration of the Trianon frontiers (1947)

ii. The postwar People's Republic: the reaction against Soviet domination in the Revolution of 1956, suppression of the revolt, the Kádár regime, introduction of the New Economic Mechanism (1968)

        iii. Deterioration of the economy in the 1980s, establishment of opposition parties, voluntary abandonment of political monopoly by the Communist Party, proclamation of the Republic of Hungary (1989), movement toward a market economy

    c. Czechoslovakia since 1914

        i. The struggle for independence under Tomáš Masaryk, establishment of the republic (1918), consolidation of internal affairs

        ii. Discontent among Sudeten German and Slovak minorities; attempts at rapprochement with Germany, the Munich agreement (1938) and German takeover (1938–39); liberation by the Soviet Union (1945); Communist rule from 1948

        iii. Developments since 1948: the People's Democracy (1948–60), collectivization of land and adjustments to the Soviet pattern; attempts at liberalization and reform ("Prague Spring") under Dubček (1968), invasion by five Warsaw Pact countries, return to orthodox Communist rule and repression of political dissent; emergence of the dissident Charter 77 movement (1977); antigovernment demonstrations, resignation of Communist government, election to presidency of dissident Vaclav Havel (1989)

    d. Poland since 1918

        i. Establishment of the Second Polish Republic (1918), the "Polish Corridor," Polish–Soviet War of 1920–21, the Piłsudski regime, social and economic problems, German invasion and joint German–Soviet partition (1939), permanent loss of territory to the Soviet Union and annexation of German territory (1945)

        ii. Postwar developments: relations with the Roman Catholic Church, agricultural and industrial growth, the 1956 uprising, the Gomułka and Gierek governments, labour unrest and the formation of Solidarity, the Kania and Jaruzelski governments, imposition of martial law (1981–82) and suppression of Solidarity, relations with the Roman Catholic Church under John Paul II

    e. The establishment (1918) of Latvia, Estonia, and Lithuania as independent states following the breakup of the Russian Empire; political and economic development in the interwar period; incorporation into the Soviet Union (1940); German occupation (1941–44); collectivization and industrialization in the postwar period

  3. The Balkans: Greece, Yugoslavia, Bulgaria, Romania, and Albania since *c.* 1920

    a. The Balkans from *c.* 1920 to *c.* 1945

        i. Settlement of the borders of Balkan states (1919–26), continued dislocation of nationality groups, civil unrest, growth of peasant political parties and Communism, land reform and industrialization, police repression and political instability

        ii. German invasion and Axis occupation (1940–45): resistance movements and Communist leadership of the partisans

    b. Postwar developments in the Balkans

        i. Greece: civil war and the defeat of Communist forces (1946–49), military dictatorship (1967–74), return to civilian rule and repudiation of the monarchy (1974), leftist government under Papandreou (1981–89), entry into the European Economic Community (1981), election of conservative government under Mitsotakis (1990)

        ii. Establishment of Communist governments in Yugoslavia, Albania, Romania, and Bulgaria; Yugoslav break with the Soviet Union (1948), establishment of collective presidency after the death of Tito (1980); Albanian expulsion of Soviet advisers (1961) and period of alignment with China (1961–78); independent Romanian foreign policy under Ceauşescu's rule (1965–89); Bulgaria's firm alliance with the Soviet bloc; Yugoslavian unrest

        iii. Political changes since the late 1980s: increasing political disintegration and emergence of separatist conflicts in Yugoslavia; popular revolt against Communist regime in Romania (1989); multiparty parliamentary elections in Romania (1990), Bulgaria (1990), and Albania (1991)

C. The arts and intellectual life in Europe since 1920: increasing concern with the problems of alienation and despair, the importance of popular culture

---

Suggested reading in the *Encyclopædia Britannica*:

MACROPAEDIA: Major articles and biographies dealing with Europe since *c.* 1920

Albania	Athens	Barcelona	Brussels
Amsterdam	Austria	Belgium	Budapest
Antwerp	Baltic States	Berlin	Bulgaria

Churchill	Hamburg	Madrid	Rome
Cologne	Hitler	Malta	Saint Petersburg
Czechoslovakia	Hungary	Manchester	Spain
Denmark	Iceland	Marseille	Stalin
Dublin	International	Milan	Sweden
Edinburgh	Relations,	Moscow	Switzerland
European History	20th-Century	Naples	Union of Soviet
and Culture	Ireland	Netherlands, The	Socialist
Finland	Italy	Norway	Republics
Florence	Kiev	Paris	United Kingdom
France	Lenin	Poland	Venice
Geneva	Lisbon	Portugal	Vienna
Germany	London	Prague	Warsaw
Greece	Luxembourg	Romania	Yugoslavia

MICROPAEDIA: Selected entries of reference information

General subjects

France:
  Action Française
  Bloc National
  Foreign Legion
  Free French
  French
    Communist Party
  Gauches,
    Cartel des
  Maginot Line
  National Centre of
    Independents and
    Peasants
  Popular
    Republican
    Movement
  Radical–Socialist
    Party
  Rally for the
    Republic
  Republican Party
  Stavisky affair
  Vichy France
Germany:
  Anschluss
  Baby Yar
  Beer Hall Putsch
  Berlin blockade
    and airlift
  Christian
    Democratic
    Union
  Christian Social
    Union
  concentration
    camp
  Dawes Plan
  Drang nach Osten
  East Prussia
  extermination
    camp
  Free Democratic
    Party
  Freikorps
  führer

German National
    People's Party
  German-Soviet
    Nonaggression
    Pact
  Gestapo
  Hitler Youth
  Holocaust
  IG Farben
  July Plot
  Kristallnacht
  Lausanne
    Conference
    (1932)
  Mein Kampf
  Memel dispute
  Munich agreement
  National
    Democratic Party
    of Germany
  National Socialism
  Nazi Party
  Nürnberg Rally
  Nürnberg trials
  Oder–Neisse Line
  Odessa
  Polish Corridor
  Red Army Faction
  Reichstag fire
  SA
  Social Democratic
    Party of Germany
  SS
  Sudetenland
  Wannsee
    Conference
  Young Plan
Ireland:
  Black and Tan
  Fianna Fáil
  Fine Gael
  Home Rule
  Irish Republican
    Army
  Labour Party
  Sinn Féin

Italy:
  Blackshirt
  Christian
    Democratic Party
  Fiume question
  Democratic Party
    of the Left
  Italian Socialist
    Party
  Italo-Ethiopian War
  Lateran Treaty
  Rome, March on
Poland:
  Auschwitz
  Curzon Line
  Katyn Massacre
  Korfanty Line
  Oder–Neisse Line
  Polish Corridor
  Poznań Riots
  Russo-Polish War
  Solidarity
  Vilnius dispute
  Warsaw Ghetto
    Uprising
  Warsaw Uprising
Spain:
  Civil Guard
  ETA
  Falange
  International
    Brigades
  Rif War
  Spanish Civil War
  Spanish Socialist
    Workers' Party
U.S.S.R.:
  Afghan War
  April Theses
  Bolshevik
  Brest-Litovsk,
    treaties of
  Chernobyl
    Accident
  Cold War
  collectivization

Cominform
  Communist Party
    of the Soviet
    Union
  Democratic
    Centralist
  Doctors' Plot
  German-Soviet
    Nonaggression
    Pact
  Gosplan
  Gulag
  July Days
  Karakhan
    Manifesto
  KGB
  kolkhoz
  Kronshtadt
    Rebellion
  kulak
  Left Communist
  Leningrad Affair
  Leninism
  Lenin's Testament
  New Economic
    Policy
  purge trials
  Russian Civil War
  Russian
    Revolution
    of 1917
  Russo-Finnish War
  Russo-Polish War
  samizdat
  soviet
  sovkhoz
  Stalinism
  Strategic Arms
    Limitation Talks
  Trotskyism
  Twentieth
    Congress of the
    Communist Party
    of the Soviet
    Union
  War Communism

Warsaw Pact
Workers'
 Opposition
United Kingdom:
 Britain, Battle of
 Conservative
 Party
 general strike
 Labour Party
 Liberal Party
 Munich agreement

Plaid Cymru
Scottish National
 Party
Social Democratic
 Party
Ulster Defence
 Association
Ulster Volunteer
 Force
Westminster,
 Statute of (1931)

Yugoslavia:
 Anti-Fascist
 Council of
 National
 Liberation of
 Yugoslavia
 Chetnik
 National
 Communism
 Serbs, Croats,
 and Slovenes,
 Kingdom of

Ustaša
other:
 Arrow Cross Party
 Baltic states
 Bulgarian Agrarian
 National Union
 EAM-ELAS
 EDES
 Iron Guard
 Zveno Group

Biographies

Balkans:
 Alexander II
 (Yugoslavia)
 Alia, Ramiz
 Boris III (Bulgaria)
 Constantine II
 (Greece)
 George II (Greece)
 Hoxha, Enver
 Metaxas, Ioannis
 Papagos,
 Alexandros
 Papandreou,
 Andreas
 Papandreou,
 Georgios
 Tito, Josip Broz
 Zhivkov, Todor
 Zog I
Czechoslovakia:
 Beneš, Edvard
 Dubček, Alexander
 Gottwald, Klemens
 Hácha, Emil
 Masaryk, Jan
 Masaryk, Tomáš
 Zapotocky,
 Antonín
France:
 Beaufre, André
 Bidault, Georges
 Blum, Léon
 Briand, Aristide
 Chaban-Delmas,
 Jacques
 Coty, René
 Couve de Murville,
 Maurice
 Daladier, Édouard
 Debré, Michel
 Decoux, Jean
 Doumergue,
 Gaston
 Faure, Edgar
 Gaulle, Charles de
 Giscard d'Estaing,
 Valéry
 Lattre de Tassigny,
 Jean de

Laval, Pierre
Mendès-France,
 Pierre
Millerand,
 Alexandre
Mitterrand,
 François
Mollet, Guy
Monnet, Jean
Painlevé, Paul
Pétain, Philippe
Pleven, René
Poincaré,
 Raymond
Pompidou,
 Georges
Poujade, Pierre
Reynard, Paul
Salan, Raoul
Schuman, Robert
Soustelle, Jacques
Tardieu, André
Thorez, Maurice
*Germany and
Austria:*
 Adenauer, Konrad
 Brandt, Willy
 Brüning, Heinrich
 Dollfuss, Engelbert
 Ebert, Friedrich
 Erhard, Ludwig
 Eichmann, Adolf
 Goebbels, Joseph
 Göring, Hermann
 Guderian, Heinz
 Hess, Rudolf
 Himmler, Heinrich
 Hindenburg,
 Paul von
 Hitler, Adolf
 Honecker, Erich
 Hugenberg, Alfred
 Kapp, Wolfgang
 Kesselring, Albert
 Kiesinger, Kurt
 Georg
 Kohl, Helmut
 Ludendorff, Erich
 Papen, Franz von

Rathenau, Walther
Ribbentrop,
 Joachim von
Roehm, Ernst
Rommel, Erwin
Rosenberg, Alfred
Rundstedt,
 Gerd von
Schacht, Hjalmar
Schleicher,
 Kurt von
Schmidt, Helmut
Schuschnigg,
 Kurt von
Seyss-Inquart,
 Arthur
Speer, Albert
Strasser, Gregor
 and Otto
Strauss, Franz
 Joseph
Stresemann,
 Gustav
Ulbricht, Walter
Hungary:
 Bethlen, István
 Gróf
 Horthy de
 Nagybánya,
 Miklós
 Kádár, János
 Nagy, Imre
 Rákosi, Matyás
Ireland:
 Cosgrave, Liam
 Cosgrave, William
 Thomas
 Costello, John A.
 de Valera, Eamon
 Fitzgerald, Garret
 Griffith, Arthur
 Haughey, Charles
 James
 Lemass, Sean F.
 Lynch, John
Italy:
 Andreotti, Giulio
 Bagdoglio, Pietro
 Berlinguer, Enrico

Ciano, Galeazzo
De Gasperi, Alcide
Moro, Aldo
Mussolini, Benito
Togliatti, Palmiro
Umberto II
Victor
 Emmanuel III
Low Countries:
 Baudouin I
 Bernhard,
 Prince of The
 Netherlands
 Juliana
 Leopold III
 (Belgium)
 Spaak, Paul-Henri
 Wilhelmina
Poland:
 Gierek, Edward
 Gomułka,
 Władysław
 Jaruzelski,
 Wojciech
 Piłsudski, Józef
 Klemens
 Sikosski,
 Władysław
 Wałęsa, Lech
*Scandinavia and
Baltic states:*
 Bernadotte, Folke,
 Greve
 Erlander, Tage
 Hammarskjöld,
 Dag
 Hansson, Per
 Albin
 Kekkonen, Urho
 Kaleva
 Palme, Olof
 Quisling, Vidkun
 Smetona, Antanas
 Ulmanis, Kārlis
 Wallenberg,
 Raoul
Spain and Portugal:
 Alfonso XIII

INDEX: See entries under all of the terms above

Section 973. The United States and Canada Since 1920

A. The United States since 1920

   1. The post-World War I Republican administrations

      a. Politics and economics under Harding and Coolidge (1921–29): favouritism toward big business, restriction of immigration, "Coolidge prosperity"

      b. Social conditions in the 1920s: prohibition, growth of organized crime, and the jazz age

      c. Hoover's administration (1929–33) and the Great Depression: the stock market crash, domestic and international repercussions, Hoover's attempts to effect economic recovery

   2. The effects of the New Deal and World War II: the presidency of Franklin D. Roosevelt (1933–45)

      a. Comprehensive New Deal measures for economic recovery, relief, and reform

      b. Reform measures of the second New Deal

         i. Judicial invalidation of New Deal legislation: power struggle between Supreme Court and President

         ii. Labour legislation and union activity: strengthening of the Democratic coalition

      c. Foreign policy between the World Wars: isolationism and neutrality, opposition to Japanese expansionism in Asia and economic sanctions against Japan, lend-lease aid to Britain (1940–41), the "good neighbor" policy in Latin America

        d. The U.S. in World War II: wartime mobilization, regulation of production and manpower, the role of U.S. forces in defeating the Axis powers in Europe and the Pacific, U.S. military occupation of Japan and participation with the Allies in occupation of Germany

  3. The U.S. after World War II: the era of the Cold War (to *c.* 1989)

      a. The Truman administration (1945–53)

          i. Foreign policy aimed at the containment of Communism: the Truman Doctrine and the Marshall Plan (1947), the Point Four Program (1949), the creation of NATO, U.S. support of Nationalist China

          ii. Programs of the Fair Deal: the conversion to a peacetime economy, labour disputes and inflation, the Taft–Hartley Act (1947), the Social Security Act (1950)

          iii. McCarthyism and the emergence of the radical right

          iv. The Korean War (1950–53): wartime mobilization of the U.S. economy, peace and bilateral security treaties with Japan (1951)

          v. Maintenance of a large postwar military establishment: collaboration of science and industry

      b. The Eisenhower administrations (1953–61)

          i. Intensification of the civil rights movement and innovative decisions of the Warren Court, passage of the Civil Rights acts of 1957 and 1960

          ii. Foreign policy during the Eisenhower years: John Foster Dulles and the Suez crisis (1956), the U.S. in the space race (1958), intervention in Lebanon (1958), continued support of Nationalist China, the U-2 affair

          iii. Social and economic problems: recessions (1953–54 and 1957–58), growing racial unrest, unemployment, labour strikes and the Landrum–Griffin Act (1959)

      c. The Kennedy administration (1961–63): the Cuban missile crisis (1962), the Nuclear Test-Ban Treaty (1963), military aid to South Vietnam, the assassination of John F. Kennedy

      d. The Johnson administrations (1963–69)

          i. Civil Rights acts of 1964 and 1968, Medicare and other social welfare legislation, inflation and increased governmental economic activity

          ii. Increasing alienation among the youth and minority groups: protests in cities and on campuses, the assassinations of Robert F. Kennedy and Martin Luther King, Jr. (1968), the anti-Vietnam War movement

          iii. Foreign policy: expansion of U.S. involvement in the Vietnam War from 1965, commencement of Paris peace talks (1968), U.S. military and economic aid to Middle Eastern and Latin-American countries

      e. The Nixon administrations (1969–74)

          i. Foreign policy: the continuing Vietnam War and the Paris peace talks, the Cambodian invasion (1970), rapprochement with the People's Republic of China, Vietnam War cease-fire agreement (1973)

          ii. Inflation, high unemployment, and temporary price and wage controls; cabinet reorganization; antiwar demonstrations

          iii. The Watergate scandal, the resignation (1973) of Vice Pres. Spiro T. Agnew and appointment of Gerald R. Ford, the resignation (1974) of Nixon

      f. The Ford administration (1974–77): presidential pardon of Nixon (1974), détente with the Soviet Union, conclusion of the Vietnam War (1975), continuing Strategic Arms Limitation Talks (SALT), celebration of the bicentennial of the Declaration of Independence (1976)

      g. The Carter administration (1977–81): foreign policy emphasis on human rights, Camp David Accords between Egypt and Israel (1978), Panama Canal treaties (1977–78), Iranian hostage crisis; Carter's efforts to alleviate the energy crisis and to reform electoral, welfare, and Social Security bureaucracies; poor relations between president and Congress

      h. The Reagan administrations (1981–89)

          i. Increased military spending, cuts in social welfare programs, reduction and simplification of personal income tax rates, rapid growth of federal deficit, Supreme Court shift to the right, Iran–*contra* scandal

          ii. Anticommunist foreign policy stance, support for anticommunist forces in Central America, invasion of Grenada (1983), decline in U.S.–Soviet relations during Reagan's first term and improvement following ascendancy of Soviet leader Gorbachev (1985)

      i. The Bush administration (1989–): continuation of conservative economic policies, war on drugs, savings and loan institutions crisis, invasion of Panama (1989), Persian Gulf War (1991)

B. Canada since 1920

   1. Canada between the World Wars

      a. The Liberal government under King (1921–30): Commonwealth relations, nationalism and the return to isolationism

      b. The Great Depression and relief measures of the Conservative government (1930–35): return of the Liberal government (1935); foreign trade, welfare legislation, financial reforms, minor political parties

   2. Canadian participation in World War II: mobilization of manpower and production, development of armed forces

   3. Canada since 1945

      a. Postwar foreign policy: North American continentalism and collective security: participation in NATO, the UN, and the Korean War; U.S.–Canadian economic relations and free-trade agreement; tension over acid rain

      b. Involvement in British Commonwealth affairs: relations with Third World nations

      c. Franco-Canadian relations and French separatism in Quebec: conflicts between French- and English-speaking Canadians

      d. Postwar prosperity: expansion of manufacturing and mining industries; economic nationalism; relations with Indians, Eskimo, and Métis

      e. Internal politics since 1945: Liberal Party control (1945–57), the Progressive Conservative coalition (1957–63), Liberal government after 1963 and the Trudeau years (1968–79, 1980–84), Canada's constitution (1982), election of Progressive Conservative government (1984)

Suggested reading in the *Encyclopædia Britannica*:

MACROPAEDIA: Major articles and a biography dealing with the United States and Canada since 1920

   Arctic, The
   Canada
   North America
   Roosevelt, Franklin D.
   United States of America

MICROPAEDIA: Selected entries of reference information; see also Sections 965 and 971

General subjects

Canada:	Agricultural	Civilian	Public Works
Canada Act	Adjustment	Conservation	Administration
Co-operative	Administration	Corps	Republican Party
Commonwealth	American Civil	Democratic Party	Sacco–Vanzetti
Federation	Liberties Union	Dixiecrat	case
Liberal Party of	American Labor	Fair Deal	Scopes Trial
Canada	Party	Farmer–Labor	Scottsboro case
New Democratic	black nationalism	Party	Social Security Act
Party	Black Panther	Hoover	Stock Market
Parti Québécois	Party	Commission	Crash of 1929
Progressive	Bonus Army	Indian	Taft–Hartley Act
Conservative	bootlegging	Reorganization	Teapot Dome
Party	Brain Trust	Act	Scandal
Social Credit Party	Brown v. Board	Liberal Party	Tennessee Valley
U.S. domestic	of Education of	National Recovery	Authority
affairs and social	Topeka	Administration	Three Mile Island
programs:	Christian Front	New Deal	Warren
Adkins v.	Civil Rights Act	Nisei	Commission
Children's	Civil Rights	Ohio Gang	Watergate Scandal
Hospital	Movement	Peace Corps	Works Progress
		Progressive Party	Administration

Section 974.   **Latin-American and Caribbean Nations Since *c.* 1920**

A. Mexico since 1920

   1. Obregón's coup and Carranza's execution (1920), land reforms during Obregón's (1920–24) and Calles' (1924–28) regimes, rule by Calles' National Revolutionary Party (1928–34)

   2. Cárdenas' Six-Year Plan (1934–40): social and economic reforms, reorganization of the National Revolutionary Party, expropriation of foreign industry (1938), election of Avila Camacho (1940)

   3. Mexico during World War II: economic and military cooperation with the United States, wartime industrialization

   4. Mexico since 1945

      a. Economic and social development: the Institutional Revolutionary Party and peaceful presidential successions, female suffrage (1958), foreign trade and industrialization, emergence as a major oil and gas producer, oil boom and financial crisis of the early 1980s, nationalization of the banks (1982)

      b. Urbanization and educational advancements, relations with the U.S. and other countries, tensions over illegal immigration to the U.S., influx of Central American refugees and efforts at peacemaking in the region, social and economic planning in the 1970s and 1980s

B. Central America and the Caribbean since *c.* 1920

   1. The Central American republics since *c.* 1920

      a. Guatemala since 1920

         i. Successive presidential governments in the 1920s, Ubico's dictatorship (1931–44), social reforms of Arévalo's regime (1945–50)

         ii. Growth of Communist influence during Arbenz' regime (1951–54), military coup (1954), anticommunist activity in Castillo Armas' regime (1954–57), domination by the armed forces from 1970, increased guerrilla and terrorist activity from 1980

      b. Honduras since 1920: political unrest in the 1920s; Carías Andino's dictatorship (1932–49); administrations of Gálvez (1949–54), Lozano Díaz (1954–56), Villeda Morales (1957–63), and successive military governments; return to civilian rule in 1982; involvement in regional conflicts

      c. El Salvador since 1920: military dictatorships to 1944, governments of Castaneda Castro (1945–48), junta rule and PRUD domination (1948–60), continued authoritarian military governments thereafter, war with Honduras (1969–70), civil war from the 1970s and U.S. involvement, civilian presidency of Duarte (1984–89) and election of Cristiani (1989)

      d. Nicaragua since 1920: continued U.S. military intervention until 1933, Sacasa's regime (1933–36), Somoza family's dominance (1937–79), popular uprising and Sandinista rule (1979–90), U.S. aid to counterrevolutionary movements, presidential election of opposition leader Chamorro (1990)

      e. Costa Rica since 1920: border disputes with Panama until 1941, orderly presidential succession, industrialization and urbanization, economic problems of the early 1980s

      f. Panama since 1920: unstable local politics and U.S. intervention, economic development, National Guard rule under Omar Torrijos (1968–78), the Panama Canal treaties with the U.S. (1977–78), U.S. invasion of Panama and overthrow of de facto ruler General Noriega

      g. Belize since 1920: progress toward independence, government of George Price (1961–84), achievement of independence in 1981

   2. The island states of the Caribbean since the end of U.S. occupation

      a. Haiti since 1934: internal struggle for power (1934–57), presidency of François Duvalier (1957–71) and succession by his son (1971–86), social and economic problems, exodus of illegal immigrants to the U.S. from the 1970s, resumption of civilian rule (1990)

      b. Dominican Republic since 1930: Trujillo's dictatorship (1930–61), economic and social services development, later repression ending with Trujillo's assassination, alternating elected governments and military juntas, the 1965 revolution and U.S. intervention, relative political stability from the mid-1970s

      c. Cuba since 1934

         i. Fulgencio Batista's first (1933–44) and second (1952–59) dictatorships, growth of the military and middle classes, the sugar industry

      ii. The Cuban Revolution of 1959: Fidel Castro's program for Cuban Socialism

     iii. Cuba under Castro: nationalization of foreign-owned property, Cuban emigration, alignment with the Soviet bloc, the 1962 missile crisis, the effort to form a Socialist society, second wave of emigration in 1980, military involvement in Africa

  d. The new nations of the Caribbean region: Antigua and Barbuda, The Bahamas, Barbados, Dominica, Grenada, Jamaica, St. Christopher and Nevis, St. Lucia, St. Vincent and the Grenadines, Trinidad and Tobago; efforts toward development and regional cooperation; U.S. involvement in the region; military intervention in Grenada (1983)

  e. U.S. and European territories and possessions in the Caribbean region: Puerto Rico and the Virgin Islands, Bermuda and other British insular possessions, French Guiana and French insular possessions, Netherlands Antilles

C. Venezuela and Colombia since *c.* 1930

  1. Venezuela since 1935

    a. Abortive attempts at democratic government amid renewed military dictatorships (1935–58), constitution of 1961, the Acción Democrática party's economic reforms, political stabilization under Acción Democrática and Social Christian (COPEI) governments

    b. Social and economic development from 1959, growing economic importance of petroleum, nationalization of the petroleum industry (1976), efforts toward development and industrial diversification

  2. Colombia since 1930

    a. Liberal Party rule (1930–46): social and land reforms during López' administrations (1934–38 and 1942–45)

    b. Reemergence of Conservative rule under Ospina Pérez (1946–50), civil unrest and political repression (1948–53), military dictatorships to 1958, coalition of Conservatives and Liberals in National Front government

    c. Economic problems in the 1960s and 1970s, return to stable government under Lleras Restrepo (1966–70) and Pastrana Borrero (1970–74), formal end of National Front arrangement in 1974 and subsequent elections, increasing activity by left-wing guerrillas and right-wing paramilitary groups, Betancur Cuartas' amnesty offer to guerrillas (1982), growth of drug trafficking and associated corruption

D. Ecuador, Peru, and Bolivia since *c.* 1930

  1. Ecuador since 1925

    a. Economic development and participation in World War II, loss of territory to Peru (1942)

    b. Various administrations of Velasco Ibarra and other presidents and military coups after 1945, constitution of 1979 and return to civilian rule, economic and social effects of the exploitation of petroleum after 1972

  2. Peru since 1930

    a. The overthrow of Leguía (1930); Sánchez Cerro's administration (1931–33); the Aprista uprising and Sánchez Cerro's assassination; Benavides' administration (1933–39), social reforms, and the outlawing of the Apristas

    b. Prado's first administration (1939–45); wartime cooperation with the U.S. and economic prosperity, legalization and re-outlawing of the Apristas during Bustamante's administration (1945–48), Odría's military dictatorship (1948–56) and suppression of Apristas

    c. Re-legalization of Apristas and economic prosperity during Prado's second term (1956–62), military seizure of power (1962), social reforms of Belaúnde Terry's administration (1963–68), military takeover in 1968, restoration of civilian rule (1980) and return of Belaúnde as president, economic difficulties of the early 1980s, rise of Sendero Luminoso guerrillas, left-of-centre government under Gárcia Pérez (1985–90), election of Fujimori (1990)

  3. Bolivia since 1930

    a. The revolt of 1930, Salamanca's presidency (1930–36), the effect of the Great Depression on the mining industry, the Chaco War (1932–35) and loss of territory to Paraguay

    b. Military coup (1936), rise of MNR and PIR political parties, 1943 military coup and the Villaroel dictatorship (1943–46), political instability to 1951, military junta (1951–52)

    c. The Bolivian National Revolution (1952), nationalization of the tin industry, electoral and land reforms, Paz Estenssoro's administrations (1952–56 and 1960–64), U.S. economic aid, civil disorders, alternating military and civilian governments in the 1960s and 1970s, return to civilian rule under Siles Zuazo (1982), foreign debt and other economic problems, effects of drug trafficking, return of Paz Estenssoro as president (1985)

E. Chile since 1920

  1. Chile from 1920 to 1938

    a. The presidency of Alessandri Palma (1920–24, 1925), military coup (1924), return to civilian rule (1925), constitution of 1925 and reduction of legislative power, political instability, military dictatorship under Ibáñez del Campo (1927–31)

    b. Economic crises during the 1930s: brief return to civilian rule under Montero Rodríguez, military coup and 100-day rule of Socialist Republic, Alessandri Palma's second administration (1932–38)

  2. Chile from 1938 to 1952: the era of the Radical Party presidencies

    a. The administrations of Cerda (1938–41) and Ríos (1942–46): agrarian reforms, Chilean neutrality until 1942, economic prosperity

    b. González Videla's administration (1946–52): strengthened economic ties with the U.S., return of Conservative Party influence

  3. Chilean politics since 1952

    a. Ibáñez del Campo's administration (1952–58) and strong presidential leadership, administration of Alessandri Rodríguez (1958–64), social and economic problems, proliferation of leftist political parties and realignment of conservative parties

    b. Frei's administration (1964–70) and nationalization of the economy, Allende's Marxist administration (1970–73), military coup (1973) and military rule under Pinochet Ugarte (1973–90), political repression, continued economic difficulties, presidential election of Aylwin (1990)

F. Argentina, Uruguay, and Paraguay since c. 1930

  1. Argentina since 1930

    a. The conservative restoration (1930–43): economic ties with Great Britain, electoral fraud and violence in the 1930s, neutrality in World War II

    b. The Perón era (1943–55): his rise to and fall from power, economic policies

    c. Argentina since 1955: attempts to restore constitutionalism, military dictatorships, civil wars and Peronista resurgence, return (1973) and death (1974) of Perón, military coup (1976), excesses and economic failures of military rule, invasion of the Falklands/Malvinas and defeat by Britain (1982), return to civilian rule under Alfonsín (1983), foreign debt problems

  2. Uruguay since 1929

    a. The Great Depression, dictatorship of Gabriel Terra (1933–38), election of Alfredo Baldomir (1938), Uruguayan neutrality until 1945, economic boom and social reforms

    b. Post-World War II developments: the constitution of 1951 and the plural executive, recession (1954–58), 1958 election of Nationalists (Blancos), return of Colorado Party and restoration of presidential powers (1966), Tupamaro insurgency, dismissal of Congress (1973) and assumption of effective control by the military, severe recession of the early 1980s, restoration of civilian government (1985)

  3. Paraguay since 1924

    a. The Great Depression, victory over Bolivia in Chaco War (1932–35), Allied alignment in World War II

    b. Political instability and economic retardation: Stroessner's dictatorship from 1954 to his overthrow in 1989

G. Brazil since 1930: the Second Republic

  1. The Getúlio Vargas dictatorship (1930–45): the revolution of 1930, the constitutions of 1934 and 1937, Vargas' consolidation of power (1937), social and economic legislation, Allied participation in World War II, Vargas' forced resignation (1945)

  2. Political, social, and economic developments in Brazil since 1945

    a. Election of Eurico Gaspar Dutra (1945) and the constitution of 1946: restoration of civil and personal liberties and representative government, outlawing of Communist Party (1947)

    b. Reelection of Vargas (1950), economic crises and governmental corruption, Vargas' forced resignation and suicide (1954)

c. Interim presidency of João Café Filho (1954), election of Juscelino Kubitschek as president and João Goulart as vice president (1955), economic development and inflation

d. Election of Jânio Quadros as president and Goulart's reelection as vice president (1960), Quadros' resignation (1961), governmental opposition to Goulart, parliamentary experiment with figurehead president and prime minister as head of state, 1963 plebiscite giving Goulart full presidential powers

e. Social and economic unrest: reemergence of Communist Party, nationalization of oil refineries, revolution and exile of Goulart (1964), Pascoal Ranieri Mazzilli as interim president and beginning of military rule

f. Castelo Branco's presidency (1964–67): the First, Second, and Third Institutional acts; suspension of existing political parties; creation of artificial two-party system; constitution of 1967

g. The presidencies of Costa e Silva, Médici, Geisel, and Figueiredo after 1967: economic growth and reduction of inflation; the constitution of 1967; moves toward democratization; end of controlled two-party system (1979) and formation of new parties; gains by the opposition party in the election of 1982; increased concentration of authority in central government (1983); recession, resurgent inflation, and foreign debt problems of the early 1980s, return to civilian government (1985)

h. Social developments since 1945: urbanization and education, increased electorate, role of the church and the military in national politics

H. Development of Latin-American literature, music, and visual arts in the 20th century: the intermingling of European, Indian, and African cultures

---

Suggested reading in the *Encyclopædia Britannica*:

MACROPAEDIA: Major articles dealing with Latin-American and Caribbean nations since *c.* 1920

Argentina	Colombia	Lima	São Paulo
Bolivia	Ecuador	Mexico	South America
Brazil	Guyana	Mexico City	Suriname
Buenos Aires	Havana	Paraguay	Uruguay
Central America	Latin America,	Peru	Venezuela
Chile	The History of	Rio de Janeiro	West Indies

MICROPAEDIA: Selected entries of reference information

General subjects

Central America and the Caribbean:	Communist Party of Cuba	*Mexico:*	Estado Novo
Bay of Pigs invasion	Cuban missile crisis	Indigenismo	Falkland Islands War
Canal Zone	Sandinista	Institutional Revolutionary	Peronist
Central American Common Market	26th of July Movement	Party	Rio de Janeiro, Protocol of
	West Indies Associated States	Sinarquism	Shining Path
		South America: Chaco War	Tupamaro

Biographies

Central America and the Caribbean:	Noriega (Morena), Manuel (Antonio)	Calles, Plutarco Elías	Frei (Montalva), Eduardo
Arias Sánchez, Oscar	Somoza Debayle, Anastasio	Cárdenas, Lázaro	Haya de la Torre, Víctor Raúl
Batista, Fulgencio	Torrijos (Herrera), Omar	Echeverría (Álvarez), Luis	Ibáñez del Campo, Carlos
Bosch, Juan	Trujillo (Molina), Rafael (Leónidas)	López Mateos, Adolfo	Perón, Eva
Castro, Fidel	Ubico (Castañeda), Jorge	Obregón, Alvaro	Perón, Juan
Duvalier, François		*South America:*	Rojas, Pinilla
Guevara, Che	*Mexico:*	Allende (Gossens), Salvador	Gustavo
Guzmán Fernández, Silvestre Antonio	Alemán, Miguel	Belaúnde Terry, Fernando	Vargas, Getúlio

INDEX: See entries under all of the terms above

Section 975.   **East Asia: China in Revolution, the Era of Japanese Hegemony, and the Influence of the United States in the 20th Century**

A. China since 1912

   1. The development of the republic (1912–20)

     a. Early power struggles: Chinese involvement in World War I

       i. Japanese gains in the early part of the war: Yüan Shih-k'ai's attempts to become emperor

       ii. Conflict over entry into the war, formation of a rival southern government, changes brought about by the war

     b. Modernization and the growth of nationalism: emergence of a new intelligentsia, riots and protests

   2. The interwar years (1920–37)

     a. The beginnings of a national revolution: the Kuomintang, the Chinese Communist Party, cooperation between the two parties

     b. Reactions to warlords and foreigners: militarism in China, the continued presence of foreign interests, reorganization of the Kuomintang

     c. Struggles within the two-party coalition: influence of Soviet Russia

       i. Outbreak of clashes with foreigners: Kuomintang opposition to the radicals

       ii. The Northern Expedition: peasant uprisings leading to the expulsion of the Communists from the Kuomintang, Communist movement into the hills and plains of central China

     d. The Nationalist government from 1928 to 1937: Chiang Kai-shek's attempts to eliminate the Communists

       i. Attempts at economic reform and failure in agriculture, educational reform, economic competition with the Japanese in Manchuria

       ii. Renewal of Japanese aggression: war between the Communists and Nationalists, the Long March, formation of the United Front against Japan

   3. The war against Japan (1937–45)

     a. Communist–Nationalist cooperation in the early stages of the war, renewed conflict between the two groups

     b. International alliance against Japan: U.S. military aid, internal conflicts, the crisis of 1944 and Nationalist deterioration, Communist growth and international efforts to prevent civil war

   4. The development of Kuomintang and Chinese Communist ideologies

     a. Origins and background of modern ideologies: social and political conditions, China's ideological heritage

     b. The political ideas of Sun Yat-sen: nationalism, democracy, and livelihood

     c. The political ideas of Chiang Kai-shek: idealization of Chinese tradition

     d. The development of Maoist ideology: the role of peasants, the "people's war," the border regions

   5. Emergence of the People's Republic of China

     a. The Civil War (1945–49): the race for territory, Communist successes and ultimate victory

     b. Economic reforms and reforms in the traditional Chinese social structure (1949–57)

       i. Reconstruction and consolidation of power (1949–52): participation in the Korean War, agrarian reform

       ii. The transition to socialism (1953–57): rural collectivization, urban nationalization

     c. The period of the Great Leap Forward and the transition to the Cultural Revolution

       i. New directions in national policy (1958–61): literature and arts for the masses, rural communes

       ii. Readjustment and reaction (1961–65): restoration of order, China as a nuclear power

      iii. The Great Proletarian Cultural Revolution (1966–76): attacks on cultural leaders and party members, resistance to Peking

      iv. Mao's "Reconstruction" (1969–71): the Chinese challenge to Soviet Communism, the Ninth Congress of the Chinese Communist Party (April 1969)

   d. International relations: UN representation (1971), rapprochement with the U.S. and Japan (1972), friction with the Soviet Union, U.S. diplomatic relations with China (1979), increased cultural and economic contacts overseas, Hong Kong agreement with Great Britain (1984)

   e. Internal affairs: the 10th Congress of the CCP (August 1973) and the fourth National People's Congress and new national constitution (January 1975), death of Zhou Enlai (January 1976) and factional strife, death of Mao Zedong (September 1976), ascendancy of Deng Xiaoping, disgrace and conviction of Maoist Gang of Four, new party and national constitutions (1982), changes in economic structure and introduction of economic incentives, forcible repression of pro-democracy movement (1989)

  6. The Nationalist government in Taiwan since 1949: initial repression and consolidation; leadership of Chiang Kai-shek until his death; alliance with the U.S. and economic growth; loss of UN representation (1971); Taiwanese separatism; loss of diplomatic support from most nations, including U.S. (1979); economic prosperity

B. Japan since *c.* 1910

  1. Japan's political, economic, and social developments in the early 20th century

   a. Constitutional government: party politics, participation by bureaucrats and business elites

   b. Social and economic changes: attempts to organize labour, cultural trends, growth of educated classes

  2. The rise and fall of Imperial Japan (*c.* 1920–45)

   a. The rise of the militarists, growth of antigovernment sentiment, the seizure of initiative in foreign policy by the military, the outbreak of war with China (1937), Axis leanings

   b. Japan's proclamation of the Greater East Asia Co-prosperity Sphere (1938), official alignment with the Axis powers (1940), and deterioration of relations with the other Western powers: Tōjō's cabinet and outbreak of war with the U.S. (1941)

   c. Initial Japanese successes in Southeast Asia and the South Pacific, the Allied counterattack culminating in the fire and atomic bombing of Japanese cities, Japan's unconditional surrender (1945)

   d. Postwar Japan: political reform, economic and social changes, international relations and cultural developments

      i. Japan under U.S. military occupation (1945–52): democratization of Japanese society; constitutional, land, and labour reforms; increased rights for women

      ii. International relations and politics; loss of Korea and other territories, relations with China and the U.S., radical political movements in the 1960s, politics of moderation

      iii. Restoration of Japanese independence (1952): great economic growth, admission to the UN (1956), return of the Bonins and Ryukyus, Japan as a major world trader, economic tensions with U.S. and the European Communities, rapprochement with China (1978), overtures toward Southeast Asia and Korea, long dominance of Liberal-Democratic Party and intra-party factionalism, government-corruption scandals

C. Korea since 1910

  1. Japanese rule (1910–45): military control, the March 1st independence movement and formation of a provisional Korean government in exile (1919), resistance movements and the end of Japanese rule

  2. Korea since 1945

   a. Division into South and North Korea (1948): U.S. and Soviet military aid to and disputes over the two Korean republics

   b. North Korean invasion (1950) of South Korea and the Korean War (1950–53): U.S. and UN intervention, Chinese participation, armistice (1953)

   c. South Korea since the armistice: the regimes of Syngman Rhee (1948–60) and Park Chung Hee (1961–79), the assassination of Park and its consequences, economic growth

   d. North Korea since the armistice: consolidation of Communist government power under Kim Il-sung, relations with the Soviet Union and the People's Republic of China, military and industrial growth

Suggested reading in the *Encyclopædia Britannica:*

MACROPAEDIA: Major articles and a biography dealing with East Asia: China in revolution, the era of Japanese hegemony, and the influence of the United States in the 20th century

Asia	Japan	Nanking	Tientsin
Canton	Korea	Peking	Tokyo–Yokohama
China	Mao Zedong	Shanghai	Metropolitan
Hong Kong	Mongolia	Taiwan	Area

MICROPAEDIA: Selected entries of reference information; see also Sections 96/10 and 971

General subjects

China:

Chinese	May Thirtieth	Japan Social	Nationalist Party
Communist	Incident	Democratic Party	Pueblo Incident
Party	Nationalist Party	kamikaze	Singanhoe
Cultural	Open Door policy	Keidanren	38th parallel
Revolution	Red Guards	Liberal-Democratic	*Sino-Japanese*
Eighth Route	Sian Incident	Party	*relations:*
Army	Sun–Joffe	Minseitō	Lytton
Gang of Four	Manifesto	Rikken Seiyūkai	Commission
Great Leap	Three Principles of	State Shintō	Marco Polo Bridge
Forward	the People	Twenty-one	Incident
Karakhan	warlord	Demands	Mukden Incident
Manifesto	*Japan:*	zaibatsu	Shantung question
Kiangsi Soviet	Clean Government	*Korea:*	Sino-Japanese
Long March	Party	Korean Provisional	War (1937–45)
Maoism	Democratic	Government	Twenty-One
May Fourth	Socialist Party	Korean War	Demands
Movement	Japan Communist	March First	United Front
	Party	Movement	

Biographies

China:

Chang Kuo-t'ao	Soong	Konoe Fumimaro,	Yoshida Shigeru
Chang Ping-lin	Ch'ing-ling	Kōshaku	Yoshino Sakuzō
Chen Boda	Sun Yat-sen	Miki Kiyoshi	*Korea:*
Chen Duxiu	Ts'ai Yüan-p'ei	Miki Takeo	Chun Doo Hwan
Chiang Ching-kuo	Tuan Ch'i-jui	Minobe Tatsukichi	Kim Chong Il
Chiang Kai-shek	Wang Ching-wei	Nagano Osami	Kim Dae Jung
Chiang K'ang-hu	Yüan Shih-k'ai	Nosaka Sanzō	Kim Il-sung
Deng Xiaoping	Zhao Ziyang	Okawa Shūmei	Kim Young Sam
Feng Yü-hsiang	Zhou Enlai	Ōkuma Shigenobu,	Park Chung Hee
Guo Moruo	Zhu De	Kōshaku	Rhee, Syngman
Hu Han-min	*Japan:*	Satō Eisaku	Roh Tae Woo
Hu Shih	Akihito	Shidehara Kijūrō	*other:*
Hu Yaobang	Araki Sadao	Taishō	Hurley, Patrick J.
Hua Guofeng	D'Aquino, Iva	Tanaka Giichi	MacArthur,
Jiang Qing	Toguri	Tanaka Kakue	Douglas
Kang Sheng	Hamaguchi Osachi	Tōjō Hideki	Reischauer,
Kuo T'ai-ch'i	Hatoyama Ichirō	Ugaki	Edwin O.
Li Dazhao	Hirohito	Kazushige	Stilwell, Joseph W.
Lin Biao	Ikeda Hayato	Yamagata	
Liu Shaoqi	Inukai Tsuyoshi	Aritomo,	
Mao Zedong	Ishibashi Tanzan	Kōshaku	
Qu Qiubai	Katō Takaaki	Yamamoto	
Soong family	Kawakami Hajime	Gonnohyōe	
Soong, T.V.	Kishi Nobusuke	Yamamoto	
		Isoroku	

INDEX: See entries under all of the terms above

Section 976. South and Southeast Asia: the Late Colonial Period and the Emergence of New Nations Since 1920

    A. India, Pakistan, Bangladesh, Ceylon, Tibet, and Nepal since 1920

        1. India *c.* 1920 to 1947

           a. Intensified agitation for Indian independence and Gandhi's *satyāgraha* movement of nonviolent resistance; Round Table Conference (1930–32), British offers of constitutional reform, the Government of India Act (1935)

           b. Increased strength of the Muslim League, movement for a separate Muslim state (Pakistan), the political and economic effects of World War II, partition and independence (1947)

        2. India since 1947

           a. Domestic affairs: establishment of a parliamentary system and reorganization of the states under Nehru and the Congress Party (1947–64); administrations of Lal Bahadur Shastri (1964–66), Indira Gandhi (1966–77, 1980–84), and Morarji Desai (1977–79); continued communal unrest; suppression of Sikh extremists in Punjab (1984), assassination of Indira Gandhi (1984); administrations of Rajiv Gandhi (1984–89), V.P. Singh (1989–90), and Chandra Shekhar (1990–91); assassination of Rajiv Gandhi (1991); election of P.V. Narasimha Rao (1991)

           b. Foreign policy: Nehru's policy of nonalignment, conflicts with Pakistan over Kashmir (1948–49 and 1965–66) and over East Pakistan (Bangladesh) in 1971, border conflict with China and Chinese incursion (1962), Indian Peace-Keeping Force in Sri Lanka (1987–1990)

        3. Pakistan since 1947

           a. National consolidation (1947–51) under Jinnah and Liaquat Ali Khan, economic and political instability

           b. Military government of Ayub Khan (1958–69); economic and political reforms; border conflict with India; administration of Yahya Khan (1969–71); civil war between East and West Pakistan, secession of East Pakistan (since 1971, Bangladesh); administrations of Zulfikar Ali Bhutto (1971–77), Mohammad Zia ul-Haq (1977–88), and Benazir Bhutto (1988–90); election of Nawaz Sharif (1990)

        4. Bangladesh since 1971: emergence of nation, administrations of President Mujibur Rahman (1971–75) and martial law administrators General Zia ur-Rahman (1975–81) and Hossain Mohammad Ershad (1982–90), election of President Begum Khaleda Zia ur–Rahman (1991)

        5. Ceylon since 1920 (after 1972, Sri Lanka)

           a. Nationalism and demands for constitutional reform (1920–31), the 1931 constitution and the granting of universal franchise

           b. Dominion status (1947); parliamentary rule by United National Party (1948–56, 1965–70, and 1977–78) and by Sri Lanka Freedom Party (1956–59, 1960–65, and 1970–77); the constitution of 1972 and the establishment of a presidential system in the constitution of 1978; presidency of J.R. Jayawardene (1978–89) and succession by Ranasinghe Premadasa (1989); Sinhalese–Tamil tensions and the movement for an independent Tamil state

        6. Tibet since 1920: defense of frontier against China; Chinese invasion (1950) and the reestablishment of Chinese hegemony, complete Chinese government control after 1959; suppression of violent protests against Chinese rule (1987)

        7. Nepal since 1920: British withdrawal (1947) and revival of Nepalese royal control under Tribhuvan (1951–55), Mahendra (1955–72), and Birendra (crowned 1975); nationwide political unrest (1990) and the establishment of a constitutional monarchy (1991)

    B. Mainland Southeast Asia since 1920

        1. Myanmar (Burma) since 1920

           a. Emergence of Myanmar nationalism and the British response (1920–37), limited constitutional government (1937–42), the Japanese occupation (1942–45)

           b. Postwar independence (1948) under U Nu, adoption of leftist–neutralist position, internal conflict and military government under U Ne Win (1962–81), continued economic problems, socialist state and new constitution (1974), minority insurgencies, victory of National League for Democracy in multiparty elections (1990)

        2. Malaya and Singapore since 1920

           a. British economic policies in Malaya, Japanese occupation (1941–45), British return to power (1945) and progress toward self-government

b. Suppression of Communist insurgents (1948–60), creation of Federation of Malaya (1957) and reestablishment as Malaysia (1963), Singapore's withdrawal (1965) from Malaysia and creation of independent Republic of Singapore, dominance of National Front in Malaysia, regime of Lee Kuan Yew in Singapore (from 1965), industrialization and growing prosperity

3. Thailand since 1920

   a. Post-World War I escape from unequal treaties, problems of kingship and repression, the coup d'etat of 1932 and the establishment of constitutional monarchy, militaristic and pro-Japanese nationalism, the Japanese occupation during World War II

   b. Loss of wartime gains and political instability, military domination (1947–68, 1971–73, and since 1976), border incursions from Cambodia and influx of refugees

4. Indochina since 1920: emergence of independent states and continued strife

   a. French direct administration of Vietnam and indirect administration of Cambodia and Laos: growth of Vietnamese nationalistic movements and Ho Chi Minh's formation of the Indochina Communist Party (1930), French administration during Japanese occupation in World War II, postwar French administration in southern Vietnam and Cambodia

   b. Ho Chi Minh's government in northern Vietnam and the French attempt to reconquer the north (1946–54), the Geneva Agreements and legal "temporary" division of Vietnam (1954), French withdrawal and U.S. limited intervention

   c. Vietnam from 1955 to 1975

      i. North Vietnam: industrialization, relations with other Communist and other Asian countries, war with South Vietnam, U.S. military intervention, cease-fire agreement (1973), conquest of South Vietnam (1975)

      ii. South Vietnam: civil war and formation of National Liberation Front (1960), U.S. military intervention, cease-fire agreement (1973), end of regime of Nguyen Van Thieu, conquest by North Vietnam (1975)

   d. Socialist Republic of Vietnam: establishment of united Vietnamese government (July 2, 1976), political and economic problems, invasion (1978) and occupation of Cambodia, exodus of ethnic Chinese refugees and border war with China (1979)

   e. Laos since 1950: civil war to 1954, Geneva Conference (1954) and creation of Laos as a neutral state, domestic instability and continued civil war between Pathet Lao and rightists, military involvement of the U.S. and North Vietnam, Pathet Lao victory and the Lao People's Democratic Republic (from 1975), domination by Vietnam

   f. Cambodia since independence (1953): Sihanouk's domestic politics and severing of relations with the U.S. (1965); deposition of Sihanouk (1970) and Lon Nol and pro-Western realignment; return, and then resignation, of Sihanouk (1975); new constitution of Democratic Kampuchea (1976); ruthless administration and designation of the Communist Party of Kampuchea as the governing body (1977); capture of Phnom Penh by Vietnamese forces (1979) and establishment of Vietnamese-dominated regime; formation of coalition government-in-exile supported by Association of Southeast Asian Nations (1982)

C. Indonesia and the Philippines

1. Indonesia since 1920

   a. Dutch administration of Indonesia from 1920 to independence in 1949

      i. Dutch administrative suppression of nationalist and Communist revolts in the 1920s and 1930s, accommodation with moderate nationalist parties, Japanese occupation in World War II

      ii. Sukarno's proclamation of Indonesian independence (1945), Dutch attempt to regain control and UN intervention, formal granting of independence in 1949

   b. Constitutional democracy (1950) and Guided Democracy (1957–65) under Sukarno; military coup (1965), purge of Communists, and Sukarno's loss of influence; administration of Suharto (from 1966); takeover of East Timor (1976); economic effects of the oil boom

2. The Philippines since 1920

   a. Economic and social policies of U.S. administration in the 1920s and 1930s, growth of nationalist political parties, establishment as a commonwealth (1935), Japanese occupation (1941–45), return of U.S. control and commonwealth status

   b. Establishment of the Republic of the Philippines (1946), political developments under successive presidents, U.S.–Philippine relations, administration of Ferdinand E. Marcos (from 1965), Communist and Muslim insurgencies, rule under martial law (1972–81), assassination of opposition leader Benigno Aquino (1983) and resulting unrest

Suggested reading in the *Encyclopædia Britannica*:

MACROPAEDIA: Major articles and a biography dealing with South and Southeast Asia: the late colonial period and the emergence of new nations since 1920

Asia	Delhi	Indonesia	Philippines
Bangkok	Gandhi	Jakarta	Southeast Asia,
Bangladesh	Hong Kong	Manila	Mainland
Bombay	India	Nepal	Sri Lanka
Calcutta		Pakistan	

MICROPAEDIA: Selected entries of reference information; see also Sections 968, 969, and 971

General subjects

Indian subcontinent:	Servants of India	Viet Nam Quoc	Hukbalahap
Delhi Pact	Society	Dan Dang	Rebellion
Donoughmore	Sinhala Maha	Vietnam War	Mandium Affair
Commission	Sabha	*Indonesia:*	Sakdal Uprising
dyarchy	Sinhala Only Bill	Hague Agreement	Tydings–
Government of	Tashkent	Linggadjati	McDuffie Act
India Acts	Agreement	Agreement	Woods–Forbes
hartal	*Indochina:*	Pancasila	Mission
Indian National	Dien Bien Phu,	Peranakan	*other:*
Congress	Battle of	Renville	Burma Road
Lee Commission	Hoa Hao	Agreement	Malayan People's
Muslim League	Indochina	Sarekat Islām	Anti-Japanese
Non-cooperation	Khmer Rouge	Sutardjo Petition	Army
Movement	National	Volksraad council	Promoters
Poona Pact	Liberation Front	*Philippines:*	Revolution
Red Shirt	Pathet Lao	Bell Trade Act	Stilwell Road
Movement	seventeenth	Hare–Hawes–	Straits Settlements
Round Table	parallel	Cutting Act	
Conference	Viet Cong		
Rowlatt Acts	Viet Minh		

Biographies

Myanmar and	Bandaranaike,	Menon, V.K.	Chu Van Tan
Thailand:	S.W.R.D.	Krishna	Cuong De
Aung San	Bhutto, Benazir	Naidu, Sarojini	Ho Chi Minh
Ba Maw	Bhutto,	Narayan, Jaya	Huyanh Tan Phat
Khuang Aphaiwong	Zulfikar Ali	Prakash	Katay Don
Ne Win, U	Bose, Subhas	Nehru, Jawaharlal	Sasorith
Nu, U	Chandra	Nehru, Motilal	Ngo Dinh Diem
Phibunsongkhram,	Desai, Morarji	Osman Ali	Nguyen Cao Ky
Luang	Fateh Singh, Sant	Pandit, Vijaya	Nguyen Huu Tho
Pridi Phanomyong	Gandhi, Indira	Lakshmi	Nguyen Van Thieu
San, Saya	Gandhi, Mohandas	Patel, Vallabhbhai	Norodom
Sarit Thanarat	Karamchand	Jhaverbhai	Sihanouk
Saw, U	Gandhi, Rajiv	Prasad, Rajendra	Phan Boi Chau
Thanom	Ghaffar Khan,	Sankaran Nair, Sir	Phetsarath
Kittikachorn	Abdul	Chettur	Ratanavongsa,
Thant, U	Giri, Varahagiri	Sastri, Srinivasa	Prince
Indian subcontinent:	Venkata	Tara Singh	Pol Pot
Abdullah, Sheikh	Jinnah,	Yahya Khan, Agha	Souphanouvong
Muhammad	Mohammed Ali	Mohammad	Souvanna Phouma
Ayub Khan,	Kamaraj,	*Indochina:*	Truong Chinh
Mohammad	Kumaraswami	Bao Dai	Vo Nguyen Giap
	Liaquat, Ali Kahn		

Indonesia:
  Agus Salim, Hadji
  Hatta, Mohammad
  Malik, Adam
  Sjahrir, Sutan
  Suharto
  Sukarno
  Tan Malaka,
    Ibrahim Datuk
Philippines:
  Aguinaldo, Emilio
  Aquino, Benigno
    Simon, Jr.

Garcia, Carlos
  Polestico
Macapagal,
  Diosdado
Magsaysay,
  Ramon
Marcos,
  Ferdinand E.
Quezon, Manuel
Quirino, Elpidio
Recto, Claro Mayo
Roxas, Manuel

other:
  Brooke Raj
  Decoux, Jean
  Lee Kuan Yew
  Linlithgow, Victor
    Alexander John
    Hope, 2nd
    marquess of
  Nūr al-Hilmī,
    Burhanuddin bin
    Muhammad
  Tan Cheng Lock

INDEX: See entries under all of the terms above

Section 977. Australia and Oceania Since 1920

A. International developments in the Pacific and the disposition of the dependent territories in Oceania since 1920

1. The post-World War I situation of the occupying powers in Oceania: the League of Nations mandate system

2. World War II in the Pacific: the rise and fall of Japanese power, effects of the war on indigenous peoples

3. Post-World War II reorganization: economic and social effects of UN trusteeship administrations, movements toward autonomy among the indigenous peoples, independent island states, dissolution of Trust Territory of the Pacific Islands (1986)

B. Australia since 1920

1. Developments to 1945: decline of the Labor Party and the Nationalist–Country coalition, industrial and rural development, the Great Depression, formation of the United Australia Party and Lyons' administrations (1931–39), military role in World War II, effects of the war on the economy

2. Political developments since 1945: alternation of Labor and Liberal-Country governments; weakening of ties with Great Britain and strengthening of ties with Asian and Pacific countries—support of Indonesian independence, recognition of China and North Vietnam; membership in Columbo Plan, ANZUS, SEATO; relations with the United States and support of U.S. troops in the wars in Korea and Vietnam; independence of Papua-New Guinea

3. Social and economic developments since 1945: rise of urban affluence and the problems of the rural areas, the effects of large-scale European and Asian immigration, development of mineral and energy resources, industrial relations problems; Aborigines' rights issues, deregulation of the economy and privatization of state-owned enterprises

C. New Zealand since *c.* 1920

1. Developments to 1945: United (Liberal)–Reform coalition governments, the Great Depression, Labour Party victory (1935) and social welfare programs, participation with Allies in World War II

2. New Zealand since 1945: National and Labour governments, increased participation in Pacific and Asian affairs, Maori nationalism, cuts in social welfare programs

Suggested reading in the *Encyclopædia Britannica:*

MACROPAEDIA: Major articles dealing with Australia and Oceania since 1920

Australia
Melbourne
New Zealand

Pacific Islands
Sydney
United States of America: Hawaii

MICROPAEDIA: Selected entries of reference information; see also Section 967

General subjects

> Australian Democrats
> Australian Labor Party
> New Zealand National Party

Biographies

Australia:

> Bruce, Stanley
>   Melbourne Bruce,
>   Viscount
> Chifley, Joseph
>   Benedict
> Curtin, John
> Fraser, Malcolm

> Gorton, Sir John
> Grey
> Hawke, Robert
> Lyons, Joseph
>   Aloysius
> Menzies, Sir
>   Robert Gordon
> Page, Sir Earle
> Whitlam, Gough

New Zealand:

> Forbes, George
>   William
> Fraser, Peter
> Holland, Sir
>   Sidney
> Holyoake, Sir
>   Keith Jacka

> Lange, David
> Muldoon, Robert
> Nash, Sir Walter
> Ngata, Sir Apirana
>   Turupa
> Savage, Michael
>   Joseph

INDEX: See entries under all of the terms above

Section 978. **Southwest Asia and Africa: the Late Colonial Period and the Emergence of New Nations in the 20th Century**

A. Turkey since 1919 and Cyprus since 1920

1. The War of Independence (1919–23) and the development of the Turkish nation under the leadership of Mustafa Kemal Atatürk

2. Atatürk's one-party government: secularization, social and economic reforms

3. Turkey since 1938: World War II and the postwar period, the republic since 1961

   a. Wartime neutrality until alignment (1945) with the Allies: postwar problems with the Soviet Union, political developments

   b. Turkey under the Democrats (1950–60): economic growth and political repression, the army coup (1960)

   c. New constitution (1961) and government under the Republican People's and Justice parties, crisis (1971) and recovery, military coup (1980), formation of civilian government (1983), urbanization and industrialization and great economic growth, mixed relations with East and West and with the Arab world

4. Cyprus since 1920: British administration to 1960, the Republic of Cyprus, political disunity over the *énosis* question, Turkish invasion (1974) and division of island, unilateral declaration of Turkish Republic of Northern Cyprus (1983)

B. Development of the Arab states and Israel in Southwest Asia and Egypt

1. The Arab lands of Southwest Asia under the mandate system

   a. Lebanon and Syria under the French mandate (1920–41): Arab demands for independence, the Druze revolt in Syria (1925–27), establishment of the Lebanese Republic (1926) and internal crises resulting in suspension of the constitution (1932), the Franco-Syrian Treaty (1936), Allied occupation in World War II, Syrian and Lebanese independence (1945)

   b. Iraq from 1918 to 1945: British occupation and mandate, independence (1932), political unrest and the role of the military, World War II and British intervention (1939–45)

   c. Palestine and Transjordan under British mandate (1920–48): the Balfour Declaration and the acceleration of Jewish settlement and conflicts with the Arabs; the Palestine Revolt (1936–39) and the Peel Commission; the Biltmore Resolution (1942); the partition of Palestine, the Palestine War, and the emergence of Israel (1948) and Jordan (1946)

2. Egypt from 1922 to 1945: Wafd-led opposition to the continued British presence, politics in the early Farouk regime, participation in World War II

3. The Arab states in the Fertile Crescent, Egypt, and Israel since 1945

   a. Lebanon: the multireligious political system, the Khuri regime (1943–52), the presidency of Chamoun and the 1958 crisis, later regimes and the civil war of 1974–76, the Israeli invasion of 1982, renewed civil war, de facto division into spheres of influence, government of national unity (1984), continuing civil disorder

   b. Syria: political instability in the postwar decade, temporary union with Egypt (1958–61), the secessionist regime (1961–63), Ba'thist Syria after 1963, conflicts with Israel, role in the Lebanese civil wars, relations with Palestine Liberation Organization, domestic unrest

   c. The League of Arab States (1945), the partition of Palestine, and the establishment of the State of Israel (1948) and the Hashemite Kingdom of Jordan (1950)

      i. The establishment of Israel (1948) and resultant conflicts with the Arabs: immigration and politics, foreign aid and economic development, renewed hostilities with the Arab states in the Suez War (1956), the Six-Day War (1967) and the diplomatic stalemate, the war of October 1973, role in the 1974–76 Lebanese civil war, treaty with Egypt (1979), invasion of Lebanon (1982) and withdrawal (1985), Palestinian *intifada* (from 1987), expansion of Jewish settlements in occupied territory and massive immigration of Soviet Jews

      ii. Economic and political problems in Jordan under King Hussein: annexation of the West Bank (1950), ambivalent foreign policy, formation of the Palestine Liberation Organization (1964), Israeli annexations (1967), Jordan's expulsion of the PLO (1970), renunciation of claims and ties to West Bank (1988)

   d. Iraq: postwar reconstruction and social upheavals (1945–58), the revolution of 1958, politics under the republic, military coups (1963–68), oil and the economy, the Ba'th regime since 1968, the Kurdish question, Iran-Iraq war (1980–88 [officially ended 1990]), invasion of Kuwait (1990) and defeat in Persian Gulf war (1991)

   e. Egyptian politics in the last years of Farouk's regime, the Egyptian revolution (1952) and Nasser's rise to power, the Suez crises (1956), the Six-Day War (1967), Sadat's presidency (1970–81), Mubarak's presidency

4. The Arabian Peninsula since *c.* 1920: the political, economic, and social effects of the discovery of oil and the resultant influx of wealth; British and other great power influences

   a. Emergence of the Kingdom of Saudi Arabia under Ibn Sa'ūd (1924); oil discoveries and exploitation; the government under Fayṣal (1964–75), Khālid (1975–82), and Fahd; foreign relations; rise as a dominant Arab power

   b. The other Arabian states: Bahrain and Qatar, Kuwait, Oman, the United Arab Emirates, Yemen (Aden), Yemen (Ṣan'ā'); Yemeni wars and union negotiations; formation of Gulf Cooperation Council (1981), unification of Yemen (1990), invasion of Kuwait and ensuing Persian Gulf war (1990–91)

C. Iran and Afghanistan since *c.* 1920

1. Iran since 1925

   a. The regime of Reza Shah (1925–41): economic and social reforms, relations with Germany and invasion by Allies during World War II

   b. The regime of Mohammad Reza Pahlavi (1941–79), nationalization of oil resources (1951), land reform (from 1962), expansion of economy from petroleum revenues

   c. The Islāmic Republic: revolution of 1978–79, the republican regime, support of Muslim fundamentalist movements, Iran-Iraq war (1980–88 [officially ended 1990])

2. Afghanistan since independence (1921): civil disorders, attempts at reform, and economic improvements; constitutional revisions; relations with other countries; the republic from 1973; Soviet invasion of 1979 and guerrilla resistance; Soviet withdrawal

D. North Africa since 1920

1. The final decades of European rule

   a. French colonial policies, the French protectorate and the Spanish zone in Morocco, the administration of Algeria and the Algerian War, Tunisian nationalist movements

   b. Libya under the domination of the Fascist Italian government (1922–43)

2. Establishment of independent states in the Maghrib

   a. Postwar British and French occupation of Libya, independence (1951), the republic (from 1969), emergence of Qaddafi (1970), disruptive role in world affairs, treaty of union with Morocco (1984) abrogated in 1986

   b. The emergence of independent Tunisia (1956): formation of republic (1957), Tunisia under Bourguiba's presidency (1957–87); rise of Islāmic fundamentalists in mid-1980s

   c. The emergence of independent Morocco (1956): government under Mohammed V (d. 1961) and Hassan II, the Spanish Zone and its reduction to Ceuta and Melilla, dispute over Spanish (now Western) Sahara, treaty of union with Libya (1984–86)

    d. The Algerian War (1954–62), French evacuation, and the emergence of independent Algeria (1962): government under Ben Bella (overthrown 1965), Boumedienne (1965–78), and Bendjedid; adoption of socialist and Islāmic National Charter (1976); support for the Polisario Front in Western Sahara

    e. Mauritania and the Spanish (Western) Sahara: independent Mauritania (from 1960), Polisario revolt in Western Sahara, division of Western Sahara between Mauritania and Morocco and Moroccan takeover of Mauritanian zone (1979)

E. The maturation of the European colonial system and the nationalist movements in sub-Saharan Africa since 1920

  1. Completion of effective occupation by the European powers: the post-World War I division of former German colonies among other colonial powers, the mandate system

  2. Administrative policies and attitudes of each colonial power: economic development, effects of colonialism on the societies and institutions of the African peoples

  3. World War II and postwar changes in colonial policies: decline of the colonial system and rise of African nationalist parties, establishment of independent African countries from 1957, the Organization of African Unity, the assertiveness of white-settled Africa

  4. West Africa since *c.* 1920

    a. Colonial rule from *c.* 1920 until independence, independent Liberia's economic ties to the U.S.

      i. Economic developments in French West Africa: Senegal, French Sudan, Upper Volta (Burkina Faso since 1984), Niger

      ii. Economic developments in British colonies: The Gambia, Sierra Leone, Gold Coast (Ghana since 1957), Nigeria

    b. Decolonization and independence

      i. Emergence of African leaders: rise of a new class of educated Africans

      ii. Formation of African independence movements, independence for all the former colonies between 1957 and 1975, the countries of West Africa after independence, problems of economic development, political instability, military coups and emergence of one-party states

  5. Ethiopia and the Nilotic Sudan since *c.* 1917

    a. Ethiopia and Eritrea since 1917: internal division and the rise of Haile Selassie, the Italian conquest (1936), Eritrea under Italian rule, federation (1952) and union (1962) with Ethiopia, establishment of the military government (1974), abolition of the monarchy and death of Haile Selassie (1975), Eritrean revolt and Somali invasion of the Ogaden, development of Socialist state under Mengistu

    b. The Anglo-Egyptian Sudan: growth of national consciousness and creation of the independent republic (1956), military coup (1958) and the Abbud government (1958–64), revolt in the southern provinces, return to civilian rule, government of Ja'afar an-Numayri (1969–85) and temporary resolution of the southern problem, renewed tension in the south following introduction of Islāmic law (1983) and administrative decentralization, military coup (1985)

  6. East Africa and Madagascar since *c.* 1920

    a. The European colonies in East Africa from *c.* 1920 to the beginning of independence (1960)

      i. The colonial economics: growth of export trade (cotton, cloves, coffee), extension of the railroads

      ii. Somalia as an Italian trust territory (1950), problems in British Somaliland

      iii. Crises of colonial rule in the 1950s: Mau Mau resistance in Kenya; independence movements in Uganda, Tanganyika, and Zanzibar

    b. Developments since independence

      i. Somalia: independence (1960), internal tensions and territorial disputes, conflict with Ethiopia, military takeover (1969) and regime of Siyad Barre, break with the Soviet Union (1977), war with Ethiopia (1977–78) and continued unrest in the Ogaden, influx of refugees

      ii. Economic cooperation among the formerly British East African nations: the East African Community and its end (1977)

      iii. Tanzania (formerly Tanganyika and Zanzibar): revolt against Arab control in Zanzibar (1964), Nyerere and introduction of *ujamaa* socialism, tension with Uganda and invasion in support of revolt against Amin (1978), economic difficulties

       iv. Uganda: independence (1962) and economic growth, the Obote and Amin governments, reign of terror and economic decline, deposition of Amin (1979), reinstatement (1980) and overthrow (1985) of Obote

       v. Kenya: independence (1963) and subsequent domestic politics and foreign relations under Kenyatta's leadership, death of Kenyatta (1978) and succession of Daniel arap Moi, establishment of one-party state (1982)

   c. Madagascar: the French administration, independence (1960) and subsequent domestic politics and foreign relations

7. Central Africa after World War II: the intensification of nationalist movements and the acquisition of independence by the former European colonies

   a. The emergence of French and Belgian colonies as republics: internal divisions and the fate of the republics

       i. The Democratic Republic of the Congo (Republic of Zaire since 1971): the Congolese nationalist movement and independence (1960), secession of Katanga province and UN intervention (1960–64), regime of Mobutu Sese Seko

       ii. Central African Republic: independence (1960), subsequent domestic politics and foreign relations, establishment and overthrow (1979) of Central African Empire under Bokassa I

       iii. The People's Republic of the Congo: independence (1960), ethnic rivalries, domestic politics and foreign relations

       iv. Gabon Republic: independence (1960), subsequent domestic politics and foreign relations

       v. Burundi and Rwanda: independence (1962), overthrow of Ntare V of Burundi (1966), warfare between Tutsi and Hutu (early 1970s)

   b. Republic of Equatorial Guinea: the Spanish administration, independence (1968), repressive regime of Macías Nguema, military coup (1979)

8. Southern Africa since *c.* 1920

   a. Southern Africa from *c.* 1920 to *c.* 1945

       i. Political and economic developments in white-settler-controlled Union of South Africa: the Hertzog administration (1924–33) and the Hertzog–Smuts coalition (1933–39), political disunity and Allied participation in World War II

       ii. White-settler control of Southern Rhodesia: relations with Northern Rhodesia and Nyasaland; colonial government economic, social, and political discrimination against black Africans; Portuguese rule in Angola and Mozambique

       iii. Indian, Coloured, and black African responses to colonial government-sanctioned discrimination: growth of local political organizations, separatist church movements, and mass nationalist movements

   b. Southern Africa since 1945: political developments in white-controlled colonies and nations, emergence of black nations

       i. Republic of South Africa (formerly the Union of South Africa): Afrikaner National Party administrations since 1948, government-sanctioned apartheid, establishment of Bantu Homelands (1959), transformation into republic (1961), antiapartheid movements and growing international isolation, Soweto riots (1976), new constitution (1983), increasing political dissent, legalization of African National Congress (1990), repeal of major apartheid laws

       ii. Namibia (formerly known as South West Africa): international and internal resistance to incorporation into South Africa, revocation of UN mandate (1966) and international efforts toward independence, independence of Namibia (1990)

       iii. Botswana, Lesotho, and Swaziland: British administration of the High Commission Territories, independence (1966, 1968), subsequent relations with South Africa

       iv. British Central Africa: postwar conditions in Northern Rhodesia, Southern Rhodesia, and Nyasaland; the Federation of Rhodesia and Nyasaland (1953–63); rise of black nationalist movements; independence of Zambia and Malaŵi (1964)

       v. Zimbabwe (formerly Southern Rhodesia): Rhodesia's unilateral declaration of independence (UDI, 1965), civil war, establishment of Zimbabwe (1980)

       vi. Developments in the Portuguese colonies of Angola and Mozambique: economic advances, nationalist movements, and independence in the mid-1970s; continued guerrilla activity; arrival of Cuban troops in Angola; border war between Angola and South Africa; Mozambique–South Africa nonaggression pact (1984)

Suggested reading in the *Encyclopædia Britannica*:

MACROPAEDIA: Major articles and a biography dealing with Southwest Asia and Africa: the late colonial period and the emergence of new nations in the 20th century

Afghanistan	Cyprus	Jordan	Sudan
Africa	Eastern Africa	Lebanon	Syria
Arabia	Egypt	North Africa	Turkey and
Asia	Iran	Palestine	Ancient Anatolia
Atatürk	Iraq	South Africa	Western Africa
Central Africa	Israel	Southern Africa	

MICROPAEDIA: Selected entries of reference information; see also Section 96/11

General subjects

central Africa:
Belgian Congo
Moyen-Congo
Ruanda-Urundi
Rwanda,
  Kingdom of
eastern Africa:
Buganda
German East
  Africa
Italian East Africa
Mau Mau
Somaliland
Ethiopia and the
Nilotic Sudan:
Anglo-Egyptian
  Condominium
Italian East Africa
Italo-Ethiopian War
Mahdist
Middle East:
Anglo-Egyptian
  Treaty
Arab Legion
Balfour
  Declaration
Ba'th Party
Camp David
  Accords

Druze revolt
Fatah
Gaza
Gaza strip
Haganah
Hashimite
Ikhwān
Iran-Iraq War
Irgun Zvai Leumi
Israel Labour Party
Jewish Agency
Likud
Mapam
Muslim
  Brotherhood
Palestine
Palestine
  Liberation
  Organization
Peel Commission
Sinai Peninsula
Stern Gang
Suez Crisis
United Arab
  Republic
Wafd
Zionism

North Africa:
Algerian Reformist
  Ulamas,
  Association of
Cyrenaica
Destour
Destourian
  Socialist Party
National Action
  Bloc
National
  Liberation Front
Polisario
Rif War
Tripolitania
Ottoman Empire and
Turkey:
Ankara, Treaty of
Greco-Turkish
  Wars
Lausanne,
  Treaty of
Moscow, Treaty of
southern Africa:
African National
  Congress
apartheid

banning
Frelimo
National Party of
  South Africa
New Republic
  Party
Pan-Africanist
  Congress of
  Azania
Progressive Federal
  Party
Rhodesia and
  Nyasaland,
  Federation of
South African
  Party
South West
  Africa People's
  Organization
United Party
western Africa:
Biafra
British West Africa
French West
  Africa
Mali Federation
Togoland
other:
EOKA

Biographies

central Africa:
Boganda,
  Barthélemy
Bokassa, Eddine
  Ahmed
Éboué, Felix
Kasavubu, Joseph
Lumumba, Patrice
M'ba, Léon
Mobutu Sese Seko
Mutesa II
Nyerere, Julius
Obote, Milton
Tshombe, Moise

eastern Africa:
Amin, Idi
Haile Selassie
Kenyatta, Jomo
Mboya, Tom
Mengistu
  Haile Mariam
Odinga, Oginga
Iran:
Khomeini,
  Ruhollah
Mohammad Reza
  Shah Pahlavi

Mosaddeq,
  Mohammad
Reza Shah Pahlavi
Middle East—Egypt:
Farouk I
Fu'ād I
Lutfī as-Sayyid,
  Ahmad
Māhir Pasha, 'Alī
Mubārak, Hosnī
Naguib,
  Muhammad
Nahhās Pasha,
  Mustafā an-

Nasser, Gamal
  Abdel
Sādāt, Anwar el-
Zaghlūl, Sa'd
Middle East—Israel
and Zionism:
Ahad Ha'am
Begin, Menachem
Ben-Gurion, David
Ben-Zvi, Itzhak
Dayan, Moshe
Herzl, Theodor
Jabotinsky,
  Vladimir

Meir, Golda
Peres, Shimon
Shamir, Yitzḥak
Sharon, Ariel
Weizman, Chaim
Middle East—other
Arab:
 ʻAflaq, Michel
 ʻArafāt, Yāsir
 Assad, Hafiz al-
 Chamoun, Camille
 (Nimer)
 Chehab, Fuad
 Fahd
 Fayṣal I
 Gemayel family
 Hawrani,
 Akram al-
 Ḥusaynī, Amīn al-
 Hussein (ibn Talal)
 Hussein, Saddam
 Ibn Saʻūd
 Kassem, Abdul
 Karim
 Nuri as-Said
North Africa:
 Abbas, Ferhat
 Abd el-Krim

Ben Bella, Ahmed
Boumedienne,
 Houari
Bourguiba, Habib
Idris I
Muhammad V
Qaddafi,
 Muammar al-
southern Africa:
 Banda, H.
 Kamuzu
 Biko, Stephen
 Buthelezi,
 Mangosuthu G.
 Hertzog, J.B.M.
 Kaunda, Kenneth
 Lutuli, Albert
 Malan, Daniel F.
 Mandela, Nelson
 Rohihlahia
 Mugabe, Robert
 Neto, Agostinho
 Nkomo, Joshua
 Nujoma, Sam
 Smith, Ian
 Smuts, Jan
 Christian

Sobhuza II
Strijdom, Johannes
 Gerhardus
Tutu, Desmond
Verwoerd, Hendrik
 Frensch
Vorster, John
Welensky, Sir Roy
Turkey:
 Atatürk, Kemal
 Bayar, Celâl
 Çakmak, Fevzi
 Demirel, Süleyman
 Ecevit, Bülent
 İnönü, İsmet
 Menderes, Adnan
western Africa:
 Awolowo, Obafemi
 Azikiwe, Nnamdi
 Balewa, Sir
 Abubaker Tafawa
 Daddah, Moktar
 Ould
 Danquah, J.B.
 Doe, Samuel K.
 Gowon, Yakubu

Guèye, Lamine
Houphouët-Boigny,
 Félix
Jawara, Sir Dawda
 Kairaba
Keita, Modibo
Margai, Sir Milton
Nkrumah, Kwame
Ojukwu,
 Odumegwu
Olympio, Sylvanus
Rawlings, Jerry J.
Senghor, Léopold
Touré, Sékou
Tubman, William
 V.S.
Zinsour, Émile
 Derlin
other:
 Amānollāh Khān
 Makarios III
 Zahir Shah,
 Mohammad

INDEX: See entries under all of the terms above

Introduction to Part Ten:
Knowledge Become Self-conscious

by Mortimer J. Adler

The words *universe* and *encyclopaedia* have an obvious similarity of meaning. Both come from words—in the one case, Latin, in the other, Greek—that mean a totality or all-inclusive whole. Whether the universe is finite or infinite, and however it is constituted or organized, it embraces everything that is. Nothing lies outside it; everything that happens occurs within it. Can one say, with equal assurance, that the encyclopaedia is a similar totality or whole? Perhaps we cannot say that of any actual, historic encyclopaedia. But that is the ideal which all encyclopaedias attempt to embody.

It is not just the similarity of the universe and the encyclopaedia as totalities or wholes that interests us, but also how these two wholes are related to each other. One of them, the universe, embraces not only everything that is, but also everything that is knowable. The other, the encyclopaedia, sets for itself the goal of reporting everything that is and can be known about the universe. The one is mirrored or reflected in the other—the macrocosm in the microcosm.

The universe includes man—man a moving body, man a living organism, man a social animal, and man not only as a doer and seeker but also as a maker and knower of things. Among the things that man seeks to know and understand is his own knowledge—his abilities, efforts, and achievements in the sphere of knowing itself. Whether or not Aristotle was correct in saying that the highest form of intellectual activity is thinking about thinking itself, it is certainly true that "knowledge become self-conscious" is a distinctive characteristic of the human enterprise of knowing. We not only seek to know whatever can be known, but we also, reflexively, turn our knowing back upon itself when we pay attention to how we know what we know, the various ways in which we know, and the divisions or branches of our knowledge.

The organization of the encyclopaedia—the way in which the branches of knowledge have been distinguished from one another and related to one another—has changed remarkably from age to age. In antiquity, before there were any real encyclopaedias, learned men envisaged the whole of human knowledge as having a certain structure of related parts or subdivisions. The organization of knowledge in medieval encyclopaedias exhibited quite a different pattern. Later encyclopaedias introduced still other changes in the picture; and that picture has changed in important respects during the last century and is undergoing further changes today.

The new *Britannica* presents us with an outline of knowledge that is radically different in its fundamental framework and its organizational scheme from the outlines that might have been constructed for an ancient encyclopaedia—if there had been any such thing—or a medieval one. The Outline of Knowledge set forth in this *Propædia* volume is divided into ten parts, each of which is broken down into divisions and sections. Division by division, from Part One through Part Nine, the outline covers what we know about the universe with the help of such sciences as physics, chemistry, astronomy, geology, meteorology, biology, medicine, psychology, anthropology, sociology, political science, economics, and technology. It also covers what we know as a result of systematic study and scholarship in such fields as education, law, the arts, religion, and history.

The knowledge of the universe that we possess by means of the disciplines mentioned above is outlined in Parts One through Nine and expounded in the articles to which the outline refers. What about Part Ten—the part to which this essay is an introduction? Where and how does that fit into the picture?

To some extent the answer has already been given. Here in Part Ten we are concerned with "knowledge become self-conscious"—with knowledge about knowledge—with our knowing turned, reflexively, back upon itself. Here it is not the knowable universe we are considering. It is, instead, the world of knowledge itself: its diverse disciplines, modes of inquiry, fields of scholarship or systematic study—in short, as the title of Part Ten indicates, the branches of knowledge. Whereas the other nine parts of the Outline of Knowledge cover *what we know* about the knowable universe, the outline of Part Ten covers what we know about the sciences or other disciplines *whereby we know* that which we know.

The answer just given is not the whole answer to the question provoked by the special character of Part Ten. What we know about the various sciences and the diverse disciplines that comprise the world of knowledge almost always includes an account of the methods of inquiry, verification or demonstration, and argument employed by scientists or scholars in a particular field of knowledge. While interest in such matters does not exhaustively represent the concerns of logic, the science of logic does provide the underpinnings for our study of the methodology of the other learned disciplines, including history and philosophy as well as the various sciences. What we know about logic itself as a science—its history and, as it were, the philosophy of it—therefore properly belongs in the outline of Part Ten, together with an indication of the scope and content of the science itself.

For a somewhat different reason mathematics is also treated here in the same way as logic. The knowledge attained by the mathematician has extraordinarily wide and diverse applicability in other spheres of inquiry and branches of knowledge—in most, if not all, of the natural sciences and in many of the social sciences. Like logic, mathematics belongs here not only for its usefulness in other sciences, but also for its own sake as a science. We are concerned with its content as well as with its method, history, and philosophy.

In addition to logic and mathematics, two other disciplines occupy a special place in any consideration of the branches of knowledge. One is history; the other, philosophy.

History as a field of study includes more than the history of peoples, of nations, of cultures, and of social institutions. It includes the history of human learning itself, of all the branches of knowledge. It includes not only the history of the natural and social sciences, but also the history of logic, of mathematics, of philosophy, and of history itself as one of the learned disciplines. And, in addition to there being a history of the study of history (*i.e.,* historiography), there is also a logic of history (its methodology) and a philosophy of history.

Like history, philosophy is operative in the study of all the other disciplines as well as of itself. Philosophy become self-conscious is concerned with questions about the nature and scope of philosophy, about whether it has a method or methods and a subject matter or subject matters peculiarly its own. Philosophy is also concerned about its own historical development and, in that history, about its changing relationship to other disciplines, especially to religion and to the sciences. As there is a history and a philosophy of history, so there is a philosophy of philosophy and a history of philosophy—a statement which probably cannot be made about any other two disciplines in the entire range of the branches of knowledge.

In addition, as each of the other disciplines has a history, so there is a philosophy of each of the other disciplines. We have already noted that there is a philosophy of logic and of mathematics. So, too, there is a philosophy of science in general and of the different sciences in particular; and also a philosophy of education, of law, of art, and of religion.

All of this, however, does not exhaust the content of philosophy, any more than the history of all the branches of knowledge exhausts the content of history, or any more than the application of logic and mathematics to other disciplines exhausts their content as disciplines with knowledge to offer. But in the case of philosophy, as not in the case of logic and mathematics, it is sometimes questioned whether it can rightly claim to offer us knowledge of the universe as well as knowledge about knowledge itself and an understanding of the various branches of knowledge. That question, together with the question of how the knowledge that philosophers claim to have stands in relation to other forms of knowledge, constitutes what is, perhaps, the most fundamental problem dealt with by philosophers when they philosophize about philosophy itself. Whether or not the knowledge they claim to have is comparable in its validity to the knowledge achieved in other spheres of inquiry, philosophy, like science, covers a wide range of subject matters and involves a large number of distinct subdivisions, each with its own problems and controversies (*e.g.,* metaphysics, philosophy of nature, epistemology, philosophy of mind, philosophy of man, ethics, political philosophy, and aesthetics).

Concerning the whole range of disciplines that are represented in an exhaustive inventory of the branches of knowledge, three questions stand out as the most challenging. Of these, the first two have been debated over and over again—in earlier epochs as well as in our own century, and in the context of organizations of knowledge quite different from that which prevails or is acceptable today.

One is the question about whether the various branches of knowledge can or should be arranged in a hierarchical order, in an ascending scale from lower to higher, or from less to more fundamental. In antiquity they were so arranged; as, for example, in Aristotle's ordering of the speculative sciences, beginning with physics and rising through mathematics to metaphysics as the science of first principles and ultimate causes; and in his characterization of politics as the architectonic or controlling discipline in the sphere of practical knowledge, directive of human action. So, too, in the Middle Ages, a hierarchical organization prevailed, in which theology was regarded as queen of the sciences, philosophy as its handmaiden, with all the other disciplines contributing their portions of knowledge for the greater glory of God and for the better understanding of man's destiny under Divine Providence. If, in accordance with the prevailing view today, a hierarchical order is rejected, is there any other order to replace it, and in terms of what criteria or principles can such an alternative be constructed? Is there, as the introductory essay in this volume suggests, a circle of learning instead of a hierarchy of the branches of knowledge—a circle in which no point is either a beginning or an end, and lines can be drawn from any point to any other?

The second question, to which different answers have been given at different times and to which conflicting answers are still being given today, asks about the coherence of the world of knowledge as a whole. Do all its constituent parts—its various component disciplines or branches of knowledge—adhere together harmoniously, each somehow complementing the other? Or, on the contrary, is the world of knowledge torn asunder by irremediable conflicts—by territorial disputes, by conflicting claims to sovereignty, by assertions and denials of legitimacy? Underlying whatever answers may be given to these questions, a deeper difference of opinion may exist concerning the unity of truth itself. If, for example, there is some truth in science and some truth in philosophy or in religion, must these diverse approximations of whatever truth man can possess be consistent with one another? Or, on the contrary, can there be some truth in science and some in philosophy or in religion, even though the truth of the one stands in sharp conflict to the truth of the other? Can there be, in short, a multiplicity of truths, each of which deserves that name, but each of which must be kept out of contact with the others, by being isolated in logic-tight compartments?

Unlike the two preceding questions, the third is one that has come to the forefront only recently. It concerns what many contemporary commentators regard as an unfortunate rift in the realm of knowledge—the chasm between the sciences, on the one hand, and the humanities, on the other. In the long history of the latter term, different disciplines have been grouped together on the side of the humanities and in contradistinction to the sciences. Today, the humanities group is generally thought to include language and literature, the fine arts, history, philosophy, and religion.

It is assumed that there are fundamental differences, in method or approach and in criteria of validity, between the humanistic disciplines, on the one hand, and the sciences, both natural and social, on the other. Of course there are, but they are not entirely clear. By reference to methodology or to criteria of validity, certain of the disciplines called humanistic closely resemble those called scientific. For example, mathematicians and logicians do their work by sitting still and thinking, not by undertaking experiments or by going out into the field to collect data or do research. Philosophy is like them in this respect; but mathematics and logic are usually regarded as sciences, whereas philosophy is grouped with the humanities. Furthermore, the criteria of validity thought to be applicable to philosophy do not operate as criteria for judging the excellence of literature or of other fine arts, yet all three are classified as humanities.

Supposing that some line can be clearly drawn to divide the humanities from the sciences, the problem that agitates those who contemplate the world of learning is whether it is one world or two—whether the rift or chasm that separates the sciences from the humanities involves an iron curtain that prevents communication between them. It is not within the purpose or the province of this essay to provide an answer to that question. Nevertheless, an answer would appear to be suggested by the conception of the encyclopaedia as a totality, as an organized whole. That conception would seem to favour the view that, in the circle of learning, there are no impenetrable barriers to communication or unbridgeable breaks in continuity. Underlying it is the faith that the whole world of knowledge is a single universe of discourse.

Part Ten. The Branches of Knowledge

Several points should be noted about the relations of this part to the preceding parts. The results of investigations in the natural and social sciences, and in medicine and technology—their content or knowledge—are set forth in Parts One through Five, and in Part Seven. Accordingly, the outlines in the seven sections of Division III in this part are confined to questions about the history of these disciplines, and about their nature, scope, structure, methods, and principal problems or tasks. Direct historical accounts of the peoples and civilizations of the world are set forth in Part Nine, whereas Section 10/41 in Division IV of this part is confined to historical and analytical studies of the discipline of history itself, treating the history of historical writing, the methods of modern historical investigation and research, speculative philosophies of history, and philosophical analyses of the specific character of historical knowledge.

The case is different with Divisions I, II, and V—on logic, mathematics, and philosophy. The results of these disciplines have not been dealt with in previous parts. In the history of each of these disciplines, substantive developments have persistently involved, and issued from, positions taken not only *within them,* but also from positions taken *about them.* Accordingly, the outlines in the sections of Divisions I, II, and V treat the substantive results of logical, mathematical, and philosophical inquiry, on the one hand, and the historical and analytical studies of the nature, scope, branches, methods, and principal problems of logic, mathematics, and philosophy, on the other.

In Part Six on the arts and Part Eight on religion, the outlines include historical and analytic studies of knowledge and inquiry concerning the arts and religion. Such studies, then, are not included separately in Part Ten. They are, however, treated in Section 10/42 of this part, insofar as the study of the arts and of religion are, together with the study of language, history, and philosophy, component disciplines of the humanities—a group of disciplines traditionally distinguished from the natural and social sciences, and traditionally considered to have, taken together, a special educational and cultural role. Section 10/42 sets forth a historical review of the changing conceptions of the humanities and of humanistic scholarship, and treats issues about the definition and scope of the humanities, about their distinction from the sciences, and about their role in education and culture.

Division I. Logic

The outlines in the two sections of Division I deal with the history and philosophy of logic and with the content of the disciplines of formal logic, metalogic, and applied logic.

The outline in Section 10/11 first treats the history of logic in the West and the history of Indian and Chinese logic; and then treats differing conceptions of the field and scope of logic, problems in the philosophy of logic concerning meaning, truth, and ontology, and the place of logic among the sciences and disciplines.

Section 10/12 deals first with formal logic, treating the propositional calculus, the predicate calculus, the theory of the syllogism, modal logic, and set theory and natural-number arithmetic. It goes on to the nature and elements of metalogic, which studies the syntax and semantics of formal languages, formal systems, and logical calculi. Finally, it deals with the applications of logic in different domains of inquiry and discourse.

Section 10/11.   History and Philosophy of Logic

A. History of logic

1. Ancient logic

a. Precursors of ancient logic: contributions of the Sophists, Socrates, and Plato to theories of language and the axiomatic method

b. Aristotle and the logic of predicates: theories of the structure of language, theories of opposition and conversion, development of syllogistic and modal logic

c. Later developments in the logic of predicates: contributions of Theophrastus and Galen

d. Founding of the logic of propositions: contributions of Theophrastus and the Megarians, Stoic logic

2. Medieval logic

a. Development of medieval logic: Arabic contributions, disputes between the "old logic" and the "new logic" after the translation of Aristotle's *Organon*, summations by William of Sherwood and Peter of Spain

b. Medieval theories of language and their relation to the development of logic: the theory of categorematic and syncategorematic terms, the theory of supposition

c. Medieval developments in formal logic: the logic of predicates, of propositions, and of modal expressions; logical fallacies and paradoxes

3. Modern logic from the Renaissance to the 20th century

a. Logic in the Renaissance: the influence of Neoplatonism and of the rise of the natural sciences, the logics of Petrus Ramus and of Port-Royal

b. The rise of mathematical logic during the Enlightenment: contributions of Leibniz (*e.g.,* his general calculus of reasoning and general methodology), the search for clarity and the use of diagrams

c. Development of mathematical logic in the 19th century: expansions of syllogistic, Boole's algebra of logic, refinements of the calculus, the study by Frege and Cantor of the relation between logic and the foundations of mathematics

4. Logic in the 20th century

a. The conflict of Logicism, the view that mathematics is a continuation of logic, with Intuitionism and Formalism: Russell's Logicism and the theory of types, Brouwer's Intuitionism, Hilbert's Formalism

b. Developments in the logic of propositions and in the logic of predicates

c. Metalogical studies: the study of the properties of axiomatized systems; syntax and semantics as metalogical disciplines

5. Logic in the East

a. Indian logic: its origins in the commentaries on the scriptural texts called *sūtra*s, special problems in grammar and special types of inference, interest in the logical implications of the notion of negation

b. Chinese logic: its origins in reflections on the characteristics of controversies between the major philosophies of Confucianism, Taoism, and Moism; its neglect after the establishment of Neo-Confucianism in the 11th century AD

B. Philosophy of logic

1. The organization of logic as a discipline

a. The nature and varieties of logic: differing conceptions of its field and scope, varieties of logical symbolism

b. Features and problems of logic: concerns with logical semantics or model theory, questions of the limitations of logic, Gödel's incompleteness theorems, the question of logic and computability

2. Issues and developments in the philosophy of logic

a. Problems in meaning and truth: logical semantics of modal concepts, logic and informativeness

b. Problems of ontology: problems concerning individuation and existence

c. Alternative logics: modal logics, intuitionistic logic

3. The place of logic among the sciences and disciplines

Suggested reading in the *Encyclopædia Britannica:*

MACROPAEDIA: Major articles dealing with the history and philosophy of logic

Logic, The History and Kinds of
Philosophies of the Branches of Knowledge

MICROPAEDIA: Selected entries of reference information

General subjects

analogy	axiom	ekthesis	thought, laws of
analytic	De Morgan laws	fallacy	types, theory of
proposition	dialectic	induction	universal

Biographies

Boole, George	Leibniz, Gottfried	Peirce, Charles	Socrates
Carnap, Rudolf	Wilhelm	Sanders	Whitehead, Alfred
Frege, Gottlob	Leśniewski,	Ramus, Petrus	North
Gödel, Kurt	Stanislaw	Russell, Bertrand	

See also Sections 10/51, 10/52, and 10/53

INDEX: See entries under all of the terms above

Section 10/12. Formal Logic, Metalogic, and Applied Logic

A. Formal logic

1. The propositional calculus: the logic of unanalyzed sentences in combination

a. General features of the propositional calculus: symbols employed for propositional connectives or operators (*i.e.,* "not," "and," "or," "if . . . then," "is equivalent to"), propositional variables

b. Special systems of the propositional calculus

2. The predicate calculus: the logic of quantified functions of terms

a. General features of the predicate calculus: individual variables and predicate variables, universal and existential quantifiers (*i.e.,* "any" or "all," "some" or "one")

b. The lower predicate calculus: the logic of individual variables

c. Higher order predicate calculi: the logics of classes of variables

3. Syllogistic: the theory of the syllogism

4. Modal logic: the logic of necessity, possibility, and contingency; systems of and validity in modal logic

5. Set theory and natural-number arithmetic

B. Metalogic: the study of the syntax and the semantics of formal languages, formal systems, and logical calculi

1. The nature and elements of metalogic

2. The nature of a formal system and of a formal language

3. Discoveries about formal mathematical systems: completeness and consistency, decidability and undecidability

4. Discoveries about logical calculi

5. Model theory: the study of the interpretations, or models, that satisfy the axioms of a given formal system

C. Applied logic

   1. The critique of forms of reasoning

      a. Theory of argumentation: the new rhetoric

      b. Analysis of logical fallacies: material, verbal, and formal fallacies

   2. Epistemic logic: logic dealing with the concepts of belief, knowledge, assertion, doubt, and question

   3. Practical logic: logic dealing with the concepts of choosing, planning, commanding, and permitting

   4. Logics of physical application

   5. Hypothetical reasoning and counterfactual conditionals: logic involving consequents whose antecedents are known to be false

---

Suggested reading in the *Encyclopædia Britannica:*

MACROPAEDIA: Major articles dealing with formal logic, metalogic, and applied logic

   Logic, The History and Kinds of
   Rhetoric

MICROPAEDIA: Selected entries of reference information

General subjects

analytic proposition	deduction	modus ponens and modus tollens	rhetoric
axiom	dichotomy	mood	set theory
axiomatic method	dilemma	predicate calculus	syllogistic
categorical proposition	enthymeme	predication	
condition	formal system	propositional calculus	
conjunction	logic	recursive function	
conversion	metalogic	reduction	
	modal logic		
	modality		

Biographies

Antiphon	Lewis, C.I.	Quintilian
Isocrates	Peano, Giuseppe	Zeno of Elea

See also Sections 10/51, 10/52, and 10/53

INDEX: See entries under all of the terms above

Division II. **Mathematics**
[For Part Ten headnote see page 479.]

The outlines in the three sections of Division II treat the history and foundations of mathematics, the branches of mathematics, and the applications of mathematics.

Section 10/21 deals first with the general history of mathematics, with the development of representative non-probabilistic areas of mathematics, and with the historical development of probabilistic areas. The treatment of the foundations of mathematics covers the axiomatic method, the genetic method, 20th-century rival formulations of the foundations of mathematics, and current investigations of the foundations of mathematics.

Section 10/22, the branches of mathematics, first treats set theory, arithmetic, elementary multivariate algebra, linear and multilinear algebra, and algebraic structures, including the subjects of homological algebra and universal algebra. It goes on to deal with Euclidean and non-Euclidean geometry, projective geometry, analytic and trigonometric geometry, differential geometry, and algebraic geometry. It then deals with the subdivisions of mathematical analysis: real analysis, complex analysis, differential equations, functional analysis, Fourier analysis, the theory of probability, and vector and tensor analysis. The outline next deals with combinatorics and combinatorial geometry, and with number theory. Finally, it treats topology: general topology, topological groups and differential topology, and algebraic topology.

Section 10/23, applications of mathematics, first treats mathematics as a calculatory science and then goes on to deal with statistics, numerical analysis, definitions and examples of automata and the development of automata theory, the mathematical theory of optimization, information theory, and the mathematical aspects of physical theories.

Section 10/21.   History and Foundations of Mathematics

A. History of mathematics

  1. The development of mathematics in general, through ancient, medieval, and modern times

    a. Ancient and medieval periods

      i. Ideas and methods originating or developing in Mesopotamia and Egypt

      ii. Greek and Hellenistic mathematics

      iii. The Middle Ages: Islāmic mathematics and its transmission to the West

    b. The modern period

      i. The 17th century: discovery of logarithms and analytic geometry, development of calculus by Newton and Leibniz

      ii. The 18th century: advances in geometry, algebra, and analysis; contributions of the Bernoulli family, Euler, Lagrange, Laplace, and others

      iii. The 19th and 20th centuries: development of non-Euclidean geometry by Bolyai, Lobachevsky, and others; contributions to the theories of groups, functions, and complex variables; development of algebraic geometry; influence of physical science on analysis; study of the foundations of mathematics

  2. Historical development of representative nonprobabilistic areas of mathematics

    a. Numerals and numeral systems
    [see also 10/23.A.1.]

      i. Simple grouping systems: ancient Egyptian, Babylonian, Greek, and Roman numerals

      ii. Development of multiplicative, ciphered, and positional numeral systems

    b. Introduction of symbolic notations to represent mathematical quantities, operations, and relationships

    c. Calculatory science
    [see also 10/23.A.]

      i. The history of mathematical tables, including tables of logarithms

      ii. The evolution of analogue devices: origins of harmonic analyzers, differential analyzers, and the slide rule

iii. The evolution of digital devices: development of computational aids from the abacus to the modern electronic digital computer
[see 10/23.A.7.]

d. Geometry
[see also 10/22.C.]

    i. Egyptian, Babylonian, and Greek geometry

    ii. The algebraic approach: development of analytic geometry

    iii. Development of projective geometry

    iv. Development of non-Euclidean geometry

    v. Philosophical aspects of geometry

    vi. Modern ideas and topics in geometry: the axiomatic method; geometrical transformations; the concept of space, differential geometry, and topology

e. Algebra
[see also 10/22.B.]

    i. Babylonian, Egyptian, and Greek contributions

    ii. Contributions from the Orient, India, and the Islāmic world

    iii. Medieval and modern European developments

    iv. Evolution of the theory of algebraic equations of one variable: solutions prior to and after Galois

3. Historical development of probabilistic areas of mathematics
[see also 10/22.D.6.]

a. Development of the mathematical theory of probability

    i. The abstract calculus of probability: the common structure of theories of probability

    ii. Alternative views of probability: the frequency theory of probability, the range theory of probability and the principle of indifference, the belief theory of probability, subjective and objective notions of probability

    iii. Bernoulli's theorem, inverse probability, and asymptotic probabilities

b. Development of mathematical statistics: the history of the theory of stochastic processes, origins of control theory

B. Foundations of mathematics

1. The axiomatic method: mathematical analysis based upon a set of axioms, or unproved statements

a. Euclidean geometry
[see also 10/22.C.1.]

b. Non-Euclidean geometry
[see also 10/22.C.2.]

c. The formal axiomatic method

2. The genetic method: mathematical analysis based upon the orderly construction or generation of objects with unknown properties from objects with known properties

a. Arithmetic and analysis
[see also 10/22.B.1.]

b. The concept of cardinal number and the theory of sets
[see also 10/22.A.2.]

3. The crisis in the foundations of mathematics after 1900: reformulations in terms of the three alternative philosophical positions of Intuitionism, Logicism, and Formalism

a. The paradoxes

b. Intuitionism

c. Logicism, Formalism, and the metamathematical method

4. Current directions in investigations of the foundations of mathematics

a. Intuitionistic studies of the foundations of mathematics: application of formalistic procedures to Intuitionism

b. Non-Intuitionistic studies of the foundations of mathematics: trends in recursion theory, proof theory, model theory, and set theory

Suggested reading in the *Encyclopædia Britannica:*

Section 10/22. Branches of Mathematics

A. Set theory

  1. Origins of set theory and the definitions of a set and a set element, or member

  2. Introduction to set theory

    a. Fundamental set concepts

    b. Essential features of Cantorian set theory

  3. Axiomatic set theory: formal analyses of set theory based upon certain fundamental assumptions or undefined notions called axioms
    [see also 10/21.B.3.a.]

    a. Postulates of axiomatic set theory: the Zermelo–Fraenkel axioms, the von Neumann–Bernays–Gödel axioms

    b. Limitations of axiomatic set theory: failure of attempts to prove the consistency of axiomatic set theory, Gödel's theorem

    c. The present status of axiomatic set theory: profound changes in axiomatic set theory as a result of recent discoveries

B. Algebra

1. Arithmetic

   a. Fundamental definitions and laws: the concepts of natural number and integer; the binary operations of addition and multiplication; the commutative and associative laws of addition; the commutative, associative, and distributive laws of multiplication

   b. Theory of divisors: extension of natural number concepts to non-integers, fractions resulting from the binary operation of division

   c. Number systems and notation: use of the positional principle and the symbol zero to specify magnitude in sequences of digits; number systems having different bases—*e.g.,* binary, decimal, and sexagesimal systems
   [see also 10/23.A.1.]

   d. Arithmetic calculation with decimals: binary operations with decimals; divisibility rules; calculation of square, cube, and higher roots

   e. Logarithms: formal definition of logarithms, use of logarithms to reduce the operations of multiplication and division to the simpler operations of addition and subtraction
   [see also 10/23.A.4.b.]

2. Elementary and multivariate algebra

   a. Algebra as an extension and generalization of arithmetic

   b. Basic algebraic properties of numbers

   c. Polynomials and rational functions

   d. Solution of equations: the principal problem of elementary algebra

3. Linear and multilinear algebra

   a. Linear algebra

      i. Vector spaces

      ii. Matrices

      iii. Linear transformations and linear operators

      iv. Linear functionals and their relation to linear transformations

      v. Inner products and inner product spaces: self-conjugate, or Hermitian, matrices; unitary and orthogonal matrices

      vi. Linear operators in an inner product space: self-adjoint, or Hermitian, operators; unitary and orthogonal operators; the spectral theorem for normal operators

   b. Multilinear algebra

4. Algebraic structures

   a. Lattices

   b. Groups

   c. Fields

   d. Rings

   e. Categories

   f. Homological algebra

   g. Universal algebra

C. Geometry

1. Euclidean geometry

   a. Geometry as an abstract doctrine: the axiomatization of the foundations of geometry; axioms of order, incidence, congruence, parallels, and continuity and results derived from them

   b. The measure of polygons and polyhedra: the theories of equivalence and measure and their relation, Euclid's contribution and its modern extension and generalization

   c. Transformation geometry: reflection, rotation, and translation of geometric figures; homotheties and similitudes

   d. Geometric constructions: the equivalence between Euclidean constructions and existence theorems, gauge constructions, ruler and compass constructions, construction with compass only

    e. Geometry of more than three dimensions: the generalization of Euclidean geometry

    f. The concept of convexity and convex sets

2. Non-Euclidean geometry
[see also 10/21.B.1.b.]

    a. Distinction between Euclidean and non-Euclidean geometry: hyperbolic geometry and elliptic geometry

    b. Geometric representations of the hyperbolic plane and hyperbolic space

    c. Coordinates in spherical and elliptical space: interpretations of four-dimensional Euclidean space

    d. Coordinates in the hyperbolic plane and hyperbolic trigonometry

    e. Transformations: hyperbolic geometry as characterized by its group of reflections

3. Projective geometry

    a. The procedure of projection as the foundation of projective geometry

    b. Homogeneous coordinates: location of points in space

    c. Complex geometry: introduction of complex numbers as homogeneous coordinates

    d. Abstract geometries: extension and generalization of projective geometry to space of any number of dimensions

4. Analytic and trigonometric geometry

    a. Plane analytic geometry: fundamental procedures and concepts

    b. Trigonometry

    c. Coordinates and transformation of coordinates

    d. Projective and solid analytic geometry: extensions of analytic geometry to the projective plane and to three or more dimensions

    e. Special curves: named curves that have been studied with regard to problems in mathematics or the physical sciences; *e.g.,* the folium of Descartes, the lemniscate of Bernoulli, the cardioid, the cycloid, the catenary, the brachistochrone

5. Combinatorial geometry
[see E.1.c., below]

6. Differential geometry
[see also F.2.e., below]

7. Algebraic geometry
[see also F.3., below]

D. Analysis

1. Real analysis

    a. Origins and concepts of real analysis

    b. Number systems and their properties

    c. Functions and differential calculus

    d. Measure and integral calculus

2. Complex analysis

    a. Theory of analytic functions of one complex variable

    b. Theory of analytic functions of several complex variables

    c. Potential theory

3. Differential equations

    a. Ordinary differential equations

    b. Partial differential equations

    c. Special functions that arise as solutions to differential equations; *e.g.,* the hypergeometric function, Legendre polynomials, spherical harmonics, Bessel functions

    d. Dynamical systems on manifolds

4. Functional analysis

          a. General features of functional analysis

          b. Calculus of variations

          c. Generalized functions: the theory of distributions

     5. Fourier analysis

          a. The theory of series

          b. Fourier series

          c. Harmonic analysis and integral transforms

          d. Representations of groups and algebras: Fourier analysis on non-Abelian groups

     6. Theory of probability

          a. Heuristic introduction to probability: the need for a mathematically precise definition of probability

          b. Probability on finite dimensional spaces

          c. Probability on infinite dimensional spaces

     7. Vector and tensor analysis

          a. Scalars, vectors, tensors, and the physical quantities that give rise to them

          b. Vector algebra and analysis

          c. Tensor algebra and analysis

E. Combinatorics and number theory

     1. Combinatorics and combinatorial geometry

          a. The nature and scope of combinatorics: the definition of combinatorics as the branch of mathematics concerned with arrangements, operations, and selections within a finite or a discrete system

          b. Methods, results, and unsolved problems of combinatorial theory, exclusive of geometric considerations

          c. Combinatorial geometry

     2. Number theory

          a. Elementary number theory: properties of the whole numbers, or integers
             [see B.1.a., above]

          b. Algebraic number theory: properties of algebraic numbers

          c. Analytic number theory

          d. Geometric number theory

          e. Probabilistic number theory

F. Topology

     1. General topology

          a. Definition and basic concepts of topology; the subject matter and applications of topology as exemplified by certain simple topological problems and their solutions

          b. Topological spaces: methods for constructing topological spaces; Euclidean n-dimensional space, Hilbert space, Cartesian-product space, and other examples of topological spaces

          c. Topological properties

          d. Topological problems of current interest; *e.g.,* the planar fixed-point problem, the polyhedral Schoenflies problem

     2. Topological groups and differential topology

          a. Interaction between analysis and topology

          b. The theorems of Tikhonov and Ascoli: embedding of a topological space as a subspace of a compact space

          c. Continuous groups

          d. Analysis on manifolds: topological implications of problems in global analysis

          e. Differential topology
             [see also C.6., above]

3. Algebraic topology
[see also C.7., above]

    a. The nature and scope of algebraic topology and its context within general topology, the basic concepts of topological spaces and maps

    b. Invariants: unchanging quantities that play a central role in the classification of spaces and maps

    c. Homotopy theory: homotopy classes and the concept of homotopy-equivalent spaces

    d. Homology and cohomology theory: definition of a simplex, axiomatic homology theory

    e. Homotopy groups: stability and suspension

    f. Definition and properties of fibres, fibre bundles, and fibrings

    g. Sheaf cohomology

    h. Spectral sequences: Serre, Rothenberg–Steenrod, and Eilenberg–Moore spectral sequences

    i. Further developments in homotopy theory: Eilenberg–MacLane spaces, the methods of killing homotopy groups, Serre's C-theory

    j. Generalized homology and cohomology theory: K-theory, the spectral sequence of G.W. Whitehead–Atiyah–Hirzebruch

    k. Recent advances in algebraic topology

Suggested reading in the *Encyclopædia Britannica*:

MACROPAEDIA: Major articles dealing with the branches of mathematics

Algebra	Geometry
Analysis (in Mathematics)	Number Theory
Arithmetic	Probability Theory
Combinatorics and Combinatorial	Set Theory
Geometry	Trigonometry

MICROPAEDIA: Selected entries of reference information

General subjects

algebra:
  algebra
  binomial theorem
  discriminant
  eigenvalue
  exponential
    function
  Gauss elimination
  harmonic function
  homotopy
  linear equation
  logarithm
  matrix
  quarter squares
  root
analysis:
  analysis
  calculus
  differential
    equation
  differentiation
  Dirichlet problem
  elliptic equation

exact equation
infinite series
integration
Laplace's equation
Markov process
mean-value
  theorem
parabolic equation
perturbation
probability theory
real number
singular solution
*combinatorics and
  number theory:*
  combinatorics
  Fermat prime
  number theory
  permutations and
    combinations
  Riemann zeta
    function

geometry:
  algebraic geometry
  analytical geometry
  catastrophe theory
  Desargues's
    theorem
  differential
    geometry
  duality
  fractal
  geometry
  hyperbolic
    geometry
  projection
  projective
    geometry
  Riemannian
    geometry
set theory:
  Boolean algebra
  measure
  set theory
  transfinite number

Zermelo-Fraenkel
  axiom
topology:
  compactness
  connectedness
  Euler characteristic
  four-colour map
    problem
  homology
  metric space
  topological space
other:
  arithmetic function
  graph
  graph theory
  mathematics
  normal
    distribution
  number system
  numeral system
  pi
  trigonometry

Biographies
  See Section 10/21

INDEX: See entries under all of the terms above

Section 10/23. Applications of Mathematics

A. Mathematics as a calculatory science

    1. Numerical notations

        a. Aggregations, or units used to assist counting or grouping of objects

        b. Ancient numerical notations

        c. Decimal notation and modern notational developments

    2. Geometrical aids

        a. Early applications of geometry

        b. Instruments for observation and navigation

        c. Mapping

        d. Applications of geometry to celestial measurement

        e. Optical instruments

        f. Drawing instruments

    3. Mathematical models: physical constructions used to aid the visualization of mathematical ideas or relationships

    4. Calculatory aspects of algebra

        a. Algebraic notation

        b. Logarithms

        c. Slide rules

    5. Calculation using tables and graphs

        a. Mathematical tables

        b. Graphs and graphical procedures

    6. Analogue computation
        [see also 735.D.]

        a. Types of problems solvable by analogue computation

        b. Analogue computers

    7. Digital computation
        [see also 735.D.]

        a. Digital calculators

        b. Punched cards

        c. Programmed machines (digital computers)

B. Statistics

    1. The basic principles of statistical inference: application of the concepts and techniques of probability theory to the analysis of data

        a. The concept of a statistical experiment: mathematical description of experiments in terms of random variables

        b. Distribution functions and their properties: the median, mean, variance, and standard deviation of a distribution; the Gaussian or normal distribution

    2. Estimation: techniques for approximating the parameters of families of distributions of random variables

    3. Hypothesis testing: techniques for determining the correctness of alternative hypotheses concerning given data and an assumed probability model

    4. Structure in data: use of regression analysis to discover systematic patterns

C. Numerical analysis

    1. Introduction: definition, origins, and basic concepts of numerical analysis

    2. Errors: round-off and truncation

    3. Approximation of functions: linear and polynomial interpolation, least squares approximation

4. Solution of equations: linear, nonlinear, and differential equations

5. Applications and implementation of numerical analysis: optimization, large-scale scientific computation, mathematical software

D. Automata theory
[see also 712.A.6.]

1. Introduction: definition and examples of automata, development of the basic concepts of automata theory, the analogy between automata and the nervous systems of living organisms

2. Neural nets and automata

3. Probabilistic questions: random effects in the operation of automata

4. Classification of automata

E. Mathematical theory of optimization

1. The theory of games: analysis of the strategic features of conflict situations

2. Linear and nonlinear programming (mathematical programming)

3. Cybernetics

4. Control theory

F. Information theory
[see also 735.A.]

1. Origins and definitions of information theory

2. Central problems of information theory

3. Principles of information theory

4. Applications of information theory to cryptography, linguistics, and other fields

G. Computer science

1. Synthesis and analysis of algorithms

2. Theory of computation

3. Computer architecture

4. Programming languages and methodology

5. Numeric computation

6. Artificial intelligence

H. Mathematical aspects of physical theories

1. Mechanics of particles and systems
[see also 126.A.]

2. Fluid mechanics
[see also 126.E.]

3. Mechanics of solids
[see also 126.C.]

4. Statistical mechanics
[see also 124.A.9.]

5. Electromagnetic theory
[see also 127.E.]

6. Relativity theory: space and time as a four-dimensional continuum
[see also 131.D.]

7. Riemannian geometry

8. Quantum mechanics
[see also 111.A.4.c.]

9. Dimensional analysis

Suggested reading in the *Encyclopædia Britannica*:

MACROPAEDIA: Major articles dealing with applications of mathematics

Automata Theory
Computer Science
Computers
Game Theory
Information Processing

Information Science
Numerical Analysis
Optimization, The
 Mathematical Theory of
Statistics

MICROPAEDIA: Selected entries of reference information

General subjects

*computers and other
 mathematical
 devices:*
  abacus
  analogue computer
  calculator
  central processing
   unit
  computer
   programming
   language
  computer
   programs
  differential
   analyzer
  differentiator
  digital computer
  harmonic analyzer

input/output
 device
integrator
microprocessor
planimeter
quipu
slide rule
supercomputer
time-sharing
numerical analysis:
 difference equation
 interpolation
 numerical analysis
optimization:
 control theory
 cybernetics
 game theory
 linear
  programming

mathematical
 programming
optimization
queuing theory
statistics:
 decision theory
 distribution
  function
 freedom, degree of
 inference
 mean
 normal
  distribution
 sampling
 standard deviation
 statistics
 Student's t-test
 variance

other:
 algorithm
 artificial
  intelligence
 automata theory
 dimensional
  analysis
 distortion
 eigenvalue
 fractal
 gamma function
 graph
 graph theory
 information theory
 mathematical
  model

Biographies

Babbage, Charles
Boole, George
Napier, John

Neumann,
 John von
Pascal, Blaise

Turing, Alan
 M(athison)
Weyl, Herman

Wiener, Norbert

INDEX: See entries under all of the terms above

Division III.   Science

[For Part Ten headnote see page 479.]

The results of investigations in the natural, social, and medical sciences and the achievements of technology are dealt with in Parts One through Five and in Part Seven. The outlines in the seven sections of Division III are concerned with inquiries that have viewed those sciences and technology as the objects of historical and analytical studies.

Section 10/31 deals with science taken generally. It first presents a synoptic history of Western and Eastern science. It then deals with the nature and scope of the philosophy of science, and with analyses of the empirical procedures and formal structures of science, of science's modes of discovery, and of validating concepts and theories.

Section 10/32 is on the physical sciences. The outline first deals with the historical evolution of astronomy and astrophysics, of physics, and of chemistry. Then, for each of them, it treats issues about the nature, scope, component disciplines, methods, and principal problems of the discipline.

Similarly, Section 10/33 first deals with the history of the several complementary Earth sciences, and then with studies of the nature, scope, methods, and principal problems of the geological, hydrologic, and atmospheric sciences.

Section 10/34 is first concerned with the historical development of the biological sciences and with issues about the methodology, scope, and conceptual structure of biology as a whole. It then sets forth the work done at four levels of biological research: the molecular, cellular, organismic, and population levels. Finally, it treats issues in the philosophy of biology: issues about the nature of biological systems, issues concerning evolution and evolutionary theory, and biological issues with ethical implications.

Section 10/35 treats the history of medicine; the many specialized fields of medical practice and research; and such affiliated disciplines as dentistry, osteopathy, nursing, and pharmacy.

Section 10/36 is on the social sciences and psychology. It first deals with the general historical development of the social sciences. It then separately treats the development, nature, scope, and methods of the particular social sciences: anthropology, sociology, economics, and political science. Finally, it deals with the history, scope, and methods of psychology.

Section 10/37 treats the history of the technological sciences; the academic and professional aspects of engineering; the nature and scope of agricultural sciences; and the nature and scope of such recently developed interdisciplinary fields as bionics, systems engineering, and cybernetics.

Section 10/31. History and Philosophy of Science

A. History of science

  1. Introduction: problems and difficulties of tracing the development of science

  2. Science in ancient and medieval Western civilization

    a. Science in Greek civilization

      i. Protoscience in Greece before the age of Pericles: empirical versus religious or mythological explanations of natural phenomena

      ii. Development of scientific attitudes: the beginning of disciplined observation, inference, definition, and classification; the Platonic versus the Aristotelian view of nature

      iii. Science during the Hellenistic Age: the emergence of Alexandria as the foremost centre of scientific research

    b. Science in Rome: the contrast between Roman success in law and technology and Roman failure in science

    c. Medieval science

  3. Science in other civilizations: Islāmic science; science in India, China, and Japan

  4. European science in the early modern period

    a. The rebirth of science in the Renaissance

      i. The state of science in Europe in the early 15th century

      ii. The influence of advances in printing, mining, metallurgy, and other areas of technology: the demands placed upon science by increases in trade and exploration

      iii. The coexistence of new scientific discoveries and old philosophical views

    b. The revolution in natural philosophy

      i. The radical reformulation of the objects, methods, and functions of natural knowledge: the work of Bacon, Descartes, and Galileo [see also 10/42.A.3.]

      ii. Results of the new philosophy: establishment of scientific societies, progress in particular fields of science

    c. Characteristics of European science

  5. Science in the age of modern revolutions

    a. Science during the Industrial Revolution

    b. Intellectual origins of revolution: the spirit of the Enlightenment

    c. The institutional organization of science under the French Revolution

    d. Romantic reaction and science: the proponents of *Naturphilosophie*

  6. Science in the 19th century: difference in styles of research; progress in physics, chemistry, and biology

7. Science in the early 20th century: the social organization and style of science, the common pattern of advance in scientific research

8. Contemporary problems and prospects: the moral, political, and environmental difficulties facing science

B. Philosophy of science
[see also 10/52.B.2.]

1. The nature and scope of the philosophy of science and its relation to other disciplines: the diverse concerns of and methods of approach to the philosophy of science

2. Historical development of the philosophy of science

   a. Classical and medieval periods: the alternative viewpoints of the Stoics and Epicureans and of the Platonists and Aristotelians

   b. The 17th century: the debate about scientific methodology, Bacon's inductive approach and Descartes's deductive approach

   c. The 18th century: Empiricist, Rationalist, and Kantian interpretations of Newtonian physics

   d. From the beginning of the 19th century through World War I: the influence of Kant's belief in the unique rationality of the classical synthesis of Euclid and Newton

   e. The 20th-century debate: responses to relativity, quantum mechanics, and other profound changes in the natural sciences; Logical Positivism versus Neo-Kantianism

3. Elements of the scientific enterprise

   a. Empirical, conceptual, and formal elements and their theoretical interpretation: diverse views of the relative importance of observation, theory, and mathematical formulation

   b. Empirical procedures of science: measurement, design of experiments, classification

   c. The formal structures of science: the problem of constructing a purely formal analysis of scientific inference, the distinction between scientific laws and empirical generalizations

   d. Conceptual change and the development of science: historical problems concerning the changing theoretical organization of science

4. Movements of scientific thought: the basic procedures of intellectual development in science

   a. Scientific discovery: the extreme positions of formalism, which emphasizes the rational elements of scientific discovery, and of irrationalism, which emphasizes the role of intuition, guesswork, and chance

   b. Validation and justification of new concepts and theories: the view that prediction is the crucial test of scientific validity; the view that coherence, consistency, and comprehensiveness are the essential requirements of a scientific theory

   c. Unification of the theories and concepts of separate sciences: attempts to construct an axiomatic system for all of natural science, the reductionist problem of achieving a consistent conceptual basis for two or more sciences

5. The philosophical status of scientific theory

   a. The status of scientific propositions and concepts of entities: diverse views of the epistemological status of scientific propositions and of the ontological status of scientific concepts

   b. The relationship between philosophical analysis and scientific practice: the application of different philosophical doctrines and approaches to different sciences

6. The relevance of scientific knowledge to other spheres of human experience and concern: the social significance of science and of scientific attitudes, limitations on the scientific endeavour

7. The relation between science and the humanities: questions of differences between scientific and humanistic methodologies
[see 10/42.B.3.]

Suggested reading in the *Encyclopædia Britannica*:

MACROPAEDIA: Major articles and biographies dealing with the history and philosophy of science

Franklin	Locke	Philosophies of	Science, The
Galileo	Measurement	the Branches of	History of
Kelvin	Theory	Knowledge	
	Newton		

MICROPAEDIA: Selected entries of reference information

General subjects

Baconian method	scientific theory
hypothetico-deductive method	typology
nature, law of	

Biographies

Albertus Magnus, Saint	Bacon, Roger	Empedocles
Anaxagoras	Bruno, Giordano	Oresme, Nicholas
Anaximenes of Miletus	Buffon, Georges-Louis Leclerc, comte de	Poincaré, Henri

INDEX: See entries under all of the terms above

Section 10/32. The Physical Sciences

A. History of the physical sciences: the evolution of astronomy, physics, and chemistry

   1. History of astronomy

      a. Ancient astronomy

         i. Time reckoning and astronomical prediction: development of lunar and solar calendars, prediction of eclipses and of first appearances of the New Moon

         ii. Early cosmologies

         iii. Ancient astronomical records, treatises, and star catalogs

      b. Medieval astronomy: European and Islāmic contributions

      c. Astronomy in the 16th and 17th centuries

         i. The geocentric and heliocentric world systems

         ii. The discovery of the laws of planetary motion

         iii. The invention and use of the telescope

         iv. The theory of universal gravitation
            [see 2.c., below]

      d. Astronomy in the 18th century

         i. Development of celestial mechanics: the calculation of orbits, the three-body problem, the dynamical stability of gravitational systems

         ii. Improvements in telescope design and increased accuracy of measurements: the discovery of the aberration of light

         iii. Speculations concerning the origin of the solar system, the nature of nebulae, and the structure of the universe

      e. Astronomy in the 19th century

         i. The discovery of Neptune and the asteroids, the search for a planet within the orbit of Mercury

         ii. Improved determinations of stellar positions and magnitudes; the first measurements of stellar parallax; the compilation of catalogs of nebulae, stars, and star clusters

         iii. Development of astronomical spectroscopy and the use of photography in observational work

      f. Astronomy in the 20th century

         i. Statistical studies of stars, nebulae, and galaxies

         ii. Theories of stellar structure and of stellar formation and evolution

         iii. Astronomical tests of general relativity: the gravitational red shift, the deflection of light, the precession of the perihelion of Mercury, the cosmological red shift

         iv. Relativistic cosmologies: the big bang model; open and closed models of the universe

         v. Major advances in solar-system astronomy: manned lunar missions; exploration of the planets and their satellites with unmanned space probes; analysis of micrometeoroids and meteorites

vi. Development of radio, X-ray, infrared, ultraviolet, and gamma-ray astronomy

vii. Identification of pulsars, quasars, cosmic background radiation, and possible black holes

viii. Advances in instrumentation and methodology: *e.g.,* use of Earth-orbiting observatories; development of electronic radiation detectors; refinement of very long baseline interferometry

2. History of physics

a. Greek physics: speculations concerning the nature of space, matter, and motion

b. Medieval physics: the influence of Aristotle

c. Physics in the 16th and 17th centuries: discoveries and theories in mechanics and optics

d. Physics in the 18th and 19th centuries

i. Development of theories of light: the wave theory versus the corpuscular theory, the search for the ether

ii. Development of the theories of electricity, magnetism, and electromagnetic waves

iii. Developments in thermodynamics: theories of heat, the laws of thermodynamics, the impossibility of perpetual motion, the kinetic theory of gases

iv. Development of the atomic theory of matter: the discovery of the electron, the discovery of radioactivity and X-rays, the discovery of spectral regularities

e. Physics in the 20th century

i. Development of the theory of relativity

ii. Development of the quantum theory, wave mechanics, statistical mechanics, and related theories

iii. Development of theories and laws concerning atomic structure, nuclear interactions, and elementary particles, including efforts to produce a unified field theory

iv. Development of condensed-matter physics and its contributions to electronics

v. Modern developments in physics: atomic beams, nuclear magnetic resonance, and electron spin resonance methods; development of nonlinear optics; the development of masers and lasers

3. History of chemistry

a. Chemistry before 1700

i. The rise of alchemy: the goal of the alchemists—to prolong life and to transmute base metals to gold

ii. The influence of the new mechanical philosophy on chemistry: the work of Boyle

b. Chemistry in the 18th century

i. Studies of combustion and respiration: the phlogiston theory, the work of Lavoisier and Cavendish

ii. Laboratory discoveries: isolation and identification of gases; discoveries of new elements, compounds, and chemical reactions

c. Chemistry in the 19th century

i. Development of the periodic table of the elements: the work of Mendeleyev and Meyer

ii. Discoveries of new elements, isotopes, and radioactive elements

iii. Development of more accurate methods of analysis

iv. Development of theories of molecular structure and chemical reaction

v. Development of organic chemistry: introduction of the concept of valence, the study of aromatic compounds, development of the structural theory

vi. Development of electrochemistry: the theory of chemical affinity in electrical terms

vii. Development of industrial chemistry: the application of chemical principles and reactions to industrial processes

   d. Chemistry in the 20th century

        i. Development of instrumental methods of chemical analysis

        ii. Explanation of chemical phenomena by principles of atomic and molecular structures

        iii. Application of quantum mechanics to chemical bonding

B. The nature and scope of astronomy and astrophysics: the major subject matters and principal problems
   [see also Part One, Division III]

   1. The nature of astronomy and methods of study

   2. Component disciplines of astronomy and their relationship to other sciences: planetary and lunar sciences; meteoritics; the study of comets, minor planets, and the origin of the solar system

   3. Investigaton of the scale of the universe and of the distribution of objects within it: the determination of positions, the measurement of distances

   4. Orbit theory: its role in astronomy

   5. Astrophysics: the study of stars, galaxies, and the universe; cosmology and cosmogony

C. The nature and scope of physics: its major subject matters, methods, and problems
   [see also Part One, Divisions I and II]

   1. The nature of physics: its concern with matter and energy and their interactions

   2. Component disciplines of physics: mechanics, thermodynamics, heat, electricity, magnetism, sound, optics, quantum mechanics, states of matter, nuclear and atomic physics

   3. The experimental and theoretical methods of physics

   4. The relationship of physics to other disciplines

   5. Interdisciplinary fields of physics: astrophysics, biophysics, geophysics

   6. Philosophical problems in physics: at the formal level, quantum level, macrophysical level, and cosmological level

D. The nature and scope of chemistry: its major subject matters and problems
   [see also 121, 122, and 123]

   1. The nature of chemistry: its concern with the composition, properties, and changes of matter

   2. The subdivisions of chemistry: analytical, inorganic, organic, physical, polymer, and industrial chemistry and biochemistry

   3. The methods of chemistry

   4. The study of chemical transformations

   5. Interdisciplinary fields of chemistry: geochemistry, chemical engineering, medicinal chemistry

---

Suggested reading in the *Encyclopædia Britannica*:

MACROPAEDIA: Major articles and biographies dealing with the physical sciences

Bohr	Helmholtz	Philosophies of	Physical
Copernicus	Kepler	the Branches of	Sciences, The
Einstein	Lavoisier	Knowledge	Planck
Faraday	Maxwell	Physical Science,	Rutherford
Galileo	Newton	Principles of	
Heisenberg	Pascal		

MICROPAEDIA: Selected entries of reference information

General subjects

major fields and	cosmology	radio and radar	*methodology and*
component	fluid mechanics	astronomy	*instrumentation:*
disciplines:	infrared astronomy	statistical	astronomical
aerodynamics	mechanics	mechanics	observatory
astronomy	optics	thermodynamics	bubble chamber
biochemistry	physics	ultraviolet	centrifuge
celestial mechanics	quantum	astronomy	chromatography
chemistry	mechanics		cloud chamber

digital computer
laser
mass spectrometry
microscope
molecular beam

nuclear magnetic
  resonance
particle
  accelerator
photometry

radio
  interferometer
radio telescope
satellite
  observatory
sounding rocket

spacecraft
spectrochemical
  analysis
star catalog
supercomputer
telescope

Biographies

astronomers:
  Ambartsumian,
    Viktor
    Amazaspovich
  Banneker,
    Benjamin
  Bessel, Friedrich
    Wilhelm
  Bradley, James
  Brahe, Tycho
  Cannon, Annie
    Jump
  Cassini, Gian
    Domenico
  Eddington, Sir
    Arthur Stanley
  Eudoxus of Cnidus
  Gamow, George
  Halley, Edmund
  Herschel, Sir John
  Herschel, Sir
    William
  Hipparchus
  Hubble, Edwin
    Powell
  Kuiper, Gerard
    Peter
  Laplace,
    Pierre-Simon,
    marquis de
  Le Verrier,
    Urbain-Jean-Joseph
  Lovell, Sir Bernard
  Messier, Charles
  Newcomb, Simon
  Ptolemy
  Russell, Henry
    Norris
  Schwarzchild, Karl
  Struve, Otto
chemists:
  Arrhenius, Svante

Berthelot,
  Marcellin
Berthollet,
  Claude-Louis,
  Comte
Berzelius, Jöns
  Jacob
Boyle, Robert
Bunsen, Robert
  Wilhelm
Cannizzaro,
  Stanislao
Cori, Carl; and
  Cori, Gerty
Crookes, Sir
  William
Curie, Marie
Curie, Pierre
Dalton, John
Davy, Sir
  Humphry
Debye, Peter
Gay-Lussac,
  Joseph-Louis
Haber, Fritz
Hahn, Otto
Hodgkin, Dorothy
  Mary
Joliot-Curie,
  Frédéric and
  Irène
Kendrew, Sir John
  Cowdery
Langmuir, Irving
Libby, Willard F.
Liebig, Justus,
  Freiherr von
Mendeleyev,
  Dmitry Ivanovich
Mulliken, Robert
  Sanderson
Pasteur, Louis

Pauling, Linus
Priestley, Joseph
Ramsay, Sir
  William
Sanger, Frederick
Scheele, Carl
  Wilhelm
Seaborg, Glenn T.
Soddy, Frederick
Stahl, Georg Ernst
Woodward, R.B.
Wöhler, Friedrich
physicists:
  Alvarez, Luis
    Walter
  Arago, François
  Bardeen, John
  Becquerel, Henri
  Bethe, Hans
    Albrecht
  Bragg,
    Sir Lawrence
  Bragg, Sir William
  Bridgman, P.W.
  Broglie,
    Louis-Victor, 7e
    duc de
  Cavendish, Henry
  Dirac, P.A.M.
  Fermi, Enrico
  Feynman, Richard
    P(hillips)
  Gell-Mann,
    Murray
  Gibbs, J. Willard
  Henry, Joseph
  Hertz, Heinrich
  Hooke, Robert
  Huygens,
    Christiaan
  Kapitsa, Pyotr
    Leonidovich

Kirchhoff, Gustav
  Robert
Landau, Lev
  Davidovich
Lee, Tsung-Dao
Lorentz, Hendrik
  Antoon
Mach, Ernst
Mayer, Maria
  Goeppert
Meitner, Lise
Michelson, A.A.
Mössbauer, Rudolf
  Ludwig
Oppenheimer, J.
  Robert
Pauli, Wolfgang
Plücker, Julius
Purcell, E.M.
Raman, Sir
  Chandrasekhara
  Venkata
Rayleigh, John
  William Strutt,
  3rd Baron
Rutherford, Ernest
Schrödinger, Erwin
Stokes, Sir George
  Gabriel
Thompson, Sir
  Benjamin
Thomson, Sir
  Joseph John
Tomonaga
  Shin'ichirō
Yang, Chen
  Ning
Young, Thomas
Yukawa Hideki

INDEX: See entries under all of the terms above

Section 10/33. The Earth Sciences

A. The history of the Earth sciences
1. The origins of the Earth sciences in prehistoric times
2. The Earth sciences from antiquity to the 16th century
   a. Geological sciences
      i. Speculations about earthquakes and volcanic eruptions
      ii. Speculations about fossils
      iii. Study of landforms and land–sea relations
   b. Hydrologic and atmospheric sciences
      i. Theories of groundwater circulation and precipitation
      ii. The origin of the Nile and the cause of its floods
      iii. Study of the tides
3. The Earth sciences in the 16th, 17th, and 18th centuries
   a. Geological sciences
      i. The beginnings of mineralogy: the study of ore deposits
      ii. The development of paleontology and stratigraphy
      iii. The controversy between the Neptunists and Plutonists: Earth history according to Werner and Hutton
   b. Hydrologic sciences
      i. Theories of spring discharge
      ii. The earliest quantitative investigations of the global water balances
   c. Atmospheric sciences
      i. The study of water vapour in the atmosphere
      ii. The study of atmospheric pressure, temperature, and circulation
4. The Earth sciences in the 19th century
   a. Geological sciences
      i. The development of crystallography and the classification of minerals and rocks
      ii. The concept of faunal succession and organic evolution: contributions of William Smith, Charles Darwin, and others
      iii. The concept of uniformitarianism: contributions of Charles Lyell and others
      iv. Evidence for an Ice Age: the work of Louis Agassiz
      v. The concept of geological time and estimates of the age of the Earth
      vi. Concepts of landform evolution
      vii. The study of gravity, isostasy, and the Earth's figure
   b. Hydrologic sciences
      i. The study of groundwater flow and surface water discharge: Darcy's law
      ii. The beginnings of oceanography as a discipline
   c. Atmospheric sciences
      i. The study of the composition of the atmosphere
      ii. The study of clouds, fog, dew, and storms
      iii. The study of weather and climate: the origin of synoptic meteorology
5. The Earth sciences in the 20th century
   a. Geological sciences
      i. Development of radiometric dating
      ii. The experimental study of rocks: experimental petrology

    iii. Development of seismology: the study of the internal structure of the Earth

    iv. Astrogeological research: the application of the Earth sciences to the investigation of the planets and their satellites

    v. Advances in paleontology: the development of paleoecology and micropaleontology, the study of Precambrian life

    vi. The theory of plate tectonics: an outgrowth of the ideas of continental drift and seafloor spreading

  b. Hydrologic sciences

    i. The study of water resources and seawater chemistry

    ii. The exploitation of oceanic resources: desalinization, tidal power, and minerals from the sea

    iii. The charting of the ocean floors: progress in bathymetry

    iv. The study of ocean circulation, currents, and waves

    v. The study of glacier motion and high-latitude ice sheets

  c. Atmospheric sciences

    i. The application of modern technology to meteorology: ground-based remote-sensing instruments, orbiting satellites, computer models simulating atmospheric features

    ii. Advances in weather forecasting and cloud physics

    iii. The study of the properties and structure of the atmosphere

    iv. The development of weather modification methods

    v. The classification of climate

B. The nature, scope, and methods of the particular Earth sciences
[see also Part Two]

  1. Physical geography: the study of the distribution and spatial patterns of soils, water, climate, landforms, and other Earth features

  2. The geological sciences: mineralogy, petrology, economic geology, and geochemistry; geodesy, geophysics, structural geology, and volcanology; geomorphology; glacial geology; engineering, environmental, and urban geology; geochronology, historical geology, paleontology, stratigraphy, and astrogeology

  3. The hydrologic sciences: hydrology, limnology, glaciology, oceanography

  4. The atmospheric sciences: meteorology, climatology, aeronomy; the study of the atmospheres of other planets
[see 223 and 723.G.5.]

Suggested reading in the *Encyclopædia Britannica*:

MACROPAEDIA: Major articles dealing with the Earth sciences

  Earth Sciences, The
  Geography

MICROPAEDIA: Selected entries of reference information

General subjects

component disciplines:	geomorphology	pedology	bathythermograph
astrogeology	geophysics	petrology	dating
bioclimatology	hydrology	sedimentology	digital computer
chemical hydrology	hydrometeorology	seismology	gravimeter
climatology	marine geology	structural geology	ionization chamber
dendrochronology	marine geophysics	tectonics	magnetometer
economic geology	meteorology	volcanology	radiosonde
environmental geology	mineralogy	*methodology and instrumentation:*	Richter scale
geochemistry	oceanography	aerial photography	seismograph
geochronology	paleoclimatology	barometer	weather map
geology	paleogeography	bathymetry	*other:*
	paleogeology	bathyscaphe	International Geophysical Year
	palynology		

Biographies

Agassiz, Louis	Goldschmidt,	Powell, John	Vernadsky,
Agricola, Georgius	Victor Moritz	Wesley	Vladimir
Bjerknes, Vilhelm	Hess, H.H.	Press, Frank	Ivanovich
F.K.	Humboldt,	Romer, Alfred	Wegener, Alfred
Buch, Leopold,	Alexander von	Sherwood	Lothar
Freiherr von	Hutton, James	Runcorn, Stanley	Werner, Abraham
Cuvier, Georges,	Köppen, Wladimir	Keith	Gottlob
Baron	Leonardi, Piero	Simpson, George	
Dana, James D.	Lyell, Sir Charles	Gaylord	
Daubré,	Maury, Matthew	Smith, William	
Gabriel-Auguste	Fontaine	Suess, Eduard	
Ekman, V. Walfrid	Mohorovičić,	Van Hise, Charles	
Gilbert,	Andrija	Richard	
Grove Karl			

Section 10/34. The Biological Sciences

A. History of the biological sciences

  1. Origin and early development of biological ideas

   a. Views of life and living things in ancient Eastern and Middle Eastern civilizations

   b. Biology in the Greco-Roman world: theories about mankind and the origin of life; Aristotelian concepts of classification, reproduction, heredity, and descent; botanical investigations; initial anatomical discoveries

   c. Biology in the Middle Ages: the influence of Arabian biologists, the development of botany and zoology as separate disciplines, further discoveries in anatomy

   d. Biology in the Renaissance: the influence of the craft of printing and artists' illustrations on the dissemination of botanical knowledge, the beginning of the scientific study of anatomy through the use of dissection

  2. Developments in the biological sciences in the 17th, 18th, and 19th centuries

   a. Biology in the 17th and 18th centuries

    i. The discovery of the circulation of blood

    ii. The establishment of scientific societies

    iii. The development of the microscope: the classical microscopists

    iv. The rise of modern taxonomy: the systematic classification of plants and animals

    v. The emergence of comparative biological studies

    vi. Experimental approaches to the origin of life: the theory of spontaneous generation

   b. Biology in the 19th century

    i. The effect of geographical explorations on the development of the biological sciences

    ii. The development of cell theory: the establishment of cellular biology

    iii. The theory of evolution: the impact of the concept of natural selection

    iv. The rise of embryology: discoveries concerning reproduction and development of organisms

    v. The emergence of genetics: the study of heredity and its mechanisms

  3. Biology in the 20th century

   a. The establishment of molecular biology

    i. The one-gene, one-enzyme theory and its effects

    ii. The discovery of the genetic significance of DNA and RNA: deciphering the genetic code

   b. The emergence of intradisciplinary specialties; *e.g.,* cell physiology, cytochemistry, ecology, population biology

  c. The application to biology of the concepts and techniques of other sciences: the development of biochemistry and biophysics, the importance of biological discoveries to medicine and agriculture

B. The nature, scope, and methodology of the biological sciences
[see also Part Three]

  1. Molecular biology: biochemistry, biophysics, genetics

  2. Cell biology: cancer research, microbiology, radiation biology, tissue culture, transplantation biology

  3. Organismic biology: botany, ecology, embryology, ethology, eugenics, genetics, gnotobiology, morphology, paleontology, physiology, zoology

  4. Population biology: biogeography, comparative psychology, ecology, population genetics

  5. Taxonomy and methods of classification

C. Philosophy of biology

  1. The range of topics in biophilosophy; *e.g.,* old questions investigated anew in the light of biological advances and new standards of philosophical rigour

  2. Issues concerning the nature of biological systems

  3. Issues concerning evolution

  4. Issues with ethical implications

Suggested reading in the *Encyclopædia Britannica*:

MACROPAEDIA: Major articles and biographies dealing with the biological sciences

Biological Sciences, The	Harvey
Darwin	Pasteur
Genetics and Heredity, The Principles of	Philosophies of the Branches of Knowledge

MICROPAEDIA: Selected entries of reference information

General subjects

component	entomology	ornithology	chromatography
disciplines:	ethology	paleontology	classification
agrostology	eugenics	palynology	electrophoresis
anatomy	exobiology	parasitology	fluoroscope
bioethics	genetic engineering	physiology	microscope
biogeography	genetics	protozoology	nuclear magnetic
biology	herpetology	synecology	resonance
biophysics	human ecology	taxonomy	radioactive isotope
biotechnology	ichthyology	teratology	spectroscopy
botany	mammalogy	zoology	testcross
cytology	microbiology	*methodology and*	
ecology	molecular biology	*instrumentation:*	
embryology	morphology	centrifuge	

Biographies

anatomists:	Huxley, Sir Julian	Watson, James	Hoagland, Dennis
Müller, Johannes	Huxley, T.H.	Dewey	Robert
Peter	Lamarck,	*botanists:*	Hooker, Sir Joseph
Sabin, Florence	Jean-Bapiste	Bentham, George	Dalton
Rena	de Monet,	Brown, Robert	Hooker, Sir
Vesalius, Andreas	chevalier de	Candolle,	William Jackson
biologists:	Loeb, Jacques	Augustin	Linnaeus, Carolus
Bateson, William	Lysenko, Trofim	Pyrame de	Nägeli, Karl
Carson, Rachel	Denisovich	Cohn, Ferdinand	Wilhelm von
Ehrenberg,	Malpighi, Marcello	Dodge, Bernard	Ray, John
Christian	*biophysicists:*	Ogilvie	Sprengel, Christian
Gottfried	Crick, Francis	Gray, Asa	Konrad
Elton, Charles	Harry Compton		

Stakman, Elvin
　Charles
embryologists:
　Baer, Karl Ernst,
　　Ritter von
　Spemann, Hans
geneticists:
　Beadle, George
　　Wells
　Dobzhansky,
　　Theodosius
　Mendel, Gregor
　Morgan, Thomas
　　Hunt
　Weismann, August
　Wright, Sewall
microbiologists:
　Dubos, René

Hérelle, Félix d'
Merchnikoff, Élie
Waksman, Selman
　Abraham
physiologists:
　Bayliss, Sir
　　William Maddock
　Bernard, Claude
　Einthoven, Willem
　Galen of
　　Pergamum
　Haller,
　　Albrecht von
　Macleod, J.J.R.
　Müller, Johannes
　　Peter
　Pavlov, Ivan
　　Petrovich

Sherrington, Sir
　Charles Scott
Spallanzani,
　Lazzaro
Starling, Ernest
　Henry
zoologists:
　Cuvier, Georges,
　　Baron
　de Beer, Sir Gavin
　Haeckel, Ernst
　Lorenz, Konrad
　Rafinesque,
　　Constantine
　　Samuel
other:
　Galton, Sir Francis
　Galvani, Luigi

Geoffroy,
　Saint-Hilaire,
　Étienne
Gesner, Conrad
Leeuwenhoek,
　Antoine van
Owen, Sir Richard
Swammerdam, Jan
Wallace, Alfred
　Russel

INDEX: See entries under all of the terms above

Section 10/35. Medicine and Affiliated Disciplines

A. History of medicine and surgery

　1. Early medicine: Western medicine before 1800, Oriental medicine before *c.* 1900

　　a. The medicine of prehistoric peoples

　　b. The practice of medicine among the Babylonians, the ancient Egyptians, and the Hebrews

　　c. Medicine and surgery in the Orient: the beginning of systematized medicine

　　　i. Medicine in India: the Vedic and Brahmanistic heritage, the influence of religious and magical beliefs, surgical practices

　　　ii. Medicine in China: the influence of the cosmic theory of Yin and Yang; the use of herbals, drugs, and acupuncture

　　　iii. Medicine in Japan: assimilation of Chinese and European practices

　　d. The beginning of systematic medicine in the Greco-Roman world

　　　i. Early influences: mythological beliefs, the investigations and theories of early philosophers

　　　ii. The work of Hippocrates: theories on the nature and treatment of disease, the charter of medical conduct

　　　iii. The spread of Greek teachings to Rome: the acceptance of Galen as a medical authority

　　e. Medicine from the fall of Rome through the Middle Ages

　　　i. Reservoirs of medical learning: the role of medieval monasteries in preserving the medical heritage of Greece and Rome, contributions of Arabian medicine

　　　ii. Establishment of the first organized medical school at Salerno

　　f. Medicine in the Renaissance

　　　i. Improvements in anatomical theory and surgery

　　　ii. The control of medical practice in Britain

　　　iii. The work of Paracelsus and Fracastoro

　　g. Medicine in the 17th century

　　　i. Discoveries concerning the circulation of the blood: use of the experimental method, importance of the microscope to medical studies

　　　ii. The iatrochemical and iatrophysical theories: the view of life as a series of chemical processes versus the view of life as a mechanism governed by physical laws

　　h. Medicine in the 18th century

      i. Genesis of the medical school and the hospital

      ii. The beginning of medical specialties: emergence of surgery, obstetrics, and pathology as separate disciplines

      iii. Improvement in techniques of vaccination and in the treatment of disease: the rise and decline of systems of animism and mesmerism

2. The rise of scientific medicine in the 19th century

  a. New doctrines, laws, and concepts; *e.g.,* the cell and cellular pathology, natural selection, homeostasis, pathogenesis, the Mendelian laws

  b. Further advances in physiology

  c. Establishment of bacteriology: verification of the germ theory, the identification of disease-producing organisms, the introduction of antisepsis

  d. The discovery and use of anesthesia

  e. Other advances: the discovery of the transmission of disease by insects, initial measures to control typhoid, the discovery of X-rays, the development of the ophthalmoscope and the stethoscope

3. Medicine in the 20th century

  a. Advances in chemotherapy: the discovery, development, and use of antibiotics and synthetic drugs in the treatment of bacterial diseases

  b. Advances in immunology

      i. Improvements in vaccines that control bacterial diseases; *e.g.,* typhoid, diphtheria, tetanus, tuberculosis

      ii. The introduction and use of vaccines to control viral diseases; *e.g.,* yellow fever, influenza, poliomyelitis, measles

  c. Developments in endocrinology: the discovery of insulin and the control of diabetes, the use of cortisone as an anti-inflammatory agent, the study and use of sex hormones

  d. Advances in other fields

      i. Nutrition: the treatment of deficiency diseases through the discovery and identification of vitamins

      ii. Cancer research: the treatment of abnormal cell growths through the application of various therapies

      iii. Tropical medicine: the treatment of yellow fever, malaria, and leprosy through the discovery and application of synthetic organic compounds derived from quinine and other sources; the application of insecticides to control malaria and yellow fever

      iv. Medical technology and biomedical instrumentation: the use of electronic devices to monitor physiological processes, to conduct automatic laboratory analyses, and to perform other diagnostic and therapeutic procedures

4. Surgery in the 20th century

  a. The state of surgery prior to 1900: the importance of antisepsis, asepsis, and anesthesia to the development of modern surgery

  b. The emergence of surgical specialties: the development of new surgical and diagnostic techniques

  c. Improvements in the treatment of wounds; *e.g.,* the development of plastic surgery, postsurgical rehabilitation

  d. The use of blood transfusions and other intravenous techniques to reduce shock, treat fluid loss, and restore electrolyte balance

  e. The introduction of inhalation anesthetic procedures; *e.g.,* improvements in thoracic surgery

B. Fields of specialized medical practice or research

  1. Hospital residency specialties

    a. Radiology

    b. Surgery
    [see also 423.C.2.a.]

    c. Obstetrics and gynecology
    [see also 423.F.5.f.]

  d. Urology
  [see also 423.F.7.]

  e. Ophthalmology and otolaryngology
  [see also 423.F.9.f. and g.]

  f. Neurology
  [see also 423.F.9.]

  g. Psychiatry

  h. Other hospital specialties; *e.g.,* anesthesiology, pathology

2. Other clinical specialties

  a. Aerospace medicine

  b. Medical jurisprudence

  c. Occupational medicine

  d. Public health

  e. Endocrinology

  f. Immunology

  g. Toxicology

  h. Tropical medicine

3. Nonclinical specialties and the basic medical sciences: medical physiology and pathological physiology, nutrition, pharmacology and experimental therapeutics, gerontology

4. Ancillary medical disciplines: cytotechnology, medical records, medical technology, X-ray technology

C. Disciplines affiliated with medicine

  1. History and practice of dentistry

  2. History and practice of osteopathy

  3. History and practice of nursing

  4. History and practice of pharmacy

Suggested reading in the *Encyclopædia Britannica:*

MACROPAEDIA: Major article dealing with medicine and affiliated disciplines

  Medicine

MICROPAEDIA: Selected entries of reference information

General subjects

aerospace medicine	gerontology and	ophthalmology	plastic surgery
anesthesiology	geriatrics	oral surgery	podiatry
cardiology	hematology	orthodontics	prosthodontics
dentistry	holistic medicine	orthopedics	psychiatry
dermatology	homeopathy	osteopathy	public health
emergency	immunology	otolaryngology	radiology
medicine	internal medicine	pathology	sports medicine
endocrinology	nephrology	pediatrics	surgery
endodontics	neurology	pedodontics	toxicology
epidemiology	nursing	peridontics	tropical medicine
family practice	obstetrics and	pharmacology	urology
forensic medicine	gynecology	pharmacy	
gastroenterology			

Biographies

Alexander, Franz	Bekhterev,	Carrel, Alexis	Fleming, Sir
Avicenna	Vladimir	Cohn, Ferdinand	Alexander
Barnard,	Mikhaylovich	De Bakey, Michael	Fracastoro,
Christiaan	Blackwell,	Ellis	Girolamo
Barnard, Claude	Elizabeth	Ehrlich, Paul	Freud, Sigmund
	Blalock, Alfred		Galvani, Luigi

Gesell, Arnold	Malpighi, Marcello	Paracelsus	Semmelweis, Ignaz
Harvey, William	Mayo family	Reed, Walter	Philipp
Hippocrates	Menninger family	Rush, Benjamin	Vesalius, Andreas
Jenner, Edward	Meyer, Adolf	Salk, Jonas	Virchow, Rudolf
Jung, Carl	Nightingale,	Edward	
Koch, Robert	Florence	Séguin, Edouard	
Lister, Joseph	Osler, Sir William		

INDEX: See entries under all of the terms above

Section 10/36.   The Social Sciences and Psychology and Linguistics

A. History of the social sciences

1. Origins of the social sciences

  a. Precursors of the social sciences in the Middle Ages and the Renaissance

  b. Heritage of the Enlightenment: social reforms and revolution

2. 19th-century developments in the social sciences

  a. The influence of new concepts in social, political, economic, and scientific theories

  b. Development of the separate disciplines; *e.g.,* economics, political science, anthropology, sociology, social statistics, human geography

3. 20th-century developments in the social sciences

  a. The influence of social upheaval in the non-Western world: the revolution of rising expectations

  b. The influence of Marxism

  c. The influence of Freudian ideas

  d. The changing character of the disciplines

    i. Specialization and cross-disciplinary approaches

    ii. The increasing professionalism of social scientists as consultants and decision makers in government and business

    iii. The introduction of mathematical and other quantitative methods: the use of computers

    iv. The influence of empiricism: the collection of data, the use of surveys and polls, the testing of theories

  e. Major theoretical influences: developmentalism, the social-systems approach, structuralism and functionalism

B. The nature of anthropology
[see also Part Five, Division I]

1. The background of anthropology

2. The scope and methods of anthropology: the division between cultural and physical anthropology

C. The nature of sociology
[see also Part Five, Division II]

1. The background of contemporary sociology

2. The methodology of contemporary sociology

3. The status of contemporary sociology

4. Emergent trends in sociology

5. Cognate disciplines: criminology, penology, social psychology, demography

D. The nature of economics
[see also Part Five, Division III]

1. Development of theories of economics

2. The scope and methods of the study of economics: microeconomics, macroeconomics

3. Cognate disciplines: mathematical economics, econometrics, accounting

E. The nature of political science
[see also Part Five, Division IV]

1. The history of political science

2. The scope and methods of contemporary political science

3. Cognate disciplines: the study of public opinion, public law, public administration, political systems, and international relations

F. The nature of geography
[see also 10/33]

1. The history of geography

2. The scope and methods of geography: the division between physical, human, and regional geography

G. History and methods of psychology
[see also Part Four, Division III]

1. The history of psychology

2. The nature and scope of psychology

3. Special branches and cognate disciplines of psychology: physiological psychology, social psychology

H. The nature of linguistics
[see also 514]

1. The history of linguistics

2. The nature and scope of linguistics

3. Linguistics and other disciplines: psycholinguistics, sociolinguistics, linguistic anthropology, linguistic geography, computational linguistics, mathematical and statistical linguistics, stylistics, and semantics

---

Suggested reading in the *Encyclopædia Britannica*:

MACROPAEDIA: Major articles and biographies dealing with the social sciences and psychology

Freud	Smith, Adam
Geography	Social Sciences, The
Marxism, Marx and	

MICROPAEDIA: Selected entries of reference information

General subjects

anthropology and allied disciplines:
anthropological linguistics
anthropology
ethnography
neoevolutionism
particularism
structuralism
economics:
Austrian school of economics
classical economics
econometrics
economics
historical school of economics
institutional economics

Keynesian economics
macroeconomics
managerial economics
welfare economics
linguistics:
anthropological linguistics
comparative linguistics
computational linguistics
dialectology
ethnolinguistics
historical linguistics
neurolinguistics
semiotics

sociolinguistics
structural linguistics
synchronic linguistics
political science:
geopolitics
political science
psychology:
analytic psychology
applied psychology
behaviourism
clinical psychology
comparative psychology
developmental psychology
educational psychology

experimental psychology
functionalism
Gestalt psychology
humanistic psychology
individual psychology
industrial psychology
physiological psychology
psychology
social psychology
other:
criminology
demography
geography
penology
sociology

Biographies

Section 10/37. The Technological Sciences

A. History of the technological sciences

B. Nature and scope of engineering

   1. Engineering as a profession

   2. Branches of engineering: civil engineering, aeronautical engineering, chemical engineering, electrical and electronics engineering, mechanical engineering, optical engineering

C. The nature and scope of agricultural sciences
[see also 731.B., C., and D.]

   1. History of the agricultural sciences
[see A., above]

   2. Subdivisions of the agricultural sciences: soil science, plant production, animal production, agricultural economics and management, agricultural engineering

D. The nature and scope of recently developed interscience disciplines

   1. Bionics

      a. Mimicry of nature as the basis for bionics; *e.g.,* design of torpedoes with surface layers similar to a dolphin's skin, construction of vehicles with articulated legs

b. The use of natural models to understand and solve engineering problems; *e.g.,* natural neural networks as models for electronic circuits, the human brain as a model for computers and information-processing devices

2. Systems engineering and operations research
[see 712.B.]

3. Cybernetics, control theory, and information science
[see 10/23]

Suggested reading in the *Encyclopædia Britannica:*

MACROPAEDIA: Major articles dealing with the technological sciences

Engineering
Optics, Principles of

MICROPAEDIA: Selected entries of reference information

General subjects

acoustical engineering	chemical engineering	industrial engineering	petroleum engineering
aerospace engineering	civil engineering	mechanical engineering	
bioengineering	electrical and electronics engineering	nuclear engineering	
bionics			

Biographies

Beach, Alfred Ely	Eads, James Buchanan	Mauchly, John W.	Steinmetz, Charles Proteus
Brunel, Isambard Kingdom	Eckert, John P.	Pierce, George Washington	Taylor, Frederick Winslow
Brunel, Sir Marc Isambard	Edison, Thomas Alva	Roebling, John Augustus	Tsiolkovsky, Konstantin Eduardovich
Burbank, Luther	Hollerith, Herman	Sikorsky, Igor	
Carver, George Washington	McCormick, Cyrus Hall	Stakman, Elvin Charles	Whitney, Eli

INDEX: See entries under all of the terms above

Division IV. **History and the Humanities**
[For Part Ten headnote see page 479.]

The outlines in the two sections of Division IV deal with historiography and the study of history, and with the humanities and humanistic scholarship.

Section 10/41 first treats the history of historical writing in the major cultures of both East and West, and the disciplines and methods involved in modern historical investigation and research. It then treats the speculative philosophies of history that have appeared in the West and the East, and philosophical analyses of the specific character of historical knowledge.

Section 10/42 first sets forth a historical review of changing conceptions of the humanities and of humanistic scholarship, covering all the major periods and mutations, from the Greek ideal of *paideia* to contemporary developments. It then treats issues about the nature and scope of the humanities; about the relation of the component disciplines to one another; and about their distinction from the sciences, their validity as ways of knowing, and their role in education.

Section 10/41. **Historiography and the Study of History**

A. Historiography: the types of historical writing

1. Development of historiography: the history of historical writing

a. In the ancient world

i. Near Eastern historiography

ii. Classical historiography: Greek and Roman

iii. Early Christian historiography

b. In the Middle Ages

i. Western Christian historiography

ii. Byzantine historiography

c. From the Renaissance to the present

i. Renaissance historiography

ii. Early modern historiography

iii. Enlightenment historiography: the 18th century

iv. 19th- and 20th-century historiography

d. Non-Western historiographical traditions

i. Islāmic historiography

ii. East Asian historiography

2. Types of historical writing: diverse ways of distinguishing or classifying kinds of historical writing by method or function

3. Factors involved in the writing of history: the background of the author and his vantage point, method of work, and purpose

B. Modern historical investigation and research: sources and methods

1. Sources for historical writing: material remains, written materials, folklore, place-names

2. Auxiliary disciplines for ascertaining and interpreting the sources

a. Anthropology

b. Archaeology

c. Bibliography

d. Chronology

e. Dendrochronology

f. Diplomatics

g. Epigraphy

h. Genealogy

i. Geography

j. Heraldry

k. Iconography and iconology

l. Linguistics

m. Paleography

n. Psychoanalysis

o. Radiometric dating

p. Sigillography

q. Textual criticism

C. Philosophy of history: speculations about the historical process, philosophical analysis of the writing of histories

1. Conceptions of the philosophy of history

2. Speculative philosophy of history: diverse explanations of the pattern of historical events

3. Critical or analytical philosophy of history: the analysis of history as a discipline

---

Suggested reading in the *Encyclopædia Britannica:*

MACROPAEDIA: Major articles dealing with historiography and the study of history

History, The Study of
Philosophies of the Branches of Knowledge

MICROPAEDIA: Selected entries of reference information

General subjects

archaeology
bibliography
diplomatics
epigraphy

genealogy
historical
geography
historiography

history
iconography
linguistics
paleography

papyrology
sigillography
textual criticism

Biographies

archaeologists:
Bingham, Hiram
Blegen, Carl
Botta, Paul-Émile
Boucher de
  Perthes, Jacques
Carter, Howard
Evans, Sir Arthur
Garstang, John
Layard, Sir Austen
  Henry
Mariette, Auguste
Petrie, Sir Flinders
Pitt-Rivers,
  Augustus Henry
  Lane-Fox
Rassam, Hormuzd
Schliemann,
  Heinrich
Squier, E.G.
Stein, Sir Aurel
Stephens, John
  Lloyd
Thompson,
  Edward Herbert
Thomsen,
  Christian
  Jürgensen
Wheeler, Sir
  Mortimer
Winckler, Hugo
Woolley, Sir
  Leonard
Worsaae, Jens
  Jacob Asmussen
historians:
Acton, John
  Emerich Edward
  Dalberg Acton,
  1st Baron

Arai Hakuseki
Aulard,
  François-Alphonse
Bancroft, George
Barros Arana,
  Diego
Beard, Charles A.
Becker, Carl
Bede the
  Venerable, Saint
Biondo, Flavio
Bloch, Marc
  Léopold
  Benjamin
Braudel, Fernand
Burckhardt, Jacob
Bury, J.B.
Clarendon, Edward
  Hyde, 1st earl of
Droysen, Johann
  Gustav
Froude, James
  Anthony
Fustel de
  Coulanges, Numa
  Denis
Geoffrey of
  Monmouth
Geyl, Pieter
Gibbon, Edward
Giovanni da Pian
  del Carpini
Guicciardini,
  Francesco
Halévy, Élie
Haskins, Charles
  Homer
Herodotus
Huizinga, Johan
Ibn Khaldūn
Jien

Klyuchevsky,
  Vasily Osipovich
Lamprecht, Karl
  Gottfried
Liutprand of
  Cremona
Livy
Ma Tuan-lin
Macaulay, Thomas
  Babington
Macaulay, Baron
McMaster, John
  Bach
Mas'ūdī, al-
Meinecke,
  Friedrich
Michelet, Jules
Mommsen,
  Theodor
Namier, Sir Lewis
  Bernstein
Niebuhr, Barthold
  Georg
Pan Ku
Parkman, Francis
Pasquier, Étienne
Pirenne, Henri
Polybius
Prescott,
  William H.
Procopius
Ranke,
  Leopold von
Robinson, James
  Harvey
Rostovtzeff,
  Michael
  Ivanovich

Sallust
Sarkar, Sir
  Jadunath
Schlesinger,
  Arthur M.
Solovyov, Sergey
  Mikhaylovich
Ssu-ma Ch'ien
Ssu-ma Kuang
Ṭabarī, aṭ-
Tacitus
Tawney, Richard
  Henry
Thierry, Augustin
Thou,
  Jacques-Auguste de
Thucydides
Tocqueville,
  Alexis de
Toynbee, Arnold
Trevelyan, G.M.
Turner, Frederick
  Jackson
Tyler, Moses Coit
Woodson,
  Carter G.
other:
Champollion,
  Jean-François
Rawlinson, Sir
  Henry Creswicke
Sayce, Archibald
Ventris, Michael

INDEX: See entries under all of the terms above

Section 10/42. The Humanities and Humanistic Scholarship

A. History of humanistic scholarship

    1. The beginnings of learning: the ideal of *paideia*

        a. Homeric education: the ideal of the hero

        b. The Sophists and Socrates: the turn to *logos*, the beginnings of rhetoric

        c. Plato and the Academy: the relation of theology to mythology, mathematics in the service of philosophy

      d. Aristotle and the Lyceum: the invention of logic, the division and organization of the sciences

      e. Hellenistic scholarship: the development of literary and textual criticism, Alexandria and Pergamum as cultural centres

      f. The Roman ideal of *humanitas*: the training of the orator

      g. The conflict of cultural ideals: the battle among rhetoric, philosophy, and science

2. Christian learning in antiquity and the Middle Ages

      a. The Christianization of pagan culture: the reconciliation of classical humanism with Christian revelation

      b. The codification of the liberal arts: the trivium and the quadrivium

      c. The founding of the universities

      d. The Scholastic method: logic and the genres of theological exposition

      e. Faith and reason: the distinction of philosophy from sacred theology

3. The development of humane letters from the Renaissance to the present

      a. The idea of Renaissance: the ideal of the classical, the rise of the vernacular, the concept of the dignity of the free individual

      b. Humanism and the new learning

      c. The search for a universal method

      d. The separation of science from philosophy: the rise and development of empirical science

      e. The quarrel between ancients and moderns: the problem of progress in learning

      f. The growth of modern humanistic scholarship: the transition from the ideal of belles lettres to the scientific investigation of antiquity through archaeology and philology

      g. The rise and development of the liberal arts college and the graduate school
[see 562.B.]

      h. The growth and proliferation of special disciplines: the knowledge explosion

      i. The organization of the contemporary university: questions of its social responsibility, the profession of learning
[see 561.C.1.c.]

4. The Jewish tradition of humanistic scholarship: its nature, methods, and development; its relation to classical and Christian learning

5. The Islāmic tradition of humanistic scholarship: its nature, methods, and development; its relation to classical and Christian learning

6. The humanities and humanistic scholarship in the East: in India, in China, in Japan

B. The humanities

1. Diverse views of the definition and scope of the humanities

2. The humanities as an educational program: the question of the humanities as a unified field of study

3. Theories of the humanities as a fundamental division of knowledge: the question of the distinction of the humanities from the sciences

4. Problems about the humanities

Suggested reading in the *Encyclopædia Britannica*:

MACROPAEDIA: Major articles and biographies dealing with the humanities and humanistic scholarship

Bacon, Francis	Humanism
Erasmus	Scholarship, Classical

MICROPAEDIA: Selected entries of reference information

General subjects

humanism	paideia	Renaissance	scholasticism
humanities	reason	Renaissance man	

Biographies

Adams, Henry	Casaubon, Isaac	Lefèvre d'Étaples,	Scaliger, Julius
Alberti, Leon	Estienne, Henri II	Jacques	Caesar
Battista	George of	Melanchthon,	Taine, Hippolyte
Alcuin	Trebizond	Philipp	Valla, Lorenzo
Bentley, Richard			Wang Wei

INDEX: See entries under all of the terms above

Division V.   Philosophy

[For Part Ten headnote see page 479.]

The outlines in the three sections of Division V treat the history of philosophy; the nature and the divisions of philosophy; and philosophical schools and doctrines.

The outline in Section 10/51 presents a synoptic history of philosophy. After treating the history of Western philosophy and of non-Western philosophies, the outline indicates other sections that treat philosophies associated with religions.

Section 10/52 first deals with theories about philosophy as a whole: theories about its nature, scope, methods, forms of exposition, and about the criteria of meaning and truth in philosophical thought. It then treats the traditional component disciplines of philosophy: metaphysics, the philosophy of nature, epistemology, the philosophy of mind, the philosophy of mankind, ethics, political philosophy, and aesthetics. In the case of each of these eight disciplines, the outline treats its historical development; its nature and scope; its relations to other branches of philosophy and other intellectual disciplines; and its principal problems. At the end, the outline of this section indicates other sections that treat disciplines involving philosophical studies of other subjects: language, logic, mathematics, art, science, religion, law, education, and history.

Section 10/53 begins by listing 25 major philosophical schools in the West. The section then deals with doctrinal differences between these schools on major philosophical issues, treating differences in theories about Being and existence; about thought, knowledge, and the faculties of the mind; and about human conduct.

Section 10/51.   History of Philosophy

A. History of Western philosophy

   1. Ancient Greek and Roman philosophy

      a. The beginnings of philosophy in Greece: the Pre-Socratic philosophers

         i. Cosmology and the metaphysics of matter: theories of the origin and nature of the physical world, monistic and pluralistic cosmologies

         ii. The rise of problems in the theory of knowledge: problems about the real and phenomenal worlds

         iii. The metaphysics of number: Pythagorean speculations about number and the nature of reality, advances toward the foundation of quantitative science

         iv. Anthropology and relativism: the Sophists' criticism of cosmological and metaphysical speculations, man as the measure of all things, the positions of the Sophists about the conventionality of law and justice

      b. The maturity of Greek philosophy

         i. The ethical concerns and positions of Socrates: the Socratic method of teaching, the influence of Socrates

         ii. The philosophy of Plato: his dialogues on issues in politics, ethics, metaphysics, epistemology, and cosmology; his emphasis on the relations of mathematics to philosophy

         iii. The philosophy of Aristotle: his criticisms of Platonic metaphysics and theory of knowledge; the corpus of his works on logic; his teleological positions in biology, ethics, and politics; his empirical researches in the natural sciences and on laws and political institutions

    c. Hellenistic and Roman philosophy: developments from the time of Alexander III the Great to the closing of the philosophical schools in Athens

        i. The philosophy of the Stoics: the teaching of Zeno of Citium concerning the basis of human happiness, the further elaboration of Stoic thought by Cleanthes and Chrysippus, the role of Stoicism during the late Roman Republic and the empire

        ii. The philosophy of the Epicureans: the teaching of Epicurus concerning the universe, the role of pleasure, and man's relationship to the gods

        iii. The philosophy of the Skeptics: the teaching of Pyrrhon of Elis concerning man's lack of certainty in knowing, the role of the Skeptics in preserving the doctrines of ancient philosophers

        iv. The philosophy of the Neo-Pythagoreans and of the Neoplatonists: the teaching of Plotinus concerning the various levels of being, Neo-Pythagorean schools in Asia Minor

        v. Jewish and Christian philosophy during the Hellenistic Age: diverse attempts to relate the teachings of the Hellenistic and Roman schools to Jewish and Christian theology

2. Philosophy in the Middle Ages

    a. Early medieval philosophy

        i. The patristic period: Augustine's use of Neoplatonist thought in his theology and his doctrine of man, the role of Boethius' translations and commentaries, Anselm's proofs of the existence of God, the methodology of Abelard

        ii. Philosophy and the liberal arts in the schools of the Christian West from the 9th to the 11th century

    b. The contribution of Arabic and Jewish philosophy: the role of the Islāmic philosophers in increasing the influence of Aristotle in the West, the teaching of Solomon ibn Gabirol and Maimonides

    c. The age of the Schoolmen: the attempt to reconcile philosophy and theology, the teaching of Bonaventure and Albertus Magnus, Thomas Aquinas' synthesis of Aristotelianism and Christian theology

    d. Philosophy in the late Middle Ages: new styles of philosophy and theology that vied with Thomism, the criticism of Aristotelian thought by Duns Scotus and Ockham, the speculative mysticism of Eckehart, Nicholas of Cusa's doctrine of the "coincidence of opposites"

3. Modern philosophy

    a. Philosophy in the Renaissance

        i. Political theory: the views of Machiavelli, Bodin, Hobbes, Grotius, and others on the nature and moral status of political power

        ii. Humanism: the influence of the writings of Plato on moral theory and literary endeavour; renewed interest in Atomistic Materialism, ancient Skepticism, and Stoicism
        [for humanistic scholarship in the Renaissance, see also 10/42.A.3.]

        iii. Philosophy of nature: the pluralistic, machinelike, and mathematically ordered character ascribed to the natural world; the influence of discoveries in anatomy, physics, and astronomy on philosophy

    b. The early modern period: the rise of Empiricism and Rationalism

        i. Developments in the Empiricist tradition: Bacon's attempt to formulate a new scientific method, Hobbes's theory of knowledge

        ii. Developments in the Rationalist tradition: the antiempirical character of Descartes's metaphysics and the dualism of his doctrine of man and the world, the speculative systems of philosophy provided by the writings of Spinoza and Leibniz

    c. Philosophy in the period of the Enlightenment, or the Age of Reason

        i. Epistemological issues: the attempt of Locke and Berkeley to inquire into the origin and nature of reason, Hume's science of man, Kant's critical examination of reason

        ii. Developments in the philosophy of science: Materialist views, the effect of scientific discoveries on philosophical thought

        iii. Social and political philosophy: the concern of Locke and Rousseau with the freedom and equality of citizens, developments in religious philosophy

    d. Philosophy in the 19th century

        i. The resurgence of the metaphysical spirit: the Idealism of Fichte, Schelling, and Hegel

       ii. Developments in the empirical and scientific tradition: Comte's Positivism and its subsequent influence on the philosophy of science, J.S. Mill's theory of knowledge and ethics, the dialectical Materialism of Marx and Engels

      iii. The reaction against Rationalism: Kierkegaard's preoccupation with the states of consciousness, Schopenhauer's doctrine of cosmic will, the writings of Nietzsche

    e. Philosophy in the 20th century

        i. Independent speculative and social philosophies: Bergson's intuitionism, Whitehead's speculative philosophy, William James's and Dewey's Pragmatism

       ii. Developments in Marxist thought: Lenin's metaphysical Materialism and his theory of knowledge, the continuing attempt to make theory serve practice

B. Non-Western philosophy

  1. Indian philosophy

    a. Early Indian philosophical thought: the role of Hindu and Buddhist sacred literature in presystematic philosophy, the concepts of Brahman and *ātman* in Hindu thought and of selflessness and Nirvāṇa in early Buddhist writings

    b. The beginning of system building in Indian philosophy: the role of the *sūtra*, metaphysical and epistemological concerns, ethical and political thought, the teaching of the Ājīvikas and Cārvākas

    c. The further developments of systematic thought in India: Realism and Idealism in metaphysical and epistemological thought, the relation of pluralistic and monistic views to various linguistic philosophies

    d. The schools of Vedānta: the contribution of Śaṅkara and Rāmānuja and their followers; the schools of Nimbārka, Vallabha, and Caitanya

    e. The Vaiṣṇava and Śaiva schools: philosophical systems based on the literature of Vaiṣṇavism and Śaivism

    f. Later Indian philosophical thought: the influence of Islāmic thought and European philosophy, recent trends

  2. Chinese philosophy

    a. The classical Chinese philosophical schools; *e.g.*, Confucianism, Taoism, Yin-Yang, Mohism, Dialecticians, the Legalist school

    b. Neo-Taoist and Buddhist thought

    c. Neo-Confucianism: the development of the concept of principle

    d. 20th-century Chinese philosophy: the effects of Western thought and of Maoism

  3. Japanese philosophy

    a. Early Japanese philosophical thought: the introduction of Buddhism and Confucianism, the Six Schools of Nara, Tendai and Shingon philosophy

    b. Developments during the Kamakura and Muromachi periods: the origins and concerns of the Zen, Jōdo (Pure Land), and Nichiren sects; tendencies in Shintō and Confucian thought

C. Philosophies associated with religion

  1. Hindu philosophy
     [see 823.B.3.]

  2. Buddhist philosophy
     [see 824.B.3.]

  3. Confucian philosophy
     [see 825.B.3.]

  4. Taoist philosophy
     [see 825.C.3.]

  5. Jewish philosophy
     [see 826.B.6.]

  6. Islāmic philosophy
     [see 828.B.4.]

  7. Christian philosophy
     [see 827.E.7.]

Suggested reading in the *Encyclopædia Britannica*:

MACROPAEDIA: Major articles and biographies dealing with the history of philosophy

Aristotelianism,	Hegelianism,	Mill, John Stuart	Smith, Adam
Aristotle and	Hegel and	Nietzsche	Socrates
Augustine	Hume	Philosophy,	Taoism
Cartesianism,	Indian Philosophy	The History of	Thomism,
Descartes and	Kantianism,	Western	Thomas
Christianity	Kant and	Platonism,	Aquinas and
Confucianism,	Locke	Plato and	
Confucius and	Marxism,	Rousseau,	
	Marx and	Jean-Jacques	

MICROPAEDIA: Selected entries of reference information

General subjects

Arabic philosophy:	epochē	māyā	*medieval Western*
Ahl al-Kitāb	first cause	Mīmāṃsā	*philosophy:*
Bāṭinīyah	form	nirguṇa	fideism
Dahrīyah	hylomorphism	Nyāya	intention
fayḍ	logos	pāramitā	Ockham's razor
ghaybah	microcosm	prajñapti	Scholasticism
ikhtilāf	Not-Being,	prakṛti	tabula rasa
kalām	denial of	pramāṇa	*modern Western*
kasb	opposites, table of	prāṇa	*philosophy:*
Māturīdīyah	paradoxes of Zeno	prāṇāyāma	a priori knowledge
Murji'ah	sensationalism	pratītya-samutpāda	antinomy
Muʿtazilah	virtue,	pratyakṣa	as if, philosophy of
Qadarīyah	teachability of	pratyaya	axiology
Rāfiḍah	*Indian philosophy:*	purusha	categorical
rahbānīyah	Abhidharmakośa	śabda	imperative
rajm	abhijñā	Śaiva-siddhānta	cogito, ergo sum
Sālimīyah	Advaita	samadhi	common sense,
shirk	ahaṃkāra	Sāṃkhya	philosophy of
tahajjud	ajīva	samsāra	concept
talbīyah	Ājīvika	samvṛti-satya	constitution theory
taqiya	akriyāvāda	skandha	deconstruction
tashbīh	ālaya-vijñāna	smṛtyupasthāna	deontological
tawḥīd	ānanda	syādvāda	ethics
ziyārah	anumāna	tat tvam asi	deus otiosus
Chinese philosophy:	Artha-śāstra	trisvabhāva	dialectical
ch'i	āsana	upādhi	materialism
Chinese	asrāva	Vaisheshika	eudaemonism
philosophy	āstika	Vedānta	good-reason theory
hsien	ātman	Viśiṣṭādvaita	humanism
hsu	bhedābheda	yama	ideal language
jen	brahma	Yoga	identity theory
Legalism	brahmavihāra	Yogācāra	innate idea
Mohism	cakra	*Japanese philosophy:*	interactionism
p'u	Cārvāka	Japanese	irrationalism
T'ai Chi	dravya	philosophy	I–Thou
tao	Dvaita	Jōjitsu	leap of faith
te	Haṭha Yoga	Kegon	mathematicism
T'ien Ming	Indian philosophy	Nichiren	metaethics
tzu-jan	indriya	Buddhism	metalanguage
wu-wei	jiva	Pure Land	methodic doubt
yin-yang	jnana	Buddhism	mind–body dualism
Greek philosophy:	kammaṭṭhāna	Ritsu	monad
apathy	karma	Shingon	natural law
cosmopolitanism	Kashmir Śaivism	Zen	normative ethics
emanationism	kuṇḍalinī		noumenon
entelechy	Mādhyamika		occasionalism

panpsychism	reductionism	sufficient reason,	theodicy
phenomenalism	revisionism	principle of	transcendental
phenomenon	secularism	superman	Idealism
protocol sentence	social contract	synthesis	unified science
radical empiricism	solipsism	teleological ethics	

Biographies

Anaximenes of	Inoue Tetsujirō	Maimonides,	Spinoza,
Miletus	Israeli, Isaac ben	Moses	Benedict de
Averroës	Solomon	Nārājunga	
Avicenna	Justin Martyr,	Nishida Kitarō	
Buber, Martin	Saint	Schopenhauer,	
Chuang-tzu	Lao-tzu	Arthur	

See also Sections 10/52 and 10/53

INDEX: See entries under all of the terms above

Section 10/52.   The Nature and the Divisions of Philosophy

A. The nature, scope, and methods of philosophy
[for the major philosophical schools in the West, see 10/53; for the development of non-Western philosophy, see 10/51.B.]

  1. Diverse conceptions of philosophy

  2. Diverse views of the methods of philosophy

  3. The forms of philosophical exposition; *e.g.*, dialogues, commentaries, histories, systematically ordered treatises

  4. Criteria of meaning and truth in philosophical thought

B. The divisions of philosophy

  1. Metaphysics, or speculative philosophy in general

    a. The history, nature, and scope of metaphysics
       [for schools of thought in metaphysics, see 10/53.B.1.]

    b. The relation of metaphysics to other parts of philosophy; *e.g.*, ethics, logic, natural theology

    c. Problems in metaphysics

  2. The philosophy of nature: the philosophical problems concerning the phenomena, laws, and theories of the natural sciences
     [see also 10/31.B.]

    a. The history, status, and scope of the philosophy of nature

    b. The relation of the philosophy of nature to science, the philosophy of science, and metaphysics

    c. The basic aspects of the natural order

    d. The philosophy of physics

    e. The philosophy of biology

  3. Epistemology, or theory of knowledge

    a. The history, nature, and scope of epistemology
       [for schools of thought in epistemology, see 10/53.C.]

    b. The relation of epistemology to metaphysics, philosophy of mind, logic, and other disciplines

    c. Problems in epistemology

  4. The philosophy of mind, or philosophical psychology

    a. The history, nature, and scope of the philosophy of mind

    b. The relation of the philosophy of mind to the empirical and mathematical sciences and to other philosophical disciplines

    c. Problems in the philosophy of mind

5. The philosophy of man, or philosophical anthropology

    a. The history, nature, and scope of philosophical anthropology
   [for schools of thought in philosophical anthropology, see 10/53.B.3.]

    b. The relation of philosophical anthropology to physical and cultural anthropology and to other disciplines in philosophy and the social sciences

    c. Problems in philosophical anthropology

6. Ethics, or moral philosophy

    a. The history, nature, and types of ethics: the distinction between metaethics and normative ethics

    b. The relation of ethics to other philosophical disciplines or to other branches of knowledge or experience

    c. Problems in ethics

7. Political philosophy

    a. The nature and scope of political philosophy: its relation to political science

    b. The form of political statements and arguments

    c. The history of political philosophy

8. Aesthetics

    a. The nature and scope of aesthetics as a discipline

    b. The development of aesthetics: approaches to the study of the aesthetic experience

    c. Problems in aesthetics

    d. The relation of aesthetics to other disciplines

9. The philosophy of language

10. The philosophy of logic
   [see 10/11.B.]

11. The philosophy of mathematics
   [see 10/21.B.]

12. The philosophy of art
   [see 611.A.]

13. The philosophy of science
   [see 10/31.B.]

14. The philosophy of religion
   [see 811.A.]

15. The philosophy of law
   [see 551.A.]

16. The philosophy of education
   [see 561.A.]

17. The philosophy of history
   [see 10/41.C.]

Suggested reading in the *Encyclopædia Britannica*:

MACROPAEDIA: Major articles and biographies dealing with the nature and the divisions of philosophy

Aesthetics	Philosophical	Political	Rousseau,
Epistemology	Anthropology	Philosophy,	Jean-Jacques
Ethics	Philosophies of	The History of	Smith, Adam
Metaphysics	the Branches of	Western	Time
Mind, The	Knowledge		
Philosophy of			

MICROPAEDIA: Selected entries of reference information

General subjects

aesthetics:
aesthetics
epistemology:
a priori knowledge
dualism
epistemology
Idéalogie
psychologism
ethics:
altruism
axiology
categorical
imperative
comparative ethics
conscience
egoism
ethical relativism
ethics
eudaemonism
good-reasons
theory

metaethics
moral theology
normative ethics
probabilism
teleological ethics
virtue
metaphysics:
appearance
dualism
creative evolution
form
Great Chain of
Being
intuition
irrationalism
metaphysics
microcosm
naturalism
ontology
phenomenon
pluralism and
monism

reason
supernaturalism
voluntarism
philosophy of mind:
belief
choice
free will
identity theory
immortality
intentionality
interactionism
mind
mind–body
dualism
psychophysical
parallelism
political philosophy:
divine right of
kings
general will
human rights
nomos

political
philosophy
powers,
separation of
social contract
other:
emergence
hylozoism
philosophical
anthropology
philosophy
spiritualism
teleology
time

Biographies

aesthetics:
Baumgarten,
Alexander
Gottlieb
Bosanquet,
Bernard
Croce, Benedetto
Gilson, Étienne
Santayana, George
epistemology:
Cassirer, Ernst
Dühring, Eugen
Locke, John
Mill, John Stuart
ethics:
Abelard, Peter
Cudworth, Ralph
Cumberland,
Richard
Hutcheson, Francis
Moore, G.E.
Scheler, Max
Whewell, William
metaphysics:
Aurobindo, Śrī
Berdyayev,
Nikolay
Aleksandrovich
Berkeley, George

Bradley, F.H.
Campanella,
Tommaso
Clauberg, Johann
Descartes, René
Feuerbach, Ludwig
Fichte, Johann
Gottlieb
Geulincx, Arnold
Green, T.H.
Hegel, Georg
Wilhelm
Friedrich
Heidegger, Martin
Husserl, Edmund
Jacobi, Friedrich
Wilhelm
Jaspers, Karl
Kant, Immanuel
Kierkegaard, Søren
Leibniz, Gottfried
Wilhelm
Lewes, George
Henry
Malebranche,
Nicolas
Marcel, Gabriel
Meinong, Alexius

Nietzsche,
Friedrich
Norris, John
Schelling, Friedrich
Wilhelm
Joseph von
Schopenhauer,
Arthur
Spinoza,
Benedict de
Whitehead, Alfred
North
political philosophy:
Bentham, Jeremy
Berlin, Sir Isaiah
Burke, Edmund
Engels, Friedrich
Han-Lei-tzu
Herzen, Aleksandr
Hobbes, Thomas
Mill, James
Machiavelli,
Niccolò
Montesquieu,
Charles-Louis de
Secondat, baron
de La Bréde et de
Paine, Thomas

other:
Adler, Mortimer J.
Alembert, Jean Le
Rond d'
Aron, Raymond
Bayle, Pierre
Collingwood, R.G.
Condillac, Étienne
Bonnot de
Cousin, Victor
Dilthey, Wilhelm
Gioberti, Vincenzo
Helvétius,
Claude-Adrien
Hoffer, Eric
Rodó, José
Enrique
Spencer, Herbert
Strauss, David
Friedrich
Swedenborg,
Emanuel
Teilhard de
Chardin, Pierre
Vico, Giambattista
Weil, Simone
Wittgenstein,
Ludwig

See also Sections 10/51 and 10/53

INDEX: See entries under all of the terms above

Section 10/53.   Philosophical Schools and Doctrines

A. Major philosophical schools in the West

   1. Philosophical schools in antiquity and in the Middle Ages

     a. Pythagoreanism

     b. The Sophists

     c. Eleaticism

     d. Atomism

     e. Platonism

     f. Aristotelianism

     g. Stoicism

     h. Epicureanism

     i. Skepticism

     j. Scholasticism

   2. Philosophical schools in the modern period

     a. Cartesianism

     b. Empiricism
       [for Empiricist tendencies in earlier philosophy, see A.1.b. and i., above; for contemporary Logical Empiricism, see A.2.i., below]

     c. Rationalism
       [for Rationalist tendencies in ancient and medieval philosophy, see A.1.a., c., e., and j., above]

     d. Materialism
       [for dialectical Materialism, see A.2.j., below]

     e. Kantianism

     f. Idealism

     g. Hegelianism

     h. Utilitarianism

     i. Positivism and Logical Empiricism
       [for metalogical studies, see 10/12.B.; for studies in the foundations of mathematics, see 10/21.B.]

     j. Marxism

     k. Realism

     l. Pragmatism

     m. Phenomenology

     n. Existentialism

     o. Analytic and Linguistic philosophy

B. Theories of Being and existence

   1. Different types of metaphysical theory: Platonism; Aristotelianism; Thomism; Cartesianism; Idealism; Materialism—dialectical Materialism, Atomism, and Naturalism; Pythagoreanism; Organismic dynamism

   2. Different views concerning the existence, attributes, and knowledge of God: agnosticism, atheism, Deism, fideism, humanism, pantheism, theism

   3. Different conceptions of man as knower, doer, and maker: Existentialism, humanism, Phenomenology, Pragmatism, rationalism, irrationalism

   4. Different views concerning the existence of the mind and its relation to the body: Materialism, dualism, immaterialism

C. Theories of thought, knowledge, and faculties of mind

   1. Different conceptions of the object of knowledge: sense-datum theory, Phenomenalism, Idealism, Realism

   2. Different conceptions of the validity of knowledge: Kantianism, Positivism, Pragmatism, Skepticism

   3. Different views of the sources or foundations of knowledge: rationalism, Empiricism

   4. Different views of the status of the universal: Realism, Conceptualism, Nominalism

   5. Different views of the epistemic status of scientific theories; *e.g.*, Realism, conventionalism, and operationalism; the Unity of Science principle; reductionism

D. Theories of conduct

   1. Metaethical theories: intuitionism, Naturalism, Noncognitivism, good reasons theories

   2. Deontological theories: rationalism, intuitionism, Existentialism

   3. Teleological theories: Eudaemonism, Utilitarianism

Suggested reading in the *Encyclopædia Britannica*:

MACROPAEDIA: Major articles dealing with Western philosophical schools and doctrines

Aristotelianism, Aristotle and	Marxism, Marx and	Religious and Spiritual Belief,
Cartesianism, Descartes and	Philosophical Schools and	Systems of Thomism, Thomas
Hegelianism, Hegel and	Doctrines, Western	Aquinas and
Kantianism, Kant and	Platonism, Plato and	

MICROPAEDIA: Selected entries of reference information

General subjects

absolute Idealism	eclecticism	Neo-Hegelianism	Skepticism
Academy	Eleaticism	nominalism	solipsism
Alexandrist	Empiricism	personalism	Sophist
Analytic philosophy	Epicureanism	phenomenology	Stoicism
Atomism	Ethical Culture	positivism	theism
Cambridge Platonists	Existentialism	pragmatism	transcendental Idealism
Cynic	idealism	process philosophy	Utilitarianism
Cyrenaic	Latin Averroism	Pythagoreanism	Vienna Circle
Deism	Logical Positivism	rationalism	
determinism	materialism	realism	
	Megarian school	scholasticism	
	naturalism	sensationalism	

Biographies

Albertus Magnus, Saint	Carnap, Rudolf	Hume, David	Pico della Mirandola,
Apuleius, Lucius	Cohen, Hermann	Husserl, Edmund	Giovanni, Conte
Athenagoras	Comte, Auguste	James, William	di Concordia
Berdyayev, Nikolay Aleksandrovich	Cousin, Victor	Jaspers, Karl	Plotinus
	Dewey, John	Kierkegaard, Søren	Royce, Josiah
	Dühring, Eugen	Lewes, George Henry	Sartre, Jean-Paul
Bernard de Chartres	Duns Scotus, John	Maine de Biran, Marie-François-Pierre	Scheler, Max
	Fichte, Johann Gottlieb		Schlick, Moritz
Boethius, Anicias Manlius Severinus	Francis of Meyronnes	Malebranche, Nicolas	Unamuno, Miguel de
	Gentile, Giovanni	Marcel, Gabriel	William de la Mare
Bosanquet, Bernard	Godfrey of Fontaines	Maritain, Jacques	
	Green, T.H.	More, Henry	
Bradley, F.H.	Heidegger, Martin	Ockham, William of	
Buridan, Jean			

   See also Sections 10/51 and 10/52

INDEX: See entries under all of the terms above

•MORTON HAMERMESH. *Professor of Physics, University of Minnesota, Minneapolis, 1975–86.*

JOSEPH J. KATZ. *Emeritus Distinguished Senior Scientist, Argonne National Laboratory, Argonne, Illinois; Senior Chemist, 1946–82.*

MALCOLM H. MACFARLANE. *Professor of Physics, Indiana University, Bloomington.*

NORMAN HARRY NACHTRIEB (d. 1991). *Professor of Chemistry, University of Chicago, 1953–86.*

EUGENE N. PARKER. *S. Chandrasekhar Distinguished Service Professor of Physics and of Astronomy and Astrophysics, University of Chicago.*

•VINCENT E. PARKER. *Emeritus Professor of Physics, California State Polytechnic University, Pomona; Dean, School of Science, 1967–77.*

SIR A. BRIAN PIPPARD. *Emeritus Professor of Physics, University of Cambridge; Cavendish Professor, 1971–82.*

STUART ALAN RICE. *Dean, Division of Physical Sciences; Frank P. Hixon Distinguished Service Professor of Chemistry, University of Chicago.*

LOCKHART B. ROGERS. *Graham Perdue Professor Emeritus of Chemistry, University of Georgia, Athens.*

ROBERT G. SACHS. *Emeritus Professor of Physics, University of Chicago.*

RUPERT WILDT (d. 1976). *Professor of Astrophysics, Yale University, 1957–73.*

•MARK W. ZEMANSKY (d. 1981). *Professor of Physics, City College, City University of New York.*

Part Two. The Earth

J HARLEN BRETZ (d. 1981). *Professor of Geology, University of Chicago, 1926–47.*

•R.J. CHORLEY. *Professor of Geography, University of Cambridge; Fellow of Sidney Sussex College, Cambridge.*

JULIAN R. GOLDSMITH. *Charles E. Merriam Distinguished Service Professor Emeritus of Geophysical Sciences, University of Chicago.*

BERNHARD KUMMEL (d. 1980). *Professor of Geology, Harvard University, 1962–80.*

PAUL EDWIN POTTER. *Professor of Geology, University of Cincinnati, Ohio.*

•WILLIAM STELLING VON ARX. *Senior Scientist, Woods Hole Oceanographic Institution, Massachusetts, 1968–78.*

BRIAN F. WINDLEY. *Professor of Geology, University of Leicester, England.*

•PETER J. WYLLIE. *Professor of Geology and Chairman, Division of Geological and Planetary Sciences, California Institute of Technology, Pasadena.*

Part Three. Life on Earth

•N.J. BERRILL. *Strathcona Professor of Zoology, McGill University, Montreal, 1946–65.*

JOHN TYLER BONNER. *George M. Moffett Professor of Biology, Princeton University.*

•V.G. DETHIER. *Gilbert L. Woodside Professor of Zoology, University of Massachusetts, Amherst.*

PETER W. FRANK. *Professor of Biology, University of Oregon, Eugene.*

•HAROLD J.F. GALL. *Emeritus Professor of Biology, University of Chicago.*

CARL GANS. *Professor of Biology, University of Michigan, Ann Arbor.*

ERNEST M. GIFFORD. *Emeritus Professor of Botany, University of California, Davis.*

•LOUIS S. GOODMAN, M.D. *Distinguished Professor of Pharmacology, University of Utah, Salt Lake City.*

•GARRETT HARDIN. *Emeritus Professor of Human Ecology, University of California, Santa Barbara.*

EMANUEL MARGOLIASH. *Professor of Biochemistry and Molecular Biology, Northwestern University, Evanston, Illinois.*

•ERNST WALTER MAYR. *Alexander Agassiz Professor Emeritus of Zoology, Harvard University.*

•JOHN ALEXANDER MOORE. *Emeritus Professor of Biology, University of California, Riverside.*

THOMAS PARK. *Emeritus Professor of Biology, University of Chicago.*

•THEODORE T. PUCK. *Professor of Biochemistry, Biophysics, and Genetics and Distinguished Professor of Medicine, University of Colorado Health Sciences Center, Denver; Director, Eleanor Roosevelt Institute for Cancer Research.*

G. LEDYARD STEBBINS. *Emeritus Professor of Genetics, University of California, Davis.*

JOHN W. THIERET. *Professor of Botany, Northern Kentucky University, Highland Heights; Chairman, Department of Biological Sciences, 1973–80.*

•BIRGIT VENNESLAND. *Head, Vennesland Research Laboratory, Max Planck Society, 1970–81; Director, Max Planck Institute for Cell Physiology, Berlin, 1968–70.*

•PAUL B. WEISZ. *Professor of Biology, Brown University, Providence, Rhode Island.*

•RALPH H. WETMORE. *Emeritus Professor of Botany, Harvard University.*

•EMIL H. WHITE. *D. Mead Johnson Professor of Chemistry, Johns Hopkins University, Baltimore, Maryland.*

Part Four. Human Life

•EMMET BLACKBURN BAY, M.D. (d. 1973). *Professor of Medicine, University of Chicago.*

DONNA BERGEN, M.D. *Associate Professor of Neurological Sciences, Rush University, Chicago.*

WILLIAM CAMERON BOWMAN. *Deputy Principal; Professor of Pharmacology, University of Strathclyde, Glasgow.*

•SIR WILFRID EDWARD LE GROS CLARK (d. 1971). *Professor of Anatomy, University of Oxford.*

MIHALY CSIKSZENTMIHALYI. *Professor of Human Development and of Education, University of Chicago.*

ELIZABETH B. CONNELL, M.D. *Professor of Gynecology and Obstetrics, Emory University, Atlanta, Georgia.*

PETER P.H. DE BRUYN, M.D. *Emeritus Professor of Anatomy, University of Chicago.*

HARVEY J. DWORKEN, M.D. *Emeritus Professor of Medicine, Case Western Reserve University, Cleveland, Ohio.*

•RUSSELL S. FISHER, M.D. (d. 1985). *Chief Medical Examiner, State of Maryland, Baltimore. Professor of Forensic Pathology, University of Maryland Medical School, Baltimore.*

MARK C. FISHMAN, M.D. *Assistant Professor of Medicine, Harvard University.*

CECIL A. GIBB. *Emeritus Professor of Psychology, Australian National University, Canberra.*

ROY R. GRINKER, SR., M.D. *Emeritus Professor of Psychiatry, University of Chicago. Director, Institute for Psychosomatic and Psychiatric Research and Training, Michael Reese Hospital and Medical Center, Chicago, 1951–76.*

NORMAN K. HOLLENBERG, M.D. *Professor of Radiology, Harvard University.*

•F. CLARK HOWELL. *Professor of Anthropology, University of California, Berkeley.*

JOHN H. HUMPHREY, M.D. (d. 1987). *Professor of Immunology, Royal Postgraduate Medical School, University of London, 1976–81.*

HOWARD F. HUNT. *Clinical Professor of Psychology in Psychiatry, Cornell University Medical College, New York City.*

AINSLEY IGGO. *Professor of Veterinary Physiology; Dean, Faculty of Veterinary Medicine, University of Edinburgh.*

JEROME P. KASSIRER, M.D. *Sara Murray Jordan Professor of Medicine, Tufts University, Boston.*

WILLIAM KESSEN. *Eugene Higgins Professor of Psychology; Professor of Pediatrics, Yale University.*

•GREGORY A. KIMBLE. *Emeritus Professor of Psychology, Duke University, Durham, North Carolina.*

•JOSEPH BARNETT KIRSNER, M.D. *Louis Block Distinguished Service Professor of Medicine, University of Chicago.*

•ERICH KLINGHAMMER. *Associate Professor of Psychology, Purdue University, West Lafayette, Indiana.*

LOUIS LASAGNA, M.D. *Dean, Sackler School of Graduate Biomedical Sciences; Dean for Academic Affairs, School of Medicine, Tufts University, Medford, Massachusetts.*

•WARREN STURGIS McCULLOCH, M.D. (d. 1969). *Neurophysiologist, cyberneticist. Staff Member, Research Laboratory of Electronics, Massachusetts Institute of Technology, Cambridge, 1952–69.*

•WILLIAM J. McGUIRE. *Professor of Psychology, Yale University.*

W. BRYAN MATTHEWS, M.D. *Emeritus Professor of Clinical Neurology, University of Oxford.*

•SIR PETER MEDAWAR (d. 1987). *Jodrell Professor of Zoology and Comparative Anatomy, University College, London, 1951–62. Director, National Institute, Mill Hill, London, 1962–71. Member, Scientific Staff, Medical Research Council, England, 1971–84. Nobel Prize for Physiology or Medicine, 1960.*

MICHAEL FRANCIS OLIVER, M.D. *Director, Wynn Institute for Metabolic Research, London. Duke of Edinburgh Professor of Cardiology, University of Edinburgh, 1979–89.*

D. KEITH PETERS. *Regius Professor of Physic, University of Cambridge.*

KEN RAWNSLEY. *Emeritus Professor of Psychological Medicine, University of Wales College of Medicine, Cardiff.*

DRUMMOND RENNIE, M.D. *Chairman of Medicine, West Suburban Hospital, Oak Park, Illinois. Professor of Medicine, Rush Medical College, Chicago.*

JAMES SCOTT ROBSON, M.D. *Emeritus Professor of Medicine, University of Edinburgh.*

FRED S. ROSEN, M.D. *James L. Gamble Professor of Pediatrics, Harvard University.*

IRVING SARNOFF. *Professor of Psychology, New York University, New York City.*

WILFRED SIRCUS, M.D. *Senior Consultant Physician, Gastrointestinal Unit; former Reader in Medicine, University of Edinburgh.*

WILLIAM H. TALIAFERRO (d. 1973). *Eliakim Hastings Moore Distinguished Service Professor of Microbiology, University of Chicago, 1954–60. Senior Immunologist, Division of Biological and Medical Research, Argonne National Laboratory, Argonne, Illinois, 1960–69.*

ILZA VEITH. *Emeritus Professor of Psychiatry and the History of Health Sciences, University of California, San Francisco.*

MAXWELL M. WINTROBE, M.D. (d. 1986). *Professor of Internal Medicine, University of Utah, Salt Lake City, 1943–70.*

Part Five. Human Society

FRANCIS A. ALLEN. *Huber C. Hurst Professor of Law, University of Florida, Gainesville. Edson R. Sunderland Professor Emeritus of Law, University of Michigan, Ann Arbor.*

CLEVELAND AMORY. *Author and lecturer. President of The Fund for Animals.*

•WILLIAM J. BAUMOL. *Professor of Economics, Princeton University and New York University, New York City.*

•DANIEL BELL. *Henry Ford II Professor of Social Science, Harvard University.*

•GIULIANO H. BONFANTE. *Former Professor of Linguistics, University of Turin, Italy.*

•KENNETH E. BOULDING. *Distinguished Professor Emeritus of Economics, University of Colorado, Boulder.*

ROBERT J. BRAIDWOOD. *Emeritus Professor of Old World Prehistory, Oriental Institute, University of Chicago.*

TIMOTHY J. COLTON. *Professor of Government, Harvard University.*

•LEWIS A. COSER. *Distinguished Professor Emeritus of Sociology, State University of New York at Stony Brook.*

MAURICE CRANSTON. *Emeritus Professor of Political Science, London School of Economics and Political Science, University of London.*

•SIGMUND DIAMOND. *Giddings Professor of Sociology, Columbia University.*

ALLISON DUNHAM. *Arnold I. Shure Professor Emeritus of Urban Law, University of Chicago.*

FRED R. EGGAN (d. 1991). *Harold H. Swift Distinguished Service Professor of Anthropology, University of Chicago, 1963–74.*

•CARL J. FRIEDRICH (d. 1984). *Eaton Professor of the Science of Government, Harvard University, 1955–71.*

DAVID A. GOSLIN. *Executive Director, Commission on Behavioral and Social Sciences and Education, National Research Council, National Academy of Sciences, Washington, D.C.*

ANDREW HACKER. *Professor of Political Science, Queens College, City University of New York, Flushing.*

JOHN HACKETT. *Consultant, Organization for Economic Cooperation and Development, Paris; Director for Financial, Fiscal, and Enterprise Affairs, 1979–89.*

ERIC P. HAMP. *Robert Maynard Hutchins Distinguished Service Professor of Linguistics, of Psychology, and of Slavic Languages; Director, Center for Balkan and Slavic Studies, University of Chicago.*

•ROBERT J. HAVIGHURST (d. 1991). *Professor of Education and of Human Development, University of Chicago, 1941–65.*

JEROME HOLTZMAN. *Author and journalist. Baseball Columnist, Chicago Tribune. Elected to the Writers' Wing, National Baseball Hall of Fame, 1990.*

•HARRY KALVEN, JR. (d. 1974). *Professor of Law, University of Chicago, 1953–74.*

EDMUND JAMES KING. *Emeritus Professor of Education, King's College, University of London.*

JOHN RICHARD KRUEGER. *Former Professor of Uralic and Altaic Studies, Indiana University, Bloomington.*

SIR JOHN LYONS. *Master of Trinity Hall, University of Cambridge.*

•RAVEN I. McDAVID, JR. (d. 1984). *Professor of English and of Linguistics, University of Chicago, 1964–77.*

DONALD GUNN MacRAE. *Martin White Professor Emeritus of Sociology, London School of Economics and Political Science, University of London.*

RUSSELL L. MATHEWS. *Emeritus Professor of Economics, Australian National University, Canberra.*

JEANNETTE R. MIRSKY (d. 1987). *Visiting Fellow, Department of East Asian Studies, Princeton University, 1970–74.*

HANS J. MORGENTHAU (d. 1980). *Leonard Davis Distinguished Professor of Political Science, City College, City University of New York, 1968–74. Albert A. Michelson Distinguished Service Professor of Political Science and Modern History, University of Chicago, 1963–68.*

•PAUL MUNDY. *Professor of Sociology; Chairman, Department of Criminal Justice, Loyola University, Chicago.*

ALEXANDER NOVE. *Emeritus Professor of Economics, University of Glasgow.*

•KENYON E. POOLE (d. 1988). *Professor of Economics, Northwestern University, Evanston, Illinois.*

•C. HERMAN PRITCHETT. *Emeritus Professor of Political Science, University of California, Santa Barbara, and University of Chicago.*

ALBERT J. REISS, JR. *William Graham Sumner Professor of Sociology; Lecturer in Law, Yale University.*

•MAX RHEINSTEIN (d. 1977). *Max Pam Professor of Comparative Law, University of Chicago, 1942–68.*

CHARLES SZLADITS (d. 1986). *Adjunct Professor of Comparative Law, Columbia University.*

•SOL TAX. *Emeritus Professor of Anthropology, University of Chicago. Director, Center for the Study of Man, Smithsonian Institution, Washington, D.C., 1968–76.*

•CHARLES RAYMOND WHITTLESEY. *Emeritus Professor of Finance and Economics, University of Pennsylvania, Philadelphia.*

AARON B. WILDAVSKY. *Professor of Political Science, University of California, Berkeley.*

TURRELL V. WYLIE (d. 1984). *Professor of Tibetan Studies, University of Washington, Seattle, 1972–84.*

Part Six. Art

•RUDOLF ARNHEIM. *Emeritus Professor of Psychology of Art, Carpenter Center for the Visual Arts, Harvard University.*

WALTER BLAIR. *Emeritus Professor of English, University of Chicago.*

JOHN ELY BURCHARD (d. 1975). *Professor of Humanities and Dean, School of Humanities and Social Science, Massachusetts Institute of Technology, Cambridge, 1948–64.*

ALBERT BUSH-BROWN. *Chairman, Barclays Bank of New York. Chancellor, Long Island University, Greenvale, New York, 1971–85.*

•ROBERT JESSE CHARLESTON. *Keeper, Department of Ceramics, Victoria and Albert Museum, London, 1963–76.*

•CLIFTON FADIMAN. *Writer and editor. Member, Board of Editors,* Encyclopædia Britannica.

•FRANCIS FERGUSSON (d. 1986). *Professor of Comparative Literature, Princeton University, 1973–81. Professor of Comparative Literature, Rutgers University, New Brunswick, New Jersey, 1953–69.*

HELMUT GERNSHEIM. *Photo-historian and author. Founder of the Gernsheim Collection. Regents Professor of Art, University of California, Riverside, 1984. Guest Professor, University of California, Santa Barbara, 1985 and 1989.*

•JOHN GLOAG (d. 1981). *Novelist and writer on architecture and industrial design.*

OLEG GRABAR. *Aga Khan Professor of Islāmic Art, Harvard University.*

•RICHARD GRIFFITH (d. 1969). *Lecturer on Motion Pictures, Wesleyan University, Middletown, Connecticut, 1967–69. Curator, Museum of Modern Art Film Library, New York City, 1951–65.*

•RICHARD HOGGART. *Warden, Goldsmiths' College, University of London, 1976–84. Professor of English, University of Birmingham, England, 1962–73.*

HANS HUTH (d. 1977). *Curator of Painting, 1944–57, Art Institute of Chicago; Curator of Decorative Arts, 1958–63.*

ARTHUR KNIGHT. *Professor of Cinema, University of Southern California, Los Angeles.*

•EDWARD LOCKSPEISER (d. 1973). *Officier d'Académie, Paris. Writer and broadcaster on music.*

•ROY McMULLEN (d. 1984). *Author, critic, and art historian.*

WILLIAM W. MELNITZ (d. 1989). *Professor of Theater Arts, University of California, Los Angeles, 1956–67; Dean, College of Fine Arts, 1961–67.*

•LEONARD B. MEYER. *Benjamin Franklin Professor of Music and Humanities, University of Pennsylvania, Philadelphia.*

•MICHAEL MORROW. *Former Music Editor,* Encyclopædia Britannica. *Director, Musica Reservatus, London.*

RAY NASH (d. 1982). *Professor of Art, Dartmouth College, Hanover, New Hampshire, 1949–70.*

BRUNO NETTL. *Professor of Music and of Anthropology, University of Illinois, Urbana.*

•BEAUMONT NEWHALL. *Emeritus Professor of Art, University of New Mexico, Albuquerque. Director, George Eastman House, Rochester, New York, 1958–71.*

DOROTHY MARGARET PARTINGTON (d. 1990). *Literary critic and historian.*

•SIR HERBERT READ (d. 1968). *Poet and critic. Watson Gordon Professor of Fine Art, University of Edinburgh, 1931–33. Editor,* The Burlington Magazine, *1933–39. Charles Eliot Norton Professor of Poetry, Harvard University, 1953–54.*

•RICHARD ROUD (d. 1989). *Film critic,* The Guardian, *Manchester, 1963–69. Program Director, London (1959–63) and New York (1963–87) Film Festivals.*

•GEORGE SAVAGE (d. 1982). *Art consultant. Author of* Porcelain Through the Ages; Pottery Through the Ages; *and others.*

NICOLAS SLONIMSKY. *Conductor, composer, writer, and editor. Lecturer in Music, University of California, Los Angeles, 1964–67.*

•WOLFGANG STECHOW (d. 1974). *Professor of Fine Arts, Oberlin College, Oberlin, Ohio, 1940–63.*

•JOSHUA C. TAYLOR (d. 1981). *Director, National Collection of Fine Arts, Smithsonian Institution, Washington, D.C., 1970–81. William Rainey Harper Professor of Humanities and Professor of Art, University of Chicago, 1963–74.*

WALTER TERRY (d. 1982). *Dance critic and editor,* Saturday Review *magazine;* New York Herald Tribune; *and others.*

•EVERARD M. UPJOHN (d. 1978). *Professor of Fine Arts, Columbia University, 1951–70.*

•PIERRE VERLET. *Chief Curator of Art Objects from the Middle Ages to the Modern Period, Louvre Museum, Paris, 1945–65. Chief Curator, National Museum of Sèvres Porcelain, Sèvres, France, 1945–65. Chief Curator, Cluny Museum, Paris, 1945–65.*

EDWARD WASIOLEK. *Avalon Foundation Distinguished Service Professor of Slavic, English, and Comparative Literature, University of Chicago.*

•RENÉ WELLEK. *Sterling Professor Emeritus of Comparative Literature, Yale University.*

•GLYNNE WILLIAM GLADSTONE WICKHAM. *Emeritus Professor of Drama, University of Bristol, England; Dean, Faculty of Arts, 1970–72.*

•RAYMOND (HENRY) WILLIAMS (d. 1988). *Professor of Drama, University of Cambridge, 1974–83; Fellow of Jesus College, Cambridge, 1961–88.*

C. BARRIE WILSON. *Vice-Principal and Professor of Architectural Science, University of Edinburgh.*

•PAUL S. WINGERT (d. 1974). *Professor of Art History and Archaeology, Columbia University.*

•BRUNO ZEVI. *Professor of Architectural History, University of Rome, 1963–79.*

Part Seven. Technology

BRIAN D.O. ANDERSON. *Professor and Head, Department of Systems Engineering, Research School of Physical Sciences, Australian National University, Canberra.*

GRACE ROGERS COOPER. *Museum consultant. Curator, Division of Textiles, National Museum of History and Technology, Smithsonian Institution, Washington, D.C., 1946–76.*

•CONSTANTINE APOSTOLOS DOXIADIS (d. 1975). *Chairman, Doxiadis Associates International, Athens; Chairman, Board of Directors, Doxiadis Associates, Inc., Washington, D.C. Chairman, Board of Directors, Athens Technological Organization. President, Athens Center of Ekistics.*

•EUGENE S. FERGUSON. *Professor of History, University of Delaware, Newark, 1969–79. Curator of Technology, Hagley Museum, Greenville, Delaware, 1969–79.*

NEAL FITZSIMONS. *Principal, Engineering Counsel, Kensington, Maryland.*

S. PAUL JOHNSTON (d. 1985). *Director, National Air and Space Museum, Smithsonian Institution, Washington, D.C., 1964–69.*

•MELVIN KRANZBERG. *Emeritus Professor of the History of Technology, Georgia Institute of Technology, Atlanta.*

WARREN PERRY MASON (deceased). *Senior Research Associate, Henry Krumb School of Mines, Columbia University, 1969–77. Head of Mechanics Research, Bell Telephone Laboratories, Murray Hill, New Jersey, 1948–65.*

•HARVEY G. MEHLHOUSE. *Chairman of the Board, Western Electric Company, New York City, 1971–72; President, 1969–71; Vice President, 1965–69.*

HARRY F. OLSON (d. 1982). *Staff Vice President, RCA Laboratories, Princeton, New Jersey, 1966–67; Director, Acoustical and Electromechanical Laboratory, 1942–66.*

•ROBERT SMITH WOODBURY (d. 1983). *Professor of the History of Technology, Massachusetts Institute of Technology, Cambridge.*

Part Eight. Religion

CHARLES JOSEPH ADAMS. *Professor of Islāmic Studies, McGill University, Montreal.*

SALO WITTMAYER BARON (d. 1989). *Professor of Jewish History, Literature, and Institutions, Columbia University, 1930–63; Director, Center of Israel and Jewish Studies, 1950–68.*

THE REV. COLMAN J. BARRY, O.S.B. *Regents Professor of History, Saint John's University, Collegeville, Minnesota; Director, Institute for Spirituality, 1977–83.*

•ARTHUR LLEWELLYN BASHAM (d. 1986). *Professor of Asian Civilizations, Australian National University, Canberra.*

J.A.B. ᴠᴀɴ BUITENEN (d. 1979). *Distinguished Service Professor of Sanskrit and Indic Studies, University of Chicago, 1974–79.*

•THE REV. JAMES T. BURTCHAELL. *Professor of Theology, University of Notre Dame, Indiana; Provost, 1970–77.*

P. JOSEPH CAHILL, S.J. *Professor of Religious Studies, University of Alberta, Edmonton.*

•THE REV. J.V. LANGMEAD CASSERLEY (d. 1978). *Professor of Apologetics, Seabury-Western Theological Seminary, Evanston, Illinois, 1959–77.*

EDWARD J.D. CONZE (d. 1979). *Visiting Professor of Religious Studies, University of Lancaster, England, 1973–75.*

H. BYRON EARHART. *Professor of Religion, Western Michigan University, Kalamazoo.*

MIRCEA ELIADE (d. 1986). *Sewell L. Avery Distinguished Service Professor, Divinity School; Professor, Committee on Social Thought, University of Chicago.*

GEORGE WOLFGANG FORELL. *Carver Professor of Religion, University of Iowa, Iowa City.*

B.A. GERRISH. *John Nuveen Professor of Historical Theology, Divinity School, University of Chicago.*

JUDAH GOLDIN. *Professor of Oriental Studies and Post-Biblical Hebrew Literature, University of Pennsylvania, Philadelphia.*

•ROBERT M. GRANT. *Carl Darling Buck Professor Emeritus of Humanities; Emeritus Professor of Early Christian History, Divinity School, University of Chicago.*

HERBERT V. GUENTHER. *Emeritus Professor of Far Eastern Studies, University of Saskatchewan, Saskatoon.*

•ICHIRO HORI (d. 1974). *Professor of the History of Religions, Seijo University and Kokugakuin University, Tokyo.*

THORKILD JACOBSEN. *Emeritus Professor of Assyriology, Harvard University.*

•JOSEPH M. KITAGAWA. *Emeritus Professor of the History of Religions and of Far Eastern Languages and Civilizations, University of Chicago; Dean, Divinity School, 1970–80.*

CHARLES H. LONG. *William Rand Kenan, Jr., Professor of the History of Religion, University of North Carolina at Chapel Hill. Professor of the History of Religions, Duke University, Durham, North Carolina.*

THE REV. GEORGE W. MᴀᴄRAE, S.J. (d. 1985). *Stillman Professor of Roman Catholic Theological Studies, Divinity School, Harvard University, 1973–85.*

MARTIN E. MARTY. *Fairfax M. Cone Distinguished Service Professor, Divinity School, University of Chicago. Senior Editor,* The Christian Century.

THE REV. JOHN MEYENDORFF. *Dean and Professor of Church History and Patristics, St. Vladimir's Orthodox Theological Seminary, Tuckahoe, New York. Professor of Byzantine and East European History, Fordham University, New York City.*

HAJIME NAKAMURA. *Founder-Director, Eastern Institute, Inc., Tokyo. Emeritus Professor of Indian and Buddhist Philosophy, University of Tokyo.*

•JAROSLAV JAN PELIKAN. *Sterling Professor of History, Yale University.*

•RABBI JAKOB JOSEF PETUCHOWSKI. *Research Professor of Judeo-Christian Studies, Hebrew Union College—Jewish Institute of Religion, Cincinnati, Ohio.*

•FAZLUR RAHMAN (d. 1988). *Professor of Islāmic Philosophy, University of Chicago, 1969–88.*

J. COERT RYLAARSDAM. *Emeritus Professor of Old Testament Theology, Divinity School, University of Chicago. Emeritus Professor of Theology, Marquette University, Milwaukee, Wisconsin.*

JONATHAN Z. SMITH. *Robert O. Anderson Distinguished Service Professor of the Humanities, University of Chicago.*

R.J. ZWI WERBLOWSKY. *Professor of Comparative Religion, Hebrew University of Jerusalem.*

Part Nine. The History of Mankind

•FREDERICK B. ARTZ (d. 1983). *Professor of History, Oberlin College, Ohio, 1934–62.*

•JACQUES BARZUN. *University Professor Emeritus, Columbia University; Dean of Faculties and Provost, 1958–67.*

DAVID BIRMINGHAM. *Professor of Modern History, University of Kent at Canterbury, England.*

JOHN A. BRINKMAN. *Charles H. Swift Distinguished Service Professor of Mesopotamian History, University of Chicago.*

JOHN F. CADY. *Distinguished Professor Emeritus of History, Ohio University, Athens.*

AINSLIE T. EMBREE. *Professor of History, Columbia University.*

JOSEPH FLETCHER (d. 1984). *Professor of Chinese and Central Asian History, Harvard University, 1972–84.*

WALTER EMIL KAEGI, JR. *Professor of Byzantine and Roman History, University of Chicago.*

HERBERT S. KLEIN. *Professor of History, Columbia University.*

•LEONARD KRIEGER. *University Professor of History, University of Chicago.*

PHILIP A. KUHN. *Professor of History; Director, John King Fairbank Center for East Asian Research, Harvard University.*

DONALD P. LITTLE. *Professor and Director, Institute of Islāmic Studies, McGill University, Montreal.*

DONALD M. LOWE. *Professor of History, San Francisco State University.*

JAMES G. LYDON. *Professor of History, Duquesne University, Pittsburgh.*

PAUL T. MASON. *Professor of History, Duquesne University, Pittsburgh.*

HERBERT GEORGE NICHOLAS. *Rhodes Professor Emeritus of American History and Institutions, University of Oxford; Fellow of New College, Oxford, 1951–78.*

DONALD MacGILLIVRAY NICOL. *Director, Gennadius Library, American School of Classical Studies at Athens. Koraës Professor Emeritus of Byzantine and Modern Greek History, Language, and Literature, King's College, University of London.*

STEWART IRVIN OOST (d. 1981). *Professor of Ancient History, University of Chicago, 1965–81.*

RICHARD E. PIPES. *Frank B. Baird, Jr., Professor of History, Harvard University.*

GORDON R. WILLEY. *Bowditch Professor Emeritus of Mexican and Central American Archaeology, Harvard University.*

GEORGE MACKLIN WILSON. *Professor of History and of East Asian Languages and Cultures, Indiana University, Bloomington.*

Part Ten. The Branches of Knowledge

MONROE C. BEARDSLEY (d. 1985). *Professor of Philosophy, Temple University, Philadelphia, 1969–84.*

•OTTO ALLEN BIRD. *Emeritus Professor of Arts and Letters, University of Notre Dame, Indiana.*

PETER G. BROWN. *Professor of Public Policy, University of Maryland, College Park.*

•WING-TSIT CHAN. *Anna R.D. Gillespie Professor Emeritus of Philosophy, Chatham College, Pittsburgh. Emeritus Professor of Chinese Philosophy and Culture, Dartmouth College, Hanover.*

RODERICK M. CHISHOLM. *Andrew Mellon Professor of the Humanities and Professor of Philosophy, Brown University, Providence, Rhode Island.*

JAMES DANIEL COLLINS (d. 1985). *Professor of Philosophy, St. Louis University, Missouri.*

ALAN DONAGAN (d. 1991). *Professor of Philosophy, California Institute of Technology, Pasadena, 1984–91.*

•WILLIAM H. DRAY. *Professor of Philosophy and of History, University of Ottawa.*

ELDON DYER. *Distinguished Professor of Mathematics, Graduate School, City University of New York.*

•NORWOOD HANSON (d. 1967). *Professor of Philosophy, Yale University, 1963–67.*

•J.H. HEXTER. *Distinguished Historian in Residence, Washington University, St. Louis, Missouri. Charles L. Stillé Professor of History, Yale University, 1967–78.*

•RICHARD P. McKEON (d. 1985). *Charles F. Grey Distinguished Service Professor of Philosophy and of Greek, University of Chicago, 1947–76.*

•THE REV. ERNAN V. McMULLIN. *Professor of Philosophy, University of Notre Dame, Indiana.*

•KARL MENGER (d. 1985). *Professor of Mathematics, Illinois Institute of Technology, Chicago, 1946–71.*

•ARTHUR NORMAN PRIOR (d. 1969). *Fellow, Balliol College, University of Oxford. Professor of Philosophy, Manchester University, 1959–66.*

•NICHOLAS RESCHER. *University Professor of Philosophy, University of Pittsburgh. Editor,* American Philosophical Quarterly.

MARK A. RONAN. *Mason Professor of Pure Mathematics, University of Birmingham, England.*

PAUL ARTHUR SCHILPP. *Emeritus Professor of Philosophy, Northwestern University, Evanston, Illinois. Distinguished Professor, Southern Illinois University, Carbondale, 1965–77.*

•SEYMOUR SCHUSTER. *Professor of Mathematics, Carleton College, Northfield, Minnesota.*

IAN NICHOLAS STEWART. *Professor of Mathematics, University of Warwich, Coventry, England.*

JULIUS R. WEINBERG (d. 1971). *Vilas Professor of Philosophy, University of Wisconsin, Madison.*

IZAAK WIRSZUP. *Emeritus Professor of Mathematics, University of Chicago.*

Geography

NATHANIEL O. ABELSON. *Former Map Librarian, Dag Hammarskjöld Library, United Nations, New York City.*

IBRAHIM A. ABU-LUGHOD. *Professor of Political Science, Northwestern University, Evanston, Illinois.*

GEORGE I. BLANKSTEN. *Emeritus Professor of Political Science, Northwestern University, Evanston, Illinois.*

NORTON S. GINSBURG. *Director, Environment and Policy Institute, East-West Center, Honolulu. Emeritus Professor of Geography, University of Chicago.*

CHAUNCY D. HARRIS. *Samuel N. Harper Distinguished Service Professor Emeritus of Geography, University of Chicago.*

HELVI A. KALMAN. *Writer and Editor, Department of Public Information, United Nations, New York City, 1958–79*

C.W. MINKEL. *Vice-Provost; Dean, Graduate School, University of Tennessee, Knoxville.*

HANS E. PANOFSKY. *Curator of Africana, Northwestern University Library, Evanston, Illinois.*

G. ETZEL PEARCY (d. 1980). *Professor of Geography, California State University, Los Angeles, 1969–73.*

IVOR G. WILKS. *Melville J. Herskovits Professor of African Studies, Northwestern University, Evanston, Illinois.*

Authors of Propædia Essays

Part One

NIGEL CALDER. *Physicist and science writer. Science Correspondent,* New Statesman, *1966–71. Editor,* New Scientist, *1962–66. Author of* Robots; Technopolis: Social Control of the Uses of Science; *and others.*

Part Two

PETER J. WYLLIE. *Petrologist, educator, and author. Professor of Geology and Chairman, Division of Geological and Planetary Sciences, California Institute of Technology, Pasadena. Author of* Ultramafic and Related Rocks; The Dynamic Earth; *and others.*

Part Three

RENÉ DUBOS (d. 1982). *Microbiologist, pathologist, and author. Professor of Pathology, Rockefeller University, New York City, 1957–71. Author of* So Human an Animal; Mirage of Health; A God Within; *and others.*

Part Four

LOREN EISELEY (d. 1977). *Anthropologist, poet, and essayist. Benjamin Franklin Professor of Anthropology and the History of Science, University of Pennsylvania, 1961–77; Curator of Early Man, University of Pennsylvania Museum, 1948–77. Author of* The Immense Journey; The Invisible Pyramid; *and others.*

Part Five

HAROLD D. LASSWELL (d. 1978). *Political scientist and author. Professor of Law, 1946–70, and of Political Science, 1952–70, Yale University. Author of* Psychopathology and Politics; Politics: Who Gets What, When, How; A Pre-View of Policy Sciences; *and others.*

Part Six

MARK VAN DOREN (d. 1972). *Poet, critic, and teacher. Professor of English, Columbia University, 1920–59. Author of lyric and narrative poems, novels, stories, plays, and works of criticism and biography.*

Part Seven

PETER RITCHIE RITCHIE-CALDER, BARON RITCHIE-CALDER (d. 1982). *Author, journalist, and educator. Senior Fellow, Center for the Study of Democratic Institutions, Santa Barbara, California, 1972–75. Montague Burton Professor of International Relations, University of Edinburgh, 1961–67. Author of* Birth of the Future; Medicine and Man; The Evolution of the Machine; *and others.*

Part Eight

WILFRED CANTWELL SMITH. *Educator and author. Emeritus Professor of the Comparative History of Religion, Harvard University. Author of* Islam in Modern History; The Meaning and End of Religion; Questions of Religious Truth; *and others.*

Part Nine

JACQUES BARZUN. *Historian, educator, and author. University Professor Emeritus, Columbia University; Dean of Faculties and Provost, 1958–67. Author of* Berlioz and the Romantic Century; Darwin, Marx, and Wagner; The House of Intellect; On Writing, Publishing, and Editing; *and others.*

Part Ten

MORTIMER J. ADLER. *Philosopher and editor. Director of the Institute for Philosophical Research. Editor of the Syntopicon of* Great Books of the Western World; *Chairman, Board of Editors,* Encyclopædia Britannica; *Director of Planning, Fifteenth Edition. Author of* The Idea of Freedom; The Conditions of Philosophy; The Common Sense of Politics; *and others.*

Initials of
Contributors

Listed are the initials signed to articles in the MACROPAEDIA and MICROPAEDIA, the names of the persons identified by the initials, a brief description of the persons so identified, and the titles of the articles with which they were involved.

A.   Morys George Lyndhurst Bruce, 4th Baron Aberdare. *Chairman of Committees, House of Lords, United Kingdom. Author of* The Story of Tennis; Willis Faber Book of Tennis and Rackets.
SPORTS, MAJOR TEAM AND INDIVIDUAL (*in part*)

A.Ad.   Anthony Adamovich. *Vice President, Byelorussian Institute of Arts and Sciences, Inc., Rutherford, New Jersey. Senior Editor, Radio Liberty. Author of* Opposition to Sovietization in Belorussian Literature.
UNION OF SOVIET SOCIALIST REPUBLICS (*in part*)

A.A.F.   Arnold A. Friedmann. *Professor of Design, University of Massachusetts, Amherst. Coauthor of* Interior Design.
DECORATIVE ARTS AND FURNISHINGS (*in part*)

A.A.G.P.   António Armando Gonçalves Pereira. *Former Professor of Commercial and Maritime Law, Technical University of Lisbon.*
SOUTHERN AFRICA (*in part*)

A.Ai.   Ayinipalli Aiyappan. *Special Officer, Tribal Research and Training Centre, Chevayur, Calicut, India. Editor of* Social Revolution in a Kerala Village.
INDIA (*in part*)

A.A.K.   Arno Artur Köörna. *Vice President, Estonian Academy of Sciences, Tallinn; former Director, Institute of Economics. Author of papers on Estonia.*
BALTIC STATES (*in part*)

A.Al-Sh.   Ahmed S. Al-Shahi. *Lecturer in Social Anthropology, University of Newcastle upon Tyne, England.*
SUDAN (*in part*)

A.A.M.   Aleksey Aleksandrovich Mints (d. 1973). *Chief, Department of Economic Geography, Institute of Geography, Academy of Sciences of the U.S.S.R., Moscow. Author of books on Transcaucasia.*
UNION OF SOVIET SOCIALIST REPUBLICS (*in part*)

A.A.Ma.   The Rev. Armand Maurer, C.S.B. *Emeritus Professor of Philosophy, Pontifical Institute of Mediaeval Studies, University of Toronto. Author of* Medieval Philosophy.
PHILOSOPHY, THE HISTORY OF WESTERN (*in part*)

A.A.P.   Alexander A. Parker (d. 1989). *Professor of Spanish Literature, University of Texas at Austin, 1970–78. Author of* The Allegorical Drama of Calderón.
CALDERÓN DE LA BARCA, PEDRO (Micropædia)

A.A.Ps.   Adamantios A. Pepelasis. *Former Professor of Economics, Virginia Polytechnic Institute and State University, Blacksburg.*
TAXATION (*in part*)

A.As.   Arthur C.V.D. Aspinall (d. 1972). *Professor of Modern History, University of Reading, England, 1947–65. Author of* The Cabinet Council, 1783–1835 *and others.*
CANNING, GEORGE (Micropædia)
FOX, CHARLES JAMES (Micropædia)
PITT, WILLIAM, THE YOUNGER (*in part*) (Micropædia)

A.A.S.   Arthur A. Siebens, M.D. *Darnall Professor of Rehabilitation Medicine and Surgery; Chief, Division of Rehabilitation Medicine, Johns Hopkins University, Baltimore. Author of* "The Mechanics of Breathing" in The Physiological Basis of Medical Practice.
RESPIRATION AND RESPIRATORY SYSTEMS (*in part*)

A.A.Si.   Andrew Annandale Sinclair. *Historian and filmmaker. Author of* Guevara *and others.*
GUEVARA, CHE (*in part*) (Micropædia)

A.B.   Alan Bullock, Baron Bullock. *Founding Master of St. Catherine's College, Oxford, 1960–1980; Vice-Chancellor, University of Oxford, 1969–73. Author of* Hitler: A Study in Tyranny *and others.*
HITLER (*in part*)

A.B.-B.   Albert Bush-Brown. *Chairman, Barclays Bank of New York. Chancellor, Long Island University, Greenvale, New York, 1971–85. Author of* Louis Sullivan; *coauthor of* The Architecture of America.
ARCHITECTURE, THE HISTORY OF WESTERN (*in part*)

A.B.C.   Andrew Barnett Christie, M.D. *Honorary Physician, Fazakerley Hospital, Liverpool. Former Head, Department of Infectious Diseases, University of Liverpool. Author of* Infectious Diseases: Epidemiology and Clinical Practice.
INFECTIOUS DISEASES (*in part*)

A.B.F.   Albert B. Friedman. William *Starke Rosecrans Professor of English Literature, Claremont Graduate School, Claremont, California. Author of* The Ballad Revival; *Editor of* Ywain and Gawain.
LITERATURE, THE ART OF (*in part*)

A.B.Fo.   Arthur B. Ford. *Geologist, Branch of Alaskan Geology, Geological Survey, U.S. Department of the Interior, Menlo Park, California. Author of* "Review of Antarctic Geology" *in* American Geophysical Union Transactions.
ANTARCTICA

A.B.G.   Ashley B. Gurney. *Research Entomologist, Systematic Entomology Laboratory, U.S. Department of Agriculture, Washington, D.C., 1955–75. Author of numerous articles on classification and distribution of insects.*
INSECTS (*in part*)

A.B.Ga.   Alfred B. Garrett. *Emeritus Professor of Chemistry, Ohio State University, Columbus.*
DALTON, JOHN (Micropædia)

A.B.Gr.   Alfred Byrd Graf. *President, Roehrs Company (horticultural publishers); Vice President, Roehrs Exotic Nurseries, Farmingdale, New Jersey. Author of* Exotica; Tropica.
GARDENING AND HORTICULTURE (*in part*)

A.Bh.   Agehananda Bharati (d. 1991). *Professor of Anthropology, Syracuse University, New York, 1961–91. Author of* The Tantric Tradition.
SACRED OFFICES AND ORDERS (*in part*)

A.B.J.   Abeodu Bowen Jones. *Professor and Chairman, Department of History, University of Liberia, Monrovia. Representative of Liberia to the United Nations, 1981–85. Coeditor of* The Official Papers of William V.S. Tubman, President of the Republic of Liberia.
WESTERN AFRICA (*in part*)

A.B.K.   Alexander B. Klots (d. 1989). *Research Associate, Department of Entomology, American Museum of Natural History, New York City. Professor of Biology, City University of New York, 1960–67. Author of* Field Guide to the Butterflies of North America *and others.*
INSECTS (*in part*)

A.B.M.   Alexander B. Murphy. *Assistant Professor of Geography, University of Oregon, Eugene. Author of* The Regional Dynamics of Language Differentiation in Belgium.
BELGIUM (*in part*)

A.B.P.   Sir A. Brian Pippard. *Professor of Physics, University of Cambridge; Cavendish Professor, 1971–82. Author of* Elements of Classical Thermodynamics.
PHYSICAL SCIENCES, PRINCIPLES OF

A.Br.   Adam Bromke. *Professor of Political Science, McMaster University, Hamilton, Ontario. Author of* Poland's Politics: Idealism vs. Realism.
GOMUŁKA, WŁADYSŁAW (Micropædia)

A.B.R.   Andreas B. Rechnitzer. *Special Deputy for International and Interagency*

Affairs, Office of the Oceanographer of the Navy, Alexandria, Virginia.
EXPLORATION (*in part*)

A.B.Ri.   A. Brewster Rickel. *President, Commutech Services (scientific and technical documentation), Boulder, Colorado. Author of manuals and articles on weather equipment.*
CLIMATE AND WEATHER (*in part*)

A.Bu.   Allison Butts (d. 1977). *Professor of Metallurgy and Materials Science, Lehigh University, Bethlehem, Pennsylvania, Editor of* Copper: The Science and Technology of the Metal, Its Alloys and Compounds.
INDUSTRIES, EXTRACTION AND
 PROCESSING (*in part*)

A.B.W.   The Rev. Allan Bernard Wolter, O.F.M. *Emeritus Professor of Philosophy, Catholic University of America, Washington, D.C. Author of* The Transcendentals and Their Function in the Metaphysics of Duns Scotus.
DUNS SCOTUS, JOHN (Micropædia)

A.By.   André Berry (d. 1986). *Author of* Florilège des troubadours; Anthologie de la poésie occitane; *and others.*
PROVENÇAL LITERATURE (Micropædia)

A.C.   Angela Codazzi. *Professor of Geography and Director, Institute of Geography, University of Milan, 1945–60.*
ITALY (*in part*)

A.C.B.   A. Craig Baird (d. 1979). *Professor of Speech, University of Iowa, Iowa City, 1928–52. Author and editor of* American Public Addresses; *coauthor of* Speech Criticism; General Speech; Communication.
ORATORY (Micropædia)

A.C.Bi.   Alan Curtis Birnholz. *Associate Professor of Art History, State University of New York at Buffalo.*
TOULOUSE-LAUTREC, HENRI DE
 (Micropædia)

A.C.Bk.   Alfred C. Beck, M.D. (deceased). *Professor of Obstetrics and Gynecology, State University of New York Downstate Medical Center at Brooklyn. Author of* Obstetrical Practice.
REPRODUCTION AND REPRODUCTIVE
 SYSTEMS (*in part*)

A.C.Br.   Armin C. Braun. (d. 1986). *Professor of Bacteriology, Rockefeller University, New York City, 1959–81; Head, Laboratory of Plant Biology, 1955–81. Editor of* Plant Tumor Research.
GROWTH AND DEVELOPMENT,
 BIOLOGICAL (*in part*)

A.C.C.   The Rev. Arthur C. Cochrane. *Emeritus Professor of Systematic Theology, Dubuque Theological Seminary, Iowa. Author of* The Existentialists and God *and others.*
BARTH, KARL (Micropædia)

A.C.D.   Alyn C. Duxbury. *Research Associate Professor of Oceanography, University of Washington, Seattle. Author of* The Earth and its Oceans; *coauthor of* An Introduction to the

World's Oceans.
OCEANS (*in part*)

A.C.G.   A.C. Grayling. *Lecturer in Philosophy, St. Anne's College, University of Oxford. Author of* An Introduction to Philosophical Logic.
METAPHYSICS (*in part*)

A.C.G.B.   Alan C.G. Best. *Associate Professor of Geography, Boston University. Coauthor of* African Survey.
SOUTHERN AFRICA (*in part*)

A.C.H.   Alan Crawford Howie. *Lecturer in Music, Victoria University of Manchester.*
BRUCKNER, ANTON (Micropædia)

A.C.Ha.   Sir Alister C. Hardy (d. 1985). *Linacre Professor of Zoology, University of Oxford, 1946–61. Author of* "Charles Elton's Influence in Ecology" in Journal of Animal Ecology.
ELTON, CHARLES (Micropædia)

A.C.M.   Adolfo C. Mascarenhas. *Director, Institute of Resource Assessment, University of Dar es Salaam, Tanzania.*
EASTERN AFRICA (*in part*)

A.Co.   Alexander Cowie. *Emeritus Professor of Mechanical and Aerospace Engineering, Illinois Institute of Technology, Chicago. Associate Editor, Technology,* Encyclopædia Britannica, *Chicago, 1967–72. Author of* Kinematics and Design of Mechanisms.
MECHANICS (*in part*)

A.C.O.   Albert Cook Outler (d. 1989). *Emeritus Professor of Theology, Southern Methodist University, Dallas, Texas, 1951–79. Author of* Who Trusts in God.
DOCTRINES AND DOGMAS, RELIGIOUS
 (*in part*)

A.C.P.S.   Andrew C.P. Sims, M.D. *Professor of Psychiatry, University of Leeds, England; Honorary Consultant, St. James's University Hospital. Author of* Symptoms in the Mind *and others.*
MENTAL DISORDERS AND THEIR
 TREATMENT (*in part*)

A.Cr.   Arthur Cronquist. *Senior Scientist, New York Botanical Garden, Bronx. Author of* An Integrated System of Classification of Flowering Plants.
ANGIOSPERMS (*in part*)

A.C.U.   Arthur Canfield Upton, M.D. *Professor and Chairman, Department of Environmental Medicine; Director, Institute of Environmental Medicine, New York University, New York City. Author of* Radiation Injury: Effects, Principles, and Perspectives.
RADIATION (*in part*)

A.C.W.M.   Adrian C.W. Mitchell. *Associate Professor of English, University of Sydney. Coeditor of* Oxford Anthology of Australian Literature.
AUSTRALIA AND NEW ZEALAND,
 LITERATURES OF (*in part*)

A.D.   Allison Danzig (d. 1987). *Sportswriter,* The New York Times, *1923–68. Author of* The History of American Football; The Racquet Game

and others.
SPORTS, MAJOR TEAM AND INDIVIDUAL
 (*in part*)

A.Da.   Adrien Dansette (d. 1976). *Member of the Academy of Moral and Political Sciences, Paris. Author of* Les Affaires de Panama.
LESSEPS, FERDINAND, VICOMTE DE
 (Micropædia)

A.D.B.   Alexander D. Baxter (d. 1988). *Engineering Consultant. Professor of Aircraft Propulsion, College of Aeronautics, Cranfield, England, 1950–57. Director, de Havilland Engine Co. Ltd., 1958–63. Author of* Design of Liquid Propellant Rocket Motors.
ENERGY CONVERSION (*in part*)

A.De.   Aleksandar R. Despić. *Professor of Physical Chemistry, University of Belgrade. Contributor to* Modern Aspects of Electrochemistry *and others.*
CHEMICAL REACTIONS (*in part*)

A. de A.-M.   Alamiro de Avila-Martel. *Professor of Roman Law and History of Law; Director of the Central Library, University of Chile, Santiago.*
COINS AND COINAGE (*in part*)

A. De C.   Alexander De Conde. *Professor of History, University of California, Santa Barbara. Author of* The Quasi-War: The Politics and Diplomacy of the Undeclared War with France, 1797–1801 *and others.*
HAMILTON, ALEXANDER (*in part*)
 (Micropædia)

A.Dem.   Abraham Demoz. *Professor of Linguistics, Northwestern University, Evanston, Illinois; Director, Program of African Studies (1974–80).*
EASTERN AFRICA (*in part*)

A.D.G.   Andrew Dewar Gibb (d. 1974). *Regius Professor of Law, University of Glasgow, 1934–58. Coauthor of* Scottish Judicial Dictionary *and others.*
LEGAL SYSTEMS, THE EVOLUTION OF
 MODERN WESTERN (*in part*)

A.D.H.B.   Adrian David Hugh Bivar. *Professor of Iranian Studies, School of Oriental and African Studies, University of London.*
IRAN (*in part*)

A.D.H.C.   Antony Dacres Hippisley Coxe (d. 1988). *Author of* A Seat at the Circus.
CIRCUS (*in part*)

A.Di.   Aubrey Diem. *Professor of Geography, University of Waterloo, Ontario. Author of* Switzerland: Land, People, Economy *and others.*
EUROPE (*in part*)

A.D.M.   Arthur D. Murphy. *Adjunct Professor of Cinema, University of Southern California, Los Angeles.*
MOTION PICTURES (*in part*)

A.D.Mo.   Arnaldo Dante Momigliano (d. 1987). *Alexander White Visiting Professor, University of Chicago, 1975–87. Professor of Ancient History, University College, University of London, 1951–75. Author of* Claudius, The Emperor and His Achievement

and others.
CLAUDIUS I (Micropædia)

A.D.N.   Arne D. Naess. *Emeritus Professor of Philosophy, University of Oslo. Author of* Four Modern Philosophers *and others.*
HEIDEGGER, MARTIN (Micropædia)

A.Do.   Andreas Dorpalen (d. 1982). *Professor of History, Ohio State University, Columbus, 1958–78. Author of* Hindenburg and the Weimar Republic.
HINDENBURG, PAUL VON (Micropædia)

A.Du.   The Rev. Avery Dulles, S.J. *Laurence J. McGinley Professor of Religion and Society, Fordham University, New York City. Author of* Models of Revelation *and others.*
DOCTRINES AND DOGMAS, RELIGIOUS (*in part*)

A.E.A.   Alfred E. Alford. *Managing Director, Media & Marketing Ltd., Belize.*
CENTRAL AMERICA (*in part*)

A.E.Ar.   Annette Elizabeth Armstrong. *Former Fellow and Tutor in Modern Languages, Somerville College, Oxford; former Lecturer in French Literature, University of Oxford. Author of* Ronsard and the Age of Gold; Robert Estienne, Royal Printer.
RONSARD, PIERRE DE (Micropædia)

A.Eb.   Arimichi Ebisawa. *Former Professor of History, International Christian University, Tokyo. Former President, Society of Historical Studies of Christianity, Japan.*
ODA NOBUNAGA (Micropædia)

A.E.Cn.   Aksel E. Christensen (d. 1981). *Professor of History, University of Copenhagen, 1948–76.*
DENMARK (*in part*)

A.E.D.   Augustus E. DeMaggio. *Professor of Biology, Dartmouth College, Hanover, New Hampshire.*
TISSUES AND FLUIDS (*in part*)

A.E.El.   Albert Edward Elsen. *Haas Professor of Art History, Stanford University, California. Author of* Origins of Modern Sculpture *and others.*
SCULPTURE, THE HISTORY OF WESTERN (*in part*)

A.E.M.   Adolphe Erich Meyer (d. 1988). *Professor of Educational History, New York University, New York City, 1946–63. Author of* An Educational History of the American People.
EDUCATION, HISTORY OF (*in part*)

A.E.S.   Alan Edouard Samuel. *Professor of Greek and Roman History, University College, University of Toronto. Author of* Ptolemaic Chronology *and others.*
EGYPT (*in part*)

A.E.Sa.   A. Edward Safarian. *Emeritus Professor of Economics; Professor of International Business, University of Toronto. Author of* Governments and Multinationals *and others.*
ECONOMIC GROWTH AND PLANNING (*in part*)

A.E.Sc.   Alfred Eric Scott. *Former Editor in Chief, Editorial and Publications Section, Commonwealth Scientific and Industrial Research Organization. Melbourne.*
AUSTRALIA (*in part*)

A.E.Si.   Akiba Ernst Simon. *Emeritus Professor of Education, Hebrew University of Jersualem. Author of* Martin Bubers lebendiges Erbe.
BUBER, MARTIN (Micropædia)

A.E.Sm.   Arthur Eltringham Smailes (d. 1984). *Professor of Geography, Queen Mary College, University of London, 1955–73.*
EUROPE (*in part*)

A.E.Ta.   Alfred Edward Taylor (d. 1945). *Professor of Moral Philosophy, University of Edinburgh, 1924–41. Author of* Plato; Socrates; *and others.*
PHILOSOPHICAL SCHOOLS AND DOCTRINES, WESTERN (*in part*)
SOCRATES

A.E.W.   Albert E. Wood. *Emeritus Professor of Biology, Amherst College, Massachusetts.*
MAMMALS (*in part*)

A.F.   Anne Foner. *Professor of Sociology, Rutgers University, New Brunswick, New Jersey. Author of* Aging and Old Age: New Perspectives.
SOCIAL DIFFERENTIATION (*in part*)

A.F.A.M.   Alice F.A. Mutton (d. 1979). *Reader in Geography, Queen Mary College, University of London. Author of* Central Europe; Western Europe.
ATLANTIC OCEAN, THE (*in part*)
EUROPE (*in part*)

A.F.B.   The Hon. Alastair Francis Buchan (d. 1976). *Montague Burton Professor of International Relations, University of Oxford, 1972–76. Founder and Director, International Institute for Strategic Studies, London, 1958–69. Author of* The Spare Chancellor: The Life of Walter Bagehot.
BAGEHOT, WALTER (Micropædia)

A.Fe.   Albert Feuerwerker. *Professor of History, University of Michigan, Ann Arbor. Author of* China's Early Industrialization.
CHINA (*in part*)

A.F.H.   Alfred F. Havighurst (d. 1991). *Professor of History, Amherst College, Massachusetts, 1954–70. Author of* Twentieth Century Britain *and others.*
UNITED KINGDOM (*in part*)

A.Fi.   Andrew Field. *Professor of Comparative Literature, Griffith University, Brisbane, Australia. Author of* Nabokov: His Life in Art; Nabokov: His Life in Part.
NABOKOV, VLADIMIR (Micropædia)

A.F.L.B.   Alfred Felix L. Beeston. *Emeritus Professor of Arabic, University of Oxford. Author of* Sabaic Grammar.
ARABIA (*in part*)

A.Fr.   Lady Antonia Fraser. *Writer. Author of* Mary, Queen of Scots.
MARY (SCOTLAND) (Micropædia)

A.F.R.   Anne F. Rockwell. *Free-lance writer and illustrator. Author of* Glass, Stones and Crown: The Abbé Suger and the Building of St. Denis *and others.*
SUGER (Micropædia)

A.F.Sh.   Arthur Frank Shore. *Brunner Professor of Egyptology, University of Liverpool, England. Author of* Portrait Painting from Roman Egypt.
PAINTING, THE HISTORY OF WESTERN (*in part*)
SCULPTURE, THE HISTORY OF WESTERN (*in part*)

A.F.St.   Adolf F. Sturmthal (d. 1986). *Professor of Labor and Industrial Relations, University of Illinois, Urbana, Author of* Left of Center: European Labor since World War II *and others.*
WORK AND EMPLOYMENT (*in part*)

A.Fu.   André Fu-Kiau kia Bunseki-L. *Director, Centre of Development and Scientific Research in African Languages, Kumba, Zaire.*
CENTRAL AFRICA (*in part*)

A.F.W.   Arthur F. Wright (d. 1976). *Charles Seymour Professor of History, Yale University, 1961–76. Author of* "The Formation of Sui Ideology" in Chinese Thought and Institutions.
WEN TI (SUI DYNASTY) (Micropædia)

A.F.We.   Arthur Frederick Wells (d. 1966). *Praelector in Classics, University College, University of Oxford.*
LUCRETIUS (Micropædia)

A.G.   Allen Guttmann. *Professor of English and American Studies, Amherst College, Massachusetts. Author of* From Ritual to Record; A Whole New Ball Game; *and others.*
SPORTS, MAJOR TEAM AND INDIVIDUAL (*in part*)

A.G.B.   Agadjan G. Babaev. *President, Turkmen S.S.R. Academy of Sciences, Ashkhabad. Editor of* Shifting Sands in the Deserts of the U.S.S.R.
ASIA (*in part*)

A.G.B.H.   Åke Gunnar Birger Hultkrantz. *Emeritus Professor of Comparative Religion, University of Stockholm. Author of* The Study of American Indian Religions *and others.*
AMERICAN INDIANS (*in part*)

A.Ge.   Arthur Gelb. *Executive Vice President, New York Times Company Foundation; Managing Editor,* The New York Times, *1986–89. Coauthor of* O'Neill.
O'NEILL, EUGENE (*in part*) (Micropædia)

A.G.G.   Alfred G. Gerteiny. *Professor of Middle-Eastern and African Studies, University of Bridgeport, Connecticut. Author of* Mauritania *and others.*
WESTERN AFRICA (*in part*)

A.G.H.   A. Gordon Hammer. *Emeritus Professor of Psychology, Macquarie University, North Ryde, Australia. Author of* Elementary Matrix Algebra for Psychologists and Social Scientists.
HYPNOSIS (*in part*) (Micropædia)

A.G.Ha.   The Rev. Adalbert G. Hamman. *Professor at Patristic Institute, Rome. Editor,* Patrologiae Latinae Supplementum. *Author of* La Prière.
RITES AND CEREMONIES, SACRED
   (*in part*)

A.Gi.   Alexander Gillies (d. 1977). *Professor of German Language and Literature, University of Leeds, England, 1945–72. Author of* Goethe's Faust: An Interpretation *and many other books on German writers and literature.*
GERMAN LITERATURE (*in part*)

A.G.J.   Adriaan G. Jongkees. *Former Professor of Medieval History, State University of Groningen, The Netherlands. Author of* Het koninkrijk Friesland in de vijftiende eeuw.
WILLIAM I (NETHERLANDS STADHOLDER)
   (*in part*) (Micropædia)

A.G.L.   Andrew George Lehmann. *Emeritus Professor, School of European Studies, University of Buckingham, England. Author of* Sainte-Beuve: A Portrait of the Critic *and others.*
SAINTE-BEUVE, CHARLES-AUGUSTIN
   (Micropædia)

A.G.Ly.   A. Gordon Lyne (deceased). *Senior Principal Research Scientist, Division of Wildlife Research, Commonwealth Scientific and Industrial Research Organization, Blacktown, Australia. Author of* Marsupials and Monotremes of Australia.
MAMMALS (*in part*)

Ag.M.   Agnes Mongan. *Emeritus Curator of Drawings, Fogg Art Museum, Harvard University. Coauthor of* Ingres Centennial Exhibition, 1867–1967; Drawings in the Fogg Museum.
INGRES, JEAN-AUGUSTE-DOMINIQUE
   (Micropædia)

A.G.M.   Alan Gibbs Massey. *Reader in Inorganic Chemistry, Loughborough University of Technology, England. Coauthor of* Inorganic Chemistry in Non-aqueous Solvents.
CHEMICAL ELEMENTS (*in part*)

A.G.Ma.   Alla Genrikhovna Massevitch. *Vice President, Astronomical Council, Academy of Sciences of the U.S.S.R., Moscow. Author of* Life of the Sun.
AMBARTSUMIAN, VIKTOR
   AMAZASPOVICH (Micropædia)

A.G.M.v.M.   Andrew G.M. van Melsen. *Emeritus Professor of Philosophy, Catholic University of Nijmegen, The Netherlands. Author of* From Atomos to Atom *and others.*
PHILOSOPHICAL SCHOOLS AND
   DOCTRINES, WESTERN (*in part*)

A.Gn.   Alfonz Gspan (d. 1977). *Scientific Adviser, Slovene Academy of Sciences and Arts, Ljubljana. Editor,* Slovenski biografski leksikon. *Coauthor of* Incunabule v Sloveniji *and others.*
YUGOSLAV LITERATURE (*in part*)

A.G.N.F.   Antony Garrard Newton Flew. *Emeritus Professor of Philosophy, University of Reading, England. Author*

of God: A Critical Enquiry; God, Freedom and Immortality.
RELIGIOUS AND SPIRITUAL BELIEF,
   SYSTEMS OF (*in part*)

A.Go.   Adam Gopnik. *Editor and staff writer,* The New Yorker.
UNITED STATES OF AMERICA (*in part*)

A.G.P.   Alexis G. Pincus. *Former Visiting Professor of Ceramics, Rutgers University, New Brunswick, New Jersey. Coauthor of* Utilization of Ceramics in Microelectronics; *compiler of* Processing in the Glass Industry (15 vol.).
INDUSTRIAL GLASS AND CERAMICS
   (*in part*)

A.G.W.   A. Geoffrey Woodhead. *Fellow of Corpus Christi College, Cambridge; Emeritus Lecturer in Classics, University of Cambridge. Adjunct Professor of Classics, Ohio State University, Columbus. Author of* The Greeks in the West *and others.*
HISTORY, THE STUDY OF (*in part*)

A.G. y B.   Antonio García y Bellido (d. 1972). *Professor of Archaeology, University of Madrid, Spain. Director, Spanish Institute of Archaeology. Member, Royal Academy of History. Author of* Las Colonizaciones Púnica y Griega en la península ibérica.
SPAIN (*in part*)

A.H.A.   A. Hilary Armstrong. *Gladstone Professor Emeritus of Greek, University of Liverpool. Editor of* The Cambridge History of Later Greek and Early Mediaeval Philosophy; *translator of* Plotinus.
PLATONISM, PLATO AND (*in part*)
PLOTINUS (Micropædia)

A.H.Ao.   The Rev. Anselm H. Amadio. *Chaplain; Instructor in Philosophy, Illinois Institute of Technology, Chicago. Staff Writer, Philosophy and Religion, Encyclopædia Britannica, Chicago, 1970–73.*
ARISTOTELIANISM, ARISTOTLE AND
   (*in part*)
PALAMAS, SAINT GREGORY
   (Micropædia)

A.H.C.   Alan H. Cook. *Master of Selwyn College, Cambridge; Jacksonian Professor of Natural Philosophy, University of Cambridge. Author of* The Interiors of the Planets *and others.*
GRAVITATION (*in part*)

A.H.Ca.   Arthur H. Cash. *Distinguished Professor of English, State University of New York College at New Paltz. Author of* Laurence Sterne: The Early and Middle Years *and others.*
STERNE, LAURENCE (Micropædia)

A.H.D.   Andrew Hutchinson Dawson. *Senior Lecturer in Geography and Modern Russian Studies, University of St. Andrews, Scotland. Author of many papers on the geography of Poland.*
POLAND (*in part*)
WARSAW (*in part*)

A.H.De.   Armand H. Delsemme. *Distinguished University Professor Emeritus of Astrophysics, University of Toledo, Ohio. Interdisciplinary Scientist,*

Comet Rendezvous and Asteroid Flyby Mission, National Aeronautics and Space Administration. *Editor of* Comets, Asteroids, Meteorites.
SOLAR SYSTEM, THE (*in part*)

A.H.E.   Archie H. Easton (d. 1988). *Professor of Mechanical and Civil Engineering, University of Wisconsin, Madison, 1953–77.*
TRANSPORTATION (*in part*)

A.H.F.   Rabbi Albert H. Friedlander. *Dean of Rabbinic Studies, Leo Baeck College, London. Minister, Westminster Synagogue, London. Author of* Leo Baeck: Teacher of Theresienstadt.
BAECK, LEO (Micropædia)

A.H.Ho.   Albert Habib Hourani. *Former Reader in the Modern History of the Middle East, University of Oxford. Author of* Arabic Thought in the Liberal Age, 1798–1939.
SYRIA (*in part*)

A.H.McD.   Alexander Hugh McDonald (d. 1979). *Lecturer in Ancient History, University of Cambridge, 1952–73. Author of* Republican Rome.
TACITUS (*in part*) (Micropædia)

A.H.M.J.   Arnold Hugh Martin Jones (d. 1970). *Professor of Ancient History, University of Cambridge, 1951–70.*
PALESTINE (*in part*)

A.H.M.K.-G.   Anthony Hamilton Millard Kirk-Greene. *Lecturer in the Modern History of Africa, University of Oxford; Fellow of St. Antony's College, Oxford. Author of* Crisis and Conflict in Nigeria, 1966–1967 *and others.*
WESTERN AFRICA (*in part*)

A.H.P.   Arnold H. Price. *Bibliographer, American Historical Association, Washington, D.C. Former Area Specialist for Central Europe, Library of Congress, Washington, D.C.*
CLAUSEWITZ, CARL VON (Micropædia)

A.H.S.   Anna Hester Smith. *Former Head Librarian, Johannesburg Public Library. Former Director, Africana Museum, Johannesburg.*
JOHANNESBURG

A.H.Sa.   A.H. Saxon. *Free-lance writer. Author of* The Life and Art of Andrew Ducrow and the Romantic Age of the English Circus; P.T. Barnum: The Legend and the Man.
CIRCUS (*in part*)

A.H.St.   Alan Howard Stratford. *Chairman, Alan Stratford and Associates (air transport consultants), Lymington, England. Author of* Air Transport Economics in the Supersonic Era *and others.*
TRANSPORTATION (*in part*)

A.I.I.   Aleksandr Ilyich Imshenetsky. *Senior Research Associate, Scientific Council on the Location of U.S.S.R. Productive Forces, Academy of Sciences of the U.S.S.R., Moscow.*
UNION OF SOVIET SOCIALIST REPUBLICS
   (*in part*)

A.I.M.   Albert I. Mendeloff, M.D. *Emeritus Physician in Chief, Sinai*

Hospital, Baltimore. *Professor of Medicine, Johns Hopkins University, Baltimore. Coauthor of* Digestive Diseases.
DIGESTION AND DIGESTIVE SYSTEMS (*in part*)

Ai.S.   Aidan William Southall. *Emeritus Professor of Anthropology, University of Wisconsin, Madison. Editor of* Social Change in Modern Africa; *coeditor of* Madagascar: Society and History.
MADAGASCAR (*in part*)

A.J.A.   A. John Arnfield. *Associate Professor of Geography, Ohio State University, Columbus.*
CLIMATE AND WEATHER (*in part*)

A.J.B.   Alan John Barnard. *Lecturer in Social Anthropology, University of Edinburgh. Coauthor of* Research Practices in the Study of Kinship.
FAMILY AND KINSHIP

A.J.C.   Arthur J. Conacher. *Associate Professor of Geography, University of Western Australia, Nedlands. Coauthor of* The Nine Unit Landsurface Model: An Approach to Pedogeomorphic Research; *editor of* Readings in Australian Geography.
AUSTRALIA (*in part*)

A.J.Ca.   A.J. Cain. *Former Derby Professor of Zoology, University of Liverpool. Editor of* Function and Taxonomic Importance.
BIOLOGICAL SCIENCES, THE (*in part*)

A.J.E.   Armand J. Eardley (d. 1972). *Professor of Geology, University of Utah, Salt Lake City, 1965–70; Dean, College of Mines and Mineral Industries, 1954–65. Author of* Structural Geology of North America.
NORTH AMERICA (*in part*)

A.J.H.   Arlen J. Hansen. *Professor of English, University of the Pacific, Stockton, California.*
LITERATURE, THE ART OF (*in part*)

A.J.I.   Aaron J. Ihde. *Emeritus Professor of Chemistry and History of Science, University of Wisconsin, Madison. Author of* The Development of Modern Chemistry.
PAULING, LINUS (Micropædia)

A.J.K.   Anthony John Kirby. *Reader in Chemistry, University of Cambridge. Coauthor of* Organic Chemistry of Phosphorus.
CHEMICAL COMPOUNDS (*in part*)

A.J.P.   Anthony J. Podlecki. *Professor of Classics, University of British Columbia, Vancouver. Author of* The Political Background of Aeschylean Tragedy *and others.*
GREEK DRAMATISTS, THE CLASSICAL (*in part*)

A.J.Sc.   Alvin J. Schumacher. *Author of* Thunder on Capitol Hill: The Life of Chief Justice Roger B. Taney.
TANEY, ROGER BROOKE (Micropædia)

A.J.So.   Alan James Southward. *Zoologist and Senior Leverhulme Fellow, Marine Biological Association of the*

United Kingdom, Plymouth. *Author of* Life on the Sea-Shore.
BIOSPHERE, THE (*in part*)

A.J.T.   Arnold Joseph Toynbee (d. 1975). *Director of Studies, Royal Institute of International Affairs, London, 1925–55. Research Professor of International History, University of London, 1925–55. Author of* A Study of History *and many others.*
CAESAR (*in part*)
TIME (*in part*)

A.J.V.   Alan John Villiers (d. 1982). *Free-lance writer. President, Society for Nautical Research, London. Author of* Captain James Cook; The Way of a Ship; *and many others.*
COOK, JAMES (Micropædia)

A.K.   Alfred Kröner. *Professor of Geology, Johannes Gutenberg University of Mainz, Germany. Editor of* Precambrian Plate Tectonics.
AFRICA (*in part*)

A.Ka.   Adrienne L. Kaeppler. *Curator of Oceanic Ethnology, National Museum of Natural History, Smithsonian Institution, Washington, D.C. Coauthor of* Hula Dahu.
OCEANIC ARTS (*in part*)

A.K.B.   Alan K. Bowman. *Lecturer in Ancient History, University of Oxford; Student and Tutor, Christ Church, Oxford. Author of* Egypt After the Pharaohs.
EGYPT (*in part*)

A.K.C.   The Rt. Rev. Albert Kenneth Cragg. *Assistant Bishop, Diocese of Oxford. Reader in Religious Studies, University of Sussex, Brighton, England, 1973–78. Author of* Counsels in Contemporary Islam *and others.*
ISLĀM, MUḤAMMAD AND THE RELIGION OF (*in part*)

A.K.Ca.   Alan K. Campbell. *Vice Chairman of the Board and Executive Vice President, Management and Public Affairs, ARA Services, Inc., Philadelphia. Dean, Maxwell Graduate School of Citizenship and Public Affairs, Syracuse University, New York, 1969–76. Author of* The States and the Urban Crisis.
UNITED STATES OF AMERICA (*in part*)

A.K.Ch.   Abdel Kader Chanderli. *Senior Adviser, the Arab Fund, Kuwait. President and General Manager, C.A.M.E.L. Petroleum Company, Algiers, 1969–75. Ambassador of Algeria to the United Nations, 1962.*
NORTH AFRICA (*in part*)

A.Ke.   Annajane Kennard. *Former Librarian, Straits Times Press, Malaysia.*
SOUTHEAST ASIA, MAINLAND (*in part*)

A.K.H.   A. Kent Hieatt. *Professor of English, University of Western Ontario, London. Author of* Chaucer, Spenser, Milton: Mythopoeic Continuities and Transformations; *coeditor of* Spenser's Selected Poetry.
SPENSER, EDMUND (*in part*) (Micropædia)

A.K.McC.   Arthur Kilgore McComb (deceased). *Author of* The Baroque Painters of Italy *and others.*
SCULPTURE, THE HISTORY OF WESTERN (*in part*)

A.Kn.   Arthur Knight. *Professor of Cinema, University of Southern California, Los Angeles. Film Critic,* The Hollywood Reporter. *Author of* The Liveliest Art; The Hollywood Style.
CHAPLIN, CHARLIE (Micropædia)

A.Ko.   Arthur Koestler (d. 1983). *Author of* The Act of Creation; Darkness at Noon; *and many others.*
HUMOUR AND WIT

A.K.P.   A. Keith Pierce. *Astronomer, Solar Division, Kitt Peak National Observatory, Tucson, Arizona.*
SOLAR SYSTEM, THE (*in part*)

A.K.Pa.   Andrew K. Pawley. *Professor of Linguistics, Research School of Pacific Studies, Australian National University, Canberra. Author of articles on the languages of Oceania.*
LANGUAGES OF THE WORLD (*in part*)

A.K.R.   A.K. Ramanujan. *William E. Colvin Professor, Departments of South Asian Languages and Civilizations and of Linguistics and Committee on Social Thought, University of Chicago. Author of* Speaking of Śiva *and others.*
SOUTH ASIAN ARTS (*in part*)

A.K.S.   Arthur K. Solomon. *Emeritus Professor of Biophysics, Medical School, Harvard University. Author of numerous scientific papers and of* Why Smash Atoms?
BIOLOGICAL SCIENCES, THE (*in part*)

A.K.Se.   Anna K. Seidel. *Member, French School of the Far East, Kyōto. Author of* La divinisation de Lao tseu dans le taoisme des Han.
TAOISM (*in part*)

Ak.W.   Akira Watanabe (deceased). *Chairman, Department of Geography, Ochanomizu Women's University, Tokyo. Editor of* Gazetteer of Japan.
JAPAN (*in part*)

A.Ky.   Ado Kyrou. *Writer and motion-picture and television director. Author of* Le Surréealisme au cinéma; Luis Buñuel; *and others.*
BUÑUEL, LUIS (*in part*) (Micropædia)

A.L.   Alberto Lecco. *Novelist, poet, essayist, and reviewer. Author of* Anteguerra *and others.*
MILAN

A.La.   Abdallah Laroui. *Professor of History, Mohammed V University, Rabat, Morocco. Author of* History of the Maghrib *and others.*
NORTH AFRICA (*in part*)

A.L. al-S.M.   Afaf Lutfi al-Sayyid Marsot. *Professor of History, University of California, Los Angeles. Author of* Egypt and Cromer.
CROMER, EVELYN BARING, 1ST EARL OF (Micropædia)

Al.B.   Alfredo Bosisio. *Former Professor of Medieval History, University* *of Pavia, Italy. Author of* Storia di Milano.

SFORZA, LUDOVICO (Micropædia)

A.L.B.   Arthur Llewellyn Basham (d. 1986). *Professor of Asian Civilizations, Australian National University, Canberra. Author of* History and Doctrines of the Ājīvikas *and others.*

HINDUISM (*in part*)

Al.Be.   Alfons Becker. *Professor of Medieval History, Johannes Gutenberg University of Mainz, Germany. Author of* Papst Urban II (1088–1099) *and others.*

URBAN II (Micropædia)

Al.Bo.   Sir Alan Bowness. *Director, Henry Moore Foundation, London. Director, Tate Gallery, London, 1980–88. Author of* Modern European Art; Recent British Painting.

COROT, CAMILLE (Micropædia)
MOORE, HENRY (*in part*) (Micropædia)

Al.C.   Alphonse Chapanis. *Human factors consultant. Professor of Psychology, Johns Hopkins University, Baltimore, 1963–83. Author of* Research Techniques in Human Engineering.

INDUSTRIAL ENGINEERING AND
   PRODUCTION MANAGEMENT (*in part*)

A.Le.   Aureliano Leite (d. 1976). *President of the São Paulo Historical and Geographical Institute. Member of the São Paulo Academy of Letters. Member of the Brazilian Historical and Geographical Institute. Author of* História da Civilização Paulista.

SÃO PAULO (*in part*)

Al.G.   Albert Goodwin. *Emeritus Professor of Modern History, Victoria University of Manchester. Author of* The French Revolution *and others.*

LOUIS XVI (FRANCE) (Micropædia)
NECKER, JACQUES (Micropædia)

A.L.G.   Arnold L. Gordon. *Professor of Oceanography, Columbia University. Editor of* Studies in Physical Oceanography (*2 vol.*).

OCEANS (*in part*)

Al.Go.   Alan Gowans. *Director, National Images of North American Living, Washington, D.C. Emeritus Professor of History in Art, University of Victoria, British Columbia. Author of* Images of American Living; The Comfortable House: North American Suburban Architecture, 1890–1930.

ARCHITECTURE, THE ART OF (*in part*)

Al.Gr.   Alan Gregg, M.D. (d. 1957). *Vice President, Rockefeller Foundation, 1951–56; Director of Medical Sciences, 1930–51.*

MEDICINE (*in part*)

A.L.-Ho.   Alexander Marie Norbert Lernet-Holenia (d. 1976). *Novelist and playwright. Author of* Prinz Eugen *and others.*

EUGENE OF SAVOY (Micropædia)

A.Li.   Assar Lindbeck. *Professor of International Economics; Director, Institute for International Economic Studies, University of Stockholm. Author of* A Study in Monetary Analysis

and others.

GOVERNMENT FINANCE (*in part*)

A.Lip.   Adolf Lippold. *Professor of History, University of Regensburg, Germany. Author of* Theodosius der Grosse und seine Zeit *and others.*

THEODOSIUS I (ROMAN AND BYZANTINE
   EMPIRE) (Micropædia)

A.L.M.   Akinlawon Ladipo Mabogunje. *Senior Partner, PAI Associates International (Nigeria) Ltd. Former Pro-Chancellor, Ogun State University, Ago-Iwoye, Nigeria. President, International Geographical Union, 1980–84. Author of* Urbanization in Nigeria.

AFRICA (*in part*)

Al.N.   Allan Nevins (d. 1971). *Historian. Senior Research Associate, Henry E. Huntington Library and Art Gallery, San Marino, California, 1958–69. Dewitt Clinton Professor of History, Columbia University, 1931–58. Author of* The American States During and After the Revolution; The Emergence of Modern America; *and many biographies.*

WASHINGTON, GEORGE (*in part*)

A.Lo.   Alan Logan. *Professor of Geology, University of New Brunswick, Saint John. Coeditor of* The Permian and Triassic Systems and Their Mutual Boundary.

GEOCHRONOLOGY (*in part*)

A.L.P.   Adolph L. Ponikvar. *Metallurgical consultant. Coauthor of* Cooperative Research and Development *and others.*

INDUSTRIES, EXTRACTION AND
   PROCESSING (*in part*)

Al.R.   Alfredo Riva. *Assistant Professor of Industrial Chemistry, University of Bologna, Italy.*

MALPIGHI, MARCELLO (*in part*)
   (Micropædia)

A.L.R.   Alexander L. Ringer. *Professor of Musicology, University of Illinois, Urbana. Author of* The Hunt as a Musical Topic: A Brief History of the Chasse.

MUSIC, THE ART OF (*in part*)

A.L.Ra.   Arthur Lionel Rawlings (d. 1959). *Chief Research Engineer, Bulova Research and Development Laboratories, Woodside, New York.*

NAVIGATION (*in part*)

Al.Re.   Albert Resis. *Associate Professor of History, Northern Illinois University, DeKalb. Author of articles on Russian and Soviet history.*

LENIN

Al.S.   Albert M. Soboul (d. 1982). *Professor of the History of the French Revolution, University of Paris I. Author of* Précis d'histoire de la révolution française *and others.*

CARNOT, LAZARE (Micropædia)
DANTON, GEORGES (Micropædia)

A.L.S.   A.L. Srivastava (deceased). *Professor of History, Āgra College, Āgra University, India. Author of* The Mughal Empire *and others.*

INDIA (*in part*)

A.L.T.   Sir A. Landsborough Thomson (d. 1977). *President, British Ornithologists' Union, 1948–55. President, Zoological Society of London, 1954–60. Chairman of Trustees, British Museum (Natural History), London, 1967–69. Author of* Problems of Bird Migration.

BIRDS (*in part*)

A.L.W.   A.L. Waddams. *Manager, Market Research and Information Division, BP Chemicals (UK) Ltd., London. Author of* Chemicals from Petroleum *and others.*

INDUSTRIES, EXTRACTION AND
   PROCESSING (*in part*)

A.M.   Abdou Moumouni. *Director, Office of Solar Energy, Niamey, Niger. Author of* L'Education en Afrique.

EDUCATION, HISTORY OF (*in part*)

A.Ma.   Andrew Henry Robert Martindale. *Professor of Visual Arts, University of East Anglia, Norwich, England. Author of* Gothic Art *and others.*

ARCHITECTURE, THE HISTORY OF
   WESTERN (*in part*)
PAINTING, THE HISTORY OF WESTERN
   (*in part*)
SCULPTURE, THE HISTORY OF WESTERN
   (*in part*)

A.M.B.   Alfred M. Beeton. *Director, Great Lakes Environmental Research Laboratory, National Oceanic and Atmospheric Administration, Ann Arbor, Michigan. Adjunct Professor of Natural Resources and Atmospheric and Oceanic Science, University of Michigan, Ann Arbor. Author of numerous scientific articles on the Great Lakes.*

NORTH AMERICA (*in part*)

A.M.-C.   Arturo Morales-Carrión (d. 1989). *Executive Director, Puerto Rican Endowment for the Humanities, San Juan, 1977–89. Author of* Puerto Rico: A Political and Cultural History *and others.*

WEST INDIES, THE (*in part*)

A.M.C.L.   Agnes M.C. Latham. *Former Reader in English, Bedford College, University of London. Editor of* The Poems of Sir Walter Ralegh *and others.*

RALEIGH, SIR WALTER (Micropædia)

A.M.C.Ş.   A.M. Celâl Şengör. *Associate Professor of Geology, Technical University of Istanbul. Author of* The Cimmeride Orogenic System and the Tectonics of Eurasia.

ASIA (*in part*)

A.M.Ga.   Aleksandr Mikhaylovich Gavrilov. *Senior Scientist, Leningrad Hydrological Institute.*

EUROPE (*in part*)

A.M.G.-G.   Angel M. García-Gómez. *Head, Department of Spanish and Latin-American Studies, University College, University of London. Author of* The Legend of the Laughing Philosopher and Its Presence in Spanish Literature, 1500–1700 *and others.*

SPANISH LITERATURE (*in part*)

A.Mi.   Arthur Mizener (d. 1988). *Mellon Foundation Professor of Humanities, Cornell University, Ithaca, New York. Author of* The Far Side of Paradise: A Biography of F. Scott Fitzgerald *and others.*
FITZGERALD, F. SCOTT (Micropædia)

A.M.K.   Albert M. Kudo. *Professor of Geology, University of New Mexico, Albuquerque.*
MINERALS AND ROCKS (*in part*)

A.M.N.   Alois M. Nagler. *Henry McCormick Professor Emeritus of Dramatic History and Criticism, Yale University. Author of* Sources of Theatrical History *and others.*
BERNHARDT, SARAH (Micropædia)
DUSE, ELEONORA (Micropædia)

A.Mo.   Alberto Monroy, M.D. (d. 1986). *Director, Zoological Station, Naples. Author of* Chemistry and Physiology of Fertilization.
REPRODUCTION AND REPRODUCTIVE SYSTEMS (*in part*)

A.Moz.   Asokendu Mozumder. *Faculty Fellow, Radiation Laboratory and Department of Chemistry, University of Notre Dame, Indiana. Coauthor of* Advances in Radiation Chemistry.
RADIATION (*in part*)

A.M.P.   Andrew M. Pullen. *Computer graphics researcher. Coauthor of* Creative Computer Graphics.
COMPUTERS (*in part*)

A.M.Q.   Anthony M. Quinton, Baron Quinton. *Chairman, British Library Board, 1985–90. President, Trinity College, Oxford, 1978–87; Lecturer in Philosophy, University of Oxford, 1950–78. Author of* The Nature of Things *and others.*
BACON, FRANCIS (*in part*)
PHILOSOPHICAL SCHOOLS AND DOCTRINES, WESTERN (*in part*)

A.M.R.   Aleksandr Maximovich Ryabchikov. *Professor of Geography; Head, Laboratory of Natural Resources, Moscow M.V. Lomonosov State University. Author of* The Changing Face of the Earth.
ASIA (*in part*)

A.M.W.   A.M. Winchester. *Emeritus Professor of Biology, University of Northern Colorado, Greeley. Author of* Genetics *and others.*
BIOLOGICAL SCIENCES, THE (*in part*)
GENETICS AND HEREDITY, THE PRINCIPLES OF (*in part*)

A.N.   Alvin Novick. *Professor of Biology, Yale University. Researcher on the biology of bats. Coauthor of* The World of Bats.
MAMMALS (*in part*)

A.Na.   Arata Naka. *Former Professor of Japanese History of Education, University of Tokyo. Author of* The Formation of the Modern Textbook System.
EDUCATION, HISTORY OF (*in part*)

A.N.A.   Antony Nicolas Allott. *Professor of African and Comparative Law, University of Buckingham, England. Emeritus Professor of African Law, School of Oriental and African Studies, University of London. Author of* New Essays in African Law *and others.*
CRIME AND PUNISHMENT (*in part*)

An.A.A.   Anwar Abdel Aleem. *Professor of Biological Oceanography; Chairman, Department of Oceanography, University of Alexandria, Egypt.*
INDIAN OCEAN, THE (*in part*)

An.B.   Anthony Burgess. *Novelist and critic. Author of* A Clockwork Orange; The Novel Now; Urgent Copy.
LITERATURE, THE ART OF (*in part*)

An.C.B.   Andrew C. Brix. *Second Secretary, International Bureau of the Universal Postal Union, Berne, Switzerland.*
POSTAL SYSTEMS (*in part*)

A.Ne.   Andries Nel. *Professor of Geography, University of Stellenbosch, South Africa. Author of* Stad en dorp; Die warm Reënstreke.
SOUTH AFRICA (*in part*)

A.N.J.   Alexander Norman Jeffares. *Emeritus Professor of English, University of Stirling, Scotland. Author of* W.B. Yeats: A New Biography *and others; editor of* Selected Poems and Prose: Whitman.
WHITMAN, WALT (Micropædia)

A.N.K.   Aleksey Nilovich Kosarev. *Professor of Oceanology, Moscow M.V. Lomonosov State University. Author of* Hydrology of the Caspian and Aral Seas.
ASIA (*in part*)

An.L.   Antonino Lombardo (d. 1985). *Inspector General of National Archives, Rome. Professor of the Study of Archives, University of Rome. Coauthor of* Documenti del commercio veneziano nei secoli XI–XIII.
DANDOLO, ENRICO (Micropædia)

A.N.L.W.   Arthur N.L. Wina. *Member of Parliament, 1962–68 and 1973– ; Minister of Finance, 1963–67; Minister of Education, 1967–68, Government of Zambia (formerly Northern Rhodesia).*
AFRICA (*in part*)

A.No.   Alexander Nove. *Emeritus Professor of Economics, University of Glasgow, Scotland. Author of* An Economic History of the U.S.S.R.
ECONOMIC GROWTH AND PLANNING (*in part*)

An.Pa.   Angel Palerm (d. 1980). *Director, Institute of Social Sciences, Universidad Iberoamericana, Mexico City.*
MEXICO (*in part*)

A.N.R.N.   Alastair N.R. Niven. *Fellow, Institute of Commonwealth Studies, University of London. Special Assistant to the Secretary-General, Association of Commonwealth Universities. Author of* D.H. Lawrence: The Novels; *editor of* The Commonwealth Writer Overseas.
AFRICAN ARTS (*in part*)

A.N.R.R.   Arthur Napoleon Raymond Robinson. *Prime Minister of Trinidad and Tobago. Author of* The Mechanics of Independence: Patterns of Political and Economic Transformation in Trinidad and Tobago.
WEST INDIES, THE (*in part*)

An.S.   Ailon Shiloh. *Professor and Director of Graduate Studies, Department of Anthropology, University of South Florida, Tampa. Editor of* Peoples and Cultures of the Middle East.
ASIAN PEOPLES AND CULTURES (*in part*)

An.Sc.   Annemarie Schimmel. *Professor of Indo-Muslim Culture, Harvard University. Author of* Gabriel's Wing; Islamic Calligraphy; Mystical Dimensions of Islam; *and others.*
ISLĀM, MUḤAMMAD AND THE RELIGION OF (*in part*)
ISLĀMIC ARTS (*in part*)
JALĀL AD-DIN AR-RŪMI (Micropædia)

An.Sh.   Ann Sheehy. *Former Research Associate, Central Asian Research Centre, London.*
UNION OF SOVIET SOCIALIST REPUBLICS (*in part*)

A.N.W.   Alfred North Whitehead (d. 1947). *Professor of Philosophy, Harvard University, 1924–36. Author of* Process and Reality *and many others.*
PHILOSOPHIES OF THE BRANCHES OF KNOWLEDGE (*in part*)

A.N.Y.   A.N. Yiannopoulos. *W.R. Irby Professor of Law, Tulane University, New Orleans. Author of* Civil Law Property *and others.*
TRANSPORTATION LAW (*in part*)

A.O.J.C.   A.O.J. Cockshut. *G.M. Young Lecturer in 19th-century English Literature, University of Oxford; Fellow of Hertford College, Oxford. Author of* The Achievement of Walter Scott; Anglican Attitudes: A Study of Victorian Religious Controversies; *and others.*
CARLYLE, THOMAS (Micropædia)

A.O.K.   Anne O. Krueger. *Arts and Sciences Professor of Economics, Duke University, Durham, North Carolina. Author of* Exchange Rate Determination.
ECONOMIC GROWTH AND PLANNING (*in part*)

A.Pa.   André Parrot (d. 1980). *Archaeologist. Director of the Louvre, Paris, 1968–72. Member of the Institute of France. Author of* Abraham and His Times *and others.*
ABRAHAM (Micropædia)

A.P.D.   Anatoly Petrovich Domanitsky. *Senior Scientist, Leningrad Hydrological Institute.*
EUROPE (*in part*)

A.P.F.   Alfred P. Fishman, M.D. *William Maul Measey Professor of Medicine; Director, Cardiovascular-Pulmonary Division, University of Pennsylvania, Philadelphia. Editor of* Handbook of Physiology, *sect. 3,* The Respiratory System *and others.*
RESPIRATION AND RESPIRATORY SYSTEMS (*in part*)

A.P.G.   Alberto Passos Guimarães. *Geography Editor,* Enciclopédia Mirador

Internacional, *Rio de Janeiro.*
RIO DE JANEIRO (*in part*)

A.P.L. Aleksandr Petrovich Lisitsin.
*Head, Laboratory of Physical Methods
of Research, Institute of Oceanology,
Academy of Sciences of the U.S.S.R.,
Moscow. Author of* Processes of Recent
Sedimentation in the Bering Sea;
Sedimentation in the World Ocean.
PACIFIC OCEAN, THE (*in part*)

A.P.M. Aleksandr Pavlovich Muranov.
*Senior Scientist, Leningrad Hydrological
Institute. Author of* Velichayshiye
reki mira.
ASIA (*in part*)

A.P.Ma. A.P. Martinich. *Professor
of Philosophy, University of Texas at
Austin. Author of* Philosophical Writing
and others.
EPISTEMOLOGY (*in part*)

A.R. Alan Ryalls. *Editor,* Camping and
Caravanning *magazine, Camping Club
of Great Britain and Ireland, 1956–75.
Author of* Modern Camping *and others.*
CAMPING (Micropædia)

Ar.B. Arnaldo Bruschi. *Professor of
the History of Architecture, University of
Rome. Author of* Bramante architetto.
BRAMANTE, DONATO (Micropædia)

A.R.B. A. Richard Baldwin. *Vice
President and Executive Director of
Research, Cargill, Inc., Minneapolis,
Minnesota, 1964–73. Former Editor,*
Journal of the American Oil Chemists'
Society.
FOOD PROCESSING (*in part*)

Ar.Br. Sir Arthur Bryant (d.
1985). *Author of* Samuel Pepys *and
many others.*
PEPYS, SAMUEL (Micropædia)

A.R.Bu. Andrew Robert Burn (d.
1991). *Visiting Professor, A College Year
in Athens, Inc., 1969–72. Reader in
Ancient History, University of Glasgow,
1965–69. Author of* Persia and the
Greeks *and others.*
THEMISTOCLES (Micropædia)

A.R.C. A. Robert Caponigri (d. 1983).
*Professor of Philosophy, University of
Notre Dame, Indiana. Author of* History
and Liberty: The Historical Writings of
Benedetto Croce.
CROCE, BENEDETTO (Micropædia)

Ar.D. Arthur J.M. Doucy. *Professor
of Social Economics; former Director,
Institute of Sociology, Free University of
Brussels. Author of* Traité d'économie
sociale.
BELGIUM (*in part*)

Ar.H. Rabbi Arthur Hertzberg.
*Professor of Religion, Dartmouth
College, Hanover, New Hampshire.
Author of* The Jews in America *and
others; editor of* The Zionist Idea.
JUDAISM (*in part*)

A.-R.H. Abdul-Rahman Hamidé.
*Professor of Geography, Damascus
University. Author of* La Région d'Alep
and others.
SYRIA (*in part*)

Ar.Hü. Arthur Hübscher. *Former
Director, Schopenhauer Archives,
Frankfurt. Senior President,
International Schopenhauer Society,
Frankfurt. Author of many books on
Schopenhauer and editor of his works.*
SCHOPENHAUER, ARTHUR (*in part*)
(Micropædia)

A.Ri. Alan Rich. *Music Critic,* Los
Angeles Herald Examiner. *Author of*
Music: Mirror of the Arts *and others.*
MUSIC, THE ART OF (*in part*)

A.R.K. Alan Roy Katritzky. *Chemical
consultant. Kenan Professor of Organic
Chemistry, University of Florida,
Gainesville. Author of* Handbook of
Heterocyclic Chemistry.
CHEMICAL COMPOUNDS (*in part*)

A.R.Ki. Albert Roland Kiralfy.
*Emeritus Professor of Law, King's
College, University of London. Author of*
The English Legal System.
LEGAL SYSTEMS, THE EVOLUTION OF
MODERN WESTERN (*in part*)

Ar.Kn. Arthur Kelman. *Emeritus
Professor of Plant Pathology, University
of Wisconsin, Madison. Visiting
Professor of Plant Pathology, North
Carolina State University, Raleigh.
Editor of* Sourcebook of Exercises in
Plant Pathology.
DISEASE (*in part*)

Ar.L.S. Arthur L. Schawlow. *Professor
of Physics, Stanford University,
California. Cowinner, Nobel Prize for
Physics, 1981, for the development of
laser spectroscopy.*
MASER (*in part*) (Micropædia)

Ar.M. Arthur Mitzman. *Professor
of History, University of Amsterdam.
Author of* The Iron Cage: An Historical
Interpretation of Max Weber.
WEBER, MAX (*in part*) (Micropædia)

A.R.M. Alexander Reginald Myers (d.
1980). *Professor of Medieval History,
University of Liverpool, 1967–80. Author
of* The Household of Edward IV.
EDWARD IV (ENGLAND AND GREAT
BRITAIN) (Micropædia)
HENRY VII (ENGLAND) (*in part*)
(Micropædia)

A.Ro. Arnold Rood. *Emeritus Professor
of Dramatic Art, Dowling College,
Oakdale, New York. Author of* Edward
Gordon Craig, Artist of the Theatre,
1872–1966; *coauthor of* Edward Gordon
Craig: A Bibliography; *editor of* Gordon
Craig on Movement and Dance.
CRAIG, EDWARD GORDON
(Micropædia)

Ar.R. Arthur Robinson, M.D. *Professor
of Biochemistry, Biophysics, and
Genetics and of Pediatrics, University of
Colorado, Denver. Director, Cytogenetics
Laboratory, National Jewish Center for
Immunology and Aspiratory Medicine,
Denver.*
GENETICS AND HEREDITY, THE
PRINCIPLES OF (*in part*)

A.R.R. Allien R. Russon. *Emeritus
Professor of Management, College of
Business, University of Utah, Salt Lake
City. Author of* Methods of Teaching
Shorthand.
WRITING (*in part*)

A.R.S. Alarich R. Schultz. *Professor
of Botany, Federal University of Rio
Grande do Sul, Pôrto Alegre, Brazil.
Author of* Estudo Prático da Botânica
Geral.
SOUTH AMERICA (*in part*)

Ar.Sp. Arnold Spekke (d. 1972).
Author of History of Latvia *and others.*
BALTIC STATES (*in part*)

A.R.T. Archie Rule Turnbull. *Chief
Executive, Edinburgh University Press.
Editor of* The Making of Classical
Edinburgh.
EDINBURGH (*in part*)

A.R.W. Almon Robert Wright. *Senior
Historian, U.S. Department of State,
Washington, D.C., 1958–66. Coeditor
of* Foreign Relations: The American
Republics, 1941–48.
CENTRAL AMERICA (*in part*)

A.S. Alvin Seiff. *Senior Research
Associate, Department of Meteorology,
San Jose State University, California.
Author of scientific papers on the
atmospheres of Mars and Venus.*
SOLAR SYSTEM, THE (*in part*)

A.S.A. Ass'ad Sulaiman Abdo.
*Professor and Chairman, Department
of Geography, King Saud University,
Riyadh, Saudi Arabia. President, Saudi
Geographical Society. Author of* Land
and Air Transport in Saudi Arabia
and others.
MECCA AND MEDINA (*in part*)

As.B. Asa Briggs, Baron Briggs.
*Provost of Worcester College, University
of Oxford. Author of* The Age of
Improvement, 1783–1867 *and others.*
COBDEN, RICHARD (Micropædia)
UNITED KINGDOM (*in part*)

A.Sc. Aaron Scharf. *Professor of Art
History, Open University, Milton Keynes,
England, 1969–82. Author of* Art and
Photography; Pioneers of Photography.
CARTIER-BRESSON, HENRI (Micropædia)

A.S.Cu. Alan S. Curtis. *Professor
of Music, University of California,
Berkeley. Author of* Sweelinck's
Keyboard Music.
RAMEAU, JEAN-PHILIPPE (Micropædia)

A.S.D. A.S. Davidsohn (deceased).
Consulting chemist. Coauthor of Soap
Manufacture; Synthetic Detergents.
INDUSTRIES, CHEMICAL PROCESS (*in part*)

A.Se. Amulya Chandra Sen. *Former
Editor,* The Indo-Asian Culture. *Author
of* Asoka's Edicts *and others.*
AŚOKA (Micropædia)

As.F. Astrid Friis (d. 1966). *Professor
of History, University of Copenhagen.*
DENMARK (*in part*)

A.S.F. Angus Stewart Fletcher.
*Distinguished Professor of English and
Comparative Literature, City University
of New York. Author of* Allegory: The
Theory of a Symbolic Mode *and others.*
LITERATURE, THE ART OF (*in part*)

A.Sg. **Alfred Steinberg.** *Writer and historian. Author of* Man from Missouri: The Life and Times of Harry S. Truman.
TRUMAN, HARRY S. (Micropædia)

A.S.G. **Arthur S. Gelston, Jr.** *Former Assistant in History, University of California, Berkeley.*
BRAZIL (*in part*)

A.Sh. **Amnon Shiloah.** *Professor of Musicology, Hebrew University of Jerusalem. Author of* The Theory of Music in Arabic Writings *and others.*
ISLĀMIC ARTS (*in part*)

A.S.K. **Arvid S. Kapelrud.** *Professor of Old Testament, University of Oslo. Author of* Israel.
AARON (Micropædia)

A.S.L. **Arthur S. Link.** *George H. Davis '86 Professor of American History; Director of the Woodrow Wilson Papers, Princeton University. Author of* Wilson; *editor of* The Papers of Woodrow Wilson.
UNITED STATES OF AMERICA (*in part*)

A.S.M. **Arve Sverre Moen** (d. 1976). *Cultural Editor,* Arbeiderbladet *(newspaper), Oslo. Member of the Board, Edvard Munch Museum, Oslo. Author of* Edvard Munch *and others.*
MUNCH, EDVARD (Micropædia)

A.So. **Angelo Solmi.** *Film critic,* Oggi *(weekly literary periodical). Former Managing Editor, Rizzoli Editore, Milan. Author of* Storia di Federico Fellini *and others.*
FELLINI, FEDERICO (*in part*) (Micropædia)

A.S.R. **Alfred S. Romer** (d. 1973). *Alexander Agassiz Professor of Zoology, Harvard University, 1947–65.*
SIMPSON, GEORGE GAYLORD (Micropædia)

A.St. **Anthony Standen.** *Executive Editor,* Kirk-Othmer Encyclopedia of Chemical Technology, *New York City, 1963–70. Author of* Science Is a Sacred Cow.
INDUSTRIES, CHEMICAL PROCESS (*in part*)

A.S.T. **A. Stewart Truswell.** *Boden Professor of Human Nutrition, University of Sydney. Author of* ABC of Nutrition.
NUTRITION (*in part*)

A.Su. **Alexander Sutulov** (d. 1991). *President, Intermet Publications, Santiago, Chile. Author of* Molybdenum Extractive Metallurgy; Molybdenum and Rhenium; *editor of* International Molybdenum Encyclopaedia, 1778–1978 (3 vol.).
INDUSTRIES, EXTRACTION AND PROCESSING (*in part*)

A.Sw. **Alfred Swenson.** *Associate Professor of Architecture, Illinois Institute of Technology, Chicago. Partner, Alfred Swenson Pao-Chi Chang Architects, Chicago.*
BUILDING CONSTRUCTION (*in part*)

A.T. **Armen Takhtajan.** *Former Director and Chief, Department of Higher Plants, Komarov Botanical Institute, Academy of Sciences of the U.S.S.R., Leningrad. Author of* Flowering Plants: Origin and Dispersal.
ANGIOSPERMS (*in part*)

A.Ta. **Allen Tate** (d. 1979). *Poet and critic. Regents' Professor of English, University of Minnesota, Minneapolis, 1966–68. Editor of* T.S. Eliot: The Man and His Work, A Critical Evaluation by Twenty-six Distinguished Writers.
ELIOT, T.S. (Micropædia)

A.Te. **Ahmet Temir.** *Emeritus Professor of Turcology and Mongolian Language, University of Ankara.*
TURKEY AND ANCIENT ANATOLIA (*in part*)

A.T.G. **Alfred Thomas Grove.** *Fellow of Downing College, Cambridge; former Director, Centre of African Studies, University of Cambridge. Author of* Geography of Changing Africa *and others.*
WESTERN AFRICA (*in part*)

A.T.L. **Anthony Thornton Luttrell.** *Former Assistant Director, British School at Rome.*
ITALY (*in part*)

A.T.T. **Alan T. Thomas.** *Technical Consultant, Distilled Spirits Council of the United States. Former Technical Director, Brown-Forman Corporation, Louisville, Kentucky.*
BEVERAGE PRODUCTION (*in part*)

A.T.v.M. **Arthur Taylor von Mehren.** *Story Professor of Law, Harvard University. Author of* The Civil Law System.
BUSINESS LAW (*in part*)

A.U. **Arne Unhjem.** *Professor of Philosophy, Wagner College, Staten Island, New York. Author of* Dynamics of Doubt: A Preface to Tillich.
TILLICH, PAUL (Micropædia)

Au.L.R. **Austin L. Rand** (d. 1982). *Research Associate, Archbold Biological Station, Lake Placid, Florida. Chief Curator of Zoology, Field Museum of Natural History, Chicago, 1955–70. Author of* Ornithology: An Introduction; *coauthor of* Birds of New Guinea.
BIRDS (*in part*)

A.Va. **Amry Vandenbosch.** *Emeritus Professor of Political Science, University of Kentucky, Lexington. Coauthor of* The United Nations.
UNITED NATIONS (*in part*)

A.V.A. **Arkady Vladimirovich Alekseev.** *Chief Deputy Director, Pacific Oceanology Institute, Academy of Sciences of the U.S.S.R., Vladivostok.*
PACIFIC OCEAN, THE (*in part*)

A.v.B. **Andres R.F.T. von Brandt.** *Emeritus Professor of Fish Catching Techniques, University of Hamburg. Director, Institute for Fish Catching Techniques, Ministry for Food and Agriculture, Hamburg, 1936–71. Author of* Fish Catching Methods of the World.
FISHING, COMMERCIAL (*in part*)

A.V.D. **A. Vibert Douglas** (d. 1988). *Professor of Astronomy, Queen's University at Kingston, Ontario, 1943–63. Author of* Arthur Stanley Eddington.
EDDINGTON, SIR ARTHUR STANLEY (Micropædia)

A.Vo. **Arthur Voyce.** *Historian of Russian art and architecture. Author of* The Art and Architecture of Medieval Russia *and others.*
ARCHITECTURE, THE HISTORY OF WESTERN (*in part*)
PAINTING, THE HISTORY OF WESTERN (*in part*)
SCULPTURE, THE HISTORY OF WESTERN (*in part*)

Av.S. **Avrum Stroll.** *Professor of Philosophy, University of California, San Diego, at La Jolla. Author of* The Emotive Theory of Ethics *and others.*
EPISTEMOLOGY (*in part*)

A.W. **Alan Walker.** *Professor of Music, McMaster University, Hamilton, Ontario. Author of* An Anatomy of Musical Criticism; A Study in Musical Analysis; *and others.*
MUSIC, THE ART OF (*in part*)

A.Wa. **Andrew Warren.** *Senior Lecturer in Geography, University College, University of London.*
CONTINENTAL LANDFORMS (*in part*)

A.W.C. **Alan William Cuthbert.** *Sheild Professor of Pharmacology, University of Cambridge.*
DRUGS AND DRUG ACTION (*in part*)

A.We. **Albert Wendt.** *Professor of English, University of Auckland, New Zealand. Author of* Leaves of the Banyan Tree *and others.*
PACIFIC ISLANDS (*in part*)

A.W.G. **Alan William Gentry.** *Principal Scientific Officer, Department of Palaeontology, British Museum (Natural History), London. Author of numerous research papers on Old World hoofed mammals.*
MAMMALS (*in part*)

A.W.Ge. **Arnold Wycombe Gomme** (d. 1959). *Professor of Greek, University of Glasgow, 1946–57. Author of* Historical Commentary on Thucydides; Greece *and others.*
THUCYDIDES (Micropædia)

A.W.Gr. **Alic William Gray** (d. 1981). *Head, Agricultural Advisory and Development Section, Electricity Council, London, 1966–70; Principal Assistant, 1948–65.*
AGRICULTURE, THE HISTORY OF (*in part*)

A.Wh. **Alwyne Wheeler.** *Former Principal Scientific Officer, Fish Section, Zoology Department, British Museum (Natural History), London. Author of* Fishes of the World *and others.*
FISHES (*in part*)

A.W.H.A. **A.W.H. Adkins.** *Edward Olson Professor of Greek, of Philosophy, and of New Testament and Early Christian Literature, University of Chicago. Author of* Merit and Responsibility: A Study in Ancient

Greek Values *and others.*
EUROPEAN RELIGIONS, ANCIENT (*in part*)

A.W.J. A. Walter James. *Principal, St. Catharine's, Windsor, England, 1974–82. Editor,* The Times *(London)* Educational Supplement, *1952–69. Author of* The Christian in Politics.
ACTON, JOHN EMERICH EDWARD
  DALBERG ACTON, 1ST BARON (*in part*)
  (Micropædia)

A.W.L. Albert William Levi (d. 1988). *David May Distinguished University Professor of Humanities, Washington University, St. Louis, Missouri, 1952–79. Author of* Philosophy and the Modern World.
PHILOSOPHY, THE HISTORY OF WESTERN
  (*in part*)

A.W.M. Anne Wood Murray. *Emeritus Curator of American Costume, Division of Costume, Department of Social and Cultural History, National Museum of American History, Smithsonian Institution, Washington, D.C.*
DRESS AND ADORNMENT (*in part*)

A.Wo. Albert Wolfson. *Professor of Biological Sciences, Northwestern University, Evanston, Illinois.*
BEHAVIOUR, ANIMAL (*in part*)

A.W.P. Alois Wilhelm Podhajsky (d. 1973). *Director, Spanish Riding School of Vienna, 1939–64. Winner, Olympic Bronze Medal for Dressage (equestrian event), 1936. Author of* The Complete Training of Horse and Rider *and others.*
HORSES AND HORSEMANSHIP (*in part*)

A.W.Po. Alan W. Powell. *Professor of History; Dean of Arts, Northern Territory University, Casuarina. Author of* Far Country: A Short History of the Northern Territory; The Shadow's Edge: Australia's Northern War.
AUSTRALIA (*in part*)

A.W.R. Alan W. Richards. *Former Development Manager, Imperial Smelting Processes Ltd., Bristol, England. Author of articles on zinc smelting and zinc metallurgy.*
INDUSTRIES, EXTRACTION AND
  PROCESSING (*in part*)

A.W.Re. Allen Walker Read. *Emeritus Professor of English, Columbia University. Author of "Approaches to Lexicography and Semantics" in* Current Trends in Linguistics.
ENCYCLOPAEDIAS AND DICTIONARIES
  (*in part*)

A.W.S. Albert Wilbur Schlechten (d. 1984). *Director, W.J. Kroll Institute for Extractive Metallurgy, Colorado School of Mines, Golden.*
INDUSTRIES, EXTRACTION AND
  PROCESSING (*in part*)

A.Y. Atsuhiko Yoshida. *Professor of Comparative Mythology, Gakushuin University, Tokyo. Author of* Origins of Japanese Myths *and others.*
LITERATURE, THE ART OF (*in part*)

Ay.Sy. Anthony Sillery (d. 1976). *Secretary to the Curators of the Taylor Institution, University of Oxford, 1951–70. Resident Commissioner, Bechuanaland Protectorate, 1947–50.*
SOUTHERN AFRICA (*in part*)

A.Zy. Antoni Zygmund. *Gustavus F. and Anne M. Swift Distinguished Service Professor Emeritus of Mathematics, University of Chicago. World authority on Fourier analysis. Author of* Trigonometric Series; *coauthor of* Analytic Functions.
ANALYSIS (IN MATHEMATICS) (*in part*)

B. Robert Norman William Blake, Baron Blake. *Provost, Queen's College, University of Oxford, 1968–87. Author of* The Conservative Party from Peel to Thatcher *and others.*
ASQUITH, H.H., 1ST EARL OF OXFORD
  AND ASQUITH (Micropædia)
DISRAELI, BENJAMIN, EARL OF
  BEACONSFIELD (*in part*) (Micropædia)
LLOYD GEORGE, DAVID (*in part*)
  (Micropædia)

B.A. Bruno Accordi (d. 1986). *Director, Geology and Paleontology Institute, University of Rome. Author of numerous publications on geology.*
EUROPE (*in part*)

B.A.B. Bruce A. Bolt. *Professor of Seismology, University of California, Berkeley. Author of* Earthquakes: A Primer *and others.*
EARTHQUAKES

B.A.C. Bruce Alan Carr. *Music Administrator, Pittsburgh Symphony Orchestra.*
MUSIC, THE ART OF (*in part*)

B.A.D. Boyce A. Drummond, Jr. *Emeritus Professor of History, Henderson State University, Arkadelphia, Arkansas. Author of* Arkansas, Politics and Government.
UNITED STATES OF AMERICA (*in part*)

B.A.F. Boris Aleksandrovich Fedorovich (d. 1981). *Senior Scientist, Institute of Geography, Academy of Sciences of the U.S.S.R., Moscow.*
ASIA (*in part*)

B.A.J. Benjamin A. Jones, Jr. *Professor of Agricultural Engineering, University of Illinois, Urbana. Coauthor of* Engineering Applications in Agriculture.
FARMING AND AGRICULTURAL
  TECHNOLOGY (*in part*)

B.Am. Barthélemy Amengual. *Editor,* Études Cinématographiques. *Author of* René Clair; Clés pour le cinéma; *and others.*
CLAIR, RENÉ (Micropædia)

B.A.M. Boyd A. Martin. *Director, Boyd and Grace Martin Peace Institute; Distinguished Borah Professor Emeritus of Political Science; Emeritus Director, Bureau of Public Affairs Research, University of Idaho, Moscow. Author of* Idaho Voting Trends *and others.*
UNITED STATES OF AMERICA (*in part*)

B.A.-S. Brian Abel-Smith. *Professor of Social Administration, London School of Economics and Political Science, University of London. Author of* The Poor and the Poorest *and others.*
SOCIAL WELFARE (*in part*)

B.As. Bernard Ashmole (d. 1988). *Lincoln Professor of Classical Archaeology and Art, University of Oxford, 1956–61.*
PAINTING, THE HISTORY OF WESTERN
  (*in part*)
SCULPTURE, THE HISTORY OF WESTERN
  (*in part*)

B.A.St. Barbara A. Standley. *Free-lance editor. Former Associate Editor,* Encyclopædia Britannica, *Chicago.*
INDIA (*in part*)

B.B. Bela Balassa (d. 1991). *Professor of Political Economy, Johns Hopkins University, Baltimore, Maryland. Consultant, International Bank for Reconstruction and Development. Author of* Trade Liberalization Among Industrial Countries: Objectives and Alternatives *and others.*
INTERNATIONAL TRADE (*in part*)

B.B.De. Barbara B. Decker. *Coauthor of* Volcanoes.
VOLCANISM (*in part*)

B.Be. Bernard Beckerman (d. 1985). *Brander Matthews Professor of Dramatic Literature, Columbia University, 1977–85. President, American Society for Theatre Research, 1973–79. Author of* Shakespeare at the Globe; Dynamics of Drama; *and others.*
THEATRICAL PRODUCTION (*in part*)

B.B.G. Bentley Brinkerhoff Gilbert. *Professor and Chairman, Department of History, University of Illinois at Chicago. Author of* David Lloyd George: A Political Life *and others.*
UNITED KINGDOM (*in part*)

B.Bl. Brand Blanshard (d. 1987). *Professor of Philosophy, Yale University, 1945–61. Author of* The Nature of Thought; Reason and Analysis.
PHILOSOPHICAL SCHOOLS AND
  DOCTRINES, WESTERN (*in part*)

B.Ble. Brebis Bleaney. *Dr. Lee's Professor Emeritus of Experimental Philosophy, University of Oxford. Coauthor of* Electricity and Magnetism *and others.*
ELECTRICITY AND MAGNETISM (*in part*)

B.Bo. Baruch Boxer. *Professor and Chair, Department of Geography and Human Ecology, Cook College, Rutgers University, New Brunswick, New Jersey. Author of "China's Environmental Prospects" in* Asian Survey *and other articles.*
CHINA (*in part*)
SHANGHAI
TIENTSIN

B.Br. Barbara Buckmaster (the Hon. Mrs. Barbara Miller) (d. 1966). *Writer on Balkan affairs. Member of the Staff, Foreign Research and Press Service, Royal Institute of International Affairs, London.*
ROMANIA (*in part*)
UNION OF SOVIET SOCIALIST REPUBLICS
  (*in part*)

B.C.B. Barry C. Bishop. *Chairman, Committee for Research and Exploration, National Geographic Society, Washington, D.C. Author of* Karnali Under Stress.

ASIA (*in part*)

B.Ch. Brian Chapman (d. 1981). *Professor of Government, Victoria University of Manchester, England, 1961–81. Author of* The Profession of Government *and others.*

PUBLIC ADMINISTRATION (*in part*)

B.C.H. Bruce C. Heezen (d. 1977). *Associate Professor of Geology, Lamont-Doherty Geological Observatory, Columbia University, Palisades, New York, 1964–77. Coauthor of* The Floors of the Oceans.

ATLANTIC OCEAN, THE (*in part*)

B.Cr. Bosley Crowther (d. 1981). *Creative consultant, Columbia Pictures, New York City, 1968–73. Screen critic and editor,* The New York Times, *1940–68. Author of* The Great Films: Fifty Golden Years of Motion Pictures.

DISNEY, WALT (*in part*) (Micropædia)

B.C.Ri. Bonham C. Richardson. *Professor of Geography, Virginia Polytechnic Institute and State University. Author of* Caribbean Migrants *and others.*

GUYANA (*in part*)

B.C.S. B. Charlotte Schreiber. *Professor of Geology, Queens College, City University of New York, Flushing. Coeditor of* Sedimentology, "Earth Science Series."

INDIAN OCEAN, THE (*in part*)

B.C.So. Brian C. Southam. *Publisher, Athlone Press, London. Author of* Jane Austen's Literary Manuscripts; Tennyson; *and others.*

AUSTEN, JANE (*in part*) (Micropædia)

B.D.H. Baxter D. Honeycutt. *Manager, Exploration Support, ARCO Oil and Gas Company, Dallas, Texas.*

ENGINEERING (*in part*)

B.Di. Bern Dibner (d. 1988). *Historian of science and technology. Founder and Director, Burndy Library, Norwalk, Connecticut, 1935–88. Author of* Heralds of Science.

GALVANI, LUIGI (Micropædia)

B.E. Blake Ehrlich (d. 1974). *Free-lance writer. Author of* Paris on the Seine; London on the Thames.

ATHENS (*in part*)
DUBLIN (*in part*)
EDINBURGH (*in part*)
FLORENCE
ISTANBUL
LISBON (*in part*)
LONDON (*in part*)
MADRID (*in part*)
MARSEILLE (*in part*)
PARIS (*in part*)
ROME (*in part*)
VIENNA (*in part*)

Be.J. Bernard Jaffe (d. 1986). *Free-lance science writer. Chairman, Science Department, James Madison High School, Brooklyn, New York,* 1944–58. *Author of* Men of Science in America *and others.*

FERMI, ENRICO (Micropædia)

Be.M. Bernd Magnus. *Professor of Philosophy; Director, Center for Intellectual History and Social Thought, University of California, Riverside. Author of* Nietzsche's Existential Imperative.

NIETZSCHE

B.E.M. Bernard E. Meland. *Emeritus Professor of Constructive Theology, University of Chicago. Author of* The Realities of Faith *and others.*

OTTO, RUDOLF (Micropædia)

B.E.Ma. Bernard Edward Matthews. *Lecturer in Zoology, University of Edinburgh. Coauthor of* Biology of Nematodes.

CIRCULATION AND CIRCULATORY SYSTEMS (*in part*)

B.E.McK. Brian E. McKnight. *Professor of History, University of Hawaii at Manoa, Honolulu. Author of* Village and Bureaucracy in Southern Sung China *and others.*

CHINA (*in part*)

Be.N. Beaumont Newhall. *Emeritus Professor of Art, University of New Mexico, Albuquerque. Director, George Eastman House, Rochester, New York, 1958–71. Author of* The History of Photography; Latent Image; *and others.*

PHOTOGRAPHY (*in part*)

B.F.S. Bradford Fuller Swan (d. 1976). *Theatre and Art Critic,* The Providence Journal and Evening Bulletin, *Rhode Island.*

UNITED STATES OF AMERICA (*in part*)

B.Fu. Bruce Furie, M.D. *Chief, Coagulation Unit, New England Medical Center; Professor of Medicine, Tufts University, Boston.*

BLOOD (*in part*)

B.F.W. Brian Frederick Windley. *Professor of Geology, University of Leicester, England. Author of* The Evolving Continents.

EARTH SCIENCES, THE (*in part*)
EUROPE (*in part*)
GEOCHRONOLOGY (*in part*)
PRECAMBRIAN TIME (Micropædia)

B.G. Branko Grünbaum. *Professor of Mathematics, University of Washington, Seattle. Author of* Convex Polytopes.

COMBINATORICS AND COMBINATORIAL GEOMETRY (*in part*)

B.Ga. Balwant Gargi. *Playwright. Former Professor and Head, Department of Indian Theatre, Panjab University, Chandīgarh, India. Author of* Folk Theater of India *and others.*

SOUTH ASIAN ARTS (*in part*)

B.Ge. Barbara Gelb. *Writer. Coauthor of* O'Neill.

O'NEILL, EUGENE (*in part*) (Micropædia)

B.G.M. Barbara G. Mertz. *Historian and writer. Author of* Temples, Tombs and Hieroglyphs *and others.*

MEMPHIS (EGYPT) (Micropædia)

B.Gr. Benny Green. *Record reviewer, British Broadcasting Corporation. Jazz Critic,* The Observer, *London, 1958–77. Author of* The Reluctant Art; Drums in My Tears; *and others.*

MUSICAL FORMS AND GENRES (*in part*)

B.G.S. Bernice Giduz Schubert. *Curator, Arnold Arboretum, Harvard University, 1969–84. Coauthor of* The Begoniaceae of Colombia.

ANGIOSPERMS (*in part*)

B.Gu. B. Gungaadash. *Senior Research Worker, Institute of Geography and Geocryology, Academy of Sciences of the Mongolian People's Republic, Ulaanbaatar.*

MONGOLIA (*in part*)

B.H.C. Ben H. Caudle. *B.J. Lancaster Professor of Petroleum Engineering, University of Texas at Austin. Author of* Reservoir Engineering Fundamentals.

INDUSTRIES, EXTRACTION AND PROCESSING (*in part*)

B.H.F. Brian Hinton Fletcher. *Bicentennial Professor of Australian History, University of Sydney. Author of* Colonial Australia before 1850 *and others.*

AUSTRALIA (*in part*)

B.-h.H. Bae-ho Hahn. *Professor of Political Science, Korea University, Seoul. Author of* Theoretical Political Science.

KOREA (*in part*)

B.H.M. Brian H. Mason. *Emeritus Curator, Department of Mineral Sciences, Smithsonian Institution, Washington, D.C. An authority on the distribution of elements in the Earth's crust. Author of* Principles of Geochemistry.

CHEMICAL ELEMENTS (*in part*)

B.H.W. Brian H. Warmington. *Former Reader in Ancient History, University of Bristol, England. Author of* The Roman North African Provinces *and others.*

NORTH AFRICA (*in part*)

B.H.We. Byron H. Webb. *Consultant in dairy technology. Former Chief, Dairy Products Laboratory, Eastern Utilization Research and Development Division, Agricultural Research Service, U.S. Department of Agriculture, Washington, D.C. Coeditor of* Fundamentals of Dairy Chemistry.

FARMING AND AGRICULTURAL TECHNOLOGY (*in part*)
FOOD PROCESSING (*in part*)

B.I.B. Boris Ivan Balinsky. *Emeritus Professor of Zoology, University of the Witwatersrand, Johannesburg, South Africa. Author of* An Introduction to Embryology.

GROWTH AND DEVELOPMENT, BIOLOGICAL (*in part*)

Bi.C.   Bin Cheng. *Emeritus Professor of Air and Space Law, University College, University of London. Author of* The Law of International Air Transport.
INTERNATIONAL LAW (*in part*)
TRANSPORTATION LAW (*in part*)

B.I.S.   Bernard I. Spinrad. *Professor and Chair, Department of Nuclear Engineering, Iowa State University, Ames. Coauthor and coeditor of* Nuclear Energy: A Sensible Alternative.
ENERGY CONVERSION (*in part*)

B.Ja.   Bernard Jacobson. *Director of Promotion, Boosey & Hawkes Ltd. (music publisher), London; Deputy Director of Publications, 1979–81. Author of* The Music of Johannes Brahms.
MUSICAL FORMS AND GENRES (*in part*)

B.J.C.   Bryant J. Cratty. *Professor of Kinesiology; Director, Perceptual-Motor Learning Laboratory, University of California, Los Angeles. Author of* Movement Behavior and Motor Learning; Perceptual and Motor Development in Infants and Children.
LEARNING AND COGNITION, HUMAN (*in part*)

B.J.D.M.   Bastiaan J.D. Meeuse. *Emeritus Professor of Botany, University of Washington, Seattle. Author of* The Story of Pollination; *coauthor of* The Sex Life of Flowers.
REPRODUCTION AND REPRODUCTIVE SYSTEMS (*in part*)

B.J.M.   Sir Basil John Mason. *President, University of Manchester Institute of Science and Technology, England. Director General, Meteorological Office, Bracknell, England, 1965–83. Author of* The Physics of Clouds; Clouds, Rain and Rainmaking.
CLIMATE AND WEATHER (*in part*)

B.J.McG.   Bernard J. McGinn. *Professor of Historical Theology and the History of Christianity, University of Chicago. Author of* The Calabrian Abbot.
CHRISTIANITY (*in part*)

B.Jo.   Bernard Joy. *Former football correspondent,* Evening Standard, *London. Author of* Soccer Tactics.
SPORTS, MAJOR TEAM AND INDIVIDUAL (*in part*)

B.J.R.   Brian James Roud (deceased). *Historian.*
SPAIN (*in part*)

B.J.T.   Brian J. Thompson. *Provost and Professor of Optics, University of Rochester, New York. Author of* Physical Optics Notebook.
OPTICS, PRINCIPLES OF (*in part*)

B.J.U.   Benton J. Underwood. *Stanley G. Harris Professor Emeritus of Social Science, Northwestern University, Evanston, Illinois. Author of* Experimental Psychology; *coauthor of* Meaningfulness and Verbal Learning.
MEMORY (*in part*)

B.K.   Benjamin Keen. *Emeritus Professor of History, Northern Illinois University, De Kalb. Editor of* Readings in Latin American Civilization, 1492 to the Present *and others.*
BALBOA, VASCO NÚÑEZ DE (Micropædia)
LATIN AMERICA, THE HISTORY OF (*in part*)

B.Ke.   Bettyann Kevles. *Consulting Editor, Stanford University Press. California. Contributor,* Los Angeles Times. *Author of* Females of the Species.
DARWIN

B.K.M.   Barrie K. Macdonald. *Reader in History, Massey University, Palmerston North, New Zealand. Author of* Cinderellas of the Empires: Towards a History of Kiribati and Tuvalu.
PACIFIC ISLANDS (*in part*)

B.K.N.   Basheer K. Nijim (d. 1991). *Professor of Geography, University of Northern Iowa, Cedar Falls, 1972–91. Coeditor of* The Arab World: A Handbook.
ARABIA (*in part*)

B.K.S.   Brian K. Smith. *Assistant Professor of Religion, Barnard College, Columbia University. Author of* Reflections on Resemblance, Ritual and Religion.
HINDUISM (*in part*)

B.L.   Barnabas Lindars. *Rylands Professor of Biblical Criticism and Exegesis, Victoria University of Manchester. Author of* Jesus Son of Man.
PAUL, THE APOSTLE

B.L.C.   Barbara Lovett Cline. *Biology teacher. Author of* The Questioners: Physicists and the Quantum Theory.
BROGLIE, LOUIS-VICTOR, 7ᵉ DUC DE (Micropædia)
DIRAC, P.A.M. (Micropædia)

B.L.G.   Burton L. Gordon. *Emeritus Professor of Geography, San Francisco State University. Author of* A Panama Forest and Shore *and others.*
CENTRAL AMERICA (*in part*)
NORTH AMERICA (*in part*)

B.L.K.   Barry L. Karger. *Professor of Chemistry, Northeastern University, Boston, Massachusetts. Coauthor of* Introduction to Separation Science.
ANALYSIS AND MEASUREMENT, PHYSICAL AND CHEMICAL (*in part*)

B.L.Kl.   B.L. Klock. *Physical Scientist, Research and Engineering Directorate, Advanced Weapons Systems Division, Defense Mapping Agency, U.S. Department of Defense, Washington, D.C. Editor of* Fundamental Star Catalogs.
TELESCOPES (*in part*)

B.L.S.   Bruce Lannes Smith. *Emeritus Professor of Political Science, Michigan State University, East Lansing. Coauthor of* Propaganda, Communication and Public Opinion.
PROPAGANDA

B.L.T.   B.L. Turner. *Professor of Botany; Director, Plant Resources Center, University of Texas at Austin.*

Author of Legumes of Texas; *coeditor of* Chemotaxonomy of the Leguminosae.
ANGIOSPERMS (*in part*)

B.L.v.d.W.   Bartel Leendert van der Waerden. *Emeritus Professor of Mathematics, University of Zürich. Author of* Science Awakening *and others.*
EUCLID (Micropædia)

B.M.   Björn Matthíasson. *Economist, Ministry of Finance, Reykjavík, Iceland.*
ICELAND (*in part*)

B.Ma.   Benjamin March (d. 1940). *Curator of Asiatic Art, Detroit Institute of Arts. Author of* The History of Chinese Painting in Outline.
DECORATIVE ARTS AND FURNISHINGS (*in part*)

B.M.A.   Bruce M. Alberts. *Professor of Biochemistry and Biophysics, University of California, San Francisco. Coauthor of* The Molecular Biology of the Cell.
CELLS (*in part*)

B.M.B.   Bridget M. Brereton. *Reader in History, University of the West Indies, St. Augustine, Trinidad. Author of* A History of Modern Trinidad *and others.*
WEST INDIES, THE (*in part*)

B.M.H.   Bernice Margaret Hamilton. *Associate of St. Edmund's College, University of Cambridge. Former Senior Lecturer in Politics, University of York, Heslington, England. Author of* Political Thought in 16th-Century Spain.
VITORIA, FRANCISCO DE (Micropædia)

B.Mo.   Brita Maud Ellen Mortensen (d. 1958). *Lecturer in Swedish, University of Cambridge, 1950–58. Coauthor of* An Introduction to Scandinavian Literature.
SCANDINAVIAN LITERATURE (*in part*)
STRINDBERG, AUGUST (Micropædia)

B.M.W.   Bernd Michael Wiese. *Lecturer in Geography, University of Cologne. Author of* Zaire *and others.*
CENTRAL AFRICA (*in part*)

B.N.   Bruno Nettl. *Professor of Music and of Anthropology, University of Illinois, Urbana. Author of* The Study of Ethnomusicology; Folk and Traditional Music of the Western Continents.
FOLK ARTS (*in part*)

B.Ne.   Bert Nelson. *Editor,* Track & Field News. *Editor of* Little Gold Book; Olympic Track & Field.
SPORTS, MAJOR TEAM AND INDIVIDUAL (*in part*)

B.Ni.   Bernard Nietschmann. *Professor of Geography, University of California, Berkeley. Author of* Between Land and Water: The Subsistence Ecology of the Miskito Indians, Eastern Nicaragua.
CENTRAL AMERICA (*in part*)

B.N.P.   Baij Nath Puri. *Emeritus Professor of Ancient Indian History and Archaeology, University of Lucknow, India. Author of* Cities of Ancient India.
TAXILA (*in part*) (Micropædia)

B.O'G.   Brendan Anthony O'Grady. *Professor of English, University of Prince Edward Island, Charlottetown.*
CANADA (*in part*)

B.O'K. **Bernard O'Kelly.** *Dean, College of Arts and Sciences; Professor of English, University of North Dakota, Grand Forks.*
UNITED STATES OF AMERICA (*in part*)

B.P.L. **Bruce Peter Luyendyk.** *Professor of Marine Geophysics; Director, Institute for Crustal Studies, University of California, Santa Barbara. Coeditor of Initial Reports of the Deep Sea Drilling Project (vol. 1 and 3).*
OCEANS (*in part*)

B.R. **Bayard Rankin.** *Associate Editor, Mathematics,* Encyclopædia Britannica, *Chicago, 1971–73. Associate Professor of Mathematics, Case Western Reserve University, Cleveland, 1960–71. Coauthor and editor of Differential Space, Quantum Systems, and Prediction.*
AUTOMATA THEORY (*in part*)

Br.M. **Brian Morton.** *Professor of Zoology, University of Hong Kong. Author of Partnerships in the Sea.*
MOLLUSKS (*in part*)

B.R.N. **B.R. Nanda.** *Former Director, Nehru Memorial Museum and Library, New Delhi. Author of Mahatma Gandhi: A Biography and others.*
GANDHI

B.R.W. **Bryan R. Wilson.** *Reader in Sociology, University of Oxford. Author of Religion in Sociological Perspective.*
MORMON (Micropædia)

B.S. **Brooke Schumm, Jr.** *President, Eagle-Cliffs, Inc. (consultants), Bay Village, Ohio. Senior Technology Associate, Eveready Battery Company, Westlake, Ohio, 1962–89. Editor of* Handbook of Manganese Dioxides.
ENERGY CONVERSION (*in part*)

B.S.B. **Benedikt Sigurdur Benedikz.** *Head of Special Collections, Library, University of Birmingham, England. Author of The Varangians of Byzantium and others.*
SCANDINAVIAN LITERATURE (*in part*)

B.S.Ba. **Bernard S. Bachrach.** *Professor of History, University of Minnesota, Minneapolis. Author of Merovingian Military Organization and others.*
FRANCE (*in part*)

B.Sc. **Bobb Schaeffer.** *Emeritus Curator of Vertebrate Paleontology, American Museum of Natural History, New York City.*
FISHES (*in part*)

B.S.-E. **Bickham A.C. Sweet-Escott.** *Group Finance Coordinator, The British Petroleum Company Ltd., 1957–72. Manager, Ionian Bank Ltd., 1950–57. Author of Greece: A Political and Economic Survey, 1939–1953.*
GREECE (*in part*)

B.S.F. **Bernard S. Finn.** *Curator, Division of Electricity and Modern Physics, Smithsonian Institution, Washington, D.C.*
TELECOMMUNICATIONS SYSTEMS (*in part*)

B.S.L. **Bruce Sween Liley.** *Professor of Physics, University of Waikato, Hamilton, New Zealand.*
MATTER (*in part*)

B.S.Lo. **Barry Steven Lorge.** *Sports Editor,* The San Diego Union, *California. Contributing Editor,* Tennis Magazine.
SPORTS, MAJOR TEAM AND INDIVIDUAL (*in part*)

B.S.M. **Basil S. Markesinis.** *Denning Professor of Comparative Law, Queen Mary College, University of London. Professor of Anglo-American Law, State University of Leiden, The Netherlands. Author of The German Law of Torts: A Comparative Introduction.*
TORTS

B.Sv. **B. Shirendev.** *Historian. Former President, Academy of Sciences of the Mongolian People's Republic, Ulaanbaatar.*
MONGOLIA (*in part*)

B.T.D. **Bernard Thomas Donovan.** *Professor of Neuroendocrinology, Institute of Psychiatry, University of London.*
REPRODUCTION AND REPRODUCTIVE SYSTEMS (*in part*)

B.T.K.B. **B.T.K. Barry.** *Director, International Tin Research Institute, Uxbridge, England. Coauthor of Tin and Its Alloys and Compounds; Technology of Tinplate.*
INDUSTRIES, EXTRACTION AND PROCESSING (*in part*)

B.T.S. **Bradley Titus Scheer.** *Emeritus Professor of Biology, University of Oregon, Eugene. Author of Animal Physiology.*
BIOLOGICAL SCIENCES, THE (*in part*)

B.T.Sh. **Byron Thomas Shaw.** *Assistant to Administrator, Agricultural Research Service, U.S. Department of Agriculture, Washington, D.C., 1965–68.*
AGRICULTURAL SCIENCES (*in part*)

Bu.H.W. **Burns H. Weston.** *Bessie Dutton Murray Distinguished Professor of Law, University of Iowa, Iowa City. Coauthor of Human Rights in the World Community: Issues and Action and others.*
HUMAN RIGHTS

B.V. **Birgit Vennesland.** *Head, Vennesland Research Laboratory, Max Planck Society, 1970–81; Director, Max Planck Institute for Cell Physiology, Berlin, 1968–70.*
BIOLOGICAL SCIENCES, THE (*in part*)

B.V.Gy. **Bo Vilhelm Gyllensvärd.** *Former Director, Museum of Far Eastern Antiquities, Stockholm. Assistant Professor, Far Eastern Section, Institute of History of Art, University of Stockholm. Author of T'ang Gold and Silver and others.*
DECORATIVE ARTS AND FURNISHINGS (*in part*)

B.V.S. **Brian Vincent Street.** *Senior Lecturer in Social Anthropology, University of Sussex, Brighton, England.*

Author of The Savage in Literature *and others.*
TYLOR, SIR EDWARD BURNETT (Micropædia)

B.W. **Basil Willey** (d. 1978). *King Edward VII Professor of English Literature, University of Cambridge, 1946–64. Author of* Darwin and Butler: Two Versions of Evolution; Nineteenth Century Studies; *and others.*
ARNOLD, MATTHEW (*in part*) (Micropædia)
BUTLER, SAMUEL (Micropædia)
WORDSWORTH, WILLIAM (*in part*) (Micropædia)

B.W.B. **Bernard Winslow Beckingsale.** *Former Senior Lecturer in Modern History, University of Newcastle upon Tyne, England. Author of Burghley: Tudor Statesman and others.*
CECIL, WILLIAM, 1ST BARON BURGHLEY (*in part*) (Micropædia)

B.-W.C. **Byong-Wuk Chong.** *Professor of Korean Literature, Seoul National University. Author of Essays on Korean Literature; Complete Anthology of Sijo.*
KOREAN LITERATURE (*in part*)

B.We. **Bruce Webster.** *Senior Lecturer in History, University of Kent at Canterbury, England.*
ROBERT I (SCOTLAND) (Micropædia)

B.W.H. **Bruce W. Halstead, M.D.** *Director, World Life Research Institute, Colton, California. Author of Poisonous and Venomous Marine Animals of the World.*
POISONS AND POISONING (*in part*)

B.W.M. **Bernard W. Minifie.** *Consultant, Richardson Researches Inc. (consultants to the candy industry), Hayward, California. Author of Chocolate, Cocoa and Confectionery: Science and Technology.*
FOOD PROCESSING (*in part*)

B.W.Ma. **B.W. Mazur.** *Lecturer in Polish Language and Literature, School of Slavonic and East European Studies, University of London. Author of Colloquial Polish.*
POLISH LITERATURE (*in part*)

B.Wn. **Brian Weinstein.** *Professor of Political Science, Howard University, Washington, D.C. Author of Eboué; coauthor of Introduction to African Politics.*
CENTRAL AFRICA (*in part*)

B.Wo. **Bernard Wood.** *Derby Professor of Anatomy, University of Liverpool. Author of Human Evolution; Evolution of Early Man.*
EVOLUTION, HUMAN (*in part*)
MUSCLES AND MUSCLE SYSTEMS (*in part*)

B.W.W. **Bruce Withington Wilshire.** *Professor of Philosophy, Rutgers University, New Brunswick, New Jersey. Author of Metaphysics: An Introduction to Philosophy and others.*
METAPHYSICS (*in part*)

B.W.Wa. **Bruce W. Watson.** *Commander, U.S. Navy (retired). Adjunct Professor of Soviet Studies,*

Defense Intelligence College, Washington, D.C., and Montgomery College, Rockville, Maryland. Author of Committed to Excellence: Systemic Problems in the U.S. Intelligence Community.
WAR, THE THEORY AND CONDUCT OF (*in part*)

B.Z.B.   Rabbi Ben Zion Bokser (d. 1984). *Rabbi, Forest Hills Jewish Center, Forest Hills, New York. Adjunct Professor of Political Science, Queens College, City University of New York. Author of* The Legacy of Maimonides.
MAIMONIDES, MOSES (Micropædia)

C.A.B.   Clifford A. Barnes. *Emeritus Professor of Oceanography, University of Washington, Seattle. Author of numerous articles on oceanography.*
ATLANTIC OCEAN, THE (*in part*)

C.A.Bl.   Conrad Alexander Blyth. *Professor of Economics, University of Auckland, New Zealand. Author of* Inflation in New Zealand *and others.*
NEW ZEALAND (*in part*)

Ca.C.   Camille Camara. *Educational Adviser, Ministry of Agriculture, Abidjan, Ivory Coast. Author of* Saint-Louis du Sénégal; Le Nigeria.
AFRICA (*in part*)
WESTERN AFRICA (*in part*)

C.A.E.   Clive Arthur Edwards. *Chairman, Department of Entomology, Ohio State University, Columbus, Ohio. Author of* Principles of Agricultural Entomology *and others.*
SOIL ORGANISMS

Ca.G.   Carlton Gamer. *Composer. Professor of Music, Colorado College, Colorado Springs.*
MUSICAL INSTRUMENTS (*in part*)

C.A.G.   Christian Antoine Girault. *Research staff member, National Centre for Scientific Research, Paris. Author of* Le Commerce du cafe en Haiti.
WEST INDIES, THE (*in part*)

C.A.G.W.   C.A.G. Wiersma (d. 1979). *Professor of Biology, California Institute of Technology, Pasadena, 1947–76. Editor of* Invertebrate Nervous Systems.
SENSORY RECEPTION (*in part*)

C.A.L.   Carl Adam Lawrence (d. 1972). *Director, Bureau of Laboratories, Los Angeles County Health Department, California, 1953–70. Author of* Surface-Active Quaternary Ammonium Germicides.
ANTIMICROBIAL AGENT (*in part*) (Micropædia)

C.-A.La.   Charles-André Laffargue. *General, French Army (retired). Author of* Foch et la Bataille de 1918 *and others.*
FOCH, FERDINAND (Micropædia)

C.A.M.   Carlile Aylmer Macartney (d. 1978). *Research Fellow, All Souls College, University of Oxford, 1936–65. Montagu Burton Professor of International Relations, University of Edinburgh, 1951–57. Author of* Hungary: A Short History *and others.*
DEÁK, FERENC (*in part*) (Micropædia)

HUNGARY (*in part*)
KOSSUTH, LAJOS (Micropædia)

C.A.McC.   Charles A. McClelland. *Emeritus Professor of International Relations, University of Southern California, Los Angeles. Author of* Theory and the International System.
SOCIAL SCIENCES, THE (*in part*)

C.A.McI.   Christopher Angus McIntosh. *Editor and writer, Mitchell Beazley (publisher), London. Author of* The Swan King: Ludwig II of Bavaria *and others.*
COLOGNE (*in part*)
HAMBURG (*in part*)

C.A.M.K.   Cuchlaine Audrey Muriel King. *Emeritus Professor of Physical Geography, University of Nottingham, England. An authority on coastal geomorphology. Author of* Beaches and Coasts; An Introduction to Oceanography.
OCEANS (*in part*)

C.A.P.   Christopher A. Pallis. *Emeritus Reader in Neurology, Royal Postgraduate Medical School, University of London. Author of* The ABC of Brain Stem Death.
DEATH

C.A.R.   Colin Alistair Ronan. *Science writer and lecturer. Secretary, East Asian History of Science Trust. Author of* The Cambridge Illustrated History of the World's Science *and many others.*
CALENDAR (*in part*)
COPERNICUS (*in part*)
HIPPARCHUS (*in part*) (Micropædia)
PTOLEMY (Micropædia)
RUSSELL, HENRY NORRIS (Micropædia)

C.A.Ro.   C. Ambrose Rogers. *Emeritus Professor of Mathematics, University College, University of London. Author of* Packing and Covering.
NUMBER THEORY (*in part*)

C.A.T.   Cornelius A. Tobias. *Professor of Biophysics and Medical Physics, University of California, Berkeley. Author of papers on radiation biophysics and cancer research.*
RADIATION (*in part*)

C.A.Tr.   Constantine Athanasius Trypanis. *Minister of Culture and Science, Government of Greece, 1974–77. Professor of Classical Languages and Literatures, University of Chicago, 1968–74. Author of* Medieval and Modern Greek Poetry *and others.*
GREEK LITERATURE (*in part*)

C.Au.   Charlotte Auerbach. *Emeritus Professor of Animal Genetics, University of Edinburgh. Author of* The Science of Genetics; Mutation Research: Problems, Results, and Perspectives.
GENETICS AND HEREDITY, THE PRINCIPLES OF (*in part*)

C.A.V.   Claude A. Villee. *Andelot Professor of Biological Chemistry, Medical School, Harvard University, Boston, Massachusetts. Author of* Biological Principles and Processes.
BIOLOGICAL SCIENCES, THE (*in part*)

C.A.W.   Charles A. Wert. *Emeritus Professor of Metallurgy, University of Illinois, Urbana. Coauthor of* Physics of Solids.
MATTER (*in part*)

C.A.Wi.   Carol Ann Winker. *Reporter, Cayman Free Press Ltd., George Town; Editor,* Cayman Islands Yearbook and Business Directory.
WEST INDIES, THE (*in part*)

C.Ba.   Clive Barker. *Senior Lecturer in Theatre Studies, University of Warwick, England. Coeditor,* New Theatre Quarterly. *Author of* Theatre Games.
THEATRICAL PRODUCTION (*in part*)

C.B.B.   Carl B. Boyer (d. 1976). *Professor of Mathematics, Brooklyn College, City University of New York, 1952–76. Author of* The History of the Calculus and Its Conceptual Development; History of Analytic Geometry; A History of Mathematics *and others.*
EULER, LEONHARD (Micropædia)
FERMAT, PIERRE DE (Micropædia)

C.B.G.   Charles Burroughs Gill. *Emeritus Professor of Metallurgical Engineering, Lafayette College, Easton, Pennsylvania. Author of* Materials Beneficiation *and others.*
INDUSTRIES, EXTRACTION AND PROCESSING (*in part*)

C.B.He.   Charles B. Heiser, Jr. *Distinguished Professor Emeritus of Botany, Indiana University, Bloomington. Author of* Seed to Civilization: The Story of Food.
ANGIOSPERMS (*in part*)

C.Bi.   Cyril Bibby (d. 1987). *Principal, Kingston upon Hull College of Education, University of Hull Institute of Education, England, 1959–76. Author of* T.H. Huxley: Scientist, Humanist, and Educator *and others.*
HUXLEY, SIR ANDREW FIELDING (Micropædia)
HUXLEY, SIR JULIAN (Micropædia)
HUXLEY, T.H. (Micropædia)

C.Bl.   Claude Blair. *Keeper of Metalwork, Victoria and Albert Museum, London, 1972–82. Author of* European Armour; European and American Arms.
DECORATIVE ARTS AND FURNISHINGS (*in part*)

C.B.MacD.   Charles B. MacDonald (d. 1990). *Deputy Chief Historian, U.S. Army Center of Military History, Washington, D.C., 1967–80. Author of* A Time for Trumpets: The Untold Story of the Battle of the Bulge *and others.*
WAR, THE TECHNOLOGY OF (*in part*)

C.B.My.   Charles B. Morrey, Jr. (d. 1984). *Professor of Mathematics, University of California, Berkeley, 1945–73. Author of* Multiple Integrals in the Calculus of Variations.
ANALYSIS (IN MATHEMATICS) (*in part*)

C.C.   Claude Cahen. *Emeritus Professor of Islāmic History, University of Paris. Author of* La Syrie du nord á l'époque des croisades *and others.*
ALP-ARSLAN (Micropædia)

C.C.A. Claude C. Albritton (d. 1988). *Hamilton Professor of Geology, Southern Methodist University, Dallas, Texas, 1955–78. Coauthor and editor of* The Fabric of Geology; Uniformity and Simplicity.
EARTH SCIENCES, THE (*in part*)

C.C.B. Charles Calvert Bayley. *Emeritus Professor of History, McGill University, Montreal. Author of* The Formation of the German College of Electors in the Mid-Thirteenth Century.
GERMANY (*in part*)

C.C.C. Catherine C. Cutbill. *Graduate student in anthropology, University of Virginia, Charlottesville. Field researcher in Djibouti, 1984 and 1987–88.*
EASTERN AFRICA (*in part*)

C.Ce. Charles Cestre (d. 1959). *Professor of American Literature and Civilization, University of Paris, 1917–42. Author of* Histoire de la littérature américaine *and others.*
POE, EDGAR ALLAN (*in part*)
  (Micropædia)

C.Ch. Charles Chadwick. *Carnegie Professor of French, University of Aberdeen, Scotland. Author of* Mallarmé, sa pensée dans sa poésie *and others.*
MALLARMÉ, STÉPHANE (Micropædia)

C.Cl. Cecil Clutton. *Secretary, Organs Advisory Committee, Council for Places of Worship, England. Fellow, Society of Antiquaries, London. Author of* The British Organ *and others.*
MUSICAL INSTRUMENTS (*in part*)

C.C.M. Claudius Cornelius Müller. *Head, East Asian Department, Museum of Ethnology, Berlin. Author of* Untersuchungen zum Erdalter she im China der Chou- und Han-Zeit.
SHIH HUANG-TI (*in part*) (Micropædia)

C.C.MacD. C.C. MacDuffee (d. 1961). *Professor of Mathematics, University of Wisconsin, Madison, 1943–61. President, Mathematical Association of America, 1945–46. Author of* The Theory of Matrices *and others.*
ARITHMETIC (*in part*)

C.C.O'B. Conor Cruise O'Brien. *Pro-Chancellor, University of Dublin. Editor in Chief,* The Observer, *London, 1978–81. Member, Seanad Eireann, Dublin, 1977–79; Dáil Eireann, 1969–77. Author of* Parnell and His Party.
PARNELL, CHARLES STEWART
  (Micropædia)

C.C.P. Cuthbert Coulson Pounder. *Marine engineering consultant. Director and Chief Technical Engineer, Harland and Wolff Ltd., Belfast, Northern Ireland, 1930–65. Coauthor of* Marine Diesel Engines.
INDUSTRIES, MANUFACTURING (*in part*)

C.C.T. Clifford Charles Townsend. *Principal Scientific Officer, Royal Botanic Gardens, Kew, England. Editor and coauthor of* Flora of Iraq.
ANGIOSPERMS (*in part*)

C.D. Carlo Diano (d. 1974). *Professor of Greek Literature, University of Padua,*

Italy. Author of Lettre di Epicuro e dei suoi; *editor of* Epicuri Ethica.
EPICURUS (Micropædia)
PHILOSOPHICAL SCHOOLS AND
  DOCTRINES, WESTERN (*in part*)

C.D.Cu. Charles D. Cuttler. *Emeritus Professor of Art History, University of Iowa, Iowa City. Author of* Northern Painting from Pucelle to Bruegel.
SLUTER, CLAUS (Micropædia)

C.D.G. C. David Gutsche. *Robert A. Welch Professor of Chemistry, Texas Christian University, Fort Worth, Texas. Former Professor of Chemistry, Washington University, St. Louis, Missouri. Author of* Chemistry of Carbonyl Compounds.
CHEMICAL COMPOUNDS (*in part*)

C.D.H. Chauncy D. Harris. *Samuel N. Harper Distinguished Service Professor Emeritus of Geography, University of Chicago. Author of* Cities of the Soviet Union: Studies in Their Functions, Size, Density, and Growth.
GEOGRAPHY
MONGOLIA (*in part*)

C.D.K. Carol D. Kiesinger. *Arts consultant. Hiker and mountain climber. Coeditor of* The Armchair Mountaineer.
MOUNTAINEERING (*in part*)
  (Micropædia)

C.D.Kl. Curtis D. Klaassen. *Professor of Pharmacology, University of Kansas Medical Center, Kansas City.*
POISONS AND POISONING (*in part*)

C.Do. Clifford Dowdey (d. 1979). *Lecturer in Creative Writing, University of Richmond, Virginia, 1958–69. Author of* Lee *and others; editor of* The Wartime Papers of Robert E. Lee.
LEE, ROBERT E. (Micropædia)

C.D.O. Clifford David Ollier. *Emeritus Professor of Geography, University of New England, Armidale, Australia.*
BIOSPHERE, THE (*in part*)

C.D.R. C.D. Ross (d. 1986). *Professor of Medieval History, University of Bristol, England. Author of* The Wars of the Roses *and others.*
HENRY V (ENGLAND) (Micropædia)

C.D.T. Conrad D. Totman. *Professor of History, Northwestern University, Evanston, Illinois. Author of* Ieyasu: Shogun *and others.*
TOKUGAWA IEYASU (Micropædia)

C.E.B.B. Charles Edmond Bradlaugh Bonner (d. 1976). *Principal Curator, Conservatory and Botanical Garden, Geneva. Author of* Index Hepaticarum.
ANGIOSPERMS (*in part*)

C.E.B.C. Charles E.B. Conybeare (d. 1982). *Reader in Geology, Australian National University, Canberra.*
INDUSTRIES, EXTRACTION AND
  PROCESSING (*in part*)

C.E.C. Charles Edward Casolani. *Lieutenant Colonel, British Army (retired). Amateur rider, show jumper, and trainer, 1919–56.*
HORSES AND HORSEMANSHIP (*in part*)

C.E.Ca. Concepción E. Castañeda. *Former Associate Professor of Spanish, Millikin University, Decatur, Illinois. Professor of Geography, University of Havana, 1960–62.*
SOUTH AMERICA (*in part*)

C.E.Co. Charles E. Cornelius, D.V.M. *Professor of Physiological Sciences, School of Veterinary Medicine, University of California, Davis; Director, California Primate Research Center, 1981–87. Editor of* Advances in Veterinary Science and Comparative Medicine.
DISEASE (*in part*)

C.E.E. Cyril Ernest Everard. *Former Senior Lecture in Geography, Queen Mary College, University of London. Editor, Physical Geography, Encyclopedia of Geography.*
ATLANTIC OCEAN, THE (*in part*)

C.E.F. C.E. Ferreira. *Lecturer in Geography, University of Pretoria, South Africa.*
AFRICA (*in part*)

C.E.G. Creighton E. Gilbert. *Professor of History of Art, Yale University. Author of* Michelangelo; *editor and translator of* Complete Poems and Selected Letters of Michelangelo.
MICHELANGELO

C.E.He. Charles E. Hecht. *Professor of Chemistry, Hunter College, City University of New York. Author of papers on physical and chemical processes occurring at very low temperatures.*
MATTER (*in part*)

C.E.I. Carroll E. Izard. *Unidel Professor of Psychology, University of Delaware, Newark. Author of* Human Emotions.
EMOTION, HUMAN

C.E.McL. Charles E. McLure, Jr. *Senior Fellow, Hoover Institution on War, Revolution and Peace, Stanford University, California. Author of* The Value Added Tax: Key to Deficit Reduction.
TAXATION (*in part*)

C.E.N. Clyde Everett Noble. *Professor of Experimental Psychology, University of Georgia, Athens. Author of* Outline of Psychological Measurement; The Psychology of Cornet and Trumpet Playing; *and others.*
LEARNING AND COGNITION, HUMAN
  (*in part*)

C.E.No. Charles E. Nowell. *Emeritus Professor of History, University of Illinois, Urbana. Author of* The Great Discoveries and the First Colonial Empires *and others.*
EUROPEAN OVERSEAS EXPLORATION AND
  EMPIRES, THE HISTORY OF (*in part*)
HENRY THE NAVIGATOR (Micropædia)

C.E.T. Cecil Edgar Tilley (d. 1973). *Professor of Mineralogy and Petrology, University of Cambridge, 1931–61. World authority on igneous petrology.*
BOWEN, NORMAN L. (Micropædia)
MINERALS AND ROCKS (*in part*)

C.Fa. **Clifton Fadiman.** *Writer and editor. Member, Board of Editors,* Encyclopædia Britannica. *Senior Editor,* Book-of-the-Month Club. *Advisory Editor,* Cricket: The Children's Magazine. *Author of* The Lifetime Reading Plan *and many others.*
LITERATURE, THE ART OF (*in part*)

C.F.A.S. **Claude Frédéric Armand Schaeffer** (d. 1982). *Professor of the Archaeology of Western Asia, College of France, Paris, 1954–69. Director of the French Archaeological Expeditions to Ras Shamra-Ugarit, Syria, and Enkomi-Alasia, Cyprus. Editor of* Ugaritica I to VII.
UGARIT (Micropædia)

C.Fe. **Cyrille Felteau.** *Journalist and historian. Former Editorial and News Writer,* La Presse, *Montreal.*
MONTREAL (*in part*)

C.F.E.R. **Clyde F.E. Roper.** *Curator of Mollusca, Department of Invertebrate Zoology, National Museum of Natural History, Smithsonian Institution, Washington, D.C. Coauthor of* Cephalopods of the World.
MOLLUSKS (*in part*)

C.F.F. **Charles F. Fuechsel** (d. 1977). *Atlantic Region Engineer, Topographic Division, Geological Survey, U.S. Department of the Interior, Washington, D.C., 1959–65. Author of numerous articles on mapping and surveys.*
MAPPING AND SURVEYING (*in part*)

C.F.K. **Carl Fred Koch.** *Professor of Geological Sciences, Old Dominion University, Norfolk, Virginia.*
GEOCHRONOLOGY (*in part*)

C.F.M. **Clovis F. Maksoud.** *Permanent Observer of the League of Arab States to the United Nations. Author of* The Crisis of the Arab Left *and others.*
LEBANON (*in part*)

C.F.O. **Christian F. Otto.** *Professor of Architecture, Cornell University, Ithaca, New York.*
BORROMINI, FRANCESCO (Micropædia)

C.F.Q. **Calvin F. Quate.** *Professor of Applied Physics and Electrical Engineering, Stanford University, California.*
MICROSCOPES (*in part*)

C.F.S. **Carl Fredrik Sandelin.** *Novelist. Former General Manager and Editor in Chief, Finnish News Agency, Helsinki.*
FINLAND (*in part*)

C.F.V. **Charles F. Voegelin** (d. 1986). *Distinguished Professor of Anthropology and of Linguistics, Indiana University, Bloomington, 1967–76. Editor,* International Journal of American Linguistics. *Coauthor of* Classification and Index of the World's Languages.
LANGUAGES OF THE WORLD (*in part*)

C.Fy. **Christopher Fyfe.** *Reader in African History, University of Edinburgh. Author of* A History of Sierra Leone.
WESTERN AFRICA (*in part*)

C.G. **Christiaan Glasz.** *Former Professor of Public Finance, State University of Leiden, The Netherlands. Royal Commissioner, De Nederlandsche Bank.*
MARKETS (*in part*)

C.Ga. **Clemente Garavito.** *Vice President, Colombian Geographical Society, Bogotá. Author of numerous articles on geography.*
COLOMBIA (*in part*)

C.G.B. **Carl G. Baker, M.D.** *Medical Director, Ludwig Institute for Cancer Research, Zurich, 1977–82. Director, National Cancer Institute, U.S. Department of Health, Education, and Welfare, Bethesda, Maryland, 1969–72.*
CANCER (*in part*)

C.G.C. **Colin Graham Clarke.** *Lecturer in Geography, University of Oxford; Official Fellow of Jesus College, Oxford. Author of* Kingston, Jamaica: Urban Development and Social Change, 1692–1962 *and others.*
WEST INDIES, THE (*in part*)

C.G.F. **Craig G. Fraser.** *Assistant Professor, Institute for the History and Philosophy of Science and Technology, University of Toronto.*
MATHEMATICS, THE HISTORY OF (*in part*)

C.G.G. **Charles Goode Gomillion.** *Emeritus Professor of Sociology, Tuskegee Institute, Alabama.*
UNITED STATES OF AMERICA (*in part*)

C.G.H. **Carl G. Hempel.** *Stuart Professor Emeritus of Philosophy, Princeton University. University Professor of Philosophy, University of Pittsburgh, Pennsylvania. Author of* Philosophy of Natural Science.
CARNAP, RUDOLF (Micropædia)

C.G.P. **Charles G. Pearson.** *Emeritus Professor of Journalism, Wichita State University, Kansas.*
UNITED STATES OF AMERICA (*in part*)

C.G.S. **Charles Gordon Smith.** *Emeritus Fellow of Keble College, Oxford; former Lecturer in Geography, University of Oxford. Editor of* Oxford Regional Economic Atlas: The Middle East and North Africa.
AFRICA (*in part*)
ARABIA (*in part*)
EGYPT (*in part*)
SYRIA (*in part*)

C.G.Se. **Claudio G. Segre.** *Associate Professor of History, University of Texas at Austin. Author of* Fourth Shore: The Italian Colonization of Libya.
ITALY (*in part*)

C.G.St. **Chester G. Starr.** *Bentley Professor of Ancient History, University of Michigan, Ann Arbor. Author of* Rise and Fall of the Ancient World.
PEISISTRATUS (Micropædia)

C.G.T. **Constantine Gennadiyevich Tikhotskiy.** *Professor, Moscow M.V. Lomonosov State University. Author of numerous articles on hydrology.*
ASIA (*in part*)

C.H. **Claude Harmel.** *Editor,* Les Études Sociales et Syndicales, *Paris.*
Former Secretary, Institute for Social History, Paris. Author of Lettre à Léon Blum sur le socialisme et la paix *and others.*
JAURÈS, JEAN (Micropædia)

C.Ha. **Carl Hanson** (d. 1985). *Pro-Vice-Chancellor, Professor of Chemical Engineering, University of Bradford, England. Editor of* Recent Advances in Liquid-Liquid Extraction.
ENGINEERING (*in part*)

C.H.A. **Clyde H. Amundson.** *Director, Aquaculture Research Center; Professor and Chairman, Department of Food Science; Professor of Oceanography and Limnology, University of Wisconsin, Madison.*
FISHING, COMMERCIAL (*in part*)

Ch.A.R. **Charles A. Ross.** *Senior Biostratigrapher, Chevron U.S.A., Inc., Houston, Texas. Editor of* Timing and Depositional History of Eustatic Sequences.
GEOCHRONOLOGY (*in part*)

Ch.C. **Christopher Chow.** *Writer on biology.*
CELLS (*in part*)

C.H.C. **Charles Henry Cotter** (deceased). *Senior Lecturer in Maritime Studies, University of Wales Institute of Science and Technology, Cardiff. Author of* The Physical Geography of the Oceans.
PACIFIC OCEAN, THE (*in part*)

Ch.D. **Charles Donahue, Jr.** *Professor of Law, Harvard University. Coauthor of* Property: An Introduction to the Concept and the Institution.
PROPERTY LAW

C.H.D. **Calaway H. Dodson.** *Senior Curator, Missouri Botanical Garden, St. Louis. Coauthor of* Orchid Flowers: Their Pollination and Evolution; The Biology of the Orchids.
ANGIOSPERMS (*in part*)

C.H.G. **Cyrus H. Gordon.** *Emeritus Professor of Hebraic and Near East Studies; Director, Center for Ebla Research, New York University, New York City. Emeritus Professor of Mediterranean Studies, Brandeis University, Waltham, Massachusetts. Author of* The Ancient Near East *and others.*
MIDDLE EASTERN RELIGIONS, ANCIENT (*in part*)
SOLOMON (Micropædia)

C.H.Gi. **Charles Hugh Giles.** *Former Reader in Surface Chemistry and Dyeing, University of Strathclyde, Glasgow, Scotland. Author of* A Laboratory Course in Dyeing.
CHEMICAL COMPOUNDS (*in part*)

C.H.G.-S. **Charles Harvard Gibbs-Smith** (d. 1981). *Research Fellow, Science Museum, London, 1976–81. Keeper, Public Relations and Education Department, Victoria and Albert Museum, London, 1947–71. Author of* Aviation: An Historical Survey; The Wright Brothers; *and others.*

WRIGHT, ORVILLE AND WILBUR
(Micropædia)

C.H.H.   Charles Harold Hayward.
Free-lance writer and artist. Editor,
Woodworker, *1939–65. Author of*
English Period Furniture *and others.*
INDUSTRIES, MANUFACTURING (*in part*)

C.H.Ha.   Cadet H. Hand, Jr. *Emeritus*
Professor of Zoology, University of
California, Berkeley; Emeritus Director,
Bodega Marine Laboratory, Bodega Bay,
California.
CNIDARIANS (*in part*)

C.H.Ho.   Cyrus Henry Hoy. *John B.*
Trevor Professor of English, University
of Rochester, New York. Author of The
Hyacinth Room: An Investigation into
the Nature of Comedy, Tragedy, and
Tragicomedy.
LITERATURE, THE ART OF (*in part*)

C.Hi.   Christopher Hibbert. *Historian*
and biographer. Author of Benito
Mussolini; The Rise and Fall of Il Duce.
MUSSOLINI, BENITO (*in part*)
(Micropædia)

Ch.L.   Chao Lin. *Former Visiting*
Associate Professor of History,
National Chung-hsing University,
Tai-chung, Taiwan. Author of Marriage,
Inheritance and Lineage Organization in
Shang-Chou China.
CALENDAR (*in part*)

C.H.L.   Clarence H. Lorig (d. 1975).
Assistant Director, Battelle Memorial
Institute, Columbus, Ohio, 1947–65.
Author of Copper as an Alloying
Element in Steel and Cast Iron.
INDUSTRIES, EXTRACTION AND
   PROCESSING (*in part*)

C.H.Li.   Carter H. Lindberg. *Professor*
of Church History, Boston University.
Author of The Third Reformation?
CHRISTIANITY (*in part*)

C.H.Lo.   Charles H. Long. *William*
Rand Kenan, Jr., Professor of the History
of Religion, University of North Carolina
at Chapel Hill. Professor of the History
of Religions, Duke University, Durham,
North Carolina. Author of Alpha: Myths
of Creation.
DOCTRINES AND DOGMAS, RELIGIOUS
   (*in part*)

C.H.P.   Clifford Hillhouse Pope (d.
1974). *Science writer. Curator, Division*
of Reptiles and Amphibians, Field
Museum of Natural History, Chicago,
1941–53. Author of The Reptile World;
Turtles of the United States and Canada.
REPTILES (*in part*)

Ch.R.   Chaim Rabin. *Former Professor*
of Hebrew Language, Hebrew University
of Jerusalem. Author of Qumran
Studies: A Short History of the Hebrew
Language.
HEBREW LITERATURE (*in part*)

Ch.S.   Charles Süsskind. *Professor*
of Engineering Science, University of
California, Berkeley. Editor of The
Encyclopedia of Electronics.
CAVENDISH, HENRY (*in part*)
(Micropædia)

Ch.Su.   Christine Sutton. *Science writer.*
Research Associate, Department of
Nuclear Physics, University of Oxford.
Author of The Particle Connection;
coauthor of The Particle Explosion.
SUBATOMIC PARTICLES

C.H.T.   Charles Henri Toupet.
Professor of Tropical Geography,
University of Lyon III. Author of
Étude du milieu physique de massif de
l'Assaba, Mauritanie.
WESTERN AFRICA (*in part*)

C.Hu.   Charles Y. Hu. *Former*
Professor of Geography, University of
Maryland, College Park. Author of
monographs on the military geography
of China.
CHINA (*in part*)

C.H.V.S.   Carol Humphrey Vivian
Sutherland (d. 1986). *Student of Christ*
Church, Oxford, 1945–75; Keeper of
the Heberden Coin Room, Ashmolean
Museum, University of Oxford,
1957–75. Author of Roman Coins
and others.
COINS AND COINAGE (*in part*)

C.H.W.   Conrad H. Waddington (d.
1975). *Buchanan Professor of Genetics,*
University of Edinburgh, Scotland,
1947–75. Author of Principles of
Embryology.
GROWTH AND DEVELOPMENT,
   BIOLOGICAL (*in part*)

C.H.Wi.   Charles Henry Wilson (d.
1991). *Professor of Modern History,*
University of Cambridge, 1965–79;
Fellow of Jesus College, Cambridge,
1938–91. Author of Anglo-Dutch
Commerce and Finance in the
Eighteenth Century *and others.*
MAURICE (NETHERLANDS)
   (Micropædia)

C.I.   Charles Issawi. *Bayard Dodge*
Professor of Near Eastern Studies,
Princeton University. Author of An Arab
Philosophy of History *and others.*
IBN KHALDŪN (Micropædia)

C.I.C.   Carleton Ivers Calkin. *Painter*
and restorer. Curator, Historic St.
Augustine Preservation Board, Florida,
1966–73.
SCULPTURE, THE HISTORY OF WESTERN
   (*in part*)

C.J.A.   Charles Joseph Adams.
Professor of Islamic Studies, McGill
University, Montreal. Editor of
A Reader's Guide to the Great
Religions.
RELIGIONS, THE STUDY AND
   CLASSIFICATION OF (*in part*)

C.J.Al.   Constantine John Alexopoulos
(d. 1986). *Professor of Botany, University*
of Texas at Austin, 1962–77. Author of
Introductory Mycology.
FUNGI (*in part*)

C.J.D.   Cornelius J. Dyck. *Professor*
of Anabaptist and Sixteenth-Century
Studies, Mennonite Biblical Seminary,
Elkhart, Indiana. Editor of A Legacy of
Faith; An Introduction to Mennonite
History *and others.*
MENNO SIMONS (Micropædia)

C.J.F.D.   Charles James Frank
Dowsett. *Calouste Gulbenkian Professor*
of Armenian Studies, University of
Oxford; Fellow of Pembroke College,
Oxford. Translator (with commentary) of
Movsēs Dasxuranci's The History of the
Caucasian Albanians *and others.*
UNION OF SOVIET SOCIALIST REPUBLICS
   (*in part*)

C.J.G.   Coleman Jett Goin (deceased).
Professor of Biological Sciences,
University of Florida, Gainesville,
1956–71. Coauthor of Introduction to
Herpetology; *author of numerous articles*
on reptiles and amphibians.
AMPHIBIANS (*in part*)

C.J.Ga.   Cyril John Gadd (d. 1969).
Professor of Ancient Semitic Languages
and Civilizations, University of London,
1955–60. Keeper, Egyptian and Assyrian
Antiquities, British Museum, London,
1948–55.
SYRIA (*in part*)

C.J.L.P.   Cecil John Layton Price.
Emeritus Professor of English Language
and Literature, University College of
Swansea, University of Wales.
SHERIDAN, RICHARD BRINSLEY
   (Micropædia)

C.J.M.   Charles John Merdinger.
Captain, Civil Engineer Corps, U.S.
Navy (retired). Deputy Director, Scripps
Institution of Oceanography, University
of California, San Diego, at La Jolla,
1974–80. Author of Civil Engineering
Through the Ages.
PUBLIC WORKS (*in part*)

C.J.Mo.   Cyril John Morley. *Former*
Honorary Secretary, British Falconers'
Club and International Association
of Falconry and Conservation of
Birds of Prey.
FALCONRY (*in part*)
   (Micropædia)

C.Jo.   Charles Joys. *Coauthor of* Vårt
folks historie.
NORWAY (*in part*)

C.J.S.   Charles J. Sippl. *Consultant*
in the computer, communications, and
video fields. Coauthor of Computer
Dictionary and Handbook.
COMPUTERS (*in part*)

C.K.   Cornelis Klein. *Professor of*
Geology, University of New Mexico,
Albuquerque. Author of Minerals and
Rocks: Exercises in Crystallography,
Mineralogy, and Hand Specimen
Petrology; *coauthor of* Manual of
Mineralogy.
MINERALS AND ROCKS (*in part*)

C.K.B.   C.K. Bertram. *President,*
Lucy Cavendish College, University of
Cambridge, 1970–79.
MAMMALS (*in part*)

C.-K.L.   Chi-Keung Leung. *Professor*
of Geography; Dean, Arts Faculty,
University of Hong Kong. Editor,
Journal of Oriental Studies *and* Asian
Geographer. *Author of* China: Railway
Patterns and National Goals.
CHINA (*in part*)
HONG KONG

C.K.S.   Carl Keenan Seyfert. *Professor of Geology, State University of New York College at Buffalo. Coauthor of* Earth History *and* Plate Tectonics.
EARTH, THE (*in part*)

C.K.St.   Christian Karlson Stead. *Emeritus Professor of English, University of Auckland, New Zealand. Author of* In the Glass Case: Essays on New Zealand Literature *and others.*
AUSTRALIA AND NEW ZEALAND, LITERATURES OF (*in part*)

C.L.C.   C. Lockard Conley, M.D. *Distinguished Service Professor Emeritus of Medicine, Johns Hopkins University and Hospital, Baltimore, Maryland; Head, Hematology Division, 1947–80. Contributor to* Medical Physiology.
BLOOD (*in part*)

C.L.Cl.   C.L. Cline. *Ashbel H. Smith Professor Emeritus of English, University of Texas at Austin. Author of* Byron, Shelley, and Their Pisan Circle; *Editor of* The Letters of George Meredith.
MEREDITH, GEORGE (Micropædia)

C.Le.   Chan Lee. *Emeritus Professor of Geography, Seoul National University, Korea.*
KOREA (*in part*)
SEOUL

C.L.F.   Charles L. Fefferman. *Professor of Mathematics, Princeton University.*
ANALYSIS (IN MATHEMATICS) (*in part*)

C.L.Ha.   C. Lowell Harriss. *Emeritus Professor of Economics, Columbia University. Coauthor of* American Public Finance *and others.*
TAXATION (*in part*)

C.Li.   Chan Lien. *Professor of Political Science, National Taiwan University, Taipei. Coauthor of* Taiwan: From Pre-history to Modern Times.
HU SHIH (Micropædia)

C.L.K.   Charlotte L. Kellner. *Former Lecturer in Physics, Imperial College of Science and Technology, University of London. Author of* Alexander von Humboldt.
HUMBOLDT, ALEXANDER VON (Micropædia)

Cl.L.   Clifford Leech. (d. 1977). *Professor of English, University of Toronto, 1963–74. Author of* The Dramatist's Experience with Other Essays in Critical Theory *and others; editor of* Marlowe: A Collection of Critical Essays.
JONSON, BEN (*in part*) (Micropædia)

C.L.Ma.   Clyde L. Manschreck. *Chavanne Professor of Religious Studies, Rice University, Houston, Texas. Emeritus Professor of the History of Christianity, Chicago Theological Seminary. Editor of* Melanchthon on Christian Doctrine *and others.*
MELANCHTHON, PHILIPP (Micropædia)

C.Lo.   Constance Lowenthal. *Executive Director, International Foundation for Art Research, New York City.*
GHIBERTI, LORENZO (Micropædia)

C.L.P.II.   Charles Lafayette Proctor II. *Associate Professor of Mechanical Engineering, University of Florida, Gainesville.*
ENERGY CONVERSION (*in part*)

C.L.Q.   Charles Loreaux Quittmeyer. *Floyd Dewey Gottwald Professor Emeritus of Business Administration, College of William and Mary, Williamsburg, Virginia. Author of* The Virginia Travel Trade *and others.*
UNITED STATES OF AMERICA (*in part*)

C.L.R.J.   C.L.R. James (d. 1989). *Star Professor of History, University of the District of Columbia, Washington, D.C., 1970–80. Secretary, West Indian Federal Labor Party, 1958–62. Author of* The Black Jacobins.
WEST INDIES, THE (*in part*)

C.L.S.   Craig L. Stark. *Technical writer and consultant. Contributing Editor,* Stereo Review *magazine. Owner, Starksonic Studio (audio testing laboratory), Montclair, New Jersey.*
SOUND (*in part*)

C.L.T.   Carol Lewis Thompson. *Editor,* Current History, *Philadelphia.*
UNITED STATES OF AMERICA (*in part*)

C.L.W.   Carl Louis Wilson (d. 1986). *Professor of Botany, Dartmouth College, Hanover, New Hampshire (1935–63). Coauthor of* Botany.
TISSUES AND FLUIDS (*in part*)

C.M.   Christopher Marriage Marsh. *Special Engineering Adviser, British Waterways Board, 1964–66; North Western Divisional Manager, 1948–64. Author of many papers on waterways.*
PUBLIC WORKS (*in part*)

C.Ma.   Carleton Mabee. *Emeritus Professor of History, State University of New York College at New Paltz. Author of* The American Leonardo: A Life of Samuel F.B. Morse.
MORSE, SAMUEL F.B. (Micropædia)

C.M.A.   Sister Consuelo Maria Aherne. *Professor of History, Chestnut Hill College, Philadelphia. Assistant Staff Editor for* Mediaeval Church History; *contributor to the* New Catholic Encyclopedia.
BONIFACE, SAINT (Micropædia)

C.McH.   Christine McHugh. *Attorney. Associate, Pellettieri, Rabstein, and Altman, Princeton, New Jersey.*
ADAMS, HENRY (Micropædia)

C.M.E.   Chester Monroe Edelmann, Jr., M.D. *Professor of Pediatrics; Associate Dean for Clinical Affairs, Albert Einstein College of Medicine, Yeshiva University, Bronx, New York. Editor of* Pediatric Kidney Disease.
CHILDHOOD DISEASES AND DISORDERS (*in part*)

C.-M.H.   Chiao-Min Hsieh. *Professor of Geography, University of Pittsburgh, Pennsylvania. Author of* China: A Geography in Perspective *and others.*
CHINA (*in part*)

C.M.K.   Cecelia M. Kenyon (d. 1990). *Clarke Professor of Government, Smith*

College, Northampton, Massachusetts, 1969–84. Editor of The Antifederalists.
JEFFERSON

C.M.-L.   Carmelo Mesa-Lago. *Distinguished Service Professor of Economics and Latin American Studies, University of Pittsburgh. Author of* The Economy of Socialist Cuba *and others.*
WEST INDIES, THE (*in part*)

C.M.N.   C.M. Naim. *Associate Professor of Urdu, University of Chicago. Editor,* Annual of Urdu Studies.
SOUTH ASIAN ARTS (*in part*)

C.M.Wi.   C. Martin Wilbur. *George Sansom Professor Emeritus of Chinese History, Columbia University. Author of* The Nationalist Revolution in China, 1923–1928 *and others.*
CHINA (*in part*)

C.M.Wo.   Christopher Montague Woodhouse. *Member of Parliament for Oxford, 1959–66, 1970–74. Author of* The Story of Modern Greece *and others; coauthor of* Rhodes.
GREECE (*in part*)
RHODES, CECIL (*in part*) (Micropædia)

C.N.   Curtis L. Newcombe. *Emeritus Professor of Marine Biology, San Francisco State University. Author of* An Experimental Study of Shock Effects on Surface and Subsurface Organisms.
BIOSPHERE, THE (*in part*)

C.N.B.   Cyril Nelson Barclay (d. 1979). *Brigadier, The Cameronians (Scottish Rifles). Editor,* The Army Quarterly and Defence Journal, *1950–66; coeditor,* Brassey's Annual: The Armed Forces Year Book, *1950–69.*
MOLTKE, HELMUTH VON (Micropædia)

C.N.C.   Charles N. Cofer. *Research Professor of Psychology, University of North Carolina at Chapel Hill. Lecturer in Psychology, Duke University, Durham, North Carolina. Author of* Human Motivation: A Guide to Information Sources *and others.*
MOTIVATION, HUMAN (*in part*).

C.N.Ca.   Cesar N. Caviedes. *Professor of Geography, University of Florida, Gainesville. Author of* The Politics of Chile *and others.*
CHILE (*in part*)

C.N.M.   Charles Nicholas Morris. *Managing Director, London Economics. Former Deputy Director, Institute for Fiscal Studies, London. Coauthor of* The Reform of Social Security.
GOVERNMENT FINANCE (*in part*)

C.O.   Carola Oman (Lady Lenanton) (d. 1978). *Biographer. Author of* David Garrick *and others.*
GARRICK, DAVID (Micropædia)

C.O.Hu.   Charles O. Hucker. *Emeritus Professor of Chinese and of History, University of Michigan, Ann Arbor. Author of* The Traditional Chinese State in Ming Times *and others.*
CHINA (*in part*)
YUNG-LO (Micropædia)

Co.L.   Colin Legum. *Associate Editor,* The Observer, *London, 1949–82; Editor,*

Africa Contemporary Record, *1968–83. Author of* Pan-Africanism *and others.*
SOUTHERN AFRICA (*in part*)

C.P.   Colin Patterson. *Curator of Fossil Fishes, British Museum (Natural History), London. Coeditor of* Fossil Vertebrates.
FISHES (*in part*)

C.P.D.   Carlos Pablo Dubois. *Head of Information Services, International Coffee Organization, London.*
URUGUAY (*in part*)

C.Pe.   Chaim Perelman (d. 1984). *Professor of Logic and Ethics, Free University of Brussels. Author of* The New Rhetoric *and others.*
RHETORIC (*in part*)

C.Pf.   Carl Pfaffmann. *Emeritus Professor of Neurobiology and Behavior, Rockefeller University, New York City. Editor of* Olfaction and Taste, *proceedings of the Third International Symposium on Olfaction and Taste.*
SENSORY RECEPTION (*in part*)

C.P.F.   Charles Patrick FitzGerald. *Emeritus Professor of Far Eastern History, Australian National University, Canberra. Author of* Son of Heaven (T'ang T'ai Tsung); The Empress Wu.
T'AI TSUNG (T'ANG DYNASTY) (Micropædia)
WU HOU (Micropædia)

C.Ra.   Chakravarthi Raghavan. *Correspondent, IPS Third World News Agency, Geneva. Chief Editor, SUNS newsletter, Nyon, Switzerland, and Rome.*
BOMBAY
INDIA (*in part*)

C.R.B.   Charles R. Bawden. *Emeritus Professor of Mongolian, University of London. Author of* The Modern History of Mongolia.
GENGHIS KHAN
KUBLAI KHAN (Micropædia)

C.R.G.   C. Robin Ganellin. *Professor of Medicinal Chemistry, University College, University of London. Coeditor of* Frontiers in Histamine Research *and others.*
DRUGS AND DRUG ACTION (*in part*)

C.R.H.   Campbell Ronald Harler (deceased). *Adviser on tea to the Central Treaty Organization. Author of* The Culture and Marketing of Tea.
FARMING AND AGRICULTURAL TECHNOLOGY (*in part*)

C.R.N.   Charles R. Noback. *Emeritus Professor of Anatomy and Cell Biology, College of Physicians and Surgeons, Columbia University. Author of* The Human Nervous System.
NERVES AND NERVOUS SYSTEMS (*in part*)

C.R.No.   Carl R. Noller (d. 1980). *Professor of Chemistry, Stanford University, California. Author of* Chemistry of Organic Compounds.
CHEMICAL COMPOUNDS (*in part*)

C.Ro.   Christopher Robinson. *Official Student in Modern Languages, Christ Church, University of Oxford. Author of*

French Literature in the 19th Century *and others.*
FRENCH LITERATURE (*in part*)

C.R.R.   Charles R. Russell. *Consulting engineer. Former Professor of Mechanical Engineering, California Polytechnic State University, San Luis Obispo. Author of* Elements of Energy Conversion.
ENERGY CONVERSION (*in part*)

C.R.S.   C. Ronald Seeger. *Professor of Geology and Geophysics, Western Kentucky University, Bowling Green. Author of* Problems for Exploration Geophysics.
CONTINENTAL LANDFORMS (*in part*)

C.R.T.   Charles Rowland Twidale. *Reader in Geology and Geophysics, University of Adelaide, Australia. Author of* Geomorphology with Special Reference to Australia *and others.*
AUSTRALIA (*in part*)
GEOMORPHIC PROCESSES (*in part*)

C.S.   Calambur Sivaramamurti. *Director, National Museum of India, New Delhi, 1966–69, 1971–75; Hony Adviser on Museums, Government of India, 1969–70. Author of* Indian Sculpture *and others.*
SOUTH ASIAN ARTS (*in part*)

C.Sa.   Claudio Sartori. *Chief, Office of Research and Indexing of the Italian Musical Funds, Braidense National Library, Milan. Author of* Puccini *and others.*
PUCCINI, GIACOMO (Micropædia)

C.S.Br.   C.S. Breed. *Geologist, Geological Survey, U.S. Department of the Interior, Flagstaff, Arizona. Coauthor of* Landscapes of Arizona: The Geological Story.
CONTINENTAL LANDFORMS (*in part*)

C.-S.Ch.   Cheng-Siang Chen. *Former Professor of Geography; former Director, Geographical Research Center, Chinese University of Hong Kong. Author of* Taiwan: An Economic and Social Geography *and several reports on Hong Kong.*
CHINA (*in part*)

C.Se.   Charles Seymour (d. 1963). *President, Yale University, 1937–50; Professor of History, 1918–37. Author of* The Diplomatic Background of the War; Woodrow Wilson and the World War.
WILSON, WOODROW (*in part*) (Micropædia)

C.S.F.   Catherine S. Fowler. *Professor of Anthropology, University of Nevada, Reno. Author of* Great Basin Anthropology: A Bibliography.
AMERICAN INDIANS (*in part*)

C.S.G.P.   Courtenay Stanley Goss Phillips. *Lecturer in Inorganic Chemistry, University of Oxford; Fellow of Merton College, Oxford. Coauthor of* Inorganic Chemistry.
CHEMICAL ELEMENTS (*in part*)

C.S.Ha.   Craig S. Harbison. *Professor of Art History, University of Massachusetts, Amherst. Author of* The

Last Judgment in Sixteenth Century Northern Europe *and others.*
GRÜNEWALD, MATTHIAS (Micropædia)
HOLBEIN, HANS, THE YOUNGER (Micropædia)

C.S.J.   Christopher Stewart Jackson. *Former Senior Lecturer in English, University of the West Indies, Cave Hill, Barbados.*
WEST INDIES, THE (*in part*)

C.Sm.   Colin Smethurst. *Marshall Professor of French, University of Glasgow, Scotland. Author of* Émile Zola, Germinal.
FRENCH LITERATURE (*in part*)

C.Sn.   Carl Sagan. *Director, Laboratory for Planetary Studies; David Duncan Professor of Astronomy, Cornell University, Ithaca, New York. Author of* The Dragons of Eden: Speculations on the Evolution of Human Intelligence; Cosmos; *and others.*
LIFE (*in part*)
SOLAR SYSTEM, THE (*in part*)

C.S.S.   Sir Charles Scott Sherrington, M.D. (d. 1952). *Waynflete Professor of Physiology, University of Oxford, 1913–35. Cowinner, Nobel Prize for Physiology or Medicine, 1932, for discoveries regarding the function of neurons. Author of* The Integrative Action of the Nervous System.
NERVES AND NERVOUS SYSTEMS (*in part*)

C.S.Sh.   Caroline Sarah Shaw. *Legal Clerk. Researcher on Cape Verde.*
WESTERN AFRICA (*in part*)

C.Su.   Chusei Suzuki. *Professor of Asian History, Aichi University, Toyohashi, Japan. Author of* A Study of Mid-Ch'ing History.
CHINA (*in part*)

C.S.W.   C. Stuart Welch, M.D. (d. 1981). *Professor of Surgery, Albany Medical College, Union University, New York. Coauthor of* The Essence of Surgery.
DIAGNOSIS AND THERAPEUTICS (*in part*)

C.S.Wh.   Charles S. Whewell. *Emeritus Professor of Textile Industries, University of Leeds, England.*
INDUSTRIES, TEXTILE (*in part*)

C.S.-y.   Chuang Shang-yen (d. 1980). *Deputy Director, National Palace Museum, Taipei, Taiwan.*
MI FEI (Micropædia)

C.-t.C.   Chen-tung Chang. *Senior Lecturer in Sociology, National University of Singapore. Author of* Fertility Transition in Singapore.
CHINA (*in part*)

C.T.Mo.   Charles Thomas Morrissey. *Director, Oral History Project, Baylor College of Medicine, Houston, Texas. Editor in Chief, International Journal of Oral History. Adjunct Professor of History, University of Vermont, Burlington. Author of* Vermont: A Bicentennial History.
UNITED STATES OF AMERICA (*in part*)

C.T.R.   C.T. Ritchie. *Historian, writer, and artist. Author of* The First Canadian:

The Story of Champlain *and others.*
CHAMPLAIN, SAMUEL DE (Micropædia)

C.T.W. Cheves T. Walling. *Distinguished Professor of Chemistry, University of Utah, Salt Lake City. Author of* Free Radicals in Solution.
RADICAL (*in part*) (Micropædia)

C.T.Wa. Chun Tsin Wang. *Senior Research Metallurgist, Teledyne Wah Chang Albany, Oregon. Coauthor of* Tungsten: Sources, Metallurgy, Properties, and Applications.
INDUSTRIES, EXTRACTION AND PROCESSING (*in part*)

C.V.B Clinton V. Black. *Archival adviser, Government of Jamaica; former Archivist, Jamaica Archives, Spanish Town. Author of* The History of Jamaica *and others.*
WEST INDIES, THE (*in part*)

C.v.d.K. C. van de Kieft. *Professor of Medieval History, University of Amsterdam. Coauthor of* 500 Jaren Staten-Generaal in de Nederlanden.
NETHERLANDS, THE (*in part*)

C.V.-F. Claudio Vita-Finzi. *Professor of Neotectonics, University College, University of London. Author of* Recent Earth History; Recent Earth Movements; *and others.*
GEOMORPHIC PROCESSES (*in part*)

C.V.N. Chakravarthi V. Narasimhan. *Senior Fellow, United Nations Institute for Training and Research, New York City; Under-Secretary-General for Inter-Agency Affairs and Coordination, United Nations, 1973–78. Author of* The United Nations: an Inside View *and others.*
ASIA (*in part*)

C.V.W. Dame C.V. Wedgwood. *Free-lance writer and historian. Fellow, University College, University of London. Author of* Thomas Wentworth, First Earl of Strafford, 1593–1641: A Revaluation.
STRAFFORD, THOMAS WENTWORTH, 1ST EARL OF (Micropædia)

C.W. Claus Westermann. *Professor of Old Testament Exegesis, University of Heidelberg. Author of* Handbook to the Old Testament.
SACRED OFFICES AND ORDERS (*in part*)

C.W.A. Charles W. Arnade. *Professor of International Studies and History, University of South Florida, Tampa. Author of* The Emergence of the Republic of Bolivia *and others.*
BOLIVIA (*in part*)

C.W.B. Curt W. Beck. *Matthew Vassar, Jr., Professor of Chemistry, Vassar College, Poughkeepsie, New York.*
STAHL, GEORG ERNST (Micropædia)

C.W.G. Carol W. Gelderman. *Research Professor of English, University of New Orleans. Author of* Henry Ford, the Wayward Capitalist *and others.*
FORD, HENRY (*in part*)

C.W.Ge. Charles William Gear. *Professor and Head, Department of Computer Science, University of Illinois at Urbana-Champaign. Author of* Numerical Initial Value Problems for Ordinary Differential Equations *and others.*
NUMERICAL ANALYSIS

C.W.H. Charles W. Hayford. *Associate, Department of History, Northwestern University, Evanston, Illinois, and Center for East Asian Studies, University of Chicago.*
LIN TSE-HSÜ (Micropædia)

C.W.H.H. C. William H. Havard, M.D. *Consultant Physician, Royal Free Hospital and Royal Northern Hospital, London. Author of* Current Medical Treatment *and others.*
DIAGNOSIS AND THERAPEUTICS (*in part*)

C.W.Ho. C. Warren Hollister. *Professor of History, University of California, Santa Barbara. Author of* The Impact of the Norman Conquest *and others.*
HENRY I (ENGLAND) (Micropædia)

C.W.J. C. Wilfred Jenks (d. 1973). *Director General of the International Labour Office, Geneva, Switzerland, 1970–73. Author of* Human Rights and International Labour Standards.
BUSINESS LAW (*in part*)

C.W.M. C.W. Minkel. *Vice-Provost; Dean, Graduate School, University of Tennessee, Knoxville. Coauthor of* Latin America.
CARACAS (*in part*)
SÃO PAULO (*in part*)

C.W.P. Clifton W. Pannell. *Director, Center for Asian Studies; Professor of Geography, University of Georgia, Athens. Coauthor of* China: Geography of Development and Modernization; *editor of* East Asia: Historical and Geographical Approaches to Foreign Area Studies.
ASIA (*in part*)

C.W.Pa. Charles William Parkin. *Fellow and Lecturer of Clare College, University of Cambridge. Author of* The Moral Basis of Burke's Political Thought.
BURKE, EDMUND (*in part*) (Micropædia)

C.W.S. Clyde William Sanger. *Visiting Lecturer, Zimbabwe Institute of Mass Communication, 1982. Director of Information, Commonwealth Secretariat, London, 1977–79. Author of* Central African Emergency.
SOUTHERN AFRICA (*in part*)

C.W.T. Charlton W. Tebeau. *Emeritus Professor of History, University of Miami, Coral Gables, Florida. Author of* A History of Florida.
JACKSON, THOMAS JONATHAN (Micropædia)

C.W.W. Charles W. Wagley. *Graduate Research Professor Emeritus of Anthropology and Latin American Studies, University of Florida, Gainesville. Author of* Introduction to Brazil *and others.*
BRAZIL (*in part*)

C.Y. Chiang Yee (d. 1977). *Painter, Professor of Chinese, Columbia University, 1968–71. Author of* Chinese Calligraphy *and others.*
WRITING (*in part*)

C.-y.C. Chu-yuan Cheng. *Professor of Economics, Ball State University, Muncie, Indiana. Consultant, National Science Foundation, Washington, D.C. Author of* China's Economic Development: Growth and Structural Change *and others.*
CHINA (*in part*)

Cy.Do. Cyril Domb. *Professor of Physics, Bar Ilan University, Ramat Gan, Israel. Editor of* Clerk Maxwell and Modern Science.
MAXWELL

C.-y.H. Cho-yun Hsu. *University Professor of History and Sociology, University of Pittsburgh. Author of* History of Western Chou Civilization.
CHINA (*in part*)

Cz.L. Czeslaw Lejewski. *Emeritus Professor of Philosophy, Victoria University of Manchester. Author of* "Logic and Existence," British Journal for the Philosophy of Science, *and numerous other journal articles.*
LOGIC, THE HISTORY AND KINDS OF (*in part*)

D.A. Dudley Andrew. *Professor of Communication Studies and of Comparative Literature; Director, Institute for Cinema and Culture, University of Iowa, Iowa City. Author of* Film in the Aura of Art *and others.*
MOTION PICTURES (*in part*)

D.A.B. Dirk Anthony Ballendorf. *Professor of History and Micronesian Studies, University of Guam. Coeditor of* Oceania Today: Towards New Directions and Political Self-Actualization.
PACIFIC ISLANDS (*in part*)

Da.Br. David Brown. *Emeritus Professor of Musicology, University of Southampton, England. Author of* Mikhail Glinka; Tchaikovsky; *and others.*
SHOSTAKOVICH, DMITRY (Micropædia)

D.A.C. David A. Cook. *Professor and Director of Film Studies Program, Emory University, Atlanta, Georgia. Author of* A History of Narrative Film.
MOTION PICTURES (*in part*)

Da.C.J. David C. Joy. *Distinguished Professor of Zoology, University of Tennessee, Knoxville. Distinguished Scientist, Oak Ridge National Laboratory, Tennessee; Director, Electron Microscopy Facility. Coeditor of* Principles of Analytical Electron Microscopy.
MICROSCOPES (*in part*)

Da.D. David Dooling, Jr. *Aerospace writer and consultant. Former Science Editor,* The Huntsville (Alabama) Times. *Coauthor of* Space Travel: A History.
EXPLORATION (*in part*)

D.A.E.S. David A.E. Spalding. *Executive Director, British Columbia Museums Association, Victoria.*

Former Head Curator of Natural History, Provincial Museum of Alberta, Edmonton. Senior editor of A Nature Guide to Alberta.
CANADA (*in part*)

Da.G.S. **David G. Scanlon** (d. 1990). *Professor of International Education, Columbia University. Editor of* Traditions of African Education *and others.*
EDUCATION, HISTORY OF (*in part*)

D.A.H. **Donald August Holm.** *Senior Geologist, Arabian American Oil Company, Dhahran, Saudi Arabia, 1946–61. Author of "Desert Geomorphology of the Arabian Peninsula" in* Science *magazine.*
ASIA (*in part*)

D.A.He. **D. Alan Heslop.** *Director, Rose Institute of State and Local Government, Claremont McKenna College, California. Editor of* Californians in Congress.
POLITICAL SYSTEMS (*in part*)

D.A.K.B. **Sir Douglas A.K. Black, M.D.** *Emeritus Professor of Medicine, Victoria University of Manchester; Physician, Manchester Royal Infirmary, 1959–77. Editor of* Renal Disease.
EXCRETION AND EXCRETORY SYSTEMS (*in part*)

D.A.L. **Daniel A. Livingstone.** *J.B. Duke Professor of Zoology, Duke University, Durham, North Carolina. Limnologist, Geological Survey, U.S. Department of the Interior, 1956–63.*
BIOSPHERE, THE (*in part*)

D.A.Lo. **D. Anthony Low.** *Smuts Professor of Commonwealth History, University of Cambridge. Author of* Buganda in Modern History.
EASTERN AFRICA (*in part*)

Da.Ma. **David Magarshack** (d. 1977). *Author of* Chekhov the Dramatist; Dostoevsky; Pushkin: A Biography.
RUSSIAN LITERATURE (*in part*)

D.An. **Donald M. Anderson.** *Emeritus Professor of Art, University of Wisconsin, Madison. Author of* The Art of Written Forms.
WRITING (*in part*)

D.A.N. **David A. Norris.** *Lecturer in Slavonic Studies, University of Nottingham, England. Translator of Edvard Kardelj's* Reminiscences.
YUGOSLAV LITERATURE (*in part*)

D.Ar. **Daniel Argov.** *Former Lecturer in Modern Indian History, Institute of Asian and African Studies, Hebrew University of Jerusalem. Author of* Moderates and Extremists in the Indian Nationalist Movement, 1883–1920.
PATEL, VALLABHBHAI JHAVERBHAI (Micropædia)

D.A.Sa. **Dawlat Ahmed Sadek.** *Chairman of the Geography Department, Faculty of Arts, Ain Shams University, Cairo, Egypt.*
ARABIA (*in part*)

D.At. **Donald Attwater** (d. 1977). *Author of* Penguin Dictionary of Saints;

St. John Chrysostom, Pastor and Preacher.
CHRYSOSTOM, SAINT JOHN (Micropædia)

D.A.T. **David A. Thomas.** *Lecturer in Criminology, University of Cambridge; Fellow of Trinity Hall, Cambridge. Author of* Principles of Sentencing.
CRIME AND PUNISHMENT (*in part*)

Da.W. **David Watts.** *Dean, School of Earth Resources, University of Hull, England. Author of* The West Indies Patterns of Development *and others.*
WEST INDIES, THE (*in part*)

D.B. **Douglas Bush** (d. 1983). *Gurney Professor of English Literature, Harvard University, 1957–66. Author of* Paradise Lost in Our Time *and others.*
MILTON (*in part*)

D.Ba. **D. Banzragch.** *Scientific Secretary, Institute of Biology, Academy of Sciences of the Mongolian People's Republic, Ulaanbaatar.*
MONGOLIA (*in part*)

D.B.C. **David B. Chan.** *Professor of History, California State University, Hayward. Author of* The Yung Lo Usurpation.
HUNG-WU (Micropædia)

D.B.E. **David Barnard Ericson.** *Research Staff Scientist, Lamont-Doherty Geological Observatory, Columbia University, 1964–73. Coauthor of* The Ever-Changing Sea.
ATLANTIC OCEAN, THE (*in part*)

D.B.En. **David B. Enfield.** *Research Oceanographer, Atlantic Oceanographic and Meteorological Laboratory, National Oceanic and Atmospheric Administration, U.S. Department of Commerce, Miami.*
EL NIÑO (Micropædia)
OCEANS (*in part*)

D.B.-G. **David Ben-Gurion** (d. 1973). *Prime Minister and Minister of Defense, Government of Israel, 1948–53, 1955–63. Author of* The Struggle *and others.*
HERZL, THEODOR (Micropædia)

D.B.H. **Dwight B. Heath.** *Professor of Anthropology, Brown University, Providence, Rhode Island. Editor of* Contemporary Cultures and Societies of Latin America.
AMERICAN INDIANS (*in part*)

D.Bi. **David Birmingham.** *Professor of Modern History, University of Kent at Canterbury, England. Author of* Trade and Conflict in Angola *and others.*
CENTRAL AFRICA (*in part*)
SOUTHERN AFRICA (*in part*)
WESTERN AFRICA (*in part*)

D.B.J.F. **David B.J. Frost.** *Subeditor and rugby writer,* The Guardian (*London*). *Author of* No Prisoners: Background to Rugby Touring.
SPORTS, MAJOR TEAM AND INDIVIDUAL (*in part*)

D.Br. **Doris Bry.** *Writer on photography, art history, and natural science. Representative for the paintings of Georgia O'Keeffe. Author of* Alfred

Stieglitz: Photographer.
STIEGLITZ, ALFRED (Micropædia)

D.B.S. **David B. Stewart.** *Research Geologist, Geological Survey, U.S. Department of the Interior, Washington, D.C.*
MINERALS AND ROCKS (*in part*)

D.B.W. **David B. Wake.** *Director, Museum of Vertebrate Zoology; Professor of Integrative Biology, University of California, Berkeley.*
AMPHIBIANS (*in part*)

D.B.Wa. **Duncan Bruce Waterson.** *Professor of History, Macquarie University, North Ryde, Australia. Coauthor of* From the Frontier: A Pictorial History of Queensland.
AUSTRALIA (*in part*)

D.C. **Douglas Cooper** (d. 1984). *Art historian and critic. Author of* Toulouse Lautrec *and many other works on French artists of the late 19th and 20th centuries.*
GAUGUIN, PAUL (Micropædia)

D.Ca. **David Carson.** *Emeritus Professor of Business Administration, Boston University. Author of* International Marketing: A Comparative Systems Approach.
MARKETING AND MERCHANDISING (in part)

D.C.A. **Dorothy C. Adkins** (d. 1975). *Psychologist. Professor of Education, University of Hawaii at Manoa, Honolulu, 1965–74. Author of* Test Construction.
PSYCHOLOGICAL TESTS AND MEASUREMENT (*in part*)

D.C.B. **Douglas C. Baxter.** *Associate Professor of History, Ohio University, Athens.*
LOUVOIS, FRANÇOIS-MICHEL LE TELLIER, MARQUIS DE (Micropædia)

D.C.C. **Donald C. Clarke.** *Assistant Professor of Law, University of Washington, Seattle.*
CRIME AND PUNISHMENT (*in part*)

D.C.G.S. **David C.G. Sibley.** *Free-lance writer and artist. Author of* With La Salle Down the Mississippi *and others.*
LA SALLE, RENÉ-ROBERT CAVELIER, SIEUR DE (Micropædia)

D.C.H. **David C. Hoaglin.** *Research Associate in Statistics, Harvard University. Senior Scientist, Abt Associates Inc., Cambridge, Massachusetts.*
STATISTICS (*in part*)

D.C.J. **D. Clayton James.** *Biggs Professor of Military History, Virginia Military Institute, Lexington. Author of* The Years of MacArthur *and others.*
MACARTHUR, DOUGLAS (Micropædia)

D.Co. **Dennis Conway.** *Associate Professor of Geography and Latin American and Caribbean Studies, Indiana University, Bloomington.*
VENEZUELA (*in part*)

D.C.P. **David C. Pieri.** *Member of the Technical Staff; Team Leader,*

Volcanology, Earth and Space Sciences Division, Jet Propulsion Laboratory, California Institute of Technology, Pasadena.

SOLAR SYSTEM, THE (*in part*)

D.C.S.   **Domingo C. Salita.** *Emeritus Professor of Geology and Geography, University of the Philippines, Quezon City; former Dean, College of Arts and Sciences.*

MANILA

D.C.T.   **Denis C. Twitchett.** *Gordon Wu Professor of Chinese Studies, Princeton University. Author of* The Financial Administration Under the T'ang Dynasty; *editor of* Cambridge History of China.

CHINA (in part)
SSU-MA CH'IEN (Micropædia)

D.C.Th.   **David Christopher Traherne Thomas.** *Former Assistant Director of Art, Arts Council of Great Britain, London. Joint compiler of* The First Hundred Years of the Royal Academy, 1769–1868 *(catalog of the Royal Academy Winter Exhibition, London, 1951–52).*

DEGAS, EDGAR (Micropædia)

D.D.   **David Diringer** (d. 1975). *Reader in Semitic Epigraphy, University of Cambridge, 1966–68. Founder and Director, Alphabet Museum, Tel Aviv, Israel. Author of* The Alphabet.

WRITING (*in part*)

D.Da.   **David Daiches.** *Emeritus Professor of English, University of Sussex, Brighton, England. Author of* Robert Burns; Robert Burns and His World; R.L. Stevenson and His World.

BURNS, ROBERT (*in part*) (Micropædia)
STEVENSON, ROBERT LOUIS (Micropædia)

D.D.B.   **Dimitry Dimitriyevich Blagoy** (d. 1984). *Professor and Head, Department of Modern Russian Literature, Institute of World Literature, Academy of Sciences of the U.S.S.R., Moscow. Author of* Tvorchesky put Pushkina *and others.*

PUSHKIN, ALEKSANDR (*in part*) (Micropædia)

D.D.Br.   **Donald Dilworth Brand** (d. 1984). *Professor of Geography, University of Texas at Austin, 1949–75. Author of* Mexico: Land of Sunshine and Shadow.

NORTH AMERICA (*in part*)

D.D.C.   **Dennis D. Cordell.** *Associate Professor of History, Southern Methodist University, Dallas, Texas. Associate Professor of Demography, University of Montreal. Coeditor of* African Population and Capitalism: Historical Perspectives.

CENTRAL AFRICA (*in part*)

D.D.F.   **Don D. Fowler.** *Professor of Anthropology; Director, Historic Preservation Program, University of Nevada, Reno. Coeditor of* Anthropology of the Numu, Smithsonian Contributions to Anthropology (*vol. 14*).

AMERICAN INDIANS (*in part*)

D.Dn.   **D. Dashtseren.** *Journalist and publicist.*

MONGOLIA (*in part*)

D.Do.   **Denis Donoghue.** *Henry James Professor of English and American Letters, New York University, New York City. Author of* Yeats; *editor of* Yeats: Memoirs.

YEATS, WILLIAM BUTLER (*in part*) (Micropædia)

D.D.R.O.   **D.D.R. Owen.** *Emeritus Professor of French, University of St. Andrews, Scotland. Author of* The Evolution of the Grail Legend *and others.*

FRENCH LITERATURE (*in part*)

D.E.   **David A. Ede.** *Associate Professor of Religion, Western Michigan University, Kalamazoo.*

ḤASAN AL-BAṢRI, AL- (Micropædia)

D.E.B.   **D. E. Berlyne** (d. 1976). *Professor of Psychology, University of Toronto. Author of* Structure and Direction in Thinking.

THOUGHT AND THOUGHT PROCESSES (*in part*)

D.E.C.   **Denis E. Cosgrove.** *Reader in Cultural Geography, Loughborough University of Technology, England. Author of* Social Formation and Symbolic Landscape.

VENICE (*in part*)

D.E.C.Y.   **David Eryl Corbet Yale.** *Reader in English Legal History, University of Cambridge; Fellow of Christ's College, Cambridge.*

HALE, SIR MATTHEW (Micropædia)

D.E.D.   **Don E. Dumond.** *Professor of Anthropology; Director, Museum of Natural History, University of Oregon, Eugene. Author of* The Eskimos and Aleuts.

ARCTIC, THE (*in part*)

D.E.G.   **David E. Gardinier.** *Professor of History, Marquette University, Milwaukee, Wisconsin. Author of* Historical Dictionary of Gabon.

CENTRAL AFRICA (*in part*)

D.E.K.   **Daniel E. Koshland, Jr.** *Professor of Biochemistry, University of California, Berkeley. Editor,* Science *magazine.*

BIOCHEMICAL COMPONENTS OF ORGANISMS (*in part*)

D.E.L.   **David Edward Luscombe.** *Professor of Medieval History, University of Sheffield, England. Author of* The School of Peter Abelard; *editor of* Peter Abelard's Ethics.

ABELARD, PETER (Micropædia)

De.M.S.   **Denis Mack Smith.** *Extraordinary Fellow, Wolfson College, University of Oxford; Senior Research Fellow, All Souls College, Oxford, 1962–87. Author of* Garibaldi; *editor of* Garibaldi.

GARIBALDI, GIUSEPPE (Micropædia)

D.E.P.   **David E. Pingree.** *Professor of the History of Mathematics, Brown University, Providence, Rhode Island. Author of* Gregory Chioniades and

Palaeologan Astronomy and others.

OCCULTISM (*in part*)

D.Er.   **Donald James Erb.** *Distinguished Professor of Composition, Cleveland Institute of Music, Ohio. Composer of "The Seventh Trumpet" and others.*

MUSIC, THE ART OF (*in part*)
MUSICAL FORMS AND GENRES (*in part*)

D.E.S.   **David Eugene Smith** (d. 1944). *Professor of Mathematics, Teachers College, Columbia University, 1901–26. Author of* History of Modern Mathematics *and others.*

ARITHMETIC (*in part*)

D.E.S.M.   **D.E.S. Maxwell.** *Professor of English, York University, Toronto. Author of* Herman Melville; American Fiction; *and others.*

MELVILLE, HERMAN (*in part*) (Micropædia)

DeW.C.R.   **DeWitt C. Reddick** (d. 1980). *Jesse H. Jones Professor of Journalism and Education, University of Texas at Austin, 1970–75.*

UNITED STATES OF AMERICA (*in part*)

D.E.W.W.   **Donald Ernest Wilson Wormell** (d. 1990). *Professor of Latin, University of Dublin, 1942–78. Coauthor of* The Delphic Oracle.

PINDAR (Micropædia)

D.F.   **David Foulkes.** *Research Scientist, Georgia Mental Health Institute, Atlanta. Author of* The Psychology of Sleep.

SLEEP AND DREAMS (*in part*)

D.F.B.   **Donald F. Bond** (d. 1987). *Emeritus Professor of English, University of Chicago, 1952–67. Editor of* The Spectator.

ADDISON, JOSEPH (Micropædia)

D.F.Br.   **Deborah Fahy Bryceson.** *Senior Member Cross-Cultural Centre for Research on Women, Queen Elizabeth House, University of Oxford. Author of* Food Insecurity and the Social Division of Labour in Tanzania, 1919–85.

EASTERN AFRICA (*in part*)

D.F.Do.   **Douglas F. Dowd.** *Professor of Economics, San Jose State University, California. Professorial Lecturer in International Economics, John Hopkins University School of Advanced Studies, Bologna Center, Italy.*

OWEN, ROBERT (*in part*) (Micropædia)

D.Fe.   **David Fellman.** *Vilas Professor Emeritus of Political Science, University of Wisconsin, Madison. Author of* The Defendant's Rights Today.

CONSTITUTIONAL LAW (*in part*)

D.F.G.   **David Frank Gordon.** *Assistant Professor of International Relations, Michigan State University, East Lansing.*

SOUTH AFRICA (*in part*)

D.Fl.   **David Flusser.** *Professor of the History of Religions, Hebrew University of Jerusalem. Author of* Jesus *and others.*

BIBLICAL LITERATURE AND ITS CRITICAL INTERPRETATION (*in part*)

D.F.R.   **Dale F. Ritter.** *Executive Director, Quaternary Sciences Center,*

Desert Research Institute, University of Nevada, Reno. Author of Process Geomorphology.
RIVERS (*in part*)

D.G.B.   David G. Browning. *Fellow, St. Cross College, University of Oxford. Author of* El Salvador: Landscape and Society.
CENTRAL AMERICA (*in part*)

D.G.Ch.   Donald Geoffrey Charlton. *Emeritus Professor of French, University of Warwick, Coventry, England. Author of* Positivist Thought in France, 1852–1870 *and others.*
TAINE, HIPPOLYTE (Micropædia)

D.G.D.   Denys G. Dyer. *Former Lecturer in German, University of Oxford; former Fellow of Exeter College, Oxford.*
GERMAN LITERATURE (*in part*)

D.Ge.   Deno John Geanakoplos. *Professor of History and Religious Studies, Yale University. Author of* Emperor Michael Palaeologus and the West *and others.*
MICHAEL VIII PALAEOLOGUS (BYZANTINE EMPIRE) (Micropædia)

D.G.F.   Donald G. Fink. *Emeritus Director, Institute of Electrical and Electronics Engineers, New York. Author of* Television Engineering.
BROADCASTING (*in part*)
ENGINEERING (*in part*)

D.G.Fa.   Daphne Gail Fautin. *Curator, Department of Invertebrate Zoology, California Academy of Sciences, San Francisco. Author of* The Clownfish Sea Anemones, *Transactions of the American Philosophical Society.*
CNIDARIANS (*in part*)

D.Gi.   Douglas Stuart Gilbert (d. 1979). *Sports columnist, Edmonton Sun, 1978–79. Sports reporter, Montreal Gazette, 1970–78.*
SPORTS, MAJOR TEAM AND INDIVIDUAL (*in part*)

D.G.J.   D. Gale Johnson. *Eliakim Hastings Moore Distinguished Service Professor Emeritus of Economics, University of Chicago. Author of* World Agriculture in Disarray *and others.*
FARMING AND AGRICULTURAL TECHNOLOGY (*in part*)

D.G.J.S.   David Grenville John Sellwood. *Principal Lecturer in Mechanical Engineering, Kingston Polytechnic, England. Author of* An Introduction to the Coinage of Parthia.
COINS AND COINAGE (*in part*)

D.G.M.   David Grier Martin, Jr. *Secretary of the University of North Carolina system, Chapel Hill.*
UNITED STATES OF AMERICA (*in part*)

D.G.MacR.   Donald Gunn MacRae. *Martin White Professor Emeritus of Sociology, London School of Economics and Political Science, University of London.*
MALTHUS, THOMAS ROBERT (Micropædia)

D.Gr.   David Greene (d. 1981). *Senior Professor, School of Celtic Studies, Dublin Institute for Advanced Studies. Author of* The Irish Language.
CELTIC LITERATURE (*in part*)
LANGUAGES OF THE WORLD (*in part*)

D.G.R.   Donald G. Rea. *Special Assistant to the Director, Jet Propulsion Laboratory, California Institute of Technology, Pasadena.*
SOLAR SYSTEM, THE (*in part*)

D.G.S.   David G. Sansing. *Professor of History, University of Mississippi, University. Author of* Mississippi: Its People and Culture.
UNITED STATES OF AMERICA (*in part*)

D.G.Sa.   D. Gregory Sanford. *Vermont State Archivist, Office of the Secretary of State, Montpelier. Editor of* Vermont Municipalities: An Index to Their Charters and Special Acts.
UNITED STATES OF AMERICA (*in part*)

D.G.Sc.   Dante G. Scarpelli, M.D. *Ernest J. and Hattie H. Magerstadt Professor and Chairman, Department of Pathology, Northwestern University, Chicago.*
CANCER (*in part*)

D.G.Ss.   D. Gail Saunders. *Director, Department of Archives, Nassau, The Bahamas. Author of* Bahamian Loyalists and Their Slaves *and others.*
WEST INDIES, THE (*in part*)

D.G.T.   David Gordon Tucker (d. 1990). *Professor and Head, Department of Electronic and Electrical Engineering, University of Birmingham, England, 1955–73.*
MEASUREMENT AND OBSERVATION, PRINCIPLES, METHODS AND INSTRUMENTS OF (*in part*)

D.H.   Derek Hopwood. *Director, Middle East Centre, University of Oxford. Author of* Egypt: Politics and Society, 1945–84.
EGYPT (*in part*)

D.H.B.   Daryle H. Busch. *Roy A. Roberts Distinguished Professor of Chemistry, University of Kansas, Lawrence.*
CHEMICAL COMPOUNDS (*in part*)

D.H.D.   David Herbert Donald. *Charles Warren Professor of American History and Professor of American Civilization, Harvard University. Author of* Lincoln Reconsidered *and others.*
UNITED STATES OF AMERICA (*in part*)

D.He.   David Herlihy (d. 1991). *Henry C. Lea Professor of Medieval History, Harvard University, 1980–86. Mary Critchfield and Barnaby Keeney Professor of History, Brown University, Providence, Rhode Island, 1986–91. Author of* Opera Muliebria: Women and Work in Medieval Europe.
EUROPEAN HISTORY AND CULTURE (*in part*)

D.H.E.   David H. Elliott. *Professor of Occupational Health, Robens Institute of Industrial and Environmental Health and Safety, University of Surrey,*

England. Coauthor and coeditor of The Physiology and Medicine of Diving.
RESPIRATION AND RESPIRATORY SYSTEMS (*in part*)

D.Hi.   Dorothy Hill. *Research Professor Emeritus of Geology, University of Queensland, St. Lucia, Brisbane, Australia. Author of* Paleozoic Corals; *coauthor of* Elements of the Stratigraphy of Queensland.
OCEANS (*in part*)

D.H.J.   Douglas Henry Jones. *Former Senior Lecturer in the History of West Africa, School of Oriental and African Studies, University of London.*
WESTERN AFRICA (*in part*)

D.H.P.   D.H. Pennington. *Former Fellow and Tutor in History, Balliol College, Oxford; former Lecturer in Modern History, University of Oxford. Author of* Seventeenth Century Europe.
LAUD, WILLIAM (*in part*) (Micropædia)

D.H.R.   Donald H. Reiman. *Editor,* Shelley and His Circle, *The Carl H. Pforzheimer Shelley and His Circle Collection, New York Public Library. General Editor,* The Bodleian Shelley Manuscripts. *Editor of* Shelley and His Circle (*vol. 5–8*).
SHELLEY, PERCY BYSSHE (*in part*) (Micropædia)

D.H.T.   David H. Tucker. *Free-lance researcher and writer. Author of* The World Health Market *and others.*
PUBLISHING (*in part*)

D.Hus.   Dyneley Hussey (d. 1972). *Music Critic,* The Times, *London, 1923–46;* The Listener, *1946–60. Author of* Verdi; Some Composers of Opera.
DONIZETTI, GAETANO (Micropædia)
VERDI, GIUSEPPE (Micropædia)

D.I.   David Irwin. *Chairman, Department of History of Art, University of Aberdeen, Scotland. Author of* English Neoclassical Art *and others.*
CANOVA, ANTONIO, MARCHESE D'ISCHIA (Micropædia)
PAINTING, THE HISTORY OF WESTERN (*in part*)
SCULPTURE, THE HISTORY OF WESTERN (*in part*)

Di.B.   Dieter Brunnschweiler (d. 1983). *Professor of Geography, Michigan State University, East Lansing. Coauthor of* Geography in Latin America: Prospect for the Seventies.
SOUTH AMERICA (*in part*)

Di.C.   Dieter Christensen. *Professor of Music; Director, Center for Ethnomusicology, Columbia University. Author of* Die Musik der Kate und Sialum; *coauthor of* Die Musik der Ellice-Inseln.
OCEANIC ARTS (*in part*)

D.I.D.   Denis Ian Duveen. *Consultant to the cosmetics industry in Brazil. President, Duveen Soap Corporation, Brooklyn, New York, 1949–69. Coauthor of* A Bibliography of the Works of Antoine Laurent Lavoisier.
LAVOISIER

Di.L. **Diouldé Laya.** *Director, Centre for Linguistic and Historical Studies by Oral Tradition, Organization of African Unity, Niamey, Niger. Author of "Tradition orale et recherche historique en Afrique,"* Journal of World History (UNESCO).
WESTERN AFRICA (*in part*)

D.J.B. **D. Joseph Bodin.** *Manager, International Sales and Marketing, Standard Manufacturing, Chicopee, Massachusetts. Editor,* Grits & Grinds *magazine, 1967–70.*
INDUSTRIAL GLASS AND CERAMICS (*in part*)

D.J.Ba. **D. James Baker.** *President, Joint Oceanographic Institutions Incorporated, Washington, D.C.*
EXPLORATION (*in part*)

D.J.Be. **David J. Bercuson.** *Professor of History, University of Calgary, Alberta; Dean, Faculty of Graduate Studies. Author of* Confrontation at Winnipeg: Labour, Industrial Relations and the General Strike.
CANADA (*in part*)

D.J.Bu. **David J. Buisseret.** *Director, Hermon Dunlap Smith Center for the History of Cartography, Newberry Library, Chicago. Professor of History, University of the West Indies, Kingston, Jamaica, 1964–80. Author of* Port Royal, Jamaica *and others.*
WEST INDIES, THE (*in part*)

D.J.F. **Douglas John Foskett.** *Director of Central Library Services and Goldsmiths' Librarian, University of London, 1978–83. Author of* Classification and Indexing in the Social Sciences *and others.*
LIBRARIES (*in part*)

D.J.Fo. **David John Fox.** *Senior Lecture in Geography, Victoria University of Manchester. Contributor to* Latin America: Geographical Perspectives, *2nd ed.*
CENTRAL AMERICA (*in part*)

D.J.G. **Douglas James Guthrie, M.D.** (d. 1975). *Medical historian. Lecturer on the History of Medicine, University of Edinburgh, 1945–56. Author of* A History of Medicine *and others.*
MEDICINE (*in part*)

D.J.H. **Donald J. Hanahan.** *Professor of Biochemistry, University of Texas Health Science Center at San Antonio. Author of* Lipide Chemistry.
BIOCHEMICAL COMPONENTS OF ORGANISMS (*in part*)

D.J.M.H. **David J.M. Higgins** (d. 1975). *Associate Professor of English, Monmouth College, West Long Branch, New Jersey. Author of* Portrait of Emily Dickinson.
DICKINSON, EMILY (Micropædia)

D.J.R. **Donald J. Reish.** *Emeritus Professor of Biology, California State University, Long Beach. Author of* Marine Life of Southern California.
ANNELIDS

D.J.Ro. **David J. Robinson.** *Dellplain Professor of Latin American Geography, Syracuse University, New York. Editor of* Studying Latin America.
LIMA

D.J.S. **Dirk Jan Struik.** *Emeritus Professor of Mathematics, Massachusetts Institute of Technology, Cambridge. Author of* Concise History of Mathematics *and others.*
FOURIER, JOSEPH, BARON (Micropædia)
LAGRANGE, JOSEPH-LOUIS, COMTE DE L'EMPIRE (Micropædia)
LOBACHEVSKY, NIKOLAY IVANOVICH (Micropædia)

D.J.W. **Donald John Wiseman.** *Emeritus Professor of Assyriology, School of Oriental and African Studies, University of London. Author of* Chronicles of Chaldaean Kings.
ASHURBANIPAL (Micropædia)
TIGLATH-PILESER III (*in part*) (Micropædia)

D.J.Wa. **David John Watkin.** *Lecturer in the History of Art, University of Cambridge. Author of* Thomas Hope 1769–1831 and the Neo-Classical Idea *and others.*
ARCHITECTURE, THE HISTORY OF WESTERN (*in part*)

D.K. **Delmar Karlen** (d. 1988). *Professor of Law, New York University, New York City, 1953–77. Author of* Judicial Administration: The American Experience *and others.*
JUDICIAL AND ARBITRATIONAL SYSTEMS (*in part*)

D.Ke. **Donald Keene.** *University Professor of Japanese, Columbia University. Translator into English of many of the great literary works in Japanese; and author of* Dawn to the West: Japanese Literature of the Modern Era *and others.*
JAPANESE LITERATURE (*in part*)

D.K.R. **David K. Rycroft.** *Former Senior Lecturer in Bantu Studies, School of Oriental and African Studies, University of London. Editor,* Galpin Society Journal. *Composer of national anthem of Swaziland. Author of* Concise siSwati Dictionary.
AFRICAN ARTS (*in part*)

D.L.D. **Decima L. Douie.** *Former Reader in Medieval History, University of Hull, England. Author of* The Nature and the Effect of the Heresy of the Fraticelli *and others.*
JOHN XXII (PAPACY) (Micropædia)

D.Le. **Dominica Legge** (d. 1986). *Professor of Anglo-Norman Studies, University of Edinburgh, 1968–73. Author of* Anglo-Norman Literature and Its Background *and others.*
ANGLO-NORMAN LITERATURE (Micropædia)

D.LeV. **David Le Vay.** *Former Consultant Surgeon, National Health Service, United Kingdom. Author of* Human Anatomy and Physiology.
EXCRETION AND EXCRETORY SYSTEMS (*in part*)

D.L.F. **Denis Llewellyn Fox** (d. 1983). *Professor of Marine Biochemistry, Scripps Institution of Oceanography, University of California, San Diego, at La Jolla, 1948–69. Author of* Animal Biochromes and Structural Colours.
COLORATION, BIOLOGICAL (*in part*)

D.L.L. **David L. Lack** (d. 1973). *Director, Edward Grey Institute of Field Ornithology, University of Oxford, 1945–73. Author of* Natural Regulation of Animal Numbers.
BIOSPHERE, THE (*in part*)

D.L.Le. **David L. Lewis.** *Professor of History, Howard University, Washington, D.C. Author of* King: A Critical Biography *and others.*
KING, MARTIN LUTHER, JR. (Micropædia)

D.L.M. **David Livingstone Mueller.** *Professor of Christian Theology, Southern Baptist Theological Seminary, Louisville, Kentucky. Author of* An Introduction to the Theology of Albrecht Ritschl *and others.*
RITSCHL, ALBRECHT (Micropædia)

D.L.N. **David Lawrence Niddrie.** *Emeritus Professor of Geography, University of Florida, Gainesville. Author of* Caribbean Geography *and others.*
WEST INDIES, THE (*in part*)

D.L.P. **David Leo Pawson.** *Curator of Echinoderms, National Museum of Natural History, Smithsonian Institution, Washington, D.C. Contributor to* Physiology of Echinodermata.
ECHINODERMS (*in part*)

D.L.S. **David Llewelyn Snellgrove.** *Emeritus Professor of Tibetan, University of London. Author of* Buddhist Himālaya *and others.*
BUDDHISM, THE BUDDHA AND (*in part*)
CENTRAL ASIAN ARTS (*in part*)

D.L.Se. **D.L. Serventy** (d. 1988). *Principal Research Scientist, Division of Wildlife Research, Commonwealth Scientific and Industrial Research Organization, Nedlands, Australia; Officer in Charge, Western Australia Station, 1951–69. Researcher on the distribution and ecology of Australian birds. Author of* Birds of Western Australia.
BIRDS (*in part*)

D.L.Sh. **D.L. Shineberg.** *Reader in History, The Faculties, Australian National University, Canberra. Author of* They Came for Sandalwood.
PACIFIC ISLANDS (*in part*)

D.Ma. **The Most Rev. David Mathew** (d. 1975). *Archbishop of Apamea; Assistant at the Pontifical Throne. Author of* James I.
JAMES I (GREAT BRITAIN) (Micropædia)

D.M.A. **David M. Armstrong.** *Professor of Natural Sciences; Director, Museum, University of Colorado, Boulder.*
MAMMALS (*in part*)

D.MacI. **David MacIsaac.** *Lieutenant Colonel, U.S. Air Force (retired). Professor of Military History, Air*

University, *Maxwell Air Force Base, Alabama.* Author of Strategic Bombing in World War II: The Story of the U.S. Strategic Bombing Survey.

WAR, THE THEORY AND CONDUCT OF (*in part*)

D.M.Ar.   Denis Midgley Arnold (d. 1986). *Heather Professor of Music, University of Oxford, 1975–86.* Author of Monteverdi *and others.*

MONTEVERDI, CLAUDIO (*in part*) (Micropædia)

D.M.B.   D. Mary Benson. *Writer.* Author of Chief Albert Lutuli of South Africa *and others.*

LUTULI, ALBERT (Micropædia)

D.M.Be.   Dewey M. Beegle. *Emeritus Professor of Old Testament, Wesley Theological Seminary, Washington, D.C.* Author of Moses, the Servant of Yahweh.

MOSES (*in part*)

D.M.Bo.   David Michael Bonavia (d. 1988). *Writer on China,* Far Eastern Economic Review, *Hong Kong. Foreign Correspondent,* The Times (*London*). Author of The Chinese: A Portrait; Hong Kong 1997; *and others.*

PEKING (*in part*)

D.M.DeL.   Dwight Moore DeLong (deceased). *Professor of Entomology, Ohio State University, Columbus.* Coauthor of An Introduction to the Study of Insects.

INSECTS (*in part*)

D.Mé.   Daniel Ménager. *Professor of French Literature, University of Paris X.* Author of Ronsard: le roi, le poète, et les hommes *and others.*

FRENCH LITERATURE (*in part*)

D.M.Ea.   David Magarey Earl. *Former Professor of History, Eastern Michigan University, Ypsilanti.* Author of Emperor and Nation in Japan: Political Thinkers of the Tokugawa Period.

SAIGŌ TAKAMORI (Micropædia)

D.M.G.   David M. Gates. *Professor of Botany; Director, Biological Station, University of Michigan, Ann Arbor.* Author of Energy Exchange in the Biosphere *and others.*

BIOSPHERE, THE (*in part*)

D.M.Gi.   Donald M. Ginsberg. *Professor of Physics, University of Illinois, Urbana. Author of many papers on superconductivity.*

MATTER (*in part*)

D.M.H.   Donald M. Hunten. *Professor of Planetary Sciences, University of Arizona, Tucson.*

ANALYSIS AND MEASUREMENT, PHYSICAL AND CHEMICAL (*in part*)

D.M.Ha.   David M. Hayne. *Emeritus Professor of French, University of Toronto.* Coauthor of Bibliographie critique du roman canadien-français, 1837–1900.

CANADIAN LITERATURE (*in part*)

D.Mi.   Dorothy Middleton. *Assistant Editor,* Geographical Journal, *1953–71.* Author of Baker of the Nile *and others.*

STANLEY, SIR HENRY MORTON (Micropædia)

D.M.J.   Dorothy M. Johnson (d. 1984). *Free-lance writer.* Author of The Hanging Tree; A Man Called Horse; Montana.

UNITED STATES OF AMERICA (*in part*)

D.M.K.   David Marcus Knight. *Reader in History of Science, University of Durham, England.* Author of Atoms and Elements *and others.*

ARRHENIUS, SVANTE (Micropædia)

D.M.Ke.   David M. Kunzle. *Professor of Art History, University of California, Los Angeles.* Author of The Early Comic Strip *and others.*

CARICATURE, CARTOON, AND COMIC STRIP (*in part*)

D.M.L.   David Malcolm Lewis. *Professor of Ancient History, University of Oxford.* Author of Sparta and Persia. *Joint Editor,* Cambridge Ancient History.

PERICLES (Micropædia)

D.M.La.   David Marshall Lang (d. 1991). *Professor of Caucasian Studies, University of London, 1964–84.* Author of A Modern History of Georgia; The Georgians; *and others.*

UNION OF SOVIET SOCIALIST REPUBLICS (*in part*)

D.M.L.-J.   David Mathias Lloyd-Jones. *Musicologist and conductor; specialist in Slavic music. Artistic Director, Opera North, Leeds, England.*

DVOŘÁK, ANTONÍN (Micropædia)

D.M.Lo.   David Morrice Low (d. 1972). *Classical Lecturer and Subdean, Arts Faculty, King's College, University of London, 1945–57.* Author of Edward Gibbon, 1737–94 *and others.*

GIBBON, EDWARD (Micropædia)

D.M.N.   Donald MacGillivray Nicol. *Director, Gennadius Library, American School of Classical Studies at Athens. Koraës Professor Emeritus of Byzantine and Modern Greek History, Language, and Literature, King's College, University of London.* Author of The Despotate of Epiros *and others.*

BYZANTINE EMPIRE, THE HISTORY OF THE (*in part*)
CONSTANTINE THE GREAT (*in part*)

D.M.Ne.   David M. Nelson. *Dean, College of Physical Education, Athletics and Recreation, University of Delaware, Newark. Former football coach.* Author of Football: Principles and Play.

SPORTS, MAJOR TEAM AND INDIVIDUAL (*in part*)

D.M.P.   Dorothy M. Pickles. *Writer, lecturer, and broadcaster.* Author of The Fifth French Republic; The Government and Politics of France; *and others.*

GAULLE, CHARLES DE (*in part*) (Micropædia)

D.M.S.   D.M. Sen. *Vice-Chancellor, University of Burdwan, West Bengal, India, 1965–69.*

INDIA (*in part*)

D.M.Sm.   Dale M. Smith. *Professor of Botany, University of California,*

Santa Barbara. Coauthor of The North American Sunflowers.

ANGIOSPERMS (*in part*)

D.M.W.   David M. Warshaw. *Associate Professor of Physiology and Biophysics, University of Vermont, Burlington.*

MUSCLES AND MUSCLE SYSTEMS (*in part*)

D.M.W.A.   Douglas M.W. Anderson. *Reader in Chemistry, University of Edinburgh. Editor of series of monographs on analysis of organic materials and functional groups.*

ANALYSIS AND MEASUREMENT, PHYSICAL AND CHEMICAL (*in part*)

D.M.Wh.   D. Maxwell White. *Emeritus Professor of Italian Language and Literature, University of Leeds, England.* Author of Zaccaria Seriman *and others.*

ITALIAN LITERATURE (*in part*)

D.N.   Dika Newlin. *Composer. Professor of Music, Virginia Commonwealth University, Richmond.* Author of Bruckner-Mahler-Schoenberg; Schoenberg Remembered.

SCHOENBERG, ARNOLD (*in part*) (Micropædia)

D.Ne.   Douglas Newton. *Evelyn A.J. Hall and John A. Friede Chairman, Department of Primitive Art, Metropolitan Museum of Art, New York City.* Author of Masterpieces of Primitive Art: The Nelson A. Rockefeller Collection *and others.*

OCEANIC ARTS (*in part*)

D.N.J.   D.N. Jeans. *Associate Professor of Geography, University of Sydney.* Author of The Open Air Museum: The Cultural Landscape of New South Wales; *editor of* Australia: A Geography (*2 vol.*).

AUSTRALIA (*in part*)

D.N.K.   David N. Keightley. *Professor of History, University of California, Berkeley.* Author of Sources of Shang History: The Oracle-Bone Inscriptions of Bronze Age China.

CHINA (*in part*)

D.N.McM.   David N. McMaster. *Former Reader in Geography, University of Edinburgh.* Coauthor of An Advanced Geography of Africa.

AFRICA (*in part*)

D.N.P.   Devavrat Nanubhai Pathak. *Former Vice-Chancellor, Saurāshtra University, Rājkot, India.* Coauthor of Three General Elections in Gujarat.

INDIA (*in part*)

D.N.W.   Donald N. Wilber. *Free-lance writer and consultant on the Middle East and Southeast Asia.* Author of Iran Past and Present *and others.*

SHĀPŪR II (PERSIA) (Micropædia)

Do.A.H.   Donald Albert Heath. *George Holt Professor of Pathology, University of Liverpool.* Coauthor of The Human Pulmonary Circulation.

RESPIRATION AND RESPIRATORY SYSTEMS (*in part*)

D.O.B.   Donald O. Bushman (d. 1973). *Associate Professor of Geography, University of South Carolina, Columbia,*

1960–73.

UNITED STATES OF AMERICA (*in part*)

D.O.D.W.   David O.D. Wurfel.
Professor of Political Science, University of Windsor, Ontario. Author of Filipino Politics: Development and Decay.

PHILIPPINES (*in part*)

D.O.E.   Dietz O. Edzard. *Professor of Assyriology, Ludwig Maximilian University of Munich. Author of* Die zweite Zwischenzeit Babyloniens.

MESOPOTAMIA, THE HISTORY OF
  ANCIENT (*in part*)

D.Ol.   Daria Olivier. *Writer, translator, book reviewer, and historian. Author of* Alexandre Ier *and others.*

ALEXANDER I (RUSSIA) (Micropædia)

D.O.L.   Deryck O. Lodrick. *Visiting Lecturer in Geography, University of California, Davis. Author of* Sacred Cows, Sacred Places: Origins and Survival of Animal Homes in India; *coeditor of* The Idea of Rajasthan: Explorations in Regional Identity.

ASIA (*in part*)

D.O.N.   David O. Norris. *Professor of Biology, University of Colorado, Boulder. Author of* Vertebrate Endocrinology.

ENDOCRINE SYSTEMS (*in part*)

D.O'N.   Denis O'Neill (d. 1981). *Under Secretary, Ministry of Transport, London, 1951–68.*

TRANSPORTATION (*in part*)

Do.S.   Donald Southgate. *Former Reader in Political and Constitutional History, University of Dundee, Scotland. Author of* The Most English Minister— The Policies and Politics of Palmerston.

PALMERSTON, HENRY JOHN TEMPLE,
  3RD VISCOUNT (*in part*) (Micropædia)

D.O.S.   David O. Siegmund. *Professor of Statistics, Stanford University, California. Author of* Sequential Analysis; Tests and Confidence Intervals.

PROBABILITY THEORY

D.P.   Dimitris Pournaras. *Former Publisher and Editor of* Eleutheros *(newspaper), Athens. Former Chairman, Greek Broadcasting Corporation. Author of* Eleuthérios Venizélos *and others.*

VENIZÉLOS, ELEUTHÉRIOS (Micropædia)

D.P.C.   Douglas Parodé Capper (d. 1979). *Commander, Royal Navy and Royal Navy Volunteer Reserve. Naval historian. Author of* Famous Sailing Ships of the World *and others.*

TRANSPORTATION (*in part*)

D.P.Ch.   David P. Chandler. *Research Director, Centre of Southeast Asian Studies, Monash University, Clayton, Australia. Author of* A History of Cambodia.

SOUTHEAST ASIA, MAINLAND (*in part*)

D.P.Cl.   Derek Plint Clifford. *Free-lance writer. Author of* A History of Garden Design *and others.*

GARDEN AND LANDSCAPE DESIGN
  (*in part*)

D.P.Ga.   David P. Gamble. *Emeritus Professor of Anthropology, San Francisco State University. Author of* The Wolof of Senegambia.

WESTERN AFRICA (*in part*)

D.Pi.   Dag Pike. *Marine surveyor and consultant. Author of* Fishing Boats and Their Equipment; Powerboats in Rough Seas.

FISHING, COMMERCIAL (*in part*)

D.P.L.   Donald P. Little. *Professor and Director, Institute of Islāmic Studies, McGill University, Montreal. Author of* An Introduction to Mamlūk Historiography *and others.*

EGYPT (*in part*)
MU'ĀWIYAH I (Micropædia)

D.P.O'C.   Daniel Patrick O'Connell (d. 1979). *Chichele Professor of International Law, University of Oxford, 1972–79. Author of* Richelieu *and others.*

RICHELIEU, ARMAND-JEAN DU PLESSIS,
  CARDINAL ET DUC DE (*in part*)
  (Micropædia)

D.P.T.   David P. Thelen. *Professor of History, Indiana University, Bloomington. Author of* Robert M. La Follette and the Insurgent Spirit.

LA FOLLETTE, ROBERT M. (Micropædia)

D.R.   Don Russell (d. 1986). *Free-lance writer. Author of* The Wild West: A History of the Wild West Shows.

RODEO (Micropædia)

D.R.C.   David R. Coffin. *Howard Crosby Butler Memorial Professor Emeritus of the History of Architecture, Princeton University. Author of* Villa d'Este at Tivoli *and others.*

ARCHITECTURE, THE HISTORY OF
  WESTERN (*in part*)

D.R.D.   Donald Reynolds Dudley (d. 1972). *Professor of Latin, University of Birmingham, England, 1955–72. Author of* The Romans.

SENECA, LUCIUS ANNAEUS
  (Micropædia)

D.Re.   Donald Read. *Professor of Modern English History, University of Kent at Canterbury, England. Author of* Cobden and Bright *and others.*

BRIGHT, JOHN (Micropædia)

D.R.G.   Denis Rolleston Gwynn (d. 1971). *Research Professor of Modern Irish History, University College, Cork, National University of Ireland, 1946–63. Author of* The History of Partition.

DE VALERA, EAMON (*in part*)
  (Micropædia)

D.R.Ha.   David Russell Harris. *Professor of Human Environment, Institute of Archaeology, University of London.*

WEST INDIES, THE (*in part*)

D.R.M.   Donald R. Morris. *Publisher,* Donald R. Morris Newsletter, *Houston, Texas. Author of* The Washing of the Spears: A History of the Rise of the Zulu Nation Under Shaka and Its Fall in the Zulu War of 1879.

SHAKA (Micropædia)

D.Ro.   Dov Ronen. *Associate, Center for International Affairs, Harvard University. Author of* Dahomey: Between Tradition and Modernity.

WESTERN AFRICA (*in part*)

D.R.O.   David R. Olson. *Professor of Applied Psychology, Ontario Institute for Studies in Education, Toronto. Director, McLuhan Program in Culture and Technology, University of Toronto. Coeditor of* Literacy, Language and Learning: The Nature and Consequences of Reading and Writing.

WRITING (*in part*)

D.R.P.   Donald Rahl Petterson (d. 1966). *Professor of Geography, East Carolina College, Greenville, North Carolina.*

WESTERN AFRICA (*in part*)

D.R.Sh.   Donald Raymond Shuster. *Associate Professor of Education, University of Guam, Mangilao. Author of articles on Palau.*

PACIFIC ISLANDS (*in part*)

D.S.D.   Donald Stephen Dugdale. *Professor of Mechanical Engineering, University of Sheffield, England. Author of* Elements of Elasticity.

MECHANICS (*in part*)

D.Še.   Drago Šega. *Scientific adviser, Institute for the Slovene Literature and Literary Sciences, Slovene Academy of Sciences and Arts, Ljubljana, Yugoslavia. Editor of* Anthologie de la poésie slovène.

YUGOSLAV LITERATURE (*in part*)

D.S.H.W.N.   Davidson S.H.W. Nicol. *Associate Lecturer, Centre of International Studies, University of Cambridge. Under-Secretary-General, United Nations, and Executive Director, United Nations Institute for Training and Research, New York City, 1972– 82. Ambassador for Sierra Leone to the United Nations, 1969–71. Editor of* Paths to Peace *and others.*

AFRICA (*in part*)
WESTERN AFRICA (*in part*)

D.Si.   Denis Sinor. *Distinguished Professor Emeritus of Uralic and Altaic Studies and of History, Indiana University, Bloomington. Author of* Inner Asia; History of Hungary; *and others.*

UNION OF SOVIET SOCIALIST REPUBLICS
  (*in part*)
HUNGARIAN LITERATURE (*in part*)

D.S.J.   David Starr Jordan, M.D. (d. 1931). *Chancellor, Stanford University, California, 1913–16; President, 1891– 1913. President, Indiana University, Bloomington, 1885–91; Professor of Zoology, 1879–85. Author of* A Guide to the Study of Fishes.

AGASSIZ, LOUIS (Micropædia)

D.S.Lr.   David Sievert Lavender. *Historian and writer. Author of* The Southwest; The Rockies; *and others.*

UNITED STATES OF AMERICA
  (*in part*)

D.So.   Dominique Sourdel. *Professor of Muslim Civilization, University of Paris IV. Author of* Le Vizirat 'abbāside de 749 à 936 *and others.*

MA'MŪN, AL- (Micropædia)

D.Sp.   David Spring. *Professor of History, Johns Hopkins University, Baltimore. Author of* The English Landed Estate in the Nineteenth Century.

RUSSELL, JOHN RUSSELL, 1ST EARL (Micropædia)

D.S.R.   Daniel Sommer Robinson (d. 1977). *Professor and Director, School of Philosophy, University of Southern California, Los Angeles, 1946–54. Author of* Royce and Hocking: American Idealists *and others.*

PHILOSOPHICAL SCHOOLS AND DOCTRINES, WESTERN (*in part*)

D.S.Ri.   D.S. Richards. *Lecturer in Arabic, University of Oxford. Coauthor of* Mamluk Jerusalem: An Architectural Study.

EGYPT (*in part*)

D.S.T.   Derick S. Thomson. *Professor of Celtic, University of Glasgow. Author of* An Introduction to Gaelic Poetry.

CELTIC LITERATURE (*in part*)

D.Su.   Denys Sutton (d. 1991). *Editor,* Apollo *magazine, 1962–87. Art Critic,* Financial Times. *Author of* Bonnard; Nocturne: The Art of James McNeill Whistler; *and others.*

BONNARD, PIERRE (Micropædia)
WHISTLER, JAMES MCNEILL (*in part*) (Micropædia)

D.T.   David Turnock. *Reader in Geography, University of Leicester, England. Author of* An Economic Geography of Romania *and others.*

ROMANIA (*in part*)

D.T.E.   Dudley Tate Easby, Jr. (d. 1973). *Secretary, Metropolitan Museum of Art, New York City, 1945–69; Chairman, Department of Primitive Art, 1969–71.*

DECORATIVE ARTS AND FURNISHINGS (*in part*)

D.T.F.   Daniel T. Finkbeiner II (d. 1986). *Professor of Mathematics, Kenyon College, Gambier, Ohio, 1956–84. Author of* Matrices and Linear Transformations.

ANALYSIS (IN MATHEMATICS) (*in part*)

D.t.H.   Dirk ter Haar. *Emeritus Reader in Theoretical Physics, University of Oxford; Emeritus Fellow of Magdalen College, Oxford. Author of* Elements of Thermostatistics.

LANDAU, LEV DAVIDOVICH (Micropædia)

D.T.J.   The Rev. Daniel T. Jenkins. *Weyerhaeuser Professor of Systematic Theology, Princeton Theological Seminary, New Jersey, 1981–84. Author of* Christian Maturity and Christian Success *and others.*

PROTESTANTISM (*in part*)

D.T.McL.   David T. McLellan. *Professor of Political Theory, University of Kent at Canterbury, England. Author of* Marxism after Marx *and others.*

MARXISM, MARX AND (*in part*)

D.T.R.   David Talbot Rice (d. 1972). *Watson-Gordon Professor of the History of Fine Art, University of Edinburgh,* 1934–72; Vice-Principal, 1968–71. *Author of* Byzantine Art *and others.*

ARCHITECTURE, THE HISTORY OF WESTERN (*in part*)
PAINTING, THE HISTORY OF WESTERN (*in part*)
SCULPTURE, THE HISTORY OF WESTERN (*in part*)

D.V.   Dora Vallier. *Art critic. Author of* Henri Rousseau: Catalogue raisonné de l'oeuvre; Henri Rousseau; *and others.*

ROUSSEAU, HENRI (Micropædia)

D.V.B.   David V. Bates, M.D. *Emeritus Professor of Medicine, University of British Columbia, Vancouver. Coauthor of* Respiratory Function in Disease.

RESPIRATION AND RESPIRATORY SYSTEMS (*in part*)

D.V.Cn.   Denis Victor Cowen. *Former Professor of Law, University of Chicago. Former Professor of Comparative Law, University of Cape Town.*

LEGAL SYSTEMS, THE EVOLUTION OF MODERN WESTERN (*in part*)

D.V.Co.   Deryck V. Cooke (d. 1976). *Musicologist. Music Presentation Editor, British Broadcasting Corporation, London, 1965–76. Author of* Mahler, 1860–1911; *Completed Mahler's unfinished* 10th Symphony.

MAHLER, GUSTAV (Micropædia)
WAGNER, RICHARD (*in part*) (Micropædia)

D.V.D.   Dimitrije V. Djordjevic. *Professor of History, University of California, Santa Barbara. Author of* Révolutions nationales des peuples balkaniques, 1804–1914 *and others.*

GREECE (*in part*)

D.W.   Dorothy Whitelock (d. 1982). *Elrington and Bosworth Professor of Anglo-Saxon, University of Cambridge, 1957–69. A leading authority on Anglo-Saxon England. Author of* Beginnings of English Society; *editor of* English Historical Documents c. 500–1042.

ALFRED (Micropædia)
CANUTE (Micropædia)
UNITED KINGDOM (*in part*)

D.Wa.   David Waines. *Lecturer in Arabic and Islāmic Studies, University of Lancaster, England. Author of* The Unholy War.

TABARI, AT- (Micropædia)

D.W.C.   David W. Crabb. *Emeritus Professor of Anthropology, Princeton University. Author of* Ekoid Bantu Languages of Ogaja (Eastern Nigeria).

LANGUAGES OF THE WORLD (*in part*)

D.We.   Donald Weinstein. *Professor of History, University of Arizona, Tucson. Author of* Savonarola and Florence; Ambassador from Venice.

EUROPEAN HISTORY AND CULTURE (*in part*)

D.W.F.   Don W. Fawcett, M.D. *Professor Emeritus of Anatomy, Harvard Medical School, Harvard University. Coauthor of* Textbook of Histology.

SUPPORTIVE AND CONNECTIVE TISSUES (*in part*)

D.W.Fi.   Donald W. Fiske. *Emeritus Professor of Psychology, University of Chicago. Author of* Measuring the Concepts of Personality *and others.*

PSYCHOLOGICAL TESTS AND MEASUREMENT (*in part*)

D.W.G.   David W. Goodall. *Honorary Fellow, Division of Wildlife and Ecology, Commonwealth Scientific and Industrial Research Organization, Perth, Australia; Senior Principal Research Scientist, Division of Land Resources Management, 1975–79. Editor in Chief,* Ecosystems of the World.

BIOSPHERE, THE (*in part*)

D.W.I.   Donald W. Insall. *Principal Architect, Donald W. Insall and Associates (architects and planning consultants), London. Commissioner, the Historic Buildings and Monuments Commission for England. Author of* The Care of Old Buildings Today *and others.*

ARTS, PRACTICE AND PROFESSION OF THE (*in part*)

D.W.K.   Daniel Wilhelmus Kruger. *Former Professor of History, University of the Transkei, Umtata. Author of* Paul Kruger.

KRUGER, PAUL (Micropædia)

D.W.K.-J.   Douglas W. Kent-Jones (d. 1978). *President, British Industrial Biological Research Association, Carshalton, England. Coauthor of* Modern Cereal Chemistry.

FARMING AND AGRICULTURAL TECHNOLOGY (*in part*)
FOOD PROCESSING (*in part*)
NUTRITION (*in part*)

D.W.L.   Donald William Lucas (d. 1985). *P.M. Laurence Reader in Classics, University of Cambridge, 1952–69. Author of* The Greek Tragic Poets; A Commentary on Aristotle's Poetics.

GREEK LITERATURE (*in part*)

D.W.M.   D.W. Maurer (d. 1981). *Professor of Linguistics, University of Louisville, Kentucky. Author of* Whiz-Mob: A Correlation of the Argot of Professional Pick-Pockets with Their Behavior Patterns *and numerous articles and papers on slang.*

LANGUAGE (*in part*)

D.Wo.   Douglas Woodruff (d. 1978). *Editor,* The Tablet, *London, 1936–67. Author of* Church and State in History.

PIUS IX (*in part*) (Micropædia)
PIUS V, SAINT (*in part*) (Micropædia)

D.W.O'C.   Daniel William O'Connor. *Charles A. Dana Professor Emeritus of Religious Studies and of Classical Languages, Saint Lawrence University, Canton, New York. Author of* Peter in Rome: The Literary, Liturgical and Archeological Evidence.

PETER THE APOSTLE, SAINT (*in part*) (Micropædia)

D.W.S.   Denis William Stevens. *President, Academia Monteverdiana. Professor of Musicology, Columbia University, 1964–76. Author of* Tudor Church Music.

MUSICAL FORMS AND GENRES (*in part*)

PALESTRINA, GIOVANNI PIERLUIGI DA (Micropædia)

D.W.S.H.   Sir David Wathen Stather Hunt. *Director, Observer Newspapers Ltd., London. High Commissioner for the U.K. in Cyprus, 1965–67; Ambassador to Brazil, 1969–73. Coauthor and editor of* Footprints in Cyprus.
CYPRUS (*in part*)

E.A.   Eric Axelson. *Emeritus Professor of History, University of Cape Town, former Assistant Principal. Author of* Congo to Cape: Early Portuguese Explorers *and others.*
CAPE TOWN

E.A.A.   Edward Alter Alpers. *Professor of History, University of California, Los Angeles.*
SOUTHERN AFRICA (*in part*)

E.A.B.   Ernest Amano Boateng. *Senior consultant and adviser to the Executive Director, United Nations Environment Programme, Nairobi, Kenya. Executive Chairman, Environmental Protection Council of Ghana, Accra, 1973–81. Vice-Chancellor, University of Cape Coast, Ghana, 1971–73. Author of* A Geography of Ghana.
WESTERN AFRICA (*in part*)

E.A.Bo.   Edmund Addison Bowles. *Instructor in the Humanities, Massachusetts Institute of Technology, Cambridge, 1951–55. Vice President, American Musical Instrument Society, 1984–88. Author of* The Timpani: A History in Pictures and Documents *and others.*
MUSICAL INSTRUMENTS (*in part*)

E.A.D.   Eugene A. Davidson. *Professor and Chairman, Department of Biochemistry and Molecular Biology, Georgetown University, Washington, D.C. Author of* Carbohydrate Chemistry.
BIOCHEMICAL COMPONENTS OF ORGANISMS (*in part*)

E.A.Ha.   Eric Alfred Havelock (d. 1988). *Sterling Professor of Classics, Yale University, 1963–71. Author of* The Lyric Genius of Catullus *and others.*
CATULLUS, GAIUS VALERIUS (Micropædia)

E.A.J.D.   Ernest Albert John Davies. *Publisher,* Traffic Engineering and Control; *Editor, 1960–76. Member of Parliament for Enfield East, England, 1945–59. Chairman, Labour Party Transport Committee, 1945–59. Author of* Traffic Engineering Practice.
PUBLIC WORKS (*in part*)
TRANSPORTATION (*in part*)

E.A.K.   E.A. Kracke, Jr. (d. 1976). *Professor of Chinese Literature and Institutions, University of Chicago, 1960–73. Author of* Civil Service in Early Sung China, 960–1067.
T'AI TSU (SUNG DYNASTY) (Micropædia)

Ea.L.   Earl Latham (d. 1977). *Joseph B. Eastman Professor of Political Science, Amherst College, Mass., 1948–73. Author of* The Group Basis of Politics *and others.*
SOCIAL SCIENCES, THE (*in part*)

E.Al.   Edward Allworth. *Professor of Turco-Soviet Studies; Director, Program on Soviet Nationality Problems; Head, Center for the Study of Central Asia, Columbia University. Author of* Soviet Asia; The Modern Uzbeks; *and others.*
UNION OF SOVIET SOCIALIST REPUBLICS (*in part*)

E.A.M.   Edith A. Müller. *Emerita Professor of Astrophysics, University of Geneva, Switzerland.*
SOLAR SYSTEM, THE (*in part*)

E.An.   Edgar Anderson (d. 1989). *Professor of History, San Jose State University, California. Author of* History of Latvia, 1920–1940 *and others.*
BALTIC STATES (*in part*)

E.A.O.   Edwin A. Olson. *Professor of Earth Science, Whitworth College, Spokane, Washington. Coeditor of* Proceedings of the Sixth International Conference on Radiocarbon and Tritium Dating.
GEOCHRONOLOGY (*in part*)

E.A.P.   Edwin A. Peel. *Professor of Education, University of Birmingham, England, 1950–78. Editor,* Educational Review. *Author of* The Psychological Basis of Education.
TEACHING (*in part*)

E.Ar.   Endel Aruja. *Author of* Estonian Books and Periodicals.
BALTIC STATES (*in part*)

E.A.R.   The Rev. Edward A. Ryan, S.J. (d. 1964). *Rector, Our Lady of Martyrs Tertianship, Auriesville, New York, 1962–64. Professor of Church History, Woodstock College, Maryland, 1936–62.*
LOYOLA, SAINT IGNATIUS OF (*in part*) (Micropædia)

E.A.R.B.   Elizabeth A.R. Brown. *Professor of History, Brooklyn College and the Graduate Center, City University of New York.*
PHILIP IV (FRANCE) (Micropædia)

E.A.T.   E.A. Thompson. *Professor of Classics, University of Nottingham, England, 1948–79. Author of* The Early Germans; A History of Attila and the Huns; *and others.*
ATTILA (Micropædia)
STILICHO, FLAVIUS (Micropædia)
THEODORIC (ITALY) (Micropædia)

E.A.U.   E. Ashworth Underwood, M.D. (d. 1980). *Director, Wellcome Institute of the History of Medicine, London, 1946–64. Editor of* Science, Medicine and History.
HIPPOCRATES (Micropædia)
MEDICINE (*in part*)
NIGHTINGALE, FLORENCE (Micropædia)
REED, WALTER (Micropædia)
VIRCHOW, RUDOLF (Micropædia)

E.A.W.   Edwin A. Winckler. *Research Associate, East Asian Institute, Columbia University. Coeditor of* Contending Approaches to the Political Economy of Taiwan.
TAIWAN (*in part*)

E.A.W.G.   Elizabeth Ann Wynne Gunner. *Lecturer in African Literature, School of Oriental and African Studies, University of London. Author of* A Handbook for Teaching African Literature.
AFRICAN ARTS (*in part*)

E.B.   Edward Bridges, 1st Baron Bridges (d. 1969). *Privy Councillor. Permanent Secretary to H.M. Treasury, London, 1945–56. Author of* Portrait of a Profession.
PUBLIC ADMINISTRATION (*in part*)

E.Ba.   E. Badian. *John Moors Cabot Professor of History, Harvard University. Author of* Roman Imperialism in the Late Republic *and others.*
GREEK AND ROMAN CIVILIZATIONS, ANCIENT (*in part*)

E.B.B.   E. Bradford Burns. *Professor of History, University of California, Los Angeles. Author of* A History of Brazil.
BRAZIL (*in part*)

E.B.D.   Edward Bronson Diethrich, M.D. *Director; Chief of Cardiovascular Surgery, Arizona Heart Institute, Phoenix.*
CIRCULATION AND CIRCULATORY SYSTEMS (*in part*)

E.Be.   Edward Kamau Brathwaite. *Poet and critic. Professor of History, University of the West Indies, Mona (Kingston), Jamaica. Author of* Rights of Passage; The Development of Creole Society in Jamaica.
CARIBBEAN LITERATURE (Micropædia)

E.B.E.   Edward B. Evenson. *Professor of Geological Sciences, Lehigh University, Bethlehem, Pennsylvania. Coeditor of* Tills and Related Deposits.
CONTINENTAL LANDFORMS (*in part*)

E.B.Fr.   Edmund B. Fryde. *Professor of History, University College of Wales, Aberystwyth, University of Wales. Coeditor of* Handbook of British Chronology.
HISTORY, THE STUDY OF (*in part*)

E.B.G.   Elizabeth Belmont Gasking (d. 1973). *Senior Lecturer in the History and Philosophy of Science, University of Melbourne, Australia. Author of* Investigations into Generation, 1651–1828.
SPALLANZANI, LAZZARO (Micropædia)

E.B.H.   Earl B. Hunt. *Professor of Psychology, University of Washington, Seattle. Author of* Concept Learning.
LEARNING AND COGNITION, HUMAN (*in part*)

E.Bi.   Elez Biberaj. *Chief, Albanian Service, Voice of America, United States Information Agency, Washington, D.C. Author of* Albania: A Socialist Maverick *and others.*
ALBANIA (*in part*)

Eb.R.   Eberhard Ruhmer. *Former Curator in Chief, Bavarian State Painting Collection, Munich. Author of* Cosimo Tura; Grünewald; *and others.*
DÜRER, ALBRECHT (*in part*) (Micropædia)

E.Br. **Ernle Bradford** (d. 1986). *Author of* The Wind Commands Me: A Life of Sir Francis Drake *and others.*
DRAKE, SIR FRANCIS (Micropædia)

E.B.R. **Elwyn B. Robinson** (d. 1985). *University Professor of History, University of North Dakota, Grand Forks, 1951–70. Author of* History of North Dakota.
NORTH AMERICA (*in part*)
UNITED STATES OF AMERICA (*in part*)

E.B.W. **E. Bright Wilson.** *Theodore William Richards Professor Emeritus of Chemistry, Harvard University. Robert A. Welch Award in Chemistry, 1978. Coauthor of* Molecular Vibrations.
ANALYSIS AND MEASUREMENT, PHYSICAL AND CHEMICAL (*in part*)

E.B.Wo. **Everett B. Woodruff.** *Former Project Engineer, A.M. Kinney, Inc., Cincinnati, Ohio. Coauthor of* Steam-Plant Operation.
ENERGY CONVERSION (*in part*)

E.Ca. **Enzo Carli.** *Director, Cathedral Museum, Siena, Italy. Author of* Duccio.
DUCCIO DI BUONINSEGNA (Micropædia)

E.C.D. **Edward C. Dimock, Jr.** *Professor of Bengali and Bengal Studies, University of Chicago. Author of* The Place of the Hidden Moon.
HINDUISM (*in part*)
SOUTH ASIAN ARTS (*in part*)

E.C.Du. **Elizabeth Corning Dudley.** *Research Associate, Department of Zoology, University of Maryland, College Park.*
ANGIOSPERMS (*in part*)

E.C.E. **Edward C. Ezell.** *Curator, Armed Forces History; Associate Chair, History of Science and Technology, National Museum of American History, Smithsonian Institution, Washington, D.C. Author of* Small Arms Today *and others; editor of* Small Arms of the World.
WAR, THE TECHNOLOGY OF (*in part*)

E.C.G. **Ernst C. Griffin.** *Professor and Chairman, Department of Geography, San Diego State University, California.*
MEXICO (*in part*)

E.C.H. **Edgar Crawshaw Holt** (d. 1975). *Author and journalist. Author of* The Making of Italy, 1815–1870.
MAZZINI, GIUSEPPE (Micropædia)

E.Cl. **Eugene Clark.** *Emeritus Professor of Economics, Washington State University, Pullman; Dean, College of Economics and Business, 1957–77.*
UNITED STATES OF AMERICA (*in part*)

E.C.LaF. **Eugene C. LaFond.** *General Manager, LaFond Oceanic Consultants, San Diego, California. President, Commission for Developing Countries, International Association for the Physical Sciences of the Ocean. Author of* Processing Oceanographic Data.
PACIFIC OCEAN, THE (*in part*)

E.C.N. **E. Clifford Nelson.** *Emeritus Professor of Religion, St. Olaf College, Northfield, Minnesota. Author of* Lutheranism in North America, 1914–70.
PROTESTANTISM (*in part*)

E.C.O. **Everett C. Olson.** *Emeritus Professor of Zoology, University of California, Los Angeles.*
ROMER, ALFRED SHERWOOD (Micropædia)

E.C.P. **Edward C. Page.** *Senior Lecturer in Politics, University of Hull, England. Author of* Political Authority and Bureaucratic Power.
PUBLIC ADMINISTRATION (*in part*)

E.C.Po. **Edgar Charles Polomé.** *Christie and Stanley E. Adams, Jr., Centennial Professor of Liberal Arts, University of Texas at Austin; Chair, Graduate Studies Committee, Department of Germanic Languages. Editor of* The Indo-Europeans, Fourth and Third Millennia *and others.*
EUROPEAN RELIGIONS, ANCIENT (*in part*)

E.C.R. **Edward C. Riley.** *Professor of Hispanic Studies, University of Edinburgh. Author of* Cervantes's Theory of the Novel *and others.*
CERVANTES

Ed. **The Editors.**

E.D.D. **Ethel Deikman Dunn.** *Executive Secretary, Highgate Road Social Science Research Station, Inc., Berkeley, California. Coauthor of* The Peasants of Central Russia.
ASIAN PEOPLES AND CULTURES (*in part*)
UNION OF SOVIET SOCIALIST REPUBLICS (*in part*)

Ed.G. **Edwin Gerow.** *Professor of Religion and Humanities, Reed College, Portland, Oregon. Author of* Indian Poetics; *coauthor of* Theatre of Memory: The Plays of Kālidāsa.
KĀLIDĀSA (*in part*) (Micropædia)

E.D.G. **Ernest Dean Gardner, M.D.** (deceased). *Professor of Neurology and Anatomy, University of California, Davis. Author of* Fundamentals of Neurology *and others.*
NERVES AND NERVOUS SYSTEMS (*in part*)

E.D.H. **Earl Dorchester Hanson.** *Professor of Biology and Science in Society, Wesleyan University, Middletown, Connecticut. Author of* Animal Diversity.
BIOLOGICAL SCIENCES, THE (*in part*).

Ed.R. **Edward Rosen** (d. 1985). *Distinguished Professor of the History of Science, City University of New York. Author of* Three Imperial Mathematicians: Kepler Trapped Between Brake and Ursus.
KEPLER (*in part*)

E.D.S. **Evgeny Dmitrievich Silaev.** *Head, Department of the North and Transcaucasus, Council for Research on Productive Forces, U.S.S.R. Planning Committee, Moscow. Author of articles on Transcaucasian republics.*
UNION OF SOVIET SOCIALIST REPUBLICS (*in part*)

E.D.T.V. **Emily D. Townsend Vermeule.** *Samuel E. Zemurray and Doris Zemurray Stone-Radcliffe Professor, Department of Classics, Harvard University. Author of* Greece in the Bronze Age.
GREEK AND ROMAN CIVILIZATIONS, ANCIENT (*in part*)

E.Du. **Enrique Dussel.** *Professor of Ethics, National Autonomous University of Mexico, Mexico City. Author of* Les Évêques hispano-américaine (1504–1620) *and others.*
LAS CASAS, BARTOLOMÉ DE (Micropædia)

E.E. **Eliahu Elath.** *Emeritus President, Hebrew University of Jerusalem. Chairman, Board of Governors, Afro-Asian Institute for Co-operative and Labour Studies, Tel Aviv, Israel. Ambassador of Israel to U.S., 1948–50, and to U.K., 1952–59. Author of* Israel and Her Neighbours *and others.*
ISRAEL (*in part*)

E.E.E. **E. Earle Ellis.** *Former Research Professor of New Testament Literature, New Brunswick Theological Seminary, New Jersey. Author of* The Gospel of Luke *and others.*
LUKE, SAINT (Micropædia)

E.Eg. **Emil Egli.** *Professor of Geography, Zürich Gymnasium. Lecturer, University of Zürich and Swiss Federal Institute of Technology, Zürich. Author of* Switzerland *and others.*
SWITZERLAND (*in part*)

E.E.La. **Eric Edwin Lampard.** *Professor of History, State University of New York at Stony Brook.*
CITIES (*in part*)

E.E.R. **Edgar Eugene Robinson** (d. 1977). *Margaret Byrne Professor of American History, Stanford University, California, 1931–52. Author of* Evolution of American Political Parties *and others.*
UNITED STATES OF AMERICA (*in part*)

E.E.S. **Eustace E. Suckling.** *Honorary Professor of Electrical Engineering, University of Auckland, New Zealand. Author of* Bioelectricity; The Living Battery.
ELECTRICITY AND MAGNETISM (*in part*)

E.E.Sn. **Esmond E. Snell.** *Ashbel Smith Professor of Chemistry and of Microbiology, University of Texas at Austin. Editor of* Pyridoxal Catalysis: Enzymes and Model Systems; Annual Review of Biochemistry (*vol. 38–52*).
NUTRITION (*in part*)

E.F. **Enno Franzius.** *Historian. Author of* History of the Byzantine Empire.
HERACLIUS (Micropædia)

E.F.C. **Eduardo F. Catalano.** *Emeritus Professor of Architecture, Massachusetts Institute of Technology, Cambridge. Author of* Structures of Warped Surfaces.
NERVI, PIER LUIGI (Micropædia)

E.F.G.D. **Emilio Fernando González Díaz.** *Professor of Geomorphology, University of Buenos Aires.*
SOUTH AMERICA (*in part*)

E.F.S. **Edward Fairbrother Strange** (d. 1925). *Keeper of Woodwork, Victoria and Albert Museum, London. Author of*

Chinese Lacquer *and others.*
DECORATIVE ARTS AND FURNISHINGS
   (*in part*)

E.F.T.   Edward F. Tedesco. *Member of the Technical Staff, Jet Propulsion Laboratory, California Institute of Technology, Pasadena.*
SOLAR SYSTEM, THE (*in part*).

E.Fu.   Edmund Fuller. *Writer and editor. Book Reviewer,* Wall Street Journal. *Coeditor of* Four American Biographies *and others.*
HOLMES, OLIVER WENDELL, JR.
   (Micropædia)

E.F.W.   Edward F. Wente. *Professor of Egyptology, Oriental Institute and Department of Near Eastern Languages and Civilizations, University of Chicago. Author of* Late Ramesside Letters.
EGYPT (*in part*)

E.F.Wo.   E.F. Wondris. *Metallurgical consultant. Former Chief Metallurgical Engineer, National Steel Corporation, Pittsburgh.*
INDUSTRIES, EXTRACTION AND
   PROCESSING (*in part*)

E.G.   Evel Gasparini (d. 1982). *Professor of Slavic Philology, University of Padova, Italy. Author of* Il matriarcato slavo.
EUROPEAN RELIGIONS, ANCIENT (*in part*)

E.G.C.   Edward Gordon Couzens (d. 1971). *Technical Director, Bexford Ltd., Manningtree, England, 1952– 62. Coauthor of* Plastics in the Modern World.
INDUSTRIES, CHEMICAL PROCESS (*in part*)

E.Ge.   Ettore Gelpi. *Director of lifelong education activities, United Nations Educational, Scientific and Cultural Organization (UNESCO), Paris. Lecturer, University of Paris I. Author of* Lifelong Education and International Relations *and others.*
EDUCATION, HISTORY OF (*in part*)

E.G.K.   E. Gordon Keith. *Emeritus Professor of Finance, University of Pennsylvania, Philadelphia. Editor of* Foreign Tax Policies and Economic Growth.
TAXATION (*in part*)

E.G.P.   Edwin G. Pulleyblank. *Emeritus Professor of Chinese, University of British Columbia, Vancouver. Author of* The Background of the Rebellion of An Lu-shan; Chinese History and World History *and others.*
AN LU-SHAN (Micropædia)

E.G.R.   The Rev. Ernest Gordon Rupp (d. 1986). *Dixie Professor of Ecclesiastical History, University of Cambridge, 1968–77. Author of* Luther's Progress to the Diet of Worms; *coauthor of* Erasmus and Luther *and others.*
LUTHER

Eg.S.   Egon Schaden. *Emeritus Professor of Anthropology, University of São Paulo, Brazil. Author of* Mitologia Heróica de Tribos Indígenas do Brasil *and others.*
AMERICAN INDIANS (*in part*)

E.G.T.   Sir Eric Gardner Turner (d. 1983). *Professor of Papyrology, University College, University of London, 1950–78; Director, Institute of Classical Studies, 1953–63. Author of* Greek Papyri *and many other works on papyri.*
WRITING (*in part*)

E.Gu.   Erna Gunther (d. 1982). *Professor of Anthropology, University of Washington, Seattle, 1941–67; Director, Thomas Burke Memorial Washington State Museum, 1929–67. Author of* Art in the Life of the Northwest Coast Indians *and others.*
AMERICAN INDIANS (*in part*)

E.G.W.   Ernest Glen Wever. *Higgins Professor Emeritus of Psychology, Auditory Research Laboratories, Princeton University. Author of* Theory of Hearing.
SENSORY RECEPTION (*in part*)

E.Ha.   Enriqueta Harris. *Honorary Fellow of the Warburg Institute, University of London. Author of* Goya; Velázquez; *and others.*
GOYA, FRANCISCO DE (Micropædia)
VELÁZQUEZ (*in part*)

E.H.B.   Edward Howland Burtt, Jr. *Professor of Zoology, Ohio Wesleyan University, Delaware, Ohio. Author of* Coloration of Wood Warblers.
COLORATION, BIOLOGICAL (*in part*)

E.H.C.   Edward H. Carr (d. 1982). *Wilson Professor of International Politics, University College of Wales, Aberystwyth, 1936–47. Author of* Michael Bakunin; A History of Soviet Russia; *and others.*
BAKUNIN, MIKHAIL ALEKSANDROVICH
   (Micropædia)

E.H.H.   Eckhard H. Hess (d. 1986). *Professor of Psychology, University of Chicago, 1959–86. Author of* Imprinting.
LORENZ, KONRAD (*in part*)
   (Micropædia)

E.H.P.B.   Sir Ernest Henry Phelps Brown. *Emeritus Professor of the Economics of Labour, University of London. Author of* The Economics of Labour.
WORK AND EMPLOYMENT (*in part*)

E.H.St.   Elmer H. Stotz (d. 1987). *Professor of Biochemistry, School of Medicine and Dentistry, University of Rochester, New York. Editor of* Comprehensive Biochemistry.
BIOLOGICAL SCIENCES, THE (*in part*)

E.H.T.   Elias H. Tuma. *Professor of Economics, University of California, Davis. Author of* Twenty-six Centuries of Agrarian Reform: A Comparative Analysis *and others.*
LAND REFORM AND TENURE

E.H.W., Jr.   Edmund H. Worthy, Jr. *Associate Director, Resident Associate Program, Smithsonian Institution, Washington, D.C. Founder,* Bulletin of Sung Yuan Studies.
WANG AN-SHIH (Micropædia)

E.Hy.   Eric Halfpenny (d. 1979). *Editor,* The Galpin Society Journal,

1963–70.
MUSICAL INSTRUMENTS (*in part*)

E.I.G.   Estill I. Green (d. 1974). *Electrical engineer. Executive Vice President, Bell Telephone Laboratories, Inc., Murray Hill, New Jersey, 1959–60.*
SOUND (*in part*)

Ei.H.   Einar Haugen. *Victor S. Thomas Professor Emeritus of Linguistics and Scandinavian, Harvard University. Author of* Norwegian Language in America; Language Conflict and Language Planning: The Case of Modern Norwegian; *and others.*
LANGUAGES OF THE WORLD (*in part*)

E.I.J.R.   Erwin I.J. Rosenthal (d. 1991). *Reader in Oriental Studies, University of Cambridge, 1959–71. Author of* Political Thought in Medieval Islam; *editor of* Averroës' Commentary on Plato's Republic.
AVERROËS (Micropædia)

E.I.U. *Economist Intelligence Unit,* The Economist, *London.*
AUSTRALIA (*in part*)
BRAZIL (*in part*)
CHINA (*in part*)
CZECHOSLOVAKIA (*in part*)
EGYPT (*in part*)
GREECE (*in part*)
INDIA (*in part*)
INDONESIA (*in part*)
ITALY (*in part*)
JAPAN (*in part*)
POLAND (*in part*)
SOUTH AFRICA (*in part*)
SPAIN (*in part*)
SUDAN (*in part*)
TURKEY AND ANCIENT ANATOLIA
   (*in part*)
UNION OF SOVIET SOCIALIST REPUBLICS
   (*in part*)
UNITED STATES OF AMERICA (*in part*)

E.J.   Emrys Jones. *Emeritus Professor of Geography, London School of Economics and Political Science, University of London. Author of* Social Geography of Belfast *and others.*
UNITED KINGDOM (*in part*)

E.J.B.   Ernest J. Briskey. *Senior Adviser, Kuwait Institute for Scientific Research, Safat. Professor of International Agriculture, Oregon State University, Corvallis. Coeditor of* The Physiology and Biochemistry of Muscle as a Food.
FOOD PROCESSING (*in part*)

E.J.Bi.   E.J. Bickerman (d. 1981). *Professor of Ancient History, Columbia University, 1952–67. Author of* Chronology of the Ancient World.
CALENDAR (*in part*)

E.J.C.   Eric J. Chaisson. *Senior Scientist, Space Telescope Science Institute, Baltimore, Maryland. Author of* Cosmic Dawn *and others.*
STARS AND STAR CLUSTERS (*in part*)

E.J.C.G.   Edward J.C. Garden. *Professor and Head, Department of Music, University of Sheffield, England. Author of* Tchaikovsky; Balakirev.

TCHAIKOVSKY, PETER ILICH (*in part*) (Micropædia)

E.J.E. Eugene J. Enrico. *Professor of Music, University of Oklahoma, Norman. Writer and producer of programs on music for public television.*
MUSICAL INSTRUMENTS (*in part*)

E.J.F. Sir Edgar John Forsdyke (d. 1979). *Director and Principal Librarian, British Museum, London, 1936–50; Keeper of Greek and Roman Antiquities, 1932–36.*
DECORATIVE ARTS AND FURNISHINGS (*in part*)

E.J.G. Elmer J. Gutherz. *Division Chief, Resource Assessment Surveys, National Marine Fisheries Service, National Oceanic and Atmospheric Administration, U.S. Department of Commerce, Pascagoula, Mississippi. Researcher on the biology of a variety of marine fishes.*
FISHES (*in part*)

E.J.J. E. Jaakko Järvinen. *Chief of Department, Finnish Institute of Leadership, Helsinki. Editor of* Contemporary Research in Psychology of Perception.
PERCEPTION, HUMAN (*in part*)

E.J.Ke. Edward John Kenney. *Kennedy Professor Emeritus of Latin, University of Cambridge; Fellow of Peterhouse, Cambridge. Author of* The Classical Text; Lucretius; *and others.*
HISTORY, THE STUDY OF (*in part*)
OVID (*in part*) (Micropædia)
PETRONIUS ARBITER, GAIUS (*in part*) (Micropædia)

E.J.M.R. Edward J.M. Rhoads. *Associate Professor of History, University of Texas at Austin. Author of* China's Republican Revolution: The Case of Kwangtung, 1895–1913.
LIN BIAO (Micropædia)

E.J.S. Sir Edward James Salisbury (d. 1978). *Director, Royal Botanic Gardens, Kew, England, 1943–56. Author of* The Living Garden *and others.*
LINNAEUS, CAROLUS (Micropædia)

E.J.Si. Ernest J. Simmons (d. 1972). *Professor of Russian Literature; Chairman, Department of Slavic Languages, Columbia University, 1946–59. Author of* Dostoyevsky: The Making of a Novelist *and others.*
DOSTOYEVSKY (*in part*)
RUSSIAN LITERATURE (*in part*)
TOLSTOY

E.J.W. Edwin J. Westermann. *Emeritus Professor of History, University of Missouri, Kansas City.*
UNITED STATES OF AMERICA (*in part*)

E.J.W.B. Ernest J.W. Barrington (d. 1985). *Professor of Zoology, University of Nottingham, England, 1949–74. Author of* Introduction to General and Comparative Endocrinology.
BIOCHEMICAL COMPONENTS OF ORGANISMS (*in part*)

E.J.Wi. E.J. Wiesenberg. *Member, Taylor-Schechter Cairo Genizah Research Unit, University of Cambridge Library. Former Reader in Hebrew, University College, University of London. Editor and translator of* Abraham Maimonides' Commentary on Genesis and Exodus.
CALENDAR (*in part*)
HISTORY, THE STUDY OF (*in part*)

E.J.Wo. Edward J. Wormley. *Products and interior designer. Former Design Director, Dunbar Furniture Corporation of Indiana, New York City.*
DECORATIVE ARTS AND FURNISHINGS (*in part*)

E.K. Edgar Kaufmann, Jr. *Emeritus Professor of the History of Architecture, Columbia University. Director, Department of Industrial Design, Museum of Modern Art, New York City, 1946–50. Coauthor and editor of* The Rise of an American Architecture; *coeditor of* Frank Lloyd Wright: Writings and Buildings.
WRIGHT, FRANK LLOYD (*in part*) (Micropædia)

E.Ka. Edwin Kashy. *Professor of Physics, Michigan State University, East Lansing.*
ELECTRICITY AND MAGNETISM (*in part*)

E.K.B. Eugene Kornel Balon. *Professor of Zoology, University of Guelph, Ontario. Editor in Chief,* Environmental Biology of Fishes.
FISHES (*in part*)

E.Ke. Elie Kedourie. *Professor of Politics, London School of Economics and Political Science, University of London. Author of* Afghani and 'Abduh: An Essay on Religious Unbelief and Political Activism in Modern Islam.
JAMĀL AD-DĪN AL-AFGHĀNĪ (Micropædia)

E.K.W. Sir Ellis K. Waterhouse (d. 1985). *Director of Studies, Paul Mellon Centre for Studies in British Art, London, 1970–73. Barber Professor of Fine Arts; Director, Barber Institute of Fine Arts, University of Birmingham, England, 1952–70. Author of* Italian Baroque Painting *and others.*
CORREGGIO (Micropædia)

E.L. Edward Lockspeiser (d. 1973). *Writer and broadcaster on music. Author of* Debussy: His Life and Mind.
DEBUSSY, CLAUDE (Micropædia)
DIAGHILEV, SERGEY (Micropædia)
MENDELSSOHN, FELIX (*in part*) (Micropædia)

E.L.B. Edward L. Bousfield. *Curator Emeritus, Zoology Division, National Museum of Natural Sciences, Ottawa.*
CRUSTACEANS (*in part*)

E.L.H. The Most Rev. Edward Louis Heston, C.S.C. (d. 1973). *Chairman, Pontifical Social Communications Commission, Vatican City, 1971–73. Author of* The Holy See at Work.
PAUL VI (PAPACY) (Micropædia)

E.Li. Edwin Lieuwen (deceased). *Professor of Latin American History, University of New Mexico, Albuquerque.* *Author of* Venezuela *and others.*
VENEZUELA (*in part*)

E.L.K. Edward Louis Keenan. *Professor and Chairman, Department of History, Harvard University. Author of* The Kurbskii-Groznyi Apocrypha: The Seventeenth-Century Genesis of the 'Correspondence' Between Ivan IV and A.M. Kurbskii.
UNION OF SOVIET SOCIALIST REPUBLICS (*in part*)

E.L.L. Emiel L. Lamberts. *Professor of Modern Political and Religious History, Catholic University of Louvain, Belgium. Author of* De Kruistocht tegen het liberalisme: facetten van het ultramontanisme in België in de 19e eeuw *and others.*
BELGIUM (*in part*)

E.Lo. Elizabeth Pakenham, Countess of Longford. *Writer. Author of* Wellington: The Years of the Sword; Wellington: The Pillar of State *and others.*
WELLINGTON

E.L.O.M. Ernesto La Orden Miracle. *Diplomat. Spanish Ambassador to Costa Rica, 1972–76, and to Nicaragua, 1966–69.*
SPAIN (*in part*)

El.R. Elliott Rudwick (d. 1985). *Professor of Sociology and of History; Senior Research Fellow, Center for Urban Regionalism, Kent State University, Ohio. Author of* W.E.B. Du Bois: Propagandist of the Negro Protest.
DU BOIS, W.E.B. (Micropædia)

E.L.T. Edward Lewis Turner, M.D. (d. 1960). *Secretary, Council on Medical Education and Hospitals, American Medical Association, Chicago, 1953–59. Professor of Medicine; Dean, School of Medicine, University of Washington, Seattle, 1945–53.*
MEDICINE (*in part*)

E.Lu. Evan Luard (d. 1991). *Fellow, St. Antony's College, University of Oxford, 1957–91. Member of Parliament, 1966–70; 1974–79. Author of* History of the United Nations (*2 vol.*).
UNITED NATIONS (*in part*)

E.L.Y. Ellen Louise Young. *Historical research specialist (manufactures).*
DECORATIVE ARTS AND FURNISHINGS (*in part*)

E.M. Eric Mendoza. *Professor of Science Teaching, Hebrew University of Jerusalem. Editor of* Sadi Carnot's Reflections on the Motive Power of Fire.
CARNOT, SADI (Micropædia)

E.Ma. Erich Matthias (d. 1983). *Professor of Contemporary History and Political Science, University of Mannheim, West Germany. Author of* Sozialdemokratie und Nation *and others.*
BEBEL, AUGUST (Micropædia)

E.M.B. Eugene M. Berkman, M.D. *Medical Director, Blood Bank, New England Medical Center Hospital; Professor of Medicine, Tufts University, Boston. Editor of* Fundamentals of a

Pheresis Program.
BLOOD (*in part*)

E.McC. Elizabeth McClintock.
*Research Associate, Herbarium,
University of California, Berkeley.*
ANGIOSPERMS (*in part*)

E.McN.E. Ernest McNeill Eller. *Rear
Admiral, U.S. Navy (retired). Author of
The Soviet Sea Challenge and others;
coeditor of Dictionary of American
Naval Fighting Ships.*
WAR, THE TECHNOLOGY OF (*in part*)

E.M.G. Ernest M. Gifford. *Emeritus
Professor of Botany, University
of California, Davis. Coauthor of
Morphology and Evolution of Vascular
Plants.*
FERNS (*in part*)
GYMNOSPERMS (*in part*)

E.M.J.C. Eila M.J. Campbell.
*Emeritus Professor of Geography,
Birkbeck College, University of London.*
GAMA, VASCO DA, 1ᵉʳ CONDE DA
  VIDIGUEIRA (Micropædia)
GIOVANNI DA PIAN DEL CARPINI
  (Micropædia)

E.M.R. Edwin M. Ripin (d. 1975).
*Assistant Curator, Musical Instruments
Department, Metropolitan Museum of
Art, New York City, 1970–73. Editor of
Keyboard Instruments.*
MUSICAL INSTRUMENTS (*in part*)

Em.Š. Emil Štampar (deceased).
*Professor of Modern Serbo-Croatian
Literature, University of Ljubljana,
Yugoslavia.*
YUGOSLAV LITERATURE (*in part*)

E.M.W. Edmund Merriman Wise (d.
1972). *Assistant to the Vice President of
Research, International Nickel Company,
New York City, 1955–61. Author
of Palladium: Recovery, Properties,
and Uses; editor of Gold: Recovery,
Properties, and Applications; coeditor of
Platinum Metals and Their Alloys.*
INDUSTRIES, EXTRACTION AND
  PROCESSING (*in part*)

E.M.Wn. Elizabeth M. Wilkinson.
*Emeritus Professor of German,
University of London. Coauthor of
Goethe: Poet and Thinker and others.*
GOETHE (*in part*)

E.N. Edward Norbeck. *Emeritus
Professor of Anthropology, Rice
University, Houston, Texas. Author of
Religion in Primitive Society and others.*
RELIGIOUS AND SPIRITUAL BELIEF,
  SYSTEMS OF (*in part*)
RITES AND CEREMONIES, SACRED
  (*in part*)

E.N.A. Edward Noah Abrahart.
*Former Assistant Research Manager,
Clayton Aniline Co. Ltd., Manchester,
England. Author of Dyes and Their
Intermediates.*
INDUSTRIES, CHEMICAL PROCESS (*in part*)
INDUSTRIES, TEXTILE (*in part*)

En.S. Enid Starkie (d. 1970). *Reader in
French Literature, University of Oxford;
Fellow, Somerville College, Oxford,
1934–65. Author of André Gide; Arthur*

Rimbaud; Baudelaire; *and others.*
BAUDELAIRE, CHARLES (Micropædia)
RIMBAUD, ARTHUR (*in part*)
  (Micropædia)

E.N.S. Eric Norman Simons (d. 1983).
*Author of The Queen and the Rebel:
Mary Tudor and Wyatt the Younger
and others.*
MARY I (ENGLAND AND GREAT BRITAIN)
  (Micropædia)

E.N.So. Estanislao Navarro Sosa.
*Manager, Advanced Development
Department, Electron Dynamics
Division, Hughes Aircraft Company,
Torrance, California.*
ELECTRONICS (*in part*)

E.O.G.T.-P. E.O.G. Turville-Petre (d.
1978). *Professor of Ancient Icelandic
Literature and Antiquities, University
of Oxford, 1953–75. Author of Myth
and Religion of the North; Origins of
Icelandic Literature; and others.*
EUROPEAN RELIGIONS, ANCIENT (*in part*)
SCANDINAVIAN LITERATURE (*in part*)

E.O.J. The Rev. Edwin Oliver James
(d. 1972). *Chaplain of All Souls College,
University of Oxford. Professor of the
History and Philosophy of Religion,
University of London. Author of Seasonal
Feasts and Festivals and numerous
other works in the comparative study of
religions.*
RITES AND CEREMONIES, SACRED
  (*in part*)
SACRED OFFICES AND ORDERS (*in part*)

E.O.W. Edwin O. Willis. *Associate
Professor of Zoology, São Paulo State
University "Julio de Mesquita Filho," Rio
Claro, Brazil. Author of The Behavior of
Bicolored Antbirds.*
BEHAVIOUR, ANIMAL (*in part*)

E.P.A. E. Paul Albury, D.D.S. (d.
1987). *Senator of The Bahamas. Author
of The Story of the Bahamas.*
WEST INDIES, THE (*in part*)

E.Pe. Edward Pessen. *Distinguished
Professor of History, Baruch College and
the Graduate Center, City University
of New York. Author of Jacksonian
America and others.*
UNITED STATES OF AMERICA (*in part*)

E.P.E. Elizabeth Pat Ebanks.
*Information Officer, Government of the
Cayman Islands, George Town.*
WEST INDIES, THE (*in part*)

E.P.G. Elias Panayiotis Gyftopoulos.
*Ford Professor of Engineering,
Massachusetts Institute of
Technology, Cambridge. Coauthor of
Thermodynamics: Foundations and
Applications and others.*
THERMODYNAMICS, PRINCIPLES
  OF (*in part*)

E.P.H. Eric P. Hamp. *Robert Maynard
Hutchins Distinguished Service Professor
of Linguistics, of Psychology, and of
Slavic Languages; Director, Center for
Balkan and Slavic Studies, University
of Chicago. Coeditor of Readings in
Linguistics, I & II.*
LANGUAGES OF THE WORLD (*in part*)
LINGUISTICS (*in part*)

E.P.Ha. Earl Parker Hanson (d.
1978). *Consultant, Department of State,
Commonwealth of Puerto Rico, 1956–
69. Professor of Geography; Chairman,
Department of Geography and Geology,
University of Delaware, Newark, 1949–
56. Author of The Amazon, a New
Frontier.*
VENEZUELA (*in part*)

E.Po. Ernesto Pontieri (deceased).
*Professor of Medieval and Modern
History, University of Naples. Author of
Tra i Normanni nell' Italia meridionale.*
ITALY (*in part*)
ROBERT (APULIA) (Micropædia)

E.P.O. Eugene P. Odum. *Alumni
Foundation Distinguished Professor of
Zoology; Director, Institute of Ecology,
University of Georgia, Athens. Author of
Fundamentals of Ecology; Ecology.*
BIOSPHERE, THE (*in part*)

E.P.S. Ellis P. Steinberg. *Director,
Chemistry Division, Argonne National
Laboratory, Argonne, Illinois, 1982–88;
Section Head, Nuclear and Inorganic
Chemistry, 1974–82.*
ATOMS (*in part*)

E.P.Y. Ernest P. Young. *Professor of
History, University of Michigan, Ann
Arbor. Author of The Presidency of Yuan
Shih-k'ai: Liberalism and Dictatorship in
Early Republican China.*
CHINA (*in part*)

E.R.A.F. Enid R.A. Forde. *Professor
of Geography, Fourah Bay College,
University of Sierra Leone, Freetown.*
WESTERN AFRICA (*in part*)

E.R.G. Edna R. Green. *Former Head,
Science Department, Philadelphia High
School for Girls. Coauthor of Biology.*
BIOLOGICAL SCIENCES, THE (*in part*)

E.R.Ha. Edward R. Hardy (d. 1981).
*Lecturer in Early Church History,
University of Cambridge, 1969–
75. Professor of Church History,
Berkeley Divinity School, New Haven,
Connecticut, 1947–69. Author of
Christian Egypt: Church and People;
editor of Christology of the Later
Fathers; Faithful Witnesses.*
ATHANASIUS, SAINT (Micropædia)
BASIL THE GREAT, SAINT (Micropædia)
GREGORY OF NAZIANZUS, SAINT
  (Micropædia)
GREGORY OF NYSSA, SAINT (Micropædia)

Er.L. Erik Lassen. *Director, Museum
of Decorative Art, Copenhagen, 1966–
82. Author of Danish Furniture of the
Classical Age and others.*
DECORATIVE ARTS AND FURNISHINGS
  (*in part*)

E.R.-M. Emir Rodríguez-Monegal (d.
1985). *Professor of Latin American and
Comparative Literature, Yale University.
Author of Borgès par lui-même.*
BORGES, JORGE LUIS (Micropædia)

E.R.S. Ernest R. Sandeen (d. 1982).
*Professor of History, Macalester College,
St. Paul, Minnesota, 1973–82. Author
of The Roots of Fundamentalism:
British and American Millenarianism
1800–1930.*

DOCTRINES AND DOGMAS, RELIGIOUS
(*in part*)
FUNDAMENTALISM (*in part*)
(Micropædia)

E.R.Se.   Elman R. Service. *Emeritus Professor of Anthropology, University of California, Santa Barbara. Investigator of the economic and social organization of primitive cultures. Author of* Primitive Social Organization.
CULTURE, THE CONCEPT AND
COMPONENTS OF (*in part*)
PARAGUAY (*in part*)

Er.St.   Erich Steingräber. *Honorary Professor, Ludwig Maximilian University of Munich. Former Director General, Bavarian State Art Galleries, Munich.*
DRESS AND ADORNMENT (*in part*)

E.Ru.   Eleanor Ruggles. *Biographer. Author of* Prince of Players: Edwin Booth *and others.*
BOOTH, EDWIN (Micropædia)

E.R.W.   Ewald R. Weibel, M.D. *Professor and Chairman, Department of Anatomy, University of Bern. Author of* The Pathway for Oxygen.
RESPIRATION AND RESPIRATORY
SYSTEMS (*in part*)

E.Sa.   Emilio Sáez (d. 1988). *Professor of Medieval Spanish History, University of Barcelona, Spain, 1959–78. Professor of Medieval History, University of Madrid, 1980–86. Author of* Colección diplomática de Sepúlveda.
ALFONSO V (SPAIN: ARAGON)
(Micropædia)
ALFONSO VI (SPAIN: CASTILE AND LEON)
(Micropædia)
JAMES I (SPAIN: ARAGON) (Micropædia)

E.S.D.   Eleanor Shipley Duckett (d. 1976). *Professor of Classical Languages and Literature, Smith College, Northampton, Massachusetts, 1928–49. Author of* The Gateway to the Middle Ages; Carolingian Portraits; *and others.*
CHARLES MARTEL (*in part*) (Micropædia)
PEPIN III (CAROLINGIAN DYNASTY)
(Micropædia)

E.S.H.   Eric S. Higgs (d. 1976). *Director of Research, Faculty of Archaeology and Anthropology, University of Cambridge. Coeditor of* Science in Archaeology.
AGRICULTURE, THE HISTORY OF (*in part*)

E.Si.   Edith Simon. *Historian, writer, and artist. Author of* The Making of Frederick the Great *and others.*
FREDERICK THE GREAT

E.S.M.   Edmund S. Muskie. *United States Secretary of State, 1980–81. U.S. Senator from Maine, 1959–80; Governor, 1955–59. Author of* Journeys.
UNITED STATES OF AMERICA (*in part*)

E.S.Mi.   Earl Schenck Miers (d. 1972). *Historian, editor, and writer. Author of* The General Who Marched to Hell; The American Civil War; *and many others.*
SHERMAN, WILLIAM TECUMSEH
(Micropædia)

E.S.P.   Edward S. Perkins, M.D. *Emeritus Professor of Ophthalmology,*

University of Iowa, Iowa City. Coauthor of *Atlas of Diseases of the Eye.*
SENSORY RECEPTION (*in part*)

E.S.R.   Evelyn S. Rawski. *Professor of History, University of Pittsburgh. Author of* Education and Popular Literacy in Ch'ing China.
CHINA (*in part*)

E.S.Ri.   Eric Stapleton Richards. *Professor of History, Flinders University of South Australia, Adelaide. Author of* A History of the Highland Clearances; *editor of* The Flinders History of South Australia.
AUSTRALIA (*in part*)

E.T.   Ettore Toffoletto, M.D. *President of the Administration Council, Arts Academy, Bologna, Italy. Author of* Discorso sul Malpighi *and others.*
MALPIGHI, MARCELLO (*in part*)
(Micropædia)

E.t.H.   Ernst ten Haaf. *Former Professor of Structural Geology, State University of Utrecht, The Netherlands.*
MINERALS AND ROCKS (*in part*)

E.Th.   Sir Eric Thompson (d. 1975). *Staff Member, Department of Archaeology, Carnegie Institution of Washington, D.C., 1935–58. Author of* The Rise and Fall of Maya Civilization.
HISTORY, THE STUDY OF (*in part*)

E.To.   Elisabeth Tooker. *Professor of Anthropology, Temple University, Philadelphia. Author of* An Ethnography of the Huron Indians, 1615–1649; The Iroquois Ceremonial of Midwinter.
AMERICAN INDIANS (*in part*)

E.Tr.   Erik Trinkaus. *Professor of Anthropology, University of New Mexico, Albuquerque. Author of* The Shanidar Neandertals.
EVOLUTION, HUMAN (*in part*)

E.T.S.   Edward Togo Salmon (d. 1988). *Messecar Professor of History, McMaster University, Hamilton, Ontario, 1954–73. Author of* A History of the Roman World from 30 B.C. to A.D. 138.
GREEK AND ROMAN CIVILIZATIONS,
ANCIENT (*in part*)

E.T.Sa.   Emilie T. Sander (d. 1976). *Associate Professor of New Testament, Yale University, 1973–75. Coeditor and translator of* The Bible and the Role of Women.
BIBLICAL LITERATURE AND ITS CRITICAL
INTERPRETATION (*in part*)

E.T.W.   Sir Edgar Trevor Williams. *Secretary, Rhodes Trust, 1959–80. Pro-Vice-Chancellor, University of Oxford, 1968–80; Emeritus Fellow of Balliol College, Oxford. Editor,* Dictionary of National Biography, *1949–80.*
VICTORIA AND THE VICTORIAN AGE
(*in part*)

Eu.M.A.   Eufronio M. Alip (deceased). *President, Philippine National Historical Society. Editor,* Journal of History *(quarterly). President and Manager, Alip & Sons, Inc. (publishing firm), Manila. Author of* Political and Cultural History

of the Philippines *and others.*
PHILIPPINES (*in part*)

E.V.   Eugene Vanderpool (d. 1989). *Professor of Archaeology, American School of Classical Studies at Athens, 1949–71.*
ATHENS (*in part*)
OLYMPIA (Micropædia)

E.Va.   Ernesto Valgiglio. *Professor of Greek and Latin Grammar, University of Genoa. Author of* Silla e la crisi repubblicana.
SULLA, LUCIUS CORNELIUS (Micropædia)

E.V.B.B.   Eric V.B. Britter (d. 1977). *Foreign Correspondent,* The Times *(London), 1944–69.*
WEST INDIES, THE (*in part*)

E.v.H.   Ernst van Heerden. *Poet. Emeritus Professor of Afrikaans and Netherlands, University of the Witwatersrand, Johannesburg. Author of* Die klop *and many others.*
SOUTH AFRICAN LITERATURE (*in part*)
(Micropædia)

E.Vi.   Eugène Vinaver (d. 1979). *Professor of French Language and Literature, Victoria University of Manchester, 1933–66. Author of* The Rise of Romance; *editor of* The Works of Sir Thomas Malory.
LITERATURE, THE ART OF (*in part*)

Ev.S.   Eva Schaper. *Professor of Philosophy, University of Glasgow, Scotland. Author of* Prelude to Aesthetics *and others.*
TROELTSCH, ERNST (Micropædia)

Ev.W.   Evert Werkman (d. 1988). *Columnist,* Het Parool, *Amsterdam. Author of* Amsterdam, 'n stad op palen *and others.*
AMSTERDAM (*in part*)

E.W.   Edward Weintal (d. 1973). *Diplomatic Correspondent, Chief European Correspondent, and Contributing Editor,* Newsweek *magazine, 1944–69. Coauthor of* Facing the Brink: An Intimate Study of Crisis Diplomacy.
DULLES, JOHN FOSTER (Micropædia)

E.W.A.   Edward W. Anderson (d. 1983). *Navigational Adviser, Aviation Division, Smiths Industries Ltd., Cheltenham, England. Author of* Principles of Navigation.
NAVIGATION (*in part*)

E.W.B.   Ernst Wilhelm Benz (d. 1978). *Professor of Church History, Philipps University of Marburg, West Germany. Author of* Evolution and Christian Hope.
CHRISTIANITY (*in part*)

E.We.   Elisabeth Weis. *Professor of Film, Brooklyn College, City University of New York. Coeditor of* Film Sound: Theory and Practice.
MOTION PICTURES (*in part*)

E.W.G.   Eric William Gray (d. 1990). *Lecturer in Ancient History, University of Oxford; Official Student and Tutor in Roman History, Christ Church, Oxford, 1939–77. Editor of* Greenidge and Clay's Sources for Roman History

(133–70 B.C.)
POMPEY THE GREAT (*in part*)
(Micropædia)

E.Wi. Edward Wichers (d. 1984).
*Associate Director, National Bureau
of Standards, U.S. Department of
Commerce, Washington, D.C., 1958–62;
Chief, Division of Chemistry, 1948–58.
Author of papers on chemical reagents,
pure substances, and atomic weights.*
ATOMIC WEIGHT (*in part*) (Micropædia)

E.Wn. Elizabeth Wiskemann (d.
1971). *Montague Burton Professor of
International Relations, University of
Edinburgh, 1958–61. Tutor in Modern
History, University of Sussex, England,
1961–64. Author of* Czechs and Germans
and others.
CZECHOSLOVAKIA (*in part*)

E.W.P. Edward W. Price. *Regents'
Professor of Aerospace Engineering,
Georgia Institute of Technology, Atlanta.*
ENERGY CONVERSION (*in part*)

E.W.Z. Ernst Walter Zeeden. *Emeritus
Professor of Modern and Medieval
History, Eberhard Karl University of
Tübingen, Germany.*
STEIN, KARL, REICHSFREIHERR VOM
UND ZUM (Micropædia)

E.Z. Erik Zürcher. *Professor of East
Asian History, State University of
Leiden, The Netherlands. Author of* The
Buddhist Conquest of China.
CHINA (*in part*)

E.Z.H. E. Zudaire Huarte. *Instructor,
Good Counsel Academy, Lecaroz, Spain.
Author of* El conde-duque y Cataluña.
OLIVARES, GASPAR DE GUZMÁN
Y PIMENTAL, CONDE-DUQUE DE
(*in part*) (Micropædia)

E.Zö Erich Zöllner. *Emeritus Professor
of Austrian History, University of
Vienna. Author of* Geschichte Österreichs
von den Anfängen bis zur Gegenwart.
AUSTRIA (*in part*)

F.A.A. Francis A. Allen. *Huber C.
Hurst Professor of Law, University
of Florida, Gainesville. Edson R.
Sunderland Professor Emeritus of
Law, University of Michigan, Ann
Arbor. Author of* The Borderland of
Criminal Justice.
BECCARIA, CESARE (Micropædia)
ERSKINE, THOMAS ERSKINE,
1ST BARON (Micropædia)

F.A.B. Frank A. Brown, Jr. (d.
1983). *Morrison Professor of Biology,
Northwestern University, Evanston,
Illinois, 1956–76. Coauthor of*
Comparative Animal Physiology; The
Biological Clock: Two Views.
BEHAVIOUR, ANIMAL (*in part*)
COLORATION, BIOLOGICAL (*in part*)

F.A.C. F. Albert Cotton. *Robert A.
Welch Professor of Chemistry, Texas
A&M University, College Station.
Author of* Chemical Applications of
Group Theory.
CHEMICAL ELEMENTS (*in part*)

F.A.L. Frank Andrew Leeming. *Senior
Lecturer in Geography, University of*

Leeds, England.
CHINA (*in part*)

F.A.P. Frederick A. Pottle. (d. 1987).
*Sterling Professor of English, Yale
University, 1944–66. Author of* James
Boswell: The Earlier Years, 1740–1769;
The Literary Career of James Boswell;
and others.
BOSWELL, JAMES (*in part*) (Micropædia)

F.A.V. Frederick Albert Valentine.
*Emeritus Professor of Mathematics,
University of California, Los Angeles.
Author of* Convex Sets.
GEOMETRY (*in part*)

F.B. François Bernard. *Conseiller
d'État, a judicial rank in the Council
of State, Paris. Director, Civil and
Military Cabinet, Ministry of Defense,
Government of France, 1981–85.*
FRANCE (*in part*)

F.Ba. Frank Barlow. *Emeritus
Professor of History, University of
Exeter, England. Author of* William I
and the Norman Conquest *and others.*
WILLIAM I (ENGLAND AND GREAT
BRITAIN) (Micropædia)

F.B.B. Frank Bagnall Bessac. *Emeritus
Professor of Anthropology, University of
Montana, Missoula. Author of* Culture
Types of Northern and Western China.
ASIAN PEOPLES AND CULTURES (*in part*)

F.B.C. Floyd Barton Chapman.
*Ecologist, Metropolitan Park District,
Columbus, Ohio. Author of* The Ruffed
Grouse and Its Management in Ohio.
FALCONRY (*in part*) (Micropædia)

F.Be. Fernando Benítez. *Writer and
editor. Former Professor of Journalism,
National Autonomous University of
Mexico, Mexico City. Author of* Los
Indios Mexicanos *and others.*
MEXICO CITY (*in part*)

F.B.G. Frank B. Gibney.
*Vice-Chairman, Board of Editors,
Encyclopædia Britannica, Inc., Chicago.
Vice-Chairman, TBS-Britannica
Company Ltd., Tokyo. Author of* The
Khrushchev Pattern.
KHRUSHCHEV, NIKITA (Micropædia)

F.Br. Friedrich Blendinger.
*Director of Archives, Augsburg,
West Germany, 1966–77. Author
of* Bevolkerungsgeschichte einer
deutschen Reichsstadt im Zeitalter der
Glaubenskämpfe.
FUGGER FAMILY (Micropædia)

F.C. Françoise Choay. *Professor of
Urban Studies, University of Paris VIII.
Author of* Le Corbusier; Planning in the
XIXth Century; *and others.*
CORBUSIER, LE (*in part*) (Micropædia)

F.C.B. Frederick C. Barghoorn.
*Emeritus Professor of Political Science,
Yale University. Author of* Politics in the
U.S.S.R.
UNION OF SOVIET SOCIALIST REPUBLICS
(*in part*)

F.C.C. Frederick C. Crews. *Professor
of English, University of California,
Berkeley. Author of* Skeptical
Engagements *and others.*

LITERATURE, THE ART OF
(*in part*)

F.C.D.III. Frederick C. Durant III.
*Aerospace historian. Assistant Director,
Astronautics, National Air and Space
Museum, Smithsonian Institution,
Washington, D.C., 1965–81.*
EXPLORATION (*in part*)
WAR, THE TECHNOLOGY OF (*in part*)

F.C.F. Sir Frank C. Francis (d. 1988).
*Director and Principal Librarian, British
Museum, London, 1959–68. Editor of*
The Bibliographical Society, 1892–1942:
Studies in Retrospect; The Treasures of
the British Museum.
HISTORY, THE STUDY OF (*in part*)
LIBRARIES (*in part*)

F.C.Gi. Frances Carney Gies.
Coauthor of Leonard of Pisa and the
New Mathematics of the Middle Ages
and others.
LEONARDO PISANO (*in part*)
(Micropædia)

F.Ch. Frank Chapman. *Former Senior
English Master, High School for Boys,
Oswestry, England. Author of "Hardy the
Novelist" in* Scrutiny.
HARDY, THOMAS (Micropædia)

F.C.H. F. Clark Howell. *Professor of
Anthropology, University of California,
Berkeley. Author of* Early Man.
EVOLUTION, HUMAN (*in part*)

F.C.Ke. Fenton Crosland Kelley.
*Emeritus Professor of Zoology, Boise
State University, Idaho.*
EXCRETION AND EXCRETORY SYSTEMS
(*in part*)

F.C.M. Frederick C. Mosher (d.
1990). *Henry L. and Grace Doherty
Foundation Professor of Government and
Foreign Affairs, University of Virginia,
Charlottesville, 1968–80. Author of*
Democracy and the Public Service.
PUBLIC ADMINISTRATION (*in part*)

F.C.O. Francis Christopher Oakley.
*President; Professor of History, Williams
College, Williamstown, Massachusetts.
Author of* Council Over Pope? Towards a
Provisional Ecclesiology *and others.*
ROMAN CATHOLICISM (*in part*)

F.C.P. Forrest C. Pogue. *Director,
Dwight D. Eisenhower Institute for
Historical Research, Smithsonian
Institution, Washington, D.C., 1974–84.
Director, George C. Marshall Research
Library, Lexington, Virginia, 1964–74.
Author of* George C. Marshall.
MARSHALL, GEORGE C. (Micropædia)

F.C.S. Frank C. Shoemaker. *Emeritus
Professor of Physics, Princeton
University. Authority on the design
of apparatus for studying subatomic
particles.*
PARTICLE ACCELERATORS (*in part*)

F.D.G. Frank Denby Gunstone.
*Honorary Research Professor of
Chemistry, University of St. Andrews,
Scotland. Author of* An Introduction to
the Chemistry and Biochemistry of the
Fatty Acids and Their Glycerides.
CHEMICAL COMPOUNDS (*in part*)

F.D.H. **F.D. Hobbs** (d. 1978). *Head, Environmental Modelling and Survey Unit, University of Birmingham, England. Author of* Traffic Planning and Engineering.
TRANSPORTATION (*in part*)

F.Do. **Filippo Donini.** *Cultural Expert, Cultural Relations Department, Italian Ministry of Foreign Affairs, Rome, 1972–76. Director, Italian Institute, London, 1961–72. Author of* Vita e poesia di Sergio Corazzini.
ITALIAN LITERATURE (*in part*)

F.D.O. **Francis D. Ommanney** (d. 1980). *Reader in Marine Biology, University of Hong Kong, 1957–60. Scientific staff member, Discovery Committee, 1929–39. Author of* South Latitude *and North Cape and others.*
BYRD, RICHARD E. (Micropædia)

F.D.P. **Franklin D. Parker.** *Emeritus Professor of History, University of North Carolina at Greensboro. Author of* The Central American Republics *and others.*
CENTRAL AMERICA (*in part*)

F.d.Pe. **Franco della Peruta.** *Professor of the History of the Risorgimento, University of Milan. Author of* I democratici e la rivoluzione italiana.
ITALY (*in part*)

F.Dr. **Franz Dölger** (d. 1968). *Professor of Byzantine and Modern Greek Studies, University of Munich. Author of* Die byzantinische Dichtung in der Reinsprache.
GREEK LITERATURE (*in part*)

F.E.B. **Frederick E. Bacon.** *Former Metallurgical Engineer, Metals Division, Union Carbide Corporation, Niagara Falls, New York.*
INDUSTRIES, EXTRACTION AND PROCESSING (*in part*)

F.E.Bl. **Floyd E. Bloom, M.D.** *Chairman, Department of Neuropharmacology, Scripps Clinic and Research Foundation, La Jolla, California. Coauthor of* Biochemical Basis of Neuropharmacology *and others.*
DRUGS AND DRUG ACTION (*in part*)

F.E.D. **Fram E. Dinshaw.** *Fellow of St. Catherine's College, University of Oxford.*
ENGLISH LITERATURE (*in part*)

F.E.G. **Frank E. Goodwin.** *Vice President, Materials Sciences, International Lead Zinc Research Organization, Research Triangle Park, North Carolina. Editor of* Engineering Properties of Zinc Alloys.
INDUSTRIES, EXTRACTION AND PROCESSING (*in part*)

F.E.K. **Frank E. Keating.** *Former Fishing Editor,* Newsday, *Garden City, New York.*
FISHING (*in part*) (Micropædia)

F.E.Ki. **F.E. Kirby.** *Professor of Music, Lake Forest College, Illinois. Author of* A Short History of Keyboard Music; An Introduction to Western Music; *and others.*
MUSICAL FORMS AND GENRES (*in part*)

F.E.M. **Frank Edward Manuel.** *Emeritus Professor of History, Brandeis University, Waltham, Massachusetts. Author of* Shapes of Philosophical History *and others.*
RELIGIOUS AND SPIRITUAL BELIEF, SYSTEMS OF (*in part*)

F.E.R. **Frank E. Reynolds.** *Professor of Buddhist Studies and History of Religions, University of Chicago. Author of* Guide to Buddhist Religion.
ANGKOR (*in part*) (Micropædia)
BUDDHISM, THE BUDDHA AND (*in part*)
JAYAVARMAN VII (Micropædia)

F.F. **Finn Fuglestad.** *Associate Professor of History, University of Oslo. Author of* A History of Niger, 1850–1960.
WESTERN AFRICA (*in part*)

F.F.B. **Frederick Fyvie Bruce** (d. 1990). *Rylands Professor of Biblical Criticism and Exegesis, Victoria University of Manchester, 1959–78. Author of* The Canon of Scripture *and others.*
BIBLICAL LITERATURE AND ITS CRITICAL INTERPRETATION (*in part*)

F.F.C. **Frederick F. Cartwright.** *Emeritus Senior Lecturer in the History of Medicine, King's College Hospital, University of London. Author of* Joseph Lister.
LISTER, JOSEPH, BARON LISTER, OF LYME REGIS (Micropædia)

F.Fe. **Fritz Fellner.** *Professor of Modern History, University of Salzburg, Austria. Author of* Schicksaljahre Österreichs.
AUSTRIA (*in part*)

F.F.E. **Fredric F. Ehrich.** *Staff Engineer, Aircraft Engine Business Group, General Electric Company, Lynn, Massachusetts.*
ENERGY CONVERSION (*in part*)

F.Fo. **Frieda Fordham** (deceased). *Training analyst, Society of Analytical Psychology, London. Author of* An Introduction to Jung's Psychology.
JUNG, CARL (*in part*) (Micropædia)

F.Fr. **Frank Freidel.** *Emeritus Professor of History, Harvard University and University of Washington, Seattle. Author of* Franklin D. Roosevelt.
ROOSEVELT, FRANKLIN D.
UNITED STATES OF AMERICA (*in part*)

F.G. **Frankdieter Grimm.** *Staff member, Institute for Geography and Geo-ecology, Academy of Sciences of the German Democratic Republic, Leipzig. Author of* Das Abflussverhalten in Europa *and others.*
EUROPE (*in part*)

F.G.A.S. **F. Gordon A. Stone.** *Professor of Inorganic Chemistry, University of Bristol, England. Editor of* Advances in Organometallic Chemistry.
CHEMICAL COMPOUNDS (*in part*)

F.Go. **Frederick Goldbeck** (d. 1981). *Critic and musicologist. Adviser for Music, Radiotélévision Française. Author of* The Perfect Conductor *and others.*
GOUNOD, CHARLES (Micropædia)

F.Gre. **Frank Greenaway.** *Keeper, Department of Chemistry, Science Museum, London, 1967–80. Author of* John Dalton and the Atom; *editor of* Lavoisier's Essays, Physical and Chemical.
MENDELEYEV, DMITRY IVANOVICH (Micropædia)

F.Gu. **The Rev. Franco Guerello, S.J.** *Professor of Italian Literature, Social Institute, Turin, Italy. Editor of* Lettere di Innocenzo IV dai cartolari notarili genovesi.
INNOCENT IV (Micropædia)

F.H. **François Haverschmidt** (deceased). *Ornithologist. Author of* Birds of Surinam *and numerous articles on neotropical birds.*
BIRDS (*in part*)

F.Ha. **Felix Haurowitz** (d. 1987). *Distinguished Professor of Chemistry, Indiana University, Bloomington. Author of* Chemistry and Function of Proteins.
BIOCHEMICAL COMPONENTS OF ORGANISMS (*in part*)

F.H.B. **Frederick Henry Boland** (d. 1985). *Chancellor, University of Dublin, 1964–82. Representative of Ireland to the United Nations, 1956–64.*
IRELAND (*in part*)

F.Hi **Finn Hiorthøy.** *Judge of the Supreme Court of Norway, Oslo, 1955–73.*
LEGAL SYSTEMS, THE EVOLUTION OF MODERN WESTERN (*in part*)

F.H.M. **Franz H. Michael.** *Emeritus Professor of Far Eastern History and International Affairs, George Washington University, Washington, D.C. Author of* The Origin of Manchu Rule in China; The Taiping Rebellion; *and others.*
NURHACHI (Micropædia)

F.H.O. **Frederick Henry Osborn** (d. 1981). *Chairman, Executive Committee, Population Council, New York City, 1930–68; President, 1952–59. Secretary-treasurer, American Eugenics Society, 1959–70. Author of* Preface to Eugenics; *coauthor of* Dynamics of Population.
BIOLOGICAL SCIENCES, THE (*in part*)
GENETICS AND HEREDITY, THE PRINCIPLES OF (*in part*)

F.H.S. **Frank Harold Spedding** (d. 1984). *Principal Scientist, U.S. Atomic Energy Commission, Ames Laboratory, Iowa State University, Ames, 1968–74; Director, Ames Laboratory, 1947–68. Coauthor of* The Rare Earths.
CHEMICAL ELEMENTS (*in part*)

F.H.Sh. **Frank H. Shu.** *Professor of Astronomy, University of California, Berkeley. Author of* The Physical Universe.
COSMOS, THE

F.Hu. **Frederick Fu Hung.** *Emeritus Professor of Geography, University of Guelph, Ontario. Author of a geography series for schools (in Chinese) and others.*
CHINA (*in part*)

F.H.W. **Fred H. Wilt.** *Professor of Cell and Developmental Biology, University of California, Berkeley. Editor of* Methods in Developmental Biology.
GROWTH AND DEVELOPMENT,
  BIOLOGICAL (*in part*)

F.İ. **Fahir İz.** *Professor of Turkish Literature, Boğaziçi University, Istanbul. Author of* Ottoman Turkish Prose; Ottoman Turkish Verse; *and others.*
CENTRAL ASIAN ARTS (*in part*)

F.J.A. **Francisco Jose Ayala.** *Donald Bren Professor of Biological Sciences, University of California, Irvine. Author of* Evolving: The Theory and Processes of Organic Evolution *and others.*
EVOLUTION, THE THEORY OF

F.J.B. **Fred J. Benson.** *Emeritus Dean, College of Engineering, Texas A&M University, College Station.*
PUBLIC WORKS (*in part*)

F.J.B.W. **Sir F.J.B. Watson.** *Director of the Wallace Collection, London, 1963–74. Surveyor of the Queen's Works of Art, 1963–72. Author of* Fragonard; Canaletto; *and others.*
FRAGONARD, JEAN-HONORÉ
  (Micropædia)

F.J.D. **Frederick J. Dockstader.** *Museum consultant and art historian. Director, Museum of the American Indian, Heye Foundation, New York City, 1960–75. Author of* Indian Art in North America; Indian Art in South America; *and others.*
AMERICAN INDIANS (*in part*)

F.J.E.R. **Frederic James Edward Raby** (d. 1966). *Fellow and Lecturer, Jesus College, University of Cambridge, 1948–54. Author of* A History of Christian Latin Poetry *and others.*
LATIN LITERATURE (*in part*)

F.J.G.E. **F. John G. Ebling.** *Emeritus Professor of Zoology; Independent Research Worker in Dermatology, University of Sheffield, England. Coeditor of and contributor to* Textbook of Dermatology.
INTEGUMENTARY SYSTEMS (*in part*)

F.J.M. **Francis J. Murray.** *Emeritus Professor of Mathematics, Duke University, Durham, North Carolina. Author of* Mathematical Machines.
ARITHMETIC (*in part*)

F.J.Ma. **Frank J. Malina** (d. 1981). *Trustee, International Academy of Astronautics, Paris, 1963–81; President, 1963. Founder–Editor,* Leonardo (*international journal of the contemporary artist*). *Editor of the first-fifth Lunar International Laboratory Symposia.*
KÁRMÁN, THEODORE VON (Micropædia)

F.J.S. **Frederick J. Streng.** *Professor of the History of Religions, Southern Methodist University, Dallas, Texas. Author of* Emptiness: A Study of Religious Meaning; Understanding Religious Life.
NĀGĀRJUNA (Micropædia)
RITES AND CEREMONIES, SACRED
  (*in part*)

F.-J.Se. **Franz-Josef Schmale.** *Professor of Medieval History, University of the Ruhr, Bochum, Germany. Editor of* Quellen zur Geschichte Kaiser Heinrichs IV.
HENRY IV (GERMANY/HOLY ROMAN
  EMPIRE) (Micropædia)
HENRY V (GERMANY/HOLY ROMAN
  EMPIRE) (Micropædia)

F.J.W. **Francis James West.** *Pro-Vice-Chancellor (Research and Development), Deakin University, Geelong, Australia. Author of* Political Advancement in the South Pacific *and others.*
PACIFIC ISLANDS (*in part*)

F.K. **The Most Rev. Franz Cardinal König.** *Archbishop of Vienna, 1956–85. Author of* Zarathustras Jenseitsvorstellungen und das Alte Testament *and others.*
ZOROASTER (Micropædia)

F.K.A. **Franklin K. Anderson.** *Senior Scientist, EG & G Idaho, Inc., Idaho Falls. Associate Editor, Life Sciences (Botany), Encyclopædia Britannica, Chicago, 1970–72. Coauthor of* Plant Stress from Air Pollution.
ANGIOSPERMS (*in part*)

F.K.H. **F. Kenneth Hare.** *Chancellor, Trent University, Peterborough, Ontario. University Professor Emeritus of Geography and of Physics, University of Toronto. An authority on world climate and its relation to other environmental conditions. Author of* The Restless Atmosphere.
CLIMATE AND WEATHER (*in part*)

F.K.L. **Fang Kuei Li** (d. 1987). *Professor of Chinese Linguistics and Anthropology, University of Washington, Seattle, 1959–69. Professor of Asian Linguistics, University of Hawaii, Honolulu, 1969–73. Authority on the languages of South China. Author of* The Tai Dialect of Lungchow.
LANGUAGES OF THE WORLD (*in part*)

F.L. **Fred Lukoff.** *Associate Professor of Korean Language and Linguistics, University of Washington, Seattle. Author of* Spoken Korean *and others.*
LANGUAGES OF THE WORLD (*in part*)

F.La. **François Lasserre.** *Emeritus Professor of Classical Greek, University of Lausanne, Switzerland. Translator and editor of* Strabon, Géographie (*books 3–6, 10–12*).
STRABO (Micropædia)

F.L.S. **Frederick L. Schwab.** *Professor of Geology, Washington and Lee University, Lexington, Virginia. Editor of* Geosynclines: Concept and Place Within Plate Tectonics.
MINERALS AND ROCKS (*in part*)

F.M. **Fosco Maraini.** *Writer. Former Lecturer in Japanese, University of Florence. Author of* Where Four Worlds Meet *and others.*
ASIA (*in part*)
POLO, MARCO (Micropædia)

F.M.B. **Fawn McKay Brodie** (d. 1981). *Professor of History, University of California, Los Angeles, 1971–77. Author of* The Devil Drives: A Life of Sir Richard Burton.
BURTON, SIR RICHARD (Micropædia)

F.M.Kg. **Felix M. Keesing** (d. 1961). *Professor of Anthropology, Stanford University, California, 1942–61. Author of* Cultural Anthropology *and others.*
PREHISTORIC PEOPLES AND CULTURES
  (*in part*)

F.M.L. **Sir Frederick M. Lea** (d. 1984). *Director of Building Research, Department of Scientific and Industrial Research, Watford, England, 1946–65. Author of* The Chemistry of Cement and Concrete *and others.*
INDUSTRIAL GLASS AND CERAMICS
  (*in part*)

F.Mo. **Francis Moran** (d. 1975). *Golf writer,* The Scotsman, *Edinburgh. President, Association of Golf Writers. Author of* Golfers' Gallery.
SPORTS, MAJOR TEAM AND INDIVIDUAL
  (*in part*)

F.M.S. **Frank M. Shipman** (deceased). *Member, Board of Directors, Brown-Forman Distillers Corporation, Louisville, Kentucky, 1951–70; Technical Director, 1940–65; Vice President, 1945–65.*
BEVERAGE PRODUCTION (*in part*)

F.M.V. **Florence M. Voegelin** (d. 1989). *Editor,* Anthropological Linguistics, *Indiana University, Bloomington; Director, Archives of Languages of the World. Coauthor of* Classification and Index of the World's Languages *and others.*
LANGUAGES OF THE WORLD (*in part*)

F.N. **Fritz Neumark.** *Emeritus Professor of Political Economy, Johann Wolfgang Goethe University of Frankfurt, Frankfurt am Main, Germany. Author of* Grundsätze gerechter und ökonomisch rationaler Steuerpolitik.
TAXATION (*in part*)

F.N.D. **Frank N. Dauster.** *Professor of Spanish, Rutgers University, New Brunswick, New Jersey. Author of* Historia del teatro hispanoamericano.
LATIN-AMERICAN LITERATURE (*in part*)

F.N.H.R. **Frank Neville H. Robinson.** *Senior Research Officer, Clarendon Laboratory, University of Oxford; Fellow and Tutor in Physics, St. Catherine's College, Oxford. Author of* Noise and Fluctuations in Electronic Devices and Circuits *and others.*
ELECTRICITY AND MAGNETISM (*in part*)

F.N.M. **Fyodor Nikolayevich Milkov.** *Professor and Head, Department of Physical Geography, Voronezh Lenin Komsomol State University, U.S.S.R.*
UNION OF SOVIET SOCIALIST REPUBLICS
  (*in part*)

F.N.S. **Fyodor Nikolayevich Sukhopara.** *Head of Section, Scientific Council on the Location of the U.S.S.R. Productive Forces, Academy of Sciences of the U.S.S.R., Moscow. Coauthor of* Development of Large Economic

Regions of the U.S.S.R.
UNION OF SOVIET SOCIALIST REPUBLICS
(*in part*)

F.N.W. Fred N. White. *Emeritus Professor of Physiology, University of California, San Diego, at La Jolla; former Director, Physiological Research Laboratory, Scripps Institution of Oceanography. Coauthor of* Animal Function: Principles and Adaptations.
RESPIRATION AND RESPIRATORY SYSTEMS (*in part*)

F.O. Frédéric Ogé. *Research staff member, National Centre for Scientific Research, Toulouse, France.*
EUROPE (*in part*)

F.Om. Farouk Omar. *Professor of History, College of Arts, University of Baghdad, Iraq. Author of* History of the Early 'Abbasids.
BARMAKIDS (Micropædia)

F.O.W. Frank Osborne Wood. *Former Technical Director, Salt Institute, Alexandria, Virginia.*
FOOD PROCESSING (*in part*)

F.O.Wa. Frederick O. Waage (d. 1985). *Professor of the History of Art and Archaeology, Cornell University, Ithaca, New York, 1945–71. Author of* Prehistoric Art *and others.*
DECORATIVE ARTS AND FURNISHINGS (*in part*)

F.P.B. Frederick P. Bargebuhr (d. 1978). *Professor of Religion, University of Iowa, Iowa City, 1962–70. Author of* The Alhambra: A Cycle of Studies on the Eleventh Century in Moorish Spain.
IBN GABIROL (Micropædia)

F.P.K. Frank P. Kolb. *Professor of Ancient History, Eberhard Karl University of Tübingen, Germany. Author of* Die Stadt im Altertum *and others.*
CARACALLA (Micropædia)

F.P.L. Fritz P. Loewe (d. 1974). *Senior Lecturer in Charge, Department of Meteorology, University of Melbourne, Australia, 1938–61. World authority on the meteorology of the Southern Hemisphere. Author of* Études de glaciologie en Terre Adélie.
CLIMATE AND WEATHER (*in part*)

F.Po. Frederik Pohl. *Author of* Tiberius (*under the pseudonym Ernst Mason*) *and of many works of science fiction.*
TIBERIUS (*in part*) (Micropædia)

F.R. Fazlur Rahman (d. 1988). *Professor of Islāmic Philosophy, University of Chicago, 1969–88. Author of* Islam; Islam and Modernity *and others.*
ISLĀM, MUḤAMMAD AND THE RELIGION OF (*in part*)

F.R.A. Francis R. Aumann. *Emeritus Professor of Political Science, Ohio State University, Columbus. Coauthor of* The Government and Administration of Ohio.
UNITED STATES OF AMERICA (*in part*)

F.R.Al. Frank Raymond Allchin. *Emeritus Reader in Indian Studies,*

University of Cambridge. Coauthor of The Rise of Civilization in India and Pakistan.
AFGHANISTAN (*in part*)
INDIA (*in part*)

Fr.H. Sir Frank Hartley. *Chairman, British Pharmacopoeia Commission, 1970–80. Vice-Chancellor, University of London, 1976–78; Dean, School of Pharmacy, 1962–76.*
MEDICINE (*in part*)

Fr.J.M. Francis J. Terence Maloney. *Product development executive. Author of* Glass in the Modern World.
INDUSTRIAL GLASS AND CERAMICS (*in part*)

Fr.L. Fred Landis. *Professor of Mechanical Engineering, University of Wisconsin, Milwaukee; Dean, College of Engineering and Applied Science, 1974–83.*
ENERGY CONVERSION (*in part*)

Fr.M. Frederick Mosteller. *Emeritus Professor of Mathematical Statistics, Harvard University. Coauthor of* Probability with Statistical Applications; Data Analysis and Regression.
STATISTICS (*in part*)

F.R.M. Frank R. Moraes (d. 1974). *Editor in Chief,* The Indian Express, *New Delhi, 1957–72. Author of* India Today; Jawaharlal Nehru: A Biography.
INDIA (*in part*)
NEHRU, JAWAHARLAL (*in part*) (Micropædia)

F.R.S. F. Richard Stephenson. *Senior Research Fellow in Physics, University of Durham, England. Coauthor of* Atlas of Historical Eclipse Maps: East Asia.
ECLIPSE, OCCULATION AND TRANSIT (*in part*)

F.S. Franklin Sherman. *Director, Institute for Jewish–Christian Understanding, Muhlenberg College, Allentown, Pennsylvania. Coauthor of* The Place of Bonhoeffer.
BONHOEFFER, DIETRICH (Micropædia)

F.Sc. Friedrich Schreyvogl (d. 1976). *Novelist and free-lance writer. Vice-Director, Vienna Burgtheater, 1954–59. Author of* Ein Jahrhundert zu früh: das Schicksal Josephs II *and others.*
JOSEPH II (GERMANY/HOLY ROMAN EMPIRE) (Micropædia)

F.So. Friedrich Solmsen (d. 1989). *Moses Slaughter Professor of Classical Studies, University of Wisconsin, Madison, 1962–74. Author of* Hesiod and Aeschylus.
HESIOD (Micropædia)

F.S.P. Francis S. Pierce. *Editor, Congressional Budget Office, Washington, D.C. Associate Editor, Economics,* Encyclopædia Britannica, *Chicago, 1967–73.*
INTERNATIONAL TRADE (*in part*)
VEBLEN, THORSTEIN (Micropædia)

F.T. Frederick Tepper. *General Manager, Instrument Division, Mine Safety Appliances Company, Pittsburgh. Coauthor of* Alkali Metal Handling and

System Operating Techniques.
CHEMICAL ELEMENTS (*in part*)

F.Th. Friedrich Thöne (deceased). *Art historian. Author of* Lucas Cranach der Ältere *and others; coauthor of* Thieme-Becker: Künstler-Lexikon.
CRANACH, LUCAS, THE ELDER (Micropædia)

F.T.M. Fred T. Mackenzie. *Professor of Oceanography, University of Hawaii at Manoa, Honolulu; Head, Marine Geochemistry Division, Hawaii Institute of Geophysics. Coauthor of* The Evolution of Sedimentary Rocks.
HYDROSPHERE, THE
OCEANS (*in part*)

F.Tr. François Treves. *Professor of Mathematics, Rutgers University, New Brunswick, New Jersey. Author of* Topological Vector Spaces, Distributions and Kernels; Basic Linear Partial Differential Equations.
ANALYSIS (IN MATHEMATICS) (*in part*)

Fu.M. Fujimura Michio. *Professor of History, Sophia University, Tokyo. Author of* Yamagata Aritomo *and others.*
YAMAGATA ARITOMO, KOSHAKU (Micropædia)

F.V.O'C. Francis Valentine O'Connor. *Director, Raphael Research Enterprises (fine arts consultants), New York City. Editor,* Federal Art Patronage Notes, *1974–86. Author of* Federal Support for the Visual Arts: The New Deal and Now *and others.*
DE KOONING, WILLEM (Micropædia)

F.V.Sn. Fernand Van Steenberghen. *Emeritus Professor of Medieval Philosophy, Catholic University of Louvain, Belgium.*
PHILOSOPHICAL SCHOOLS AND DOCTRINES, WESTERN (*in part*)

F.W.C. Francis William Carter. *Chairman, Department of Social Sciences, School of Slavonic and East European Studies, University of London. Editor of* An Historical Geography of the Balkans.
BULGARIA (*in part*)
CZECHOSLOVAKIA (*in part*)
PRAGUE (*in part*)

F.W.G. Frederick William Gibbs (d. 1966). *Deputy Secretary and Editor, Royal Institute of Chemistry, London.*
DAVY, SIR HUMPHRY, BARONET (Micropædia)

F.Wh. Frederick Whitehead (d. 1971). *Reader in Old French Language and Literature, Victoria University of Manchester. Editor of* La Chanson de Roland; La Chastelaine de Vergi.
LITERATURE, THE ART OF (*in part*)

F.Wi. Frank Willett. *Director and Titular Professor, Hunterian Museum and Art Gallery, University of Glasgow. Author of* African Art; Ife in the History of West African Sculpture.
AFRICAN ARTS (*in part*)

F.W.K. Francis W. Karasek. *Professor of Chemistry, University of Waterloo, Ontario.*

MEASUREMENT AND OBSERVATION, PRINCIPLES, METHODS, AND INSTRUMENTS OF (*in part*)

F.W.Kn. **Franklin W. Knight.** *Professor of Latin American and Caribbean History, Johns Hopkins University, Baltimore, Maryland. Author of* Slave Society in Cuba during the Nineteenth Century *and others.*

WEST INDIES, THE (*in part*)

F.W.W. **Frank W. Walbank.** *Rathbone Professor Emeritus of Ancient History and Classical Archaeology, University of Liverpool. Author of* A Historical Commentary on Polybius *and others.*

ALEXANDER THE GREAT (*in part*)
PLUTARCH (*in part*) (Micropædia)
POLYBIUS (Micropædia)

F.W.We. **Frits W. Went.** *Emeritus Professor of Botany, Desert Research Institute, University of Nevada System, Reno. Author of* The Experimental Control of Plant Growth.

BIOSPHERE, THE (*in part*)

F.W.W.-S. **Francis William Wentworth-Sheilds** (d. 1969). *Artist. Principal Lecturer, Department of Printing and Graphic Design, Twickenham College of Technology, England, 1966–69.*

PAINTING, THE HISTORY OF WESTERN (*in part*)

F.X.H. **The Rev. Francis X. Hezel, S.J.** *Director, Micronesian Seminar, Truk, Federated States of Micronesia. Author of* The First Taint of Civilization: A History of the Caroline and Marshall Islands in Pre-Colonial Days, 1521–1885.

PACIFIC ISLANDS (*in part*)

F.X.M. **The Rev. Francis Xavier Murphy, C.SS.R.** *Emeritus Professor of Patristic Moral Theology, Academia Alfonsiana, Rome. Staff editor for* Patrology, New Catholic Encyclopedia.

ALEXANDER VI (PAPACY) (Micropædia)
PAUL III (PAPACY) (Micropædia)

G.A. **Giovanni Aquilecchia.** *Emeritus Professor of Italian, University College, University of London. Author of* Giordano Bruno *and others.*

ARIOSTO, LUDOVICO (Micropædia)
BRUNO, GIORDANO (Micropædia)
ITALIAN LITERATURE (*in part*)
TASSO, TORQUATO (*in part*) (Micropædia)

G.A.B. **Georg A. Borgstrom** (d. 1990). *Professor of Food Science, 1956–81, and of Geography, 1960–81, Michigan State University, East Lansing. Editor of* Fish as Food.

FISHING, COMMERCIAL (*in part*)

G.A.C. **G. Arthur Cooper.** *Emeritus Paleobiologist, Smithsonian Institution, Washington, D.C. Author of* Chazyan and Related Brachiopods.

LAMP SHELLS

G.A.C.H. **Geoffrey A.C. Herklots** (d. 1986). *Colombo Plan Botanical Adviser to Government of Nepal, 1961–63. Principal and Director of Research, Imperial College of Tropical Agriculture, Trinidad, 1953–60. Author of* Vegetables

in South-East Asia *and others.*

GARDENING AND HORTICULTURE (*in part*)

G.A.F.K. **George Angus Fulton Knight.** *President, Pacific Theological College, Suva, Fiji, 1965–72. Author of* A Christian Theology of the Old Testament; Deutero-Isaiah, a Theological Commentary; *and others.*

MACCABEES (*in part*) (Micropædia)

G.A.G.M. **G.A.G. Mitchell.** *Professor of Anatomy; Director, Anatomical Laboratories, Victoria University of Manchester, 1946–74. Author of* The Anatomy of the Autonomic Nervous System *and others.*

EXCRETION AND EXCRETORY SYSTEMS (*in part*)

G.A.H. **Geoffrey Alan Hosking.** *Professor of Russian History, School of Slavonic and East European Studies, University of London. Author of* Beyond Socialist Realism: Soviet Fiction Since Ivan Denisovich *and others.*

RUSSIAN LITERATURE (*in part*)

G.Ak. **George Akita.** *Professor of History, University of Hawaii at Manoa, Honolulu. Author of* Foundations of Constitutional Government.

ITŌ HIROBUMI, KOSHAKU (Micropædia)

G.A.K. **Gregory A. Kimble.** *Emeritus Professor of Psychology, Duke University, Durham, North Carolina. Editor of* Hilgard and Marquis' Conditioning and Learning.

LEARNING AND COGNITION, HUMAN (*in part*)

G.A.L. **George Arthur Lindbeck.** *Pitkin Professor of Historical Theology, Yale University. Author of* The Nature of Doctrine: Religion and Theology in a Post-Liberal Age *and others.*

RITES AND CEREMONIES, SACRED (*in part*)

G.An. **George Anastaplo.** *Professor of Law, Loyola University, Chicago. Lecturer in the Liberal Arts, University of Chicago. Emeritus Professor of Political Science and of Philosophy, Rosary College, River Forest, Illinois. Author of* The Constitutionalist.

CENSORSHIP
GREECE (*in part*)

G.A.O. **George A. Olah.** *Professor of Chemistry, University of Southern California, Los Angeles. Coeditor of* Carbonium Ions.

CARBONIUM ION (*in part*) (Micropædia)

Ga.P. **Gary William Poole.** *Associate Editor, Encyclopædia Britannica, Chicago, 1970–72.*

CHAMBERLAIN, JOSEPH (Micropædia)
JOSEPHUS, FLAVIUS (Micropædia)

G.A.P. **George A. Pettitt** (d. 1976). *Assistant to the President, University of California, Berkeley, 1936–66; Lecturer in Anthropology, 1940–66. Author of* Prisoners of Culture.

GESNER, CONRAD (Micropædia)

G.A.Po. **Gary A. Polis.** *Associate Professor of Biology, Vanderbilt*

University, Nashville, Tennessee. Author of Biology of Scorpions *and others.*

ARACHNIDS (*in part*)

Ga.S. **Gabriel Smith.** *Barrister-at-Law. Departmental Editor,* Journal of Business Law.

TAXATION (*in part*)

G.A.S. **George Albert Shepperson.** *William Robertson Professor Emeritus of Commonwealth and American History, University of Edinburgh. Author of* David Livingstone and the Rovuma.

LIVINGSTONE, DAVID (Micropædia)

G.A.Sa. **George A. Sacher** (d. 1981). *Senior Biologist, Division of Biological and Medical Research, Argonne National Laboratory, Argonne, Illinois, 1959–80. President, Gerontological Society, 1978–79. Coeditor of* Aging and Levels of Biological Organization.

GROWTH AND DEVELOPMENT, BIOLOGICAL (*in part*)

G.A.Sm. **George Alan Smith.** *Arts consultant. Hiker and mountain climber. Author of* Introduction to Mountaineering; The Armchair Mountaineer.

MOUNTAINEERING (*in part*) (Micropædia)

G.A.So. **G. Alan Solem** (d. 1990). *Curator of Invertebrates, Field Museum of Natural History, Chicago, 1959–90. Author of* The Shell Makers *and others.*

MOLLUSKS (*in part*)

G.B. **Giovanni Bognetti.** *Professor of Public Law, University of Milan. Author of* Costituzione economica e Corte costituzionale *and others.*

CONSTITUTIONAL LAW (*in part*)

G.Ba. **George Barany.** *Professor of History, University of Denver, Colorado. Author of* Stephen Széchenyi and the Awakening of Hungarian Nationalism, 1791–1841.

HUNGARY (*in part*)

G.B.Cl. **George B. Clark.** *Former Professor of Mining Engineering, University of Missouri, Rolla; Director, Rock Mechanics and Explosives Research Center, 1964–76. Coauthor of* Elements of Mining.

INDUSTRIES, EXTRACTION AND PROCESSING (*in part*)

G.B.D. **George B. Dantzig.** *Professor of Operations Research and Computer Science, Stanford University, California. Author of* Linear Programming and Extensions.

OPTIMIZATION, THE MATHEMATICAL THEORY OF (*in part*)

G.Be. **George Benneh.** *Professor of Geography and Resource Development, University of Ghana, Legon.*

WESTERN AFRICA (*in part*)

G.Bh. **Geoffrey Barraclough** (d. 1984). *Chichele Professor of Modern History, University of Oxford, 1970–73. President, The Historical Association, 1964–67.*

HOLY ROMAN EMPIRE, THE HISTORY OF THE (*in part*)

G.Bi. **Garrett Birkhoff.** *George Putnam Professor Emeritus of Pure and Applied Mathematics, Harvard University. Coauthor of* Algebra.
ALGEBRA (*in part*)

G.B.K. **George Briscoe Kerferd.** *Hulme Professor Emeritus of Greek, Victoria University of Manchester.*
PHILOSOPHICAL SCHOOLS AND
DOCTRINES, WESTERN (*in part*)

G.Bl. **Georges Blond** (d. 1989). *Novelist and historian. Author of* Pétain, 1856–1951.
PÉTAIN, PHILIPPE (Micropædia)

G.B.L. **Gerhart B. Ladner.** *Emeritus Professor of History, University of California, Los Angeles. Author of* Die Papstbildnisse des Altertums und des Mittelalters.
BONIFACE VIII (PAPACY) (Micropædia)
INNOCENT III (Micropædia)

G.Bor. **Günther Bornkamm** (d. 1990). *Professor of New Testament Studies, Rupert Charles University of Heidelberg, 1949–71. Author of* Jesus of Nazareth.
JESUS (*in part*)

G.Br. **Günter Bräuer.** *Professor of Anthropology, University of Hamburg.*
EVOLUTION, HUMAN (*in part*)

G.C. **Guido Calogero** (deceased). *Professor of Theoretical Philosophy, University of Rome. Author of* Studi sull'eleatismo.
PHILOSOPHICAL SCHOOLS AND
DOCTRINES, WESTERN (*in part*)

G.Car. **Giovanni Carsaniga.** *Professor of Italian, University of Sydney, Australia.*
ITALIAN LITERATURE (*in part*)

G.C.B. **Gregorio C. Borlaza** (d. 1987). *Editorial Consultant, Philippine Christian University, Manila. Former President, Philippine Normal College.*
PHILIPPINES (*in part*)

G.C.Bo. **Geoffrey C. Bolton.** *Professor and Head, Department of History, University of Queensland, Brisbane, Australia. Author of* The Oxford History of Australia: Modern Australia, 1942–1986; *general editor,* The Oxford History of Australia.
AUSTRALIA (*in part*)

G.C.C. **George C. Cromer.** *Former Manager, Administrative Services, General Motors Corporation, Warren, Michigan.*
TRANSPORTATION (*in part*)

G.C.E. **George C. Engerrand** (d. 1961). *Graduate Professor of Anthropology, University of Texas at Austin. Chief Geologist, Mexican Geological Survey, 1907–15.*
NORTH AMERICA (*in part*)

G.C.G. **George C. Gorman.** *Director, Tropical Programs, Center for Conservation Biology, Stanford University, California. Researcher on the evolution, behaviour, and systematics of lizards.*
REPTILES (*in part*)

G.C.H. **Gerald C. Hickey.** *Former Research Fellow, East–West Center, Honolulu. Research Anthropologist, the RAND Corporation, Saigon, 1964–73. Author of* Village in Vietnam *and others.*
SOUTHEAST ASIA, MAINLAND (*in part*)

G.C.Ha. **Gladys Cox Hansen.** *City Archivist, San Francisco. Author of* San Francisco Almanac; *editor of* San Francisco: The Bay and Its Cities.
SAN FRANCISCO (*in part*)

G.C.H.B. **Göran C.H. Bauer, M.D.** *Professor and Chairman, Department of Orthopedic Surgery, Medical School, University of Lund, Sweden.*
SUPPORTIVE AND CONNECTIVE
TISSUES (*in part*)

G.C.I. **George C. Izenour.** *Emeritus Professor of Theater Design and Technology, Yale University.*
THEATRICAL PRODUCTION (*in part*)

G.C.K. **George C. Kent, Jr.** *Alumni Professor Emeritus of Zoology, Louisiana State University, Baton Rouge. Author of* Comparative Anatomy of the Vertebrates.
REPRODUCTION AND REPRODUCTIVE
SYSTEMS (*in part*)

G.C.L.B. **G.C.L. Bertram.** *Former Senior Tutor, St. John's College, University of Cambridge. Author of* In Search of Mermaids: The Manatees of Guiana *and others.*
MAMMALS (*in part*)

G.Cr. **Gerhard Croll.** *Professor of Musicology, University of Salzburg, Austria. General editor of* Christoph Willibald Gluck, Complete Edition of His Works.
GLUCK, CHRISTOPH WILLIBALD
(Micropædia)

G.C.R. **George Clarence Robinson** (d. 1976). *Professor of Political Science, University of Northern Iowa, Cedar Falls. Editor of* Dictionary of Presidential Disapprovals.
POLK, JAMES K. (Micropædia)

G.d'A. **Guido d'Agostino.** *Associate in Institutional Parliamentary History, University of Naples.*
ITALY (*in part*)

G.D.B. **Georgy Dmitriyevich Bessarabov.** *Head, Department of Agrarian Resources, Government Research Institute of Agrarian Resources, Moscow.*
ASIA (*in part*)

G.D.C. **Gerson D. Cohen** (d. 1991). *Chancellor, 1972–86; Jacob H. Schiff Professor of History, 1970–86, Jewish Theological Seminary of America, New York City. Editor and translator of* Abraham ibn Daud's Sefer ha-Kabbala.
JUDAISM (*in part*)

G.De. **George G. Dekker.** *Professor of English, Stanford University, California. Author of* James Fenimore Cooper: The Novelist *and others.*
COOPER, JAMES FENIMORE (Micropædia)

G. de S. **Giorgio D. de Santillana** (d. 1974). *Professor of the History and*

Philosophy of Science, Massachusetts Institute of Technology, Cambridge. Author of The Crime of Galileo *and others.*
GALILEO (*in part*)

G.Det. **Georges Dethan.** *Archivist, French Foreign Ministry Archives, Paris, 1947–88. Chief Editor,* Revue d'Histoire Diplomatique. *Author of* Mazarin et ses amis *and others.*
MAZARIN, JULES, CARDINAL
(Micropædia)

G.D.G. **George D. Garland.** *Emeritus Professor of Physics, University of Toronto. Author of* The Earth's Shape and Gravity *and others.*
EARTH, THE (*in part*)

G.Di. **Gérard Diffloth.** *Professor of Linguistics and Asian Studies, Cornell University, Ithaca, New York.*
LANGUAGES OF THE WORLD (*in part*)

G.D.J. **Gary Dean Johnson.** *Professor of Geology, Dartmouth College, Hanover, New Hampshire.*
GEOCHRONOLOGY (*in part*)

G.D.L. **Geoffrey D. Lewis.** *Former Director of Museum Studies, University of Leicester, England. Coeditor of* Manual of Curatorship: A Guide to Museum Practice.
MUSEUMS

G.D.M. **George Daniel Mostow.** *Henry Ford II Professor of Mathematics, Yale University. Author of* Strong Rigidity of Locally Symmetric Spaces.
ALGEBRA (*in part*)
GEOMETRY (*in part*)

G.D.P. **George Duncan Painter.** *Assistant Keeper in charge of incunabula, Department of Printed Books, British Library, London, 1954–74. Author of* Proust: The Early Years; Proust: The Later Years; *and others.*
PROUST, MARCEL (*in part*) (Micropædia)

G.D.W. **G. Donald Whedon, M.D.** *Medical research consultant. Director, National Institute of Arthritis, Metabolism, and Digestive Diseases, U.S. Department of Health and Human Services, Bethesda, Maryland, 1962–81.*
SUPPORTIVE AND CONNECTIVE
TISSUES (*in part*)

G.Dy. **George Dykhuizen.** *Emeritus Professor of Philosophy, University of Vermont, Burlington. Author of* The Life and Mind of John Dewey.
DEWEY, JOHN (Micropædia)

G.E. **Gordon Epperson.** *Professor of Music, University of Arizona, Tucson. Author of* The Musical Symbol: A Study of the Philosophic Theory of Music.
MUSIC, THE ART OF (*in part*)

G.E.A. **Godfrey Edward Arnold, M.D.** (d. 1989). *Professor and Director, Division of Otolaryngology, University of Mississippi Medical Center, Jackson, 1963–79. Coauthor of* Voice, Speech, Language; Clinical Communicology.
SPEECH (*in part*)

G.E.Al. **Garland Edward Allen.** *Professor of Biology, Washington*

University, St. Louis, Missouri. Author of Thomas Hunt Morgan: The Man and His Science.
MORGAN, THOMAS HUNT (*in part*) (Micropædia)

Ge.B. Gerald Bonner. *Emeritus Reader in Theology, University of Durham, England.*
ARTS, PRACTICE AND PROFESSION OF THE (*in part*)

G.Ec. Garrett Eckbo. *Landscape architect and consultant in urban and environmental planning and design. Emeritus Professor of Landscape Architecture, University of California, Berkeley. Author of* Landscape for Living *and others.*
GARDEN AND LANDSCAPE DESIGN (*in part*)

Ge.Ca. George Cardona. *Professor of Linguistics, University of Pennsylvania, Philadelphia. Author of* Studies in Indian Grammarians *and others; coeditor of* Indo-European and Indo-Europeans.
LANGUAGES OF THE WORLD (*in part*)

G.E.D. Glyn Edmund Daniel (d. 1986). *Disney Professor of Archaeology, University of Cambridge, 1974–81; Fellow of St. John's College, Cambridge. Author of* The First Civilizations; A Hundred and Fifty Years of Archaeology; *and others.*
HISTORY, THE STUDY OF (*in part*)
SCHLIEMANN, HEINRICH (Micropædia)

Ge.E. Brother George Every, S.S.M. (deceased). *Lecturer, Kelham Theological College, Newark, England. Author of* The Byzantine Patriarchate, 451–1204 *and others.*
PHOTIUS, SAINT (Micropædia)

G.E.F. George Edwin Fussell (d. 1990). *President, British Agricultural History Society. Author of* The Farmer's Tools; Farming Technique from Prehistoric to Modern Times.
AGRICULTURE, THE HISTORY OF (*in part*)

G.E.F.C. Guy Edward Farquhar Chilver (d. 1982). *Professor of Classical Studies, University of Kent at Canterbury, England, 1964–76. Author of* "Vespasian" *in* Oxford Classical Dictionary.
DOMITIAN (Micropædia)
ROMANIA (*in part*)
VESPASIAN (Micropædia)

G.E.Fo. Gary Edward Forsythe. *Assistant Professor of Classical Languages and Literatures, University of Chicago.*
GREEK AND ROMAN CIVILIZATIONS, ANCIENT (*in part*)

G.E.H. The Rev. G.E. Hughes. *Professor of Philosophy, Victoria University of Wellington, New Zealand, 1951–84. Coauthor of* The Elements of Formal Logic *and others.*
LOGIC, THE HISTORY AND KINDS OF (*in part*)

G.E.H.A. Gerald E.H. Abraham (d. 1988). *President, Royal Musical Association, 1970–74. Assistant Controller of Music, British Broadcasting Corporation, London, 1962–67. James and Constance Alsop Professor of Music, University of Liverpool, 1947–62. Author of* A Hundred Years of Music; Slavonic and Romantic Music; *and others.*
SCHUMANN, ROBERT (Micropædia)

G.E.Ma. Gene E. Martin. *Professor of Geography, California State University, Chico. Author of* La división de la tierra en Chile central.
SOUTH AMERICA (*in part*)

G.E.Me. George Emery Mendenhall. *Emeritus Professor of Ancient and Biblical Studies, University of Michigan, Ann Arbor. Author of* Law and Covenant in Israel and the Ancient Near East *and others.*
DOCTRINES AND DOGMAS, RELIGIOUS (*in part*)

G.E.Mi. Gordon E. Misner. *Professor of Criminal Justice, University of Illinois, Chicago. Coauthor of* The Police and Society: An Environment for Collaboration and Confrontation.
POLICE (*in part*)

G.E.M.M. Gladstone E.M. Mills. *Professor of Public Administration; Dean, Faculty of Social Sciences, University of the West Indies, Kingston, Jamaica. Coeditor of* The Role of Small Nations in a Big World.
WEST INDIES, THE (*in part*)

Ge.Mo. Gerald Moore. *Former Professor of English, University of Jos, Nigeria. Author of* Seven African Writers *and others.*
AFRICAN ARTS (*in part*)

Ge.S. George Savage (d. 1982). *Free-lance writer. Author of* Concise History of Interior Decoration; French Decorative Art; Porcelain Through the Ages; *and many other works on the decorative arts.*
DECORATIVE ARTS AND FURNISHINGS (*in part*)

G.Es. Gerald Eskenazi. *Sportswriter,* The New York Times. *Free-lance writer. Author of* Hockey; A Thinking Man's Guide to Pro Hockey; *and others.*
SPORTS, MAJOR TEAM AND INDIVIDUAL (*in part*)

G.E.S. George E. Shambaugh, Jr., M.D. *Emeritus Professor of Otolaryngology, Northwestern University, Chicago. Chief Editor,* Archives of Otolaryngology, *1960–70. Author of* Surgery of the Ear.
SENSORY RECEPTION (*in part*)

Ge.St. Gerald Strauss. *Distinguished Professor of History, Indiana University, Bloomington. Author of* Law, Resistance, and the State in Reformation Germany.
GERMANY (*in part*)

G.E.T. Gordon Ernest Taylor. *Senior Scientific Officer, Royal Greenwich Observatory, Herstmonceux, England. President of the British Astronomical Association, 1968–70.*
SOLAR SYSTEM, THE (*in part*)

G.Ev. Graham Evans. *Reader in Sedimentology, Imperial College of Science, Technology, and Medicine, University of London.*
INDIAN OCEAN, THE (*in part*)

G.E.W. Glen E. Woolfenden. *Professor of Zoology, University of South Florida, Tampa.*
BIRDS (*in part*)

G.E.Wh. Geoffrey Edleston Wheeler (d. 1990). *Lieutenant Colonel, Indian Army. Director, Central Asian Research Centre, London, 1953–68. Author of* The Modern History of Soviet Central Asia *and others.*
UNION OF SOVIET SOCIALIST REPUBLICS (*in part*)

G.F.A. Geoffrey Freeman Allen. *Free-lance writer on rail transportation. Editor,* Jane's World Railways. *Author of* Railways in the Twentieth Century *and others.*
TRANSPORTATION (*in part*)

G.F.B. George F. Bertsch. *Hannah Professor of Physics, Michigan State University, East Lansing. Author of* Practitioner's Shell Model.
ATOMS (*in part*)

G.F.E. George F. Ekstrom (deceased). *Professor of Agricultural Education, University of Missouri, Columbia.*
AGRICULTURAL SCIENCES (*in part*)

G.F.H. Gregory F. Herzog. *Professor of Chemistry, Rutgers University, New Brunswick, New Jersey.*
ATOMS (*in part*)

G.Fi. Gilbert Fielder. *Emeritus Reader in Environmental Sciences, University of Lancaster, England; former Head, Lunar and Planetary Unit. Author of* Lunar Geology; *editor of* Geology and Physics of the Moon.
SOLAR SYSTEM, THE (*in part*)

G.Fo. Gabriel Fournier. *Professor of Medieval History, University of Clermont-Ferrand, France. Author of* Les Mérovingiens *and others.*
FRANCE (*in part*)

G.F.P. Gabor F. Peterdi. *Painter and printmaker. Emeritus Professor of Printmaking, Yale University. Author of* Printmaking; Great Prints of the World.
PRINTMAKING

G.F.S. Gilles François Sautter. *Professor of Geography, University of Paris I (Panthéon-Sorbonne). Author of* De l'Atlantique au fleuve Congo.
AFRICA (*in part*)

G.F.W. Gilbert F. White. *Gustavson Distinguished Professor Emeritus of Geography, University of Colorado, Boulder. Coauthor of* The Lower Mekong.
ASIA (*in part*)

G.G. George Gömöri. *Lecturer in Slavonic Studies, University of Cambridge. Author of* Polish and Hungarian Poetry, 1945 to 1956.
HUNGARIAN LITERATURE (*in part*)

G.Ge. Gino Germani (d. 1979). *Monroe Gutman Professor of Latin American*

Studies, Harvard University. Author of Política y sociedad en una época de transición.
SOUTH AMERICA (*in part*)

G.Gr. Guido Gregorietti. *Former Director, Poldi Pezzoli Museum, Milan. Author of* Jewelry Through the Ages.
DRESS AND ADORNMENT (*in part*)

G.G.V.D. Glyndon G. Van Deusen (deceased). *Professor of History, University of Rochester, New York, 1947–62. Author of* The Life of Henry Clay.
CLAY, HENRY (Micropædia)

G.G.Wd. Guido Gustav Weigend. *Professor of Geography, Arizona State University, Tempe.*
ATLANTIC OCEAN, THE (*in part*)

G.Ha. Georg Hazai. *Corresponding Member; Deputy Director, Oriental Studies Research Group, Hungarian Academy of Sciences, Budapest; General Manager, Akadémiai Kiadó és Nyomda (publishing house of the academy). Author of* Sovietico-Turcica.
LANGUAGES OF THE WORLD (*in part*)

G.H.B. Geoffrey H. Beale. *Royal Society Research Professor of Genetics, University of Edinburgh, Scotland, 1963–78. Author of* The Genetics of Paramecium Aurelia.
WEISMANN, AUGUST (Micropædia)

G.H.Bl. Gerald Henry Blake. *Reader in Geography, University of Durham, England; Director, International Boundaries Research Unit. Coauthor of* The Cambridge Atlas of the Middle East and North Africa; The Middle East: A Geographical Study.
IRAQ (*in part*)

G.H.D. George Harry Dury. *Emeritus Professor of Geography and Geology, University of Wisconsin, Madison. World authority on fluvial processes in geomorphology. Author of* The Face of the Earth.
RIVERS (*in part*)

G.He. George Hendricks (d. 1979). *Professor of Social Sciences, Georgia Institute of Technology, Atlanta, 1962–69. Author of* Union Army Occupation of the Southern Seaboard, 1861–1865.
UNITED STATES OF AMERICA (*in part*)

G.Hi. Gilbert Highet (d. 1978). *Anthon Professor of Latin Language and Literature, Columbia University, 1950–72. Author of* Juvenal the Satirist; The Classical Tradition: Greek and Roman Influences on Western Literature.
JUVENAL (Micropædia)

G.H.J. Gareth H. Jones. *Downing Professor of the Laws of England, University of Cambridge; Fellow of Trinity College, Cambridge.*
COKE, SIR EDWARD (Micropædia)

G.H.K. George Hall Kirby. *Free-lance writer, editor, and translator. Author of* Looking at Germany *and others.*
GERMANY (*in part*)

G.H.S. Genjun H. Sasaki. *Professor of Buddhism, Otani University,*

Kyōto. Author of A Study of Buddhist Psychology.
SHINRAN (Micropædia)

G.H.S.B. Geoffrey H.S. Bushnell (d. 1978). *Reader in New World Archaeology, University of Cambridge, 1966–70; Fellow of Corpus Christi College, Cambridge; Curator, University Museum of Archaeology and Ethnology, 1948–70. Author of* Peru *and others.*
PRE-COLUMBIAN CIVILIZATIONS (*in part*)

G.H.T.K. George H.T. Kimble. *Director, Survey of Tropical Africa, Twentieth Century Fund, New York City, 1953–60. Professor of Geography, Indiana University, Bloomington, 1957–66. Author of* Tropical Africa.
AFRICA (*in part*)

G.I.A. Gordon I. Atwater (d. 1973). *Founder and Senior Member, Atwater, Cowan, Carter, Miller, and Heffner (geological and petroleum consultants), New Orleans.*
FUELS, FOSSIL (*in part*)

G.I.B. George I. Blanksten. *Emeritus Professor of Political Science, Northwestern University, Evanston, Illinois. Author of* Perón's Argentina; Ecuador: Constitutions and Caudillos *and others.*
BRAZIL (*in part*)
URUGUAY (*in part*)

G.I.Bk. George I. Back (d. 1972). *Major General, U.S. Army.*
WAR, THE TECHNOLOGY OF (*in part*)

Gi.M. Giovanni Macchia. *Professor of French Language and Literature, University of Rome. Author of* L'opera completa di Watteau *and others.*
WATTEAU, ANTOINE (Micropædia)

Gi.Ma. Giuseppe Martini. *Former Professor of Medieval History; Director, Institute of Medieval and Modern History, University of Milan. Author of* Cattolicesimo e storicismo *and others.*
ITALY (*in part*)

Gi.T. Giuseppe Tucci (d. 1984). *Professor of Oriental Religion and Philosophy, University of Rome, 1933–65. Author of* Il buddhismo; Minor Buddhist Texts; *and others.*
BUDDHISM, THE BUDDHA AND (*in part*)

G.J. Gordon Jackson. *Reader in Economic History, University of Strathclyde, Glasgow. Author of* The British Whaling Trade *and others.*
FISHING, COMMERCIAL (*in part*)

G.J.A. George J. Annas. *Edward R. Utley Professor of Health Law; Chief, Health Law Section, Schools of Medicine and of Public Health, Boston University. Author of* The Rights of Patients.
MEDICINE (*in part*).

G.J.B. Gilbert James Butland. *Emeritus Professor of Geography, University of New England, Armidale, Australia.*
PARAGUAY (*in part*)
SPAIN (*in part*)

G.J.G. George J. Goodman. *Regents Professor Emeritus of Botany, University*

of Oklahoma, Norman. Author of Spring Flora of Central Oklahoma.
ANGIOSPERMS (*in part*)

G.J.N. Gareth Jon Nelson. *Chairman and Curator, Department of Ichthyology, American Museum of Natural History, New York City. Author of articles on the anatomy and systematics of fishes.*
FISHES (*in part*)

G.J.P. Gray Johnson Poole. *Free-lance writer. Author of* Architects and Man's Skyline; *coauthor of* Men Who Dig Up History *and others.*
PETRIE, SIR FLINDERS (Micropædia)

G.J.S. George J. Stigler. *Charles R. Walgreen Distinguished Service Professor Emeritus of American Institutions, University of Chicago. Nobel Prize for Economics, 1982. Author of* The Theory of Price.
ECONOMIC THEORY (*in part*)

G.J.Si. Gustavus J. Simmons. *Senior Fellow, National Security Studies, Sandia National Laboratories, Albuquerque, New Mexico. Researcher in command and control of nuclear weapons. Author of numerous articles on cryptology and authentication.*
CRYPTOLOGY

G.J.T. Gerald J. Toomer. *Professor of the History of Mathematics, Brown University, Providence, Rhode Island. Author of* Diocles on Burning Mirrors.
ARCHIMEDES

G.J.W. Gerald James Whitrow. *Emeritus Professor of the History and Applications of Mathematics, Imperial College of Science and Technology, University of London. Author of* The Natural Philosophy of Time *and others.*
HAMILTON, SIR WILLIAM ROWAN (Micropædia)
LAPLACE, PIERRE-SIMON, MARQUIS DE (Micropædia)
POINCARÉ, HENRI (Micropædia)

G.K. Gerhard Kubik. *Cultural Anthropologist, Institute of Ethnology, University of Vienna. Author of* Theory of African Music (3 vol.) *and other works on African music.*
AFRICAN ARTS (*in part*)

G.Ka. George Kazantzis. *Professor of Occupational Medicine, London School of Hygiene and Tropical Medicine, University of London. Contributor to* Handbook on the Toxicology of Metals.
OCCUPATIONAL DISEASES AND DISORDERS

G.Ke. Gavin Kennedy. *Professor of Defence Finance, Heriot–Watt University, Edinburgh. Author of* Defence Economics *and others.*
WAR, THE THEORY AND CONDUCT OF (*in part*)

G.K.E. Geoffrey Kenyon Elliott. *Former Senior Lecturer in Forestry, University College of North Wales, University of Wales, Bangor.*
BIOSPHERE, THE (*in part*)

G.K.G. G.K. Ghori. *Former Professor of Geography, University of Mysore,*

India.
INDIA (*in part*)

G.K.Ge. Gerald K. Geerlings. *Architect, etcher, and writer. Author of* Wrought Iron in Architecture; Metal Crafts in Architecture; *and others.*
DECORATIVE ARTS AND FURNISHINGS
  (*in part*)

G.Kh. George Kish (d. 1989). *Professor of Geography, University of Michigan, Ann Arbor.*
ITALY (*in part*)

G.K.L. George Knowlton Lewis. *Emeritus Professor of Geography, Boston University. Coauthor of* Boston: A Geographical Portrait.
BOSTON (*in part*)

G.K.P. George Kerlin Park. *Professor of Anthropology, Memorial University of Newfoundland, St. John's. Author of* The Idea of Social Structure; An Afterpiece to Peasantry.
OCCULTISM (*in part*)
RELIGIOUS AND SPIRITUAL BELIEF,
  SYSTEMS OF (*in part*)

G.K.S.R. Gotthold K.S. Rhode. *Emeritus Professor of East European and Russian History, Johannes Gutenberg University of Mainz, Germany; former Director, Institute for East European Research. Author of* Kleine Geschichte Polens.
CASIMIR III (Micropædia)
CASIMIR IV (Micropædia)
JOHN III SOBIESKI (POLAND)
  (Micropædia)
WŁADYSŁAW II JAGIEŁŁO (Micropædia)

G.L. George Lang. *International hotel, restaurant, and food consultant. Columnist,* Travel & Leisure *magazine. Author of* The Cuisine of Hungary *and others; consulting editor of* Time-Life Foods of the World.
GASTRONOMY (*in part*)
RESTAURANT (*in part*) (Micropædia)

G.L.C. Gerhard L. Closs. *A.A. Michelson Distinguished Service Professor of Chemistry, University of Chicago. Author of numerous papers on transient intermediates in chemical reactions.*
CARBANION (*in part*) (Micropædia)
CARBENE (Micropædia)

G.L.Ca. George Law Cawkwell. *Former Lecturer in Ancient History, University of Oxford; Emeritus Fellow of University College, Oxford.*
ISOCRATES (Micropædia)

G.L.D. Gwenda Louise Davis. *Former Associate Professor of Botany, University of New England, Armidale, Australia. Author of* Systematic Embryology of the Angiosperms.
ANGIOSPERMS (*in part*)

G.L.G. George L. Gooberman. *Senior Lecturer in Electrical Engineering, University of Limerick, Ireland. Author of* Ultrasonics.
SOUND (*in part*)

G.Li. Gillian Lindt. *Professor of Religion, Columbia University. Author of* Moravians in Two Worlds.
ZINZENDORF, NIKOLAUS LUDWIG, GRAF
  VON (Micropædia)

G.L.K. Sir Geoffrey Langdon Keynes, M.D. (d. 1982). *Honorary Librarian, Royal College of Surgeons of England. Consulting Surgeon, St. Bartholomew's Hospital, London. Author of* The Life of William Harvey; A Bibliography of the Writings of Dr. William Harvey.
HARVEY (*in part*)

G.L.Ke. George L. Kelling. *Professor of Criminal Justice, Northeastern University, Boston. Research Fellow, John F. Kennedy School of Government, Harvard University. Coauthor of* Newark Foot Patrol Experiment.
POLICE (*in part*)

G.L.S. Gordon Leslie Squires. *Lecturer in Physics, University of Cambridge; Fellow of Trinity College, Cambridge. Author of* Introduction to the Theory of Thermal Neutron Scattering.
MECHANICS (*in part*)

G.Lu. Georg Hans Luck. *Professor of Classics, Johns Hopkins University, Baltimore. Author of* The Latin Love-Elegy *and others.*
PROPERTIUS, SEXTUS (Micropædia)

G.L.V. Gilbert L. Voss (d. 1989). *Professor of Marine Science, University of Miami, Florida, 1961–88. Author of* Cephalopods of the Philippine Islands.
MOLLUSKS (*in part*)

G.M. George Makdisi. *Professor of Arabic and Islamic Studies; Director, Center of Medieval Studies, University of Pennsylvania, Philadelphia. Author of* The Rise of Humanism in Classical Islam and the Christian West *and others.*
AḤMAD IBN ḤANBAL (Micropædia)

G.Ma. Golo Mann. *Writer. Professor of History and Political Science, Technical University, Stuttgart, West Germany, 1960–64. Author of* Friedrich von Gentz *and others.*
GENTZ, FRIEDRICH (Micropædia)

G.M.A. Glenda M. Abramson. *Fellow, Oxford Centre for Hebrew Studies; Cowley Lecturer in Post-Biblical Hebrew, University of Oxford. Author of* The Writing of Yehuda Amichai.
HEBREW LITERATURE (*in part*)

G.M.A.R. Gisela Marie Augusta Richter (d. 1972). *Curator, Greek and Roman Department, Metropolitan Museum of Art, New York City. Author of* Engraved Gems of the Greeks, Etruscans, and Romans *and others.*
DRESS AND ADORNMENT (*in part*)

G.M.C. Gerald M. Capers. *Emeritus Professor of History, Tulane University, New Orleans. Author of* John C. Calhoun, Opportunist: A Reappraisal *and others.*
CALHOUN, JOHN C. (Micropædia)

G.McC.McB. George McCutchen McBride (d. 1971). *Professor of Geography, University of California, Los Angeles. Visiting Professor, Carnegie Endowment for International Peace,* South America, 1929–30; Central America 1938. *Author of* Agrarian Indian Communities of Highland Bolivia *and others.*
BOLIVIA (*in part*)

G.M.Ce. Gerald M. Clemence (d. 1974). *Professor of Astronomy, Yale University, 1966–74. Coauthor of* Methods of Celestial Mechanics.
NEWCOMB, SIMON (Micropædia)

G.McK.H. Graham McK. Hughes. *Editor,* Arts Review *magazine. Former Art Director, Worshipful Company of Goldsmiths, London. Head of Design, Royal Mint, London. Author of* Modern Silver.
DECORATIVE ARTS AND FURNISHINGS
  (*in part*)

G.Me. Gustav Mensching (d. 1978). *Professor of Comparative Religion, Rhenish Friedrich Wilhelm University of Bonn, West Germany. Author of* Die Religion, Erscheinungsformen, Strukturtypen und Lebensgesetze; Soziologie der Religion; *and others.*
DOCTRINES AND DOGMAS, RELIGIOUS
  (*in part*)

G.Mn. Georges Mongrédien (d. 1980). *Historian. Director of the Municipal Council of Paris and General Council of the Seine, 1947–67. Author of* Le Grand Condé; Colbert; *and many others.*
CONDÉ, LOUIS II DE BOURBON, 4ᵉ PRINCE
  DE (Micropædia)

G.Mo. Gaston Monnerville. *Member, Constitutional Council of France, 1974–83. President, Senate of France, 1958–68. Author of* Clemenceau *and others.*
CLEMENCEAU, GEORGES (*in part*)
  (Micropædia)

G.M.W. George M. Woodwell. *Director and President, Woods Hole Research Center, Massachusetts. Lecturer in Ecology, School of Forestry and Environmental Studies, Yale University. Editor of* The Earth in Transition.
PLANTS (*in part*)

G.Na. Giuseppe Nangeroni. *Emeritus Professor of Geography, Catholic University of Milan. Author of* Geografia e geomorfologia.
ITALY (*in part*)

G.N.G. George N. Gordon. *Professor of Communications, Fordham University, Bronx, New York. Author of* The Languages of Communication; The Communications Revolution; *and others.*
COMMUNICATION

G.N.Ha. George N. Hatsopoulos. *President, Thermo Electron Corporation, Waltham, Massachusetts. Coauthor of* Principles of General Thermodynamics.
THERMODYNAMICS, PRINCIPLES
  OF (*in part*)

G.O. George Ordish (d. 1991). *Editor,* Tropical Science, *London, 1966–72. Author of* Untaken Harvest; The Constant Pest; *and others.*
AGRICULTURE, THE HISTORY OF (*in part*)

G.P.   Gerhardt Preuschen. *Emeritus Director, Max Planck Institute for Agricultural Labour and Scientific Farming, Bad Kreuznach, Germany. Author of* Die Technik im landwirtschaftlichen Betrieb.
AGRICULTURAL SCIENCES (*in part*)

G.Pa.   Günter Passavant. *Editor,* Mitteilungen, *Institute for the Study of the History of Art, Florence. Author of* Andrea del Verrocchio: Sculptures, Paintings, and Drawings *and others.*
VERROCCHIO, ANDREA DEL (Micropædia)

G.Pan.   Guido Pannain (d. 1977). *Professor of the History of Music, S. Pietro a Maiella Conservatory of Music, Naples. Author of* Lineamento di storia della musica *and others.*
CORELLI, ARCANGELO (Micropædia)

G.Pe.   George Pendle (d. 1977). *Managing Director, Pendle & Rivett Ltd., London. Author of* A History of Latin America *and others.*
URUGUAY (*in part*)

G.P.G.   Georges Paul Gusdorf. *Former Professor of Philosophy, University of Strasbourg, France. Author of* Les Sciences humaines et la conscience occidentale; La Découverte de soi; Mémoire et personne.
PHILOSOPHICAL ANTHROPOLOGY (*in part*)

G.P.Gi.   Giovanni Pietro Giorgetti. *Lecturer in Italian, Birkbeck College, University of London.*
ITALIAN LITERATURE (*in part*)

G.Pi.   Sir George Pickering, M.D. (d. 1980). *Master of Pembroke College, Oxford, 1968–74; Regius Professor of Medicine, University of Oxford, 1956–68. Author of* High Blood Pressure.
OSLER, SIR WILLIAM, BARONET (Micropædia)

G.P.K.   Gertrude Prokosch Kurath. *Research Fellow, Wenner-Gren Foundation for Anthropological Research, New York City. Former Coordinator, Dance Research Center, Ann Arbor, Michigan. Author of* Iroquois Music and Dance *and others.*
AMERICAN INDIANS (*in part*)
FOLK ARTS (*in part*)

G.P.L.   Gilbert P. Laue. *Former Chief Copy Editor, Richard D. Irwin, Inc., Homewood, Illinois. Former Associate Editor,* Sports, *Encyclopædia Britannica, Chicago.*
SPORTS, MAJOR TEAM AND INDIVIDUAL (*in part*)

G.P.Ma.   The Rev. Germain P. Marc'hadour. *Professor of Philology, Catholic University of the West, Angers, France. Director,* Moreana Quarterly. *Author of* L'Univers de Thomas More *and other works on Thomas More.*
MORE, SIR THOMAS (*in part*) (Micropædia)

G.P.R.   Gerald P. Rodnan, M.D. (d. 1983). *Professor of Medicine, University of Pittsburgh, 1967–83. Editor of* Primer on the Rheumatic Diseases.
SUPPORTIVE AND CONNECTIVE TISSUES (*in part*)

G.P.Ri.   G. Philip Rightmire. *Professor of Anthropology, State University of New York at Binghamton.*
EVOLUTION, HUMAN (*in part*)

G.P.T.   Sir George Paget Thomson (d. 1975). *Professor of Physics, University of London, 1930–52. Cowinner, Nobel Prize for Physics, 1937. Author of* J.J. Thomson and the Cavendish Laboratory.
THOMSON, SIR J.J. (Micropædia)

G.R.   Graham Reynolds. *Keeper, Departments of Prints and Drawings, 1961–74, and of Paintings, 1959–74, Victoria and Albert Museum, London. Author of* Constable, the Natural Painter.
CONSTABLE, JOHN (Micropædia)

G.Ra.   Graham Ratcliff. *Neuropsychologist, Harmarville Rehabilitation Center, Pittsburgh. Clinical Assistant Professor of Psychiatry, Neurology, and Psychology, University of Pittsburgh.*
NERVES AND NERVOUS SYSTEMS (*in part*)

G.R.B.   Glenn Richard Bugh. *Associate Professor of Ancient History, Virginia Polytechnic Institute and State University, Blacksburg. Author of* The Horsemen of Athens.
LEBANON (*in part*)
PALESTINE (*in part*)

G.R.C.   Gerald Roe Crone (d. 1982) *Librarian and Map Curator, Royal Geographical Society, London, 1945–66. Author of* Maps and Their Makers *and others.*
HAKLUYT, RICHARD (Micropædia)
MACKINDER, SIR HALFORD JOHN (Micropædia)

G.R.Co.   George R. Collins. *Emeritus Professor of Art History, Columbia University. Author of* Antonio Gaudí *and others; coauthor of* The Designs and Drawings of Antonio Gaudí.
GAUDÍ, ANTONI (Micropædia)

G.Re.   George S. Rentz. *Emeritus Curator of the Middle East Collection, Hoover Institution on War, Revolution and Peace, Stanford, California. Emeritus Lecturer in Islāmic History, Stanford University. Coauthor and editor of* Oman and the Southern Shore of the Persian Gulf.
ARABIA (*in part*)

G.R.E.   Sir Geoffrey R. Elton. *Regius Professor Emeritus of Modern History, University of Cambridge; Fellow of Clare College, Cambridge. Author of* The Tudor Revolution in Government: Administrative Changes in the Reign of Henry VIII *and others.*
CRANMER, THOMAS (*in part*) (Micropædia)
CROMWELL, THOMAS, EARL OF ESSEX (Micropædia)
HENRY VIII (ENGLAND) (*in part*) (Micropædia)

G.R.F.   Gizella Rochelle Fowler. *Free-lance writer and consultant.*
DRESS AND ADORNMENT (*in part*)

G.R.G.H.   Gavin R.G. Hambly. *Professor of History, University of Texas at Dallas. Coauthor and editor of* Central Asia.
UNION OF SOVIET SOCIALIST REPUBLICS (*in part*)

G.R.H.   G.R. Hawting. *Senior Lecturer in the History of the Near and Middle East, School of Oriental and African Studies, University of London.*
MANṢŪR, AL- (Micropædia)

G.R.M.B.   Germain René Michel Bazin (d. 1990). *Research Professor of Fine Arts, York University, Toronto, 1970–75. Chief Curator of Paintings and Drawings, the Louvre Museum, Paris, 1951–65. Author of* History of World Sculpture.
RODIN, AUGUSTE (Micropædia)

G.Ro.   Gloria Robinson. *Research Affiliate in the History of Medicine, Yale University.*
HAECKEL, ERNST (Micropædia)

G.R.P.   George Richard Potter (d. 1981). *Professor of Medieval History, University of Sheffield, England. Coauthor of* A Short History of Switzerland.
SWITZERLAND (*in part*)

G.R.R.   George Richard Rumney. *Emeritus Professor of Geography, University of Connecticut, Storrs. Author of* Climatology and the World's Climates.
KÖPPEN, WLADIMIR (Micropædia)

G.R.R.T.   Geoffrey Russell Richards Treasure. *Senior Master, Harrow School, England. Author of* Seventeenth Century France; The Making of Modern Europe.
EUROPEAN HISTORY AND CULTURE (*in part*)

G.R.S.   G. Ralph Strohl. *Market Researcher, Journals Division, University of Chicago Press. Author of* "The Ephemeral and the Immortal" *in* India and Greece: Connections and Parallels.
JAINISM (*in part*)

G.R.Sl.   Gordon R. Slemon. *Professor of Electrical Engineering, University of Toronto. Coauthor of* Electric Machines.
ENERGY CONVERSION (*in part*)

G.R.T.   George Raynor Thompson. *Historian, U.S. Army Strategic Communications Command, 1964–72.*
WAR, THE TECHNOLOGY OF (*in part*)

G.R.W.   Gordon R. Willey. *Bowditch Professor Emeritus of Mexican and Central American Archaeology, Harvard University. Author of* An Introduction to American Archaeology.
MEXICO (*in part*)
PRE-COLUMBIAN CIVILIZATIONS (*in part*)

G.R.We.   Gerald Raymond Webster. *Assistant Professor of Geography, University of Alabama, University. Assistant Professor of Geography, University of Wyoming, Laramie, 1985–89.*
UNITED STATES OF AMERICA (*in part*)

Gr.W.K.   Gregory W. Knapp. *Assistant Professor of Geography, University of*

Texas at Austin. Author of Ecología Cultural Prehispánica del Ecuador.
ECUADOR (*in part*)

G.R.Z.   George R. Zug. *Curator, Department of Vertebrate Zoology, National Museum of Natural History, Smithsonian Institution, Washington, D.C.*
BEHAVIOUR, ANIMAL (*in part*)

G.S.   Geoffrey Sawer. *Emeritus Professor of Law, Australian National University, Canberra. Author of* Law in Society.
LAW, THE PROFESSION AND PRACTICE OF (*in part*)

G.Sa.   Gudmund Sandvik. *Professor of Legal History, University of Oslo. Author of* Det gamle veldet: Norske finansar 1760–79 *and others.*
DENMARK (*in part*)
NORWAY (*in part*)
SWEDEN (*in part*)

G.S.A.   Guy S. Alitto. *Associate Professor of Modern Chinese History, University of Chicago. Author of* The Last Confucian.
ASIA (*in part*)

G.Sc.   Georg Schwarzenberger. *Emeritus Professor of International Law, University of London. Vice President, London Institute of World Affairs. Author of* A Manual of International Law.
INTERNATIONAL LAW (*in part*)

G.S.E.   Gary S. Elbow. *Professor of Geography; Director of Latin American Area Studies, Texas Tech University, Lubbock. Contributor to* Middle America: Its Lands and Peoples (*3rd ed.*).
CENTRAL AMERICA (*in part*)

G.Sh.   Gordon Shillinglaw. *Professor of Accounting, Columbia University. Author of* Managerial Cost Accounting.
ACCOUNTING

G.S.H.   Gerald S. Hawkins. *Astronomer, Smithsonian Astrophysical Observatory, Cambridge, Massachusetts, 1962–74. Author of* Mindsteps to the Cosmos *and others.*
BRADLEY, JAMES (Micropædia)

G.S.Ha.   Gordon S. Haight (d. 1985). *Professor of English, Yale University 1950–68. Author of* George Eliot: A Biography; *editor of* The George Eliot Letters.
ELIOT, GEORGE (Micropædia)

G.Si.   George Bertrand Silberbauer. *Senior Lecturer in Anthropology and Sociology, Monash University, Clayton, Australia. Author of* Hunter and Habitat in the Central Kalahari Desert *and others.*
AFRICA (*in part*)
SOUTHERN AFRICA (*in part*)

G.S.K.   Geoffrey S. Kirk. *Regius Professor Emeritus of Greek, University of Cambridge. Author of* The Songs of Homer *and others.*
HOMERIC EPICS, THE

G.S.Ke.   G. Stuart Keith. *Research Associate, Department of Ornithology, American Museum of Natural History, New York City. Author of numerous scientific and popular articles on cranes.*
BIRDS (*in part*)

G.S.L.   George S. Lane (d. 1981). *Kenan Professor of Germanic and Comparative Linguistics, University of North Carolina at Chapel Hill, 1950–72. Author of* Studies in Kuchean Grammar I.
LANGUAGES OF THE WORLD (*in part*)

G.S.Lo.   George S. Losey. *Professor of Zoology; Associate Director, Hawaii Institute of Marine Biology, University of Hawaii at Manoa, Honolulu.*
COLORATION, BIOLOGICAL (*in part*)

G.S.O.   Glenn S. Orton. *Member of the Technical Staff, Earth and Space Sciences Division, Jet Propulsion Laboratory, California Institute of Technology, Pasadena.*
SOLAR SYSTEM, THE (*in part*)

G.S.P.F.-G.   Greville Stewart Parker Freeman-Grenville. *Honorary Fellow, University of York, Heslington, England. Professor of African History, State University of New York College at New Paltz, 1969–74. Author of* The Medieval History of the Coast of Tanganyika *and others.*
SAʿĪD IBN SULṬĀN (Micropædia)

G.St.   George Speaight. *Former Editorial Director, George Rainbird Ltd. Author of* The History of the English Puppet Theatre; Punch and Judy: A History; *and others.*
PUPPETRY

G.T.G.   Guy Thompson Griffith (d. 1985). *Laurence Reader in Classics, University of Cambridge, 1951–75; Fellow of Gonville and Caius College, Cambridge. Coauthor of* A History of Macedonia.
PHILIP II (MACEDONIA) (Micropædia)

G.Ts.   George Thomas Tsoumis. *Professor of Forest Utilization, Aristotelian University of Thessaloníki, Greece. Author of* Science and Technology of Wood *and others.*
FORESTRY AND WOOD PRODUCTION (*in part*)

G.T.S.   Glenn T. Seaborg. *University Professor of Chemistry; Associate Director, Lawrence Berkeley Laboratory; Chairman, Lawrence Hall of Science, University of California, Berkeley; Chancellor, 1958–61. Chairman, Atomic Energy Commission, 1961–71. Cowinner, Nobel Prize for Chemistry, 1951. Author of* Man-Made Transuranium Elements.
CHEMICAL ELEMENTS (*in part*)

G.T.Se.   Giles Timothy Severin. *Free-lance writer. Author of* Explorers of the Mississippi.
NORTH AMERICA (*in part*)

G.Tu.   Glenn Tucker (d. 1976). *Free-lance writer and historian. Author of* Tecumseh: Vision of Glory.
TECUMSEH (Micropædia)

G.U.   George Unwin. *Free-lance reader, editor, and translator; formerly with George Allen & Unwin Ltd., London. Translator of* Sign, Symbol and Script *and others.*
PUBLISHING (*in part*)

Gu.A.   Gustavo Anguizola. *Assistant Professor of History, University of Texas at Arlington. Author of* One Hundred Years of Isthmian Political Instability *and others.*
CENTRAL AMERICA (*in part*)

Gu.K.   Gunnar Karlsson. *Professor of History, University of Iceland, Reykjavík. Author of* Sjálfstæði íslendinga *and others.*
ICELAND (*in part*)

Gü.P.   Günther Patzig. *Professor of Philosophy and Director, Philosophical Seminar, Georg August University of Göttingen, Germany. Author of* Aristotle's Theory of the Syllogism.
LOGIC, THE HISTORY AND KINDS OF (*in part*)

Gu.S.   Gunnar Schlieder. *Instructor in Geology, Lehigh University, Bethlehem, Pennsylvania.*
CONTINENTAL LANDFORMS (*in part*)

Gu.W.   Gunther Wolf. *Professor of History, University of Stuttgart, Germany. Coauthor and editor of* Stupor Mundi: Zur Geschichte Friedrichs II von Hohenstaufen.
FREDERICK II (GERMANY/HOLY ROMAN EMPIRE) (Micropædia)

G.V.   Georges Vajda (d. 1981). *Director of Studies, École pratique des Hautes études (Institute for Advanced Research), Paris. Author of* Recherches sur la philosophie et la Kabbale dans la pensée juive du Moyen-Âge *and others.*
JUDAISM (*in part*)

G.v.B.   Gerhardt von Bonin, M.D. (d. 1979). *Consultant in Neuroanatomy, Neurological Institute, Mt. Zion Hospital, San Francisco. Professor of Anatomy, University of Illinois, Chicago, 1939–58. Author of* Essay on the Cerebral Cortex.
NERVES AND NERVOUS SYSTEMS (*in part*)

G.V.G.   Gerald V. Gibbs. *University Distinguished Professor of Mineralogy, Virginia Polytechnic Institute and State University, Blacksburg.*
MINERALS AND ROCKS (*in part*)

G.V.K.   German Viktorovich Kopanev. *Head, Central Asian Section, Council for Research on Productive Forces, U.S.S.R. Planning Committee, Moscow. Coauthor of* Central Asian Economic Region.
UNION OF SOVIET SOCIALIST REPUBLICS (*in part*)

G.V.M.   Gerard V. Middleton. *Professor of Geology, McMaster University, Hamilton, Ontario. A leading advocate of quantitative methods in studies of sediments.*
OCEANS (*in part*)

G.V.T.M.   Geoffrey Vernon Townsend Matthews. *Director of Research and Conservation, The Wildfowl and*

Wetlands Trust, Slimbridge, England, 1955–88. Author of Bird Navigation.
BIRDS (*in part*)

G.W. **George Woodcock.** *Free-lance writer. Editor,* Canadian Literature (*quarterly*), *University of British Columbia, Vancouver, 1959–77. Author of* Anarchism; The Crystal Spirit: A Study of George Orwell; Pierre-Joseph Proudhon; *and others.*
ORWELL, GEORGE (Micropædia)
PROUDHON, PIERRE-JOSEPH (Micropædia)
SOCIO-ECONOMIC DOCTRINES AND
  REFORM MOVEMENTS, MODERN
  (*in part*)

G.W.A. **Gösta W. Ahlström.** *Emeritus Professor of Old Testament and Ancient Palestinian Studies, University of Chicago. Author of* Aspects of Syncretism in the Israelite Religion *and others.*
DOCTRINES AND DOGMAS, RELIGIOUS
  (*in part*)

G.W.B. **Geoffrey W. Bromiley.** *Senior Professor of Church History and Historical Theology, Fuller Theological Seminary, Pasadena, California. Editor and translator of* Zwingli and Bullinger (*Library of Christian Classics*).
ZWINGLI, HULDRYCH (Micropædia)

G.W.Ba. **Glen W. Baxter.** *Senior Lecturer on East Asian Studies, Harvard University, 1956–80; Associate Director, Harvard-Yenching Institute, 1964–80. Author of* Index to the Imperial Register of Tz'u Prosody.
PAN KU (Micropædia)

G.W.Bo. **G.W. Bowersock.** *Professor of Ancient History, Institute for Advanced Study, Princeton, New Jersey. Author of* Greek Sophists in the Roman Empire; Augustus and the Greek World; *and others.*
AGRIPPA, MARCUS VIPSANIUS
  (Micropædia)
GALEN OF PERGAMUM (Micropædia)
HADRIAN (*in part*) (Micropædia)

G.W.H. **Gerard Willem Huygens.** *Professor of History and Dutch Literature, Rotterdam Lyceum, The Netherlands. Author of* The Dutch Writer and His Public.
DUTCH LITERATURE (*in part*)

G.Win. **Gustaf Wingren.** *Emeritus Professor of Systematic Theology, University of Lund, Sweden. Author of* Man and the Incarnation: A Study in the Biblical Theology of Irenaeus *and others.*
IRENAEUS, SAINT (Micropædia)

G.W.Kn. **George W. Knepper.** *Distinguished Professor of History, University of Akron, Ohio. Author of* An Ohio Portrait *and others.*
UNITED STATES OF AMERICA (*in part*)

G.W.P. **Giles William Playfair.** *Free-lance writer. Professor of Drama, Williams College, Williamstown, Massachusetts, 1956–63. Author of* Kean *and others.*
KEAN, EDMUND (Micropædia)

G.Wr. **Gordon Wright.** *William H. Bonsall Professor Emeritus of History,*

Stanford University, California. Author of France in Modern Times *and others.*
FRANCE (*in part*)

G.W.R. **Gar W. Rothwell.** *Professor of Botany, Ohio University, Athens.*
PLANTS (*in part*)

G.W.S.B. **Geoffrey Wallis Steuart Barrow.** *Sir William Fraser Professor of Scottish History and Palaeography, University of Edinburgh. Author of* Feudal Britain *and others.*
RICHARD I (ENGLAND) (Micropædia)

G.W.We. **George W. Wetherill.** *Director, Department of Terrestrial Magnetism, Carnegie Institution of Washington, D.C.*
SOLAR SYSTEM, THE (*in part*)

H.A. **Henri Arvon.** *Professor, University of Paris X. Author of* Le Bouddhisme *and others.*
FA-HSIEN (*in part*) (Micropædia)

Ha.A. **Hans Aurenhammer.** *Former Director, Austrian State Gallery, Vienna. Author of* J.B. Fischer von Erlach *and others.*
FISCHER VON ERLACH, JOHANN
  BERNHARD (Micropædia)

H.A.A. **Hamza A. Alavi.** *Former Reader in Sociology, Victoria University of Manchester. Author of numerous articles on Pakistan; coeditor of* Rural Development in Pakistan.
PAKISTAN (*in part*)

H.A.B.R. **Helen Anne B. Rivlin.** *Emerita Professor of History, State University of New York at Binghamton. Author of* The Agricultural Policy of Muḥammad ʿAlī in Egypt *and others.*
MUḤAMMAD ʿALĪ (EGYPT) (Micropædia)

Ha.D. **Harry Davis.** *President, Systems Review Associates, Arlington, Virginia. Deputy Undersecretary of the Air Force (Systems Review), U.S. Department of Defense, Washington, D.C., 1968–73.*
WAR, THE TECHNOLOGY OF (*in part*)

H.A.D. **Harl Adams Dalstrom.** *Professor of History, University of Nebraska at Omaha. Author of* A.V. Sorenson and the New Omaha.
UNITED STATES OF AMERICA (*in part*)

H.A.Da. **Hugh Alistair Davies.** *Lecturer in English, University of Sussex, Brighton, England.*
ENGLISH LITERATURE (*in part*)

Ha.G. **Harvey S. Gross.** *Professor of Comparative Literature, State University of New York at Stony Brook. Author of* Sound and Form in Modern Poetry *and others.*
LITERATURE, THE ART OF (*in part*)

H.A.G. **Harry A. Gailey.** *Professor of History, San Jose State University, California. Author of* A History of The Gambia *and others.*
WESTERN AFRICA (*in part*)

H.Ah. **Hélène Ahrweiler.** *Chancellor, University of Paris, 1982–89; former Professor of the History of Byzantine Civilization, University of Paris I. Author of* Recherches sur l'administration de

l'empire byzantin aux IXᵉ–XIᵉ siècles.
NICEPHORUS II PHOCAS (Micropædia)

Ha.He. **Hans Herzfeld** (d. 1982). *Professor of Modern History, Free University of Berlin, 1950–60. Author of* Die moderne Welt, 1789–1945.
FREDERICK WILLIAM IV (PRUSSIA)
  (Micropædia)

Ha.K. **Harold Kurtz** (d. 1972). *Author of* The Trial of Marshal Ney: His Last Years and Death *and others.*
NEY, MICHEL, DUC D'ELCHINGEN
  (Micropædia)

Ha.Ko. **Sir Hans Kornberg.** *Sir William Dunn Professor of Biochemistry, University of Cambridge; Master of Christ's College, Cambridge. Coauthor of* Energy Transformations in Living Matter; *editor of* Essays in Cell Metabolism.
METABOLISM (*in part*)

Ha.M. **Hans Moldenhauer.** *Musicologist. Director, Moldenhauer Archives. President, Spokane Conservatory of Music and Allied Arts, Inc., Washington. Author of* Anton von Webern: A Chronicle of His Life and Work *and others.*
WEBERN, ANTON VON (Micropædia)

H.A.M. **Henry A. Millon.** *Dean, Center for Advanced Study in the Visual Arts, National Gallery of Art, Washington, D.C. Author of* Baroque and Rococo Architecture *and others.*
ARCHITECTURE, THE HISTORY OF
  WESTERN (*in part*)

Ha.Ma. **Harry Magdoff.** *Coeditor, Monthly Review. Author of* The Age of Imperialism *and others.*
EUROPEAN OVERSEAS EXPLORATION AND
  EMPIRES, THE HISTORY OF (*in part*)

Ha.P. **Hans H. Penner.** *Professor of Religion, Dartmouth College, Hanover, New Hampshire. Author of articles on structuralism, myth, and ritual.*
RITES AND CEREMONIES, SACRED
  (*in part*)

H.Ar. **Hassan Arfa.** *Major General, Iranian Army (retired). Author of* Under Five Shahs *and others.*
REZA SHAH PAHLAVI (Micropædia)

Ha.Ro. **Hans Roos** (d. 1984). *Professor of East European History, University of the Ruhr, Bochum, West Germany. Author of* A History of Modern Poland.
POLAND (*in part*)

Ha.S. **Hans Saner.** *Free-lance writer. Personal Assistant to Professor Karl Jaspers, 1962–69. Author of* Karl Jaspers *and others.*
JASPERS, KARL (Micropædia)

H.A.S. **H. Arthur Steiner.** *Emeritus Professor of Political Science, University of California, Los Angeles. Editor of* Report on China; Chinese Communism in Action.
CHINA (*in part*)

Ha.Sc. **Harold Scarborough** (d. 1988). *Professor of Medicine; Provost, College of Medical Sciences, University of Maiduguri, Nigeria, 1979–84.*

Coauthor of Textbook of Physiology and Biochemistry.
MEDICINE (*in part*)

H.A.T. Henry Ashby Turner, Jr. *Bass Professor of History, Yale University. Author of* The Two Germanies since 1945 *and others.*
GERMANY (*in part*)

H.Au. Hermann Aubin (d. 1969). *Professor of History, University of Hamburg, 1946–54.*
EUROPEAN HISTORY AND CULTURE
   (*in part*)

Ha.We. Hans Fritz Welzel (deceased). *Professor of Penal Law and of the Philosophy of Law, Rhenish Friedrich Wilhelm University of Bonn. Author of* Die Naturrechtslehre Samuel Pufendorfs.
PUFENDORF, SAMUEL, FREIHERR VON
   (Micropædia)

H.B. Hans Bobek (d. 1990). *Professor of Geography, University of Vienna. Author of* Iran: Probleme eines unterentwickelten Landes alter Kultur.
ELBURZ MOUNTAINS (Micropædia)

H.B.A. Harry Burrows Acton (d. 1974). *Professor of Moral Philosophy, University of Edinburgh, 1964–74.*
CONDORCET, MARIE-JEAN-ANTOINE-
   NICOLAS DE CARITAT, MARQUIS DE
   (Micropædia)
SPENCER, HERBERT (Micropædia)

H.Bi. Haralds Biezais. *Former Professor of the History of Comparative Religions, Swedish University of Åbo, Finland. Author of* Die himmlische Götterfamilie der alten Letten *and others.*
EUROPEAN RELIGIONS, ANCIENT
   (*in part*)

H.B.K. Herbert B. Knechtel (d. 1987). *President, Knechtel Laboratories, Inc. (consultants to the candy industry), Skokie, Illinois.*
FOOD PROCESSING (*in part*)

H.B.-M. Hubert Beuve-Méry (d. 1989). *Journalist. Founder of* Le Monde. *Author of* Le Suicide de la IVᵉ République.
FRANCE (*in part*)

H.B.P. Henry Bamford Parkes (d. 1972). *Professor of History, New York University, New York City, 1949–72. Author of* A History of Mexico.
MEXICO (*in part*)

H.Br. Hugh Brogan. *Reader in History, University of Essex, Colchester, England. Author of* Longman History of the United States of America.
GOVERNMENT, THE FORMS OF

H.B.Ro. H.B. Rodgers. *Professor of Geography, Victoria University of Manchester. Coauthor of* Lancashire, Cheshire and Isle of Man.
MANCHESTER

H.C. The Rev. Henri Chambre, S.J. *Professor, Institute of Social Studies, Catholic Institute of Paris, 1947–78. Associate Director of the Laboratory, College of France, Paris, 1968–73. Author of* De Karl Marx à Lénine et

Mao Tsé-toung *and others.*
MARXISM, MARX AND (*in part*)

H.Ca. Harold Carter. *Emeritus Professor of Geography, University College of Wales, Aberystwyth, University of Wales. Coauthor of* The Towns of Wales: A Study in Urban Geography *and others.*
UNITED KINGDOM (*in part*)

H.C.B. Harold C. Bold (d. 1987). *Professor of Systematic Botany, University of Texas at Austin, 1957– 78. Author of* Morphology of Plants *and others.*
REPRODUCTION AND REPRODUCTIVE
   SYSTEMS (*in part*)

H.C.C. H.C. Casey, Jr. *Professor and Chairman, Department of Electrical Engineering, Duke University, Durham, North Carolina. Coauthor of* Heterostructure Lasers (*2 vol.*).
ELECTRONICS (*in part*)

H.C.G. Howard C. Goldblatt. *Professor of Chinese, University of Colorado, Boulder. Author of* Hsiao Hung; *editor of* Chinese Literature for the 1980s *and others.*
CHINESE LITERATURE (*in part*)

H.Ch. Hoklam Chan. *Professor of Chinese History, University of Washington, Seattle. Coeditor of and contributor to* Yüan Thought: Chinese Thought and Religion Under the Mongols.
CHINA (*in part*)

H.Cha. The Very Rev. Henry Chadwick. *Master of Peterhouse, Cambridge; Regius Professor Emeritus of Divinity, University of Cambridge. Author of* The Early Church; Origen contra Celsum; *and others.*
CHRISTIANITY (*in part*)
JOHN THE APOSTLE, SAINT (Micropædia)
ORIGEN (Micropædia)

H.D. Hariprasanna Das. *Former Professor of Geography, Gauhāti University, Assam, India. Author of* Geography of Assam.
INDIA (*in part*)

H.Da. Hugh Davson. *Honorary Research Associate and Fellow, Department of Physiology, University College, University of London. Author of* Physiology of the Eye; *editor of* The Eye.
SENSORY RECEPTION (*in part*)

H.D.F.K. H.D.F. Kitto (d. 1982). *Professor of Greek, University of Bristol, England, 1944–62. Author of* Greek Tragedy; Form and Meaning in Drama.
GREEK DRAMATISTS, THE CLASSICAL
   (*in part*)

H.-D.H.W. Hans-Dietrich H. Weigmann. *Associate Director of Research, Textile Research Institute, Princeton, New Jersey.*
FARMING AND AGRICULTURAL
   TECHNOLOGY (*in part*)

H.Di. Heide Dienst. *Assistant, Institute of Austrian History Research, University of Vienna. Author of* Babenberger Studien *and others.*

LEOPOLD I (GERMANY/HOLY ROMAN
   EMPIRE) (*in part*) (Micropædia)

H.D.I. Hans Dietrich Irmscher. *Professor of Modern German Literary Criticism, University of Cologne. Author of* Probleme der Herder-Forschung *and others.*
HERDER, JOHANN GOTTFRIED VON
   (Micropædia)

H.D.L. Hywel David Lewis. *Emeritus Professor of History and Philosophy of Religion, King's College, University of London. Chairman of the Council of the Royal Institute of Philosophy. Author of* Our Experience of God; The Elusive Mind; *and others.*
RELIGIOUS AND SPIRITUAL BELIEF,
   SYSTEMS OF (*in part*)

H.D.S. Helmut Dietmar Starke. *Free-lance writer on modern European history.*
GERMANY (*in part*)
LUXEMBURG, ROSA (Micropædia)

H.E. Heinz Eulau. *Emeritus Professor of Political Science, Stanford University, California. Author of* The Politics of Representation *and others.*
POLITICAL SYSTEMS (*in part*)

He.B. Hellmut Brunner. *Emeritus Professor of Egyptology, Eberhard Karl University of Tübingen, Germany. Author of* An Outline of Middle Egyptian Grammar *and others.*
WRITING (*in part*)

He.Ba. Hélène J. Balfet. *Teaching assistant, University of Aix-Marseille II, Aix-en-Provence, France. Former staff member for comparative technology, Musée de l'Homme, Paris. Author of* "Basketry: A Proposed Classification" *in* Papers on Californian Archaeology.
DECORATIVE ARTS AND FURNISHINGS
   (*in part*)

H.E.C. Henk E. Chin. *Associate Professor of Economics, University of Amsterdam. Coauthor of* Surinam: Politics, Economics and Society.
SURINAME

He.F. Herbert Friedmann (d. 1987). *Director, Los Angeles County Museum of Natural History, 1961–70. Researcher on the evolution and ecology of brood parasites among birds. Author of* The Honey-Guides; The Symbolic Goldfinch.
BIRDS (*in part*)

He.Gu. Henri Guillemin. *Emeritus Professor of History of French Literature, University of Geneva. Author of* Lamartine, l'homme et l'oeuvre; Lamartine en 1848; *and others.*
LAMARTINE, ALPHONSE DE (*in part*)
   (Micropædia)

He.H. Heinz Heinen. *Professor of Ancient History, University of Trier, Germany. Author of* Untersuchungen zur hellenistischen Geschichte des 3. Jahrhunderts vor Chr. *and others.*
PTOLEMY II PHILADELPHUS (Micropædia)

H.E.H. Hans Egon Holthusen. *Professor of German, Northwestern University, Evanston, Illinois, 1968–81.*

Author of A Portrait of Rilke.
RILKE, RAINER MARIA (Micropædia)

H.E.Ht.   Harold Edwin Hurst (d. 1978). Hydrological Consultant, Ministry of Irrigation, *Egypt; Director General, Physical Department, Ministry of Public Works, 1919–46. Author of* The Nile.
AFRICA (*in part*)

H.E.K.   Harry Edward Korab. *Executive Director, Society of Soft Drink Technologists. Former Technical Director, National Soft Drink Association, Washington, D.C.*
BEVERAGE PRODUCTION (*in part*)

H.E.L.-H.   Hellmut E. Lehmann-Haupt. *Emeritus Professor of Bibliography and Rare Book Consultant, University of Missouri, Columbia. Author of* Gutenberg and the Master of the Playing Cards.
GUTENBERG, JOHANNES (*in part*)
   (Micropædia)

He.M.   Hershel Markovitz. *Professor of Chemistry and Polymer Science, Carnegie-Mellon University, Pittsburgh. Coauthor of* Viscometric Flows of Non-Newtonian Fluids.
MECHANICS (*in part*)

H.E.Mo.   Harold E. Moore, Jr. (d. 1980). *Professor of Botany, L.H. Bailey Hortorium, New York State College of Agriculture and Life Sciences, Cornell University, Ithaca, 1960–80. Author of several articles on the palm order.*
ANGIOSPERMS (*in part*)

H.En.   Henrik Enander. *Former Lecturer in History, University of Stockholm.*
DENMARK (*in part*)
EUROPE (*in part*)
NORWAY (*in part*)
SWEDEN (*in part*)

He.Ni.   Henri Nicolaï. *Professor and Head, Department of Human Geography, Free University of Brussels.*
CENTRAL AFRICA (*in part*)

He.P.   Hermann Pálsson. *Professor of Icelandic, University of Edinburgh. Author of* Art and Ethics in Hrafnkel's Saga; *translator of* Hrafnkel's Saga *and other Icelandic stories.*
LITERATURE, THE ART OF (*in part*)

He.R.   Helmuth Rogge. *Chief Archivist, National Records Office, Potsdam, Germany, 1921–45. Author of* Friedrich von Holstein, Lebensbekenntnis in Briefen an eine Frau *and several other books on Holstein.*
HOLSTEIN, FRIEDRICH VON
   (Micropædia)

H.E.R.   Hugh E. Richardson. *Member, Indian Civil Service, 1930–50; Indian Trade Agent, Gyantse, and Officer in Charge, Indian Mission, Lhasa, 1936–40 and 1946–50. Author of* Tibet and Its History *and others.*
CHINA (*in part*)

H.E.R.G.   Helmut Erich Robert Gernsheim. *Photo-historian and author. Founder of the Gernsheim Collection. Regents Professor of Art, University of California, Riverside, 1984. Guest Professor, University of California, Santa Barbara, 1985 and 1989. Author of* The History of Photography *and many others.*
PHOTOGRAPHY (*in part*)

He.S.   Henri Stern. *Director of Research, National Centre for Scientific Research, Paris. Author of* Le Calendrier de 354; L'Art byzantin.
ARCHITECTURE, THE HISTORY OF
WESTERN (*in part*)
PAINTING, THE HISTORY OF WESTERN (*in part*)
SCULPTURE, THE HISTORY OF WESTERN (*in part*)

He.Th.   Helmuth Thomsen (d. 1978). *Principal Curator, Museum for the History of Hamburg, 1957–71. Author of* Liebes altes Hamburg; *editor of* Hamburg.
HAMBURG (*in part*)

He.W.   Hellmut Wilhelm. *Emeritus Professor of Chinese History and Literature, University of Washington, Seattle. Author of* Change: Eight Lectures on the I Ching *and others.*
CHINESE LITERATURE (*in part*)

H.E.W.   Harold E. Wethey (d. 1984). *Professor of the History of Art, University of Michigan, Ann Arbor, 1946–72. Author of* Colonial Architecture and Sculpture in Peru; El Greco and His School; The Complete Paintings of Titian.
ARCHITECTURE, THE HISTORY OF
   WESTERN (*in part*)
GIORGIONE (Micropædia)
GRECO, EL (Micropædia)
TITIAN

H.Ey.   Henry Eyring (d. 1981). *Distinguished Professor of Chemistry and Professor of Metallurgy, University of Utah, Salt Lake City, 1967–81. Coauthor of* Quantum Chemistry; Theory of Rate Processes.
CHEMICAL REACTIONS (*in part*)

H.F.   Hermann Friedrich. *Former Director, Overseas Museum, Bremen, West Germany. Author of* Marine Biology.
EUROPE (*in part*)

H.F.A.   Héctor Fernando Avila. *Division Chief, International Monetary Fund Institute, Washington, D.C.*
SOUTH AMERICA (*in part*)

H.F.A.V.d.W.   Herman F.A. Van der Wee. *Professor of Social and Economic History, Catholic University of Louvain, Belgium. Author of* The Growth of the Antwerpen Market and the European Economy.
BELGIUM (*in part*)

H.F.C.   Howard F. Cline (d. 1971). *Director, Hispanic Foundation, Library of Congress, Washington, D.C., 1952–71. Author of* Mexico: Revolution to Evolution, 1940–1960 *and others.*
MEXICO (*in part*)

H.F.D.   Hugh F. Denman. *Lecturer in Yiddish, University College, University of London.*
YIDDISH LITERATURE

H.Fe.   Herbert Feigl (d. 1988). *Professor of Philosophy, University of Minnesota, Minneapolis, 1941–71; Director, Minnesota Center for Philosophy of Science, 1953–71. Original member of the Vienna Circle, which developed the Positivist movement. Author of "The Wiener Kreis in America" in* The Intellectual Migration: Europe and America, 1930–1960.
PHILOSOPHICAL SCHOOLS AND
   DOCTRINES, WESTERN (*in part*)

H.F.G.   Hessle Filmore Garner. *Emeritus Professor of Geology, Rutgers University, Newark, New Jersey. Author of* The Origin of Landscapes.
CONTINENTAL LANDFORMS (*in part*)

H.F.Gr.   Hugh F. Graham. *Emeritus Professor of History, California State University, Bakersfield.*
EDUCATION, HISTORY OF (*in part*)

H.F.J.   Herbert Felix Jolowicz (d. 1954). *Regius Professor of Civil Law, University of Oxford, 1948–54. Professor of Roman Law, University of London, 1931–48; Dean, Faculty of Law, 1937–38. Author of* Historical Introduction to the Study of Roman Law.
LEGAL SYSTEMS, THE EVOLUTION OF
   MODERN WESTERN (*in part*)

H.F.K.   H.F. Koeper. *Professor of Architectural History, California State Polytechnic University, Pomona. Author of* American Architecture, 1607–1976.
AALTO, ALVAR (Micropædia)
GROPIUS, WALTER (Micropædia)
SAARINEN, EERO (Micropædia)
SULLIVAN, LOUIS (Micropædia)

H.F.L.   Harvey F. Lodish. *Professor of Biology, Massachusetts Institute of Technology, Cambridge. Member, Whitehead Institute for Biomedical Research, Cambridge, Massachusetts. Coauthor of* Molecular Cell Biology.
CELLS (*in part*)

H.F.M.   Herman F. Mark. *Emeritus Dean, Polytechnic Institute of New York, Brooklyn. Director, Polymer Research Institute, 1946–64. World authority on polymers and polymerization processes. Editor of* Encyclopedia of Polymer Science and Technology.
CHEMICAL COMPOUNDS (*in part*)

H.F.P.   H.F. Pearson (deceased). *Author of* A Popular History of Singapore; This Other India: A Biography of Sir Thomas Stamford Raffles.
RAFFLES, SIR STAMFORD (Micropædia)

H.Fr.   Herbert Franke. *Emeritus Professor of Far Eastern Studies, Ludwig Maximilian University of Munich. Author of* Geld und Wirtschaft in China unter der Mongolen *and others.*
CHINA (*in part*)

H.Fra.   Heinrich Fraenkel (d. 1986). *Free-lance writer. Author of* The Other Germany; *coauthor of* Hermann Göring.
GÖRING, HERMANN (*in part*)
   (Micropædia)

H.F.W. **Harold F. Walton.** *Emeritus Professor of Chemistry, University of Colorado, Boulder. Coauthor of* Ion Exchange in Analytical Chemistry.
CHEMICAL REACTIONS (*in part*)

H.F.We. **Heinz Fritz Wermuth.** *Former Curator of Herpetology, State Museum of Natural History, Ludwigsburg, West Germany. Coauthor of* Schildkröten, Krokodile, Brückenechsen.
REPTILES (*in part*)

H.G. **Herbert V. Guenther.** *Emeritus Professor of Far Eastern Studies, University of Saskatchewan, Saskatoon. Author of* The Life and Teaching of Nāropa; Tibetan Buddhism Without Mystification; *and others.*
BUDDHISM, THE BUDDHA AND (*in part*)

H.G.D. **H. Grady Davis** (d. 1975). *Professor of Functional Theology, Lutheran School of Theology at Chicago. Coauthor of* The Gospels in Study and Preaching.
BIBLICAL LITERATURE AND ITS CRITICAL INTERPRETATION (*in part*)

H.G.Do. **Herndon G. Dowling.** *Professor of Biology, New York University, New York City. Curator of Reptiles, New York Zoological Park, 1960–67.*
REPTILES (*in part*)

H.G.E. **Heinrich Gustav Euler.** *Professor of Modern History, University of Würzburg, Germany. Author of* Napoleon III. in seiner Zeit, (*vol. 1*).
NAPOLEON III (FRANCE) (Micropædia)

H.G.F. **Henry George Forder** (d. 1981). *Professor of Mathematics, University of Auckland, New Zealand, 1934–55. Author of* The Foundations of Euclidean Geometry *and others.*
GEOMETRY (*in part*)

H.G.G. **Hans G. Güterbock.** *Tiffany and Margaret Blake Distinguished Service Professor Emeritus of Hittitology, Oriental Institute, University of Chicago. Author of* Siegel aus Boğazköy.
BOĞAZKÖY (Micropædia)

H.G.K. **Helmut Georg Koenigsberger.** *Emeritus Professor of History, King's College, University of London. Author of* Medieval Europe, 400–1500; Early Modern Europe, 1500–1789; *and others.*
ALBA, FERNANDO ALVAREZ DE TOLEDO Y PIMENTEL, 3ᵉʳ DUQUE DE (Micropædia)
JIMÉNEZ DE CISNEROS, FRANCISCO, CARDENAL (Micropædia)
PHILIP II (SPAIN) (Micropædia)
SPAIN (*in part*)

H.G.M. **Harold G. Marcus.** *Professor of History and African Studies, Michigan State University, East Lansing. Author of* The Life and Times of Menelik II; Haile Selassie I.
EASTERN AFRICA (*in part*)

H.G.N. **Herbert G. Nicholas.** *Rhodes Professor Emeritus of American History and Institutions, University of Oxford. Author of* Britain and the U.S.A.
CHURCHILL

H.Go. **Hermann Goetz** (d. 1976). *Director, Baroda Museum and Picture Gallery, Baroda, India, 1940–53. Curator, National Gallery of Modern Art, New Delhi, 1953–55. Author of* The Art of India *and others.*
DECORATIVE ARTS AND FURNISHINGS (*in part*)

H.G.R. **Henry Godfrey Roseveare.** *Professor of History, King's College, University of London. Author of* The Treasury: The Evolution of a British Institution.
CHARLES II (GREAT BRITAIN) (Micropædia)

H.Gu. **Henri Guitton.** *Emeritus Professor of Economics, University of Paris I. Editor in Chief,* La Revue d'Économie Politique.
ECONOMIC THEORY (*in part*)

H.G.W. **Harris Gaylord Warren.** *Emeritus Professor of History, Miami University, Oxford, Ohio. Author of* Paraguay and the Triple Alliance: The Postwar Decade, 1869–1878.
PARAGUAY (*in part*)

H.Ha. **Harold Hart.** *Emeritus Professor of Chemistry, Michigan State University, East Lansing. Author of* Organic Chemistry.
CHEMICAL COMPOUNDS (*in part*)

H.H.A. **H. Harvard Arnason** (d. 1986). *Art historian. Vice President for Art Administration, Solomon R. Guggenheim Foundation, New York City, 1961–69. Author of* History of Modern Art; *coauthor of two books on Alexander Calder; and others.*
CALDER, ALEXANDER (Micropædia)

H.H.A.B. **Hans H.A. Bielenstein.** *Dean Lung Professor of Chinese, Columbia University. Author of* "The Restoration of the Han Dynasty" *in* Bulletin of the Museum of Far Eastern Antiquities.
WANG MANG (Micropædia)

H.H.B.-S. **Haim Hillel Ben-Sasson** (d. 1977). *Professor of Jewish Medieval History, Hebrew University of Jerusalem. Editor of* Peraqim be-toldot ha-Yehudim bi-yeme ha-benayim, (*3 vol.*); *author of vol. 2.*
ELIJAH BEN SOLOMON (Micropædia)

H.He. **Herbert Hensel** (d. 1983). *Professor of Physiology; Director, Institute of Physiology, Philipps University of Marburg, West Germany. Coauthor of* Temperatur und Leben.
SENSORY RECEPTION (*in part*)

H.Hei. **Helmut Heiber.** *Assistant, Institute for Contemporary History, Munich. Author of* Joseph Goebbels.
GOEBBELS, JOSEPH (Micropædia)

H.H.Hu. **Herbert Henry Huxley.** *Emeritus Professor of Classics, University of Victoria, British Columbia. Supervisor in Classics, St. John's College, University of Cambridge. Editor of* Virgil's Georgics (*Books I and IV*).
MARTIAL (Micropædia)

H.Hj. **Hakon Hjelmqvist.** *Associate Professor of Botany, University of Lund,*

Sweden, 1960–71. *Author of* Studies on the Floral Morphology and Phylogeny of the Amentiferae.
ANGIOSPERMS (*in part*)

H.-H.J. **Hans-Heinrich Jescheck.** *Emeritus Professor of Law, Albert Ludwig University of Freiburg, Freiburg im Breisgau, Germany. Emeritus Director, Max Planck Institute for Foreign and International Criminal Law, Freiburg. Author of* Lehrbuch des Strafrechts.
CRIMINAL LAW
PROCEDURAL LAW (*in part*)

H.H.K. **Howard H. Kendler.** *Emeritus Professor of Psychology, University of California, Santa Barbara. Author of* Historical Foundations of Modern Psychology *and others.*
LEARNING AND COGNITION, HUMAN (*in part*)

H.H.L. **Hubert Horace Lamb.** *Former Director, Climatic Research Unit, School of Environmental Sciences, University of East Anglia, Norwich, England. Investigator of climatic variation from the viewpoint of general atmospheric circulation. Author of* Climate: Present, Past and Future *and others.*
CLIMATE AND WEATHER (*in part*)

H.Hn. **Herbert Hoffmann.** *Former Curator of Ancient Art, Museum of Art and Industry, Hamburg.*
ARCHITECTURE, THE HISTORY OF WESTERN (*in part*)

H.Ho. **Harmannus Hoetink.** *Professor of Cultural Anthropology and Comparative Sociology of Latin America and the Caribbean, Institute of Cultural Anthropology, University of Utrecht, The Netherlands. Author of* Slavery and Race Relations in the Americas *and others.*
WEST INDIES, THE (*in part*)

H.H.R. **Harry Howe Ransom.** *Professor of Political Science, Vanderbilt University, Nashville, Tennessee. Author of* The Intelligence Establishment.
INTELLIGENCE AND COUNTERINTELLIGENCE

H.H.S. **Howard Hayes Scullard** (d. 1983). *Professor of Ancient History, King's College, University of London, 1959–70. Author of* Roman Politics, 220–150 B.C. *and others.*
GREEK AND ROMAN CIVILIZATIONS, ANCIENT (*in part*)
SCIPIO AFRICANUS THE ELDER (*in part*) (Micropædia)
SCIPIO AFRICANUS THE YOUNGER (*in part*) (Micropædia)
SYRIA (*in part*)

H.I. **Halil Inalcik.** *University Professor Emeritus of History, University of Chicago. Author of* "Mehmed the Conqueror (1432–1481) and His Time" *in* Speculum *and others.*
MEHMED II (Micropædia)

Hi.K. **Hideomi Kodama.** *Senior Research Scientist (soil mineralogy); Land Resource Research Centre, Agriculture Canada, Ottawa.*
MINERALS AND ROCKS (*in part*)

H.-I.M. Henri-Irénée Marrou (d. 1977). *Professor of the History of Ancient Christianity, University of Paris, 1945–75. Author of* De la connaissance historique.
EDUCATION, HISTORY OF (*in part*)

Hi.Mo. Hiroyuki Momo. *Emeritus Professor and former Director, Historiographical Institute, University of Tokyo.*
HISTORY, THE STUDY OF (*in part*)

H.Is. Hildebert İsnard (d. 1983). *Professor of Geography, University of Nice, France. Professor of Geography, University of Aix-Marseille II, Aix-en-Provence, France, 1947–70. Author of* Géographie du Maghreb; Afrique tropicale; *and others.*
AFRICA (*in part*)

H.I.S. Harold I. Sharlin. *Consultant on science policy. Former Professor of History, Iowa State University, Ames. Author of* The Making of the Electrical Age; Lord Kelvin: Dynamic Victorian.
KELVIN

H.J.Bi. Harold J. Bissell. *Emeritus Professor of Geology, Brigham Young University, Provo, Utah.*
MINERALS AND ROCKS (*in part*)

H.J.Bl. Henry J. Blumenthal. *Reader in Greek, University of Liverpool. Coeditor of* Soul and the Structure of Being in Late Neoplatonism.
PLATONISM, PLATO AND (*in part*)

H.J.Bn. Henry J. Bruman. *Emeritus Professor of Geography, University of California, Los Angeles.*
NORTH AMERICA (*in part*)

H.J.C. Henry J. Cadbury (d. 1974). *Hollis Professor of Divinity, Harvard University, 1934–54. Chairman, American Friends Service Committee, 1928–34; 1944–60.*
FOX, GEORGE (Micropædia)

H.J.Cr. Howard J. Critchfield. *Professor of Geography, Western Washington University, Bellingham. Author of* General Climatology.
UNITED STATES OF AMERICA (*in part*)

H.J.D. Hubert Jules Deschamps (d. 1979). *Professor of Modern History of Black Africa, University of Paris, 1962–70. Colonial Administrator, Madagascar, 1926–36. Author of* History of Madagascar *and others.*
MADAGASCAR (*in part*)
WESTERN AFRICA (*in part*)

H.J.De. Henri J. Delporte. *Honorary Inspector General, Museums of France; former Chief Curator, Museum of National Antiquities, Saint-Germain-en-Laye, France. Author of* Archéologie et réalité *and others.*
EVOLUTION, HUMAN (*in part*)

H.J. de B. Harm J. de Blij. *Professor of Geography, University of Miami, Coral Gables, Florida. Author of* Mozambique *and others.*
SOUTHERN AFRICA (*in part*)

H.J. de V. Herman Jean de Vleeschauwer. *Emeritus Professor of Philosophy, University of South Africa, Pretoria. Author of* L'Évolution de la pensée kantienne; *editor of* Kantstudien.
KANTIANISM, KANT AND (*in part*)

H.J.Dw. Harvey J. Dworken, M.D. *Emeritus Professor of Medicine, Case Western Reserve University, Cleveland, Ohio. Author of* Gastroenterology: Pathophysiology and Clinical Applications *and others.*
DIGESTION AND DIGESTIVE SYSTEMS (*in part*)

H.J.Er. Hubert Joseph Erb. *Berlin Correspondent, Associated Press.*
BERLIN (*in part*)

H.-J.I. Heinz-Jürgen Ipfling. *Professor of Educational Theory, University of Regensburg, Germany. Author and editor of works on education.*
EDUCATION, HISTORY OF (*in part*)

H.-J.K. Hans-Joachim Kramm. *Professor of Economic Geography, College of Education, Potsdam, Germany. Author of* Ökonomische Geographie der DDR.
GERMANY (*in part*)

H.J.S. Howard James Stains. *Emeritus Professor of Zoology, Southern Illinois University, Carbondale. Author of* "Carnivores and Pinnipeds" *in* Recent Mammals of the World.
MAMMALS (*in part*)

H.J.Sp. Herbert John Spiro. *Professor of Government, University of Texas at Austin. U.S. Ambassador to Cameroon, 1975–77. Author of* Government by Constitution *and others.*
CONSTITUTION AND CONSTITUTIONAL GOVERNMENT (*in part*)

H.J.Wi. Howard J. Wiarda. *Professor of Political Science, University of Massachusetts, Amherst. Associate, Center for International Affairs, Harvard University. Author of* The Politics of External Influence in the Dominican Republic *and others.*
WEST INDIES, THE (*in part*)

H.K. Hans Kohn (d. 1971). *Professor of History, City College, City University of New York, 1949–62. Author of* Political Ideologies of the Twentieth Century.
ISRAEL (*in part*)
SOCIO-ECONOMIC DOCTRINES AND REFORM MOVEMENTS, MODERN (*in part*)

H.Ka. Harry Kalven, Jr. (d. 1974). *Harry A. Bigelow Professor of Law, University of Chicago, 1953–74. Coauthor of* The American Jury.
JUDICIAL AND ARBITRATIONAL SYSTEMS (*in part*)

H.K.B. Howard Kent Birnbaum. *Professor of Materials Science and Engineering; Director, Materials Research Laboratory, University of Illinois at Urbana-Champaign. Author of numerous papers on the physics and mechanics of solids.*
MATTER (*in part*)

H.Ke. Hugh Kennedy. *Reader in Mediaeval History, University of St. Andrews, Scotland. Author of* The Prophet and the Age of the Caliphates.
IRAQ (*in part*)

H.K.G. Harry K. Girvetz (d. 1974). *Professor of Philosophy, University of California, Santa Barbara, 1951–74. Author of* The Evolution of Liberalism.
SOCIO-ECONOMIC DOCTRINES AND REFORM MOVEMENTS, MODERN (*in part*)

H.K.M.S. H.K. Manmohan Singh. *Vice-Chancellor; former Professor of Economics, Punjabi University, Patiala, India.*
INDIA (*in part*)

H.Ko. Horst Koegler. *Music Editor, Stuttgarter Zeitung. Editor,* Ballett (*annual*), 1965–83. *Author of* Concise Oxford Dictionary of Ballet.
DANCE, THE HISTORY OF WESTERN (*in part*)

H.Kü. Hans Kühner (d. 1986). *Historian and free-lance writer. Specialist on the history of the Roman Catholic Church and the Papacy. Author of* Encyclopedia of the Papacy *and others.*
GREGORY I, SAINT (PAPACY) (Micropædia)
JULIUS II (Micropædia)

H.K.V. Hans K. Vogt (deceased). *Professor of General Linguistics, University of Oslo. Author of* Grammaire du géorgien moderne.
LANGUAGES OF THE WORLD (*in part*)

H.L. Henri Laoust (d. 1983). *Professor of Sociology of Islām, College of France, Paris, 1956–76. Editor and translator of* Le Traité de droit public d'Ibn Taimīya.
IBN TAYMĪYAH (Micropædia)

H.L.A.H. Herbert Lionel Adolphus Hart. *Principal of Brasenose College, Oxford, 1973–78; Professor of Jurisprudence, University of Oxford, 1952–68. Author of* The Concept of Law; Law, Liberty and Morality.
AUSTIN, JOHN (Micropædia)

H.L.B. Henry Lewis Barnett, M.D. *Emeritus Professor of Pediatrics, Albert Einstein College of Medicine, Yeshiva University, Bronx, New York. Medical Director, Children's Aid Society, New York City.*
CHILDHOOD DISEASES AND DISORDERS (*in part*)

H.L.C. Hampton L. Carson. *Emeritus Professor of Genetics, University of Hawaii at Manoa, Honolulu. Author of* Heredity and Human Life.
GENETICS AND HEREDITY, THE PRINCIPLES OF (*in part*)

H.L.C.J. Hans L.C. Jaffé. *Professor of Modern Art History, University of Amsterdam. Author of* Piet Mondrian; Picasso.
MONDRIAN, PIET (*in part*) (Micropædia)

H.L.E. Herbert Leeson Edlin (d. 1976). *Publications Officer, Forestry Commission of Great Britain, London.*

Author of Trees, Woods and Man.
FORESTRY AND WOOD PRODUCTION
(*in part*)

**H.-L.-É.T. Henri-Louis-Étienne
Terrasse** (d. 1971). *Curator, Historic
Monuments of Morocco, 1935–57.
Director, Institute for Advanced
Moroccan Studies, Rabat, Morocco,
1941–57. Chairman, Department of
Islāmic Archaeology, University of
Algiers, 1945–57. Director, Casa de
Velázquez, Ciudad University, Madrid,
1957–65. Author of* Histoire du Maroc.
ʿABD AL-MUʾMIN (Micropædia)
NORTH AFRICA (*in part*)

H.Li. Heinz Lieberich. *General
Director, Bavarian State Archives,
Munich. Author of* Ludwig der Bayer als
Gesetzgeber *and others.*
LOUIS IV (GERMANY/HOLY ROMAN
EMPIRE) (Micropædia)

H.L.-J. Sir Hugh Lloyd-Jones. *Regius
Professor of Greek, University of Oxford,
1960–89. Author of* The Justice of Zeus
and others.
SCHOLARSHIP, CLASSICAL

H.L.Ke. Herbert Leon Kessler.
*Professor and Chairman, Department
of the History of Art, Johns Hopkins
University, Baltimore. Author of* French
and Flemish Illuminated Manuscripts in
Chicago Collections *and others.*
EYCK, JAN VAN (Micropædia)
WEYDEN, ROGIER VAN DER (Micropædia)

H.L.M. Hanns Leo Mikoletzky (d.
1978). *General Director, Austrian State
Archives, Vienna. Professor of History,
University of Vienna. Author of* Kaiser
Heinrich II und die Kirche *and others.*
HENRY III (GERMANY/HOLY ROMAN
EMPIRE) (Micropædia)

H.L.Ms. Hallam L. Movius, Jr.
(d. 1987). *Professor of Anthropology,
Harvard University; Curator of
Paleolithic Archaeology, Peabody
Museum.*
PREHISTORIC PEOPLES AND CULTURES
(*in part*)

H.L.P. Herbert L. Petri. *Professor of
Psychology, Towson State University,
Maryland. Author of* Motivation:
Theory, Research, and Applications.
MOTIVATION, HUMAN (*in part*)

H.M. Hermann Mannheim (d. 1974).
*Reader in Criminology, University
of London, 1946–55. Author of*
Comparative Criminology.
SOCIAL SCIENCES, THE (*in part*)

H.M.A. Harold Maurice Abrahams
(d. 1978). *Broadcaster and journalist.
Chairman, British Amateur Athletic
Board. Olympic Gold Medalist
(100-metre dash), 1924. Author of* The
Olympic Games, 1896–1952.
OLYMPIC GAMES (*in part*)

H.Me. Henk Meijer. *Director,
Information and Documentation Centre
for the Geography of the Netherlands,
State University of Utrecht. Author of* A
Compact Geography of the Netherlands.
NETHERLANDS, THE (*in part*)

H.M.K. Horace M. Kallen (d. 1974).
*Professor of Social Philosophy, New
School for Social Research, New York
City, 1919–52. Author of the introduction
to* The Philosophy of William James,
Drawn from His Own Works.
JAMES, WILLIAM (Micropædia)

H.M.L. Henry M. Leicester (d. 1991).
*Professor of Biochemistry, University
of the Pacific, San Francisco, 1948–77.
Coauthor of* Source Book in Chemistry
1400–1900.
LIEBIG, JUSTUS, FREIHERR VON
(Micropædia)
WÖHLER, FRIEDRICH (Micropædia)

H.M.La. Hugh Michael Laracy.
*Associate Professor of History, University
of Auckland, New Zealand.*
PACIFIC ISLANDS (*in part*)

H.M.M. Harold M. Mayer. *Professor
of Geography, University of Wisconsin,
Milwaukee. Author of* The Port of
Chicago and the St. Lawrence Seaway;
coauthor of Chicago, Growth of a
Metropolis.
CHICAGO (*in part*)

H.M.P. Henri M. Peyre (d. 1988).
*Distinguished Professor of French,
Graduate Center, City University of
New York, 1969–81. Sterling Professor
of French, Yale University, 1938–69.
Author of* Literature and Sincerity *and
many others.*
DURKHEIM, ÉMILE (Micropædia)
LITERATURE, THE ART OF (*in part*)

H.M.S. Harold M. Somers. *Emeritus
Professor of Economics, University of
California, Los Angeles; Dean, Division
of Social Sciences, 1967–70. Author of*
Capital Gains, Death and Gift Taxation.
TAXATION (*in part*)

H.Mu. Hugo Munsterberg. *Professor of
Oriental Art, Bard College, Annandale-
on-Hudson, New York. Author of* The
Arts of Japan *and others.*
OGATA KŌRIN (Micropædia)
SESSHŪ (Micropædia)
SŌTATSU (Micropædia)

H.M.V.D. Hobart Merritt Van Deusen
(d. 1976). *Archbold Assistant Curator,
Department of Mammalogy, American
Museum of Natural History, New York
City, 1958–75. Coauthor of* "Marsupials"
in Recent Mammals of the World.
MAMMALS (*in part*)

H.M.W. Helen Margaret Wallis.
*Former Map Librarian, British Library,
London. Editor of* Carteret's Voyage
Round the World *and others.*
TASMAN, ABEL JANSZOON (Micropædia)

H.My. Hla Myint. *Emeritus
Professor of Economics, London
School of Economics and Political
Science, University of London.
Author of* Economic Theory and the
Underdeveloped Countries.
ECONOMIC GROWTH AND PLANNING
(*in part*)

H.N. Heinrich Nagel. *Emeritus
Professor of Civil and International Civil
Procedure, Georg August University of
Göttingen, Germany. Former Presiding*

*Judge, Hanseatic Court of Appeals,
Bremen. Author of* Internationales
Zivilprozessrecht *and others.*
PROCEDURAL LAW (*in part*)

H.Na. Hajime Nakamura. *Director,
Eastern Institute, Inc., Tokyo. Emeritus
Professor of Indian and Buddhist
Philosophy, University of Tokyo. Author
of* Ways of Thinking of Eastern Peoples
and others.
BUDDHISM, THE BUDDHA AND (*in part*)

H.Ne. Howard Nemerov (d. 1991).
*Poet and novelist. Edward Mallinckrodt
Distinguished Professor of English,
Washington University, St. Louis,
Missouri, 1976–90. Poet Laureate of the
U.S., 1988–90. Author of* Poetry and
Fiction: Essays; Reflexions on Poetry
and Poetics; *and others.*
LITERATURE, THE ART OF (*in part*)

H.N.G. Harry Norwood Ginns (d.
1981). *Deputy Chief Engineer, Highways
Engineering Division, Ministry of
Transport, London, 1963–69.*
TRANSPORTATION (*in part*)

H.O. Harold Oldroyd (deceased).
*Senior Principal Scientific Officer, British
Museum (Natural History), London,
1964–73. Author of* The Natural History
of Flies *and others.*
INSECTS (*in part*)

Ho.B. Howard Bay (d. 1986). *Stage
and film designer. Professor of Theatre
Arts, Brandeis University, Waltham,
Massachusetts. Author of* Stage Design.
THEATRICAL PRODUCTION (*in part*)

Ho.I.P. Hovhanness Israel Pilikian.
*Theatre director. Founder and Artistic
Director of Hano-no Mask-Theatre
Company. Author of* The Prince of
Darkness *and others.*
REINHARDT, MAX (Micropædia)

H.O.Sc. Hans Otto Schmitt. *Senior
Adviser, International Monetary Fund,
Washington, D.C.; Division Chief,
1971–80.*
ECONOMIC THEORY (*in part*)

H.P. Heinrich Potthoff. *Contributor,
Commission for the History of
Parliamentarism and Political Parties,
Bonn. Author of* Die deutsche Politik
Beusts *and others.*
BEUST, FRIEDRICH FERDINAND, GRAF
VON (Micropædia)

H.Pa. Hans Patze. *Professor of
German History; Director, Institute
for Historical Research, Georg August
University of Göttingen, Germany.
Author of* Die Entstehung der
Landesherrschaft in Thüringen.
FREDERICK I (GERMANY/HOLY ROMAN
EMPIRE) (Micropædia)

H.Pe. Harry Perry. *Energy consultant.
Senior Specialist, Congressional
Research Service, Library of Congress,
Washington, D.C., 1970–72.*
INDUSTRIES, EXTRACTION AND
PROCESSING (*in part*)

H.P.La. Harriet Pratt Lattin.
Historian. Author of The Peasant Boy
Who Became Pope; *translator of* The

Letters of Gerbert, with His Papal Privileges as Sylvester II.
SYLVESTER II (Micropædia)

H.Pr. Helmut Preidel. *Historian. Author of* Das grossmährische Reich im Spiegel der Bodenfunde; Handel und Handwerk im frühgeschichtlichen Mitteleuropa; *and others.*
CHARLES IV (GERMANY/HOLY ROMAN EMPIRE) (Micropædia)

H.P.R. Humphrey P. Rang. *Director, Sandoz Institute for Medical Research, London. Coauthor of* Pharmacology.
DRUGS AND DRUG ACTION (*in part*)

H.P.Tr. Hamilton P. Traub (d. 1983). *Editor,* Plant Life, *American Plant Life Society, La Jolla, California. Author of* The Amaryllis Manual *and others.*
ANGIOSPERMS (*in part*)

H.P.V. Homero Pozo Vélez. *Professor of History and Geography, National University of Loja, Ecuador. President, National High School "Adolfo Valarezo," Loja.*
ECUADOR (*in part*)

H.R. Helmer Ringgren. *Emeritus Professor of Old Testament Exegesis, University of Uppsala, Sweden. Author of* Israelite Religion; Messiah in the Old Testament; *and various articles on theological concepts in the Qur'ān.*
ISLĀM, MUḤAMMAD AND THE RELIGION OF (*in part*)

H.Ra. Hassanein Muhammad Rabie. *Professor of History, University of Cairo. Author of* The Financial System of Egypt: A.H. 564–741/A.D. 1169–1341.
BAYBARS I (Micropædia)

H.Re. Hans Reichardt. *Emeritus Professor of Mathematics, Humboldt University of Berlin. Editor of* C.F. Gauss Gedenkband anlässlich des 100. Todestages am 23. Februar 1855.
GAUSS

H.R.H. Heribert R. Hutter. *Director, Gallery of the Academy of Fine Arts, Vienna. Author of* Drawing: History and Technique *and others.*
DRAWING (*in part*)

H.Ro. Herbert H. Rowen. *Emeritus Professor of History, Rutgers University, New Brunswick, New Jersey. Author of* The Princess of Orange *and others.*
NETHERLANDS, THE (*in part*)

H.R.T. Hugh Russell Tinker. *Emeritus Professor of Politics, University of Lancaster, England. Author of* India and Pakistan: A Political Analysis; Experiment with Freedom, India and Pakistan; *and others.*
BANGLADESH (*in part*)
PAKISTAN (*in part*)

H.R.W. Henry R. West. *Professor of Philosophy, Macalester College, St. Paul, Minnesota. Coeditor of* Moral Philosophy: Classic Texts and Contemporary Problems.
PHILOSOPHICAL SCHOOLS AND DOCTRINES, WESTERN (*in part*)

H.S. Helmut Sick. *Naturalist, Brazilian Academy of Sciences, Rio de Janeiro. Author of numerous papers on neotropical birds.*
BIRDS (*in part*)

H.Sa. Heinrich Satter. *Free-lance writer. Author of* Paul Ehrlich, Begründer der Chemotherapie *and others.*
EHRLICH, PAUL (Micropædia)

H.Se. Humphrey Searle (d. 1982). *Composer. Professor of Composition, Royal College of Music, London. Author of* The Music of Liszt *and others.*
LISZT, FRANZ (*in part*) (Micropædia)

H.S.H. Helen Sawyer Hogg. *Emeritus Professor of Astronomy, University of Toronto. Astronomy columnist,* Toronto Daily Star, *1951–81.*
STARS AND STAR CLUSTERS (*in part*)

H.Sm. Harlan James Smith. *Randall Professor of Astronomy, University of Texas at Austin; Director, McDonald Observatory, 1963–89. Coeditor of* Planetary Atmospheres.
SOLAR SYSTEM, THE (*in part*)

H.S.M. H.S. Morris. *Former Reader in Anthropology, London School of Economics and Political Science, University of London. Author of* Indians in Uganda.
SOCIAL DIFFERENTIATION (*in part*)

H.S.MacD.C. H.S. MacDonald Coxeter. *Emeritus Professor of Mathematics, University of Toronto. Author of* Non-Euclidean Geometry.
GEOMETRY (*in part*)

H.S.N. H.S. Narayana. *Former Professor of Botany, University of Rājasthān, Jaipur, India.*
ANGIOSPERMS (*in part*)

H.Sp. Herbert Spiegelberg (d. 1990). *Professor of Philosophy, Washington University, St. Louis, Missouri, 1963–71. Author of* The Phenomenological Movement.
PHILOSOPHICAL SCHOOLS AND DOCTRINES, WESTERN (*in part*)

H.S.P. H. Steffen Peiser. *Chief, Office of International Relations, National Bureau of Standards, U.S. Department of Commerce, Washington, D.C., 1969–79. Author of* X-Ray Diffraction by Polycrystalline Materials.
ATOMIC WEIGHT (*in part*) (Micropædia)

H.Sr. Hugo Stehkämper. *Director, Historical Archives, Cologne.*
COLOGNE (*in part*)

H.S.R. Hans Siegbert Reiss. *Emeritus Professor of German, University of Bristol, England. Author of* Goethe's Novels *and others.*
GERMAN LITERATURE (*in part*)

H.Ss. Halsey Stevens (d. 1989). *Composer. Professor of Music, University of Southern California, Los Angeles, 1951–76. Author of* The Life and Music of Béla Bartók.
BARTÓK, BÉLA (Micropædia)

H.S.Sc. Herbert S. Schell. *Emeritus Dean of the Graduate School, University of South Dakota, Vermillion; Emeritus Professor of History. Author of* South Dakota, Its Beginning and Growth; History of South Dakota.
UNITED STATES OF AMERICA (*in part*)

H.S.-Sm. Sir Hubert Shirley-Smith (d. 1981). *Consulting Engineer to W.V. Zinn & Associates, London, 1969–78. President, Institute of Civil Engineers, 1967. Author of* The World's Great Bridges.
PUBLIC WORKS (*in part*)

H.St. Hans Sturmberger. *Former Director, Upper Austrian Provincial Archives, Linz. Author of* Kaiser Ferdinand II *and others.*
FERDINAND II (GERMANY/HOLY ROMAN EMPIRE) (Micropædia)

H.S.T. H.S. Thayer. *Professor of Philosophy, City College, City University of New York. Author of* Meaning and Action: A Critical History of Pragmatism.
PHILOSOPHICAL SCHOOLS AND DOCTRINES, WESTERN (*in part*)

H.S.Ta. Sir Hugh S. Taylor (d. 1974). *Professor of Chemistry, 1922–58; Dean of the Graduate School, 1945–58, Princeton University. Coauthor of* Catalysis in Theory and Practice.
CHEMICAL REACTIONS (*in part*)

H.St.J.B.P. Harry St. John Bridger Philby (d. 1960). *Explorer in Arabia. Author of* The Heart of Arabia.
ARABIA (*in part*)

H.S.-W. Hugh Seton-Watson (d. 1984). *Professor of Russian History, University of London, 1951–83. Author of* The Russian Empire, 1801–1917.
UNION OF SOVIET SOCIALIST REPUBLICS (*in part*)

H.T. Holger Thesleff. *Emeritus Professor of Greek, University of Helsinki. Author of* An Introduction to the Pythagorean Writings of the Hellenistic Period *and others.*
PHILOSOPHICAL SCHOOLS AND DOCTRINES, WESTERN (*in part*)

H.Ta. Hugh Tait. *Deputy Keeper, Department of Medieval and Later Antiquities, British Museum, London. Author of* Porcelain *and others.*
DECORATIVE ARTS AND FURNISHINGS (*in part*)

H.T.C. Hiden T. Cox. *Emeritus Professor of Biology, California State University, Long Beach.*
ANGIOSPERMS (*in part*)

H.T.D. Harry T. Dickinson. *Professor of History, University of Edinburgh. Author of* Bolingbroke *and others.*
BOLINGBROKE, HENRY SAINT JOHN, 1ST VISCOUNT (Micropædia)

Ht.F. Hellmut Fritzsche. *Louis Block Professor of Physics, University of Chicago. Coauthor and editor of* Advances in Disordered Semiconductors (*2 vol.*).
ELECTROMAGNETIC RADIATION (*in part*)

H.T.F. Harold T. Friermood. *Former Chairman, Education Council, United States Olympic Committee. Editor of*

Handball: Official, Unified-Playing
Rules; When Volleyball Began;
and others.
HANDBALL (Micropædia)

H.Th. Helmut Thielicke (d. 1986).
*Professor of Systematic Theology,
University of Hamburg, 1954–74. Author
of* Theological Ethics *and others.*
THEOLOGY

H.T.H. Herbert T. Hoover. *Professor
of History, University of South Dakota,
Vermillion. Author of* The Yankton
Sioux *and others.*
UNITED STATES OF AMERICA (*in part*)

H.T.M. Haydn T. Mason. *Professor
of French Language and Literature,
University of Bristol, England. Author of*
French Writers and their Society 1715–
1800 *and others.*
FRENCH LITERATURE (*in part*)

H.T.P. Hugh T. Patrick. *R.D. Calkins
Professor of International Business;
Director, Center on Japanese Economy
and Business, Columbia University.
Author of* Monetary Policy and Central
Banking in Contemporary Japan.
MARKETS (*in part*)

H.U. Homer Ulrich (d. 1987).
*Professor and Head, Department of
Music, University of Maryland, College
Park, 1953–72. Editor,* American Music
Teacher, *1973–87. Author of* Chamber
Music *and others.*
MUSICAL FORMS AND GENRES (*in part*)

H.-U.H. Hanns-Ulrich Haedeke.
*Director, German Sword Museum,
Solingen, Germany. Author of* Metalwork
and others.
DECORATIVE ARTS AND FURNISHINGS
(*in part*)

Hu.M. Hugh Sinclair Morrison (d.
1978). *Leon E. Williams Professor of
Art, Dartmouth College, Hanover, New
Hampshire, 1963–69. Author of* Early
American Architecture; Louis Sullivan.
ARCHITECTURE, THE HISTORY OF
WESTERN (*in part*)

Hu.S. Hudson Strode (d. 1976).
*Professor of English, University of
Alabama, Tuscaloosa, 1924–63. Author
of* Jefferson Davis *and others.*
DAVIS, JEFFERSON (Micropædia)

H.U.S. Harald Ulrik Sverdrup (d.
1957). *Director, Norwegian Polar
Research Institute, Oslo, 1948–57.
Director, Scripps Institution of
Oceanography, University of California,
San Diego, at La Jolla, 1936–48. Author
of* Oceanography for Meteorologists
and others.
ATLANTIC OCEAN, THE (*in part*)
NANSEN, FRIDTJOF (Micropædia)

Hu.Wa. Hugh Wakefield (d. 1984).
*Keeper, Department of Circulation,
Victoria and Albert Museum, London,
1960–75. Author of* Nineteenth Century
British Glass; Victorian Pottery.
DECORATIVE ARTS AND FURNISHINGS
(*in part*)

H.V. Hans Volkmann (deceased).
Professor of Ancient History, University

of Cologne.
ANTIGONUS I MONOPHTHALMUS
(Micropædia)
ANTIGONUS II GONATAS (Micropædia)
ANTIOCHUS III (Micropædia)
ANTIOCHUS IV EPIPHANES (Micropædia)

H. van W. H. van Werveke (d. 1974).
*Professor of the History of Belgium,
State University of Ghent.*
ARTEVELDE, JACOB VAN (Micropædia)

H.V.L. Harold V. Livermore. *Emeritus
Professor of Spanish and Portuguese,
University of British Columbia,
Vancouver. Author of* Origins of Spain
and Portugal *and others.*
ALBUQUERQUE, AFONSO DE, THE GREAT
(Micropædia)
COVILHÃ, PÊRO DA (Micropædia)
DIAS, BARTOLOMEU (Micropædia)
JOHN I (PORTUGAL) (Micropædia)
JOHN II (PORTUGAL) (Micropædia)
MANUEL I (PORTUGAL) (Micropædia)
PORTUGAL (*in part*)

H.Wa. Hao Wang. *Professor of Logic,
Rockefeller University, New York City.
Author of* Logic, Computers and Sets
and others.
LOGIC, THE HISTORY AND KINDS
OF (*in part*)

H.W.B. Hendrik W. Bode (d. 1982).
*Gordon McKay Professor of Systems
Engineering, Harvard University, 1967–
74. Author of* Network Analysis and
Feedback Amplifier Design.
INDUSTRIAL ENGINEERING AND
PRODUCTION MANAGEMENT (*in part*)

H.W.Br. Harold Whitman Bradley (d.
1990). *Professor of History, Vanderbilt
University, Nashville, Tennessee, 1954–
72. Member, Tennessee House of
Representatives, 1964–72. Author of* The
United States, 1492–1877 *and others.*
JACKSON, ANDREW (*in part*)
(Micropædia)
UNITED STATES OF AMERICA (*in part*)

H.We. Herbert Weinstock (d. 1971).
*Consulting Editor, Alfred A. Knopf, Inc.,
New York City, 1963–71; Executive
Editor, 1943–59. Author of* The Opera;
Music as an Art; *and many biographies
of composers.*
MUSICAL FORMS AND GENRES (*in part*)

H.W.F. Hubert William Frings.
*David Ross Boyd Professor Emeritus
of Zoology, University of Oklahoma,
Norman. Coauthor of* Animal
Communication.
SENSORY RECEPTION (*in part*)

H.W.F.S. Henry W.F. Saggs. *Emeritus
Professor of Semitic Languages,
University College, Cardiff, University
of Wales. Author of* The Greatness That
Was Babylon *and others.*
BABYLON (Micropædia)
NEBUCHADREZZAR II (Micropædia)
SENNACHERIB (Micropædia)

H.W.G. Herman W. Goult (d. 1977).
Editor, Cyprus Mail, *Nicosia. Cyprus
correspondent,* The Times (*London*).
CYPRUS (*in part*)

H.Wi. Hermann Wiesflecker. *Professor
of Austrian History, University of*

Graz, Austria. Author of Maximilian I,
Österreich, das Reich und Europa an der
Wende zur Neuzeit (*vol. 1–3*) *and others.*
MAXIMILIAN I (GERMANY/HOLY ROMAN
EMPIRE) (Micropædia)

H.W.J. H.W. Janson (d. 1982).
*Professor of Fine Arts, Washington
Square College of Arts and Science,
New York University, New York City,
1949–79. Author of* The Sculpture of
Donatello; History of Art.
DONATELLO (*in part*) (Micropædia)

H.W.L. Herbert W. Levi. *Agassiz
Professor of Zoology; Curator of
Arachnology, Museum of Comparative
Zoology, Harvard University. Coauthor
of* A Guide to Spiders and Their Kin;
cotranslator and coeditor of Invertebrate
Zoology *by A. Kaestner.*
ARACHNIDS (*in part*)

H.W.M. Horace Winchell Magoun (d.
1991). *Professor of Anatomy, University
of California, Los Angeles; 1950–72;
Dean, Graduate Division, 1962–72.
Author of* The Waking Brain *and others.*
NERVES AND NERVOUS SYSTEMS (*in part*)

H.W.P. Herbert William Parke (d.
1986). *Professor of Ancient History,
Trinity College, University of Dublin,
1934–73. Author of* Greek Mercenary
Soldiers.
EPAMINONDAS (Micropædia)

H.W.W. Harold W. Wardman.
*Emeritus Professor of French Studies,
University of Lancaster, England. Author
of* Ernest Renan: A Critical Biography;
Renan Historien Philosophe.
RENAN, ERNEST (Micropædia)

Hy.K. Hyman Kaufman. *Professor
of Mathematics, McGill University,
Montreal, 1952–80. Coauthor of* Table of
Laplace Transforms.
ANALYSIS (IN MATHEMATICS) (*in part*)

H.Z. Hans Zeisel. *Emeritus Professor
of Law and Sociology, University of
Chicago. Coauthor of* The American
Jury.
JUDICIAL AND ARBITRATIONAL
SYSTEMS (*in part*)

H.Z.D. Haim Zalman Dimitrovsky.
*Professor of Talmud, Hebrew University
of Jerusalem. Editor and translator of*
Bava metzia.
JUDAISM (*in part*)

I.A. Isaac Asimov. *Science writer.
Professor of Biochemistry, Boston
University. Author of* Asimov's
Biographical Encyclopedia of Science
and Technology *and many others.*
MICHELSON, A.A. (Micropædia)

I.A.Y. Ivan Alekseyevich Yerofeyev.
*Head Geography Editor, Prosveshcheniye
(educational publishers), Moscow. Author
of* Southwestern Economic Region;
coauthor of Kiev.
UNION OF SOVIET SOCIALIST REPUBLICS
(*in part*)

I.Be. Ian D. Bent. *Professor of Music,
Columbia University. Author of* Musical
Analysis in the Nineteenth Century; *text
editor of* The New Grove Dictionary of

Music and Musicians, (6th ed.).
MUSIC, THE ART OF (*in part*)

I.Bo.   Ira Bornstein. *Nuclear Engineer, Office of the Director, Argonne National Laboratory, Illinois.*
ENGINEERING (*in part*)

I.Bt.   Irving Brant (d. 1976). *Member, Advisory Board, James Madison Papers, University of Chicago. Council Member, Institute of Early American History and Culture, 1959–62. Author of* James Madison (6 vol.) *and others.*
MADISON, JAMES (*in part*)
    (Micropædia)

I.C.B.   The Rev. Ignatius Charles Brady, O.F.M. *Director of the theological section, College of St. Bonaventura, Grottaferrata, Italy, 1961–82. Coeditor and cotranslator of* Francis and Clare: The Complete Works.
FRANCIS OF ASSISI, SAINT (Micropædia)

I.C.C.   Ian C. Clingan. *Former Engineer in Chief, Trinity House Lighthouse Service, London.*
PUBLIC WORKS (*in part*)

I.C.Cn.   Ivor Cecil Coffin. *Regional Economist, Economics Department, Lloyds Bank Group, London.*
URUGUAY (*in part*)

I.C.L.   Iñigo Cavero Lataillade. *Minister of Education and Science, 1977–79, of Justice, 1979–80, and of Culture, 1980–81, Government of Spain.*
SPAIN (*in part*)

I.C.M.   Iseabail C. Macleod. *Editorial Director, Scottish National Dictionary Association, Edinburgh. Coeditor of* Concise Scots Dictionary.
UNITED KINGDOM (*in part*)

I.D.E.   Ian David Edge. *Lecturer in Islamic Law; Director, Centre for Islamic and Middle-East Law, School of Oriental and African Studies, University of London.*
CRIME AND PUNISHMENT (*in part*)

I.D'O.E.   Sir Ivo D'Oyly Elliott (d. 1961). *Indian Civil Service, 1906–32.*
TURENNE, HENRI DE LA TOUR
    D'AUVERGNE, VICOMTE DE
    (Micropædia)

I.E. *Specialists, Institute of Economics, University of Havana.*
WEST INDIES, THE (*in part*)

I.F.B.   Ivor F. Burton. *Professor of Social Policy, Bedford College, University of London. Author of* The Captain-General: The Career of John Churchill, Duke of Marlborough, from 1702–1711 *and others.*
MARLBOROUGH, JOHN CHURCHILL, 1ST
    DUKE OF (*in part*) (Micropædia)
PIUS IX (*in part*) (Micropædia)
PIUS V, SAINT (*in part*) (Micropædia)

I.F.G.B.   Ian F.G. Baxter. *Emeritus Professor of Law, University of Toronto; former Director of Family Law Study.*
FAMILY LAW

I.G.   Isabella Gordon (d. 1988). *Head, Crustacea Section, British Museum (Natural History), London, 1928–66.*

Coeditor of Crustaceana.
CRUSTACEANS (*in part*)

I.G.S.   Irwin G. Sarason. *Professor of Psychology, University of Washington, Seattle. Author of* Personality: An Objective Approach.
PERSONALITY (*in part*)

I.H.   Igor Hájek. *Senior Lecturer in Czechoslovak Studies, University of Glasgow. Coauthor and coeditor of* Dictionary of Czech Writers, 1948–1979.
CZECHOSLOVAK LITERATURE (*in part*)

I.Hr.   Ivan Hrbek. *Member, Oriental Institute, Czechoslovak Academy of Sciences, Prague. Author of* "The Chronology of Ibn Battute's Travels" *in* Archiv Orientalni.
IBN BAṬṬŪṬAH (Micropædia)

I.Hy.   Isabelle Hyman. *Professor of Fine Arts, Washington Square and University College of Arts and Science, New York University, New York City.*
BRUNELLESCHI, FILIPPO (*in part*)
    (Micropædia)

I.J.   Ivar K. Johansson (d. 1988). *Professor of Animal Breeding, Agricultural College of Sweden, Uppsala. Author of* Genetic Aspects of Dairy Cattle Breeding; *coauthor of* Genetics and Animal Breeding.
FARMING AND AGRICULTURAL
    TECHNOLOGY (*in part*)

I.J.G.   Ignace J. Gelb (d. 1985). *Frank P. Hixon Distinguished Service Professor, Oriental Institute and Departments of Linguistics and of Near Eastern Languages and Civilizations, University of Chicago, 1965–79. Author of* A Study of Writing *and many others.*
LANGUAGES OF THE WORLD (*in part*)
LINGUISTICS (*in part*)

I.J.S.   Irving J. Stolberg. *Speaker of the House of Representatives of Connecticut. Former Assistant Professor of Geography, Southern Connecticut State College, New Haven.*
UNITED STATES OF AMERICA (*in part*)

I.K.   Irving Kaplansky. *Director, Mathematical Sciences Research Institute, Berkeley, California. Author of* Commutative Rings.
GALOIS, ÉVARISTE (Micropædia)
HILBERT, DAVID (Micropædia)
NUMBER THEORY (*in part*)

I.K.P.   Ismail K. Poonawala. *Professor of Arabic and Islāmic Studies, University of California, Los Angeles.*
ʿALĪ (Micropædia)

I.M.D.   Igor Mikhailovich Diakonoff. *Chief scientific collaborator; former Head, Near Eastern Department and Ancient Oriental Languages Group, Institute of Oriental Studies, Academy of Sciences of the U.S.S.R., Leningrad. Author of* Semito-Hamitic Languages *and others.*
LANGUAGES OF THE WORLD (*in part*)

I.M.J.   Ingrid Margareta Jonsson. *Staff Research Editor, Encyclopædia Britannica, Chicago, 1969–73.*
ATLANTIC OCEAN, THE (*in part*)

I.M.L.   Ioan M. Lewis. *Professor of Anthropology, London School of Economics and Political Science, University of London. Author of* A Pastoral Democracy; A Modern History of Somalia from Nation to State.
EASTERN AFRICA (*in part*)

I.M.P. do A.   Ilídio Melo Peres do Amaral. *Professor of Geography, University of Lisbon. Rector, International University, Lisbon. Author of numerons publications on the geography of Portugal and its former colonies.*
PORTUGAL (*in part*)

I.N.   Ivan Niven. *Emeritus Professor of Mathematics, University of Oregon, Eugene. Coauthor of* Introduction to the Theory of Numbers *and others.*
NUMBER THEORY (*in part*)

I.N.S.   Ian Naismith Sneddon. *Emeritus Professor of Mathematics, University of Glasgow. Author of* Elements of Partial Differential Equations *and others.*
ANALYSIS (IN MATHEMATICS) (*in part*)

I.P.   Indra Pal. *Professor and Head, Department of Geography, University of Rājasthān, Jaipur, India. Coauthor of* World in Its Natural Regions.
INDIA (*in part*)

I.P.C.   Ioan Petru Culianu (d. 1991). *Visiting Professor of the History of Religions and the History of Christianity, University of Chicago. Author of* Eros and Magic in the Renaissance *and others.*
EUROPEAN RELIGIONS, ANCIENT (*in part*)

I.P.G.   Innokentii Petrovich Gerasimov (d. 1985). *Director, Institute of Geography, Academy of Sciences of the U.S.S.R., Moscow. An authority on geomorphology and soil science.*
GEOMORPHIC PROCESSES (*in part*)

I.P.H.   Ian P. Howard. *Professor of Psychology, York University, Toronto. Coauthor of* Human Spatial Orientation.
PERCEPTION, HUMAN (*in part*)

I.P.S.   Ivan Peter Shaw. *Former Fellow and Secretary, King's College, University of London. Author of* Nationality and the Western Church Before the Reformation.
EDWARD THE BLACK PRINCE
    (Micropædia)

I.R.C.   Ian R. Christie. *Astor Professor Emeritus of British History, University College, University of London. Author of* Wilkes, Wyvill and Reform *and others.*
WILKES, JOHN (Micropædia)

Ir.W.   Irving Wallace (d. 1990). *Novelist and biographer. Author of* The Fabulous Showman: The Life and Times of P.T. Barnum; The Man; *and many others.*
BARNUM, P.T. (Micropædia)

I.S.   Isaac Schapera. *Emeritus Professor of Anthropology, London School of Economics and Political Science, University of London. Author of* The Tswana *and others.*
SOUTHERN AFRICA (*in part*)

I.S.C.   Ivan Stoddard Coggeshall.
*Fellow, Institute of Electrical and
Electronics Engineers. Assistant
Vice President, Western Union
Telegraph Company, New York
City, 1959; Director of International
Communications, 1951–58.*
TELECOMMUNICATIONS SYSTEMS
   (*in part*)

I.S. de S.   Isbelia M. Sequera Segnini.
*President, National Academy of
Economic Sciences, Caracas, Venezuela.
Author of* Dinámica de la agricultura.
VENEZUELA (*in part*)

I.S.S.   Irvin S. Snyder. *Professor and
Chairman, Department of Microbiology
and Immunity, West Virginia University,
Morgantown. Contributor to* Modern
Pharmacology.
DRUGS AND DRUG ACTION (*in part*)

I.Su.   Ilmari Sundblad. *Foreign Editor,
Finnish News Agency (STT-FNB),
Helsinki.*
FINLAND (*in part*)

I.T.   Isadore Twersky. *Littauer
Professor of Hebrew Literature and
Philosophy, Harvard University. Author
of* Rabad of Posquières *and others.*
RASHI (*in part*) (Micropædia)

**I.T.R.   The Rt. Rev. Ian Thomas
Ramsey** (d. 1972). *Lord Bishop of
Durham, England, 1966–72. Nolloth
Professor of the Philosophy of Christian
Religion, University of Oxford, 1951–66.
Author of* Religious Language; Christian
Discourse.
PHILOSOPHIES OF THE BRANCHES OF
   KNOWLEDGE (*in part*)

I.V.H.   Ian Vernon Hogg. *Free-lance
writer. Editor,* Jane's Infantry Weapons;
Jane's Security and Counter-Insurgency
Yearbook. *Author of* A History of
Artillery; Illustrated Encyclopedia of
Artillery.
WAR, THE TECHNOLOGY OF (*in part*)

**I.V.Ko.   Innokenty Varfolomeevich
Kozlov.** *Deputy Principal Editor,
Geography, Mysl Publishing House,
Moscow. Author of* Sovetskiye subtropiki.
UNION OF SOVIET SOCIALIST REPUBLICS
   (*in part*)

I.V.N.   Israel Vladimirovich Nestyev.
*Chief Scientist, Research Institute of
History of Arts, Moscow. Author of*
Prokofiev.
PROKOFIEV, SERGEY (*in part*)
   (Micropædia)

I.V.P.   Igor Vladimirovich Popov.
*Senior Scientist, Leningrad Hydrological
Institute. Author of* Basic Methods for
the Study of Riverbed Processes.
ASIA (*in part*)

I.W.   Immanuel Wallerstein.
*Distinguished Professor of Sociology,
State University of New York at
Binghamton. Author of* Africa: The
Politics of Independence.
LUMUMBA, PATRICE (*in part*)
   (Micropædia)

I.W.H.   Inez Whitaker Hunt (d. 1983).
Lecturer and free-lance writer. Teacher of

creative writing, University of Colorado
extension, Colorado Springs, 1963–66.
Coauthor of Lightning in His Hand: The
Life Story of Nikola Tesla.
TESLA, NIKOLA (Micropædia)

I.Wo.   Isser Woloch. *Professor of
History, Columbia University. Author
of* Jacobin Legacy: The Democratic
Movement under the Directory
and others.
FRANCE (*in part*)

I.Z.   Imre Zoltán, M.D. *Professor of
Gynecology and Obstetrics, Semmelweis
Medical University, Budapest, Hungary.
Coauthor of* Semmelweis élete és
munkássága.
SEMMELWEIS, IGNAZ PHILIPP
   (Micropædia)

J.A.A.   J.A. Andrups. *Author of*
Latvian Literature *and others.*
LATVIAN LITERATURE (Micropædia)

J.A.B.   James Alan Bassham. *Senior
Scientist, Chemical Biodynamics
Division, Lawrence Berkeley Laboratory,
University of California, Berkeley,
1978–85; Research Chemist, 1949–77.
Coauthor of* Photosynthesis of Carbon
Compounds; The Path of Carbon in
Photosynthesis.
PHOTOSYNTHESIS

J.A.Ba.   John A. Bailey. *President,
Transportation Systems Associates,
Philadelphia. Director, Transportation
Center, Northwestern University,
Evanston, Illinois, 1967–75.*
TRANSPORTATION (*in part*)

Ja.Be.   Jane Bergerol. *Free-lance
journalist based in Angola.*
SOUTHERN AFRICA (*in part*)

J.A.Bo.   John Andrew Boyle (d. 1978).
*Professor of Persian Studies, Victoria
University of Manchester, 1966–78.
Editor of and contributor to* Cambridge
History of Iran, (*vol. 5*).
FERDOWSĪ (Micropædia)
GHĀZĀN, MAḤMŪD (Micropædia)

J.A.B.v.B.   J.A.B. van Buitenen (d.
1979). *Distinguished Service Professor
of Sanskrit and Indic Studies, University
of Chicago, 1974–79. Author of* Tales of
Ancient India.
CALENDAR (*in part*)
HINDUISM (*in part*)
RĀMĀNUJA (Micropædia)
SOUTH ASIAN ARTS (*in part*)

Ja.C.   Jan Christensen. *Assistant
Foreign Editor, Verdens Gang, Oslo.
Author of* Kort om Stortinget.
NORWAY (*in part*)

J.A.C.   James A. Charles. *Emeritus
Reader in Process Metallurgy, University
of Cambridge. Coauthor of* Selection and
Use of Engineering Materials.
INDUSTRIES, EXTRACTION AND
   PROCESSING (*in part*)

J.A.Ca.   Jorge A. Camacho (d. 1989).
*Free-lance writer. Staff member, British
Broadcasting Corporation, 1938–69;
Head of Talks and Current Affairs
(Radio), 1961–69.*
BROADCASTING (*in part*)

**J.A.C.A.   John Anthony Charles
Ardagh.** *Free-lance writer and journalist.
Author of* France Today *and others.*
PARIS (*in part*)

J.A.C.B.   J.A.C. Brown (d. 1984).
*Professor of Applied Economics,
University of Oxford, 1970–84. Coauthor
of* The Lognormal Distribution.
ECONOMIC THEORY (*in part*)

J.A.Cr.   John Anthony Crook. *Professor
of Ancient History, University of
Cambridge, 1979–84. Author of* Law and
Life of Rome.
MARCUS AURELIUS (Micropædia)

Ja.D.   Janusz Durko. *Director,
Historical Museum of Warsaw. Editor of*
Bibliography of Warsaw.
WARSAW (*in part*)

J.Ad.   Jean Adhémar (d. 1987). *Curator
of Prints, Bibliothèque Nationale, Paris,
1961–87. Editor in Chief,* Gazette des
Beaux Arts, *1955–87. Author of* Honoré
Daumier *and others.*
DAUMIER, HONORÉ (Micropædia)

Ja.F.   James E. Faller. *Fellow, Joint
Institute for Laboratory Astrophysics,
University of Colorado, Boulder.*
GRAVITATION (*in part*)

Ja.F.D.   Jane F. Desforges, M.D.
*Professor of Medicine, Tufts University,
Boston.*
BLOOD (*in part*)

J.A.G.   Jeffrey Allman Gritzner.
*Research Professor of Geography;
Director, Public Policy Research
Institute, University of Montana,
Missoula. Author of* The West
African Sahel: Human Agency and
Environmental Change *and others.*
AFRICA (*in part*)

Ja.H.   Jay Higginbotham. *Archivist,
Mobile Municipal Archives, Alabama.
Author of* Old Mobile: Fort Louis de la
Louisiane, 1702–1711 *and others.*
IBERVILLE (ET D'ARDILLIÈRES), PIERRE
   LE MOYNE D' (Micropædia)

J.A.H.   John A. Haywood. *Reader in
Arabic, University of Durham, England,
1967–78. Author of* Arabic Lexicography.
FAKHR AD-DĪN AR-RĀZĪ (Micropædia)
JAʿFAR IBN MUḤAMMAD (Micropædia)
MASʿŪDĪ, AL- (Micropædia)

J.A.Ha.   John A. Harrison. *Emeritus
Professor of History, University of
Miami, Coral Gables, Florida. Editor,*
The Journal of Asian Studies, *1969–
72. Author of* New Light on Early and
Medieval Japanese History.
HŌJŌ FAMILY (Micropædia)

Ja.H.B.   James H. Bready. *Former
editorial writer and book columnist,* The
Sun *newspapers, Baltimore. Author of*
The Home Team.
UNITED STATES OF AMERICA (*in part*)

J.A.Ho.   James A. Hodges. *Professor
of History, Wooster College, Wooster,
Ohio.*
UNITED STATES OF AMERICA (*in part*)

Ja.J.P.   James J. Parsons. *Emeritus
Professor of Geography, University*

of California, Berkeley. Author of Antioqueño Colonization in Western Colombia and others.
COLOMBIA (in part)

Ja.J.S.   James Joseph Stilwell. Rear Admiral, U.S. Navy (retired). Labour arbitrator and consulting engineer.
TRANSPORTATION (in part)

Ja.K.   Jan Kazimour. President, Federal Statistical Office of Czechoslovakia, Prague, 1969–81.
PRAGUE (in part)

J.A.K.   Jerzy A. Kondracki. Emeritus Professor of Physical Geography, University of Warsaw. Author of Geografia fizyczna Polski.
EUROPE (in part)
POLAND (in part)

J.A.Ka.   John Anderson Kay. Director, Centre for Business Strategy; Professor of Industrial Economics, London Business School. Coauthor of The British Tax System and others.
GOVERNMENT FINANCE (in part)

J.A.Ke.   The Rev. John Arthur Kemp, S.J. (d. 1963). Professor of Medieval History, Loyola University, Chicago, 1959–63. Author of History of Europe to 1500.
ANSELM OF CANTERBURY, SAINT (Micropædia)

Ja.L.   James Laver (d. 1975). Keeper, Departments of Engraving, Illustration and Design, and of Paintings, Victoria and Albert Museum, London, 1938–59. Author of A Concise History of Costume.
DRESS AND ADORNMENT (in part)

J.Al.   John Allan (d. 1955). Keeper, Department of Coins and Medals, British Museum, London, 1931–49.
COINS AND COINAGE (in part)

J.A.L.   Joseph Albert Lauwerys (d. 1981). Director, Atlantic Institute of Education, Halifax, Nova Scotia, 1970–76. Professor of Comparative Education, University of London, 1947–70. Coeditor, World Year Book of Education, 1947–70.
EDUCATION, HISTORY OF (in part)

Ja.La.   Janko Lavrin (d. 1986). Professor of Russian Literature, University of Nottingham, England, 1923–53. Author of Gogol; Russian Writers; and others.
GOGOL, NIKOLAY (Micropædia)

J.A.Le.   James A. Lee (d. 1981). Consultant, Brick Institute of America, Atlanta, Georgia. Author of articles in American Ceramic Journal and other journals.
INDUSTRIAL GLASS AND CERAMICS (in part)

Ja.L.S.   Jason Lewis Saunders. Professor of Philosophy, City College, City University of New York. Author of Early Stoic Philosophy.
PHILOSOPHICAL SCHOOLS AND DOCTRINES, WESTERN (in part)

Ja.M.   Jacques Millot (d. 1980). Professor, National Museum of Natural History, Paris, 1943–67. Researcher on the anatomy of coelacanths and their fossil relatives.
FISHES (in part)

J.A.Ma.   J. Alan Mackie. Free-lance writer.
ALEXANDRIA (in part)

J.A.McG.   Joseph A. McGeough. Regius Professor of Engineering; Head, Department of Mechanical Engineering, University of Edinburgh. Author of Advanced Methods of Machining.
TOOLS (in part)

J.A.M.K.I.   Jozef A.M.K. IJsewijn. Professor of Neo-Latin, Catholic University of Louvain, Belgium. Editor, Humanistica Lovaniensia.
GROTIUS, HUGO (Micropædia)

J.A.Mn.   J. Alden Mason (d. 1967). Curator, American Section, University Museum, University of Pennsylvania, 1926–55.
PERU (in part)

J.A.Mo.   John A. Monick (d. 1981). Research Associate, Colgate-Palmolive Company, Piscataway, New Jersey. Author of Alcohols: Their Chemistry, Properties and Manufacture.
CHEMICAL COMPOUNDS (in part)

J.A.Mu.   John A. Munroe. H. Rodney Sharp Professor Emeritus of History, University of Delaware, Newark. Editor, Delaware History. Author of History of Delaware and others.
UNITED STATES OF AMERICA (in part)

J.A.P.   James A. Peters (d. 1972). Curator and Supervisor, Division of Reptiles and Amphibians, National Museum of Natural History, Smithsonian Institution, Washington, D.C., 1966–72. Specialist on the taxonomy of snakes. Author of Dictionary of Herpetology.
REPTILES (in part)

J.A.R.   James Arthur Ramsay (d. 1988). Professor of Comparative Physiology, University of Cambridge, 1969–76. Joint Editor, Journal of Experimental Biology, 1952–74. Author of Physiological Approach to the Lower Animals.
EXCRETION AND EXCRETORY SYSTEMS (in part)

Ja.S.   Jacques Soustelle (d. 1990). Director of Studies, School of Advanced Studies in the Social Sciences, Paris, 1969–85. Author of La Vie quotidienne des Aztèques and others.
PRE-COLUMBIAN CIVILIZATIONS (in part)

J.A.S.   Jorge A. Suárez (d. 1985). Professor of Amerindian Linguistics and of Contemporary Linguistics, National Autonomous University of Mexico, Mexico City. Coauthor of A Description of Colloquial Guaraní.
LANGUAGES OF THE WORLD (in part)

Ja.Se.   Jane Selverstone. Associate Professor of Geology, Harvard University.
MINERALS AND ROCKS (in part)

J.A.S.G.   John A.S. Grenville. Professor of Modern History, University of Birmingham, England. Author of Lord Salisbury and Foreign Policy and others.
SALISBURY, ROBERT CECIL, 3RD MARQUESS OF (Micropædia)

J.A.Sh.   Jerome A. Shaffer. Professor and Head, Department of Philosophy, University of Connecticut, Storrs. Author of Philosophy of Mind.
MIND, THE PHILOSOPHY OF

J.A.T.   John A. Thomas. Vice President for Academic Services; Professor of Pharmacology, University of Texas Health Science Center at San Antonio. Coauthor of Principles of Endocrine Pharmacology and others.
DRUGS AND DRUG ACTION (in part)

J.Au.   Jeannine Auboyer (d. 1990). Curator in Chief, Museum Guimet, Paris, 1965–80. Author of La Vie quotidienne dans l'Inde ancienne.
RITES AND CEREMONIES, SACRED (in part)

Ja.W.   Jan Wojnowski. Senior Editor, Polish Scientific Publishers, Warsaw. Editor, Wielka Encyklopedia Powszechna, Warsaw, 1962–70. Editor of Literatura polska: Przewodnik encyklopedyczny.
POLISH LITERATURE (in part)

J.A.W.   Sir Jack Allan Westrup (d. 1975). Professor of Music, University of Oxford, 1946–71; Fellow of Wadham College, Oxford, 1947–71. Author of Purcell and many others.
MUSICAL INSTRUMENTS (in part)
PURCELL, HENRY (Micropædia)

J.A.Y.   Jay A. Young. Consultant on chemical safety and health. Manager, Technical Publications, Manufacturing Chemists Association, Washington, D.C., 1976–80. Hudson Professor of Chemistry, Auburn University, Alabama, 1970–75.
CHEMICAL REACTIONS (in part)

J.B.   Jonathan Barnes. Fellow of Balliol College, University of Oxford. Author of Aristotle; coeditor of Articles on Aristotle.
PLATONISM, PLATO AND (in part)

J.Ba.   Jacques Barzun. University Professor Emeritus, Columbia University; Dean of Faculties and Provost, 1958–67. Author of Berlioz and the Romantic Century; Darwin, Marx, Wagner; and others.
BERLIOZ, HECTOR (Micropædia)
EUROPEAN HISTORY AND CULTURE (in part)
FLAUBERT, GUSTAVE (in part) (Micropædia)
POE, EDGAR ALLAN (in part) (Micropædia)

J.B.A.   John B. Allcock. Head, Research Unit in Yugoslav Studies, University of Bradford, England. Coeditor of Yugoslavia in Transition.
YUGOSLAVIA (in part)

J.B.B.   John Bernard Beer. Fellow of Peterhouse, Cambridge; Professor of English Literature, University of Cambridge. Author of Coleridge, the Visionary and others.

ENGLISH LITERATURE (*in part*)
FORSTER, E.M. (Micropædia)

J.-B.Ba.   Jean-Bertrand Barrère (d. 1985). *Professor of French Literature, University of Cambridge, 1954–82; Fellow of St. John's College, Cambridge. Author of* Hugo, l'homme et l'oeuvre *and other works on Victor Hugo.*
HUGO, VICTOR (*in part*) (Micropædia)

J.B.Bd.   J. Brian Bird. *Professor of Geography, McGill University, Montreal. Author of* The Physiography of Arctic Canada *and others.*
ARCTIC, THE (*in part*)

J.B.B.T.   John B.B. Trussell. *Chief, Division of History, Pennsylvania Historical and Museum Commission, Harrisburg.*
PHILADELPHIA (*in part*)

J.B.C.   J.B. Condliffe (d. 1981). *Senior Economist, Stanford Research Institute, Menlo Park, California, 1961–67. Professor of Economics, University of California, Berkeley, 1940–58. Author of* The Commerce of Nations.
UNITED NATIONS (*in part*)

J.B.Co.   Jerome B. Cohen. *Frank C. Engelhart Professor of Materials Science and Engineering; Dean, McCormick School of Engineering, Northwestern University, Evanston, Illinois. Author of* Diffraction Methods in Materials Science.
MATTER (*in part*)

J.Be.   Jeremy Bernstein. *Professor of Physics, Stevens Institute of Technology, Hoboken, New Jersey. Author of* Elementary Particles and Their Currents.
SCHRÖDINGER, ERWIN (*in part*) (Micropædia)
YANG, CHEN NING (Micropædia)

J.B.F.   John Bailey Fernald (d. 1985). *Theatre director. Principal, Royal Academy of Dramatic Art, London, 1955–65. Professor of Dramatic Art, Oakland University, Rochester, Michigan, 1966–70. Author of* Sense of Direction.
THEATRE, THE ART OF THE (*in part*)

J.B.-G.   Jacqueline Beaujeu-Garnier. *Emeritus Professor of Geography, University of Paris I. President, Society of Geography, Paris. Author of* Géographie de la population *and others.*
FRANCE (*in part*)

J.B.Gl.   Sir John Bagot Glubb (d. 1986). *Lieutenant General; Chief of General Staff, The Arab Legion, Amman, Jordan, 1939–56. Author of* War in the Desert *and others.*
ARABIA (*in part*)
IBN SAʿŪD (Micropædia)
MECCA AND MEDINA (*in part*)

J.B.He.   James B. Hendrickson. *Professor of Chemistry, Brandeis University, Waltham, Massachusetts. Author of* The Molecules of Nature; *coauthor of* Organic Chemistry.
WOODWARD, R.B. (Micropædia)

J.B.Ho.   Joseph Bixby Hoyt. *Emeritus Professor of Geography, Southern Connecticut State College, New Haven. Author of* The Connecticut Story.
UNITED STATES OF AMERICA (*in part*)

J.B.-J.   John Buettner-Janusch. *Former Professor and Chairman, Department of Anthropology, New York University, New York City. Author of* Origins of Man.
EVOLUTION, HUMAN (*in part*)

J.B.M.   John Barron Mays (d. 1987). *Eleanor Rathbone Professor of Sociology, University of Liverpool, 1965–80. Author of* The Young Pretenders: Teenage Culture in Contemporary Society *and others.*
SOCIAL DIFFERENTIATION (*in part*)

J.B.Mi.   Jean Brown Mitchell. *Fellow, Newnham College, Cambridge, 1934–68; Lecturer in Geography, University of Cambridge, 1945–68. Author of* Historical Geography.
EUROPEAN OVERSEAS EXPLORATION AND EMPIRES, THE HISTORY OF (*in part*)

J.Bo.   James Bowen. *Professor of Education, University of New England, Armidale, Australia. Author of* A History of Western Education (*3 vol.*).
EDUCATION, HISTORY OF (*in part*)

J.B.P.   J. Bruce Pluckhahn. *Bowling historian. Former Curator, National Bowling Hall of Fame and Museum, St. Louis, Missouri. Coauthor of* Pins and Needlers.
SPORTS, MAJOR TEAM AND INDIVIDUAL (*in part*)

J.B.Ra.   John Bell Rae (d. 1988). *Professor of the History of Technology, Harvey Mudd College, Claremont, California, 1959–76. Author of* American Automobile Manufacturers: The First Forty Years *and others.*
INDUSTRIES, MANUFACTURING (*in part*)

J.Bru.   Jean Bruhat. *Former Professor, Institute of Political Science of Paris. Former Instructor, University of Paris VIII. Author of* Les Journées de février 1848 *and others.*
BLANQUI, AUGUSTE (Micropædia)

J.B.Sm.   J(enkyn) Beverley Smith. *Professor of Welsh History, University College of Wales, Aberystwyth, University of Wales. Author of* Llywelyn ap Gruffydd, Tywysog Cymru.
UNITED KINGDOM (*in part*)

J.B.Sp.   J. Brookes Spencer. *Associate Professor of the History of Science, Oregon State University, Corvallis. Editor of* The Collected Works of Niels Bohr.
PHYSICAL SCIENCES, THE (*in part*)

J.Bu.   Joseph Buttinger. *Free-lance writer. Author of* Vietnam: A Dragon Embattled *and others.*
SOUTHEAST ASIA, MAINLAND (*in part*)

J.B.Wi.   John Bernard Wilkinson. *Former Head, Unilever Research Laboratory, Isleworth, England. Editor of* Harry's Cosmeticology.
DRESS AND ADORNMENT (*in part*)

J.C.A.   John C. Ayres (d. 1982). *D.W. Brooks Distinguished Professor of Food Science, University of Georgia, Athens. Coeditor of* Chemical and Biological Hazards in Foods *and others.*
FOOD PROCESSING (*in part*)

J.C.B.   Jon Charles Barlow. *Curator, Department of Ornithology, Royal Ontario Museum, Toronto. Professor of Zoology; Director, Museum Studies Program, University of Toronto. Researcher of the biology and taxonomy of vireos. Author of* "Xenarthrans and Pholidotes" *in* Recent Mammals of the World.
MAMMALS (*in part*)

J.C.Be.   The Rev. John C. Bennett. *Emeritus President, Union Theological Seminary, New York City. Senior Contributing Editor,* Christianity and Crisis. *Author of* Christians and the State.
NIEBUHR, REINHOLD (Micropædia)

J.C.D.   John C. Dewdney. *Professor of Geography, University of Durham, England. Author of* A Geography of the Soviet Union *and others.*
UNION OF SOVIET SOCIALIST REPUBLICS (*in part*)

J.C. de C.   Jacques Chastenet de Castaing (d. 1978). *Historian and journalist. Member of the French Academy. Author of* Léon Gambetta *and others.*
GAMBETTA, LÉON (Micropædia)

J.C. de G.-J.   John Coleman de Graft-Johnson (d. 1977). *Editor,* Economic Bulletin of Ghana. *Research Associate Professor of Economics, University of Ghana. Author of* African Glory: The Story of Vanished Negro Civilizations.
MŪSĀ (Micropædia)

J.C.F.   Jean Claude Froelich (d. 1972). *Director, Center for Advanced Studies on Modern Africa and Asia, University of Paris. Author of* Les Musulmans d'Afrique noire; *"al-Ḥādjdj ʿUmar b. Saʿīd b. ʿUthmān Tāl" in* The Encyclopedia of Islam.
ʿUMAR TALL (Micropædia)

J.C.G.   John Charles Godbey. *Professor of Church History, Meadville/Lombard Theological School, Chicago.*
PROTESTANTISM (*in part*)

J.C.Gi.   J. Calvin Giddings. *Professor of Chemistry, University of Utah, Salt Lake City. Author of* Dynamics of Chromatography.
ANALYSIS AND MEASUREMENT, PHYSICAL AND CHEMICAL (*in part*)

J.C.Gr.   Jerald C. Graue (d. 1982). *Associate Professor of Musicology and Music History, Eastman School of Music, University of Rochester, New York.*
MUSIC, THE ART OF (*in part*)

J.Ch.   John Cherry. *Deputy Keeper, Department of Medieval and Later Antiquities, British Museum, London.*
HISTORY, THE STUDY OF (*in part*)

J.C.H.   J.C. Holt. *Emeritus Professor of Medieval History, University of Cambridge. Author of* King John

and others.
JOHN (ENGLAND) (Micropædia)

J.C.J.   John Calhoun Jamieson
(d. 1983). *Professor of Geophysics,
University of Chicago, 1965–83.*
MATTER (*in part*)

**J.C.J.M.   John Callan James
Metford.** *Emeritus Professor of Spanish,
University of Bristol, England. Author of*
San Martín the Liberator *and others.*
SAN MARTÍN, JOSÉ DE (Micropædia)

J.C.K.   John C. Krantz, Jr. (d. 1983).
*Professor of Pharmacology, University
of Maryland, Baltimore, 1935–65.
Coauthor of* Pharmacologic Principles of
Medical Practice.
MEDICINE (*in part*)

J.C.Ki.   Joseph C. Kiger. *Editor in
Chief,* International Encyclopedia of
Learned Societies and Academies.
Author of American Learned Societies;
Historiographic Review of Foundation
Literature; *editor of* International
Encyclopedia of Foundations.
PHILANTHROPIC FOUNDATIONS
   (Micropædia)

J.C.L.   Joseph Collins Lawrence.
*Assistant Professor of History, University
of British Columbia, Vancouver. Author
of* A Brief History of Sooke and
District.
CANADA (*in part*)

J.C.Mi.   James Clyde Mitchell. *Official
Fellow of Nuffield College, University of
Oxford. Professor of Urban Sociology,
Victoria University of Manchester,
1966–74.*
SOUTHERN AFRICA (*in part*)

J.Co.   Jean L. Comhaire. *Emeritus
Professor of Social Anthropology,
University of Juba, The Sudan. Former
Sociologist, United Nations Economic
Commission for Africa. Author of* Urban
Administration in Africa *and others.*
WESTERN AFRICA (*in part*)

J.Cr.   John Cruickshank. *Emeritus
Professor of French, University of Sussex,
Brighton, England. Author of* Albert
Camus and the Literature of Revolt *and
others; editor of* French Literature and
Its Background.
CAMUS, ALBERT (Micropædia)

J.C.-R.   Jules-Marie Chaix-Ruy.
*Professor of Philosophy, University of
Nice, France, 1965–67. Author of* J.-B.
Vico et l'illuminisme athée; Vie de
J.-B. Vico.
VICO, GIAMBATTISTA (Micropædia)

J.C.Rd.   John Cowie Reid (d. 1972).
*Professor of English, University of
Auckland, New Zealand. Author of* Mind
and Art of Coventry Patmore; Francis
Thompson: Man and Poet; *and others.*
HOPKINS, GERARD MANLEY
   (Micropædia)

J.C.Re.   John C. Reilly, Jr. *Historian,
Naval History Division, Office of
the Chief of Naval Operations, U.S.
Department of the Navy, Washington,
D.C. Coauthor of* Capital Ships: A
Handbook of United States Battleships

and Battle Cruisers 1896–1969.
WAR, THE TECHNOLOGY OF (*in part*)

J.C.Ry.   J. Coert Rylaarsdam. *Emeritus
Professor of Old Testament Theology,
University of Chicago. Emeritus
Professor of Theology, Marquette
University, Milwaukee. Author of*
Revelation in Jewish Wisdom Literature.
BIBLICAL LITERATURE AND ITS CRITICAL
   INTERPRETATION (*in part*)
DAVID (ISRAEL) (Micropædia)

J.C.S.   James C. Spalding. *Professor
of Religion, University of Iowa, Iowa
City. Author of* The Demise of English
Presbyterianism.
PROTESTANTISM (*in part*)

J.C.Sa.   John C. Sainsbury. *Professor
and Head, Department of Oceanography
and Ocean Engineering, Florida Institute
of Technology, Melbourne. Author of*
Commercial Fishing Methods: An
Introduction to Vessels and Gears.
FISHING, COMMERCIAL (*in part*)

J.C.T.   James Chase Tyler. *Deputy
Director, National Museum of Natural
History, Smithsonian Institution,
Washington, D.C. Author of* Osteology,
Phylogeny, and Higher Classification
of the Fishes of the Order Plectognathi
(Tetraodontiformes).
FISHES (*in part*)

J.C.Ta.   John Campbell Taylor.
*President, Jan H. Reimers and
Associates Inc. (metallurgical consulting
engineers), Oakville, Ontario. Editor of
or contributor to numerous papers on
extraction, smelting, by-product recovery,
plant safety, and environmental issues
related to metallurgy.*
INDUSTRIES, EXTRACTION AND
   PROCESSING (*in part*)

J.Cul.   James Cullen. *Director, Stanley
Smith Horticultural Trust. Coauthor of*
The Identification of Flowering Plant
Families.
ANGIOSPERMS (*in part*)

J.C.V.   J. Charles Verlinden. *Emeritus
Professor of History, State University
of Ghent. Director, Belgian Historical
Institute, Rome. Author of* En Flandre
sous Philippe II *and others.*
BELGIUM (*in part*)

J.D.A.   Jean Daniel Anthony. *Professor,
Laboratory of Comparative Anatomy,
National Museum of Natural History,
Paris. Coauthor of* Anatomie de
Latimeria Chalumnae.
FISHES (*in part*)

J.D.Ad.   Jeremy D. Adler. *Reader in
German, Queen Mary and Westfield
College, University of London.*
GERMAN LITERATURE (*in part*)

J.D.An.   John Duke Anthony.
*President, National Council on U.S.–
Arab Relations, Washington, D.C.
Author of* The Sultanate of Oman
and the Emirates of Eastern Arabia
and others.
ARABIA (*in part*)

J.D.B.   John D. Bell. *Professor of
History, University of Maryland,*

Baltimore County, Baltimore. Author of
The Bulgarian Communist Party from
Blagoev to Zhivkov *and others.*
BULGARIA (*in part*)

J.D.C.   Jesse Dunsmore Clarkson (d.
1973). *Professor of History, Brooklyn
College, City University of New York,
1945–67. Author of* A History of Russia.
SPERANSKY, MIKHAIL MIKHAYLOVICH,
   GRAF (Micropædia)

J.D.Co.   James Daniel Collins (d.
1985). *Professor of Philosophy, St. Louis
University, Missouri. Author of* The
Emergence of Philosophy of Religion.
THOMISM, THOMAS AQUINAS AND
   (*in part*)

J.D.F.   John D. Fage. *Emeritus
Professor of African History,
University of Birmingham, England;
Pro-Vice-Chancellor, 1979–84;
Vice-Principal, 1981–84. Author of* A
History of Africa *and others.*
WESTERN AFRICA (*in part*)

J.D.-G.   Jacques Duchesne-Guillemin.
*Emeritus Professor of Indo-Iranian
Studies, University of Liège, Belgium.
Author of* The Religion of Ancient Iran
and others.
ZOROASTRIANISM AND PARSIISM

J.D.H.   John D. Hargreaves. *Emeritus
Professor of History, University
of Aberdeen, Scotland. Author of*
Decolonization in Africa *and others.*
WESTERN AFRICA (*in part*)

J.Di.   James Dickie. *Lecturer in
Islāmic Studies, University of Lancaster,
England, 1969–74. Editor of* Dīwān Ibn
Shuhaid al-Andalusi.
RITES AND CEREMONIES, SACRED
   (*in part*)

J.D.K.   John D. Kesby. *Lecturer in
Social Anthropology, University of Kent
at Canterbury, England. Author of* The
Cultural Regions of East Africa.
EASTERN AFRICA (*in part*)

J.D.L.   John David Legge. *Emeritus
Professor of History, Monash University,
Clayton, Australia; Dean, Faculty of
Arts, 1978–86. Author of* Intellectuals
and Nationalism in Indonesia
and others.
INDONESIA (*in part*)

J.D.M.   Jürgen D. Moltmann. *Professor
of Systematic Theology, Eberhard Karl
University of Tübingen, Germany.
Author of* Theology of Hope *and others.*
DOCTRINES AND DOGMAS, RELIGIOUS
   (*in part*)

J.D.Ma.   John D. Martz. *Professor of
Political Science, Pennsylvania State
University, University Park. Author of*
Acción Democratica: Evolution of a
Modern Political Party in Venezuela
and others.
VENEZUELA (*in part*)

J.D.Mo.   Janet D. Momsen. *Senior
Lecturer in Geography, University of
Newcastle upon Tyne, England. Coeditor
of* Land and Development in the
Caribbean.
WEST INDIES, THE (*in part*)

J.D.Mu. J. Derral Mulholland. *Research Scientist, McDonald Observatory and Department of Astronomy, University of Texas at Austin, and Centre for the Study and Research of Geodynamics and Astronomy, Grasse, France.*
SOLAR SYSTEM, THE (*in part*)

J.D.Pr. John Douglas Pringle. *Editor,* Sydney Morning Herald, *1965–70. Author of* Australian Accent.
SYDNEY

J.D.Pro. Jules David Prown. *Paul Mellon Professor of the History of Art, Yale University. Author of* American Painting from Its Beginnings to the Armory Show *and others.*
EAKINS, THOMAS (Micropædia)
HOMER, WINSLOW (Micropædia)

J.D.R. John D. Ryder. *Emeritus Professor of Electrical Engineering, Michigan State University, East Lansing. Author of* Engineering Electronics.
ENGINEERING (*in part*)

J.D.Ri. John David Rickard. *Reader in History, Monash University, Clayton, Victoria, Australia. Author of* Australia: A Cultural History *and others.*
AUSTRALIA (*in part*)

J.D.Ro. Jack D. Rollin. *Soccer Columnist,* Sunday Telegraph, *London. Editor,* Rothmans Football Yearbook. *Author of* The Guinness Book of Soccer Facts & Feats *and others.*
SPORTS, MAJOR TEAM AND INDIVIDUAL (*in part*)

J.D.S. James Duane Squires (d. 1981). *Professor of History, Colby-Sawyer College, New London, New Hampshire, 1933–70. Chairman, New Hampshire American Revolution Bicentennial Commission. Member, Governor's Task Force for Study of New Hampshire, 1970.*
UNITED STATES OF AMERICA (*in part*)

J.D.Sc. John D. Schmidt. *Assistant Professor of History, Columbia University.*
CALENDAR (*in part*)

J.D.Sm. James Desmond Smyth. *Emeritus Professor of Parasitology, London School of Hygiene and Tropical Medicine, University of London. Author of* Introduction to Animal Parasitology.
FLATWORMS

J.D.T. James D. Tracy. *Professor of History, University of Minnesota, Minneapolis. Author of* Erasmus: The Growth of a Mind *and others.*
ERASMUS

J.D.W. John D. Weaver. *Free-lance writer. Former West Coast Editor,* Travel & Leisure. *Author of* Los Angeles: The Enormous Village *and others.*
LOS ANGELES

J.E. Jens Engberg. *Professor of History, University of Århus, Denmark. Author of* Det slesvigske spørgsmål 1850–1853 *and others.*
CHRISTIAN IV (DENMARK) (Micropædia)

Je.B. Jean Bouvier (d. 1987). *Professor of Economics, University of Paris I. Author of* Les Rothschild *and others.*
ROTHSCHILD FAMILY (Micropædia)
TURGOT, ANNE-ROBERT-JACQUES, BARON DE L'AULNE (Micropædia)

J.E.B. John Edward Bowle (d. 1985). *Professor of Political Theory, College of Europe, Brugge, Belgium, 1950–67. Author of* Politics and Opinion in the 19th Century.
POLITICAL PHILOSOPHY, THE HISTORY OF WESTERN

J.E.Bu. John Everett Butt (d. 1965). *Regius Professor of Rhetoric and English Literature, University of Edinburgh, 1959–65. Author of* Pope's Poetical Manuscripts; *coeditor of* Letters of Alexander Pope; *and others.*
POPE, ALEXANDER (*in part*) (Micropædia)

Je.C. Jean Cousin (deceased). *Professor of Latin Language and Literature, University of Besançon, France. Author of* Études sur Quintilien; Destin de Rome; *and others.*
DIOCLETIAN (Micropædia)

J.E.C. John E. Carruthers. *Assistant General Manager, Refineries Department, British Petroleum Company Ltd., London, 1964–69.*
INDUSTRIES, EXTRACTION AND PROCESSING (*in part*)

J.E.Ca. James Edward Canright. *Emeritus Professor of Botany, Arizona State University, Tempe. Author of* Fossil Plants of Indiana.
ANGIOSPERMS (*in part*)

Je.Ch. Jerome Ch'en. *Emeritus Professor of East Asian History, York University, Toronto. Author of* Yuan Shih-k'ai, 1859–1916.
YÜAN SHIH-K'AI (Micropædia)

J.E.C.H. J.E. Christopher Hill. *Master of Balliol College, University of Oxford, 1965–78. Author of* Intellectual Origins of the English Revolution.
PYM, JOHN (Micropædia)

J.E.Co. J.E. Coates (d. 1973). *Professor of Chemistry, University College of Swansea, University of Wales, 1920–48. Author of the Chemical Society memorial lecture on Haber.*
HABER, FRITZ (Micropædia)

J.E.C.W. J.E. Caerwyn Williams. *Emeritus Professor of Irish, University College of Wales, Aberystwyth, University of Wales; Director, Centre for Advanced Welsh and Celtic Studies, 1979–85. Editor,* Studia Celtica (*annual*); Y Traethodydd (*quarterly*); *and* Ysgrifau Beirniadol (*annual*). *Author of* Traddodiad Llenyddol Iwerddon.
CELTIC LITERATURE (*in part*)

Je.D. Jean Dresch. *Emeritus Professor of Geography, University of Paris VII. Author of* Recherches sur l'évolution du relief dans le Haut-Atlas *and others.*
MADAGASCAR (*in part*)

J.E.E. John E. Englekirk (deceased). *Professor of Spanish and Portuguese,*

University of California, Los Angeles, 1958–73. Author of Poe in Hispanic Literature; *coauthor of* La narrativa uruguaya.
LATIN-AMERICAN LITERATURE (*in part*)

J.E.Ec. James Emory Eckenwalder. *Associate Professor of Botany, University of Toronto.*
GYMNOSPERMS (*in part*)

J.E.F. John E. Fagg. *Emeritus Professor of History, New York University, New York City. Author of* Cuba, Haiti, and the Dominican Republic *and others.*
TOUSSAINT-LOUVERTURE (Micropædia)

J.E.H. Joseph E. Hawkins. *Emeritus Professor of Otorhinolaryngology (Physiological Acoustics), Medical School, University of Michigan, Ann Arbor. Editor of* Otophysiology.
SENSORY RECEPTION (*in part*)

J.E.He. Judith Eleanor Herrin. *Stanley J. Seeger Professor of Byzantine History, Princeton University. Author of* The Formation of Christendom; *editor of* Constantinople in the Early Eighth Century.
EUROPEAN HISTORY AND CULTURE (*in part*)

Je.Ho. Jerome Holtzman. *Baseball columnist,* Chicago Tribune. *Elected to the Writers' Wing, National Baseball Hall of Fame, 1990. Coauthor of* Three and Two; *editor of* No Cheering in the Press Box; Fielder's Choice.
SPORTS, MAJOR TEAM AND INDIVIDUAL (*in part*)

J.E.I. Joseph E. Illick. *Professor of History, San Francisco State University. Author of* William Penn the Politician *and others.*
PENN, WILLIAM (*in part*) (Micropædia)

Je.M. Jean Mitry. *Professor and Director, Cinema Division, Institute of Art and Archaeology, University of Paris I. Author of* Esthétique et psychologie du cinéma; Histoire du cinéma; S.M. Eisenstein; *and others.*
EISENSTEIN, SERGEY (Micropædia)
RAY, SATYAJIT (*in part*) (Micropædia)

J.E.M. John E. Miller. *Chief Curator, Indian River Coastal Zone Museum; Assistant Research Scientist, Harbor Branch Oceanographic Institution, Inc., Ft. Pierce, Florida.*
ECHINODERMS (*in part*)

Jé.Ma. José Maceda. *Emeritus Professor of Music, University of the Philippines, Quezon City. Author of* The Music of the Magindanao in the Philippines.
SOUTHEAST ASIAN ARTS (*in part*)

J.E.McM. James Edward McMurtrey, Jr. *Collaborator, Tobacco and Sugar Crops Research Branch, Agricultural Research Service, U.S. Department of Agriculture, Plant Science Research Division, Beltsville, Maryland; formerly Leader of Tobacco Investigations.*
FARMING AND AGRICULTURAL TECHNOLOGY (*in part*)

J.-E.-M.-G.D. **Joseph-Edouard-Marie-Ghislain Delmelle.** *Poet, essayist, and critic of art and literature. Member, International Academy of French Culture.*
BELGIAN LITERATURE (*in part*)

J.E.M.L.-P. **Johanna E.M. Laybourn-Parry.** *Senior Lecturer, Institute of Environmental and Biological Sciences, University of Lancaster, England. Author of* A Functional Biology of Free-living Protozoa.
PROTOZOA

Je.P. **Jerzy Pruchnicki.** *Deputy Director for Research, Institute for Meteorology and Water Management, Warsaw. Author of* Methods of Climatological Analysis.
EUROPE (*in part*)

J.E.P. **J.E. Peterson.** *Writer and consultant. Adjunct Fellow, Center for Strategic and International Studies, Washington, D.C. Author of* Oman in the Twentieth Century *and others.*
ARABIA (*in part*)

Je.-P.H. **Jean-Paul Harroy.** *Emeritus Professor of Zairian, Rwandan and Burundian Economics, Free University of Brussels. Author of* Afrique, terre qui meurt.
AFRICA (*in part*)

Je.S. **Jean Selz.** *Art historian and critic. Member, International Association of Art Critics, Paris. Author of* Modern Sculpture: Origins and Evolution; Matisse; *and others.*
BRANCUSI, CONSTANTIN (Micropædia)

J.E.S. **John E. Shelton.** *Consultant. Former Supervisory Physical Scientist, Bureau of Mines, U.S. Department of the Interior, Washington, D.C.*
INDUSTRIES, EXTRACTION AND PROCESSING (*in part*)

J.E.Sa. **John E. Sadler.** *Head, Education Department, City of Birmingham College of Education, University of Birmingham, England, 1950–67. Author of* J.A. Comenius and the Concept of Universal Education.
COMENIUS, JOHN AMOS (Micropædia)

Je.Si. **Jerome Silbergeld.** *Professor of the History of Chinese Art, University of Washington, Seattle. Author of* Chinese Painting Style.
CHINA (*in part*)

J.E.Sm. **John Edwin Smith.** *Clark Professor of Philosophy, Yale University. Author of* Experience and God.
RELIGIOUS EXPERIENCE (*in part*)

J.E.Sn. **James E. Snyder** (d. 1990). *Professor of Art History, Bryn Mawr College, Pennsylvania. Author of* Northern Renaissance Art *and others.*
MEMLING, HANS (Micropædia)

Je.St. **Jerry Stannard** (d. 1988). *Professor of History, University of Kansas, Lawrence, 1967–88.*
PLINY THE ELDER (Micropædia)

J.E.St. **John E. Stark, M.D.** *Physician, Addenbrookes Hospital, Cambridge,* England.
DIAGNOSIS AND THERAPEUTICS (*in part*)

J.Ev. **Dame Joan Evans** (d. 1977). *President, Society of Antiquaries, London, 1959–64. Author of* John Ruskin *and many others.*
RUSKIN, JOHN (*in part*) (Micropædia)

J.E.W. **John E. Woods.** *Associate Professor of Middle Eastern History, University of Chicago. Author of* The Agguyunlu: Clan, Confederation, and Empire.
IRAQ (*in part*)

J.F.A.A. **J.F. Ade Ajayi.** *Professor of History, University of Ibadan, Nigeria. Author of* Milestones in Nigerian History *and others.*
WESTERN AFRICA (*in part*)

J.F.B. **John Fleming Brock, M.D.** (d. 1983). *Professor of Medicine, University of Cape Town, South Africa, 1938–70. Author of* Recent Advances in Human Nutrition, with Special Reference to Clinical Medicine.
NUTRITION (*in part*)

J.F.Br. **John Fleetwood Baker, Baron Baker** (d. 1985). *Professor of Mechanical Sciences, University of Cambridge, 1943–68; Fellow of Clare College, Cambridge. Author of* Differential Equations of Engineering Science *and others; coauthor of* The Analysis of Engineering Structures.
ENGINEERING (*in part*)

J.F.C. **James F. Cahill.** *Professor of the History of Art, University of California, Berkeley. Author of* Chinese Painting; Hills Beyond a River; *and others.*
HSIA KUEI (Micropædia)

J.F.C.C. **J.F.C. Conn.** *Emeritus Professor of Naval Architecture, University of Glasgow.*
INDUSTRIES, MANUFACTURING (*in part*)

J.F.D. **John F. Due.** *Emeritus Professor of Economics, University of Illinois at Urbana-Champaign. Author of* Government Finance.
GOVERNMENT FINANCE (*in part*)

J.F.De. **John F. Devlin.** *Free-lance writer, lecturer, and consultant on Middle East affairs. Author of* Syria: Modern State in an Ancient Land *and others.*
DAMASCUS (*in part*)

J.F.Dr. **John Frederick Drinkwater.** *Lecturer in Ancient History, University of Nottingham, England. Author of* Roman Gaul: The Three Provinces, 58 B.C.–A.D. 260 *and others.*
FRANCE (*in part*)

J.Fe. **John Ferguson** (d. 1989). *President, Selly Oak Colleges, Birmingham, England, 1979–86. Professor, Dean, and Director of Studies in Arts, The Open University, Milton Keynes, England, 1969–79. Author of* The Heritage of Hellenism *and others.*
CICERO, MARCUS TULLIUS (*in part*) (Micropædia)
GREEK AND ROMAN CIVILIZATIONS, ANCIENT (*in part*)

J.F.G. **John F. Guilmartin, Jr.** *Associate Professor of History, Ohio State University, Columbus. Author of* Gunpowder and Galleys: Changing Technology and Mediterranean Warfare at Sea in the Sixteenth Century.
WAR, THE TECHNOLOGY OF (*in part*)

J.F.Ha. **John F. Hayward** (d. 1983). *Associate Director, Sotheby Parke-Bernet and Company, London and New York City. Deputy Keeper, Victoria and Albert Museum, London, 1946–65. Author of* Virtuoso Goldsmiths; Art of the Gunmaker; *and others.*
DECORATIVE ARTS AND FURNISHINGS (*in part*)

J.Fi. **James Smith Findley.** *Professor of Biology; Director, Museum of Southwestern Biology, University of New Mexico, Albuquerque. Author of* Natural History of New Mexican Mammals.
MAMMALS (*in part*)

J.F.I. **John F. Iaboni.** *Former Director of Communications, Canadian Football League, Toronto; former Editor,* Facts, Figures, and Records (*annual*).
SPORTS, MAJOR TEAM AND INDIVIDUAL (*in part*)

J.F.M. **John F.M. Middleton.** *Professor of Anthropology, Yale University. Author of* Lugbara Religion *and others; editor of* Magic, Witchcraft and Curing.
AFRICA (*in part*)
OCCULTISM (*in part*)

J.F.Ma. **J.F. Matthews.** *Lecturer in the Middle and Late Roman Empire, University of Oxford; Official Fellow of Queen's College, Oxford.*
CONSTANTINE THE GREAT (*in part*)

J.F.McD. **James F. McDivitt.** *Advisor, ASEAN Federation of Mining Associations, Jakarta, Indonesia. Former Coordinator, United Nations Economic and Social Commission for Asia and the Pacific (ESCAP) Regional Mineral Resources Development Centre, Bandung, Indonesia.*
INDONESIA (*in part*)

J.F.Me. **John F. Mee** (d. 1985). *Mead Johnson Professor of Management, Indiana University, Bloomington. Author of* Management Thought in a Dynamic Economy.
TAYLOR, FREDERICK W. (Micropædia)

J.F.N.B. **John F.N. Bradley.** *Visiting Professor, University of Bordeaux I, France. Fellow, Victoria University of Manchester, England. Author of* Politics in Czechoslovakia, 1945–1971 *and others.*
CZECHOSLOVAKIA (*in part*)

J.Fo. **Jean Fourastié** (d. 1990). *Professor of Economics, National Conservatory of Arts and Crafts, Paris, 1940–78. Member of the Academy of Moral and Political Sciences, Institute of France, 1968–90. Author of* The Causes of Wealth.
WORK AND EMPLOYMENT (*in part*)

J.F.O'C. **Joseph F. O'Callaghan.** *Professor of Medieval History, Fordham*

University, New York City.
SPAIN (*in part*)

J.F.O'G.   James Francis O'Gorman.
*Grace Slack McNeil Professor of the
History of American Art, Wellesley
College, Massachusetts. Author of* H.H.
Richardson: Architectural Forms for an
American Society.
RICHARDSON, HENRY HOBSON
   (Micropædia)

J.F.P.B.   Jean F.P. Blondel. *Professor
of Political Science, European
University Institute, Florence. Author of*
Comparative Government *and others.*
FRANCE (*in part*)

J.F.P.H.   John Francis Price Hopkins.
*Fellow of Corpus Christi College,
Cambridge; former Lecturer in Modern
Arabic, University of Cambridge.*
AFRICA (*in part*)

Jf.Pi.   Josef Pieper. *Emeritus Professor
of Philosophical Anthropology, University
of Münster, Germany. Author of*
Scholasticism *and others.*
PHILOSOPHICAL SCHOOLS AND
   DOCTRINES, WESTERN (*in part*)

J.F.Q.   John Francis Quinn. *Professor
of Philosophy, Pontifical Institute of
Mediaeval Studies, Toronto. Author
of* "The Historical Constitution of St.
Bonaventure's Philosophy," *in* Medieval
Texts and Studies.
BONAVENTURE, SAINT (Micropædia)

J.Fr.   Joseph Frankel (d. 1989).
*Professor of Politics, University of
Southampton, England, 1963–78. Author
of* The Making of Foreign Policy.
WAR, THE THEORY AND CONDUCT
   OF (*in part*)

J.F.S.   Joseph Frederick Scott
(d. 1971). *Vice-Principal; Principal
Lecturer in Mathematics, St. Mary's
College, Strawberry Hill, England.
Author of* A History of Mathematics.
NAPIER, JOHN (Micropædia)

J.F.Sk.   John Francis Skone, M.D.
*Honorary Lecturer in Epidemiology
and Community Medicine, University of
Wales College of Medicine, Cardiff.*
MEDICINE (*in part*)

J.F.W.   J. Fred Weston. *Emeritus
Professor of Managerial Economics
and Finance, University of California,
Los Angeles. Author of* The Scope and
Methodology of Finance *and others.*
BUSINESS ORGANIZATION (*in part*)

J.G.   John Gergely, M.D. *Director,
Department of Muscle Research,
Boston Biomedical Research Institute.
Biochemist, Massachusetts General
Hospital, Boston. Associate Professor
of Biological Chemistry, Harvard
University.*
MUSCLES AND MUSCLE SYSTEMS (*in part*)

J.G.B.   J. Guthrie Brown (d. 1976).
*Senior Consultant, Sir Alexander Gibb
& Partners, Consulting Engineers.
President, International Commission
on Large Dams, 1964–67. Coauthor of*
Power from Water.
PUBLIC WORKS (*in part*)

J.G.Co.   James Gordon Cook. *Director,
Merrow Publishing Company Ltd.,
Shildon, England. Author of* Handbook
of Textile Fibres.
INDUSTRIES, CHEMICAL PROCESS (*in part*)

J.G.Cr.   J.G. Crowther (d. 1983).
Author of Famous American Men of
Science; Science in Modern Society
and others.
GIBBS, J. WILLARD (Micropædia)

J.G.D.   The Rev. J. Gordon Davies
(d. 1990). *Edward Cadbury Professor
and Head, Department of Theology,
University of Birmingham, England,
1960–86. Author of* The Early Christian
Church *and others.*
NESTORIUS (Micropædia)

J.G.G.   John G. Gallaher. *Professor
of History, Southern Illinois University,
Edwardsville. Author of* "Leo X" *in* New
Catholic Encyclopedia.
LEO X (PAPACY) (Micropædia)

J.G.H.   John G. Hargrave (d. 1982).
Author of The Life and Soul of
Paracelsus *and others.*
PARACELSUS (Micropædia)

J.Gi.   The Rev. Joseph Gill, S.J. (d.
1989). *Former Professor of Byzantine
Greek Language and of Byzantine
History, Pontifical Oriental Institute,
Rome, 1946–67. Author of* The Council
of Florence *and others.*
NICHOLAS V (PAPACY) (Micropædia)
PIUS II (Micropædia)

J.Go.   Jacques Godechot (d. 1989).
*Professor of Modern and Contemporary
History, 1945–80; Dean, Faculty
of Letters, University of Toulouse
II, France, 1961–71. Author of* Les
Révolutions, 1770–1799; Napoléon.
NAPOLEON
TALLEYRAND, CHARLES-MAURICE
   DE, PRINCE DE BENEVENT (*in part*)
   (Micropædia)

J.Gol.   Judah Goldin. *Professor of
Oriental Studies and Post-Biblical
Hebrew Literature, University of
Pennsylvania, Philadelphia. Author
of* The Fathers According to Rabbi
Nathan; *articles on Hillel and Johanan
ben Zakkai.*
HILLEL (*in part*) (Micropædia)
JOHANAN BEN ZAKKAI (Micropædia)

J.G.P.   John Graham Pollard. *Former
Deputy Director and Keeper, Department
of Coins and Medals, Fitzwilliam
Museum, University of Cambridge.
Coeditor of* Renaissance Medals from
the Samuel H. Kress Collection at the
National Gallery.
COINS AND COINAGE (*in part*)

J.Gre.   James Green. *Professor of
Zoology, Queen Mary and Westfield
College, University of London. Author of*
The Biology of Estuarine Animals.
CRUSTACEANS (*in part*)

J.Gt.   Jean Guiart. *Professor of
Ethnology, Museum of Man, National
Museum of Natural History, Paris.
Author of* Oceania.
OCEANIC ARTS (*in part*)

J.G.Th.   John Gareth Thomas (d.
1987). *Registrar, University of Wales,
Cardiff. Coauthor of* Wales.
UNITED KINGDOM (*in part*)

J.G.W.   J. Garth Watson. *Secretary,
Institution of Civil Engineers, London,
1967–79.*
ENGINEERING (*in part*)

J.H.   Jakob Houtgast (d. 1981).
*Associate Professor of Astronomy,
Astronomical Institute, Utrecht
University, The Netherlands. Coauthor of*
Photometric Atlas of the Solar Spectrum.
ECLIPSE, OCCULTATION, AND TRANSIT
   (*in part*)

J.Ha.   Jack Halpern. *Louis Block
Distinguished Service Professor of
Chemistry, University of Chicago. Author
of papers on transition metal ions and
complexes.*
CHEMICAL COMPOUNDS (*in part*)

J.H.A.   John H. Adler (d. 1980).
*Director, Programming and Budgeting
Department, International Bank for
Reconstruction and Development,
Washington, D.C., 1968–76. Coauthor of*
Public Finance in a Developing Country.
UNITED NATIONS (*in part*)

J.H.A.J.   Jörg H.A. Janzen. *Academic
counselor, Centre for Development
Studies, Faculty of Geosciences, Free
University of Berlin. Author of* Nomads
in the Sultanate of Oman.
EASTERN AFRICA (*in part*)

J.-H.B.   Jacques-Henry Bornecque.
*Professor of Modern and Contemporary
French Literature, University of
Paris XIII. Author of* Les Années
d'apprentissage d'Alphonse Daudet;
Verlaine par lui-même; *and others.*
DAUDET, ALPHONSE (Micropædia)

J.H.Be.   John Herbert Beynon. *Royal
Society Research Professor, University
College of Swansea, University of Wales.
Author of* Mass Spectrometry and Its
Application to Organic Chemistry.
ANALYSIS AND MEASUREMENT,
   PHYSICAL AND CHEMICAL (*in part*)

J.H.Bo.   John H. Bounds. *Professor
of Geography, Sam Houston State
University, Huntsville, Texas. Author
of* Tahiti.
WEST INDIES, THE (*in part*)

J.H.Br.   John H. Bryant, M.D.
*Professor and Chairman, Department of
Community Health Sciences, Aga Khan
University, Karachi, Pakistan. Author of*
Health and the Developing World.
MEDICINE (*in part*)

J.H.D.   James H. Downing.
*Metallurgical consultant. Senior Fellow,
Elkem Metals, Niagara Falls, New York,
1986–91.*
INDUSTRIES, EXTRACTION AND
   PROCESSING (*in part*)

J.He.   John Herivel. *Former Reader in
the History and Philosophy of Science,
Queen's University of Belfast, Northern
Ireland. Author of* The Background to
Newton's Principia.
HUYGENS, CHRISTIAAN (Micropædia)

J.H.H. **John H. Holmes.** *Professor of Geography, University of Queensland, Brisbane. Editor of* Queensland: A Geographical Interpretation; *coeditor of* Settlement Systems in Sparsely Populated Regions.
AUSTRALIA (*in part*)

J.H.-H. **John Heslop-Harrison.** *Royal Society Research Professor, Welsh Plant-Breeding Station, University College of Wales, Aberystwyth, University of Wales. Author of numerous papers on development in plants.*
GROWTH AND DEVELOPMENT, BIOLOGICAL (*in part*)

J.H.Hi. **John Hugh Hill.** *Emeritus Professor of Medieval History, University of Houston, Texas. Coauthor of* Raymond IV, Count of Toulouse *and others.*
BOHEMOND I (*in part*) (Micropædia)

J.H.Hy. **John H. Humphrey, M.D.** (d. 1987). *Professor of Immunology, Royal Postgraduate Medical School, University of London, 1976–81. Coeditor of* Advances in Immunology.
IMMUNITY

J.Hi. **John Hick.** *Danforth Professor of the Philosophy of Religion, Claremont Graduate School, California. Author of* Death and Eternal Life *and others.*
CHRISTIANITY (*in part*)

J.H.J. **John Holmes Jellett** (d. 1971). *Civil engineer. Director, Anglo Dutch Dredging Company Ltd., Beaconsfield, England. Docks engineer, Southampton, England, 1946–66.*
PUBLIC WORKS (*in part*)

J.H.K. **Joseph Henry Keenan** (d. 1977). *Professor of Mechanical Engineering, Massachusetts Institute of Technology, Cambridge, 1939–66. Author of* Thermodynamics; *coauthor of* Principles of General Thermodynamics.
THERMODYNAMICS, PRINCIPLES OF (*in part*)

J.H.L. **J.H. Larson.** *Senior Sculpture Conservator, Victoria and Albert Museum, London. Author of* Guan Yin: A Masterpiece Revealed.
ARTS, PRACTICE AND PROFESSION OF THE (*in part*)

J.Hm. **James Holderbaum.** *Professor of Art, Smith College, Northampton, Massachusetts.*
SCULPTURE, THE HISTORY OF WESTERN (*in part*)

J.H.McM.S. **John Hearsey McMillan Salmon.** *Marjorie Walter Goodhart Professor of History, Bryn Mawr College, Pennsylvania. Author of* Renaissance and Revolt: Essays in the Intellectual and Social History of Early Modern France *and others.*
EUROPEAN HISTORY AND CULTURE (*in part*)

J.Ho. **James Houston.** *Former Chancellor, Regent College, Vancouver, British Columbia. Author of* The Western Mediterranean World.
SPAIN (*in part*)

J.H.O. **John H. Ostrom.** *Professor of Geology; Curator of Vertebrate Paleontology, Peabody Museum of Natural History, Yale University. Coauthor of* Marsh's Dinosaurs: The Collections from Como Bluff.
DINOSAURS

J.H.Py. **John Horace Parry** (d. 1982). *Gardiner Professor of Oceanic History and Affairs, Harvard University, 1965–82. Author of* A Short History of the West Indies *and others.*
WEST INDIES, THE (*in part*)

J.H.R. **John H. Rizley.** *Consulting engineer. Former Manager, Materials Research and Process Engineering, General Dynamics Corporation, Pomona, California. Coauthor of* Metals Handbook.
INDUSTRIES, EXTRACTION AND PROCESSING (*in part*)

J.H.Ro. **Jonathan H. Robbins, M.D.** *Director, Cardiology Section, Leominster Hospital, Massachusetts.*
DISEASE (*in part*)

J.H.Sh. **J.H. Shennan.** *Pro-Vice-Chancellor and Professor of European History, University of Lancaster, England. Author of* Government and Society in France, 1461–1661 *and others.*
FRANCE (*in part*)

J.H.Sm. **The Rev. James Hutchinson Smylie.** *Ernest Trice Thompson Professor of Church History, Union Theological Seminary, Richmond, Virginia. Editor,* Journal of Presbyterian History.
ADVENTIST (Micropædia)

J.H.-s.S. **The Rev. Joseph Hsing-san Shih.** *Professor of Missions and Sinology, Pontifical Gregorian University, Rome, Italy. Contributor to* Studia Missionalia.
RICCI, MATTEO (Micropædia)

J.Hud. **Joseph Hudnut** (d. 1968). *Professor of Architecture and Dean, Graduate School of Design, Harvard University, 1935–53. Author of* Modern Sculpture *and others.*
SCULPTURE, THE HISTORY OF WESTERN (*in part*)

J.H.W. **John Humphreys Whitfield.** *Serena Professor Emeritus of Italian Language and Literature, University of Birmingham, England. Author of* Petrarch and the Renascence; A Short History of Italian Literature; *and others.*
PETRARCH (*in part*) (Micropædia)
PIRANDELLO, LUIGI (Micropædia)

J.H.Wa. **James Hamilton Ware, Jr.** *Professor of Philosophy and Religion; Chairman, Asian Studies Program, Austin College, Sherman, Texas. Author of* Chinese Religions.
CHUANG-TZU (Micropædia)

J.H.We. **John H. Wellington.** *Emeritus Professor of Geography, University of the Witwatersrand, Johannesburg. Author of* Southern Africa.
AFRICA (*in part*)

J.H.Wi. **John Hoyt Williams.** *Professor of History, Indiana State University, Terre Haute. Author of* The Rise and Fall of the Paraguayan Republic, 1800–1870.
PARAGUAY (*in part*)

J.H.Y. **John H. Yopp.** *Professor of Plant Biology; Associate Vice President for Academic Affairs and Research; Dean, Graduate School, Southern Illinois University, Carbondale. Coeditor of* Symmetries in Science IV *and* Bioassays and Other Special Techniques for Plant Hormomes and Plant Growth Regulators.
PLANTS (*in part*)

J.H.Z. **James Herbert Zumberge.** *President, University of Southern California, Los Angeles. Author of* Elements of Geology *and others.*
GEOMORPHIC PROCESSES (*in part*)

Ji.B. **Jillian Becker.** *Director, Institute for the Study of Terrorism, London. Author of* Hitler's Children: The Story of the Baader-Meinhof Terrorist Gang.
CRIME AND PUNISHMENT (*in part*)

J.I.C. **John Innes Clarke.** *Emeritus Professor of Geography, University of Durham, England. Coeditor of* Population and Development Projects in Africa.
AFRICA (*in part*)

J.I.D. **Jorge I. Domínguez.** *Professor of Government; Member, Center for International Affairs, Harvard University. Author of* Cuba: Order and Revolution.
CASTRO, FIDEL (*in part*) (Micropædia)

J.I.M.S. **John I.M. Stewart.** *Reader in English Literature, University of Oxford, 1969–73. Author of* Rudyard Kipling.
KIPLING, RUDYARD (Micropædia)
SHAW, GEORGE BERNARD (*in part*) (Micropædia)

J.I.S. **James Irvine Smith.** *Advocate. Sheriff of North Strathclyde; former Sheriff of Glasgow.*
LEGAL SYSTEMS, THE EVOLUTION OF MODERN WESTERN (*in part*)

J.J. **Jules Janick.** *James Troop Distinguished Professor of Horticulture, Purdue University, West Lafayette, Indiana. Author of* Horticultural Science.
GARDENING AND HORTICULTURE (*in part*)

J.-J.C. **Jean-Jacques Chevallier.** *Emeritus Professor of the History of Political Thought, University of Paris. Member of the Institute of France. Author of* Mirabeau *and others.*
MIRABEAU, HONORÉ-GABRIEL RIQUETI, COMTE DE (Micropædia)

J.J.Ca. **John J. Cahir.** *Professor of Meteorology; Associate Dean, College of Earth and Mineral Sciences, Pennsylvania State University, University Park. Coauthor of* Principles of Climatology *and others.*
CLIMATE AND WEATHER (*in part*)

J.J.Ch. **J.J. Chambliss.** *Professor of Education, Rutgers University, New Brunswick, New Jersey. Author* *of* Educational Theory as Theory of Conduct.

EDUCATION, HISTORY OF (*in part*)

J.J.C.S. **John Jamieson Carswell Smart.** *Emeritus Professor of Philosophy, Institute of Advanced Studies, Australian National University, Canberra. Emeritus Professor of Philosophy, University of Adelaide, Australia. Author of* Philosophy and Scientific Realism *and others; editor of* Problems of Space and Time.

PHILOSOPHICAL SCHOOLS AND DOCTRINES, WESTERN (*in part*)
TIME (*in part*)

J.J.G. **Jeremy John Gray.** *Senior Lecturer in Mathematics, Open University, Milton Keynes, England. Author of* Linear Differential Equations and Group Theory from Riemann to Poincaré *and others.*

MATHEMATICS, THE HISTORY OF (*in part*)

J.J.Ha. **James J. Haggerty.** *Free-lance writer, specializing in aviation and space technology. Editor,* Aerospace Year Book, *1957–70. Author of* Apollo: Lunar Landing.

INDUSTRIES, MANUFACTURING (*in part*)

J.J.Ho. **John J. Honigmann** (d. 1977). *Professor of Anthropology, University of North Carolina at Chapel Hill, 1955–77. Author of* World of Man.

AMERICAN INDIANS (*in part*)

J.J.J. **Joy Juanita Jackson.** *Professor of History and Archivist, Southeastern Louisiana University, Hammond; Director, Center for Regional Studies. Author of* New Orleans in the Gilded Age.

NEW ORLEANS

J.J.Jo. **John J. Johnson.** *Emeritus Professor of History, Stanford University, California. Author of* Political Change in Latin America *and others.*

CHILE (*in part*)
LATIN AMERICA, THE HISTORY OF (*in part*)
MEXICO (*in part*)

J.J.L. **J.J. Lagowski.** *Professor of Chemistry, University of Texas at Austin. Author of* The Chemical Bond.

CHEMICAL ELEMENTS (*in part*)

J.J.M. **James J. Murphy.** *Professor of Rhetoric, University of California, Davis. Editor of* Demosthenes' On the Crown: A Critical Case Study of a Masterpiece of Ancient Oratory.

DEMOSTHENES (Micropædia)

J.J.M.T. **Jan Joseph Marie Timmers.** *Former Professor of the History of Art, Jan van Eyck Academy, Maastricht, The Netherlands. Author of* Dutch Life and Art; A Handbook of Romanesque Art.

ARCHITECTURE, THE HISTORY OF WESTERN (*in part*)
SCULPTURE, THE HISTORY OF WESTERN (*in part*)

J.J.No. **J. Jeremy Noble.** *Professor of Music, State University of New York at Buffalo.*

BYRD, WILLIAM (Micropædia)

J.J.P. **Jan J. Poelhekke.** *Emeritus Professor of Modern History, Catholic University of Nijmegen, The Netherlands. Author of* De Vrede van Munster *and others.*

FREDERICK HENRY, PRINCE OF ORANGE (Micropædia)
OLDENBARNEVELT, JOHAN VAN (Micropædia)

J.J.Pe. **Jaroslav Jan Pelikan.** *Sterling Professor of History, Yale University. Author of* The Christian Tradition: A History of the Development of Doctrine; The Riddle of Roman Catholicism.

CHRISTIANITY (*in part*)
JESUS (*in part*)
MARY (MOTHER OF JESUS) (*in part*) (Micropædia)
ROMAN CATHOLICISM (*in part*)

J.J.S. **John J. Stoudt.** *Professor of Philosophy, Kutztown State College, Pennsylvania, 1965–70. Free-lance writer and researcher. Author of* Jacob Boehme: His Life and Thought *and others.*

BÖHME, JAKOB (Micropædia)

J.J.Se. **Jean J. Seznec** (d. 1983). *Marshal Foch Professor of French Literature, University of Oxford, 1950–72. Author of* Marcel Proust et les dieux *and others.*

MICHELET, JULES (Micropædia)

J.J.Sp. **Joseph J. Spengler** (d. 1991). *James B. Duke Professor of Economics, Duke University, Durham, North Carolina, 1955–71. Author of* Population Economics *and others.*

RICARDO, DAVID (Micropædia)

J.J.V. **John J. Veevers.** *Associate Professor of Earth Sciences, Macquarie University, Sydney. Editor of* Phanerozoic Earth History of Australia.

AUSTRALIA (*in part*)

J.J.W. **John J. Winberry.** *Professor of Geography, University of South Carolina, Columbia. Coauthor of* South Carolina: A Geography.

UNITED STATES OF AMERICA (*in part*)

J.Ke. **James Kerney, Jr.** (deceased). *Editor,* Trenton Times Newspapers, *New Jersey, 1965–74; Publisher, 1962–73.*

UNITED STATES OF AMERICA (*in part*)

J.K.-G. **Joan Kelly-Gadol** (d. 1982). *Professor of History, City College, City University of New York, 1972–82. Author of* Leon Battista Alberti.

ALBERTI, LEON BATTISTA (Micropædia)

J.Ki. **Jay Kinsbruner.** *Professor of History, Queens College, City University of New York. Author of* Bernardo O'Higgins *and others.*

O'HIGGINS, BERNARDO (Micropædia)

J.K.J. **J. Knox Jones, Jr.** *Paul Whitfield Horn Distinguished Professor of Biological Sciences and Museum Science, Texas Tech University, Lubbock. Coeditor of* Orders and Families of Recent Mammals of the World.

MAMMALS (*in part*)

J.K.L. **John K. Loosli.** *Emeritus Professor of Animal Nutrition, Cornell University, Ithaca, New York. Visiting Professor of Animal Science, University of Florida, Gainesville. Coauthor of* Animal Nutrition.

FARMING AND AGRICULTURAL TECHNOLOGY (*in part*)

J.K.La. **John Kingsley Lattimer, M.D.** *Emeritus Professor of Urology, Columbia University. Director, Squier Urological Clinic, Presbyterian Hospital, New York City.*

REPRODUCTION AND REPRODUCTIVE SYSTEMS (*in part*)

J.Kr. **Julian Krzyżanowski** (d. 1976). *Professor of the History of Polish Literature, University of Warsaw, 1934–66. President, Mickiewicz Literary Society. Author of* Polish Romantic Literature *and others.*

POLISH LITERATURE (*in part*)

J.K.Sh. **John K.G. Shearman.** *Professor and Chairman, Department of Fine Arts, Harvard University. Author of* Andrea del Sarto.

ANDREA DEL SARTO (Micropædia)

J.Ku. **Job Kuijt.** *Professor of Biology, University of Victoria, British Columbia. Author of* The Biology of Parasitic Flowering Plants.

ANGIOSPERMS (*in part*)

J.K.W. **James King West** (d. 1984). *Professor of Religion and Philosophy, Catawba College, Salisbury, North Carolina. Author of* Introduction to the Old Testament.

SAUL (Micropædia)

J.La. **Jean Lacouture.** *Former Professor, Institute for Political Studies, University of Paris. Adviser, Éditions du Seuil, Paris. Author of* Ho Chi Minh *and others.*

HO CHI MINH (Micropædia)

J.L.A.F. **Jean L.A. Filliozat** (d. 1982). *Professor of Indian Languages and Literatures, College of France, Paris. Member, Institute of France. Author of* Inde classique *and others.*

HISTORY, THE STUDY OF (*in part*)

J.L.A.-L. **Janet L. Abu-Lughod.** *Emerita Professor of Sociology, Northwestern University, Evanston, Illinois. Professor of Sociology, New School for Social Research, New York City. Author of* Cairo: 1001 Years of the City Victorious *and others.*

CAIRO

J.L.B. **J.L. Berggren.** *Professor of Mathematics, Simon Fraser University, Burnaby, British Columbia. Author of* Episodes in the Mathematics of Medieval Islam.

MATHEMATICS, THE HISTORY OF (*in part*)

J.L.C. **John L. Cornwall.** *Professor of Economics, Dalhousie University, Halifax, Nova Scotia. Author of* The Theory of Economic Breakdown *and others.*

ECONOMIC GROWTH AND PLANNING (*in part*)

J.-L.Ca. **Jean-Louis Caussou.** *Former Editor,* Opéra (*journal*), *Paris. Author*

of Rossini.
ROSSINI, GIOACCHINO (Micropædia)

J.-L.Ch. Jean-Léon Charles. *Professor of Military History, Belgian Royal Military Academy, Brussels. Author of* La ville de Saint-Trond au moyen-âge.
FARNESE, ALESSANDRO, DUCA DI PARMA E PIACENZA (Micropædia)

J.L.Cl. James Lowry Clifford (d. 1978). *Professor of English, Columbia University, 1946–69. Author of* Young Sam Johnson *and others.*
JOHNSON, SAMUEL (*in part*)

J.L.D. Jack L. Dull. *Associate Professor of History, University of Washington, Seattle. Editor of* Han Social Structure; Han Agriculture.
CHINA (*in part*)
WU-TI (HAN DYNASTY) (Micropædia)

J.L.Di. John L. Dietz. *Professor of Geography, University of Northern Colorado, Greeley.*
NORTH AMERICA (*in part*)
UNITED STATES OF AMERICA (*in part*)

J.Le. Jacques Levron. *Honorary Chief Curator, Archives of France, Paris. Author of* Saint-Louis ou l'apogée du moyen-âge *and others.*
LOUIS IX (FRANCE) (Micropædia)

J.L.Fi. John L. Fischer (deceased). *Professor of Anthropology, Tulane University, New Orleans. Coauthor of* The Eastern Carolines.
PACIFIC ISLANDS (*in part*)

J.L.G. Judson Linsley Gressitt (d. 1982). *Director, Wau Ecology Institute, Papua New Guinea. Distinguished Chair of Zoology, Bernice P. Bishop Museum, Honolulu. Coauthor of* Chrysomelidae of China; Insects of Campbell Island.
INSECTS (*in part*)

J.L.Gi. James L. Gibbons, M.D. *Professor of Psychiatry, University of Southampton, England. Editor of* Psychiatry.
MENTAL DISORDERS AND THEIR TREATMENT (*in part*)

J.L.H. John Lawrance Howard. *Head, Magnetic Division, Admiralty Compass Observatory, Slough, England. Author of several compass manuals.*
NAVIGATION (*in part*)

J.L.H.K. John L.H. Keep. *Emeritus Professor of Russian History, University of Toronto. Author of* The Russian Revolution: A Study in Mass Mobilization.
MILYUKOV, PAVEL NIKOLAYEVICH (*in part*) (Micropædia)
NICHOLAS II (RUSSIA) (Micropædia)

J.-L.Hu. Jean-Louis Huot. *Professor of Oriental Archaeology, University of Paris I. Author of* Iran.
XERXES I (PERSIA) (Micropædia)

J.L.I.F. John Lister Illingworth Fennell. *Emeritus Professor of Russian, University of Oxford. Author of* Ivan the Great of Moscow *and others.*
IVAN III (*in part*) (Micropædia)

J.L.Ki. John Louis King, Jr. *Former Assistant Professor of History, University of the District of Columbia, Washington, D.C.*
CARVER, GEORGE WASHINGTON (Micropædia)

J.L.M. John Lawrence Mero. *President, Ocean Resources, Inc., La Jolla, California. Author of* The Mineral Resources of the Sea.
OCEANS (*in part*)

J.L.McK. The Rev. John L. McKenzie, S.J. *Emeritus Professor of Theology, De Paul University, Chicago. Author of* The World of the Judges; Dictionary of the Bible; *and others.*
ROMAN CATHOLICISM (*in part*)
SAMUEL (Micropædia)

J.L.Me. Julian Louis Meltzer (d. 1977). *Executive Vice-Chairman, Yad Chaim Weizmann National Memorial, and Director, Weizmann Archives, Rehovot, Israel, 1966–75. Managing editor of* Weizmann Letters and Papers.
WEIZMANN, CHAIM (Micropædia)

J.L.Ra. John Lang Rawlinson. *Professor of History, Hofstra University, Hempstead, New York. Author of* China's Struggle for Naval Development, 1839–1895.
LI HUNG-CHANG (Micropædia)

J.L.Ro. J. Lewis Robinson. *Emeritus Professor of Geography, University of British Columbia, Vancouver. Author of* Concepts and Themes in the Regional Geography of Canada *and others.*
NORTH AMERICA (*in part*)

J.L.S. J.L. Styan. *Franklyn Bliss Snyder Professor Emeritus of English Literature and Theatre, Northwestern University, Evanston, Illinois. Author of* The Elements of Drama; Shakespeare's Stagecraft; Chekhov in Performance; *and others.*
LITERATURE, THE ART OF (*in part*)

J.L.Sa. Jeffrey L. Sammons. *Professor of German, Yale University. Author of* Heinrich Heine: A Modern Biography.
HEINE, HEINRICH (Micropædia)

J.L.Sp. Jay L. Spaulding. *Associate Professor of History, Kean College of New Jersey, Union. Coauthor of* Kingdoms of the Sudan.
SUDAN (*in part*)

J.L.T. John L. Thomas. *Professor of History, Brown University, Providence, Rhode Island. Author of* The Liberator: William Lloyd Garrison.
GARRISON, WILLIAM LLOYD (Micropædia)

J.L.Te. John L. Teall (d. 1979). *Professor of History, Mount Holyoke College, South Hadley, Massachusetts, 1968–79. Coauthor of* Atlas of World History.
BYZANTINE EMPIRE, THE HISTORY OF THE (*in part*)

J.L.W. James L. Wescoat, Jr. *Assistant Professor of Geography, University of Colorado at Boulder. Author of* Integrated Water Development; Water Use and Conservation Practice in Western Colorado.
NORTH AMERICA (*in part*)

J.Ly. John Lyman (d. 1977). *Professor of Oceanography; Marine Sciences Coordinator, University of North Carolina at Chapel Hill, 1968–73. Coauthor of* Ocean Sciences.
MAPPING AND SURVEYING (*in part*)

J.Lyo. Sir John Lyons. *Master of Trinity Hall, University of Cambridge. Professor of Linguistics, University of Sussex, Brighton, England, 1976–84. Author of* Introduction to Theoretical Linguistics; Language and Linguistics; *and others.*
LINGUISTICS (*in part*)

J.M. The Rev. John Meyendorff. *Dean, St. Vladimir's Orthodox Theological Seminary,Tuckahoe, New York; Professor of Church History and Patristics. Professor of Byzantine and East European History, Fordham University, New York City. Author of* The Orthodox Church, Its Past and Its Role in the World Today.
EASTERN ORTHODOXY (*in part*)

J.Ma. Joseph Machlis. *Emeritus Professor of Music, Queens College, City University of New York. Author of* The Enjoyment of Music *and others.*
COPLAND, AARON (*in part*) (Micropædia)

J.MacG. Janet MacGaffey. *Assistant Professor of Anthropology, Bucknell University, Lewisburg, Pennsylvania.*
KINSHASA (*in part*)

J.M.Bo. James M. Borders. *Assistant Professor of Musical History and Musicology; Curator, Stearns Collection of Musical Instruments, University of Michigan, Ann Arbor. Author of* European and American Wind and Percussion Instruments.
MUSICAL INSTRUMENTS (*in part*)

J.M.-Br. Josef Müller-Brockmann. *Graphic designer, lecturer, and writer. IBM European Design Consultant. Author of* The Graphic Artist and His Design Problems *and others.*
MARKETING AND MERCHANDISING (*in part*)

J.M.Bu. Julian Medforth Budden. *Former External Services Music Organizer, British Broadcasting Corporation, London. Author of* The Operas of Verdi.
BEETHOVEN

J.M.C. John M. Crowley. *Professor of Geography, University of Montana, Missoula.*
UNITED STATES OF AMERICA (*in part*)

J.M.Ca. Janet M. Cartwright. *Chairman, Board of Trustees, Black Hawk College, Moline, Illinois.*
UNITED STATES OF AMERICA (*in part*)

J.McL. John McLaughlin. *Former Political Writer, Trenton Times Newspapers, New Jersey.*
UNITED STATES OF AMERICA (*in part*)

J.M.C.T. Jocelyn M.C. Toynbee (d. 1985). *Laurence Professor of Classical Archaëology, University of Cambridge, 1951–62. Author of* The Art of the Romans.
PAINTING, THE HISTORY OF WESTERN (*in part*)
SCULPTURE, THE HISTORY OF WESTERN (*in part*)

J.M.F.P. José M.F. Pastor. *Town and regional planning expert. President, Town Planning Council, Buenos Aires. Author of* Urbanismo con planeamiento.
BUENOS AIRES (*in part*)

J.M.G. Jean Marie Gehring. *Lecturer in Geography, University of Metz, France. Author of* Le Luxembourg un espace ouvert de l'Europe rhénane.
LUXEMBOURG (*in part*)

J.M.H. Joan Mervyn Hussey. *Emeritus Professor of History, Royal Holloway College, University of London. Author of* The Byzantine World; The Orthodox Church in the Byzantine Empire; *and others.*
ALEXIUS I COMNENUS (Micropædia)
BASIL I (BYZANTINE EMPIRE) (Micropædia)
BASIL II (BYZANTINE EMPIRE) (Micropædia)
GREECE (*in part*)
JUSTINIAN I (*in part*) (Micropædia)

J.M.Ha. J.M. Hayes. *Distinguished Professor of Biogeochemistry, Indiana University, Bloomington. Coauthor of* Chemical Separations and Measurements.
ATMOSPHERE (*in part*)

J.M.Hi. John M. Hills. *Emeritus Professor of Geological Sciences, University of Texas at El Paso. Author of numerous articles on the petroleum and saline deposits of the Permian basin of Texas and New Mexico.*
FOOD PROCESSING (*in part*)

J.Mi. Jacques Miège. *Professor of Systematic Botany, University of Geneva. Former Director, Conservatory and Botanical Garden, Geneva. Editor of* Candollea *and* Boissiera.
ANGIOSPERMS (*in part*)

J.Mir. Jeannette Mirsky (d. 1987). *Visiting Fellow, Department of East Asian Studies, Princeton University, 1970–74. Coauthor of* The World of Eli Whitney.
WHITNEY, ELI (*in part*) (Micropædia)

J.M.J.M. Jan Maria Juul Materné. *Research Assistant, National Foundation for Scientific Research, Brussels.*
BELGIUM (*in part*)

J.M.J.v.H. Baron Jean M.J. van Houtte. *Minister of State, Government of Belgium, 1966; Minister of Finance, 1950–52, 1958–61; Prime Minister, 1952–54. Emeritus Professor of Fiscal Law, State University of Ghent. Emeritus Professor of Penal Law, State University of Liège.*
TAXATION (*in part*)

J.M.K. Joseph M. Kitagawa. *Emeritus Professor of the History of Religions and of Far Eastern Languages and Civilizations, University of Chicago; Dean, Divinity School, 1970–80. Author of* Religions of the East *and others.*
BUDDHISM, THE BUDDHA AND (*in part*)

J.M.K.S. J.M.K. Spalding, M.D. *Former Consultant Neurologist, Radcliffe Infirmary, Oxford. Former Senior Research Fellow, St. Peter's College, University of Oxford. Coauthor of* Disorders of the Autonomic Nervous System; Neurocardiology.
NERVES AND NERVOUS SYSTEMS (*in part*)

J.M.L. Jacob M. Landau. *Professor of Political Sciences, Hebrew University of Jerusalem. Author of* Studies in the Arab Theatre and Cinema *and others.*
ISLĀMIC ARTS (*in part*)

J.M.Lu. Joseph M. Lucker (d. 1980). *Editor in Chief,* De Tijd, *Amsterdam. Editorial Chairman of* The Netherlands Newsreel, *Polygoon. The Netherlands Delegate to UNESCO.*
NETHERLANDS, THE (*in part*)

J.M.M.-R. J.M. Munn-Rankin (d. 1981). *Lecturer in Near Eastern History, University of Cambridge, 1949–81. Contributor to* The Cambridge Ancient History.
DARIUS I (Micropædia)

J.M.N.-D. John M. Newsom-Davis. *Professor of Clinical Neurology, University of Oxford. Coauthor of* Respiratory Muscles: Mechanics and Neural Control.
MUSCLES AND MUSCLE SYSTEMS (*in part*)

J.Mo. The Rev. Jacques Monet, S.J. *Professor of History, Regis College, Toronto School of Theology, University of Toronto. Author of* The Last Cannon Shot: A Study of French-Canadian Nationalism.
LAURIER, SIR WILFRID (Micropædia)

J.M.O. Jane M. Oppenheimer. *Emeritus Professor of Biology and the History of Science, Bryn Mawr College, Pennsylvania. Author of* Essays in the History of Embryology and Biology.
BAER, KARL ERNST, RITTER VON, ELDER VON HUTHORN (Micropædia)
DRIESCH, HANS ADOLF EDUARD (Micropædia)

J.M.P. John M. Prausnitz. *Professor of Chemical Engineering, University of California, Berkeley. Author of* Molecular Thermodynamics of Fluid-Phase Equilibria.
MATTER (*in part*)

J.M.Po. James M. Powell. *Professor of Medieval History, Syracuse University, New York. Author of* Anatomy of a Crusade, 1213–21.
ALEXANDER III (PAPACY) (Micropædia)
GREGORY IX (PAPACY) (Micropædia)

J.M.R. Johannes M. Renger. *Professor of Assyriology, Free University of Berlin.*
HAMMURABI (Micropædia)

J.-M.-R.N. Jacques-M.-R. Nicolle (d. 1972). *Director, Laboratory of Isomeric Biochemistry, Collège de France, Paris. Author of* Louis Pasteur, a Master of Scientific Inquiry.
PASTEUR (*in part*)

J.M.S. John M. Simpson. *Senior Lecturer in Scottish History, University of Edinburgh.*
UNITED KINGDOM (*in part*)

J.M.T. James M. Tanner, M.D. *Emeritus Professor of Child Health and Growth, Institute of Child Health, University of London. Author of* A History of the Study of Human Growth *and others.*
GROWTH AND DEVELOPMENT, BIOLOGICAL (*in part*)

J.Mu. Joachim Müller. *Professor of German Literature, Friedrich Schiller University of Jena, Germany.*
LESSING, GOTTHOLD EPHRAIM (*in part*) (Micropædia)

J.M.W.-H. John Michael Wallace-Hadrill (d. 1985). *Chichele Professor of Modern History, University of Oxford, 1974–83; Fellow of All Souls College, Oxford. Author of* The Long-Haired Kings *and others.*
CLOVIS I (Micropædia)
GERMANY (*in part*)

J.M.Ws. James M. Wells. *Former Vice President and Emeritus Custodian, John M. Wing Foundation on the History of Printing, Newberry Library, Chicago. Author of* The Scholar Printers; "Book Typography in the U.S.A." *in* Book Typography in Europe and the U.S.
PRINTING, TYPOGRAPHY, AND PHOTOENGRAVING (*in part*)

J.M.W.S. Jonathan M.W. Slack. *Principal Research Scientist, Developmental Biology Unit, Imperial Cancer Research Fund, University of Oxford. Author of* From Egg to Embryo.
CELLS (*in part*)

J.N. Josef Nadler (d. 1963). *Professor of the History of Literature, University of Vienna, 1931–45.*
GERMAN LITERATURE (*in part*)

J.Na. Jerome Namias. *Research Meteorologist, Scripps Institution of Oceanography, University of California at San Diego, La Jolla. Chief, Extended Forecast Division, National Weather Service, National Oceanic and Atmospheric Administration, U.S. Department of Commerce, Washington, D.C., 1941–71. Author of* "30-Day Forecasting," American Meteorological Society Monograph.
ATLANTIC OCEAN, THE (*in part*)

J.N.B. John N. Burrus. *Distinguished University Professor Emeritus of Sociology and Anthropology, University of Southern Mississippi, Hattiesburg. Author of* Life Opportunities: An Analysis of Differential Mortality in Mississippi *and others.*
UNITED STATES OF AMERICA (*in part*)

J.N.C. John N. Cole. *Cofounder and Editor,* Maine Times, *Topsham, 1968–82. Author of* In Maine *and others.*
UNITED STATES OF AMERICA (*in part*)

J.N.D.   James Norman Davidson (d. 1972). *Gardiner Professor of Biochemistry, University of Glasgow, 1957–72. Author of* Biochemistry of the Nucleic Acids.
BIOCHEMICAL COMPONENTS OF ORGANISMS (*in part*)

J.N.D.K.   The Rev. John N.D. Kelly. *Principal of St. Edmund Hall, Oxford, 1951–79; Lecturer in Patristic Studies, University of Oxford, 1948–76. Author of* Early Christian Creeds; Early Christian Doctrines; *and others.*
CHRISTIANITY (*in part*)

J.N.G.   James Nelson Goodsell. *Latin America Correspondent, "World Monitor" (TV news program),* The Christian Science Monitor, *Boston. Editor of* Fidel Castro's Personal Revolution in Cuba: 1959–1973 *and others.*
HAVANA

J.N.H.   John N. Hazard. *Nash Professor Emeritus of Law, Columbia University. Author of* Communists and Their Law; Managing Change in the U.S.S.R.; *and others.*
LEGAL SYSTEMS, THE EVOLUTION OF MODERN WESTERN (*in part*)

J.N.M.   Jitendra N. Mohanty. *George Lynn Cross Research Professor of Philosophy, University of Oklahoma, Norman. Author of* Gaṅgeśa's Theory of Truth *and others.*
INDIAN PHILOSOPHY

J.N.S.   Johannes Nicolaas Scheepers. *Emeritus Professor of Geography, Rand Afrikaans University, Johannesburg; former Dean of Research. Author of* A Cartographic Analysis of the Man-Land Ratio: An Adventure into the Population Geography of the Transvaal.
SOUTH AFRICA (*in part*)

J.N.T.   John N. Tuppen. *Professor of Intercultural Communication and Linguistics, Lyon College of Business, France. Author of* The Economic Geography of France *and others.*
FRANCE (*in part*)

J.Nu.   Jack Nutting. *Metallurgical consultant. Emeritus Professor of Metallurgy, University of Leeds, England. Former President, Historical Metallurgy Society, London. Author of* Microstructure of Metals.
INDUSTRIES, EXTRACTION AND PROCESSING (*in part*)

J.O.   The Rev. Joseph Owens, C.SS.R. *Professor of Philosophy, Pontifical Institute of Mediaeval Studies, University of Toronto. Author of* The Doctrine of Being in the Aristotelian Metaphysics.
PHILOSOPHICAL SCHOOLS AND DOCTRINES, WESTERN (*in part*)

J.O.A.   James Oladipo Adejuwon. *Professor of Geography, Obafemi Awolowo University, Ile-Ife, Nigeria.*
KINSHASA (*in part*)

Jo.A.W.   John A. Wilson (d. 1976). *Andrew MacLeish Distinguished Service Professor of Egyptology, University of Chicago, 1953–68. Author of* The Burden of Egypt *and others.*
AKHENATON (Micropædia)

Jo.B.   José Bonilla. *Town and regional planning expert. Codirector, Regional and Urban Planning Institute, Buenos Aires, 1952–82.*
BUENOS AIRES (*in part*)

Jo.Be.   John Beresford Bentley. *Former Managing Editor,* Air-Cushion Vehicles *(bimonthly); former Editor,* Hoverfoil News.
TRANSPORTATION (*in part*)

Jo.B.M.   John Burnett Mitchell. *Lecturer in the History of Art, University of East Anglia, Norwich, England. Coeditor of* San Vincenzo al Volturno: The Archaeology, Art and Territory of an Early Medieval Monastery.
PAINTING, THE HISTORY OF WESTERN (*in part*)

Jo.Bo.   Sir John Boardman. *Lincoln Professor of Classical Art and Archaeology, University of Oxford. Fellow of the British Academy. Author of* Greek Art; The Greeks Overseas.
ARCHITECTURE, THE HISTORY OF WESTERN (*in part*)
PAINTING, THE HISTORY OF WESTERN (*in part*)
SCULPTURE, THE HISTORY OF WESTERN (*in part*)

Jo.Br.   John Bright. *Emeritus Professor of Hebrew and the Interpretation of the Old Testament, Union Theological Seminary, Richmond, Virginia. Author of* A History of Israel *and others.*
EZRA (Micropædia)

Jo.O'B.R.   John O'Beirne Ranelagh. *Television producer. Deputy Chief Executive and Director of Programmes, TV 2 Denmark, 1988. Commissioning Editor, Channel Four Television, London, 1981–87. Author of* A Short History of Ireland *and others.*
DUBLIN (*in part*)
IRELAND (*in part*)

Jo.Bu.   The Rev. John Burnaby (d. 1978). *Regius Professor of Divinity, University of Cambridge, 1952–58. Author of* Amor Dei: A Study in the Religion of St. Augustine *and others.*
AUGUSTINE (*in part*)

Jo.C.   John Cogley (d. 1976). *Senior Fellow, Center for the Study of Democratic Institutions, Santa Barbara, California, 1967–76; Editor,* The Center Magazine, *1967–74. Author of* The Layman and the Council *and others.*
JOHN XXIII (PAPACY) (Micropædia)

Jo.O.C.   John O. Corliss. *Emeritus Professor of Zoology, University of Maryland, College Park. Author of* The Ciliated Protozoa.
PROTISTS

Jo.Ch.   Joan Chissell. *Music critic. Assistant Music Critic,* The Times, *London, 1947–79. Author of* Chopin; Schumann *and others.*
CHOPIN, FRÉDÉRIC (*in part*) (Micropædia)

Jo.Co.   Johann Cooks. *Professor of Geography, University of Pretoria, South Africa. Author of* Exogenetic Landforms.
AFRICA (*in part*)

Jo.E.B.   John E. Bardach. *Senior Marine Advisor, Environment and Policy Institute, East-West Center, Honolulu. Author of* Harvest of the Sea *and others.*
PACIFIC OCEAN, THE (*in part*)

Jo.E.C.   John Edwards Caswell. *Emeritus Professor of History, California State College, Stanislaus, Turlock, California. Author of* Arctic Frontiers: U.S. Explorations in the Far North.
HUDSON, HENRY (Micropædia)

Jo.E.F.   John E. Flower. *Professor of French, University of Exeter, England. Author of* Literature and the Left in France.
FRANCE (*in part*)

Jo.E.S.   Joseph E. Spencer (d. 1984). *Emeritus Professor of Geography, University of California, Los Angeles. Coauthor of* Asia, East by South.
ASIA (*in part*)

J.O.Fl.   Joseph O. Fletcher. *Director, Environmental Research Laboratories, National Oceanic and Atmospheric Administration, U.S. Department of Commerce, Boulder, Colorado.*
ATLANTIC OCEAN, THE (*in part*)

Jo.H.   Josef Haekel (deceased). *Professor of Ethnology; Director, Institute for Ethnology, University of Vienna. Author of* Zum Individual- und Geschlechtstotemismus in Australien.
RELIGIONS AND SPIRITUAL BELIEF, SYSTEMS OF (*in part*)

Jo.Ha.   Joseph Hashisaki (deceased). *Professor of Mathematics, Western Washington University, Bellingham. Coauthor of* Theory of Arithmetic.
SET THEORY (*in part*)

Jo.Hac.   John Hackett. *Consultant, Organization for Economic Cooperation and Development, Paris; Director for Financial, Fiscal, and Enterprise Affairs, 1979–89. Author of* Economic Planning in France.
ECONOMIC GROWTH AND PLANNING (*in part*)

Jo.Ho.   John Hospers. *Emeritus Professor of Philosophy, University of Southern California, Los Angeles. Author of* Understanding the Arts *and others.*
PHILOSOPHIES OF THE BRANCHES OF KNOWLEDGE (*in part*)

Jo.La.   Jorgen Laessoe. *Professor of Assyriology, University of Copenhagen. Author of* People of Ancient Assyria *and others.*
SARGON II (ASSYRIA) (Micropædia)

Jo.Ly.   John Lynch. *Emeritus Professor of Latin American History, University of London. Author of* Spain Under the Habsburgs *and others.*
CHARLES III (SPAIN) (Micropædia)

Jo.M.   John Mitchell. *Free-lance writer and translator.*
ITALIAN LITERATURE (*in part*)

Jo.Ma. **John Marlowe.** *Free-lance writer. Author of* Anglo-Egyptian Relations, 1800–1953; Cromer in Egypt.
ZAGHLŪL, SAʿD (Micropædia)

J.O'M.B. **John O'M. Bockris.** *Distinguished Professor of Chemistry, Texas A&M University, College Station. Coauthor of* Fuel Cells: Their Electrochemistry; Modern Electrochemistry.
CHEMICAL REACTIONS (*in part*)

Jo.M.P. **Joseph Michael Powell.** *Reader in Geography, Monash University, Clayton, Victoria, Australia. Author of* An Historical Geography of Modern Australia *and others.*
AUSTRALIA (*in part*)

Jo.Ms. **John Markakis.** *Professor of African Studies, University of Crete, Réthimnon, Greece. Author of* Ethiopia: Anatomy of a Traditional Polity *and others.*
EASTERN AFRICA (*in part*)

Jo.N. **John Naisbitt.** *Social forecaster, lecturer, and writer. Author of* Megatrends *and others.*
UNITED STATES OF AMERICA (*in part*)

Jo.Pl. **Sir John Plumb.** *Professor of Modern English History, University of Cambridge, 1966–74; Master of Christ's College, Cambridge, 1978–82. Fellow of the British Academy. Author of* England in the Eighteenth Century; Sir Robert Walpole; *and others.*
WALPOLE, ROBERT, 1ST EARL OF ORFORD (Micropædia)

Jo.Pr. **Joshua Prawer** (d. 1990). *Professor of Medieval History, Hebrew University of Jerusalem, 1958–90. Editor in Chief,* Encyclopaedia Hebraica. *Author of* The History of the Jews in the Latin Kingdom of Jerusalem.
JERUSALEM (*in part*)

Jo.R. **John A. Rowe.** *Associate Professor of African History, Northwestern University, Evanston, Illinois.*
KENYATTA, JOMO (*in part*) (Micropædia)

J.Or. **Jean Orcibal.** *Director of Studies, Religious Sciences Division, Institute for Advanced Research, Paris.*
PASCAL (*in part*)

J.O.R. **John O. Rasmussen, Jr.** *Professor of Chemistry, University of California, Berkeley. Author of* "Models of Heavy Nuclei" *in* Nuclear Spectroscopy *and others.*
ATOMS (*in part*)

Jo.S. **The Rev. John Stacey.** *Secretary, Local Preachers' Office, British Methodist Church, London; Editor, Epworth Press. Author of* John Wyclif and Reform *and others.*
WYCLIFFE, JOHN (Micropædia)

J.O.S. **John Oliver Stoner, Jr.** *Professor of Physics, University of Arizona, Tucson.*
ANALYSIS AND MEASUREMENT, PHYSICAL AND CHEMICAL (*in part*)

Jo.Si. **Joseph Silverman.** *Professor of Chemical and Nuclear Engineering;* Director, Laboratory for Radiation and Polymer Science, University of Maryland, College Park. Coeditor of Radiation Processing: Transactions of the First International Meeting on Radiation Processing.
RADIATION (*in part*)

Jo.S.R. **John Shipley Rowlinson.** *Dr. Lee's Professor of Chemistry, University of Oxford. Author of* Liquids and Liquid Mixtures.
MATTER (*in part*)

Jo.St. **John Strugnell.** *Professor of Christian Origins, Harvard University.*
JOHN THE BAPTIST, SAINT (Micropædia)

J.O'T. **James Joseph O'Toole.** *University Associates' Professor of Management and Organization, University of Southern California, Los Angeles. Author of* Vanguard Management.
FUTUROLOGY (*in part*) (Micropædia)

Jö.We. **Jörgen Weibull.** *Emeritus Professor of History, Göteborg University, Sweden. Author of* Carl Johan och Norge 1810–1814 *and others.*
DENMARK (*in part*)
FINLAND (*in part*)
NORWAY (*in part*)
SWEDEN (*in part*)

Jo.W.H. **Sir John Wardle Houlton** (d. 1973). *President of the Swaziland Senate, 1968–73.*
SOUTHERN AFRICA (*in part*)

Jo.W.P. **John Whitney Pickersgill.** *President, Canadian Transport Commission, Ottawa, 1967–72. Member, House of Commons, Parliament of Canada, 1953–67. Coauthor of* The Mackenzie King Record.
KING, W.L. MACKENZIE (Micropædia)

J.P. **Jan Pen.** *Professor of Economics, State University of Groningen, The Netherlands. Author of* Income Distribution *and others.*
ECONOMIC THEORY (*in part*)

J.Pa. **Juan Papadakis.** *Member, Academy of Athens. Former Professor, University of Buenos Aires. Author of* Soils of the World.
SOILS

J.P.A.G. **Johannes P.A. Gruijters.** *Mayor of Lelystad, The Netherlands. Minister of Housing and Physical Planning, Government of The Netherlands, 1973–77.*
NETHERLANDS, THE (*in part*)

J.P.D. **Jean P. Dorst.** *Professor, National Museum of Natural History, Paris. Author of* The Migration of Birds *and others.*
BEHAVIOUR, ANIMAL (*in part*)
SOUTH AMERICA (*in part*)

J.P.Do. **Jean P. Doresse.** *Research Master, National Centre for Scientific Research, Paris. Author of* Ethiopia *and others.*
EASTERN AFRICA (*in part*)

J.P.-H. **Sir John Pope-Hennessy.** *Professor of Fine Arts, New York University. Consultative Chairman,* Department of European Paintings, Metropolitan Museum of Art, New York City, 1977–86. Author of Italian Renaissance Sculpture; Cellini; and others.
CELLINI, BENVENUTO (Micropædia)

J.P.Hy. **J. Philip Hyatt** (d. 1972). *Professor of Old Testament, Vanderbilt University, Nashville, Tennessee, 1944–72. Author of* Jeremiah: Prophet of Courage and Hope *and others.*
JEREMIAH (*in part*) (Micropædia)

J.Pi. **John Picton.** *Lecturer in African Art, School of Oriental and African Studies, University of London. Coauthor of* African Textiles.
AFRICAN ARTS (*in part*)

J.Piv. **Jean Piveteau.** *Professor of Palaeontology, University of Paris. Editor of* Oeuvres philosophiques de Buffon.
BUFFON, GEORGES-LOUIS LECLERC, COMTE DE (Micropædia)

J.P.K. **John P. Kenyon.** *Joyce and Elizabeth Hall Distinguished Professor of Early Modern British History, University of Kansas, Lawrence. Professor of Modern History, University of St. Andrews, Scotland, 1981–87. Author of* The Stuarts.
JAMES II (GREAT BRITAIN) (Micropædia)

J.-p.L. **Jung-pang Lo** (d. 1981). *Professor of History, University of California, Davis, 1969–76. Author of* K'ang Yu-wei: A Biography and a Symposium.
CHENG HO (Micropædia)
K'ANG YU-WEI (Micropædia)

J.Pl. **Jaan Puhvel.** *Professor of Classics and Indo-European Studies, University of California, Los Angeles.*
HISTORY, THE STUDY OF (*in part*)
WRITING (*in part*)

J.P.M. **John Preston Moore.** *Emeritus Professor of History, Louisiana State University, Baton Rouge. Author of* The Cabildo in Peru Under the Bourbons *and others.*
PERU (*in part*)

J.P.Mo. **J. Philip Mosley.** *Assistant Professor of English and Comparative Literature, Pennsylvania State University, Worthington Scranton Campus, Dunmore.*
BELGIAN LITERATURE (*in part*)

J.P.M.S. **J. Patricia Morgan Swenson.** *Free-lance writer and editor. Author of* Hawaii: A Book to Begin On *and others.*
UNITED STATES OF AMERICA (*in part*)

J.P.P. **Justo Pastor Prieto** (d. 1982). *Former Minister of Foreign Affairs, Paraguay, 1939; Minister of Justice and Public Education, 1931–36. Rector, National University of Asunción, 1929–31. Author of* Paraguay, la provincia gigante de las Indias *and others.*
PARAGUAY (*in part*)

J.P.Pl. **John P. Plamenatz** (d. 1975). *Chichele Professor of Social and Political Theory, University of Oxford, 1967–75; Fellow of All Souls College, Oxford.*

Author of The English Utilitarians.
BENTHAM, JEREMY (*in part*)
  (Micropædia)

J.P.P.R. J.P. Perry Robinson. *Senior Fellow, Science Policy Research Unit, University of Sussex, Brighton, England. Coauthor of* The Problem of Chemical and Biological Warfare (6 *vol.*).
WAR, THE TECHNOLOGY OF (*in part*)

J.Pr. Jean Prevost. *Professor of Biology, French University of the Pacific, Nouméa, New Caledonia. Author of* Le Manchot empereur; *coeditor of* Biologie antarctique.
BIRDS (*in part*)

J.P.R. Jean Pierre Rouch. *Director of Research, National Centre for Scientific Research, Paris. Author of* Les Songhay.
MUḤAMMAD I ASKIA (Micropædia)

J.P.Ri. Joseph P. Riva, Jr. *Specialist in Earth Sciences (geologist), Congressional Research Service, Library of Congress, Washington, D.C. Author of* World Petroleum Resources and Reserves.
FUELS, FOSSIL (*in part*)

J.P.S. James Patrick Saville. *Former Manager, Information Services, The Metals Society, London.*
BESSEMER, SIR HENRY (Micropædia)

J.P.-V. Javier Pulgar-Vidal. *Emeritus Professor of Geography, National University of San Marcos, Lima. Author of* Geografía del Perú: Las ocho regiones naturales *and others.*
PERU (*in part*)

J.P.V.D.B. John P.V. Dacre Balsdon (d. 1977). *Fellow of Exeter College, University of Oxford, 1928–69. Author of* Life and Leisure in Ancient Rome.
CICERO, MARCUS TULLIUS (*in part*)
  (Micropædia)
MARIUS, GAIUS (Micropædia)

J.R. Jacques Ryckmans. *Professor of Medieval Studies, Catholic University of Louvain, Belgium. Author of* La Persécution des Chrétiens Himyarites au Sixième Siècle *and others.*
MIDDLE EASTERN RELIGIONS, ANCIENT
  (*in part*)

J.R.B. James R. Brandon. *Professor of Drama and Theatre, University of Hawaii, at Manoa, Honolulu. Author of* Kabuki: Five Classic Plays; Theatre in Southeast Asia; *and others.*
EAST ASIAN ARTS (*in part*)
SOUTHEAST ASIAN ARTS (*in part*)

J.R.Ba. John R. Baines. *Professor of Egyptology, University of Oxford. Coauthor of* Atlas of Ancient Egypt.
EGYPT (*in part*)
MIDDLE EASTERN RELIGIONS, ANCIENT
  (*in part*)

J.R.Br. John Russell Brown. *Professor of Theatre, University of Michigan, Ann Arbor. Author of* Shakespeare's Dramatic Style *and others.*
SHAKESPEARE (*in part*)

J.R.C. John R. Campbell. *President, Oklahoma State University, Stillwater. Dean, College of Agriculture, University* of Illinois at Urbana-Champaign, 1983–88. *Coauthor of* The Science of Animals That Serve Humanity.
AGRICULTURAL SCIENCES (*in part*)

J.R.D. Jere R. Daniell. *Professor of History, Dartmouth College, Hanover, New Hampshire. Author of* Colonial New Hampshire: A History *and others.*
UNITED STATES OF AMERICA (*in part*)

J.R.G. James R. Giles. *Professor of English, Northern Illinois University, De Kalb. Author of* Confronting the Horror: The Novels of Nelson Algren *and others.*
AMERICAN LITERATURE (*in part*)

J.R.Go. John Ross Goodner. *Senior Editor,* Golf Digest. *Author of* Golf's Greatest *and others.*
SPORTS, MAJOR TEAM AND INDIVIDUAL
  (*in part*)

J.R.Kr. John Richard Krueger. *Former Professor of Uralic and Altaic Studies, Indiana University, Bloomington. Coauthor of* Introduction to Classical Mongolian.
CENTRAL ASIAN ARTS (*in part*)

J.R.L.H. J.R.L. Highfield. *Emeritus Fellow of Merton College, Oxford; former Lecturer in Modern History, University of Oxford. Editor of* Spain in the Fifteenth Century; *coeditor of* Europe in the Late Middle Ages.
EDWARD III (ENGLAND AND GREAT
  BRITAIN) (*in part*) (Micropædia)
ISABELLA I (SPAIN) (Micropædia)

J.R.M. John Richard Meyer. *Associate Professor of Education, University of Windsor, Ontario.*
BERNARD DE CLAIRVAUX, SAINT
  (Micropædia)

J.R.Ma. Judith R. Mackrell. *Dance critic,* The Independent, *London.*
DANCE, THE ART OF

J.R.Me. José Ramón Medina. *Poet and writer. Professor, Faculty of Law, Central University of Venezuela, Caracas. Comptroller General of Venezuela; former Ambassador to Greece and Attorney General. Author of* Ochenta años de literatura venezolana *and others.*
CARACAS (*in part*)

J.R.Mn. J. Ronald Munson. *Professor of Philosophy, University of Missouri, St. Louis. Author of* Reasoning in Medicine.
PHILOSOPHIES OF THE BRANCHES OF
  KNOWLEDGE (*in part*)

J.R.Mo. Joseph R. Morgan. *Associate Professor of Geography, University of Hawaii at Manoa, Honolulu. Research Associate, Environment and Policy Institute, East-West Center, Honolulu. Coeditor of* Atlas for Marine Policy in Southeast Asian Seas.
INDIAN OCEAN, THE (*in part*)
PACIFIC OCEAN, THE (*in part*)

J.R.M.R. J. Roberto Moncada R. *President, MONDAI Engineers (engineering and architectural consultants), Tegucigalpa, Honduras. Director General of the National Geographic Institute, Tegucigalpa,* 1969–71.
CENTRAL AMERICA (*in part*)

J.R.N. J.R. Napier (d. 1987). *Director, Unit of Primate Biology, Birkbeck College, University of London. Coauthor of* A Handbook of Living Primates; The Natural History of the Primates.
MAMMALS (*in part*)

J.Ro. Joan Violet Robinson (d. 1983). *Professor of Economics, University of Cambridge, 1965–71. Author of* Theory of Imperfect Competition *and others.*
MARKETS (*in part*)

J.R.P. John R. Pierce. *Emeritus Professor of Engineering, California Institute of Technology, Pasadena. Author of* The Beginnings of Satellite Communications *and others.*
TELECOMMUNICATIONS SYSTEMS
  (*in part*)

J.R.Po. J.R. Pole. *Rhodes Professor Emeritus of American History and Institutions, University of Oxford. Author of* Political Representation in England and the Origins of the American Republic.
UNITED STATES OF AMERICA (*in part*)

J.R.P.R. June R.P. Ross. *Professor and Chair, Department of Biology, Western Washington University, Bellingham. Editor of* Bryozoa: Present and Past.
GEOCHRONOLOGY (*in part*)

J.R.-S. John Graham Royde-Smith (d. 1986). *Associate Editor, History, Encyclopædia Britannica, London.*
BOURBON, THE HOUSE OF (*in part*)
HABSBURG, THE HOUSE OF
WORLD WARS, THE (*in part*)

J.R.Sp. John R. Spencer. *Professor of Art, Duke University, Durham, North Carolina. Editor of L.B. Alberti's* On Painting.
CIMABUE (Micropædia)
PAINTING, THE HISTORY OF WESTERN
  (*in part*)
SCULPTURE, THE HISTORY OF WESTERN
  (*in part*)

J.R.T. John Russell Taylor. *Art Critic,* The Times (*London*); *Film Critic, 1962–73. Professor of Cinema, University of Southern California, Los Angeles, 1972–78. Author of* Cinema Eye, Cinema Ear: Some Key Film-Makers of the Sixties.
ANTONIONI, MICHELANGELO
  (Micropædia)
BERGMAN, INGMAR (Micropædia)

J.R.T.P. John Richard Thornhill Pollard. *Former Senior Lecturer in Classics, University College of North Wales, University of Wales, Bangor. Author of* Birds in Greek Life and Myth; Helen of Troy; *and others.*
EUROPEAN RELIGIONS, ANCIENT (*in part*)

J.R.V.P. John R.V. Prescott. *Professor of Geography, University of Melbourne. Author of* Political Frontiers and Boundaries *and others.*
AUSTRALIA (*in part*)
MELBOURNE

J.S. John Scarne (d. 1985). *President, John Scarne Games, Inc., North Bergen,*

New Jersey. Authority on gambling. Author of Scarne's Complete Guide to Gambling; Scarne on Dice; *and others.*
ROULETTE (Micropædia)

J.S.A.   James Stephen Atherton (deceased). *Lecturer in English Literature, Wigan and District Mining and Technical College, England. Author of* The Books at the Wake.
JOYCE, JAMES (*in part*) (Micropædia)

J.S.Ac.   James S. Ackerman. *Arthur Kingsley Porter Professor of Fine Arts, Harvard University. Author of* The Architecture of Michelangelo; Palladio.
ARCHITECTURE, THE ART OF (*in part*)

J.S.B.   Joe S. Bain (d. 1991). *Professor of Economics, University of California, Berkeley, 1949–75. Author of* Industrial Organization; Barriers to New Competition.
ECONOMIC THEORY (*in part*)

J.S.Bo.   John S. Bowman. *Free-lance writer and editor. Editor, "Monuments of Civilization" Series. Author of* Traveler's Guide to Crete.
GREECE (*in part*)

J.S.Br.   The Rev. Joseph Stanislaus Brusher, S.J. (d. 1972). *Professor of History, University of San Francisco, 1968–72. Author of* Popes Through the Ages.
GREGORY VII, SAINT (PAPACY) (Micropædia)

J.Sc.   Jefim H. Schirmann (d. 1981). *Professor of Hebrew Literature, Hebrew University of Jerusalem. Member, Israel National Academy of Sciences. Author of* The Hebrew Poetry in Spain and Provence.
JUDAH HA-LEVI (Micropædia)

J.Sch.   Johannes Schregle. *Honorary President, International Society for Labour Law and Social Security. Honorary Professor of International and Comparative Labour Law, University of Salzburg, Austria. Former Director of Industrial Relations, International Labour Office, International Labour Organisation, Geneva. Author of* Negotiating Development: Labour Relations in Southern Asia.
BUSINESS LAW (*in part*)

J.S.D.   John S. Driscoll. *Editor, Boston Globe.*
UNITED STATES OF AMERICA (*in part*)

J.Se.   Jakob Seibert. *Professor of Ancient History, Ludwig Maximilian University of Munich. Author of* Historische Beiträge zu den dynastischen Verbindungen in hellenistischer Zeit.
SELEUCUS I NICATOR (Micropædia)

J.S.E.   John S. Ezell. *David Ross Boyd Professor Emeritus of History, University of Oklahoma, Norman. Author of* The South Since 1865.
UNITED STATES OF AMERICA (*in part*)

J.S.F.   Jeffrey S. Fedan. *Research Pharmacologist, National Institute for Occupational Safety and Health, Morgantown, West Virginia. Professor of Pharmacology and Toxicology, West Virginia University, Morgantown.*
DRUGS AND DRUG ACTION (*in part*)

J.S.G.W.   John Stuart Gladstone Wilson. *Emeritus Professor of Economics and Commerce, University of Hull, England. Author of* Banking Policy and Structure.
BANKS AND BANKING (*in part*)

J.Sh.   Jose Shercliff (deceased). *Lisbon Correspondent of* The Times (*London*), *and the British Broadcasting Corporation.*
PORTUGAL (*in part*)

J.Shi.   James Shiel. *Former Reader in the History of Hellenic Thought, University of Sussex, Brighton, England. Author of* Greek Thought and the Rise of Christianity.
BOETHIUS, ANICIUS MANLIUS SEVERINUS (Micropædia)

J.Si.   Josef Silverstein. *Professor of Political Science, Rutgers University, New Brunswick, New Jersey. Author of* Burma: Military Rule and the Politics of Stagnation *and others.*
SOUTHEAST ASIA, MAINLAND (*in part*)

J.S.K.   James S. Kus. *Professor and Chairman, Department of Geography, California State University, Fresno.*
PERU (*in part*)

J.S.M.   John S. Mathis. *Professor of Astronomy, University of Wisconsin, Madison.*
NEBULA

J.S.Ma.   John S. Marshall (d. 1979). *Professor of Philosophy, University of the South, Sewanee, Tennessee, 1946–68. Author of* Hooker's Polity in Modern English; Hooker and the Anglican Tradition.
HOOKER, RICHARD (Micropædia)

J.S.McE.   The Rev. James Stevenson McEwen. *Professor of Church History, University of Aberdeen, Scotland, 1958–77. Author of* The Faith of John Knox.
KNOX, JOHN (*in part*) (Micropædia)

J.Sn.   Joshua Stern. *Lecturer in Physics, University of Maryland, College Park. Associate Editor,* Review of Scientific Instruments.
MEASUREMENT AND OBSERVATION, PRINCIPLES, METHODS, AND INSTRUMENTS OF (*in part*)

J.So.   Jacob Solinger. *Management consultant. Author of* Apparel Manufacturing Analysis; Apparel Manufacturing Handbook.
INDUSTRIES, MANUFACTURING (*in part*)

J.S.O.   Jerry S. Olson. *Senior Ecologist, Environmental Sciences Division, Oak Ridge National Laboratory, Tennessee. Professor of Botany, University of Tennessee, Knoxville. Editor of* Ecological Studies.
BIOSPHERE, THE (*in part*)

J.S.R.   John S. Ryland. *Professor of Marine Biology, University College of Swansea, University of Wales. Author of* Bryozoans.
MOSS ANIMALS

J.S.Ro.   James Scott Robson, M.D. *Emeritus Professor of Medicine, University of Edinburgh; Consultant Physician, Edinburgh Royal Infirmary. Author of numerous articles on acid-base and electrolyte metabolism and renal disorders.*
EXCRETION AND EXCRETORY SYSTEMS (*in part*)
TISSUES AND FLUIDS (*in part*)

J.S.-Sm.   James Stuart-Smith. *Judge Advocate General of the United Kingdom. President, International Society for Military Law and the Law of War. Contributor to* Law Quarterly Review.
WAR, THE THEORY AND CONDUCT OF (*in part*)

J.S.Sz.   Joseph S. Szyliowicz. *Professor of International Relations, University of Denver, Colorado. Author of* Education and Modernization in the Middle East.
EDUCATION, HISTORY OF (*in part*)

J.S.T.   Joseph S. Tulchin. *Professor of History, University of North Carolina at Chapel Hill. Coeditor of* Latin America in World Politics.
BUENOS AIRES (*in part*)

J.Ste.   Johannes Steudel (d. 1973). *Professor of the History of Medicine, Rhenish Friedrich Wilhelm University of Bonn.*
MÜLLER, JOHANNES PETER (Micropædia)

J.Sum.   Sir John Summerson. *Curator, Sir John Soane's House and Museum, London, 1945–84. Author of* Inigo Jones; Sir Christopher Wren; Architecture in Britain, 1530–1830; *and others.*
JONES, INIGO (Micropædia)
WREN, SIR CHRISTOPHER (*in part*) (Micropædia)

J.S.W.   John Steven Watson (d. 1986). *Principal and Vice-Chancellor, University of St. Andrews, Scotland, 1966–86. Author of* The Reign of George III.
GEORGE III (GREAT BRITAIN) (Micropædia)

J.T.   John Taylor. *Senior Research Fellow, Centre for Aboriginal Economic Policy Research, Australian National University, Canberra. Author of* Aboriginal People in the Northern Territory; *coauthor of* A Social Atlas of Darwin.
AUSTRALIA (*in part*)

J.T.B.   Joseph T. Butler. *Senior Museum Director, Historic Hudson Valley, Tarrytown, New York. Professor, Fashion Institute of Technology, New York City. Author of* American Antiques 1800–1900 *and others.*
DECORATIVE ARTS AND FURNISHINGS (*in part*)

J.T.Bo.   John Tyler Bonner. *George M. Moffett Professor of Biology, Princeton University. Author of* The Evolution of Complexity by Means of Natural Selection *and others.*
REPRODUCTION AND REPRODUCTIVE SYSTEMS (*in part*)

J.T.C.   J. Terry Copp. *Professor of History, Wilfrid Laurier University,*

Waterloo, Ontario. Coauthor of Confederation: 1867 *and others.*
BORDEN, SIR ROBERT (Micropædia)

J.T.C.L.   James T.C. Liu. *Professor of History and of East Asian Studies, Princeton University. Author of* China Turning Inward *and others.*
CHINA (*in part*)

J.T.G.O.   Jan Theodoor Gerard Overbeek. *Emeritus Professor of Physical Chemistry, Utrecht University, The Netherlands. Coauthor of* Theory of the Stability of Lyophobic Colloids.
MATTER (*in part*)

J.Th.   John Patrick Thomas. *Singer and composer. Former Assistant Professor of Music, State University of New York at Buffalo.*
MUSIC, THE ART OF (*in part*)

J.T.H.   James T. Harris. *Former Regional Representative for West Africa (Lagos, Nigeria) for the African-American Institute, New York City.*
UNITED STATES OF AMERICA (*in part*)

J.T.M.   Joe T. Marshall. *Zoologist, National Fish and Wildlife Laboratory, National Museum of Natural History, Washington, D.C. Coauthor of* Birds of Arizona.
BIRDS (*in part*)

J.T.Mi.   John T. Mickel. *Curator of Ferns, New York Botanical Garden, Bronx. Author of* The Home Gardener's Book of Ferns; How to Know the Ferns and Fern Allies.
FERNS (*in part*)

J.T.Pa.   John T. Paoletti. *Professor of Art History, Wesleyan University, Middletown, Connecticut.*
UCCELLO, PAOLO (Micropædia)

J.T.S.   James T. Staley. *Senior Technical Consultant, Advanced Alloys and Processes, Alcoa Laboratories, Aluminum Company of America, Pittsburgh.*
INDUSTRIES, EXTRACTION AND PROCESSING (*in part*)

J.T.Sc.   Jacob T. Schwartz. *Chairman, Department of Computer Science, Courant Institute of Mathematical Sciences, New York University, New York City. Author of* Mathematical Methods in Analytical Economics; *coauthor of* Linear Operators.
ANALYSIS (IN MATHEMATICS) (*in part*)

J.U.   Jürgen Untermann. *Professor of Comparative Philology, University of Cologne. Author of* Die venetischen Personennamen.
LANGUAGES OF THE WORLD (*in part*)

Ju.H.   Julius S. Held. *Emeritus Professor of Art History, Barnard College, Columbia University. Author of* Flemish Painting *and others.*
VAN DYCK, SIR ANTHONY (Micropædia)

Ju.S.   Julius Stone (d. 1985). *Professor of Law, University of New South Wales, Kensington, Australia. Distinguished Professor of Jurisprudence and International Law, University of*

California Hastings College of Law, San Francisco. Challis Professor of Jurisprudence and International Law, University of Sydney, Australia, 1942–72. Author of The Province and Function of Law *and others.*
PHILOSOPHIES OF THE BRANCHES OF KNOWLEDGE (*in part*)

Ju.S.B.   Julia S. Berrall. *Free-lance lecturer and writer. Author of* Flowers and Table Settings; The Garden: An Illustrated History; A History of Flower Arrangement.
DECORATIVE ARTS AND FURNISHINGS (*in part*)

J.v.E.   Josef van Ess. *Professor of Islamic Studies and Semitic Languages, Eberhard Karl University of Tübingen, Germany. Author of* Die Erkenntnislehre des 'Aḍudaddīn al-Ícī.
MUḤĀSIBĪ, AL- (Micropædia)

J.V.F.   J. Valerie Fifer. *Honorary Research Fellow, Institute of Latin American Studies, University of London, 1986–89. Author of* Bolivia: Land, Location, and Politics since 1825.
BOLIVIA (*in part*)

J.V.G.   Juan Vernet Ginés. *Emeritus Professor of Arabic, University of Barcelona. Author of* Los Musulmanes españoles *and others.*
SPAIN (*in part*)

J.v.H.   Jan S.F. van Hoogstraten. *Former Chief of Mission, Intergovernmental Committee for Migration, Bonn. Former Church World Service Director, Africa Department, National Council of the Churches of Christ in the U.S.A.*
CENTRAL AFRICA (*in part*)

J.Vi.   Jean Vidalenc. *Former Professor of Contemporary History, University of Rouen, France. Author of* Louis Blanc; La Restauration (1814–1830).
BLANC, LOUIS (Micropædia)
MARAT, JEAN-PAUL (Micropædia)
THIERS, ADOLPHE (Micropædia)

J.V.K.   John V. Killheffer. *Associate Editor, Science,* Encyclopædia Britannica, *Chicago, 1971–88.*
CHEMICAL COMPOUNDS (*in part*)
INDUSTRIES, CHEMICAL PROCESS (*in part*)

J.V.M.   John V. Murra. *President, Institute of Andean Research, New York City. Emeritus Professor of Anthropology, Cornell University, Ithaca, New York. Author of* The Economic Organization of the Inka State *and others.*
AMERICAN INDIANS (*in part*)
PRE-COLUMBIAN CIVILIZATIONS (*in part*)

J.V.N.   Joseph Veach Noble. *Emeritus Director, Museum of the City of New York, New York City. Author of* The Techniques of Painted Attic Pottery; *coauthor of* An Inquiry into the Forgery of the Etruscan Terracotta Warriors in the Metropolitan Museum of Art.
ARTS, PRACTICE AND PROFESSION OF THE (*in part*)

J.Vo.   Jack Vowles. *Lecturer in Political Studies, University of Auckland,*

New Zealand.
NEW ZEALAND (*in part*)

J.V.R.   Jan L.R. Van Roey. *Honorary Archivist, City Archives, Antwerp.*
ANTWERP (*in part*)

J.V.W.   James V. Warren, M.D. (d. 1990). *Professor of Medicine, Ohio State University, Columbus, 1961–86. Contributor to* Textbook of Medicine; The Heart.
CIRCULATION AND CIRCULATORY SYSTEMS (*in part*)

J.W.B.   James W. Byrkit. *Professor of Interdisciplinary Studies and Research Associate, Northern Arizona University, Flagstaff. Author of* Forging the Copper Collar: Arizona's Labor-Management War, 1901–1921.
UNITED STATES OF AMERICA (*in part*)

J.W.Ba.   John Walton Barker, Jr. *Professor of History, University of Wisconsin, Madison. Author of* Justinian and the Later Roman Empire *and others.*
BELISARIUS (Micropædia)

J.W.C.   John W. Caughey. *Emeritus Professor of American History, University of California, Los Angeles. Author of* McGillivray of the Creeks.
MCGILLIVRAY, ALEXANDER (Micropædia)

J.We.   Jac Weller. *Weapons engineer, military historian, and free-lance writer. Author of* Weapons and Tactics; *coauthor of* Firearms Investigation, Identification, and Evidence.
WAR, THE TECHNOLOGY OF (*in part*)

J.W.F.   J.W. Fiegenbaum. *Professor of Religion, Mount Holyoke College, South Hadley, Massachusetts.*
ḤALLĀJ, AL- (Micropædia)
IBN ḤAZM (Micropædia)

J.W.H.   Joseph W. Harpster. *President, Intek Inc., Columbus, Ohio.*
ENERGY CONVERSION (*in part*)

J.W.Ha.   John W. Harbaugh. *Professor of Applied Earth Sciences, Stanford University, California. Coauthor of* Computer Simulation in Geology.
EARTH SCIENCES, THE (*in part*)

J.W.Hu.   John W. Huffman, M.D. (d. 1989). *Emeritus Professor of Obstetrics and Gynecology, Medical School, Northwestern University, Chicago, 1962–73. Author of* Gynecology and Obstetrics.
REPRODUCTION AND REPRODUCTIVE SYSTEMS (*in part*)

J.Wi.   J. Williams. *Former Deputy Director, Atomic Energy Research Establishment, United Kingdom Atomic Energy Authority, Harwell, England.*
INDUSTRIES, EXTRACTION AND PROCESSING (*in part*)

J.W.J.   Jeffrey W. Jacobs. *Research Assistant, Research and Applications Information Center, Institute of Behavioral Science, University of Colorado at Boulder.*
ASIA (*in part*)

J.W.Ja.   John W. James. *Associate Professor of Geography, University of Nevada, Reno. State Climatologist for*

Nevada. An authority on the alpine environment.
NORTH AMERICA (*in part*)

J.W.K.   John W. Kendrick. *Emeritus Professor of Economics, George Washington University, Washington, D.C. Former Chief Economist, U.S. Department of Commerce. Author of* Productivity Trends in the United States.
ECONOMIC GROWTH AND PLANNING (*in part*)

J.W.L.   Justin W. Leonard (d. 1975). *Professor of Natural Resources and of Zoology; Research Associate, Museum of Zoology, University of Michigan, Ann Arbor, 1964–75. Coauthor of* Mayflies of Michigan Trout Streams.
INSECTS (*in part*)

J.W.Le.   John Wilson Lewis. *William Haas Professor of Chinese Politics, Stanford University, California. Author of* Leadership in Communist China.
CHINA (*in part*)
TAIWAN (*in part*)

J.W.McF.   James Walter McFarlane. *Emeritus Professor of European Literature, University of East Anglia, Norwich, England. Author of* Ibsen and the Temper of Norwegian Literature; *editor and translator of* The Oxford Ibsen.
SCANDINAVIAN LITERATURE (*in part*)

J.Wo.   John Woodward (d. 1988). *Keeper, Birmingham City Museum and Art Gallery, Birmingham, England. Author of* A Picture History of British Painting.
REYNOLDS, SIR JOSHUA (Micropædia)

J.W.O.   John W. Osborne. *Professor of History, Rutgers University, New Brunswick, New Jersey. Author of* William Cobbett: His Thoughts and His Times *and others.*
COBBETT, WILLIAM (Micropædia)

J.W.R.   James Wilmot Rowe. *Economic and international consultant. Former Executive Director, New Zealand Employers' Federation, Wellington. Coauthor of* New Zealand.
NEW ZEALAND (*in part*)

J.W.R.T.   John W.R. Taylor. *Emeritus Editor,* Jane's All the World's Aircraft. *Author of* Combat Aircraft of the World; History of Aerial Warfare; *and others.*
WAR, THE TECHNOLOGY OF (*in part*)

J.W.T.   John Walford Todd, M.D. (d. 1989). *Consultant Physician, Frimley Park and Farnham Hospitals, Farnham, England. Author of* Health and Humanity.
MEDICINE (*in part*)

J.W.Th.   John W. Thieret. *Professor of Botany, Northern Kentucky University, Highland Heights. Coauthor of* Trees.
ANGIOSPERMS (*in part*)

J.W.W.   James Wreford Watson (d. 1990). *Professor of Geography, University of Edinburgh, 1954–82. Author of* North America: Its Countries and Regions *and others.*
NORTH AMERICA (*in part*)

J.W.Wr.   John Wilfrid Wright. *Land surveyor; free-lance writer and lecturer. Author of* Ground and Air Survey for Field Scientists.
MAPPING AND SURVEYING (*in part*)

J.Y.S.   John Y. Simon. *Professor of History, Southern Illinois University, Carbondale. Executive Director, Ulysses S. Grant Association. Editor of* The Papers of Ulysses S. Grant.
GRANT, ULYSSES S. (Micropædia)

J.Z.S.   Jonathan Z. Smith. *Robert O. Anderson Distinguished Service Professor of the Humanities, University of Chicago. Author of* To Take Place: Toward Theory in Ritual *and others.*
EUROPEAN RELIGIONS, ANCIENT (*in part*)
MYTH AND MYTHOLOGY (*in part*)

J.Z.V.   Josefina Zoraida Vázquez. *Professor of History, College of Mexico, Mexico City. Author of* Nacionalismo y educación en México.
EDUCATION, HISTORY OF (*in part*)

K.A.B.   Kenneth A. Ballhatchet. *Former Professor of the History of South Asia, School of Oriental and African Studies, University of London. Author of* Race, Sex and Class under the Raj.
AKBAR (Micropædia)
DALHOUSIE, JAMES ANDREW BROUN RAMSAY, MARQUESS AND 10TH EARL OF (Micropædia)

K.A.H.   Keith Arnold Hitchins. *Professor of History, University of Illinois at Urbana-Champaign. Author of* Orthodoxy and Nationality.
UNION OF SOVIET SOCIALIST REPUBLICS (*in part*)

K.A.J.W.   Keith Arthur John Wise. *Entomologist, Auckland Institute and Museum, New Zealand.*
INSECTS (*in part*)

K.A.M.   Kazimieras Antano Meškauskas. *Department Chief, Institute of Economics, former Chief Learned Secretary of the Presidium, Lithuanian Academy of Sciences. Author of* Soviet Lithuania: An Economic Survey *and others.*
BALTIC STATES (*in part*)

K.A.S.   Kaj Aa. Strand. *Scientific Director, U.S. Naval Observatory, Washington, D.C., 1963–77. Editor of* Basic Astronomical Data; Vistas in Astronomy.
PARALLAX (*in part*) (Micropædia)

K.A.Sc.   Karl A. Schleunes. *Professor of History, University of North Carolina at Greensboro. Author of* The Twisted Road to Auschwitz.
GERMANY (*in part*)

K.A.Si.   Karl A. Sinnhuber. *Emeritus Professor of Economic Geography, Vienna University of Commerce. Author of* Germany, Its Geography and Growth.
EUROPE (*in part*)

K.A.St.   Kaydon Al Stanzione. *Senior Engineer, Advanced Vehicle Aerodynamics, Boeing Vertol Company, Philadelphia.*
ENGINEERING (*in part*)

K.A.W.C.   Keith A.W. Crook. *Reader in Geology, Australian National University, Canberra. Coauthor of* Geological Evolution of Australia and New Zealand.
MINERALS AND ROCKS (*in part*)

K.B.   Knut Bergsland. *Emeritus Professor of Finno-Ugric Languages, University of Oslo. Scholar who proved the connection between the Eskimo and Aleut languages. Author of* "Aleut Dialects of Atka and Attu" *in* Transactions of the American Philosophical Society.
LANGUAGES OF THE WORLD (*in part*)

K.Ba.   Kurt Badt (d. 1973). *Art historian. Author of* Die Kunst des Nicolas Poussin; John Constable's Clouds; The Art of Cézanne; *and others.*
POUSSIN, NICOLAS (Micropædia)

K.B.D.   Kwamina Busumafi Dickson. *Vice-Chancellor, University of Cape Coast, Ghana. Author of* A Historical Geography of Ghana.
AFRICA (*in part*)

K.Be.   Karl Beckson. *Professor of English, Brooklyn College, City University of New York. Editor of* Aesthetes and Decadents of the 1890's; Oscar Wilde: The Critical Heritage.
WILDE, OSCAR (Micropædia)

K.-b.L.   Ki-baik Lee. *Professor of History, Sogang University, Seoul, Korea. Author of* Hankuksa sillon.
KOREA (*in part*)

K.B.M.   Kathleen Berton Murrell. *Researcher on the history of Moscow. Author of* Moscow: An Architectural History.
MOSCOW (*in part*)

K.Br.   Sir Kenneth Bradley (d. 1977). *Director, Commonwealth Institute, London, 1953–69.*
SOUTHERN AFRICA (*in part*)

K.C.B.   Kevin Charles Beck. *Associate Professor of Geophysical Sciences, Georgia Institute of Technology, Atlanta. Coauthor of* Clay Water Diagenesis During Burial: How Mud Becomes Gneiss.
MINERALS AND ROCKS (*in part*)

K.C.C.   Karine Carole Chemla. *Research staff member, National Centre for Scientific Research, Paris. Editor of* "Démarches mathématique" *in* Encyclopédie Philosophique.
MATHEMATICS, THE HISTORY OF (*in part*)

K.-c.H.   Kung-chuan Hsiao (d. 1981). *Professor of the History of Chinese Thought, University of Washington, Seattle, 1959–68. Author of* Rural China: Imperial Control in the 19th Century.
HAN-FEI-TZU (Micropædia)

K.C.P.   Kenneth C. Parkes. *Senior Curator of Birds, Carnegie Museum of Natural History, Pittsburgh, Pennsylvania. Author of numerous articles on the biology and systematics of birds.*
BIRDS (*in part*)

K.-D.G.   Karl-Dietrich Gundermann. *Emeritus Professor of Organic Chemistry, Technical University of Clausthal, Germany. Author of* Chemilumineszenz organischer Verbindungen.
LIGHT (*in part*)

Ke.B.   Kenneth Barkin. *Professor of History, University of California, Riverside. Author of* The Controversy over German Industrialization, 1890–1902.
BISMARCK
GERMANY (*in part*)

K.E.Bo.   Kenneth E. Boulding. *Distinguished Professor Emeritus of Economics, University of Colorado, Boulder. Author of* Economics as a Science; Ecodynamics: A New Theory of Societal Evolution.
ECONOMIC THEORY (*in part*)

K.E.C.   Kathleen Elizabeth Conlan. *Assistant Curator of Crustacea, Zoology Division, National Museum of Natural Sciences, Ottawa.*
CRUSTACEANS (*in part*)

K.E.H.   Kenneth E. Hofer, Jr. *Vice President, L. J. Broutman and Associates, Ltd., Chicago. Former Senior Research Engineer, Materials Engineering, IIT Research Institute, Chicago.*
ANALYSIS AND MEASUREMENT, PHYSICAL AND CHEMICAL (*in part*)

K.E.N.   Kai E. Nielsen. *Professor of Philosophy, University of Calgary, Alberta. Author of* Scepticism.
RELIGIOUS AND SPIRITUAL BELIEF, SYSTEMS OF (*in part*)

K.E.P.   Kenyon Edwards Poole (d. 1988). *Professor of Economics, Northwestern University, Evanston, Illinois. Author of* Public Finance and Economic Welfare.
GOVERNMENT FINANCE (*in part*)

Ke.S.   Sir Keith Sinclair. *Emeritus Professor of History, University of Auckland, New Zealand. Author of* A History of New Zealand *and others.*
NEW ZEALAND (*in part*)

K.G.   Karl Geiringer (d. 1989). *Professor of Music, University of California, Santa Barbara, 1962–73. Coauthor of* Haydn: A Creative Life in Music.
HAYDN, JOSEPH (*in part*) (Micropædia)

K.Ga.   Kenneth Garrad. *Professor of Spanish, Flinders University of South Australia, Bedford Park (Adelaide).*
SPAIN (*in part*)

K.G.L.   Kenneth G. Lieberthal. *Professor of Political Science; Research Associate, Center for Chinese Studies, University of Michigan, Ann Arbor. Author of* Central Documents and Politburo Politics in China *and others.*
CHINA (*in part*)
CULTURAL REVOLUTION (Micropædia)

K.G.R.   Kenneth Grahame Rea. *Lecturer and Tutor in Drama, Guildhall School of Music and Drama, London.*

Theatre Critic and writer, The Guardian.
THEATRE, THE HISTORY OF WESTERN

K.G.T.   Kennedy G. Tregonning. *Headmaster, Hale School, Wembley Downs, Western Australia. Raffles Professor of History, University of Singapore, 1958–66. Author of* A History of Modern Malaysia and Singapore.
SOUTHEAST ASIA, MAINLAND (*in part*)

K.Hä.   Karl H. Häuser. *Professor of Political Economy, Johann Wolfgang Goethe University of Frankfurt, Frankfurt am Main, Germany. Coauthor of* The German Economy, 1870 to the Present.
TAXATION (*in part*)

K.H.C.   Kenneth H. Cooper, M.D. *President and Founder, The Aerobics Center, Dallas, Texas. Author of* The Aerobics Program for Total Well-being.
EXERCISE AND PHYSICAL CONDITIONING (*in part*)

K.H.D.H.   K.H.D. Haley. *Emeritus Professor of Modern History, University of Sheffield, England. Author of* The First Earl of Shaftesbury.
SHAFTESBURY, ANTHONY ASHLEY COOPER, 1ST EARL OF (Micropædia)

K.H.L.   Karl Heinz Lüling (d. 1984). *Chairman, Department of Ichthyology, Zoological Research Institute and Alexander Koenig Museum, Bonn. Researcher on the physiology and behaviour of lungfishes.*
FISHES (*in part*)

Kh.Mo.   Khosrow Mostofi. *Emeritus Professor of Political Science, University of Utah, Salt Lake City; former Director, Middle East Languages and Area Center. Author of* Aspects of Nationalism: A Sociology of Colonial Revolt.
IRAN (*in part*)

K.Ho.   Keigo Hogetsu. *Honorary Professor of Literature, University of Tokyo. Author of* Nihon shi gairon *and others.*
TAIRA FAMILY (Micropædia)

K.I.K.   Kenneth I. Kellermann. *Senior Scientist, National Radio Astronomy Observatory, Charlottesville, Virginia. Coeditor of* Galactic and Extragalactic Radio Astronomy.
TELESCOPES (*in part*)

K.In.   Kenneth Ingham. *Emeritus Professor of History, University of Bristol, England. Author of* East Africa *and others.*
EASTERN AFRICA (*in part*)
SOUTHERN AFRICA (*in part*)

K.Iw.   Kenkichi Iwasawa. *H.B. Fine Professor Emeritus of Mathematics, Princeton University. Author of* Lectures on p-adic L-functions.
ANALYSIS (IN MATHEMATICS) (*in part*)

K.J.   Karl H.E. Jordan (d. 1984). *Professor of Medieval and Modern History, Christian Albrecht University of Kiel, West Germany. Editor of* Die Urkunden Heinrichs des Löwen.
HENRY III (Saxony) (Micropædia)

K.J.B.   Keith J. Beven. *Reader in Environmental Science, University of Lancaster, England.*
EARTH SCIENCES, THE (*in part*)

K.J.DeW.   Kenneth J. DeWoskin. *Professor of Chinese and Chair, Department of Asian Languages and Cultures, University of Michigan, Ann Arbor. Author of* A Song for One or Two: Music and the Concept of Art in Early China *and others.*
CHINA (*in part*)

K.J.Hi.   K. Jaakko J. Hintikka. *Professor of Philosophy, Boston University. Author of* Logic, Language-Games and Information.
PHILOSOPHIES OF THE BRANCHES OF KNOWLEDGE (*in part*)

K.J.L.   K.J. Leyser. *Chichele Professor Emeritus of Medieval History, University of Oxford. Author of* Medieval Germany and Its Neighbours, 900–1250.
GERMANY (*in part*)

K.J.N.   Karl J. Narr. *Emeritus Professor of Prehistory and Protohistory, University of Münster, Germany.*
PREHISTORIC PEOPLES AND CULTURES (*in part*)

K.J.No.   Knut J. Norstog. *Research Associate, Fairchild Tropical Garden, Miami. Coauthor of* Plant Biology.
GYMNOSPERMS (*in part*)

K.J.R.   Kenneth John Rea. *Professor of Economics, University of Toronto. Author of* The Political Economy of the Canadian North.
CANADA (*in part*)

K.K.   Kumar Krishna. *Research Associate, Department of Entomology, American Museum of Natural History, New York City. Professor of Biology, City College, City University of New York. Coeditor of* Biology of Termites.
INSECTS (*in part*)

K.Ku.   Karthigesapillai Kularatnam (deceased). *Professor and Head, Department of Geography, University of Sri Lanka, Colombo. Author of* "Ceylon" *in* Developing Countries of the World.
SRI LANKA (*in part*)

K.La.   Kenneth Lamott (d. 1979). *Novelist and journalist. Author of* Anti-California *and numerous other books and magazine articles.*
SAN FRANCISCO (*in part*)

K.L.K.L.   Kai L.K. Laitinen. *Associate Professor of Finnish Literature, University of Helsinki, 1982–89. Author of* Literature of Finland *and others.*
FINNISH LITERATURE (Micropædia)

K.L.N.   Kenneth L. Nordtvedt, Jr. *Professor of Physics, Montana State University, Bozeman.*
GRAVITATION (*in part*)

K.Lo.   Dame Kathleen Lonsdale (d. 1971). *Professor of Chemistry, University of London, 1949–68. Editor of and part author of Vol. I, II, III,* International Tables for X-Ray Crystallography.

BRAGG, SIR LAWRENCE (Micropædia)
BRAGG, SIR WILLIAM (Micropædia)

K.L.W.   King Lit Wong. *Senior Research Scientist in Toxicology, Krug International, Lyndon B. Johnson Space Center, Houston, Texas.*
POISONS AND POISONING (*in part*)

K.M.   Kathy Mezei. *Associate Professor of English, Simon Fraser University, Burnaby, British Columbia. Author of* Bibliography of Criticism on English and French Literary Translations in Canada.
CANADIAN LITERATURE (*in part*)

K.Ma.   Kitajima Masamoto. *Former Professor of Japanese History, Tokyo Metropolitan University. Author of* Structure of Power in the Edo Shogunate.
JAPAN (*in part*)

K.M.A.G.   Kurt Moritz Artur Goldammer. *Professor of Comparative History of Religions and of the History of Religious Art, Philipps University of Marburg, Germany. Author of* Kultsymbolik des Protestantismus.
RELIGIOUS SYMBOLISM AND ICONOGRAPHY

K.M.B.   Kathleen M. Baker. *Lecturer in Geography, School of Oriental and African Studies, University of London. Author of* Agricultural Change in Nigeria.
WESTERN AFRICA (*in part*)

K.Me.   Kenneth Mellanby. *Director, Monks Wood Experimental Station, Huntingdon, England, 1961–74. Author of* Farming and Wildlife *and others.*
AGRICULTURE, THE HISTORY OF (*in part*)

K.M.G.P.   Kings Mbacazwa G. Phiri. *Associate Professor of History, University of Malaŵi, Zomba.*
SOUTHERN AFRICA (*in part*)

K.M.K.   Dame Kathleen Mary Kenyon (d. 1978). *Principal, St. Hugh's College, University of Oxford, 1962–73. Director, British School of Archaeology in Jerusalem, 1951–66. Author of* Archaeology in the Holy Land; Digging Up Jericho; *and others.*
PALESTINE (*in part*)

K.M.L.   Kathleen Marguerite Lea. *Emeritus Fellow of Lady Margaret Hall, University of Oxford; Vice-Principal of Lady Margaret Hall, Oxford, 1947–71.*
BACON, FRANCIS (*in part*)

K.M.S.   Kazimierz Maciej Smogorzewski. *Free-lance writer on contemporary history. London Correspondent,* Kurier Polski (*Warsaw*), *1957–81. Founder and Editor,* Free Europe, *1939–45. Author of* Joseph Pilsudski, soldat de la Pologne restaurée; Poland's Access to the Sea; *and others.*
PIŁSUDSKI, JÓZEF (Micropædia)
POLAND (*in part*)
ROMANIA (*in part*)
BALTIC STATES (*in part*)

K.M.W.   Karl M. Waage. *Emeritus Professor of Geology; Emeritus Curator of Invertebrate Paleontology, Peabody Museum of Natural History, Yale University. Coauthor of* Historical Geology.

DANA, JAMES D. (Micropædia)

K.N.   Keiji Nagahara. *Professor of History, Hitotsubashi University, Tokyo. Author of* Minamoto no Yoritomo.
MINAMOTO YORITOMO (Micropædia)

K.Na.   Kusum Nair. *Former Visiting Professor, Department of Economics, University of Maryland, College Park. Author of* The Lonely Furrow: Farming in the United States, Japan, and India.
AGRICULTURE, THE HISTORY OF (*in part*)

K.N.L.   Karl Nickerson Llewellyn (d. 1962). *Professor of Law, University of Chicago, 1951–62.*
MANSFIELD, WILLIAM MURRAY, 1ST EARL OF (Micropædia)

K.Ob.   Kalervo Oberg (d. 1973). *Professor of Anthropology, Oregon State University, Corvallis. Author of* Indian Tribes of Northern Mato Grosso, Brazil.
AMERICAN INDIANS (*in part*)

K.O.v.A.   Karl Otmar, Baron von Aretin. *Head Editor,* Neue Deutsch Biographie. *Emeritus Professor of Contemporary History, Technical University of Darmstadt, Germany. Director, Institute for European History, Mainz, Germany.*
FRANCIS JOSEPH (Micropædia)
METTERNICH, KLEMENS, FURST VON (*in part*) (Micropædia)

K.P.S.   Karl Patterson Schmidt (d. 1957). *Chief Curator of Zoology, Field Museum of Natural History, Chicago, 1941–55.*
CHINA (*in part*)
UNITED STATES OF AMERICA (*in part*)

K.Re.   Kenneth Rexroth (d. 1982). *Poet, writer, and painter. Special Lecturer, University of California, Santa Barbara. Author of* Classics Revisited *and others.*
LITERATURE, THE ART OF (*in part*)

Kr.K.   Krishan Kumar. *Professor of Social Thought, University of Kent at Canterbury, England. Author of* Prophecy and Progress *and others.*
MODERNIZATION AND INDUSTRIALIZATION

K.-r.L.   Kwang-rin Lee. *Professor of History, Sogang University, Seoul, Korea. Author of* History of Enlightenment in Korea.
KOREA (*in part*)

K.R.S.   Kenneth Reginald Sturley, *Professor of Telecommunications, Ahmadu Bello University, Zaria, Nigeria, 1968–71. Chief Engineer, External Broadcasting, British Broadcasting Corporation, London, 1963–68. Author of* Radio Receiver Design *and others.*
BROADCASTING (*in part*)

K.R.St.   Karl R. Stadler (d. 1987). *Professor and Head, Institute of Modern and Contemporary History, Johannes Kepler University of Linz, Austria. Author of* The Birth of the Austrian Republic.
AUSTRIA (*in part*)

K.R.V.H.   Kent R. Van Horn (d. 1989). *Vice President, Research and Development, Aluminum Company of America, Pittsburgh, 1962–70; Director of Research, 1952–62; Research Metallurgist, 1929–62. Coauthor of* Aluminum in Iron and Steel; *editor of* Aluminum.
INDUSTRIES, EXTRACTION AND PROCESSING (*in part*)

K.S.   Khushwant Singh. *Free-lance journalist. Member, Rajya Sabha* (*upper house of the Indian Parliament*). *Author of* A History of the Sikhs *and others.*
SIKHISM

K.S.A.J.   Kamel S. Abu Jaber. *Professor of Political Science, University of Jordan, Amman. Author of* The Jordanians and the People of Jordan.
JORDAN (*in part*)

K.S.B.   Karl S. Bottigheimer. *Associate Professor of History, State University of New York at Stony Brook. Author of* Ireland and the Irish *and others.*
UNITED KINGDOM (*in part*)

K.S.C.   Ken S. Coates. *Associate Professor of History, University of Victoria, British Columbia. Coauthor of* Manitoba: The Province and the People.
CANADA (*in part*)

K.S.D.   Keith S. Donnellan. *Professor of Philosophy, University of California, Los Angeles. Author of articles in various philosophical journals, particularly on the theory of reference.*
PHILOSOPHICAL SCHOOLS AND DOCTRINES, WESTERN (*in part*)

K.Si.   Kate Silber (deceased). *Senior Lecturer in German, University of Edinburgh, 1963–73. Author of* Pestalozzi: The Man and His Work.
PESTALOZZI, JOHANN HEINRICH (*in part*) (Micropædia)

K.S.L.   Kenneth S. Lane. *Consulting engineer for dams and tunnels, and soils and rock engineering. Editor of* Proceedings *of the North American Rapid Excavating and Tunneling Conference, 1972;* Proceedings *of the ASCE symposium on Underground Rock Chambers, 1971.*
PUBLIC WORKS (*in part*)

K.S.N.   Kenneth Stafford Norris. *Professor of Natural History, University of California, Santa Cruz. Director, Oceanic Institute, Waimanalo, Hawaii, 1968–71. Editor of* Whales, Dolphins and Porpoises.
MAMMALS (*in part*)

K.S.S.   Kamal Suleiman Salibi. *Professor of History, American University of Beirut. Author of* The Modern History of Lebanon *and others.*
BEIRUT (*in part*)
ISRAEL (*in part*)
SYRIA (*in part*)

K.St.   The Rev. Krister Stendahl. *Bishop of Stockholm, 1984–88. Andrew W. Mellon Professor of Divinity, Harvard University, 1981–84; Dean, Divinity School, 1968–79. Author of* Paul Among Jews and Gentiles *and others.*

BIBLICAL LITERATURE AND ITS CRITICAL
INTERPRETATION (*in part*)

K.S.W.   Kathrine Sorley Walker.
*Free-lance writer, editor, and dance
critic. Author of* Dance and Its Creators
and others.
BALANCHINE, GEORGE (Micropædia)
FOKINE, MICHEL (Micropædia)
PAVLOVA, ANNA (Micropædia)

**K.T.B.   Konstantin Trifonovich
Bogdanov.** *Head, Thermic and Dynamic
Ocean Department, Pacific Oceanology
Institute, Academy of Sciences of the
U.S.S.R., Vladivostok.*
PACIFIC OCEAN, THE (*in part*)

Ku.N.   Kurt Nassau. *Professor,
Princeton University. Former Research
Scientist, AT&T Bell Laboratories,
Murray Hill, New Jersey. Author of* The
Physics and Chemistry of Color.
COLOUR

Ku.R.   Kurt Reindel. *Professor of
History, University of Regensburg,
Germany.*
OTTO I (GERMANY/HOLY ROMAN
EMPIRE) (Micropædia)

K.v.Fr.   Kurt von Fritz (d. 1985).
*Professor of Classical Philosophy,
Ludwig Maximilian University of
Munich. Author of* Die griechische
Geschichtesschreibung (*vol. 1) and
numerous others.*
PHILOSOPHY, THE HISTORY OF WESTERN
(*in part*)

K.V.J.v.F.   Kai V.J. von Fieandt.
*Emeritus Professor of Psychology,
University of Helsinki. Author of* The
World of Perception.
PERCEPTION, HUMAN (*in part*)

K.V.Su.   K.V. Sundaram. *Consultant,
Food and Agriculture Organization,
United Nations, Rome.*
DELHI (*in part*)

K.V.Z.   Kamil V. Zvelebil. *Professor of
Dravidology, State University of Utrecht,
The Netherlands. Author of* Comparative
Dravidian Phonology.
LANGUAGES OF THE WORLD (*in part*)

K.W.B.   Karl W. Butzer. *Dickson
Centennial Professor of Liberal Arts,
University of Texas at Austin. Specialist
on the interrelationships among
environment, prehistoric cultures, and
human evolution. Author of* Environment
and Archeology; *coauthor of* Desert and
River in Nubia.
CLIMATE AND WEATHER (*in part*)

K.W.Bo.   Kees W. Bolle. *Professor of
History, University of California, Los
Angeles. Author of* The Freedom of Man
in Myth.
MYTH AND MYTHOLOGY (*in part*)

K.W.Br.   Kenneth W. Britt. *Senior
Research Associate, Empire State Paper
Research Institute, State University of
New York College of Environmental
Science and Forestry, Syracuse. Editor
of* Handbook of Pulp and Paper
Technology.
INDUSTRIES, CHEMICAL PROCESS
(*in part*)

K.W.P.   Ken W. Purdy (d. 1972).
Free-lance writer. Author of Kings of the
Road; Motorcars of the Golden Past.
TRANSPORTATION (*in part*)

La.B.   Larissa Bonfante. *Professor of
Classics, New York University, New
York City. Author of* Etruscan Dress.
DRESS AND ADORNMENT (*in part*)

La.B.S.   Lacey Baldwin Smith. *Peter
B. Ritzma Professor of Humanities,
Northwestern University, Evanston,
Illinois. Author of* Treason in Tudor
England *and others.*
UNITED KINGDOM (*in part*)

L.A.C.   Lewis A. Coser. *Distinguished
Professor Emeritus of Sociology, State
University of New York at Stony Brook.
Author of* The Functions of Social
Conflict.
SOCIO-ECONOMIC DOCTRINES AND
REFORM MOVEMENTS, MODERN
(*in part*)

L.A.Cr.   Lawrence A. Cremin (d. 1990).
*Frederick A.P. Barnard Professor of
Education, Teachers College, Columbia
University, 1961–90. Author of* American
Education: The National Experience
and others.
MANN, HORACE (Micropædia)

La.G.   Sir Lawrence Gowing (d. 1991).
*Slade Professor of Fine Art, University
College, University of London, 1975–85.
Author of* Vermeer; Turner; Imagination
and Reality.
PAINTING, THE HISTORY OF WESTERN
(*in part*)
SCULPTURE, THE HISTORY OF WESTERN
(*in part*)

La.L.   Laurence Elliot Libin. *Frederick
P. Rose Curator of Musical Instruments,
Metropolitan Museum of Art, New
York City. Author of* American Musical
Instruments in The Metropolitan
Museum of Art.
MUSICAL FORMS AND GENRES (*in part*)
MUSICAL INSTRUMENTS (*in part*)

L.-A.L.   Luce-Andrée Langevin.
*Honorary Professor; former teacher of
physical science, Lycée Fénelon, Paris.
Author of* Lomonosov.
LOMONOSOV, MIKHAIL VASILYEVICH
(Micropædia)

L.A.M.   Leslie A. Marchand. *Emeritus
Professor of English, Rutgers University,
New Brunswick, New Jersey. Author of*
Byron: A Biography *and others; editor of*
Byron's Letters and Journals.
BYRON, GEORGE GORDON BYRON, 6TH
BARON (*in part*) (Micropædia)

L.A.Ma.   L. Andrew Mannheim.
*Technical editor, writer, and consultant.
Author of* Leica Way *and others; editor
of* Focal Encyclopedia of Photography.
PHOTOGRAPHY (*in part*)

L.A.N.   Leonid Alekseyevich Nikiforov.
*Senior Scientific Associate, Institute
of History of the U.S.S.R., Academy
of Sciences of the U.S.S.R., Moscow.
Author of* Anglo-Russian Relations in the
Reign of Peter I.
PETER I THE GREAT, OF RUSSIA
(*in part*)

L.A.P.G.   L.A. Peter Gosling. *Professor
of Geography, University of Michigan;
Director, Center for South and Southeast
Asian Studies, 1962–66 and 1977–
80. Executive Officer, Association for
Asian Studies.*
SOUTHEAST ASIA, MAINLAND (*in part*)

L.A.R.   Lionel A. Rogg. *Professor of
Organ, Counterpoint, Styles, and Form,
Geneva Conservatory.*
MUSICAL FORMS AND GENRES (*in part*)

La.S.   Lawrence Sternstein. *Senior
Lecturer in Geography, Australian
National University, Canberra.
Former Municipal Advisor, Bangkok
Municipality, Thailand. Author of
Portrait of Bangkok* and others.
BANGKOK

L.A.S.   Lionel Astor Sheridan.
*Professor of Law, University College,
University of Wales, Cardiff. Coauthor
of* Equity.
LAW, THE PROFESSION AND PRACTICE
OF (*in part*)

L.A.Si.   Larry A. Silver. *Professor of
Art History, Northwestern University,
Evanston, Illinois. Author of* The
Paintings of Quinten Massys.
REMBRANDT

L.A.St.   L. Andrew Staehelin. *Professor
of Cell Biology, University of Colorado,
Boulder. Coeditor of* Encyclopedia of
Plant Physiology (*vol. 19*).
CELLS (*in part*)

L.A.W.   Leslie A. White (d. 1975).
*Professor of Anthropology, University
of Michigan, Ann Arbor. Author of*
The Science of Culture; The Evolution
of Culture.
CULTURE, THE CONCEPT AND
COMPONENTS OF (*in part*)

L.A.Wa.   Lionel A. Walford (d.
1979). *Director, Sandy Hook Marine
Laboratory, Highlands, New Jersey,
1960–71; Senior Scientist, 1971–74.
Author of* Living Resources of the Sea.
FISHES (*in part*)

L.B.   Liliana Brisby. *Free-lance editor
and writer on East European affairs.
Former Editor,* The World Today.
Author of Les Relations russo-bulgares,
1878–1886.
BULGARIAN LITERATURE (*in part*)
(Micropædia)

L.Ba.   Lawrence Badash. *Professor
of the History of Science, University of
California, Santa Barbara. Author of*
Radioactivity in America.
BECQUEREL, HENRI (Micropædia)

L.B.A.   Leslie B. Arey (d. 1988).
*Robert L. Reu Professor and Chairman,
Department of Anatomy, Medical School,
Northwestern University, Chicago,
1925–56. Author of* Developmental
Anatomy.
GROWTH AND DEVELOPMENT,
BIOLOGICAL (*in part*)

L.B.As.   Larned B. Asprey. *Former
Staff Member, Los Alamos National
Laboratory, New Mexico. Author
of numerous papers on the actinide,*

rare-earth, transuranium, and halogen elements.
CHEMICAL ELEMENTS (*in part*)

L.Be.   Lyman Benson. *Emeritus Professor of Botany, Pomona College, Claremont, California. Author of* The Cacti of the United States and Canada *and others.*
ANGIOSPERMS (*in part*)

L.B.S.   Leonard Bertram Schapiro (d. 1983). *Professor of Political Science (Russian Studies), London School of Economics and Political Science, University of London, 1963–75. Author of* The Communist Party of the Soviet Union *and others.*
SOCIO-ECONOMIC DOCTRINES AND
    REFORM MOVEMENTS, MODERN
    (*in part*)

L.B.Sm.   Lyman B. Smith. *Emeritus Botanist, Smithsonian Institution, Washington, D.C. Author of* Bromeliaceae—North American Flora; Flora Neotropica.
ANGIOSPERMS (*in part*)

L.C.   Leonard W. Conversi. *Former Lecturer in English, Yale University.*
LITERATURE, THE ART OF (*in part*)

L.Ca.   Luigi Carluccio. *Member of the arts editorial staff,* La Gazzetta del popolo, *Turin, Italy. Author of* Giacometti: A Sketchbook of Interpretative Drawings.
CARAVAGGIO (Micropædia)

L.C.B.   Lawrence C. Bliss. *Professor of Botany, University of Washington, Seattle. Author of* Alpine Zone of the Presidential Range.
BIOSPHERE, THE (*in part*)

L.C.Br.   L. Carl Brown. *Garrett Professor of Foreign Affairs; Director, Program in Near Eastern Studies, Princeton University. Author of* The Tunisia of Ahmad Bey.
NORTH AFRICA (*in part*)
WESTERN AFRICA (*in part*)

L.C.D.   L.C. Dunn (d. 1974). *Professor of Zoology, 1928–62; Senior Research Associate in Biological Sciences, 1962–74, Columbia University, New York City. Author of* Heredity and Evolution in Human Populations *and others.*
GROWTH AND DEVELOPMENT,
    BIOLOGICAL (*in part*)
MENDEL, GREGOR (*in part*) (Micropædia)

L.C.F.   Louis C. Faron. *Professor of Anthropology, State University of New York at Stony Brook. Author of* Hawks of the Sun *and others.*
AMERICAN INDIANS (*in part*)

L.Ch.   Luciano Chiappini. *Teacher. President, Ferrarese Delegation for the History of Italy. Committeeman, Antonio Frizzi Institute for the History of Ferrara. Author of* Eleonora d'Aragona, prima duchessa di Ferrara *and others.*
ESTE, HOUSE OF (Micropædia)

L.C.H.   Lois Chapman Houghton. *Staff member, Middle East Institute, Washington, D.C.*
DAMASCUS (*in part*)

L.C.O.   Leonard C. Overton. *Country Representative, Asia Foundation, Phnom Penh, Cambodia, 1955–59, 1961–64; Saigon, South Vietnam, 1965–67.*
SOUTHEAST ASIA, MAINLAND (*in part*)

L.C.P.   Linus C. Pauling. *Research Professor, Linus Pauling Institute of Science and Medicine, Palo Alto, California. Professor of Chemistry, Stanford University, California, 1969–74. Nobel Prize for Chemistry, 1954; Nobel Prize for Peace, 1962. Author of* The Nature of the Chemical Bond *and others.*
CHEMICAL ELEMENTS (*in part*)

L.D.   Lovat Dickson (d. 1987). *Writer. Director, Macmillan & Company Ltd., London, 1941–64. Author of* H.G. Wells.
WELLS, H.G. (Micropædia)

L.D.A.   Larry D. Agenbroad. *Professor of Geology; Director, Quaternary Studies Program, Northern Arizona University, Flagstaff. Author of* The Hudson-Meng Site: An Alberta Bison Kill in the Nebraska High Plains.
GEOCHRONOLOGY (*in part*)

L.De.   Ludwig Denecke. *Director, Murhard Library of the City of Kassel and State Library, and Head of the Brothers Grimm Museum, Kassel, West Germany, 1959–68. Author of* Jacob Grimm und sein Bruder Wilhelm; *editor of* Brüder Grimm Gedenken.
GRIMM, JACOB LUDWIG CARL AND
    WILHELM CARL (Micropædia)

L. de R.   Leendert de Ruiter. *Former Professor of Comparative Animal Physiology, State University of Groningen, The Netherlands.*
BEHAVIOUR, ANIMAL (*in part*)

L. de S.R.   Luís de Sousa Rebelo. *Emeritus Reader in Portuguese Studies; Calouste Gulbenkian Senior Fellow, King's College, University of London. Author of* A tradição clássica na Literatura portuguesa *and others.*
LISBON (*in part*)
PORTUGUESE LITERATURE (*in part*)

L.DeV.   Louis De Vorsey. *Emeritus Professor of Geography, University of Georgia, Athens. Coauthor of* A Panorama of Georgia.
UNITED STATES OF AMERICA (*in part*)

L.D.F.   Larry D. Faller. *Associate Professor, Department of Medicine, University of California, Los Angeles. Author of papers on the application of relaxation techniques to rapid chemical processes.*
CHEMICAL REACTIONS (*in part*)

L.D.Fr.   Lawrence D. Freedman. *Professor and Head, Department of War Studies, King's College, University of London. Author of* The Evolution of Nuclear Strategy *and others.*
WAR, THE THEORY AND CONDUCT OF
    (*in part*)

L.Du.   Louis Dupree (d. 1989). *Anthropologist. Visiting Professor and Senior Research Associate, Islamic and Arabian Studies, Duke University, Durham, North Carolina, 1985–89.*

Field researcher in Afghanistan, India, Pakistan, and Bangladesh. Author of Afghanistan.
AFGHANISTAN (*in part*)
ASIAN PEOPLES AND CULTURES (*in part*)

L.Ed.   Leon Edel. *Henry James Professor Emeritus of English and American Letters, New York University, New York City. Citizens' Professor Emeritus of English Literature, University of Hawaii at Manoa. Author of* The Life of Henry James *and others; editor of* The Complete Tales of Henry James *and others.*
JAMES, HENRY (*in part*) (Micropædia)

L.-E.H.   Louis-Edmond Hamelin. *Geographer, University of Quebec at Trois-Rivières; Rector, 1978–83. Author of* Canada.
NORTH AMERICA (*in part*)

L.E.Hu.   Lawrence E. Hussman. *Professor of English, Wright State University, Dayton, Ohio. Author of* Dreiser and His Fiction: A Twentieth-Century Quest.
DREISER, THEODORE (Micropædia)

L.El.   Lajos Elekes. *Former Professor of the Medieval History of Hungary, Eötvös Loránd University, Budapest. Author of* Hunyadi; Mátyás és kora.
HUNYADI, JÁNOS (Micropædia)
MATTHIAS I (HUNGARY) (Micropædia)

Le.M.   Leonard Mosley. *Author of* Curzon: The End of an Epoch *and others.*
CURZON, GEORGE NATHANIEL CURZON,
    MARQUESS (Micropædia)

L.E.M.   Leonard E. Mason. *Consultant in Pacific Islands affairs. Emeritus Professor of Anthropology, University of Hawaii at Manoa, Honolulu. Author of* Relocation of the Bikini Marshallese.
PACIFIC ISLANDS (*in part*)

L.E.R.   Leo E. Rose. *Former Adjunct Professor of Political Science, University of California, Berkeley. Author of* Nepal: Strategy for Survival *and others.*
NEPAL (*in part*)

Le.S.   Lee Strasberg (d. 1982). *Artistic Director, Actors Studio, 1948–82. Head, Lee Strasberg Theatre Institute, New York City. Author of* Strasberg at the Actors Studio.
THEATRE, THE ART OF THE (*in part*)

L.E.S.   Lawrence E. Sullivan. *Associate Professor of the History of Religions, University of Chicago. Author of* Icanchu's Drum: South American Religions, an Orientation to Meaning.
CHRISTIANITY (*in part*)

L.E.Si.   Leighton E. Sissom. *Professor of Mechanical Engineering, Tennessee Technological University, Cookeville. Coauthor of* Elements of Transport Phenomena *and others.*
ENERGY CONVERSION (*in part*)

L.F.   Linwood Fredericksen. *Undersecretary and Manager, Program Development Division, Rotary International. Associate Editor, Religion, Encyclopædia Britannica, Chicago,*

1969–73. Author of A Christian Witness in a Non-Christian Culture According to Clement of Alexandria.
BIBLICAL LITERATURE AND ITS CRITICAL INTERPRETATION (*in part*)
CHRISTIANITY (*in part*)
CLEMENT OF ALEXANDRIA, SAINT (*in part*) (Micropædia)
DOCTRINES AND DOGMAS, RELIGIOUS (*in part*)
RITES AND CEREMONIES, SACRED (*in part*)

L.F. de B.   Lieven Ferdinand de Beaufort (d. 1968). *Professor of Zoogeography, University of Amsterdam, 1929–49. Director, Zoological Museum, Amsterdam, 1922–49. Author of* Zoogeography of the Land and Inland Waters.
ASIA (*in part*)

L.F.K.W.   Lothar F.K. Wickert (d. 1989). *Professor of Ancient History, University of Cologne. Author of* Theodor Mommsen: Eine Biographie; Drei Vorträge über Theodor Mommsen.
MOMMSEN, THEODOR (Micropædia)

L.Fo.   Lukas Foss. *Composer and pianist. Music Director, 1971–90, and Conductor Laureate, Brooklyn (New York) Philharmonic. Music Director, 1982–86, and Conductor Laureate, Milwaukee Symphony Orchestra. Composer of* Time Cycle *and many other works.*
MUSIC, THE ART OF (*in part*)

L.F.R.W.   Laurence Frederic Rushbrook Williams (d. 1978). *Editorial Adviser, The Pakistan Society, London. Vice President, Indo-British Historical Association. Editorial Staff member, The Times (London), 1944–55. Author of* The State of Pakistan *and others.*
PAKISTAN (*in part*)

L.G.D.   Lawrence G. Duggan. *Associate Professor of History, University of Delaware, Newark. Author of* Bishop and Chapter: The Governance of the Bishopric of Speyer to 1552.
GERMANY (*in part*)

L.G.J.B.   Ludwig G.J. Bieler (d. 1981). *Professor of Paleography and Late Latin, University College, Dublin, National University of Ireland. Author of* Boethii Philosophiae Consolatio *and others.*
IGNATIUS OF ANTIOCH, SAINT (Micropædia)

L.Go.   Ludwig Goldscheider. *Art historian. Former director and designer of books for Phaidon Press Ltd., London. Author of* Kokoschka; Michelangelo; *and numerous other classic works on the art of antiquity, the Italian Renaissance, the Baroque, and the late 19th and early 20th centuries.*
KOKOSCHKA, OSKAR (Micropædia)

L.G.P.   Leslie Gilbert Pine (d. 1987). *Writer and lecturer. Editor, Burke's Peerage. Author of* The Genealogist's Encyclopedia; The Story of Heraldry; *and many others.*
HERALDRY
HISTORY, THE STUDY OF (*in part*)

L.G.S.   Lloyd Grenfell Stevenson, M.D. (deceased). *William H. Welch Professor of the History of Medicine; Director, Institute of the History of Medicine, Johns Hopkins University, Baltimore, 1968–83.*
KOCH, ROBERT (Micropædia)

L.H.   Leslie Harris. *President and Vice-Chancellor, Memorial University of Newfoundland, St. John's. Author of* A Short History of Newfoundland and Labrador.
CANADA (*in part*)

L.H.A.   Lawrence Hugh Aller. *Emeritus Professor of Astronomy, University of California, Los Angeles. Author of* Atoms, Stars, and Nebulae.
STARS AND STAR CLUSTERS (*in part*)

L.H.B.   Leslie Hilton Brown (d. 1980). *Ornithologist, naturalist, and consultant on range management, land use, and planning. Specialist on the ecology of birds and mammals of East Africa. Author of* Africa: A Natural History; African Birds of Prey; Eagles; *coauthor of* Eagles, Hawks and Falcons of the World.
AFRICA (*in part*)
BIRDS (*in part*)

L.H.Bu.   Lyman H. Butterfield (d. 1982). *Editor in Chief,* The Adams Papers, *Massachusetts Historical Society, Boston, 1954–75. Editor of* Letters of Benjamin Rush.
RUSH, BENJAMIN (Micropædia)

L.H.E.   Luther Harris Evans (d. 1981). *Director, International Collections, Columbia University, 1962–71. Director General, UNESCO, 1953–58. Librarian of Congress, 1945–53. Author of* The Virgin Islands from Naval Base to New Deal.
WEST INDIES, THE (*in part*)

L.H.F.   Louis H. Feldman. *Professor of Classics, Yeshiva University, New York City. Author of* Josephus and Modern Scholarship; *editor and translator of* Josephus, *vol. 9,* Jewish Antiquities.
JUDAISM (*in part*)

L.H.H.   Ludwig Heinrich Heydenreich (d. 1978). *Director, Central Institute for the History of Art, Munich, 1947–70. Author of* Leonardo da Vinci; Leonardo architetto.
LEONARDO DA VINCI (*in part*)

L.Hi.   Lejaren Hiller. *Composer. Birge-Cary Professor of Composition, State University of New York at Buffalo, 1981–89. Author of* Informationstheorie und Computermusik; *coauthor of* Experimental Music.
MUSICAL FORMS AND GENRES (*in part*)

L.H.S.   Lou Hackett Silberman. *Hillel Professor Emeritus of Jewish Literature and Thought, Vanderbilt University, Nashville, Tennessee. Author of* Listening to the Text; *editor of* Rabbinic Essays.
JUDAISM (*in part*)

L.H.St.   Lawrence H. Starkey. *Lecturer in Philosophy, University of Missouri, Rolla, 1986–87. Associate Editor,* Philosophy, *Encyclopædia Britannica, Chicago, 1968–72.*
PHILOSOPHICAL SCHOOLS AND DOCTRINES, WESTERN (*in part*)

Li.L.   Libero Lenti. *Emeritus Professor of Statistics, University of Milan. Author of* L'economia degli anni Ottanta.
ITALY (*in part*)

L.J.   Lucien Jerphagnon. *Emeritus Professor of Philosophy, University of Caen, France. Author of* Le Caractère de Pascal.
PASCAL (*in part*)

L.J.A.   Leonard James Arrington. *Former Lemuel H. Redd Professor of Western American History, Brigham Young University, Provo, Utah. Author of* Great Basin Kingdom: An Economic History of the Latter-day Saints.
UNITED STATES OF AMERICA (*in part*)

L.J.B.   Louis J. Battan (d. 1986). *Professor of Atmospheric Sciences, University of Arizona, Tucson, 1958–86. World authority on radar meteorology and its applications. Author of* Radar Meteorology; The Nature of Violent Storms; *and others.*
CLIMATE AND WEATHER (*in part*)

L.J.C.   Lawrence James Chisholm. *Metric consultant. Former Special Assistant, Bureau of Product Safety, Food and Drug Administration, U.S. Department of Health, Education, and Welfare, Washington, D.C. Author of* Units of Weight and Measure.
MEASUREMENT SYSTEMS (*in part*)

L.J.Co.   Linda J. Colley. *Associate Professor of History, Yale University. Author of* In Defiance of Oligarchy: The Tory Party, 1714–60.
UNITED KINGDOM (*in part*)

L.J.D.   Larry James Doyle. *Professor of Marine Science, University of South Florida at St. Petersburg. Coeditor of* Continental Slopes *and contributor to many publications on marine science.*
OCEANS (*in part*)

L.J.S.   Lewis Judson Stannard, Jr. (d. 1988). *Taxonomist, Illinois Natural History Survey, Urbana, 1961–77. Author of* The Phylogeny and Classification of the North American Genera of the Suborder Tubulifera (Thysanoptera).
INSECTS (*in part*)

L.J.T.   L.J. Trinterud. *Emeritus Professor of Church History, San Francisco Theological Seminary, San Anselmo, California. Editor of* Elizabethan Puritanism.
BUCER, MARTIN (Micropædia)

L.J.W.   Louis Jolyon West, M.D. *Professor of Psychiatry, University of California, Los Angeles; former Director, Neuropsychiatric Institute; former Psychiatrist in Chief, UCLA Hospital and Clinics. Author of* Hallucinations.
PERCEPTION, HUMAN (*in part*)

L.K.   Lawrence Kaplan. *Professor of Biology, University of Massachusetts, Boston.*
GROWTH AND DEVELOPMENT, BIOLOGICAL (*in part*)

L.Kl.   Larry Klein. *Audio Editor,* Radio-Electronics *magazine. Former Technical Director,* Stereo Review *magazine. Coauthor of* Electronic Test Equipment.
SOUND (*in part*)

L.K.L.   Lawrence K. Lustig. *Former Vice President and Editor in Chief, Aretê Publishing Company, Princeton, New Jersey. Senior Editor, Earth Sciences,* Encyclopædia Britannica, *Chicago, 1968–73; Managing Editor, Yearbooks, 1974–77. An authority on fluvial processes in arid regions.*
BIOSPHERE, THE (*in part*)
RIVERS (*in part*)

L.K.M.   Liliya Konstantinovna Malik. *Senior Scientist, Institute of Geography, Academy of Sciences of the U.S.S.R., Moscow. Author of* The Characteristic of the Snow Cover as One of the Factors of the Formation of High Waters in the Basin of the Ob River.
ASIA (*in part*)

L.Ko.   Lionel Kochan. *Bearsted Reader in Jewish History, University of Warwick, England. Author of* Russia in Revolution, 1890–1918 *and others.*
WITTE, SERGEY YULYEVICH, GRAF (Micropædia)

L.Kr.   Lawrence Krader. *Emeritus Director, Ethnological Institute, Free University of Berlin. Author of* Peoples of Central Asia; Social Organization of Mongol-Turkic Pastoral Nomads.
ASIAN PEOPLES AND CULTURES (*in part*)
UNION OF SOVIET SOCIALIST REPUBLICS (*in part*)

L.L.H.   Laurita L. Hill (deceased). *Writer and editor. Instructor in History, University of Texas at Austin, 1963–68. Coauthor of* Raymond IV, Count of Toulouse *and others.*
BOHEMOND I (*in part*) (Micropædia)

L.L.S.   Lester L. Short. *Lamont Curator of Birds, Department of Ornithology, American Museum of Natural History, New York City.*
BIRDS (*in part*)

L.M.   Luis Michelena (d. 1987). *Professor of Indo-European and Basque Linguistics, University of the Basque Country, Vitoria, Spain. Author of* Fonética histórica vasca; *editor of* Textos arcaicos vascos.
LANGUAGES OF THE WORLD (*in part*)

L.Ma.   Leopold Marquard (deceased). *Publisher. President, South African Institute of Race Relations, 1957–58, 1968. Author of* The Story of South Africa *and others.*
SMUTS, JAN CHRISTIAN (Micropædia)

L.M.A.   Lewis M. Alexander. *Professor of Marine Affairs, University of Rhode Island, Kingston. Author of* Offshore Geography of Northwestern Europe *and others.*
ATLANTIC OCEAN, THE (*in part*)

L.M.At.   Lewis Malcolm Atherden (d. 1973). *Lecturer in Pharmaceutical Chemistry, University of Bath, England.*

Editor of Bentley and Driver's Textbook of Pharmaceutical Chemistry.
INDUSTRIES, CHEMICAL PROCESS (*in part*)

L.M.B.   Laurie M. Brown. *Professor of Physics and Astronomy, Northwestern University, Evanston, Illinois. Coeditor of* The Birth of Particle Physics.
PHYSICAL SCIENCES, THE (*in part*)

L.M.F.   Luch Mikhaylovich Fomin. *Head, Laboratory of Sea Currents, Southern Division, Institute of Oceanography, Academy of Sciences of the U.S.S.R., Gelendzhik.*
ATLANTIC OCEAN, THE (*in part*)

L.M.G.   Leland Matthew Goodrich (d. 1990). *Professor of Political Science, Columbia University, 1950–68. Author of* The United Nations; *coauthor of* Charter of the United Nations: Commentary and Documents.
UNITED NATIONS (*in part*)

L.M.K.   Lewis M. Killian. *Faculty Associate, University of West Florida, Pensacola. Emeritus Professor of Sociology, University of Massachusetts, Amherst. Author of* The Impossible Revolution; *coauthor of* Collective Behavior.
COLLECTIVE BEHAVIOUR (*in part*)

L.M.L.   Ludwig M. Landgrebe. *Professor of Philosophy, University of Cologne. Director of the Husserl Archives, Cologne. Member of the International Institute of Philosophy, Paris. Author of* Phaenomenologie und Geschichte *and others.*
HUSSERL, EDMUND (Micropædia)

L.M.M.   Leonard M. Marcus. *Editor in Chief,* High Fidelity *magazine and* Musical America, *1968–80.*
MUSIC, THE ART OF (*in part*)

L.Mo.   Lynn Montross (d. 1961). *Historian, United States Marine Corps, 1950–61. Author of* War Through the Ages *and others.*
WAR, THE THEORY AND CONDUCT OF (*in part*)

L.M.Ö.   The Rev. Ladislas M. Örsy, S.J. *Professor of Canon Law, Catholic University of America, Washington, D.C. Author of* Marriage in Canon Law *and others.*
CHRISTIANITY (*in part*)

L.M.-P.   Lorenzo Minio-Paluello (d. 1986). *Reader in Mediaeval Philosophy, University of Oxford, 1956–75. Director of Aristoteles Latinus, 1959–72. Editor of numerous works of Aristotle.*
ARISTOTELIANISM, ARISTOTLE AND (*in part*)

L.Ms.   Luciano Martins. *Assistant Professor, Federal University of Rio de Janeiro. Research Assistant, National Centre of Scientific Research, Paris. Author of* Industrialização, Burguesia Nacional e Desenvolvimento.
BRAZIL (*in part*)

L.M.T.   Leonard Monteath Thompson. *Charles H. Stillé Professor Emeritus of History, Yale University; Director, Yale*

Southern African Research Program. Author of The Political Mythology of Apartheid.
SOUTH AFRICA (*in part*)

L.M.V.V.   Leigh M. Van Valen. *Professor of Ecology and Evolution, University of Chicago.*
ANIMALS (*in part*)

L.M.W.   Lillian M. Weber. *Chief Horticulture Assistant to the Senior Horticulture Specialist, New York Botanical Garden, Bronx. Collaborating Editor of* New Illustrated Encyclopedia of Gardening.
TREES (*in part*)

L.N.F.   Lee Nathan Feigon. *Associate Professor of History; Director, East Asian Studies, Colby College, Waterville, Maine. Staff Writer, East Asian Affairs,* Encyclopædia Britannica, *Chicago, 1970–73.*
HUNG HSIU-CH'ÜAN (Micropædia)

L.O.H.   Lauri O. Honko. *Professor of Folkloristics and Comparative Religion, University of Turku, Finland. Author of* Geisterglaube in Ingermanland.
EUROPEAN RELIGIONS, ANCIENT (*in part*)

Lo.J.B.   Lowell John Bean. *Professor of Anthropology, California State University, Hayward. Author of* Temalpah: An Ethnobotany of the Cahuilla Indians of Southern California; Mukat's People: An Ecological Study of the Cahuilla Indians of Southern California.
AMERICAN INDIANS (*in part*)

L.P.   László Péter. *Reader in Hungarian History, School of Slavonic and East European Studies, University of London.*
BUDAPEST (*in part*)

L.P.L.   Lawrence P. Lessing. *Member, Board of Editors,* Fortune *magazine, New York City, 1941–52; 1965–74. Author of* Man of High Fidelity: Edwin Howard Armstrong.
ARMSTRONG, EDWIN H. (Micropædia)

L.P.Le.   Lucile P. Leone. *Chief Nurse Officer, Public Health Service, U.S. Department of Health, Education, and Welfare, Washington, D.C., 1949–66. Associate Dean, College of Nursing, Texas Women's University, 1968–71. Author of* Statewide Planning for Nursing Education.
MEDICINE (*in part*)

L.P.L.K.   Leendert P. Louwe Kooijmans. *Professor of Prehistory, State University of Leiden, The Netherlands. Author of* The Rhine/Meuse Delta; Verleden Land.
NETHERLANDS, THE (*in part*)

L.P.V.   Lalita P. Vidyarthi (d. 1985). *Professor and Head, Department of Anthropology, University of Rānchī, India, 1968–85. Author of* Socio-Cultural Implication of Industrialization in India *and others.*
ASIAN PEOPLES AND CULTURES (*in part*)

L.P.W.   L. Pearce Williams. *John Stambaugh Professor of the History*

of Science; Director, Program in the History and Philosophy of Science and Technology, Cornell University, Ithaca, New York. Author of Michael Faraday.
FARADAY
HELMHOLTZ
SCIENCE, THE HISTORY OF

L.P.Wi.   Lancelot Patrick Wilkinson (d. 1985). *Brereton Reader in Classics, University of Cambridge, 1969–74; Fellow of King's College, Cambridge. Author of* Ovid Recalled *and others.*
LATIN LITERATURE (*in part*)

L.R.C.   L. Russell Cook (d. 1978). *President, Chocolate and Confectionery Division, W.R. Grace & Company, New York City, 1965–73. Author of* Chocolate Production and Use.
FARMING AND AGRICULTURE
   TECHNOLOGY (*in part*)
FOOD PROCESSING (*in part*)

L.R.L.   Lorna R. Levi. *Coauthor of* A Guide to Spiders and Their Kin; *cotranslator and coeditor of* Invertebrate Zoology *by A. Kaestner.*
ARACHNIDS (*in part*)

L.R.M.   Laurence Reginald (Bob) Mernagh (d. 1980). *Director, Institution of the Rubber Industry, London, 1966–70. Formerly Chief Chemist and Manager of Product Engineering, Firestone Tyre and Rubber Company Ltd. Editor of* Engineering Design—Rubber.
INDUSTRIES, CHEMICAL PROCESS (*in part*)

L.R.R.   Leonard R. Rogers. *Sculptor and writer. Former Head, Faculty of Three-Dimensional Design, College of Art and Design, Loughborough, England. Author of* Sculpture: Appreciation of the Arts; Relief Sculpture.
SCULPTURE, THE ART OF

L.S.   Leon Sokoloff, M.D. *Professor of Pathology, State University of New York at Stony Brook. Author of* The Biology of Degenerative Joint Disease.
SUPPORTIVE AND CONNECTIVE
   TISSUES (*in part*)

L.S.B.   Louis Stanley Berenson. *Owner and Chairman of the Board, Berensons' Hartford Jai-Alai, Connecticut.*
JAI ALAI (Micropædia)

L.S.El H.   Laila Shukry El Hamamsy. *Director, Social Research Center, American University in Cairo.*
EGYPT (*in part*)

L.S.F.   Lewis S. Feuer. *University Professor Emeritus of Sociology and Government, University of Virginia, Charlottesville. Author of* Marx and the Intellectuals *and others.*
MARXISM, MARX AND (*in part*)

L.S.Fe.   Luis Suárez Fernández. *Former Professor of History, University of Valladolid, Spain.*
SPAIN (*in part*)

L.Si.   Les Sirkin. *Professor of Earth Sciences, Adelphi University, Garden City, New York. Coauthor of* Earth History and Plate Tectonics.
GEOCHRONOLOGY (*in part*)

L.S.K.   Lester S. King, M.D. *Professorial Lecturer in the History of Medicine, University of Chicago. Author of* The Growth of Medical Thought.
JENNER, EDWARD (Micropædia)

L.S.M.   Lee S. Motteler. *President, GeoMap Corporation, Kaneohe, Hawaii. Coauthor of* Kaneohe: A History of Change.
UNITED STATES OF AMERICA (*in part*)

L.Sur.   Leo Suryadinata. *Former Research Associate, Centre for Southeast Asian Studies, Kyōto University, Japan. Author of* The Pre-World War II Peranakan Chinese Press of Java: A Preliminary Survey.
GAJAH MADA (Micropædia)
KERTANAGARA (Micropædia)

L.S.V.   Lalgudi Sivasubramanian Venkataramanan (deceased). *Director, Institute for Social and Economic Change, Bangalore, India. Author of* The Theory of Futures Trading.
MARKETS (*in part*)

L.T.   Lewis Thorpe (d. 1977). *Professor of French, University of Nottingham, England, 1958–77. Editor and translator of* Two Lives of Charlemagne.
LOUIS I (GERMANY/HOLY ROMAN
   EMPIRE) (Micropædia)

L.T.C.R.   L.T.C. Rolt (d. 1974). *Member, Executive Committee, American Society for the History of Technology. Chairman, Talyllyn Railway Company, England, 1963–68. Author of* Great Engineers *and many others.*
TREVITHICK, RICHARD (Micropædia)

L.Th.   Laura Thompson. *Consultant in applied anthropology. Field researcher on Hopi, Pagogo, Zuni, Navaho, and Sioux reservations. Author of* Culture in Crisis: A Study of the Hopi Indians *and others.*
AMERICAN INDIANS (*in part*)

L.T.N.   Lennart T. Norman. *Archivist and historian.*
MARGARET I (DENMARK/NORWAY/
   SWEDEN) (Micropædia)
SWEDEN (*in part*)

L.V.   Leo Vroman. *Senior Research Scientist, Department of Chemical Engineering, Columbia University. Physiologist, Medical Research Department, Veterans Administration Hospital, Brooklyn, New York, 1961–86. Author of* Blood.
TISSUES AND FLUIDS (*in part*)

L.V.A.   Lloyd Van Horn Armstrong (d. 1977). *Chief Engineer, Diesel Engine Department, Ingersoll Rand Company. Coauthor of* The Diesel Engine.
ENERGY CONVERSION (*in part*)

L.Ve.   Louis Verniers. *Honorary Secretary, General Ministry of Education, Belgium. Author of* Un millénaire d'historie de Bruxelles, des origines à 1830 *and others.*
BRUSSELS (*in part*)

L.v.G.   Ludwig von Gogolák. *Author of* Csehszlovákia; "T.G. Masaryks slowakische und ungarländische Politik: Ein Beitrag zur Vorgeschichte

des Zerfalls Ungarns im Jahre 1918" in Bohemia, Jahrbuch des Collegium Carolinum; *and others.*
MASARYK, TOMÁŠ (Micropædia)

L.Vi.   Luigi Villari (deceased). *Official in the Italian Foreign Office. Author of* Italian Life in Town and Country.
ITALY (*in part*)

L.V.M.   Leen Van Molle. *Research Associate of the National Fund for Scientific Research, Catholic University of Louvain, Belgium. Author of* Chacun pour tous: Le Boerenbond Belge 1890–1990.
BELGIUM (*in part*)

L.v.S.-P.   Luitfried von Salvini-Plawen. *Professor of Zoology, University of Vienna.*
MOLLUSKS (*in part*)

L.W.B.   Lewis W. Bealer. *Former Assistant Professor of History, University of Oklahoma, Norman.*
BRAZIL (*in part*)

L.W.D.   Larry W. Donald. *Editor and Publisher,* Basketball Times.
SPORTS, MAJOR TEAM AND INDIVIDUAL
   (*in part*)

L.We.   Leo Weaver. *Environmental engineering consultant. Executive Director and Chief Engineer, Ohio River Valley Water Sanitation Commission, Cincinnati, 1974–87. Technical editor of* Municipal Refuse Disposal; Refuse Collection Practice.
PUBLIC WORKS (*in part*)

L.Wy.   Sir Leonard Woolley (d. 1960). *Archaeologist; excavated at Ur, 1922–34, and many other sites. Major contributor to knowledge of the Sumerians. Author of* Digging Up the Past; Excavations at Ur.
UR (*in part*) (Micropædia)

L.Y.B.   Louay Y. Bahry. *Adjunct Professor of Political Science, University of Tennessee, Knoxville. Author of* Die Bagdad-Bahn: A Study in the Development and Diplomacy of the Baghdad Railway Question.
BAGHDAD (*in part*)

L.Z.   Lev Zetlin. *President, Zetlin-Argo Structural Investigations, Inc., New York City. Author of structural and civil engineering handbooks on concrete and suspension structures.*
STADIUM (*in part*) (Micropædia)

L.Zg.   Ladislav Zgusta. *Professor of Linguistics and of Classics; Member, Center for Advanced Studies, University of Illinois, Urbana. Author of* Kleinasiatische Personennamen; Personennamen griechischer Staedte; *and others.*
NAMES

M.A.   Marcelle Auclair (d. 1983). *Writer. Author of* Enfances et mort de Garcia Lorca; La Vie de Sainte Thérèse d'Avila; Le Livre du bonheur; *and others.*
GARCÍA LORCA, FEDERICO
   (Micropædia)

Ma.A.   Maurice Allais. *Professor of Economic Analysis, National College of

Mines of Paris. Professor of Monetary Analysis, University of Paris X, 1970–85. Nobel Prize for Economics, 1988. Author of Traité d'économie pure.
INTERNATIONAL TRADE (*in part*)

M.A.A.   Maynard A. Amerine. *Emeritus Professor of Enology, University of California, Davis; Emeritus Enologist at the Agricultural Experiment Station. Coauthor of* The Technology of Wine Making.
BEVERAGE PRODUCTION (*in part*)

Ma.A.C.   Margret A. Carey. *Former Assistant Keeper, Department of Ethnography, British Museum, London. Author of* Beads and Beadwork of East and South Africa *and others.*
AFRICAN ARTS (*in part*)

M.A.Al.   The Rev. Michel Adrien Allard, S.J. (d. 1976). *Director, Institute of Oriental Studies, St. Joseph University, Beirut, Lebanon. Author of* Le problème des attributs divins en théologie musulmane *and others.*
ASHʿARĪ, ABU AL-ḤASAN AL- (*in part*)
   (Micropædia)

Ma.B.   Marino Berengo. *Professor of Modern History, University of Venice. Author of* La società veneta alla fine del 700 *and others.*
ITALY (*in part*)

Ma.Br.   Martin Brett. *Fellow and Lecturer of Robinson College, University of Cambridge. Author of* English Church under Henry I.
EUROPEAN HISTORY AND CULTURE (*in part*)

Ma.Bu.   Martin Butlin. *Former Keeper of the British Collection, Tate Gallery, London. Author of* Turner Watercolours; *coauthor of* The Paintings of J.M.W. Turner.
TURNER, J.M.W. (*in part*) (Micropædia)

Ma.C.   Malcolm Cowley (d. 1989). *Literary Adviser, The Viking Press, 1948–85. President, National Institute of Arts and Letters, New York City, 1956–59, 1961–64. Literary Editor,* The New Republic, *1929–44. Author of* The Faulkner-Cowley File; *editor of* The Portable Faulkner.
FAULKNER, WILLIAM (Micropædia)

M.A.Ca.   Marcello A. Carmagnani. *Professor of Latin American History, University of Turin, Italy. Author of* El salariado minero en Chile colonial.
CHILE (*in part*)

M.A.E.   M. Albert Evans. *Mining consultant. Coauthor of* Demonstration Mine Using Longwall Mining Techniques; Technical Manual on Longwall Mining Systems.
INDUSTRIES, EXTRACTION AND
   PROCESSING (*in part*)

Ma.E.O.   Mario E. Occhialino. *Professor of Law, University of New Mexico, Albuquerque.*
PROCEDURAL LAW (*in part*)

Ma.F.   Marvin Frankel. *Professor of Economics, University of Illinois, Urbana. Author of* British and American

Manufacturing Productivity: A Comparison and Interpretation.
ECONOMIC GROWTH AND PLANNING
   (*in part*)

Ma.Fu.   Masutani Fumio. *Former Professor of the History of Religion, Taisho University, Tokyo.*
HŌNEN (Micropædia)

M.Ag.   Margarita Aguirre. *Writer. Author of* Las vidas de Pablo Neruda.
NERUDA, PABLO (Micropædia)

M.A.G.   Mahmud Ali Ghul (deceased). *Professor of Arabic and Semitic Languages, American University of Beirut.*
ARABIA (*in part*)

M.A.Gl.   Mary Ann Glendon. *Professor of Law, Harvard University. Author of* The New Family and the New Property.
INHERITANCE AND SUCCESSION (*in part*)
LAW, THE PRACTICE AND PROFESSION
   OF (*in part*)
LEGAL SYSTEMS, THE EVOLUTION OF
   MODERN WESTERN (*in part*)

Ma.H.   Marshall Hall, Jr. *Professor of Mathematics, Emory University, Atlanta, Georgia. IBM Professor Emeritus of Mathematics, California Institute of Technology, Pasadena. Author of* The Theory of Groups; Combinatorial Theory.
ALGEBRA (*in part*)

M.A.H.   Michael Anthony Hoskin. *President of Churchill College, University of Cambridge. Author of* William Herschel and the Construction of the Heavens.
LOVELL, SIR BERNARD (*in part*)
   (Micropædia)

Ma.Ha.   Mamie Harmon. *Contributor to* Dictionary of Folklore, Mythology and Legend; *contributor and advisory editor to* Encyclopedia of World Art.
FOLK ARTS (*in part*)

Ma.J.   Marsden Jones. *Professor of Arabic Studies, American University in Cairo. Editor of* Kitāb al-maghāzī lil-Wāgidī.
EGYPT (*in part*)

Ma.J.M.   Matthew James Moulton. *Former Chief Editorial Writer,* The Scotsman, *Edinburgh.*
UNITED KINGDOM (*in part*)

Ma.K.   Max Kaltenmark. *Director of Studies, École Pratique des Hautes Études (Institute for Advanced Research), Paris, 1957–78. Author of* Lao Tzu and Taoism.
LAO-TZU (Micropædia)

M.A.K.   Mark A. Kishlansky. *Professor of History, University of Chicago. Author of* Parliamentary Selection *and others.*
UNITED KINGDOM (*in part*)

Ma.Ko.   Margaret Kohl. *Free-lance writer and translator. Staff member, English Department, University of Munich, 1962–68; 1978–80.*
COLOGNE (*in part*)

M.Al.   Mohammad Ali (deceased). *Professor and Head, Department of*

History, Kābul University, Afghanistan. Author of *A Cultural History of Afghanistan;* Afghanistan: Land of Glorious Past; *and numerous other works on the history of Afghanistan, its culture, and its economy.*
AFGHANISTAN (*in part*)
MAḤMŪD (GHAZNA) (Micropædia)

Ma.M.   Maurice Matloff. *Adjunct Professor of History, Georgetown University, Washington, D.C. Chief Historian, Center of Military History, U.S. Department of the Army, Washington, D.C., 1973–81. Author of* Strategic Planning for Coalition Warfare, 1943–1944; *editor of* American Military History.
WAR, THE THEORY AND CONDUCT OF
   (*in part*)

M.A.M.   Maurice Alfred Millner. *Emeritus Professor of Law, University College, University of London. Author of* Negligence in Modern Law.
LEGAL SYSTEMS, THE EVOLUTION OF
   MODERN WESTERN (*in part*)

M.A.MacC.   Michael A. MacConaill (d. 1987). *Professor of Anatomy, University College, Cork, National University of Ireland. Coauthor of* Synovial Joints; Muscles and Movements.
SUPPORTIVE AND CONNECTIVE
   TISSUES (*in part*)

Ma.Me.   Matthew Meselson. *Professor of Biochemistry and Molecular Biology, Harvard University. Editor of* Chemical Weapons and Chemical Arms Control.
WAR, THE TECHNOLOGY OF (*in part*)

Ma.N.   Manning Nash. *Professor of Anthropology, University of Chicago. Specialist on economic development and cultural change. Author of* Machine-Age Maya.
AMERICAN INDIANS (*in part*)

Ma.P.   Maurizio Parotto. *Professor of Geology, University of Rome. Coauthor and coeditor of* Structural Model of Italy.
EUROPE (*in part*)

Ma.R.   Mary Rowlatt (d. 1983). *Free-lance writer on Egypt. Author of* Founders of Modern Egypt.
ALEXANDRIA (*in part*)

M.Ar.   Michael Argyle. *Reader in Social Psychology, University of Oxford; Fellow of Wolfson College, Oxford. Author of* Social Interaction; The Psychology of Interpersonal Behaviour.
SOCIAL SCIENCES, THE (*in part*)

M.A.R.   Margaret Ann Richardson. *Assistant Curator, Sir John Soane's Museum, London.*
PALLADIO, ANDREA (Micropædia)

M.A.Ro.   Margaret Ann Rowe. *Lecturer in English, Palmerston North Teachers' College, New Zealand. Coauthor of* New Zealand.
NEW ZEALAND (*in part*)

M.As.   Maurice Ashley. *Research Fellow, Loughborough University of Technology, England, 1967–70. Editor,* The Listener, *1958–67. Author of* The

Greatness of Oliver Cromwell.
CHARLES I (GREAT BRITAIN)
(Micropædia)

M.A.S.   M.A. Screech. *Senior Research Fellow, All Souls College, University of Oxford. Fielden Professor of French Language and Literature, University College, University of London, 1971–84. Author of* Rabelais *and others.*
RABELAIS, FRANÇOIS (*in part*)
(Micropædia)

M.A.Sa.   Michael Anthony Samuels. *Senior Vice President, Hill and Knowlton, Inc., Washington, D.C. Deputy U.S. Trade Representative and Ambassador, General Agreements on Tariffs and Trade, Geneva, 1986–89. U.S. Ambassador to Sierra Leone, 1974–77. Author of* Education in Angola, 1878–1914.
SOUTHERN AFRICA (*in part*)

M.A.Su.   Margaret Ann Sumner. *Lecturer in Physiology, University of Melbourne, Australia, and University College, University of London. Author of* Thought for Food.
DRUGS AND DRUG ACTION (*in part*)

M.A.v.M.   M.A. van Meerhaeghe. *Emeritus Professor of Economics, State University of Ghent, Belgium. Author of* International Economics *and others.*
INTERNATIONAL TRADE (*in part*)

M.B.   Minodhar Barthakur. *Visiting Professor, Manipur University, India. Former Professor of Geography, Gauhāti University, India. Author of numerous articles on geography.*
INDIA (*in part*)

M.Ba.   Michael Bar-Zohar. *Free-lance writer. Member of the Knesset. Lecturer in Political Science, Haifa University, Israel, 1970–73. Author of* Ben-Gurion: The Armed Prophet *and others.*
BEN-GURION, DAVID (Micropædia)

M.B.C.   Malcolm Breckenridge Carpenter, M.D. *Emeritus Professor of Anatomy, Uniformed Services University of the Health Sciences, Bethesda, Maryland. Author of* Core Text of Neuroanatomy.
NERVES AND NERVOUS SYSTEMS (*in part*)

M.Be.   Manfred Bensing. *Emeritus Professor of History, University of Leipzig. Author of* Thomas Müntzer.
MÜNTZER, THOMAS (Micropædia)

M.B.F.   Manuel Basas Fernández. *Former Professor, Faculty of Economic Sciences, University of Valladolid, Spain. Author of* Breve Historia de la ria y noble Villa de Bilbao.
SPAIN (*in part*)

M.Bg.   Mark Blaug. *Consultant Professor of Economics, University of Buckingham, England. Emeritus Professor of the Economics of Education, Institute of Education, University of London. Author of* Economic Theory in Retrospect.
SOCIAL SCIENCES, THE (*in part*)

M.B.G.   Manuel Ballesteros Gaibrois. *Professor and Head, Section of American History, University of Madrid. Author of* Francisco Pizarro *and others.*
PIZARRO, FRANCISCO (*in part*)
(Micropædia)

M.Bi.   Margarete Bieber (d. 1978). *Associate Professor of Art History and Archaeology, Columbia University, 1937–48; Special Lecturer, School of General Studies, 1949–54. Author of* The History of the Greek and Roman Theater; The Sculpture of the Hellenistic Age.
DRESS AND ADORNMENT (*in part*)

M.B.J.   Marius B. Jansen. *Professor of History, Princeton University. Author of* Sakamoto Ryōma and the Meiji Restoration *and others.*
JAPAN (*in part*)

M.Bl.   Miroslav Blažek. *Former Professor of Human Geography and of Regional Economy, School of Economics, Prague. Author of* Economic Geography of Czechoslovakia.
CZECHOSLOVAKIA (*in part*)

M.B.McE.   Michael B. McElroy. *Abbott Lawrence Rotch Professor of Atmospheric Sciences; Chairman, Department of Earth and Planetary Sciences, Harvard University.*
ATMOSPHERE (*in part*)

M.Bo.   Marc Bouloiseau. *Former Secretary, Commission for the Economic and Social History of the French Revolution. Emeritus Teaching Assistant in History of the French Revolution, University of Paris. Author of* Robespierre *and others.*
ROBESPIERRE, MAXIMILIEN-FRANÇOIS-MARIE-ISIDORE DE (Micropædia)

M.B.R.   Michael B. Rowton (d. 1986). *Professor of Near Eastern Languages and Civilizations, Oriental Institute, University of Chicago.*
HISTORY, THE STUDY OF (*in part*)

M.B.T.   Martin B. Thorp. *Senior Lecturer in Geography, University College, Dublin, National University of Ireland. Coauthor of* An Advanced Geography of Africa.
WESTERN AFRICA (*in part*)

M.Bu.   Milton Burton (d. 1985). *Professor of Chemistry, University of Notre Dame, Indiana, 1945–71; Director, Radiation Laboratory, 1946–71. Coeditor of* Advances in Radiation Chemistry.
RADIATION (*in part*)

M.C.   Maurice Cranston. *Emeritus Professor of Political Science, London School of Economics and Political Science, University of London. Biographer of Locke and Rousseau.*
GENEVA (*in part*)
HUME (*in part*)
IDEOLOGY
ROUSSEAU, JEAN-JACQUES

M.Car.   Max Cary (d. 1958). *Reader, then Professor of Ancient History, University of London, 1908–46. Author of* The Geographic Background of Greek and Roman History.

GREEK AND ROMAN CIVILIZATIONS, ANCIENT (*in part*)

M.C.G.   M. Charles Gilbert. *Professor of Geology, Texas A&M University, College Station.*
MINERALS AND ROCKS (*in part*)

McG.G.   McGuire Gibson. *Professor of Mesopotamian Archaeology, University of Chicago. Author of* The City and Area of Kish; *editor of* The Organization of Power; Aspects of Bureaucracy in the Ancient Near East.
ASIA (*in part*)

M.Ch.   Mary Chamot. *Assistant Keeper, Tate Gallery, London, 1950–65. Author of* Modern Painting in England.
TURNER, J.M.W. (*in part*)
(Micropædia)

M.C.J.   Marshall C. Johnston. *Professor of Botany; Associate Director, Plant Resources Center, University of Texas at Austin. Coauthor of* Manual of the Vascular Plants of Texas.
ANGIOSPERMS (*in part*)

Mc.M.   McKim Marriott. *Professor of Anthropology, University of Chicago. Author of* Caste Ranking and Community Structure in Five Regions of India and Pakistan *and others.*
SOCIAL DIFFERENTIATION (*in part*)

M.C.M.   Michael C. Meyer. *Professor of History, University of Arizona, Tucson. Coauthor of* The Course of Mexican History.
MEXICO (*in part*)

M.C.Ma.   Michael C. Malin. *Professor of Geology, Arizona State University, Tempe. Coauthor of* Earthlike Planets.
SOLAR SYSTEM, THE (*in part*)

M.Co.   Michael Cordner. *Senior Lecturer in English and Related Literature, University of York, England. Editor of* The Plays of Sir George Etherege.
ENGLISH LITERATURE (*in part*)

M.C.P.   Michael Charles Prestwich. *Professor of History, University of Durham, England. Author of* The Three Edwards *and others.*
UNITED KINGDOM (*in part*)

M.C.R.   Marvin Chauncey Ross (d. 1977). *Curator, Hillwood (art collections of Mrs. Merriweather Post), Washington, D.C. Chief Curator, Los Angeles County Museum of Art, 1952–55.*
DECORATIVE ARTS AND FURNISHINGS (*in part*)

M.C.S.   Malcolm C. Shurtleff. *Professor of Plant Pathology; Extension Plant Pathologist, University of Illinois, Urbana. Author of* How to Control Plant Diseases in Home and Garden.
DISEASE (*in part*)

M.Cu.   Michael Cuffe. *Writer on biology.*
CELLS (*in part*)

M.C.U.   Melvyn C. Usselman. *Associate Professor of Chemistry, University of Western Ontario, London.*
PHYSICAL SCIENCES, THE (*in part*)

M.D. **Myles Dillon** (d. 1972). *Senior Professor of Celtic Studies, Dublin Institute for Advanced Studies, 1949–72. Author of* Early Irish Society.
EUROPEAN RELIGIONS, ANCIENT
(*in part*)

M.Da. **Monique Dacharry.** *Professor of Geography, University of Lille I, France. Author of* Hydrologie de la Loire *and others.*
EUROPE (*in part*)

M.D.B. **Marvin David Bernstein.** *Emeritus Professor of History, State University of New York at Buffalo. Author of* The Mexican Mining Industry, 1890–1950.
MEXICO (*in part*)

M.D.C. **Michael Douglas Coe.** *Professor of Anthropology, Yale University. Author of* The Maya.
PRE-COLUMBIAN CIVILIZATIONS (*in part*)

M.-D.Ch. **The Rev. Marie-Dominique Chenu, O.P.** (d. 1990). *Lecturer, École pratique des hautes études, Paris, 1945–51. Author of* Toward Understanding St. Thomas *and others.*
THOMISM, THOMAS AQUINAS AND
(*in part*)

M.D.D. **Morton D. Davis.** *Professor of Mathematics, City College, City University of New York. Author of* Game Theory: A Nontechnical Introduction.
GAME THEORY

M.De. **Mary Delane.** *Free-lance writer. Women's Editor,* The Times (*London*), *1954–64. Author of* Sardinia: The Undefeated Island.
ITALY (*in part*)

M. de F. **Michael de Ferdinandy.** *Emeritus Professor of Humanities, University of Puerto Rico, Río Piedras. Author of* El emperador Carlos V: semblanza de un hombre *and others.*
CHARLES V (GERMANY/HOLY ROMAN
EMPIRE) (*in part*) (Micropædia)

M. Del V. **Mario Del Viscovo.** *Professor of Economics and Politics of Transport, University of Rome. Director, Centre for Studies of Transportation Systems, Rome. Author of* Il conto nazionale dei trasporti.
ITALY (*in part*)

M.D.H.M. **Mark D.H. Miller.** *Research Associate, Syracuse University, New York.*
SOUTH AMERICA (*in part*)

M.D.K. **The Rev. Michael David Knowles, O.S.B.** (d. 1974). *Regius Professor of Modern History, University of Cambridge, 1954–63. Author of* The Benedictines: A Digest for Moderns; The Evolution of Medieval Thought; Thomas Becket; *and others.*
BECKET, SAINT THOMAS (Micropædia)
BENEDICT OF NURSIA, SAINT
(Micropædia)
HENRY II (ENGLAND) (Micropædia)
MACAULAY, THOMAS
BABINGTON MACAULAY, BARON
(Micropædia)
ROMAN CATHOLICISM (*in part*)

M.Do. **Martin Domke** (d. 1980). *Adjunct Professor of Law, New York University, New York City. Consultant on commercial and international arbitration. Author of* The Law and Practice of Commercial Arbitration.
JUDICIAL AND ARBITRATIONAL
SYSTEMS (*in part*)

M.Dr. **Moira Dunbar.** *Acting Director, Division of Earth Sciences, Defence Research Board, Ottawa, Canada, 1975–77.*
ARCTIC, THE (*in part*)

M.D.R. **Milton D. Rafferty.** *Professor and Head, Department of Geosciences, Southwest Missouri State University, Springfield. Author of* Missouri: A Geography *and others.*
UNITED STATES OF AMERICA (*in part*)

M.Du. **Maurice Duverger.** *Emeritus Professor of Political Science, University of Paris I. Member, European Parliament. Author of* Les Partis politiques.
POLITICAL PARTIES AND INTEREST
GROUPS (*in part*)

M. Du P.C. **Martin Du Pré Cooper** (d. 1986). *Music Editor,* Daily Telegraph, *London, 1954–76. Author of* French Music, 1869–1924; Georges Bizet.
BIZET, GEORGES (Micropædia)
FRANCK, CÉSAR (Micropædia)

M.E. **Marcel Emerit.** *Emeritus Professor of History; Member, Academy of Ethics and Politics, Institute of France. Author of* L'Algérie à l'époque d' Abd-el-Kader.
ABDELKADER (Micropædia)

M.E.Bl. **Milton E. Bliss.** *Farmer and agricultural communications specialist. Author of* A Handbook on Farm Broadcasting for the Developing Countries.
FARMING AND AGRICULTURAL
TECHNOLOGY (*in part*)

M.Ec. **Myron Echenberg.** *Associate Professor of History, McGill University, Montreal.*
WESTERN AFRICA (*in part*)

M.E.D. **M. Edward Davis, M.D.** (d. 1978). *Joseph Bolivar De Lee Professor of Obstetrics and Gynecology, University of Chicago, 1947–66. Coauthor of* De Lee's Obstetrics for Nurses.
REPRODUCTION AND REPRODUCTIVE
SYSTEMS (*in part*)

M.E.DeB. **Michael E. DeBakey, M.D.** *Chancellor, Baylor College of Medicine; Professor and Chairman, Department of Surgery. Director, DeBakey Heart Center, Methodist Hospital, Houston, Texas. Coauthor of* Blood Transfusion.
CIRCULATION AND CIRCULATORY
SYSTEMS (*in part*)

M.e.D.S. **Mohy el Din Sabr.** *Director General, Arab League Educational, Cultural and Scientific Organization, Cairo. Minister of Education, Republic of The Sudan, 1969–72. Author of* Cultural Change and Community Development.
SUDAN (*in part*)

M.Ee. **Mircea Eliade** (d. 1986). *Sewell L. Avery Distinguished Service Professor, Divinity School; Professor, Committee on Social Thought, University of Chicago.*
SACRED OFFICES AND ORDERS (*in part*)

Me.F. **Menso Folkerts.** *Director, Institute for the History of Science, Ludwig Maximilian University of Munich. Author of* "Boethius" Geometrie II: ein mathematisches Lehrbuch des Mittelalters.
MATHEMATICS, THE HISTORY OF (*in part*)

Me.F.G. **Mercedes Fermín Gómez.** *Professor of Geography, Central University of Venezuela, Caracas. Author of* The Orinoco Basin.
SOUTH AMERICA (*in part*)

M.E.H. **Melvin E. Hecht** (deceased). *Professor of Geography and Regional Development, University of Arizona, Tucson.*
UNITED STATES OF AMERICA (*in part*)

M.E.Ho. **Sir Michael E. Howard.** *Robert E. Lovett Professor of Military and Naval History, Yale University. Regius Professor of Modern History, University of Oxford, 1980–89. Author of* War in European History *and others.*
WAR, THE THEORY AND CONDUCT OF
(*in part*)

M.E.J. **Martin Evan Jay.** *Professor of History, University of California, Berkeley. Author of* The Dialectical Imagination *and others.*
FREUD

M.E.Jo. **Markes E. Johnson.** *Professor of Geology, Williams College, Williamstown, Massachusetts.*
GEOCHRONOLOGY (*in part*)

M.E.M. **Martin E. Marty.** *Fairfax M. Cone Distinguished Service Professor, Divinity School, University of Chicago. Senior Editor,* The Christian Century. *Author of* Religion & Republic: The American Circumstance *and others.*
CHRISTIANITY (*in part*)
PROTESTANTISM (*in part*)
ROMAN CATHOLICISM (*in part*)

M.E.Ma. **Martin E. Malia.** *Professor of History, University of California, Berkeley. Author of* Alexander Herzen and the Birth of Russian Socialism, 1812–1855.
HERZEN, ALEKSANDR (Micropædia)

M.E.O. **Milton Edgeworth Osborne.** *Head, Asia—Pacific Branch, Office of National Assessments, Canberra, Australia. Author of* Southeast Asia: An Illustrated Introductory History.
SOUTHEAST ASIA, MAINLAND (*in part*)

M.E.P. **Maynard E. Pirsig.** *Emeritus Professor of Law, University of Minnesota, Minneapolis. Professor of Law, William Mitchell College of Law, St. Paul, Minnesota. Coauthor of* Cases and Materials on Professional Responsibility.
LAW, THE PROFESSION AND PRACTICE
OF (*in part*)

M.E.R. **Marjorie E. Reeves.** *Honorary Fellow and former Vice-Principal, St.*

Anne's College, Oxford; former Lecturer in Modern History, University of Oxford. Author of The Influence of Prophecy in the Later Middle Ages: A Study in Joachimism and others.
JOACHIM OF FIORE (Micropædia)

M.E.Ro.   M. Elizabeth Rogers. Lecturer in Zoology, University of Edinburgh. Author of Looking at Vertebrates.
CIRCULATION AND CIRCULATORY SYSTEMS (in part)

M.E.T.   Mary Elizabeth Tiles. Associate Professor of Philosophy, University of Hawaii at Manoa, Honolulu. Author of Bachelard: Science and Objectivity and others.
PHILOSOPHICAL ANTHROPOLOGY (in part)

M.E.Y.   Malcolm Edward Yapp. Professor of the Modern History of Western Asia, School of Oriental and African Studies, University of London.
TURKEY AND ANCIENT ANATOLIA (in part)

M.F.   Merle Fainsod (d. 1972). Carl H. Pforzheimer Professor of Government; Director of the Library, Harvard University, 1965–72; Director, Russian Research Center, 1959–64. Author of How Russia Is Ruled and others.
UNION OF SOVIET SOCIALIST REPUBLICS (in part)

M.F.A.   Sir Michael Francis Atiyah. Master, Trinity College, University of Cambridge. Royal Society Research Professor, Mathematical Institute, University of Oxford, 1973–90. Author of K-Theory; coauthor of Introduction to Commutative Algebra.
GEOMETRY (in part)

M.F.Go.   Morris F. Goodman. Associate Professor of Linguistics, Northwestern University, Evanston, Illinois. Author of several articles on African languages and A Comparative Study of Creole French Dialects.
LANGUAGES OF THE WORLD (in part)

M.Fl.   Marcel Florkin, M.D. (d. 1979). Professor of Biochemistry, State University of Liège, Belgium. Author of L'Evolution biochimique.
VESALIUS, ANDREAS (in part) (Micropædia)

M.F.M.   Mark F. Meier. Director, Institute of Arctic and Alpine Research; Professor of Geological Sciences, University of Colorado, Boulder.
ICE AND ICE FORMATIONS (in part)

M.F.Mo.   Maynard F. Moseley, Jr. Professor of Botany, University of California, Santa Barbara. Author of a series of morphological studies on the family Nymphaeaceae.
ANGIOSPERMS (in part)

M.Fo.   Murray Fowler. Emeritus Professor of Linguistics, University of Wisconsin, Madison. Coeditor of Materials for the Study of the Etruscan Language.
LANGUAGES OF THE WORLD (in part)

M.F.O.   Michael Francis Oliver, M.D. Director, Wynn Institute for Metabolic Research, London. Duke of Edinburgh Professor of Cardiology, University of Edinburgh, 1979–89. Editor of Coronary Heart Disease in Young Women.
CIRCULATION AND CIRCULATORY SYSTEMS (in part)

M.Fr.   Milton Friedman. Paul Snowden Russell Distinguished Service Professor Emeritus of Economics, University of Chicago. Senior Research Fellow, Hoover Institution, Stanford University, California. Nobel Prize for Economics, 1976. Author of Price Theory and others.
MONEY

M.Fre.   Michael Freund (d. 1973). Professor of Political Theory and History, Christian Albrecht University of Kiel, West Germany. Author of Deutsche Geschichte; "Friedrich Ebert" in Die grossen Deutschen; and others.
EBERT, FRIEDRICH (Micropædia)

M.F.S.   Mark F. Schwartz. Research and Clinical Associate; Director of Educational Programs, Masters and Johnson Institute, St. Louis, Missouri.
SEX AND SEXUALITY (in part)

M.G.   Marija Gimbutas. Professor of European Archaeology, University of California, Los Angeles. Author of The Bronze Age Cultures of Central and Eastern Europe; The Language of the Goddess; and others.
BALTIC STATES (in part)
PREHISTORIC PEOPLES AND CULTURES (in part)

M.Ga.   Mikael Gam (d. 1982). Minister for Greenland, 1960–64. Author of Den grønlandske kvinde.
ARCTIC, THE (in part)

M.G.A.V.   Malcolm G.A. Vale. Fellow and Tutor in History, St. John's College, Oxford; Lecturer in Modern History, University of Oxford. Author of War and Chivalry and others.
JOAN OF ARC (in part)

M.G.B.   Michael Graham Balfour. Emeritus Professor of European History, University of East Anglia, Norwich, England. Author of The Kaiser and His Times.
WILLIAM II (GERMAN EMPIRE) (Micropædia)

M.Gi.   Martin Gimm. Professor of Sinology, University of Cologne.
DORGON (Micropædia)

M.G.Ma.   Maxwell Gay Marwick. Reader in Humanities, Griffith University, Brisbane, Australia, 1976–81. Professor of Sociology, University of Stirling, Scotland, 1969–74. Author of Sorcery in Its Social Setting: A Study of the Northern Rhodesian Ceŵa.
OCCULTISM (in part)

M.Gr.   Michael Grant. President and Vice-Chancellor, Queen's University of Belfast, Northern Ireland, 1959–66. Author of History of Rome; Myths of the Greeks and Romans; and others; editor of Latin Literature and others.
ANTONY, MARK (Micropædia)

AUGUSTUS
EUROPEAN RELIGIONS, ANCIENT (in part)
HORACE (Micropædia)

M.G.W.   M. Gordon Wolman. Professor and Chairman, Department of Geography and Environmental Engineering, Johns Hopkins University, Baltimore, Maryland. An authority on fluvial processes and ecological problems concerning rivers. Coauthor of Fluvial Processes in Geomorphology.
GEOMORPHIC PROCESSES (in part)

M.H.   Maureen Heneghan Tripp. Costume Designer, Stratford-on-Avon Shakespeare Company, BBC-TV, and Stratford Festival, Ontario. Associate Professor of Costume Design, Brandeis University, Waltham, Massachusetts.
THEATRICAL PRODUCTION (in part)

M.Ha.   Mason Hammond. Pope Professor Emeritus of Latin Language and Literature; former Professor of Roman History, Harvard University. Author of The Antonine Monarchy.
TRAJAN (Micropædia)

M.H.A.   Marvin H. Alisky. Professor of Political Science, Arizona State University, Tempe. Author of Uruguay: A Contemporary Survey and others.
URUGUAY (in part)

M.Has.   Margaret Hastings (d. 1979). Professor of History, Douglass College, Rutgers University, New Brunswick, New Jersey, 1960–75. Author of The Court of Common Pleas in Fifteenth Century England and others.
UNITED KINGDOM (in part)

M.H.Au.   Maung Htin Aung (d. 1978). Associate Fellow, St. Antony's College, University of Oxford. Burmese Ambassador to Ceylon, 1959–63. Rector and Vice-Chancellor, University of Rangoon, 1946–59. Author of Burmese Drama; A History of Burma; and others.
SOUTHEAST ASIA, MAINLAND (in part)
SOUTHEAST ASIAN ARTS (in part)

M.H.B.   M.H. Butler. Lecturer in English, University of Leeds, England. Author of Theatre and Crisis, 1632–1642.
ENGLISH LITERATURE (in part)

M.H.Bo.   Marc H. Bornstein. Head, Child and Family Research, National Institute of Child Health and Human Development, U.S. Department of Health and Human Services, Bethesda, Maryland. Author of Development in Infancy: An Introduction and others.
BEHAVIOR, THE DEVELOPMENT OF HUMAN (in part)

M.H.C.   Mary Heimerdinger Clench. Assistant Professor (Research), Department of Internal Medicine, University of Texas Medical Branch at Galveston. Research Associate, Carnegie Museum of Natural History, Pittsburgh. Author and coauthor of numerous articles on birds.
BIRDS (in part)

M.H.D.   Michael H. Day. Staff member, Department of Palaeontology, British Museum (Natural History),

London. Emeritus Professor of Anatomy, United Medical and Dental Schools of Guy's and St. Thomas's Hospitals, University of London. Author of Guide to Fossil Man.

EVOLUTION, HUMAN (*in part*)

M.H.K.   Malcolm H. Kerr (d. 1984). *President, American University of Beirut, 1982–84. Professor of Political Science, University of California, Los Angeles, 1967–82. Author of* Islamic Reform: The Political and Legal Theories of Muhammad 'Abduh and Rashid Rida.

'ABDUH, MUḤAMMAD (Micropædia)

M.H.S.   The Rev. Massey H. Shepherd, Jr. *Hodges Professor Emeritus of Liturgics, Church Divinity School of the Pacific, Berkeley, California. Author of* The Worship of the Church *and others.*

CHRISTIANITY (*in part*)

M.Hu.   Mahmud Husain (d. 1975). *Vice-Chancellor, University of Karāchi, Pakistan. Editor of* History of the Freedom Movement.

JINNAH, MOHAMMED ALI (Micropædia)

M.H.W.   Michael Henry Woodford. *Secretary, British Falconers' Club, London, 1956–67. Author of* A Manual of Falconry.

FALCONRY (*in part*) (Micropædia)

M.H.Wo.   Milford H. Wolpoff. *Professor of Anthropology, University of Michigan, Ann Arbor. Author of* Paleoanthropology.

EVOLUTION, HUMAN (*in part*)

M.H.Z.   Martin Huldrych Zimmermann (d. 1984). *Charles Bullard Professor of Forestry, Harvard University; Director, Harvard Forest, Petersham, 1970–84. Coauthor of* Trees: Structure and Function.

TISSUES AND FLUIDS (*in part*)

M.I.A.L.   Michael I.A. Linton. *Assistant Professor of History, University of Aarhus, Denmark.*

DENMARK (*in part*)

M.I.B.   Michael I. Bruce. *Angas Professor of Chemistry, University of Adelaide, Australia. Coeditor of* Progress in Organometallic Chemistry.

CHEMICAL COMPOUNDS (*in part*)

M.I.C.   Dame Margaret I. Cole (d. 1980). *Honorary President, Fabian Society, England. Author of* Beatrice Webb *and others; editor of* The Webbs and Their Work.

WEBB, SIDNEY AND BEATRICE (Micropædia)

Mi.D.   Michael A.E. Dummett. *Wykeham Professor of Logic, University of Oxford; Fellow of New College, Oxford. Author of* Frege: Philosophy of Language *and others.*

FREGE, GOTTLOB (Micropædia)

M.I.H.   Marvin Irving Herzog. *Atran Professor Emeritus of Linguistics and Yiddish Studies, Columbia University. Director, Language and Culture Atlas of Ashkenazic Jewry. Author of* The Yiddish Language in Northern Poland;

coeditor of The Field of Yiddish, *Third and Fourth Collections.*

LANGUAGES OF THE WORLD (*in part*)

Mi.He.   Markku Ilmari Henriksson. *Co-Director, North American Studies Program; Assistant for Non-European History, Renvall Institute of Historical Research, University of Helsinki.*

FINLAND (*in part*)

Mi.L.   Michael Levi. *Reader in Criminology, University of Wales College of Cardiff. Author of* Regulating Fraud: White-collar Crime and the Criminal Process *and others.*

CRIME AND PUNISHMENT (*in part*)

Mi.Ma.   Michael Edward Mallett. *Professor of History, University of Warwick, England. Author of* The Borgias *and others.*

BORGIA, CESARE, DUC DE VALENTINOIS (Micropædia)

M.I.R.   Mikhail Ivanovich Rostovtsev. *Senior Research Associate, Institute of Geography, Academy of Sciences of the U.S.S.R., Moscow. Coauthor of* Belorussian S.S.R.

UNION OF SOVIET SOCIALIST REPUBLICS (*in part*)

Mi.Ro.   Michel Rouzé. *Former producer in French broadcasting. Author of* Robert Oppenheimer and the Atomic Bomb; Robert Oppenheimer: The Man and His Theories.

OPPENHEIMER, J. ROBERT (Micropædia)

M.I.S.   Merrill I. Skolnik. *Superintendent, Radar Division, Naval Research Laboratory, Office of Naval Research, U.S. Department of the Navy, Washington, D.C. Author of* Introduction to Radar Systems.

RADAR

Mi.T.   Michael Talbot. *Professor of Music, University of Liverpool, England. Author of* Vivaldi.

VIVALDI, ANTONIO (Micropædia)

Mi.V.   Michele Vishny. *Art historian and critic. Author of* Mordcai Ardon; *contributor to* Arts Magazine.

PISSARRO, CAMILLE (Micropædia)

M.I.V.   Milton I. Vanger. *Emeritus Professor of History, Brandeis University, Waltham, Massachusetts; Chairman of Latin American Studies, 1971–81. Author of* José Batlle y Ordoñez of Uruguay (*2 vol.*).

URUGUAY (*in part*)

M.I.W.   Matthew Immanuel Wiencke. *Professor of Classics, Dartmouth College, Hanover, New Hampshire.*

WINCKELMANN, JOHANN (Micropædia)

M.I.Wr.   Marion I. Wright. *Emerita Professor of Geography, Rhode Island College, Providence. Author of* Providence: A Metropolitan Region.

UNITED STATES OF AMERICA (*in part*)

M.J.   Madeleine Jarry (d. 1982). *Principal Inspector, Mobilier National (state furniture collection); National Factories of Gobelins and Beauvais (tapestry); and of the Savonnerie (carpet factory), Ministry of Cultural Affairs,*

France. Author of World Tapestry.

DECORATIVE ARTS AND FURNISHINGS (*in part*)

M.J.B.   Margaret J. Baigent. *Associate Professor of Nutrition, University of Toronto.*

BIOCHEMICAL COMPONENTS OF ORGANISMS (*in part*)

M.J.D.   Mário José Domingues. *Author of* O Marquês de Pombal *and others.*

POMBAL, SEBASTIÃO DE CARVALHO, MARQUÊS DE (Micropædia)

M.J.Dr.   Mark J. Dresden (d. 1986). *Professor of Iranian Studies, University of Pennsylvania, Philadelphia, 1960–80. Editor of* Modern Persian Reader.

IRAN (*in part*)

M.J.Du.   Maxwell John Dunbar. *Emeritus Professor of Oceanography, McGill University, Montreal; Chairman, Marine Sciences Center, 1963–77. Author of* Ecological Development in Polar Regions.

ARCTIC, THE (*in part*)

M.J.E.   Martin J. Esslin. *Emeritus Professor of Drama, Stanford University, California. Head of Radio Drama, British Broadcasting Corporation, London, 1963–77. Author of* Brecht: The Man and His Work; The Theatre of the Absurd.

BECKETT, SAMUEL (*in part*) (Micropædia)

M.J.E.B.   Maurice J.E. Brown (d. 1975). *Author of* Schubert: A Critical Biography; Essays on Schubert.

SCHUBERT, FRANZ (*in part*) (Micropædia)

M.J.G.   Michael James Godman. *Senior Lecturer in Child Life and Health, University of Edinburgh. Consultant Paediatric Cardiologist, Royal Hospital for Sick Children, Edinburgh. Coeditor of* Heart Disease in the Newborn.

CIRCULATION AND CIRCULATORY SYSTEMS (*in part*)

M.J.K.   Martin J. Klein. *Eugene Higgins Professor of the History of Physics, Yale University.*

BOHR (*in part*)

M.J.Ke.   Martin J. Kemp. *Professor of Fine Arts, University of St. Andrews, Scotland.*

ARCHITECTURE, THE HISTORY OF WESTERN (*in part*)
PAINTING, THE HISTORY OF WESTERN (*in part*)
SCULPTURE, THE HISTORY OF WESTERN (*in part*)

M.J.L.   Margaret Jean Legum. *Free-lance journalist. Editor,* X-Ray on Current Affairs in Southern Africa. *Coauthor of* South Africa: Crisis for the West.

SOUTH AFRICA (*in part*)

M.J.Lo.   M. John Loeffler. *Emeritus Professor of Geography, University of Colorado, Boulder. Author of several articles on Colorado.*

UNITED STATES OF AMERICA (*in part*)

M.J.MacL.   Murdo J. MacLeod. *Graduate Research Professor of History,*

University of Florida, Gainesville. Author of Spanish Central America.
ECUADOR (*in part*)
WEST INDIES, THE (*in part*)

M.J.Mo. Michel J. Mollat. *Emeritus Professor of History, University of Paris. Author of* Genèse médiévale de la France moderne; Les Affaires de Jacques Coeur.
CHARLES (BURGUNDY) (Micropædia)
COEUR, JACQUES (Micropædia)
LOUIS XI (FRANCE) (Micropædia)

M.Jo. Matthew Josephson (d. 1978). *Author of* Edison: A Biography.
EDISON (*in part*)

M.J.O. Margaret J. Osler. *Associate Professor of History, University of Calgary, Alberta.*
PHYSICAL SCIENCES, THE (*in part*)

M.J.Pi. Mark Jeffrey Pietka. *Technical Director, Cadbury Beverages Latin America, Inc., Fort Lauderdale, Florida.*
BEVERAGE PRODUCTION (*in part*)

M.J.S.B. Michael J.S. Belton. *Astronomer, Kitt Peak National Observatory, Tucson, Arizona.*
SOLAR SYSTEM, THE (*in part*)

M.J.V. Mark J. Valencia. *Research Associate, Resource Systems Institute, East-West Center, Honolulu. Author of* South-East Asian Seas: Oil Under Troubled Waters; *Coeditor of* Atlas for Marine Policy in East Asia.
PACIFIC OCEAN, THE (*in part*)

M.K. Michael Kennedy. *Chief Music Critic, Sunday Telegraph (London). Author of* Richard Strauss.
STRAUSS, RICHARD (Micropædia)

M.Ke. Mark Keller. *Emeritus Professor, Rutgers University, New Brunswick, New Jersey; Emeritus Editor,* Journal of Studies on Alcohol. *Editor of* International Bibliography of Studies on Alcohol.
ALCOHOL AND DRUG CONSUMPTION (*in part*)

M.Kh. Majid Khadduri. *Emeritus Professor of Middle East Studies, School of Advanced International Studies, Johns Hopkins University, Washington, D.C. Author of* Independent Iraq; Republican Iraq; Socialist Iraq; *and others.*
IRAQ (*in part*)

M.Ki. Martin Kilson. *Professor of Government, Harvard University; Research Associate, Harvard Center for International Affairs. Author of* Political Change in a West African State.
KAUNDA, KENNETH (Micropædia)

M.K.L. Mildred K. Lehman. *Researcher on* This High Man: The Life of Robert H. Goddard.
GODDARD, ROBERT HUTCHINGS (*in part*) (Micropædia)

M.K.N. Mehdi K. Nakosteen (d. 1982). *Professor of the History and Philosophy of Education, University of Colorado, Boulder. Author of* The History and Philosophy of Education.
EDUCATION, HISTORY OF (*in part*)

M.Ko. Mieczyslaw Kolinski (d. 1981). *Composer, ethnomusicologist, and author of numerous musicological and ethnomusicological articles.*
MUSIC, THE ART OF (*in part*)

M.K.P. Macaire K. Pedanou. *Director, Office of the Commissioner for Namibia, United Nations, New York City.*
WESTERN AFRICA (*in part*)

M.Kr. Melvin Kranzberg. *Emeritus Professor of the History of Technology, Georgia Institute of Technology, Atlanta. Editor in Chief,* Technology and Culture *(quarterly), 1958–81. Coauthor of* By the Sweat of Thy Brow: Work in the Western World.
WORK AND EMPLOYMENT (*in part*)

M.K.Sp. Monroe K. Spears. *Moody Professor of English, Rice University, Houston, Texas. Author of* The Poetry of W.H. Auden; Dionysus and the City; *editor of* W.H. Auden: A Collection of Critical Essays.
AUDEN, W.H. (Micropædia)

M.K.W. Marcus K. Williams. *Senior member of sports staff,* The Times *(London). Editor of* Double Century: 200 Years of Cricket in The Times.
SPORTS, MAJOR TEAM AND INDIVIDUAL (*in part*)

M.L.-B. Massimo Livi-Bacci. *Professor of Demography, University of Florence. President, International Union for the Scientific Study of Population. Author of* A History of Italian Fertility *and others.*
ITALY (*in part*)

M.L.C. Martin Lowther Clarke. *Former Professor of Latin, University College of North Wales, Bangor, University of Wales. Author of* Rhetoric at Rome; Higher Education in the Ancient World.
QUINTILIAN (Micropædia)

M.L.Cl. Martha L. Clark. *Special Assistant to the Archivist, Massachusetts State Archives, Boston.*
UNITED STATES OF AMERICA (*in part*)

M.L.D. Mikhail Leonidovich Djibladze. *Journalist.*
UNION OF SOVIET SOCIALIST REPUBLICS (*in part*)

M.Le. Michel Lejeune. *Director of Research, National Center for Scientific Research, Paris, 1963–78. Author of* Phonétique historique du mycénien et du grec ancien *and others.*
LANGUAGES OF THE WORLD (*in part*)

M.L.Go. Marie Louise Goodnight. *Free-lance writer and researcher. Instructor in Biological Sciences, Purdue University, West Lafayette, Indiana, 1946–65. Coauthor of* General Zoology.
ARACHNIDS (*in part*)

M.Li. Martin Lindauer. *Emeritus Professor of Zoology and Comparative Physiology; Emeritus Director, Zoological Institute, University of Würzburg, Germany. Author of* Communication Among Social Bees.
INSECTS (*in part*)

Ml.J. Michael Jaffé. *Professor of the History of Western Art; Director, Fitzwilliam Museum, University of Cambridge; Fellow of King's College, Cambridge. Author of* Rubens and Italy *and others.*
RUBENS, PETER PAUL (*in part*) (Micropædia)

M.Ln. Milton Lehman (d. 1966). *Free-lance writer. Author of* This High Man: The Life of Robert H. Goddard.
GODDARD, ROBERT HUTCHINGS (*in part*) (Micropædia)

Ml.R. Michael Roe. *Professor of History, University of Tasmania, Hobart, Australia. Author of* Nine Australian Progressives *and others.*
AUSTRALIA (*in part*)

M.L.R. The Hon. Miriam Louisa Rothschild. *Coauthor of* An Illustrated Catalogue of the Rothschild Collection of Fleas (Siphonaptera) in the British Museum (Natural History) *and author of many papers on fleas and other insects.*
INSECTS (*in part*)

M.L.S. Maurice L. Schwartz. *Dean, Graduate Affairs and Research, Western Washington University, Bellingham. Editor of* The Encyclopedia of Beaches and Coastal Environments.
OCEANS (*in part*)

M.-L.S.S. Marie-Louise Stig Sørensen. *Assistant Lecturer in Anthropology and Archaeology, University of Cambridge; Fellow, Jesus College, Cambridge. Coeditor of* The Transition from Bronze to Iron Age in Europe.
EUROPEAN HISTORY AND CULTURE (*in part*)

M.Lu. Myron Luntz. *Professor of Physics, State University of New York College at Fredonia.*
RADIATION (*in part*)

M.McA. Mary McAuley. *Fellow and Tutor in Politics, St. Hilda's College, University of Oxford. Author of* Politics and the Soviet Union *and others.*
SAINT PETERSBURG (*in part*)

M.McC. Malcolm McChesney. *Former Director, Schools of Engineering Science; former Senior Lecturer in Mechanical Engineering, University of Liverpool. Coauthor of* The Dynamics of Relaxing Gases.
MATTER (*in part*)

M.McCu. Marilyn McCully. *Free-lance writer. Coauthor of* Der Junge Picasso; *editor of* A Picasso Anthology.
PICASSO

M.Me. Manuel Medina. *Professor of International Law and International Relations, University of Madrid.*
SPAIN (*in part*)

M.M.E. Marc Marie Escholier (d. 1972). *Judge, Supreme Court of Appeal, Paris. Author of* Port-Royal *and others.*
JANSEN, CORNELIUS OTTO (Micropædia)

M.M.El-K. Magdi M. El-Kammash (deceased). *Associate Professor of Economics, North Carolina State University at Raleigh. Author of*

Economic Development and Planning
in Egypt.
AFRICA (*in part*)

M.Mi.   Mairin Mitchell. *Free-lance
writer. Author of* The Odyssey of Acurio
Who Sailed with Magellan *and others.*
MAGELLAN, FERDINAND (Micropædia)

M.Ml.   Michel Michel. *Lecturer in
Geography, University of Paris I.*
BRAZIL (*in part*)

M.M.M.   Maynard M. Miller.
*Professor of Geology; Emeritus Dean,
College of Mines and Earth Resources;
Director, Glaciological and Arctic
Sciences Institute, University of Idaho,
Moscow. Director, Foundation for
Glacier and Environmental Research,
Pacific Science Center, Seattle,
Washington. Author of* The Juneau
Icefield, Alaska *and others.*
UNITED STATES OF AMERICA (*in part*)

M.Mn.   Sir Max Mallowan (d.
1978). *Professor of Western Asiatic
Archaeology, University of London,
1947–62. President, British School
of Archaeology in Iraq, 1970–78.
Archaeologist on staff of the British
Museum Expedition to Nineveh,
1931–32; later leader of many other
archaeological expeditions. Author of*
Nimrud and Its Remains *and others.*
NINEVEH (Micropædia)

M.M.Sa.   Mostafa Moh. Salah. *Former
Director, Institute of Oceanography
and Fisheries, Kayed Bey, Alexandria,
Egypt. Author of numerous articles on
oceanography.*
ATLANTIC OCEAN, THE (*in part*)

M.M.W.   Maxwell M. Wintrobe, M.D.
(d. 1986). *Professor of Internal Medicine,
University of Utah, Salt Lake City,
1943–70. Author of* Clinical Hematology.
BLOOD (*in part*)

M.N.   Max Neutze. *Deputy
Vice-Chancellor, Australian National
University, Canberra. Author of*
Australian Urban Policy; Urban
Development in Australia.
AUSTRALIA (*in part*)

M.Na.   Maurice Nadeau. *Editor,*
Lettres Nouvelles *and* La Quinzaine
Littéraire, *Paris. Author of* Histoire du
surréalisme: *editor of the Marquis de
Sade's* Oeuvres; *and others.*
SADE, MARQUIS DE (Micropædia)

M.N.B.   Marjorie Nice Boyer. *Emerita
Professor of History, York College, City
University of New York, Jamaica. Author
of* "Medieval Suspended Carriages" *in*
Speculum; "Medieval Pivoted Axles" *in*
Technology and Culture.
TRANSPORTATION (*in part*)

M.N.D.   Manmath Nath Das. *Former
Vice-Chancellor; former Professor and
Head, Department of History, Utkal
University, Bhubaneswar, Orissa, India.*
INDIA (*in part*)

M.N.v.L.   Maurits N. van Loon.
*Professor of Prehistory and Archaeology
of Western Asia, University of
Amsterdam. Research Associate*

in Archaeology, Oriental Institute,
University of Chicago. Author of*
Urartian Art.
DRESS AND ADORNMENT (*in part*)

Mo.Gr.   Moshe Greenberg. *Professor of
Bible, Hebrew University of Jerusalem.
Author of* The Hab/piru *and others;
editor and translator of* The Religion of
Israel *by Yehezkel Kaufmann.*
JUDAISM (*in part*)

M.P.   Malcolm Potts. *President,
Family Health International, Research
Triangle Park, North Carolina. Coauthor
of* The Textbook of Contraceptive
Practice *and others.*
BIRTH CONTROL

M.Pa.   Marcel Pacaut. *Professor of the
History of the Middle Ages; Emeritus
Director, Institute of Political Studies,
University of Lyon. Author of* Louis VII
et son royaume *and others.*
PHILIP II (FRANCE) (Micropædia)

M.P.B.   Michael Parker Banton.
*Professor of Sociology, University
of Bristol, England. Author of* The
Policeman in the Community.
POLICE (*in part*)

M.P.G.   Mikell P. Groover. *Professor
of Industrial Engineering, Lehigh
University, Bethlehem, Pennsylvania.
Author of* Automation, Production
Systems, and Computer-Integrated
Manufacturing.
AUTOMATION (*in part*)

M.Ph.   Melba Phillips. *Emerita
Professor of Physics, University of
Chicago. Coauthor of* Classical Electricity
and Magnetism.
ELECTROMAGNETIC RADIATION (*in part*)

M.Pl.   Maurice Platnauer (d. 1974).
*Principal of Brasenose College,
University of Oxford, 1956–60. Author of*
Latin Elegiac Verse *and others; editor of*
Aristophanes' *Peace.*
GREEK DRAMATISTS, THE CLASSICAL
  (*in part*)

M.Pm.   Dame Margery Perham (d.
1982). *Fellow of Nuffield College,
Oxford, 1939–63; Reader in Colonial
Administration, University of Oxford,
1939–48. Author of* Lugard; *coeditor of*
The Diaries of Lord Lugard.
LUGARD OF ABINGER, FREDERICK JOHN
  DEALTRY LUGARD, BARON
  (Micropædia)

**M.P.Pe.   Mikhail Platonovich
Petrov** (d. 1978). *Professor of Physical
Geography, Leningrad A.A. Zhdanov
State University. Author of* Pustyni
Tsentralnoy Azi ("Deserts of Central
Asia").
ASIA (*in part*)

M.Py.   E. Michael Pye. *Professor of
Comparative Religion, University of
Marburg, Germany. Author of* The Study
of Kanji *and others.*
RITES AND CEREMONIES, SACRED
  (*in part*)

M.R.   Mario Rossi (deceased). *Professor
of the History of Philosophy, University
of Siena, Italy. Author of* Marx e la

dialettica hegeliana.
HEGELIANISM, HEGEL AND (*in part*)

M.Ra.   Marc Raeff. *Bakhmeteff
Professor Emeritus of Russian Studies,
Columbia University. Author of* Origins
of the Russian Intelligentsia *and others.*
UNION OF SOVIET SOCIALIST REPUBLICS
  (*in part*)

M.R.B.   Merton R. Bernfield, M.D.
*Clement A. Smith Professor of Pediatrics;
Director, Joint Program in Neonatology,
Harvard University. Chairman, Ciba
Foundation Symposium:* Basement
Membranes and Cell Movement.
CELLS (*in part*)

M.R.D.   Mary R. Dawson. *Curator,
Vertebrate Fossils, Carnegie Museum
of Natural History, Pittsburgh. Active in
research on the biology and paleontology
of rabbits.*
MAMMALS (*in part*)

M.R.Da.   Milton Rockwood Daniels
(deceased). *Commodore, U.S.
Coast Guard.*
NAVIGATION (*in part*)

**M.R.D.F.   Michael Richard Daniell
Foot.** *Professor of History, Victoria
University of Manchester, 1967–
73. Editor of* The Gladstone Diaries
(*vol. 1–4*).
GLADSTONE, WILLIAM EWART (*in part*)
  (Micropædia)

M.Re.   Marcel Reinhard (d. 1973).
*Professor of History, University of
Paris. Author of* Le Grand Carnot;
Paris pendant la révolution française;
and others.
SAINT-JUST, LOUIS DE (Micropædia)

M.R.G.   Mark Richard Greene.
*Distinguished Professor Emeritus of
Insurance, University of Georgia, Athens.
Author of* Risk and Insurance.
INSURANCE

M.Rh.   Max Rheinstein (d. 1977).
*Max Pam Professor of Comparative
Law, University of Chicago, 1942–68.
Coauthor of* Law of Decedents' Estates.
INHERITANCE AND SUCCESSION (*in part*)
LEGAL SYSTEMS, THE EVOLUTION OF
  MODERN WESTERN (*in part*)
PROCEDURAL LAW (*in part*)

M.R.H.   Michael R. House. *Professor
of Geology, University of Southampton,
England. Author of* Continental Drift
and the Devonian System *and others.*
GEOCHRONOLGY (*in part*)

M.-R.Ho.   Michel-Rostislav Hofmann.
Musicologist. Author of Moussorgski;
Histoire de la musique en Russie.
MUSSORGSKY, MODEST (Micropædia)

M.Ro.   Michael Roberts. *Professor of
Modern History, Queen's University
of Belfast, Northern Ireland, 1954–73.
Author of* Gustavus Adolphus: A History
of Sweden, 1611–1632; The Early Vasas:
A History of Sweden, 1523–1611.
GUSTAV II ADOLF (Micropædia)
OXENSTIERNA (AF SODERMORE), AXEL,
  GREVE (Micropædia)

M.R.W.   Marilyn R. Waldman.
Professor of History; Director, Center

for Comparative Studies, Ohio State University, Columbus. Author of Toward a Theory of Historical Narrative: A Case Study in Perso-Islamicate Historiography.
ISLĀMIC WORLD, THE

M.Sa. **Michele Sarà.** *Professor of Zoology; Director, Institute of Zoology, University of Genoa. Author of* Zoologia; Biologia generale.
SPONGES (*in part*)

M.S.A. **Mikhail S. Arlazorov.** *Staff member, Union of Cinematographers, Moscow. Author of* Tsiolkovsky.
TSIOLKOVSKY, KONSTANTIN
  EDUARDOVICH (Micropædia)

M.Sal. **Mario Salmi** (d. 1980). *Professor of the History of Medieval and Modern Art, University of Rome. Author of* Il Beato Angelico *and many monographs on Italian Renaissance artists.*
ANGELICO, FRA (Micropædia)

M.S.C. **Maria S. Cox.** *Former Assistant Professor of Economics, University of Wisconsin, Madison.*
TAXATION (*in part*)

M.Sch. **Mischa Schwartz.** *Charles Batchelor Professor of Electrical Engineering, Columbia University. Author of* Information Transmission, Modulation, and Noise; Telecommunication Networks.
TELECOMMUNICATIONS SYSTEMS (*in part*)

M.S.D. **Margaret Stefana Drower.** *Fellow of University College, London; former Reader in Ancient History, University of London. Author of* Nubia: A Drowning Land *and others.*
THUTMOSE III (Micropædia)

M.S.F.H. **M. Sinclair F. Hood.** *Archaeologist. Director, British School at Athens, 1954–62. Author of* The Minoans: Crete in the Bronze Age *and others.*
GREEK AND ROMAN CIVILIZATIONS,
  ANCIENT (*in part*)

M.Sh. **Minoru Shinoda.** *Emeritus Professor of History, University of Hawaii at Manoa, Honolulu. Author of* The Founding of the Kamakura Shogunate 1180–1185.
DAIGO, GO- (Micropædia)
FUJIWARA FAMILY (Micropædia)

M.S.H. **Muhammad Shamsul Huq.** *President, Foundation for Research on Educational Planning and Development. Foreign Minister, Bangladesh, 1978– 82. Minister for Education and Scientific Research, Pakistan, 1969–71. Author of* Education and Manpower Development in South and Southeast Asia *and others.*
EDUCATION, HISTORY OF (*in part*)

M.S.Ki. **M. Semakula M. Kiwanuka.** *Director of Planning, Makerere University, Kampala, Uganda; former Professor of History. Author of* A History of Buganda.
EASTERN AFRICA (*in part*)

M.S.M. **Muhsin S. Mahdi.** *James Richard Jewett Professor of Arabic,*

Harvard University. Author of Ibn Khaldun's Philosophy of History *and others.*
ISLĀM, MUḤAMMAD AND THE RELIGION
  OF (*in part*)

M.S.Ma. **Matthew S. Magda.** *Adjunct Instructor in History, Sacred Heart University, Fairfield, Connecticut. Former Associate Historian, Division of History, Pennsylvania Historical and Museum Commission, Harrisburg.*
PHILADELPHIA (*in part*)

M.S.M.F. **Michael S.M. Fordham.** *Analytical psychologist. Coeditor of* The Collected Works of C.G. Jung.
JUNG, CARL (*in part*)
  (Micropædia)

M.Sp. **Matthew Spinka** (d. 1972). *Professor of Church History, Hartford Seminary Foundation, Connecticut, 1943–58. Author of* John Hus: A Biography *and others.*
HUS, JOHN (Micropædia)

M.S.S. **Mark S. Slobin.** *Professor of Music, Wesleyan University, Middletown, Connecticut. Author of* Music in the Culture of Northern Afghanistan *and others.*
CENTRAL ASIAN ARTS (*in part*)

M.St. **Michel Strickmann.** *Associate Professor of Oriental Languages, University of California, Berkeley. Author of* Le Taoïsme du Mao Chan *and others.*
TAOISM (*in part*)

M.S.T. **Michael S. Teitelbaum** *Program Officer, Alfred P. Sloan Foundation, New York City. Author of* The British Fertility Decline: Demographic Transition in the Crucible of the Industrial Revolution.
POPULATION

M.Su. **Michael Sullivan.** *Christensen Professor Emeritus of Oriental Art, Stanford University, California. Author of* The Birth of Landscape Painting in China; The Arts of China.
MA YÜAN (Micropædia)
EAST ASIAN ARTS (*in part*)

M.T. **Morris Tanenbaum.** *Vice-Chairman and Chief Financial Officer, AT&T Company, New York City. Coeditor of* Superconductors.
AUTOMATION (*in part*)
INDUSTRIAL ENGINEERING AND
  PRODUCTION MANAGEMENT (*in part*)

M.Ta. **Mohamed Talbi.** *Emeritus Professor, Faculty of Letters and Human Sciences, University of Tunis. Author of* L'Emirat aghlabide, histoire politique 800–909.
NORTH AFRICA (*in part*)

M.T.C. **Marjorie Tuainekore Crocombe.** *Director, Centre for Pacific Studies, University of Auckland, New Zealand. Author of* They Came for Sandalwood *and others.*
PACIFIC ISLANDS (*in part*)

M.T.F. **Michael T. Florinsky** (d. 1981). *Professor of Economics, Columbia University, 1956–63. Author of* Russia: A

History and an Interpretation *and others.*
ALEXANDER III (RUSSIA) (Micropædia)

M.T.G. **Michael T. Ghiselin.** *Senior Research Fellow, California Academy of Sciences, San Francisco. Author of* The Triumph of the Darwinian Method *and others.*
CHORDATES (*in part*)

M.T.J. **Malcolm T. Jollie.** *Professor of Biological Sciences, Northern Illinois University, DeKalb, 1965–88. Author of* Chordate Morphology.
CHORDATES (*in part*)

M.T.O. **Martin T. Orne, M.D.** *Professor of Psychiatry, University of Pennsylvania, Philadelphia; Director, Unit for Experimental Psychiatry, Institute of Pennsylvania Hospital.*
HYPNOSIS (*in part*) (Micropædia)

M.Tu. **Martin Turnell** (d. 1979). *Writer. Head, Programme Contracts Department, British Broadcasting Corporation, London, 1959–69. Author of* The Art of French Fiction.
MAUPASSANT, GUY DE (Micropædia)
ZOLA, ÉMILE (Micropædia)

M.T.V. **M. Tulio Velásquez.** *Director, Institute of Andean Biology, National University of San Marcos, Lima. Coauthor of* Physiological Effects of High Altitude.
SOUTH AMERICA (*in part*)

M.U. **Michitaka Uda.** *Emeritus Professor, Tokyo University of Fisheries. Author of* Umi *and numerous articles on oceanography.*
PACIFIC OCEAN, THE (*in part*)

Mu.B. **Mukhtar Mustafa Buru.** *Professor of Geography, Al-Fatah University, Tripoli, Libya. Author of* Atlas of Libyan Arab Republic.
NORTH AFRICA (*in part*)

Mu.McC. **Murray McCaskill.** *Professor of Geography, Flinders University of South Australia, Adelaide. Author of* Patterns on the Hand; *coeditor of* Atlas of South Australia.
AUSTRALIA (*in part*)

Mu.S. **Murray Schumach.** *Former Reporter,* The New York Times. *Author of* The Face on the Cutting Room Floor.
NEW YORK CITY

M.V. **Meredith Veldman.** *Assistant Professor of History, Louisiana State University, Baton Rouge.*
VICTORIA AND THE VICTORIAN AGE
  (*in part*)

M.V.F. **Marion Valerie Friedmann** (d. 1980). *Editor and translator. Author of* The Slap; *editor of* I Will Still Be Moved: Reports from South Africa.
SOUTH AFRICAN LITERATURE (*in part*)
  (Micropædia)

M.Vi. **Marcelle Vioux** (deceased). *Free-lance writer. Author of* Francois I; Henri IV; *and others.*
FRANCIS I (FRANCE) (Micropædia)

M.V.O. **Maynard V. Olson.** *Professor of Genetics, Washington University, St. Louis. Author of papers on mechanisms*

of reactions of transition-metal compounds.
CHEMICAL REACTIONS (*in part*)

M.V.S.-W. M.V. Seton-Williams. *Former Honorary Research Fellow in Egyptian and Coptic, University College, University of London. Former director of archaeological expeditions in Turkey, Syria, Jordan, Egypt, and Cyprus. Author of* Britain and the Arab States *and others.*
JORDAN (*in part*)

M.W.B. Marshall W. Baldwin (d. 1975). *Professor of History, New York University, New York City, 1954–72. Coeditor of* A History of the Crusades.
CRUSADES, THE (*in part*)

M.W.DeL. Mark W. DeLancey. *Professor of Government and International Studies, University of South Carolina, Columbia. Author of* Cameroon: Dependence and Independence; *editor of* Aspects of International Relations in Africa.
WESTERN AFRICA (*in part*)

M.W.F. Marvin W. Formo. *Manager, Oil and Protein Research, Cargill Inc., Minneapolis, Minnesota. Contributor to* Industrial Fatty Acids.
FOOD PROCESSING (*in part*)

M.W.Fo. Michael W. Fox. *Vice President, The Humane Society of the United States, Washington, D.C. Author of* Superdog.
CATS, DOMESTIC (*in part*)
DOGS

M.W.Fr. Michael Wulf Friedlander. *Professor of Physics, Washington University, St. Louis, Missouri. Author of* Astronomy: From Stonehenge to Quasars *and others.*
COSMIC RAY (Micropædia)
PHYSICAL SCIENCES, THE (*in part*)

M.W.G. Malcolm W. Greaves. *Professor of Dermatology, Institute of Dermatology, St. Thomas's Hospital, University of London. Editor of* The Urticarias.
INTEGUMENTARY SYSTEMS (*in part*)

M.W.H. Marcus Willem Heslinga. *Emeritus Professor of Human Geography, Free University, Amsterdam.*
NETHERLANDS, THE (*in part*)

M.Wi. Mitchell Wilson (d. 1973). *Science writer and novelist. Author of* American Science and Invention.
MCCORMICK, CYRUS HALL (Micropædia)

M.W.L. Maung Wai Lin. *Research Editor, Biology,* Encyclopædia Britannica, *Chicago, 1970–72.*
FISHES (*in part*)

M.W.L.K. Michael William Lely Kitson. *Professor of the History of Art; Director of Studies, Paul Mellon Centre for Studies in British Art, London. Author of* The Art of Claude Lorrain *and others.*
CLAUDE LORRAIN (*in part*) (Micropædia)

M.W.M. Marvin W. Mikesell. *Professor of Geography, University of Chicago. Author of* Northern Morocco:

A Cultural Geography.
AFRICA (*in part*)

M.Wo. Mary Woodall (d. 1988). *Director, City Museum and Art Gallery, Birmingham, England, 1956–64. Author of* Gainsborough's Landscape Drawings; *editor of* The Letters of Thomas Gainsborough.
GAINSBOROUGH, THOMAS (Micropædia)

M.W.R. Matilda White Riley. *Associate Director, Social and Behavioral Sciences Research, National Institute on Aging, National Institutes of Health, U.S. Department of Health and Human Services, Bethesda, Maryland. Coauthor of* Aging and Society (*vol. 1–3*).
SOCIAL DIFFERENTIATION (*in part*)

M.W.Ri. Michael William Richey. *Former Director, Royal Institute of Navigation, London. Coauthor of* The Geometrical Seaman; The Encyclopedia of Sailing.
NAVIGATION (*in part*)

M.W.W. Manfred W. Wenner. *Associate Professor of Political Science, Northern Illinois University, DeKalb. Author of* Modern Yemen, 1918–1966.
ARABIA (*in part*)

M.Y.S. Margaret Yvonne Stant. *Principal Scientific Officer in Plant Anatomy, Jodrell Laboratory, Royal Botanic Gardens, Kew, England. Author of* Anatomy of the Butomaceae.
ANGIOSPERMS (*in part*)

M.Z. Moses Zucker (d. 1987). *Professor of Biblical Exegesis, Jewish Theological Seminary of America, New York City. Author of* Rav Saadya Gaon's Translation of the Torah.
SA'ADIA BEN JOSEPH (Micropædia)

M.Zu. Matinuzzaman Zuberi. *Senior Fellow and Head, Centre for International Politics and Organization, Jawaharlal Nehru University, New Delhi.*
NEPAL (*in part*)

N. John Julius Cooper, 2nd Viscount Norwich. *Writer and broadcaster. Author of* The Normans in the South; The Kingdom in the Sun.
ROGER II (SICILY) (Micropædia)

N.A. Nafis Ahmad (deceased). *Professor of Geography, University of Dacca, Bangladesh. Author of* Economic Geography of East Pakistan; *editor of* Oriental Geographer.
ASIA (*in part*)

N.Ab. Nicola Abbagnano. *Emeritus Professor of History of Philosophy, University of Turin, Italy. Foremost Italian Existentialist philosopher. Author of* Critical Existentialism *and others.*
PHILOSOPHICAL SCHOOLS AND DOCTRINES, WESTERN (*in part*)

N.A.Ba. Nicholas A. Barr. *Senior Lecturer in Economics, London School of Economics and Political Science, University of London. Author of* The Economics of the Welfare State.
UNITED KINGDOM (*in part*)

N.A.C. Nancy A. Curtin. *Senior Lecturer in Physiology, Charing Cross*

and Westminster Medical School, University of London.
MUSCLES AND MUSCLE SYSTEMS (*in part*)

N.A.Ct. Nathan Altshiller Court (d. 1968). *Professor of Mathematics, University of Oklahoma, Norman, 1935–51. Author of* College Geometry; Mathematics in Fun and in Earnest.
GEOMETRY (*in part*)

N.A.F. Nabih Amin Faris (d. 1968). *Professor of Arab History and Director, Arab Studies Programme, American University of Beirut.*
PALESTINE (*in part*)

N.A.G. Nikolay Andreyevich Gvozdetsky. *Emeritus Professor of Geography, Moscow M.V. Lomonosov State University. Author of* Kavkaz.
ASIA (*in part*)

N.A.J. Nazir Ali Jairazbhoy. *Professor of Ethnomusicology, University of California, Los Angeles. Author of* The Rāgs of North Indian Music: Their Structure and Evolution.
SOUTH ASIAN ARTS (*in part*)

Na.M. Nancy Mitford (d. 1973). *Writer. Author of* Madame de Pompadour *and others.*
POMPADOUR, JEANNE-ANTOINETTE POISSON, MARQUISE DE (Micropædia)

N.A.M. Norman A. Malcolm (d. 1990). *Susan Linn Sage Professor of Philosophy, Cornell University, Ithaca, New York, 1964–78. Author of* Ludwig Wittgenstein: A Memoir.
WITTGENSTEIN, LUDWIG (*in part*) (Micropædia)

Na.Mo. Naoaki Maeno. *Emeritus Professor of Chinese Literature, University of Tokyo. Author of* Poets in the T'ang Dynasty.
LITERATURE, THE ART OF (*in part*)

N.An. Nikolay Andreyev (d. 1982). *Reader in Russian Studies, University of Cambridge; Fellow of Clare Hall, Cambridge. Author of* Studies in Muscovy *and others.*
IVAN IV (Micropædia)

N.A.O. Ned Allen Ostenso. *Assistant Administrator for Oceanic and Atmospheric Research, National Oceanic and Atmospheric Administration, U.S. Department of Commerce, Rockville, Maryland. Leader or participant in several polar expeditions. Author of* Geophysical Investigations of the Arctic Ocean Basin.
ARCTIC, THE (*in part*)

N.A.R. Nesca A. Robb (d. 1976). *Free-lance writer and lecturer. Author of* William of Orange: A Personal Portrait.
WILLIAM III (ENGLAND AND GREAT BRITAIN) (Micropædia)

N.A.Ro. Nicholas A. Romas, M.D. *Director of Urology, St. Luke's-Roosevelt Hospital Center, New York City.*
REPRODUCTION AND REPRODUCTIVE SYSTEMS (*in part*)

N.A.W. Nixon A. Wilson. *Professor of Biology, University of Northern Iowa, Cedar Falls. Author of numerous papers*

on mites and ticks.
ARACHNIDS (*in part*)

N.A.Z.   Nicola Abdo Ziadeh. *Emeritus Professor of Arab History, American University of Beirut. Author of* Origins of Nationalism—Tunisia *and others.*
BOURGUIBA, HABIB (*in part*)
   (Micropædia)
CALENDAR (*in part*)
HISTORY, THE STUDY OF (*in part*)

N.B.   Nevill Barbour (d. 1972). *Assistant Head, Eastern Services, British Broadcasting Corporation, 1944–56. Author of* Morocco; *editor of* A Survey of North West Africa.
NORTH AFRICA (*in part*)
WESTERN AFRICA (*in part*)

N.B.P.   Nicholas B. Penny. *Keeper of Western Art, Ashmolean Museum of Art and Archaeology, University of Oxford. Author of* Church Monuments in Romantic England.
PAINTING, THE HISTORY OF WESTERN
   (*in part*)
SCULPTURE, THE HISTORY OF WESTERN
   (*in part*)

N.C.   Norman Crossland (d. 1991). *Bonn correspondent,* The Economist, *London. Author of* The German Electoral System.
BERLIN (*in part*)

N.C.G.   Neil C. Gustafson. *President, Anticipatory Management, Inc., Minneapolis. Coauthor and editor of* Report of the Commission on Minnesota's Future; *coauthor of* Atlas of Minnesota Resources and Settlement.
UNITED STATES OF AMERICA (*in part*)

N.Ch.   Ned Chaillet. *Editor, Radio Drama, British Broadcasting Corporation, London.*
THEATRE, THE ART OF THE (*in part*)

N.C.H.   Nicholas Carr Hightower, M.D. *Senior Consultant, Department of Gastroenterology, Scott and White Clinic and Scott and White Memorial Hospital, Temple, Texas. Contributor of "Digestion" in Best and Taylor,* The Physiological Basis of Medical Practice *(8th ed.).*
DIGESTION AND DIGESTIVE SYSTEMS
   (*in part*)

N.C.N.   N. Chandrasekharan Nair. *Former Joint Director, Botanical Survey of India, Coimbatore. Author of* Flora of the Punjab Plains *and others.*
ANGIOSPERMS (*in part*)

N.Co.   Nigel Collins. *Editor in Chief,* The Ring, *1985–89. Editor,* Boxing Illustrated, *1984.*
SPORTS, MAJOR TEAM AND INDIVIDUAL
   (*in part*)

N.C.P.   Norman C. Polmar. *Consultant. Editor, U.S. sections,* Jane's Fighting Ships, *1967–77. Author of* Atomic Submarines; The Ships and Aircraft of the U.S. Fleet; *and others.*
WAR, THE TECHNOLOGY OF (*in part*)

N.C.W.   Neil C. Wells. *Lecturer in Meteorology and Physical Oceanography, University of Southampton, England.*

Author of The Atmosphere and Ocean.
OCEANS (*in part*)

N.D.   Norman Davies. *Professor of Polish History, School of Slavonic and East European Studies, University of London. Author of* God's Playground: A History of Poland.
POLAND (*in part*)
WARSAW (*in part*)

N.E.L.   Nancy Ellen Lawler. *Professor of History and Economics, Oakton Community College, Des Plaines, Illinois.*
WESTERN AFRICA (*in part*)

N.E.S.   Neil E. Salisbury. *Professor of Geography, University of Oklahoma, Norman. Coauthor of "Growth and Decline of Iowa Villages" and "The Valleys of Iowa,"* Iowa Studies in Geography.
UNITED STATES OF AMERICA (*in part*)

N.E.W.   Neil E. Wiseman. *Lecturer in Computer Science, University of Cambridge. Coauthor of* Creative Computer Graphics.
COMPUTERS (*in part*)

N.F.   Norman Friedman. *Defense consultant. Visiting Professor of Operations Research, University College, University of London. Author of* The Postwar Naval Revolution *and many others.*
WAR, THE TECHNOLOGY OF (*in part*)

N.F.C.   Norman F. Childers. *Adjunct Professor, Department of Fruit Crops, University of Florida, Gainesville. M.A. Blake Professor Emeritus of Horticulture, Rutgers University, New Brunswick, New Jersey. Author of* Modern Fruit Science.
FARMING AND AGRICULTURAL
   TECHNOLOGY (*in part*)

N.G.   Norman Gash. *Emeritus Professor of History, University of St. Andrews, Scotland. Author of* Sir Robert Peel *and others.*
CASTLEREAGH, ROBERT STEWART,
   VISCOUNT (Micropædia)
GREY, CHARLES GREY, 2ND EARL
   (Micropædia)
PEEL, SIR ROBERT, 2ND BARONET
   (Micropædia)

N.G.J.   Norman Gardner Johnson (d. 1973). *Industry Manager, Explosives Department, Du Pont de Nemours and Company, Wilmington, Delaware, 1960–67; Technical Specialist, Technical Service Section, 1943–60. Author of* Safety in the Transportation, Storage, Handling and Use of Explosives.
INDUSTRIES, CHEMICAL PROCESS (*in part*)

N.G.L.H.   Nicholas G.L. Hammond. *Henry Overton Wills Professor Emeritus of Greek, University of Bristol, England. Author of* A History of Greece to 322 B.C.; *editor of* Cambridge Ancient History *(3rd ed.).*
GREECE (*in part*)
XENOPHON (Micropædia)

N.Go.   Noël Goodwin. *Associate Editor,* Dance and Dancers, *London. Overseas News Editor,* Opera. *London Correspondent,* Opera News. *Assistant*

Music Critic, The Times *(London). Area Editor,* The New Grove Dictionary of Music and Musicians. *Coauthor of* London Symphony: Portrait of an Orchestra.
MUSICAL FORMS AND GENRES (*in part*)

N.G.P.   N. Geoffrey Parker. *Charles E. Nowell Distinguished Professor of History, University of Illinois at Urbana-Champaign. Author of* The Thirty Years' War; The Military Revolution 1500–1800.
EUROPEAN HISTORY AND CULTURE
   (*in part*)

N.G.S.   Neal Griffith Smith. *Biologist, Smithsonian Tropical Research Institute, Balboa, Panama.*
BEHAVIOUR, ANIMAL (*in part*)

N.H.   Naofusa Hirai. *Professor of Shintō Studies, Kokugakuin University, Tokyo. Author of* Japanese Shinto.
SHINTŌ

N.H.C.   Nigel Hardy Copperthwaite. *Lecturer in Geography, University of Bradford, England. Coauthor of* Local Government in the Community.
YUGOSLAVIA (*in part*)

N.H.D.   Nancy Hatch Dupree. *Executive Director, Aebar Resource and Information Centre, Peshawar, Pakistan. Author of* An Historical Guide to Afghanistan.
AFGHANISTAN (*in part*)

N.H.R.   Norman H. Russell. *Former Professor of Biology, Central State University, Edmond, Oklahoma. Author of* An Introduction to the Plant Kingdom.
ANGIOSPERMS (*in part*)

N.I.   Nobutaka Ike. *Emeritus Professor of Political Science, Stanford University, California. Author of* The Beginnings of Political Democracy in Japan *and others.*
II NAOSUKE (Micropædia)

N.I.M.   Nikolay Ivanovich Mikhaylov. *Professor of Geography, Moscow M.V. Lomonosov State University. Author of* Gory Yuzhnoy Sibiri.
ASIA (*in part*)

N.It.   Norman Itzkowitz. *Professor of Near Eastern Studies, Princeton University. Author of* Ottoman Emrire and Islamic Tradition; *coauthor of* The Immortal Ataturk.
ATATÜRK

N.J.B.   N.J. Berrill. *Strathcona Professor of Zoology, McGill University, Montreal, 1946–65. Author of* Sex and the Nature of Things *and others.*
SEX AND SEXUALITY (*in part*)

N.J.C.   Noel James Coulson (d. 1986). *Professor of Oriental Laws, University of London, 1967–86. Author of* A History of Islamic Law.
ISLĀM, MUḤAMMAD AND THE RELIGION
   OF (*in part*)

N.J.H.   Nicholas Joseph Healy. *Adjunct Professor of Law, New York University. Attorney, Healy & Baillie, New York City. Vice President, International Maritime Committee.*

Editor, Journal of Maritime Law and Commerce. *Coauthor of* Healy & Sharpe's Cases and Materials on Admiralty.

TRANSPORTATION LAW *(in part)*

N.J.L.   Norman Jones Lamb. *Former Senior Lecturer in Portuguese and Spanish, University of Liverpool.*

PORTUGUESE LITERATURE *(in part)*

N.J.M.   Nicholas John Mackintosh. *Professor of Experimental Psychology, University of Cambridge. Author of* Psychology of Animal Learning; Conditioning and Associative Learning.

LEARNING, ANIMAL

N.J.Mo.   Nic J. Money. *Director, Geological Survey Department, Lusaka, Zambia. Author of* The Geology of Western Zambia.

AFRICA *(in part)*

N.J.R.A.   Nigel John Roger Allan. *Associate Professor of Geography, University of California, Davis. Editor of* Human Impact on Mountains.

ASIA *(in part)*

N.J.S.   Neil J. Smelser. *University Professor of Sociology, University of California, Berkeley. Author of* Theory of Collective Behavior *and others.*

COLLECTIVE BEHAVIOUR *(in part)*

N.Ka.   Nobuo Kanda. *Professor of East Asian History, Meiji University, Tokyo. Coauthor of* Glory of the Forbidden City in Peking.

K'ANG-HSI (Micropædia)

N.K.G.   Nikolai Kallinikovich Gudzii (d. 1965). *Professor of Old Russian Language and Literature, Moscow M.V. Lomonosov State University. Member, Academy of Sciences of the U.S.S.R. Author of* History of Early Russian Literature *and others.*

RUSSIAN LITERATURE *(in part)*

N.K.S.   N.K. Sinha (d. 1974). *Professor and Head, Department of History, University of Calcutta, 1955–68. Author of* Rise of the Sikh Power.

BOSE, SUBHAS CHANDRA (Micropædia)
CALCUTTA *(in part)*

N.L.G.   Nancie L. González. *Professor of Anthropology, University of Maryland, College Park. Author of* Sojourners of the Caribbean *and others.*

WEST INDIES, THE *(in part)*

N.L.N.   Norman L. Nicholson. *Senior Professor of Geography, University of Western Ontario, London. Author of* The Boundaries of the Canadian Confederation *and others.*

CANADA *(in part)*

N.M.   Nobuhiro Matsumoto. *Emeritus Professor of Oriental History, Keio University, Tokyo. Author of* Essai sur la mythologie japonaise.

JAPANESE LITERATURE *(in part)*

N.M.C.   Nydia María Cardoze. *Professor of Geography, University of Panama, Panama City. Author of* Notas de geografía.

CENTRAL AMERICA *(in part)*

N.Mo.   Neil Morgan. *Editor,* San Diego *(California)* Tribune. *Author of* The California Syndrome; Westward Tilt.

UNITED STATES OF AMERICA *(in part)*

N.M.S.   Nicholas M. Short. *Research Scientist, Geophysics Branch, Laboratory for Earth Sciences, Goddard Space Flight Center, National Aeronautics and Space Administration, Greenbelt, Maryland. Author of* Planetary Geology.

CONTINENTAL LANDFORMS *(in part)*

N.M.Sa.   Nahum M. Sarna. *Golding Professor Emeritus of Biblical Studies, Brandeis University, Waltham, Massachusetts. Author of* Understanding Genesis *and others.*

BIBLICAL LITERATURE AND ITS CRITICAL
   INTERPRETATION *(in part)*

N.M.Su.   N.M. Sutherland. *Emeritus Professor of Early Modern History, Royal Holloway and Bedford New College, University of London. Author of* Princes, Politics, and Religion, 1547–1589 *and others.*

CATHERINE DE MÉDICIS (Micropædia)

N.N.A.   Nina Nikolaevna Alexeeva. *Researcher, Geography Faculty, Moscow M.V. Lomonosov State University. Coauthor of* Ecological Aspects of Hydromelioration.

ASIA *(in part)*

N.N.G.   Nahum N. Glatzer (d. 1990). *Professor of Jewish History, Brandeis University, Waltham, Massachusetts, 1956–73. Author of* Franz Rosenzweig: His Life and Thought *and others.*

AKIBA BEN JOSEPH (Micropædia)
ROSENZWEIG, FRANZ (Micropædia)

N.O.S.   Norman Obed Smith. *Emeritus Professor of Chemistry, Fordham University, New York City. Coauthor of* The Phase Rule and Its Applications.

MATTER *(in part)*

N.P.   Norman Perrin (d. 1976). *Professor of New Testament, University of Chicago, 1969–76. Author of* The Promise of Bultmann.

BULTMANN, RUDOLF (Micropædia)

N.Pa.   Ntsomo Payanzo. *Former Assistant Professor of Sociology, National University of Zaire, Lubumbashi.*

CENTRAL AFRICA *(in part)*

N.P.A.   Nagarajan Panchapagesan Ayyar (d. 1979). *Professor of Geography, Shivaji University, Kolhāpur, India, 1977–79.*

INDIA *(in part)*

N.P.As.   N. Philip Ashmole. *Senior Lecturer in Zoology, University of Edinburgh. Author of numerous papers on the ecology of seabirds.*

BIRDS *(in part)*

N.Po.   Nicholas Polunin. *President, Foundation for Environmental Conservation; Secretary-General and Editor, International Conferences on Environmental Future; Founder and Editor,* Environmental Conservation. *Author of* Circumpolar Arctic Flora *and others.*

BIOSPHERE, THE *(in part)*

N.R.   Nicholas Rescher. *University Professor of Philosophy, University of Pittsburgh. Author of* Topics in Philosophical Logic.

LOGIC, THE HISTORY AND KINDS OF
   (in part)

N.R.A.   Norman R. Alpert. *Professor and Chairman, Department of Physiology and Biophysics, University of Vermont, Burlington.*

MUSCLES AND MUSCLE SYSTEMS *(in part)*

N.Ru.   Nicolai Rubinstein. *Emeritus Professor of History, Westfield College, University of London. Author of* The Government of Florence Under the Medici, 1434–1494, *and others.*

GUICCIARDINI, FRANCESCO (Micropædia)
ITALY *(in part)*

N.R.W.   Nelson Raymond Williams. *Principal Technical Adviser to Assistant Director, U.S. Air Force Technical Applications Center, Virginia, 1961–63. Meteorologist, U.S. Weather Bureau, 1940–46. Contributor to* The Encyclopedia of Atmospheric Sciences and Astrogeology.

CLIMATE AND WEATHER *(in part)*

N.S.   Nobuo Shimahara. *Professor of the Anthropology of Education and Associate Dean, Graduate School of Education, Rutgers University, New Brunswick, New Jersey. Author of* Adaptation and Education in Japan.

EDUCATION, HISTORY OF *(in part)*

N.S.B.   Norman Spencer Brommelle (d. 1989). *Secretary-General, International Institute for Conservation of Historic and Artistic Works, 1957–64 and 1966–87. Director, Hamilton Kerr Institute, Fitzwilliam Museum, University of Cambridge, 1978–83. Keeper, Department of Conservation, Victoria and Albert Museum, London, 1960–77.*

ARTS, PRACTICE AND PROFESSION OF
   THE *(in part)*

N.S.C.   Neil S. Cherniack, M.D. *Professor of Medicine and Physiology; Associate Dean for Academic Programs, Case Western Reserve University, Cleveland, Ohio. Coeditor of* Handbook of Physiology, *sect. 3,* The Respiratory System, *vol. 2,* Control of Breathing.

RESPIRATION AND RESPIRATORY
   SYSTEMS *(in part)*

N.S.G.   Norton S. Ginsburg. *Director, Environment and Policy Institute, East-West Center, Honolulu. Emeritus Professor of Geography, University of Chicago. Author of* An Atlas of Economic Development; *editor of* The Pattern of Asia.

TAIWAN *(in part)*

N.Sh.   Nicholas Shrimpton. *Fellow and Tutor in English Literature, Lady Margaret Hall, University of Oxford.*

ENGLISH LITERATURE *(in part)*

N.Sl.   Nicolas Slonimsky. *Conductor, composer, writer, and editor. Lecturer in Music, University of California, Los Angeles, 1964–67. Author of* Music Since 1900; Music of Latin America; *editor of* Baker's Biographical Dictionary of

Musicians.

RIMSKY-KORSAKOV, NIKOLAY (Micropædia)

N.Sm.   Ninian Smart. *J.F. Rowny Professor of Comparative Religions, University of California, Santa Barbara. Author of* The Religious Experience of Mankind; Philosophers and Religious Truth; *and others.*

RELIGIONS, THE STUDY AND CLASSIFICATION OF (*in part*)

RELIGIOUS AND SPIRITUAL BELIEF, SYSTEMS OF (*in part*)

N.St.   Noel Stock. *Professor of English, University of Toledo, Ohio. Author of* The Life of Ezra Pound; Reading the Cantos; *and others.*

POUND, EZRA (Micropædia)

N.T.   Nicholas Temperley. *Professor of Musicology, University of Illinois, Urbana. Editor of Berlioz'* Symphonie fantastique.

MUSIC, THE ART OF (*in part*)

N.T.deG.   Nancy Thomson de Grummond. *Professor of Classics, Florida State University, Tallahassee. Author and editor of* A Guide to Etruscan Mirrors.

GREEK AND ROMAN CIVILIZATIONS (*in part*)

N.V.He.   Norman V. Henfrey. *Lecturer in English, University of Bristol, England. Editor of* Selected Critical Writings of George Santayana.

SANTAYANA, GEORGE (Micropædia)

N.V.R.   Nicholas V. Riasanovsky. *Sidney Hellman Ehrman Professor of European History, University of California, Berkeley. Author of* The History of Russia *and others.*

NICHOLAS I (RUSSIA) (Micropædia)

N.W.   Norman Ward (d. 1990). *Britnell Professor of Political Science, University of Saskatchewan, Saskatoon, 1967–85. Author of* The Government of Canada *and others.*

CANADA (*in part*)

N.W.D.   Norman Wilfred Desrosier. *Former Director of Research, National Biscuit Company, New York City. Author of* The Technology of Food Preservation.

FOOD PROCESSING (*in part*)

N.Wi.   Nico Wilterdink. *Lecturer in Sociology, University of Amsterdam. Author of* Vermogensverhoudingen in Nederland.

SOCIAL STRUCTURE AND CHANGE

N.W.S.   Nathan Wetherill Shock (d. 1989). *Chief, Gerontology Research Center, National Institute on Aging, U.S. Department of Health, Education, and Welfare, Baltimore, 1941–76. Author of* Trends in Gerontology; *editor of* Perspectives in Experimental Gerontology.

GROWTH AND DEVELOPMENT, BIOLOGICAL (*in part*)

N.Z.   Nicolas M. Zernov (d. 1980). *Spalding Lecturer in Eastern Orthodox Culture, University of Oxford, 1947–*

66. Author of The Russian Religious Renaissance of the Twentieth Century *and others.*

KHOMYAKOV, ALEKSEY STEPANOVICH (*in part*) (Micropædia)

O.A.   Oskar Anweiler. *Professor of Education, University of the Ruhr, Bochum, Germany. Author of* Geschichte der Schule und Pädagogik in Russland, vom Ende des Zarenreiches bis zum Beginn der Stalin-Ära.

EDUCATION, HISTORY OF (*in part*)

O.A.B.   Otto Allen Bird. *Emeritus Professor of Arts and Letters, University of Notre Dame, Indiana. Author of* Cultures in Conflict: An Essay in the Philosophy of the Humanities.

KANTIANISM, KANT AND (*in part*)
LEŚNIEWSKI, STANISŁAW (Micropædia)

O.A.O.   Oscar A. Ornati. *Professor of Manpower Management, New York University, New York City. Author of* Transportation Needs of the Poor: A Case Study of New York City.

WORK AND EMPLOYMENT (*in part*)

O.B.G.   O. Benjamin Gerig (d. 1976). *Director, Office of Dependent Area Affairs, U.S. Department of State, 1945–62.*

UNITED NATIONS (*in part*)

O.C.   Otis Cary. *Professor of History, Doshisha University, Kyōto; Representative of Amherst College. Coauthor and editor of* War-Wasted Asia.

KYŌTO

O.C.C.   Orville C. Cromer (d. 1980). *Professor of Mechanical Engineering, Purdue University, West Lafayette, Indiana, 1954–63. Coauthor of* Elementary Heat Power.

ENERGY CONVERSION (*in part*)
TRANSPORTATION (*in part*)

O.C.K.   Otto C. Kopp. *Professor of Geological Sciences, University of Tennessee, Knoxville. Coauthor of* Laboratory Exercises in Physical Geology.

FUELS, FOSSIL (*in part*)

O.D.   Oliver Davies (deceased). *Associate Professor of Archaeology, University of Ghana, 1952–66.*

WESTERN AFRICA (*in part*)

O.E.Z.   Oleksa Eliseyovich Zasenko. *Head, Department of the History of Ukrainian Prerevolutionary Literature, Institute of Literature, Ukrainian S.S.R. Academy of Sciences, Kiev. Coauthor of* History of Ukrainian Literature (*vol. 8*).

UKRAINIAN LITERATURE (*in part*) (Micropædia)

O.F.B.   Otto Friedrich Bollnow. *Emeritus Professor of Philosophy and Education, Eberhard Karl University of Tübingen, Germany. Author of* Dilthey: Eine Einführung in seine Philosophie.

DILTHEY, WILHELM (Micropædia)

O.G.   Owen Gingerich. *Professor of Astronomy and of the History of Science, Harvard University. Senior Astronomer, Smithsonian Astrophysical Observatory,*

Cambridge, Massachusetts. Coauthor of Solar and Planetary Longitudes for Years −2500 to +2000.

STARS AND STAR CLUSTERS (*in part*)

O.Gr.   Oleg Grabar. *Aga Khan Professor of Islamic Art, Harvard University. Author of* The Formation of Islamic Art; *coauthor of* The Art and Architecture of Islam 650–1250.

ISLĀMIC ARTS (*in part*)

O.H.   Oscar Handlin. *Carol M. Loeb University Professor Emeritus, Harvard University. Author of* History of Liberty in America; The Americans; *and others.*

UNITED STATES OF AMERICA (*in part*)

O.H.H.   Oscar H. Horst. *Emeritus Professor of Geography, Western Michigan University, Kalamazoo. Editor of* New Themes in Instruction for Latin American Geography *and others.*

CENTRAL AMERICA (*in part*)

O.H.K.   Omari H. Kokole. *Assistant Professor of Political Science, State University of New York at Binghamton.*

EASTERN AFRICA (*in part*)

O.J.   Oswald Jacoby (d. 1984). *Author of* Oswald Jacoby on Poker *and many other works on card playing.*

POKER (Micropædia)

O.J.B.   Ooi Jin Bee. *Professor of Geography, National University of Singapore. Editor,* Singapore Journal of Tropical Geography. *Author of* Peninsular Malaysia *and others.*

SOUTHEAST ASIA, MAINLAND (*in part*)

O.J.E.   Olin Jeuck Eggen. *Senior Astronomer, Cerro Tololo Interamerican Observatory, La Serena, Chile.*

BRAHE, TYCHO (Micropædia)
HALLEY, EDMOND (Micropædia)

O.J.H.   Oscar J. Hammen. *Emeritus Professor of History, University of Montana, Missoula. Author of* The Red '48ers: Karl Marx and Friedrich Engels.

ENGELS, FRIEDRICH (Micropædia)

O.K.   Olin Kalmbach (d. 1979). *President, Tipton and Kalmbach, Inc., Consulting Engineers, Denver.*

PUBLIC WORKS (*in part*)

O.K.-J.   Ole Klindt-Jensen (d. 1980). *Professor of Prehistory, University of Århus, Denmark, 1961–80. Author of* Foreign Influences in Denmark's Early Iron Age; Denmark Before the Vikings.

PAINTING, THE HISTORY OF WESTERN (*in part*)

O.K.L.   Oleg Konstantinovich Leontiev (d. 1988). *Professor and Head, Department of Geomorphology, Moscow M.V. Lomonosov State University.*

ASIA (*in part*)

O.L.   Otto Leichter (d. 1973). *Correspondent for United Nations and U.S. Affairs, Arbeiter-Zeitung, Vienna; and* Neue Ruhr-Zeitung, *Essen, West Germany. Author of* Zwischen zwei Diktaturen.

AUSTRIA (*in part*)

O.La.   Owen Lattimore (d. 1989). *Professor of Chinese Studies, University*

620 Initials of contributors

of Leeds, England, 1963–70. Author of Mongols of Manchuria; Inner Asian Frontiers of China; *and others.*
MONGOLIA (*in part*)

O.L.A.   Oliver L. Austin, Jr. (d. 1988). *Curator in Ornithology, Florida State Museum, University of Florida, Gainesville, 1957–73. Author of* Birds of the World *and of numerous papers.*
BIRDS (*in part*)

O.L.Z.   Oliver Louis Zangwill (d. 1987). *Professor of Experimental Psychology, University of Cambridge, 1952–81. Author of* An Introduction to Modern Psychology; *coeditor of* Amnesia.
MEMORY (*in part*)

O.N.B.   O. Nigel Bolland. *Professor of Sociology, Colgate University, Hamilton, New York. Author of* Belize: A New Nation in Central America *and others.*
CENTRAL AMERICA (*in part*)

O.O.   Otakar Odlozilik (d. 1973). *Professor of European History, University of Pennsylvania, Philadelphia, 1955–70. Author of* Bohemia in European Affairs, 1440–1471.
CZECHOSLOVAKIA (*in part*)

O.O.W.   Oscar O. Winther (d. 1970). *University Professor of History, Indiana University, Bloomington, 1965–70. Author of* The Great Northwest *and others.*
UNITED STATES OF AMERICA (*in part*)

O.R.A.K.   Oswin R.A. Köhler. *Emeritus Professor of African Studies; former Director, Institute for African Studies, University of Cologne. Author of* Die Kxoe-Buschleute und ihre ethnische Umgebung *and others.*
LANGUAGES OF THE WORLD (*in part*)

O.R.G.   Oliver Robert Gurney. *Professor of Assyriology, University of Oxford, 1965–78. Author of* The Hittites *and others.*
MIDDLE EASTERN RELIGIONS, ANCIENT (*in part*)

O.Sh.   O. Shagdarsuren. *Director, Institute of General and Experimental Biology, Academy of Sciences of the Mongolian People's Republic, Ulaanbaatar.*
MONGOLIA (*in part*)

O.T.   Oliver Taplin. *Fellow and Tutor of Magdalen College, Oxford; Lecturer in Classical Languages and Literature, University of Oxford. Author of* Greek Tragedy in Action; Greek Fire.
GREEK DRAMATISTS, THE CLASSICAL (*in part*)

O.W.   Owen Williams. *Emeritus Professor of Geography, University of Natal, Pietermaritzburg, South Africa. Coauthor of* The Economic Framework of South Africa.
SOUTH AFRICA (*in part*)

O.W.W.   Oliver W. Wolters. *Goldwin Smith Professor of Emeritus Southeast Asian History, Cornell University, Ithaca, New York. Author of* Early

Indonesian Commerce *and others.*
INDONESIA (*in part*)

P.A.   Paul Avrich. *Distinguished Professor of History, Queens College, City University of New York, Flushing. Author of* The Russian Anarchists.
KROPOTKIN, PETER (Micropædia)

P.A.C.   Paul A. Crow, Jr. *President, Council on Christian Unity of the Christian Church (Disciples of Christ), Indianapolis, Indiana. Author of* Christian Unity: Matrix for Mission.
CHRISTIANITY (*in part*)

P.A.H.   Patrick Aidan Heelan. *Professor of Philosophy, State University of New York at Stony Brook. Author of* Quantum Mechanics and Objectivity.
HEISENBERG

Pa.M.   Paul Mercier (d. 1976). *Professor of Ethnology, University of Paris V. Director of Studies, Institute for Advanced Research, Paris. Author of* Historie de l'anthropologie.
SOCIAL SCIENCES, THE (*in part*)

P.A.M.   Peter A. Mackridge. *Lecturer in Modern Greek, University of Oxford. Author of* The Modern Greek Language; Dionysios Solomos.
GREEK LITERATURE (*in part*)

P.A.Ma.   Phebe A. Marr. *Senior Fellow, National Defense University, Washington, D.C. Former Associate Professor of History, University of Tennessee, Knoxville. Author of* The Modern History of Iraq.
BAGHDAD (*in part*)

Pa.N.   Paul Nash. *Professor of Philosophy and Education, Boston University. Author of* Authority and Freedom in Education.
PHILOSOPHIES OF THE BRANCHES OF KNOWLEDGE (*in part*)

Pa.S.   Pauline Simmons. *Associate Curator of Far Eastern Art, Metropolitan Museum of Art, New York City, 1928–58. Author of* Chinese Patterned Silks.
DRESS AND ADORNMENT (*in part*)

P.A.S.   Paul A. Schwartz. *Research Associate, Rancho Grande Biological Research Station, Ministry of the Environment and Renewable Natural Resources, Venezuela.*
BIRDS (*in part*)

P.A.S.S.   Peter A.S. Smith. *Professor of Chemistry, University of Michigan, Ann Arbor. Author of* Derivatives of Hydrazine and Other Hydronitrogens.
CHEMICAL COMPOUNDS (*in part*)

P.A.V.   Philomene A. Verlaan. *Editor, Professional Correspondence Series of the Law of the Sea Institute, University of Hawaii at Manoa, Honolulu. Author of* South Asian Seas: A Review of the Oceanography, Resources and Environment.
INDIAN OCEAN, THE (*in part*)

P.B.Ca.   Philip B. Calkins. *Former Assistant Professor of History, Duke University, Durham, North Carolina.*
INDIA (*in part*)

P.B.C.M.   Peter B.C. Matthews, M.D. *Professor of Sensorimotor Physiology, University of Oxford. Author of* Mammalian Muscle Receptors and Their Central Actions.
NERVES AND NERVOUS SYSTEMS (*in part*)

P.B.D. de la M.   Peter B.D. de la Mare (d. 1989). *Professor of Chemistry, University of Auckland, New Zealand. Author of* Electrophilic Halogenation.
CHEMICAL REACTIONS (*in part*)

P.-B.L.   Pierre-Bernard Lafont. *Director of Studies, Division of Historical and Philological Sciences, École Pratique des Hautes Études (Institute for Advanced Research), Paris. Author of* Bibliographie du Laos *and others.*
SOUTHEAST ASIA, MAINLAND (*in part*)

P.C.   Pierre Camu. *Senior Consultant, Lavalin Inc., Ottawa. Professor of Economic Geography, Laval University, Quebec, 1956–60. President, St. Lawrence Seaway Authority, 1965–73. Author of* Economic Geography of Canada.
NORTH AMERICA (*in part*)

P.Ca.   Pedro Calmon (d. 1985). *President, Brazilian Historical and Geographical Institute, Rio de Janeiro. Author of* História do Brasil.
CABRAL, PEDRO ÁLVARES (Micropædia)

P.C.-B.   Peter Cannon-Brookes. *Museum consultant. Keeper, Department of Art, National Museum of Wales, Cardiff, 1978–86. Author of* Lombard Paintings; Czech Sculpture, 1800–1938; *and others.*
ARCHITECTURE, THE HISTORY OF WESTERN (*in part*)
PAINTING, THE HISTORY OF WESTERN (*in part*)
SCULPTURE, THE HISTORY OF WESTERN (*in part*)

P.-C.C.   Pao-Chi Chang. *Associate Professor of Architecture, Illinois Institute of Technology, Chicago. Partner, Alfred Swenson Pao-Chi Chang Architects, Chicago. Coauthor of* Architectural Education at IIT, 1938–1978.
BUILDING CONSTRUCTION (*in part*)

P.Ch.   Pramod Chandra. *George P. Bickford Professor of Indian Art, Harvard University. Author of* Stone Sculpture in the Allahabad Museum; Bundi Painting.
SOUTH ASIAN ARTS (*in part*)

P.C.-H.   Peter Crossley-Holland. *Emeritus Professor of Music, University of California, Los Angeles. Author of* Pelican History of Music (*vol. 1, part I*).
MUSIC, THE ART OF (*in part*)

P.-c.K.   Ping-chia Kuo. *Emeritus Professor of History, Southern Illinois University, Carbondale. Senior Fellow, National Endowment for the Humanities, 1973–74. Author of* China; China: New Age and New Outlook.
CANTON (*in part*)
CHINA (*in part*)
CHUNGKING (*in part*)
NANKING (*in part*)

P.Cla.   Peter Classen (deceased). *Professor of Medieval and Modern History, Rupert Charles University of Heidelberg. Author of* Karl der Grosse, das Papsttum und Byzanz.
CHARLEMAGNE

P.Co.   Pierre Courthion. *Vice President, Syndicate of the French Artistic Press, 1965–78. Author of* Klee; Manet; Seurat; *and many other monographs on modern European artists.*
KLEE, PAUL (Micropædia)
MANET, ÉDOUARD (*in part*) (Micropædia)
SEURAT, GEORGES (Micropædia)

P.C.R.   Philip C. Ritterbush. *Historian of science. Program Director, Institute for Cultural Progress, Washington, D.C. Author of* Overtures to Biology; The Speculations of Eighteenth-Century Naturalists; *and others.*
LAMARCK, JEAN-BAPTISTE DE MONTE, CHEVALIER DE (Micropædia)

P.D.   P. Dayal. *Professor and Head, Department of Geography, Patna University, India, 1951–75; 1978–82. Author of* Bihar in Maps.
INDIA (*in part*)

P.De.   Pierre Descargues. *Art historian and critic. Author of* Frans Hals; Jan Vermeer; *and other monographs.*
HALS, FRANS (Micropædia)
VERMEER, JAN (Micropædia)

P.de L.   Pierre de Latil. *Scientific Editor,* Le Figaro, *Paris. Coauthor of* Le Professeur Auguste Piccard; Man and the Underwater World; *and others.*
PICCARD, AUGUSTE (*in part*) (Micropædia)

P.D.O.   Peter D. Owen. *Painter and printmaker. Former Senior Lecturer, Croydon College of Design and Technology, England. Author of* Painting: Appreciation of the Arts.
PAINTING, THE ART OF

P.Dr.   Philip Drucker (d. 1982). *Professor of Anthropology, University of Kentucky, Lexington, 1968–78. Author of* The Native Brotherhoods: Modern Inter-Tribal Organizations of the Northwest Coast.
AMERICAN INDIANS (*in part*)

P.Du V.   Patrick Du Val. *Former Professor of Geometry, University of Istanbul. Author of* Homographies, Quaternions, and Rotations; Elliptic Functions and Elliptic Curves.
GEOMETRY (*in part*)

P.D.V.   Paul D. Vignaux (d. 1987). *President, Section of Religious Sciences, École Pratique des Hautes Études (Institute for Advanced Research), Paris, 1961–72. Author of* Philosophy in the Middle Ages: An Introduction.
OCKHAM, WILLIAM OF (Micropædia)

P.E.   Peter Ellis. *Consultant. Former Senior Lecturer in Textiles, University of Bradford, England. Author of* The Geometry of the Plain-Square Weave.
INDUSTRIES, MANUFACTURING (*in part*)

Pe.C.   Peter Collins (d. 1981). *Professor of Architecture, McGill University,* Montreal. Author of Changing Ideals in Modern Architecture; Concrete: The Vision of a New Architecture *and others.*
ARCHITECTURE, THE ART OF (*in part*)

Pe.G.   Peter Gray (deceased). *Andrey Avinoff Professor of Biology, University of Pittsburgh, Pennsylvania, 1964–78. Author of* Microtomist's Formulary and Guide; *editor of* Encyclopedia of Biological Sciences.
TISSUES AND FLUIDS (*in part*)

P.E.H.   Peter E. Herzog. *Crandall Melvin Professor of Law, Syracuse University, New York. Author of* Civil Procedure in France.
PROCEDURAL LAW (*in part*)

Pe.He.   Peter Herde. *Professor of History; Director of the Historical Institute, University of Würzburg, Germany. Author of* Beiträge zum päpstlichen Kanzlei und Urkundenwesen im Dreizehnten Jahrhundert *and others.*
HISTORY, THE STUDY OF (*in part*)

P.E.J.   Preston E. James (d. 1986). *Maxwell Professor of Geography, Syracuse University, New York, 1964–70. Author of* All Possible Worlds: A History of Geographical Ideas; Latin America.
BRAZIL (*in part*)
URUGUAY (*in part*)

P.E.K.   Paul E. Klopsteg (d. 1991). *Professor of Applied Science, Northwestern University, Evanston, Illinois, 1944–54. Author of* Turkish Archery and the Composite Bow.
ARCHERY (*in part*) (Micropædia)

P.E.L.   Peter Erik Lasko. *Professor of the History of Art, Courtauld Institute, University of London, 1974–85. Author of* Ars Sacra, 800–1200.
DECORATIVE ARTS AND FURNISHINGS (*in part*)

P.E.P.   Phillip E. Pope. *Professor of Forestry, Purdue University, West Lafayette, Indiana. Coauthor of* Environmental Impacts of Harvesting Wood for Energy.
FORESTRY AND WOOD PRODUCTION (*in part*)

P.E.P.D.   Paul E. Pieris Deraniyagala (d. 1973). *Director, National Museums of Ceylon, 1939–63. Dean, Faculty of Arts, Vidyodaya University of Ceylon, 1961–64. Specialist on fossil and recent animals of the Indian subcontinent, including extinct human populations. Author of* Some Extinct Elephants, Their Relatives and the Two Living Species.
MAMMALS (*in part*)

P.Er.   Philippe Erlanger (d. 1987). *Head, Artistic Exchange Department, Ministry of Foreign Affairs, Paris, 1946–68. Author of* Louis XIV *and others.*
LOUIS XIV (FRANCE) (Micropædia)

P.E.R.   Peter Edward Russell. *King Alfonso XIII Professor Emeritus of Spanish Studies, University of Oxford; Fellow of Exeter College, Oxford. Author of* The English Intervention in Spain and Portugal in the Time of Edward III and Richard II *and others.*
CID, THE (Micropædia)
SPAIN (*in part*)

Pe.S.G.   Peter Spence Gilchrist, Jr. (d. 1985). *President, Gilchem Corporation, Charlotte, North Carolina.*
UNITED STATES OF AMERICA (*in part*)

Pe.V.   Peter Viereck. *Emeritus Professor of History, Mount Holyoke College, South Hadley, Massachusetts. Author of* Conservatism Revisited *and others.*
SOCIO-ECONOMIC DOCTRINES AND REFORM MOVEMENTS, MODERN (*in part*)

P.E.W.   Paul Edward Waggoner. *Distinguished Scientist, Connecticut Agricultural Experiment Station, New Haven; Director, 1972–87. Author of* Agricultural Meteorology.
CLIMATE AND WEATHER (*in part*)

P.F.   Paul Fraisse. *Emeritus Professor of Experimental Psychology, University of Paris V. Author of* Psychology of Time.
PERCEPTION, HUMAN (*in part*)

P.F.B.   Paul F. Borth. *Technical Director, International Prepress Association, South Holland, Illinois. Author of numerous articles on engraving processes.*
PRINTING, TYPOGRAPHY, AND PHOTOENGRAVING (*in part*)

P.F.F.   Philip F. Flemion. *Associate Professor of History, San Diego State University, California. Author of* Historical Dictionary of El Salvador.
CENTRAL AMERICA (*in part*)

P.F.H.   Paul F. Hoffman. *Research Scientist, Continental Geoscience Division, Geological Survey of Canada, Ottawa.*
NORTH AMERICA (*in part*)

P.F.L.   Peirce F. Lewis. *Professor of Geography, Pennsylvania State University, University Park. Author of* New Orleans: The Making of an Urban Landscape.
UNITED STATES OF AMERICA (*in part*)

P.F.P.   Philip F. Purrington (d. 1989). *Curator, Whaling Museum, New Bedford, Massachusetts. Editor of* Returns of Whaling Vessels Sailing from American Ports, 1876–1928.
FISHING, COMMERCIAL (*in part*)

P.F.V.   Paul F. Vincent. *Free-lance translator. Former Senior Lecturer in Dutch, University College, University of London. Coeditor of* European Context: Studies in the History and Literature of the Netherlands.
AMSTERDAM (*in part*)
DUTCH LITERATURE (*in part*)

P.F.W.   Paul F. Watson. *Associate Professor of the History of Art, University of Pennsylvania, Philadelphia. Author of* The Garden of Love in Tuscan Art.
PIERO DELLA FRANCESCA (Micropædia)

P.G.   Paul Guichonnet. *Honorary Professor of Human Geography, University of Geneva. Author of* Genève, Reflexions sur un destin urbain; *general*

editor of Histoire de Genève.
GENEVA (*in part*)

P.Ga.   Philippe Garigue. *Professor of Political Science, Glendon College, York University, Toronto. Professor of Political Science, University of Montreal, 1957–80. Author of* La Vie familiale des Canadiens français *and others.*
CANADA (*in part*)

P.G.B.   Peter G. Bietenholz. *Professor of History, University of Saskatchewan, Saskatoon. Author of* History and Biography in the Work of Erasmus of Rotterdam *and others.*
BURCKHARDT, JACOB
  (Micropædia)

P.G.Be.   Peter G. Bergmann. *Emeritus Professor of Physics, Syracuse University, New York. Research Professor of Physics, New York University, New York City. Author of* Introduction to the Theory of Relativity.
RELATIVITY

P.G.C.   Pablo González Casanova. *Professor, Institute of Social Research, National Autonomous University of Mexico, Mexico City. Author of* La democracia en México.
MEXICO (*in part*)

P.Go.   Peter Godman. *Fellow and Tutor, Pembroke College, University of Oxford. Author of* Poetry and the Carolingian Renaissance *and others.*
LATIN LITERATURE (*in part*)

P.G.P.   Peter Georgiev Penčev. *Professor of Hydrology, University of Sofia, Bulgaria. Chairman, National Committee for the International Hydrologic Program. Author of* Hydrologic Regionalization of Bulgaria.
EUROPE (*in part*)

P.Gr.   Pier Groen. *Former Professor of Meteorology and Physical Oceanography, Free University, Amsterdam. Author of* The Waters of the Sea.
OCEANS (*in part*)

P.G.S.   Peter G. Stein. *Regius Professor of Civil Law, University of Cambridge; Fellow of Queens' College, Cambridge. Author of* Regulæ Iuris: From Juristic Rules to Legal Maxims *and others.*
LEGAL SYSTEMS, THE EVOLUTION OF
  MODERN WESTERN (*in part*)

P.Gu.   Pierre Gourou. *Honorary Professor, College of France, Paris. Emeritus Professor of Geography, Free Univerity of Brussels. Author of* L'Asie.
ASIA (*in part*)

P.G.W.   Patrick Chrestien Gordon Walker, Baron Gordon-Walker (d. 1980). *Member of Parliament (Labour) for Leyton, 1966–74. Author of* The Cabinet; The Commonwealth *and others.*
UNITED KINGDOM (*in part*)

P.H.   Peggy Harper. *Former Senior Research Fellow in Dance, Institute of African Studies, University of Ife, Nigeria. Author of numerous articles on African dance.*
AFRICAN ARTS (*in part*)

P.H.B.   Peter H. Burri. *Professor of Anatomy, Histology, and Embryology; Head, Section of Developmental Biology, Institute of Anatomy, University of Bern.*
RESPIRATION AND RESPIRATORY
  SYSTEMS (*in part*)

Ph.C.   Philip Collins. *Emeritus Professor of English, University of Leicester, England. Author of* Dickens and Crime; Dickens and Education.
DICKENS (*in part*)

Ph.D.   Philip Drew. *Former Professor of English Literature, University of Glasgow. Author of* The Poetry of Browning: A Critical Introduction; *editor of* Robert Browning: A Collection of Critical Essays.
BROWNING, ROBERT (*in part*)
  (Micropædia)

P.He.   Sir Philip Hendy (d. 1980). *Adviser to the Israel Museum, Jerusalem, 1968–71. Director, National Gallery, London, 1946–67. Author of* Giovanni Bellini; Piero della Francesca and the Early Renaissance.
BELLINI, GIOVANNI (Micropædia)

P.H.G.   Peter Humphry Greenwood. *Deputy Chief Scientific Officer, Department of Zoology, British Museum (Natural History), London. Author of* The Fishes of Uganda; *coauthor of the major modern classification of the bony fishes.*
FISHES (*in part*)

P.H.Ge.   Paul Henry Gebhard. *Emeritus Professor of Anthropology, Indiana University, Bloomington; former Director, Institute for Sex Research. Coauthor of* Pregnancy, Birth and Abortion; Sex Offenders.
SEX AND SEXUALITY (*in part*)

P.H.Gu.   Pierre H. Guiguemde. *Former Director of Public Relations for the Parliament of Upper Volta.*
WESTERN AFRICA (*in part*)

P.H.H.   Perry H. Howard. *Emeritus Professor of Sociology, Louisiana State University, Baton Rouge. Author of* Political Tendencies in Louisiana.
UNITED STATES OF AMERICA (*in part*)

Ph.H. J.H.t.C.   Philo H.J. Houwink ten Cate. *Professor of Ancient Near Eastern History and Languages, University of Amsterdam. Author of* The Luwian Population Groups of Lycia and Cilicia Aspera during the Hellenistic Period; The Records of the Early Hittite Empire (c. 1450–1380 BC).
LANGUAGES OF THE WORLD (*in part*)
TURKEY AND ANCIENT ANATOLIA
  (*in part*)

P.Hi.   Patrice Louis-René Higonnet. *Goelet Professor of French History, Harvard University. Author of* Class, Ideology, and the Rights of Nobles During the French Revolution.
FRANCE (*in part*)

P.H.J.C.   Peter Henry John Castle. *Reader in Zoology, Victoria University of Wellington, New Zealand. Author of numerous papers on eels.*
FISHES (*in part*)

P.H.L.   Peter H. Lee. *Professor and Chairman, Department of East Asian Languages and Cultures, University of California, Los Angeles. Author of* Songs of Flying Dragons: A Critical Reading.
KOREAN LITERATURE (*in part*)

P.H.M.   Peter H. Molnar. *Senior Research Associate, Department of Earth, Atmospheric, and Planetary Sciences, Massachusetts Institute of Technology, Cambridge.*
CONTINENTAL LANDFORMS (*in part*)

P.H.O.   Paul H. Oehser. *Editor of Scientific Publications, National Geographic Society, 1966–78. Chief, Editorial and Publications Division, Smithsonian Institution, Washington, D.C., 1950–66.*
UNITED STATES OF AMERICA (*in part*)

P.H.S.   Peter H. Solomon, Jr. *Professor of Political Science, University of Toronto. Author of* Soviet Criminologists and Criminal Policy *and others.*
CRIME AND PUNISHMENT (*in part*)

P.Hu.   Peter J. Huizing. *Professor of Canon Law and History of Canon Law, Catholic University of Nijmegen, The Netherlands. Author of* The Sacraments in Theology and Canon Law.
CHRISTIANITY (*in part*)

P.I.   Pavle Ivić. *Former Professor of Serbo-Croatian Language, History, and Dialectology, University of Belgrade. Author of* Die serbokroatischen Dialekte; *coauthor of* Accent in Serbocroatian.
LANGUAGE (*in part*)
LINGUISTICS (*in part*)

P.J.C.   Peter John Callaghan. *Lecturer in Classics, University of Cambridge.*
PAINTING, THE HISTORY OF WESTERN
  (*in part*)

P.J.G.   Patrick J. Geary. *Professor of History, University of Florida, Gainesville. Author of* Before France *and others.*
GERMANY (*in part*)

P.J.H.   Peter John Hilton. *Distinguished Professor of Mathematics, State University of New York at Binghamton. Coauthor of* Homology Theory; A Course in Modern Algebra; *and others.*
ALGEBRA (*in part*)

P.J.He.   Peter John Heather. *Murray Research Fellow in History, Worcester College, University of Oxford. Author of* The Emergence of the Goths and the Decline of Rome.
GERMANY (*in part*)

P.J.I.   Pascal James Imperato, M.D. *Professor and Chairman, Department of Preventive Medicine and Community Health, State University of New York Health Science Center at Brooklyn. Editor,* New York State Journal of Medicine. *Author of* Historical Dictionary of Mali *and others.*
WESTERN AFRICA (*in part*)

P.J.M.   P.J. Marshall. *Rhodes Professor of Imperial History, King's College, University of London. Author of*

The Impeachment of Warren Hastings *and others.*
HASTINGS, WARREN (Micropædia)

P.J.Mu. Peter J. Murray. *Emeritus Professor of the History of Art, Birkbeck College, University of London. Author of* Architecture of the Italian Renaissance; *coauthor of* A Dictionary of Art and Artists.
GHIRLANDAJO, DOMENICO (Micropædia)
GIOTTO DI BONDONE (Micropædia)
PERUGINO (Micropædia)

P.J.N. Per Jonas Nordhagen. *Professor of in Art History, University of Bergen, Norway. Coauthor of* Mosaics.
DECORATIVE ARTS AND FURNISHINGS (*in part*)

P.J.P. Peter J. Pollack (d. 1978). *Photographer and lecturer. Author of* The Picture History of Photography *and others.*
STEICHEN, EDWARD (Micropædia)

P.J.R. Peter John Rowe. *Professor of Law, University of Liverpool. Author of* Defence: The Legal Implications.
WAR, THE THEORY AND CONDUCT OF (*in part*)

P.J.S. Phillip J. Smith. *Professor of Atmospheric Science, Purdue University, West Lafayette, Indiana.*
CLIMATE AND WEATHER (*in part*)

P.J.Sc. Paul Joseph Scudiere. State Historian of New York.
UNITED STATES OF AMERICA (*in part*)

P.J.S.L. Philip James Stopford Law. *Senior Lecturer in Marketing, London Business School. Editor of* Product Management Readings.
MARKETING AND MERCHANDISING (*in part*)

P.K. Philip Kissam (d. 1978). *Professor of Civil Engineering, Princeton University, 1948–65. Author of* Surveying Practice.
MEASUREMENT AND OBSERVATION, PRINCIPLES, METHODS, AND INSTRUMENTS OF (*in part*)

P.K.E. Peter K. Endress. *Professor of Systematic Botany, Institute for Systematic Botany, University of Zürich.*
ANGIOSPERMS (*in part*)

P.K.K. Peter K. King. *Former Director, Institute of Modern Dutch Studies, University of Hull, England. Author of* Dawn Poetry in the Netherlands *and others.*
DUTCH LITERATURE (*in part*)

P.L. Philip Longworth. *Professor of History, McGill University, Montreal. Author of* The Art of Victory: The Life and Achievements of Generalissimo Suvorov *and others.*
SUVOROV, ALEKSANDR VASILYEVICH, GRAF (Micropædia)

P.Le. Pierre Leprohon. *Writer and journalist. Author of* Jean Renoir; Charles Chaplin; Antonioni; *and others.*
RENOIR, JEAN (Micropædia)

P.L.G. Patrick Lancaster Gardiner. *Fellow and Tutor in Philosophy,*

Magdalen College, University of Oxford. Author of The Nature of Historical Explanation *and others.*
PHILOSOPHIES OF THE BRANCHES OF KNOWLEDGE (*in part*)

P.L.Kl. Paul Lincoln Kleinsorge. *Emeritus Professor of Economics, University of Oregon, Eugene.*
ECONOMIC THEORY (*in part*)

P.L.v.d.B. Pierre Louis van den Berghe. *Professor of Sociology, University of Washington, Seattle. Author of* Race and Racism.
SOCIAL DIFFERENTIATION (*in part*)

P.Ma. Philip Mason. *Writer. Director, Institute of Race Relations, London, 1958–69. Indian Civil Service, 1928–47. Author of* The Founders; The Guardians; The Birth of a Dilemma; The Men Who Ruled India; *and many others.*
BENTINCK, LORD WILLIAM (Micropædia)

P.Mac C. Proinsias Mac Cana. *Senior Professor, School of Celtic Studies, Dublin Institute for Advanced Studies. Author of* Celtic Mythology *and others.*
EUROPEAN RELIGIONS, ANCIENT (*in part*)

P.M.C. Paul M. Cohn. *Emeritus Professor of Mathematics, University College, University of London. Author of* Universal Algebra; Algebra *(3 vol.); and others.*
ALGEBRA (*in part*)

P.McC. Patrick McCarthy. *Former Associate Professor of French, Haverford College, Pennsylvania. Author of* Céline; Camus.
FRENCH LITERATURE (*in part*)

P.McG.R. Peter McGregor Ross (d. 1974). *Professor of Engineering, University of Cambridge, 1970–74.*
ENGINEERING (*in part*)

P.McL. Peter McLintock (deceased). *Editor,* Winnipeg Free Press, *Manitoba.*
CANADA (*in part*)

P.Me. Pierre Mertz (d. 1982). *Chairman, Board of Editors,* Journal of the Society of Motion Picture and Television Engineers, *1954–77. Coauthor of* Communication System Engineering Handbook.
MOTION PICTURES (*in part*)

P.M.F. Peter Marshall Fraser. *Emeritus Fellow of All Souls College, Oxford; Reader in Hellenistic History, University of Oxford, 1964–85.*
PALESTINE (*in part*)

P.M.Ho. Peter M. Holt. *Emeritus Professor of the History of the Near and Middle East, University of London. Author of* Egypt and the Fertile Crescent, 1516–1922 *and others.*
EGYPT (*in part*)

P.Mi. Peter Michelmore. *Roving Editor,* Reader's Digest. *Author of* Einstein: Profile of the Man.
EINSTEIN
TELLER, EDWARD (*in part*) (Micropædia)

P.M.K. Paul Murray Kendall (d. 1973). *Professor of English, University of Kansas, Lawrence. Author of* The

Art of Biography; Richard the Third; *and others.*
LITERATURE, THE ART OF (*in part*)

P.Mo. Patrick Moore. *President, British Astronomical Association. Author of* The Unfolding Universe *and many others.*
SOLAR SYSTEM, THE (*in part*)

P.M.R. Pierre M. Rosenberg. *Chief Curator, Department of Paintings, Louvre Museum, Paris. Author of* Chardin: Étude biographique et critique; Dessins français du 17ème siècle.
CHARDIN, JEAN-BAPTISTE-SIMÉON (Micropædia)

P.M.Sy. Patrick Millington Synge (d. 1982). *Editor, Publications of the Royal Horticultural Society, London, 1945–70. Author of* Collins Guide to Bulbs; *coauthor of* The Dictionary of Garden Plants in Colour.
GARDENING AND HORTICULTURE (*in part*)

P.Mu. Peter Munz. *Emeritus Professor of History, Victoria University of Wellington, New Zealand. Author of* The Origin of the Carolingian Empire *and others.*
CONRAD II (GERMANY/HOLY ROMAN EMPIRE) (Micropædia)
HENRY II (SAXONY) (Micropædia)

P.M.U. Peter Michael Urbach. *Lecturer in Philosophy, London School of Economics and Political Science, University of London. Author of* Francis Bacon's Philosophy of Science: An Account and a Reappraisal.
BACON, FRANCIS (*in part*)

P.M.Y. Percy Marshall Young. *Composer. Director of Music, Wolverhampton College of Technology, England, 1944–66. Author of* A History of British Music; Handel.
HANDEL, GEORGE FRIDERIC (*in part*) (Micropædia)

P.N.L. Peter N. Ladefoged. *Professor of Phonetics, University of California, Los Angeles. Author of* A Course in Phonetics *and others.*
SPEECH (*in part*)

P.N.S. Peter N. Stearns. *Heinz Professor and Head, Department of History, Carnegie-Mellon University, Pittsburgh. Author of* European Society in Upheaval: Social History Since 1750.
EUROPEAN HISTORY AND CULTURE (*in part*)

P.O. Paul Oliver. *Former Associate Head, Department of Architecture, Oxford Polytechnic, England. Editor of* Shelter in Africa *and others.*
AFRICAN ARTS (*in part*)

P.O.W. Peter O. Wacker. *Professor of Geography, Rutgers University, New Brunswick, New Jersey. Author of* Land and People: An Historical Cultural Geography of Preindustrial New Jersey.
UNITED STATES OF AMERICA (*in part*)

P.P. Paul Petit (d. 1981). *Professor of Ancient History, University of Grenoble II, France. Author of* Histoire général de

l'Empire romaine *and others*.
GREEK AND ROMAN CIVILIZATIONS, ANCIENT (*in part*)

P.P.A.   Phoon Phon Asanachinta. *Colonel, Royal Thai Army. Emeritus Professor of Geography, Chiang Mai University, Chiang Mai, Thailand.*
SOUTHEAST ASIA, MAINLAND (*in part*)

P.P.B.   Patrick Paul Billingsley. *Professor of Mathematics and of Statistics, University of Chicago. Author of* Convergence of Probability Measures *and others*.
NUMBER THEORY (*in part*)

P.P. del C.   Pier Paolo del Campana. *Professor of Comparative Religion, Sophia University, Tokyo. Author of* Shinran and Nichiren.
NICHIREN (Micropædia)

P.P.E.   Paul P. Ewald (d. 1985). *Professor of Physics, Polytechnic Institute of Brooklyn, New York, 1949–59.*
BETHE, HANS ALBRECHT (*in part*) (Micropædia)

P.P.G.   Pedro P. Geiger. *Professor of Geography, Pontifical Catholic University of Rio de Janeiro. Author of* Evolução da Rede Urbana do Brasil.
RIO DE JANEIRO (*in part*)

P.P.H.   Philip Prichard Henderson (d. 1977). *Free-lance writer and editor. Author of* William Morris: His Life, Work and Friends; *editor of* The Letters of William Morris *and others*.
MORRIS, WILLIAM (Micropædia)

P.P.K.   Pradyumna P. Karan. *Distinguished Professor of Geography, University of Kentucky, Lexington. Author of* Nepal: A Physical and Cultural Geography; Bhutan: Environment, Culture and Development Strategy; *and others*.
BHUTAN
NEPAL (*in part*)

Pp.M.   Philip Merlan (d. 1968). *Professor of German Philosophy and Literature, Scripps College, Claremont, California, 1942–68. Author of* From Platonism to Neoplatonism *and others*.
PHILOSOPHICAL SCHOOLS AND DOCTRINES, WESTERN (*in part*)

P.P.M.   Philip P. Micklin. *Professor of Geography, Western Michigan University, Kalamazoo.*
ASIA (*in part*)
EUROPE (*in part*)

P.P.R.   Peter P. Rohde (d. 1978). *Free-lance writer. Author of* Søren Kierkegaard; *editor of* Kierkegaard's works.
KIERKEGAARD, SØREN (*in part*) (Micropædia)

P.R.   Pierre Riché. *Professor of Medieval History, University of Paris X. Author of* Education and Culture in the Barbarian West *and others*.
EDUCATION, HISTORY OF (*in part*)

P.R.A.   Pierre Robert Angel. *Former Professor and Head, Department of Classical and Modern Languages, Literature and Civilizations, University of Tours, France. Author of* Eduard Bernstein et l'évolution du socialisme allemand *and others*.
BERNSTEIN, EDUARD (Micropædia)

P.R.B.   Peter R. Bridenbaugh. *Vice President, Research and Development, Alcoa Laboratories, Aluminum Company of America, Pittsburgh.*
INDUSTRIES, EXTRACTION AND PROCESSING (*in part*)

P.R.C.   Peter Raymond Creevey. *Free-lance writer and journalist. Managing Editor,* The Samoa Times, *Pago Pago, American Samoa, 1963–70.*
PACIFIC ISLANDS (*in part*)

P.R.Cd.   Paul R. Clifford. *Department Head, Environmental Chemistry and Biology, Metrek Division, Mitre Corporation, McLean, Virginia. Coauthor of* Fundamentals of Organic Chemistry.
CARBONIUM ION (*in part*) (Micropædia)

P.R.G.   Peter R. Grant. *Professor of Biology, University of Michigan, Ann Arbor.*
BIOSPHERE, THE (*in part*)

P.R.Go.   Peter R. Goethals. *Writer, consultant, and research specialist on Southeast Asia. Author of* Aspects of Local Government in a Sumbawan Village.
ASIAN PEOPLES AND CULTURES (*in part*)

P.Rh.   Philip Rhodes. *Regional Postgraduate Dean of Medical Studies; Professor of Postgraduate Medical Education, University of Southampton, England, 1980–87. Author of* An Outline History of Medicine *and others*.
MEDICINE (*in part*)

P.R.L.B.   Peter R.L. Brown. *Rollins Professor of History, Princeton University. Author of* Religion and Society in the Age of Saint Augustine.
AMBROSE, SAINT (Micropædia)

P.R.P.   Peter R. Prifti. *Free-lance writer and translator, specializing in Albanian studies. Author of* Socialist Albania Since 1944.
ALBANIA (*in part*)

P.Ru.   Peter Rudge. *Consultant Neurologist, National Hospital for Nervous Diseases, London. Author of* Clinical Neuro-otology.
NERVES AND NERVOUS SYSTEMS (*in part*)

P.S.   Pierre Samuel. *Professor of Mathematics, University of Paris XI. Author of* Théorie algébrique des nombres.
ALGEBRA (*in part*)

P.S.Ba.   Peter S. Baker. *Associate Professor of English, Emory University, Atlanta, Georgia. Coeditor of* The Correspondence of James Boswell with David Garrick, Edmund Burke, and Edmond Malone.
ENGLISH LITERATURE (*in part*)

P.Sc.   Peter Scott. *Emeritus Professor of Geography, University of Tasmania, Hobart.*
AUSTRALIA (*in part*)

P.S.C.   Philip S. Corbet. *Emeritus Professor of Zoology, University of Dundee, Scotland. Author of* A Biology of Dragonflies.
INSECTS (*in part*)

P.S.F.   Philip S. Foner. *Independence Foundation Professor Emeritus of History, Lincoln University, Pennsylvania. Editor of* The Complete Writings of Thomas Paine.
PAINE, THOMAS (Micropædia)

P.S.G.   Peter S. Green. *Honorary Research Associate, Royal Botanic Gardens, Kew, England; former Deputy Director. Coeditor of* Wild Flowers of the World.
ANGIOSPERMS (*in part*)

P.S.H.   Philip S. Holzman. *Esther and Sidney R. Rabb Professor of Psychology, Harvard University. Coauthor of* Assessing Schizophrenic Thinking *and others*.
PERSONALITY (*in part*)

P.S.Ha.   Phillip S. Hattingh. *Professor and Head, Department of Geography, University of Pretoria, South Africa. Coauthor of* Black Homelands in South Africa.
AFRICA (*in part*)

P.Si.   Peter Singer. *Professor of Philosophy; Director, Centre for Human Bioethics, Monash University, Victoria, Australia. Author of* Practical Ethics.
ETHICS

P.S.K.   Pavel Sergeyevich Kuzin (d. 1976). *Senior Scientist, Leningrad Hydrological Institute. Author of* Volga Zavtra.
EUROPE (*in part*)

P.S.M.   P.S. Messenger (d. 1976). *Professor of Entomology, University of California, Berkeley, 1965–76. Author of many research papers on entomology.*
BIOSPHERE, THE (*in part*)

P.S.R.   Philip S. Rawson. *Dean, School of Art and Design, Goldsmiths' College, London, 1981–84. Curator, Gulbenkian Museum of Oriental Art and Archaeology, University of Durham, England, 1960–79. Author of* The Arts of Southeast Asia *and others*.
PAGAN (Micropædia)
SOUTHEAST ASIAN ARTS (*in part*)

P.Su.   Patrick Suppes. *Lucie Stern Professor of Philosophy; Director, Institute for Mathematical Studies in the Social Sciences, Stanford University, California. Coauthor of* Foundations of Measurement.
MEASUREMENT THEORY (*in part*)

P.S.W.   Paul S. Wingert (d. 1974). *Professor of Art History and Archaeology, Columbia University. Author of* Primitive Art, Its Traditions and Styles *and others*.
MASKS

P.T.   Piero Treves. *Professor of Ancient History, University of Venice, Italy. Author of biography of Miltiades in* Oxford Classical Dictionary.
MILTIADES THE YOUNGER (Micropædia)

P.U.   Philip Soundy Unwin (d. 1981). *Free-lance editor. Senior Director, George Allen & Unwin Ltd., London. Author of* Book Publishing as a Career.
PUBLISHING (*in part*)

P.V.   Paul Veyret (deceased). *Professor of Mountain Geography, University of Grenoble I, France. Coauthor of* Au coeur de l'Europe: Les Alpes *and others.*
EUROPE (*in part*)

P.V.G.   Peteris V. Gulyans. *Assistant Director, Institute of Economics, Latvian Academy of Sciences, Riga. Author of* Latvia in the System of the U.S.S.R. National Economy.
BALTIC STATES (*in part*)

P.Vi.   Paul Viallaneix. *Emeritus Professor of French Literature, University of Clermont-Ferrand, France. Author of* Vigny par lui-même; *editor of Vigny's* Oeuvres complètes.
VIGNY, ALFRED-VICTOR, COMTE DE (Micropædia)

P.V.T.   Phillip Vallentine Tobias. *Professor and Head, Department of Anatomy and Human Biology, University of the Witwatersrand, Johannesburg. Author of* Olduvai Gorge: Cranium of Zinjanthropus (*vol. 2 and 4*).
EVOLUTION, HUMAN (*in part*)

P.W.   Paul E. Walker. *Former Associate Professor of Islamic Studies, McGill University, Montreal.*
SALADIN (Micropædia)

P.Wa.   Peggy Wagner. *Staff member, Houghton Mifflin Company, Boston. Editorial Assistant, Arts,* Encyclopædia Britannica, *Chicago, 1971–73.*
AFRICAN ARTS (*in part*)

P.W.A.   Peter William Avery. *Lecturer in Persian, University of Cambridge; Fellow of King's College, Cambridge. Author of* Modern Iran.
IRAN (*in part*)

P.W.D.   Paul W. Drake. *Professor of Political Science, University of California, San Diego, at La Jolla. Author of* Socialism and Populism in Chile, 1932–52.
CHILE (*in part*)

P.W.F.   Peter W. Frank. *Professor of Biology, University of Oregon, Eugene.*
GROWTH AND DEVELOPMENT, BIOLOGICAL (*in part*)

P.W.H.   Paul W. Hodge. *Professor of Astronomy, University of Washington, Seattle. Author of* Galaxies *and others.*
GALAXIES

P.W.J.   Pascual W. Jordon (d. 1980). *Professor of Theoretical Physics, University of Hamburg, 1953–70. Author of* Verdrängung und Komplementarität: Eine philosophische Untersuchung.
PHILOSOPHIES OF THE BRANCHES OF KNOWLEDGE (*in part*)

P.W.K.   Peter W. Kingsford. *Tutor, Extra Mural Department, University of London. Author of* Engineers, Inventors, and Workers; Victorian Railwaymen *and others.*
WATT, JAMES (Micropædia)

P.W.N.   Peter W. Nathan. *Former External Scientific Worker of Medical Research Council, National Hospital for Nervous Diseases, London. Author of* The Nervous System.
NERVES AND NERVOUS SYSTEMS (*in part*)

P.Wo.   Paul Wonnacott. *Professor of Economics, University of Maryland, College Park. Author of* The United States and Canada: The Quest for Free Trade *and others.*
INTERNATIONAL TRADE (*in part*)

P.W.R.   Paul Westmacott Richards. *Emeritus Professor of Botany, University College of North Wales, University of Wales, Bangor. Author of* The Tropical Rain Forest *and others.*
BIOSPHERE, THE (*in part*)

P.Y.   Philip Young. *Evan Pugh Professor of English, Pennsylvania State University, University Park. Author of* Ernest Hemingway; *coauthor of* The Hemingway Manuscripts.
HEMINGWAY, ERNEST (Micropædia)

P.Y.K.   Pekka Yrjö Korkala. *Former Lecturer in Psychometrics, Institute of Psychology, University of Helsinki. Coauthor of* Introduction to Psychometrics; *coeditor of* Contemporary Research in the Psychology of Perception.
PERCEPTION, HUMAN (*in part*)

Q.W.   Quincy Wright (d. 1970). *Professor of International Law, University of Chicago, 1931–56. Author of* Study of International Relations.
UNITED NATIONS (*in part*)

Q.Z.   Quido Záruba. *Professor of Geology, Czech Technical University in Prague, 1946–71. Member of the Czechoslovak Academy of Sciences. Coauthor of* Landslides and Their Control *and others.*
GEOMORPHIC PROCESSES (*in part*)

R.A.   Rosendo Arguello. *Former President, Academy of the Geography and History of Nicaragua, Managua. Author of* Nueva Nicaragua.
CENTRAL AMERICA (*in part*)

R.Aa.   Richard I. Aaron (d. 1987). *Emeritus Professor of Philosophy, University College of Wales, Aberystwyth, University of Wales, 1932–69. Author of* John Locke; Knowing and the Function of Reason.
LOCKE (*in part*)

R.A.A.   Ralph A. Austen. *Professor of History, University of Chicago; Chairman, Committee on African Studies, 1974–79 and 1984–89. Author of* African Economic History *and others.*
EASTERN AFRICA (*in part*)

R.A.An.   Robert A. Andersen. *Director, Provasoli-Guillard Center for Culture of Marine Phytoplankton, Bigelow Laboratory for Ocean Sciences, West Boothbay Harbor, Maine. Coeditor of* Chrysophytes: Aspects and Problems.
ALGAE

R.A.B.   Roland A. Budenholzer. *Emeritus Professor of Mechanical Engineering; Chairman, American Power Conference, Illinois Institute of Technology, Chicago.*
ENERGY CONVERSION (*in part*)

R.A.Bu.   Robert Angus Buchanan. *Reader in the History of Technology; Director, Centre for the History of Technology, Science, and Society, University of Bath, England. Author of* Technology and Social Progress.
TECHNOLOGY, THE HISTORY OF

R.A.-C.   René Albrecht-Carrié (d.1978). *Professor of History, Barnard College, 1945–69, and Columbia University, 1953–69. Author of* A Diplomatic History of Europe Since the Congress of Vienna.
EUROPE (*in part*)

R.A.Co.   Ralph A. Connor, D.D.S. *Professor of Pediatric and Community Dentistry, Dalhousie University, Halifax, Nova Scotia, 1971–72. Chief, Dental Health Division, Canadian Department of National Health and Welfare, Ottawa, 1963–71.*
MEDICINE (*in part*)

R.Ad.   Ron Adams. *Principal Lecturer in Social and Cultural Studies, Victoria University of Technology, Melbourne. Author of* In the Land of Strangers: A Century of European Contact with Tanna, 1774–1874.
PACIFIC ISLANDS (*in part*)

R.A.D.   Richard A Davis, Jr. *Professor of Geology, University of South Florida, Tampa. Author of* Depositional Systems *and others.*
CONTINENTAL LANDFORMS (*in part*)

R.A.E.   Robert A. East. *Emeritus Professor of History, Brooklyn College, City University of New York. Author of* John Adams *and others.*
ADAMS, JOHN (Micropædia)

R.A.F.   Richard Antony French. *Senior Lecturer in the Geography of the U.S.S.R., University College and School of Slavonic and East European Studies, University of London. Author of* The U.S.S.R. and Eastern Europe.
KIEV (*in part*)
MOSCOW (*in part*)
SAINT PETERSBURG (*in part*)
UNION OF SOVIET SOCIALIST REPUBLICS (*in part*)

R.A.G.   Richard A. Geyer. *Emeritus Professor of Oceanography, Texas A&M University, College Station.*
ATLANTIC OCEAN, THE (*in part*)

R.A.Gi.   Robert Andrew Gilbert. *Antiquarian bookseller. Author of* The Golden Dawn: Twilight of the Magicians; *coeditor of* The Oxford Book of English Ghost Stories.
OCCULTISM (*in part*)

R.A.H.   Robert A. Hall, Jr. *Emeritus Professor of Linguistics and Italian, Cornell University, Ithaca, New York. Author of* Pidgin and Creole Languages.
LANGUAGES OF THE WORLD (*in part*)

R.A.He. Ronald A. Henson, M.D. *Physician and Neurologist, London Hospital, 1949–81. Physician, National Hospital for Nervous Diseases, 1952–81.*
MUSCLES AND MUSCLE SYSTEMS (*in part*)

R.A.Hi. Reynold Alleyne Higgins. *Deputy Keeper of Greek and Roman Antiquities, British Museum, London, 1965–77. Author of* Minoan and Mycenaean Art *and others.*
PAINTING, THE HISTORY OF WESTERN (*in part*)
SCULPTURE, THE HISTORY OF WESTERN (*in part*)

Ra.Ho. Ralph Holmes. *Stage lighting designer. Senior Lighting Director, Columbia Broadcasting System, New York City.*
THEATRICAL PRODUCTION (*in part*)

R.A.Ho. R.A. Horne. *Former Senior Scientist, Energy and Environmental Engineers, Inc., Cambridge, Massachusetts. Author of* Marine Chemistry *and others; editor of* Water and Aqueous Solutions.
CHEMICAL COMPOUNDS (*in part*)

R.A.J.McD. Robert A.J. McDonald. *Assistant Professor of History, University of British Columbia, Vancouver. Coeditor of* Vancouver Past: Essays in Social History; British Columbia: Historical Readings.
CANADA (*in part*)

R.A.K. Raymond A. Kliphardt. *Emeritus Professor of Engineering Sciences, Northwestern University, Evanston, Illinois. Author of* Program Design in Fortran IV.
DRAFTING

R.A.Ka. Robert A. Kann (d. 1981). *Professor of History, Rutgers University, New Brunswick, New Jersey, 1956–76. Author of* The Habsburg Empire.
AUSTRIA (*in part*)

R.A.Kl. Robert A. Klocke, M.D. *Professor of Medicine and Physiology; Chief, Pulmonary Division, State University of New York at Buffalo. Coauthor of* Normal and Abnormal Lung Function.
RESPIRATION AND RESPIRATORY SYSTEMS (*in part*)

R.Al. Rex Alston. *Broadcaster and journalist. Staff Sports Commentator and Reporter, British Broadcasting Corporation, 1942–61. Cricket Reporter,* Daily *and* Sunday Telegraph (*London*), *1961–88. Author of* Watching Cricket.
SPORTS, MAJOR TEAM AND INDIVIDUAL (*in part*)

R.A.L. Robert A. Laudise. *Director, Materials Chemistry Research Laboratory, Bell Telephone Laboratories, Inc., Murray Hill, New Jersey. Author of* The Growth of Single Crystals.
MATTER (*in part*)

R.A.La. Ronald A. Laskey. *Charles Darwin Professor of Animal Embryology, University of Cambridge. Editor of* Higher Order Structure in the Nucleus.
CELLS (*in part*)

R.A.M. Robert A. Moog. *Research Professor of Music, University of North Carolina at Asheville.*
MUSICAL INSTRUMENTS (*in part*)

R.A.Mu. Robert A. Muller. *Professor of Geography and Anthropology; Director, Southern Regional Climate Center, Louisiana State University, Baton Rouge. Coauthor of* Physical Geography Today *and others.*
NORTH AMERICA (*in part*)

Ra.N. Ray Nash (d. 1982). *Professor of Art, Dartmouth College, Hanover, New Hampshire, 1949–70. Author of* American Penmanship, 1800–1850; *editor and translator of* Calligraphy and Printing in the Sixteenth Century.
WRITING (*in part*)

R.A.N. Robert A. Nisbet. *Albert Schweitzer Professor Emeritus of Humanities, Columbia University. Noted for contributions to social theory and organization. Author of* Social Change and History *and others.*
SOCIAL SCIENCES, THE (*in part*)

R.A.P. Robert A. Pinker. *Professor of Social Work Studies, London School of Economics and Political Science, University of London. Author of* The Idea of Welfare *and others.*
SOCIAL WELFARE (*in part*)

R.A.Pi. Roger Alvin Pielke. *Professor of Atmospheric Science, Colorado State University, Ft. Collins. Author of* Mesoscale Meteorological Modeling.
EARTH SCIENCES, THE (*in part*)

R.A.Pr. Ralph Anthony Palmer. *Assistant Secretary, American Society of Agricultural Engineers, 1927–69.*
AGRICULTURAL SCIENCES (*in part*)

R.A.R. Richard A. Robison. *Gulf-Hedberg Professor of Geology, University of Kansas, Lawrence. Coauthor of* Fossil Invertebrates.
GEOCHRONOLOGY (*in part*)

R.A.R.T. Ronald A.R. Tricker (d. 1984). *Staff Inspector for Science, Ministry of Education, U.K., 1946–62. Author of* Bores, Breakers, Waves and Wakes; The Contributions of Faraday and Maxwell to Electrical Science.
MECHANICS (*in part*)
OCEANS (*in part*)

R.Au. Robert Austerlitz. *Professor of Linguistics and Uralic Studies, Columbia University. Coeditor of* Readings in Linguistics I and II; *compiler of* Finnish Reader and Glossary (*2nd ed.*).
LANGUAGES OF THE WORLD (*in part*)

R.A.W. Richard A. Watson. *Professor of Philosophy, Washington University, St. Louis, Missouri. Author of* The Breakdown of Cartesian Metaphysics *and others.*
CARTESIANISM, DESCARTES AND

R.A.Wa. Robert Austin Warner (d. 1986). *Professor of Music History and Musicology; Director, Stearns Collection of Musical Instruments, University of Michigan, Ann Arbor.*
MUSICAL INSTRUMENTS (*in part*)

R.A.We. Richard A. Webster. *Professor of History, University of California, Berkeley. Author of* Industrial Imperialism in Italy, 1908–1915.
EUROPEAN OVERSEAS EXPLORATION AND EMPIRES, THE HISTORY OF (*in part*)

R.A.Wo. Ralph A. Wooster. *Associate Vice President; Dean of Faculties, Lamar University, Beaumont, Texas. Author of* Secession Conventions of the South *and others.*
UNITED STATES OF AMERICA (*in part*)

R.B. Robert Browning. *Emeritus Professor of Classics and Ancient History, Birkbeck College, University of London. Author of* The Byzantine Empire *and others.*
EDUCATION, HISTORY OF (*in part*)
GREEK LITERATURE (*in part*)

R.Ba. Ruth Barbour. *Lecturer in Greek Palaeography, University of Oxford, 1960–67.*
WRITING (*in part*)

R.B.A. Robert Brown Asprey. *Military historian and biographer. Author of* The Panther's Feast; War in the Shadows; *and others.*
WAR, THE THEORY AND CONDUCT OF (*in part*)

R.B.Ba. Ronald B. Ballinger (d. 1981). *Professor of History, Rhode Island College, Providence. Author of* South West Africa: The Case Against the Union *and others.*
SOUTH AFRICA (*in part*)
SOUTHERN AFRICA (*in part*)

R.B.C. Raymond Brazenor Clayton. *Professor of Biochemistry in Psychiatry, Stanford University, California. Editor of* Steroids and Terpenoids.
CHEMICAL COMPOUNDS (*in part*)

R.B.D. Robert Bruce Davidson. *Historical resources consultant. Former Curator of History, Provincial Museum of Alberta, Edmonton.*
CANADA (*in part*)

R.B.G. Richard B. Goode. *Director, Fiscal Affairs Department, International Monetary Fund, Washington, D.C., 1965–81. Author of* The Corporation Income Tax.
TAXATION (*in part*)

R.B.I. Ronald B. Inden. *Associate Professor of History, University of Chicago. Author of* Marriage and Rank in Bengali Culture: A History of Caste and Clan in Middle Period Bengal.
SOCIAL DIFFERENTIATION (*in part*)

R.Bl. Raymond Bloch. *Professor, École Pratique des Hautes Études (Institute for Advanced Research), Paris. Author of* The Etruscans; The Origins of Rome.
ARCHITECTURE, THE HISTORY OF WESTERN (*in part*)
PAINTING, THE HISTORY OF WESTERN (*in part*)
SCULPTURE, THE HISTORY OF WESTERN (*in part*)

R.B.L. R. Bruce Lindsay (d. 1985). *Hazard Professor of Physics, Brown*

University, Providence, Rhode Island, 1936–71. Editor in Chief, Acoustical Society of America. Author of Lord Rayleigh: The Man and His Work.

MECHANICS (*in part*)

RAYLEIGH, JOHN WILLIAM STRUTT, 3RD BARON (Micropædia)

SOUND (*in part*)

R.B.N.   Robert Bradford Newman (d. 1983). *Senior Vice President, Bolt Beranek and Newman Inc., Cambridge, Massachusetts. Adjunct Professor of Architecture, Massachusetts Institute of Technology, 1976–83. Professor of Architectural Technology, Harvard University, 1971–83.*

SOUND (*in part*)

R.B.Ni.   Robert Brayton Nichols. *Landscape architect.*

PARK (Micropædia)

R.Br.   Reginald Brill. *Free-lance writer and historian. Author of* Terror of the French: John, Lord Talbot, *c. 1388–1453 and several articles on the period of the Hundred Years' War.*

RICHEMONT, ARTHUR, CONSTABLE DE (Micropædia)

R.B.S.   Richard B. Sewall. *Emeritus Professor of English, Yale University. Author of* The Vision of Tragedy; *coeditor of* Tragedy: Modern Essays in Criticism.

LITERATURE, THE ART OF (*in part*)

R.B.Se.   Robert Bertram Serjeant. *Sir Thomas Adams's Professor Emeritus of Arabic, University of Cambridge; Director, Middle East Centre, 1965–82. Author of* The Portuguese off the South Arabian Coast *and others.*

ARABIA (*in part*)

R.C.   René Coste. *President, French Institute of Coffee and Cocoa, Paris; General Director, 1958–78. Author of* Les Caféiers et les cafés dans le monde.

BEVERAGE PRODUCTION (*in part*)

FARMING AND AGRICULTURAL TECHNOLOGY (*in part*)

R.Ca.   Sir Raymond Carr. *Warden of St. Antony's College, University of Oxford, 1968–87. Author of* Spain, 1808–1939.

SPAIN (*in part*)

R.C.A.   Raymond Clare Archibald (d. 1955). *Professor of Mathematics, Brown University, Providence, Rhode Island, 1923–43. Author of* Outline of the History of Mathematics *and others.*

GEOMETRY (*in part*)

R.C.At.   Ralph Charles Atkins. *Staff reporter,* Financial Times, *London.*

UNITED KINGDOM (*in part*)

R.C.B.   Robert C. Bailey. *Assistant Professor of Anthropology, University of California, Los Angeles.*

AFRICA (*in part*)

R.C.Bi.   R.C. Bigalke. *Professor of Nature Conservation, University of Stellenbosch, South Africa. Coauthor of* The Evolution of Mammals on the Southern Continents.

MAMMALS (*in part*)

R.C.Bo.   Raj C. Bose (deceased). *Professor of Mathematics and Statistics, Colorado State University, Fort Collins, 1971–80. Coeditor of* Proceedings of the Conference on Combinatorial Mathematics and Its Applications.

COMBINATORICS AND COMBINATORIAL GEOMETRY (*in part*)

R.C.Br.   Robert C. Brasted (d. 1986). *Professor of Chemistry, University of Minnesota, Minneapolis. Coauthor and editor of* Comprehensive Inorganic Chemistry (*8 vol.*).

CHEMICAL ELEMENTS (*in part*)

R.C.Bu.   Robin Caron Buss. *Writer. Lecturer in French, Woolwich College of Further Education, London. Author of* The French Through Their Films *and others.*

FRENCH LITERATURE (*in part*)

MARSEILLE (*in part*)

R.C.C.   Ralph C. Croizier. *Professor of History, University of Victoria, British Columbia. Author of* Traditional Medicine in Modern China.

CHENG CH'ENG-KUNG (Micropædia)

R.Ce.   Roberto Cessi (d. 1969). *Professor of History, University of Padua, Italy, 1922–60. Deputy in the Italian Parliament, 1948–53.*

ITALY (*in part*)

VENICE (*in part*)

R.C.E.   Robert C. Elliott (d. 1981). *Professor of English Literature, University of California, San Diego, at La Jolla, 1964–81. Author of* The Power of Satire: Magic, Ritual, Art; The Shape of Utopia.

LITERATURE, THE ART OF (*in part*)

R.C.Ei.   Robert C. Eidt (d. 1987). *Professor of Geography, University of Wisconsin, Milwaukee, 1967–87; Director, State Soils Laboratory, 1981–87. Author of* Pioneer Settlement in Northeast Argentina.

ARGENTINA (*in part*)

R.C.F.   Richard Charles Froeschner. *Curator, Hemiptera Section, Department of Entomology, Smithsonian Institution, Washington, D.C.*

INSECTS (*in part*)

R.C.K.   Roy Clement Knight. *Emeritus Professor of French, University College of Swansea, University of Wales. Author of* Racine et la Grèce *and others.*

RACINE, JEAN (Micropædia)

R.C.Ki.   Robert C. Kiste. *Director and Professor, Center for Pacific Islands Studies, University of Hawaii at Manoa, Honolulu. Author of* The Bikinians: A Study in Forced Migration.

PACIFIC ISLANDS (*in part*)

R.C.L.   Richard C. Latham. *Former coauthor of* United States Polo Association Annual.

POLO (*in part*) (Micropædia)

R.C.N.   Robert C. North. *Emeritus Professor of Political Science, Stanford University, California. Author of* Moscow and Chinese Communists *and others.*

LIU SHAOQI (Micropædia)

R.Co.   Robert Cornevin (d. 1988). *Permanent Secretary, Academy of Overseas Sciences, Paris. Head, Centre of Studies and Documentation on Africa and Overseas, Paris. Author of* Histoire de l'Afrique *and others.*

WEST INDIES, THE (*in part*)

R.Cog.   Raymond Cogniat (d. 1977). *Principal Inspector of Fine Arts, 1943–67. Head of the arts section,* Le Figaro, *Paris, 1957–77. Author of* Renoir *and other works on 20th-century artists of the school of Paris.*

RENOIR, PIERRE-AUGUSTE (Micropædia)

R.C.R.   Reed C. Rollins. *Asa Gray Professor Emeritus of Systematic Botany, Harvard University; Director, Gray Herbarium, 1948–78. Coauthor of* Edible Wild Plants of Eastern North America.

ANGIOSPERMS (*in part*)

UNITED STATES OF AMERICA (*in part*)

R.C.Sm.   Robert C. Smith (d. 1975). *Professor of the History of Art, University of Pennsylvania, Philadelphia, 1956–75. Author of* The Art of Portugal *and others.*

DECORATIVE ARTS AND FURNISHINGS (*in part*)

R.C.Su.   Robert Carl Suggs. *Anthropologist. Conductor of anthropological and archaeological field research in Polynesia, 1956–58. Author of* Island Civilizations of Polynesia; The Hidden Worlds of Polynesia; *and others.*

PACIFIC ISLANDS (*in part*)

R.C.-W.   Rupert Crawshay-Williams (d. 1977). *Author of* Russell Remembered; Methods and Criteria of Reasoning.

RUSSELL, BERTRAND (Micropædia)

R.C.Y.   Richard Charles York. *Instructor of Horticulture and Education, McHenry County College, Crystal Lake, Illinois, Former Associate Editor,* Biology, *Encyclopædia Britannica, Chicago.*

PHILOSOPHIES OF THE BRANCHES OF KNOWLEDGE (*in part*)

R.D.   Robert Dorfman. *Emeritus Professor of Economics, Harvard University. Author of* The Price System.

ECONOMIC THEORY (*in part*)

R.Da.   René David. *Professor of Comparative Law, University of Aix-Marseille III, Aix-en-Provence, France, 1970–76. Author of* Les Grands Systèmes de droit contemporains.

SOCIAL SCIENCES, THE (*in part*)

R.D.B.   Richard David Barnett (d. 1986). *Keeper, Department of Western Asiatic Antiquities, British Museum, London, 1955–74.*

LEBANON (*in part*)

R.D.Ba.   Robert D. Barnes. *Professor of Biology, Gettysburg College, Pennsylvania. Author of* Invertebrate Zoology.

ARTHROPODS

R.D.C.   Rosalind D. Cartwright. *Chairman, Department of Psychology; Director, Sleep Disorder Service,*

Rush-Presbyterian St. Lukes Medical Center, Chicago. Author of Night Life: Explorations in Dreaming *and others.*
SLEEP AND DREAMS (*in part*)

R.D.D.G.   Robert Donald Davidson Gibson. *Professor of French, University of Kent at Canterbury, England. Author of* Modern French Poets on Poetry.
VALÉRY, PAUL (Micropædia)

R.De.   Robert Descloitres. *Former President and Director of Research, Centre of Applied Human Sciences, Aix-en-Provence, France. Coauthor of* L'Algérie des bidonvilles.
NORTH AFRICA (*in part*)

R.D.F.   Ralph D. Feigin, M.D. *J.S. Abercrombie Professor and Chairman, Department of Pediatrics, Baylor College of Medicine, Houston. Physician-in-Chief, Texas Children's Hospital. Coeditor and coauthor of* Textbook of Pediatric Infectious Diseases.
INFECTIOUS DISEASES (*in part*)

R.D.Fo.   Raymond D. Fogelson. *Professor of Anthropology, University of Chicago. Editor of* Handbook of North American Indians, *vol. 14, Southeast.*
AMERICAN INDIANS (*in part*)

R.D.H.   Robert D. Herman. *Professor of Sociology, Pomona College, Claremont, California. Author of* Gamblers and Gambling.
LOTTERY (Micropædia)

R.D.L.   R. Duncan Luce. *Victor S. Thomas Professor Emeritus of Psychology, Harvard University. Distinguished Professor of Cognitive Science, University of California, Irvine. Coauthor of* Foundations of Measurement.
MEASUREMENT THEORY (*in part*)

R.D.M.   Robert Douthat Meade (d. 1974). *Professor of History, Randolph-Macon Woman's College, Lynchburg, Virginia, 1939–71. Author of* Patrick Henry, Patriot in the Making *and others.*
HENRY, PATRICK (Micropædia)

R.D.Mi.   Robin David Middleton. *Professor of Art History and Archaeology, Columbia University.*
ARCHITECTURE, THE HISTORY OF WESTERN (*in part*)

R.Do.   Ron Dorfman. *Director of Publications, Field Museum of Natural History, Chicago.*
CHICAGO (*in part*)

R.Du.   Raymond E. Durgnat. *Lecturer, Department of Three-Dimensional Design, Kingston Polytechnic, Kingston upon Thames, England. Author of* Films and Feelings; Buñuel; Jean Renoir *and others.*
GODARD, JEAN-LUC (Micropædia)
RESNAIS, ALAIN (*in part*) (Micropædia)
TRUFFAUT, FRANÇOIS (*in part*) (Micropædia)

R.Dum.   René Dumesnil (d. 1967). *Literary and music critic. Member, Academy of Fine Arts, Institute of France, 1965–67. Author of* Gustave Flaubert, l'homme et l'oeuvre; Guy de Maupassant; *and others.*
FLAUBERT, GUSTAVE (*in part*) (Micropædia)

R.D.W.   Robert Deryck Williams (d. 1986). *Professor of Classics, University of Reading, England. Author of* Virgil; *editor of* Aeneid.
VIRGIL (*in part*)

R.D.Wa.   Robert Donald Walker. *Training Manager, Allied Steel and Wire, Cardiff, Wales. Author of* Modern Ironmaking Methods *and others.*
INDUSTRIES, EXTRACTION AND PROCESSING (*in part*)

R.E.Be.   Ronald E. Bedford. *Principal Research Officer, Division of Physics; Head Photometry and Radiometry Section, National Research Council of Canada, Ottawa.*
MEASUREMENT AND OBSERVATION, PRINCIPLES, METHODS, AND INSTRUMENTS OF (*in part*)

R.E.Bn.   Ray E. Brown (d. 1974). *Professor of Administration and Executive Vice President, Northwestern University Medical Center, Chicago, 1970–74.*
MEDICINE (*in part*)

R.E.C.   Roy Eugene Cameron. *Senior Staff Scientist, Office of Environmental Programs, Lockheed Engineering & Sciences Company, Las Vegas, Nevada.*
NORTH AMERICA (*in part*)

R.E.Co.   Robert E. Conot. *Editor, Los Angeles Times. Senior Lecturer in Journalism, University of Southern California, Los Angeles. Author of* A Streak of Luck: The Life and Legend of Thomas Alva Edison *and others.*
EDISON (*in part*)

R.E.Cr.   Raymond E. Crist. *Research Professor Emeritus of Geography, University of Florida, Gainesville. Author of* The Cauca Valley, Colombia.
SOUTH AMERICA (*in part*)
VENEZUELA (*in part*)
WEST INDIES, THE (*in part*)

R.E.D.   The Rev. Rupert E. Davies. *Principal, Wesley College, Bristol, England, 1967–73. Author of* Methodism; *coeditor of* The History of the Methodist Church in Great Britain.
PROTESTANTISM (*in part*)

R.E.Da.   Robert E. Davies. *Benjamin Franklin Professor of Molecular Biology and University Professor, School of Veterinary Medicine, University of Pennsylvania, Philadelphia.*
MUSCLES AND MUSCLE SYSTEMS (*in part*)

R.E.E.   Ronald Eric Emmerick. *Professor and Director, Department of Iranian Studies, University of Hamburg. Author of* Saka Grammatical Studies; *editor and translator of several Khotanese works.*
LANGUAGES OF THE WORLD (*in part*)

R.E.F.   Ralph E. Fuhrman. *Consultant, Black & Veatch, consulting engineers, Washington, D.C. Special Assistant to the Director, Municipal Wastewater Systems Division, Environmental Protection Agency, 1972–73.*
PUBLIC WORKS (*in part*)

R.E.Fi.   Raymond E. Fielding. *Professor of Communication, University of Houston, Texas. Editor of* A Technological History of Motion Pictures and Television.
DE FOREST, LEE (Micropædia)

Re.G.   Renu Garg, M.D. *Pediatrician.*
INFECTIOUS DISEASES (*in part*)

R.E.G.   Ralph E. Grim (d. 1989). *Research Professor of Geology, University of Illinois, Urbana, 1948–67. Scholar whose outstanding synthesis of clay mineralogy served as a guide for a generation of research scientists. Author of* Clay Mineralogy *and others.*
MINERALS AND ROCKS (*in part*)

R.E.Ga.   Rosemary Elizabeth Galli. *Visiting Fulbright Professor, Institute of Social Science, University of Lisbon, and Centre for International Relations Studies, University of the Azores, Ponta Delgada. Coauthor of* Guinea Bissau: Politics, Economics and Society.
WESTERN AFRICA (*in part*)

R.E.Gi.   Reginald E. Gillmor (d. 1960). *Vice President, Sperry Gyroscope Company, Inc., Brooklyn, New York, 1932–45.*
NAVIGATION (*in part*)

Re.H.   Reinhold D. Hohl. *Art historian. Author of* Giacometti *and others.*
GIACOMETTI, ALBERTO (Micropædia)

R.E.H.   Richard E. Holttum. *Honorary Research Associate, Royal Botanic Gardens, Kew, England. Director, Botanic Gardens, Singapore, 1925–49. Professor of Botany, University of Malaya, Singapore, 1949–54. Author of* A Revised Flora of Malaya *and others.*
ANGIOSPERMS (*in part*)

R.E.H.M.   Roy E.H. Mellor. *Emeritus Professor of Geography, University of Aberdeen, Scotland. Author of* Eastern Europe *and others.*
GERMANY (*in part*)

R.E.K.   Rudolf E. Kalman. *Graduate Research Professor of Mathematics; Director, Center for Mathematical System Theory, University of Florida, Gainesville. Professor of Mathematical System Theory, Swiss Federal Institute of Technology, Zürich, Switzerland. Coauthor of* Topics in Mathematical System Theory.
OPTIMIZATION, THE MATHEMATICAL THEORY OF (*in part*)

Re.L.   René Lemarchand. *Professor of Political Science, University of Florida, Gainesville. Author of* Rwanda and Burundi *and others.*
CENTRAL AFRICA (*in part*)

R.E.L.F.   Robert E.L. Faris. *Emeritus Professor of Sociology, University of Washington, Seattle. Editor of* Handbook of Modern Sociology.
SOCIAL SCIENCES, THE (*in part*)

R.E.O.   The Rev. Ronald E. Osborn. *Emeritus Professor of American Church History, School of Theology at Claremont, California. Author of* The Faith We Affirm *and others.*
PROTESTANTISM (*in part*)

R.E.Or.   Richard Edmonds Orville. *Professor and Chairman, Department of Atmospheric Science, State University of New York at Albany. Investigator of electrical phenomena in the atmosphere through photographs and their interpretation.*
CLIMATE AND WEATHER (*in part*)

Re.P.   Rebecca Posner. *Professor of Romance Languages, University of Oxford. Author of* Consonantal Dissimilation in the Romance Languages; The Romance Languages: A Linguistic Introduction.
LANGUAGES OF THE WORLD (*in part*)

R.E.P.   Rollie E. Poppino. *Professor of History, University of California, Davis. Author of* Brazil; The Land and People.
BRAZIL (*in part*)
VARGAS, GETÚLIO (Micropædia)

R.E.Pi.   Richard E. Pipes. *Frank B. Baird, Jr., Professor of History, Harvard University. Author of* The Russian Revolution *and others.*
NIKON (Micropædia)

R.Es.   Robert Escarpit. *Emeritus Professor of Information and Communication Sciences, University of Bordeaux III, France. Author of* L'Angleterre dans l'oeuvre de Madame de Staël *and others.*
STAËL-HOLSTEIN, ANNE-LOUISE-GERMAINE NECKER, BARONNE DE (Micropædia)

R.E.S.   Robert E. Stewart. *Distinguished Professor Emeritus of Agricultural Engineering, Texas A&M University, College Station.*
FARMING AND AGRICULTURAL TECHNOLOGY (*in part*)

R.E.Sh.   Robert E. Sheriff. *Professor of Geophysics, University of Houston, Texas. Author of* Encyclopedic Dictionary of Exploration Geophysics.
EXPLORATION (*in part*)

R.F.   Robert L. Faherty. *Director of Publications, Brookings Institution, Washingon, D.C. Staff editor, Religion,* Encyclopædia Britannica, *1969–72.*
BIBLICAL LITERATURE AND ITS CRITICAL INTERPRETATION (*in part*)
RITES AND CEREMONIES, SACRED (*in part*)

R.F.B.   Robert F. Byrnes. *Distinguished Professor of History, Indiana University, Bloomington. Author of* Pobedonostsev: His Life and Thought.
POBEDONOSTSEV, KONSTANTIN PETROVICH (*in part*) (Micropædia)

R.F.D.   Raymond F. Dasmann. *Emeritus Professor of Ecology, University of California, Santa Cruz. Author of* Environmental Conservation *and others.*
CONSERVATION OF NATURAL RESOURCES

R.F.G.A.   R.F.G. Alford. *Cassel Reader in Economics, London School of Economics and Political Science, University of London.*
MARKETS (*in part*)

R.F.H.   Sir Roy Forbes Harrod (d. 1978). *Nuffield Reader in Economics, University of Oxford, 1952–67. Author of* International Economics *and others.*
INTERNATIONAL TRADE (*in part*)

R.F.-He.   Regina Flannery-Herzfeld. *Emeritus Professor of Anthropology, Catholic University of America, Washington, D.C. Author of* The Gros Ventre of Montana, *Part 1,* Social Life.
AMERICAN INDIANS (*in part*)

R.F.Hi.   Ronald Francis Hingley. *Fellow of St. Antony's College, Oxford; Lecturer in Russian, University of Oxford. Author of* Chekhov: A Biographical and Critical Study; Russian Writers and Society; Nihilists; *and others; editor and translator of* The Oxford Chekhov.
CHEKHOV, ANTON (*in part*) (Micropædia)
GORKY, MAKSIM (*in part*) (Micropædia)
STALIN (*in part*)

R.Fi.   Ross Fitzgerald. *Senior Lecturer in History and Politics, Griffith University, Brisbane, Australia. Author of* A History of Queensland (*2 vol.*).
AUSTRALIA (*in part*)

R.Fl.   Ronald Fletcher. *Emeritus Professor of Sociology, University of Reading, England. Author of* Auguste Comte and the Making of Sociology *and others.*
COMTE, AUGUSTE (*in part*) (Micropædia)

R.F.L.   Robert Frederic Lawson. *Chair, Department of Educational Policy and Leadership, Ohio State University, Columbus. Coauthor of* Studies in Educational Change.
EDUCATION, HISTORY OF (*in part*)

R.F.Li.   René Felix Lissens. *Emeritus Professor of Dutch and General Literature, St. Ignatius University Faculty, Antwerp. Member, Royal Flemish Academy of Language and Literature. Author of* De Vlaamse letterkunde van 1780 tot heden.
BELGIAN LITERATURE (*in part*)

R.F.Lo.   Richard F. Logan. *Emeritus Professor of Geography, University of California, Los Angeles. Author of* The Central Namib Desert.
AFRICA (*in part*)

R.-F.-M.A.   Roger-François-Marie Aubert. *Emeritus Professor of Church History, Catholic University of Louvain, Belgium. Author of* Le Pontificat de Pie IX *and others.*
LEO XIII (PAPACY) (Micropædia)

R.F.Pe.   Ronald Francis Peel (d. 1985). *Professor of Geography, University of Bristol, England, 1957–77. Chairman, Commission on Arid Lands, International Geographical Union. Author of* Physical Geography.
AFRICA (*in part*)

R.F.T.   René Frédéric Thom. *Mathematician and philosopher, Institut des Hautes Études Scientifiques (Institute of Advanced Scientific Research), Bures-sur-Yvette, France. Author of* Stabilité structurelle et morphogénèse.
GEOMETRY (*in part*)

R.F.Th.   Robert Folger Thorne. *Emeritus Taxonomist and Curator, Rancho Santa Ana Botanic Garden, Claremont, California. Emeritus Professor of Botany, Claremont Graduate School.*
ANGIOSPERMS (*in part*)

R.F.Tr.   Reginald Francis Treharne (d. 1967). *Professor of History, University College of Wales, Aberystwyth, University of Wales, 1930–67. Author of* The Baronial Plan of Reform, 1258–1263 *and others.*
EDWARD I (ENGLAND AND GREAT BRITAIN) (Micropædia)
MONTFORT, SIMON DE, EARL OF LEICESTER (Micropædia)

R.G.   Roger Gibbins. *Professor of Political Science, University of Calgary, Alberta.*
POLITICAL SYSTEMS (*in part*)

R.G.A.   Raymond George Ayoub. *Professor of Mathematics, Pennsylvania State University, University Park. Author of* An Introduction to the Analytic Theory of Numbers.
NUMBER THEORY (*in part*)

R.G.A.B.   Richard G.A. Buxton. *Senior Lecturer in Classics, University of Bristol, England. Author of* Persuasion in Greek Tragedy: A Study of Peitho.
MYTH AND MYTHOLOGY (*in part*)

R.G.C.   Ronald G. Crocombe. *Emeritus Professor of Pacific Studies, University of the South Pacific, Rarotonga, Cook Islands. Author of* The Cook Islands *and others.*
PACIFIC ISLANDS (*in part*)

R.G.F.   Richard G. Fox. *Professor of Anthropology, Duke University, Durham, North Carolina. Author of* Gandhian Utopia: Experiments with Culture *and others.*
CULTURE, THE CONCEPTS AND COMPONENTS OF (*in part*)

R.G.G.   Robert G. Gallager. *Fujitsu Professor of Electrical Engineering, Massachusetts Institute of Technology, Cambridge; Codirector, Laboratory for Information and Decision Systems. Author of* Information Theory and Reliable Communication *and others.*
INFORMATION THEORY

R.Gh.   Roman Ghirshman (d. 1979). *Archaeologist. Director General, French Archaeological Delegation to Iran, 1946–67.*
IRAN (*in part*)

R.G.Lo.   Robert G. Logan. *Sportswriter, Chicago Tribune. Author of* The Bulls and Chicago: A Stormy Affair.
SPORTS, MAJOR TEAM AND INDIVIDUAL (*in part*)

R.Gr. **Ronald Grimsley.** *Emeritus Professor of French, University of Bristol, England. Author of* Jean d'Alembert.
ALEMBERT, JEAN LE ROND D'
(Micropædia)

R.G.R. **Robert G. Richardson.** *Consultant medical editor. Former Editor,* Abbottempo *(international medical journal). Author of* Surgery: Old and New Frontiers *and others.*
MEDICINE *(in part)*

R.G.S. **Ralph G. Sanger** (d. 1968). *Professor of Mathematics, Kansas State University, Manhattan, 1946–68. Author of* Synthetic Projective Geometry.
GEOMETRY *(in part)*

R.H.A.J. **Richard H.A. Jenkyns.** *Fellow of Lady Margaret Hall, University of Oxford. Author of* Three Classical Poets: Sappho, Catullus, and Juvenal *and others.*
LATIN LITERATURE *(in part)*

R.H.B. **Roland H. Bainton** (d. 1984). *Titus Street Professor of Church History, Yale University, 1936–62. Author of* The Reformation of the Sixteenth Century *and others.*
PROTESTANTISM *(in part)*

R.H.Bi. **R.H. Bing** (d. 1986). *Professor of Mathematics, University of Texas at Austin. Author of* Elementary Point Set Topology.
GEOMETRY *(in part)*

R.H.By. **Robert Howard Byrne.** *Professor of Marine Science, University of South Florida at St. Petersburg.*
OCEANS *(in part)*

R.H.C. **Robin Huw Crompton.** *Lecturer in Anatomy, University of Liverpool. Coauthor of* Lifestyles and Anatomies in Prosimians.
MUSCLES AND MUSCLE SYSTEMS *(in part)*

R.He. **Richard Hellie.** *Professor of Russian History, University of Chicago. Author of* Slavery in Russia, 1450–1725 *and others.*
ALEXANDER NEVSKY, SAINT
(Micropædia)
SLAVERY
UNION OF SOVIET SOCIALIST REPUBLICS
(in part)

R.H.E. **Richard H. Eastman.** *Emeritus Professor of Chemistry, Stanford University, California. Author of* General Chemistry—Experiment and Theory.
CHEMICAL COMPOUNDS *(in part)*

R.H.Fl. **Richard Howell Fleming** (d. 1989). *Professor of Oceanography and Marine Studies, University of Washington, Seattle, 1951–80. Coauthor of* The Oceans.
ATLANTIC OCEAN, THE *(in part)*

R.H.Fr. **Richard H. Freeborn.** *Emeritus Professor of Russian Literature, School of Slavonic and East European Studies, University of London. Author of* Turgenev, a Study *and others.*
RUSSIAN LITERATURE *(in part)*
TURGENEV, IVAN *(in part)* (Micropædia)

R.H.Fu. **Robert H. Fuson.** *Emeritus Professor of Geography, University*

of South Florida, Tampa. Author of Fundamental Place-Name Geography.
UNITED STATES OF AMERICA *(in part)*

R.H.G. **Richard Harold Greenwood.** *Professor of Geography, University College of Swansea, University of Wales, 1970–80. Professor of Geography, University of Queensland, Brisbane, Australia, 1958–70.*
AUSTRALIA *(in part)*

R.H.Ga. **Ralph Henry Gabriel** (d. 1987). *Professor of History, Yale University, 1928–58. Author of* The Course of American Democratic Thought *and others.*
UNITED STATES OF AMERICA *(in part)*

R.H.H. **Robert H. Hardie** (d. 1989). *Professor of Physics and Astronomy, Vanderbilt University, Nashville, Tennessee; Director, Dyer Observatory, 1961–72.*
ANALYSIS AND MEASUREMENTS,
PHYSICAL AND CHEMICAL *(in part)*
SOLAR SYSTEM, THE *(in part)*

R.H.I. **Ralph Hammond Innes.** *Novelist and writer on history and travel. Author of* The Conquistadors.
CORTÉS, HERNÁN, MARQUES DEL VALLE
DE OAXACA (Micropædia)

R.H.J. **Richard H. Jahns** (d. 1983). *Crook Professor of Geology and Applied Earth Sciences, Stanford University, California; Dean, School of Earth Sciences, 1965–79. Editor and coauthor of* Geology of Southern California.
MINERALS AND ROCKS *(in part)*

R.H.K. **Richard H. Kesel.** *Professor of Geomorphology, Louisiana State University, Baton Rouge.*
NORTH AMERICA *(in part)*

R.H.M. **Richard H. Manske** (d. 1977). *Director of Research, Dominion Rubber Company Ltd., Guelph, Ontario, 1943–66. Editor of* The Alkaloids.
CHEMICAL COMPOUNDS *(in part)*

R.H.O. **Richard Horsley Osborne.** *Emeritus Professor of Geography, University of Nottingham, England. Author of* East-Central Europe: A Geographical Introduction to Seven Socialist States.
CZECHOSLOVAKIA *(in part)*
PRAGUE *(in part)*

R.H.P. **Richard H. Popkin.** *Emeritus Professor of Philosophy, Washington University, St. Louis, Missouri. Author of* History of Scepticism from Erasmus to Spinoza.
PHILOSOPHICAL SCHOOLS AND
DOCTRINES, WESTERN *(in part)*

R.H.Po. **René Henry Pomeau.** *Former Professor of French Literature, University of Paris IV. Author of* La Religion de Voltaire *and others.*
VOLTAIRE

R.H.P.-W. **Ralph H. Pinder-Wilson.** *Former Deputy Keeper, Department of Oriental Antiquities, British Museum, London. Author of* Persian Painting in the Fifteenth Century.
WRITING *(in part)*

R.H.Ra. **Robert H. Ralston.** *Former Senior Research Chemist, Hercules Inc., Wilmington, Delaware.*
FOOD PROCESSING *(in part)*

R.H.S. **Roger Henry Simpson.** *Historian and lecturer.*
MITHRADATES VI EUPATOR (PONTUS)
(Micropædia)

R.H.Sc. **Robert H. Schmidt.** *Professor of Geological Sciences, University of Texas at El Paso. Author of various papers on the geography and climate of Mexico.*
NORTH AMERICA *(in part)*

R.H.St. **Roger H. Stuewer.** *Professor of the History of Science and Technology, University of Minnesota, Minneapolis. Author of* The Compton Effect: Turning Point in Physics.
PLANCK

R.H.T. **Ralph H. Turner.** *Professor of Sociology and Anthropology, University of California, Los Angeles. Coauthor of* Collective Behavior.
COLLECTIVE BEHAVIOUR *(in part)*

R.H.T.E. **Richard Humphrey Tudor Edwards.** *Professor and Head, Department of Medicine, University of Liverpool; Director, Muscle Research Centre. Author of* Muscle Weakness.
MUSCLES AND MUSCLE SYSTEMS *(in part)*

R.Hu. **René Huyghe.** *Professor of Art, College of France, Paris, 1950–76. President, Council of Museums, Paris, 1974–88. Author of* Cézanne; Delacroix ou le combat solitaire; *and others.*
CÉZANNE, PAUL *(in part)* (Micropædia)
DELACROIX, EUGÈNE (Micropædia)

R.H.W. **Robert H. Whittaker** (d. 1980). *Charles A. Alexander Professor of Biology, Cornell University, Ithaca, New York, 1976–80. Author of* Communities and Ecosystems; Ordination and Classification of Communities.
BIOSPHERE, THE *(in part)*

Ri.B. **Richard Beadle.** *Fellow in English, St. John's College, University of Cambridge. Editor of* York Mystery Plays.
ENGLISH LITERATURE *(in part)*

Ri.G. **Richard David Greenfield.** *Former Director of General Studies, University of Benin, Nigeria. Author of* Ethiopia: A New Political History.
MENELIK II *(in part)* (Micropædia)

Ri.H. **Richard Hamilton Hobson.** *Public Relations Adviser, Zal Holdings Ltd., London; formerly with Zambia Consolidated Copper Mines Ltd., Lusaka, Zambia.*
SOUTHERN AFRICA *(in part)*

Ri.J.H. **Richard J. Hathaway.** *Consultant on Michigan history and literature. Editor of* Michigan: Visions of Our Past; Literary Michigan: A Sense of Place, A Sense of Time.
UNITED STATES OF AMERICA
(in part)

Ri.L. **Richard Lane.** *Research Associate, Honolulu Academy of Arts.*

Author of Masters of the Japanese Print; Hokusai: Life and Work; *and others.*
HOKUSAI (Micropædia)

Ri.L.C.   Richard L. Chambers. *Associate Professor of Near Eastern Languages and Civilizations, University of Chicago. Coeditor of and contributor to* Beginnings of Modernization in the Middle East.
IRAQ (*in part*)

Ri.M.L.   Richard M. Lerner. *Professor of Child and Adolescent Development, Pennsylvania State University, University Park. Author of* Concepts and Theories of Human Development *and others.*
BEHAVIOUR, THE DEVELOPMENT OF
  HUMAN (*in part*)

Ri.P.   Richard Pittioni (d. 1985). *Emeritus Professor of Prehistory and Protohistory, University of Vienna. Author of* Ergebnisse und Probleme des urzeitlichen Metallhandels *and others.*
PREHISTORIC PEOPLES AND CULTURES
  (*in part*)

R.I.S.   Robert I. Scace. *Deputy Director, Center for Electronics and Electrical Engineering, National Institute of Standards and Technology, Gaithersburg, Maryland.*
ELECTRONICS (*in part*)

Ri.W.S.   Richard Walton Stephens. *Professor of Sociology, George Washington University, Washington, D.C. Coauthor of* Power, Presidents, and Professors.
WASHINGTON, D.C.

R.J.   Raymond Jeanloz. *Professor of Geology and Geophysics, University of California, Berkeley.*
EARTH, THE (*in part*)

R.J.A.   Richard J. Andrew. *Professor of Animal Behaviour, University of Sussex, Brighton, England. Author of numerous papers on behaviour of birds and primates.*
BEHAVIOUR, ANIMAL (*in part*)

R.J.Al.   Robert J. Alexander. *Professor of Economics and Political Science, Rutgers University, New Brunswick, New Jersey. Author of* Prophets of the Revolution: Profiles of Latin American Political Leaders.
CÁRDENAS, LÁZARO (Micropædia)

R.J.B.   Robert John Behnke. *Fisheries consultant. Professor of Fishery Biology, Colorado State University, Fort Collins.*
FISHES (*in part*)

R.J.Br.   Robert J. Braidwood. *Emeritus Professor of Old World Prehistory, Oriental Institute, University of Chicago. Author of* Prehistoric Men *and others.*
PREHISTORIC PEOPLES AND CULTURES
  (*in part*)

R.J.Ch.   Robert Jesse Charleston. *Keeper, Department of Ceramics, Victoria and Albert Museum, London, 1963–76. Author of* Masterpieces of Glass *and others.*
DECORATIVE ARTS AND FURNISHINGS
  (*in part*)

R.J.Da.   R.J. Davies. *Professor of Geography, University of Cape Town.*
SOUTH AFRICA (*in part*)

R.J.F.   Robert J. Fernier (d. 1977). *President, The Friends of Gustave Courbet, Paris. Author of* Gustave Courbet, peintre de l'art vivant.
COURBET, GUSTAVE (Micropædia)

R.J.G.   Richard Johnson Goss. *Professor of Biology, Brown University, Providence, Rhode Island. Author of* Principles of Regeneration.
GROWTH AND DEVELOPMENT,
  BIOLOGICAL (*in part*)

R.J.Gl.   Reginald John Gladstone, M.D. (d. 1947). *Reader in Anatomy and Lecturer in Embryology, King's College, University of London.*
NERVES AND NERVOUS SYSTEMS (*in part*)

R.J.H.   Robert J. Havighurst (d. 1991). *Professor of Education and of Human Development, University of Chicago, 1941–65. Specialist on the social psychology of education and human development. Author of* Comparative Perspectives on Education *and others.*
TEACHING (*in part*)

R.J.Ha.   Richard J. Harrison, M.D. *Emeritus Professor of Anatomy, University of Cambridge. Author of* Reproduction and Man *and others.*
REPRODUCTION AND REPRODUCTIVE
  SYSTEMS (*in part*)

R.J.H.-C.   Ronald James Harrison-Church. *Emeritus Professor of Geography, London School of Economics and Political Science, University of London. Author of* West Africa.
AFRICA (*in part*)
WESTERN AFRICA (*in part*)

R.J.Hi.   Roland John Hill. *Former London Correspondent,* Die Presse *(Vienna) and* Stuttgarter Zeitung, *Stuttgart, West Germany.*
VIENNA (*in part*)

R.J.J.   Roland John Jackson. *Professor of Music, Claremont Graduate School, California. Editor of* Neapolitan Keyboard Composers c. 1600.
MUSIC, THE ART OF (*in part*)

R.J.K.   Robert J. Kadner. *Professor of Microbiology, University of Virginia, Charlottesville. Coauthor of* Essentials of Medical Microbiology.
BACTERIA AND OTHER MONERANS

R.J.M.   Ronald James Morley. *Former Technical Director, Coal Products Division, National Coal Board, Harrow, England.*
INDUSTRIES, EXTRACTION AND
  PROCESSING (*in part*)

R.J.Ma.   Richard J. Mayne. *Contributing Editor,* Encounter. *Author of* The Recovery of Europe; Postwar: The Dawn of Today's Europe.
EUROPEAN HISTORY AND CULTURE
  (*in part*)

R.J.Me.   Robert James Menzies (d. 1976). *Professor of Oceanography, Florida State University, Tallahassee, 1967–76. Panel Chairman in Marine

Biology, Gulf University Research Corporation.
ATLANTIC OCEAN, THE (*in part*)

R.J.N.   Robert J. Nelson. *Professor of French, University of Illinois at Urbana-Champaign. Author of* Corneille: His Heroes and Their Worlds.
CORNEILLE, PIERRE (Micropædia)

R.J.Ne.   R.J. Nelson. *Truman P. Handy Professor Emeritus of Philosophy, Case Western Reserve University, Cleveland. Author of* Introduction to Automata.
AUTOMATA THEORY (*in part*)

R.J.No.   Robert J. Norrell. *Associate Professor of History; Director, Center for Southern History and Culture, University of Alabama, Tuscaloosa. Author of* Reaping the Whirlwind: The Civil Rights Movement in Tuskegee.
UNITED STATES OF AMERICA (*in part*)

R.J.Q.   Ricardo J. Quinones. *Professor of English and Comparative Literature; Director, Center for Renaissance and Modernity, Claremont McKenna College, Califonia. Author of* Dante Alighieri.
DANTE

R.J.S.   R.J. Stephenson (d. 1973). *William F. Harn Professor of Physics, College of Wooster, Ohio, 1959–71.*
NAVIGATION (*in part*)

R.J.Sc.   Randall John Schaetzl. *Assistant Professor of Geography, Michigan State University, East Lansing.*
NORTH AMERICA (*in part*)

R.J.Sm.   Ralph J. Smith. *Emeritus Professor of Electrical Engineering, Stanford University, California. Author of* Engineering as a Career.
ENGINEERING (*in part*)

R.J.St.   Robert J. Sternberg. *IBM Professor of Psychology and Education, Yale University. Author of* Beyond IQ; Intelligence Applied.
INTELLIGENCE, HUMAN

R.J.T.   Roger John Tayler. *Professor of Astronomy; Director, Astronomy Centre, University of Sussex, Brighton, England. Author of* The Origin of the Chemical Elements *and others.*
CHEMICAL ELEMENTS (*in part*)

R.J.Ta.   Robert J. Tata. *Professor of Geography, Florida Atlantic University, Boca Raton. Author of* Structural Changes in Puerto Rico's Economy, 1947–1976 *and others.*
WEST INDIES, THE (*in part*)

R.J.Th.   Robert James Thornton. *Senior Lecturer in Anthropology, University of Cape Town. Author of* The Iraqw of Northern Tanzania.
EASTERN AFRICA (*in part*)

R.J.Z.   Roman J. Zorn. *Emeritus Professor of American History, University of Nevada, Las Vegas. Author of numerous articles on U.S. history and political science.*
UNITED STATES OF AMERICA (*in part*)

R.J.Z.W.   R.J. Zwi Werblowsky. *Professor of Comparative Religion,*

Hebrew University of Jerusalem. Author of Joseph Karo, Lawyer and Mystic *and others.*
DOCTRINES AND DOGMAS, RELIGIOUS (*in part*)

R.K.   Rudolf Kingslake. *Emeritus Professor of Optics, University of Rochester. Director of Optical Design, Eastman Kodak Company, Rochester, New York, 1939–69. Author of* Optical System Design *and others; editor of* Applied Optics and Optical Engineering.
OPTICS, PRINCIPLES OF (*in part*)

R.K.A.G.   Robert K.A. Gardiner. *Commissioner for Economic Planning, Ghana, 1975–78. Executive Secretary, United Nations Economic Commission for Africa, Addis Ababa, Ethiopia, 1962–75. Author of* A World of Peoples.
AFRICA (*in part*)

R.Ki.   Ralph Kirkpatrick (d. 1984). *Harpsichordist. Professor of Music, Yale University, 1965–76. Author of* Domenico Scarlatti *and others.*
SCARLATTI, DOMENICO (Micropædia)

R.K.K.   Raymond K. Kent. *Professor of History, University of California, Berkeley. Author of* Early Kingdoms in Madagascar, 1500–1700 *and many others.*
MADAGASCAR (*in part*)

R.K.L.   Robert K. Lane. *Regional Director, Western and Northern Region, Environmental Protection Service, Environment Canada, Edmonton, Alberta. Head, Physical Limnology Section, Canada Centre for Inland Water, Burlington, Ontario, 1967–72.*
LAKES (*in part*)

R.K.M.   Ronald K. Murton (d. 1978). *Senior Principal Scientific Officer, Institute of Terrestrial Ecology, Monks Wood Experimental Station, Huntingdon, England. Researcher on the population dynamics and behaviour of pigeons and doves. Author of* The Woodpigeon.
BIRDS (*in part*)

R.Kr.   Richard Kroner (d. 1974). *Professor of the Philosophy of Religion, Union Theological Seminary, New York City, 1941–55. Author of* Von Kant bis Hegel.
FICHTE, JOHANN GOTTLIEB (Micropædia)

R.K.U.   Reuben Kenrick Udo. *Professor of Geography, University of Ibadan, Nigeria. Member, National Population Commission, Lagos. Author of* Geographical Regions of Nigeria.
WESTERN AFRICA (*in part*)

R.L.   Robert Lekachman (d. 1989). *Distinguished Professor of Economics, Herbert H. Lehman College, City University of New York, 1973–89. Author of* The Age of Keynes *and others.*
KEYNES, JOHN MAYNARD (*in part*) (Micropædia)

R.La.   Robin Law. *Reader in History, University of Stirling, Scotland. Author of* The Horse in West African History *and others.*
WESTERN AFRICA (*in part*)

R.L.A.   Russell L. Ackoff. *Chairman, Interact: The Institute for Interactive Management, Philadelphia. Anheuser-Busch Professor Emeritus of Management Science, Wharton School, University of Pennsylvania, Philadelphia. Coauthor of* Fundamentals of Operations Research.
INDUSTRIAL ENGINEERING AND PRODUCTION MANAGEMENT (*in part*)

R.L.B.   The Rev. Robert L. Bireley, S.J. *Professor of History, Loyola University, Chicago.*
XAVIER, SAINT FRANCIS (Micropædia)

R.L.C.   Robert L. Collison (d. 1989). *Professor of Library Science and Information Studies, University of California, Los Angeles, 1968–73. Author of* Encyclopaedias: Their History Throughout the Ages *and others.*
ENCYCLOPAEDIAS AND DICTIONARIES (*in part*)

R.L.C.F.   Raymond-Louis-Charles Furon. *Former Professor of Geology, University of Paris. Author of* Géologie de l'Afrique *and others.*
AFRICA (*in part*)

R.L.D.   R.L. Dwivedi. *Former Professor and Head, Department of Geography, University of Allāhābād, Uttar Pradesh, India.*
INDIA (*in part*)

R.Le.   Robert Lebel (d. 1986). *Art expert, critic, and writer. Author of* On Marcel Duchamp *and others.*
DUCHAMP, MARCEL (Micropædia)

R.L.F.   Robert Louis Folk. *Dave P. Carlton Professor Emeritus of Geology, University of Texas at Austin. An authority on the classification and interpretation of sedimentary rocks. Author of* Petrology of Sedimentary Rocks.
MINERALS AND ROCKS (*in part*)

R.L.Fr.   Richard L. Frey (d. 1988). *Editor in Chief,* Official Encyclopedia of Bridge, *1964–76. Editor,* The Contract Bridge Bulletin, *1958–70. President, International Bridge Press Association, 1970–81. Author of* According to Hoyle *and others.*
CRIBBAGE (Micropædia)

R.L.G.   Roger Lancelyn Green (d. 1987). *Author of* The Story of Lewis Carroll *and others; editor of* The Diaries of Lewis Carroll.
CARROLL, LEWIS (Micropædia)

R.L.Ge.   Robert Louis Gilmore. *Emeritus Professor of History, University of Kansas, Lawrence.*
COLOMBIA (*in part*)

R.L.Ha.   Rosemary Lois Harris. *Reader in Anthropology, University College, University of London. Author of* The Political Organization of the Mbembe of South-East Nigeria *and others.*
WESTERN AFRICA (*in part*)

R.L.He.   Robert L. Heilbroner. *Norman Thomas Professor Emeritus of Economics, New School for Social Research, New York City. Author of* The Worldly Philosophers; The Nature and Logic of Capitalism; *and others.*
ECONOMIC SYSTEMS
SMITH, ADAM

R.L.Hi.   Richard Leslie Hill. *Professor of History, Abdullahi Bayero College, Ahmadu Bello University, Kano, Nigeria, 1968–69. Lecturer in Modern Near Eastern History, University of Durham, England, 1949–66. Author of* The Europeans in Sudan, 1834–78 *and others.*
MAHDI, AL- (Micropædia)

R.L.M.   Robert L. McPherron. *Professor of Geophysics and Space Physics, University of California, Los Angeles.*
EARTH, THE (*in part*)

R.L.Mo.   Richard Lee Morton (d. 1974). *Professor of History, College of William and Mary, Williamsburg, Virginia, 1921–59. Author of* Colonial Virginia.
UNITED STATES OF AMERICA (*in part*)

R.L.Ne.   Ray L. Newburn, Jr. *Leader, International Halley Watch and Cometary Science Team, Earth and Space Sciences Division, Jet Propulsion Laboratory, California Institute of Technology, Pasadena.*
SOLAR SYSTEM, THE (*in part*)

R.L.N.S.   R.L.N. Sastri. *Former Deputy Director, Teluga Academy, Hyderābād, India. Author of a series of studies of the Laurales.*
ANGIOSPERMS (*in part*)

R.L.P.   Robert Lewis Parkinson (d. 1991). *Chief Librarian and Historian, Circus World Museum, Baraboo, Wisconsin, 1965–91. Author of* The First 100 Years of the Greatest Show on Earth.
CIRCUS (*in part*)

R.L.S.   Robert L. Scranton. *Emeritus Professor of Classical Art and Archaeology, University of Chicago. Author of* Aesthetic Aspects of Ancient Art; Corinth (*vol. 1, 3, and 16*) *and others.*
ARCHITECTURE, THE HISTORY OF WESTERN (*in part*)

R.L.Sc.   Robert L. Scheina. *Historian, U.S. Coast Guard, Washington, D.C. Author of* U.S. Coast Guard Cutters and Craft of World War II; *coauthor of* American Battleships, 1886–1923.
WAR, THE TECHNOLOGY OF (*in part*)

R.L.Se.   Robert L. Seale. *Professor of Nuclear and Energy Engineering, University of Arizona, Tucson. Coeditor of* Water Production Using Nuclear Energy.
ENERGY CONVERSION (*in part*)

R.L.Sm.   Robert Leo Smith. *Professor of Wildlife Biology and Ecology, West Virginia University, Morgantown. Author of* Ecology and Field Biology.
BIOLOGICAL SCIENCES, THE (*in part*)

R.L.S.-R.   Reginald Leslie Smith-Rose (d. 1980). *Secretary-General, Inter-Union*

Commission on Frequency Allocations for Radio Astronomy and Space Science, 1961–73. Director, Radio Research, Department of Scientific and Industrial Research, London, 1948–60.
MARCONI, GUGLIELMO (Micropædia)
POPOV, ALEKSANDR STEPANOVICH (Micropædia)

R.L.Su.   Robert Lee Suettinger. *Author of "The Political Process" in* China: A Country Study.
CHINA (*in part*)

R.L.Sw.   Roland Lee Swink. *Former Director, Adult Evening Education Program, 10th Combat Support Group, United States Air Forces in Europe. Former Lecturer in Education, University of Maryland, Overseas Division. Author of* A Comparison of the Academic Achievement of English and American School Boys and Girls, Ages 12 and 17.
EDUCATION, HISTORY OF (*in part*)

R.L.W.   Ralph Lee Woodward, Jr. *Professor of Latin American History, Tulane University, New Orleans. Author of* Central America: A Nation Divided *and others.*
CENTRAL AMERICA (*in part*)

R.L.Z.   Richard L. Zusi. *Curator, Division of Birds, National Museum of Natural History, Smithsonian Institution, Washington, D.C. Author of* Structural Adaptations of the Head and Neck in the Black Skimmer, Rynchops nigra Linnaeus.
BIRDS (*in part*)

R.M.   Roger Manvell (d. 1987). *Biographer and film historian. University Professor of Film, Boston University. Director, British Film Academy, 1947–59. Author of* Ellen Terry; *coauthor of* Hermann Göring; The Technique of Film Animation; *and many others.*
BROADCASTING (*in part*)
GÖRING, HERMANN (*in part*) (Micropædia)
MOTION PICTURES (*in part*)
TERRY, ELLEN (Micropædia)

R.Ma.   Roger Martinot. *Engineer in Chief, Rural Lands, Water, and Forests, National Institute of Agricultural Research, Paris. Coauthor of* La Stabulation libre des bovins Eyrolles.
FARMING AND AGRICULTURAL TECHNOLOGY (*in part*)

R.M.A.   Robert M. Adams. *Emeritus Professor of English, University of California, Los Angeles. Author of* The Land and Literature of England.
IBSEN, HENRIK (Micropædia)

R.MacM.   Ramsay MacMullen. *Dunham Professor of History and Classics, Yale University. Author of* Roman Social Relations; Corruption and the Decline of Rome.
GREEK AND ROMAN CIVILIZATIONS, ANCIENT (*in part*)

R.M.As.   Robert McCormick Adams. *Secretary, Smithsonian Institution, Washington, D.C. Provost, University of Chicago, 1982–84; Harold H.*

Swift Distinguished Service Professor of Anthropology, 1975–84; Director, Oriental Institute, 1962–68 and 1981–82.
PREHISTORIC PEOPLES AND CULTURES (*in part*)

R.M.B.   Ronald M. Berndt (d. 1990). *Foundation Professor of Anthropology, University of Western Australia, Nedlands, 1963–81. Coauthor of* The World of the First Australians *and others.*
AUSTRALIA (*in part*)

R.McD.   Raven I. McDavid, Jr. (d. 1984). *Professor of English and of Linguistics, University of Chicago, 1964–77. Coauthor of* The Pronunciation of English in the Atlantic States; *editor of H.L. Mencken's* The American Language.
WEBSTER, NOAH (Micropædia)

R.McMu.   Roy Donald McMullen (d. 1984). *Art historian. Author of* Art, Affluence, and Alienation; The World of Marc Chagall; *and others.*
BRAQUE, GEORGES (Micropædia)
CHAGALL, MARC (Micropædia)
DAVID, JACQUES-LOUIS (Micropædia)
FOLK ARTS (*in part*)
KANDINSKY, WASSILY (*in part*) (Micropædia)
LÉGER, FERNAND (Micropædia)
MATISSE, HENRI (*in part*) (Micropædia)
ROUAULT, GEORGES (Micropædia)

R.McN.A.   Robert McNeill Alexander. *Professor of Zoology, University of Leeds, England. Author of* Elastic Mechanisms in Animal Movement *and others.*
MUSCLES AND MUSCLE SYSTEMS (*in part*)

R.M.D.   Richard M. Dorson (d. 1981). *Director, Folklore Institute; Professor of History and Folklore, Indiana University, Bloomington, 1957–81. Author of* American Folklore; Folklore and Fakelore; *and others; editor of* Journal of American Folklore.
FOLK ARTS (*in part*)

R.Me.   Reinhold Merkelbach. *Professor of Classics, University of Cologne. Author of* Roman und Mysterium in der Antike *and others.*
MYSTERY RELIGIONS

R.M.G.   Robert M. Grant. *Carl Darling Buck Professor Emeritus of Humanities; Emeritus Professor of Early Christian History, Divinity School, University of Chicago. Author of* Historical Introduction to the New Testament; Early Christianity and Society; *and others.*
BIBLICAL LITERATURE AND ITS CRITICAL INTERPRETATION (*in part*)

R.M.H.   Ragnhild Marie Hatton. *Emeritus Professor of International History, London School of Economics and Political Science, University of London. Author of* Charles XII of Sweden *and others.*
CHARLES XII (SWEDEN) (Micropædia)

R.M.He.   Robert M. Henderson. *Chief, General Library and Museum of*

the Performing Arts, New York Public Library at Lincoln Center, New York City. Author of D.W. Griffith, the Years at Biograph; D.W. Griffith, His Life and Times; *and others.*
GRIFFITH, D.W. (Micropædia)

R.M.Hi.   Richard M. Highsmith, Jr. *Emeritus Professor of Geography, Oregon State University, Corvallis. Coauthor of* Conservation in the United States.
UNITED STATES OF AMERICA (*in part*)

R.M.Ke.   Roger M. Keesing. *Professor and Head, Department of Anthropology, Research School of Pacific Studies, Australian National University, Canberra. Author of* Melanesian Pidgin and The Oceanic Substrate *and others.*
PACIFIC ISLANDS (*in part*)

R.M.L.   R.M. Lockley. *Naturalist. Author of* Shearwaters; Puffins; *and others; coauthor of* Sea Birds of the North Atlantic.
BIRDS (*in part*)

R.M.Le.   Richard M. Leighton. *Military historian and consultant. Professor of National Security Affairs, National Defense University, U.S. Department of Defense, Washington, D.C., 1965–78. Coauthor of* Global Logistics and Strategy 1940–45.
WAR, THE THEORY AND CONDUCT OF (*in part*)

R.M.Lu.   R.M. Lumiansky (d. 1987). *President, American Council of Learned Societies, 1974–82. Professor of English, New York University, New York City, 1975–83. Author of* Of Sondry Folk: The Dramatic Principle in the Canterbury Tales *and others.*
CHAUCER (*in part*)

R.Mo.   Rudolf Morsey. *Professor of Modern History, Postgraduate School for Administrative Sciences, Speyer, Germany. Author of* Die deutsche Zentrumspartei, 1917–1923 *and others.*
STRESEMANN, GUSTAV (Micropædia)

R.M.O.   Richard Marian Ogorkiewicz. *Professor, Royal Military College of Science, Cranfield Institute of Technology, Shrivenham, England. Author of* Armour *and others.*
WAR, THE TECHNOLOGY OF (*in part*)

R.M.Og.   Robert Maxwell Ogilvie (d. 1981). *Professor of Humanity, University of St. Andrews, Scotland. Editor of* A Commentary on Livy, Books 1–5.
LIVY (Micropædia)

R.M.P.   Raghawendra Mukund Pai. *Professor and Head, Department of Botany, Marathwada University, Aurangabad, India.*
ANGIOSPERMS (*in part*)

R.M.Sa.   Roger M. Savory. *Emeritus Professor of Middle East and Islāmic Studies, University of Toronto. Translator of* The History of Shah ʿAbbas.
ʿABBĀS I (PERSIA) (Micropædia)

R.M.T.   R. Murray Thomas. *Professor of Education and Head, Program in*

International Education, University of California, Santa Barbara. Author of Comparing Theories of Child Development.
EDUCATION, HISTORY OF (*in part*)

R.My.   Rollo H. Myers (d. 1985). *Writer on music. Author of* Modern French Music; Ravel: Life and Works; *and others.*
RAVEL, MAURICE (Micropædia)

R.Na.   Raghavan Narasimhan. *Professor of Mathematics, University of Chicago. Author of* Analysis on Real and Complex Manifolds; Several Complex Variables.
ANALYSIS (IN MATHEMATICS) (*in part*)

R.N.Bu.   Robert N. Burr. *Emeritus Professor of History, University of California, Los Angeles. Author of* Troubled Hemisphere *and others.*
PERU (*in part*)

R.N.C.   Richard N. Current. *University Distinguished Professor Emeritus of History, University of North Carolina, Greensboro. Author of* Daniel Webster and the Rise of National Conservatism; The Lincoln Nobody Knows; *and others.*
LINCOLN
WEBSTER, DANIEL (Micropædia)

R.N.DeJ.   Russell N. DeJong, M.D. (d. 1990). *Professor of Neurology, University of Michigan Medical School, Ann Arbor, 1950–76. Author of* The Neurological Examination *and others.*
TISSUES AND FLUIDS (*in part*)

R.N.F.   Richard N. Frye. *Aga Khan Professor of Iranian, Harvard University. Director, Asia Institute, Pahlavi University, Shīrāz, Iran, 1969–74. Author of* The History of Ancient Iran *and others.*
CYRUS II (Micropædia)
KHOSROW I (Micropædia)
MESOPOTAMIA, THE HISTORY OF
   ANCIENT (*in part*)

R.Ni.   Romola Nijinsky (d. 1978). *Author of* Nijinsky; The Last Years of Nijinsky; *editor of* The Diary of Vaslav Nijinsky.
NIJINSKY, VASLAV (Micropædia)

R.N.S.   The Rev. R. Norman Sharp. *Assistant Professor of Old Persian and Pahlavi, Pahlavi University, Shīrāz, Iran, 1962–67. Author of* The Inscriptions of the Achaemenian Emperors in Old Persian Cuneiform *and others.*
PERSEPOLIS (Micropædia)

R.O.   Ron Olver. *British correspondent,* The Ring. *Former Assistant Editor,* Boxing World *and* Boxing News. *Coauthor of* Boxing.
SPORTS, MAJOR TEAM AND INDIVIDUAL
   (*in part*)

Ro.A.   Roberto Almagià (d. 1962). *Professor of Geography, University of Rome, 1915–59. Author of* Il mondo attuale *and many others.*
VESPUCCI, AMERIGO (Micropædia)

Ro.A.K.   Roy A. Keller. *Professor of Chemistry, State University of New York College at Fredonia. Former Editor,* Journal of Chromatographic Science.

ANALYSIS AND MEASUREMENT,
   PHYSICAL AND CHEMICAL (*in part*)

Ro.Au.   Robert Auty (d. 1978). *Professor of Comparative Slavonic Philology, University of Oxford, 1965–78; Fellow of Brasenose College, Oxford.*
CZECHOSLOVAK LITERATURE (*in part*)

R.O.C.   Robert O. Collins. *Professor of History, University of California, Santa Barbara. Author of* Shadows in the Grass: Britain in the Southern Sudan, 1918–1956 *and others.*
SUDAN (*in part*)

R.O.C.N.   Sir Richard O.C. Norman. *Rector, Exeter College, University of Oxford. Professor of Chemistry, University of York, England, 1956–87. Author of* Principles of Organic Synthesis.
CHEMICAL COMPOUNDS (*in part*)

Ro.D.   Roger Davies. *Associate Professor of Meteorology, McGill University, Montreal.*
CLIMATE AND WEATHER (*in part*)

R.O.F.   Raymond Oliver Faulkner (deceased). *Fellow of University College, London; Lecturer in Ancient Egyptian, University College, University of London, 1955–67. Author of* Egypt: From the Inception of the Nineteenth Dynasty to the Death of Ramesses III *and others.*
RAMSES II (Micropædia)

Ro.G.   Robert Grudin. *Professor of English, University of Oregon, Eugene. Author of* The Grace of Great Things *and others.*
HUMANISM

R.O.H.   Raymond O. Harrison. *Architect. Former Director, Provincial Museum and Archives, Edmonton, Alberta.*
CANADA (*in part*)

Ro.H.R.   Robert Henry Robins. *Emeritus Professor of General Linguistics, University of London. Author of* General Linguistics: An Introductory Survey.
LANGUAGE (*in part*)

Ro.L.   Robert Lechêne. *Journalist and popular science writer. Author of* L'Imprimerie, de Gutenberg à l'électron.
PRINTING, TYPOGRAPHY, AND
   PHOTOENGRAVING (*in part*)

Ro.M.   Robert Merle. *Novelist. Author of* Ahmed Ben Bella *and others.*
BEN BELLA, AHMED (Micropædia)

Ro.Ma.   Robert L. Marshall. *Sachar Professor of Music, Brandeis University, Waltham, Massachusetts. Author of* The Compositional Process of J.S. Bach.
BACH (*in part*)

Ro.N.   Robert Niklaus. *Emeritus Professor of French, University of Exeter, England. Author of* A Literary History of France: The Eighteenth Century; *editor of Diderot's* Pensées philosophiques; Lettre sur les aveugles.
DIDEROT, DENIS (Micropædia)

Ro.P.   Roy Perrott. *Free-lance book editor and consultant. Fellow of the*

Royal Horticultural Society, London. Author of The Aristocrats.
GARDENING AND HORTICULTURE
   (*in part*)

Ro.Pa.   Roy Pascal (d. 1980). *Professor of German, University of Birmingham, England, 1939–69. Author of* The German Novel *and others.*
MANN, THOMAS (Micropædia)

Ro.P.B.   Robert Percy Beckinsale. *Senior Lecturer in Geography, University of Oxford, 1945–75.*
SPAIN (*in part*)

Ro.Pe.   Roger Pélissier (d. 1972). *Assistant Director, Centre for Far East Documentation, École Pratique des Hautes Études (Institute for Advanced Research), Paris. Author of* The Awakening of China, 1793–1949 *and others.*
CH'IEN-LUNG (Micropædia)

Ro.Po.   Roland Pourtier. *Professor of Geography, University of Paris I. Author of* Le Gabon (*vol. 1–2*).
AFRICA (*in part*)

Ro.R.   Rollin C. Richmond. *Professor and Chairman, Department of Biology, Indiana University, Bloomington.*
GENETICS AND HEREDITY, THE
   PRINCIPLES OF (*in part*)

Ro.Ri.   Roberto Ridolfi. *Member of Accademia Nazionale dei Lincei. Director of "National Editions of the Works of Savonarola." Director,* La Bibliofilia, *1944–82. Author of* Life of Machiavelli *and others.*
MACHIAVELLI, NICCOLÒ (*in part*)
   (Micropædia)
SAVONAROLA, GIROLAMO (Micropædia)

Ro.S.   Ronald Strahan. *Executive Officer, National Photographic Index of Australian Wildlife, Australian Museum, Sydney. Director, Taronga Zoological Park, Sydney, 1967–74. Coauthor of* The Biology of Myxine.
FISHES (*in part*)

Ro.Sc.   Roger Scruton. *Professor of Aesthetics, Birkbeck College, University of London. Author of* The Aesthetics of Architecture *and others.*
AESTHETICS (*in part*)

Ro.Si.   Roy Sieber. *Rudy Professor of Fine Arts, Indiana University, Bloomington. Associate Director, National Musuem of African Art, Smithsonian Institution, Washington, D.C. Author of* African Art in the Cycle of Life *and others.*
DECORATIVE ARTS AND FURNISHINGS
   (*in part*)

Ro.T.   Robert Tonkinson. *Professor of Anthropology, University of Western Australia, Nedlands.* The Mardu Aborigines: Living the Dream in Australia's Desert.
AUSTRALIA (*in part*)

Ro.W.   Robert L. Wilken. *Professor of the History of Christianity, University of Notre Dame, Indiana. Author of* The Myth of Christian Beginnings.
TERTULLIAN (Micropædia)

Ro.W.C.   Robert W. Conn. *Professor of Engineering and Applied Science; Director, Institute of Plasma and Fusion Research, University of California, Los Angeles. Editor,* Fusion Engineering and Design.
ATOMS (*in part*)

Ro.W.F.   Robert W. Finley. *Emeritus Professor of Geography, University of Wisconsin, Madison. Author of* Geography of Wisconsin: A Content Outline.
UNITED STATES OF AMERICA (*in part*)

Ro.W.St.   Robert Walter Steel. *Principal, University College of Swansea, 1974–82; Vice-Chancellor, University of Wales, 1979–81. John Rankin Professor of Geography, University of Liverpool, 1957–74. Director, Commonwealth Geographical Bureau, 1972–81.*
AFRICA (*in part*)
SOUTHERN AFRICA (*in part*)

R.O.Wt.   Sir Richard Olof Winstedt (d. 1966). *Reader in Malay, University of London, 1937–47. Author of* A History of Malay Literature; Malaya and Its History; *and others.*
SOUTHEAST ASIA, MAINLAND (*in part*)

R.P.   René Pélissier. *Authority on Portuguese- and Spanish-speaking Africa. Author of* Los territorios españoles de Africa; Études hispano-guinéennes; *and others.*
WESTERN AFRICA (*in part*)

R.Pa.   Reginald Passmore. *Former Reader in Physiology, University of Edinburgh. Coauthor of* Human Nutrition and Dietetics.
NUTRITION (*in part*)

R.P.A.   Richard Paul Aulie. *Former Lecturer in Natural Science, Loyola University, Chicago. Associate Editor,* Encyclopædia Britannica, *Chicago, 1971–72.*
EUDOXUS OF CNIDUS (Micropædia)

R.Pal.   Rodolfo Pallucchini (d. 1989). *Director, Institute of Art History, Giorgio Cini Foundation, Venice, 1972–89. Author of* Disegni di Giambattista Tiepolo; La giovinezza del Tintoretto; Veronese; *and others.*
TIEPOLO, GIOVANNI BATTISTA (Micropædia)
TINTORETTO (*in part*) (Micropædia)
VERONESE, PAOLO (Micropædia)

R.P.An.   Richard Paul Anschutz. *Emeritus Professor of Philosophy, University of Auckland, New Zealand. Author of* Philosophy of J.S. Mill.
MILL, JOHN STUART (*in part*)

R.P.B.   Ronald Percy Bell. *Emeritus Professor of Chemistry, University of Stirling, Scotland. Honorary Research Professor of Physical Chemistry, University of Leeds, England, 1976–82. Author of* Acid-Base Catalysis *and others.*
CHEMICAL REACTIONS (*in part*)

R.P.C.M.   Reginald P.C. Mutter. *Emeritus Professor of English Literature, University of Sussex, Brighton, England.*

Editor of The History of Tom Jones.
DEFOE, DANIEL (*in part*) (Micropædia)
ENGLISH LITERATURE (*in part*)
STEELE, SIR RICHARD (Micropædia)

R.Pe.   Régine Pernoud. *Keeper, Joan of Arc Centre, Orléans, France. Author of* Aliénor d'Aquitaine; Héloïse and Abélard; Histoire de la bourgeoisie en France; *and others.*
ELEANOR OF AQUITAINE (Micropædia)
VILLON, FRANÇOIS (Micropædia)

R.P.He.   Robert Proulx Heaney, M.D. *John A. Creighton University Professor, Creighton University, Omaha, Nebraska; Vice President for Health Sciences, 1971–84. Coauthor of* Skeletal Renewal and Metabolic Bone Diseases.
SUPPORTIVE AND CONNECTIVE TISSUES (*in part*)

R.Pi.   Robert Pick (d. 1978). *Free-lance writer and editor. Author of* Empress Maria Theresa.
MARIA THERESA (Micropædia)

R.P.M.   Robert P. Multhauf. *Senior Historian, Smithsonian Institution, Washington, D.C. Author of* The Origins of Chemistry; Neptune's Gift.
OCCULTISM (*in part*)

R.P.Mo.   Richard P. Momsen, Jr. *Emeritus Professor of Geography, University of Calgary, Alberta. Author of* Brazil: A Giant Stirs.
BRAZIL (*in part*)

R.Po.   Raphael Powell (d. 1965). *Professor of Roman Law, University of London, 1955–64.*
LEGAL SYSTEMS, THE EVOLUTION OF MODERN WESTERN (*in part*)

R.P.S.   Robert P. Scharlemann. *Commonwealth Professor of Religious Studies, University of Virginia, Charlottesville. Author of* Reflection and Doubt in the Thought of Paul Tillich.
PROTESTANTISM (*in part*)
SCHLEIERMACHER, FRIEDRICH (Micropædia)

R.P.Sa.   Richard P. Saller. *Professor of History and Classics, University of Chicago. Author of* Personal Patronage Under the Early Empire; The Roman Empire: Economy, Society and Culture.
GREEK AND ROMAN CIVILIZATIONS, ANCIENT (*in part*)

R.P.Sp.   Robert Phillip Sharp. *Emeritus Professor of Geology, California Institute of Technology, Pasadena. Author of* Glaciers.
GEOMORPHIC PROCESSES (*in part*)

R.P.T.   Ronald P. Toby. *Professor of History and East Asian Studies, University of Illinois at Urbana-Champaign. Author of* State and Diplomacy in Early Modern Japan.
ŌSAKA-KŌBE METROPOLITAN AREA (*in part*)

R.Q.   Ricardo Quintana. *Emeritus Professor of English, University of Wisconsin, Madison. Author of* Mind and Art of Jonathan Swift; Oliver Goldsmith: A Georgian Study.
SWIFT, JONATHAN (*in part*) (Micropædia)

R.R.   Romney Robinson. *Professor of Economics, University of Toronto, 1967–70. Associate Professor of Economics, Brandeis University, Waltham, Massachusetts, 1955–67.*
INTERNATIONAL TRADE (*in part*)

R.R.B.   Richard R. Beeman. *Professor and Chairman, Department of History, University of Pennsylvania, Philadelphia. Author of* The Old Dominion and the New Nation, 1788–1801 *and others.*
UNITED STATES OF AMERICA (*in part*)

R.R.D.   Ranjit Ramchandra Desai. *Agriculturist and writer. Author of* Śrīmāna Yogī: the Life of Śivajī in Marathi *and others.*
ŚIVAJĪ (Micropædia)

R.Ri.   Raymond Ritter (d. 1974). *Attorney. Editor in Chief of the review* Pyrénées. *Author of* Henry IV lui-même; *editor of* Lettres du cardinal de Florence sur Henri IV et sur la France (1596–1598).
HENRY IV (FRANCE) (Micropædia)

R.R.K.   Ralph R. Krueger. *Professor of Geography, University of Waterloo, Ontario. Coauthor of* Canada: A New Geography.
CANADA (*in part*)

R.R.M.   Raymond R. Myers. *University Professor Emeritus of Chemistry, Kent State University, Ohio. Former Editor,* Journal of Rheology. *Coeditor of* Treatise on Coatings.
INDUSTRIES, CHEMICAL PROCESS (*in part*)

R.R.Pr.   Richard Riseley Proud (d. 1975). *Lieutenant Colonel, Indian Army.*
NEPAL (*in part*)

R.R.R.   Richard R. Ring. *Former Assistant Professor of History, Ripon College, Wisconsin.*
ROME (*in part*)

R.R.S.   Robert R. Stoll. *Emeritus Professor of Mathematics, Cleveland State University. Author of* Set Theory and Logic.
SET THEORY (*in part*)

R.R.Sh.   Robert R. Shannon. *Director, Optical Sciences Center; Professor of Optical Sciences, University of Arizona, Tucson. Coeditor of* Applied Optics and Optical Engineering (*vol. 7–10*).
MICROSCOPES (*in part*)

R.R.W.   Robert R. Wagner, M.D. *Marion McNulty and Malvin C. Weaver Professor of Oncology and Microbiology and Chairman, Department of Microbiology, University of Virginia, Charlottesville. Coeditor of* Comprehensive Virology (*19 vol.*)
VIRUSES

R.S.   Roger Sharrock (d. 1991). *Professor of English Language and Literature, King's College, University of London, 1968–81. Author of* John Bunyan *and others; editor of* Oxford Bunyan.
BUNYAN, JOHN (Micropædia)

R.S.B.   Rupert Stevenson Bradley. *Former Reader in Inorganic and Structural Chemistry, University of*

Leeds, England. Coauthor and editor of High Pressure Physics and Chemistry.
BRIDGMAN, P.W. (*in part*) (Micropædia)

R.S.Be.   R. Stephen Berry. *James Franck Distinguished Service Professor of Chemistry, University of Chicago. Coauthor of* Physical Chemistry *and others.*
CHEMICAL REACTIONS (*in part*)

R.Sc.   R.A.M. Schmidt. *Consulting geologist. Chairman, Geology Department, Anchorage Community College, University of Alaska. Geologist, Geological Survey, U.S. Department of the Interior, 1943–56; District Geologist, Anchorage, 1956–63.*
NORTH AMERICA (*in part*)

R.S.C.   Richard S. Cowan. *Director, National Museum of Natural History, Smithsonian Institution, Washington, D.C., 1965–73; Senior Scientist, Department of Botany, 1973–85.*
ANGIOSPERMS (*in part*)

R.S.Ca.   Robert S. Carmichael. *Professor of Geophysics and Geology, University of Iowa, Iowa City. Editor of* Handbook of Physical Properties of Rocks *(3 vol.).*
MINERALS AND ROCKS (*in part*)

R.Sch.   Reiner Schürmann. *Professor of Philosophy, Graduate Faculty, New School for Social Research, New York City. Author of* Meister Eckhart, Mystic and Philosopher *and others.*
ECKEHART, MEISTER (Micropædia)

R.S.Co. Robin Sinclair Cormack. *Reader in the History of Art, Courtauld Institute of Art, University of London. Author of* Writing in Gold; The Byzantine Eye.
PAINTING, THE HISTORY OF WESTERN (*in part*)

R.S.De.   The Most Rev. Ralph Stanley Dean. (d. 1987). *Executive Officer, Anglican Communion, 1964–69. Archbishop of Cariboo and Metropolitan of the Anglican Province of British Columbia, 1971–73. Rector, Church of the Redeemer; Greenville, South Carolina, 1979–87. Author of* In the Light of the Cross.
PROTESTANTISM (*in part*)

R.S.Du.   Richard S. Dunn. *Professor of History, University of Pennsylvania, Philadelphia. Author of* Puritans and Yankees *and others.*
WINTHROP, JOHN (Micropædia)

R.Sh.   Robert Shackleton. (d. 1986). *Marshal Foch Professor of French Literature, University of Oxford, 1979–86; Bodley's Librarian, 1966–79. Author of* Montesquieu: A Critical Biography.
MONTESQUIEU, CHARLES-LOUIS DE SECONDAT, BARON DE LA BREDE ET DE (*in part*) (Micropædia)

R.S.H.   Richard S. Hartenberg. *Emeritus Professor of Mechanical Engineering, Northwestern University, Evanston, Illinois. Coauthor of* Kinematic Synthesis of Linkages.
FULTON, ROBERT (Micropædia)
TOOLS (*in part*)

R.S.L.   Robert Sabatino Lopez (d. 1986). *Professor of History, Yale University, 1955–71. Author of* The Birth of Europe *and others.*
CONSTANTINE VII PORPHYROGENITUS (BYZANTINE EMPIRE) (Micropædia)

R.S.N.   Robert S. Norris. *Senior Research Associate, Natural Resources Defense Council, Inc., Washington, D.C. Coauthor and coeditor of* Nuclear Weapons Databook *(vol. 2–4).*
WAR, THE TECHNOLOGY OF (*in part*)

R.So.   Robert W. Sowers. *Stained-glass artist. Author of* The Language of Stained Glass *and others.*
DECORATIVE ARTS AND FURNISHINGS (*in part*)

R.Sp.   Robert Spence (d. 1976). *Master of Keynes College; Professor of Applied Chemistry, University of Kent at Canterbury, England, 1968–73. Director, Atomic Energy Research Establishment, Harwell, England, 1964–68. Author of the obituary memoir on Otto Hahn for the Royal Society.*
HAHN, OTTO (Micropædia)

R.S.Q.   Robert S. Quimby. *Emeritus Professor of Humanities, Michigan State University, East Lansing. Author of* The Background of Napoleonic Warfare.
VAUBAN, SÉBASTIEN LE PRESTRE DE (Micropædia)

R.S.S.   Robert S. Schwartz, M.D. *Professor of Medicine, Tufts University, Boston; former Chief, Division of Hematology-Oncology, New England Medical Center.*
BLOOD (*in part*)

R.St.   Ralph Stephenson. *Former Director, Paris Pullman Cinema, London. Author of* The Animated Film; *coauthor of* The Cinema as Art.
MOTION PICTURES (*in part*)

R.St.J.   Robert St. John. *Journalist, lecturer, and foreign affairs radio commentator. Author of* The Boss *and others.*
NASSER, GAMAL ABDEL (Micropædia)

R.S.-U.   Rivka Schatz-Uffenheimer. *Edmonton Professor of Jewish Mysticism, Hebrew University of Jerusalem. Author of* ha-Ḥasidut ke-misṭiqa *("Ḥasidism as Mysticism").*
BAʿAL SHEM ṬOV (*in part*) (Micropædia)
LURIA, ISAAC BEN SOLOMON (*in part*) (Micropædia)

R.S.V.   René Santamaria Varela. *Director, R.V. y Asociados (management consultants), San Salvador, El Salvador.*
CENTRAL AMERICA (*in part*)

R.S.W.   Richard S. Westfall. *Professor of History of Science, Indiana University, Bloomington. Author of* The Construction of Modern Science; Never at Rest: A Biography of Isaac Newton.
NEWTON (*in part*)
RAY, JOHN (Micropædia)

R.S.Y.   Roland S. Young (d. 1988). *Consulting chemical engineer. Author of* Cobalt in Biology and Biochemistry *and others; editor of* Cobalt: Its Chemistry,

Metallurgy, Uses.
INDUSTRIES, EXTRACTION AND PROCESSING (*in part*)

R.T.   Robert Traub. *Colonel (retired), U.S. Army. Professor of Microbiology, University of Maryland, Baltimore. Author of numerous scientific papers, including many on fleas.*
INSECTS (*in part*)

R.T.A.   Robert T. Anderson. *Professor of Anthropology, Mills College, Oakland, California. Author of* Traditional Europe: A Study in Anthropology and History; Denmark: Suecess of A Developing Nation.
DENMARK (*in part*)
EUROPE (*in part*)

R.T.C.   Robert Thomas Coupland. *Emeritus Professor of Plant Ecology, University of Saskatchewan, Saskatoon.*
BIOSPHERE, THE (*in part*)

R.T.D.   Ralph Thomas Daniel (d. 1985). *Professor of Music History, Indiana University, Bloomington. Coauthor of* The Harvard Brief Dictionary of Music *and others.*
MUSIC, THE HISTORY OF WESTERN

R.T.F.   Raymond T. Fonash. *Free-lance writer specializing in historical subject matter.*
ENERGY CONVERSION (*in part*)

Rt.H.   Robert Ho (d. 1972). *Senior Fellow, Department of Human Geography, Australian National University, Canberra. Author of* Farmers of Central Malaya; *editor of* Studies in the Geography of Southeast Asia.
SOUTHEAST ASIA, MAINLAND (*in part*)

R.Th.   Romila Thapar. *Professor of Ancient Indian History, Jawaharlal Nehru University, New Delhi. Author of* Aśoka and the Decline of the Mauryas *and others.*
INDIA (*in part*)

R.T.H.   Robert Thomas Harms. *Professor of Linguistics, University of Texas at Austin. Author of* Estonian Grammar; Finnish Structural Sketch.
LANGUAGES OF THE WORLD (*in part*)

R.T.J.   Richard T. Jackson. *Professor of Geography, James Cook University of North Queensland, Townsville, Australia. Coauthor of* Geography Through Papua New Guinea.
PACIFIC ISLANDS (*in part*)

R.T.L.   Richard T. Lockhart. *President, Social Engineering Associates, Inc., Chicago; Publisher and Editor,* Illinois Political Reporter, *1961–86.*
UNITED STATES OF AMERICA (*in part*)

R.T.La.   Robert Terence Lange. *Senior Visiting Fellow, National Key Centre for Teaching and Research in Dryland Agriculture and Land Use Systems, Roseworty Campus, University of Adelaide, Australia; former Reader in Botany. Contributor to* A History of Australasian Vegetation *and others.*
AUSTRALIA (*in part*)

R.To.   Richard Tolson. The Times *(London) Correspondent, Leeward*

Islands, 1954–56.
WEST INDIES, THE (*in part*)

R.T.S.   R. Thomas Sanderson (d. 1990).
Professor of Chemistry, Arizona State University, Tempe, 1963–78. Author of Simple Inorganic Substances: A New Approach *and others.*
CHEMICAL ELEMENTS (*in part*)

R.T.V.   Richard T. Vann. *Professor of History and Letters, Wesleyan University, Middletown, Connecticut. Author of* The Social Development of English Quakerism, 1655–1755.
PROTESTANTISM (*in part*)

R.T.We.   Richard Tilghman Weidner. *Emeritus Professor of Physics, Rutgers University, New Brunswick, New Jersey. Coauthor of* Elementary Modern Physics *and others.*
PHYSICAL SCIENCES, THE (*in part*)

Ru.M.   Russell Meiggs (d. 1989). *Fellow of Balliol College, Oxford; Lecturer in Ancient History, University of Oxford, 1939–70. Author of* Ostia; *editor of J.M. Bury's* History of Greece.
ALCIBIADES (Micropædia)
CLEISTHENES OF ATHENS (Micropædia)

Ru.S.   Ruth Stephan (d. 1974). *Writer. Author of* My Crown, My Love *and others.*
CHRISTINA (Micropædia)

Ru.Sc.   Rudolf Schmid. *Associate Professor of Integrative Biology, University of California, Berkeley.*
PLANTS (*in part*)

Ru.V.   Rudolf Vierhaus. *Professor and Director, Max Planck Institute for History, Göttingen, Germany. Author of* Ranke und die soziale Welt *and others.*
RANKE, LEOPOLD VON (Micropædia)

R.V.   Randolph Vigne. *Writer. Author of* The Transkei: A South African Tragedy; A Dwelling Place of Our Own: The Story of the Namibian Nation.
SOUTH AFRICA (*in part*)

R.Va.   Richard Vaughan. *Former Professor of History, University of Hull, England. Author of* Philip the Good; John the Fearless.
JOHN (BURGUNDY) (Micropædia)
PHILIP III (BURGUNDY) (Micropædia)

R.V.D.   Robert V. Daniels. *Emeritus Professor of History, University of Vermont, Burlington. Author of* Russia: Roots of Confrontation *and others.*
TROTSKY, LEON (*in part*) (Micropædia)
UNION OF SOVIET SOCIALIST REPUBLICS (*in part*)

R.V.Di.   R.V. Dietrich. *Emeritus Professor of Geology, Central Michigan University, Mount Pleasant. Author of* Stones; *coauthor of* Gems, Gravels and Granites.
MINERALS AND ROCKS (*in part*)

R.Vi.   Reino Virtanen (d. 1987). *Professor of Modern Languages, University of Nebraska, Lincoln, 1957–78. Author of* Claude Bernard and His Place in the History of Ideas.
BERNARD, CLAUDE (Micropædia)

R.V.R.   Robert Vincent Roosa. *Partner, Brown Brothers, Harriman and Company, New York City. Under Secretary for Monetary Affairs, U.S. Department of the Treasury, 1961–64. Author of* Federal Reserve Operations in the Money and Government Securities Markets.
MARKETS (*in part*)

R.V.R.C.R.   R.V.R. Chandrasekhara Rao. *Professor and Head, Department of Political Science; Dean, School of Social Sciences, University of Hyderabad, India. Author of* From Innocence to Strength: India Through Cold War, Detente and Entente.
INDIA (*in part*)

R.W.   Rex Wailes (d. 1986). *Consultant, U.K. Department of the Environment and National Trust on Industrial Monuments. Author of* The English Windmill *and others.*
ENERGY CONVERSION (*in part*)

R.W.A.   R.W. Allard. *Emeritus Professor of Genetics, University of California, Davis. Author of* Principles of Plant Breeding.
FARMING AND AGRICULTURAL TECHNOLOGY (*in part*)

R.W.B.   Roger William Benedict. *Managing Editor,* Petroleum Intelligence Weekly, *London.*
NORTH AMERICA (*in part*)

R.W.Bd.   Raymond Walter Barnard (d. 1962). *Associate Professor of Mathematics, University of Chicago, 1932–62.*
TRIGONOMETRY (*in part*)

R.W.C.   Robert W. Cahn. *Former Professor of Materials Science, University of Sussex, Brighton, England. Editor of* Physical Metallurgy.
AGRICOLA, GEORGIUS (Micropædia)

R.W.Co.   Richard W. Cottle. *Professor of Operations Research, Stanford University, California.*
OPTIMIZATION, THE MATHEMATICAL THEORY OF (*in part*)

R.W.D.   Ronald Walter Douglas. *Emeritus Professor of Glass Technology, University of Sheffield, England. Former editor,* Glass Technology *and* Physics and Chemistry of Glasses.
MATTER (*in part*)

R.W.De. Robert W. Decker. *Professor of Geophysics, University of Hawaii at Hilo. Coauthor of* Volcanoes.
VOLCANISM (*in part*)

R.W.D.E.   Robert Walter Dudley Edwards (d. 1988). *Professor of Modern Irish History, University College, Dublin, National University of Ireland, 1945–79. Author of* Church and State in Tudor Ireland.
IRELAND (*in part*)

R.W.Di.   Robert William Ditchburn (d. 1987). *Professor of Physics, University of Reading, England, 1946–68. Author of* Light.
LIGHT (*in part*)

R.We.   Robert Werner. *Emeritus Professor of Ancient History, Friedrich Alexander University of Erlangen-Nürnberg, Germany. Author of* Der Beginn der römischen Republik.
PTOLEMY I SOTER (Micropædia)

R.W.E.   Richard W. Everett. *Vice President, Economic Research Division, Chase Manhattan Bank, New York City, 1967–87.*
ECONOMIC GROWTH AND PLANNING (*in part*)

R.W.F.   Rhodes W. Fairbridge. *Professor of Geology, Columbia University, 1955–82. World authority on Quaternary history, events, and processes. Editor of* Encyclopedia of Geomorphology; Encyclopedia of World Regional Geology.
GEOCHRONOLOGY (*in part*)

R.W.Fi.   Sir Raymond William Firth. *Emeritus Professor of Anthropology, University of London. Internationally known for his contributions in social anthropology. Author of* Man and Culture: An Evaluation of the Work of Bronislaw Malinowski.
MALINOWSKI, BRONISŁAW (*in part*) (Micropædia)

R.W.Fo.   Roland Wynfield Force. *President and Director, Museum of the American Indian, New York City. Coeditor of* Polynesian Culture History.
PACIFIC ISLANDS (*in part*)

R.W.L.   Robert Warden Lee (d. 1958). *Rhodes Professor of Roman-Dutch Law, University of Oxford, 1921–56. Author of* Introduction to Roman-Dutch Law *and others.*
LEGAL SYSTEMS, THE EVOLUTION OF MODERN WESTERN (*in part*)

R.W.M.   Robert W. Marks. *Former Lecturer, New School for Social Research, New York City. Author of* The Dymaxion World of Buckminster Fuller.
FULLER, R. BUCKMINSTER (Micropædia)

R.W.Ma.   Richard W. Macomber. *Professor of Physics, Brooklyn Center, Long Island University, New York.*
LYELL, SIR CHARLES, BARONET (Micropædia)
SMITH, WILLIAM (Micropædia)

R.W.P.   Richard W. Pohl. *Distinguished Professor of Botany; Curator of the Herbarium, Iowa State University, Ames. Author of* How to Know the Grasses *and others.*
ANGIOSPERMS (*in part*)

R.W.St.   Robert W. Storer. *Emeritus Professor of Zoology, University of Michigan, Ann Arbor; Curator of Birds, Museum of Zoology, 1956–85.*
BIRDS (*in part*)

R.W.Y.   Ralph W. Yerger. *Emeritus Professor of Biology, Florida State University, Tallahassee.*
FISHES (*in part*)

R.Y.C.   Sir Roy Yorke Calne. *Professor of Surgery, University of Cambridge. Author of* Renal Transplantation.
TRANSPLANTS, ORGAN AND TISSUE

R.Y.T.   Robert Young Thomson. *Senior Lecturer in Biochemistry, University of Glasgow, Scotland.*
BIOCHEMICAL COMPONENTS OF ORGANISMS (*in part*)

S.   Subramani. *Professor of Literature, University of the South Pacific, Suva, Fiji. Author of* South Pacific Literature; The Fantasy Eaters: Stories from Fiji.
OCEANIC ARTS (*in part*)

S.A.Kr.   Stepan Andriyovich Kryzhanivsky. *Professor, Institute of Literature, Ukrainian S.S.R. Academy of Sciences, Kiev. Coauthor of* History of Ukrainian Literature (*vol. 8*).
UKRAINIAN LITERATURE (*in part*) (Micropædia)

Sa.M.   Sally Marks. *Historian. Former Professor of History, Rhode Island College, Providence. Author of* The Illusion of Peace: International Relations in Europe, 1918–1933.
DIPLOMACY

S.A.M.   Samuel A. Matz. *President, Pan-Tech International, Inc., McAllen, Texas. Vice President, Research and Development, Ovaltine Food Products, Villa Park, Illinois, 1971–82. Author of* Bakery Technology.
FOOD PROCESSING (*in part*)

S.A.R.   Sh. Abdur Rashid. *Adviser, Research Society of Pakistan, Lahore. Director, Historical Research Institute; Head, Department of History, University of the Punjab, Lahore, 1960–65. Author of* History of Muslims of India and Pakistan *and others.*
MUḤAMMAD IBN TUGHLUQ (Micropædia)

S.Ara.   Sinnappah Arasaratnam. *Professor of History, University of New England, Armidale, Australia. Author of* Ceylon *and others.*
SRI LANKA (*in part*)

S.A.Ri.   Stefan Albrecht Riesenfeld. *Emmanuel S. Heller Professor Emeritus of Law, University of California, Berkeley. Professor of Law, Hastings College of the Law, San Francisco. Author of* Creditors' Remedies and Debtors' Protection.
BUSINESS LAW (*in part*)

S.A.S.   Stanley A. Schumm. *Professor of Geology, Colorado State University, Fort Collins.*
RIVERS (*in part*)

S.A.V.   Sergey Arsentyevich Vodovozov (*d. 1983*). *Head, Section of Economics of North Caucasus, Central Economics Institute, R.S.F.S.R. Planning Committee, Moscow.*
UNION OF SOVIET SOCIALIST REPUBLICS (*in part*)

S.A.W.   Stephen A. Wurm. *Professor of Linguistics, Research School of Pacific Studies, Australian National University, Canberra. Author of* Languages of Australia and Tasmania; Papuan Languages of Oceania; *and others.*
LANGUAGES OF THE WORLD (*in part*)

S.A.Wo.   Stanley A. Wolpert. *Professor of History, University of California, Los Angeles. Author of* A New History of India *and others.*
INDIA (*in part*)

S.B.   Suri Balakrishna. *Former Acting Director, National Geophysical Research Institute, Council of Scientific and Industrial Research, Hyderābād, India. Author of* Earth.
INDIAN OCEAN, THE (*in part*)

S.Be.   Staffan Bergsten. *Novelist. Docent in Literary History, University of Uppsala, Sweden. Author of several works on 19th- and 20th-century Swedish poetry.*
SCANDINAVIAN LITERATURE (*in part*)

S.B.-G.   Swapna Banerjee-Guha. *Senior Lecturer in Geography, University of Bombay. Coauthor of* Declining City-core of an Indian Metropolis.
CALCUTTA (*in part*)

S.Bh.   The Rev. Sebastian Bullough, O.P. (*d. 1967*). *Lecturer in Hebrew, University of Cambridge.*
DOMINIC, SAINT (*in part*) (Micropædia)

S.Bl.   Solomon Bluhm. *Professor of Education, Hunter College, City University of New York, 1930–59.*
FROEBEL, FRIEDRICH (Micropædia)

S.B.O.   Sherry B. Ortner. *Professor of Anthropology, University of Michigan, Ann Arbor. Author of* High Religion: A Cultural and Political History of Sherpa Buddhism.
RITES AND CEREMONIES, SACRED (*in part*)

S.B.P.   Simon B. Parker. *Associate Professor of Hebrew Bible, Boston University. Author of* The Pre-Biblical Narrative Tradition.
MIDDLE EASTERN RELIGIONS, ANCIENT (*in part*)

S.Br.   Savile Bradbury. *Lecturer in Human Anatomy, University of Oxford; Fellow of Pembroke College, Oxford. Author of* The Evolution of the Microscope.
MICROSCOPES (*in part*)

S.Bu.   Salvino Busuttil. *Director General, Foundation for International Studies, Valletta, Malta. Author of* Fiscal Policy in Malta.
MALTA

S.C.   Seymour Cain. *Fellow, National Endowment for the Humanities, Washington, D.C., 1979–80. Senior Editor, Religion,* Encyclopædia Britannica, *Chicago, 1967–73. Author of* Gabriel Marcel.
BIBLICAL LITERATURE AND ITS CRITICAL INTERPRETATION (*in part*)
MARCEL, GABRIEL (*in part*) (Micropædia)

S.C.E.   Søren Christian Egerod. *Professor of East Asian Languages, University of Copenhagen. Editor,* Acta Orientalia *and* Acta Lingvistica Hafniensia. *Author of* Atayal-English Dictionary *and others.*
LANGUAGES OF THE WORLD (*in part*)

S.Ch.   Sripati Chandrasekhar. *Vice-Chancellor, Annamalai University, India, 1975–78. Member, Rajya Sabha (upper house of the Indian Parliament), 1964–70. Minister of Health, Family Planning, and Urban Development, Government of India, 1966–70. Author of* Asia's Population Problems *and others.*
ASIA (*in part*)

S.C.K.   Stephen Cole Kleene. *Emeritus Dean of Letters and Science; Emeritus Professor of Mathematics and Computer Science, University of Wisconsin, Madison. Author of* Introduction to Metamathematics; Mathematical Logic.
MATHEMATICS, THE FOUNDATIONS OF (*in part*)

S.C.O.C.   Sten C.O. Carlsson (*deceased*). *Professor of History, University of Uppsala, Sweden. Author of* Svensk historia *and others.*
CHARLES XIV JOHN (SWEDEN) (Micropædia)

S.C.P.   Stewart C. Prager. *Professor of Physics, University of Wisconsin, Madison.*
ENERGY CONVERSION (*in part*)

S.D.   Stanley Dufford. *Film and theatre make-up artist. Make-up and Wig Designer, Lyric Opera of Chicago.*
THEATRICAL PRODUCTION (*in part*)

S.-d.C.   Sen-dou Chang. *Professor of Geography, University of Hawaii at Manoa, Honolulu. Author of "Peking: The Growing Metropolis of Communist China" in* Geographical Review.
PEKING (*in part*)

S.De.   Samuel Decalo. *Professor of African Government, University of Natal, Durban, South Africa. Author of* Historical Dictionary of Togo.
WESTERN AFRICA (*in part*)

S.D.E.   Solomon D. Erulkar. *Professor of Pharmacology, University of Pennsylvania, Philadelphia.*
NERVES AND NERVOUS SYSTEMS (*in part*)

S.Der N.   Sirarpie Der Nersessian. *Emeritus Professor of Byzantine Art, Dumbarton Oaks Research Library and Collection, Washington, D.C. Author of* L'Illustration des psautiers grecs du moyen-âge; L'Art arménien.
PAINTING, THE HISTORY OF WESTERN (*in part*)

S.Di.   Sven Dijkgraaf. *Emeritus Professor of Comparative Physiology, State University of Utrecht, The Netherlands.*
SENSORY RECEPTION (*in part*)

S.Dr.   Seymour Drescher. *University Professor of History, University of Pittsburgh. Author of* Tocqueville and England *and others.*
TOCQUEVILLE, ALEXIS DE (Micropædia)

S.E.   Samuel Eilon. *Senior Research Fellow, Imperial College of Science and Technology, University of London; Professor of Management Science, 1963–89. Author of* Elements of Production Planning and Control *and others.*
INDUSTRIAL ENGINEERING AND PRODUCTION MANAGEMENT (*in part*)

S.E.B.   Susan Elizabeth Benenson. *Former Assistant Keeper, Department*

of Western Art, Ashmolean Museum, University of Oxford.
HOGARTH, WILLIAM (*in part*) (Micropædia)
PAINTING, THE HISTORY OF WESTERN (*in part*)
SCULPTURE, THE HISTORY OF WESTERN (*in part*)

S.E.C.   Sam E. Clagg. *Emeritus Professor of Geography, Marshall University, Huntington, West Virginia. Author of* West Virginia Historical Almanac *and others.*
UNITED STATES OF AMERICA (*in part*)

S.E.Cu.   Stanley Evan Curtis. *Professor of Animal Science, University of Illinois at Urbana-Champaign. Author of* Environmental Management in Animal Agriculture.
AGRICULTURAL SCIENCES (*in part*)

S.E.F.   Samuel Edward Finer. *Gladstone Professor Emeritus of Government and Public Administration, University of Oxford. Author of* Anonymous Empire: A Study of the Lobby in Great Britain *and others.*
POLITICAL PARTIES AND INTEREST GROUPS (*in part*)

S.E.H.   Svend E. Holsoe. *Associate Professor of Anthropology, University of Delaware, Newark. Coauthor of* Historical Dictionary of Liberia.
WESTERN AFRICA (*in part*)

Se.M.   Sengaku Mayeda. *Professor of Indian Philosophy, University of Tokyo. Editor of* Śaṅkara's Upadeśasāhasrī.
ŚAṄKARA (Micropædia)

S.E.McG.   Samuel Emmett McGregor (d. 1980). *Apiculturist, Bee Research Laboratory, U.S. Department of Agriculture, Tucson, Arizona. Coauthor of* Beekeeping in the United States.
FARMING AND AGRICULTURAL TECHNOLOGY (*in part*)

S.E.P.   Stephen E. Patterson. *Professor of History, University of New Brunswick, Fredericton. Author of* Political Parties in Revolutionary Massachusetts.
CANADA (*in part*)

S.Er.   Sirri Erinc. *Director, Institute of Marine Sciences and Geography, University of Istanbul. Author of* Geography of Eastern Anatolia.
TURKEY AND ANCIENT ANATOLIA (*in part*)

S.E.T.   Stephen E. Toulmin. *Avalon Professor in the Humanities, Northwestern University, Evanston, Illinois. Author of* Philosophy of Science.
PHILOSOPHIES OF THE BRANCHES OF KNOWLEDGE (*in part*)

S.F.Be.   Samuel Flagg Bemis (d. 1973). *Sterling Professor of Diplomatic History and Inter-American Relations, Yale University, 1945–61. Author of* John Quincy Adams and the Foundations of American Foreign Policy *and others.*
ADAMS, JOHN QUINCY (Micropædia)
MONROE, JAMES (Micropædia)

S.Fe.   Solomon Feferman. *Professor of Mathematics and Philosophy, Stanford University, California. Author of* The Number Systems: Foundations of Algebra and Analysis.
MATHEMATICS, THE FOUNDATIONS OF (*in part*)

S.F.W.   S.F. Wise. *Dean of Graduate Studies and Research, Carleton University, Ottawa. Coauthor of* Canada Views the United States: 19th Century Political Attitudes.
CANADA (*in part*)

S.F.We.   Stephen F. Weiss. *Professor and Chairman, Department of Computer Science, University of North Carolina at Chapel Hill.*
COMPUTERS (*in part*)

S.G.   Samy Gorgy. *Former Director General, Institute of Oceanography and Fisheries, Alexandria. Author of numerous articles on oceanography.*
ATLANTIC OCEAN, THE (*in part*)

S.G.B.   Stephen G. Brush. *Professor of the History of Science, University of Maryland, College Park. Author of* The History of Modern Science: A Guide to the Second Scientific Revolution, 1800–1950.
PHYSICAL SCIENCES, THE (*in part*)

S.G.C.   Sir Stanley George Clayton, M.D. (d. 1986). *Professor of Obstetrics and Gynecology, King's College Hospital Medical School, University of London, 1967–76.*
REPRODUCTION AND REPRODUCTIVE SYSTEMS (*in part*)

S.Ge.   Saul Genuth, M.D. *Professor of Medicine, Case Western Reserve University, Cleveland, Ohio.*
METABOLISM (*in part*)

S.G.F.B.   The Rev. Samuel G.F. Brandon (d. 1971). *Professor of Comparative Religion, Victoria University of Manchester, 1951–71. Author of* Man and His Destiny in the Great Religions *and others.*
DOCTRINES AND DOGMAS, RELIGIOUS (*in part*)
RITES AND CEREMONIES, SACRED (*in part*)

S.Gh.   Sisirkumar Ghose. *Professor of English, Visva-Bharati, Santiniketan, India. Author of* Mystics and Society.
RELIGIOUS EXPERIENCE (*in part*)

S.G.H.   Stephen G. Handzo. *Motion picture projectionist. Audiovisual technician, American Museum of Natural History, New York City. Contributor to* Film Sound: Theory and Practice.
MOTION PICTURES (*in part*)

S.G.K.   Samir G. Khalaf. *Former Professor of Sociology, American University of Beirut. Coauthor of* Hamra of Beirut: A Case of Rapid Urbanization.
BEIRUT: *Bibliography*
LEBANON (*in part*)

S.Gl.   Sidney Glazer (d. 1983). *Professor of History, Wayne State University, Detroit, 1955–76. Coauthor of* Michigan: From Primitive Wilderness to Industrial Commonwealth.
UNITED STATES OF AMERICA (*in part*)

S.Go.   Stephen Gottschalk. *Associate Professor of History, U.S. Naval Postgraduate School, Monterey, California, 1972–75. Author of* The Emergence of Christian Science in American Religious Life.
CHRISTIAN SCIENCE (Micropædia)

S.G.P.   Stanley G. Payne. *Professor of History, University of Wisconsin, Madison. Author of* The Franco Regime, 1936–75 *and others.*
FRANCO, FRANCISCO (Micropædia)

S.G.S.   Stanwyn G. Shetler. *Curator, Department of Botany, Smithsonian Institution, Washington, D.C.*
ANGIOSPERMS (*in part*)

S.G.W.   Stephen Graham Wright. *Former Adviser at the National Library of Ethiopia and at Haile Selassie I University, Addis Ababa.*
ETHIOPIAN LITERATURE (Micropædia)

S.H.   Simon Hornblower. *Lecturer in Ancient History, University of Oxford; Fellow and Tutor in Ancient History, Oriel College, Oxford. Author of* The Greek World, 479–323 B.C.; Thucydides.
GREEK AND ROMAN CIVILIZATIONS, ANCIENT (*in part*)

S.Ha.   Shirō Hattori. *Director, Tokyo Institute for Advanced Studies of Language. Emeritus Professor of Linguistics, University of Tokyo. Author of* Methods in Linguistics; Genealogy of Japanese; *and others.*
LANGUAGES OF THE WORLD (*in part*)

S.H.B.   Samuel H. Baron. *Professor of History, University of North Carolina at Chapel Hill. Author of* Plekhanov: The Father of Russian Marxism *and others.*
PLEKHANOV, GEORGY VALENTINOVICH (Micropædia)

Sh.Bi.   Sh. Bira. *Head of Section, Institute of History, Academy of Sciences of the Mongolian People's Republic, Ulaanbaatar.*
MONGOLIA (*in part*)

S.H.Bl.   Sheldon H. Blank (d. 1989). *Professor of Bible, Hebrew Union College-Jewish Institute of Religion, Cincinnati, Ohio, 1926–78. Author of* Prophetic Faith in Isaiah *and others.*
ISAIAH (Micropædia)

S.He.   Stanislaw Herbst (d. 1973). *Professor of Pre-18th Century Polish History, University of Warsaw. President, Polish Historic Society, Warsaw. Coauthor of* A Thousand Years of Polish History.
KOŚCIUSZKO, TADEUSZ (Micropædia)

S.H.F.L.   Seton H.F. Lloyd. *Emeritus Professor of Western Asiatic Archaeology, University of London. Author of* Early Highland Peoples of Anatolia; Twin Rivers; Ancient Turkey; *and others.*
ASIA (*in part*)
INDIA (*in part*)
MIDDLE EASTERN ARTS AND ARCHITECTURE, ANCIENT (*in part*)
TURKEY AND ANCIENT ANATOLIA (*in part*)

Sh.H.   Shigeru Hayashi (d. 1985). *Professor, Institute of Social Science, University of Tokyo. Author of* The Pacific War.
KONOE FUMIMARO, KOSHAKU (Micropædia)

Sh.Ha.   Shirley Hazzard. *Novelist and writer on Italian cultural themes. Author of* The Transit of Venus; The Bay of Noon; *and others.*
NAPLES

S.H.J.   Susan Heyner Joshi. *Former Professor of Biology, Philadelphia College of Pharmacy and Science.*
BIOLOGICAL SCIENCES, THE (*in part*)

S.H.L.   Sandra H. Levinson. *Executive Director, Center for Cuban Studies, Inc., New York City. Coeditor of* Venceremos Brigade.
WEST INDIES, THE (*in part*)

Sh.M.   Shula E. Marks. *Director and Professor of Commonwealth History, Institute of Commonwealth Studies, University of London. Author of* Reluctant Rebellion: The 1906–08 Disturbances in Natal *and others.*
SOUTHERN AFRICA (*in part*)

S.H.N.   Seyyed Hossein Nasr. *University Professor of Islamic Studies, George Washington University, Washington, D.C. Author of* Three Muslim Sages.
AVICENNA (Micropædia)

S.H.O.   Simeon Hongo Ominde. *Professor of Geography; Director, Population Studies and Research Institute, University of Nairobi, Kenya. Author of* Land and Population Movements in Kenya.
EASTERN AFRICA (*in part*)

S.H.P.   Stewart Henry Perowne (d. 1989). *Orientalist, historian, and lecturer. Author of* The Life and Times of Herod the Great; The End of the Roman World; The Political Background of the New Testament; *and others.*
CLEOPATRA VII THEA PHILOPATOR (Micropædia)
HEROD (Micropædia)
JERUSALEM (*in part*)
JULIAN (Micropædia)

S.H.S.   Stephen H. Schneider. *Senior Scientist and Head, Natural Systems Group, National Center for Atmospheric Research, Boulder, Colorado. Editor,* Climatic Change. *Author of* Global Warming: Are We Entering the Greenhouse Century?
CLIMATE AND WEATHER (*in part*)

S.H.St.   S. Henry Steinberg (d. 1969). *Editor,* The Statesman's Year-Book, *1946–69. Author of* The Thirty Years' War and the Conflict for European Hegemony, 1600–1660 *and others.*
WALLENSTEIN, ALBRECHT WENZEL EUSEBIUS VON, HERZOG VON FRIEDLAND (Micropædia)

Sh.Ts.   Sh. Tsevegmid. *Director, Institute of Geography and Geocryology,* Academy of Sciences of the Mongolian People's Republic, Ulaanbaatar.
MONGOLIA (*in part*)

S.H.W.   Stanley H. Weitzman. *Curator of Fishes, Division of Fishes, National Museum of Natural History, Smithsonian Institution, Washington, D.C. Author of numerous articles on fishes.*
FISHES (*in part*)

S.I.B.   Solomon Ilich Bruk. *Chief researcher, Institute of Ethnography, Academy of Sciences of the U.S.S.R., Moscow. Coauthor and editor of* Ethnographic Maps of Asian Countries.
ASIA (*in part*)

S.I.F.   Stanley I. Fischler. *Broadcaster, Sports Channel TV, New York City. Columnist,* The Hockey News. *Coauthor of* The Hockey Encyclopedia; Everybody's Hockey Book.
SPORTS, MAJOR TEAM AND INDIVIDUAL (*in part*)

Si.L.   The Rev. Sione Lātūkefu. *Principal, Pacific Theological College, Suva, Fiji. Author of* Church and State in Tonga.
PACIFIC ISLANDS (*in part*)

Si.T.   Sidney Thomas. *Emeritus Professor of Fine Arts, Syracuse University, New York. Editor of* Images of Man; *coeditor of* The Nature of Art.
ARTS, PRACTICE AND PROFESSION OF THE (*in part*)

S.J.B.   Shahid Javed Burki. *Director, International Bank for Reconstruction and Development, Washington, D.C. Author of* Pakistan Under Bhutto *and others.*
PAKISTAN (*in part*)

S.J.F.   Stephen Joseph Fonash. *Alumni Professor of Engineering Sciences; Director, Center for Electronic Materials and Processing, Pennsylvania State University, University Park. Author of* Solar Cell Device Physics.
ENERGY CONVERSION (*in part*)

S.J.G.   Stephen J. Greenblatt. *Class of 1932 Professor of English Literature, University of California, Berkeley. Author of* Renaissance Self-Fashioning: From More to Shakespeare *and others.*
ELIZABETH I OF ENGLAND

S.J.K.B.   Samuel John Kenneth Baker. *Emeritus Professor of Geography, Makerere University, Kampala, Uganda. Honorary Lecturer in Geography, University of Leicester, England, 1968–74.*
AFRICA (*in part*)

S.J.S.   Stanford Jay Shaw. *Professor of History, University of California, Los Angeles. Editor in Chief,* International Journal of Middle East Studies. *Author of* History of the Ottoman Empire and Modern Turkey *and others.*
TURKEY AND ANCIENT ANATOLIA (*in part*)

S.K.   Shinzo Kiuchi. *Emeritus Professor of Geography, University of Tokyo. Coeditor of* Japanese Cities.

ŌSAKA-KŌBE METROPOLITAN AREA (*in part*)
TOKYO-YOKOHAMA METROPOLITAN AREA

S.Ka.   Sidney Karin. *Director, San Diego Supercomputer Center, California. Coauthor of* The Supercomputer Era.
SUPERCOMPUTER (Micropædia)

S.Kh.   Stella Kramrisch. *Emeritus Curator, Indian and Himalayan Art, Philadelphia Museum of Art. Adjunct Professor of Indian Art, Institute of Fine Arts, New York University, New York City. Author of* The Art of Nepal; The Presence of Siva; *and others.*
CENTRAL ASIAN ARTS (*in part*)

S.K.S.   Sylvester K. Stevens (d. 1974). *Executive Director, Pennsylvania Historical and Museum Commission, Harrisburg, 1956–72. Author of* Pennsylvania: Birthplace of a Nation.
PHILADELPHIA (*in part*)

S.La.   Sylvia Dorothy Lawler, M.D. *Emeritus Professor of Human Genetics, Institute of Cancer Research, University of London. Former Honorary Consultant in Immunology and Cytogenetics, Royal Marsden Hospital, London. Coauthor of* Human Blood Groups and Inheritance.
BLOOD (*in part*)

S.L.D.   S. Lawrence Dingman. *Professor of Hydrology and Water Resources, University of New Hampshire, Durham.*
ICE AND ICE FORMATIONS (*in part*)

S.Lr.   Samuel Leiter. *Former Seminary Professor of Hebrew Literature, Jewish Theological Seminary of America, New York City. Editor of* Selected Stories of S.Y. Agnon.
HEBREW LITERATURE (*in part*)

S.L.R.   Stanley L. Robbins, M.D. *Visiting Professor of Pathology, Harvard University. Senior Pathologist, Brigham and Womens Hospital, Boston. Author of* Pathologic Basis of Disease *and others.*
DISEASE (*in part*)

S.L.Sm.   Sigmund L. Smith. *Emeritus Professor of Metallurgical Engineering, University of Arizona, Tucson. Author of* Ore Microscopy.
INDUSTRIES, EXTRACTION AND PROCESSING (*in part*)

S.Ma.   Sibyl Marcuse. *Curator, Yale University Collection of Musical Instruments, 1952–60. Author of* Musical Instruments: A Comprehensive Dictionary; A Survey of Musical Instruments.
MUSICAL INSTRUMENTS (*in part*)

S.M.B.   Surinder M. Bhardwaj. *Professor of Geography, Kent State University, Ohio.*
ASIA (*in part*)

S.McC.H.   Sarah McCanless Howell. *Professor of History, Middle Tennessee State University, Murfreesboro.*
UNITED STATES OF AMERICA (*in part*)

S.McD.   Sheila D. McDonough. *Professor of Religion, Sir George Williams University, Montreal. Author*

of Muhammad Ali Jinnah, Maker of Modern Pakistan *and others.*
IQBĀL, SIR MUḤAMMAD (Micropædia)

S.McG.   Sharon McGrayne. *Science writer; former journalist.*
ATOMS (*in part*)
ELECTRICITY AND MAGNETISM (*in part*)

S.M.Ci.   Sima M. Čirković. *Professor of the Medieval History of Yugoslavia, University of Belgrade. Author of* Duke Stefan Vukčić Kosača and His Time; Istorija srednjovekovne bosanske države.
STEFAN, DUŠAN (Micropædia)

S.M.D.   Stephanie Mary Dalley. *Senior Research Fellow, Somerville College, Oxford; Shillito Fellow in Assyriology, Oriental Institute, University of Oxford.*
SARGON (AKKAD) (Micropædia)

S.M.G.   Stanley M. Garn. *Professor of Human Nutrition and of Anthropology; Fellow of the Center for Human Growth and Development, University of Michigan, Ann Arbor. Author of* Human Races.
EVOLUTION, HUMAN (*in part*)

S.M.H.   Sigismund M. Herschdoerfer. *Consultant and former Chief Chemist and Quality Controller, T. Wall & Sons Ltd. (ice cream), London. Editor of* Quality Control in the Food Industry.
FOOD PROCESSING (*in part*)

S.Mi.   Sandra Millikin. *Free-lance architectural historian. Lecturer in the History of Art, Open University, Walton, England. 1971–73.*
ADAM, ROBERT (Micropædia)
ARCHITECTURE, THE HISTORY OF WESTERN (*in part*)

S.M.I.   S.M. Ikram (d. 1973). *Director, Institute of Islāmic Culture, Lahore, Pakistan. Author of* History of Muslim Civilisation in India and Pakistan *and others.*
AHMAD KHAN, SIR SAYYID (*in part*) (Micropædia)

S.M.M.   Sidnie M. Manton (d. 1979). *Reader in Zoology, King's College, University of London, 1949–60.*
SUPPORTIVE AND CONNECTIVE TISSUES (*in part*)

S.Mo.   Sitanshu Mookerjee. *President, Indian Institute of Geography. Principal, Morris College, Nāgpur University, India.*
INDIA (*in part*)

S.M.R.   Sidney Martin Robbins. *Chase Manhattan Professor Emeritus of Financial Institutions, Columbia University. Author of* Securities Markets *and others.*
MARKETS (*in part*)

S.M.S.   Shekou M. Sesay. *Deputy Secretary-General, Mano River Union, Freetown, Sierra Leone. Coauthor of* Sierra Leone in Maps.
WESTERN AFRICA (*in part*)

S.M.Sn.   Samuel Miklos Stern (d. 1969). *Fellow of All Souls College, University of Oxford, 1957–69. Author of* Les Chansons mozarabes; Fatimid Decrees; *and others.*
COINS AND COINAGE (*in part*)

S.M.Sz.   S.M. Sze. *Member of the technical staff, AT&T Bell Laboratories, Murray Hill, New Jersey. Author of* Physics of Semiconductor Devices.
ELECTRONICS (*in part*)

S.N.B.   Steven N. Blair. *Director, Epidemiology, Institute for Aerobics Research, The Aerobics Center, Dallas, Texas. Vice President for Basic and Applied Sciences, American College of Sports Medicine.*
EXERCISE AND PHYSICAL CONDITIONING (*in part*)

S.N.M.   S.N. Mukerji. *Dean, Faculty of Education, Maharaja Sayajirao University of Baroda, India, 1949–65. Dean of Studies, National Institute of Education, New Delhi, 1965–68. Author of* History of Education in India *and others.*
EDUCATION, HISTORY OF (*in part*)

S.N.R.   Sergey Nikolayevich Ryazantsev (d. 1980). *Professor of Economic Geography, Moscow Oblast Pedagogical Institute. Author of* Kirgizskaya S.S.R. *and many others.*
UNION OF SOVIET SOCIALIST REPUBLICS (*in part*)

S.N.W.   S. Nicholas Woodward. *Fellow, Templeton College—the Oxford Centre for Management Studies, University of Oxford. Coauthor of* Finance for Managers.
BUSINESS ORGANIZATION (*in part*)

S.O.F.   Stephen Oliver Fought. *Professor, U.S. Naval War College, Newport, Rhode Island. Author of* SDI: A Policy Analysis.
WAR, THE TECHNOLOGY OF (*in part*)

So.T.   Sol Tax. *Emeritus Professor of Anthropology, University of Chicago. Director, Center for the Study of Man, Smithsonian Institution, Washington, D.C., 1968–76. Editor,* Current Anthropology, *1957–74. Authority noted for his work in American Indian ethnology and in the theory of social anthropology.*
BOAS, FRANZ (Micropædia)

S.P.   Simeon Potter (d. 1976). *Bains Professor of English Language and Philology, University of Liverpool, 1945–65. Author of* Our Language; Changing English; *and others.*
LANGUAGES OF THE WORLD (*in part*)

S.P.A.   Sara Prince Anastaplo. *Researcher. Author of* Alexander The Great: King of Asia.
GREECE (*in part*)

S.P.C.   Shiba P. Chatterjee (d. 1989). *Professor of Geography, University of Calcutta. Author of* Physiography of India *and others; editor of* Selected Papers of the 21st International Geographical Congress (*vol. 1–4*).
ASIA (*in part*)
INDIA (*in part*)

S.P.D.   Stephen Porter Dunn. *Director of Research, Highgate Road Social Science Research Station, Inc., Berkeley, California. Coauthor of* The Peasants of Central Russia.
ASIAN PEOPLES AND CULTURES (*in part*)
UNION OF SOVIET SOCIALIST REPUBLICS (*in part*)

S.Pi.   Shlomo Pines (d. 1990). *Professor of General and Jewish Philosophy, Hebrew University of Jerusalem, 1952–77. Author of* Scholasticism after Thomas Aquinas and the Teachings of Hasdai Crescas and his Predecessors; *translator of* Maimonides' Guide of the Perplexed.
JUDAISM (*in part*)

S.P.J.   S. Paul Johnston (d. 1985). *Director, National Air and Space Museum, Smithsonian Institution, Washington, D.C., 1964–69. Author of* Horizons Unlimited *and others.*
SIKORSKY, IGOR (Micropædia)
TRANSPORTATION (*in part*)

S.P.Jn.   Stanley Percival Jackson. *Emeritus Professor of Geography, University of the Witwatersrand, Johannesburg; Deputy Vice-Chancellor, 1965–73.*
SOUTHERN AFRICA (*in part*)

S.P.V.   Shanti Prasad Varma. *Former Director, Institute of Development Studies, Jaipur, India. Former Chairman, Department of Political Science; former Director, South Asia Studies Centre, University of Rājasthān, Jaipur. Author of* A Study of Maratha Diplomacy: Anglo-Maratha Relations, 1772–1783 *and others.*
INDIA (*in part*)

S.R.   Sydney Ross. *Emeritus Professor of Chemistry, Rensselaer Polytechnic Institute, Troy, New York. Coauthor of* On Physical Adsorption; Colloids and Interfaces.
PRIESTLEY, JOSEPH (Micropædia)

S.Ra.   Sheila Ralphs. *Former Senior Lecturer in Italian, Victoria University of Manchester, England.*
ITALIAN LITERATURE (*in part*)

S.R.M.   S. Roy Meadow. *Professor and Head, Department of Paediatrics and Child Health, St. James's Hospital, University of Leeds, England. Coauthor of* The Child and His Symptoms.
CHILDHOOD DISEASES AND DISORDERS (*in part*)

S.Rs.   Sir Sydney Roberts (d. 1966). *Vice-Chancellor, University of Cambridge, 1949–51; Master of Pembroke College, Cambridge, 1948–58. A noted Johnson scholar. Author of* Doctor Johnson *and others; editor of* Samuel Johnson, Writer; *and many other works on Johnson.*
JOHNSON, SAMUEL (*in part*)

S.R.S.   Stuart Reynolds Schram. *Emeritus Professor of Politics, School of Oriental and African Studies, University of London. Author of* The Thought of Mao Tse-tung *and others.*
MAO TSE-TUNG

S.R.Se.   Stan R. Seagle. *Vice President, Research and Technical Development, RMI Titanium Company, Niles, Ohio.*

INDUSTRIES, EXTRACTION AND
PROCESSING (*in part*)

S.R.T.   Steven R. Tannenbaum.
*Professor of Chemistry and of
Toxocology, Massachusetts Institute of
Technology, Cambridge. Coeditor of
Single-Cell Protein and others.*
FOOD PROCESSING (*in part*)

S.S.   Sergio Sarmiento. *Editor in
Chief, Spanish-language publications,
Encyclopædia Britannica Publishers,
Inc., Mexico City. Author of
Lucubraciones: Ensayos económicos y
políticos.*
MEXICO CITY (*in part*)

S.Sa.   Stanley Sadie. *Editor,* The
New Grove Dictionary of Music and
Musicians, *London. Editor,* The Musical
Times, *1967–87. Music Critic,* The
Times (*London*), *1964–81.*
MOZART

S.S.A.   Stanislas Spero Adotevi.
*Director, Institute of Applied Research,
Porto-Novo, Benin. Author of* Demain
la veille.
WESTERN AFRICA (*in part*)

S.S.C.   S.S. Chern. *Emeritus Professor
of Mathematics, University of California,
Berkeley. Author of* Complex Manifolds
Without Potential Theory.
GEOMETRY (*in part*)

S.S.Ch.   Sukhdev Singh Chib. *Reader
and Head, Geography Department,
Directorate of Correspondence Courses,
Panjab University, Chandigarh, India.
Author of* Nineteen Fateful Months: A
Socio-economic Study *and others.*
INDIA (*in part*)

S.S.D.J.   S.S.D. Jones (d. 1990).
*Navigation consultant. Former Head,
Navigation and Guidance Division,
Royal Aircraft Establishment,
Farnborough, England. Author of
"Recent Developments in Radio
Navigation" in* Encyclopaedic Dictionary
of Physics.
NAVIGATION (*in part*)

S.S.F.   Sheppard Sunderland Frere.
*Emeritus Professor of the Archaeology
of the Roman Empire, University of
Oxford. Author of* Britannia: A History
of Roman Britain *and others.*
UNITED KINGDOM (*in part*)

S.S.H.   Syed Sajjad Husain. *Professor
of English, Umm al-Qūrah University,
Mecca, 1975–85. Vice-Chancellor,
University of Rājshāhi, Bangladesh,
1969–71. Author of* Descriptive
Catalogue of Bengali Manuscripts.
BANGLADESH (*in part*)

S.Si.   Sinnathurai Sivasubramaniam.
*Senior Lecturer in Agronomy, Eastern
University, Chenkaladi, Sri Lanka.
Project Coordinator, Agricultural
Research Project, Tea Research Institute
of Sri Lanka, Talawakelle, 1988.*
BEVERAGE PRODUCTION (*in part*)

S.Sk.   Stephan Skalweit. *Emeritus
Professor of Modern History, Rhenish
Friedrich Wilhelm University of Bonn.
Author of* Frankreich und Friedrich der

Grosse *and others.*
FREDERICK WILLIAM (BRANDENBURG)
(Micropædia)

S.Sm.   Stephen Smale. *Professor of
Mathematics, University of California,
Berkeley. Coeditor of* Global Analysis.
ANALYSIS (IN MATHEMATICS) (*in part*)

S.Sp.   The Rev. Sidney Spencer
(deceased). *Minister, Bath and
Trowbridge Unitarian Churches,
England. Principal of Manchester
College, University of Oxford, 1951–56.
Author of* Mysticism in World Religion.
CHRISTIANITY (*in part*)

S.St.   Sewell Stokes (d. 1979). *Author
and dramatist. Author of* Isadora: An
Intimate Portrait *and others.*
DUNCAN, ISADORA (Micropædia)

S.T.   Stith Thompson (d. 1976).
*Distinguished Service Professor
of English and Folklore, Indiana
University, Bloomington, 1953–55.
Author of* Motif-Index of Folk-Literature
(6 vol.); The Folktale; *and others.*
FOLK ARTS (*in part*)

S.Ta.   Shin'ichi Tani. *Former
Professor of the History of Japanese
Art, Tokyo University of Arts. Author of*
Muromachi-jidai bijutsushiron ("A Study
on Arts of the Muromachi Period");
Bijutsushi ("History of Japanese Art").
EAST ASIAN ARTS (*in part*)

S.Tr.   Stanley Trapido. *Lecturer in the
Government of New States, University
of Oxford.*
SOUTHERN AFRICA (*in part*)

S.V.A.   Stanley Victor Anderson.
*Professor of Political Science, University
of California, Santa Barbara. Author of*
The Nordic Council.
DENMARK (*in part*)

S.V.G.   Stephen Vincent Grancsay
(d. 1980). *Curator of Arms and Armor,
Metropolitan Museum of Art, New York
City, 1929–64. Author of classic studies
on arms and metalwork.*
DECORATIVE ARTS AND FURNISHINGS
(*in part*)

S.V.U.   Sergei Vasilievich Utechin.
*Former Professor of Russian History,
Pennsylvania State University, University
Park. Author of* Everyman's Concise
Encyclopædia of Russia *and others.*
UNION OF SOVIET SOCIALIST REPUBLICS
(*in part*)

S.W.B.   Salo Wittmayer Baron (d.
1989). *Professor of Jewish History,
Literature, and Institutions, Columbia
University, 1930–63. Author of* A Social
and Religious History of the Jews.
JUDAISM (*in part*)

S.We.   Stanley Weintraub. *Evan Pugh
Professor of Arts and Humanities,
Pennsylvania State University, University
Park. Author of* Private Shaw and Public
Shaw: A Dual Portrait of Lawrence of
Arabia and G.B.S.; *coeditor of* Evolution
of a Revolt: Early Postwar Writings of
T.E. Lawrence.
LAWRENCE, T.E. (*in part*) (Micropædia)

SHAW, GEORGE BERNARD (*in part*)
(Micropædia)

S.W.F.   Sidney W. Fox. *Distinguished
Research Professor of Plant Biology
and of Electrical Engineering, Southern
Illinois University, Carbondale. Former
Director, Institute for Molecular and
Cellular Evolution; former Research
Professor, University of Miami, Coral
Gables. Coauthor of* Molecular Evolution
and the Origin of Life.
OPARIN, ALEKSANDR IVANOVICH
(Micropædia)

S.W.Fi.   Shirley W. Fischler. *Adjunct
Lecturer in Journalism, Columbia
University. Coauthor of* The Hockey
Encyclopedia; Everybody's Hockey
Book.
SPORTS, MAJOR TEAM AND INDIVIDUAL
(*in part*)

S.W.J.   Stanley W. Jacob, M.D.
*Gerlinger Professor of Surgery, Oregon
Health Sciences University, Portland.
Author of* Structure and Function in
Man.
CIRCULATION AND CIRCULATORY
SYSTEMS (*in part*)

**S.W.K.M.   Stephen William Kenneth
Morgan.** *Former Director, Imperial
Smelting Processes Limited, Avonmouth,
England.*
CHEMICAL ELEMENTS (*in part*)

S.Y.C.   Shou Yi Chen (d. 1978).
*Professor of Chinese Culture, Pomona
College, Claremont, California, 1941–
67. Author of* Chinese Literature: A
Historical Introduction.
CHINESE LITERATURE (*in part*)

S.-y.H.   Shan-yüan Hsieh. *Former
Assistant Professor of Philosophy,
Haverford College, Pennsylvania.*
TSENG KUO-FAN (Micropædia)

S.Z.L.   Sid Z. Leiman. *Professor
of Jewish History and Literature;
Chairman, Department of Judaic
Studies, Brooklyn College, City
University of New York.*
BA'AL SHEM ṬOV (*in part*) (Micropædia)
JUDAISM (*in part*)

T.A.J.   Thomas Athol Joyce (d. 1942).
*Subkeeper, Department of Ethnography,
British Museum, London, 1902–38.*
SOUTH AMERICA (*in part*)

T.A.K.   Thomas A. Kochan. *Professor
of Industrial Relations, Massachusetts
Institute of Technology, Cambridge.
Coauthor of* The Transformation of
American Industrial Relations.
WORK AND EMPLOYMENT (*in part*)

T.A.S.   Thomas A. Schafer. *Emeritus
Professor of Church History, McCormick
Theological Seminary, Chicago.*
EDWARDS, JONATHAN (Micropædia)

T.A.Sa.   Tilde A. Sankovitch.
*Professor and Chair, Department of
French and Italian, Northwestern
University, Evanston, Illinois. Author of*
French Women Writers and the Book
and others.
ANTWERP (*in part*)
MONTAIGNE

T.B.B.   Thomas B. Bottomore.
*Emeritus Professor of Sociology,
University of Sussex, Brighton, England.
Author of* Classes in Modern Society;
Elites and Society.
SOCIAL DIFFERENTIATION (*in part*)

T.B.C.   Thomas B. Cochran. *Senior
Staff Scientist, Natural Resources
Defense Council, Inc., Washington,
D.C. Coauthor and coeditor of* Nuclear
Weapons Databook (*vol. 1–4*).
WAR, THE TECHNOLOGY OF (*in part*)

T.B.H.   Thomas B. Hinton (d. 1976).
*Associate Professor of Anthropology,
University of Arizona, Tucson. Author
of* A Survey of Indian Assimilation in
Eastern Sonora.
AMERICAN INDIANS (*in part*)

**T.B.S.   Theodore B. Schwartz,
M.D.** *Clinical Professor of Medicine,
University of Washington, Seattle.
Editor,* Year Book of Endocrinology,
1964–86.
ENDOCRINE SYSTEMS (*in part*)

T.B.T.   Terence Barrington Thomas.
*Director, Gladding International Ltd.
Angling correspondent,* The Field, *and
others. Presenter of "Angling Today,"
Associated Television, Birmingham,
England. Author of* Casting.
FISHING (*in part*) (Micropædia)

T.C.   Theresa Clay. *Former Senior
Principal Scientific Officer, Department
of Entomology, British Museum (Natural
History), London.*
INSECTS (*in part*)

T.C.C.   Timothy C. Champion. *Senior
Lecturer in Archaeology, University of
Southampton, England. Coauthor of*
Prehistoric Europe.
EUROPEAN HISTORY AND CULTURE
    (*in part*)

T.C.M.   Terence Croft Mitchell.
*Keeper, Department of Western Asiatic
Antiquities, British Museum, London,
1985–89.*
HISTORY, THE STUDY OF (*in part*)

T.C.McC.   T.C. McCaskie. *Lecturer
in the Social History of West Africa,
University of Birmingham, England.*
WESTERN AFRICA (*in part*)

T.C.O.   Tobias Chant Owen. *Professor
of Astronomy, University of Hawaii at
Manoa, Honolulu. Coauthor of* The
Planetary System.
SOLAR SYSTEM, THE (*in part*)

T.C.P.   Thomas C. Patterson. *Professor
of Anthropology and History, Temple
University, Philadelphia. Author of* The
Inca Empire *and others.*
PRE-COLUMBIAN CIVILIZATIONS (*in part*)

**T.Cr.   The Rev. Theodore Crowley,
O.F.M.** (d. 1990). *Professor of Scholastic
Philosophy, Queen's University of
Belfast, Northern Ireland. Author of*
Roger Bacon: The Problem of the Soul
in His Philosophical Commentaries.
BACON, ROGER (*in part*) (Micropædia)

T.C.R.   Thomas C. Reeves. *Professor
of History, University of Wisconsin,
Parkside. Author of* Freedom and the

Foundation: The Fund for the Republic
in the Era of McCarthyism *and others.*
EISENHOWER, DWIGHT D. (Micropædia)

T.C.S.   Thomas Clark Shedd. *Editorial
Director,* Modern Railroads, *Chicago.*
TRANSPORTATION (*in part*)

T.C.W.   T. Carroll Wilson. *Company
Historian, Hills Bros. Coffee, Inc.,
San Francisco; Director, 1964–68;
Vice President, 1945–66. Author of*
The Art of Coffee Making.
BEVERAGE PRODUCTION (*in part*)

T.C.Y., Jr.   T. Cuyler Young, Jr.
*Curator, West Asian Department, Royal
Ontario Museum, Toronto. Professor
of Near Eastern Studies, University of
Toronto. Author of "A Comparative
Ceramic Chronology for Western Iran,
1500–500* B.C." *in* Iran.
IRAN (*in part*)

T.D.   Theodosius Dobzhansky (d.
1975). *Professor of Biology, Rockefeller
University, New York City, 1962–
71. Adjunct Professor of Genetics,
University of California, Davis, 1971–75.
Author of* Mankind Evolving; Genetics
of the Evolutionary Process; *author
of numerous papers on evolutionary
genetics.*
GENETICS AND HEREDITY, THE
    PRINCIPLES OF (*in part*)

T.d.A.   The Rev. Tarsicio de Azcona.
*Former Professor of Theology, University
of Navarre, Pamplona, Spain. Author of*
Isabel la Católica.
FERDINAND II (SPAIN: ARAGON)
    (Micropædia)

T.De.   T. Delevoryas. *Professor of
Botany, University of Texas at Austin.
Author of* Morphology and Evolution of
Fossil Plants *and others.*
GYMNOSPERMS (*in part*)

T.E.A.   Thomas Edward Allibone.
*External Professor Emeritus of Electrical
Engineering, University of Leeds,
England. Robert Kitchin Research
Professor of Physics, City University,
London. Director, Research Laboratory,
Associated Electrical Industries,
Aldermaston, England, 1946–63. Author
of* The Release and Use of Nuclear
Energy *and others.*
RUTHERFORD

T.E.Ar.   Terence Edward Armstrong.
*Emeritus Reader in Arctic Studies, Scott
Polar Research Institute, University
of Cambridge. Coauthor of* The
Circumpolar North.
ARCTIC, THE (*in part*)

T.E.F.   Thomas E. Faber. *Lecturer in
Physics, University of Cambridge; Fellow
of Corpus Christi College, Cambridge.
Author of* Introduction to the Theory of
Liquid Metals.
MECHANICS (*in part*)

T.E.G.   T.E. Gudava (deceased).
*Professor of Linguistics, Tbilisi State
University, Georgian S.S.R.*
LANGUAGES OF THE WORLD (*in part*)

T.E.Je.   Thomas Edmund Jessop (d.
1980). *Ferens Professor of Philosophy,*

*University of Hull, England, 1928–61.
Editor of* Bibliography of David Hume
and of Scottish Philosophy.
HUME (*in part*)

Te.K.   Terrence Kaufman. *Professor of
Anthropology and Linguistics, University
of Pittsburgh. Coauthor of* Language
Contact, Creolization, and Genetic
Linguistics.
LANGUAGES OF THE WORLD (*in part*)

T.E.K.   Thomas Edward Keys.
*Emeritus Professor of the History of
Medicine, Mayo Graduate School of
Medicine, University of Minnesota,
Rochester. Emeritus Librarian, Mayo
Foundation. Author of* The History of
Surgical Anesthesia *and others.*
MAYO FAMILY (Micropædia)

T.E.Kr.   Thomas Edvard Krogh.
*Director, Geochronology Laboratory,
Royal Ontario Museum, Toronto.*
GEOCHRONOLOGY (*in part*)

T.E.O'T.   Thomas E. O'Toole.
*Associate Professor of Interdisciplinary
Studies; Director of African Studies,
St. Cloud State University, Minnesota.
Author of* Historical Dictionary of
Guinea; Central African Republic: The
Continent's Hidden Heart.
CENTRAL AFRICA (*in part*)
WESTERN AFRICA (*in part*)

T.F.B.   Thomas F. Budinger, M.D.
*Professor of Research Medicine,
Donner Laboratory, Lawrence
Berkeley Laboratory; Professor of
Bioinstrumentation, University of
California, Berkeley. Operations Officer,
International Ice Patrol, 1959–60.*
ICE AND ICE FORMATIONS (*in part*)

T.F.McG.   Thomas F. McGann (d.
1982). *Professor of History, University
of Texas at Austin. Author of* Argentina,
the Divided Land; Argentina, the United
States, and the Inter-American System,
1880–1914.
PERÓN, JUAN (*in part*) (Micropædia)

T.F.T.   Thomas Frederick Tout (d.
1929). *President, Royal Historical
Society, 1925–28. Professor of History,
Victoria University of Manchester, 1890–
1925. Author of* Edward the First; The
Place of the Reign of Edward II in
English History; *and others.*
EDWARD III (ENGLAND AND GREAT
    BRITAIN) (*in part*) (Micropædia)

T.G.   Sir Tyrone Guthrie (d. 1971).
*Theatrical director. Chancellor, Queen's
University of Belfast, Northern Ireland,
1963–70. Author of* A Life in the
Theatre; New Theatre; *and others.*
THEATRE, THE ART OF THE (*in part*)

T.G.B.   Thomas G. Benedek, M.D.
*Professor of Medicine; Adjunct Professor
of History, University of Pittsburgh.
Former Chief, Outpatient Department
and Rheumatology Section, Veterans
Administration Hospital, Pittsburgh.*
SUPPORTIVE AND CONNECTIVE
    TISSUES (*in part*)

**T.G.H.J.   Thomas Garnet Henry
James.** *Former Keeper, Department of
Egyptian Antiquities, British Museum,*

London. *Editor of* The Hekanakhte Papers, *and* Other Middle Kingdom Documents.
EGYPTIAN ARTS AND ARCHITECTURE, ANCIENT

T.G.Ms. **Thomas G. Mathews.** *Secretary-General, Association of Caribbean Universities and Research Institutes, San Juan, Puerto Rico. Research Professor of History, University of Puerto Rico, 1969–80. Author of* Puerto Rican Politics and the New Deal.
WEST INDIES, THE (*in part*)

T.G.P.S. **T.G. Percival Spear** (d. 1982). *Fellow of Selwyn College, Cambridge; Lecturer in History, University of Cambridge, 1963–69. Author of* India: A Modern History *and others; coauthor and editor of* Oxford History of India (3rd ed.).
AURANGZEB (Micropædia)
BĀBUR (Micropædia)
CLIVE, ROBERT, 1ST BARON CLIVE OF PLASSEY (Micropædia)
INDIA (*in part*)

T.Gr. **Theodore C. Grame.** *Author of* Folk Music; America's Ethnic Music; *and others.*
MUSICAL INSTRUMENTS (*in part*)

T.H.B. **Thornton Howard Bridgewater.** *Chief Engineer, Television, British Broadcasting Corporation, 1962–68.*
BROADCASTING (*in part*)

T.H.C. **Theodore Hsi-en Chen.** *Emeritus Professor of Education and Asian Studies, University of Southern California, Los Angeles. Author of* The Maoist Educational Revolution.
EDUCATION, HISTORY OF (*in part*)

T.H.D. **Tulio Halperin Donghi.** *Professor of History, University of California, Berkeley. Author of* Historia contemporánea de América Latina.
ARGENTINA (*in part*)

T.H.E. **Thomas H. Everett** (d. 1986). *Director of Horticulture, New York Botanical Garden, Bronx. Author of* Living Trees of the World.
TREES (*in part*)

T.H.El. **Thomas Henry Elkins.** *Honorary Professor of Geography, University of Sussex, Brighton, England. Author of* Germany *and others.*
FRANCE (*in part*)
GERMANY (*in part*)

T.H.G. **Theodor H. Gaster.** *Emeritus Professor of Religion, Barnard College, Columbia University. Author of* Myth, Legend, and Custom in the Old Testament; Thespis: Ritual, Myth, and Drama in the Ancient Near East.
JUDAISM (*in part*)

Th.H. **Thor Heyerdahl.** *Member, Norwegian Academy of Science and Letters, Oslo. Organizer and leader of Norwegian Archaeological Expedition to Easter Island and the East Pacific, 1955–56, and many other expeditions. Author of* Aku-Aku: The Secret of Easter Island; The Kon-Tiki Expedition; *and others.*
PACIFIC ISLANDS (*in part*)

Th.Ho. **Thomas Howarth.** *Emeritus Professor of Architecture, University of Toronto.*
TORONTO

Th.M. **Thomas Munro** (d. 1974). *Curator of Education, Cleveland Museum of Art, 1931–67. Professor of Art, Case Western Reserve University, Cleveland. Author of* The Arts and Their Interrelations *and others.*
AESTHETICS (*in part*)

T.Hn. **Tom Harrisson** (d. 1976). *Government Ethnologist and Curator, Sarawak Museum, 1947–66. Author of* The Malays of Sarawak *and others.*
SOUTHEAST ASIA, MAINLAND (*in part*)

T.Ho. **Thomas Hodgkin** (d. 1982). *Writer. Fellow of Balliol College, Oxford; Lecturer in the Government of New States, University of Oxford, 1965–70. Author of* Nationalism in Colonial Africa *and others.*
USMAN DAN FODIO (Micropædia)

T.Hor. **Theodore Hornberger** (d. 1975). *John Welsh Centennial Professor of History and English Literature, University of Pennsylvania, Philadelphia, 1968–75. Author of* Benjamin Franklin.
FRANKLIN (*in part*)

T.H.v.A. **Tjeerd H. van Andel.** *Wayne Loel Professor of Earth Sciences, Stanford University, California. Author of* New Views on an Old Planet: Continental Drift and the History of the Earth.
PLATE TECTONICS

Th.V.G. **Thomas V. Gamkrelidze.** *Director, Oriental Institute, Academy of Sciences of the Georgian S.S.R., Tbilisi. Author of* Alphabetic System of Writing and the Old Georgian Script *and others.*
LANGUAGES OF THE WORLD (*in part*)

T.I. **Toshihiko Izutsu.** *Professor of Islāmic Studies, McGill University, Montreal, 1969–75. Author of* A Comparative Study of the Key Philosophical Concepts in Sufism and Taoism.
IBN AL'ARABĪ (Micropædia)

T.Ic. **Takashi Ichiye.** *Professor of Oceanography, Texas A&M University, College Station.*
EKMAN, V. WALFRID (Micropædia)

T.In. **Tim Ingold.** *Professor of Social Anthropology, Victoria University of Manchester. Author of* Hunters, Pastoralists, and Ranchers: Reindeer Economics and Their Transformations *and others.*
ARCTIC, THE (*in part*)

T.Io. **Teiji Ichiko.** *Former Director General, National Institute of Japanese Literature, Tokyo. Author of* History of Japanese Literature *and others.*
LITERATURE, THE ART OF (*in part*)

T.J. **Thorkild Jacobsen.** *Emeritus Professor of Assyriology, Harvard University. Author of* The Sumerian Kinglist; "Mesopotamia" *in* The Intellectual History of Ancient Man; *and others.*

MIDDLE EASTERN RELIGIONS, ANCIENT (*in part*)

T.J.B. **Trent J. Bertrand.** *Senior Economist, International Bank for Reconstruction and Development, Washington, D.C. Former Professor of Economics, State University of New York at Binghamton.*
INTERNATIONAL TRADE (*in part*)

T.J.Br. **T. Julian Brown** (d. 1987). *Professor of Palaeography, University of London, 1961–84. Coauthor of* Codex Lindisfarnensis.
WRITING (*in part*)

T.J.C. **Theodore John Cadoux.** *Former Senior Lecturer in Ancient History, University of Edinburgh.*
CIMON (Micropædia)
SOLON (Micropædia)

T.J.Co. **Timothy John Connell.** *Principal Lecturer in Hispanic Studies, Ealing College of Higher Education, London. Coauthor of* Spain after Franco *and others.*
BARCELONA
MADRID (*in part*)

T.J.H. **Theo Jozef Hermans.** *Reader in Dutch, University College, University of London. Author of* The Structure of Modernist Poetry.
BELGIAN LITERATURE (*in part*)
BRUSSELS (*in part*)

T.Jo. **Thomas Jones** (d. 1972). *Professor of Welsh Language and Literature, University College of Wales, Aberystwyth, University of Wales, 1952–70. Editor of* Brut y Tywysogion; *cotranslator of* The Mabinogion.
CELTIC LITERATURE (*in part*)

T.K.B. **T. Keilor Bentley.** *Director, Owens Art Gallery, Mount Allison University, Sackville, New Brunswick, 1976–89. Superintendent, Alexander Graham Bell Museum, Baddeck. Nova Scotia, 1959–64.*
BELL, ALEXANDER GRAHAM (Micropædia)

T.K.F. **Thea K. Flaum.** *Producer, WTTW (public television), Chicago. Former Editor, Urban Research Corporation, Chicago.*
UNITED STATES OF AMERICA (*in part*)

T.Kh. **Tarif Khalidi.** *Professor of History and Archaeology, American University of Beirut.*
'ABD AL-MALIK (Micropædia)
'ABD AR-RAḤMĀN III (Micropædia)

T.Kl. **Tibor Klaniczay.** *Director, Institute of Literary Studies, Hungarian Academy of Sciences, Budapest.*
HUNGARIAN LITERATURE (*in part*)

T.Ku. **Tadachika Kuwata.** *Emeritus Professor of Japanese History, Kokugakuin University, Tokyo. Author of* Toyotomi Hideyoshi *and others.*
TOYOTOMI HIDEYOSHI (Micropædia)

T.K.Z. **Tatyana Konstantinovna Zakharova.** *Senior Science Editor, Sovetskaya entsiklopediya (publisher).*
ASIA (*in part*)

T.L.K. **Thomas L. Karnes.** *Emeritus Professor of History, Arizona State University, Tempe. Author of* Failure of Union: Central America, 1824–1975.
CENTRAL AMERICA (*in part*)

T.L.L. **Thomas L. Lentz, M.D.** *Professor of Cell Biology, School of Medicine, Yale University, New Haven, Connecticut. Author of* Primitive Nervous Systems.
NERVES AND NERVOUS SYSTEMS (*in part*)

T.L.Pe. **Troy L. Péwé.** *Emeritus Professor of Geology, Arizona State University, Tempe. President, International Permafrost Association. An authority on the geomorphology of polar regions. Editor of* The Periglacial Environment: Past and Present.
ICE AND ICE FORMATIONS (*in part*)

T.L.S. **T. Lynn Smith** (d. 1976). *Graduate Research Professor of Sociology, University of Florida, Gainesville, 1959–74. Author of* Brazil: People and Institutions; Latin American Population Studies; *and others.*
BRAZIL (*in part*)

T.M.A. **Tom M. Apostol.** *Professor of Mathematics, California Institute of Technology, Pasadena. Author of* Introduction to Analytic Number Theory *and others.*
NUMBER THEORY (*in part*)

T.M.D. **Thomas M. Davies, Jr.** *Professor of History; Chairman of Latin American Studies; Director, Center for Latin American Studies, San Diego State University, California. Author of* Indian Integration in Peru: A Half Century of Experience, 1900–1948.
PERU (*in part*)

T.M.K. **Sir T. Malcolm Knox** (d. 1980). *Principal of the University of St. Andrews, Scotland, 1953–66. Translator of Hegel's* Political Writings, Early Theological Writings, *and* Aesthetics.
HEGELIANISM, HEGEL AND (*in part*)

T.Mo. **Therald Moeller.** *Emeritus Professor of Chemistry, Arizona State University, Tempe. Author of* Inorganic Chemistry: A Modern Introduction.
CHEMICAL ELEMENTS (*in part*)

T.M.P. **Thomas M. Poulsen.** *Professor and Head, Department of Geography, Portland State University, Oregon. Coauthor of* A Geography of Europe.
EUROPE (*in part*)

T.N.B. **T.N. Bisson.** *Henry Charles Lea Professor of Medieval History, Harvard University. Author of* The Medieval Crown of Aragon *and others.*
FRANCE (*in part*)

T.O.M. **Thomas Ollive Mabbott** (d. 1968). *Professor of English, Hunter College, City University of New York, 1946–66. Editor of* Complete Works of Poe.
POE, EDGAR ALLAN (*in part*) (Micropædia)

T.O'R. **Tarlach O'Raifeartaigh** (deceased). *Chairman, Cultural Relations Committee, Dublin. Editor of* Genealogical Tracts I.
PATRICK, SAINT (Micropædia)

T.O.S. **Thomas O. Sloane.** *Professor of Rhetoric, University of California, Berkeley. Author of* Donne, Milton, and the End of Humanist Rhetoric; *coeditor* The Rhetoric of Renaissance Poetry.
RHETORIC (*in part*)

T.P. **Tatiana Proskouriakoff** (d. 1985). *Curator of Maya Art, Peabody Museum, Harvard University. Staff member, Carnegie Institution of Washington, D.C., 1939–58. Author of* An Album of Maya Architecture.
CALENDAR (*in part*)

T.P.A. **Thomas P. Anderson.** *Professor and Chair, Department of History, Eastern Connecticut State University, Willimantic. Author of* Politics in Central America *and others.*
CENTRAL AMERICA (*in part*)

T.Po. **Tom Pocock.** *Special writer,* The Standard (*London*), *1982–88; Defense Correspondent, 1960–73; Travel Editor, 1973–82. Author of* Nelson and His World; Horatio Nelson; *and others.*
NELSON, HORATIO NELSON, VISCOUNT (*in part*) (Micropædia)

T.P.v.B. **Theodorus P. van Baaren.** *Former Professor of Science of Religions, State University of Groningen, The Netherlands. Author of* Menschen wie wir *and others.*
DOCTRINES AND DOGMAS, RELIGIOUS (*in part*)
RELIGIOUS AND SPIRITUAL BELIEF, SYSTEMS OF (*in part*)

T.R.L. **Thomas R. Leinbach.** *Professor of Geography, University of Kentucky, Lexington. Coauthor of* Development and Environment in Malaysia; Southeast Asian Transport: Issues in Development.
ASIA (*in part*)
INDONESIA (*in part*)

T.R.T. **Thomas R. Tregear** (deceased). *Warden, Woodbrooke College, Selly Oak, Birmingham, England, 1959–63. Lecturer in Geography, University of Hong Kong, 1951–59. Author of* A Geography of China *and others.*
CHINA (*in part*)

T.S. **Tadao Sato.** *Writer. Chairman, Japan Film P.E.N. Club. Author of* Kurosawa Akira no sekai *and others.*
KUROSAWA AKIRA (Micropædia)

T.Sa. **Taro Sakamoto** (d. 1987). *Historian. Professor, University of Tokyo. Author of* History of Japan *and others.*
JAPAN (*in part*)

T.S.Bu. **Thomas S. Buechner.** *Artist. President, Corning Museum of Glass, Corning, New York, 1971–87; Director, 1951–60. Chairman, Corning Glass Works Foundation and Steuben Glass, Inc., 1971–86. Author of* Guide to the Collections of the Corning Museum of Glass *and others.*
DECORATIVE ARTS AND FURNISHINGS (*in part*)

T.S.H. **Theodore S. Hamerow.** *Professor of History, University of Wisconsin, Madison. Author of* The Social Foundations of German Unification, 1858–71 *and others.*
GERMANY (*in part*)

T.S.McL. **Thomas S. McLeod.** *Former Director of Design Technology, Plessey Company Ltd., Ilford, England. Author of* Management of Research Development and Design in Industry.
INDUSTRIAL ENGINEERING AND PRODUCTION MANAGEMENT (*in part*)

T.Sp. **Terence John Bew Spencer** (d. 1978). *Professor of English Language and Literature, 1958–78; Director, Shakespeare Institute, 1961–78, University of Birmingham, England. General Editor,* The New Penguin Shakespeare *and the* Penguin Shakespeare Library, *1964–78. Author of* The Tyranny of Shakespeare; Shakespeare: The Roman Plays.
SHAKESPEARE (*in part*)

T.T. **Takeshi Toyoda.** *Historian. Professor, Tohoku University, Sendai, Japan, and Hōsei University, Tokyo. Author of* A History of Pre-Meiji Commerce in Japan *and others.*
JAPAN (*in part*)

T.-t.C. **Tse-tsung Chow.** *Professor of East Asian Languages, Literature, and History, University of Wisconsin, Madison. Author of* The May Fourth Movement: Intellectual Revolution in Modern China *and others.*
CHEN DUXIU (Micropædia)

T.T.M. **T.T. Macan.** *Former Naturalist, Freshwater Biological Association, Windermere Laboratory, Ambleside, England. Author of* Freshwater Ecology.
BIOSPHERE, THE (*in part*)

T.T.P. **Theodore Thomas Puck.** *Director, Eleanor Roosevelt Institute for Cancer Research; Professor of Biochemistry, Biophysics, and Genetics and Distinguished Professor of Medicine, University of Colorado Health Sciences Center, Denver. Author of* The Mammalian Cell as a Microorganism: Genetic and Biochemical Studies in Vitro.
TISSUE CULTURE (*in part*)

T.T.R. **Tamara Talbot Rice.** *Author of* Ancient Arts of Central Asia; The Scythians; Russian Art; *and others.*
CENTRAL ASIAN ARTS (*in part*)

T.V.W. **Turrell V. Wylie** (d. 1984). *Professor of Tibetan Studies, University of Washington, Seattle, 1972–84. Author of* The Geography of Tibet According to the 'Dzam-gling-rgyas-bshad.
CENTRAL ASIAN ARTS (*in part*)
CHINA (*in part*)

T.W. **Thomas M. Woodard.** *Writer and researcher. Instructor in Classics, Princeton University, 1962–64. Editor of* Sophocles: A Collection of Critical Essays.
GREEK DRAMATISTS, THE CLASSICAL (*in part*)

T.W.B. **Thomas W. Burns, M.D.**
*Director, Cosmopolitan International
Diabetes Center, Columbia, Missouri.
Distinguished Professor of Medicine;
Director, Division of Endocrinology and
Metabolism, University of Missouri,
Columbia. Author of* Endocrine Lecture
Syllabus.
ENDOCRINE SYSTEMS (*in part*)

T.W.D.S. **Tsepon W.D. Shakabpa** (d.
1989). *Historian. Minister of Finance,
Tibet, 1939–51. Chief Representative
of the Dalai Lama to the Government
of India, 1959–66. Author of* Tibet: A
Political History.
CHINA (*in part*)

T.We. **Thomas Weigend.** *Professor
of Law, University of Cologne. Author
of "Criminal Procedure: Comparative
Aspects" in* Encyclopedia of Crime
and Justice.
PROCEDURAL LAW (*in part*)

T.W.J.G. **Theodorus W.J. Gadella.**
*Lecturer in Systematic Botany, Utrecht
University, The Netherlands. Author of*
Cytotaxonomic Studies in the Genus
Campanula.
ANGIOSPERMS (*in part*)

T.W.-m. **Tu Wei-ming.** *Professor
of Chinese History and Philosophy,
Harvard University. Author of* Confucian
Thought: Selfhood as Creative
Transformation *and others.*
CONFUCIANISM, CONFUCIUS AND

T.W.Wa. **Thomas W. Walker.**
*Professor of Political Science; Director,
Latin American Studies, Ohio
University, Athens. Author of* Nicaragua:
The Land of Sandino *and others.*
CENTRAL AMERICA (*in part*)

T.W.Y. **Thomas W. Young.** *Lecturer in
Biochemistry, University of Birmingham,
England. Coauthor of* Malting and
Brewing Science.
BEVERAGE PRODUCTION (*in part*)

T.Y. **Takeo Yamane.** *Former Professor
of Food Manufacture, Showa Women's
University, Tokyo. Author of* Cane Sugar
Handbook.
FARMING AND AGRICULTURAL
TECHNOLOGY (*in part*)
FOOD PROCESSING (*in part*)

T.-y.L. **Tien-yi Li.** *Mershon Professor
Emeritus of Chinese Literature and
History, Ohio State University,
Columbus. Editor of* Readings in
Contemporary Chinese Literature;
Chinese Historical Literature.
CHINESE LITERATURE (*in part*)

T.Y.S. **Tatyana Yosifovna Supranovich.**
*Senior Scientist and Head, Division
of Sea Dynamics, For Eastern
Hydrometeorological Research Institute,
Vladivostok, U.S.S.R.*
PACIFIC OCEAN, THE (*in part*)

U.A.U. **Urho A. Uotila.** *Emeritus
Professor of Geodesy, Ohio State
University, Columbus.*
EARTH, THE (*in part*)

U.B. **Ugo Bianchi.** *Professor of the
History of Religions, University of Rome.*

Author of Il dualismo religioso; *editor of*
The Origins of Gnosticism.
RELIGIONS AND SPIRITUAL BELIEF,
SYSTEMS OF (*in part*)

U.Ba. **Umberto Baldini.** *Art historian.
Director, International University of Art,
Florence. Author of* Il Rinascimento nell'
Italia centrale *and others.*
MASACCIO (*in part*) (Micropædia)

U.Be. **Ulli Beier.** *Director, Iwalewa
House Centre for Contemporary Arts
from Africa and the Third World,
University of Bayreuth, Germany.
Research Professor and Director,
Institute of African Studies, University of
Ife, Ile-Ife, Nigeria, 1971–74. Founder of
Black Orpheus. Author of* African Poetry
and others; editor of Introduction to
African Literature.
AFRICAN ARTS (*in part*)

U.M. **Umberto Marcelli.** *Lecturer in
History, University of Bologna, Italy.
Author of* Cavour diplomatico.
CAVOUR, CAMILLO BENSO, CONTE DI
(*in part*) (Micropædia)

U.M.D. **Ulrich M. Drobnig.** *Director,
Max Planck Institute for Foreign
Private and Private International
Law, Hamburg. Professor of Law,
University of Hamburg. Author of*
American-German Private International
Law *and others.*
BUSINESS LAW (*in part*)
PROCEDURAL LAW (*in part*)

U.M.S. **Ulric M. Spencer.** *Economic
Statistician, National Economic
Development Office, London. Coauthor
of* Profit and Personality in Retailing.
UNITED KINGDOM (*in part*)

U.P.B. **Ulick Peter Burke.** *Reader in
History, University of Cambridge; Fellow
of Emmanuel College, Cambridge.
Author of* The Renaissance Sense of the
Past *and others.*
VALLA, LORENZO (Micropædia)

U.P.S. **Umakant Premanand Shah**
(d. 1988). *Deputy Director, Oriental
Institute, Maharaja Sayajirao University
of Baroda, India. Author of* Studies in
Jaina Art: Akota Bronzes.
JAINISM
MAHĀVĪRA (*in part*) (Micropædia)

V.A. **Vernon Ahmadjian.** *Professor of
Botany, Clark University, Worcester,
Massachusetts. Author of* The Lichen
Symbiosis; *coeditor of* The Lichens.
FUNGI (*in part*)

Va.K. **Valdimar Kristinsson.** *Editor,
Fjarmalatidindi (Financial Times),
Central Bank of Iceland, Reykjavík.*
ICELAND (*in part*)

V.Al. **Victor Alba.** *Emeritus
Professor of Political Science, Kent
State University, Ohio. Author of* The
Mexicans *and others.*
ZAPATA, EMILIANO (Micropædia)

V.A.U. **Victor Andrade U.** *Minister
of Foreign Affairs of Bolivia, 1958–
60. Ambassador of Bolivia to the U.S.,
1944–46; 1952–58; 1960–62. Author of*

Problemas sociales de Bolivia *and others.*
BOLIVIA (*in part*)

V.B. **Victor Barna** (d. 1972). *World
table tennis champion, men's singles,
1930, 1932–35; men's doubles, 1929–35;
mixed doubles, 1932, 1935. Author of*
Table Tennis Today.
TABLE TENNIS (*in part*) (Micropædia)

V.Br. **Victor Brombert.** *Henry Putnam
University Professor of Romance and
Comparative Literature, Princeton
University. Editor of* Stendhal: A
Collection of Critical Essays.
STENDHAL (Micropædia)

V.B.W. **Sir Vincent Brian
Wigglesworth.** *Emeritus Professor
of Biology, University of Cambridge;
Director, Agricultural Research Council
Unit of Insect Physiology, 1943–67.
Author of* The Principles of Insect
Physiology; The Life of Insects.
INSECTS (*in part*)

V.B.Z. **Viktor Borisovich Zhmuida.**
*Former Head, Central Asian Section,
Council for Research on Productive
Forces, U.S.S.R. Planning Committee,
Moscow. Author of numerous
publications on Turkmen S.S.R.*
UNION OF SOVIET SOCIALIST REPUBLICS
(*in part*)

V.C. **Vincent Cronin.** *Free-lance
writer. Author of* The Flowering of the
Renaissance *and others.*
SARPI, PAOLO (Micropædia)

V.C.F. **Victor C. Falkenheim** *Associate
Professor and Chairman, Department
of East Asian Studies, University of
Toronto. Editor of* Citizens and Groups
in Contemporary China.
CHINA (*in part*)

V.C.M. **Virginia C. Maiorana.**
*Research Associate, Department of
Ecology and Evolution, University of
Chicago.*
ANIMALS (*in part*)

V.D. **Vilmos Diószegi** (d. 1971).
*Research Fellow, Hungarian Academy
of Sciences, Budapest. Author of* Tracing
Shamans in Siberia; *editor of* Popular
Beliefs and Folklore Tradition in Siberia.
SACRED OFFICES AND ORDERS
(*in part*)

V.D.S. **Vicki D. Sebela.** *Executive
Administrator, Social Engineering
Associates, Inc., Chicago.*
UNITED STATES OF AMERICA (*in part*)

V.E.I. **Verity Elizabeth Irvine.** *Writer
and researcher.*
ARABIA (*in part*)
JORDAN (*in part*)
SYRIA (*in part*)

V.F.K. **Viktor Filipovich Kanayev.**
*Senior Scientist, Moscow M.V.
Lomonosov State University. Coauthor of*
Reléf dna Indiïskogo okeana *and others.*
INDIAN OCEAN, THE (*in part*)

V.F.Ko. **Vladimir Fyodorovich Kosov.**
*Head, Kazakhstan Section, Scientific
Council on the Location of U.S.S.R.
Productive Forces, Academy of Sciences
of the U.S.S.R., Moscow. Coauthor of*

Development of National Economy of the U.S.S.R. Eastern Regions.
UNION OF SOVIET SOCIALIST REPUBLICS (*in part*)

V.G. Viktor Gutmann. *Professor of Inorganic Chemistry, Technical University of Vienna. Author of* Halogen Chemistry *and others.*
CHEMICAL ELEMENTS (*in part*)

V.G.N. Viktor Grigoryevich Neyman. *Deputy Head, Department of Oceanology, Atmospheric Physics, and Geography, Academy of Sciences of the U.S.S.R., Moscow. Author of several articles on oceanology.*
INDIAN OCEAN, THE (*in part*)

V.G.S. Victor G. Szebehely. *Professor of Aerospace Engineering, University of Texas at Austin. Coeditor of* Methods in Astrodynamics and Celestial Mechanics.
MECHANICS (*in part*)

V.I.S. Victor Ilyich Seroff (d. 1979). *Writer. Author of* Rachmaninoff.
RACHMANINOFF, SERGEY (Micropædia)

V.J.M. Vytautas J. Mažiulis. *Professor of Baltic Languages, Vilnius V. Kapsukas State University, Lithuania.*
LANGUAGES OF THE WORLD (*in part*)

V.J.P. V.J. Parry (d. 1974). *Reader in the History of the Near and Middle East, School of Oriental and African Studies, University of London. Contributor to* The New Cambridge Modern History; Encyclopædia of Islam.
BAYEZID II (Micropædia)
SÜLEYMAN I (Micropædia)

V.J.T. Vello Julius Tarmisto. *Former Director, Institute of Economics, Estonian S.S.R. Academy of Sciences, Tallinn. Coauthor of* Estonian S.S.R.
BALTIC STATES (*in part*)

V.K. Viola Klein (d. 1973). *Reader in Sociology, University of Reading, England, 1971–73. Coauthor of* Women's Two Roles: At Home and Work *and others.*
SOCIAL DIFFERENTIATION (*in part*)

V.Ka. Vytautas Kavolis. *Charles A. Dana Professor of Comparative Civilizations and Professor of Sociology, Dickinson College, Carlisle, Pennsylvania. Author of* Artistic Expression: A Sociological Analysis; History on Art's Side: Social Dynamics in Artistic Efflorescences.
ARTS, PRACTICE AND PROFESSION OF THE (*in part*)

V.L. Véronique Lambert. *Editor and researcher in the literary and church history of the southern Low Countries.*
LUXEMBOURG (*in part*)

V.Lo. Victor Lowe (d. 1988). *Professor of Philosophy, Johns Hopkins University, Baltimore, 1961–73. Author of* Understanding Whitehead; The Life of Alfred North Whitehead.
WHITEHEAD, ALFRED NORTH (*in part*) (Micropædia)

V.L.S.P.R. Vaddiparti Lova Surya Prakasa Rao. *Senior Fellow, Centre for Economic and Social Studies, Hyderabad, India.*
DELHI (*in part*)

V.L.T. Victor-Lucien Tapié (d. 1974). *Member, Academy of Moral and Political Sciences, Institute of France, Paris, 1963–74. Professor of Modern History, University of Paris IV, 1949–70. Author of* La France de Louis XIII et de Richelieu *and others.*
COLBERT, JEAN-BAPTISTE (Micropædia)

V.M. Valerio Mariani (deceased). *Professor of the History of Art, University of Naples. Author of* Pittori protagonisti della crisi del quattrocento; Giotto.
LIPPI, FRA FILIPPO (Micropædia)

V.M.S. Vasily Mikhaylovich Sinitsyn (d. 1977). *Professor and Head, Laboratory of Paleogeography, Leningrad A.A. Zhdanov State University, 1961–77; Dean, Department of Geology, 1965–72.*
ASIA (*in part*)

V.M.St. Valery Mikhailovich Strygin. *Head of Section, Geographical Books, Mysl Publishing House, Moscow. Author of numerous papers on the geography of the Soviet Union.*
UNION OF SOVIET SOCIALIST REPUBLICS (*in part*)

V.M.W. Vera Muriel White. *Former Extramural Lecturer, University of Cambridge.*
PITT, WILLIAM, THE ELDER (Micropædia)

V.N. Victor Nachtergaele. *Professor of French Literature, Catholic University of Louvain, Belgium.*
BELGIAN LITERATURE (*in part*)

V.N.D. Vladimir Nikolaevich Dunaev. *Correspondent, Novosti Press Agency, Moscow. Author of numerous papers on administrative and social conditions in the Soviet Union.*
UNION OF SOVIET SOCIALIST REPUBLICS (*in part*)

V.N.K. Victor Nikolaevich Kondratiev. *Assistant Director, Institute of Chemical Physics; Member, Academy of Sciences of the U.S.S.R., Moscow. Author of* Chemical Kinetics of Gas Reactions.
CHEMICAL REACTIONS (*in part*)

V.P.G. Vladimir Petrovich Goncharov. *Head, Geology of the Southern Seas Laboratory, Southern Division, Institute of Oceanography, Academy of Sciences of the U.S.S.R., Gelendzhik. Coauthor of* Reléf dna i glubinnoe stroenie Chernomoskoĭ vpadiny.
ATLANTIC OCEAN, THE (*in part*)

V.P.P. Victor P. Petrov. *Professor of Geography, California State University, Los Angeles, 1970–74, Author of* China: Emerging World Power *and others.*
AFGHANISTAN (*in part*)

V.P.U. Vernon Philip Underwood (d. 1988). *Professor of French, University College, University of London. Author of* Verlaine et l'Angleterre; *editor of* Verlaine's Carnet personnel *and others.*
VERLAINE, PAUL (Micropædia)

V.P.Z. Vsevolod Pavlovich Zenkovich. *Former Head of Shore Department, Institute of Oceanology, Academy of Sciences of the U.S.S.R., Moscow. An authority on near-shore oceanography and attendant physical processes.*
OCEANS (*in part*)

V.R. Vernon Ram. *Arts Editor*, Hong Kong Standard.
DELHI (*in part*)

V.R.B. Victor R. Baker. *Regents Professor of Geosciences and of Planetary Sciences; University of Arizona, Tucson. Author of* The Channels of Mars.
CONTINENTAL LANDFORMS (*in part*)

V.R.F. Vernon R. Fryburger, Jr. *Professor of Advertising and Marketing; Chairman, Department of Advertising, Northwestern University, Evanston, Illinois. Coauthor of* Advertising Theory and Practice.
MARKETING AND MERCHANDISING (*in part*)

V.R.L. Val R. Lorwin (d. 1982). *Professor of History, University of Oregon, Eugene, 1958–75.*
UNITED NATIONS (*in part*)

V.R.P. V.R. Pillai. *Member, Kerala State Planning Board. Former Professor of Economics, University of Kerala, India. Coauthor of* Land Reclamation in Kerala *and others.*
INDIA (*in part*)

V.S.C. Vasile S. Cucu. *Professor of Geography, University of Bucharest. Author of* Geografia României.
ROMANIA (*in part*)

V.Sl. Vladimir Slamecka. *Emeritus Professor of Information and Computer Science, Georgia Institute of Technology, Atlanta. Coauthor of* National Information Systems.
INFORMATION PROCESSING AND INFORMATION SYSTEMS (*in part*)

V.S.M. V. Standish Mallory. *Emeritus Professor of Geological Sciences; Curator of Invertebrate Paleontology, Burke Washington State Museum, University of Washington, Seattle.*
GEOCHRONOLOGY (*in part*)

V.T.P. Vladimir T. Pashuto (d. 1983). *Professor, Institute of History of the U.S.S.R., Academy of Sciences of the U.S.S.R., Moscow. Author of* Vneshnyaya politika drevney Rusi.
ALGIRDAS (Micropædia)

V.U. Valev Uibopuu. *Novelist. Editor, Estonian Writers' Cooperative, Lund, Sweden. Author of* Keegi ei kuule meid.
ESTONIAN LITERATURE (Micropædia)

V.V.I. Vyacheslav Vsevolodovich Ivanov. *Head, Department of Structural Typology, Institute of Slavonic and Balkan Studies, Academy of Sciences of the U.S.S.R., Moscow.*
LANGUAGES OF THE WORLD (*in part*)

V.V.P. Vladimir V. Pokshishevsky (d. 1984). *Staff member, Institute of Ethnography, Academy of Sciences of the U.S.S.R., Moscow.*

UNION OF SOVIET SOCIALIST REPUBLICS (*in part*)

V.V.Z.   Vladimir Viktorovich Zhdanov. *Literary critic. Assistant to the Chief Editor,* Kratkaya Literaturnaya Entsiklopediya, *Moscow. Author of* M. Yu. Lermontov *and other works on Russian writers.*

LERMONTOV, MIKHAIL (Micropædia)

V.W.v.H.   Victor Wolfgang von Hagen. *Director, Roman Road Expeditions in Europe and North Africa, 1961–70. Director, Inca Highway Expedition to Peru, Bolivia, and Ecuador, 1953–55. Author of* Realm of the Incas *and others; editor of* The Incas.

PRE-COLUMBIAN CIVILIZATIONS (*in part*)

V.Z.   Vice Zaninović. *Professor of Serbian Literature, University of Zagreb, Yugoslavia. Author of* August Cesarec, Life and Work.

YUGOSLAV LITERATURE (*in part*)

V.Zw.   Vladimir Zwass. *Professor of Computer Science, Fairleigh Dickinson University, Teaneck, New Jersey. Editor in Chief,* Journal of Management Information Systems. *Author of* Introduction to Computer Science.

COMPUTER SCIENCE

W.A.   Warren Andrew, M.D. (d. 1982). *Professor of Anatomy, Indiana University, Indianapolis, 1958–82. Author of* Textbook of Comparative Histology.

SUPPORTIVE AND CONNECTIVE TISSUES (*in part*)

Wa.B.   Walter Blair. *Emeritus Professor of English, University of Chicago. Author of* Mark Twain and "Huck Finn"; *coauthor of* America's Humor; Poor Richard to Doonesbury.

AMERICAN LITERATURE (*in part*)

W.A.B.   Warren A. Beck. *Professor of History, California State University, Fullerton. Author of* New Mexico: A History of Four Centuries; *coauthor of* An Historical Atlas of New Mexico.

UNITED STATES OF AMERICA (*in part*)

W.A.Be.   William A. Berggren. *Senior Scientist, Woods Hole Oceanographic Institution, Massachusetts. Coeditor of* Catastrophies and Earth History.

GEOCHRONOLOGY (*in part*)

W.A.Bl.   Wilford A. Bladen. *Associate Professor of Geography, University of Kentucky, Lexington. Author of* Geography of Kentucky.

UNITED STATES OF AMERICA (*in part*)

W.A.Br.   William Arthur Brown. *Montague Burton Professor of Industrial Relations, University of Cambridge. Author of* Piecework Bargaining.

WORK AND EMPLOYMENT (*in part*)

W.A.C.   William A. Chaney. *George McKendree Steele Professor of Western Culture, Lawrence University, Appleton, Wisconsin. Author of* The Cult of Kingship in Anglo-Saxon England: The Transition from Paganism to Christianity.

UNITED KINGDOM (*in part*)

Wa.E.M.   Wayne E. Manning. *Emeritus Professor of Botany, Bucknell University, Lewisburg, Pennsylvania. Author of numerous articles on the walnut family.*

ANGIOSPERMS (*in part*)

W.A.H.   Walter A. Harrison. *Professor of Applied Physics, Stanford University, California, Author of* Pseudopotentials in the Theory of Metals.

MATTER (*in part*)

W.A.Ha.   Willard A. Hanna. *Senior Associate, Universities Field Staff International, Hanover, New Hampshire. Author of* Bung Karno's Indonesia.

SUKARNO (Micropædia)

W.A.K.   Walid Ahmed Khalidi. *Professor of Political Studies and Public Administration, American University of Beirut.*

PALESTINE (*in part*)

W.Am.   Winslow Ames (d. 1990). *Associate Professor of Art, University of Rhode Island, Kingston, 1966–75. Curator, Gallery of Modern Art, New York City, 1957–61. Author of* Great Drawings of All Time, *vol. 1,* Italian Drawings *and others.*

CARICATURE, CARTOON, AND COMIC STRIP (*in part*)

Wa.M.   Wang Mingye. *Professor of Geomorphology, Ch'eng-tu Institute of Geography, Chinese Academy of Sciences. Author of* The Mountains in China *and others.*

CHUNGKING (*in part*)

W.A.McD.   Walter A. McDougall. *Alloy-Ansin Professor of International Relations, University of Pennsylvania, Philadelphia. Author of* The Heavens and the Earth: A Political History of the Space Age *and others.*

INTERNATIONAL RELATIONS, 20TH-CENTURY

W.A.N.   William Anderson Newman. *Professor of Biological Oceanography, Scripps Institution of Oceanography, University of California, San Diego, at La Jolla. Author of* "Evolution of Cirripedes and Their Major Groups" *in* Barnacle Biology.

CRUSTACEANS (*in part*)

W.A.P.   The Rev. William Arthur Purdy. *Secretary for Anglican and Methodist Relations, Secretariat for Promoting Christian Unity, Vatican. Author of* The Church on the Move: The Characters and Policies of Pius XII and John XXIII.

PIUS XII (Micropædia)

W.A.Po.   William A. Poucher (d. 1988). *Chief Perfumer, Yardley and Company, Ltd., London, 1929–59. Author of* Perfumes, Cosmetics & Soaps.

DRESS AND ADORNMENT (*in part*)

Wa.R.   Walpola Rāhula. *Supervisor, University of Oxford. Chancellor, University of Kelaniya, Sri Lanka. Author of* What the Buddha Taught.

BUDDHISM, THE BUDDHA AND (*in part*)

W.A.R.   William Alexander Robson (d. 1980). *Professor of Public Administration, University of London, 1947–62. Author of* Justice and Administrative Law; *coauthor of* Great Cities of the World: Their Government, Politics and Planning.

CITIES (*in part*)
PUBLIC ADMINISTRATION (*in part*)

W.A.Ri.   William Andrew Ringler, Jr. (d. 1987). *Professor of English, University of Chicago, 1962–1980. Editor of* The Poems of Sir Philip Sidney.

SIDNEY, SIR PHILIP (Micropædia)

W.A.W.   Warid A. Warid. *Former Professor of Agriculture, University of Al Fateh, Tripoli, Libya. Coauthor of* Vegetable Production.

FARMING AND AGRICULTURAL TECHNOLOGY (*in part*)

W.B.   Wim Blockmans. *Professor of Medieval History, State University of Leiden, The Netherlands. Coauthor of* The Burgundian Netherlands.

NETHERLANDS, THE (*in part*)

W.Ba.   William Barr. *Professor and Head, Department of Geography, University of Saskatchewan, Saskatoon. Author of* The Expeditions of the First International Polar Year, 1882–83.

ARCTIC, THE (*in part*)

W.B.B.   William B. Bean, M.D. (d. 1989). *Professor of Medicine, University of Iowa, Iowa City, 1948–70. Editor in Chief,* Archives of Internal Medicine, *1962–67. Author of* Rare Diseases and Lesions: Their Contributions to Clinical Medicine.

DIAGNOSIS AND THERAPEUTICS (*in part*)

W.B.F.   W. Beall Fowler. *Professor of Physics, Lehigh University, Bethlehem, Pennsylvania.*

MATTER (*in part*)

W.B.Fi.   William B. Fisher (d. 1984). *Principal, Graduate Society, 1965–81; Professor of Geography, University of Durham, England, 1956–81. Author of* The Middle East; *editor of* Cambridge History of Iran (*vol. 1*).

AFRICA (*in part*)

W.B.F.R.   William B.F. Ryan. *Senior Research Scientist, Lamont-Doherty Geological Observatory, Columbia University.*

INDIAN OCEAN, THE (*in part*)

W.Bi.   Walter Biemel. *Emeritus Professor of Philosophy, State Academy of Art of Düsseldorf, Germany.*

PHILOSOPHICAL SCHOOLS AND DOCTRINES, WESTERN (*in part*)

W.B.McM.   William B. McMahon. *Law enforcement and privacy consultant. Coeditor of* Law Enforcement Science and Technology III.

POLICE (*in part*)

W.B.N.B.   William B.N. Berry. *Professor of Integrative Biology, University of California, Berkeley; Marine Scientist, Lawrence Berkeley Laboratory. Author of* Growth of a

Prehistoric Time Scale.
GEOCHRONOLOGY (*in part*)

W.B.S.   Wilfred Borden Schofield.
*Professor of Botany, University of
British Columbia, Vancouver. Author of*
Introduction to Bryology *and others.*
BRYOPHYTES

W.B.Si.   William B. Simmons.
*Professor of Mineralogy, University of
New Orleans. Coauthor of* Rare-Earth
Pegmatites of the South Platte District.
MINERALS AND ROCKS (*in part*)

W.Bu.   William Burrows (d. 1978).
*Professor of Microbiology, University of
Chicago, 1947–73. Author of* Textbook
of Microbiology.
DISEASE (*in part*)

W.B.W.   Wilse B. Webb. *Graduate
Research Professor of Psychology,
University of Florida, Gainesville. Author
of* Sleep: An Experimental Analysis.
SLEEP AND DREAMS (*in part*)

W.B.Wh.   William B. White. *Professor
of Geochemistry, Pennsylvania State
University, University Park. Author of*
Hydrology and Geomorphology of Karst
Terrains.
CONTINENTAL LANDFORMS (*in part*)

W.C.   Warren Cowgill (d. 1985).
*Professor of Indo-European Linguistics,
Yale University, 1972–85. Author
of several articles on Indo-European
languages.*
LANGUAGES OF THE WORLD (*in part*)

W.C.A.   William C. Atkinson. *Professor
of Hispanic Studies, University of
Glasgow, 1932–72; Director, Institute
of Latin-American Studies, 1966–
72. Author of* A History of Spain
and Portugal; *translator of Camões'*
The Lusiads.
PORTUGUESE LITERATURE (*in part*)
SPANISH LITERATURE (*in part*)

W.C.B.   William Charles Brice.
*Emeritus Professor of Geography,
Victoria University of Manchester.*
NORTH AFRICA (*in part*)
PALESTINE (*in part*)

W.C.Be.   Wendell Clark Bennett (d.
1953). *Professor of Anthropology, Yale
University, 1945–53.*
SOUTH AMERICA (*in part*)

W.C.D.   William C. Dickison. *Professor
of Biology, University of North Carolina
at Chapel Hill. Coauthor of* Vascular
Plant Systematics.
PLANTS (*in part*)

W.C.Di.   William C. Dilger. *Associate
Professor of Ethology, Cornell
University, Ithaca, New York. Author of*
Psychobiology; 39 Steps to Biology.
BEHAVIOUR, ANIMAL (*in part*)

W.C.F.   Warren Curtis Freihofer. *Field
Associate, Department of Ichthyology,
California Academy of Sciences, San
Francisco. Author of research papers on
the anatomy and systematics of fishes.*
FISHES (*in part*)

W.C.H.   Walther C. Hubatsch.
Professor of Medieval and Modern

History, Rhenish Friedrich Wilhelm
University of Bonn. Author of Die Åra
Tirpitz *and others.*
TIRPITZ, ALFRED VON (Micropædia)

W.C.Ho.   William Coffeen Holton.
*Director, Semiconductor Research
Corporation, Research Triangle Park,
North Carolina.*
ELECTRONICS (*in part*)

W.C.McC.   W. Cheyne McCallum.
*Senior Research Fellow in Psychology,
Burden Neurological Institute and
University of Bristol, England. Coeditor
of* The Responsive Brain.
ATTENTION

W.Cr.   William Cruse. *Technical
Consultant, Uris Theatre Complex,
New York City, and New Orleans
Cultural Center. Former Supervisor of
Scenic Services, American Broadcasting
Company, New York City. Former
Technical Director, Ahmandson Theatre,
Los Angeles.*
THEATRICAL PRODUCTION (*in part*)

W.C.Se.   William C. Seitz (d. 1974).
*George R. Kenan, Jr., Professor of the
History of Art, University of Virginia,
Charlottesville, 1971–74. Author of*
Claude Monet.
MONET, CLAUDE (*in part*) (Micropædia)

W.C.St.   William Campbell Steere (d.
1989). *Professor of Botany, Columbia
University, 1958–75. President, New
York Botanical Garden, Bronx, 1970–72;
Director, 1958–70. Editor of* Fifty Years
of Botany.
BIOLOGICAL SCIENCES, THE (*in part*)

W.Cu.   William Culican (d. 1984).
*Reader in History, University of
Melbourne, 1972–84. Author of* The
Medes and Persians *and others.*
ARCHITECTURE, THE HISTORY OF
   WESTERN (*in part*)
HANNIBAL (Micropædia)
KHOSROW II (*in part*) (Micropædia)
SCULPTURE, THE HISTORY OF WESTERN
   (*in part*)

W.D.   Wilma Dykeman. *Adjunct
Professor of English, University of
Tennessee, Knoxville. State Historian of
Tennessee. Author of* The French Broad;
coauthor of The Appalachian Mountains
and others.
NORTH AMERICA (*in part*)
UNITED STATES OF AMERICA (*in part*)

W.De.   Wilfrid Desan. *Emeritus
Professor of Philosophy, Georgetown
University, Washington, D.C. Author of*
The Tragic Finale *and others.*
SARTRE, JEAN-PAUL (Micropædia)

W.D.H.   William Driver Howarth.
*Former Professor of French, University of
Bristol, England. Author of* Sublime and
Grotesque: A Study of French Romantic
Drama *and others.*
FRENCH LITERATURE (*in part*)

W.D.J.   William D. Jackson.
*President and Technical Director, HMJ
Corporation, Chevy Chase, Maryland.
Editor in Chief,* Magnetohydrodynamics:
An International Journal.
ENERGY CONVERSION (*in part*)

W.D.L.R.   W.D.L. Ride. *Visiting
Fellow, Australian National University,
Canberra. Head, School of Applied
Science, Canberra College of Advanced
Education, 1982–87. Author of* A Guide
to the Native Mammals of Australia;
coeditor of Species at Risk: Research in
Australia.
AUSTRALIA (*in part*)

W.Do.   Wendy Doniger. *Mircea Eliade
Professor of the History of Religions,
University of Chicago. Author of* Dreams,
Illusion, and Other Realities *and others.*
HINDUISM (*in part*)

W.D.P.   W. Douglas Piercey, M.D. (d.
1972). *Associate Professor of Hospital
Administration, University of Toronto,
1954–65. Executive Director, Canadian
Hospital Association, Toronto; Editor,*
The Canadian Hospital Journal,
1954–65.
MEDICINE (*in part*)

W.D.R.   Wayne D. Rasmussen.
*Executive Secretary, Agricultural History
Society, Washington, D.C. Historian,
Agricultural History Branch, Economic
Research Service, U.S. Department of
Agriculture, Washington, D.C., 1940–
86. Editor of* Agriculture in the United
States: A Documentary History.
AGRICULTURE, THE HISTORY OF
   (*in part*)

W.D.S.   Wilfred D. Stein. *Professor
of Biophysics, Hebrew University of
Jerusalem. Author of* Transport and
Diffusion Across Cell Membranes.
CELLS (*in part*)

W.E.   William Epstein. *Professor of
Psychology, University of Wisconsin,
Madison. Author of* Varieties of
Perceptual Learning.
PERCEPTION, HUMAN (*in part*)

W.E.A.   Walter E. Allen. *Professor
of English Studies, New University of
Ulster, Coleraine, Northern Ireland,
1968–73. Author of* The English Novel.
FIELDING, HENRY (*in part*)
   (Micropædia)
SMOLLETT, TOBIAS (Micropædia)

W.E.D.   William E. Duellman. *Curator,
Division of Herpetology, Museum of
Natural History; Professor of Systematics
and Ecology, University of Kansas,
Lawrence. Researcher on the biology
and systematics of frogs, with particular
emphasis on the New World tropics.
Author of* The Hylid Frogs of Middle
America.
AMPHIBIANS (*in part*)

W.E.K.   Walter Emil Kaegi, Jr.
*Professor of Byzantine and Roman
History, University of Chicago. Author of*
Byzantine Military Unrest *and others.*
LEO III (BYZANTINE EMPIRE)
   (Micropædia)

W.Em.   Walter Emery (d. 1974).
*Director, Novello and Company Ltd.,
London. Specialist on the work of Bach.
Author of* Bach's Ornaments.
BACH (*in part*)

W.E.M.   William Edward May (d.
1989). *Commander, Royal Navy. Deputy*

Director, National Maritime Museum, Greenwich, England, 1951–68. Naval Assistant to the Director, Compass Department, Admiralty, 1929–51. Author of Compass Adjustment.

NAVIGATION (in part)

W.E.Mo. **W.E. Mosse.** Emeritus Professor of European History, University of East Anglia, Norwich, England. Author of Alexander II and the Modernization of Russia and others.

ALEXANDER II (RUSSIA) (Micropædia)

W.E.M.P.-P. **William E.M. Pryse-Phillips, M.D.** Professor of Medicine (Neurology), Memorial University of Newfoundland, St. John's. Coauthor of Essential Neurology.

NERVES AND NERVOUS SYSTEMS (in part)

W.E.P. **Warren E. Preece.** Member, Board of Editors, Encyclopædia Britannica, Chicago; Vice-Chairman, 1975–79; The Editor, 1964–75. Coauthor of The Technological Order.

ENCYCLOPAEDIAS AND DICTIONARIES (in part)
PRINTING, TYPOGRAPHY, AND PHOTOENGRAVING (in part)

W.Er. **Walter Erben** (d. 1981). Professor of Art Education, College of Education of the Ruhr, Dortmund, West Germany. Author of Joan Miró; Chagall.

MIRÓ, JOAN (in part) (Micropædia)

W.E.S. **William Edward Stubbs** (d. 1973). Assistant Judge Advocate General, Office of the Judge Advocate General of the British Forces in Germany, London.

WAR, THE THEORY AND CONDUCT OF (in part)

W.E.T. **William E. Thomson.** Professor of Music Theory and Composition, University of Southern California, Los Angeles. Author of Materials and Structure of Music; Introduction to Music as Structure; and others.

MUSIC, THE ART OF (in part)

W.E.V. **W. Edgar Vinacke.** Emeritus Professor of Psychology, State University of New York at Buffalo. Author of The Psychology of Thinking.

THOUGHT AND THOUGHT PROCESSES (in part)

W.F. **Wallace Fowlie.** James B. Duke Professor Emeritus of French Literature, Duke University, Durham, North Carolina. Author of Jean Cocteau; Stendhal; A Guide to Contemporary French Literature; Age of Surrealism.

COCTEAU, JEAN (Micropædia)

W.F.A. **William Foxwell Albright** (d. 1971). Professor of Semitic Languages, Johns Hopkins University, Baltimore, Maryland, 1929–58. Author of Archæology of Palestine; From the Stone Age to Christianity.

PALESTINE (in part)
PREHISTORIC PEOPLES AND CULTURES (in part)

W.F.K. **William F. Kieffer.** Emeritus Professor of Chemistry, Wooster College, Ohio. Author of The Mole Concept in Chemistry; Chemistry Today; and others.

CHEMICAL COMPOUNDS (in part)

W.F.Kn. **Wilfrid F. Knapp.** Fellow and Tutor in Politics, St. Catherine's College, Oxford; Lecturer in Politics, University of Oxford. Author of A History of War and Peace, 1939–65.

HITLER (in part)

W.Ft. **Wesley Frost** (d. 1968). U.S. Ambassador to Paraguay, 1942–44.

SOUTH AMERICA (in part)

W.F.V. **Walter F. Vella** (d. 1984). Professor of History, University of Hawaii at Manoa, Honolulu. Author of Siam under Rama III, 1824–1851; A History of Modern Thailand; and others.

SOUTHEAST ASIA, MAINLAND (in part)

W.F.W. **Warren F. Walker, Jr.** Emeritus Professor of Biology, Oberlin College, Ohio. Author of Vertebrate Dissection.

MUSCLES AND MUSCLE SYSTEMS (in part)

W.F.Wh. **William Foote Whyte.** Emeritus Professor of Industrial and Labour Relations, Cornell University, Ithaca, New York. Author of Organizational Behavior: Theory and Application and others.

WORK AND EMPLOYMENT (in part)

W.Ga. **William Gaunt** (d. 1980). Art historian. Special correspondent on art subjects, The Times, London. Author of The Pre-Raphaelite Tragedy; The Aesthetic Adventure.

ROSSETTI, CHRISTINA (Micropædia)
ROSSETTI, DANTE GABRIEL (Micropædia)
ROSSETTI, GABRIELE (Micropædia)
ROSSETTI, WILLIAM MICHAEL (Micropædia)

W.G.A. **W. Geoffrey Arnott.** Professor of Greek Language and Literature, University of Leeds, England.

TERENCE (Micropædia)

W.G.B. **Walter G. Bergmann** (d. 1988). Editor, Schott and Co. Ltd., Music Publishers, London. Author of several articles on Telemann.

TELEMANN, GEORG PHILIPP (Micropædia)

W.G.Br. **Walter G. Bradley, M.D.** Professor and Chairman, Department of Neurology, University of Vermont, Burlington. Author of Disorders of Peripheral Nerves; coeditor of Recent Advances in Myology.

MUSCLES AND MUSCLE SYSTEMS (in part)

W.G.C. **William G. Constable** (d. 1976). Curator of Paintings, Boston Museum of Fine Arts, 1938–57. Author of Canaletto: Giovanni Antonio Canal, 1697–1768.

CANALETTO (Micropædia)

W.G.C.-S. **William Gervase Clarence-Smith.** Reader in the Economic History of Asia and Africa, School of Oriental and African Studies, University of London. Author of The Third Portuguese Empire: A Study in Economic Imperialism, 1826–1975.

CENTRAL AFRICA (in part)

W.G.E. **W. Gordon East.** Emeritus Professor of Geography, Birkbeck College, University of London. Author of

An Historical Geography of Europe.

EUROPE (in part)

W.G.J. **Walton Glyn Jones.** Professor of Scandinavian Studies, University of East Anglia, Norwich, England. Author of Denmark; Tove Jansson; and others.

SCANDINAVIAN LITERATURE (in part)

W.G.M. **William George Mokray** (d. 1974). Editor and Publisher, Basketball's Best. Writer for Converse Basketball Yearbook. U.S. correspondent on basketball for European publications. Elected to the Basketball Hall of Fame, 1965.

SPORTS, MAJOR TEAM AND INDIVIDUAL (in part)

W.G.Mo. **Will G. Moore** (d. 1978). Reader in French Literature, University of Oxford. Author of La Rochefoucauld: His Mind and Art and others.

LA ROCHEFOUCAULD, FRANÇOIS VI, DUC DE (Micropædia)
MOLIÈRE (in part)

W.Go. **Walter Otto Julius Görlitz.** Journalist; Editorial Staff, Die Welt, Hamburg. Author of History of the German General Staff, 1657–1945.

LUDENDORFF, ERICH (Micropædia)
ROMMEL, ERWIN (Micropædia)

W.G.Pr. **W.G. Prout.** Consultant Surgeon, Portsmouth Group Hospitals, England.

CIRCULATION AND CIRCULATORY SYSTEMS (in part)

W.G.St. **William Glenn Steiner.** Professor of Psychology, Bradley University, Peoria, Illinois.

ALCOHOL AND DRUG CONSUMPTION (in part)

W.G.U. **William G. Urry** (d. 1981). Reader in Medieval Western Paleography, University of Oxford; Fellow of St. Edmund Hall, Oxford, 1969–81.

HISTORY, THE STUDY OF (in part)

W.H. **Wolfgang Helck.** Professor of Egyptology, University of Hamburg. Author of Manetho und die ägyptischen Königslisten and others.

HISTORY, THE STUDY OF (in part)

W.Ha. **Walter Harrelson.** Distinguished Professor Emeritus of Hebrew Bible, Vanderbilt University, Nashville, Tennessee. Author of From Fertility Cult to Worship and others.

RITES AND CEREMONIES, SACRED (in part)

W.H.B. **William H. Baumer** (d. 1989). Major General, U.S. Army Reserve. President, International General Industries, Inc., Washington, D.C., 1963–72. Coauthor of The Little Wars of the United States.

WAR, THE TECHNOLOGY OF (in part)

W.H.Br. **Walter Henry Breen.** Former Coeditor, Standard Catalogue of United States Coins. Author of Walter Breen's Complete Encyclopedia of U.S. and Colonial Coins and others.

COINS AND COINAGE (in part)

W.H.C.   Walter Houston Clark. *Professor of the Psychology of Religion, Andover Newton Theological School, Newton Centre, Massachusetts, 1962–67. Author of* Chemical Ecstasy: Psychedelic Drugs and Religion.
ALCOHOL AND DRUG CONSUMPTION (*in part*)

W.H.C.F.   The Rev. William Hugh Clifford Frend. *Emeritus Professor of Ecclesiastical History, University of Glasgow. Author of* The Rise of Christianity *and others.*
CYPRIAN, SAINT (Micropædia)

W.H.D.   William Henry Dawbin. *Honorary Research Associate, Australian Museum, Sydney. Former Reader in Biology, University of Sydney. Author of papers on tuataras.*
REPTILES (*in part*)

W.He.   Walter Heinemeyer. *Professor of Medieval History, Philipps University of Marburg, Germany. Coeditor of* Politisches Archiv des Landgrafen Philipps.
PHILIPP (HESSE) (Micropædia)

W.H.G.   W. Horsley Gantt, M.D. (d. 1980). *Associate Professor of Psychiatry, 1932–58; Director, Pavlovian Laboratory, School of Medicine, Johns Hopkins University, Baltimore. Senior Scientist, Pavlovian Laboratory, Veterans Administration Hospital, Perry Point, Maryland.*
PAVLOV, IVAN PETROVICH (Micropædia)

W.H.G.A.   Walter Harry Green Armytage. *Emeritus Professor of Education, University of Sheffield, England. Author of* A Social History of Engineering.
EADS, JAMES B. (Micropædia)
EVANS, OLIVER (Micropædia)

W.H.I.   William Harold Ingrams (d. 1973). *Adviser on Overseas Information to the Secretary of State for the Colonies, United Kingdom, 1950–54. Author of* Arabia and the Isles *and others.*
ARABIA (*in part*)

W.H.J.   W. Hilton Johnson. *Professor of Geology, University of Illinois at Urbana-Champaign.*
GEOCHRONOLOGY (*in part*)

W.H.M.   William H. Miller, M.D. *Professor of Ophthalmology and Visual Science, School of Medicine, Yale University.*
SENSORY RECEPTION (*in part*)

W.H.McL.   William Hewat McLeod. *Professor of History, University of Otago, Dunedin, New Zealand. Author of* Gurū Nānak and the Sikh Religion.
NĀNAK (Micropædia)

W.H.McN.   William H. McNeill. *Robert A. Millikan Distinguished Service Professor Emeritus of History, University of Chicago. Author of* The Rise of the West *and others.*
STEPPE, THE HISTORY OF THE EURASIAN

W.H.N.   William H. Nienhauser, Jr. *Professor of East Asian Languages and Literature, University of Wisconsin,* Madison. *Author of* P'i Jih-hsiu; *editor of* Indiana Companion to Traditional Chinese Literature.
CHINESE LITERATURE (*in part*)

W.H.O.   William Hosking Oliver. *Editor, Dictionary of New Zealand Biography. Author of* The Story of New Zealand *and others.*
NEW ZEALAND (*in part*)

W.H.T.   William Homan Thorpe (d. 1986). *Professor of Animal Ethology, University of Cambridge, 1966–69. Author of* Learning and Instinct in Animals.
BEHAVIOUR, ANIMAL (*in part*)

W.H.Th.   William Harford Thomas. *Journalist. Former Deputy Editor,* The Guardian, *London. Author of* Crisis in the British Press.
UNITED KINGDOM (*in part*)

W.H.W.   William Henry Walsh (d. 1986). *Professor of Logic and Metaphysics, University of Edinburgh, 1960–79. Author of* Reason and Experience; Metaphysics.
METAPHYSICS (*in part*)

W.H.Wa.   Warren H. Wagner, Jr. *Professor of Botany; Curator of Pteridophytes, University Herbarium, University of Michigan, Ann Arbor. Author of* The Fern Genus Diellia.
FERNS (*in part*)

Wi.G.M.   William G. Moulton. *Professor of Linguistics, Princeton University, 1960–79. Professor of Germanic Linguistics, Cornell University, Ithaca, New York, 1949–60. Author of* The Sounds of English and German.
LANGUAGES OF THE WORLD (*in part*)

Wi.M.   Wilhelm Matull (deceased). *Senior Civil Servant, National Centres for Political Education, Hannover, Bonn, and Düsseldorf, West Germany, 1954–68. Author of* Ferdinand Lassalle *and others.*
LASSALLE, FERDINAND (Micropædia)

W.J.   Walter John. *Research Scientist, Air and Industrial Hygiene Laboratory, California Department of Health Services, Berkeley.*
MECHANICS (*in part*)

W.J.Al.   Wybe Jappe Alberts. *Former Professor of History, University of Utrecht, The Netherlands.*
LOW COUNTRIES, THE (*in part*)

W.J.Ar.   W.J. Argyle. *Professor of Social Anthropology, University of Natal, Durban, South Africa. Author of* The Fon of Dahomey.
SOUTHERN AFRICA (*in part*)

W.J.B.   William J. Baumol. *Professor of Economics, Princeton University and New York University, New York City. Author of* Superfairness: Applications and Theory *and others.*
ECONOMIC THEORY (*in part*)

W.J.Bo.   William J. Bouwsma. *Sather Professor of History, University of California, Berkeley. Author of* Venice and the Defense of Republican Liberty; John Calvin: A Sixteenth-Century Portrait.
CALVINISM, CALVIN AND ITALY (*in part*)

W.J.Br.   William J. Breed. *Consulting geologist. Head, Geology Department, Museum of Northern Arizona, Flagstaff, 1978–80; Curator of Geology, 1960–78.*
CONTINENTAL LANDFORMS (*in part*)

W.J.Bu.   The Rev. Walter John Burghardt, S.J. *Theologian in Residence, Georgetown University, Washington, D.C. Editor,* Theological Studies. *Author of* The Image of God in Man According to Cyril of Alexandria.
JEROME, SAINT (Micropædia)

W.J.C.   Willie J. Chevalier. *Journalist. Editor,* Le Droit (Ottawa), *1963–67. Managing Editor,* Le Petit Journal (Montreal), *1959–63.*
MONTREAL (*in part*)

W.J.E.   W.J. Eccles. *Emeritus Professor of History, University of Toronto. Author of* France in America; Frontenac *and others.*
CARTIER, JACQUES (Micropædia)
FRONTENAC, LOUIS DE BUADE, COMTE DE PALLUAU ET DE (Micropædia)

W.J.F.   W.J. Frank. *Senior Staff, Lawrence Livermore National Laboratory, University of California, Livermore.*
WAR, THE TECHNOLOGY OF (*in part*)

W.J.G.   Willis John Gertsch. *Emeritus Curator, Arachnida, Department of Entomology, American Museum of Natural History, New York City. Author of* American Spiders.
ARACHNIDS (*in part*)

W.J.Gr.   William J. Griffith. *Emeritus Professor of History, University of Kansas, Lawrence; Director, Center of Latin American Studies, 1970–74. Author of* Empires in the Wilderness: Foreign Colonization and Development in Guatemala, 1834–1844.
CENTRAL AMERICA (*in part*)

W.J.H.   William James Hamilton, M.D. (d. 1975). *Professor of Anatomy, Charing Cross Hospital Medical School, University of London, 1947–70. Editor of* Textbook of Human Anatomy.
SUPPORTIVE AND CONNECTIVE TISSUES (*in part*)

W.J.He.   Wilfrid James Hemp (d. 1962). *Inspector of Ancient Monuments for Wales in H.M. Office of Works, United Kingdom. Secretary to the Royal Commission on Ancient Monuments for Wales and Monmouth.*
SPAIN (*in part*)

W.J.H.W.   Wolfgang J.H. Wickler. *Director, Max Planck Institute for Behavioral Physiology, Seewiesen, Germany. Editor in Chief,* Ethology. *Author of* Mimicry in Plants and Animals *and others.*
MIMICRY

W.J.LeV.   William Judson LeVeque. *Executive Director, American Mathematical Society, Providence, Rhode Island, 1977–88. Professor of*

Mathematics, Claremont Graduate School, California, 1970–77. Author of Topics in Number Theory; Introduction to Number Theory; *and others.*
ARITHMETIC (*in part*)

W.J.M.   Wolfgang J. Mommsen. *Professor of Modern History, University of Düsseldorf, Germany. Chairman, Union of German Historians. Author of* Max Weber und die deutsche Politik 1890–1920.
GERMANY (*in part*)

W.J.McC.   Willard J. McCarthy. *Associate Professor of Industrial Technology, Illinois State University, Normal. Coauthor of* Machine Tool Technology.
TOOLS (*in part*)

W.J.S.   W. John Smith. *Professor of Biology and Psychology, University of Pennsylvania, Philadelphia. Author of* The Behavior of Communicating.
BEHAVIOUR, ANIMAL (*in part*)

W.J.T.   William John Talbot. *Emeritus Professor of Geography, University of Cape Town. Coauthor of* Atlas of the Union of South Africa.
SOUTH AFRICA (*in part*)

W.J.Tu.   William Julian Tuttle. *Motion picture makeup artist. Adjunct Professor, School of Cinema-Television, University of Southern California, Los Angeles. President, Custom Color Cosmetics, Pacific Palisades, California. Winner of a special Academy Award, 1965.*
DRESS AND ADORNMENT (*in part*)

W.Jw.   Wadie Jwaideh. *Emeritus Professor of History and Arabic, Indiana University, Bloomington.*
IDRĪSĪ, ASH-SHARĪF AL- (Micropædia)

W.J.W.   Willem Johan Wawaroentoe. *Professor of Regional and Urban Planning, Bandung Institute of Technology, Java, Indonesia. Rector, Sam Ratulangi University, Manado. Author of* Recent Urban Growth in Indonesia and Its Regional Development Implications.
JAKARTA

W.K.H.   William K. Holstein. *Professor of Management Science, State University of New York at Albany. Coauthor of* Casebooks in Production Management.
INDUSTRIAL ENGINEERING AND PRODUCTION MANAGEMENT (*in part*)

W.Ki.   William Kirk (deceased). *Professor and Head, Department of Geography, Queen's University of Belfast, Northern Ireland. Author of various articles on southern Asia.*
INDIA (*in part*)

W.K.M.   Woodville K. Marshall. *Professor of History, University of the West Indies, Cave Hill, Barbados.*
WEST INDIES, THE (*in part*)

W.K.R.M.   William K.R. Musgrave. *Emeritus Professor of Organic Chemistry, University of Durham, England. Author of numerous articles on halogen-containing organic compounds.*
CHEMICAL COMPOUNDS (*in part*)

W.L.J.   William Lee Jolly. *Professor of Chemistry, University of California, Berkeley. Author of* The Synthesis and Characterization of Inorganic Compounds *and others.*
CHEMICAL ELEMENTS (*in part*)

W.L.M.   William Lewis Morton (d. 1980). *Vanier Professor of Canadian History, Trent University, Peterborough, Ontario, 1969–75. Author of* The Kingdom of Canada *and others.*
CANADA (*in part*)

W.L.Ma.   Walter L. Manger. *Professor of Geology, University of Arkansas, Fayetteville. Coeditor of* The Atokan Series, Pennsylvanian, and Its Boundaries: A Symposium.
GEOCHRONOLOGY (*in part*)

W.L.N.   Warwick L. Nicholas. *Reader in Zoology, Australian National University, Canberra. Author of* The Biology of Free-Living Nematodes.
ASCHELMINTHS

W.L.O.   William L. Ochsenwald. *Professor of History, Virginia Polytechnic Institute and State University, Blacksburg. Author of* Religion, Society, and the State in Arabia.
ARABIA (*in part*)
ASIA (*in part*)
ISRAEL (*in part*)
JORDAN (*in part*)
LEBANON (*in part*)
PALESTINE (*in part*)
SYRIA (*in part*)

W.L.O'N.   William L. O'Neill. *Professor of History, Rutgers University, New Brunswick, New Jersey. Author of* Coming Apart: An Informal History of America in the 1960's *and others.*
UNITED STATES OF AMERICA (*in part*)

W.L.Re.   William L. Reese. *Professor of Philosophy, State University of New York at Albany. Author of* Dictionary of Philosophy and Religion: Eastern and Western Thought.
RELIGIOUS AND SPIRITUAL BELIEF, SYSTEMS OF (*in part*)

W.L.S.   William L. Schaaf. *Emeritus Professor of Mathematical Education, Brooklyn College, City University of New York. Author of* Bibliography of Recreational Mathematics.
NUMBER GAMES AND OTHER MATHEMATICAL RECREATIONS

W.L.Sa.   The Rev. William L. Sachs. *Assistant Rector, St. Stephen's Episcopal Church, Richmond, Virginia. Author of* The Transformation of Anglicanism.
PROTESTANTISM (*in part*)

W.L.St.   William Louis Stern. *Professor of Botany, University of Florida, Gainesville. Coauthor of* Humanistic Botany.
ANGIOSPERMS (*in part*)

W.M.   William Montagna. *Emeritus Professor of Dermatology, Oregon Health Sciences University, Portland. Author of* The Structure and Function of Skin.
INTEGUMENTARY SYSTEMS (*in part*)

W.Ma.   William Markowitz. *Adjunct Professor of Physics, Nova University, Fort Lauderdale, Florida. Astronomer, U.S. Naval Observatory, Washington, D.C., 1936–66; Director, Time Service, 1953–66. Coeditor of* Continental Drift, Secular Motion of the Pole, and Rotation of the Earth.
TIME (*in part*)

W.MacG.   Wyatt MacGaffey. *Professor of Anthropology, Haverford College, Pennsylvania. Author of* Custom and Government in the Lower Congo.
KINSHASA (*in part*)

W.Man.   William Manchester. *Adjunct Professor of History; Writer-in-Residence, Wesleyan University, Middletown, Connecticut. Author of* The Death of a President; The Arms of Krupp.
KENNEDY, JOHN F. (*in part*) (Micropædia)
KENNEDY, JOSEPH P. (*in part*) (Micropædia)
KENNEDY, ROBERT F. (*in part*) (Micropædia)

Wm.A.R.T.   William Archibald Robson Thomson, M.D. (d. 1983). *Editor,* The Practitioner, *1944–73. Author of* The Searching Mind in Medicine *and others; coeditor of* Black's Medical Dictionary.
MEDICINE (*in part*)

W.M.B.   W. Mary Bannerman (d. 1984). *Coauthor of* The Birds of the Atlantic Islands (*4 vol.*).
WESTERN AFRICA (*in part*)

W.M.Cl.   Wayne M. Clegern. *Professor of History, Colorado State University, Fort Collins. Author of* British Honduras: Colonial Dead End, 1859–1900.
CENTRAL AMERICA (*in part*)

W.M.E.   Walter M. Elsasser. *Adjunct Professor of Geophysics, Johns Hopkins University, Baltimore.*
SOLAR SYSTEM, THE (*in part*)

Wm.F.   William Fleming. *Emeritus Professor of Fine Arts, Syracuse University, New York.*
ARCHITECTURE, THE HISTORY OF WESTERN (*in part*)

W.M.-F.   Wolfram Müller-Freienfels. *Professor of International Civil Law; Director, Institute of Foreign and International Civil Law, Albert Ludwig University of Freiburg, Germany. Author of* Die Vertretung beim Rechtsgeschälft *and others.*
BUSINESS LAW (*in part*)

W.Mi.   Wesley Milgate. *Emeritus Professor of English, Australian National University, Canberra. Editor of* John Donne: The Satires, Epigrams and Verse Letters; John Donne: A Life.
DONNE, JOHN (Micropædia)

W.Mo.   Warren Moran. *Professor of Geography, University of Auckland, New Zealand. Editor of* Auckland and the Central North Island.
NEW ZEALAND (*in part*)

W.Mr.   William Miller (d. 1945). *Author of* Greece; The Ottoman Empire

and Its Successors (1801–1936).
GREECE (*in part*)

W.M.S.   William Merritt Sale, Jr.
(d. 1981). *Goldwin Smith Professor of English, Cornell University, Ithaca, New York. Author of* Samuel Richardson: A Biographical Record; Samuel Richardson: Master Printer.
RICHARDSON, SAMUEL (Micropædia)

W.M.W.   William Montgomery Watt. *Professor of Arabic and Islāmic Studies, University of Edinburgh, 1964–79. Author of* Muhammad: Prophet and Statesman; Muslim Intellectual: A Study of al-Ghazālī; *general editor of* Islāmic Surveys.
GHAZĀLĪ, AL- (Micropædia)
HĀRŪN AR-RASHĪD (Micropædia)
ISLĀM, MUḤAMMAD AND THE RELIGION OF (*in part*)

W.M.Wa.   Willard M. Wallace. *Emeritus Professor of History, Wesleyan University, Middletown, Connecticut. Author of* Appeal to Arms: A Military History of the American Revolution.
UNITED STATES OF AMERICA (*in part*)

W.M.Wh.   Walter Muir Whitehill (d. 1978). *Director and Librarian, Boston Athenaeum, 1946–73. Author of* Boston: A Topographical History *and others.*
BOSTON (*in part*)

W.M.Yo.   Warren Melvin Young. *Professor and Chairman, Department of Physics and Astronomy, Youngstown State University, Ohio.*
STARS AND STAR CLUSTERS (*in part*)

W.N.D.   William N. Dember. *Professor of Psychology, University of Cincinnati, Ohio. Author of* The Psychology of Perception.
PERCEPTION, HUMAN (*in part*)

W.O.   Wilfred Owen. *Former Senior Fellow, Brookings Institution, Washington, D.C. Author of* The Accessible City *and others.*
UNITED STATES OF AMERICA (*in part*)

W.O.B.   William O. Bright. *Emeritus Professor of Linguistics and Anthropology, University of California, Los Angeles. Author of* American Indian Linguistics and Literature.
LANGUAGES OF THE WORLD (*in part*)

W.O.C.   W. Owen Chadwick. *Regius Professor of Modern History, University of Cambridge, 1968–83; Dixie Professor of Ecclesiastical History, 1958–68. Author of* The Reformation *and others.*
GREGORY OF TOURS, SAINT (Micropædia)
NEWMAN, JOHN HENRY (Micropædia)
PROTESTANTISM (*in part*)

W.P.   Wilhelm Pauck (d. 1981). *Professor of Church History, Union Theological Seminary, New York City, 1953–67. Author of* Harnack and Troeltsch *and others.*
HARNACK, ADOLF VON (Micropædia)

W.Pa.   Władysław Parczewski (d. 1981). *Professor of Physics of the Atmosphere, Technical University of Warsaw. Director, National Institute for Hydrology and Meteorology, Warsaw,*

1966–69.
EUROPE (*in part*)

W.P.D.   W. Phillips Davison. *Emeritus Professor of Sociology and Journalism, Columbia University. Author of* International Political Communication.
PUBLIC OPINION

W.P.G.   Wesley Patterson Garrigus (d. 1985). *Professor of Animal Husbandry, University of Kentucky, Lexington, 1941–74. Author of* Introductory Animal Science.
FARMING AND AGRICULTURAL TECHNOLOGY (*in part*)

W.P.H.   Capt. Wayne P. Hughes, Jr. *Captain, U.S. Navy (retired). Professor of Operations Research, Naval Postgraduate School, Monterey, California. Author of* Fleet Tactics: Theory and Practice.
WAR, THE THEORY AND CONDUCT OF (*in part*)

W.Ph.C.   W.Ph. Coolhaas (deceased). *Professor of Colonial History, Utrecht University, The Netherlands. Coauthor of* Jan Pieterszoon Coen *and others.*
COEN, JAN PIETERSZOON (Micropædia)

W.P.M.   William P. Malm. *Professor of Musicology, University of Michigan, Ann Arbor. Author of* Japanese Music and Musical Instruments; Six Hidden Views of Japanese Music.
EAST ASIAN ARTS (*in part*)

W.P.McG.   William Paul McGreevey. *Senior Economist, International Bank for Reconstruction and Development, Washington, D.C. Author of* An Economic History of Colombia, 1845–1930.
COLOMBIA (*in part*)

W.R.   Willi Reich (d. 1980). *Music critic. Author of* The Life and Work of Alban Berg *and many others.*
BERG, ALBAN (Micropædia)

W.Ra.   William Ravenhill. *Reardon Smith Professor Emeritus of Geography, University of Exeter, England. Author of* Ben Donn's Map of Devon, 1765; *coauthor of* South-West England.
UNITED KINGDOM (*in part*)

W.R.C.   William R. Chaney. *Professor of Tree Physiology, Purdue University, West Lafayette, Indiana.*
FORESTRY AND WOOD PRODUCTION (*in part*)

W.R.H.   William Richey Hogg. *Emeritus Professor of World Christianity, Southern Methodist University, Dallas, Texas. Author of* One World, One Mission.
CHRISTIANITY (*in part*)

W.R.J.   Wilbur R. Jacobs. *Professor of History, University of California, Santa Barbara. Editor of* The Letters of Francis Parkman.
PARKMAN, FRANCIS (Micropædia)
PRESCOTT, WILLIAM H. (Micropædia)

W.R.K.   Wilbur R. Knorr. *Associate Professor of the History of Science, Stanford University, California. Author of* Ancient Tradition of Geometric

problems *and others.*
MATHEMATICS, THE HISTORY OF (*in part*)

W.R.P.   William Roe Polk. *Historian. Professor of Middle Eastern History, University of Chicago, 1965–75. Author of* The United States and the Arab World.
ISRAEL (*in part*)
SYRIA (*in part*)

W.R.S.   Walter R. Sharp (d. 1977). *Professor of International Relations, Yale University, 1951–64. Author of* Field Administration in the United Nations System *and others.*
UNITED NATIONS (*in part*)

W.S.   Wilfred Sircus, M.D. *Senior Consultant Physician, Gastrointestinal Unit; former Reader in Medicine, University of Edinburgh. Coeditor of* Scientific Foundations of Gastroenterology.
DIGESTION AND DIGESTIVE SYSTEMS (*in part*)

W.Sc.   Walter Schulz. *Emeritus Professor of Philosophy, Eberhard Karl University of Tübingen, Germany. Member of the F.W.J. Schelling Commission of the Bavarian Academy of Sciences. Author of* Schelling.
SCHELLING, FRIEDRICH WILHELM JOSEPH VON (*in part*) (Micropædia)

W.S.-cg.   Wu Shih-ch'ang. *Former Senior Lecturer in Chinese, University of Oxford.*
HISTORY, THE STUDY OF (*in part*)

W.S.F.   William S. Fyfe. *Professor of Geology, University of Western Ontario, London. Coauthor of* The Earth.
MINERALS AND ROCKS (*in part*)

W.S.H.   Winthrop S. Hudson. *Adjunct Professor of Religion, University of North Carolina at Chapel Hill. James B. Colgate Professor of the History of Christianity, Colgate Rochester Divinity School, Rochester, New York, 1948–77. Author of* Religion in America.
PROTESTANTISM (*in part*)

W.S.L.   William S. Laughlin. *Professor of Ecology and Evolutionary Biology, University of Connecticut, Storrs.*
BIOLOGICAL SCIENCES (*in part*)

W.S.MacNu.   W. Stewart MacNutt (d. 1976). *Professor of History, University of New Brunswick, Fredericton. Author of* New Brunswick: A History, 1784–1867.
CANADA (*in part*)

W.S.N.   William S. Newman. *Alumni Distinguished Professor Emeritus of Music, University of North Carolina at Chapel Hill. Author of* A History of the Sonata Idea *and others.*
MUSICAL FORMS AND GENRES (*in part*)

W.S.Sh.   Wendy Stedman Sheard. *Art historian. Author of* Antiquity in the Renaissance; *coeditor of* Collaboration in Italian Renaissance Art.
MANTEGNA, ANDREA (Micropædia)

W.T.   Walter Terry (d. 1982). *Dance critic and editor,* Saturday Review *magazine;* New York Herald Tribune;

and others. Author of The Dance in America *and many others.*
GRAHAM, MARTHA (Micropædia)

W.Ta.   William Taylor. *Principal, University of London; Director, Institute of Education, 1973–83. Author of* Society and the Education of Teachers.
TEACHING (*in part*)

W.-t.C.   Wing-tsit Chan. *Anna R.D. Gillespie Professor Emeritus of Philosophy, Chatham College, Pittsburgh. Emeritus Professor of Chinese Philosophy and Culture, Dartmouth College, Hanover, New Hampshire. Author of* A Source Book in Chinese Philosophy *and others.*
WANG YANG-MING (Micropædia)

W.T.G.   Wassil Todorov Gjuzelev. *Professor of Bulgarian Medieval History, University of Sofia. Author of* Knjaz Boris Parvi *and others.*
BORIS I (Micropædia)

W.T.Ke.   William T. Keeton (d. 1980). *Liberty Hyde Bailey Professor of Biology, Cornell University, Ithaca, New York, 1969–80. Author of* Biological Science; Elements of Biological Science.
DIGESTION AND DIGESTIVE SYSTEMS (*in part*)

W.T.Sa.   William T. Sanders. *Evan Pugh Professor of Anthropology, Pennsylvania State University, University Park. Coauthor of* Mesoamerica: The Evolution of a Civilization *and others.*
PRE-COLUMBIAN CIVILIZATIONS (*in part*)

W.T.v.S.   Wolfram Th. von Soden. *Emeritus Professor of Ancient Semitic Philology and Ancient Oriental History, University of Münster, Germany.*
MESOPOTAMIA, THE HISTORY OF ANCIENT (*in part*)

W.T.W.M.   William Thomas Wilson Morgan. *Senior Lecturer in Geography, University of Durham, England. Author of* East Africa; *editor of* East Africa: Its Peoples and Resources.
EASTERN AFRICA (*in part*)

W.U.   Walter Ullmann (d. 1983). *Professor of Medieval History, University of Cambridge, 1972–78; Professor of Ecclesiastical History, 1965–72. Author of* The Growth of Papal Government in the Middle Ages *and others.*
LEO IX, SAINT (Micropædia)

W.V.D'A.   William Vincent D'Antonio. *Executive Officer, American Sociological Association, Washington, D.C. Professor and Chairman, Department of Sociology, University of Connecticut, Storrs, 1971–76. Coauthor of* Influentials in Two Border Cities.
UNITED STATES OF AMERICA (*in part*)

W.V.E.   Wolf Von Eckardt. *Design Critic,* Time *magazine, 1981–85. Architecture Critic,* The Washington Post, *1963–81. Author of* A Place to Live: The Crisis of the Cities *and others.*
MIES VAN DER ROHE, LUDWIG (Micropædia)

W.V.M.   William Vernon Mayer (d. 1989). *Professor of Biology, University of*

Colorado, Boulder. Director, Biological Sciences Curriculum Study. Author of Hibernation.
BEHAVIOUR, ANIMAL (*in part*)

W.V.P.   William V. Porter. *Professor of Music History and Literature, Northwestern University, Evanston, Illinois.*
MUSICAL FORMS AND GENRES (*in part*)

W.V.S.   Walter V. Scholes (d. 1975). *Professor of History, University of Missouri, Columbia, 1954–75. Author of* Mexican Politics During the Juárez Regime, 1855–1872 *and others.*
JUÁREZ, BENITO (Micropædia)

W.W.   William Watson. *Emeritus Professor of Chinese Art and Archaeology; Head, Percival David Foundation of Chinese Art, 1966–83, School of Oriental and African Studies, University of London. Author of* China Before the Han Dynasty *and others.*
HISTORY, THE STUDY OF (*in part*)

W.W.Bu.   Warren W. Burggren. *Professor of Zoology, University of Massachusetts, Amherst. Editor, Physiological Zoology. Coeditor of* New Directions in Ecological Physiology.
RESPIRATION AND RESPIRATORY SYSTEMS (*in part*)

W.W.C.   W. Walker Chambers (d. 1985). *William Jacks Professor of German, University of Glasgow, 1954–79. Coauthor of* A Short History of the German Language.
GERMAN LITERATURE (*in part*)

W.W.H.   Warren W. Hassler, Jr. *Emeritus Professor of American History, Pennsylvania State University, University Park. Author of* Commanders of the Army of the Potomac *and others.*
UNITED STATES OF AMERICA (*in part*)

W.Wi.   William Witte. *Emeritus Professor of German, University of Aberdeen, Scotland. Author of* Schiller; *editor of several works of Schiller's works.*
HÖLDERLIN, FRIEDRICH (Micropædia)
SCHILLER, FRIEDRICH VON (*in part*) (Micropædia)

W.W.M.   William W. Malandra. *Associate Professor of Indo-Iranian Philology, University of Minnesota, Minneapolis. Author of* An Introduction to Ancient Iranian Religion.
MIDDLE EASTERN RELIGIONS, ANCIENT (*in part*)

W.W.R.   William Wallace Robson. *Masson Professor of English Literature, University of Edinburgh. Author of* Critical Essays: Modern English Literature.
LAWRENCE, D.H. (*in part*) (Micropædia)
TENNYSON, ALFRED TENNYSON, 1ST BARON (Micropædia)

W.W.W.   William Walter Watts (d. 1948). *Keeper, Department of Metal Work, Victoria and Albert Museum, London, 1879–1923. Author of* Old English Silver *and others.*
DECORATIVE ARTS AND FURNISHINGS (*in part*)

W.-Y.K.   Won-Yong Kim. *Emeritus Professor of Archaeology, Seoul National University. Author of* Art and Archaeology of Ancient Korea *and others.*
EAST ASIAN ARTS (*in part*)
WRITING (*in part*)

W.Y.W.   William Young Willetts. *Former Curator, Museum of Asian Art, University of Malaya, Kuala Lumpur. Author of* Chinese Art.
DECORATIVE ARTS AND FURNISHINGS (*in part*)

W.Z.   Warren Zeiller. *Vice President and General Manager, Miami Seaquarium. Author of* Tropical Marine Fishes of South Florida and the Bahamas *and others.*
FISHES (*in part*)

W.Ze.   Wilbur Zelinsky. *Emeritus Professor of Geography, Pennsylvania State University, University Park. Author of* The Cultural Geography of the United States *and others.*
NORTH AMERICA (*in part*)
UNITED STATES OF AMERICA (*in part*)

Y.A.C.   Yehudi A. Cohen. *Professor of Anthropology, Rutgers University, New Brunswick, New Jersey. Editor of* Man in Adaptation.
RITES AND CEREMONIES, SACRED (*in part*)

Y.B.   Yvon Belaval (d. 1988). *Professor of Philosophy, University of Paris I, 1965–79. Vice President, Leibniz Society, Hanover, West Germany. Author of* Leibniz: Initiation à sa philosophie *and many others.*
LEIBNIZ, GOTTFRIED WILHELM (*in part*) (Micropædia)

Y.-c.K.   Yu-chin Kang. *Professor of Atmospheric Sciences, National Taiwan University, Taipei.*
TAIWAN (*in part*)

Y.C.W.   Yi Chu Wang. *Emeritus Professor of History, Queens College, City University of New York. Author of* Chinese Intellectuals and the West.
CHANG CHIH-TUNG (Micropædia)
SUN YAT-SEN (Micropædia)

Y.-G.G.H.   Yueh-Gin Gung Hu. *Researcher in Chinese studies. Assistant Librarian, University of Chicago, 1938–43.*
CHINA (*in part*)

Y.J.   Yette Jeandet. *Former Editor,* Literary News, Bayard-Presse, *Paris. Author of* Blanche de Castille, reine de l'unité française *and others.*
BLANCHE OF CASTILE (Micropædia)

Y.K.Y.   Yury Konstantinovich Yefremov. *Former Senior Scientist, Geographical Museum, Moscow M.V. Lomonosov State University.*
ASIA (*in part*)

Y.L.   Yvonne Lanhers. *Curator, National Archives, Paris. Coeditor of* La Réhabilitation de Jeanne la Pucelle.
CHARLES VII (FRANCE) (Micropædia)
JOAN OF ARC (*in part*)

Y.-L.W.   Yoke-Lan Wicks. *Deputy Director, National Library, Singapore.*
INFORMATION PROCESSING AND
    INFORMATION SYSTEMS (*in part*)

Y.M.   Yasuo Masai. *Professor of Geography, Rissho University, Tokyo. Editor of* Atlas Tokyo.
JAPAN (*in part*)

Y.M.A.   Yuri M. Ado. *Professor, Accelerator Division, Institute for High Energy Physics, State Committee for Utilization of Atomic Energy of the U.S.S.R., Protvino. Coauthor of* "Coherent Radiation from the Electrons in a Synchrotron" *in* Atomnaya energiya.
PARTICLE ACCELERATORS (*in part*)

Y.M.D.   Yelena Matveyevna Doroshinskaya. *Journalist. Coauthor of* Leningrad.
SAINT PETERSBURG (*in part*)

Y.-m.Y.   Yue-man Yeung. *Professor of Geography, Chinese University of Hong Kong.*
CHINA (*in part*)

Y.P.M.   Yi Pao Mei. *Henry Luce Professor of Humanities, Tunghai University, T'ai-chung, Taiwan, 1973–77. Professor of Oriental Studies, University of Iowa, Iowa City, 1955–70. Author of* Motse: The Neglected Rival of Confucius.
MENCIUS (Micropædia)
MO-TZU (Micropædia)

Y.T.   Yoshinori Takeuchi. *Emeritus Professor of Philosophy of Religion, Kyōto University. Author of* Philosophy of Shinran; The Heart of Buddhism.
NISHIDA KITARŌ (Micropædia)

Y.T.T.   Youssef T. Toni. *Professor of Geography, Laurentian University of Sudbury, Ontario. Author of* Lexique de Geographie.
ARABIA (*in part*)

Y.V.Y.   Yevgeny V. Yastrebov. *Former Assistant Professor of Geography, Moscow Oblast Pedagogical Institute. Author of* How the Urals Have Been Discovered *and others.*
EUROPE (*in part*)

Y.Y.R.   Yelizaveta Yakovlevna Rantsman. *Senior Scientist, Institute of Geography, Academy of Sciences of the U.S.S.R., Moscow. Author of numerous articles on geography.*
ASIA (*in part*)

Z.A.B.Z.   Z.A.B. Zeman. *Research Professor of European History, University of Oxford; Fellow of St. Edmund Hall, Oxford. Author of* The Break-up of the Habsburg Empire, 1914–1918 *and others.*
CZECHOSLOVAKIA (*in part*)

Z.A.K.   Zafar Ahmad Khan. *Professor of Geography, Government College, Rāwalpindi, Pakistan. Author of* Karachi: An Urban Profile.
KARĀCHI

Z.D.K.   Zimani David Kadzamira. *Reader in Government; Principal, Chancellor College, University of Malawi, Zomba. Contributor to* Malawi Past and Present.
SOUTHERN AFRICA (*in part*)

Z.G.   Zhong Gongfu. *Professor, Guangzhou Institute of Geography, China.*
CANTON (*in part*)

Z.I.A.   Zafar Ishaq Ansari. *Former Professor of History, University of Petroleum and Minerals, Dhahran, Saudi Arabia.*
ABŪ ḤANĪFAH (*in part*)
    (Micropædia)

Z.O.   Zoé Oldenbourg-Idalie. *Novelist and free-lance writer. Author of* Catherine the Great *and others.*
CATHERINE II (Micropædia)

Z.V.   Zeno Vendler. *Emeritus Professor of Philosophy, University of California, San Diego, at La Jolla. Author of* Linguistics in Philosophy; Adjectives and Nominalizations; *and others.*
LINGUISTICS (*in part*)

Z.Z.   Zeng Zungu. *Professor of Geography, Nanking University, China. Coauthor of* World Geography.
NANKING (*in part*)

Names of
Contributors

Listed below, with initials that identify them, are the names of persons who have written articles or sections of articles. For brief summaries of their positions and the titles of all articles contributed, see under authors' initials in the list on pages 531–655.

Aaron, Richard I.   R.Aa.
Abbagnano, Nicola.   N.Ab.
Abdo, Ass'ad Sulaiman.   A.S.A.
Abel-Smith, Brian.   B.A.-S.
Aberdare, Morys George Lyndhurst Bruce, 4th Baron.   A.
Abraham, Gerald E.H.   G.E.H.A.
Abrahams, Harold Maurice.   H.M.A.
Abrahart, Edward Noah.   E.N.A.
Abramson, Glenda M.   G.M.A.
Abu Jaber, Kamel S.   K.S.A.J.
Abu-Lughod, Janet L.   J.L.A.-L.
Accordi, Bruno.   B.A.
Ackerman, James S.   J.S.Ac.
Ackoff, Russell L.   R.L.A.
Acton, Harry Burrows.   H.B.A.
Adamovich, Anthony.   A.Ad.
Adams, Charles Joseph.   C.J.A.
Adams, Robert M.   R.M.A.
Adams, Robert McCormick.   R.M.As.
Adams, Ron.   R.Ad.
Adejuwon, James Oladipo.   J.O.A.
Adhémar, Jean.   J.Ad.
Adkins, A.W.H.   A.W.H.A.
Adkins, Dorothy C.   D.C.A.
Adler, Jeremy D.   J.D.Ad.
Adler, John H.   J.H.A.
Ado, Yuri M.   Y.M.A.
Adotevi, Stanislas Spero.   S.S.A.
Agenbroad, Larry D.   L.D.A.
Agostino, Guido d'.   G.d'A.
Aguirre, Margarita.   M.Ag.
Aherne, Sister Consuelo Maria.   C.M.A.
Ahlström, Gösta W.   G.W.A.
Ahmad, Nafis.   N.A.
Ahmadjian, Vernon.   V.A.
Ahrweiler, Hélène.   H.Ah.
Aiyappan, Ayinipalli.   A.Ai.
Ajayi, J.F. Ade.   J.F.A.A.
Akita, George.   G.Ak.
Alavi, Hamza A.   H.A.A.
Alba, Victor.   V.Al.
Alberts, Bruce M.   B.M.A.
Alberts, Wybe Jappe.   W.J.Al.
Albrecht-Carrié, René.   R.A.-C.
Albright, William Foxwell.   W.F.A.
Albritton, Claude C.   C.C.A.
Albury, E. Paul.   E.P.A.
Aleem, Anwar Abdel.   An.A.A.
Alekseev, Arkody Vladimirovich.   A.V.A.
Alexander, Lewis M.   L.M.A.
Alexander, Robert J.   R.J.Al.
Alexander, Robert McNeill.   R.McN.A.
Alexeeva, Nina Nikolaevna.   N.N.A.
Alexopoulos, Constantine John.   C.J.Al.
Alford, Alfred E.   A.E.A.

Alford, R.F.G.   R.F.G.A.
Ali, Mohammad.   M.Al.
Alip, Eufronio M.   Eu.M.A.
Alisky, Marvin H.   M.H.A.
Alitto, Guy S.   G.S.A.
Allais, Maurice.   Ma.A.
Allan, John.   J.Al.
Allan, Nigel John Roger.   N.J.R.A.
Allard, The Rev. Michel Adrien.   M.A.Al.
Allard, R.W.   R.W.A.
Allchin, Frank Raymond.   F.R.Al.
Allcock, John B.   J.B.A.
Allen, Francis A.   F.A.A.
Allen, Garland Edward.   G.E.Al.
Allen, Geoffrey Freeman.   G.F.A.
Allen, Walter E.   W.E.A.
Aller, Lawrence Hugh.   L.H.A.
Allibone, Thomas Edward.   T.E.A.
Allott, Antony Nicolas.   A.N.A.
Allworth, Edward.   E.Al.
Almagià, Roberto.   Ro.A.
Alpers, Edward Alter.   E.A.A.
Alpert, Norman R.   N.R.A.
Al-Shahi, Ahmed S.   A.Al-Sh.
Alston, Rex.   R.Al.
Amadio, The Rev. Anselm H.   A.H.Ao.
Amaral, Ilídio Melo Peres do.   I.M.P. do A.
Amengual, Barthélemy.   B.Am.
Amerine, Maynard A.   M.A.A.
Ames, Winslow.   W.Am.
Amundson, Clyde H.   C.H.A.
Anastaplo, George.   G.An.
Anastaplo, Sara Prince.   S.P.A.
Andersen, Robert A.   R.A.An.
Anderson, Donald M.   D.An.
Anderson, Douglas M.W.   D.M.W.A.
Anderson, Edgar.   E.An.
Anderson, Edward W.   E.W.A.
Anderson, Franklin K.   F.K.A.
Anderson, Robert T.   R.T.A.
Anderson, Stanley Victor.   S.V.A.
Anderson, Thomas P.   T.P.A.
Andrade U., Victor.   V.A.U.
Andrew, Dudley.   D.A.
Andrew, Richard J.   R.J.A.
Andrew, Warren.   W.A.
Andreyev, Nikolay.   N.An.
Andrups, J.A.   J.A.A.
Angel, Pierre Robert.   P.R.A.
Anguizola, Gustavo.   Gu.A.
Annas, George J.   G.J.A.
Ansari, Zafar Ishaq.   Z.I.A.
Anschutz, Richard Paul.   R.P.An.
Anthony, Jean Daniel.   J.D.A.
Anthony, John Duke.   J.D.An.
Anweiler, Oskar.   O.A.
Apostol, Tom M.   T.M.A.
Aquilecchia, Giovanni.   G.A.
Arasaratnam, Sinnappah.   S.Ara.
Archibald, Raymond Clare.   R.C.A.
Ardagh, John Anthony Charles.   J.A.C.A.
Aretin, Karl Otmar, Baron von.   K.O.v.A.
Arey, Leslie B.   L.B.A.

Arfa, Maj. Gen. Hassan.   H.Ar.
Argov, Daniel.   D.Ar.
Arguello, Rosendo.   R.A.
Argyle, Michael.   M.Ar.
Argyle, W.J.   W.J.Ar.
Arlazorov, Mikhail S.   M.S.A.
Armstrong, A. Hilary.   A.H.A.
Armstrong, Annette Elizabeth.   A.E.Ar.
Armstrong, David M.   D.M.A.
Armstrong, Lloyd Van Horn.   L.V.A.
Armstrong, Terence Edward.   T.E.Ar.
Armytage, Walter Harry Green.   W.H.G.A.
Arnade, Charles W.   C.W.A.
Arnason, H. Harvard.   H.H.A.
Arnfield, A. John.   A.J.A.
Arnold, Denis Midgley.   D.M.Ar.
Arnold, Godfrey Edward.   G.E.A.
Arnott, W. Geoffrey.   W.G.A.
Arrington, Leonard James.   L.J.A.
Aruja, Endel.   E.Ar.
Arvon, Henri.   H.A.
Asanachinta, Col. Phoon Phon.   P.P.A.
Ashley, Maurice.   M.As.
Ashmole, Bernard.   B.As.
Ashmole, N. Philip.   N.P.As.
Asimov, Isaac.   I.A.
Aspinall, Arthur C.V.D.   A.As.
Asprey, Larned B.   L.B.As.
Asprey, Robert Brown.   R.B.A.
Atherden, Lewis Malcolm.   L.M.At.
Atherton, James Stephen.   J.S.A.
Atiyah, Sir Michael Francis.   M.F.A.
Atkins, Ralph Charles.   R.C.At.
Atkinson, William C.   W.C.A.
Attwater, Donald.   D.At.
Atwater, Gordon I.   G.I.A.
Aubert, Roger-François-Marie.   R.-F.-M.A.
Aubin, Hermann.   H.Au.
Auboyer, Jeannine.   J.Au.
Auclair, Marcelle.   M.A.
Auerbach, Charlotte.   C.Au.
Aulie, Richard Paul.   R.P.A.
Aumann, Francis R.   F.R.A.
Aurenhammer, Hans.   Ha.A.
Austen, Ralph A.   R.A.A.
Austerlitz, Robert.   R.Au.
Austin, Oliver L., Jr.   O.L.A.
Auty, Robert.   Ro.Au.
Avery, Peter William.   P.W.A.
Avila, Héctor Fernando.   H.F.A.
Avila-Martel, Alamiro de.   A.de A.-M.
Avrich, Paul.   P.A.
Axelson, Eric.   E.A.
Ayala, Francisco Jose.   F.J.A.
Ayoub, Raymond George.   R.G.A.
Ayres, John C.   J.C.A.
Ayyar, Nagarajan Panchapagesan.   N.P.A.
Azcona, The Rev. Tarsicio de.   T.d.A.

Baaren, Theodorus P. van.   T.P.v.B.
Babaev, Agadjan G.   A.G.B.
Bachrach, Bernard S.   B.S.Ba.
Back, George I.   G.I.Bk.

Bode, Hendrik W.   H.W.B.
Bodin, D. Joseph.   D.J.B.
Bogdanov, Konstantin Trifonovich.
   K.T.B.
Bognetti, Giovanni.   G.B.
Bokser, Rabbi Ben Zion.   B.Z.B.
Boland, Frederick Henry.   F.H.B.
Bold, Harold C.   H.C.B.
Bolland, O. Nigel.   O.N.B.
Bolle, Kees W.   K.W.Bo.
Bollnow, Otto Friedrich.   O.F.B.
Bolt, Bruce A.   B.A.B.
Bolton, Geoffrey C.   G.C.Bo.
Bonavia, David Michael.   D.M.Bo.
Bond, Donald F.   D.F.B.
Bonfante, Larissa.   La.B.
Bonilla, José.   Jo.B.
Bonin, Gerhardt von.   G.v.B.
Bonner, Charles Edmond Bradlaugh.
   C.E.B.B.
Bonner, Gerald.   Ge.B.
Bonner, John Tyler.   J.T.Bo.
Borders, James M.   J.M.Bo.
Borgstrom, Georg A.   G.A.B.
Borlaza, Gregorio C.   G.C.B.
Bornecque, Jacques-Henry.   J.-H.B.
Bornkamm, Günther.   G.Bor.
Bornstein, Ira.   I.Bo.
Bornstein, Marc H.   M.H.Bo.
Borth, Paul F.   P.F.B.
Bose, Raj C.   R.C.Bo.
Bosisio, Alfredo.   Al.B.
Bottigheimer, Karl S.   K.S.B.
Bottomore, Thomas B.   T.B.B.
Boulding, Kenneth E.   K.E.Bo.
Bouloiseau, Marc.   M.Bo.
Bounds, John H.   J.H.Bo.
Bousfield, Edward L.   E.L.B.
Bouvier, Jean.   Je.B.
Bouwsma, William J.   W.J.Bo.
Bowen, James.   J.Bo.
Bowersock, G.W.   G.W.Bo.
Bowle, John Edward.   J.E.B.
Bowles, Edmund Addison.   E.A.Bo.
Bowman, Alan K.   A.K.B.
Bowman, John S.   J.S.Bo.
Bowness, Sir Alan.   Al.Bo.
Boxer, Baruch.   B.Bo.
Boyer, Carl B.   C.B.B.
Boyer, Marjorie Nice.   M.N.B.
Boyle, John Andrew.   J.A.Bo.
Bradbury, Savile.   S.Br.
Bradford, Ernle.   E.Br.
Bradley, Harold Whitman.   H.W.Br.
Bradley, John F.N.   J.F.N.B.
Bradley, Sir Kenneth.   K.Br.
Bradley, Rupert Stevenson.   R.S.B.
Bradley, Walter G.   W.G.Br.
Brady, The Rev. Ignatius Charles.
   I.C.B.
Braidwood, Robert J.   R.J.Br.
Brand, Donald Dilworth.   D.D.Br.
Brandon, James R.   J.R.B.
Brandon, The Rev. Samuel G.F.
   S.G.F.B.
Brandt, Andres R.F.T. von.   A.v.B.
Brant, Irving.   I.Bt.
Brasted, Robert C.   R.C.Br.
Brathwaite, Edward Kamau.   E.Be.
Bräuer, Günter.   G.Br.
Braun, Armin C.   A.C.Br.
Bready, James H.   Ja.H.B.
Breed, C.S.   C.S.Br.
Breed, William J.   W.J.Br.
Breen, Walter Henry.   W.H.Br.
Brereton, Bridget M.   B.M.B.

Brett, Martin.   Ma.Br.
Brice, William Charles.   W.C.B.
Bridenbaugh, Peter R.   P.R.B.
Bridges, Edward Bridges, 1st Baron.
   E.B.
Bridgewater, Thornton Howard.   T.H.B.
Briggs, Asa Briggs, Baron.   As.B.
Bright, John.   Jo.Br.
Bright, William O.   W.O.B.
Brill, Reginald.   R.Br.
Brisby, Liliana.   L.B.
Briskey, Ernest J.   E.J.B.
Britt, Kenneth W.   K.W.Br.
Britter, Eric V.B.   E.V.B.B.
Brix, Andrew C.   An.C.B.
Brock, John Fleming.   J.F.B.
Brodie, Fawn McKay.   F.M.B.
Brogan, Hugh.   H.Br.
Brombert, Victor.   V.Br.
Bromiley, Geoffrey W.   G.W.B.
Bromke, Adam.   A.Br.
Brommelle, Norman Spencer.   N.S.B.
Brown, David.   Da.Br.
Brown, Elizabeth A.R.   E.A.R.B.
Brown, Frank A., Jr.   F.A.B.
Brown, J.A.C.   J.A.C.B.
Brown, J. Guthrie.   J.G.B.
Brown, John Russell.   J.R.Br.
Brown, L. Carl.   L.C.Br.
Brown, Laurie M.   L.M.B.
Brown, Leslie Hilton.   L.H.B.
Brown, Maurice J.E.   M.J.E.B.
Brown, Peter R.L.   P.R.L.B.
Brown, Ray E.   R.E.Bn.
Brown, T. Julian.   T.J.Br.
Brown, William Arthur.   W.A.Br.
Browning, David G.   D.G.B.
Browning, Robert.   R.B.
Bruce, Frederick Fyvie.   F.F.B.
Bruce, Michael I.   M.I.B.
Bruhat, Jean.   J.Bru.
Bruk, Solomon Ilich.   S.I.B.
Bruman, Henry J.   H.J.Bn.
Brunner, Hellmut.   He.B.
Brunnschweiler, Dieter.   Di.B.
Bruschi, Arnaldo.   Ar.B.
Brush, Stephen G.   S.G.B.
Brusher, The Rev. Joseph Stanislaus.
   J.S.Br.
Bry, Doris.   D.Br.
Bryant, Sir Arthur.   Ar.Br.
Bryant, John H.   J.H.Br.
Bryceson, Deborah Fahy.   D.F.Br.
Buchan, The Hon. Alastair Francis.
   A.F.B.
Buchanan, Robert Angus.   R.A.Bu.
Buckmaster, Barbara.   B.Br.
Budden, Julian Medforth.   J.M.Bu.
Budenholzer, Roland A.   R.A.B.
Budinger, Thomas F.   T.F.B.
Buechner, Thomas S.   T.S.Bu.
Buettner-Janusch, John.   J.B.-J.
Bugh, Glenn Richard.   G.R.B.
Buisseret, David J.   D.J.Bu.
Buitenen, J.A.B. van.   J.A.B.v.B.
Bullock, Alan Bullock, Baron.   A.B.
Bullough, The Rev. Sebastian.   S.Bh.
Burgess, Anthony.   An.B.
Burggren, Warren W.   W.W.Bu.
Burghardt, The Rev. Walter John.
   W.J.Bu.
Burke, Ulick Peter.   U.P.B.
Burki, Shahid Javed.   S.J.B.
Burn, Andrew Robert.   A.R.Bu.
Burnaby, The Rev. John.   Jo.Bu.
Burns, E. Bradford.   E.B.B.

Burns, Thomas W.   T.W.B.
Burr, Robert N.   R.N.Bu.
Burri, Peter H.   P.H.B.
Burrows, William.   W.Bu.
Burrus, John N.   J.N.B.
Burton, Ivor F.   I.F.B.
Burton, Milton.   M.Bu.
Burtt, Edward Howland, Jr.   E.H.B.
Buru, Mukhtar Mustafa.   Mu.B.
Busch, Daryle H.   D.H.B.
Bush, Douglas.   D.B.
Bush-Brown, Albert.   A.B.-B.
Bushman, Donald O.   D.O.B.
Bushnell, Geoffrey H.S.   G.H.S.B.
Buss, Robin Caron.   R.C.Bu.
Busuttil, Salvino.   S.Bu.
Butland, Gilbert James.   G.J.B.
Butler, Joseph T.   J.T.B.
Butler, M.H.   M.H.B.
Butlin, Martin.   Ma.Bu.
Butt, John Everett.   J.E.Bu.
Butterfield, Lyman H.   L.H.Bu.
Buttinger, Joseph.   J.Bu.
Butts, Allison.   A.Bu.
Butzer, Karl W.   K.W.B.
Buxton, Richard G.A.   R.G.A.B.
Byrkit, James W.   J.W.B.
Byrne, Robert Howard.   R.H.By.
Byrnes, Robert F.   R.F.B.

Cadbury, Henry J.   H.J.C.
Cadoux, Theodore John.   T.J.C.
Cahen, Claude.   C.C.
Cahill, James F.   J.F.C.
Cahir, John J.   J.J.Ca.
Cahn, Robert W.   R.W.C.
Cain, A.J.   A.J.Ca.
Cain, Seymour.   S.C.
Calkin, Carleton Ivers.   C.I.C.
Calkins, Philip B.   P.B.Ca.
Callaghan, Peter John.   P.J.C.
Calmon, Pedro.   P.Ca.
Calne, Sir Roy Yorke.   R.Y.C.
Calogero, Guido.   G.C.
Camacho, Jorge A.   J.A.Ca.
Camara, Camille.   Ca.C.
Cameron, Roy Eugene.   R.E.C.
Campana, Pier Paolo del.   P.P. del C.
Campbell, Alan K.   A.K.Ca.
Campbell, Eila M.J.   E.M.J.C.
Campbell, John R.   J.R.C.
Camu, Pierre.   P.C.
Cannon-Brookes, Peter.   P.C.-B.
Canright, James Edward.   J.E.Ca.
Capers, Gerald M.   G.M.C.
Caponigri, A. Robert.   A.R.C.
Capper, Comdr. Douglas Parodé.
   D.P.C.
Cardona, George.   Ge.Ca.
Cardoze, Nydia María.   N.M.C.
Carey, Margret A.   Ma.A.C.
Carli, Enzo.   E.Ca.
Carlsson, Sten C.O.   S.C.O.C.
Carluccio, Luigi.   L.Ca.
Carmagnani, Marcello A.   M.A.Ca.
Carmichael, Robert S.   R.S.Ca.
Carpenter, Malcolm Breckenridge.
   M.B.C.
Carr, Bruce Alan.   B.A.C.
Carr, Edward H.   E.H.C.
Carr, Sir Raymond.   R.Ca.
Carruthers, John E.   J.E.C.
Carsaniga, Giovanni.   G.Car.
Carson, David.   D.Ca.
Carson, Hampton L.   H.L.C.

Carter, Francis William.   F.W.C.
Carter, Harold.   H.Ca.
Cartwright, Frederick F.   F.F.C.
Cartwright, Janet M.   J.M.Ca.
Cartwright, Rosalind D.   R.D.C.
Cary, Max.   M.Car.
Cary, Otis.   O.C.
Casey, H.C., Jr.   H.C.C.
Cash, Arthur H.   A.H.Ca.
Casolani, Lieut. Col. Charles Edward.
   C.E.C.
Castañeda, Concepción E.   C.E.Ca.
Castle, Peter Henry John.   P.H.J.C.
Caswell, John Edwards.   Jo.E.C.
Catalano, Eduardo F.   E.F.C.
Caudle, Ben H.   B.H.C.
Caughey, John W.   J.W.C.
Caussou, Jean-Louis.   J.-L.Ca.
Cavero Lataillade, Iñigo.   I.C.L.
Caviedes, Cesar N.   C.N.Ca.
Cawkwell, George Law.   G.L.Ca.
Cessi, Roberto.   R.Ce.
Cestre, Charles.   C.Ce.
Chadwick, Charles.   C.Ch.
Chadwick, The Very Rev. Henry.
   H.Cha.
Chadwick, W. Owen.   W.O.C.
Chaillet, Ned.   N.Ch.
Chaisson, Eric J.   E.J.C.
Chaix-Ruy, Jules-Marie.   J.C.-R.
Chambers, Richard L.   Ri.L.C.
Chambers, W. Walker.   W.W.C.
Chambliss, J.J.   J.J.Ch.
Chambre, The Rev. Henri.   H.C.
Chamot, Mary.   M.Ch.
Champion, Timothy C.   T.C.C.
Chan, David B.   D.B.C.
Chan, Hoklam.   H.Ch.
Chan, Wing-tsit.   W.-t.C.
Chanderli, Abdel Kader.   A.K.Ch.
Chandler, David P.   D.P.Ch.
Chandra, Pramod.   P.Ch.
Chandrasekhar, Sripati.   S.Ch.
Chaney, William A.   W.A.C.
Chaney, William R.   W.R.C.
Chang, Chen-tung.   C.-t.C.
Chang, Pao-Chi.   P.-C.C.
Chang, Sen-dou.   S.-d.C.
Chao Lin.   Ch.L.
Chapanis, Alphonse.   Al.C.
Chapman, Brian.   B.Ch.
Chapman, Floyd Barton.   F.B.C.
Chapman, Frank.   F.Ch.
Charles, James A.   J.A.C.
Charles, Jean-Léon.   J.-L.Ch.
Charleston, Robert Jesse.   R.J.Ch.
Charlton, Donald Geoffrey.   D.G.Ch.
Chastenet de Castaing, Jacques.
   J.C. de C.
Chatterjee, Shiba P.   S.P.C.
Chemla, Karine Carole.   K.C.C.
Chen, Cheng-Siang.   C.-S.Ch.
Ch'en, Jerome.   Je.Ch.
Chen, Shou Yi.   S.Y.C.
Chen, Theodore Hsi-en.   T.H.C.
Cheng, Bin.   Bi.C.
Cheng, Chu-yuan.   C.-y.C.
Chenu, The Rev. Marie-Dominique.
   M.-D.Ch.
Chern, S.S.   S.S.C.
Cherniack, Neil S.   N.S.C.
Cherry, John.   J.Ch.
Chevalier, Willie J.   W.J.C.
Chevallier, Jean-Jacques.   J.-J.C.
Chiang Yee.   C.Y.
Chiappini, Luciano.   L.Ch.

Chib, Sukhdev Singh.   S.S.Ch.
Childers, Norman F.   N.F.C.
Chilver, Guy Edward Farquhar.
   G.E.F.C.
Chin, Henk E.   H.E.C.
Chisholm, Lawrence James.   L.J.C.
Chissell, Joan.   Jo.Ch.
Choay, Françoise.   F.C.
Chong, Byong-Wuk.   B.-W.C.
Chow, Christopher.   Ch.C.
Chow, Tse-tsung.   T.-t.C.
Christensen, Aksel E.   A.E.Cn.
Christensen, Dieter.   Di.C.
Christensen, Jan.   Ja.C.
Christie, Andrew Barnett.   A.B.C.
Christie, Ian R.   I.R.C.
Chuang Shang-yen.   C.S.-y.
Ćirković, Sima M.   S.M.Ci.
Clagg, Sam E.   S.E.C.
Clarence-Smith, William Gervase.
   W.G.C.-S.
Clark, Eugene.   E.Cl.
Clark, George B.   G.B.Cl.
Clark, Martha L.   M.L.Cl.
Clark, Walter Houston.   W.H.C.
Clarke, Colin Graham.   C.G.C.
Clarke, Donald C.   D.C.C.
Clarke, John Innes.   J.I.C.
Clarke, Martin Lowther.   M.L.C.
Clarkson, Jesse Dunsmore.   J.D.C.
Classen, Peter.   P.Cla.
Clay, Theresa.   T.C.
Clayton, Raymond Brazenor.   R.B.C.
Clayton, Sir Stanley George.   S.G.C.
Clegern, Wayne M.   W.M.Cl.
Clemence, Gerald M.   G.M.Ce.
Clench, Mary Heimerdinger.   M.H.C.
Clifford, Derek Plint.   D.P.Cl.
Clifford, James Lowry.   J.L.Cl.
Clifford, Paul R.   P.R.Cd.
Cline, Barbara Lovett.   B.L.C.
Cline, C.L.   C.L.Cl.
Cline, Howard F.   H.F.C.
Clingan, Ian C.   I.C.C.
Closs, Gerhard L.   G.L.C.
Clutton, Cecil.   C.Cl.
Coates, J.E.   J.E.Co.
Coates, Ken S.   K.S.C.
Cochran, Thomas B.   T.B.C.
Cochrane, The Rev. Arthur C.   A.C.C.
Cockshut, A.O.J.   A.O.J.C.
Codazzi, Angela.   A.C.
Coe, Michael Douglas.   M.D.C.
Cofer, Charles N.   C.N.C.
Coffin, David R.   D.R.C.
Coffin, Ivor Cecil.   I.C.Cn.
Coggeshall, Ivan Stoddard.   I.S.C.
Cogley, John.   Jo.C.
Cogniat, Raymond.   R.Cog.
Cohen, Gerson D.   G.D.C.
Cohen, Jerome B.   J.B.Co.
Cohen, Yehudi A.   Y.A.C.
Cohn, Paul M.   P.M.C.
Cole, Dame Margaret I.   M.I.C.
Cole, John N.   J.N.C.
Colley, Linda J.   L.J.C.
Collins, George R.   G.R.Co.
Collins, James Daniel.   J.D.Co.
Collins, Nigel.   N.Co.
Collins, Peter.   Pe.C.
Collins, Philip.   Ph.C.
Collins, Robert O.   R.O.C.
Collison, Robert L.   R.L.C.
Comhaire, Jean L.   J.Co.
Conacher, Arthur J.   A.J.C.
Condliffe, J. B.   J.B.C.

Conlan, Kathleen Elizabeth.   K.E.C.
Conley, C. Lockard.   C.L.C.
Conn, J.F.C.   J.F.C.C.
Conn, Robert W.   Ro.W.C.
Connell, Timothy John.   T.J.Co.
Connor, Ralph A.   R.A.Co.
Conot, Robert E.   R.E.Co.
Constable, William G.   W.G.C.
Conversi, Leonard W.   L.C.
Conway, Dennis.   D.Co.
Conybeare, Charles E.B.   C.E.B.C.
Cook, Alan H.   A.H.C.
Cook, David A.   D.A.C.
Cook, James Gordon.   J.G.Co.
Cook, L. Russell.   L.R.C.
Cooke, Deryck V.   D.V.Co.
Cooks, Johann.   Jo.Co.
Coolhaas, W.Ph.   W.Ph.C.
Cooper, Douglas.   D.C.
Cooper, G. Arthur.   G.A.C.
Cooper, Kenneth H.   K.H.C.
Cooper, Martin Du Pré.   M. Du P.C.
Copp, J. Terry.   J.T.C.
Copperthwaite, Nigel Hardy.   N.H.C.
Corbet, Philip S.   P.S.C.
Cordell, Dennis D.   D.D.C.
Cordner, Michael.   M.Co.
Corliss, John O.   J.O.C.
Cormack, Robin Sinclair.   R.S.Co.
Cornelius, Charles E.   C.E.Co.
Cornevin, Robert.   R.Co.
Cornwall, John L.   J.L.C.
Coser, Lewis A.   L.A.C.
Cosgrove, Denis E.   D.E.C.
Coste, René.   R.C.
Cotter, Charles Henry.   C.H.C.
Cottle, Richard W.   R.W.Co.
Cotton, F. Albert.   F.A.C.
Coulson, Noel James.   N.J.C.
Coupland, Robert Thomas.   R.T.C.
Court, Nathan Altshiller.   N.A.Ct.
Courthion, Pierre.   P.Co.
Cousin, Jean.   Je.C.
Couzens, Edward Gordon.   E.G.C.
Cowan, Richard S.   R.S.C.
Cowen, Denis Victor.   D.V.Cn.
Cowgill, Warren.   W.C.
Cowie, Alexander.   A.Co.
Cowley, Malcolm.   Ma.C.
Cox, Hiden T.   H.T.C.
Cox, Maria S.   M.S.C.
Coxe, Antony Dacres Hippisley.
   A.D.H.C.
Coxeter, H.S. MacDonald.   H.S.MacD.C.
Crabb, David W.   D.W.C.
Cragg, The Rt. Rev. Albert Kenneth.
   A.K.C.
Cranston, Maurice.   M.C.
Cratty, Bryant J.   B.J.C.
Crawshay-Williams, Rupert.   R.C.-W.
Creevey, Peter Raymond.   P.R.C.
Cremin, Lawrence A.   L.A.Cr.
Crews, Frederick C.   F.C.C.
Crist, Raymond E.   R.E.Cr.
Critchfield, Howard J.   H.J.Cr.
Crocombe, Marjorie Tuainekore.   M.T.C.
Crocombe, Ronald G.   R.G.C.
Croizier, Ralph C.   R.C.C.
Croll, Gerhard.   G.Cr.
Cromer, George C.   G.C.C.
Cromer, Orville C.   O.C.C.
Crompton, Robin Huw.   R.H.C.
Crone, Gerald Roe.   G.R.C.
Cronin, Vincent.   V.C.
Cronquist, Arthur.   A.Cr.
Crook, John Anthony.   J.A.Cr.

Crook, Keith A.W.   K.A.W.C.
Crossland, Norman.   N.C.
Crossley-Holland, Peter.   P.C.-H.
Crow, Paul A., Jr.   P.A.C.
Crowley, John M.   J.M.C.
Crowley, The Rev. Theodore.   T.Cr.
Crowther, Bosley.   B.Cr.
Crowther, J.G.   J.G.Cr.
Cruickshank, John.   J.Cr.
Cruse, William.   W.Cr.
Cucu, Vasile S.   V.S.C.
Cuffe, Michael.   M.Cu.
Culianu, Ioan Petru.   I.P.C.
Culican, William.   W.Cu.
Cullen, James.   J.Cul.
Current, Richard N.   R.N.C.
Curtin, Nancy A.   N.A.C.
Curtis, Alan S.   A.S.Cu.
Curtis, Stanley Evan.   S.E.Cu.
Cutbill, Catherine C.   C.C.C.
Cuthbert, Alan William.   A.W.C.
Cuttler, Charles D.   C.D.Cu.

Dacharry, Monique.   M.Da.
Daiches, David.   D.Da.
Dalley, Stephanie Mary.   S.M.D.
Dalstrom, Harl Adams.   H.A.D.
Daniel, Glyn Edmund.   G.E.D.
Daniel, Ralph Thomas.   R.T.D.
Daniell, Jere R.   J.R.D.
Daniels, Milton Rockwood.   M.R.Da.
Daniels, Robert V.   R.V.D.
Dansette, Adrien.   A.Da.
D'Antonio, William Vincent.   W.V.D'A.
Dantzig, George B.   G.B.D.
Danzig, Allison.   A.D.
Das, Hariprasanna.   H.D.
Das, Manmath Nath.   M.N.D.
Dashtseren, D.   D.Dn.
Dasmann, Raymond F.   R.F.D.
Dauster, Frank N.   F.N.D.
David, René.   R.Da.
Davidsohn, A.S.   A.S.D.
Davidson, Eugene A.   E.A.D.
Davidson, James Norman.   J.N.D.
Davidson, Robert Bruce.   R.B.D.
Davies, Ernest Albert John.   E.A.J.D.
Davies, Hugh Alistair.   H.A.Da.
Davies, The Rev. J. Gordon.   J.G.D.
Davies, Norman.   N.D.
Davies, Oliver.   O.D.
Davies, R.J.   R.J.Da.
Davies, Robert E.   R.E.Da.
Davies, Roger.   Ro.D.
Davies, The Rev. Rupert E.   R.E.D.
Davies, Thomas M., Jr.   T.M.D.
Davis, Gwenda Louise.   G.L.D.
Davis, Harry.   Ha.D.
Davis, H. Grady.   H.G.D.
Davis, M. Edward.   M.E.D.
Davis, Morton D.   M.D.D.
Davis, Richard A., Jr.   R.A.D.
Davison, W. Phillips.   W.P.D.
Davson, Hugh.   H.Da.
Dawbin, William Henry.   W.H.D.
Dawson, Andrew Hutchinson.   A.H.D.
Dawson, Mary R.   M.R.D.
Day, Michael H.   M.H.D.
Dayal, P.   P.D.
Dean, The Most Rev. Ralph Stanley.
   R.S.De.
DeBakey, Michael E.   M.E.DeB.
de Blij, Harm J.   H.J. de B.
Decalo, Samuel.   S.De.
Decker, Barbara B.   B.B.De.

Decker, Robert W.   R.W.De.
De Conde, Alexander.   A. De C.
de Graft-Johnson, John Coleman.
   J.C. de G.-J.
de Grummond, Nancy Thomson.
   N.T.de G.
DeJong, Russell N.   R.N.DeJ.
Dekker, George G.   G.De.
de la Mare, Peter B.D.   P.B.D. de la M.
DeLancey, Mark W.   M.W.DeL.
Delane, Mary.   M.De.
Delevoryas, T.   T.De.
Delmelle, Joseph-Edouard-Marie-
   Ghislain.   J.-E.-M.-G.D.
DeLong, Dwight Moore.   D.M.DeL.
Delporte, Henri J.   H.J.De.
Delsemme, Armand H.   A.H.De.
DeMaggio, Augustus E.   A.E.D.
Dember, William N.   W.N.D.
Demoz, Abraham.   A.Dem.
Denecke, Ludwig.   L.De.
Denman, Hugh F.   H.F.D.
Deraniyagala, Paul E. Pieris.   P.E.P.D.
Der Nersessian, Sirarpie.   S. Der N.
Desai, Ranjit Ramchandra.   R.R.D.
Desan, Wilfrid.   W.De.
de Santillana, Giorgio D.   G. de S.
Descargues, Pierre.   P.De.
Deschamps, Hubert Jules.   H.J.D.
Descloitres, Robert.   R.De.
Desforges, Jane F.   Ja.F.D.
Despić, Aleksandar R.   A.De.
Desrosier, Norman Wilfred.   N.W.D.
Dethan, Georges.   G.Det.
de Vleeschauwer, Herman Jean.
   H.J. de V.
Devlin, John F.   J.F.De.
De Vorsey, Louis.   L.De.V.
Dewdney, John C.   J.C.D.
DeWoskin, Kenneth J.   K.J.DeW.
Diakonoff, Igor Mikhailovich.   I.M.D.
Diano, Carlo.   C.D.
Dibner, Bern.   B.Di.
Dickie, James.   J.Di.
Dickinson, Harry T.   H.T.D.
Dickison, William C.   W.C.D.
Dickson, Kwamina Busumafi.   K.B.D.
Dickson, Lovat.   L.D.
Diem, Aubrey.   A.Di.
Dienst, Heide.   H.Di.
Diethrich, Edward Bronson.   E.B.D.
Dietrich, R.V.   R.V.Di.
Dietz, John L.   J.L.Di.
Diffloth, Gérard.   G.Di.
Dijkgraaf, Sven.   S.Di.
Dilger, William C.   W.C.Di.
Dillon, Myles.   M.D.
Dimitrovsky, Haim Zalman.   H.Z.D.
Dimock, Edward C., Jr.   E.C.D.
Dingman, S. Lawrence.   S.L.D.
Dinshaw, Fram E.   F.E.D.
Diószegi, Vilmos.   V.D.
Diringer, David.   D.D.
Ditchburn, Robert William.   R.W.Di.
Djibladze, Mikhail Leonidovich.   M.L.D.
Djordjevic, Dimitrije V.   D.V.D.
Dobzhansky, Theodosius.   T.D.
Dockstader, Frederick J.   F.J.D.
Dodson, Calaway H.   C.H.D.
Dölger, Franz.   F.Dr.
Domanitsky, Anatoly Petrovich.   A.P.D.
Domb, Cyril.   Cy.Do.
Domingues, Mário José.   M.J.D.
Domínguez, Jorge I.   J.I.D.
Domke, Martin.   M.Do.
Donahue, Charles, Jr.   Ch.D.

Donald, David Herbert.   D.H.D.
Donald, Larry W.   L.W.D.
Doniger, Wendy.   W.Do.
Donini, Filippo.   F.Do.
Donnellan, Keith S.   K.S.D.
Donoghue, Denis.   D.Do.
Donovan, Bernard Thomas.   B.T.D.
Dooling, David, Jr.   Da.D.
Doresse, Jean P.   J.P.Do.
Dorfman, Robert.   R.D.
Dorfman, Ron.   R.Do.
Doroshinskaya, Yelena Matveyevna.
   Y.M.D.
Dorpalen, Andreas.   A.Do.
Dorson, Richard M.   R.M.D.
Dorst, Jean P.   J.P.D.
Doucy, Arthur J.M.   Ar.D.
Douglas, A. Vibert.   A.V.D.
Douglas, Ronald Walter.   R.W.D.
Douie, Decima L.   D.L.D.
Dowd, Douglas F.   D.F.Do.
Dowdey, Clifford.   C.Do.
Dowling, Herndon G.   H.G.Do.
Downing, James H.   J.H.D.
Dowsett, Charles James Frank.   C.J.F.D.
Doyle, Larry James.   L.J.D.
Drake, Paul W.   P.W.D.
Dresch, Jean.   Je.D.
Drescher, Seymour.   S.Dr.
Dresden, Mark J.   M.J.Dr.
Drew, Philip.   Ph.D.
Drinkwater, John Frederick.   J.F.Dr.
Driscoll, John S.   J.S.D.
Drobnig, Ulrich M.   U.M.D.
Drower, Margaret Stefana.   M.S.D.
Drucker, Philip.   P.Dr.
Drummond, Boyce A., Jr.   B.A.D.
Dubois, Carlos Pablo.   C.P.D.
Duchesne-Guillemin, Jacques.   J.D.-G.
Duckett, Eleanor Shipley.   E.S.D.
Dudley, Donald Reynolds.   D.R.D.
Dudley, Elizabeth Corning.   E.C.Du.
Due, John F.   J.F.D.
Duellman, William E.   W.E.D.
Dufford, Stanley.   S.D.
Dugdale, Donald Stephen.   D.S.D.
Duggan, Lawrence G.   L.G.D.
Dull, Jack L.   J.L.D.
Dulles, The Rev. Avery.   A.Du.
Dumesnil, René.   R.Dum.
Dummett, Michael A.E.   Mi.D.
Dumond, Don E.   D.E.D.
Dunaev, Vladimir Nikolaevich.   V.N.D.
Dunbar, Maxwell John.   M.J.Du.
Dunbar, Moira.   M.Dr.
Dunn, Ethel Deikman.   E.D.D.
Dunn, L.C.   L.C.D.
Dunn, Richard S.   R.S.Du.
Dunn, Stephen Porter.   S.P.D.
Dupree, Louis.   L.Du.
Dupree, Nancy Hatch.   N.H.D.
Durant, Frederick C., III.   F.C.D.III.
Durgnat, Raymond E.   R.Du.
Durko, Janusz.   Ja.D.
Dury, George Harry.   G.H.D.
Dussel, Enrique.   E.Du.
Du Val, Patrick.   P. Du V.
Duveen, Denis Ian.   D.I.D.
Duverger, Maurice.   M.Du.
Duxbury, Alyn C.   A.C.D.
Dwivedi, R.L.   R.L.D.
Dworken, Harvey J.   H.J.Dw.
Dyck, Cornelius J.   C.J.D.
Dyer, Denys G.   D.G.D.
Dykeman, Wilma.   W.D.
Dykhuizen, George.   G.Dy.

Eardley, Armand J.   A.J.E.
Earl, David Magarey.   D.M.Ea.
Easby, Dudley Tate, Jr.   D.T.E.
East, Robert A.   R.A.E.
East, W. Gordon.   W.G.E.
Eastman, Richard H.   R.H.E.
Easton, Archie H.   A.H.E.
Ebanks, Elizabeth Pat.   E.P.E.
Ebisawa, Arimichi.   A.Eb.
Ebling, F. John G.   F.J.G.E.
Eccles, W.J.   W.J.E.
Echenberg, Myron.   M.Ec.
Eckbo, Garrett.   G.Ec.
Eckenwalder, James Emory.   J.E.Ec.
Ede, David A.   D.E.
Edel, Leon.   L.Ed.
Edelmann, Chester Monroe, Jr.   C.M.E.
Edge, Ian David.   I.D.E.
Edlin, Herbert Leeson.   H.L.E.
Edwards, Clive Arthur.   C.A.E.
Edwards, Richard Humphrey Tudor.
   R.H.T.E.
Edwards, Robert Walter Dudley.
   R.W.D.E.
Edzard, Dietz O.   D.O.E.
Egerod, Søren Christian.   S.C.E.
Eggen, Olin Jeuck.   O.J.E.
Egli, Emil.   E.Eg.
Ehrich, Fredric F.   F.F.E.
Ehrlich, Blake.   B.E.
Eidt, Robert C.   R.C.Ei.
Eilon, Samuel.   S.E.
Ekstrom, George F.   G.F.E.
Elath, Eliahu.   E.E.
Elbow, Gary S.   G.S.E.
Elekes, Lajos.   L.El.
El Hamamsy, Laila Shukry.   L.S.El H.
Eliade, Mircea.   M.Ee.
El-Kammash, Magdi M.   M.M.El-K.
Elkins, Thomas Henry.   T.H.El.
Eller, Ernest McNeill.   E.McN.E.
Elliott, David H.   D.H.E.
Elliott, Geoffrey Kenyon.   G.K.E.
Elliott, Sir Ivo D'Oyly.   I.D'O.E.
Elliott, Robert C.   R.C.E.
Ellis, E. Earle.   E.E.E.
Ellis, Peter.   P.E.
Elsasser, Walter M.   W.M.E.
Elsen, Albert Edward.   A.E.El.
Elton, Sir Geoffrey R.   G.R.E.
Emerit, Marcel.   M.E.
Emery, Walter.   W.Em.
Emmerick, Ronald Eric.   R.E.E.
Enander, Henrik.   H.En.
Endress, Peter K.   P.K.E.
Enfield, David B.   D.B.En.
Engberg, Jens.   J.E.
Engerrand, George C.   G.C.E.
Englekirk, John E.   J.E.E.
Enrico, Eugene J.   E.J.E.
Epperson, Gordon.   G.E.
Epstein, William.   W.E.
Erb, Donald James.   D.Er.
Erb, Hubert Joseph.   H.J.Er.
Erben, Walter.   W.Er.
Ericson, David Barnard.   D.B.E.
Erinc, Sirri.   S.Er.
Erlanger, Philippe.   P.Er.
Erulkar, Solomon D.   S.D.E.
Escarpit, Robert.   R.Es.
Escholier, Marc Marie.   M.M.E.
Eskenazi, Gerald.   G.Es.
Ess, Josef van.   J.v.E.
Esslin, Martin J.   M.J.E.
Eulau, Heinz.   H.E.
Euler, Heinrich Gustav.   H.G.E.

Evans, Graham.   G.Ev.
Evans, Dame Joan.   J.Ev.
Evans, Luther Harris.   L.H.E.
Evans, M. Albert.   M.A.E.
Evenson, Edward B.   E.B.E.
Everard, Cyril Ernest.   C.E.E.
Everett, Richard W.   R.W.E.
Everett, Thomas H.   T.H.E.
Every, Brother George.   Ge.E.
Ewald, Paul P.   P.P.E.
Eyring, Henry.   H.Ey.
Ezell, Edward C.   E.C.E.
Ezell, John S.   J.S.E.

Faber, Thomas E.   T.E.F.
Fadiman, Clifton.   C.Fa.
Fage, John D.   J.D.F.
Fagg, John E.   J.E.F.
Faherty, Robert L.   R.F.
Fainsod, Merle.   M.F.
Fairbridge, Rhodes W.   R.W.F.
Falkenheim, Victor C.   V.C.F.
Faller, James E.   Ja.F.
Faller, Larry D.   L.D.F.
Faris, Nabih Amin.   N.A.F.
Faris, Robert E.L.   R.E.L.F.
Faron, Louis C.   L.C.F.
Faulkner, Raymond Oliver.   R.O.F.
Fautin, Daphne Gail.   D.G.Fa.
Fawcett, Don W.   D.W.F.
Fedan, Jeffrey S.   J.S.F.
Fedorovich, Boris Aleksandrovich.
   B.A.F.
Feferman, Solomon.   S.Fe.
Fefferman, Charles L.   C.L.F.
Feigin, Ralph D.   R.D.F.
Feigl, Herbert.   H.Fe.
Feigon, Lee Nathan.   L.N.F.
Feldman, Louis H.   L.H.F.
Fellman, David.   D.Fe.
Fellner, Fritz.   F.Fe.
Felteau, Cyrille.   C.Fe.
Fennell, John Lister Illingworth.
   J.L.I.F.
Ferdinandy, Michael de.   M. de F.
Ferguson, John.   J.Fe.
Fermín Gómez, Mercedes.   Me.F.G.
Fernald, John Bailey.   J.B.F.
Fernier, Robert J.   R.J.F.
Ferreira, C.E.   C.E.F.
Feuer, Lewis S.   L.S.F.
Feuerwerker, Albert.   A.Fe.
Fieandt, Kai V.J. von.   K.V.J.v.F.
Fiegenbaum, J.W.   J.W.F.
Field, Andrew.   A.Fi.
Fielder, Gilbert.   G.Fi.
Fielding, Raymond E.   R.E.Fi.
Fifer, J. Valerie.   J.V.F.
Filliozat, Jean L.A.   J.L.A.F.
Findlay, James Smith.   J.Fi.
Finer, Samuel Edward.   S.E.F.
Fink, Donald G.   D.G.F.
Finkbeiner, Daniel T., II.   D.T.F.
Finley, Robert W.   Ro.W.F.
Finn, Bernard S.   B.S.F.
Firth, Sir Raymond William.
   R.W.Fi.
Fischer, John L.   J.L.Fi.
Fischler, Shirley W.   S.W.Fi.
Fischler, Stanley I.   S.I.F.
Fisher, William B.   W.B.Fi.
Fishman, Alfred P.   A.P.F.
Fiske, Donald W.   D.W.Fi.
FitzGerald, Charles Patrick.   C.P.F.
Fitzgerald, Ross.   R.Fi.

Flannery-Herzfeld, Regina.   R.F.-He.
Flaum, Thea K.   T.K.F.
Fleming, Richard Howell.   R.H.Fl.
Fleming, William.   Wm.F.
Flemion, Philip F.   P.F.F.
Fletcher, Angus Stewart.   A.S.F.
Fletcher, Brian Hinton.   B.H.F.
Fletcher, Joseph O.   J.O.Fl.
Fletcher, Ronald.   R.Fl.
Flew, Antony Garrard Newton.
   A.G.N.F.
Florinsky, Michael T.   M.T.F.
Florkin, Marcel.   M.Fl.
Flower, John E.   Jo.E.F.
Flusser, David.   D.Fl.
Fogelson, Raymond D.   R.D.Fo.
Folk, Robert Louis.   R.L.F.
Folkerts, Menso.   Me.F.
Fomin, Luch Mikhaylovich.   L.M.F.
Fonash, Raymond T.   R.T.F.
Fonash, Stephen Joseph.   S.J.F.
Foner, Anne.   A.F.
Foner, Philip S.   P.S.F.
Foot, Michael Richard Daniell.
   M.R.D.F.
Force, Roland Wynfield.   R.W.Fo.
Ford, Arthur B.   A.B.Fo.
Forde, Enid R.A.   E.R.A.F.
Forder, Henry George.   H.G.F.
Fordham, Frieda.   F.Fo.
Fordham, Michael S.M.   M.S.M.F.
Formo, Marvin W.   M.W.F.
Forsdyke, Sir Edgar John.   E.J.F.
Forsythe, Gary Edward.   G.E.Fo.
Foskett, Douglas John.   D.J.F.
Foss, Lukas.   L.Fo.
Fought, Stephen Oliver.   S.O.F.
Foulkes, David.   D.F.
Fourastié, Jean.   J.Fo.
Fournier, Gabriel.   G.Fo.
Fowler, Catherine S.   C.S.F.
Fowler, Don D.   D.D.F.
Fowler, Gizella Rochelle.   G.R.F.
Fowler, Murray.   M.Fo.
Fowler, W. Beall.   W.B.F.
Fowlie, Wallace.   W.F.
Fox, David John.   D.J.Fo.
Fox, Denis Llewellyn.   D.L.F.
Fox, Michael W.   M.W.Fo.
Fox, Richard G.   R.G.F.
Fox, Sidney W.   S.W.F.
Fraenkel, Heinrich.   H.Fra.
Fraisse, Paul.   P.F.
Francis, Sir Frank C.   F.C.F.
Frank, Peter W.   P.W.F.
Frank, W.J.   W.J.F.
Franke, Herbert.   H.Fr.
Frankel, Joseph.   J.Fr.
Frankel, Marvin.   Ma.F.
Franzius, Enno.   E.F.
Fraser, Lady Antonia.   A.Fr.
Fraser, Craig G.   C.G.F.
Fraser, Peter Marshall.   P.M.F.
Fredericksen, Linwood.   L.F.
Freeborn, Richard H.   R.H.Fr.
Freedman, Lawrence D.   L.D.Fr.
Freeman-Grenville, Greville Stewart
   Parker.   G.S.P.F.-G.
Freidel, Frank.   F.Fr.
Freihofer, Warren Curtis.   W.C.F.
French, Richard Antony.   R.A.F.
Frend, The Rev. William Hugh Clifford.
   W.H.C.F.
Frere, Sheppard Sunderland.   S.S.F.
Freund, Michael.   M.Fre.
Frey, Richard L.   R.L.Fr.

Friedlander, Rabbi Albert H.   A.H.F.
Friedlander, Michael Wulf.   M.W.Fr.
Friedman, Albert B.   A.B.F.
Friedman, Milton.   M.Fr.
Friedman, Norman.   N.F.
Friedmann, Arnold A.   A.A.F.
Friedmann, Herbert.   He.F.
Friedmann, Marion Valerie.   M.V.F.
Friedrich, Hermann.   H.F.
Friermood, Harold T.   H.T.F.
Friis, Astrid.   As.F.
Frings, Hubert William.   H.W.F.
Fritz, Kurt von.   K.v.Fr.
Fritzsche, Hellmut.   Ht.F.
Froelich, Jean Claude.   J.C.F.
Froeschner, Richard Charles.   R.C.F.
Frost, David B.J.   D.B.J.F.
Frost, Wesley,   W.Ft.
Fryburger, Vernon R., Jr.   V.R.F.
Fryde, Edmund B.   E.B.Fr.
Frye, Richard N.   R.N.F.
Fuechsel, Charles F.   C.F.F.
Fuglestad, Finn.   F.F.
Fuhrman, Ralph E.   R.E.F.
Fujimura Michio.   Fu.M.
Fu-Kiau kia Bunseki-L., André.   A.Fu.
Fuller, Edmund.   E.Fu.
Furie, Bruce.   B.Fu.
Furon, Raymond-Louis-Charles.
   R.L.C.F.
Fuson, Robert H.   R.H.Fu.
Fussell, George Edwin.   G.E.F.
Fyfe, Christopher.   C.Fy.
Fyfe, William S.   W.S.F.

Gabriel, Ralph Henry.   R.H.Ga.
Gadd, Cyril John.   C.J.Ga.
Gadella, Theodorus W.J.   T.W.J.G.
Gailey, Harry A.   H.A.G.
Gallager, Robert G.   R.G.G.
Gallaher, John G.   J.G.G.
Galli, Rosemary Elizabeth.   R.E.Ga.
Gam, Mikael.   M.Ga.
Gamble, David P.   D.P.Ga.
Gamer, Carlton.   Ca.G.
Gamkrelidze, Thomas V.   Th.V.G.
Ganellin, C. Robin.   C.R.G.
Gantt, W. Horsley.   W.H.G.
Garavito, Clemente.   C.Ga.
García-Gómez, Angel M.   A.M.G.-G.
García y Bellido, Antonio.   A.G. y B.
Garden, Edward J.C.   E.J.C.G.
Gardiner, Patrick Lancaster.   P.L.G.
Gardinier, David E.   D.E.G.
Gardiner, Robert K.A.   R.K.A.G.
Gardner, Ernest Dean.   E.D.G.
Garg, Renu.   Re.G.
Gargi, Balwant.   B.Ga.
Garigue, Philippe.   P.Ga.
Garland, George D.   G.D.G.
Garn, Stanley M.   S.M.G.
Garner, Hessle Filmore.   H.F.G.
Garrad, Kenneth.   K.Ga.
Garrett, Alfred B.   A.B.Ga.
Garrigus, Wesley Patterson.   W.P.G.
Gash, Norman.   N.G.
Gasking, Elizabeth Belmont.   E.B.G.
Gasparini, Evel.   E.G.
Gaster, Theodor H.   T.H.G.
Gates, David M.   D.M.G.
Gaunt, William.   W.Ga.
Gavrilov, Aleksandr Mikhaylovich.
   A.M.Ga.
Geanakoplos, Deno John.   D.Ge.
Gear, Charles William.   C.W.Ge.

Geary, Patrick J.   P.J.G.
Gebhard, Paul Henry.   P.H.Ge.
Geerlings, Gerald K.   G.K.Ge.
Gehring, Jean Marie.   J.M.G.
Geiger, Pedro P.   P.P.G.
Geiringer, Karl.   K.G.
Gelb, Arthur.   A.Ge.
Gelb, Barbara.   B.Ge.
Gelb, Ignace J.   I.J.G.
Gelderman, Carol W.   C.W.G.
Gelpi, Ettore.   E.Ge.
Gelston, Arthur S., Jr.   A.S.G.
Gentry, Alan William.   A.W.G.
Genuth, Saul.   S.Ge.
Gerasimov, Innokentii Petrovich.   I.P.G.
Gergely, John.   J.G.
Gerig, O. Benjamin.   O.B.G.
Germani, Gino.   G.Ge.
Gernsheim, Helmut Erich Robert.
   H.E.R.G.
Gerow, Edwin.   Ed.G.
Gerteiny, Alfred G.   A.G.G.
Gertsch, Willis John.   W.J.G.
Geyer, Richard A.   R.A.G.
Ghirshman, Roman.   R.Gh.
Ghiselin, Michael T.   M.T.G.
Ghori, G.K.   G.K.G.
Ghose, Sisirkumar.   S.Gh.
Ghul, Mahmud Ali.   M.A.G.
Gibb, Andrew Dewar.   A.D.G.
Gibbins, Roger.   R.G.
Gibbons, James L.   J.L.Gi.
Gibbs, Frederick William.   F.W.G.
Gibbs, Gerald V.   G.V.G.
Gibbs-Smith, Charles Harvard.
   C.H.G.-S.
Gibney, Frank B.   F.B.G.
Gibson, McGuire.   McG.G.
Gibson, Robert Donald Davidson.
   R.D.D.G.
Giddings, J. Calvin.   J.C.Gi.
Gies, Frances Carney.   F.C.Gi.
Gifford, Ernest M.   E.M.G.
Gilbert, Bentley Brinkerhoff.   B.B.G.
Gilbert, Creighton E.   C.E.G.
Gilbert, Douglas Stuart.   D.Gi.
Gilbert, M. Charles.   M.C.G.
Gilbert, Robert Andrew.   R.A.Gi.
Gilchrist, Peter Spence, Jr.   Pe.S.G.
Giles, Charles Hugh.   C.H.Gi.
Giles, James R.   J.R.G.
Gill, Charles Burroughs.   C.B.G.
Gill, The Rev. Joseph.   J.Gi.
Gillies, Alexander.   A.Gi.
Gillmor, Reginald E.   R.E.Gi.
Gilmore, Robert Louis.   R.L.Ge.
Gimbutas, Marija.   M.G.
Gimm, Martin.   M.Gi.
Gingerich, Owen.   O.G.
Ginns, Harry Norwood.   H.N.G.
Ginsberg, Donald M.   D.M.Gi.
Ginsburg, Norton S.   N.S.G.
Giorgetti, Giovanni Pietro.   G.P.Gi.
Girault, Christian Antoine.   C.A.G.
Girvetz, Harry K.   H.K.G.
Gjuzelev, Wassil Todorov.   W.T.G.
Gladstone, Reginald John.   R.J.Gl.
Glasz, Christiaan.   C.G.
Glatzer, Nahum N.   N.N.G.
Glazer, Sidney.   S.Gl.
Glendon, Mary Ann.   M.A.Gl.
Glubb, Sir John Bagot.   J.B.Gl.
Godbey, John Charles.   J.C.G.
Godechot, Jacques.   J.Go.
Godman, Michael James.   M.J.G.
Godman, Peter.   P.Go.

Goethals, Peter R.   P.R.Go.
Goetz, Hermann.   H.Go.
Gogolák, Ludwig von.   L.v.G.
Goin, Coleman Jett.   C.J.G.
Goldammer, Kurt Moritz Artur.
   K.M.A.G.
Goldbeck, Frederick.   F.Go.
Goldblatt, Howard C.   H.C.G.
Goldin, Judah.   J.Gol.
Goldscheider, Ludwig.   L.Go.
Gomillion, Charles Goode.   C.G.G.
Gomme, Arnold Wycombe.   A.W.Ge.
Gömöri, George.   G.G.
Gonçalves Pereira, António Armando.
   A.A.G.P.
Goncharov, Vladimir Petrovich.   V.P.G.
González, Nancie L.   N.L.G.
González Casanova, Pablo.   P.G.C.
González Díaz, Emilio Fernando.
   E.F.G.D.
Gooberman, George L.   G.L.G.
Goodall, David W.   D.W.G.
Goode, Richard B.   R.B.G.
Goodman, George J.   G.J.G.
Goodman, Morris F.   M.F.Go.
Goodner, John Ross.   J.R.Go.
Goodnight, Marie Louise.   M.L.Go.
Goodrich, Leland Matthew.   L.M.G.
Goodsell, James Nelson.   J.N.G.
Goodwin, Albert.   Al.G.
Goodwin, Frank E.   F.E.G.
Goodwin, Noël.   N.Go.
Gopnik, Adam.   A.Go.
Gordon, Arnold L.   A.L.G.
Gordon, Burton L.   B.L.G.
Gordon, Cyrus H.   C.H.G.
Gordon, David Frank.   D.F.G.
Gordon, George N.   G.N.G.
Gordon, Isabella.   I.G.
Gordon-Walker, Patrick Chrestien
   Gordon Walker, Baron.   P.G.W.
Gorgy, Samy.   S.G.
Görlitz, Walter Otto Julius.   W.Go.
Gorman, George C.   G.C.G.
Gosling, L.A. Peter.   L.A.P.G.
Goss, Richard Johnson.   R.J.G.
Gottschalk, Stephen.   S.Go.
Goult, Herman W.   H.W.G.
Gourou, Pierre.   P.Gu.
Gowans, Alan.   Al.Go.
Gowing, Sir Lawrence.   La.G.
Grabar, Oleg.   O.Gr.
Graf, Alfred Byrd.   A.B.Gr.
Graham, Hugh F.   H.F.Gr.
Grame, Theodore C.   T.Gr.
Grancsay, Stephen Vincent.   S.V.G.
Grant, Michael.   M.Gr.
Grant, Peter R.   P.R.G.
Grant, Robert M.   R.M.G.
Graue, Jerald C.   J.C.Gr.
Gray, Alic William.   A.W.Gr.
Gray, Eric William.   E.W.G.
Gray, Jeremy John.   J.J.G.
Gray, Peter.   Pe.G.
Grayling, A.C.   A.C.G.
Greaves, Malcolm W.   M.W.G.
Green, Benny.   B.Gr.
Green, Edna R.   E.R.G.
Green, Estill I.   E.I.G.
Green, James.   J.Gre.
Green, Peter S.   P.S.G.
Green, Roger Lancelyn.   R.L.G.
Greenaway, Frank.   F.Gre.
Greenberg, Moshe.   Mo.Gr.
Greenblatt, Stephen J.   S.J.G.
Greene, David.   D.Gr.

Greene, Mark Richard. M.R.G.
Greenfield, Richard David. Ri.G.
Greenwood, Peter Humphry. P.H.G.
Greenwood, Richard Harold. R.H.G.
Gregg, Alan. Al.Gr.
Gregorietti, Guido. G.Gr.
Grenville, John A.S. J.A.S.G.
Gressitt, Judson Linsley. J.L.G.
Griffin, Ernst C. E.C.G.
Griffith, Guy Thompson. G.T.G.
Griffith, William J. W.J.Gr.
Grim, Ralph E. R.E.G.
Grimm, Frankdieter. F.G.
Grimsley, Ronald. R.Gr.
Gritzner, Jeffrey Allman. J.A.G.
Groen, Pier. P.Gr.
Groover, Mikell P. M.P.G.
Gross, Harvey S. Ha.G.
Grove, Alfred Thomas. A.T.G.
Grudin, Robert. Ro.G.
Gruijters, Johannes P.A. J.P.A.G.
Grünbaum, Branko. B.G.
Gspan, Alfonz. A.Gn.
Gudava, T.E. T.E.G.
Gudzii, Nikolai Kallinikovich. N.K.G.
Guenther, Herbert V. H.G.
Guerello, The Rev. Franco. F.Gu.
Guiart, Jean. J.Gt.
Guichonnet, Paul. P.G.
Guiguemde, Pierre H. P.H.Gu.
Guillemin, Henri. He.Gu.
Guilmartin, John F., Jr. J.F.G.
Guimarães, Alberto Passos. A.P.G.
Guitton, Henri. H.Gu.
Gulyans, Peteris V. P.V.G.
Gundermann, Karl-Dietrich. K.-D.G.
Gungaadash, B. B.Gu.
Gunner, Elizabeth Anne Wynne.
 E.A.W.G.
Gunstone, Frank Denby. F.D.G.
Gunther, Erna. E.Gu.
Gurney, Ashley B. A.B.G.
Gurney, Oliver Robert. O.R.G.
Gusdorf, Georges Paul. G.P.G.
Gustafson, Neil C. N.C.G.
Güterbock, Hans G. H.G.G.
Gutherz, Elmer J. E.J.G.
Guthrie, Douglas James. D.J.G.
Guthrie, Sir Tyrone. T.G.
Gutmann, Viktor. V.G.
Gutsche, C. David. C.D.G.
Guttmann, Allen. A.G.
Gvozdetsky, Nikolay Andreyevich.
 N.A.G.
Gwynn, Denis Rolleston. D.R.G.
Gyftopoulos, Elias Panayiotis. E.P.G.
Gyllensvärd, Bo Vilhelm. B.V.Gy.

Haaf, Ernst ten. E.t.H.
Haar, Dirk ter. D.t.H.
Hackett, John. Jo.Hac.
Haedeke, Hanns-Ulrich. H.-U.H.
Haekel, Josef. Jo.H.
Haggerty, James S. J.J.Ha.
Hahn, Bae-ho. B.-h.H.
Haight, Gordon S. G.S.Ha.
Hájek, Igor. I.H.
Haley, K.H.D. K.H.D.H.
Halfpenny, Eric. E.Hy.
Hall, Marshall, Jr. Ma.H.
Hall, Robert A., Jr. R.A.H.
Halperin Donghi, Tulio. T.H.D.
Halpern, Jack. J.Ha.
Halstead, Bruce W. B.W.H.
Hambly, Gavin R.G. G.R.G.H.

Hamelin, Louis-Edmond. L.-E.H.
Hamerow, Theodore S. T.S.H.
Hamidé, Abdul-Rahman. A.-R.H.
Hamilton, Bernice Margaret. B.M.H.
Hamilton, William James. W.J.H.
Hamman, The Rev. Adalbert G.
 A.G.Ha.
Hammen, Oscar J. O.J.H.
Hammer, A. Gordon. A.G.H.
Hammond, Mason. M.Ha.
Hammond, Nicholas G.L. N.G.L.H.
Hammond Innes, Ralph. R.H.I.
Hamp, Eric P. E.P.H.
Hanahan, Donald J. D.J.H.
Hand, Cadet H., Jr. C.H.Ha.
Handlin, Oscar. O.H.
Handzo, Stephen G. S.G.H.
Hanna, Willard A. W.A.Ha.
Hansen, Arlen J. A.J.H.
Hansen, Gladys Cox. G.C.Ha.
Hanson, Carl. C.Ha.
Hanson, Earl Dorchester. E.D.H.
Hanson, Earl Parker. E.P.Ha.
Harbaugh, John W. J.W.Ha.
Harbison, Craig S. C.S.Ha.
Hardie, Robert H. R.H.H.
Hardy, Sir Alister C. A.C.Ha.
Hardy, Edward R. E.R.Ha.
Hare, F. Kenneth. F.K.H.
Hargrave, John G. J.G.H.
Hargreaves, John D. J.D.H.
Harler, Campbell Ronald. C.R.H.
Harmel, Claude. C.H.
Harmon, Mamie. Ma.Ha.
Harms, Robert Thomas. R.T.H.
Harper, Peggy. P.H.
Harpster, Joseph W. J.W.H.
Harrelson, Walter. W.Ha.
Harris, Chauncy D. C.D.H.
Harris, David Russell. D.R.Ha.
Harris, Enriqueta. E.Ha.
Harris, James T. J.T.H.
Harris, Leslie. L.H.
Harris, Rosemary Lois. R.L.Ha.
Harrison, John A. J.A.Ha.
Harrison, Raymond O. R.O.H.
Harrison, Richard J. R.J.Ha.
Harrison, Walter A. W.A.H.
Harrison-Church, Ronald James.
 R.J.H.-C.
Harriss, C. Lowell. C.L.Ha.
Harrisson, Tom. T.Hn.
Harrod, Sir Roy Forbes. R.F.H.
Harroy, Jean-Paul. Je.-P.H.
Hart, Harold. H.Ha.
Hart, Herbert Lionel Adolphus.
 H.L.A.H.
Hartenberg, Richard S. R.S.H.
Hartley, Sir Frank. Fr.H.
Hashisaki, Joseph. Jo.Ha.
Hassler, Warren W., Jr. W.W.H.
Hastings, Margaret. M.Has.
Hathaway, Richard J. Ri.J.H.
Hatsopoulos, George N. G.N.Ha.
Hattingh, Phillip S. P.S.Ha.
Hatton, Ragnhild Marie. R.M.H.
Hattori, Shirō. S.Ha.
Haugen, Einar. Ei.H.
Haurowitz, Felix. F.Ha.
Häuser, Karl H. K.Hä.
Havard, C. William H. C.W.H.H.
Havelock, Eric Alfred. E.A.Ha.
Haverschmidt, François. F.H.
Havighurst, Alfred F. A.F.H.
Havighurst, Robert J. R.J.H.
Hawkins, Gerald S. G.S.H.

Hawkins, Joseph E. J.E.H.
Hawting, G.R. G.R.H.
Hayashi, Shigeru. Sh.H.
Hayes, J.M. J.M.Ha.
Hayford, Charles W. C.W.H.
Hayne, David M. D.M.Ha.
Hayward, Charles Harold. C.H.H.
Hayward, John F. J.F.Ha.
Haywood, John A. J.A.H.
Hazai, Georg. G.Ha.
Hazard, John N. J.N.H.
Hazzard, Shirley. Sh.Ha.
Healy, Nicholas Joseph. N.J.H.
Heaney, Robert Proulx. R.P.He.
Heath, Donald Albert. Do.A.H.
Heath, Dwight B. D.B.H.
Heather, Peter John. P.J.He.
Hecht, Charles E. C.E.He.
Hecht, Melvin E. M.E.H.
Heelan, Patrick Aidan. P.A.H.
Heerden, Ernst van. E.v.H.
Heezen, Bruce C. B.C.H.
Heiber, Helmut. H.Hei.
Heilbroner, Robert L. R.L.He.
Heinemeyer, Walter. W.He.
Heinen, Heinz. He.H.
Heiser, Charles B., Jr. C.B.He.
Helck, Wolfgang. W.H.
Held, Julius S. Ju.H.
Hellie, Richard. R.He.
Hemp, Wilfrid James. W.J.He.
Hempel, Carl G. C.G.H.
Henderson, Philip Prichard. P.P.H.
Henderson, Robert M. R.M.He.
Hendricks, George. G.He.
Hendrickson, James B. J.B.He.
Hendy, Sir Philip. P.He.
Henfrey, Norman V. N.V.He.
Henriksson, Markku Ilmari. M.I.He.
Hensel, Herbert. H.He.
Henson, Ronald A. R.A.He.
Herbst, Stanislaw. S.He.
Herde, Peter. Pe.He.
Herivel, John. J.He.
Herklots, Geoffrey A.C. G.A.C.H.
Herlihy, David. D.He.
Herman, Robert D. R.D.H.
Hermans, Theo Jozef. T.J.H.
Herrin, Judith Eleanor. J.E.He.
Herschdoerfer, Sigismund M. S.M.H.
Hertzberg, Rabbi Arthur. Ar.H.
Herzfeld, Hans. Ha.He.
Herzog, Gregory F. G.F.H.
Herzog, Marvin Irving. M.I.H.
Herzog, Peter E. P.E.H.
Heslinga, Marcus Willem. M.W.H.
Heslop, D. Alan. D.A.He.
Heslop-Harrison, John. J.H.-H.
Hess, Eckhard H. E.H.H.
Heston, The Most Rev. Edward Louis.
 E.L.H.
Heydenreich, Ludwig Heinrich. L.H.H.
Heyerdahl, Thor. Th.H.
Hezel, The Rev. Francis X. F.X.H.
Hibbert, Christopher. C.Hi.
Hick, John. J.Hi.
Hickey, Gerald C. G.C.H.
Hieatt, A. Kent. A.K.H.
Higginbotham, Jay. Ja.H.
Higgins, David J.M. D.J.M.H.
Higgins, Reynold Alleyne. R.A.Hi.
Higgs, Eric S. E.S.H.
Highet, Gilbert. G.Hi.
Highfield, J.R.L. J.R.L.H.
Highsmith, Richard M., Jr. R.M.Hi.
Hightower, Nicholas Carr. N.C.H.

Higonnet, Patrice Louis-René.   P.Hi.
Hill, Dorothy.   D.Hi.
Hill, J.E. Christopher.   J.E.C.H.
Hill, John Hugh.   J.H.Hi.
Hill, Laurita L.   L.L.H.
Hill, Richard Leslie.   R.L.Hi.
Hill, Roland John.   R.J.Hi.
Hiller, Lejaren.   L.Hi.
Hills, John M.   J.M.Hi.
Hilton, Peter John.   P.J.H.
Hingley, Ronald Francis.   R.F.Hi.
Hintikka, K. Jaakko J.   K.J.Hi.
Hinton, Thomas B.   T.B.H.
Hiorthøy, Finn.   F.Hi.
Hirai, Naofusa.   N.H.
Hitchins, Keith Arnold.   K.A.H.
Hjelmqvist, Hakon.   H.Hj.
Ho, Robert.   Rt.H.
Hoaglin, David C.   D.C.H.
Hobbs, F.D.   F.D.H.
Hobson, Richard Hamilton.   Ri.H.
Hodge, Paul W.   P.W.H.
Hodges, James A.   J.A.Ho.
Hodgkin, Thomas.   T.Ho.
Hoetink, Harmannus.   H.Ho.
Hofer, Kenneth E., Jr.   K.E.H.
Hoffman, Paul F.   P.F.H.
Hoffmann, Herbert.   H.Hn.
Hofmann, Michel-Rostislav.   M.-R.Ho.
Hogetsu, Keigo.   K.Ho.
Hogg, Helen Sawyer.   H.S.H.
Hogg, Ian Vernon.   I.V.H.
Hogg, William Richey.   W.R.H.
Hohl, Reinhold D.   Re.H.
Holderbaum, James.   J.Hm.
Hollister, C. Warren.   C.W.Ho.
Holm, Donald August.   D.A.H.
Holmes, John H.   J.H.H.
Holmes, Ralph.   Ra.Ho.
Holsoe, Svend E.   S.E.H.
Holstein, William K.   W.K.H.
Holt, Edgar Crawshaw.   E.C.H.
Holt, J.C.   J.C.H.
Holt, Peter M.   P.M.Ho.
Holthusen, Hans Egon.   H.E.H.
Holton, William Coffeen.   W.C.Ho.
Holttum, Richard E.   R.E.H.
Holtzman, Jerome.   Je.Ho.
Holzman, Philip S.   P.S.H.
Honeycutt, Baxter D.   B.D.H.
Honigmann, John J.   J.J.Ho.
Honko, Lauri O.   L.O.H.
Hood, M. Sinclair F.   M.S.F.H.
Hoogstraten, Jan S.F. van.   J.v.H.
Hoover, Herbert T.   H.T.H.
Hopkins, John Francis Price.   J.F.P.H.
Hopwood, Derek.   D.H.
Hornberger, Theodore.   T.Hor.
Hornblower, Simon.   S.H.
Horne, R.A.   R.A.Ho.
Horst, Oscar H.   O.H.H.
Hoskin, Michael Anthony.   M.A.H.
Hosking, Geoffrey Alan.   G.A.H.
Hospers, John.   Jo.Ho.
Houghton, Lois Chapman.   L.C.H.
Houlton, Sir John Wardle.   Jo.W.H.
Hourani, Albert Habib.   A.H.Ho.
House, Michael R.   M.R.H.
Houston, James.   J.Ho.
Houtgast, Jakob.   J.H.
Houtte, Baron Jean M.J. van.   J.M.J.v.H.
Houwink ten Cate, Philo H.J.
    Ph.H.J.H.t.C.
Howard, Ian P.   I.P.H.
Howard, John Lawrance.   J.L.H.
Howard, Perry H.   P.H.H.

Howard, Sir Michael E.   M.E.Ho.
Howarth, Thomas.   Th.Ho.
Howarth, William Driver.   W.D.H.
Howell, F. Clark.   F.C.H.
Howell, Sarah McCanless.   S.McC.H.
Howie, Alan Crawford.   A.C.H.
Hoy, Cyrus Henry.   C.H.Ho.
Hoyt, Joseph Bixby.   J.B.Ho.
Hrbek, Ivan.   I.Hr.
Hsiao, Kung-chuan.   K.-c.H.
Hsieh, Chiao-Min.   C.-M.H.
Hsieh, Shan-yüan.   S.-y.H.
Hsu, Cho-yun.   C.-y.H.
Htin Aung, Maung.   M.H.Au.
Hu, Charles Y.   C.Hu.
Hu, Yueh-Gin Gung.   Y.-G.G.H.
Hubatsch, Walther C.   W.C.H.
Hübscher, Arthur.   Ar.Hü.
Hucker, Charles O.   C.O.Hu.
Hudnut, Joseph.   J.Hud.
Hudson, Winthrop S.   W.S.H.
Huffman, John W.   J.W.Hu.
Hughes, The Rev. G.E.   G.E.H.
Hughes, Graham McK.   G.McK.H.
Hughes, Capt. Wayne P., Jr.   W.P.H.
Huizing, Peter J.   P.Hu.
Hultkrantz, Åke Gunnar Birger.
    Å.G.B.H.
Humphrey, John H.   J.H.Hy.
Hung, Frederick Fu.   F.Hu.
Hunt, Sir David Wathen Stather.
    D.W.S.H.
Hunt, Earl B.   E.B.H.
Hunt, Inez Whitaker.   I.W.H.
Hunten, Donald M.   D.M.H.
Huot, Jean-Louis.   J.-L.Hu.
Huq, Muhammad Shamsul.   M.S.H.
Hurst, Harold Edwin.   H.E.Ht.
Husain, Mahmud.   M.Hu.
Husain, Syed Sajjad.   S.S.H.
Hussey, Dyneley.   D.Hus.
Hussey, Joan Mervyn.   J.M.H.
Hussman, Lawrence C.   L.E.Hu.
Hutter, Heribert R.   H.R.H.
Huxley, Herbert Henry.   H.H.Hu.
Huygens, Gerard Willem.   G.W.H.
Huyghe, René.   R.Hu.
Hyatt, J. Philip.   J.P.Hy.
Hyman, Isabelle.   I.Hy.

Iaboni, John F.   J.F.I.
Ichiko, Teiji.   T.Io.
Ichiye, Takashi.   T.Ic.
Ihde, Aaron J.   A.J.I.
IJsewijn, Jozef A.M.K.   J.A.M.K.I.
Ike, Nobutaka.   N.I.
Ikram, S.M.   S.M.I.
Illick, Joseph E.   J.E.I.
Imperato, Pascal James.   P.J.I.
Imshenetsky, Aleksandr Ilyich.   A.I.I.
Inalcik, Halil.   H.I.
Inden, Ronald B.   R.B.I.
Ingham, Kenneth.   K.In.
Ingold, Tim.   T.In.
Ingrams, William Harold.   W.H.I.
Insall, Donald W.   D.W.I.
Ipfling, Heinz-Jürgen.   H.-J.I.
Irmscher, Hans Dietrich.   H.D.I.
Irvine, Verity Elizabeth.   V.E.I.
Irwin, David.   D.I.
İsnard, Hildebert.   H.İs.
Issawi, Charles.   C.I.
Itzkowitz, Norman.   N.It.
Ivanov, Vyacheslav Vsevolodovich.
    V.V.I.

Ivić, Pavle.   P.I.
Iwasawa, Kenkichi,   K.Iw.
İz, Fahir.   F.İ.
Izard, Carroll E.   C.E.I.
Izenour, George C.   G.C.I.
Izutsu, Toshihiko.   T.I.

Jackson, Christopher Stewart.   C.S.J.
Jackson, Gordon.   G.J.
Jackson, Joy Juanita.   J.J.J.
Jackson, Richard T.   R.T.J.
Jackson, Roland John.   R.J.J.
Jackson, Stanley Percival.   S.P.Jn.
Jackson, William D.   W.D.J.
Jacob, Stanley W.   S.W.J.
Jacobs, Jeffrey W.   J.W.J.
Jacobs, Wilbur R.   W.R.J.
Jacobsen, Thorkild.   T.J.
Jacobson, Bernard.   B.Ja.
Jacoby, Oswald.   O.J.
Jaffe, Bernard.   Be.J.
Jaffé, Hans L.C.   H.L.C.J.
Jaffé, Michael.   Ml.J.
Jahns, Richard H.   R.H.J.
Jairazbhoy, Nazir Ali.   N.A.J.
James, A. Walter.   A.W.J.
James, C.L.R.   C.L.R.J.
James, D. Clayton.   D.C.J.
James, The Rev. Edwin Oliver.   E.O.J.
James, John W.   J.W.Ja.
James, Preston E.   P.E.J.
James, Thomas Garnet Henry.   T.G.H.J.
Jamieson, John Calhoun.   J.C.J.
Janick, Jules.   J.J.
Jansen, Marius B.   M.B.J.
Janson, H.W.   H.W.J.
Janzen, Jörg H.A.   J.H.A.J.
Jarry, Madeleine.   M.J.
Järvinen, E. Jaakko.   E.J.J.
Jay, Martin Evan.   M.E.J.
Jeandet, Yette.   Y.J.
Jeanloz, Raymond.   R.J.
Jeans, D.N.   D.N.J.
Jeffares, Alexander Norman.   A.N.J.
Jellett, John Holmes.   J.H.J.
Jenkins, The Rev. Daniel T.   D.T.J.
Jenks, C. Wilfred.   C.W.J.
Jenkyns, Richard H.A.   R.H.A.J.
Jerphagnon, Lucien.   L.J.
Jescheck, Hans-Heinrich.   H.-H.J.
Jessop, Thomas Edmund.   T.E.Je.
Johansson, Ivar K.   I.J.
John, Walter.   W.J.
Johnson, D. Gale.   D.G.J.
Johnson, Dorothy M.   D.M.J.
Johnson, Gary Dean.   G.D.J.
Johnson, John J.   J.J.Jo.
Johnson, Markes E.   M.E.Jo.
Johnson, Norman Gardner.   N.G.J.
Johnson, W. Hilton.   W.H.J.
Johnston, Marshall C.   M.C.J.
Johnston, S. Paul.   S.P.J.
Jollie, Malcolm T.   M.T.J.
Jolly, William Lee.   W.L.J.
Jolowicz, Herbert Felix.   H.F.J.
Jones, Abeodu Bowen.   A.B.J.
Jones, Arnold Hugh Martin.   A.H.M.J.
Jones, Benjamin A., Jr.   B.A.J.
Jones, Douglas Henry.   D.H.J.
Jones, Emrys.   E.J.
Jones, Gareth H.   G.H.J.
Jones, J. Knox, Jr.   J.K.J.
Jones, Marsden.   Ma.J.
Jones, S.S.D.   S.S.D.J.
Jones, Thomas.   T.Jo.

Lack, David L. D.L.L.
Lacouture, Jean. J.La.
Ladefoged, Peter N. P.N.L.
Ladner, Gerhart B. G.B.L.
Laessoe, Jorgen. Jo.La.
Laffargue, Gen. Charles-André. C.-A.La.
LaFond, Eugene C. E.C.LaF.
Lafont, Pierre-Bernard. P.-B.L.
Lagowski, J.J. J.J.L.
Laitinen, Kai L.K. K.L.K.L.
Lamb, Hubert Horace. H.H.L.
Lamb, Norman Jones. N.J.L.
Lambert, Véronique. V.L.
Lamberts, Emiel L. E.L.L.
Lamott, Kenneth. K.La.
Lampard, Eric Edwin. E.E.La.
Landau, Jacob M. J.M.L.
Landgrebe, Ludwig M. L.M.L.
Landis, Fred. Fr.L.
Lane, George S. G.S.L.
Lane, Kenneth S. K.S.L.
Lane, Richard. Ri.L.
Lane, Robert K. R.K.L.
Lang, David Marshall. D.M.La.
Lang, George. G.L.
Lange, Robert Terence. R.T.La.
Langevin, Luce-Andrée. L.-A.L.
Lanhers, Yvonne. Y.L.
La Orden Miracle, Ernesto. E.L.O.M.
Laoust, Henri. H.L.
Laracy, Hugh Michael. H.M.La.
Laroui, Abdallah. A.La.
Larson, J.H. J.H.L.
Laskey, Ronald A. R.A.La.
Lasko, Peter Erik. P.E.L.
Lassen, Erik. Er.L.
Lasserre, François. F.La.
Latham, Agnes M.C. A.M.C.L.
Latham, Earl. Ea.L.
Latham, Richard C. R.C.L.
Latil, Pierre de. P. de L.
Lattimer, John Kingsley. J.K.La.
Lattimore, Owen. O.la.
Lattin, Harriet Pratt. H.P.La.
Lātūkefu, The Rev. Sione. Si.L.
Laudise, Robert A. R.A.L.
Laue, Gilbert P. G.P.L.
Laughlin, William S. W.S.L.
Lauwerys, Joseph Albert. J.A.L.
Lavender, David Sievert. D.S.Lr.
Laver, James. Ja.L.
Lavrin, Janko. Ja.La.
Law, Philip James Stopford. P.J.S.L.
Law, Robin. R.La.
Lawler, Nancy Ellen. N.E.L.
Lawler, Sylvia Dorothy. S.La.
Lawrence, Carl Adam. C.A.L.
Lawrence, Joseph Collins. J.C.L.
Lawson, Robert Frederic. R.F.L.
Laya, Diouldé. Di.L.
Laybourn-Parry, Johanna E.M.
    J.E.M.L.-P.
Lea, Sir Frederick M. F.M.L.
Lea, Kathleen Marguerite. K.M.L.
Lebel, Robert. R.Le.
Lecco, Alberto. A.L.
Lechêne, Robert. Ro.L.
Lee, Chan. C.Le.
Lee, James A. J.A.Le.
Lee, Ki-baik. K.-b.L.
Lee, Kwang-rin. K.-r.L.
Lee, Peter H. P.H.L.
Lee, Robert Warden. R.W.L.
Leech, Clifford. Cl.L.
Leeming, Frank Andrew. F.A.L.
Legge, Dominica. D.Le.

Legge, John David. J.D.L.
Legum, Colin. Co.L.
Legum, Margaret Jean. M.J.L.
Lehman, Mildred K. M.K.L.
Lehman, Milton. M.Ln.
Lehmann, Andrew George. A.G.L.
Lehmann-Haupt, Hellmut E. H.E.L.-H.
Leicester, Henry M. H.M.L.
Leichter, Otto. O.L.
Leighton, Richard M. R.M.Le.
Leiman, Sid Z. S.Z.L.
Leinbach, Thomas R. T.R.L.
Leite, Aureliano. A.Le.
Leiter, Samuel. S.Lr.
Lejeune, Michel. M.Le.
Lejewski, Czeslaw. Cz.L.
Lekachman, Robert. R.L.
Lemarchand, René. Re.L.
Lenti, Libero. Li.L.
Lentz, Thomas L. T.L.L.
Leonard, Justin W. J.W.L.
Leone, Lucile P. L.P.Le.
Leontiev, Oleg Konstantinovich. O.K.L.
Leprohon, Pierre. P.Le.
Lerner, Richard M. Ri.M.L.
Lernet-Holenia, Alexander Marie
    Norbert. A.L.-Ho.
Lessing, Lawrence P. L.P.L.
Leung, Chi-Keung. C.-K.L.
Le Vay, David. D. Le V.
LeVeque, William Judson. W.J.LeV.
Levi, Albert William. A.W.L.
Levi, Herbert W. H.W.L.
Levi, Lorna R. L.R.L.
Levi, Michael. Mi.L.
Levinson, Sandra H. S.H.L.
Levron, Jacques. J.Le.
Lewis, David L. D.L.Le.
Lewis, David Malcolm. D.M.L.
Lewis, Geoffrey D. G.D.L.
Lewis, George Knowlton. G.K.L.
Lewis, Hywel David. H.D.L.
Lewis, Ioan M. I.M.L.
Lewis, John Wilson. J.W.Le.
Lewis, Peirce F. P.F.L.
Leyser, K.J. K.J.L.
Li, Fang Kuei. F.K.L.
Li, Tien-yi. T.-y.L.
Libin, Laurence Elliot. La.L.
Lieberich, Heinz. H.Li.
Lieberthal, Kenneth G. K.G.L.
Lien, Chan. C.Li.
Lieuwen, Edwin. E.Li.
Liley, Bruce Sween. B.S.L.
Lin, Maung Wai. M.W.L.
Lindars, Barnabas. B.L.
Lindauer, Martin. M.Li.
Lindbeck, Assar. A.Li.
Lindbeck, George Arthur. G.A.L.
Lindberg, Carter H. C.H.Li.
Lindsay, R. Bruce. R.B.L.
Lindt, Gillian. G.Li.
Link, Arthur S. A.S.L.
Linton, Michael I.A. M.I.A.L.
Lippold, Adolf. A.Lip.
Lisitsin, Aleksandr Petrovich. A.P.L.
Lissens, René Felix. R.F.Li.
Little, Donald P. D.P.L.
Liu, James T.C. J.T.C.L.
Livermore, Harold V. H.V.L.
Livi-Bacci, Massimo. M.L.-B.
Livingstone, Daniel A. D.A.L.
Llewellyn, Karl Nickerson. K.N.L.
Lloyd, Seton H.F. S.H.F.L.
Lloyd-Jones, David Mathias. D.M.L.-J.
Lloyd-Jones, Hugh. H.L.-J.

Lo, Jung-pang. J.-p.L.
Lockhart, Richard T. R.T.L.
Lockley, R.M. R.M.L.
Lockspeiser, Edward. E.L.
Lodish, Harvey F. H.F.L.
Lodrick, Deryck O. D.O.L.
Loeffler, M. John. M.J.Lo.
Loewe, Fritz P. F.P.L.
Logan, Alan. A.Lo.
Logan, Richard F. R.F.Lo.
Logan, Robert G. R.G.Lo.
Lombardo, Antonino. An.L.
Long, Charles H. C.H.Lo.
Longford, Elizabeth Pakenham,
    Countess of. E.Lo.
Longworth, Philip. P.L.
Lonsdale, Dame Kathleen. K.Lo.
Loon, Maurits N. van. M.N.v.L.
Loosli, John K. J.K.L.
Lopez, Robert Sabatino. R.S.L.
Lorge, Barry Steven. B.S.Lo.
Lorig, Clarence H. C.H.L.
Lorwin, Val R. V.R.L.
Losey, George S. G.S.Lo.
Louwe Kooÿmans, Leendert P.
    L.P.L.K.
Low, D. Anthony. D.A.Lo.
Low, David Morrice. D.M.Lo.
Lowe, Victor. V.Lo.
Lowenthal, Constance. C.Lo.
Luard, Evan. E.Lu.
Lucas, Donald William. D.W.L.
Luce, R. Duncan. R.D.L.
Luck, Georg Hans. G.Lu.
Lucker, Joseph M. J.M.Lu.
Lukoff, Fred. F.L.
Lüling, Karl Heinz. K.H.L.
Lumiansky, R.M. R.M.Lu.
Luntz, Myron. M.Lu.
Luscombe, David Edward. D.E.L.
Lustig, Lawrence K. L.K.L.
Lutfi al-Sayyid Marsot, Afaf.
    A.L.al-S.M.
Luttrell, Anthony Thornton. A.T.L.
Luyendyk, Bruce Peter. B.P.L.
Lyman, John. J.Ly.
Lynch, John. Jo.Ly.
Lyne, A. Gordon. A.G.Ly.
Lyons, Sir John. J.Lyo.

Mabbott, Thomas Ollive. T.O.M.
Mabee, Carleton. C.Ma.
Mabogunje, Akinlawon Ladipo. A.L.M.
Macan, T.T. T.T.M.
Macartney, Carlile Aylmer. C.A.M.
McAuley, Mary. M.McA.
McBride, George McCutchen.
    G.McC.McB.
McCallum, W. Cheyne. W.C.McC.
Mac Cana, Proinsias. P.Mac C.
McCarthy, Patrick. P.McC.
McCarthy, Willard J. W.J.McC.
McCaskie, T.C. T.C.McC.
McCaskill, Murray. Mu.McC.
McChesney, Malcolm. M.McC.
Macchia, Giovanni. Gi.M.
McClelland, Charles A. C.A.McC.
McClintock, Elizabeth. E.McC.
McComb, Arthur Kilgore. A.K.McC.
MacConaill, Michael A. M.A.MacC.
McCully, Marilyn. M.McCu.
McDavid, Raven I., Jr. R.McD.
McDivitt, James F. J.F.McD.
McDonald, Alexander Hugh. A.H.McD.
Macdonald, Barrie K. B.K.M.

MacDonald, Charles B.   C.B.MacD.
McDonald, Robert A.J.   R.A.J.McD.
McDonough, Sheila D.   S.McD.
McDougall, Walter A.   W.A.McD.
MacDuffee, C.C.   C.C.MacD.
Maceda, José.   Jé.Ma.
McElroy, Michael B.   M.B.McE.
McEwen, The Rev. James Stevenson.   J.S.McE.
McFarlane, James Walter.   J.W.McF.
MacGaffey, Janet.   J.MacG.
MacGaffey, Wyatt.   W.MacG.
McGann, Thomas F.   T.F.McG.
McGeough, Joseph A.   J.A.McG.
McGinn, Bernard J.   B.J.McG.
McGrayne, Sharon.   S.McG.
McGreevey, William Paul.   W.P.McG.
McGregor, Samuel Emmett.   S.E.McG.
Machlis, Joseph.   J.Ma.
McHugh, Christine.   C.McH.
McIntosh, Christopher Angus.   C.A.McI.
MacIsaac, Lt. Col. David.   D.MacI.
Mackenzie, Fred T.   F.T.M.
McKenzie, The Rev. John L.   J.L.McK.
Mackie, J. Alan.   J.A.Ma.
Mackintosh, Nicholas John.   N.J.M.
McKnight, Brian E.   B.E.McK.
Mackrell, Judith R.   J.R.Ma.
Mackridge, Peter A.   P.A.M.
Mack Smith, Denis.   De.M.S.
McLaughlin, John.   J.McL.
McLellan, David T.   D.T.McL.
Macleod, Iseabail C.   I.C.M.
MacLeod, Murdo J.   M.J.MacL.
McLeod, Thomas S.   T.S.McL.
McLeod, William Hewat.   W.H.McL.
McLintock, Peter.   P.McL.
McLure, Charles E., Jr.   C.E.McL.
McMahon, William B.   W.B.McM.
McMaster, David N.   D.N.McM.
MacMullen, Ramsay.   R.MacM.
McMullen, Roy Donald.   R.McMu.
McMurtrey, James Edward, Jr.   J.E.McM.
McNeill, William H.   W.H.McN.
MacNutt, W. Stewart.   W.S.MacNu.
Macomber, Richard W.   R.W.Ma.
McPherron, Robert L.   R.L.M.
MacRae, Donald Gunn.   D.G.MacR.
Maeno, Naoaki.   Na.Mo.
Magarshack, David.   Da.Ma.
Magda, Matthew S.   M.S.Ma.
Magdoff, Harry.   Ha.Ma.
Magnus, Bernd.   Be.M.
Magoun, Horace Winchell.   H.W.M.
Mahdi, Muhsin S.   M.S.M.
Maiorana, Virginia C.   V.C.M.
Makdisi, George.   G.M.
Maksoud, Clovis F.   C.F.M.
Malandra, William W.   W.W.M.
Malcolm, Norman A.   N.A.M.
Malia, Martin E.   M.E.Ma.
Malik, Liliya Konstantinovna.   L.K.M.
Malin, Michael C.   M.C.Ma.
Malina, Frank J.   F.J.Ma.
Mallett, Michael Edward.   Mi.Ma.
Mallory, V. Standish.   V.S.M.
Mallowan, Sir Max.   M.Mn.
Malm, William P.   W.P.M.
Maloney, Francis J. Terence.   Fr.J.M.
Manchester, William.   W.Man.
Manger, Walter L.   W.L.Ma.
Mann, Golo.   G.Ma.
Mannheim, Hermann.   H.M.
Mannheim, L. Andrew.   L.A.Ma.
Manning, Wayne E.   Wa.E.M.

Manschreck, Clyde L.   C.L.Ma.
Manske, Richard H.   R.H.M.
Manton, Sidnie M.   S.M.M.
Manuel, Frank Edward.   F.E.M.
Manvell, Roger.   R.M.
Maraini, Fosco.   F.M.
Marcelli, Umberto.   U.M.
March, Benjamin.   B.Ma.
Marc'hadour, The Rev. Germain P.   G.P.Ma.
Marchand, Leslie A.   L.A.M.
Marcus, Harold G.   H.G.M.
Marcus, Leonard M.   L.M.M.
Marcuse, Sibyl.   S.Ma.
Mariani, Valerio.   V.M.
Mark, Herman F.   H.F.M.
Markokis, John.   Jo.Ms.
Markesinis, Basil S.   B.S.M.
Markovitz, Hershel.   He.M.
Markowitz, William.   W.Ma.
Marks, Robert W.   R.W.M.
Marks, Sally.   Sa.M.
Marks, Shula E.   Sh.M.
Marlowe, John.   Jo.Ma.
Marquard, Leopold.   L.Ma.
Marr, Phebe A.   P.A.Ma.
Marriott, McKim.   Mc.M.
Marrou, Henri-Irénée.   H.-I.M.
Marsh, Christopher Marriage.   C.M.
Marshall, Joe T.   J.T.M.
Marshall, John S.   J.S.Ma.
Marshall, P.J.   P.J.M.
Marshall, Robert L.   Ro.Ma.
Marshall, Woodville K.   W.K.M.
Martin, Boyd A.   B.A.M.
Martin, David Grier, Jr.   D.G.M.
Martin, Gene E.   G.E.Ma.
Martindale, Andrew Henry Robert.   A.Ma.
Martini, Giuseppe.   Gi.Ma.
Martinich, A.P.   A.P.Ma.
Martinot, Roger.   R.Ma.
Martins, Luciano.   L.Ms.
Marty, Martin E.   M.E.M.
Martz, John D.   J.D.Ma.
Marwick, Maxwell Gay.   M.G.Ma.
Masai, Yasuo.   Y.M.
Mascarenhas, Adolfo C.   A.C.M.
Mason, Sir Basil John.   B.J.M.
Mason, Brian H.   B.H.M.
Mason, Haydn T.   H.T.M.
Mason, J. Alden.   J.A.Mn.
Mason, Leonard E.   L.E.M.
Mason, Philip.   P.Ma.
Massevitch, Alla Genrikhovna.   A.G.Ma.
Massey, Alan Gibbs.   A.G.M.
Masutani Fumio.   Ma.Fu.
Materné, Jan Maria Juul.   J.M.J.M.
Mathew, The Most Rev. David.   D.Ma.
Mathews, Thomas G.   T.G.Ms.
Mathis, John S.   J.S.M.
Matloff, Maurice.   Ma.M.
Matsumoto, Nobuhiro.   N.M.
Matthews, Bernard Edward.   B.E.Ma.
Matthews, Geoffrey Vernon Townsend.   G.V.T.M.
Matthews, J.F.   J.F.Ma.
Matthews, Peter B.C.   P.B.C.M.
Matthias, Erich.   E.Ma.
Matthíasson, Björn.   B.M.
Matull, Wilhelm.   Wi.M.
Matz, Samuel A.   S.A.M.
Maurer, The Rev. Armand.   A.A.Ma.
Maurer, D.W.   D.W.M.
Maxwell, D.E.S.   D.E.S.M.
May, Comdr. William Edward.   W.E.M.

Mayeda, Sengaku.   Se.M.
Mayer, Harold M.   H.M.M.
Mayer, William Vernon.   W.V.M.
Mayne, Richard J.   R.J.Ma.
Mays, John Barron.   J.B.M.
Mažiulis, Vytautas J.   V.J.M.
Mazur, B.W.   B.W.Ma.
Meade, Robert Douthat.   R.D.M.
Meadow, S. Roy.   S.R.M.
Medina, José Ramón.   J.R.Me.
Medina, Manuel.   M.Me.
Mee, John F.   J.F.Me.
Meerhaeghe, M.A. van.   M.A.v.M.
Meeuse, Bastiaan J.D.   B.J.D.M.
Mehren, Arthur Taylor von.   A.T.v.M.
Mei, Yi Pao.   Y.P.M.
Meier, Mark F.   M.F.M.
Meiggs, Russell.   Ru.M.
Meijer, Henk.   H.Me.
Meland, Bernard E.   B.E.M.
Mellanby, Kenneth.   K.Me.
Mellor, Roy E.H.   R.E.H.M.
Melsen, Andrew G.M. van.   A.G.M.v.M.
Meltzer, Julian Louis.   J.L.Me.
Ménager, Daniel.   D.Mé.
Mendeloff, Albert I.   A.I.M.
Mendenhall, George Emery.   G.E.Me.
Mendoza, Eric.   E.M.
Mensching, Gustav.   G.Me.
Menzies, Robert James.   R.J.Me.
Mercier, Paul.   Pa.M.
Merdinger, Capt. Charles John.   C.J.M.
Merkelbach, Reinhold.   R.Me.
Merlan, Philip.   Pp.M.
Merle, Robert.   Ro.M.
Mernagh, Laurence Reginald.   L.R.M.
Mero, John Lawrence.   J.L.M.
Mertz, Barbara G.   B.G.M.
Mertz, Pierre.   P.Me.
Mesa-Lago, Carmel.   C.M.-L.
Meselson, Matthew.   Ma.Me.
Meškauskas, Kazimieras Antano.   K.A.M.
Messenger, P.S.   P.S.M.
Metford, John Callan James.   J.C.J.M.
Meyendorff, The Rev. John.   J.M.
Meyer, Adolphe Erich.   A.E.M.
Meyer, John Richard.   J.R.M.
Meyer, Michael C.   M.C.M.
Mezei, Kathy.   K.M.
Michael, Franz H.   F.H.M.
Michel, Michel.   M.Ml.
Michelena, Luis.   L.M.
Michelmore, Peter.   P.Mi.
Mickel, John T.   J.T.Mi.
Micklin, Philip P.   P.P.M.
Middleton, Dorothy.   D.Mi.
Middleton, Gerard V.   G.V.M.
Middleton, John F.M.   J.F.M.
Middleton, Robin David.   R.D.Mi.
Miège, Jacques.   J.Mi.
Miers, Earl Schenck.   E.S.Mi.
Mikesell, Marvin W.   M.W.M.
Mikhaylov, Nikolay Ivanovich.   N.I.M.
Mikoletzky, Hanns Leo.   H.L.M.
Milgate, Wesley.   W.Mi.
Milkov, Fyodor Nikolayevich.   F.N.M.
Miller, John E.   J.E.M.
Miller, Mark D.H.   M.D.H.M.
Miller, Maynard M.   M.M.M.
Miller, William.   W.Mr.
Miller, William H.   W.H.M.
Millikin, Sandra.   S.Mi.
Millner, Maurice Alfred.   M.A.M.
Millon, Henry A.   H.A.M.
Millot, Jacques.   Ja.M.

Mills, Gladstone E.M.   G.E.M.M.
Minifie, Bernard W.   B.W.M.
Minio-Paluello, Lorenzo.   L.M.-P.
Minkel, C.W.   C.W.M.
Mints, Aleksey Aleksandrovich.   A.A.M.
Mirsky, Jeannette.   J.Mir.
Misner, Gordon E.   G.E.Mi.
Mitchell, Adrian C.W.   A.C.W.M.
Mitchell, G.A.G.   G.A.G.M.
Mitchell, James Clyde.   J.C.Mi.
Mitchell, Jean Brown.   J.B.Mi.
Mitchell, John.   Jo.M.
Mitchell, John Burnett.   Jo.B.M.
Mitchell, Mairin.   M.Mi.
Mitchell, Terence Croft.   T.C.M.
Mitford, Nancy.   Na.M.
Mitry, Jean.   Je.M.
Mitzman, Arthur.   Ar.M.
Mizener, Arthur.   A.Mi.
Moeller, Therald.   T.Mo.
Moen, Arve Sverre.   A.S.M.
Mohanty, Jitendra N.   J.N.M.
Mokray, William George.   W.G.M.
Moldenhauer, Hans.   Ha.M.
Mollat, Michel J.   M.J.Mo.
Molnar, Peter H.   P.H.M.
Moltmann, Jürgen D.   J.D.M.
Momigliano, Arnaldo Dante.   A.D.Mo.
Mommsen, Wolfgang J.   W.J.M.
Momo, Hiroyuki.   Hi.Mo.
Momsen, Janet D.   J.D.Mo.
Momsen, Richard P., Jr.   R.P.Mo.
Moncada R., J. Roberto.   J.R.M.R.
Monet, The Rev. Jacques.   J.Mo.
Money, Nic J.   N.J.Mo.
Mongan, Agnes.   Ag.M.
Mongrédien, Georges.   G.Mn.
Monick, John A.   J.A.Mo.
Monnerville, Gaston.   G.Mo.
Monroy, Alberto.   A.Mo.
Montagna, William.   W.M.
Montross, Lynn.   L.Mo.
Moog, Robert A.   R.A.M.
Mookerjee, Sitanshu.   S.Mo.
Moore, Gerald.   Ge.Mo.
Moore, Harold E., Jr.   H.E.Mo.
Moore, John Preston.   J.P.M.
Moore, Patrick.   P.Mo.
Moore, Will G.   W.G.Mo.
Moraes, Frank R.   F.R.M.
Morales-Carrión, Arturo.   A.M.-C.
Moran, Francis.   F.Mo.
Moran, Warren.   W.Mo.
Morgan, Joseph R.   J.R.Mo.
Morgan, Neil.   N.Mo.
Morgan, Stephen William Kenneth.
   S.W.K.M.
Morgan, William Thomas Wilson.
   W.T.W.M.
Morley, Cyril John.   C.J.Mo.
Morley, Ronald James.   R.J.M.
Morrey, Charles B., Jr.   C.B.My.
Morris, Charles Nicholas.   C.N.M.
Morris, Donald R.   D.R.M.
Morris, H.S.   H.S.M.
Morrison, Hugh Sinclair.   Hu.M.
Morrissey, Charles Thomas.   C.T.Mo.
Morsey, Rudolf.   R.Mo.
Mortensen, Brita Maud Ellen.   B.Mo.
Morton, Brian.   Br.M.
Morton, Richard Lee.   R.L.Mo.
Morton, William Lewis.   W.L.M.
Moseley, Maynard F., Jr.   M.F.Mo.
Mosher, Frederick C.   F.C.M.
Mosley, J. Philip.   J.P.Mo.
Mosley, Leonard.   Le.M.

Mosse, W.E.   W.E.Mo.
Mosteller, Frederick.   Fr.M.
Mostofi, Khosrow.   Kh.Mo.
Mostow, George Daniel.   G.D.M.
Motteler, Lee S.   L.S.M.
Moulton, Matthew James.   Ma.J.M.
Moulton, William G.   Wi.G.M.
Moumouni, Abdou.   A.M.
Movius, Hallam L., Jr.   H.L.Ms.
Mozumder, Asokendu.   A.Moz.
Mueller, David Livingstone.   D.L.M.
Mukerji, S.N.   S.N.M.
Mulholland, J. Derral.   J.D.Mu.
Müller, Claudius Cornelius.   C.C.M.
Müller, Edith A.   E.A.M.
Müller, Joachim.   J.Mu.
Muller, Robert A.   R.A.Mu.
Müller-Brockmann, Josef.   J.M.-Br.
Müller-Freienfels, Wolfram.   W.M.-F.
Multhauf, Robert P.   R.P.M.
Munn-Rankin, J.M.   J.M.M.-R.
Munro, Thomas.   Th.M.
Munroe, John A.   J.A.Mu.
Munson, J. Ronald.   J.R.Mn.
Munsterberg, Hugo.   H.Mu.
Munz, Peter.   P.Mu.
Muranov, Aleksandr Pavlovich.   A.P.M.
Murphy, Alexander B.   A.B.M.
Murphy, Arthur D.   A.D.M.
Murphy, The Rev. Francis Xavier.
   F.X.M.
Murphy, James J.   J.J.M.
Murra, John V.   J.V.M.
Murray, Anne Wood.   A.W.M.
Murray, Francis J.   F.J.M.
Murray, Peter J.   P.J.Mu.
Murrell, Kathleen Berton   K.B.M.
Murton, Ronald K.   R.K.M.
Musgrave, William K.R.   W.K.R.M.
Muskie, Edmund S.   E.S.M.
Mutter, Reginald P.C.   R.P.C.M.
Mutton, Alice F.A.   A.F.A.M.
Myers, Alexander Reginald.   A.R.M.
Myers, Raymond R.   R.R.M.
Myers, Rollo H.   R.My.
Myint, Hla.   H.My.

Nachtergaele, Victor.   V.N.
Nadeau, Maurice.   M.Na.
Nadler, Josef.   J.N.
Naess, Arne D.   A.D.N.
Nagahara, Keiji.   K.N.
Nagel, Heinrich.   H.N.
Nagler, Alois M.   A.M.N.
Naim, C.M.   C.M.N.
Nair, Kusum.   K.Na.
Nair, N. Chandrasekharan.   N.C.N.
Naisbitt, John.   Jo.N.
Naka, Arata.   A.Na.
Nakamura, Hajime.   H.Na.
Nakosteen, Mehdi K.   M.K.N.
Namias, Jerome.   J.Na.
Nanda, B.R.   B.R.N.
Nangeroni, Giuseppe.   G.Na.
Napier, J.R.   J.R.N.
Narasimhan, Chakravarthi V.   C.V.N.
Narasimhan, Raghavan.   R.Na.
Narayana, H.S.   H.S.N.
Narr, Karl J.   K.J.N.
Nash, Manning.   Ma.N.
Nash, Paul.   Pa.N.
Nash, Ray.   Ra.N.
Nasr, Seyyed Hossein.   S.H.N.
Nassau, Kurt.   Ku.N.
Nathan, Peter W.   P.W.N.

Nel, Andries.   A.Ne.
Nelson, Bert.   B.Ne.
Nelson, David M.   D.M.Ne.
Nelson, E. Clifford.   E.C.N.
Nelson, Gareth Jon.   G.J.N.
Nelson, R.J.   R.J.Ne.
Nelson, Robert J.   R.J.N.
Nemerov, Howard.   H.Ne.
Nestyev, Israel Vladimirovich.   I.V.N.
Nettl, Bruno.   B.N.
Neumark, Fritz.   F.N.
Neutze, Max.   M.N.
Nevins, Allan.   Al.N.
Newburn, Ray L., Jr.   R.L.Ne.
Newcombe, Curtis L.   C.N.
Newhall, Beaumont.   Be.N.
Newlin, Dika.   D.N.
Newman, Robert Bradford.   R.B.N.
Newman, William Anderson.   W.A.N.
Newman, William S.   W.S.N.
Newsom-Davis, John M.   J.M.N.-D.
Newton, Brian E.   B.E.N.
Newton, Douglas.   D.Ne.
Neyman, Viktor Grigoryevich.   V.G.N.
Nicholas, Herbert G.   H.G.N.
Nicholas, Warwick L.   W.L.N.
Nichols, Robert Brayton.   R.B.Ni.
Nicholson, Norman L.   N.L.N.
Nicol, Davidson S.H.W.   D.S.H.W.N.
Nicol, Donald MacGillivray.   D.M.N.
Nicolaï, Henri.   He.Ni.
Nicolle, Jacques-M.-R.   J.-M.-R.N.
Niddrie, David Lawrence.   D.L.N.
Nielsen, Kai E.   K.E.N.
Nienhauser, William H., Jr.   W.H.N.
Nietschmann, Bernard.   B.Ni.
Nijim, Basheer K.   B.K.N.
Nijinsky, Romola.   R.Ni.
Nikiforov, Leonid Alekseyevich.
   L.A.N.
Niklaus, Robert.   Ro.N.
Nisbet, Robert A.   R.A.N.
Niven, Alastair N.R.   A.N.R.N.
Niven, Ivan,   I.N.
Noback, Charles R.   C.R.N.
Noble, Clyde Everett.   C.E.N.
Noble, J. Jeremy.   J.J.No.
Noble, Joseph Veach.   J.V.N.
Noller, Carl R.   C.R.No.
Norbeck, Edward.   E.N.
Nordhagen, Per Jonas.   P.J.N.
Nordtvedt, Kenneth L., Jr.   K.L.N.
Norman, Lennart T.   L.T.N.
Norman, Sir Richard O.C.   R.O.C.N.
Norrell, Robert J.   R.J.No.
Norris, David A.   D.A.N.
Norris, David O.   D.O.N.
Norris, Kenneth Stafford.   K.S.N.
Norris, Robert S.   R.S.N.
Norstog, Knut J.   K.J.No.
North, Robert C.   R.C.N.
Norwich, John Julius Cooper, 2nd
   Viscount.   N.
Nove, Alexander.   A.No.
Novick, Alvin.   A.N.
Nowell, Charles E.   C.E.No.
Nutting, Jack.   J.Nu.

Oakley, Francis Christopher.   F.C.O.
O'Beirne Ranelagh, John.   J.O'B.R.
Oberg, Kalervo.   K.Ob.
O'Brien, Conor Cruise.   C.C.O'B.
O'Callaghan, Joseph F.   J.F.O'C.
Occhialino, Mario E.   Ma.E.O.
Ochsenwald, William L.   W.L.O.

O'Connell, Daniel Patrick. D.P.O'C.
O'Connor, Daniel William. D.W.O'C.
O'Connor, Francis Valentine. F.V.O'C.
Odlozilik, Otakar. O.O.
Odum, Eugene P. E.P.O.
Oehser, Paul H. P.H.O.
Ogé, Frédéric. F.O.
Ogilvie, Robert Maxwell. R.M.Og.
Ogorkiewicz, Richard Marian. R.M.O.
O'Gorman, James Francis. J.F.O'G.
O'Grady, Brendan Anthony. B.O'G.
O'Kelly, Bernard. B.O'K.
Olah, George A. G.A.O.
Oldenbourg-Idalie, Zoé. Z.O.
Oldroyd, Harold. H.O.
Oliver, Michael Francis. M.F.O.
Oliver, Paul P.O.
Oliver, William Hosking. W.H.O.
Olivier, Daria. D.Ol.
Ollier, Clifford David. C.D.O.
Olson, David R. D.R.O.
Olson, Edwin A. E.A.O.
Olson, Everett C. E.C.O.
Olson, Jerry S. J.S.O.
Olson, Maynard V. M.V.O.
Olver, Ron. R.O.
Oman, Carola (Lady Lenanton). C.O.
Omar, Farouk. F.Om.
Ominde, Simeon Hongo. S.H.O.
Ommanney, Francis D. F.D.O.
O'Neill, Denis. D.O'N.
O'Neill, William L. W.L.O'N.
Ooi Jin Bee. O.J.B.
Oppenheimer, Jane M. J.M.O.
O'Raifeartaigh, Tarlach. T.O'R.
Orcibal, Jean. J.Or.
Ordish, George. G.O.
Ornati, Oscar A. O.A.O.
Orne, Martin T. M.T.O.
Örsy, The Rev. Ladislas M. L.M.Ö.
Ortner, Sherry B. S.B.O.
Orton, Glenn S. G.S.O.
Orville, Richard Edmonds. R.E.Or.
Osborn, Frederick Henry. F.H.O.
Osborn, The Rev. Ronald E. R.E.O.
Osborne, John W. J.W.O.
Osborne, Milton Edgeworth. M.E.O.
Osborne, Richard Horsley. R.H.O.
Osler, Margaret J. M.J.O.
Ostenso, Ned Allen. N.A.O.
Ostrom, John H. J.H.O.
O'Toole, James Joseph. J.O'T.
O'Toole, Thomas E. T.E.O'T.
Otto, Christian F. C.F.O.
Outler, Albert Cook. A.C.O.
Overbeek, Jan Theodoor Gerard.
    J.T.G.O.
Overton, Leonard C. L.C.O.
Owen, D.D.R. D.D.R.O.
Owen, Peter D. P.D.O.
Owen, Tobias Chant. T.C.O.
Owen, Wilfred. W.O.
Owens, The Rev. Joseph. J.O.

Pacaut, Marcel. M.Pa.
Page, Edward C. E.C.P.
Pai, Raghawendra Mukund. R.M.P.
Painter, George Duncan. G.D.P.
Pal, Indra. I.P.
Palerm, Angel. An.Pa.
Pallis, Christopher A. C.A.P.
Pallucchini, Rodolfo. R.Pal.
Palmer, Ralph Anthony. R.A.Pr.
Pálsson, Hermann. He.P.
Pannain, Guido. G.Pan.

Pannell, Clifton W. C.W.P.
Paoletti, John T. J.T.Pa.
Papadakis, Juan. J.Pa.
Parczewski, Władysław. W.Pa.
Park, George Kerlin. G.K.P.
Parke, Herbert William. H.W.P.
Parker, Alexander A. A.A.P.
Parker, Franklin D. F.D.P.
Parker, N. Geoffrey. N.G.P.
Parker, Simon B. S.B.P.
Parkes, Henry Bamford. H.B.P.
Parkes, Kenneth C. K.C.P.
Parkin, Charles William. C.W.Pa.
Parkinson, Robert Lewis. R.L.P.
Parotto, Maurizio. Ma.P.
Parrot, André. A.Pa.
Parry, John Horace. J.H.Py.
Parry, V.J. V.J.P.
Parsons, James J. Ja.J.P.
Pascal, Roy. Ro.Pa.
Pashuto, Vladimir T. V.T.P.
Passavant, Günter. G.Pa.
Passmore, Reginald. R.Pa.
Pastor, José M.F. J.M.F.P.
Pathak, Devavrat Nanubhai. D.N.P.
Patrick, Hugh T. H.T.P.
Patterson, Colin. C.P.
Patterson, Stephen E. S.E.P.
Patterson, Thomas C. T.C.P.
Patze, Hans. H.Pa.
Patzig, Günther. Gü.P.
Pauck, Wilhelm. W.P.
Pauling, Linus C. L.C.P.
Pawley, Andrew K. A.K.Pa.
Pawson, David Leo. D.L.P.
Payanzo, Ntsomo. N.Pa.
Payne, Stanley G. S.G.P.
Pearson, Charles G. C.G.P.
Pearson, H.F. H.F.P.
Pedanou, Macaire K. M.K.P.
Peel, Edwin A. E.A.P.
Peel, Ronald Francis. R.F.Pe.
Peiser, H. Steffen. H.S.P.
Pelikan, Jaroslav Jan. J.J.Pe.
Pélissier, René. R.P.
Pélissier, Roger. Ro.Pe.
Pen, Jan. J.P.
Penčev, Peter Georgiev. P.G.P.
Pendle, George. G.Pe.
Penner, Hans H. Ha.P.
Pennington, D.H. D.H.P.
Penny, Nicholas B. N.B.P.
Pepelasis, Adamantios A. A.A.Ps.
Perelman, Chaim. C.Pe.
Perham, Dame Margery. M.Pm.
Perkins, Edward S. E.S.P.
Pernoud, Régine. R.Pe.
Perowne, Stewart Henry. S.H.P.
Perrin, Norman. N.P.
Perrott, Roy. Ro.P.
Perry, Harry. H.Pe.
Perry Robinson, J.P. J.P.P.R.
Peruta, Franco della. F.d.Pe.
Pessen, Edward. E.Pe.
Péter, László. L.P.
Peterdi, Gabor F. G.F.P.
Peters, James A. J.A.P.
Peterson, J.E. J.E.P.
Petit, Paul. P.P.
Petri, Herbert L. H.L.P.
Petrov, Mikhail Platonovich. M.P.Pe.
Petrov, Victor P. V.P.P.
Petterson, Donald Rahl. D.R.P.
Pettitt, George A. G.A.P.
Péwé, Troy L. T.L.Pe.
Peyre, Henri M. H.M.P.

Pfaffmann, Carl. C.Pf.
Phelps Brown, Ernest Henry. E.H.P.B.
Philby, Harry St. John Bridger.
    H.St.J.B.P.
Phillips, Courtenay Stanley Goss.
    G.S.G.P.
Phillips, Melba. M.Ph.
Phiri, Kings Mbacazwa G. K.M.G.P.
Pick, Robert. R.Pi.
Pickering, Sir George. G.Pi.
Pickersgill, John Whitney. Jo.W.P.
Pickles, Dorothy M. D.M.P.
Picton, John. J.Pi.
Pielke, Roger Alvin. R.A.Pi.
Pieper, Josef. Jf.Pi.
Pierce, A. Keith. A.K.P.
Pierce, Francis S. F.S.P.
Pierce, John R. J.R.P.
Piercey, W. Douglas. W.D.P.
Pieri, David C. D.C.P.
Pietka, Mark Jeffrey. M.J.Pi.
Pike, Dag. D.Pi.
Pilikian, Hovhanness Israel. Ho.I.P.
Pillai, V.R. V.R.P.
Pincus, Alexis G. A.G.P.
Pinder-Wilson, Ralph H. R.H.P.-W.
Pine, Leslie Gilbert. L.G.P.
Pines, Shlomo. S.Pi.
Pingree, David E. D.E.P.
Pinker, Robert A. R.A.P.
Pipes, Richard E. R.E.Pi.
Pippard, Sir A. Brian. A.B.P.
Pirsig, Maynard E. M.E.P.
Pittioni, Richard. Ri.P.
Piveteau, Jean. J.Piv.
Plamenatz, John P. J.P.Pl.
Platnauer, Maurice. M.Pl.
Playfair, Giles William. G.W.P.
Pluckhahn, J. Bruce. J.B.P.
Plumb, Sir John. Jo.Pl.
Pocock, Tom. T.Po.
Podhajsky, Alois Wilhelm. A.W.P.
Podlecki, Anthony J. A.J.P.
Poelhekke, Jan J. J.J.P.
Pogue, Forrest C. F.C.P.
Pohl, Frederik. F.Po.
Pohl, Richard W. R.W.P.
Pokshishevsky, Vladimir V. V.V.P.
Pole, J.R. J.R.Po.
Polis, Gary A. G.A.Po.
Polk, William Roe. W.R.P.
Pollack, Peter J. P.J.P.
Pollard, John Graham. J.G.P.
Pollard, John Richard Thornhill.
    J.R.T.P.
Polmar, Norman C. N.C.P.
Polomé, Edgar Charles. E.C.Po.
Polunin, Nicholas. N.Po.
Pomeau, René Henry. R.H.Po.
Ponikvar, Adolph L. A.L.P.
Pontieri, Ernesto. E.Po.
Poole, Gary William. Ga.P.
Poole, Gray Johnson. G.J.P.
Poole, Kenyon Edwards. K.E.P.
Poonawala, Ismail K. I.K.P.
Pope, Clifford Hillhouse. C.H.P.
Pope, Phillip E. P.E.P.
Pope-Hennessy, Sir John. J.P.-H.
Popkin, Richard H. R.H.P.
Popov, Igor Vladimirovich. I.V.P.
Poppino, Rollie E. R.E.P.
Porter, William V. W.V.P.
Posner, Rebecca. Re.P.
Potter, George Richard. G.R.P.
Potter, Simeon. S.P.
Potthoff, Heinrich. H.P.

Pottle, Frederick A.   F.A.P.
Potts, Malcolm.   M.P.
Poucher, William A.   W.A.Po.
Poulsen, Thomas M.   T.M.P.
Pounder, Cuthbert Coulson.   C.C.P.
Pournaras, Dimitris.   D.P.
Pourtier, Roland.   Ro.Po.
Powell, Alan W.   A.W.Po.
Powell, James M.   J.M.Po.
Powell, Joseph Michael.   Jo.M.P.
Powell, Raphael.   R.Po.
Pozo Vélez, Homero.   H.P.V.
Prager, Stewart C.   S.C.P.
Prakasa Rao, Vaddiparti Lova Surya.
   V.L.S.P.R.
Prausnitz, John M.   J.M.P.
Prawer, Joshua.   Jo.Pr.
Preece, Warren E.   W.E.P.
Preidel, Helmut.   H.Pr.
Prescott, John R.V.   J.R.V.P.
Prestwich, Michael Charles.   M.C.P.
Preuschen, Gerhardt.   G.P.
Prevost, Jean.   J.Pr.
Price, Arnold H.   A.H.P.
Price, Cecil John Layton.   C.J.L.P.
Price, Edward W.   E.W.P.
Prieto, Justo Pastor.   J.P.P.
Prifti, Peter R.   P.R.P.
Pringle, John Douglas.   J.D.Pr.
Proctor, Charles Lafayette, II.   C.L.P.II.
Proskouriakoff, Tatiana.   T.P.
Proud, Lieut. Col. Richard Riseley.
   R.R.Pr.
Prout, W.G.   W.G.Pr.
Prown, Jules David.   J.D.Pro.
Pruchnicki, Jerzy.   Je.P.
Pryse-Phillips, William E.M.
   W.E.M.P.-P.
Puck, Theodore Thomas.   T.T.P.
Puhvel, Jaan.   J.Pl.
Pulgar-Vidal, Javier.   J.P.-V.
Pullen, Andrew M.   A.M.P.
Pulleyblank, Edwin G.   E.G.P.
Purdy, Ken W.   K.W.P.
Purdy, The Rev. William Arthur.
   W.A.P.
Puri, Baij Nath.   B.N.P.
Purrington, Philip F.   P.F.P.
Pye, E. Michael.   M.Py.

Quate, Calvin F.   C.F.Q.
Quimby, Robert S.   R.S.Q.
Quinn, John Francis.   J.F.Q.
Quinones, Ricardo J.   R.J.Q.
Quintana, Ricardo.   R.Q.
Quinton, Anthony M. Quinton,
   Baron.   A.M.Q.
Quittmeyer, Charles Loreaux.   C.L.Q.

Rabie, Hassanein Muhammad.   H.Ra.
Rabin, Chaim.   Ch.R.
Raby, Frederic James Edward.
   F.J.E.R.
Rae, John Bell.   J.B.Ra.
Raeff, Marc.   M.Ra.
Rafferty, Milton D.   M.D.R.
Raghavan, Chakravarthi.   C.Ra.
Rahman, Fazlur.   F.R.
Rāhula, Walpola.   Wa.R.
Ralphs, Sheila.   S.Ra.
Ralston, Robert H.   R.H.Ra.
Ram, Vernon.   V.R.
Ramanujan, A.K.   A.K.R.
Ramsay, James Arthur.   J.A.R.

Ramsey, The Rt. Rev. Ian Thomas.
   I.T.R.
Rand, Austin L.   Au.L.R.
Rang, Humphrey P.   H.P.R.
Rankin, Bayard.   B.R.
Ransom, Harry Howe.   H.H.R.
Rantsman, Yelizaveta Yakovlevna.
   Y.Y.R.
Rao, R.V.R. Chandrasekhara.
   R.V.R.C.R.
Rashid, Sh. Abdur.   S.A.R.
Rasmussen, John O., Jr.   J.O.R.
Rasmussen, Wayne D.   W.D.R.
Ratcliff, Graham.   G.Ra.
Ravenhill, William.   W.Ra.
Rawlings, Arthur Lionel.   A.L.Ra.
Rawlinson, John Lang.   J.L.Ra.
Rawski, Evelyn S.   E.S.R.
Rawson, Philip S.   P.S.R.
Rea, Donald G.   D.G.R.
Rea, Kenneth Grahame.   K.G.R.
Rea, Kenneth John.   K.J.R.
Read, Allen Walker.   A.W.Re.
Read, Donald.   D.Re.
Rebelo, Luís de Sousa.   L.de S.R.
Rechnitzer, Andreas B.   A.B.R.
Reddick, DeWitt C.   DeW.C.R.
Reese, William L.   W.L.Re.
Reeves, Marjorie E.   M.E.R.
Reeves, Thomas C.   T.C.R.
Reich, Willi.   W.R.
Reichardt, Hans.   H.Re.
Reid, John Cowie.   J.C.Rd.
Reilly, John C., Jr.   J.C.Re.
Reiman, Donald H.   D.H.R.
Reindel, Kurt.   Ku.R.
Reinhard, Marcel.   M.Re.
Reish, Donald J.   D.J.R.
Reiss, Hans Siegbert.   H.S.R.
Renger, Johannes M.   J.M.R.
Rentz, George S.   G.Re.
Rescher, Nicholas.   N.R.
Resis, Albert.   Al.Re.
Rexroth, Kenneth.   K.Re.
Reynolds, Frank E.   F.E.R.
Reynolds, Graham.   G.R.
Rheinstein, Max.   M.Rh.
Rhoads, Edward J.M.   E.J.M.R.
Rhode, Gotthold K.S.   G.K.S.R.
Rhodes, Philip.   P.Rh.
Riasanovsky, Nicholas V.   N.V.R.
Rich, Alan.   A.Ri.
Richards, Alan W.   A.W.R.
Richards, D.S.   D.S.Ri.
Richards, Eric Stapleton.   E.S.Ri.
Richards, Paul Westmacott.   P.W.R.
Richardson, Bonham C.   B.C.Ri.
Richardson, Hugh E.   H.E.R.
Richardson, Margaret Ann.   M.A.R.
Richardson, Robert G.   R.G.R.
Riché, Pierre.   P.R.
Richey, Michael William.   M.W.Ri.
Richmond, Rollin C.   Ro.R.
Richter, Gisela Marie Augusta.
   G.M.A.R.
Rickard, John David.   J.D.Ri.
Rickel, A. Brewster.   A.B.Ri.
Ride, W.D.L.   W.D.L.R.
Ridolfi, Roberto.   Ro.Ri.
Riesenfeld, Stefan Albrecht.   S.A.Ri.
Rightmire, G. Philip.   G.P.Ri.
Riley, Edward C.   E.C.R.
Riley, Matilda White.   M.W.R.
Ring, Richard R.   R.R.R.
Ringer, Alexander L.   A.L.R.
Ringgren, Helmer.   H.R.

Ringler, William Andrew, Jr.   W.A.Ri.
Ripin, Edwin M.   E.M.R.
Ritchie, C.T.   C.T.R.
Ritter, Dale F.   D.F.R.
Ritter, Raymond.   R.Ri.
Ritterbush, Philip C.   P.C.R.
Riva, Alfredo.   Al.R.
Riva, Joseph P., Jr.   J.P.Ri.
Rivlin, Helen Anne B.   H.A.B.R.
Rizley, John H.   J.H.R.
Robb, Nesca A.   N.A.R.
Robbins, Jonathan H.   J.H.Ro.
Robbins, Sidney Martin.   S.M.R.
Robbins, Stanley L.   S.L.R.
Roberts, Michael.   M.Ro.
Roberts, Sir Sydney.   S.Rs.
Robins, Robert Henry.   Ro.H.R.
Robinson, Arthur.   Ar.R.
Robinson Arthur Napoleon Raymond.
   A.N.R.R.
Robinson, Christopher.   C.Ro.
Robinson, Daniel Sommer.   D.S.R.
Robinson, David J.   D.J.Ro.
Robinson, Edgar Eugene.   E.E.R.
Robinson, Elwyn B.   E.B.R.
Robinson, Frank Neville H.   F.N.H.R.
Robinson, George Clarence.   G.C.R.
Robinson, Gloria.   G.Ro.
Robinson, J. Lewis.   J.L.Ro.
Robinson, Joan Violet.   J.Ro.
Robinson, Romney.   R.R.
Robison, Richard A.   R.A.R.
Robson, James Scott.   J.S.Ro.
Robson, William Alexander.   W.A.R.
Robson, William Wallace.   W.W.R.
Rockwell, Anne F.   A.F.R.
Rodgers, H.B.   H.B.Ro.
Rodnan, Gerald P.   G.P.R.
Rodríguez-Monegal, Emir.   E.R.-M.
Roe, Michael.   Ml.R.
Roey, Jan L.R. Van.   J.V.R.
Rogers, C. Ambrose.   C.A.Ro.
Rogers, Leonard R.   L.R.R.
Rogers, M. Elizabeth.   M.E.Ro.
Rogg, Lionel A.   L.A.R.
Rogge, Helmuth.   He.R.
Rohde, Peter P.   P.P.R.
Rollin, Jack D.   J.D.Ro.
Rollins, Reed C.   R.C.R.
Rolt, L.T.C.   L.T.C.R.
Romas, Nicholas A.   N.A.Ro.
Romer, Alfred S.   A.S.R.
Ronan, Colin Alistair.   C.A.R.
Ronen, Dov.   D.Ro.
Rood, Arnold.   A.Ro.
Roos, Hans.   Ha.Ro.
Roosa, Robert Vincent.   R.V.R.
Roper, Clyde F.E.   C.F.E.R.
Rose, Leo E.   L.E.R.
Rosen, Edward.   Ed.R.
Rosenberg, Pierre M.   P.M.R.
Rosenthal, Erwin I.J.   E.I.J.R.
Roseveare, Henry Godfrey.   H.G.R.
Ross, C.D.   C.D.R.
Ross, Charles A.   Ch.A.R.
Ross, June R.P.   J.R.P.R.
Ross, Marvin Chauncey.   M.C.R.
Ross, Peter McGregor.   P.McG.R.
Ross, Sydney.   S.R.
Rossi, Mario.   M.R.
Rostovtsev, Mikhail Ivanovich.   M.I.R.
Rothschild, The Hon. Miriam Louisa.
   M.L.R.
Rothwell, Gar W.   G.W.R.
Rouch, Jean Pierre.   J.P.R.
Roud, Brian James.   B.J.R.

Rouzé, Michel. Mi.Ro.
Rowe, James Wilmot. J.W.R.
Rowe, John A. Jo.R.
Rowe, Margaret Ann. M.A.Ro.
Rowe, Peter John. P.J.R.
Rowen, Herbert H. H.Ro.
Rowlatt, Mary. Ma.R.
Rowlinson, John Shipley. Jo.S.R.
Rowton, Michael B. M.B.R.
Royde-Smith, John Graham. J.R.-S.
Rubinstein, Nicolai. N.Ru.
Rudge, Peter. P.Ru.
Rudwick, Elliott. El.R.
Ruggles, Eleanor. E.Ru.
Ruhmer, Eberhard. Eb.R.
Ruiter, Leendert de. L. de R.
Rumney, George Richard. G.R.R.
Rupp, The Rev. Ernest Gordon. E.G.R.
Rushbrook Williams, Laurence Frederic.
    L.F.R.W.
Russell, Charles R. C.R.R.
Russell, Don. D.R.
Russell, Norman H. N.H.R.
Russell, Peter Edward. P.E.R.
Russon, Allien R. A.R.R.
Ryabchikov, Aleksandr Maximovich.
    A.M.R.
Ryalls, Alan. A.R.
Ryan, The Rev. Edward A. E.A.R.
Ryan, William B.F. W.B.F.R.
Ryazantsev, Sergey Nikolayevich.
    S.N.R.
Ryckmans, Jacques. J.R.
Rycroft, David K. D.K.R.
Ryder, John D. J.D.R.
Rylaarsdam, J. Coert. J.C.Ry.
Ryland, John S. J.S.R.

Sabr, Mohy el Din. M.e.D.S.
Sacher, George A. G.A.Sa.
Sachs, The Rev. William L. W.L.Sa.
Sadek, Dawlat Ahmed. D.A.Sa.
Sadie, Stanley. S.Sa.
Sadler, John E. J.E.Sa.
Sáez, Emilio. E.Sa.
Safarian, A. Edward. A.E.Sa.
Sagan, Carl. C.Sn.
Saggs, Henry W.F. H.W.F.S.
Sainsbury, John C. J.C.Sa.
St. John, Robert. R.St.J.
Sakamoto, Taro. T.Sa.
Salah, Mostafa Moh. M.M.Sa.
Sale, William Merritt, Jr. W.M.S.
Salibi, Kamal Suleiman. K.S.S.
Salisbury, Sir Edward James. E.J.S.
Salisbury, Neil E. N.E.S.
Salita, Domingo C. D.C.S.
Saller, Richard P. R.P.Sa.
Salmi, Mario. M.Sal.
Salmon, Edward Togo. E.T.S.
Salmon, John Hearsey McMillan.
    J.H.McM.S.
Salvini-Plawen, Luitfried von. L.v.S.-P.
Sammons, Jeffrey L. J.L.Sa.
Samuel, Alan Edouard. A.E.S.
Samuel, Pierre. P.S.
Samuels, Michael Anthony. M.A.Sa.
Sandeen, Ernest R. E.R.S.
Sandelin, Carl Fredrik. C.F.S.
Sander, Emilie T. E.T.Sa.
Sanders, William T. W.T.Sa.
Sanderson, R. Thomas. R.T.S.
Sandvik, Gudmund. G.Sa.
Saner, Hans. Ha.S.
Sanford, D. Gregory. D.G.Sa.

Sanger, Clyde William. C.W.S.
Sanger, Ralph G. R.G.S.
Sankovitch, Tilde A. T.A.Sa.
Sansing, David G. D.G.S.
Sarà, Michele. M.Sa.
Sarason, Irwin G. I.G.S.
Sarmiento, Sergio. S.S.
Sarna, Nahum M. N.M.Sa.
Sartori, Claudio. C.Sa.
Sasaki, Genjun H. G.H.S.
Sastri, R.L.N. R.L.N.S.
Sato, Tadao. T.S.
Satter, Heinrich. H.Sa.
Saunders, D. Gail. D.G.Ss.
Saunders, Jason Lewis. Ja.L.S.
Sautter, Gilles François. G.F.S.
Savage, George. Ge.S.
Saville, James Patrick. J.P.S.
Savory, Roger M. R.M.Sa.
Sawer, Geoffrey. G.S.
Saxon, A.H. A.H.Sa.
Scanlon, David G. Da.G.S.
Scarborough, Harold. Ha.Sc.
Scarne, John. J.S.
Scarpelli, Dante G. D.G.Sc.
Scace, Robert I. R.I.S.
Schaaf, William L. W.L.S.
Schaden, Egon. Eg.S.
Schaeffer, Bobb. B.Sc.
Schaeffer, Claude Frédéric Armand.
    C.F.A.S.
Schaetzl, Randall John. R.J.Sc.
Schafer, Thomas A. T.A.S.
Schaper, Eva. Ev.S.
Schapera, Isaac. I.S.
Schapiro, Leonard Bertram. L.B.S.
Scharf, Aaron. A.Sc.
Scharlemann, Robert P. R.P.S.
Schatz-Uffenheimer, Rivka. R.S.-U.
Schawlow, Arthur L. Ar.L.S.
Scheepers, Johannes Nicolaas. J.N.S.
Scheer, Bradley Titus. B.T.S.
Scheina, Robert L. R.L.Sc.
Schell, Herbert S. H.S.Sc.
Schimmel, Annemarie. An.Sc.
Schirmann, Jefim H. J.Sc.
Schlechten, Albert Wilbur. A.W.S.
Schleunes, Karl A. K.A.Sc.
Schlieder, Gunnar. Gu.S.
Schmale, Franz-Josef. F.-J.Se.
Schmid, Rudolf. Ru.Sc.
Schmidt, John D. J.D.Sc.
Schmidt, Karl Patterson. K.P.S.
Schmidt, R.A.M. R.Sc.
Schmidt, Robert H. R.H.Sc.
Schmitt, Hans Otto. H.O.Sc.
Schneider, Stephen H. S.H.S.
Schofield, Wilfred Borden. W.B.S.
Scholes, Walter V. W.V.S.
Schram, Stuart Reynolds. S.R.S.
Schregle, Johannes. J.Sch.
Schreiber, B. Charlotte. B.C.S.
Schreyvogl, Friedrich. F.Sc.
Schubert, Bernice Giduz. B.G.S.
Schultz, Alarich R. A.R.S.
Schulz, Walter. W.Sc.
Schumach, Murray. Mu.S.
Schumacher, Alvin J. A.J.Sc.
Schumm, Brooke, Jr. B.S.
Schumm, Stanley A. S.A.S.
Schürmann, Reiner. R.Sch.
Schwab, Frederick L. F.L.S.
Schwartz, Jacob T. J.T.Sc.
Schwartz, Mark F. M.F.S.
Schwartz, Maurice L. M.L.S.
Schwartz, Mischa. M.Sch.

Schwartz, Paul A. P.A.S.
Schwartz, Robert S. R.S.S.
Schwartz, Theodore B. T.B.S.
Schwarzenberger, Georg. G.Sc.
Scott, Alfred Eric. A.E.Sc.
Scott, Joseph Frederick. J.F.S.
Scott, Peter. P.Sc.
Scranton, Robert L. R.L.S.
Screech, M.A. M.A.S.
Scruton, Roger. Ro.Sc.
Scudiere, Paul Joseph. P.J.Sc.
Scullard, Howard Hayes. H.H.S.
Seaborg, Glenn T. G.T.S.
Seagle, Stan R. S.R.Se.
Seale, Robert L. R.L.Se.
Searle, Humphrey. H.Se.
Sebela, Vicki D. V.D.S.
Seeger, C. Ronald. C.R.S.
Šega, Drago. D.Še.
Segre, Claudio G. C.G.Se.
Seibert, Jakob. J.Se.
Seidel, Anna K. A.K.Se.
Seiff, Alvin. A.S.
Seitz, William C. W.C.Se.
Sellwood, David Grenville John.
    D.G.J.S.
Selverstone, Jane. Ja.Se.
Selz, Jean. Je.S.
Sen, Amulya Chandra. A.Se.
Sen, D.M. D.M.S.
Şengör, A.M. Celâl. A.M.C.Ş.
Sequera Segnini, Isbelia M. I.S. de S.
Serjeant, Robert Bertram. R.B.Se.
Seroff, Victor Ilyich. V.I.S.
Serventy, D.L. D.L.Se.
Service, Elman R. E.R.Se.
Sesay, Shekou M. S.M.S.
Seton-Watson, Hugh. H.S.-W.
Seton-Williams, M.V. M.V.S.-W.
Severin, Giles Timothy. G.T.Se.
Sewall, Richard B. R.B.S.
Seyfert, Carl Keenan. C.K.S.
Seymour, Charles. C.Se.
Seznec, Jean J. J.J.Se.
Shackleton, Robert. R.Sh.
Shaffer, Jerome A. J.A.Sh.
Shagdarsuren, O. O.Sh.
Shah, Umakant Premanand. U.P.S.
Shakabpa, Tsepon W.D. T.W.D.S.
Shambaugh, George E., Jr. G.E.S.
Shannon, Robert R. R.R.Sh.
Sharlin, Harold I. H.I.S.
Sharp, The Rev. R. Norman. R.N.S.
Sharp, Robert Phillip. R.P.Sp.
Sharp, Walter R. W.R.S.
Sharrock, Roger. R.S.
Shaw, Byron Thomas. B.T.Sh.
Shaw, Caroline Sarah. C.S.Sh.
Shaw, Ivan Peter. I.P.S.
Shaw, Stanford Jay. S.J.S.
Sheard, Wendy Stedman. W.S.Sh.
Shearman, John K.G. J.K.Sh.
Shedd, Thomas Clark. T.C.S.
Sheehy, Ann. An.Sh.
Shelton, John E. J.E.S.
Shennan, J.H. J.H.Sh.
Shepherd, The Rev. Massey H., Jr.
    M.H.S.
Shepperson, George Albert. G.A.S.
Shercliff, Jose. J.Sh.
Sheridan, Lionel Astor. L.A.S.
Sheriff, Robert E. R.E.Sh.
Sherman, Franklin. F.S.
Sherrington, Sir Charles Scott. C.S.S.
Shetler, Stanwyn G. S.G.S.
Shiel, James. J.Shi.

Shih, The Rev. Joseph Hsing-san. J.H.-s.S.
Shillinglaw, Gordon. G.Sh.
Shiloah, Amnon. A.Sh.
Shiloh, Ailon. An.S.
Shimahara, Nobuo. N.S.
Shineberg, D.L. D.L.Sh.
Shinoda, Minoru. M.Sh.
Shipman, Frank M. F.M.S.
Shirendev, B. B.Sv.
Shirley-Smith, Sir Hubert. H.S.-Sm.
Shock, Nathan Wetherill. N.W.S.
Shoemaker, Frank C. F.C.S.
Shore, Arthur Frank. A.F.Sh.
Short, Lester L. L.L.S.
Short, Nicholas M. N.M.S.
Shrimpton, Nicholas. N.Sh.
Shu, Frank H. F.H.Sh.
Shurtleff, Malcolm C. M.C.S.
Shuster, Donald Raymond. D.R.Sh.
Sibley, David C.G. D.C.G.S.
Sick, Helmut. H.S.
Siebens, Arthur A. A.A.S.
Sieber, Roy. Ro.Si.
Siegmund, David O. D.O.S.
Silaev, Evgeny Dmitrievich. E.D.S.
Silber, Kate. K.Si.
Silberbauer, George Bertrand. G.Si.
Silbergeld, Jerome. Je.Si.
Silberman, Lou Hackett. L.H.S.
Sillery, Anthony. Ay.Sy.
Silver, Larry A. L.A.Si.
Silverman, Joseph. Jo.Si.
Silverstein, Josef. J.Si.
Simmons, Ernest J. E.J.Si.
Simmons, Gustavus J. G.J.Si.
Simmons, Pauline. Pa.S.
Simmons, William B. W.B.Si.
Simon, Akiba Ernst. A.E.Si.
Simon, Edith. E.Si.
Simon, John Y. J.Y.S.
Simons, Eric Norman. E.N.S.
Simpson, John M. J.M.S.
Simpson, Roger Henry. R.H.S.
Sims, Andrew C.P. A.C.P.S.
Sinclair, Andrew Annandale. A.A.Si.
Sinclair, Sir Keith. Ke.S.
Singer, Peter. P.Si.
Singh, H.K. Manmohan. H.K.M.S.
Singh, Khushwant. K.S.
Sinha, N.K. N.K.S.
Sinitsyn, Vasily Mikhaylovich. V.M.S.
Sinnhuber, Karl A. K.A.Si.
Sinor, Denis. D.Si.
Sippl, Charles J. C.J.S.
Sircus, Wilfred. W.S.
Sirkin, Les. L.Si.
Sissom, Leighton E. L.E.Si.
Sivaramamurti, Calambur. C.S.
Sivasubramaniam, Sinnathurai. S.Si.
Skalweit, Stephan. S.Sk.
Skolnik, Merrill I. M.I.S.
Skone, John Francis. J.F.Sk.
Slack, Jonathan M.W. J.M.W.S.
Slamecka, Vladimir. V.Sl.
Slemon, Gordon R. G.R.Sl.
Sloane, Thomas O. T.O.S.
Slobin, Mark S. M.S.S.
Slonimsky, Nicolas. N.Sl.
Smailes, Arthur Eltringham. A.E.Sm.
Smale, Stephen. S.Sm.
Smart, John Jamieson Carswell. J.J.C.S.
Smart, Ninian. N.Sm.
Smelser, Neil J. N.J.S.
Smethurst, Colin. C.Sm.
Smith, Anna Hester. A.H.S.

Smith, Brian K. B.K.S.
Smith, Bruce Lannes. B.L.S.
Smith, Charles Gordon. C.G.S.
Smith, Dale M. D.M.Sm.
Smith, David Eugene. D.E.S.
Smith, Gabriel. Ga.S.
Smith, George Alan. G.A.Sm.
Smith, Harlan James. H.Sm.
Smith, James Irvine. J.I.S.
Smith, J. Beverley. J.B.Sm.
Smith, John Edwin. J.E.Sm.
Smith, Jonathan Z. J.Z.S.
Smith, Lacey Baldwin. La.B.S.
Smith, Lyman B. L.B.Sm.
Smith, Neal Griffith. N.G.S.
Smith, Norman Obed. N.O.S.
Smith, Peter A.S. P.A.S.S.
Smith, Phillip J. P.J.S.
Smith, Ralph J. R.J.Sm.
Smith, Robert C. R.C.Sm.
Smith, Robert Leo. R.L.Sm.
Smith, Sigmund L. S.L.Sm.
Smith, T. Lynn. T.L.S.
Smith, W. John. W.J.S.
Smith-Rose, Reginald Leslie. R.L.S.-R.
Smogorzewski, Kazimierz Maciej. K.M.S.
Smylie, The Rev. James Hutchinson. J.H.Sm.
Smyth, James Desmond. J.D.Sm.
Sneddon, Ian Naismith. I.N.S.
Snell, Esmond E. E.E.Sn.
Snellgrove, David Llewelyn. D.L.S.
Snyder, Irvin S. I.S.S.
Snyder, James E. J.E.Sn.
Soboul, Albert M. Al.S.
Soden, Wolfram Th. von. W.T.v.S.
Sokoloff, Leon. L.S.
Solem, G. Alan. G.A.So.
Solinger, Jacob. J.So.
Solmi, Angelo. A.So.
Solmsen, Friedrich. F.So.
Solomon, Arthur K. A.K.S.
Solomon, Peter H., Jr. P.H.S.
Somers, Harold M. H.M.S.
Sørensen, Marie-Louise Stig. M.-L.S.S.
Sorley Walker, Kathrine. K.S.W.
Sosa, Estanislao Navarro. E.N.So.
Sourdel, Dominique. D.So.
Soustelle, Jacques. Ja.S.
Southall, Aidan William. Ai.S.
Southam, Brian C. B.C.So.
Southgate, Donald. Do.S.
Southward, Alan James. A.J.So.
Sowers, Robert W. R.So.
Spalding, David A.E. D.A.E.S.
Spalding, James C. J.C.S.
Spalding, J.M.K. J.M.K.S.
Spaulding, Jay L. J.L.Sp.
Speaight, George. G.St.
Spear, T.G. Percival. T.G.P.S.
Spears, Monroe K. M.K.Sp.
Spedding, Frank Harold. F.H.S.
Spekke, Arnold. Ar.Sp.
Spence, Robert. R.Sp.
Spencer, J. Brookes. J.B.Sp.
Spencer, John R. J.R.Sp.
Spencer, Joseph E. Jo.E.S.
Spencer, The Rev. Sidney. S.Sp.
Spencer, Terence John Bew. T.Sp.
Spencer, Ulric M. U.M.S.
Spengler, Joseph J. J.J.Sp.
Spiegelberg, Herbert. H.Sp.
Spinka, Matthew. M.Sp.
Spinrad, Bernard I. B.I.S.

Spiro, Herbert John. H.J.Sp.
Spring, David. D.Sp.
Squires, Gordon Leslie. G.L.S.
Squires, James Duane. J.D.S.
Srivastava, A.L. A.L.S.
Stacey, The Rev. John. Jo.S.
Stadler, Karl R. K.R.St.
Staehelin, L. Andrew. L.A.St.
Stains, Howard James. H.J.S.
Staley, James T. J.T.S.
Štampar, Emil. Em.Š.
Standen, Anthony. A.St.
Standley, Barbara A. B.A.St.
Stannard, Jerry. Je.St.
Stannard, Lewis Judson, Jr. L.J.S.
Stant, Margaret Yvonne. M.Y.S.
Stanzione, Kaydon Al. K.A.St.
Stark, Craig L. C.L.S.
Stark, John E. J.E.St.
Starke, Helmut Dietmar. H.D.S.
Starkey, Lawrence H. L.H.St.
Starkie, Enid. En.S.
Starr, Chester G. C.G.St.
Stead, Christian Karlson. C.K.St.
Stearns, Peter N. P.N.S.
Steel, Robert Walter. Ro.W.St.
Steere, William Campbell. W.C.St.
Stehkämper, Hugo. H.Sr.
Stein, Peter G. P.G.S.
Stein, Wilfred D. W.D.S.
Steinberg, Alfred. A.Sg.
Steinberg, Ellis P. E.P.S.
Steinberg, S. Henry. S.H.St.
Steiner, H. Arthur. H.A.S.
Steiner, William Glenn. W.G.St.
Steingräber, Erich. Er.St.
Stendahl, The Rev. Krister. K.St.
Stephan, Ruth. Ru.S.
Stephens, Richard Walton. Ri.W.S.
Stephenson, F. Richard. F.R.S.
Stephenson, Ralph. R.St.
Stephenson, R.J. R.J.S.
Stern, Henri. He.S.
Stern, Joshua. J.Sn.
Stern, Samuel Miklos. S.M.Sn.
Stern, William Louis. W.L.St.
Sternberg, Robert J. R.J.St.
Sternstein, Lawrence. La.S.
Steudel, Johannes. J.Ste.
Stevens, Denis William. D.W.S.
Stevens, Halsey. H.Ss.
Stevens, Sylvester K. S.K.S.
Stevenson, Lloyd Grenfell. L.G.S.
Stewart, David B. D.B.S.
Stewart, John I.M. J.I.M.S.
Stewart, Robert E. R.E.S.
Stigler, George J. G.J.S.
Stilwell, Rear Adm. James Joseph. Ja.J.S.
Stock, Noel. N.St.
Stokes, Sewell. S.St.
Stolberg, Irving J. I.J.S.
Stoll, Robert R. R.R.S.
Stone, F. Gordon A. F.G.A.S.
Stone, Julius. Ju.S.
Stoner, John Oliver, Jr. J.O.S.
Storer, Robert W. R.W.St.
Stotz, Elmer H. E.H.St.
Stoudt, John J. J.J.S.
Strahan, Ronald. Ro.S.
Strand, Kaj Aa. K.A.S.
Strange, Edward Fairbrother. E.F.S.
Strasberg, Lee. Le.S.
Stratford, Alan Howard. A.H.St.
Strauss, Gerald. Ge.St.
Street, Brian Vincent. B.V.S.

Streng, Frederick J.   F.J.S.
Strickmann, Michel.   M.St.
Strode, Hudson.   Hu.S.
Strohl, G. Ralph.   G.R.S.
Stroll, Avrum.   Av.S.
Strugnell, John.   Jo.St.
Struik, Dirk Jan.   D.J.S.
Strygin, Valery Mikhailovich.   V.M.St.
Stuart-Smith, James.   J.S.-Sm.
Stubbs, William Edward.   W.E.S.
Stuewer, Roger H.   R.H.St.
Sturley, Kenneth Reginald.   K.R.S.
Sturmberger, Hans.   H.St.
Sturmthal, Adolf F.   A.F.St.
Styan, J.L.   J.L.S.
Suárez, Jorge A.   J.A.S.
Suárez Fernández, Luis.   L.S.Fe.
Subramani.   S.
Suckling, Eustace E.   E.E.S.
Suettinger, Robert Lee.   R.L.Su.
Suggs, Robert Carl.   R.C.Su.
Sukhopara, Fyodor Nikolayevich.
    F.N.S.
Sullivan, Lawrence E.   L.E.S.
Sullivan, Michael.   M.Su.
Summerson, Sir John.   J.Sum.
Sumner, Margaret Ann.   M.A.Su.
Sunblad, Ilmari.   I.Su.
Sundaram, K.V.   K.V.Su.
Suppes, Patrick.   P.Su.
Supranovich, Tatyana Yosifovna.
    T.Y.S.
Suryadinata, Leo.   L.Sur.
Süsskind, Charles.   Ch.S.
Sutherland, Carol Humphrey Vivian.
    C.H.V.S.
Sutherland, N.M.   N.M.Su.
Sutton, Christine.   Ch.Su.
Sutton, Denys.   D.Su.
Sutulov, Alexander.   A.Su.
Suzuki, Chusei.   C.Su.
Sverdrup, Harald Ulrik.   H.U.S.
Swan, Bradford Fuller.   B.F.S.
Sweet-Escott, Bickham A.C.   B.S.-E.
Swenson, Alfred.   A.Sw.
Swenson, J. Patricia Morgan.   J.P.M.S.
Swink, Roland Lee.   R.L.Sw.
Synge, Patrick Millington.   P.M.Sy.
Sze, S.M.   S.M.Sz.
Szebehely, Victor G.   V.G.S.
Szyliowicz, Joseph S.   J.S.Sz.

Tait, Hugh.   H.Ta.
Takeuchi, Yoshinori.   Y.T.
Takhtajan, Armen.   A.T.
Talbi, Mohamed.   M.Ta.
Talbot, Michael.   Mi.T.
Talbot, William John.   W.J.T.
Talbot Rice, David.   D.T.R.
Talbot Rice, Tamara.   T.T.R.
Tanenbaum, Morris.   M.T.
Tani, Shin'ichi.   S.Ta.
Tannenbaum, Steven R.   S.R.T.
Tanner, James M.   J.M.T.
Tapié, Victor-Lucien.   V.L.T.
Taplin, Oliver.   O.T.
Tarmisto, Vello Julius.   V.J.T.
Tata, Robert J.   R.J.Ta.
Tate, Allen.   A.Ta.
Tax, Sol.   So.T.
Tayler, Roger John.   R.J.T.
Taylor, Alfred Edward.   A.E.Ta.
Taylor, Gordon Ernest.   G.E.T.
Taylor, Sir Hugh S.   H.S.Ta.
Taylor, John.   J.T.

Taylor, John Campbell.   J.C.Ta.
Taylor, John Russell.   J.R.T.
Taylor, John W.R.   J.W.R.T.
Taylor, William.   W.Ta.
Teall, John L.   J.L.Te.
Tebeau, Charlton W.   C.W.T.
Tedesco, Edward F.   E.F.T.
Teitelbaum, Michael S.   M.S.T.
Temir, Ahmet.   A.Te.
Temperley, Nicholas.   N.T.
Tepper, Frederick.   F.T.
Terrasse, Henri-Louis-Étienne.
    H.-L.-É.T.
Terry, Walter.   W.T.
Thapar, Romila.   R.Th.
Thayer, H.S.   H.S.T.
Thelen, David P.   D.P.T.
Thesleff, Holger.   H.T.
Thielicke, Helmut.   H.Th.
Thieret, John W.   J.W.Th.
Thom, René Frédéric.   R.F.T.
Thomas, Alan T.   A.T.T.
Thomas, David A.   D.A.T.
Thomas, David Christopher Traherne.
    D.C.Th.
Thomas, John A.   J.A.T.
Thomas, John Gareth.   J.G.Th.
Thomas, John L.   J.L.T.
Thomas, John Patrick.   J.Th.
Thomas, R. Murray.   R.M.T.
Thomas, Sidney.   Si.T.
Thomas, Terence Barrington.   T.B.T.
Thomas, William Harford.   W.H.Th.
Thompson, Brian J.   B.J.T.
Thompson, Carol Lewis.   C.L.T.
Thompson, E.A.   E.A.T.
Thompson, Sir Eric.   E.Th.
Thompson, George Raynor.   G.R.T.
Thompson, Laura.   L.Th.
Thompson, Leonard Monteath.   L.M.T.
Thompson, Stith.   S.T.
Thomsen, Helmuth.   He.Th.
Thomson, Sir A. Landsborough.   A.L.T.
Thomson, Derick S.   D.S.T.
Thomson, Sir George Paget.   G.P.T.
Thomson, Robert Young.   R.Y.T.
Thomson, William Archibald Robson.
    Wm.A.R.T.
Thomson, William E.   W.E.T.
Thöne, Friedrich.   F.Th.
Thorne, Robert Folger.   R.F.Th.
Thornton, Robert James.   R.J.Th.
Thorp, Martin B.   M.B.T.
Thorpe, Lewis.   L.T.
Thorpe, William Homan.   W.H.T.
Tikhotskiy, Constantine Gennadiyevich.
    C.G.T.
Tiles, Mary Elizabeth.   M.E.T.
Tilley, Cecil Edgar.   C.E.T.
Timmers, Jan Joseph Marie.   J.J.M.T.
Tinker, Hugh Russell.   H.R.T.
Tobias, Cornelius A.   C.A.T.
Tobias, Phillip Vallentine.   P.V.T.
Toby, Ronald P.   R.P.T.
Todd, John Walford.   J.W.T.
Toffoletto, Ettore.   E.T.
Tolson, Richard.   R.To.
Toni, Youssef T.   Y.T.T.
Tonkinson, Robert.   Ro.T.
Tooker, Elisabeth.   E.To.
Toomer, Gerald J.   G.J.T.
Totman, Conrad D.   C.D.T.
Toulmin, Stephen E.   S.E.T.
Toupet, Charles Henri.   C.H.T.
Tout, Thomas Frederick.   T.F.T.
Townsend, Clifford Charles.   C.C.T.

Toynbee, Arnold Joseph.   A.J.T.
Toynbee, Jocelyn M.C.   J.M.C.T.
Toyoda, Takeshi.   T.T.
Tracy, James D.   J.D.T.
Trapido, Stanley.   S.Tr.
Traub, Hamilton P.   H.P.Tr.
Traub, Col. Robert.   R.T.
Treasure, Geoffrey Russell
    Richards.   G.R.R.T.
Tregear, Thomas R.   T.R.T.
Tregonning, Kennedy G.   K.G.T.
Treharne, Reginald Francis.   R.F.Tr.
Treves, François.   F.Tr.
Treves, Piero.   P.T.
Tricker, Ronald A.R.   R.A.R.T.
Trinkaus, Erik.   E.Tr.
Trinterud, L.J.   L.J.T.
Tripp, Maureen Heneghan.   M.H.
Trussell, John B.B.   J.B.B.T.
Truswell, A. Stewart.   A.S.T.
Trypanis, Constantine Athanasius.
    C.A.Tr.
Tsevegmid, Sh.   Sh.Ts.
Tsoumis, George Thomas.   G.Ts.
Tucci, Giuseppe.   Gi.T.
Tucker, David Gordon.   D.G.T.
Tucker, David H.   D.H.T.
Tucker, Glenn.   G.Tu.
Tulchin, Joseph S.   J.S.T.
Tuma, Elias H.   E.H.T.
Tuppen, John N.   J.N.T.
Turnbull, Archie Rule.   A.R.T.
Turnell, Martin.   M.Tu.
Turner, B.L.   B.L.T.
Turner, Edward Lewis.   E.L.T.
Turner, Sir Eric Gardner.   E.G.T.
Turner, Henry Ashby, Jr.   H.A.T.
Turner, Ralph H.   R.H.T.
Turnock, David.   D.T.
Turville-Petre, E.O.G.   E.O.G.T.-P.
Tuttle, William Julian.   W.J.Tu.
Tu Wei-ming.   T.W.-m.
Twersky, Isadore.   I.T.
Twidale, Charles Rowland.   C.R.T.
Twitchett, Denis C.   D.C.T.
Tyler, James Chase.   J.C.T.

Uda, Michitaka.   M.U.
Udo, Reuben Kenrick.   R.K.U.
Uibopuu, Valev.   V.U.
Ullmann, Walter.   W.U.
Ulrich, Homer.   H.U.
Underwood, Benton J.   B.J.U.
Underwood, E. Ashworth.   E.A.U.
Underwood, Vernon Philip.   V.P.U.
Unhjem, Arne.   A.U.
Untermann, Jürgen.   J.U.
Unwin, George.   G.U.
Unwin, Philip Soundy.   P.U.
Uotila, Urho A.   U.A.U.
Upton, Arthur Canfield.   A.C.U.
Urbach, Peter Michael.   P.M.U.
Urry, William G.   W.G.U.
Usselman, Melvyn C.   M.C.U.
Utechin, Sergei Vasilievich.   S.V.U.

Vajda, Georges.   G.V.
Vale, Malcolm G.A.   M.G.A.V.
Valencia, Mark J.   M.J.V.
Valentine, Frederick Albert.   F.A.V.
Valgiglio, Ernesto.   E.Va.
Vallier, Dora.   D.V.
van Andel, Tjeerd H.   T.H.v.A.
Vandenbosch, Amry.   A.Va.

Vanderpool, Eugene.   E.V.
Van der Wee, Herman F.A.
   H.F.A.V.d.W.
Van Deusen, Glyndon G.   G.G.V.D.
Van Deusen, Hobart Merritt.   H.M.V.D.
Vanger, Milton I.   M.I.V.
Van Horn, Kent R.   K.R.V.H.
Van Molle, Leen.   L.V.M.
Vann, Richard T.   R.T.V.
Van Steenberghen, Fernand.   F.V.Sn.
Van Valen, Leigh M.   L.M.V.V.
Varela, René Santamaria.   R.S.V.
Varma, Shanti Prasad.   S.P.V.
Vaughan, Richard.   R.Va.
Vázquez, Josefina Zoraida.   J.Z.V.
Veevers, John J.   J.J.V.
Velásquez, M. Tulio.   M.T.V.
Veldman, Meredith.   M.V.
Vella, Walter F.   W.F.V.
Vendler, Zeno.   Z.V.
Venkataramanan, Lalgudi S.   L.S.V.
Vennesland, Birgit.   B.V.
Verlaan, Philomene A.   P.A.V.
Verlinden, J. Charles.   J.C.V.
Vermeule, Emily D. Townsend.
   E.D.T.V.
Vernet Ginés, Juan.   J.V.G.
Verniers, Louis.   L.Ve.
Veyret, Paul.   P.V.
Viallaneix, Paul.   P.Vi.
Vidalenc, Jean.   J.Vi.
Vidyarthi, Lalita P.   L.P.V.
Viereck, Peter.   Pe.V.
Vierhaus, Rudolf.   Ru.V.
Vignaux, Paul D.   P.D.V.
Vigne, Randolph.   R.V.
Villari, Luigi.   L.Vi.
Villee, Claude A.   C.A.V.
Villiers, Alan John.   A.J.V.
Vinacke, W. Edgar.   W.E.V.
Vinaver, Eugène.   E.Vi.
Vincent, Paul F.   P.F.V.
Vioux, Marcelle.   M.Vi.
Virtanen, Reino.   R.Vi.
Viscovo, Mario Del.   M. Del V.
Vishny, Michele.   Mi.V.
Vita-Finzi, Claudio.   C.V.-F.
Vodovozov, Sergey Arsentyevich.
   S.A.V.
Voegelin, Charles F.   C.F.V.
Voegelin, Florence M.   F.M.V.
Vogt, Hans K.   H.K.V.
Volkmann, Hans.   H.V.
Von Eckardt, Wolf.   W.V.E.
von Hagen, Victor Wolfgang.   V.W.v.H.
Voss, Gilbert L.   G.L.V.
Vowles, Jack.   J.Vo.
Voyce, Arthur.   A.Vo.
Vroman, Leo.   L.V.

Waage, Frederick O.   F.O.Wa.
Waage, Karl M.   K.M.W.
Wacker, Peter O.   P.O.W.
Waddams, A.L.   A.L.W.
Waddington, Conrad H.   C.H.W.
Waerden, Bartel Leendert van der.
   B.L.v.d.W.
Waggoner, Paul Edward.   P.E.W.
Wagley, Charles W.   C.W.W.
Wagner, Peggy.   P.Wa.
Wagner, Robert R.   R.R.W.
Wagner, Warren H., Jr.   W.H.Wa.
Wailes, Rex.   R.W.
Waines, David.   D.Wa.
Wake, David B.   D.B.W.

Wakefield, Hugh.   Hu.Wa.
Walbank, Frank W.   F.W.W.
Waldman, Marilyn R.   M.R.W.
Walford, Lionel A.   L.A.Wa.
Walker, Alan.   A.W.
Walker, Paul E.   P.W.
Walker, Robert Donald.   R.D.Wa.
Walker, Thomas W.   T.W.Wa.
Walker, Warren F., Jr.   W.F.W.
Wallace, Irving.   Ir.W.
Wallace, Willard M.   W.M.Wa.
Wallace-Hadrill, John Michael.
   J.M.W.-H.
Wallerstein, Immanuel.   I.W.
Walling, Cheves T.   C.T.W.
Wallis, Helen Margaret.   H.M.W.
Walsh, William Henry.   W.H.W.
Walton, Harold F.   H.F.W.
Wang, Chun Tsin.   C.T.Wa.
Wang, Hao.   H.Wa.
Wang, Yi Chu.   Y.C.W.
Wang Mingye.   Wa.M.
Ward, Norman.   N.W.
Wardman, Harold W.   H.W.W.
Ware, James Hamilton, Jr.   J.H.Wa.
Warid, Warid A.   W.A.W.
Warmington, Brian H.   B.H.W.
Warner, Robert Austin.   R.A.Wa.
Warren, Andrew.   A.Wa.
Warren, Harris Gaylord.   H.G.W.
Warren, James V.   J.V.W.
Warshaw, David M.   D.M.W.
Watanabe, Akira.   Ak.W.
Waterhouse, Sir Ellis K.   E.K.W.
Waterson, Duncan Bruce.   D.B.Wa.
Watkin, David John.   D.J.Wa.
Watson, Comdr. Bruce W.   B.W.Wa.
Watson, Sir F.J.B.   F.J.B.W.
Watson, J. Garth.   J.G.W.
Watson, James Wreford.   J.W.W.
Watson, John Steven.   J.S.W.
Watson, Paul F.   P.F.W.
Watson, Richard A.   R.A.W.
Watson, William.   W.W.
Watt, William Montgomery.   W.M.W.
Watts, David.   Da.W.
Watts, William Walter.   W.W.W.
Waworoentoe, Willem Johan.   W.J.W.
Weaver, John D.   J.D.W.
Weaver, Leo.   L.We.
Webb, Byron H.   B.H.We.
Webb, Wilse B.   W.B.W.
Weber, Lillian M.   L.M.W.
Webster, Bruce.   B.We.
Webster, Gerald Raymond.   G.R.We.
Webster, Richard A.   R.A.We.
Wedgwood, Dame C.V.   C.V.W.
Weibel, Ewald R.   E.R.W.
Weibull, Jörgen.   Jö.We.
Weidner, Richard Tilghman.   R.T.We.
Weigend, Guido Gustav.   G.G.Wd.
Weigend, Thomas.   T.We.
Weigmann, Hans-Dietrich H.
   H.-D.H.W.
Weinstein, Brian.   B.Wn.
Weinstein, Donald.   D.We.
Weinstock, Herbert.   H.We.
Weintal, Edward.   E.W.
Weintraub, Stanley.   S.We.
Weis, Elisabeth.   E.We.
Weiss, Stephen F.   S.F.We.
Weitzman, Stanley H.   S.H.W.
Welch, C. Stuart.   C.S.W.
Weller, Jac.   J.We.
Wellington, John H.   J.H.We.
Wells, Arthur Frederick.   A.F.We.

Wells, James M.   J.M.Ws.
Wells, Neil C.   N.C.W.
Welzel, Hans Fritz.   Ha.We.
Wendt, Albert.   A.We.
Wenner, Manfred W.   M.W.W.
Went, Frits W.   F.W.We.
Wente, Edward F.   E.F.W.
Wentworth-Sheilds, Francis William.
   F.W.W.-S.
Werblowsky, R.J. Zwi.   R.J.Z.W.
Werkman, Evert.   Ev.W.
Wermuth, Heinz Fritz.   H.F.We.
Werner, Robert.   R.We.
Wert, Charles A.   C.A.W.
Werveke H. van.   H. van W.
Wescoat, James L., Jr.   J.L.W.
West, Francis James.   F.J.W.
West, Henry R.   H.R.W.
West, James King.   J.K.W.
West, Louis Jolyon.   L.J.W.
Westermann, Claus.   C.W.
Westermann, Edwin J.   E.J.W.
Westfall, Richard S.   R.S.W.
Weston, Burns H.   Bu.H.W.
Weston, J. Fred.   J.F.W.
Westrup, Sir Jack Allan.   J.A.W.
Wetherill, George W.   G.W.We.
Wethey, Harold E.   H.E.W.
Wever, Ernest Glen.   E.G.W.
Whedon, G. Donald.   G.D.W.
Wheeler, Alwyne.   A.Wh.
Wheeler, Geoffrey Edleston.   G.E.Wh.
Whewell, Charles S.   C.S.Wh.
White, D. Maxwell.   D.M.Wh.
White, Fred N.   F.N.W.
White, Gilbert F.   G.F.W.
White, Leslie A.   L.A.W.
White, Vera Muriel.   V.M.W.
White, William B.   W.B.Wh.
Whitehead, Alfred North.   A.N.W.
Whitehead, Frederick.   F.Wh.
Whitehill, Walter Muir.   W.M.Wh.
Whitelock, Dorothy.   D.W.
Whitfield, John Humphreys.   J.H.W.
Whitrow, Gerald James.   G.J.W.
Whittaker, Robert H.   R.H.W.
Whyte, William Foote.   W.F.Wh.
Wiarda, Howard J.   H.J.Wi.
Wichers, Edward.   E.Wi.
Wickert, Lothar F.K.   L.F.K.W.
Wickler, Wolfgang J.H.   W.J.H.W.
Wicks, Yoke-Lan.   Y.-L.W.
Wiencke, Matthew Immanuel.   M.I.W.
Wiersma, C.A.G.   C.A.G.W.
Wiese, Bernd Michael.   B.M.W.
Wiesenberg, E.J.   E.J.Wi.
Wiesflecker, Hermann.   H.Wi.
Wigglesworth, Sir Vincent Brian.
   V.B.W.
Wilber, Donald N.   D.N.W.
Wilbur, C. Martin.   C.M.Wi.
Wilhelm, Hellmut.   He.W.
Wilken, Robert L.   Ro.W.
Wilkinson, Elizabeth M.   E.M.Wn.
Wilkinson, John Bernard.   J.B.Wi.
Wilkinson, Lancelot Patrick.   L.P.Wi.
Willett, Frank.   F.Wi.
Willetts, William Young.   W.Y.W.
Willey, Basil.   B.W.
Willey, Gordon R.   G.R.W.
Williams, Sir Edgar Trevor.   E.T.W.
Williams, J.   J.Wi.
Williams, J.E. Caerwyn.   J.E.C.W.
Williams, John Hoyt.   J.H.Wi.
Williams, L. Pearce.   L.P.W.
Williams, Marcus K.   M.K.W.

Williams, Nelson Raymond. N.R.W.
Williams, Owen. O.W.
Williams, Robert Deryck. R.D.W.
Willis, Edwin O. E.O.W.
Wilshire, Bruce Withington. B.W.W.
Wilson, Bryan R. B.R.W.
Wilson, Carl Louis. C.L.W.
Wilson, Charles Henry. C.H.Wi.
Wilson, E. Bright. E.B.W.
Wilson, John A. Jo.A.W.
Wilson, John Stuart Gladstone.
   J.S.G.W.
Wilson, Mitchell. M.Wi.
Wilson, Nixon A. N.A.W.
Wilson, T. Carroll. T.C.W.
Wilt, Fred H. F.H.W.
Wilterdink, Nico. N.Wi.
Wina, Arthur N.L. A.N.L.W.
Winberry, John J. J.J.W.
Winchester, A.M. A.M.W.
Winckler, Edwin A. E.A.W.
Windley, Brian Frederick. B.F.W.
Wingert, Paul S. P.S.W.
Wingren, Gustaf. G.Win.
Winker, Carol Ann. C.A.Wi.
Winstedt, Sir Richard Olof. R.O.Wt.
Winther, Oscar O. O.O.W.
Wintrobe, Maxwell M. M.M.W.
Wise, Edmund Merriman. E.M.W.
Wise, Keith Arthur John. K.A.J.W.
Wise, S.F. S.F.W.
Wiseman, Donald John. D.J.W.
Wiseman, Neil E. N.E.W.
Wiskemann, Elizabeth. E.Wn.
Witte, William. W.Wi.
Wojnowski, Jan. Ja.W.
Wolf, Gunther. Gu.W.
Wolfson, Albert. A.Wo.
Wolman, M. Gordon. M.G.W.
Woloch, Isser. I.Wo.
Wolpert, Stanley A. S.A.Wo.
Wolpoff, Milford H. M.H.Wo.
Wolter, The Rev. Allan Bernard.
   A.B.W.
Wolters, Oliver W. O.W.W.
Wondris, E.F. E.F.Wo.
Wong, King Lit. K.L.W.
Wonnacott, Paul. P.Wo.

Wood, Albert E. A.E.W.
Wood, Bernard. B.Wo.
Wood, Frank Osborne. F.O.W.
Woodall, Mary. M.Wo.
Woodard, Thomas M. T.W.
Woodcock, George. G.W.
Woodford, Michael Henry. M.H.W.
Woodhead, A. Geoffrey. A.G.W.
Woodhouse, Christopher Montague.
   C.M.Wo.
Woodruff, Douglas. D.Wo.
Woodruff, Everett B. E.B.Wo.
Woods, John E. J.E.W.
Woodward, John. J.Wo.
Woodward, Ralph Lee, Jr. R.L.W.
Woodward, S. Nicholas. S.N.W.
Woodwell, George M. G.M.W.
Woolfenden, Glen E. G.E.W.
Woolley, Sir Leonard. L.Wy.
Wooster, Ralph A. R.A.Wo.
Wormell, Donald Ernest Wilson.
   D.E.W.W.
Wormley, Edward J. E.J.Wo.
Worthy, Edmund H., Jr. E.H.W., Jr.
Wright, Almon Robert. A.R.W.
Wright, Arthur F. A.F.W.
Wright, Gordon. G.Wr.
Wright, John Wilfrid. J.W.Wr.
Wright, Marion I. M.I.Wr.
Wright, Quincy. Q.W.
Wright, Stephen Graham. S.G.W.
Wurfel, David O.D. D.O.D.W.
Wurm, Stephen A. S.A.W.
Wu Shih-ch'ang. W.S.-cg.
Wylie, Turrell V. T.V.W.

Yale, David Eryl Corbet. D.E.C.Y.
Yamane, Takeo. T.Y.
Yapp, Malcolm Edward. M.E.Y.
Yastrebov, Yevgeny V. Y.V.Y.
Yefremov, Yury Konstantinovich.
   Y.K.Y.
Yerger, Ralph W. R.W.Y.
Yerofeyev, Ivan Alekseyevich. I.A.Y.
Yeung, Yue-man. Y.-m.Y.
Yiannopoulos, A.N. A.N.Y.
Yopp, John H. J.H.Y.

York, Richard Charles. R.C.Y.
Yoshida, Atsuhiko. A.Y.
Young, Ellen Louise. E.L.Y.
Young, Ernest P. E.P.Y.
Young, Jay A. J.A.Y.
Young, Percy Marshall. P.M.Y.
Young, Philip. P.Y.
Young, Roland S. R.S.Y.
Young, T. Cuyler, Jr. T.C.Y., Jr.
Young, Thomas W. T.W.Y.
Young, Warren Melvin. W.M.Yo.

Zakharova, Tatyana Konstantinovna.
   T.K.Z.
Zangwill, Oliver Louis. O.L.Z.
Zaninović, Vice. V.Z.
Záruba, Quido. Q.Z.
Zasenko, Oleksa Eliseyovich. O.E.Z.
Zeeden, Ernst Walter. E.W.Z.
Zeiller, Warren. W.Z.
Zeisel, Hans. H.Z.
Zelinsky, Wilbur. W.Ze.
Zeman, Z.A.B. Z.A.B.Z.
Zeng Zungu. Z.Z.
Zenkovich, Vsevolod Pavlovich. V.P.Z.
Zernov, Nicolas M. N.Z.
Zetlin, Lev. L.Z.
Zgusta, Ladislav. L.Zg.
Zhdanov, Vladimir Viktorovich.
   V.V.Z.
Zhmuida, Viktor Borisovich. V.B.Z.
Zhong Gongfu. Z.G.
Ziadeh, Nicola Abdo. N.A.Z.
Zimmermann, Martin Huldrych. M.H.Z.
Zöllner, Erich. E.Zö.
Zoltán, Imre. I.Z.
Zorn, Roman J. R.J.Z.
Zuberi, Matinuzzaman. M.Zu.
Zucker, Moses. M.Z.
Zudaire Huarte, E. E.Z.H.
Zug, George R. G.R.Z.
Zumberge, James Herbert. J.H.Z.
Zürcher, Erik. E.Z.
Zusi, Richard L. R.L.Z.
Zvelebil, Kamil V. K.V.Z.
Zwass, Vladimir. V.Zw.
Zygmund, Antoni. A.Zy.

Authorities for the Micropædia
volumes 1–12

Material in these volumes was written by or is based on material or advice submitted by the following authorities.

Part One. Matter and Energy

George Ogden Abell (d. 1983). *Professor of Astronomy, University of California, Los Angeles; 1967–83.*

Anatole Abragam. *Professor of Nuclear Magnetism, Collège de France, Paris.*

Roger Adams (d. 1971). *Professor of Organic Chemistry, University of Illinois, Urbana, 1919–57.*

Henry Gavin Alexander. *Headmaster, Hampton School, England. Editor of the Leibniz-Clarke correspondence.*

Lawrence Hugh Aller. *Emeritus Professor of Astronomy, University of California, Los Angeles.*

Douglas M.W. Anderson. *Reader in Chemistry, University of Edinburgh.*

Edward Neville da Costa Andrade (d. 1971). *Quain Professor of Physics, University of London, 1928–50.*

Isaac Asimov. *Science writer. Professor of Biochemistry, Boston University.*

Larned B. Asprey. *Former Staff Member, Los Alamos National Laboratory, N.M.*

Lawrence Badash. *Professor of the History of Science, University of California, Santa Barbara.*

Donald Baim. *Free-lance writer on physics.*

Robert Horace Baker (d. 1964). *Professor of Astronomy, University of Illinois, 1923–51.*

Virginia Bartow. *Associate Professor Emerita of Chemistry, University of Illinois, Urbana.*

Curt W. Beck. *Matthew Vassar, Jr., Professor of Chemistry, Vassar College, Poughkeepsie, N.Y.*

J.M. Beckers. *Experimental Astrophysicist, European Southern Observatory, Garching, Ger.*

Jeremy Bernstein. *Professor of Physics, Stevens Institute of Technology, Hoboken, N.J.*

Robert H. Bernstein. *Research Assistant, Department of Physics, Columbia University.*

R. Byron Bird. *Vilas Research Professor of Chemical Engineering, University of Wisconsin, Madison.*

William John Bishop (d. 1961). *Editor, Medical History. Librarian, Wellcome Historical Medical Library, London, 1946–53.*

Bart Bok (d. 1983). *Professor of Astronomy, University of Arizona, Tucson, 1966–74.*

Rupert Stevenson Bradley. *Former Reader in Inorganic and Structural Chemistry, University of Leeds, Eng.*

John C. Brandt. *Chief, Laboratory for Astronomy and Solar Physics, Goddard Space Flight Center, National Aeronautics and Space Administration, Greenbelt, Md.*

J.W. Buchta (d. 1966). *Professor of Physics, University of Minnesota, Minneapolis, 1938–62.*

Anton B. Burg. *Emeritus Professor of Chemistry, University of Southern California, Los Angeles.*

Joseph A. Burns. *Professor of Mechanics and Astronomy, Cornell University, Ithaca, N.Y.*

Horace R. Byers. *Emeritus Professor of Meteorology, Texas A&M University, College Station.*

Eric Dungan Carlson. *Senior Astronomer, Adler Planetarium, Chicago.*

Michael H. Carr. *Member, Voyager and Galileo Imaging Teams, Geological Survey, U.S. Department of the Interior, Menlo Park, Calif.*

Joseph M. Chamberlain. *Director, Adler Planetarium, Chicago.*

James W. Christy. *Physicist, Hughes Aircraft, Tucson, Ariz.*

Francis Edward Cislak (d. 1990). *Director of Research, Reilly Tar and Chemical Corporation, Indianapolis, Ind., 1937–73.*

Norman Clarke. *Secretary and Registrar, Institute of Mathematics and Its Applications, Southend-on-Sea, Eng.*

Paul R. Clifford. *Department Head, Environmental Chemistry and Biology, Metrek Division, Mitre Corporation, McLean, Va.*

Barbara Lovett Cline. *Biology teacher. Author of* The Questioners: Physicists and the Quantum Theory.

Gerhard L. Closs. *A.A. Michelson Distinguished Service Professor of Chemistry, University of Chicago.*

J.E. Coates (d. 1973). *Professor of Chemistry, University College of Swansea, University of Wales, 1920–48.*

Alexander Cowie. *Emeritus Professor of Mechanical and Aerospace Engineering, Illinois Institute of Technology, Chicago. Associate Editor, Technology, Encyclopædia Britannica, Chicago, 1967–72.*

Frank Donald Drake. *Professor of Astronomy and Astrophysics; Dean, Division of Natural Sciences, University of California, Santa Cruz.*

Raynor Duncombe. *Professor of Aerospace Sciences, University of Texas at Austin.*

Edward W. Dunham. *Research Associate, Department of Earth, Atmospheric, and Planetary Sciences, Massachusetts Institute of Technology, Cambridge.*

Richard H. Eastman. *Emeritus Professor of Chemistry, Stanford University, Calif.*

Olin Jeuck Eggen. *Senior Astronomer, Cerro Tololo Interamerican Observatory, La Serena, Chile.*

Farouk El-Baz. *Director, Center for Remote Sensing, Boston University.*

James L. Elliot. *Professor of Astronomy and Physics; Director, Wallace Astrophysical Observatory, Massachusetts Institute of Technology, Cambridge.*

Paul P. Ewald (d. 1985). *Professor of Physics, Polytechnic Institute of Brooklyn, N.Y., 1949–59.*

Henry Eyring (d. 1981). *Distinguished Professor of Chemistry and Professor of Metallurgy, University of Utah, Salt Lake City, 1967–81.*

Henry Feuer. *Emeritus Professor of Chemistry, Purdue University, West Lafayette, Ind.*

Henry Michael Foley (d. 1982). *Professor of Physics, Columbia University, 1954–82.*

Alfred B. Garrett. *Emeritus Professor of Chemistry, Ohio State University, Columbus.*

Tom Gehrels. *Professor, Lunar and Planetary Laboratory, University of Arizona, Tucson.*

Thomas R.P. Gibb, Jr. *Emeritus Professor of Chemistry, Tufts University, Medford, Mass.*

Frederick William Gibbs (d. 1966). *Deputy Secretary and Editor, Royal Institute of Chemistry, London.*

Henry Lee Giclas. *Astronomer, Lowell Observatory, Flagstaff, Ariz., 1942–81.*

Peter J. Gierasch. *Professor of Astronomy, Cornell University, Ithaca, N.Y.*

Owen Gingerich. *Professor of Astronomy and of the History of Science, Harvard University. Senior Astronomer, Smithsonian Astrophysical Observatory, Cambridge, Mass.*

676

Leo Goldberg (d. 1987). *Director, Kitt Peak National Observatory, Tucson, Ariz., 1971–77. Higgins Professor of Astronomy, Harvard University, 1960–73.*

Donald Goldsmith. *President, Interstellar Media, Berkeley, Calif.*

Murray Goodman. *Professor of Chemistry, University of California, San Diego.*

Lois Graham. *Professor of Mechanical Engineering, Illinois Institute of Technology, Chicago.*

Frank Greenaway. *Keeper, Department of Chemistry, Science Museum, London, 1967–80.*

Edward F. Greene. *Jesse H. and Louisa D. Sharpe Metcalf Professor of Chemistry, Brown University, Providence, R.I.*

Earle Covington Gregg (d. 1983). *Professor of Radiology, School of Medicine, Case Western Reserve University, Cleveland.*

Dirk ter Haar. *Emeritus Reader in Theoretical Physics, University of Oxford; Emeritus Fellow of Magdalen College, Oxford.*

Wayne B. Hadley. *Engineering Scientist, AMP Incorporated, Harrisburg, Pa.*

Dalziel Llewellyn Hammick (d. 1966). *Fellow of Oriel College, Oxford, 1921–52; Aldrichian Praelector in Chemistry, University of Oxford, 1949–52.*

Edward Robert Harrison. *Professor of Astrophysics, University of Massachusetts, Amherst.*

William K. Hartmann. *Senior Scientist, Planetary Science Institute, Science Applications, Inc., Tucson, Ariz.*

George N. Hatsopoulos. *President, Thermo Electron Corporation, Waltham, Mass.*

Gerald S. Hawkins. *Astronomer, Smithsonian Astrophysical Observatory, Cambridge, Mass., 1962–74.*

Eleanor Kay Helin. *Member of the technical staff, Jet Propulsion Laboratory, California Institute of Technology, Pasadena.*

Wilfried Heller (deceased). *Professor of Chemistry, Wayne State University, Detroit, 1953–73.*

James B. Hendrickson. *Professor of Chemistry, Brandeis University, Waltham, Mass.*

G.H. Herbig. *Professor of Astronomy, Lick Observatory, University of California, Santa Cruz.*

John Herivel. *Former Reader in the History and Philosophy of Science, Queen's University of Belfast, N.Ire.*

Reuben Hersh. *Professor of Mathematics, University of New Mexico, Albuquerque.*

Max H. Hey. *Senior Principal Scientific Officer, Department of Mineralogy, British Museum (Natural History), London, 1951–69.*

Christopher T. Hill. *Scientist I, Fermi National Accelerator Laboratory, Batavia, Ill.*

William B. Hubbard. *Professor of Planetary Sciences, University of Arizona, Tucson.*

Maurice Loyal Huggins. *Research consultant. Senior Research Associate, Arcadia Institute for Scientific Research, Woodside, Calif., 1968–75.*

Merkel Henry Jacobs (d. 1970). *Professor of General Physiology, University of Pennsylvania, Philadelphia, 1923–35.*

Stanley Eric Janson (d. 1974). *Keeper, Department of Astronomy and Geophysics, Science Museum, London, 1967–69; Keeper, Department of Chemistry, 1959–67.*

Hamilton Moore Jeffers (d. 1976). *Astronomer, Lick Observatory, Mount Hamilton, Calif., 1938–61.*

Flora Johnson. *Free-lance writer on technical subjects.*

William J. Kaufmann. *Adjunct Professor of Physics, San Diego State University, Calif.*

Richard Kimmel. *Free-lance writer on physics.*

George B. Kistiakowsky (d. 1982). *Abbot and James Lawrence Professor of Chemistry, Harvard University.*

Martin Jesse Klein. *Eugene Higgins Professor of the History of Physics, Yale University.*

Charles T. Kowal. *Staff Scientist, Computer Sciences Corp., Space Telescope Science Institute, Baltimore, Md.*

Sonja Krause. *Professor of Physical Chemistry, Rensselaer Polytechnic Institute, Troy, N.Y.*

Polykarp Kusch. *Regental Professor Emeritus of Physics, University of Texas at Dallas. Cowinner, Nobel Prize for Physics, 1955.*

Juliet Lee-Franzini. *Professor of Physics; Director, Lepton-Photon Spectrometer Group, State University of New York at Stony Brook.*

Henry M. Leicester (d. 1991). *Professor of Biochemistry, University of the Pacific, San Francisco, 1948–77.*

Dame Kathleen Lonsdale (d. 1971). *Professor of Chemistry, University of London, 1949–68.*

Raymond Arthur Lyttleton. *Emeritus Professor of Theoretical Astronomy, University of Cambridge; Fellow of St. John's College, Cambridge.*

Douglas McKie (d. 1967). *Professor of History and Philosophy of Science, University of London, 1957–64.*

William Marshall MacNevin (deceased). *Professor and Chairman, Department of Chemistry, Ohio State University, Columbus.*

William Markowitz. *Adjunct Professor of Physics, Nova University, Fort Lauderdale, Fla. Astronomer, U.S. Naval Observatory, Washington, D.C., 1936–66; Director, Time Service, 1953–66.*

Ladislaus L. Marton (d. 1979). *Chief, Office of International Relations, National Bureau of Standards, Washington, D.C., 1962–70; Chief, Electron Physics Section, 1948–62.*

Alla Genrikhovna Massevitch. *Vice President, Astronomical Council, Academy of Sciences of the U.S.S.R., Moscow.*

Gary Mechler. *Astronomy consultant and writer.*

Henry Jay Melosh. *Professor of Planetary Sciences and Geosciences, University of Arizona, Tucson.*

Eric Mendoza. *Professor of Science Teaching, Hebrew University of Jerusalem.*

Paul Willard Merrill (d. 1961). *President, American Astronomical Society. Member of staff, Mt. Wilson and Palomar Observatories, Pasadena, Calif., 1929–52.*

Allan H. Morrish. *Distinguished Professor of Physics, University of Manitoba, Winnipeg.*

Frederick C. Nachod. *Consultant. Director of Special Projects, Sterling-Winthrop Research Institute, Rensselaer, N.Y., 1974–78; Chemical Liaison Staff Director, 1964–74.*

Gerald C. Nelson. *Member of the Technical Staff, Sandia Laboratories, Albuquerque, N.M.*

Francis Netter. *Head, Department of the Linear Accelerator, Nuclear Research Centre, Saclay, Fr.*

The Rev. Daniel J.K. O'Connell, S.J. (d. 1982). *Director of the Vatican Observatory, Castel Gandolfo, 1952–70.*

Charles Robert O'Dell. *Professor of Space Physics and Astronomy, Rice University, Houston, Texas.*

Peter Oesper. *Professor of Chemistry, St. Lawrence University, Canton, N.Y.*

Ralph Edward Oesper (d. 1977). *Professor of Analytical Chemistry, University of Cincinnati, Ohio, 1937–51.*

John A. O'Keefe. *Astronomer, Laboratory for Astronomy and Solar Physics, Goddard Space Flight Center, National Aeronautics and Space Administration, Greenbelt, Md.*

George A. Olah. *Professor of Chemistry, University of Southern California, Los Angeles.*

Donald E. Osterbrock. *Professor of Astronomy, Lick Observatory, University of California, Santa Cruz.*

Thornton Leigh Page. *Research Astrophysicist, Lyndon B. Johnson Space Center, National Aeronautics and Space Administration, Houston, Texas. Professor of Astronomy, Wesleyan University, Middletown, Conn., 1958–68.*

Bernard E.J. Pagel. *Deputy Chief Scientific Officer, Royal Greenwich Observatory, Herstmonceux, Eng. Visiting Professor of Astronomy, University of Sussex, Brighton, Eng.*

James Bayard Parsons (d. 1985). *Professor of Chemistry, University of Chicago, 1958–61.*

H. Steffen Peiser. *Chief, Office of International Relations, National Bureau of Standards, U.S. Department of Commerce, Washington, D.C., 1969–79.*

Melba Phillips. *Emerita Professor of Physics, University of Chicago.*

Herman Pines. *Vladimir Ipatieff Professor Emeritus of Chemistry, Northwestern University, Evanston, Ill.*

Michael Polanyi, M.D. (d. 1976). *Professor of Social Studies, 1948–58; Professor of Physical Chemistry, 1933–48, Victoria University of Manchester.*

Ernest Rabinowicz. *Professor of Mechanical Engineering, Massachusetts Institute of Technology, Cambridge.*

John O. Rasmussen, Jr. *Professor of Chemistry, University of California, Berkeley.*

Donald G. Rea. *Special Assistant to the Director, Jet Propulsion Laboratory, California Institute of Technology, Pasadena.*

Franklin Evans Roach. *Physicist, U.S. National Bureau of Standards, 1954–65.*

Frank Neville H. Robinson. *Senior Research Officer, Clarendon Laboratory, University of Oxford.*

Colin Alistair Ronan. *Science writer and lecturer. Secretary, East Asian History of Science Trust.*

Carl (Edward) Sagan. *Director, Laboratory for Planetary Studies; David Duncan Professor of Astronomy, Cornell University, Ithaca, N.Y.*

Edwin Ernest Salpeter. *J.G. White Distinguished Professor of Physical Science, Cornell University, Ithaca, N.Y.*

Bernard G. Saunders. *Associate Editor, Physics, Encyclopædia Britannica, Chicago, 1970–73, Physicist, Lawrence Radiation Laboratory, University of California, Livermore, 1959–70.*

Arthur L. Schawlow. *Professor of Physics, Stanford University, Calif. Cowinner, Nobel Prize for Physics, 1981.*

Aurelia Keith Townes Schawlow (Mrs. Arthur L. Schawlow).

Hermann I(rving) Schlesinger (d. 1960). *Professor of Chemistry, University of Chicago.*

Maarten Schmidt. *Professor of Astronomy, California Institute of Technology, Pasadena.*

Robert L. Seale. *Professor of Nuclear and Energy Engineering, University of Arizona, Tucson.*

Frederick Hanley Seares (d. 1964). *Assistant Director, Mount Wilson Observatory of the Carnegie Institution of Washington, Pasadena, Calif., 1925–40.*

Emilio Gino Segrè (d. 1989). *Professor of Physics, University of California, Berkeley, 1946–72. Nobel Prize for Physics, 1959.*

Ralph Pray Seward. *Emeritus Professor of Chemistry, Pennsylvania State University, University Park.*

Charles Donald Shane (d. 1983). *Director, Lick Observatory, University of California, Santa Cruz, 1945–58.*

Steven Soter. *Senior Research Associate, Center for Radiophysics and Space Research, Cornell University, Ithaca, N.Y.*

Robert Spence (d. 1976). *Master of Keynes College; Professor of Applied Chemistry, University of Kent at Canterbury, Eng., 1968–73. Director, Atomic Energy Research Establishment, Harwell, Eng., 1964–68.*

Steven W. Squyres. *National Research Council Associate, Ames Research Center, National Aeronautics and Space Administration, Moffett Field, Calif.*

Vernon Arthur Stenger. *Consultant, Dow Chemical Company, Midland, Mich.*

Kaj Aa. Strand. *Scientific Director, U.S. Naval Observatory, Washington, D.C., 1963–77.*

Yervant Terzian. *Professor and Chairman, Department of Astronomy, Cornell University, Ithaca, N.Y.*

Saul Arno Teukolsky. *Professor of Physics and Astronomy, Cornell University, Ithaca, N.Y.*

Sir George Paget Thomson (d. 1975). *Professor of Physics, University of London, 1930–52. Cowinner, Nobel Prize for Physics, 1937.*

Peter van de Kamp. *Edward Hicks Magill Professor Emeritus of Astronomy, Swarthmore College, Pa.*

Birgit Vennesland. *Head, Vennesland Research Laboratory, Max Planck Society, 1970–81; Director, Max Planck Institute for Cell Physiology, Berlin, 1968–70.*

Joseph Veverka. *Associate Professor of Astronomy, Cornell University, Ithaca, N.Y.*

Robert Vernon Wagoner, Jr. *Professor of Physics, Stanford University, Calif.*

Robert M. Wald. *Professor of Physics, University of Chicago.*

Cheves T. Walling. *Distinguished Professor of Chemistry, University of Utah, Salt Lake City.*

Charles A. Wert. *Emeritus Professor of Metallurgy, University of Illinois, Urbana.*

Gunther K. Wertheim. *Member, Chemical Physics Research Laboratory, AT&T Bell Laboratories, Murray Hill, N.J.*

F. Wesemael. *Research Assistant in Physics, University of Montreal.*

George Willard Wheland (d. 1972). *Professor of Chemistry, University of Chicago.*

Donald H. White. *Professor of Physics, Western Oregon State College, Monmouth.*

Gerald James Whitrow. *Emeritus Professor of the History and Applications of Mathematics, Imperial College of Science and Technology, University of London.*

Edward Wichers (d. 1984). *Associate Director, National Bureau of Standards, U.S. Department of Commerce, Washington, D.C., 1958–62; Chief, Division of Chemistry, 1948–58.*

John A. Wood, Jr. *Geologist, Smithsonian Astrophysical Observatory, Cambridge, Mass.*

Sir Richard Woolley (d. 1986). *Director, South African Astronomical Observatory, 1972–76.*

Fritz Zwicky (d. 1973). *Professor of Astrophysics, California Institute of Technology, Pasadena, 1942–68. Staff Astronomer, Mt. Wilson and Palomar Observatories.*

Part Two. The Earth

Ernst (Valdemar) Antevs. *Private research geologist.*

Clifford A. Barnes. *Emeritus Professor of Oceanography, University of Washington, Seattle.*

Michel J. Batisse. *President, Regional Activities Centre for the Blue Plan for the Mediterranean, UNESCO, Paris.*

Louis J. Battan (d. 1986). *Professor of Atmospheric Sciences, University of Arizona, Tucson, 1958–86.*

Werner A. Baum. *Professor of Meteorology; Dean, College of Arts and Sciences, Florida State University, Tallahassee.*

Kenneth O. Bennington. *Research Chemist, Thermodynamics Laboratory, Albany Metallurgy Research Center, Bureau of Mines, U.S. Department of the Interior, Albany, Ore.*

Marland P. Billings. *Emeritus Professor of Geology, Harvard University.*

F. Donald Bloss. *Alumni Distinguished Professor of Mineralogy, Virginia Polytechnic Institute and State University, Blacksburg.*

William Frank Bradley (d. 1973). *Professor of Chemical Engineering, University of Texas at Austin.*

George William Brindley (d. 1983). *Professor of Mineral Sciences, Pennsylvania State University, University Park, 1962–73.*

Max Edwin Britton. *Biological Scientist, Geological Survey, U.S. Department of the Interior, Reston, Va., 1974–80.*

Edward Morgan Brooks. *Professor of Geology and Geophysics, Boston College, Chestnut Hill, Mass., 1968–81 and 1985.*

Arthur C. Barrington Brown. *Consulting oil geologist.*

Franklin Becker Brown. *Former Director of Research and Development, Union Carbide Corporation, Chemicals and Plastics Operations Division, South Charleston, W.Va.*

Wesley Carr Calef. *Emeritus Professor of Geography, Illinois State University, Normal.*

Carleton Abramson Chapman. *Former Professor of Geology, University of Illinois at Urbana-Champaign.*

Felix Chayes. *Former Petrologist, Geophysical Laboratory, Carnegie Institution of Washington, D.C.*

Robert Griffin Coleman. *Professor of Geology, Stanford University, Calif.*

Paul E. Damon. *Professor of Geosciences; Chief Scientist, Laboratory of Isotope Geochemistry, University of Arizona, Tucson.*

Hubert G. Davis. *Staff Scientist and Principal Investigator, Energy and Environment Division, Lawrence Berkeley Laboratory, University of California.*

George A. Dawson. *Professor of Atmospheric Sciences, University of Arizona, Tucson.*

George W. DeVore. *Professor of Geology, Florida State University, Tallahassee.*

Ernest George Ehlers. *Emeritus Professor of Mineralogy, Ohio State University, Columbus.*

David B. Enfield. *Research Oceanographer, Atlantic Oceanographic and Meteorological Laboratory, National Oceanic and Atmospheric Administration, U.S. Department of Commerce, Miami.*

Richard Kempton Estelow. *Former Business Manager, Columbian Carbon Company, Princeton, N.J.*

George Tobias Faust. *Former Mineralogist-Petrologist, Division of Experimental Geochemistry and Mineralogy, Geological Survey, U.S. Department of the Interior, Washington, D.C.*

Carroll Lane Fenton (d. 1969). *Author of* Our Amazing Earth *and others.*

Mildred Adams Fenton. *Coauthor of* Story of the Great Geologists *and others.*

Robert G. Fleagle. *Emeritus Professor of Atmospheric Sciences, University of Washington, Seattle.*

Robert Louis Folk. *Dave P. Carlton Professor Emeritus of Geology, University of Texas at Austin.*

Clifford Frondel. *Professor of Mineralogy, Harvard University, 1954–77.*

Fritiof Melvin Fryxell (d. 1986). *Professor of Geology, Augustana College, Rock Island, Ill., 1929–73.*

Julian R. Goldsmith. *Charles E. Merriam Distinguished Service Professor Emeritus of Geochemistry, University of Chicago.*

Allan Grierson. *Former Senior Lecturer in Mining, Royal School of Mines, Imperial College of Science and Technology, University of London.*

John W. Harbaugh. *Professor of Applied Earth Sciences, Stanford University, Calif.*

Walter Brian Harland. *Fellow of Gonville and Caius College, Cambridge; former Reader in Tectonic Geology, University of Cambridge.*

Herbert Edwin Hawkes, Jr. *Professor of Mineral Exploration, University of California, Berkeley, 1957–65.*

E. William Heinrich. *Emeritus Professor of Geological Science, University of Michigan, Ann Arbor.*

Donald Munro Henderson. *Professor of Geology, University of Illinois at Urbana-Champaign.*

Benjamin M. Herman. *Professor of Atmospheric Sciences, University of Arizona, Tucson.*

Jörgen Holmboe (deceased). *Professor of Meteorology, University of California, Los Angeles, 1943–70.*

Floyd Allen Hummel. *Emeritus Professor of Ceramic Science, Pennsylvania State University, University Park.*

Charles B. Hunt. *Professor of Geology, Johns Hopkins University, Baltimore, Md., 1961–73.*

Cornelius Searle Hurlbut. *Emeritus Professor of Mineralogy, Harvard University.*

Takashi Ichiye. *Professor of Oceanography, Texas A&M University, College Station.*

Richard H. Jahns (d. 1983). *Crook Professor of Geology and Applied Earth Sciences, Stanford University, Calif.*

George Clayton Kennedy. *Professor of Geology and Geochemistry, University of California, Los Angeles, 1969–80.*

Léo F. Laporte. *Professor of Earth Sciences, University of California, Santa Cruz.*

Austin Long. *Professor of Geosciences, University of Arizona, Tucson.*

Duncan McConnell. *Emeritus Professor of Dentistry and of Mineralogy, Ohio State University, Columbus.*

Wayne Anthony McCurdy. *Former Head, Division of Mining and Preparation, Office of Coal Research, U.S. Department of the Interior, Washington, D.C.*

D. Clay McDowell. *Former Professor of Meteorology; former Director, Institute of Tropical Meteorology, University of Puerto Rico, Río Piedras.*

Wayne E. McGovern. *Mesoscale Branch Chief, National Weather Service, National Oceanic and Atmospheric Administration, U.S. Department of Commerce, Silver Spring, Md.*

Richard W. Macomber. *Professor of Physics, Brooklyn Center, Long Island University, Brooklyn, N.Y.*

Rolland Lee Mays. *Director of Research, Linde Division, Union Carbide Corporation, Tarrytown, N.Y., 1978–81.*

J. Robert Moore. *Director, Marine Science Institute; Professor of Marine Studies, University of Texas at Austin.*

Paul B. Moore. *Professor of Mineralogy and Crystallography, University of Chicago.*

Morris Neiburger (deceased). *Professor of Meteorology, University of California, Los Angeles, 1954–78.*

Jehuda Neumann. *Emeritus Professor of Atmospheric Sciences, Hebrew University of Jerusalem.*

Bert E. Nordlie. *Professor of Geology and Chairman, Department of Earth Sciences, Iowa State University, Ames.*

Frederick J. North. *Formerly Keeper of the Department of Geology, National Museum of Wales.*

John Claud Trewinard Oates (d. 1990). *Reader in Historical Bibliography, University of Cambridge, 1972–79; Fellow of Darwin College, Cambridge, 1964–79.*

Gerald D. O'Brien. *Staff Geologist, Shell Oil Company.*

Charles W. Ott. *Free-lance writer.*

Robert Joseph Pafford, Jr. *Regional Director, Bureau of Reclamation, U.S. Department of the Interior, Sacramento, Calif., 1963–73.*

Hans Arnold Albert Panofsky (d. 1988). *Evan Pugh Research Professor of Atmospheric Sciences, Pennsylvania State University, University Park, 1966–82.*

Ralph Brazelton Peck. *Emeritus Professor of Foundation Engineering, University of Illinois at Urbana-Champaign.*

Márton Pécsi. *Director, Geographical Research Institute, Hungarian Academy of Sciences, Budapest.*

F.J. Pettijohn. *Emeritus Professor of Geology, Johns Hopkins University, Baltimore.*

Hans Ramberg. *Professor and Head, Department of Mineralogy and Petrology, University of Uppsala, Swed.*

Lewis S. Ramsdell (d. 1975). *Professor of Mineralogy, University of Michigan, Ann Arbor, 1945–61.*

Kelvin S. Rodolfo. *Associate Professor of Geological Sciences, University of Illinois at Chicago.*

Edwin Woods Roedder. *Associate, Department of Earth and Planetary Sciences, Harvard University. Geologist, Experimental Geochemistry and Mineralogy Branch, Geological Survey, U.S. Department of the Interior, Reston, Va., 1962–87.*

Della Roy. *Professor of Materials Science, Pennsylvania State University, University Park.*

Rustum Roy. *Evan Pugh Professor of the Solid State; Director, Science, Technology, and Society Program, Pennsylvania State University, University Park.*

George Richard Rumney. *Emeritus Professor of Geography, University of Connecticut, Storrs.*

Maurice L. Schwartz. *Professor of Geology, Western Washington University, Bellingham.*

William D. Sellers. *Professor and Head, Department of Atmospheric Sciences; Director, Institute of Atmospheric Physics, University of Arizona, Tucson.*

Nicholas M. Short. *Research Scientist, Geophysics Branch, Laboratory for Earth Sciences, Goddard Space Flight Center, National Aeronautics and Space Administration, Greenbelt, Md.*

Sol Robert Silverman. *Senior Research Associate, Chevron Oil Field Research Company, La Habra, Calif.*

Joseph V. Smith. *Louis Block Professor of Physical Sciences, University of Chicago.*

Ian M. Steele. *Senior Research Associate, Department of Geophysical Sciences, University of Chicago.*

John S. Sumner. *Emeritus Professor of Geosciences, University of Arizona, Tucson.*

Reginald C. Sutcliffe (d. 1991). *Professor of Meteorology, University of Reading, Eng., 1965–70.*

Sir Graham Sutton (d. 1977). *Vice President, University College of Wales, Aberystwyth, 1967–77. Director General, Meteorological Office, London, 1953–65.*

George S. Switzer. *Emeritus Curator, Department of Mineral Sciences, Smithsonian Institution, Washington, D.C.*

John M. Teal. *Senior Scientist, Woods Hole Oceanographic Institution, Mass.*

Thomas Prence Thayer. *Former Geologist, Eastern Mineral Resources Branch, Geological Survey, U.S. Department of the Interior, Washington, D.C.*

James Burleigh Thompson, Jr. *Sturgis Hooper Professor of Geology, Harvard University.*

Charles Warren Thornthwaite (d. 1963). *Director, Laboratory of Climatology, Centerton, N.J. Principal Climatologist, U.S. Soil Conservation Service, 1935–46.*

Cecil Edgar Tilley (d. 1973). *Professor of Mineralogy and Petrology, University of Cambridge, 1931–61.*

Karl M. Waage. *Emeritus Professor of Geology; Emeritus Curator of Invertebrate Paleontology, Peabody Museum of Natural History, Yale University.*

Howel Williams (d. 1980). *Professor of Geology, University of California, Berkeley, 1945–70.*

Richard F. Wilson. *Former Associate Professor of Geosciences, University of Arizona, Tucson.*

Donald Wolberg. *Paleontologist, New Mexico Bureau of Mines and Mineral Resources, Socorro.*

W.A. Wooster. *Former Director, Crystal Structures Ltd., Cambridge, Eng.*

Jerome J. Wright. *Chief Hydrologist, Metropolitan Utilities Management Agency, Tucson, 1974–78. Associate Professor of Geosciences, University of Arizona, Tucson, 1966–74.*

Vsevolod Pavlovich Zenkovich. *Former Head of Shore Department, Institute of Oceanology, Academy of Sciences of the U.S.S.R., Moscow.*

Part Three. Life on Earth

Constantine John Alexopoulos (d. 1986). *Professor of Botany, University of Texas at Austin, 1962–77.*

Garland Edward Allen. *Professor of Biology, Washington University, St. Louis, Mo.*

Angeles Alvariño. *Fishery Research Biologist, National Marine Fisheries Service, National Oceanic and Atmospheric Administration, U.S. Department of Commerce, La Jolla, Calif., 1970–87.*

George Sherman Avery. *Emeritus Director, Brooklyn Botanic Garden, N.Y.*

Edward William Baker. *Acarologist, Agricultural Research Service, U.S. Department of Agriculture, Beltsville, Md.*

Fred Alexander Barkley. *Former Professor of Biology, Northeastern University, Boston.*

J. Laurens Barnard. *Curator, Division of Crustacea, Smithsonian Institution, Washington, D.C.*

Roger Lyman Batten. *Professor of Geology, Columbia University. Curator, American Museum of Natural History, New York City.*

Dmitri Konstantinovich Belyaev. *Director, Institute of Cytology and Genetics; Chief of the Laboratory of Evolution Genetics, Siberian Department, Academy of Sciences of the U.S.S.R., Novosibirsk.*

Lyman Benson. *Emeritus Professor of Botany, Pomona College, Claremont, Calif.*

Victor Rickman Boswell. *Assistant Director, Crops Research Division, U.S. Department of Agriculture, Plant Industry Station, Beltsville, Md., 1965–68.*

Andrew Gavin Brown. *Former Senior Experimental Officer, Department of Applied Genetics, John Innes Institute, Norwich, Eng.*

Frank A. Brown, Jr. (d. 1983). *Morrison Professor of Biology, Northwestern University, Evanston, Ill., 1956–76.*

John Bonner Buck. *Chief, Section of Comparative Physiology, National Institutes of Health, Bethesda, Md., 1975–85.*

F.M. Carpenter. *Fisher Professor Emeritus of Natural History, Harvard University; Curator of Fossil Insects, Museum of Comparative Zoology, 1936–72.*

Jackson Leaphart Cartter. *Director, U.S. Regional Soybean Laboratory, U.S. Department of Agriculture, Urbana, Ill., 1950–65.*

Robert H. Catlett. *Former Associate Professor of Zoology, San Diego State College, Calif.*

Ailsa McGowan Clark. *Principal Scientific Officer, Department of Zoology, British Museum (Natural History), London.*

Phil Clark. *Free-lance writer on botany.*

Arthur L. Cohen. *Emeritus Professor of Botany and of Biological Sciences, Washington State University, Pullman; Director, Electron Microscope Center, 1962–79.*

Ira Judson Condit (d. 1981). *Professor of Subtropical Horticulture, University of California, Citrus Research Center, Riverside.*

Patricia L. Cook. *Principal Scientific Officer, Department of Zoology, British Museum (Natural History), London.*

Charles E. Cornelius, D.V.M. *Professor of Physiological Sciences, School of Veterinary Medicine, University of California, Davis; Director, California Primate Research Center, 1981–87.*

Paul F.S. Cornelius. *Principal Scientific Officer, Department of Zoology, British Museum (Natural History), London.*

Donovan Stewart Correll (d. 1983). *Program Director, Division of Biological and Medical Sciences, National Science Foundation. Chief Botanist; Head of Botanical Laboratory, Texas Research Foundation, Renner, Texas, 1956–71.*

Francis E.G. Cox. *Professor of Zoology, King's College, University of London.*

Alistair Cameron Crombie. *Senior Lecturer in the History of Science, University of Oxford, 1953–83.*

Frank P. Cullinan. *Collaborator, U.S. National Arboretum, Washington, D.C.*

R.L. Cushing. *Vice President and Secretary, Hawaiian Sugar Planters Association, Honolulu; Director, Experiment Station, 1963–79.*

George McMillan Darrow. *Principal Horticulturist in Charge of Small Fruit Investigations, U.S. Department of Agriculture, Beltsville, Md., 1954–57.*

Charles C. Davis. *Emeritus Professor of Biology, Memorial University of Newfoundland, St. John's.*

Robert H. Denison. *Associate, Museum of Comparative Zoology, Harvard University. Curator of Fossil Fishes, Field Museum of Natural History, Chicago, 1948–71.*

Bernard Dixon. *Science writer. Editor, New Scientist, 1969–79.*

Elizabeth C. Dudley. *Research Associate, Zoology, University of Maryland, College Park.*

L.C. Dunn (d. 1974). *Professor of Zoology, 1928–62; Senior Research Associate in Biological Sciences, 1962–74, Columbia University.*

Stephen Porter Dunn. *Director of Research, Highgate Road Social Science Research Station, Inc., Berkeley, Calif.*

O.J. Eigsti. *Emeritus Professor of Botany, Chicago State University.*

Alfred E. Emerson (d. 1976). *Professor of Biology, University of Chicago, 1934–62.*

Richard Fifield. *Managing Editor, New Scientist.*

Claudio Gilberto Froehlich. *Associate Professor of Zoology, Institute of Biosciences, University of São Paulo, Braz.*

Marshall Gates. *Charles Frederick Houghton Professor Emeritus of Chemistry, University of Rochester, N.Y.*

J. Whitfield Gibbons. *Associate Director, Savannah River Ecology Laboratory, University of Georgia, Aiken, S.C.*

David Ian Gibson. *Principal Scientific Officer, Department of Zoology, British Museum (Natural History), London.*

Ray Gibson. *Senior Lecturer in Biology, Liverpool Polytechnic, Eng.*

Ernest M. Gifford. *Emeritus Professor of Botany, University of California, Davis.*

Clarence James Goodnight (d. 1987). *Professor of Biology, Western Michigan University, Kalamazoo, 1965–84.*

Marie Louise Goodnight. *Free-lance writer and researcher. Instructor in Biological Sciences, Purdue University, West Lafayette, Ind., 1946–65.*

Andres Goth, M.D. *Former Professor of Pharmacology, University of Texas Southwestern Medical School at Dallas.*

Edna R. Green. *Former Head, Science Department, Philadelphia High School for Girls.*

James Green. *Professor of Zoology, Queen Mary College, University of London.*

Per H.H. Halldal. *Professor of Plant Physiology, University of Oslo.*

Yata Haneda. *Curator, Yokosuka City Museum, Japan. Coeditor of Bioluminescence in Progress.*

Sir Alister C. Hardy (d. 1985). *Linacre Professor of Zoology, University of Oxford, 1946–61.*

Ellwood Scott Harrar (d. 1975). *James B. Duke Professor of Wood Science, Duke University, Durham, N.C., 1967–74.*

Hudson Thomas Hartmann. *Emeritus Professor of Pomology, University of California, Davis.*

Joel W(alker) Hedgpeth. *Emeritus Professor of Oceanography, Oregon State University, Newport; Head, Yaquina Biological Laboratory, Marine Science Center, 1965–74.*

Edward Hindle (d. 1973). *Scientific Director, Zoological Society of London, 1944–51. Regius Professor of Zoology, University of Glasgow, 1935–43.*

Cecil Arthur Hoare (d. 1984). *Wellcome Research Fellow, Wellcome Laboratories of Tropical Medicine, London, 1957–70; Head, Protozoological Department, 1923–57.*

Walter Henricks Hodge. *Section Head for Ecological and Systematic Botany, National Science Foundation, Washington, D.C., 1970–73.*

Richard Lawrence Hoffman. *Professor of Biology, Radford University, Va.*

Turner Harcourt Hopper. *Chief, Oilseed Crops Laboratory, Southern Utilization Research and Development Division, Agricultural Research Service, New Orleans, 1958–65.*

Carl L. Hubbs (d. 1979). *Professor of Biology, Scripps Institution of Oceanography, University of California, San Diego, at La Jolla, 1944–69.*

Clark Hubbs. *Professor of Zoology, University of Texas at Austin.*

Hilary Mary Hughes. *Horticulturalist, Ministry of Agriculture, Wolverhampton, Eng.*

Laurence Irving (d. 1979). *Professor of Zoophysiology, University of Alaska, Fairbanks, 1962–74; Advisory Scientific Director, Institute of Arctic Biology, 1966–74.*

Artemy V. Ivanov. *Former Head, Laboratory of Evolutionary Morphology, Zoological Institute, Academy of Sciences of the U.S.S.R., Leningrad. Former Professor of Zoology, Leningrad A.A. Zhdanov State University.*

David Starr Jordan, M.D. (d. 1931). *Chancellor, Stanford University, Calif., 1913–16; President, 1891–1913. President, Indiana University, Bloomington, 1885–91; Professor of Zoology, 1879–85.*

Theodor (Karl) Just (d. 1960). *Chief Curator, Department of Botany, Field Museum of Natural History, Chicago.*

Chester Scott Keefer, M.D. (d. 1972). *Wade Professor of Medicine, Boston University, 1940–64.*

Keith R. Kelson. *Former Acting Assistant Director for Education and Executive Assistant, National Science Foundation, Washington, D.C. Coauthor of The Mammals of North America.*

Vera V. Khvostova (d. 1977). *Chief, Laboratory of Cytogenetics, Institute of Cytology and Genetics, Siberian Department, Academy of Sciences of the U.S.S.R., Novosibirsk.*

James Edward Knott (deceased). *Professor and Chairman, Department of Vegetable Crops, University of California, Davis, 1940–64.*

Paulden Ford Knowles. *Emeritus Professor of Agronomy, University of California, Davis.*

Barry Koffler. *Free-lance writer on zoology and ecology.*

Sir Hans (Adolf) Krebs (d. 1981). *Whitley Professor of Biochemistry, University of Oxford, 1954–67. Cowinner, Nobel Prize for Physiology or Medicine, 1953.*

Christine Laning. *Free-lance writer on botany.*

Carl Adam Lawrence (d. 1972). *Director, Bureau of Laboratories, Los Angeles County Health Department, Calif., 1953–70.*

Morris Cecil Leikind (d. 1976). *Scientist Administrator, National Clearinghouse for Mental Health Information, National Institutes of Health, Bethesda, Md., 1963–66.*

Roger John Lincoln. *Principal Scientific Officer, Department of Zoology, British Museum (Natural History), London.*

Thomas D. Luckey. *Professor of Biochemistry, University of Missouri, Columbia, 1954–84.*

Joseph Colvin McDaniel. *Former Assistant Professor of Horticulture (Research), University of Illinois, Urbana.*

John Robert Magness. *Chief, Fruit and Nut Crops Research Branch, U.S. Department of Agriculture, U.S. Plant Industry Station, Beltsville, Md., 1953–59.*

Leonard Harrison Matthews (d. 1986). *Scientific Director, Zoological Society of London, 1951–66.*

Florence Moog. *Rebstock Professor Emeritus of Biology, Washington University, St. Louis, Mo.*

Thomas Edwin Moore. *Curator of Insects, Museum of Zoology; Professor of Zoology, University of Michigan, Ann Arbor.*

Ernst Trier Mörch, M.D. *Anesthesiologist, Nassau General Hospital, Fernandina Beach, Fla. Former Clinical Professor of Surgery, University of Illinois at Chicago.*

James William Moulder. *Emeritus Professor of Molecular Genetics and Cell Biology, University of Chicago.*

Walter Conrad Muenscher (d. 1963). *Professor of Botany, Cornell University, Ithaca, N.Y.*

Carl F.W. Muesebeck. *Honorary Collaborator, U.S. Department of Agriculture and U.S. National Museum, 1954–65. Chief, Division of Insect Identification, U.S. Department of Agriculture, 1935–54.*

John Spangler Nicholas (d. 1963). *Sterling Professor of Biology, Yale University, 1939–63.*

George Torao Okita. *Professor of Pharmacology, Northwestern University, Chicago.*

Everett C. Olson. *Emeritus Professor of Zoology, University of California, Los Angeles.*

Jane M. Oppenheimer. *Emeritus Professor of Biology and the History of Science, Bryn Mawr College, Pa.*

Gilbert Fred Otto. *Professor of Zoology, University of Maryland, College Park, 1966–72.*

Thomas G. Overmire. *Head, Office of Project Management, Kuwait Institute for Scientific Research. Author of* Homeostatic Regulation.

Richard Tudor Owen. *Advisory Pharmacologist, Scientific Services Division, Wellcome Foundation Ltd., Crewe, Eng.*

Gordon Paterson. *Higher Scientific Officer, Department of Zoology, British Museum (Natural History), London.*

Fernandus Payne (deceased). *Professor of Zoology, Indiana University, Bloomington, 1919–51.*

Michael J. Pelczar, Jr. *Emeritus Vice President for Graduate Studies and Research; Emeritus Professor of Microbiology, University of Maryland, College Park.*

Bernard George Peters (d. 1967). *Professor of Parasitology, Imperial College of Science and Technology, University of London, 1955–67.*

Sir Rudolph Albert Peters (d. 1982). *Whitley Professor of Biochemistry, University of Oxford, 1923–54. Head, Biochemistry Department, Agricultural Research Council, Institute of Animal Physiology, Babraham, Cambridge, Eng., 1954–59.*

Richard W. Pohl. *Distinguished Professor of Botany; Curator of the Herbarium, Iowa State University, Ames.*

(Frederick) Wilson Popenoe. *Director Emeritus, Escuela Agrícola Panamericana, Tegucigalpa, Honduras, Author of* Manual of Tropical and Subtropical Fruits *and others.*

John Ramsbottom (d. 1974). *Keeper, Department of Botany, British Museum (Natural History), London, 1930–50.*

Austin L. Rand (d. 1982). *Research Associate, Archbold Biological Station, Lake Placid, Fla. Chief Curator of Zoology, Field Museum of Natural History, Chicago, 1955–70.*

Gloria Robinson. *Research Affiliate in the History of Medicine, Yale University.*

Alfred S. Romer (d. 1973). *Alexander Agassiz Professor of Zoology, Harvard University, 1947–65.*

Anthony H. Rose. *Professor of Microbiology, University of Bath, Eng.*

Herbert Holdsworth Ross (d. 1978). *Professor of Entomology, University of Georgia, Athens.*

Bradley Titus Scheer. *Emeritus Professor of Biology, University of Oregon, Eugene.*

Aaron J. Sharp. *Alumni Distinguished Service Professor Emeritus of Botany, University of Tennessee, Knoxville.*

Malcolm C. Shurtleff, Jr. *Professor of Plant Pathology; Extension Plant Pathologist, University of Illinois, Urbana.*

Reginald W. Sims. *Head, Annelida Section, Department of Zoology, British Museum (Natural History), London.*

Walton B. Sinclair (deceased). *Professor of Biochemistry, University of California, Riverside, 1946–68.*

Robert Leo Smith. *Professor of Wildlife Biology and Ecology, West Virginia University, Morgantown.*

Howard James Stains. *Professor of Zoology, Southern Illinois University, Carbondale.*

William Campbell Steere (d. 1988). *Professor of Botany, Columbia University, 1958–75. President, New York Botanical Garden, Bronx, 1970–72; Director, 1958–70.*

C.D. Stein, V.M.D. (d. 1965). *Consultant, Animal Disease Eradication Division, Agricultural Research Service, U.S. Department of Agriculture.*

William Louis Stern. *Professor of Botany, University of Florida, Gainesville.*

Robert W. Storer. *Emeritus Professor of Zoology, University of Michigan, Ann Arbor; Curator of Birds, Museum of Zoology, 1956–85.*

William Cofield Summers, M.D. *Professor of Therapeutic Radiology, Molecular Biophysics and Biochemistry, and Human Genetics, Yale University.*

William H. Taliaferro (d. 1973). *Eliakim Hastings Moore Distinguished Service Professor of Microbiology, University of Chicago, 1954–60. Senior Immunologist, Division of Biological and Medical Research, Argonne National Laboratory, Argonne, Ill., 1960–69.*

John David Taylor. *Head, Mollusca Section, Zoology Department, British Museum (Natural History), London.*

Norman Taylor (d. 1967). *Assistant Curator, New York Botanical Garden, 1905–11. Author of* Guide to Garden Flowers *and others.*

John W. Thieret. *Professor of Botany, Northern Kentucky University, Highland Heights.*

Frederick Ichiro Tsuji. *Research Biochemist, Marine Biology Research Division, Scripps Institution of Oceanography, University of California, San Diego, at La Jolla.*

Robert Templeton Van Tress. *Former Horticulturist, Chicago Park District.*

Paul Dirks Voth. *Emeritus Professor of Botany, University of Chicago.*

David B. Wake. *Director, Museum of Vertebrate Zoology; Professor of Integrative Biology, University of California, Berkeley.*

Lionel A. Walford (d. 1979). *Director, Sandy Hook Marine Laboratory, Highlands, N.J., 1960–71; Senior Scientist, 1971–74.*

Stanley H. Weitzman. *Curator of Fishes, Division of Fishes, National Museum of Natural History, Smithsonian Institution, Washington, D.C.*

Rupert L. Wenzel. *Emeritus Curator of Insects, Field Museum of Natural History, Chicago; Chairman, Department of Zoology, 1970–77.*

Geoffrey Buckle West (d. 1991). *Reader in Pharmacology, North East London Polytechnic, 1970–82.*

George W. Wharton (d. 1990). *Professor of Entomology, Ohio State University, Columbus, 1961–76; Director, Acarology Laboratory, 1969–76.*

Donald Walter Wilkie. *Director, Aquarium-Museum, Scripps Institution of Oceanography, University of California, San Diego.*

Gordon Roy Williams. *Head, New Zealand Wildlife Service, Department of Internal Affairs, Wellington.*

Louis O. Williams. *Emeritus Curator of Botany, Field Museum of Natural History, Chicago.*

A.J. Winkler. *Emeritus Professor of Viticulture and Emeritus Viticulturist, College of Agriculture, University of California, Davis.*

Keith Arthur John Wise. *Entomologist, Auckland Institute and Museum, N.Z.*

Dorothea Woodruff. *Herbarium Associate and Research Assistant, Department of Biology, University of Utah, Salt Lake City.*

A.H. Wright (d. 1966). *Professor of Agronomy, University of Wisconsin, Madison, 1931–57.*

Kanichiro Yashiroda. *Proprietor, Yashiroda Acclimatization Garden, Tonosho, Japan. Author of* Bonsai: Japanese Miniature Trees.

Richard Charles York. *Instructor of Horticulture and Education, McHenry County College, Crystal Lake, Ill. Former Associate Editor, Biology, Encyclopædia Britannica, Chicago.*

Wolfram Winfried Zillig. *Director, Max Planck Institute for Biochemistry, Munich.*

Martin Huldrych Zimmermann (d. 1984). *Charles Bullard Professor of Forestry, Harvard University; Director, Harvard Forest, Petersham, 1970–84.*

Solly Zuckerman, Baron Zuckerman. *Sands Cox Professor Emeritus of Anatomy, University of Birmingham, Eng. President, Zoological Society of London, 1977–84.*

Part Four. Human Life

Fred Lyman Adair, M.D. (d. 1972). *Mary Campau Ryerson Professor of Obstetrics and Gynecology, University of Chicago, 1931–42.*

Rodolfo Almeida Pintos (deceased). *Phthisiologist, Institute of Epidemiology and Contagious Diseases, School of Medicine, University of Montevideo, Uruguay.*

W.A.D. Anderson, M.D. *Emeritus Professor of Pathology, School of Medicine, University of Miami.*

Alfred Alvin Angrist, M.D. (d. 1984). *Professor of Pathology, Albert Einstein College of Medicine, Yeshiva University, Bronx, N.Y.*

(Edith Kathleen) Charlotte Banks. *Former Lecturer in Psychology, University College, University of London.*

M. Robert Barnett. *Consultant, American Foundation for the Blind, New York City; Executive Director, 1949–74.*

Edward W. Barrett (d. 1989). *Dean, Graduate School of Journalism, Columbia University, 1956–68. Founder, Columbia Journalism Review.*

Frank X. Barron. *Professor of Psychology, University of California, Santa Cruz.*

Sir Frederic Charles Bartlett (d. 1969). *Professor of Experimental Psychology, University of Cambridge, 1931–52; Director, Psychological Laboratory, 1922–52.*

S. Howard Bartley (d. 1988). *Professor of Psychology, Michigan State University, East Lansing, 1947–71.*

David V. Bates, M.D. *Emeritus Professor of Medicine, University of British Columbia, Vancouver.*

William B. Bean, M.D. (d. 1989). *Professor of Medicine, University of Iowa, Iowa City, 1948–70. Editor in Chief, Archives of Internal Medicine, 1962–67.*

Marc Oliver Beem, M.D. *Emeritus Professor of Pediatrics, University of Chicago.*

Walter Reginald Bett. *Medical Editor, Wm. Douglas McAdams, Inc., New York City. Author of* The Infirmities of Genius *and others.*

Emma Mary Birch. *Head Occupational Therapist, Royal Free Hospital Group, London.*

Edwin Garrigues Boring (d. 1968). *Edgar Pierce Professor of Psychology, Harvard University, 1956–57; Professor of Psychology, 1928–56.*

Arthur Hills Brayfield. *Emeritus Professor of Psychology, Claremont Graduate School, Calif.*

Henry W. Brosin, M.D. *Professor of Psychiatry, University of Arizona, Tucson.*

Carroll L. Bryant. *Director, Office of Publications, American National Red Cross, 1954–60.*

William Burrows (d. 1978). *Professor of Microbiology, University of Chicago, 1947–73.*

Sir Cyril Lodowic Burt (d. 1971). *Professor of Psychology, University College, University of London, 1931–50.*

Douglas E. Busby, M.D. *Medical Director, Downtown Healthcare Services, Lutheran Medical Center, Cleveland.*

Donald E. Cassels, M.D. (d. 1981). *Professor of Pediatrics, University of Chicago.*

Andrew Barnett Christie, M.D. *Honorary Physician, Fazakerley Hospital, Liverpool. Former Head, Department of Infectious Diseases, University of Liverpool.*

Conrad Chyatte. *Associate Professor of Psychology, De Paul University, Chicago, 1952–76.*

Leighton E. Cluff, M.D. *President, Robert Wood Johnson Foundation, Princeton, N.J. Professor and Chairman, Department of Medicine, University of Florida, Gainesville, 1966–76.*

David W. Crabb. *Emeritus Professor of Anthropology, Princeton University.*

Paul Frederic Cranefield. *Professor of Physiology, Rockefeller University, New York City.*

Jean-Marie Crépin. *Electroradiologist, Léopold Bellan Hospital, Paris.*

Edward P. Crowell, D.O. *Former Executive Director, American Osteopathic Association, Chicago.*

Liza Dahlby. *Translator and free-lance writer.*

Robert Croly Darling, M.D. *Simon Baruch Professor Emeritus of Rehabilitation Medicine, Columbia University.*

Henry P. David. *Director, Transnational Family Research Institute, Bethesda, Md. Associate Clinical Professor of Psychology, School of Medicine, University of Maryland, Baltimore.*

Peter P.H. De Bruyn, M.D. *Emeritus Professor of Anatomy, University of Chicago.*

Susan J. Decker. *Free-lance writer on medical topics. Electron Microscopist, Department of Biology, University of Illinois, Chicago.*

William N. Dember. *Professor of Psychology, University of Cincinnati, Ohio.*

Helen Aird Dickie, M.D. *Professor of Medicine, University of Wisconsin, Madison.*

John Holmes Dingle, M.D. (d. 1973). *Elisabeth Severance Prentiss Professor of Preventive Medicine and Professor of Medicine, Case Western Reserve University, Cleveland.*

Joseph Lewi Donhauser (d. 1964). *Professor of Surgery, Albany Medical College, N.Y. Senior Surgeon, Albany Medical Center Hospital.*

Roy Melvin Dorcus (d. 1968). *Professor of Psychology, 1944–65; Dean, Division of Life Sciences, University of California, Los Angeles, 1950–63.*

James Russell Eckman. *Senior Consultant, Section of Publications, Mayo Clinic, Rochester, Minn.*

Lillian Eichelberger. *Emeritus Professor of Biochemistry, University of Chicago.*

Kendall Emerson, Jr., M.D. *Emeritus Professor of Medicine, Harvard University.*

William Fisher Enneking, M.D. *Distinguished Service Professor of Orthopaedic Surgery, University of Florida, Gainesville.*

George Hoben Estabrooks (d. 1974). *Professor of Psychology, Colgate University, Hamilton, N.Y., 1935–64.*

Hans Jurgen Eysenck. *Emeritus Professor of Psychology, Institute of Psychiatry, University of London.*

Ernest Carroll Faust (d. 1978). *Professor of Parasitology, Tulane University, New Orleans.*

Louis B. Flexner, M.D. *Emeritus Professor of Anatomy, University of Pennsylvania, Philadelphia.*

Anna Freud (d. 1982). *Director of the Hampstead Child Therapy Course and Clinic, London, 1952–82. Author of* The Ego and the Mechanisms of Defence *and others.*

William F. Ganong, M.D. *Lange Professor of Physiology, University of California, San Francisco.*

Esther Garvey. *Registered Nurse, specializing in geriatric care.*

Jacob Warren Getzels. *R. Wendell Harrison Distinguished Service Professor Emeritus of Educational Psychology, University of Chicago.*

Edward Girden. *Emeritus Professor of Psychology, Brooklyn College, City University of New York.*

Francis Byron Gordon, M.D. (d. 1973). *Director, Department of Microbiology, Naval Medical Research Institute, Bethesda, Md., 1962–72.*

Ashton Graybiel, M.D. *Chief Scientific Advisor, Naval Aerospace Medical Research Laboratory, Naval Air Station, Pensacola, Fla.; Director of Research, 1945–70.*

Douglas James Guthrie, M.D. (d. 1975). *Medical historian. Lecturer on the History of Medicine, University of Edinburgh, 1945–56.*

Ward Campbell Halstead (d. 1969). *Professor, Department of Psychology and Medicine, University of Chicago, 1946–69.*

A. Gordon Hammer. *Emeritus Professor of Psychology, Macquarie University, North Ryde, Australia.*

Henry Nelson Harkins, M.D. (d. 1967). *Professor of Surgery, University of Washington, 1947–67; Surgeon-in-Chief, University Hospital, Seattle, 1957–64.*

Donald F.N. Harrison, M.D. *Professor of Laryngology and Otology, University of London.*

Réjane M. Harvey, M.D. *Richards Professor Emeritus of Medicine, Columbia University.*

A. Waller Hastings. *Medical writer and editor.*

R.L. Hay. *Professor of Geology, University of California, Berkeley. Author of* Geology of the Olduvai Gorge.

Ralph William Heine. *Emeritus Professor of Psychology, University of Michigan, Ann Arbor; Director, Institute for Human Adjustment, 1974–78.*

Roger Moss Herriott. *Emeritus Professor of Biochemistry, School of Hygiene and Public Health, Johns Hopkins University, Baltimore.*

Nicholas Carr Hightower, M.D. *Senior Consultant, Department of Gastroenterology, Scott and White Clinic and Scott and White Memorial Hospital, Temple, Texas.*

Constance Holden. *Staff writer,* Science *magazine.*

Howard Francis Hunt. *Clinical Professor of Psychology in Psychiatry, Cornell University Medical College, New York City.*

Stanley W. Jacob, M.D. *Gerlinger Professor of Surgery, Oregon Health Sciences University, Portland.*

Saul Jarcho, M.D. *Medical historian. Former Consultant to the Surgeon General of the U.S. Army and to the National Institutes of Health, Bethesda, Md.*

Herbert Henry Jasper, M.D. *Emeritus Professor of Neurophysiology, University of Montreal.*

Franklin Davis Johnston, M.D. (d. 1971). *Professor of Internal Medicine, University of Michigan, Ann Arbor.*

J.R. Kantor (d. 1984). *Professor of Psychology, Indiana University, Bloomington, 1923–59.*

George Alexander Kelly (d. 1967). *Professor of Psychology, Brandeis University, Waltham, Mass., 1965–67.*

Pearl L. Kendrick (d. 1980). *Lecturer, Department of Epidemiology, School of Public Health, University of Michigan, Ann Arbor, 1951–60.*

Meave Kenny, M.D. *Former University Reader in Obstetrics and Gynecology, Postgraduate Medical School of London.*

John Franklin Kenward, M.D. (d. 1989). *Associate Professor of Pediatrics and Psychiatry, University of Chicago, 1957–78.*

Thomas Edward Keys. *Emeritus Professor of the History of Medicine, Mayo Graduate School of Medicine, University of Minnesota, Rochester.*

Joseph Barnett Kirsner, M.D. *Louis Block Distinguished Service Professor of Medicine, University of Chicago.*

Arthur Paul Klotz, M.D. *Director of Research, Biogerontology Research Institute, Boswell Memorial Hospital, Sun City, Ariz. Professor of Medicine, University of Kansas, Kansas City, 1962–75; Head of Section of Gastroenterology, 1954–75.*

Heinrich Klüver (d. 1979). *Sewell L. Avery Distinguished Service Professor of Biological Psychology, University of Chicago, 1957–62.*

John Knowelden, M.D. *Professor of Community Medicine, University of Sheffield, Eng, 1960–84.*

Helen Lois Koch (d. 1977). *Professor of Child Psychology, University of Chicago, 1945–60.*

Sigmund Koch. *Professor of Psychology and Philosophy, Boston University.*

Dieter Koch-Weser, M.D. *Professor of Preventive and Social Medicine; Associate Dean for International Programs, Medical School, Harvard University.*

Sheldon Jerome Korchin. *Professor of Psychology, University of California, Berkeley.*

Raymond G. Kuhlen (d. 1967). *Professor of Psychology, Syracuse University, N.Y.*

Karen Landahl. *Associate Professor of Linguistics, University of Chicago.*

Olof Larsell (d. 1964). *Professor of Neuroanatomy, University of Minnesota, Minneapolis.*

Gabriel W. Lasker. *Emeritus Professor of Anatomy, School of Medicine, Wayne State University, Detroit.*

Richard Last. *Television critic,* Daily Telegraph *(London).*

James P. Leake, M.D. (d. 1973). *Medical Director, U.S. Public Health Service, Washington, D.C., 1935–45.*

Mary Leakey. *Director of Research, Olduvai Gorge, Tanzania.*

W.R. Lee, M.D. *Professor of Occupational Health, Victoria University of Manchester, Eng.*

Benedict Leerburger. *Free-lance science writer.*

Edwin Herman Lennette, M.D. *Emeritus Chief, Viral and Rickettsial Disease Laboratory, California State Department of Public Health. Lecturer in Epidemiology and Virology, University of California, Berkeley, 1948–78.*

David Le Vay. *Former Consultant Surgeon, National Health Service, United Kingdom.*

Max Levin, M.D. (d. 1974). *Neurologist and psychiatrist. Clinical Professor of Neurology, New York Medical College, New York City.*

Dorothy C.H. Ley, M.D. *Director, Palliative Care Foundation, Toronto. Former Director, Laboratory Certification and Proficiency Testing Program, Ontario Medical Association.*

Allan L. Lorincz, M.D. *Professor of Dermatology, University of Chicago.*

Douglas McAlpine, M.D. (d. 1981). *Consulting Physician, Middlesex Hospital and Maida Vale Hospital, London.*

Morton McCutcheon, M.D. (d. 1962). *Professor of Pathology, University of Pennsylvania, Philadelphia.*

William J. McGuire. *Professor of Psychology, Yale University.*

Ralph Hermon Major, M.D. (d. 1970). *Professor of Medicine and of the History of Medicine, University of Kansas, Kansas City.*

Judd Marmor, M.D. *Franz Alexander Professor Emeritus of Psychiatry, University of Southern California, Los Angeles.*

Jonathan Meader. *Free-lance writer on entertainment.*

Harold Merskey, M.D. *Professor of Psychiatry, University of Western Ontario, London.*

Heino F.L. Meyer-Bahlburg. *Associate Clinical Professor of Medical Psychology, Columbia University.*

William James Mills, Jr., M.D. *Orthopedic Surgeon. Professor and Director, Center of High Latitude Health Research, University of Alaska, Anchorage. Rear Admiral (retired), Medical Corps, U.S. Naval Reserve.*

John Edgar Morison, M.D. *Honorary Professor of Histopathology, Queen's University of Belfast, N.Ire. Consultant in Histopathology, Belfast City Hospital.*

John Douglas Newth. *Former Honorary Secretary, British Council for Doctor Schweitzer's Hospital.*

Charles R. Noback. *Emeritus Professor of Anatomy and Cell Biology, College of Physicians and Surgeons, Columbia University.*

Norman H. Olsen, D.D.S. *Dean, Dental School, Northwestern University, Chicago.*

Charles Donald O'Malley (d. 1970). *Professor of Medical History, University of California Medical Center, Los Angeles.*

Martin T. Orne, M.D. *Professor of Psychiatry, University of Pennsylvania, Philadelphia; Director, Unit for Experimental Psychiatry, Institute of Pennsylvania Hospital.*

Thomas Parran, M.D. (d. 1968). *Surgeon General, U.S. Public Health Service, 1936–48. Dean, Graduate School of Public Health, University of Pittsburgh, 1948–58.*

Donald G. Paterson (d. 1961). *Professor of Psychology; Member of Staff, Industrial Relations Center, University of Minnesota, Minneapolis.*

Sir George (White) Pickering, M.D. (d. 1980). *Master of Pembroke College, Oxford, 1968–74; Regius Professor of Medicine, University of Oxford, 1956–68.*

Fred Plum, M.D. *Anne Parrish Titzell Professor of Neurology, Medical College, Cornell University, New York City. Neurologist in Chief, New York Hospital.*

C. Stanford Read, M.D. *Former Lecturer in Psychological Medicine, Bethlem Royal Hospital, London. Former Clinical Psychologist, West End Hospital for Nervous Diseases, London.*

Robert G. Richardson. *Consultant medical editor. Former Editor, Abbottempo (international medical journal).*

J. Alfred Rider, M.D. *Director, Gastrointestinal Research Laboratory, Franklin Hospital, San Francisco.*

Walther Riese, M.D. (d. 1976). *Associate Professor of the History of Medicine and of Neurology and Psychiatry, Medical College of Virginia, Richmond, 1958–60.*

Austin Herbert Riesen. *Emeritus Professor of Psychology, University of California, Riverside.*

H. Rocke Robertson, M.D. *Principal and Vice-Chancellor, McGill University, Montreal, 1962–70.*

Arthur Robinson, M.D. *Professor of Biochemistry, Biophysics, and Genetics and of Pediatrics, University of Colorado, Denver.*

Nicholas A. Romas, M.D. *Director of Urology, St. Luke's-Roosevelt Hospital Center, New York City.*

Arturo Stearns Rosenblueth, M.D. (d. 1970). *Director, Centre for Investigation and Advanced Studies, National Polytechnic Institute, Mexico City.*

Paul Farr Russell, M.D. (d. 1983). *Visiting Professor, Harvard University School of Public Health, 1960–63. Staff member, Rockefeller Foundation, 1923–59.*

Heinrich Satter. *Free-lance writer. Author of* Paul Ehrlich, Begründer der Chemotherapie *and others.*

T.C. Schneirla (d. 1968). *Curator of Animal Behaviour, American Museum of Natural History, New York City, 1947–68.*

Sidney Schulman, M.D. *Ellen C. Manning Professor of Neurology, University of Chicago.*

Laurance F. Shaffer (d. 1976). *Professor of Psychology and Education, Teachers College, Columbia University.*

Leon Sokoloff, M.D. *Professor of Pathology, State University of New York at Stony Brook.*

Walter Graham Spector (d. 1982). *Professor of Pathology, St. Bartholomew's Hospital Medical College, University of London, 1962–82.*

William Spector. *Senior Editor, Human Life, Encyclopædia Britannica, Chicago, 1967–72. Editor of* Handbook of Biological Data *and others.*

Wesley William Spink, M.D. (d. 1988). *Regents' Professor of Medicine, University of Minnesota, Minneapolis, 1967–73.*

Howard Burnham Sprague, M.D. (d. 1970). *Honorary Physician to the Massachusetts General Hospital. Lecturer in Medicine, Harvard University, 1956–59.*

Ross Stagner. *Emeritus Professor of Psychology, Wayne State University, Detroit.*

Mario Stefanini, M.D. *Director of the Laboratories, St. Elizabeth's Hospital, Danville, Ill.*

Robert Henry Thouless (d. 1984). *Reader in Educational Psychology, University of Cambridge, 1945–61; Fellow of Corpus Christi College, Cambridge.*

Bettey Tomasi. *Free-lance writer on medical topics.*

Richard Tuttle. *Researcher, Trudeau Institute, Saranac Lake, N.Y.*

Leroy Vail. *Free-lance writer.*

Ilza Veith. *Emeritus Professor of Psychiatry and the History of Health Sciences, University of California, San Francisco.*

Reino Virtanen (d. 1987). *Professor of Modern Languages, University of Nebraska, Lincoln, 1957–78.*

Nancy Theilgaard Watts. *Professor and Director, Graduate Program in Physical Therapy, MGH Institute of Health Professions, Boston.*

Louis Weinstein, M.D. *Professor of Medicine, Tufts University, Medford, Mass., 1957–75.*

Michael M. Wertheimer. *Professor of Psychology, University of Colorado, Boulder.*

Emil Witschi (d. 1971). *Senior Scientist, Bio-Medical Division of the Population Council, Rockefeller University, New York City, 1967–71.*

Henry D. von Witzleben, M.D. *Emeritus Director of Professional Education, Veterans Administration Hospital, Palo Alto, Calif. Associate Clinical Professor Emeritus of Psychiatry, Stanford University, Calif.*

Robert E. Wood, M.D. *Associate Professor of Pediatrics, University of North Carolina at Chapel Hill.*

John H. Wykert. *Medical and psychiatric writer.*

Robert Henry Yager, V.M.D. *Former Executive Secretary, Institute on Laboratory Animal Resources, National Research Council, National Academy of Sciences, Washington, D.C.*

Leo M. Zimmerman, M.D. (d. 1980). *Professor of Surgery, Chicago Medical School, 1948–80. Senior Attending Surgeon, Michael Reese Hospital, Chicago.*

Imre Zoltán, M.D. *Professor of Gynecology and Obstetrics, Semmelweis Medical University, Budapest, Hung.*

Part Five. Human Society

John C. Abbott. *Deputy Director, Economic Analysis Division, Food and Agriculture Organization of the United Nations, Rome.*

George Plimpton Adams, Jr. *Emeritus Professor of Economics, Cornell University, Ithaca, N.Y.*

John H. Adler (d. 1980). *Director, Programming and Budgeting Department, International Bank for Reconstruction and Development, Washington, D.C., 1968–76.*

Joseph C. Agrella. *Correspondent,* The Blood-Horse *magazine.*

Leslie Ronald Aldous. *Head of Information Department, United Nations Association of Great Britain and Northern Ireland, 1947–66. Editor,* United Nations Association Yearbook *and* New World.

Maurice Allais. *Professor of Economic Analysis, National College of Mines of Paris. Professor of Monetary Analysis, University of Paris X, 1970–85. Nobel Prize for Economics, 1988.*

Francis A. Allen. *Huber C. Hurst Professor of Law, University of Florida, Gainesville. Edson R. Sunderland Professor Emeritus of Law, University of Michigan, Ann Arbor.*

Rex Alston. *Broadcaster and journalist. Staff Sports Commentator and Reporter, British Broadcasting Corporation, 1942–61. Cricket Reporter,* Daily *and* Sunday Telegraph *(London), 1961–88.*

John Thomas Amber. *Emeritus Editor in Chief, D.B.I. Books, Inc., Northfield, Illinois; editor of* Gun Digest, Handloader's Digest, Single Shot Actions and Rifles, *and others.*

Robert T. Anderson. *Professor of Anthropology, Mills College, Oakland, Calif.*

Jack Andresen. *Consulting Engineer. Underwater Photographer. World Champion Trick Water Skier, 1950.*

Pierre Robert Angel. *Former Professor and Head, Department of Classical and Modern Languages, Literature and Civilizations, University of Tours, Fr.*

John Armitage (d. 1980). *London Editor,* Encyclopædia Britannica, *1949–65, President, Rugby Fives Association, London, 1955–60.*

Michael Austin. *Rugby and cricket writer,* Daily Telegraph *(London).*

Robert Auty (d. 1978). *Professor of Comparative Slavonic Philology, University of Oxford, 1965–78.*

Paul Avrich. *Distinguished Professor of History, Queens College, City University of New York, Flushing.*

Hans Herman Baerwald. *Professor of Political Science, University of California, Los Angeles; Director, Study Center of the University of California, Tokyo, 1965–67; 1969–70.*

B. Devereux Barker III. *Associate, Brewer & Lord (insurance), Boston. Former Associate Editor,* Yachting *magazine.*

Victor Barna (d. 1972). *World table tennis champion, men's singles, 1930, 1932–35; men's doubles, 1929–35; mixed doubles, 1932, 1935. Author of* Tennis Today.

Harry Elmer Barnes (d. 1968). *Historian, sociologist, and writer. Author of* A History of Historical Writing *and others.*

Samuel H. Baron. *Professor of History, University of North Carolina at Chapel Hill.*

Howard Bass. *Winter sports correspondent,* Daily Telegraph *and* Sunday Telegraph *(London). Sports broadcaster, British Broadcasting Corporation World Service.*

Richard Reeve Baxter (d. 1980). *Judge, International Court of Justice, The Hague, 1979–80. Professor of Law, Harvard University, 1959–80.*

Lowell John Bean. *Professor of Anthropology, California State University, Hayward.*

Charles-Louis de Beaumont (d. 1972). *President, Amateur Fencing Association of Great Britain. President, British Commonwealth Fencing Federation. Deputy Chairman, British Olympic Association.*

John Matthew Beck. *Executive Director, Chicago Consortium of Colleges and Universities.*

Cyril S(hirley) Belshaw. *Professor of Anthropology, University of British Columbia, Vancouver.*

Ernest Bender. *Professor of Indo-Aryan Languages and Literatures, University of Pennsylvania, Philadelphia. General Editor,* Journal of the American Oriental Society.

George C.S. Benson. *Emeritus President and Professor of Political Science, Claremont Men's College, Calif.*

Ellen M. Bentsen. *Director for Development Communications, Northwestern University. Former Assistant Director for One Design Racing, U.S. Yacht Racing Union, Evanston, Ill.; Former Editor,* USYRU News.

Louis Stanley Berenson. *Owner and Chairman of the Board, Berensons' Hartford Jai-Alai, Conn.*

Stanley F. Bergstein. *Executive Vice President, Harness Tracks of America, Morristown, N.J. Vice President, Publicity—Public Relations, U.S. Trotting Association, and Executive Editor,* Hoof Beats *magazine, 1968–75.*

Ronald M. Berndt (d. 1990). *Foundation Professor of Anthropology, University of Western Australia, Nedlands, 1963–81.*

Siegfried F. Bethke. *Marketing Economist, Food and Agriculture Organization of the United Nations, Rome.*

David Bidney (d. 1987). *Professor of Anthropology and of Philosophy of Education, Indiana University, Bloomington, 1965–74.*

George W. Bishop, Jr. (d. 1974). *Professor and Head, Department of Finance, Northern Illinois University, De Kalb, 1965–74.*

Max Black (d. 1988). *Susan Linn Sage Professor of Philosophy, Cornell University, Ithaca, N.Y., 1946–77.*

Mark Blaug. *Consultant Professor of Economics, University of Buckingham, Eng. Emeritus Professor of the Economics of Education, Institute of Education, University of London.*

Friedrich Blendinger. *Director of Archives, Augsburg, W.Ger., 1966–77.*

Solomon Bluhm. *Professor of Education, Hunter College, City University of New York, 1930–59.*

George Gleason Bogert (d. 1977). *James Parker Hall Professor of Law, University of Chicago.*

Marc Bouloiseau. *Former Secretary, Commission for the Economic and Social History of the French Revolution. Emeritus Teaching Assistant in the History of the French Revolution, University of Paris.*

Marjorie Boulton. *Principal, Charlotte Mason College, Ambleside, Eng., 1962–70. Member of the Esperanto Academy, Author of* Zamenhof, Creator of Esperanto *and others.*

Jean Bouvier (d. 1987). *Professor of Economics, University of Paris I.*

William W. Brickman (d. 1986). *Professor of Educational History and Comparative Education, University of Pennsylvania, Philadelphia, 1962–81.*

Lloyd Vernet Bridges. *Actor. Author of* Masks and Flippers.

William O(liver) Bright. *Emeritus Professor of Linguistics and Anthropology, University of California, Los Angeles.*

Colin Fraser Brockington, M.D. *Emeritus Professor of Social and Preventive Medicine, Victoria University of Manchester, Eng.*

Dorothy Margaret Brodie. *Editor of Edmund Dudley's* Tree of Commonwealth.

Martin Bronfenbrenner. *Kenan Professor Emeritus of Economics, Duke University, Durham, N.C.*

Arthur Joseph Brown. *Emeritus Professor of Economics, University of Leeds, Eng.*

Lionel Neville Brown. *Professor of Comparative Law, University of Birmingham, Eng.*

William Francis Brown. *Editor,* American Field, *Chicago. Author of* How to Train Hunting Dogs *and others.*

James Robert Browning. *Chief Judge, United States Court of Appeals for the Ninth Circuit, San Francisco.*

Jean Bruhat. *Former Professor, Institute of Political Science of Paris. Former Instructor, University of Paris VIII.*

Avery Brundage (d. 1975). *President, International Olympic Committee, 1952–72.*

The Hon. Alastair Francis Buchan (d. 1976). *Montague Burton Professor of International Relations, University of Oxford, 1972–76. Founder and Director, International Institute for Strategic Studies, London, 1958–69.*

Arthur F. Burns (d. 1987). *U.S. Ambassador to the Federal Republic of Germany, 1981–85. John Bates Clark Professor of Economics, Columbia University, 1959–69. Chairman, Board of Governors, Federal Reserve System, Washington, D.C., 1970–78.*

Thomas Ferrier Burns. *Chairman of Burns and Oates Ltd., Publishers, London, 1948–67. Editor,* The Tablet.

Asa S. Bushnell (d. 1975). *Commissioner, Eastern College Athletic Conference, 1938–70.*

Robin Buss. *Lecturer in French, Woolwich College of Further Education, London.*

R. Freeman Butts. *William F. Russell Professor Emeritus in the Foundations of Education, Teachers College, Columbia University; Associate Dean for International Studies, 1964–75.*

Raoul C. van Caenegem. *Professor of Medieval History, State University of Ghent, Belgium.*

Joseph R. Caldwell. *Professor of Anthropology, University of Georgia, Athens.*

Robert Graham Caldwell. *Professor of Criminology, University of Iowa, Iowa City, 1948–72.*

Charles Clifford Callahan. *Professor of Law, Ohio State University, Columbus.*

Schuyler van Rensselaer Cammann. *Professor of East Asian Studies, University of Pennsylvania, Philadelphia.*

Archibald Hunter Campbell. *Regius Professor of Public Law, University of Edinburgh, 1945–72.*

Guillaume Cardascia. *Professor of the History of Ancient Private Law, University of Paris II.*

George Cardona. *Professor of Linguistics, University of Pennsylvania, Philadelphia.*

Michael Carey. *Cricket writer,* Daily Telegraph (*London*).

Edward H. Carr (d. 1982). *Wilson Professor of International Politics, University College of Wales, Aberystwyth, 1936–47.*

George Barr Carson, Jr. *Professor of History, Oregon State University, Corvallis.*

John Philip Carter. *Emeritus Professor of Business Administration, University of California, Berkeley.*

Joseph Cataio. *Free-lance writer.*

David Gawen Champernowne. *Professor of Economics and Statistics, University of Cambridge, 1969–78; Fellow of Trinity College, Cambridge.*

Brian Chapman (d. 1981). *Professor of Government, Victoria University of Manchester, 1961–81.*

Floyd Barton Chapman. *Ecologist, Metropolitan Park District, Columbus, Ohio.*

Elliott E. Cheatham (d. 1972). *Charles Evans Hughes Professor of Law, Columbia University, 1950–57. Research Professor of Law, Vanderbilt University, Nashville, Tenn., 1968–72.*

Charles Edward Clark (d. 1963). *Judge, 1939–63. Chief Judge, U.S. Court of Appeals, 2nd Circuit, 1954–59. Dean, Law School, Yale University, 1929–39.*

James D. Clarkson. *Research Associate, Center for South and Southeast Asian Studies, University of Michigan, Ann Arbor.*

Inis Lothair Claude, Jr. *Edward R. Stettinius, Jr., Professor of Government and Foreign Affairs, University of Virginia, Charlottesville.*

Susan Clinton. *Free-lance writer on public administration.*

Luella Cole (Mrs. R.H. Lowie) (deceased). *Author of* History of Education, from Socrates to Montessori *and others.*

Dame Margaret I. Cole (d. 1980). *Honorary President, Fabian Society, England. Author of* Beatrice Webb *and others.*

J(ohn) B. Condliffe (d. 1981). *Senior Economist, Stanford Research Institute, Menlo Park, Calif., 1961–67. Author of* The Commerce of Nations *and others.*

Bernard Earl Conor. *Corporate Vice President and President, AMF International Trade Operations, AMF, Incorporated, Stamford, Conn.*

William Stewart Cornyn (d. 1971). *Professor of Slavic and Southeast Asian Linguistics, Yale University.*

Frank A. Cowell. *Lecturer in Economics, London School of Economics and Political Science, University of London.*

Denis Victor Cowen. *Former Professor of Law, University of Chicago. Former Professor of Comparative Law, University of Cape Town, S.Af.*

Robert Cowen. *Senior Lecturer in Comparative Education, Institute of Education, University of London.*

Warren Cowgill (d. 1985). *Professor of Indo-European Linguistics, Yale University, 1972–85.*

Robert L. Crain. *Senior Social Scientist, Rand Corporation, at the Center for the Social Organization of Schools, Johns Hopkins University, Baltimore.*

Lawrence A. Cremin (d. 1990). *Frederick A.P. Barnard Professor of Education, Teachers College, Columbia University, 1961–90.*

Robert A. Cromie. *Host, "Book Beat," National Educational Television. Daily Columnist,* Chicago Tribune, *1969–74.*

Brainerd Currie (d. 1965). *Professor of Law, Duke University, Durham, N.C., 1961–65.*

Stanley James Curtis (deceased). *Reader in Education, University of Leeds, Eng., 1955–58; Honorary Lecturer in Medieval Philosophy, 1934–58.*

Allison Danzig (d. 1987). *Sportswriter,* The New York Times, *1923–68. Author of* The History of American Football *and others.*

Bernard Darwin (d. 1961). *Golf Correspondent,* Country Life, *1907–61, and* The Times (*London*), *1919–58.*

John P. Davis (d. 1973). *Editor of Special Publications, Phelps-Stokes Fund, N.Y. Editor of* The American Negro Reference Book.

Alan Charles Lynn Day. *Professor of Economics, London School of Economics and Political Science, University of London.*

George Henry John Daysh (d. 1987). *Professor of Geography, University of Newcastle upon Tyne, Eng., 1963–66.*

Martin Dell (d. 1966). *Cartoonist and Puzzle Maker, Chicago Tribune Syndicate.*

Carl Thomas Devine. *Professor of Accounting, Florida State University, Tallahassee.*

Dudley Dillard (d. 1991). *Professor and Head, Department of Economics, University of Maryland, College Park.*

Mary Earhart Dillon. *Emerita Professor of Political Science, Queens College, City University of New York.*

William H. Dodge. *Professor of Business, University of Wisconsin, Madison.*

Michael Hugh Donovan. *Free-lance economic journalist. Former Editor,* Retail Business (*monthly*), Economist Intelligence Unit, London.

Joseph Dorfman (d. 1991). *Professor of Economics, Columbia University, 1948–70.*

Robert Dorfman. *Emeritus Professor of Economics, Harvard University.*

Douglas F. Dowd. *Professor of Economics, San Jose State University, Calif. Professorial Lecturer in International Economics, Johns Hopkins University School of Advanced International Studies, Bologna Center, Italy.*

Harold Edson Driver. *Emeritus Professor of Anthropology, Indiana University, Bloomington.*

John W. Dudderidge. *President of Honour, British Canoe Union. Honorary Member, International Canoe Federation. Vice President, British Olympic Association.*

Ralph Craigon Dudrow, Jr. *Former Director for the Red Cross Centenary, League of Red Cross Societies, Geneva.*

John F. Due. *Emeritus Professor of Economics, University of Illinois at Urbana-Champaign.*

Allison Dunham. *Arnold I. Shure Professor Emeritus of Urban Law, University of Chicago.*

Charles Émile Durand. *Former Professor of Constitutional Law, University of Aix-Marseille, Aix-en-Provence, France.*

Isidore Dyen. *Professor of Comparative Linguistics and Austronesian Languages, Yale University.*

John K. Dyer, Jr. *Independent Actuary.*

George Dykhuizen. *Emeritus Professor of Philosophy, University of Vermont, Burlington.*

Karl August Eckhardt. *Former Professor of Law, University of Berlin.*

John Percy Eddy (d. 1975). *Queen's Counsel; Recorder of West Ham, 1936–49; Stipendiary Magistrate for East and West Ham, 1949–54.*

Robert Romain Edge. *Former Associate Editor,* Sports Afield. *Outdoor Editor, American Broadcasting Company.*

Fred R. Eggan (d. 1991). *Harold H. Swift Distinguished Service Professor of Anthropology, University of Chicago, 1963–74.*

Paul Einzig (d. 1973). *London Correspondent,* The Commercial and Financial Chronicle (*New York*), *1945–73.*

Daniel Judah Elazar. *Director, Center for the Study of Federalism; Professor of Political Science, Temple University, Philadelphia. Senator N.M. Paterson Professor of Intergovernmental Relations, Bar-Ilan University, Ramat Gan, Israel.*

Adolphus Peter Elkin (d. 1979). *Professor of Anthropology, University of Sydney, 1934–56.*

Norman Robson Elliott. *Senior Lecturer in Geography, University of Edinburgh.*

Manuel C(onrad) Elmer (deceased). *Professor and Head, Department of Sociology, University of Pittsburgh.*

Alex Elson. *Attorney. Coauthor of* Illinois Civil Practice Forms *and others.*

Linn Emrich. *Manager, Skyport Airfield, Issaquah, Washington. Professional balloonist, parachutist, and pilot.*

Ralph Erickson. *Physical Education Instructor; Swimming and Water Polo Coach, Loyola University, Chicago.*

Emory Gibbons Evans. *Professor and Chairman, Department of History, University of Maryland, College Park.*

Gordon Page Evans (d. 1991). *Secretary, Standing Conference on the Economic and Social Work of the United Nations, 1952–68.*

Gwynfor Evans. *Member of Parliament for Carmarthen, Wales, 1966–70; 1974–79. President, Plaid Cymru, 1945–81.*

Frank Fairfax. *Visiting Lecturer, Center for Afro-American and African Studies, University of Michigan, Ann Arbor.*

Charles Fairman. *Emeritus Professor of Law, Harvard University.*

David I. Fand. *Professor of Economics, Wayne State University, Detroit.*

Dan Farley. *Managing Editor,* The Thoroughbred Record.

Louis C. Faron. *Professor of Anthropology, State University of New York at Stony Brook.*

David Fellman. *Vilas Professor Emeritus of Political Science, University of Wisconsin, Madison.*

Charles G. Fenwick (d. 1973). *Director, Department of International Law, Pan American Union, Washington, D.C., 1948–62. Professor of Political Science, Bryn Mawr College, Pa., 1918–40.*

Cornelia Van Hook Ferber. *Economist, Office of Programs and Research, Export-Import Bank of the United States.*

John Henry Webb Fingleton (d. 1981). *Journalist. International Cricketer, 1931–38. Author of* Cricket Crisis *and others.*

Lawrence E. Fisher. *Director of Graduate Studies, Department of Anthropology, Loyola University, Chicago.*

Ossip K. Flechtheim. *Emeritus Professor of Political Science, Free University, Berlin.*

Henry Hubbard Foster, Jr. (d. 1988). *Professor of Law, New York University, New York City, 1962–77.*

Robert Allen Fowkes. *Emeritus Professor of Germanic Languages, New York University, New York City.*

Henry Waller Fowler, Jr. *Securities trader. Author of* Kites *and others.*

Michel François. *Professor of the History of French Institutions, École Nationale des Chartes, Paris. Secretary General, International Committee of Historical Sciences.*

Phyllis Frederick. *Toy and game designer, Mattel Inc., Hawthorne, Calif.*

Richard L(incoln) Frey (d. 1988). *Editor in Chief,* Official Encyclopædia of Bridge, *1964–76. Editor,* The Contract Bridge Bulletin, *1958–70. President, International Bridge Press Association, 1970–81.*

(Jerome) Ed(ison) Friel. *Sportswriter,* Newark (*N.J.*) News. *Former President, New York Track Writers Association.*

Harold T. Friermood. *Former Chairman, Education Council, United States Olympic Committee. Editor of* When Volleyball Began *and others.*

Lon L. Fuller (d. 1978). *Carter Professor of General Jurisprudence, Harvard University, 1948–72.*

Joseph William Garbarino. *Professor of Business Administration, University of California, Berkeley.*

Charles Garratt-Holden. *Former Secretary, The Building Societies Association, London.*

Paul Henry Gebhard. *Emeritus Professor of Anthropology, Indiana University, Bloomington; former Director, Institute for Sex Research.*

Ignace J. Gelb (d. 1985). *Frank P. Hixon Distinguished Service Professor, Oriental Institute and Departments of Linguistics and of Near Eastern Languages and Civilizations, University of Chicago, 1965–79.*

David George. *Journalist and free-lance writer on sports.*

O. Benjamin Gerig (d. 1976). *Director, Office of Dependent Area Affairs, U.S. Department of State, 1945–62.*

Colin Gibson. *Rugby League writer,* Daily Telegraph (*London*).

Douglas Stuart Gilbert (d. 1979). *Sports columnist*, Edmonton Sun, *1978–79. Sports reporter*, Montreal Gazette, *1970–78.*

Peter Robin Gimbel (d. 1987). *Film Producer and Director*, Blue Water, White Death *and others.*

Alexander Hayden Girard. *Architect.*

Geoffrey R. Gleeson. *International judo consultant. Executive Officer, British Association of National Coaches. Author of* Judo for the West *and others.*

Oscar R. Goodman (d. 1985). *Professor of Ecomonics and Finance, Roosevelt University, Chicago, 1966–85.*

Charles H. Goren (d. 1991). *Author and lecturer. Bridge Editor, Chicago Tribune-New York News Syndicate. Author of* Contract Bridge Complete *and others.*

E. Kathleen Gough Aberle (d. 1990). *Research Associate in Anthropology, University of British Columbia, Vancouver. Professor of Anthropology, Simon Fraser University, Burnaby, B.C., 1967–70.*

Frank Graner. *Professor of Finance, University of Wisconsin, Madison.*

Leo Gross (d. 1990). *Professor of International Law, Tufts University, Medford, Mass, 1943–80.*

David Lawrence Grove. *President, U.S. Council, International Chamber of Commerce. Vice President and Chief Economist, International Business Machines Corp., Armonk, N.Y., 1969–78.*

Seli Groves. *Free-lance writer.*

Claude William Guillebaud (d. 1971). *Lecturer in Economics, University of Cambridge, 1926–56.*

Lealand Roger Gustavson (d. 1966). *Artist and illustrator. Author of* Winning Badminton *and others.*

Harry G. Guthmann. *Morrison Professor Emeritus of Finance, Northwestern University, Evanston, Ill.*

Gottfried Haberler. *Emeritus Professor of International Trade, Harvard University.*

Green H. Hackworth (d. 1973). *Judge, International Court of Justice, The Hague, 1946–61.*

Eric P. Hamp. *Robert Maynard Hutchins Distinguished Service Professor of Linguistics, of Psychology, and of Slavic Languages; Director, Center for Balkan and Slavic Studies, University of Chicago.*

Moffatt Hancock. *Kirkwood Professor Emeritus of Law, Stanford University, Calif.*

Frank Hamilton Hankins (d. 1970). *Professor of Sociology, Smith College, Northampton, Mass., 1922–46.*

Jerry F. Hardy. *Coordinator for Gymnastics, Amateur Athletic Union of the United States. Member, Board of Directors, U.S. Gymnastics Federation. Member, U.S. Men's Olympic Gymnastic Committee, 1940; 1952–72.*

Fred Harvey Harrington. *Vilas Research Professor of American Diplomatic History, University of Wisconsin, Madison; President of the University of Wisconsin, 1962–70.*

Herbert Lionel Adolphus Hart. *Principal of Brasenose College, Oxford, 1973–78; Professor of Jurisprudence, University of Oxford, 1952–68.*

Joseph R. Hartley. *Professor of Business Administration, Indiana University, Bloomington.*

Nancy Kymn Harvin. *Free-lance writer.*

Harlan Henthorne Hatcher. *President Emeritus, University of Michigan, Ann Arbor.*

Robert J. Havighurst (d. 1991). *Professor of Education and of Human Development, University of Chicago, 1941–65.*

Robert D. Herman. *Professor of Sociology, Pomona College, Claremont, Calif.*

D. Alan Heslop. *Director, Rose Institute of State and Local Government, Claremont McKenna College, Calif.*

Forest Garrett Hill. *Professor of Economics, University of Texas at Austin.*

J. E. Christopher Hill. *Master, Balliol College, University of Oxford, 1965–78.*

Norman Llewellyn Hill (d. 1976). *Professor of International Law and Relations, University of Nebraska, Lincoln, 1935–63.*

Finn Hiorthøy. *Judge of the Supreme Court of Norway, Oslo, 1955–73.*

Frank Hole. *Professor and Chairman, Department of Anthropology, Yale University.*

(George) Kenneth Holland (d. 1977). *President, Institute of International Education, Inc., New York City, 1950–73.*

Bert Frank Hoselitz. *Emeritus Professor of the Social Sciences and Economics, University of Chicago.*

Cyril O. Houle. *Emeritus Professor of Education, University of Chicago.*

Ralph Gordon Hoxie. *President, Center for the Study of the Presidency, New York City. Chancellor, Long Island University, Greenvale, N.Y., 1964–68.*

Edward M. Hutchinson. *Educational consultant. Secretary, National Institute of Adult Education, London, 1947–71; Editor,* Adult Education *journal, 1949–71.*

Ford Hutchinson. *Free-lance writer.*

Terence Wilmot Hutchison. *Emeritus Professor of Economics, University of Birmingham, Eng.*

John Henry Hutton (d. 1968). *William Wyse Professor of Social Anthropology, University of Cambridge, 1937–50.*

James Nevins Hyde. *Lawyer.*

Jozef A.M.K. IJsewijn. *Professor of Neo-Latin, Catholic University of Louvain, Belg.*

Jacques André Istel. *President, Parachutes Incorporated, Orange, Mass. Captain, U.S. parachuting team, 1956 and 1958.*

Elmore Jackson (d. 1989). *Vice President, United Nations Association of the U.S.A., 1966–73. Special Assistant for Policy Planning to the Assistant Secretary of State for International Organization Affairs, U.S. Department of State, 1961–64.*

William Turrentine Jackson. *Professor of American History, University of California, Davis.*

Per Jacobsson (d. 1963). *Managing Director, International Monetary Fund, Washington, D.C., 1956–63.*

Oswald Jacoby (d. 1984). *Author of* Oswald Jacoby's Complete Canasta *and many other works on card playing.*

Fred W. Jameson (deceased). *Manager of Educational Services, Public Relations Department, Montgomery Ward and Company, Chicago.*

Philip C. Jessup (d. 1986). *Judge, International Court of Justice, The Hague, The Netherlands, 1961–70.*

John E. Jeuck. *Robert Law Professor of Business Administration, University of Chicago.*

Gareth H. Jones. *Downing Professor of the Laws of England, University of Cambridge; Fellow of Trinity College, Cambridge.*

Bernard Joy. *Former football correspondent,* Evening Standard, *London. Author of* Soccer Tactics.

Milton Z. Kafoglis. *Professor of Economics, Emory University, Atlanta, Ga.*

Jerome Kagan. *Professor of Human Development, Harvard University.*

Nicholas deBelleville Katzenbach. *Chairman, First American Bankshares, Inc., Washington, D.C., Vice President and General Counsel, International Business Machines Corporation, Armonk, N.Y., 1969–84. Attorney General, U.S. Department of Justice, 1965–66. Under Secretary, U.S. Department of State, 1966–68.*

Terrence Kaufman. *Professor of Anthropology and Linguistics, University of Pittsburgh.*

Frank E. Keating. *Former Fishing Editor,* Newsday, *Garden City, N.Y.*

George Williams Keeton (d. 1989). *President, London Institute of World Affairs, 1952–89. Professor of English Law, University of London, 1937–69.*

William H. Kelly (d. 1980). *Professor of Anthropology, University of Arizona, Tucson, 1952–74.*

Howard H. Kendler. *Emeritus Professor of Psychology, University of California, Santa Barbara.*

Raymond P. Kent (d. 1983). *Professor of Finance and Business Economics, University of Notre Dame, Ind.*

Marshall D. Ketchum (d. 1989). *Professor of Finance, University of Chicago, 1951–71.*

V.O. Key, Jr. (d. 1963). *Jonathan Trumbull Professor of American History and Government, Harvard University, 1955–63.*

Frank Leroy Kidner. *Vice President of Educational Relations; Professor of Economics, University of California, Berkeley.*

Carol D. Kiesinger. *Arts consultant. Hiker and mountain climber. Coeditor of* The Armchair Mountaineer.

Joseph C. Kiger. *Editor in Chief, International Encyclopedia of Learned Societies and Academies.*

Charles P. Kindleberger. *Emeritus Professor of Economics, Massachusetts Institute of Technology, Cambridge.*

Vernon Kinietz. *Educator. Author of* Chippewa Village *and others.*

Clyde Vernon Kiser. *Former Senior Research Demographer, Office of Population Research, Princeton, N. J.*

Lawrence R. Klein. *Benjamin Franklin Professor of Economics, University of Pennsylvania, Philadelphia. Nobel Prize for Economics, 1980.*

Paul Lincoln Kleinsorge. *Emeritus Professor of Economics, University of Oregon, Eugene.*

Paul E. Klopsteg (d. 1991). *Professor of Applied Science, Northwestern University, Evanston, Ill., 1944–54.*

George Frederick Kneller. *Emeritus Professor of Education, University of California, Los Angeles.*

Ole Ferdinand Knudsen. *Editor, Export Council of Norway, Oslo.*

Herman Kogan (d. 1989). *Journalist. Corporate Historian, Field Enterprises, Inc., 1977–89. Author of* The Great EB.

Omari Kokole. *Assistant Professor of Political Science, State University of New York at Binghamton.*

Walter Korn. *Author of* The Brilliant Touch in Chess; Modern Chess Openings; *and others.*

John Richard Krueger. *Former Professor of Uralic and Altaic Studies, Indiana University, Bloomington.*

Philip B. Kurland. *William R. Kenan, Jr., Distinguished Service Professor of Law, University of Chicago. Editor of* The Supreme Court Review.

Peter N. Ladefoged. *Professor of Phonetics, University of California, Los Angeles.*

Harry Wellington Laidler (d. 1970). *Executive Director, League for Industrial Democracy.*

Clay Lancaster. *Author of* Japanese Influence in America; Architectural Follies in America; *and others.*

Gerard Eduard Langemeijer. *Attorney General, Supreme Court of the Netherlands, The Hague, 1957–73.*

Luce-Andrée Langevin. *Honorary Professor; former teacher of physical science, Lycée Fénelon, Paris. Author of* Lomonossov.

George E. Lardner (deceased). *Associate Editor, Bell-McClure Syndicate, Inc., New York City.*

Richard C. Latham. *Partner, Seay & Latham Investments, Dallas, Texas. Coauthor of* United States Polo Association Annual.

Gilbert P. Laue. *Former Chief Copy Editor, Richard D. Irwin, Inc., Homewood, Ill. Former Associate Editor, Sports,* Encyclopædia Britannica, Chicago.

Elihu Lauterpacht. *Barrister-at-Law. Fellow of Trinity College, Cambridge; Reader in International Law, University of Cambridge.*

Sir Edmund Ronald Leach (d. 1989). *Provost of King's College, Cambridge, 1966–79; Professor of Social Anthropology, University of Cambridge, 1972–78.*

James Elzar Lebensohn, M.D. *Associate Professor Emeritus of Ophthalmology, Northwestern University, Chicago.*

Colin Legum. *Associate Editor,* The Observer, London, *1949–82. Editor,* Africa Contemporary Record, *1968–83.*

Richard M. Leighton. *Military historian and consultant. Professor of National Security Affairs, National Defense University, U.S. Department of Defense, Washington, D.C., 1965–78.*

George Eidt Lent. *Assistant Director, Tax Policy Division, International Monetary Fund, Washington, D.C., 1964–75.*

Don Divance Lescohier (d. 1961). *Professor of Economics, University of Wisconsin, Madison, 1918–61.*

Robert Alan LeVine. *Roy E. Larsen Professor of Education and Human Development, Harvard University.*

David L. Lewis. *Professor of History, Howard University, Washington, D.C.*

Choh-Ming Li (d. 1991). *Professor of Business Administration, University of California, Berkeley, 1958–64. Vice-Chancellor, Chinese University of Hong Kong, 1964–78.*

Fang Kuei Li (d. 1987). *Professor of Chinese Linguistics and Anthropology, University of Washington, Seattle, 1959–69. Professor of Asian Linguistics, University of Hawaii, Honolulu, 1969–73.*

Alfred Lief. *Biographer and business historian.*

Joseph Colville Lincoln. *Author of* Soaring for Diamonds.

Genevieve Collins Linebarger. *Associate Professor of Political Science, Trinity College, Washington, D.C., 1967–68.*

Paul M.A. Linebarger (d. 1966). *Professor of Asiatic Politics, School of Advanced International Studies, Johns Hopkins University, Washington, D.C., 1946–66.*

Kwang-Ching Liu. *Professor of History, University of California, Davis.*

Karl Nickerson Llewellyn (d. 1962). *Professor of Law, University of Chicago, 1951–62.*

Laurence Lockhart (d. 1975). *Member of the Faculty of Oriental Studies, University of Cambridge.*

Erwin Hugo Loewenfeld (deceased). *Solicitor of the Supreme Court, Great Britain. Member of the Faculty of Law, University of Cambridge. Legal Adviser, Liechtenstein Government.*

James Rubert Longstreet. *Professor of Finance, University of South Florida, Tampa.*

Jo Desha Lucas. *Arnold I. Shure Professor of Law, University of Chicago.*

Alma Lutz (d. 1973). *Author of* Susan B. Anthony, Rebel, Crusader, Humanitarian *and others.*

John P. Lyall. *Marine Information Specialist and Sailing Directions Writer, Sailing Directions Branch, U.S. Naval Oceanographic Office, Washington, D.C.*

Sir John Lyons. *Master of Trinity Hall, University of Cambridge. Professor of Linguistics, University of Sussex, Brighton, Eng., 1976–84.*

John Dennis McCallum (d. 1988). *Author of* That Kelly Family; The Tiger Wore Spikes; Big Eight Football; *and others.*

Wendell McClean. *Research Assistant, Institute of Social and Economic Research, University of the West Indies, Kingston, Jamaica.*

John McDowell (d. 1974). *Director for Social Welfare, National Council of the Churches of Christ in the U.S.A., 1967–73.*

Joseph E. McGrath. *Professor of Psychology, University of Illinois, Urbana.*

James Angell MacLachlan (d. 1967). *Professor of Law, Harvard University, 1927–60.*

Charles R. McLoud. *Head, Sailing Directions Branch, U.S. Naval Oceanographic Office, Washington, D.C.*

(Ardee) Wayne McMillen. *General Consultant, Bay Area Social Planning Council, Oakland, Calif. Professor of Social Service Administration, University of Chicago, 1936–60.*

Arnold Duncan McNair, 1st Baron McNair (d. 1975). *President, International Court of Justice, 1952–55; Judge, 1946–55.*

Edward McWhinney. *Queen's Counsel. Professor of Constitutional and International Law, Simon Fraser University, Burnaby, B.C.*

Norris Dewar McWhirter. *Television commentator, Olympic Games, British Broadcasting Corporation, 1960–72. Compiler,* Guinness Book of World Records; Dunlop Book of Facts.

Philip Maher. *Free-lance writer.*

Janice Grow Maienza. *Free-lance writer.*

Reginald Francis Malcolmson. *Professor of Architecture, University of Michigan, Ann Arbor.*

Martin E. Malia. *Professor of History, University of California, Berkeley.*

Yakov Malkiel. *Professor of Linguistics and Romance Philology, University of California, Berkeley.*

Sir James Gow Mann (d. 1962). *Surveyor of the Queen's Works of Art, 1946–62. Master of the Armouries, The Tower of London, 1939–62.*

Benigno Mantilla Pineda. *Professor of the Sociology and Philosophy of Law, University of Antioquia, Medellín, Colom.*

Julius Margolis. *Professor of Economics, University of California, Irvine.*

McKim Marriott. *Professor of Anthropology, University of Chicago.*

John C. Martin. *Director, Navigational Information Services Division, U.S. Naval Oceanographic Office, Washington, D.C.*

Roscoe C. Martin (d. 1972). *Professor of Political Science, Syracuse University, N.Y., 1949–72.*

Erich Matthias (d. 1983). *Professor of Contemporary History and Political Science, University of Mannheim, W.Ger.*

Wilhelm Matull (deceased). *Senior Civil Servant, National Centres for Political Education, Hannover, Bonn, and Düsseldorf, W.Ger., 1954–68.*

Harold M. Mayer. *Professor of Geography, University of Wisconsin, Milwaukee.*

John F. Mee (d. 1985). *Mead Johnson Professor of Management, Indiana University, Bloomington.*

Ben Scudder Meeker. *Chief U.S. Probation Officer and Director of Training Center, Chicago.*

Patrick Denis Mehigan (deceased). *Author of* History of Hurling; History of Irish Athletics; *and others.*

Lois Bannister Merk. *Lecturer in History, Northeastern University, Boston, 1956–68.*

Ford Messamore (d. 1962). *Professor of Stockton College, Canton, Mo.*

Michael Charles Meston. *Professor of Scots Law, University of Aberdeen, Scot.*

Adolphe Erich Meyer (d. 1988). *Professor of Educational History, New York University, New York City, 1946–63.*

Karl W. Meyer. *Chancellor, University of Wisconsin, Superior.*

Karl B. Michael. *Emeritus Swimming Coach, Dartmouth College, Hanover, N.H. U.S. Olympic Team Men's Diving Coach, 1956.*

John Francis Marchment Middleton. *Professor of Anthropology, Yale University.*

Elmer Mayse Million (d. 1990). *Professor of Law, University of Oklahoma, Norman, 1970–83.*

Aron Leonard Minkes. *Professor of Business Organization, University of Birmingham, Eng.*

Broadus Mitchell (d. 1988). *Professor of Economics, Rutgers University, New Brunswick, N.J., 1949–58.*

Laura Molzahn. *Free-lance writer.*

Ashley Montagu. *Biological and cultural anthropologist. Professor and Chairman, Department of Anthropology, Rutgers University, New Brunswick, N.J., 1949–55.*

Patrick Wykeham Montague-Smith. *Consulting Editor,* Debrett's Peerage; *Editor, 1962–80.*

John Michael Montias. *Professor of Economics, Yale University.*

Lynn Montross (d. 1961). *Historian, United States Marine Corps, 1950–61.*

The Rev. E. Garth Moore. *Barrister-at-Law. Chancellor, Dioceses of Durham, Southwark and Gloucester. Fellow of Corpus Christi College, University of Cambridge.*

Albert H. Morehead (d. 1966). *Writer and editor. Bridge editor,* The New York Times, *1935–63.*

Hans J. Morgenthau (d. 1980). *Albert A. Michelson Distinguished Service Professor of Political Science and Modern History, University of Chicago, 1963–68. Leonard Davis Distinguished Professor of Political Science, City College, City University of New York, 1968–74.*

Cyril John Morley. *Former Honorary Secretary, British Falconers' Club and International Association of Falconry and Conservation of Birds of Prey.*

James William Morley. *Professor of Government, Columbia University.*

Geoffrey Mott-Smith (d. 1960). *Editor,* The Bridge World, *1936–46;* Games Digest, *1938–39, Author of* Book of Hobbies *and others.*

Nicos Panayiotou Mouzelis. *Senior Lecturer in Sociology, London School of Economics and Political Science, University of London.*

George Peter Murdock (d. 1985). *Andrew Mellon Professor of Social Anthropology, University of Pittsburgh, 1960–73.*

Lawrence Nabers. *Professor of Economics, University of Utah, Salt Lake City.*

Manning Nash. *Professor of Anthropology, University of Chicago.*

Phil Caldwell Neal. *Harry A. Bigelow Professor Emeritus of Law, University of Chicago.*

Carl Leroy Nelson. *George O. May Professor of Financial Accounting, Columbia University.*

Jeannette Paddock Nichols. *Historian, University of Pennsylvania, Philadelphia, 1969–78; Associate Professor of History, 1957–61.*

Maurice Nockles. *Press and Information Officer, Board of Customs and Excise, London.*

Val Nolan, Jr. *Emeritus Professor of Law and of Biology, Indiana University, Bloomington.*

Jan P. Norbye. *Free-lance writer on automobiles. Former International Editor,* Automotive News.

Douglass Cecil North. *Professor of Economics, University of Washington, Seattle.*

Robert C. North. *Emeritus Professor of Political Science, Stanford University, Calif.*

D.P. O'Brien. *Professor of Economics, University of Durham, Eng.*

A.C. Olshen. *Actuarial consultant. Former Senior Vice President and Director, West Coast Life Insurance Company, San Francisco.*

Morris Edward Opler. *Emeritus Professor of Anthropology, Cornell University, Ithaca, N.Y.*

Keith Langford Osborne. *Honorary Editor of* British Rowing Almanack.

Herbert L. Packer (d. 1972). *Professor of Law, Stanford University, Calif.*

Roland Palmedo (d. 1977). *President, Amateur Ski Club of New York. Cofounder, National Ski Patrol.*

Robert Parienté. *Editor in Chief, L'Équipe (daily sports newspaper), Paris.*

Ralph Halstead Parker. *Emeritus Dean, School of Library and Information Science, University of Missouri, Columbia.*

Charles William Parkin. *Fellow and Lecturer of Clare College, University of Cambridge.*

Cyril Northcote Parkinson. *Raffles Professor of History, University of Malaya, 1950–58.*

Maureen L.P. Patterson. *Former Associate Professor of South Asian Languages and Civilizations; former South Asia Bibliographic Specialist, University of Chicago.*

Kosta Stevan Pavlowitch. *Librarian, Department of Slavonic Studies, University of Cambridge. Yugoslav diplomat, 1928–45.*

Andrew K. Pawley. *Professor of Linguistics, Research School of Pacific Studies, Australian National University, Canberra.*

Adamantios A. Pepelasis. *Former Professor of Economics, Virginia Polytechnic Institute and State University, Blacksburg.*

R. Scott Perry. *Free-lance writer on education.*

Frederick William Pethick-Lawrence, 1st Baron Pethick-Lawrence (d. 1961). *Secretary of State for India and Burma, 1945–47. Privy Councillor.*

James L. Phillips. *Associate Professor of Archaeology; Director, Graduate Studies in Archaeology, University of Illinois, Chicago.*

Joseph Dexter Phillips. *Research Professor, Bureau of Economic and Business Research, University of Illinois, Urbana.*

Donald L. Piccard. *Balloon designer and manufacturer.*

Jean Felix Piccard (d. 1963). *Professor of Aeronautical Engineering, University of Minnesota, Minneapolis. F.A.I. Balloon Pilot.*

Jeannette Piccard (d. 1981). *Consultant to the Director, National Aeronautical and Space Administration Manned Spacecraft Center, Houston, Texas, 1964–70.*

Francis S. Pierce. *Editor, Congressional Budget Office, Washington, D.C. Associate Editor, Economics, Encyclopædia Britannica, Chicago, 1967–73.*

George Wilson Pierson. *Larned Professor Emeritus of History, Yale University.*

John Pincus. *Economic consultant. Former Manager, California Program, Rand Corporation, Santa Monica.*

William M. Pinkerton. *Former News Officer for the University, Harvard University.*

Frederick P. Pittera. *Chairman, International Exposition Consultants Co. President, Frederick Pittera and Associates, Inc. Author of* The Art and Science of International Fairs and Exhibitions *and others.*

Cecil Wilson Plant. *Honorary Secretary, International Water Polo Board.*

Earl Edward Pollock. *Member of the law firm of Sonnenschein, Carlin, Nath & Rosenthal, Chicago.*

David Morris Potter (d. 1971). *William R. Coe Professor of American History, Stanford University, Calif., 1961–71.*

Pitman Benjamin Potter (d. 1981). *Grozier Professor of International Law, American University, Washington, D.C., 1944–57.*

Raphael Powell (d. 1965). *Professor of Roman Law, University of London, 1955–64.*

Arnold H. Price. *Bibliographer, American Historical Association, Washington, D.C. Former Area Specialist for Central Europe, Library of Congress, Washington, D.C.*

Francis Douglas Price. *Former Lecturer in Modern History, University of Oxford.*

Jack H. Prost. *Associate Professor of Physical Anthropology, University of Illinois, Chicago.*

Roy Pryce. *Visiting Professor, European Institute of Public Administration, Maastricht, Neth. Director, Directorate General for Information, Commission of the European Communities, Brussels, 1973–78.*

Jean Puhvel. *Professor of Classics and Indo-European Studies, University of California, Los Angeles.*

Ernst Pulgram. *Hayward Keniston Distinguished Professor Emeritus of Romance and Classical Linguistics, University of Michigan, Ann Arbor.*

Peter George Julius Pulzer. *Gladstone Professor of Government and Public Administration, University of Oxford.*

Nathan Marsh Pusey. *President of Harvard University, 1953–71.*

Robert Mantle Rattenbury (d. 1970). *Registrary, University of Cambridge, 1953–69.*

Helen B. Redl. *Professor of Early Child Education, North Adams State College, Mass.*

Jerry Reedy. *Free-lance writer.*

David Allen Revzan. *Emeritus Professor of Marketing, University of California, Berkeley.*

Max Rheinstein (d. 1977). *Max Pam Professor of Comparative Law, University of Chicago, 1942–68.*

Madeleine Hooke Rice. *Emeritus Professor of History, Hunter College, City University of New York.*

Ivor Armstrong Richards (d. 1979). *Professor of English, Harvard University, 1944–63.*

John Henry Richardson (d. 1970). *United Nations Technical Assistance Adviser (International Labour Office), 1956–65. President, Aden Industrial Court, 1960–66. Professor of Industrial Relations, University of Leeds, Eng., 1930–55.*

Jack L. Roach. *Professor of Sociology, University of Connecticut, Storrs.*

Janet K. Roach. *Instructor in Sociology, Eastern Connecticut State College, Willimantic.*

Allen Roberts. *Former Professor of Anthropology, University of Michigan, Ann Arbor.*

Benjamin Charles Roberts. *Emeritus Professor of Industrial Relations, London School of Economics and Political Science, University of London.*

John Morris Roberts. *Warden, Merton College, University of Oxford.*

Sir Dennis Holme Robertson (d. 1963). *Professor of Political Economy, University of Cambridge, 1944–57.*

William H.P. Robertson (deceased). *Editor-Publisher,* The Thoroughbred Record; *Chairman, Record Publishing Company, Inc., Lexington, Kentucky.*

Robert Robson. *Fellow and Tutor of Trinity College, University of Cambridge. Author of* The Attorney in Eighteenth Century England.

William Alexander Robson (d. 1980). *Professor of Public Administration, University of London, 1947–62.*

C.H. Rolph. *Director, New Statesman, London, 1965–80; staff writer, 1946–70. Author of* Law and the Common Man *and others.*

Raymond de Roover (d. 1972). *Professor of History, Brooklyn College, City University of New York.*

Rabbi Samuel Rosenblatt. *Former Professor of Oriental Languages, Johns Hopkins University, Baltimore.*

Margaret Keeney Rosenheim. *Helen Ross Professor of Social Service Administration, University of Chicago.*

Elliot Rudwick (d. 1985). *Professor of Sociology and of History; Senior Research Fellow, Center for Urban Regionalism, Kent State University, Ohio.*

Raymond A. Ruge. *President, Eastern Ice Yachting Association, 1948, 1959–60; Secretary, 1938–42.*

Don Russell (d. 1986). *Free-lance writer. Author of* The Wild West: A History of the Wild West Shows *and others.*

Alan Ryalls. *Editor,* Camping and Caravanning *magazine, Camping Club of Great Britain and Ireland, 1956–75. Author of* Modern Camping *and others.*

M.J. Ryan. *Former Professor of Constitutional Law, University College, Dublin.*

John E. Sadler. *Head, Education Department, City of Birmingham College of Education, University of Birmingham, Eng., 1950–67.*

Wolfgang Sauer. *Professor of History, University of California, Berkeley.*

Donald Sayenga. *Author of "The Oldest Sport," a series of articles on the history of wrestling, in* Amateur Wrestling News.

John Scarne (d. 1985). *President, John Scarne Games, Inc., North Bergen, N.J. Author of* Scarne's Complete Guide to Gambling *and others.*

Joseph B. Schechtman (d. 1970). *President, United Zionist Revisionists of America.*

Donald Schiffer (d. 1964). *Editor, Sport and Outdoor Book Division, Thos. Nelson and Sons, New York City.*

Elmer Schmierer. *Colonel, U.S. Army, Infantry (retired).*

Helmut Schoeck. *Professor of Sociology, Johannes Gutenberg University, Mäinz, Ger.*

Albert Schoenfield. *Swimmer.*

G. Richard Schreiber. *President, National Automatic Merchandising Association, Chicago.*

Gerhard Schulz. *Professor of Contemporary History; Director, Seminar of Contemporary History, University of Tübingen, Ger.*

Georg Schwarzenberger. *Emeritus Professor of International Law, University of London. Vice President, London Institute of World Affairs.*

Egon Schwelb (d. 1979). *Principal Officer, Office of Legal Affairs, United Nations, New York City; Deputy Director, Division of Human Rights, 1947–62. Senior Fellow and Lecturer in Law, Yale University, 1962–68.*

Austin Wakeman Scott, Jr. (d. 1966). *Professor of Law, University of Colorado, Boulder.*

Thomas A. Sebeok. *Distinguished Professor of Linguistics and Semiotics; Professor of Anthropology and of Folklore; Chairman, Research Center for Language and Semiotic Studies, Indiana University, Bloomington.*

Melvin Seeman. *Professor of Sociology, University of California, Los Angeles.*

Odell Shepard (d. 1967). *Author of* Pedlar's Progress, The Life of Bronson Alcott *and others.*

Kate Silber (deceased). *Senior Lecturer in German, University of Edinburgh, 1963–73.*

David L. Sills. *Executive Associate, Social Science Research Council, New York City.*

Stanley C. Silverberg. *Director of Research, Federal Deposit Insurance Corporation, Washington, D.C.*

Helen Silving. *Professor of Law, University of Puerto Rico, 1957–76.*

Edwin Howard Simmons. *Brigadier General, U.S. Marine Corps; Director, Marine Corps History and Museums, Arlington, Va.*

Denis Sinor. *Distinguished Professor Emeritus of Uralic and Altaic Studies and of History, Indiana University, Bloomington.*

Gabriel Smith. *Barrister-at-Law. Departmental Editor,* Journal of Business Law.

George Alan Smith. *Arts consultant. Hiker and mountain climber. Author of* Introduction to Mountaineering.

Jack Smith. *Senior Editor,* Yachting *magazine, Cos Cobb, Conn.*

Theodore H. Smith. *Emeritus Professor of Marketing, California State College, Fullerton.*

Pincus Sober (d. 1980). *Chairman, National A.A.U. Law and Legislation Committee; Track and Field Committee, 1956–61. Chairman, U.S. Olympic Track and Field Committee, 1957–61.*

Ernst Frithiof Söderlund. *Emeritus Professor of Economic History, University of Stockholm.*

Wallace Sokolsky. *Associate Professor of History, Bronx Community College, City University of New York. Lecturer, New York University and New School for Social Research, New York City.*

Ezra Solomon. *Dean Witter Professor of Finance, Graduate School of Business, Stanford University, Calif.*

Dorothy Mary Spencer. *Visiting Lecturer in South Asia Regional Studies, University of Pennsylvania, Philadelphia.*

Joseph J. Spengler (d. 1991). *James B. Duke Professor of Economics, Duke University, Durham, N.C., 1955–71.*

Edward H. Spicer (d. 1983). *Professor of Anthropology, University of Arizona, Tucson.*

Sybille van der Sprenkel. *Former Lecturer in Sociology, University of Leeds, Eng.*

Mysore Narasimhachar Srinivas. *Professor and Head, Department of Sociology, Institute for Social and Economic Change, Bangalore, India.*

W.J. Stankiewicz. *Professor of Political Science, University of British Columbia, Vancouver.*

Helmut Dietmar Starke. *Free-lance writer on modern European history.*

Oscar State. *Former General Secretary, International Weightlifting Federation and Commonwealth Weightlifting Federation.*

Michael Steed. *Senior Lecturer in Government, Victoria University of Manchester.*

Erwin Stengel, M.D. (d. 1973). *Professor of Psychiatry, University of Sheffield, Eng.*

Wilson Stephens. *Former Editor,* The Field, *London. Coeditor of* In Praise of Hunting.

Walter Marcel Stern. *Former Senior Lecturer in Economic History, London School of Economics and Political Science, University of London.*

Henry Noel Cochrane Stevenson. *Managing Director, Scottish Television Ltd., 1961–66. Lecturer in Social Anthropology, University of Glasgow, 1950–57. Burma Frontier Service, 1926–47.*

Omer C. Stewart. *Emeritus Professor of Anthropology, University of Colorado, Boulder.*

Marcel Henri Stijns (d. 1967). *President of Honour, International Federation of Journalists. Editor in Chief,* Het Laatste Nieuws, *Brussels.*

John E. Stoner. *Emeritus Professor of Government, Indiana University, Bloomington.*

John Ford Stover. *Emeritus Professor of History, Purdue University, West Lafayette, Ind.*

Ruth Strang (d. 1971). *Professor of Education, Teachers College, Columbia University, 1940–60.*

Robert Strausz-Hupé. *U.S. Ambassador to Turkey. Emeritus Professor of Political Science, University of Pennsylvania, Philadelphia.*

Donald Stuart Strong. *Emeritus Professor of Political Science, University of Alabama, Tuscaloosa.*

Roland Stucki. *Emeritus Professor of Banking and Finance, University of Utah, Salt Lake City.*

William C. Sturtevant. *Curator, Department of Anthropology, Smithsonian Institution, Washington, D.C.*

Ernst W. Swanson. *Emeritus Professor of Economics, North Carolina State University at Raleigh.*

L.E. Sweet. *Professor of Anthropology, University of Manitoba, Winnipeg.*

Philip Taft (d. 1976). *Professor of Economics, Brown University, Providence, R.I.*

Lawrence Edward Tanner (d. 1979). *Librarian, Westminster Abbey, London, 1956–72; Keeper of the Muniments, 1926–66.*

Sol Tax. *Emeritus Professor of Anthropology, University of Chicago. Director, Center for the Study of Man, Smithsonian Institution, Washington, D.C., 1968–76.*

Sheldon Tefft. *James Parker Hall Professor Emeritus of Law, University of Chicago.*

Georges Tessier (d. 1967). *Professor of Diplomacy, École Nationale des Chartes (School of Paleography), Paris, 1930–61.*

Brinley Thomas. *Professor of Economics, University College, Cardiff, University of Wales, 1946–73.*

Bruce R. Thomas. *Free-lance writer on labour matters.*

Joseph Anthony Charles Thomas (d. 1981). *Professor of Roman Law, University of London, 1965–81.*

Terence Barrington Thomas. *Director, Gladding International Ltd. Angling correspondent,* The Field *and others. Presenter of "Angling Today," Associated Television, Birmingham, Eng.*

William Miles Webster Thomas, Baron Thomas (d. 1980). *Chairman, Britannia Airways Ltd.; Neumo Ltd.; and other companies. Director, Sun Insurance Office, Ltd. President, National Savings Committee, 1965–72.*

David Thomson (d. 1970). *Master, Sidney Sussex College, University of Cambridge, 1957–70. Author of* Europe Since Napoleon *and others.*

Lynn Thorndike (d. 1965). *Professor of History, Columbia University, 1924–52.*

Samuel Edmund Thorne. *Fairchild Professor Emeritus of Legal History, Harvard University.*

Fred J. Tickner (d. 1980). *Professor of Political Science, State University of New York at Albany.*

Nicholas S. Timasheff (d. 1970). *Professor of Sociology, Fordham University, New York City, 1949–57.*

Mischa Titiev. *Emeritus Professor of Anthropology, University of Michigan, Ann Arbor.*

Bursley Howland Titus. *Former Analyst, Department of the Army, Washington, D.C.*

Frederick Porter Todd (d. 1977). *Colonel, U.S. Army Reserve. Director, West Point Museum, U.S. Military Academy, 1953–65.*

Frederick B. Tolles (d. 1975). *Howard M. Jenkins Professor of Quaker History, Swarthmore College, Pa., 1954–70; Director, Friends Historical Library, 1941–70.*

Stanley Trapido. *Lecturer in the Government of New States, University of Oxford.*

Philip N(orton) Tucker. *Military Intelligence Research Specialist, Office of Assistant Chief of Staff, Intelligence, Department of the Army, Washington, D.C.*

Will C. Turnbladh. *Former Commissioner of Corrections, State of Minnesota.*

Lorenzo Dow Turner (d. 1972). *Professor of English, Roosevelt University, Chicago, 1946–69.*

Arthur Walter Tyler. *Former President, TYCO, Inc., Waltham, Mass.*

Frederick John Underhill. *Secretary, National Greyhound Racing Club Ltd., London.*

Dorothy Firman Van Ess (Mrs. John Van Ess) (d. 1975). *Missionary, Arabian Mission of the Reformed Church in America; Educational and social worker, Basra, Iraq, 1909–55.*

Harold Goodhue Vatter. *Professor of Economics, Portland State University, Ore.*

Francis Joseph Violich. *Professor of City Planning and of Landscape Architecture, University of California, Berkeley.*

Charles De Visscher (d. 1973). *Honorary President of the Institute of International Law. Judge, International Court of Justice, 1945–52.*

Sir Claud Humphrey Meredith Waldock (d. 1981). *Chichele Professor of Public International Law, University of Oxford, 1947–72.*

Pat Ward-Thomas. *Writer on golf.*

Donovan W.M. Waters. *Queen's Counsel. Professor of Law, University of Victoria, B.C. Associate Counsel, Douglas, Symes & Brissenden, Vancouver.*

Nathan A. Waxman. *Scholar of Caucasian languages.*

Hans W. Weigert (d. 1983). *Director, Georgetown Research Project; Research Professor of Political Geography, Georgetown University, Washington, D.C.*

Joseph Sidney Weiner (d. 1982). *Professor of Environmental Physiology, 1965–80; Director, Medical Research Council Environmental Physiology Unit, 1962–80, London School of Hygiene and Tropical Medicine, University of London.*

William Thomas Wells (d. 1990). *Queen's Counsel. Member of Parliament for Walsall, Eng., 1945–55; Walsall North, 1955–74. General Staff Officer, 2nd Grade, Directorate of Military Training, War Office, London, 1942–45.*

Hans Fritz Welzel (deceased). *Professor of Penal Law and of the Philosophy of Law, Rhenish Friedrich Wilhelm University of Bonn, W.Ger.*

Roger J.R. Whistler. *Major; Regimental Secretary, Regimental Headquarters, Royal Military Police, Roussillon Barracks, Chichester, Eng.*

Harry George Whiteman. *Writer and critic.*

Trevor Williamson. *Chief Sports Subeditor,* Daily Telegraph (*London*).

Neill Compton Wilson. *Author of* Treasure Express: Epic Days of Wells Fargo *and others.*

Robert Renbert Wilson. *James B. Duke Professor Emeritus of Political Science, Duke University, Durham, N.C.*

Hans Julius Wolff (d. 1983). *Professor of Roman Law, Albert Ludwig University of Freiburg, Freiburg im Breisgau, W.Ger.*

William Lower Wonderly. *Translations Coordinator for Latin America, United Bible Societies, Mexico City.*

Arthur Evans Wood (d. 1960). *Professor of Sociology, University of Michigan, Ann Arbor.*

Michael Henry Woodford. *Secretary, British Falconers' Club, London, 1956–67.*

Ruth Frances Woodsmall (d. 1963). *United Nations Representative of International Alliance of Women. Chief of Women's Affairs, U.S. High Commission of Germany, 1948–52. General Secretary, World YWCA, 1934–48.*

Quincy Wright (d. 1970). *Professor of International Law, University of Chicago, 1931–56.*

Frederick S. Wyle. *Attorney.*

David Eryl Corbet Yale. *Reader in English Legal History, University of Cambridge; Fellow of Christ's College, Cambridge.*

Dale Yoder (d. 1990). *Professor and Director, Bureau of Business Services and Research, California State University, Long Beach, 1967–75. Professor of Industrial Relations, Stanford University, California, 1959–66.*

Kimball Young (d. 1973). *Professor of Sociology, Northwestern University, Evanston, Ill., 1947–62.*

Carle Clark Zimmerman (deceased). *Associate Professor of Sociology, Harvard University.*

Robert Walter Zimmermann. *Retired foreign service officer, U.S. Department of State; Director, East Coast Affairs, 1976–79.*

George William Zinke. *Emeritus Professor of Economics, University of Colorado, Boulder.*

Roman J. Zorn. *Professor of History, University of Nevada, Las Vegas.*

Part Six. Art

Gerald E.H. Abraham. *President, Royal Musical Association, 1970–74. Assistant Controller of Music, British Broadcasting Corporation, London, 1962–67. James and Constance Alsop Professor of Music, University of Liverpool, Eng., 1947–62.*

Irving Abrahamson. *Associate Professor of English, Kennedy-King College, City Colleges of Chicago.*

Percy G. Adams. *Professor of English, University of Tennessee, Knoxville.*

Robert M. Adams. *Emeritus Professor of English, University of California, Los Angeles.*

Jean Adhémar (d. 1987). *Curator of Prints, Bibliothèque Nationale, Paris, 1961–87.*

Margarita Aguirre. *Writer. Author of* Las vidas de Pablo Neruda *and others.*

Walter E. Allen. *Professor of English Studies, New University of Ulster, Coleraine, N.Ire., 1968–73.*

Barthélemy Amengual. *Editor,* Études Cinématographiques. *Author of* René Clair; Clés pour le cinéma.

Reed Anderson. *Assistant Professor of Spanish and Portuguese, University of California, Davis.*

J.A. Andrups. *Author of* Latvian Literature *and others.*

Noel Gilroy Annan, Baron Annan. *Vice-Chancellor, University of London, 1978–81; Provost of University College, 1966–78. Author of* Leslie Stephen.

Joseph Anthony. *Former Special Assignments Editor,* Encyclopædia Britannica, *Chicago.*

Giovanni Aquilecchia. *Emeritus Professor of Italian, University College, University of London.*

Arthur John Arberry (d. 1969). *Sir Thomas Adams Professor of Arabic, University of Cambridge, 1947–69.*

Annette Elizabeth Armstrong. *Former Fellow and Tutor in Modern Languages, Somerville College, Oxford; former Lecturer in French Literature, University of Oxford.*

H. Harvard Arnason (d. 1986). *Art historian. Vice President for Art Administration, Solomon R. Guggenheim Foundation, New York City, 1961–69.*

Denis Midgley Arnold (d. 1986). *Heather Professor of Music, University of Oxford, 1975–86.*

Steven Arnold. *Free-lance writer on African literature.*

W. Geoffrey Arnott. *Professor of Greek Language and Literature, University of Leeds, Eng.*

Elizabeth Mary Aslin (d. 1989). *Keeper, Bethnal Green Museum, Victoria and Albert Museum, London, 1974–81.*

James Stephen Atherton (deceased). *Lecturer in English Literature, Wigan and District Mining and Technical College, England. Author of* The Books at the Wake.

Marcelle Auclair (d. 1983). *Writer. Author of* Enfances et mort de Garcia Lorca *and others.*

Hans Aurenhammer. *Former Director, Austrian State Gallery, Vienna.*

Kurt Badt (d. 1973). *Art historian. Author of* Die Kunst des Nicolas Poussin *and others.*

Anthony Cuthbert Baines. *Curator of the Bate Collection of historical wind instruments, University of Oxford, 1970–80.*

A. Craig Baird (d. 1979). *Professor of Speech, University of Iowa, Iowa City, 1928–52.*

Peter P. Baldass. *Author of* Romanische Kunst in Österreich *and others.*

Umberto Baldini. *Art historian. Director, International University of Art, Florence.*

The Rev. John Francis Bannon, S.J. (d. 1986). *Professor of History, St. Louis University, Mo., 1949–73.*

Eric Arthur Barber (d. 1965). *Rector of Exeter College, University of Oxford, 1943–56.*

Frederick P. Bargebuhr (d. 1978). *Professor of Religion, University of Iowa, Iowa City, 1962–70.*

Henry James Baron. *Professor of English, Calvin College, Grand Rapids, Mich.*

William Barr. *Senior Lecturer in Latin, University of Liverpool.*

Jean-Bertrand Barrère (d. 1985). *Professor of French Literature, University of Cambridge, 1954–82; Fellow of St. John's College, Cambridge.*

Eleanor Dodge Barton. *Former Professor and Chairman, Department of Art History, University of Hartford, West Hartford, Conn. Professor and Chairman, Department of Art, Sweet Briar College, Va., 1952–71.*

Jacques Barzun. *University Professor Emeritus, Columbia University; Dean of Faculties and Provost, 1958–67.*

Annette K. Baxter. *Professor of History, Barnard College, Columbia University. Author of* Henry Miller, Expatriate.

Germain René Michel Bazin (d. 1990). *Research Professor of Fine Arts, York University, Toronto, 1970–75. Chief Curator of Paintings and Drawings, the Louvre Museum, Paris, 1951–65.*

William Beare (d. 1963). *Professor of Latin, University of Bristol, Eng., 1931–63.*

Alexander Munro Beattie. *Emeritus Professor of English, Carleton University, Ottawa.*

Bernard Beckerman (d. 1985). *Brander Matthews Professor of Dramatic Literature, Columbia University, 1977–85.*

Karl Beckson. *Professor of English, Brooklyn College, City University of New York.*

John Bernard Beer. *Fellow of Peterhouse, Cambridge; Professor of English Literature, University of Cambridge.*

Charles G. Bell. *Poet and novelist. Tutor, St. John's College, Santa Fe, N.M. Author of* Delta Return; The Married Land; *and others.*

Benedikt Sigurdur Benedikz. *Head of Special Collections, Library, University of Birmingham, Eng.*

Susan Elizabeth Benenson. *Former Assistant Keeper, Department of Western Art, Ashmolean Museum, University of Oxford.*

Michel N. Benisovich (d. 1963). *Art historian. Instructor, New York University.*

Albert S. Bennett. *Free-lance writer. Senior Editor and Biographies Editor,* The American Heritage Dictionary of the English Language, *1966–68.*

Joan Bennett (d. 1986). *Fellow of Girton College, Cambridge; Lecturer in English, University of Cambridge, 1936–64.*

Ian D. Bent. *Professor of Music, Columbia University.*

Harry Beran. *Senior Lecturer in Philosophy, University of Wollongong, Australia.*

Walter G. Bergmann (d. 1988). *Editor, Schott and Co. Ltd., Music Publishers, London.*

John Dagfinn Bergsagel. *Musicologist, Institute of Musicology, University of Copenhagen.*

Joshua Berrett. *Assistant Professor of Humanities, Wayne State University, Detroit.*

Brenda Berrian. *Free-lance writer on African literature.*

André Berry (d. 1986). *Author of* Florilège des troubadours; Anthologie de la poésie occitane; *and others.*

Albert Bettex. *Author and lecturer. Editor,* Librarium.

Alan Curtis Birnholz. *Associate Professor of Art History, State University of New York at Buffalo.*

Easley Blackwood. *Professor of Music, University of Chicago.*

James Blades. *Lecturer on music. Professional Timpanist, formerly with the English Opera Group and English Chamber Orchestra.*

Dimitry Dimitriyevich Blagoy (d. 1984). *Professor and Head, Department of Modern Russian Literature, Institute of World Literature, Academy of Sciences of the U.S.S.R., Moscow.*

Claude Blair. *Keeper of Metalwork, Victoria and Albert Museum, London, 1972–82.*

Walter Blair. *Emeritus Professor of English, University of Chicago.*

José Manuel Blecua. *Professor of the History of Spanish Language and Literature, University of Barcelona.*

Carl Bode. *Emeritus Professor of English, University of Maryland, College Park.*

Joseph Sullivan Bolt. *Professor of Art History, University of Alabama, Tuscaloosa.*

Donald F. Bond (d. 1987). *Professor of English, University of Chicago, 1952–67.*

Jacques-Henry Bornecque. *Professor of Modern and Contemporary French Literature, University of Paris XIII.*

Marvin Sidney Borowsky (d. 1969). *Professor of Theatre Arts, University of California, Los Angeles.*

Umberto Bosco. *Emeritus Professor of Italian Language and Literature, University of Rome. Director, Enciclopedia italiana.*

Margaret Innes Bouton. *Curator in Charge of Educational Work, National Gallery of Art, Washington, D.C.*

Alan Bowness. *Director, Henry Moore Foundation, London. Director, Tate Gallery, London, 1980–88.*

Charles Ralph Boxer. *Camoens Professor Emeritus of Portuguese, King's College, University of London.*

Muriel Clara Bradbrook. *Professor of English Literature, University of Cambridge, 1965–76; Mistress of Girton College, Cambridge, 1968–76.*

Johannes Christiaan Brandt Corstius. *Former Professor of Comparative Literature, State University of Utrecht, Neth.*

Edward Kamau Brathwaite. *Poet and critic. Professor of History, University of the West Indies, Mona (Kingston), Jamaica.*

Otto J. Brendel (d. 1973). *Professor of Art History and Archaeology, Columbia University, 1956–69.*

Liliana Brisby. *Free-lance editor and writer on East-European affairs. Former Editor,* The World Today. *Author of* Les Relations russo-bulgares, 1878–1886.

Oscar Gross Brockett. *Waggener Professor of Drama, University of Texas at Austin.*

Victor Brombert. *Henry Putnam University Professor of Romance and Comparative Literature, Princeton University.*

Bernard Jocelyn Brooke (d. 1966). *Author of* The Military Orchid *and others.*

Anita Brookner. *Reader in the History of Art, Courtauld Institute of Art, University of London.*

Conrad Brown. *Emeritus Chief Editor, Adult Books, Grosset and Dunlap Inc., New York City.*

David Brown. *Emeritus Professor of Musicology, University of Southampton, Eng.*

Maurice J.E. Brown (d. 1975). *Author of* Schubert: A Critical Biography; Essays on Schubert.

Reginald Francis Brown (d. 1985). *Cowdray Professor of Spanish Language and Literature, University of Leeds, Eng., 1953–75.*

Robert Browning. *Emeritus Professor of Classics and Ancient History, Birkbeck College, University of London.*

Charlotte H. Bruner. *Professor of French, Iowa State University, Ames.*

Arnaldo Bruschi. *Professor of the History of Architecture, University of Rome.*

Doris Bry. *Writer on photography, art history, and natural science. Representative for the paintings of Georgia O'Keeffe.*

Sir Arthur Bryant (d. 1985). *Author of* Samuel Pepys *and many others.*

J.A.B. Van Buitenen (d. 1979). *Distinguished Service Professor of Sanskrit and Indic Studies, University of Chicago, 1974–79.*

Donald Burness. *Professor of English, Franklin Pierce College, Rindge, N.H.*

John Burton-Page. *Reader in the Art and Archaeology of South Asia, School of Oriental and African Studies, University of London.*

Douglas Bush (d. 1983). *Gurney Professor of English Literature, Harvard University, 1957–66.*

Joseph T. Butler. *Senior Museum Director, Historic Hudson Valley, Tarrytown, N.Y. Professor, Fashion Institute of Technology, New York City.*

Martin Butlin. *Former Keeper of the British Collection, Tate Gallery, London.*

John Everett Butt (d. 1965). *Regius Professor of Rhetoric and English Literature, University of Edinburgh, 1959–65.*

James F. Cahill. *Professor of the History of Art, University of California, Berkeley.*

Henry Seidel Canby (d. 1961). *Literary critic. Founder and Editor,* Saturday Review of Literature, *1924–36.*

Peter Cannon-Brookes. *Museum consultant. Keeper, Department of Art, National Museum of Wales, Cardiff, 1978–86.*

Harry Caplan (d. 1980). *Goldwin Smith Professor of the Classical Languages and Literature, Cornell University, Ithaca, N.Y., 1941–67.*

Sir Neville Cardus (d. 1975). *Music Critic,* The Guardian (*London*).

Margret A. Carey. *Former Assistant Keeper, Department of Ethnography, British Museum, London.*

Enzo Carli. *Director, Cathedral Museum, Siena, Italy.*

Luigi Carluccio. *Member of the arts editorial staff,* La Gazzetta del popolo, *Turin, Italy.*

Arthur H. Cash. *Distinguished Professor of English, State University of New York College at New Paltz.*

Pierre-Georges Castex. *Emeritus Professor of Modern French Literature, University of Paris.*

Homero Castillo. *Professor of Spanish, University of California, Davis.*

James Caswell. *Associate Professor of Art History, University of British Columbia, Vancouver.*

Eduardo F. Catalano. *Emeritus Professor of Architecture, Massachusetts Institute of Technology, Cambridge.*

Jean-Louis Caussou. *Former Editor,* Opéra (*journal*), *Paris. Author of* Rossini.

Charles Cestre (d. 1959). *Professor of American Literature and Civilization, University of Paris, 1917–42.*

Charles Chadwick. *Carnegie Professor of French, University of Aberdeen, Scot.*

John Chalker. *Professor of English Language and Literature, Westfield College, University of London.*

Mary Chamot. *Assistant Keeper, Tate Gallery, London, 1950–65.*

Moti Chandra. *Former Director, Prince of Wales Museum of Western India, Bombay.*

Pramod Chandra. *George P. Bickford Professor of Indian Art, Harvard University.*

Frank Chapman. *Former Senior English Master, High School for Boys, Oswestry, Eng. Author of "Hardy the Novelist" in* Scrutiny.

Joan Chissell. *Assistant Music Critic,* The Times, *London, 1947–79.*

Françoise Choay. *Professor of Urban Studies, University of Paris VIII. Author of* Le Corbusier *and others.*

Chuang Shang-yen (d. 1980). *Deputy Director, National Palace Museum, Taipei, Taiwan.*

Charles Manning Hope Clark (d. 1991). *Professor of History, Australian National University, Canberra, 1949–75.*

James Midgley Clark (d. 1961). *Professor of German, University of Glasgow, 1951–54.*

Derek Plint Clifford. *Free-lance writer. Author of* A History of Garden Design *and others.*

C.L. Cline. *Ashbel H. Smith Professor Emeritus of English, University of Texas at Austin.*

Raymond Cogniat (d. 1977). *Principal Inspector of Fine Arts, 1943–67. Head of the arts section,* Le Figaro, *Paris, 1957–77.*

Pierre Cogny. *Senior Lecturer in French Literature, University of Caen, France.*

John Michael Cohen. *Writer, critic, and translator. Editor of* More Comic and Curious Verse; A History of Western Literature; *and others.*

George R. Collins. *Emeritus Professor of Art History, Columbia University.*

Peter Collins (d. 1981). *Professor of Architecture, McGill University, Montreal.*

Carl Wilbur Condit. *Professor of Art and Urban Affairs, Northwestern University, Evanston, Ill.*

William G. Constable (d. 1976). *Curator of Paintings, Boston Museum of Fine Arts, 1938–57.*

Deryck V. Cooke (d. 1976). *Musicologist. Music Presentation Editor, British Broadcasting Corporation, London, 1965–76.*

Douglas Cooper (d. 1984). *Art historian and critic. Author of* Courtauld Collection, a Catalogue *and others.*

Martin Du Pré Cooper (d. 1986). *Music Editor,* Daily Telegraph, *London, 1954–76.*

Wayne F. Cooper. *Free-lance writer. Editor of* The Passion of Claude McKay.

Gertrude Mary-Anne Coor (d. 1962). *Art historian. Assistant, Institute for Advanced Study, Princeton, N.J., 1959–62.*

Solange Corbin. *Professor of Musicology, University of Poitiers, Fr.*

Charles Philip Corney. *Deputy Librarian, British Library of Political and Economic Science, University of London.*

Robert B. Costello. *Publications Editor, Museum of Modern Art, New York City.*

Pierre Courthion. *Vice President, Syndicate of the French Artistic Press, 1965–78. Author of* Klee; Manet; *and many other monographs on modern European artists.*

David Cowan. *Senior Lecturer in Arabic, School of Oriental and African Studies, University of London.*

Malcolm Cowley (d. 1989). *Literary Adviser, The Viking Press, 1948–85. President, National Institute of Arts and Letters, New York City, 1956–59, 1961–64.*

Edward Croft-Murray (d. 1980). *Keeper, Department of Prints and Drawings, British Museum, London, 1954–73.*

Gerhard Croll. *Professor of Musicology, University of Salzburg, Austria.*

Anthony Cronin. *Poet and critic.*

Bosley Crowther (d. 1981). *Creative consultant, Columbia Pictures, New York City, 1968–73. Screen critic and editor,* The New York Times, *1940–68.*

John Cruickshank. *Emeritus Professor of French, University of Sussex, Brighton, Eng.*

Margaret Campbell Crum. *Assistant, Department of Western Manuscripts, Bodleian Library, University of Oxford.*

Charles Cudworth (d. 1977). *Curator, Pendlebury Library of Music, University of Cambridge.*

Alan S. Curtis. *Professor of Music, University of California, Berkeley.*

Charles D. Cuttler. *Emeritus Professor of Art History, University of Iowa, Iowa City.*

David Daiches. *Emeritus Professor of English, University of Sussex, Brighton, Eng.*

Mary L. Daniel. *Professor of Portuguese, University of Wisconsin, Madison.*

William Aubrey Darlington (d. 1979). *Chief Drama Critic,* London Daily Telegraph, *1920–68. London Theatre Correspondent,* The New York Times, *1939–60.*

O.R. Dathorne. *Professor of English and Director, Caribbean, African, and Afro-American Studies, University of Miami, Coral Gables, Florida.*

Ronald Austin Davey. *Professor of Art, University of Alberta, Edmonton.*

Donald Alfred Davie. *Andrew W. Mellon Professor of Humanities, Vanderbilt University, Nashville, Tenn.*

Harold Hess Davis (d. 1964). *Phebe Estelle Spalding Professor of English Literature, Pomona College, Claremont, Calif.*

J. Cary Davis. *Emeritus Professor of Romance Languages, Southern Illinois University, Carbondale.*

Margaret Josephine Dean-Smith. *Author of* A Guide to English Folk Song Collections *and others.*

William A. DeGregorio. *Free-lance writer and editor. Author of* The Complete Book of U.S. Presidents.

George G. Dekker. *Professor of English, Stanford University, Calif.*

Joseph-Edouard-Marie-Ghislain Delmelle. *Poet, essayist, and critic of art and literature. Member, International Academy of French Culture.*

Frederic Paul Deloffre. *Professor of French Literature, University of Paris III.*

Ludwig Denecke. *Director, Murhard Library of the City of Kassel and State Library, and Head of the Brothers Grimm Museum, Kassel, W.Ger., 1959–68.*

Bernard Denvir. *Principal Lecturer, Ravensbourne College of Art and Design, Bromley, Eng.*

Wilfrid Desan. *Emeritus Professor of Philosophy, Georgetown University, Washington, D.C.*

Pierre Descargues. *Art historian and critic. Author of* Frans Hals; Jan Vermeer; *and other monographs.*

Hugues de Varine-Bohan. *Director, France-Portuguese Institute, Lisbon. Former Director, International Council of Museums, Paris.*

Leon Townsend Dickinson. *Professor of English, University of Missouri, Columbia.*

Lovat Dickson (d. 1987). *Writer. Director, Macmillan & Company Ltd., London, 1941–64. Author of* H.G. Wells *and others.*

Paul Dinnage. *Free-lance writer, translator, and book reviewer. Formerly reviewer for literature,* The Times (London) *Literary Supplement, and for art,* The Spectator.

Maurice Willson Disher (d. 1969). *Author of* Blood and Thunder; Clowns and Pantomimes; *and others.*

Armel Hugh Diverres. *Professor of French; Head, Department of Romance Studies, University College of Swansea, University of Wales, 1974–81.*

Frederick J. Dockstader. *Museum consultant and art historian. Director, Museum of the American Indian, Heye Foundation, New York City, 1960–75.*

John V. Dodge (d. 1991). *Assistant and Managing Editor, 1938–60; Executive Editor, 1960–64; Senior Vice President, Editorial, 1964–70; Vice President, International Editorial, 1970–72, Encyclopædia Britannica, Inc., Chicago.*

Charles Reginald Dodwell. *Pilkington Professor of the History of Art; Director, Whitworth Art Gallery, Victoria University of Manchester.*

Frank Doeringer. *Assistant Professor of History, Lawrence University, Appleton, Wis.*

Robert Donington (d. 1990). *Musician and musicologist. Professor of Music, University of Iowa, Iowa City, 1964–73.*

Filippo Donini. *Cultural Expert, Cultural Relations Department, Italian Ministry of Foreign Affairs, Rome, 1972–76. Director, Italian Institute, London, 1961–72.*

Denis Donoghue. *Henry James Professor of English and American Letters, New York University, New York City.*

David F. Dorsey, Jr. *Associate Dean, School of Arts and Sciences, Atlanta University, Ga.*

Richard M. Dorson (d. 1981). *Director, Folklore Institute; Professor of History and Folklore, Indiana University, Bloomington, 1957–81.*

Brian Westerdale Downs (d. 1984). *Master of Christ's College, Cambridge, 1950–63; Professor of Scandinavian Studies, University of Cambridge, 1950–60.*

Kandioura Drame. *Free-lance writer on African literature.*

Philip Drew. *Professor of English Literature, University of Glasgow.*

Laura Dru. *Records and Archives Department, Madame Tussaud's Ltd., London.*

Donald Reynolds Dudley (d. 1972). *Professor of Latin, University of Birmingham, Eng., 1955–72.*

Anne Schley Duggan (d. 1973). *Professor and Dean, College of Health, Physical Education and Recreation, Texas Woman's University, Denton.*

René Dumesnil (d. 1967). *Literary and music critic. Member, Academy of Fine Arts, Institute of France, 1965–67.*

Archibald A.M. Duncan. *Professor of Scottish History and Literature, University of Glasgow.*

Lowell Dunham. *Distinguished Regents Professor of Modern Languages, University of Oklahoma, Norman.*

Raymond E. Durgnat. *Lecturer, Department of Three-Dimensional Design, Kingston Polytechnic, Kingston upon Thames, Eng. Author of* Films and Feelings; Jean Renoir; *and others.*

Wilma Robb Ebbitt. *Professor of English, Pennsylvania State University, University Park.*

Edwin Harold Eby. *Emeritus Professor of English, University of Washington, Seattle.*

Leon Edel. *Henry James Professor Emeritus of English and American Letters, New York University, New York City. Citizens' Professor Emeritus of English Literature, University of Hawaii at Manoa, Honolulu.*

Christopher Edmunds (d. 1990). *Composer. Examiner for the Trinity College of Music, London, 1940–78.*

Hugh Edwards. *Former Curator of Photography and Associate Curator, Department of Prints and Drawings, Art Institute of Chicago.*

Tudor Edwards. *Formerly Investigating Officer of Historic Buildings, Ministry of Town and Country Planning, England.*

Lorenz E.A. Eitner. *Professor and Chairman, Department of Art, Stanford University, Calif.*

Sverker Ek (d. 1981). *Professor of Literary History, Göteborg University, Swed., 1931–55.*

Charles Grant Ellis. *Research Associate, The Textile Museum, Washington, D.C.*

Elmer Ellis (d. 1989). *President, 1955–66; Professor of History, University of Missouri, Columbia.*

Angna Enters (d. 1989). *Dancer, mime, and artist. Originator of phase dance mime. Author of* On Mime.

Walter Erben (d. 1981). *Professor of Art Education, College of Education of the Ruhr, Dortmund, W.Ger.*

Robert Escarpit. *Emeritus Professor of Information and Communication Sciences, University of Bordeaux III, France.*

Martin J. Esslin. *Emeritus Professor of Drama, Stanford University, Calif. Head of Radio Drama, British Broadcasting Corporation, London, 1963–77.*

Joan Evans (d. 1977). *President, Society of Antiquaries, London, 1959–64. Author of* John Ruskin *and many others.*

David Fagan. *Former Assistant Professor of Spanish and Portuguese, Indiana University, Bloomington.*

Alison (Anna Bowie) Fairlie. *Professorial Fellow of Girton College, Cambridge; Professor of French, University of Cambridge.*

Dennis Larry Ashwell Farr. *Director, Courtauld Institute Galleries, London.*

Suzanne Pier Fauteux. *Free-lance writer.*

John Bailey Fernald (d. 1985). *Theatre Director. Principal, Royal Academy of Dramatic Art, London, 1955–65. Professor of Dramatic Art, Oakland University, Rochester, Mich., 1966–70.*

Robert J. Fernier (d. 1977). *President, The Friends of Gustave Courbet, Paris. Author of* Gustave Courbet, peintre de l'art vivant.

Andrew Field. *Professor of Comparative Literature, Griffith University, Brisbane, Australia.*

Roger Elwyn Fiske (d. 1987). *Musicologist and composer. Author of* English Theatre Music in the Eighteenth Century; Ballet Music; *and others.*

Ian Fletcher (d. 1988). *Professor of English Literature, University of Reading, Eng., 1978–82.*

Louis-Fernand Flutre. *Emeritus Professor of Old French Language and Literature, University of Lyon.*

John Stuart Forbes. *Deputy Warden, The Worshipful Company of Goldsmiths, London.*

Patrick K. Ford. *Director, Center for the Study of Comparative Folklore and Mythology, University of California, Los Angeles.*

Nigel Fortune. *Reader in Music, University of Birmingham, Eng.*

Wallace Fowlie. *James B. Duke Professor Emeritus of French Literature, Duke University, Durham, N.C.*

George Sutherland Fraser (d. 1980). *Poet and critic. Reader in Modern English Literature, University of Leicester, Eng., 1964–79.*

Richard H. Freeborn. *Emeritus Professor of Russian Literature, School of Slavonic and East European Studies, University of London.*

Marion Valerie Friedmann (d. 1980). *Editor and translator. Author of* The Slap; *editor of* I Will Still Be Moved: Reports from South Africa.

Oluf Anker Friis (d. 1979). *Professor of Literature, University of Copenhagen, 1957–64.*

Holger Elof Uno Frykenstedt. *Lecturer in Literary History with Poetics, University of Stockholm.*

David Fuller. *Professor of Music, State University of New York at Buffalo.*

Jean Overton Fuller. *Codirector, Fuller d'Arch Smith Ltd., Rare Books, London. Author of* Swinburne: A Critical Biography *and others.*

Richard Clair Gabriel. *Senior History Master, King's School, Worcester, Eng. Former Research Assistant, Institute of Historical Research, University of London.*

Hans Gal (d. 1987). *Composer and musicologist. Lecturer on Music, University of Edinburgh, 1945–65. Director of Municipal College of Music, Mainz, Ger., 1929–33.*

Edward J.C. Garden. *Professor and Head, Department of Music, University of Sheffield, Eng.*

John F. Garganigo. *Professor of Spanish and Chairman, Department of Latin American Studies, Washington University, St. Louis, Mo.*

William Gaunt (d. 1980). *Art historian. Special correspondent on art subjects,* The Times (*London*).

Robert Gayre of Gayre and Nigg. *Editor,* Armorial, *Edinburgh.*

Karl Geiringer (d. 1989). *Professor of Music, University of California, Santa Barbara, 1962–73.*

Willi Geismeier. *Former Director, National Gallery, National Museum of Berlin.*

Arthur Gelb. *Executive Vice President, New York Times Company Foundation; Managing Editor,* The New York Times, *1986–89. Coauthor of* O'Neill.

Barbara Gelb. *Writer. Coauthor of* O'Neill.

Margaret Oliver Gentles. *Former Keeper of the Buckingham Collection of Japanese Prints; former Associate Curator of Oriental Art, Art Institute of Chicago.*

Albert S. Gerard. *Professor of Comparative Literature, State University of Liège, Belg.*

Edwin Gerow. *Professor of Religion and Humanities, Reed College, Portland, Ore.*

Giuseppe Giangrande. *Professor of Classics, Birkbeck College, University of London.*

Robert Donald Davidson Gibson. *Professor of French, University of Kent at Canterbury, Eng.*

Alexander Gillies (d. 1977). *Professor of German Language and Literature, University of Leeds, Eng., 1945–72.*

Giovanni Pietro Giorgetti. *Lecturer in Italian, Birkbeck College, University of London.*

Cuthbert Morton Girdlestone (d. 1975). *Professor of French, Universities of Durham and Newcastle upon Tyne, Eng., 1926–60.*

Nina C. Gitz. *Free-lance writer and translator.*

Kurt Moritz Artur Goldammer. *Professor of Comparative History of Religions and of the History of Religious Art, Philipps University of Marburg, Ger.*

Frederick Goldbeck (d. 1981). *Critic and musicologist. Adviser for Music, Radiotélévision Française.*

Ludwig Goldscheider. *Art historian. Former director and designer of books for Phaidon Press Ltd., London. Author of* Kokoschka *and many others.*

Dale Good. *Editor,* Compton's Encyclopedia. *Librarian, Music Division, New York Public Library's Research Center for the Performing Arts at Lincoln Center, New York City, 1970–77.*

Robert Marshall Goodwin. *Racing correspondent, London.*

Sydney Charles Gould. *Former Reader in French and Comparative Literature, University of Bristol, Eng.*

Andrew Sydenham Farrar Gow (d. 1978). *Fellow of Trinity College, University of Cambridge; Brereton Reader in Classics, 1947–51.*

Alan Gowans. *Director, National Images of North American Living, Washington, D.C. Emeritus Professor of History in Art, University of Victoria, B.C.*

Philip Graham (d. 1967). *Professor of American Literature, University of Texas at Austin.*

Theodore C. Grame. *Author of* Folk Music; America's Ethnic Music; *and others.*

Serge Grandjean. *Keeper, Department of Objets d'Art, Louvre Museum, Paris.*

Benny Green. *Record reviewer, British Broadcasting Corporation. Jazz Critic,* The Observer (*London*), *1958–77.*

Roger Lancelyn Green (d. 1987). *Author of* The Story of Lewis Carroll *and others; editor of* The Diaries of Lewis Carroll.

David Greene (d. 1981). *Senior Professor, School of Celtic Studies, Dublin Institute for Advanced Studies.*

Mark Gridley. *Lecturer in Music, Case Western Reserve University, Cleveland, Ohio.*

F. Grossmann (d. 1984). *Senior Professor of Art History, University of Washington, Seattle.*

Henri Guillemin. *Emeritus Professor of History of French Literature, University of Geneva.*

Masakatsu Gunji. *Professor of Kabuki Drama, Waseda University, Tokyo.*

Gordon S. Haight (d. 1985). *Professor of English, Yale University, 1950–68.*

Eric Halfpenny (d. 1979). *Editor,* The Galpin Society Journal, *1963–70.*

Frieda F. Halpern. *Consultant on needlework.*

Charles E. Hamm. *Composer. Arthur Virgin Professor of Music, Dartmouth College, Hanover, N.H.*

Craig S. Harbison. *Professor of Art History, University of Massachusetts, Amherst.*

Enriqueta Harris. *Honorary Fellow of the Warburg Institute, University of London. Author of* Spanish Painting; Goya.

Francis Llewellyn Harrison (d. 1987). *Professor of Ethnomusicology, University of Amsterdam, 1970–76. Reader in the History of Music, University of Oxford, 1962–70.*

William J. Harrison. *Consultant on industrial design.*

Kenneth Harrow. *Professor of Humanities, Michigan State University, East Lansing.*

Arnold Lionel Haskell (d. 1980). *Director, 1946–65, and Governor, 1966–77, Royal Ballet School; Governor, Royal Ballet, London, 1957–80.*

David Hately. *Critic and consultant on literature.*

Eric Alfred Havelock (d. 1988). *Sterling Professor of Classics, Yale University, 1963–71.*

David M. Hayne. *Emeritus Professor of French, University of Toronto.*

John A. Haywood. *Reader in Arabic, University of Durham, Eng., 1967–78.*

Ernst van Heerden. *Poet. Emeritus Professor of Afrikaans and Netherlands, University of the Witwatersrand, Johannesburg.*

Julius S. Held. *Emeritus Professor of Art History, Barnard College, Columbia University.*

Ruth P. Hellman. *Consultant on lace, Metropolitan Museum of Art, New York City.*

Philip Prichard Henderson (d. 1977). *Free-lance writer and editor. Author of* William Morris: His Life, Work and Friends.

Robert M. Henderson. *Chief, General Library and Museum of the Performing Arts, New York Public Library at Lincoln Center, New York City.*

Sir Philip Hendy (d. 1980). *Adviser to the Israel Museum, Jerusalem, 1968–71. Director, National Gallery, London, 1946–67.*

Julian Herbage (d. 1976). *Free-lance musicologist, broadcaster, and writer.*

Don Herdeck. *Free-lance writer on African literature.*

Barnard Hewitt. *Emeritus Professor of Theatre, University of Illinois, Urbana.*

Howard Hibbard (d. 1984). *Professor of Art History, Columbia University, 1966–84.*

A. Kent Hieatt. *Professor of English, University of Western Ontario, London.*

David J.M. Higgins (d. 1975). *Associate Professor of English, Monmouth College, West Long Branch, N.J.*

Gilbert Highet (d. 1978). *Anthon Professor of Latin Language and Literature, Columbia University, 1950–72.*

Ronald Francis Hingley. *Fellow of St. Antony's College, Oxford; Lecturer in Russian, University of Oxford.*

André Hodeir. *Composer, conductor, and writer. Author of* Jazz: Its Evolution and Its Essence.

Michel-Rostislav Hofmann. *Musicologist. Author of* Moussorgski; Histoire de la musique en Russie.

Reinhold D. Hohl. *Art historian. Author of* Giacometti *and others.*

Christina Stanley Hole. *Honorary Editor,* Folklore. *Author of* English Custom and Usage; English Folklore; *and others.*

Hans Egon Holthusen. *Professor of German, Northwestern University, Evanston, Ill., 1968–81.*

Yasuji Honda. *Former Professor of Drama, Waseda University, Tokyo. Member, Japanese Society for Theatre Research.*

Kenneth Hopkins (d. 1988). *Novelist and poet. Professor of English, Southern Illinois University, Carbondale, 1964–72.*

John Horden. *Author of* Francis Quarles: A Bibliography of His Works to the Year 1800.

Paul Horgan. *Emeritus Professor of English; Author in Residence, Wesleyan University, Middleton, Conn.*

Louis Horst (d. 1964). *Teacher of Dance Composition, Juilliard School of Music. Managing Editor,* Dance Observer.

William Driver Howarth. *Former Professor of French, University of Bristol, Eng.*

Alan Crawford Howie. *Lecturer in Music, Victoria University of Manchester.*

Ivan Hrbek. *Member, Oriental Institute, Czechoslovak Academy of Sciences, Prague.*

Garfield Hopkin Hughes (d. 1969). *Senior Lecturer in Welsh Language and Literature, University College of Wales, Aberystwyth, 1960–69.*

G(eorge) Haydn Huntley. *Emeritus Professor of Art, Northwestern University, Evanston, Ill.*

Jethro Hurt. *Former Instructor in the History of Art and Architecture, University of Illinois, Chicago.*

Dyneley Hussey (d. 1972). *Music Critic, The Times (London), 1923–46; The Listener, 1946–60. Author of Verdi; Some Composers of Opera.*

Lawrence E. Hussman. *Professor of English, Wright State University, Dayton, Ohio.*

Hans Huth (d. 1977). *Curator of Decorative Arts, Art Institute of Chicago, 1958–63.*

Herbert Henry Huxley. *Emeritus Professor of Classics, University of Victoria, B.C. Supervisor in Classics, St. John's College, University of Cambridge.*

Gerard Willem Huygens. *Professor of History and Dutch Literature, Rotterdam Lyceum.*

René Huyghe. *Professor of Art, College of France, Paris, 1950–76. President, Council of Museums, Paris, 1974–88.*

Stuart Wallace Hyde. *Professor of Broadcast Communication Arts, San Francisco State University.*

Isabelle Hyman. *Professor of Fine Arts, Washington Square and University College of Arts and Science, New York University, New York City.*

Catherine Mills Ing (d. 1983). *Fellow of St. Hilda's College, Oxford; Senior Lecturer in English Literature, University of Oxford.*

Hans Dietrich Irmscher. *Professor of Modern German Literary Criticism, University of Cologne.*

John H.B. Irving. *Director, Education Division, WGBH Educational Foundation, Boston.*

David Irwin. *Chairman, Department of History of Art, University of Aberdeen, Scot.*

Elizabeth Jachimowicz. *Curator of Costumes, Chicago Historical Society.*

Ian Jack. *Fellow of Pembroke College, Cambridge; Professor of English Literature, University of Cambridge.*

Stephen W. Jacobs. *Professor of Architecture, Cornell University, Ithaca, N.Y.*

Hans L.C. Jaffé. *Professor of Modern Art History, University of Amsterdam.*

Michael Jaffé. *Professor of the History of Western Art; Director, Fitzwilliam Museum, University of Cambridge; Fellow of King's College, Cambridge.*

Richard Edward Warwick James. *Assistant Curator, Barber Institute of Fine Arts; Lecturer in History of Art, University of Birmingham, Eng.*

William Louis G. James. *Reader in English, University of Kent at Canterbury, Eng.*

H.W. Janson (d. 1982). *Professor of Fine Arts, Washington Square College of Arts and Science, New York University, New York City, 1949–79.*

Alexander Norman Jeffares. *Emeritus Professor of English, University of Stirling, Scot.*

Harold Jenkins. *Emeritus Professor of Rhetoric and English Literature, University of Edinburgh.*

Romilly James Heald Jenkins (d. 1969). *Professor of Byzantine History and Director of Studies, Harvard University Dumbarton Oaks Research Library and Collection, 1960–69.*

Frederick L. Jones (d. 1973). *Professor of English, University of Pennsylvania, Philadelphia.*

Joseph Jay Jones. *Emeritus Professor of English, University of Texas at Austin.*

Bertram Leon Joseph (d. 1981). *Professor of Drama; Chairman, Department of Theatre, Queens College, City University of New York, 1970–81.*

Wayne Kamin. *Research Associate in African and Afro-American Studies, University of Texas at Austin.*

Maxine Kanter. *Free-lance writer on music.*

Ben Zion Kaplan. *President, Universal Hairpieces, New York City.*

Edgar Kaufmann, Jr. *Emeritus Professor of the History of Architecture, Columbia University. Director, Department of Industrial Design, Museum of Modern Art, New York City, 1946–50.*

Martin J. Kemp. *Professor of Fine Arts, University of St. Andrews, Scot.*

Elspeth Mary Kennedy. *Lecturer in French, University of Oxford; Fellow of St. Hilda's College, Oxford.*

Michael Kennedy. *Chief Music Critic, Sunday Telegraph, London.*

Edward John Kenney. *Kennedy Professor Emeritus of Latin, University of Cambridge; Fellow of Peterhouse, Cambridge.*

Herbert Leon Kessler. *Professor and Chairman, Department of the History of Art, Johns Hopkins University, Baltimore.*

Arnold Charles Kettle (d. 1986). *Professor of Literature, Open University, Walton, Eng., 1970–81.*

Heinz Kindermann (d. 1985). *Professor of Drama, University of Vienna. Chairman, Commission for the History of the Austrian Theatre, Austrian Academy of Sciences, Vienna. Vice President, International Institute for Theatrical Research, Vienna.*

Donald King. *Deputy Keeper, Victoria and Albert Museum, London.*

Peter K. King. *Former Director, Institute of Modern Dutch Studies, University of Hull, Eng.*

A.M. Kinghorn. *Professor of English. University of Qatar, Doha.*

Romas Kinka. *Former Lecturer in Lithuanian, University of Chicago. Vice-Director of the Lithuanian Institute of Education, Chicago.*

The Rev. James Kinsley (d. 1984). *Professor and Head, Department of English Studies, University of Nottingham, Eng., 1961–84. General Editor, Oxford English Novels, 1967–77.*

F.E. Kirby. *Professor of Music, Lake Forest College, Ill.*

Ralph Kirkpatrick (d. 1984). *Harpsichordist. Professor of Music, Yale University, 1965–76.*

Lincoln Edward Kirstein. *General Director Emeritus, New York City Ballet Company.*

Michael William Lely Kitson. *Professor of the History of Art; Director of Studies, Paul Mellon Centre for Studies in British Art, London.*

Tibor Klaniczay. *Director, Institute of Literary Studies, Hungarian Academy of Sciences, Budapest.*

Margaret Brown Klapthor. *Former Associate Curator, Division of Political History, National Museum of History and Technology, Smithsonian Institution, Washington, D.C.*

Carl Frederick Klinck. *Emeritus Professor of Canadian Literature, University of Western Ontario, London.*

Jan Knappert. *Former Lecturer in Bantu, School of Oriental and African Studies, University of London.*

Arthur Knight. *Professor of Cinema, University of Southern California, Los Angeles. Film Critic, The Hollywood Reporter.*

Roy Clement Knight. *Emeritus Professor of French, University College of Swansea, University of Wales.*

Dorothy Knowles. *Historian of modern French drama. Honorary Research Fellow, Bedford College, University of London.*

H.F. Koeper. *Professor of Architectural History, California State Polytechnic University, Pomona.*

Dame Leonie Judith Kramer. *Chancellor and Emeritus Professor of Australian Literature, University of Sydney.*

Sven Møller Kristensen. *Professor of Scandinavian Literature, University of Copenhagen, Den., 1964–79.*

Stepan Andriyovich Kryzhanivsky. *Professor, Institute of Literature, Ukrainian S.S.R. Academy of Sciences, Kiev.*

George Alexander Kubler. *Sterling Professor of the History of Art, Yale University.*

Daniel P. Kunene. *Professor of African Languages and Literature, University of Wisconsin, Madison.*

David M. Kunzle. *Professor of Art History, University of California, Los Angeles.*

Ado Kyrou. *Writer, motion-picture and television director. Author of* Luis Buñuel *and others.*

Kai L.K. Laitinen. *Professor of Finnish Literature, University of Helsinki, 1982–89.*

Basil Raymond Lam (d. 1984). *Conductor and harpsichordist. Organizer of Pre-Classical Music Programmes, British Broadcasting Corporation.*

Norman Jones Lamb. *Former Senior Lecturer in Portuguese and Spanish, University of Liverpool.*

Richard Lane. *Research Associate, Honolulu Academy of Arts. Author of* Masters of the Japanese Print.

Paul M. Laporte. *Emeritus Professor of Art History, Immaculate Heart College, Los Angeles.*

Mary Madge Lascelles. *Fellow of the British Academy. Reader in English Literature, University of Oxford, 1966–67.*

Jan Lauts. *Director, Karlsruhe Art Gallery, W.Ger., 1956–73.*

Pierre Lavedan. *Director, Institute of Town Planning, University of Paris, 1940–65; Professor, Faculty of Letters, 1930–55.*

Janko Lavrin (d. 1986). *Professor of Russian Literature, University of Nottingham, Eng., 1923–53.*

Reginald Norcom Lawrence (d. 1967). *Playwright. Lecturer in Speech, City College, City University of New York.*

Frederick Laws (d. 1976). *Free-lance journalist and art critic.*

Luis Leal. *Emeritus Professor of Spanish, University of Illinois, Urbana.*

Lewis Leary (d. 1990). *William Rand Kenan, Jr., Professor of English, University of North Carolina at Chapel Hill, 1968–76.*

Raymond Lebègue (d. 1984). *Professor of 16th- and 17th-Century French Literature, University of Paris. Officer of the Legion of Honour.*

Robert Lebel (d. 1986). *Art expert, critic, and writer. Author of* On Marcel Duchamp *and others.*

Eileen Le Breton. *Reader in French, Bedford College, University of London.*

Clifford Leech (d. 1977). *Professor of English, University of Toronto, 1963–74.*

Trevor LeGassick. *Professor of Arabic, University of Michigan, Ann Arbor.*

Dominica Legge (d. 1986). *Professor of Anglo-Norman Studies, University of Edinburgh, 1968–73.*

Andrew George Lehmann. *Emeritus Professor, School of European Studies, University of Buckingham, Eng.*

Richard Lepine. *Free-lance writer on African literature.*

Pierre Leprohon. *Writer and journalist. Author of* Jean Renoir; Charles Chaplin; Antonioni; *and others.*

Laurence Elliot Libin. *Frederick P. Rose Curator of Musical Instruments, Metropolitan Museum of Art, New York City.*

Ronald William Lightbown. *Keeper of the Library, Victoria and Albert Museum, London; Assistant Keeper, Department of Metalwork, 1964–73.*

Bernth Lindfors. *Professor of English and African Literatures, University of Texas at Austin.*

Sten Hjalmar Lindroth. *Professor of the History of Science and Ideas, University of Uppsala, Swed.*

Anne Lippert. *Professor of French, Ohio Northern University, Ada.*

Ian Littlewood. *Lecturer in English, University of Sussex, Brighton, England.*

René Felix Lissens. *Emeritus Professor of Dutch and General Literature, St. Ignatius University Faculty, Antwerp.*

David Mathias Lloyd-Jones. *Musicologist and conductor. Artistic Director, Opera North, Leeds, Eng.*

Edward Lockspeiser (d. 1973). *Writer and broadcaster on music. Author of* Debussy: His Life and Mind *and others.*

David Loshak. *Assistant Professor of Art History, University of Wisconsin, Madison, 1958–64.*

John Evelyn Lowe. *Director, Weald and Downland Open Air Museum, Sussex, Eng., 1969–74. Principal, West Dean College, 1972–78.*

Constance Lowenthal. *Executive Director, International Foundation for Art Research, New York City.*

Bates Lowry. *Director, National Building Museum, Washington, D.C. Professor of Art History, University of Massachusetts, Boston, 1971–80.*

Wilfrid Irvine Lucas (d. 1973). *Professor of German, University of Southampton, Eng., 1954–71.*

Georg Hans Luck. *Professor of Classics, Johns Hopkins University, Baltimore.*

Henry Julius Philip Maas. *Joint Head of Academic Staff and Tutor in Classics, Moreton Hall, Oswestry, Eng. Coeditor of* The Letters of Ernest Dowson *and others.*

Thomas Ollive Mabbott (d. 1968). *Professor of English, Hunter College, City University of New York, 1946–66.*

Richard Dyer MacCann. *Professor of Film, University of Iowa, Iowa City.*

Giovanni Macchia. *Professor of French Language and Literature, University of Rome.*

Ivy Lilian McClelland. *Former Reader in Spanish, University of Glasgow.*

Arthur Kilgore McComb (deceased). *Author of* The Baroque Painters of Italy *and others.*

Raven I. McDavid, Jr. (d. 1984). *Professor of English and of Linguistics, University of Chicago, 1964–77.*

The Rev. Eric McDermott, S.J. *Associate Professor Emeritus of History, Georgetown University, Washington, D.C.*

Sheila D. McDonough. *Professor of Religion, Sir George Williams University, Montreal.*

Robert Law McDougall. *Professor of English; Carleton University, Ottawa; General Editor,* The Carleton Library.

James Walter McFarlane. *Emeritus Professor of European Literature, University of East Anglia, Norwich, Eng.*

Sheila Roberts McGuire. *Professor of English and African Studies, Michigan State University, East Lansing.*

Joseph Machlis. *Emeritus Professor of Music, Queens College, City University of New York.*

Christine McHugh. *Attorney. Associate, Pellettieri, Rabstein, and Altman, Princeton, N.J.*

Roy Donald McMullen (d. 1984). *Art historian. Author of* Art, Affluence, and Alienation; The World of Marc Chagall; *and others.*

Hugo A. McPherson. *Professor of English, McGill University, Montreal. Chairman and Commissioner, National Film Board of Canada, Montreal, 1967–70.*

Walter James Macqueen-Pope (d. 1960). *Writer on the theatre. Author of* Haymarket: Theatre of Perfection *and others.*

David Magarshack (d. 1977). *Author of* Chekhov the Dramatist; Dostoevsky; Pushkin: A Biography *and many other works on Russian writers.*

Claude-Edmonde Magny (d. 1966). *Teacher of Philosophy, University of Paris.*

Francis Peabody Magoun, Jr. (d. 1979). *Professor of English, Harvard University, 1951–61.*

Jean Mallion. *Lecturer, Faculty of Literature and Humane Studies, University of Grenoble, France.*

William P. Malm. *Professor of Musicology, University of Michigan, Ann Arbor.*

Charles Mancuso. *Associate Professor of the Performing Arts, State University of New York College at Buffalo.*

William Somervell Mann (d. 1989). *Chief Music Critic,* The Times (*London*), *1960–82.*

Roger Manvell (d. 1987). *Biographer and film historian. University Professor of Film, Boston University. Director, British Film Academy, 1947–59.*

Leslie A. Marchand. *Emeritus Professor of English, Rutgers University, New Brunswick, N.J.*

Valerio Mariani (deceased). *Professor of the History of Art, University of Naples.*

Sidney Marrat. *Journalist, literary critic, and theatre historian.*

Leonard Cyril Martin (d. 1976). *King Alfred Professor of English Literature, University of Liverpool, 1929–51.*

Colin Mason (d. 1971). *Music critic. Editor,* Tempo, *1964–71.*

D.E.S. Maxwell. *Professor of English, York University, Toronto.*

Claude Albert Mayer. *Former Professor and Head, Department of French, University of Liverpool.*

Ralph Mayer (d. 1979). *Painter. Director, Artists Technical Research Institute. Lecturer in Painting, Columbia University, 1944–64.*

El-Hadji Mbengue. *Associate Professor of African Studies, Howard University, Washington, D.C.*

Wesley Milgate. *Emeritus Professor of English, Australian National University, Canberra.*

John Miller. *Researcher and writer on music.*

Sandra Millikin. *Free-lance architectural historian. Lecturer in the History of Art, Open University, Walton, Eng., 1971–73.*

Henry A. Millon. *Dean, Center for Advanced Study in the Visual Arts, National Gallery of Art, Washington, D.C.*

William Mishler. *Associate Professor of Scandinavian, University of Minnesota, Minneapolis.*

Donald (Charles Peter) Mitchell. *Music critic and publisher. Chairman, Faber Music Ltd., London.*

Jean Mitry. *Professor and Director, Cinema Division, Institute of Art and Archaeology, University of Paris I.*

Arthur Mizener (d. 1988). *Mellon Foundation Professor of Humanities, Cornell University, Ithaca, N.Y.*

Arve Sverre Moen (d. 1976). *Cultural Editor,* Arbeiderbladet (*newspaper*), *Oslo. Member of the Board, Edvard Munch Museum, Oslo.*

Hans Moldenhauer. *Musicologist. Director, Moldenhauer Archives. President, Spokane Conservatory of Music and Allied Arts, Inc., Wash.*

Agnes Mongan. *Emeritus Curator of Drawings, Fogg Art Museum, Harvard University.*

Lillian Moore (d. 1967). *Dancer. Member of Faculty, American Ballet Center, New York City.*

Sonia Moore. *Founder and President, American Center for Stanislavski Theatre Art, Inc., New York City. Founder and Artistic Director, American Stanislavski Theatre.*

Will G. Moore (d. 1978). *Reader in French Literature, University of Oxford.*

Albert Mordell (deceased). *Author of* Quaker Militant: John Greenleaf Whittier *and others.*

Anne-Marie de Moret. *Free-lance writer on African literature.*

Edwin George Morgan. *Poet. Titular Professor of English, University of Glasgow, 1975–80.*

Brita Maud Ellen Mortensen (d. 1958). *Lecturer in Swedish, University of Cambridge, 1950–58.*

Charles Moseley. *Free-lance writer.*

Frank Luther Mott (d. 1964). *Dean, School of Journalism, University of Missouri, Columbia, 1942–51.*

Joachim Müller. *Professor of German Literature, Friedrich Schiller University of Jena, Ger.*

Hugo Munsterberg. *Professor of Oriental Art, Bard College, Annandale-on-Hudson, N.Y.*

Peter J. Murray. *Emeritus Professor of the History of Art, Birkbeck College, University of London.*

Reginald P.C. Mutter. *Emeritus Professor of English Literature, University of Sussex, Brighton, Eng.*

Bernard S. Myers. *Art historian. Editor in Chief and Manager, Art Books Department, McGraw-Hill Book Company, New York City, 1958–70.*

Rollo H. Myers (d. 1985). *Writer on music. Author of* Music in the Modern World; Ravel: Life and Works *and others.*

Maurice Nadeau. *Editor,* Lettres Nouvelles *and* La Quinzaine Littéraire, *Paris.*

Alois M. Nagler. *Henry McCormick Professor Emeritus of Dramatic History and Criticism, Yale University.*

James Thompson Nardin. *Professor of English, Louisiana State University, Baton Rouge.*

Ray Nash (d. 1982). *Professor of Art, Dartmouth College, Hanover, N.H., 1949–70.*

Robert J. Nelson. *Professor of French Literature, University of Illinois at Urbana-Champaign.*

Israel Vladimirovich Nestyev. *Chief Scientist, Research Institute of History of Arts, Moscow.*

Arthur Hobart Nethercot. *Franklyn Bliss Snyder Professor Emeritus of English, Northwestern University, Evanston, Ill.*

Dika Newlin. *Composer. Professor of Music, Virginia Commonwealth University, Richmond.*

Robert Brayton Nichols. *Landscape architect.*

Norman Cornthwaite Nicholson (d. 1987). *Poet and critic. Author of* H.G. Wells *and others.*

Romola Nijinsky (d. 1978). *Author of* Nijinsky; The Last Years of Nijinsky.

Robert Niklaus. *Emeritus Professor of French, University of Exeter, Eng.*

Arnoldus Noach (d. 1976). *Professor of the History of Art and Architecture, University of Leeds, Eng.*

J. Jeremy Noble. *Professor of Music, State University of New York at Buffalo.*

Linda Weinberg Nochlin. *Distinguished Professor of Art History, Graduate Center, City University of New York.*

Paul F. Norton. *Professor of Art, University of Massachusetts, Amherst.*

Bonnie Oberman. *Free-lance writer.*

Francis Valentine O'Connor. *Director, Raphael Research Enterprises (fine arts consultants), New York City. Editor,* Federal Art Patronage Notes, *1974–86.*

Donald Mitchell Oenslager (d. 1975). *Designer of scenery and theatre consultant. Professor of Scene Design, Yale University.*

James Francis O'Gorman. *Grace Slack McNeil Professor of the History of American Art, Wellesley College, Mass.*

Kenneth O'Leary. *Former Associate Professor of English, Seton Hall University, South Orange, N.J.*

Aladar Olgyay (d. 1963). *Architect. Author of* Solar Control and Shading Devices *and others.*

Carola Oman (Lady Lenanton) (d. 1978). *Biographer. Author of* David Garrick *and others.*

Peter M. Opie (d. 1982). *Coauthor of* The Oxford Dictionary of Nursery Rhymes; The Lore and Language of Schoolchildren; Children's Games in Street and Playground.

Masako Osako. *Free-lance writer on Japanese literature and affairs.*

Christian F. Otto. *Professor of Architecture, Cornell University, Ithaca, N.Y.*

Peter D. Owen. *Painter and printmaker. Former Senior Lecturer, Croydon College of Design and Technology, Eng.*

Oyekan Owomoyela. *Professor of Literature and Drama, University of Nebraska, Lincoln.*

(William Cyril) Desmond Pacey (d. 1975). *Vice President; Professor of English, University of New Brunswick, Fredericton.*

Sir Denys (Lionel) Page (d. 1978). *Regius Professor of Greek, University of Cambridge, 1950–73.*

George Duncan Painter. *Assistant Keeper in charge of incunabula, Department of Printed Books, British Library, London, 1954–74.*

Rodolfo Pallucchini (d. 1989). *Director, Institute of Art History, Giorgio Cini Foundation, Venice, 1972–89.*

Guido Pannain (d. 1977). *Professor of the History of Music, S. Pietro a Maiella Conservatory of Music, Naples.*

John T. Paoletti. *Professor of Art History, Wesleyan University, Middletown, Conn.*

Alexander A. Parker (d. 1989). *Professor of Spanish Literature, University of Texas at Austin, 1970–78.*

Robert Lewis Parkinson (d. 1991). *Chief Librarian and Historian, Circus World Museum, Baraboo, Wis., 1965–91.*

Dorothy Margaret Partington (d. 1990). *Literary historian and critic.*

Roy Pascal (d. 1980). *Professor of German, University of Birmingham, Eng., 1939–69.*

Günter Passavant. *Editor, Mitteilungen, Institute for the Study of the History of Art, Florence.*

David Patterson. *President, Oxford Centre for Post-Graduate Hebrew Studies; Cowley Lecturer in Post-Biblical Hebrew, University of Oxford; Fellow of St. Cross College, Oxford.*

Damião António Peres. *Former Professor of History, University of Coimbra, Port. Member, Portuguese Academy of History.*

Roy Perrott. *Free-lance book editor and consultant. Author of* The Aristocrats.

Lino Pertile. *Reader in Italian, University of Sussex, Brighton, Eng.*

Gabor F. Peterdi. *Painter and printmaker. Emeritus Professor of Printmaking, Yale University.*

Helene Peters. *Professor of French, Macalester College, St. Paul, Minn.*

Edwin Burr Pettet. *Former Schulman Professor of Theatre Arts, Brandeis University, Waltham, Mass.*

Friedrich Pfister (deceased). *Professor of Classical Philology, University of Würzburg, W.Ger.*

James Smith Pierce. *Professor of Art History, University of Kentucky, Lexington.*

André Pierre (d. 1966). *Member of Editorial Staff,* Le Monde, *Paris, 1944–58.*

Hovhanness Israel Pilikian. *Theatre director. Founder and Artistic Director of Hana-no Mask-Theatre Company.*

Vivian de Sola Pinto (d. 1969). *Professor of English, University of Nottingham, Eng., 1938–61.*

Henry C. Pitz (d. 1976). *Writer and painter. Professor of Art, Philadelphia College of Art, 1934–60.*

Adolf K. Placzek. *Avery Librarian Emeritus, Columbia University.*

Giles William Playfair. *Free-lance writer. Professor of Drama, Williams College, Williamstown, Mass., 1956–63.*

Henry A. Pochmann (d. 1973). *Professor of English, University of Wisconsin, Madison, 1938–71.*

Georg Poensgen. *Formerly Director of the Palatinate Museum, Heidelberg, W.Ger.*

Peter J. Pollack (d. 1978). *Photographer and lecturer. Author of* The Picture History of Photography *and others.*

Sir John Pope-Hennessy. *Professor of Fine Arts, New York University. Consultative Chairman, Department of European Paintings, Metropolitan Museum of Art, New York City, 1977–86.*

William V. Porter. *Professor of Music History and Literature, Northwestern University, Evanston, Ill.*

Frederick A. Pottle (d. 1987). *Sterling Professor of English, Yale University, 1944–66.*

John Povey. *Professor of English, University of California, Los Angeles.*

Anthony Powell. *Novelist, playwright, and literary critic.*

Mario Praz (d. 1982). *Professor of English Language and Literature, University of Rome, 1934–66.*

Joseph Prescott. *Emeritus Professor of English, Wayne State University, Detroit.*

Cecil John Layton Price. *Emeritus Professor of English Language and Literature, University College of Swansea, University of Wales.*

Brian Priestman. *Orchestral conductor. Former Dean, Faculty of Music, University of Cape Town.*

Jules David Prown. *Paul Mellon Professor of the History of Art, Yale University.*

Ricardo Quintana. *Emeritus Professor of English, University of Wisconsin, Madison.*

Regula B. Qureshi. *Mactaggart Fellow, Department of Music, University of Alberta, Edmonton.*

Chaim Rabin. *Former Professor of Hebrew Language, Hebrew University of Jerusalem.*

Frederic James Edward Raby (d. 1966). *Fellow and Lecturer, Jesus College, University of Cambridge, 1948–54. Author of* A History of Christian Latin Poetry *and others.*

Kathleen Raine. *Poet and scholar. Author of* Collected Poems; Blake and Tradition; *and others.*

Gilbert Reaney. *Professor of Musicology, University of California, Los Angeles.*

Frederick Stephen Reckert. *Former Camoens Professor of Portuguese, King's College, University of London.*

Willi Reich (d. 1980). *Music critic. Author of* The Life and Work of Alban Berg *and many others.*

John Cowie Reid (d. 1972). *Professor of English, University of Auckland, New Zealand.*

Donald H. Reiman. *Editor,* Shelley and His Circle, The Carl H. Pforzheimer Shelley and His Circle Collection, New York Public Library. *General Editor,* The Bodleian Shelley Manuscripts.

Hans Siegbert Reiss. *Emeritus Professor of German, University of Bristol, Eng.*

Graham Reynolds. *Keeper, Departments of Prints and Drawings, 1961–74, and of Paintings, 1959–74, Victoria and Albert Museum, London.*

Edgar Preston Richardson (d. 1985). *President, Pennsylvania Academy of the Fine Arts, 1968–70. Director, Detroit Institute of Arts, 1945–62, and Winterthur Museum, Wilmington, Del., 1962–66.*

Margaret Ann Richardson. *Assistant Curator, Sir John Soane's Museum, London.*

Gisela Marie Augusta Richter (d. 1972). *Curator, Greek and Roman Department, Metropolitan Museum of Art, New York City.*

Christopher Bruce Ricks. *Professor of English, Boston University.*

Alexander L. Ringer. *Professor of Musicology, University of Illinois, Urbana.*

William Andrew Ringler, Jr. (d. 1987). *Professor of English, University of Chicago, 1962–80.*

Charles Martin Robertson. *Lincoln Professor of Classical Archaeology and Art, University of Oxford, 1961–78.*

Jean Robertson (d. 1990). *Senior Lecturer in English Literature, University of Southampton, Eng.*

Charles Alan Robson. *Former Reader in French Philology and Old French Literature, University of Oxford.*

William Wallace Robson. *Masson Professor of English Literature, University of Edinburgh.*

Jerome Laurence Alexander Roche. *Senior Lecturer in Music, University of Durham, Eng.*

Anne F. Rockwell. *Free-lance writer and illustrator. Author of* Glass, Stones and Crown: The Abbé Suger and the Building of St. Denis *and others.*

Emir Rodríguez-Monegal (d. 1985). *Professor of Latin American and Comparative Literature, Yale University.*

Leonard R. Rogers. *Sculptor and writer. Former Head, Faculty of Three-Dimensional Design, College of Art and Design, Loughborough, Eng.*

Arnold Rood. *Emeritus Professor of Dramatic Art, Dowling College, Oakdale, N.Y.*

Pierre M. Rosenberg. *Chief Curator, Department of Paintings, Louvre Museum, Paris.*

Sybil (Marion) Rosenfeld. *Theatre historian and writer. Coeditor,* Theatre Notebook, *1945–85.*

Marion Dean Ross. *Emeritus Professor of Architecture, University of Oregon, Eugene.*

Ronald Rossner. *Free-lance writer on African literature.*

Cecil Roth (d. 1970). *Editor in Chief,* Encyclopaedia Judaica. *Reader in Jewish Studies, University of Oxford, 1939–64.*

The Rev. Erik Reginald Routley (d. 1982). *Professor of Church Music, Westminster Choir College, Princeton, N.J., 1975–82.*

Eleanor Ruggles. *Biographer. Author of* Prince of Players: Edwin Booth *and others.*

Eberhard Ruhmer. *Former Curator in Chief, Bavarian State Painting Collection, Munich.*

Harold Rutland (d. 1977). *Music critic. Examiner, Trinity College of Music, London. Editor,* The Musical Times, *1957–60.*

Elizabeth Sabiston. *Academic Adviser, Stong College, York University, Downsview, Ont.*

Stanley Sadie. *Editor,* The New Grove Dictionary of Music and Musicians, *London.*

William Merritt Sale, Jr. (d. 1981). *Goldwin Smith Professor of English, Cornell University, Ithaca, N.Y.*

Mario Salmi (d. 1980). *Professor of the History of Medieval and Modern Art, University of Rome.*

Kaarlo Salo. *Former Attaché for Press and Cultural Affairs, Finnish Embassy, London.*

Lionel Salter. *Harpsichordist, pianist, and conductor. Assistant Controller of Music, British Broadcasting Corporation, London, 1967–74.*

Jeffrey L. Sammons. *Professor of German, Yale University.*

Claudio Sartori. *Chief, Office of Research and Indexing of the Italian Musical Funds, Braidense National Library, Milan.*

Angiola Sartorio. *Choreographer. Director of International Summer Dance School, Corona Del Mar, Calif. Former Head of the Dance Department, Sullins College, Bristol, Va.*

Tadao Sato. *Writer. Chairman, Japan Film P.E.N. Club. Author of* Kurosawa Akira no sekai *and others.*

Richard Anthony Sayce (d. 1977). *Fellow of Worcester College, Oxford; Reader in French Literature, University of Oxford.*

Byron Schaeffer, Jr. *Free-lance writer.*

Aaron Scharf. *Professor of Art History, Open University, Milton Keynes, Eng., 1969–82.*

Jefim H. Schirmann (d. 1981). *Professor of Hebrew Literature, Hebrew University of Jerusalem.*

Paul Schlueter. *Writer, editor, and lecturer on literary topics.*

Laurence E. Schmeckebier. *Emeritus Professor of Fine Arts and Emeritus Dean, School of Art, Syracuse University, N.Y.*

Nancy Schmidt. *Free-lance writer on African literature.*

Paul Waldo Schwartz. *Art Critic in Paris for* The New York Times *and* Studio International. *Author of* The Sculptor in His Studio.

Alexander Mackie Scott (d. 1989). *Reader in Scottish Literature, University of Glasgow.*

M.A. Screech. *Senior Research Fellow, All Souls College, University of Oxford. Fielden Professor of French Language and Literature, University College, University of London, 1971–84.*

Humphrey Searle (d. 1982). *Composer. Professor of Composition, Royal College of Music, London.*

Nancy Seeger. *Free-lance writer on visual arts.*

Edward G. Seidensticker. *Professor of Japanese, Columbia University.*

William C. Seitz (d. 1974). *George R. Kenan, Jr., Professor of the History of Art, University of Virginia, Charlottesville, 1971–74.*

Charles Coleman Sellers. *Librarian, Dickinson College, Carlisle, Pa., 1956–68. Author of* Charles Willson Peale *and others.*

Jean Selz. *Art historian and critic. Member, International Association of Art Critics, Paris.*

Victor Ilyich Seroff (d. 1979). *Writer. Author of* Rachmaninoff *and others.*

Alexandrino E. Severino. *Professor of Portuguese, Vanderbilt University, Nashville, Tenn.*

Charles Seymour, Jr. (d. 1977). *Professor of the History of Art, Yale University, 1954–77.*

Isaac Avi Shapiro. *Honorary Fellow, Shakespeare Institute, University of Birmingham, Eng.; former Senior Lecturer in English.*

Claude L. Shaver. *Alumni Professor Emeritus of Speech, Louisiana State University, Baton Rouge.*

Donald Leslie Shaw. *Professor of Latin American Studies, University of Edinburgh.*

Wendy Stedman Sheard. *Art historian. Author of* Antiquity in the Renaissance.

John K.G. Shearman. *Professor and Chairman, Department of Fine Arts, Harvard University.*

Sin-yan Shen. *President, Chinese Music Society of North America, Woodridge, Ill.*

David Julian Silverman. *Former Lecturer on Music, University of London.*

João Gaspar Simões. *Literary Critic, Diario de Noticias, Lisbon.*

Denis Sinor. *Distinguished Professor Emeritus of Uralic and Altaic Studies and of History, Indiana University, Bloomington.*

Otto Skutsch (d. 1990). *Professor of Latin, University College, University of London, 1951–72.*

Nicolas Slonimsky. *Conductor, composer, writer, and editor. Lecturer in Music, University of California, Los Angeles, 1964–67.*

F. Basil R. Smallman. *Alsop Professor Emeritus of Music, University of Liverpool.*

Arthur J(ames) M(arshall) Smith (d. 1980). *Professor of English and Poet-in-Residence, Michigan State University, East Lansing, 1960–72.*

Gilbert G. Smith. *Associate Professor of Spanish, North Carolina State University, Raleigh.*

Sheila Mary Smith. *Senior Lecturer in English, University of Nottingham, Eng.*

Whitney Smith. *Executive Director, Flag Research Center; Editor,* The Flag Bulletin, *Winchester, Mass.*

William Stevenson Smith (d. 1969). *Curator, Department of Egyptian Art, Museum of Fine Arts, Boston, 1956–69. Lecturer in Fine Arts, Harvard University, 1948–69.*

Craig Hugh Smyth. *Director, Villa I Tatti, Harvard Center for Italian Renaissance Studies, Florence; Professor of Fine Arts, Harvard University.*

M.R. Snodin. *Curatorial staff member, Department of Metalwork, Victoria and Albert Museum, London.*

Wilbert Snow (d. 1977). *Professor of English, Wesleyan University, Middletown, Conn., 1929–72.*

James E. Snyder (d. 1990). *Professor of Art History, Bryn Mawr College, Pa.*

David Sokol. *Professor of the History of Art and Architecture, University of Illinois at Chicago.*

Angelo Solmi. *Film critic,* Oggi (*weekly literary periodical*). *Former Managing Editor, Rizzoli Editore, Milan.*

Friedrich Solmsen (d. 1989). *Moses Slaughter Professor of Classical Studies, University of Wisconsin, Madison, 1962–74.*

Kathrine Sorley Walker. *Free-lance writer, editor, and dance critic. Author of* Dance and Its Creators *and others.*

Brian C. Southam. *Publisher, Athlone Press, London. Author of* Jane Austen's Literary Manuscripts *and others.*

John Sparrow. *Warden of All Souls College, University of Oxford, 1952–77.*

George Speaight. *Former Editorial Director, George Rainbird Ltd. Author of* The History of the English Puppet Theatre *and others.*

Robert (William) Speaight (d. 1976). *Actor, biographer, critic, and fiction writer. Author of* Life of Hilaire Belloc *and others.*

Monroe K. Spears. *Moody Professor of English, Rice University, Houston, Texas.*

John R. Spencer. *Professor of Art, Duke University, Durham, N.C.*

Albert Sperisen. *Vice President in Charge of Production, Foote, Cone & Belding, San Francisco.*

Radcliffe Squires. *Poet. Professor of English, University of Michigan, Ann Arbor, 1963–81.*

William Bedell Stanford (d. 1984). *Chancellor, University of Dublin, 1982–84; Regius Professor of Greek, 1940–80.*

Jerry Stannard (d. 1988). *Professor of History, University of Kansas, Lawrence, 1967–88.*

Enid Starkie (d. 1970). *Reader in French Literature, University of Oxford; Fellow, Somerville College, Oxford, 1934–65.*

Wolfgang Stechow (d. 1974). *Professor of Fine Arts, Oberlin College, Ohio, 1940–63.*

Richard G. Stern. *Professor of English, University of Chicago.*

Frederick William Sternfeld. *Former Reader in the History of Music, University of Oxford.*

Denis William Stevens. *President, Academia Monteverdiana. Professor of Musicology, Columbia University, 1964–76.*

Halsey Stevens (d. 1989). *Composer. Professor of Music, University of Southern California, Los Angeles, 1951–76.*

John I.M. Stewart. *Reader in English Literature, University of Oxford, 1969–73.*

Noel Stock. *Professor of English, University of Toledo, Ohio.*

Göran Stockenström. *Professor and Chairman, Department of Scandinavian Studies, University of Minnesota, Minneapolis.*

Sewell Stokes (d. 1979). *Author and dramatist. Author of* Isadora: An Intimate Portrait *and others.*

Eric Stone. *Lecturer in Modern History, University of Oxford; Fellow and Tutor in Medieval History, Keble College, Oxford.*

Gleb Struve (d. 1985). *Professor of Slavic Languages and Literatures, University of California, Berkeley, 1947–67.*

Michael Sullivan. *Christensen Professor Emeritus of Oriental Art, Stanford University, Calif.*

Sir John Summerson. *Curator, Sir John Soane's House and Museum, London, 1945–84.*

Denys Sutton (d. 1991). *Editor,* Apollo *magazine, 1962–87. Art Critic,* Financial Times. *Author of* The Art of James McNeill Whistler *and others.*

Frederick A. Sweet. *Curator of American Painting and Sculpture, Art Institute of Chicago, 1952–68.*

Jean-Guy Sylvestre. *National Librarian of Canada, Library of Parliament, Ottawa, 1968–83.*

Charles Johnson Taggart. *Free-lance writer.*

Stanley Taikeff. *Playwright and poet.*

Michael Talbot. *Professor of Music, University of Liverpool, Eng.*

James S. Tassie. *Adjunct Professor of French, Carleton University, Ottawa.*

Allen Tate (d. 1979). *Poet and critic. Regents' Professor of English, University of Minnesota, Minneapolis, 1966–68.*

Abdallah at-Tayib. *Vice-Chancellor; Professor of Arabic, University of Khartoum, Sudan.*

John Russell Taylor. *Art Critic,* The Times (*London*); *Film Critic, 1962–73. Professor of Cinema, University of Southern California, Los Angeles, 1972–78.*

Owen Reece Taylor (d. 1983). *Professor of French, Queen Mary College, University of London, 1969–77.*

Ronald Jack Taylor. *Professor of German, University of Sussex, Brighton, Eng.*

Walter Terry (d. 1982). *Dance critic and editor,* Saturday Review *magazine;* New York Herald Tribune; *and others.*

David Christopher Traherne Thomas. *Former Assistant Director of Art, Arts Council of Great Britain, London. Joint compiler of* The First Hundred Years of the Royal Academy, 1769–1868 (*catalog of Royal Academy Winter Exhibition, London, 1951–52*).

Lawrance R. Thompson (d. 1973). *Holmes Professor of Belles-Lettres, Princeton University, 1968–73; Professor of English, 1951–73.*

Friedrich Thöne (deceased). *Art historian. Author of* Lucas Cranach der Ältere *and others.*

Anthony Thwaite. *Poet and critic. Coeditor,* Encounter. *Author of* Contemporary English Poetry *and others.*

Marion Rose Tinling. *Coeditor of* The Secret Diary of William Byrd of Westover *and others.*

Joyce M.S. Tompkins (d. 1986). *Reader in English, University of London, 1948–65.*

Louis Tremaine. *Free-lance writer on African literature.*

Brian Lewis Trowell. *King Edward Professor of Music, King's College, University of London.*

C.H. Truman. *Curatorial staff member, Victoria and Albert Museum, London.*

Constantine Athanasius Trypanis. *Minister of Culture and Science, Government of Greece, 1974–77. Professor of Classical Languages and Literatures, University of Chicago, 1968–74.*

Martin Turnell (d. 1979). *Writer. Head, Programme Contracts Department, BBC, London, 1959–69.*

Arlin Turner (d. 1980). *James B. Duke Professor of English, Duke University, Durham, N.C., 1974–79.*

Darwin T. Turner (d. 1991). *University of Iowa Foundation Professor of English, University of Iowa, Iowa City, 1981–91; Chairman, African-American World Studies.*

Valev Uibopuu. *Novelist. Editor, Estonian Writers' Cooperative, Lund, Sweden.*

Vernon Philip Underwood (d. 1988). *Professor of French, University College, University of London.*

Dora Vallier. *Art critic. Author of* Henri Rousseau: Catalogue raisonné de l'oeuvre; Henri Rousseau; *and others.*

Norman Vance. *Lecturer in English, University of Sussex, Brighton, Eng.*

Eugene Vanderpool (d. 1989). *Professor of Archaeology, American School of Classical Studies at Athens, 1949–71.*

Milos Velimirovic. *Professor of Music, University of Virginia, Charlottesville.*

Paul Viallaneix. *Emeritus Professor of French Literature, University of Clermont-Ferrand, Fr.*

Michele Vishny. *Art historian and critic.* Contributor to Arts Magazine.

Wolf Von Eckardt. *Design Critic,* Time *magazine, 1981–85. Architecture Critic,* The Washington Post, *1963–81.*

Klaus Philipp Wachsmann. *Emeritus Professor of Music, Northwestern University, Evanston, Ill.*

John Wain. *Novelist, poet, and critic. Professor of Poetry, University of Oxford, 1973–78.*

Hugh Wakefield (d. 1984). *Keeper, Department of Circulation, Victoria and Albert Museum, London, 1960–75.*

Frank Walker (d. 1962). *Musicologist and broadcaster.*

David Harold Wallace. *Chief, Branch of Reference Services, National Park Service, U.S. Department of the Interior, Harpers Ferry, W.Va., 1974–80.*

Irving Wallace (d. 1990). *Novelist and biographer. Author of* The Fabulous Showman: The Life and Times of P.T. Barnum; The Man; *and many others.*

Francis James Warne. *Former Senior Lecturer in French, University of Bristol, Eng.*

Sir Ellis K. Waterhouse (d. 1985). *Director of Studies, Paul Mellon Centre for Studies in British Art, London, 1970–73. Barber Professor of Fine Arts; Director, Barber Institute of Fine Arts, University of Birmingham, Eng., 1952–70.*

Sir F.J.B. Watson. *Director of the Wallace Collection, London, 1963–74. Surveyor of the Queen's Works of Art, 1963–72.*

Paul F. Watson. *Associate Professor of the History of Art, University of Pennsylvania, Philadelphia.*

Max Wehrli. *Professor of the History of German Literature, University of Zürich.*

Sharon Weiner. *Free-lance writer.*

Stanley Weintraub. *Evan Pugh Professor of Arts and Humanities, Pennsylvania State University, University Park.*

John S. Weissmann. *Musicologist.*

David Welch. *Assistant Professor of Music, Ramapo College, Mahwah, N.J.*

Arthur Frederick Wells (d. 1966). *Praelector in Classics, University College, University of Oxford.*

James M. Wells. *Former Vice President and Custodian Emeritus, John M. Wing Foundation on the History of Printing, Newberry Library, Chicago.*

Enid Elder Hancock Welsford (d. 1981). *Lecturer in English, University of Cambridge, 1923–59. Author of* The Court Masque; The Fool; *and others.*

Francis William Wentworth-Sheilds (d. 1969). *Artist. Principal Lecturer, Department of Printing and Graphic Design, Twickenham College of Technology, Middlesex, Eng., 1966–69.*

Algot Werin (d. 1975). *Professor of Literature, University of Lund, Sweden.*

Carroll W. Westfall. *Associate Professor of the History of Art and Architecture, University of Illinois, Chicago.*

Geoffrey Weston. *Editorial staff member,* The Times (*London*). *Former Senior Subeditor,* Country Life.

Sir Jack Allan Westrup (d. 1975). *Professor of Music, University of Oxford, 1946–71; Fellow of Wadham College, Oxford, 1947–71.*

Harold E. Wethey (d. 1984). *Professor of the History of Art, University of Michigan, Ann Arbor, 1946–72.*

Margaret Dickens Whinney (d. 1975). *Reader in the History of Art, University of London, 1950–64.*

D. Maxwell White. *Emeritus Professor of Italian Language and Literature, University of Leeds, Eng.*

David White. *Faculty member, Department of Visual Arts, Trinity College, University of Dublin.*

E.B. White (d. 1985). *Writer. Contributing Editor,* The New Yorker.

Dorothy Whitelock (d. 1982). *Elrington and Bosworth Professor of Anglo-Saxon, University of Cambridge; Fellow of Newnham College, Cambridge, 1957–69.*

John Humphreys Whitfield. *Serena Professor Emeritus of Italian Language and Literature, University of Birmingham, Eng.*

Richard Whittingham. *Free-lance writer.*

David S. Wiley. *Director, African Studies Program, Michigan State University, East Lansing.*

John Ritchie Wilkie. *Emeritus Professor of German, University of Aberdeen, Scot.*

Frank Willett. *Director and Titular Professor, Hunterian Museum and Art Gallery, University of Glasgow.*

John William Mills Willett. *Writer and editor. Planning Editor,* The Times (*London*) Literary Supplement, *1969–71.*

Basil Willey (d. 1978). *King Edward VII Professor of English Literature, University of Cambridge, 1946–64.*

Geoffrey Wills. *Free-lance writer on antiques. Author of "Automata" in* The Concise Encyclopedia of Antiques.

Marjorie Winters. *Free-lance writer on African literature.*

William Witte. *Emeritus Professor of German, University of Aberdeen, Scot.*

Rudolf Wittkower (d. 1971). *Professor of the History of Art, Columbia University, 1956–68.*

Friedrich Wilhelm Wodtke (d. 1973). *Professor of German Literature, Kiel University, W.Ger., and Athens University, Greece.*

Mary Woodall (d. 1988). *Director, City Museum and Art Gallery, Birmingham, Eng., 1956–64.*

George Woodcock. *Free-lance writer. Editor,* Canadian Literature (*quarterly*), *University of British Columbia, Vancouver, 1959–77.*

Raymond Bernard Wood-Jones. *Reader in Architecture, Victoria University of Manchester.*

John E. Woods. *Associate Professor of History, University of Chicago.*

John Woodward (d. 1988). *Keeper, Birmingham City Museum and Art Gallery, Eng.*

Edward J. Wormley. *Products and interior designer. Former Design Director, Dunbar Furniture Corporation of Indiana, New York City.*

Robert M. Wren. *Professor of English, University of Houston, Texas.*

Stephen Graham Wright. *Former Adviser at the National Library of Ethiopia and at Haile Selassie I University, Addis Ababa.*

Patrick Maurice Yarker. *Former Senior Lecturer in English Literature, King's College, University of London.*

Percy Marshall Young. *Composer. Director of Music, Wolverhampton College of Technology, Eng., 1944–66.*

Philip Young. *Evan Pugh Professor of English, Pennsylvania State University, University Park.*

Oleksa Eliseyovich Zasenko. *Head, Department of the History of Ukrainian Prerevolutionary Literature, Institute of Literature, Ukrainian S.S.R. Academy of Sciences, Kiev.*

Nicolas M. Zernov (d. 1980). *Spalding Lecturer in Eastern Orthodox Culture, University of Oxford, 1947–66.*

Vladimir Viktorovich Zhdanov. *Literary critic. Assistant to the Chief Editor, Kratkaya Literaturnaya Entsiklopediya, Moscow.*

Leon M. Zolbrod. *Professor of Asian Studies, University of British Columbia, Vancouver.*

Part Seven. Technology

Samuel Roy Aldrich. *Emeritus Professor of Agronomy, University of Illinois, Urbana.*

Robert Theodore Alexander. *Captain, U.S. Coast Guard (retired); former Chief, Civil Engineering Division, U.S. Coast Guard Headquarters, Washington, D.C.*

Bruce E. Anderson. *Former Head, (gun) Propellant Research, U.S. Army Ordnance, Research and Development Division.*

Joseph Chapman Anderson. *Professor of Electrical Materials, Imperial College of Science and Technology, University of London.*

Walter Harry Green Armytage. *Emeritus Professor of Education, University of Sheffield, Eng. Author of* A Social History of Engineering.

A. Richard Baldwin. *Vice President and Executive Director of Research, Cargill, Inc., Minneapolis, Minn., 1964–73.*

Stanley S. Ballard. *Emeritus Professor of Physics, University of Florida, Gainesville.*

Karl A. Bauer. *Former President, Carl Zeiss, Inc., New York City.*

Sir Frederick Charles Bawden (d. 1972). *Director of Rothamsted Experimental Station, Harpenden, Eng., 1958–72.*

Roy E. Beal. *Manager, Welding Research, Illinois Institute of Technology Research Institute, Chicago.*

Jesse W. Beams (d. 1977). *Professor of Physics, University of Virginia, Charlottesville, 1930–69.*

T. Keilor Bentley. *Director, Owens Art Gallery, Mount Allison University, Sackville, N.B., 1976–89. Superintendent, Alexander Graham Bell Museum, Baddeck, Nova Scotia, 1959–64.*

Don H. Berkebile. *Associate Curator, Division of Transportation, Smithsonian Institution, Washington, D.C., 1974–81.*

Henry H. Billings. *Free-lance writer, illustrator, and mural painter. Author of* Bridges *and others.*

Raymond C. Binder (d. 1978). *Professor of Mechanical Engineering, University of Southern California, Los Angeles, 1960–78.*

Orlan William Boston. *Emeritus Professor of Mechanical and Production Engineering, University of Michigan, Ann Arbor.*

John Boyd. *Consulting Engineer, Electro Mechanical Division, Westinghouse Electric Corporation, Cheswick, Pa.*

John E. Brekke. *Former Head, Hawaii Fruit Laboratory, U.S. Department of Agriculture, University of Hawaii, Honolulu.*

Benjamin Arthur Brock. *Director and Factory Manager, Brock's Fireworks Ltd., England.*

Matthew Joseph Bruccoli. *Jefferies Professor of English, University of South Carolina, Columbia.*

Nelson Hitchcock Budd. *Former Information and Public Relations Director, National Canners Association.*

Willem Burger. *Former Senior Lecturer in Maritime Studies, University of Wales Institute of Science and Technology, Cardiff.*

Thomas Burnett. *Research Officer, Ottawa Research Station, Canada Department of Agriculture.*

Henry R. Clauser. *Consultant,* Materials Engineering *magazine; Editor-Publisher, 1965–69; Editor, 1958–64; Associate Editor and Managing Editor, 1946–57.*

Donald George Coleman. *Compiler, Computerized Information Retrieval System,* Wood Science and Forest Products Journal, *Forest Products Research Society, Madison, Wis.*

John Paul Comstock. *Former Naval Architect, Newport News Shipbuilding and Dry Dock Company, Va.*

Grace Rogers Cooper. *Museum consultant. Curator, Division of Textiles, Smithsonian Institution, Washington, D.C., 1946–76.*

André George Corbet. *Lecturer in Maritime Studies, University of Wales Institute of Science and Technology, Cardiff.*

Edwin Alfred Course. *Senior Lecturer in Adult Education, University of Southampton, Eng. Author of* London Railways.

Alden S. Crafts (d. 1990). *Professor of Botany, University of California, Davis, 1946–64.*

Daniel B. Dallas. *Editorial Director, Society of Manufacturing Engineers, Dearborn, Mich.; Editor in Chief,* The Tool and Manufacturing Engineers Handbook.

Milton Rockwood Daniels (deceased). *Commodore, U.S. Coast Guard.*

C.W. Dannatt (d. 1962). *Professor, Royal School of Mines, University of London.*

Donald de Carle. *Author of* Horology; Practical Watch Repairing; *and many others.*

Nigel T.M. Dennis. *Technical Manager, Edwards High Vacuum (Division of BOC Ltd.), Crawley, Eng.*

Charles Dollfus (d. 1981). *Aeronautical historian. Founder and Director, Museum of the Air, Paris.*

Francis Donaldson (d. 1970). *Vice President, Mason & Hanger—Silas Mason, Inc., New York City. Author of* Practical Shaftsinking.

George Dubpernell. *Consultant, M & T Chemicals Inc., Southfield, Mich.; technical adviser, 1955–66.*

Peter Duff. *Former Editor,* The Shipping World, *London.*

LeRoy Dugan. *Emeritus Professor of Food Science, Michigan State University, East Lansing.*

Frederick C. Durant III. *Aerospace historian. Assistant Director, Astronautics, National Air and Space Museum, Smithsonian Institution, Washington, D.C., 1965–81.*

Ernst R.G. Eckert. *Regents' Professor Emeritus of Mechanical Engineering, University of Minnesota, Minneapolis; Director, Thermodynamics and Heat Transfer Division, 1955–73.*

John F. Elliott (d. 1991). *Professor of Metallurgy, Massachusetts Institute of Technology, Cambridge, 1960–91.*

Victor A. Endersby. *Consulting civil engineer.*

Barbara Ensrud. *Writer and editor on food and wine.*

Daniel Snell Eppelsheimer (d. 1988). *Professor of Metallurgical and Nuclear Engineering, University of Missouri, Rolla, 1947–78.*

Valeska Evertsbusch. *Biochemist and Technical Editor, Biomedical Research Division, Lawrence Radiation Laboratory, University of California, Livermore.*

Gordon Maskew Fair (d. 1970). *Abbott and James Lawrence Professor of Engineering; Gordon McKay Professor of Sanitary Engineering, Harvard University.*

Raymond E. Fielding. *Professor of Communication, University of Houston, Texas.*

Gerald Reginald Mansel Garratt. *Keeper, Department of Aeronautics and Marine Transport, Science Museum, London, 1966–71.*

Wesley Patterson Garrigus. *Emeritus Professor of Animal Husbandry, University of Kentucky, Lexington.*

Alan H. Gayfer. *Editorial consultant and technical adviser,* Cycling World, *London. Editor,* Cycling, *1964–69.*

Lucien Albert Gerardin. *Research Director, Future Studies, Groupe Thomson, Paris.*

Frank Gerrard. *President, Institute of Meat, London, 1960–62. Head of Department, National College of Food Technology, Smithfield, London, 1947–61.*

George Sweet Gibb. *Former Director of Communications, Balfour Company, Attleboro, Mass.*

Charles Harvard Gibbs-Smith (d. 1981). *Research Fellow, Science Museum, London, 1976–81. Keeper, Public Relations and Education Department, Victoria and Albert Museum, London, 1947–71.*

Keith Reginald Gilbert (d. 1973). *Keeper, Department of Mechanical and Civil Engineering, Science Museum, London.*

John B. Gordon (d. 1964). *Secretary, Bureau of Raw Materials for American Vegetable Oils and Fats Industries, Washington, D.C.*

Linton E. Grinter. *Emeritus Dean, Graduate School, University of Florida, Gainesville; Executive Vice President, 1969–70. Author of* Design of Modern Steel Structures *and others.*

Harold James Grossman (d. 1967). *Marketing consultant on beverages. Author of* Grossman's Guide to Wines, Spirits and Beers *and others.*

Hagiwara Takahiro. *Emeritus Professor of Earthquake Research Institute, University of Tokyo.*

Andrew Edward Hahn. *Former Managing Editor,* Quality of Sheffield, *Sheffield, Eng.*

Robert W. Hamilton. *Consultant in environmental physiology. Research Supervisor, Research and Development Laboratory, Ocean Systems, Inc., Tarrytown, N.Y., 1969–74.*

Stanley Baines Hamilton. *Chartered civil and structural engineer. Writer and editor on engineering history.*

Francis Hamit. *Free-lance writer.*

Carl Hanson (d. 1985). *Pro-Vice-Chancellor; Professor of Chemical Engineering, University of Bradford, Eng.*

Wayne V. Harsha. *Editor,* Inland Printer/American Lithographer, *1951–70; Executive Editor, 1970–75.*

Richard S. Hartenberg. *Emeritus Professor of Mechanical Engineering, Northwestern University, Evanston, Ill.*

Alden Hatch (d. 1975). *Novelist, biographer, and historian. Author of* Remington Arms in American History *and others.*

John M. Hayes. *Emeritus Professor of Structural Engineering, Purdue University, West Lafayette, Ind.*

John F. Hayward (d. 1983). *Associate Director, Sotheby Parke-Bernet and Company, London and New York City. Deputy Keeper, Victoria and Albert Museum, London, 1946–65.*

Phyllis West Heathcote (d. 1990). *Paris fashion editor,* The Guardian (*Manchester*), *1946–68.*

John B. Heffernan (d. 1978). *Rear Admiral, U.S. Navy. Secretary, Naval Historical Foundation, Washington, D.C. Director of Naval History, Navy Department, 1946–56.*

Philip Heiberger. *Research Associate, E.I. du Pont de Nemours & Company, Inc., Philadelphia, 1976–83.*

Russell W. Henke. *Consulting engineer. Education Consultant, Institute for Fluid Power Education.*

David Himmelfarb. *Former Superintendent, U.S. Navy Ropewalk, Boston Naval Shipyard, Charlestown, Mass.*

Frederick Anthony Holland. *Professor and Chairman, Department of Chemical Engineering, University of Salford, Eng. Partner in Saldrem Associates (consulting chemical engineers).*

Solomon Cady Hollister (d. 1982). *Professor of Civil Engineering, Cornell University, Ithaca, N.Y.; Dean of Engineering, 1937–59.*

W.E. Howland (deceased). *Professor of Sanitary Engineering, Purdue University, West Lafayette, Ind.*

Inez Whitaker Hunt (d. 1983). *Lecturer and free-lance writer. Teacher of creative writing, University of Colorado, Colorado Springs, 1963–66.*

John Cyril Herbert Hurd. *Textiles consultant. Former Head, School of Textiles, Leicester College of Technology and Commerce, Eng.*

William G. Ibberson. *Chairman, Sheffield Testing Works Ltd. and Sheffield Assay Office, Eng. Former Chairman, George Ibberson and Company Ltd., Sheffield, Eng.*

Miles Hopkins Imlay. *Rear Admiral (retired), U.S. Coast Guard.*

William Thorton Innes (d. 1969). *Founder and Director, Typothetae Printing Trade School, Philadelphia.*

Emerson C. Itschner. *Lieutenant General, U.S. Army (retired); Chief of Engineers, U.S. Army Corps of Engineers, 1956–61.*

Jules Janick. *James Troop Distinguished Professor of Horticulture, Purdue University, West Lafayette, Ind.*

S. Paul Johnston (d. 1985). *Director, National Air and Space Museum, Smithsonian Institution, Washington, D.C., 1964–69.*

C. Clyde Jones. *Professor of Business Administration, Kansas State University, Manhattan.*

Sidney Karin. *Director, San Diego Supercomputer Center, California.*

Ralph Kenyon Kilbon. *Director, Creative Services, RCA Corporation, New York City.*

John Louis King, Jr. *Former Assistant Professor of History, University of the District of Columbia, Washington, D.C.*

Peter W. Kingsford. *Tutor, Extra Mural Department, University of London. Author of* Engineers, Inventors, and Workers.

Rudolf Kingslake. *Emeritus Professor of Optics, University of Rochester. Director of Optical Design, Eastman Kodak Company, Rochester, N.Y., 1939–69.*

D.C. Kiplinger (deceased). *Professor of Horticulture, Ohio State University, Columbus.*

Arthur Koehler (d. 1967). *Wood consultant, 1948–67. Chief, Division of Silvicultural Relations, Forest Products Laboratory, U.S. Forest Service, 1927–48. Lecturer, School of Forestry, Yale University, 1951–53.*

Dietrich Küchemann (d. 1976). *Consultant, Aerodynamics Department, Royal Aircraft Establishment, Farnborough, Eng.; Head of Department, 1966–71.*

George Lang. *International hotel, restaurant, and food consultant. Columnist,* Travel & Leisure *magazine.*

Pierre de Latil. *Scientific Editor,* Le Figaro, *Paris. Coauthor of* Le Professeur Auguste Piccard *and others.*

Mildred K. Lehman. *Researcher on* This High Man: The Life of Robert H. Goddard.

Milton Lehman (d. 1966). *Free-lance writer. Author of* This High Man: The Life of Robert H. Goddard.

Hellmut E. Lehmann-Haupt. *Emeritus Professor of Bibliography and Rare Book Consultant, University of Missouri, Columbia.*

Irwin Solomon Lerner. *President, Lerner Laboratories, New Haven, Conn.*

Lawrence P. Lessing. *Member, Board of Editors,* Fortune *magazine, New York City, 1941–52; 1965–74.*

Donald S. Lopez. *Chairman, Department of Aeronautics, National Air and Space Museum, Smithsonian Institution, Washington, D.C.*

Carleton Mabee. *Emeritus Professor of History, State University of New York College at New Paltz.*

Alexander McDonald (d. 1968). *Secretary, The Institution of Civil Engineers, London, 1954–67.*

James McDonald. *Free-lance writer.*

Fred Devereux McHugh. *Editor for the Office, Chief of Ordnance (Army), Washington, D.C.*

Donald LeCrone McMurry. *Author of* The Great Burlington Strike of 1888 *and others.*

L. Andrew Mannheim. *Technical editor, writer, and consultant. Author of* Leica Way *and others; editor of* Focal Encyclopedia of Photography.

Clarence Thomas Marek. *Emeritus Professor of Metal Processing, Purdue University, West Lafayette, Ind.*

Robert W. Marks. *Former Lecturer, New School for Social Research, New York City.*

George Peterkin Meade (d. 1975). *Vice President, International Commission for Uniform Methods of Sugar Analysis. Manager, Colonial Sugars Company, Gramercy, La., 1928–56.*

John Lawrence Mero. *President, Ocean Resources, Inc., La Jolla, Calif.*

Peter Michelmore. *Roving Editor, Reader's Digest. Author of* Einstein: Profile of the Man.

Jeannette Mirsky (d. 1987). *Visiting Fellow, Department of East Asian Studies, Princeton University, 1970–74. Coauthor of* The World of Eli Whitney.

Malcolm Monroe (d. 1988). *Vice President, Monroe Calculating Machine Company, Orange, N.J.*

John D. Moorhead. *Free-lance writer on military and technical subjects.*

James Charles Moran. *Former Editor,* Graphic Technology (*London*).

Michael James Moylan. *Director, Moylubes Ltd., Farnham, Eng.*

William Alvin Mudge. *Assistant to the President, International Nickel Company, Inc., New York City, 1955–58; Director, Technical Service, 1947–55.*

Herbert Lownds Nichols, Jr. *Publisher, Greenwich, Conn. Author of* Moving the Earth *and others.*

St. John Cousins Nixon. *Author of* The Invention of the Automobile; Wolseley: A Saga of the Motor Industry; *and others.*

Richard Marian Ogorkiewicz. *Professor, Royal Military College of Science, Cranfield Institute of Technology, Shrivenham, Eng.*

William David Ollis. *Professor of Organic Chemistry, University of Sheffield, Eng.*

Christabel Susan Orwin. *Coauthor of* The Open Fields; History of British Agriculture, 1846–1914.

A.S. Osley (d. 1987). *Head of Naval Scientific Administration Department, Ministry of Defence, United Kingdom.*

Robert P. Pace. *Account Executive, R. Hoe & Company, Inc., New York City.*

John Bingham Parkinson. *Former Chief, Aerodynamics, Aeronautical Vehicles, National Aeronautics and Space Administration, Washington, D.C.*

John W. Parry (d. 1976). *Author of* Spices; The Spice Handbook.

Harold Leslie Peterson (d. 1978). *Chief Curator, National Park Service, U.S. Department of the Interior, 1964–77. Author of* Arms and Armor in Colonial America, 1526–1783 *and others.*

William G. Pfann (d. 1982). *Department Head, Materials Research Laboratory, Bell Telephone Laboratories, Inc., Murray Hill, N.J.*

Jack Pickthall. *Consultant to International Flavours and Fragrances Ltd., Enfield, Eng. Former President, Society of Cosmetic Chemists, Great Britain, and British Society of Perfumers.*

Norman C. Polmar. *Consultant. Editor, U.S. sections,* Jane's Fighting Ships, *1967–77.*

John Bell Rae (d. 1988). *Professor of the History of Technology, Harvey Mudd College, Claremont, Calif., 1959–76.*

Deborah Robbins. *Free-lance writer.*

L.T.C. Rolt (d. 1974). *Member, Executive Committee, American Society for the History of Technology. Chairman, Talyllyn Railway Company, England, 1963–68.*

John Kerr Rose (d. 1974). *Senior Specialist in Natural Resources and Conservation, Library of Congress, 1955–73.*

Richard D. Ross. *Eastern Area Manager, Chemical Waste Management, Inc., Norristown, Pa.*

Hunter Rouse. *Carver Professor Emeritus of Hydraulics, University of Iowa, Iowa City.*

Michel Rouzé. *Former producer in French broadcasting. Author of* Robert Oppenheimer: The Man and His Theories.

Charles R. Russell. *Former Professor of Mechanical Engineering, California Polytechnic State University, San Luis Obispo.*

Sir (Edward) John Russell (d. 1965). *Director, Rothamsted Experimental Station, Harpenden, Eng., 1912–43.*

Harold Eugene Saunders (d. 1961). *Captain, U.S. Navy; Technical Assistant to Chief of Bureau of Ships, Navy Department.*

James Patrick Saville. *Former Manager, Information Services, The Metals Society, London.*

Julian L. Schueler (d. 1962). *Consultant, Continental Steel Corporation, Kokomo, Ind.*

Bernard Sylvester Schweigert. *Professor and Chairman, Department of Food Science and Technology, University of California, Davis.*

Donald Shannon. *Former Manager, Public Relations Department, Otis Elevator Company, New York City.*

Mitchell R. Sharpe. *Science writer and rocketry historian. Author of* Living in Space: The Astronaut and His Environment *and others.*

Orson Cutler Shepard. *Emeritus Professor of Metallurgy, Stanford University, Calif.*

Charles Ely Rose Sherrington. *Secretary, British Railways Research Service, 1924–62.*

Thomas Mortimer Simmons. *Former Deputy Keeper, Department of Transport and Mining, Science Museum, London.*

Alec Westley Skempton. *Emeritus Professor of Civil Engineering, Imperial College of Science and Technology, University of London.*

Albert Lewis Slover. *Former Technical Assistant to the Chief, Naval Engineering Division, U.S. Coast Guard.*

F.D. Smith. *Consultant, Monsanto Chemical Company, St. Louis, Mo.; Manager, University Development, Research and Engineering Division, 1956–63.*

Reginald Leslie Smith-Rose (d. 1980). *Secretary-General, Inter-Union Commission on Frequency Allocations for Radio Astronomy and Space Science, 1961–73. Director, Radio Research, Department of Scientific and Industrial Research, London, 1948–60.*

Edward W. Smykay. *Professor and Chairman, Department of Marketing, University of Baltimore.*

Harry J. Solberg. *Director of Corporate Planning, American Express Company. Former Associate Professor of Commerce, University of Wisconsin, Madison.*

Hereward Philip Spratt. *Deputy Keeper, Science Museum, London, 1930–67.*

Anthony Standen. *Executive Editor, Kirk-Othmer Encyclopedia of Chemical Technology, New York City, 1963–70.*

Joshua Stern. *Lecturer in Physics, University of Maryland, College Park. Associate Editor,* Review of Scientific Instruments.

Robert E. Stewart. *Distinguished Professor Emeritus of Agricultural Engineering, Texas A&M University, College Station.*

Arthur Stowers (d. 1977). *Keeper, Department of Mechanical and Civil Engineering, Science Museum, London, 1950–62.*

George R. Strakosch. *Associate, Jaros, Baum and Bolles (consulting engineers), New York City. Former Manager, Elevators, General Sales, Otis Elevator Company, New York City.*

Frank Whitworth Stubbs, Jr. (d. 1967). *Professor of Civil Engineering, Purdue University, West Lafayette, Ind.*

Charles Süsskind. *Professor of Engineering Science, University of California, Berkeley.*

Harry C. Thomson. *Former Chairman, Political Science Department, De Paul University, Chicago. Assistant Editor, Encyclopædia Britannica, Chicago, 1959–66.*

Samuel Tolansky (d. 1973). *Professor of Physics, Royal Holloway College, University of London, 1947–73.*

Forrest Glenn Tucker (deceased). *Emeritus Professor of Physics, Oberlin College, Ohio, 1926–60.*

William Arthur Vine (d. 1966). *Professor and Head, Department of Mining Engineering, Montana College of Mineral Science and Technology.*

Francis Walley. *Consulting Engineer. Under Secretary, Director of Civil Engineering Development, Department of the Environment, London, 1973–78.*

J. Garth Watson. *Secretary, Institution of Civil Engineers, London, 1967–79.*

Leon H. Weaver. *Former Professor of Criminal Justice, Michigan State University, East Lansing.*

Frederick Victor Wells. *Former Editor,* Soap, Perfumery and Cosmetics, *London. Founder-President, Society of Cosmetic Chemists of Great Britain.*

Charles S. Whewell. *Emeritus Professor of Textile Industries, University of Leeds, Eng.*

Theodore J. Williams. *Professor of Engineering; Director, Purdue Laboratory for Applied Industrial Control, Purdue University, West Lafayette, Ind.*

Harold Francis Williamson. *Professor of Economics, Northwestern University, Evanston, Ill., 1948–69. Author of* Winchester: The Gun That Won the West.

George Bulkeley Laird Wilson. *Former Deputy Keeper, Department of Mechanical and Civil Engineering, Science Museum, London.*

Mitchell Wilson (d. 1973). *Science writer and novelist. Author of* American Science and Invention *and others.*

Melville Lawrence Wolfrom (d. 1969). *Regents' Professor of Chemistry, Ohio State University, Columbus, 1965–69.*

Ellen Louise Young. *Historical research specialist (manufactures).*

R. Eric Young. *Consultant in high technology systems engineering and instrumentation.*

Lev Zetlin. *President, Zetlin-Argo Structural Investigations, Inc., New York City.*

Part Eight. Religion

Nigel James Abercrombie (d. 1986). *Chief Regional Adviser, Arts Council of Great Britain, London, 1968–73; Secretary-General, 1963–68.*

Charles Joseph Adams. *Professor of Islāmic Studies, McGill University, Montreal.*

The Rev. Joseph Denis Agius, O.S.B. *Monk of Downside Abbey, England.*

Sister Consuelo Maria Aherne. *Professor of History, Chestnut Hill College, Philadelphia. Assistant Staff Editor for* Mediaeval Church History; *Contributor to the* New Catholic Encyclopedia.

Sydney Eckman Ahlstrom (d. 1984). *Professor of Modern Religious History and American History, Yale University, 1964–83.*

Kye-hyon Ahn. *Director, Dong-kook University Museum, Seoul.*

Kurt Aland. *Professor of Church History, University of Münster, Ger.*

Hamilcar S. Alivisatos (d. 1969). *State Procurator of the Holy Synod of the Church of Greece. Professor of Canon Law and Pastoral Theology, University of Athens, 1918–56.*

The Rev. Michel Adrien Allard, S.J. (d. 1976). *Director, Institute of Oriental Studies, St. Joseph University, Beirut.*

The Rev. Arthur MacDonald Allchin. *Residentiary Canon of Canterbury Cathedral, Eng.*

Robert W. Allison. *Former Manuscript Research Specialist, Department of Special Collections, University of Chicago Library.*

The Rev. Anselm H. Amadio. *Chaplain; Instructor in Philosophy, Illinois Institute of Technology, Chicago. Staff Writer,* Philosophy and Religion, Encyclopædia Britannica, *Chicago, 1970–73.*

Milton Vasil Anastos. *Emeritus Professor of Byzantine Greek and History, University of California, Los Angeles.*

The Rev. George Wishart Anderson, D.D. *Professor of Hebrew and Old Testament Studies, University of Edinburgh.*

The Very Rev. Laurence Thomas Anderson, C.R.P. *President, St. Norbert's College, Kilnacrott, Cavan, Ire.*

William Scovil Anderson. *Professor of Latin and Comparative Literature, University of California, Berkeley.*

Zafar Ishaq Ansari. *Former Professor of History, University of Petroleum and Minerals, Dhahran, Saudi Arabia.*

Michio Araki. *Professor of Asian Studies, Tokyo Science University.*

Henri Arvon. *Professor, University of Paris X.*

Max Arzt (d. 1975). *Vice-Chancellor, Jewish Theological Seminary of America, New York City, 1951–75.*

Donald Attwater (d. 1977). *Author of* Penguin Dictionary of Saints; St. John Chrysostom, Pastor and Preacher.

Roger-François-Marie Aubert. *Emeritus Professor of Church History, Catholic University of Louvain, Belg.*

Peter William Avery. *Lecturer in Persian, University of Cambridge; Fellow of King's College, Cambridge.*

Roland H. Bainton (d. 1984). *Titus Street Professor of Church History, Yale University, 1936–62.*

The Rev. Msgr. Joseph W. Baker. *Officialis, Archdiocese of Saint Louis, Mo.*

Ernst Bammel. *Reader in Early Christian and Jewish Studies, University of Cambridge.*

The Rev. Wade Crawford Barclay (d. 1965). *Historian, Board of Missions, Methodist Church, New York City.*

The Rt. Rev. Msgr. John Mackintosh Tilney Barton (d. 1977). *Priest-in-Charge, SS. Peter and Edward, London, 1950–75. English Consultor, Pontifical Biblical Commission.*

František M. Bartoš (d. 1972). *Professor of Church History, Comenius Protestant Theological Faculty, Prague.*

Robert Pierce Beaver (d. 1987). *Professor of Missions, Divinity School, University of Chicago, 1955–71.*

The Very Rev. Msgr. Henry G.J. Beck. *Emeritus Professor of Church History, Immaculate Conception Seminary, Darlington, N.J.*

Alfons Becker. *Professor of Medieval History, Johannes Gutenberg University of Mainz, Ger.*

David Ben-Gurion (d. 1973). *Prime Minister and Minister of Defense, government of Israel, 1948–53, 1955–63.*

The Rev. John C. Bennett. *Emeritus President, Union Theological Seminary, New York City.*

Haim Hillel Ben-Sasson (d. 1977). *Professor of Jewish Medieval History, Hebrew University of Jerusalem.*

Manfred Bensing. *Emeritus Professor of History, University of Leipzig.*

Alan Lewis Berger. *Instructor in Religion, Miami University, Oxford, Ohio.*

Reginald Robert Betts (d. 1961). *Masaryk Professor of Central European History, University of London, 1946–61.*

The Rev. Maurice Bévenot, S.J. (d. 1980). *Professor of Ecclesiology, Heythrop College, University of London.*

Stephen Beyer. *Free-lance writer.*

Agehananda Bharati (d. 1991). *Professor of Anthropology, Syracuse University, N.Y., 1961–91.*

Jean Elfride Bickersteth. *Lecturer in Theology, University of Hull, Eng.*

Ludwig G.J. Bieler (d. 1981). *Professor of Palaeography and Late Latin, University College, Dublin, National University of Ireland.*

The Rev. Anselm Gordon Biggs, O.S.B. *Professor of History, Belmont Abbey College, N.C.*

Katharine Bird. *Free-lance writer on religion.*

The Rev. Robert L. Bireley, S.J. *Professor of History, Loyola University, Chicago.*

The Rev. Nicholas Frederick Bisheimer, S.V.D. (d. 1966). *President, Society of the Divine Word, Western Province.*

Ernst Bizer (d. 1975). *Professor of Church History, Rhenish Friedrich Wilhelm University of Bonn.*

William Barnett Blakemore (d. 1975). *Professor of Ecumenical Christianity, 1971–75; Dean, Disciples Divinity House, University of Chicago.*

Sheldon H. Blank (d. 1989). *Professor of Bible, Hebrew Union College–Jewish Institute of Religion, Cincinnati, Ohio, 1926–78.*

Edwin Boardman (d. 1968). *Professor of Church History and Senior Counselor, Ashland Theological Seminary, Ohio.*

Pieter Arie Hendrik de Boer (d. 1989). *Professor of Old Testament, State University of Leiden, Neth., 1938–78.*

Rabbi Ben Zion Bokser (d. 1984). *Rabbi, Forest Hills Jewish Center, Forest Hills, N.Y. Adjunct Professor of Political Science, Queens College, City University of New York.*

Arthur Stanley Bolster, Jr. *Professor of Education, Harvard University.*

Gerald Bonner. *Emeritus Reader in Theology, University of Durham, Eng.*

The Rev. William Joseph Bosch, S.J. *Associate Professor of History, LeMoyne College, Syracuse, N.Y.*

Carroll Julian Bourg. *Associate Professor of Sociology, Fisk University, Nashville, Tenn. Director, Office of Social Research, Maryland Province of Jesuits, Baltimore, 1966–68.*

The Rev. Charles Samuel Braden (d. 1970). *Resident Scholar, Perkins School of Theology, Southern Methodist University. Professor of History and Literature of Religions, Northwestern University, Evanston, Ill., 1943–54.*

The Rev. Ignatius Charles Brady, O.F.M. *Director of the theological section, College of St. Bonaventura, Grottaferrata, Italy, 1961–82.*

Paul Breidenbach. *Associate Professor of Anthropology, Loyola University, Chicago.*

Keith Richard Bridston. *Professor of Systematic Theology, Pacific Lutheran Theological Seminary and the Graduate Theological Union, Berkeley, Calif.*

John Bright. *Emeritus Professor of Hebrew and the Interpretation of the Old Testament, Union Theological Seminary, Richmond, Va.*

Harmon Hartzell Bro. *Codirector, Pilgrim Institute, Clinton, Wash.*

The Rev. John Francis Broderick, S.J. *Emeritus Professor of Ecclesiastical History, Weston College, Mass.*

The Rev. James Patrick Brodrick, S.J. *Author of* Origin of the Jesuits *and others.*

Geoffrey W. Bromiley. *Senior Professor of Church History and Historical Theology, Fuller Theological Seminary, Pasadena, Calif.*

The Rev. Victor John Knight Brook (d. 1974). *Fellow of All Souls College, Oxford, 1938–59; Lecturer in Reformation Theology, University of Oxford, 1929–34.*

Christopher Nugent Lawrence Brooke. *Dixie Professor of Ecclesiastical History, University of Cambridge.*

Peter R.L. Brown. *Rollins Professor of History, Princeton University.*

Frederick Fyvie Bruce (d. 1990). *Rylands Professor of Biblical Criticism and Exegesis, Victoria University of Manchester, 1959–78.*

The Rev. Joseph Stanislaus Brusher, S.J. (d. 1972). *Professor of History, University of San Francisco, 1968–72.*

The Rev. Erwin Buck. *Pastor, St. Peter Lutheran Church, Medicine Hat, Alberta.*

Robert J. Buck. *Professor of Classics, University of Alberta, Edmonton.*

J.A.B. van Buitenen (d. 1979). *Distinguished Service Professor of Sanskrit and Indic Studies, University of Chicago, 1974–79.*

The Rev. Sebastian Bullough, O.P. (d. 1967). *Lecturer in Hebrew, University of Cambridge.*

The Rev. Walter John Burghardt, S.J. *Theologian in Residence, Georgetown University, Washington, D.C. Editor, Theological Studies.*

The Rev. Ernest Joseph Burrus, S.J. *Historian of Jesuit Order, Jesuit Historical Institute, Rome, Italy, and St. Louis, Mo.*

Harold Butcher. *Free-lance writer.*

Theodore Vern Buttrey, Jr. *Professor of Classics, University of Michigan, Ann Arbor.*

Charles Robert Byrnes. *Former Executive Director, International Association of Auditorium Managers, Chicago Heights, Ill.*

The Rev. William James Byron, S.J. *President, Catholic University of America, Washington, D.C.*

Henry J. Cadbury (d. 1974). *Hollis Professor of Divinity, Harvard University, 1934–54. Chairman, American Friends Service Committee, 1928–34; 1944–60.*

The Rev. Carnegie Samuel Calian. *President and Professor of Theology, Pittsburgh Theological Seminary.*

Mother Louise Callan, R.S.C.J. (d. 1966). *Professor of History, Maryville College of the Sacred Heart, St. Louis, Mo.*

Pier Paolo del Campana. *Professor of Comparative Religion, Sophia University, Tokyo.*

The Rev. Philip Caraman, S.J. *Editor, The Month, 1948–63.*

Clifford M. Carey. *Assistant Executive Director, National Council of the Young Men's Christian Associations, New York City.*

John Carey. *Merton Professor of English Literature, University of Oxford.*

William David James Cargill Thompson (d. 1978). *Professor of Ecclesiastical History, King's College, University of London, 1976–78.*

The Rev. Edward Wilson Carlile. *Liaison Officer, East Africa Appeal, Church Army, London; Chief Secretary, 1949–60.*

Henry Stewart Carter (deceased). *Minister, Memorial Church, Cambridge, Eng.*

Ernest Cassara. *Professor of History, George Mason University, Fairfax, Va.*

The Very Rev. Henry Chadwick. *Master of Peterhouse, Cambridge; Regius Professor Emeritus of Divinity, University of Cambridge.*

Nora Kershaw Chadwick (d. 1972). *University Lecturer, University of Cambridge, 1950–58. Editor and contributor,* Studies in Early British History *and others.*

W. Owen Chadwick. *Regius Professor of Modern History, University of Cambridge, 1968–83; Dixie Professor of Ecclesiastical History, 1958–68.*

Wing-tsit Chan. *Emeritus Professor of Chinese Philosophy and Culture, Dartmouth College, Hanover, N.H. Anna R.D. Gillespie Professor Emeritus of Philosophy, Chatham College, Pittsburgh.*

Helen McCaig Chandra. *Free-lance writer on Asian religions.*

Byong-gil Chang. *Professor of Religion, Seoul National University.*

Kenneth K.S. Chen. *Emeritus Professor of Oriental Languages, University of California, Los Angeles.*

The Rev. Sok-u Choe. *Pastor, Myong-dong Catholic Cathedral, Seoul.*

Francis P(almer) Clarke. *Emeritus Professor of Philosophy, University of Pennsylvania, Philadelphia.*

The Rev. Arthur C. Cochrane. *Emeritus Professor of Systematic Theology, Dubuque Theological Seminary, Iowa.*

A.O.J. Cockshut. *G.M. Young Lecturer in 19th Century English Literature, University of Oxford; Fellow of Hertford College, Oxford. Author of* Anglican Attitudes: A Study of Victorian Religious Controversies *and others.*

John Cogley (d. 1976). *Senior Fellow, Center for the Study of Democratic Institutions, Santa Barbara, Calif., 1967–76; Editor,* The Center Magazine, *1967–74. Author of* The Layman and the Council *and others.*

The Rev. Louis Cognet. *Director of Studies, Collège de Juilly, France.*

Gerson D. Cohen (d. 1991). *Chancellor, Jewish Theological Seminary of America, New York City, 1972–86; Jacob H. Schiff Professor of History, 1970–86.*

The Very Rev. Francis J. Connell (d. 1967). *Dean for Religious Communities, Catholic University of America, Washington, D.C., 1957–67; Professor of Moral Theology, 1949–58.*

Thomas L. Coonan. *Former Professor of History, St. Louis University, Mo.*

Patricia Louise Cox. *Free-lance writer on religion.*

Vincent Cronin. *Free-lance writer. Author of* The Flowering of the Renaissance *and others.*

The Rev. Frank Leslie Cross (d. 1968). *Lady Margaret Professor of Divinity, University of Oxford, 1944–68. Editor of* The Oxford Dictionary of the Christian Church.

Alice Curtayne (d. 1981). *Author of* St. Catherine of Siena; The Irish Story; *and others.*

Jean Dagens. *Former Professor of Classical French Literature, University of Strasbourg, Fr.*

Horton Marlais Davies. *Henry W. Putman Professor of the History of Christianity, Princeton University.*

The Rev. J. Gordon Davies (d. 1990). *Edward Cadbury Professor and Head, Department of Theology, University of Birmingham, Eng., 1960–86.*

The Rev. Victor Cyril De Clercq, C.I.C.M. *Former Professor of Patrology and Church History, Pontifical College Josephinum, Worthington, Ohio.*

Count Michael de la Bedoyere (d. 1973). *Editor,* Search *newsletter, 1962–68;* Catholic Herald, *1934–62.*

The Rt. Rev. Carl Gustav Diehl. *Bishop of Tranquebar, Tamil Evangelical Lutheran Church, South India, 1967–72.*

The Rev. Godfrey Leo Diekmann, O.S.B. *Regents Professor of Theology, St. John's University, Collegeville, Minn. Editor of* Worship.

George Edward Dimock, Jr. *Professor of Classical Languages and Literatures, Smith College, Northampton, Mass.*

Decima L. Douie. *Former Reader in Medieval History, University of Hull, Eng.*

Jacques Duchesne-Guillemin. *Emeritus Professor of Indo-Iranian Studies, State University of Liège, Belg.*

The Rev. George H. Dunne, S.J. *Secretary, Committee on Society, Development and Peace, World Council of Churches and the Pontifical Commission for Justice and Peace, Ecumenical Centre, Geneva, Switz., 1967–72.*

The Very Rev. Joseph William Dunne (deceased). *Canon of Metropolitan Chapter of Birmingham; Parish Priest, St. Mary's, The Mount, Walsall, Eng.*

Donald F. Durnbaugh. *Professor of Church History, Bethany Theological Seminary, Oak Brook, Ill.*

Cornelius J. Dyck. *Professor of Anabaptist and Sixteenth-century Studies, Mennonite Biblical Seminary, Elkhart, Ind.*

H. Byron Earhart. *Professor of Religion, Western Michigan University, Kalamazoo.*

David A. Ede. *Associate Professor of Religion, Western Michigan University, Kalamazoo.*

E. Earle Ellis. *Former Research Professor of New Testament Literature, New Brunswick Theological Seminary, N.J.*

The Rt. Rev. John Tracy Ellis. *Emeritus Professor of Church History, University of San Francisco.*

Gracia Fay Ellwood. *Free-lance writer on religion, mythology, and the occult.*

Robert S. Ellwood, Jr. *Bishop James W. Bashford Professor of Oriental Studies, University of Southern California, Los Angeles.*

The Rev. John Adney Emerton. *Regius Professor of Hebrew, University of Cambridge.*

Marc Marie Escholier (d. 1972). *Judge, Supreme Court of Appeal, Paris. Author of* Port-Royal *and others.*

Josef van Ess. *Professor of Islamic Studies and Semitic Languages, Eberhard Karl University of Tübingen, Ger.*

The Rev. Carl Evans. *Pastor, Door Village United Methodist Church, La Porte, Ind.*

The Rev. Edward Every. *Canon, St. George's Collegiate Church, Jerusalem.*

Brother George Every, S.S.M. (deceased). *Lecturer, Kelham Theological College, Newark, Eng.*

The Rev. Eugene Rathbone Fairweather. *Keble Professor of Divinity, Trinity College, University of Toronto.*

Andrea Faste. *Free-lance writer on religion.*

J.W. Fiegenbaum. *Professor of Religion, Mount Holyoke College, South Hadley, Mass.*

Floyd V. Filson. *Emeritus Dean and Emeritus Professor of New Testament, McCormick Theological Seminary, Chicago.*

Louis Finkelstein. *Emeritus Chancellor, Jewish Theological Seminary of America, New York City.*

Thomas Fish. *Professor of Mesopotamian Studies, Victoria University of Manchester, 1948–60.*

The Rev. Joseph Augustine Fitzmyer, S.J. *Professor of New Testament, Catholic University of America, Washington, D.C.*

The Ven. Charles Robert Forder. *Emeritus Archdeacon of York, Eng.; Canon and Prebendary of Fenton in York Minster, 1957–72.*

A. Durwood Foster. *Professor of Christian Theology, Pacific School of Religion, Berkeley, Calif.*

The Rev. Kenelm Francis Foster, O.P. (d. 1986). *Reader in Italian, University of Cambridge.*

Brian Fothergill (d. 1990). *Chairman, Royal Society of Literature, 1986–89. Author of* The Cardinal King *and others.*

Linwood Fredericksen. *Undersecretary and Manager, Program Development Division, Rotary International. Associate Editor, Religion,* Encyclopædia Britannica, *Chicago, 1969–73.*

The Rev. Walter Freitag. *Professor of the Church in Historic Witness and Biblical Interpretation, Lutheran Theological Seminary, University of Saskatchewan, Saskatoon.*

The Rev. Reginald Michael French. *Vicar of St. James', London, 1930–55.*

The Rev. William Hugh Clifford Frend. *Emeritus Professor of Ecclesiastical History, University of Glasgow.*

Rabbi Albert H. Friedlander. *Dean of Rabbinic Studies, Leo Baeck College, London. Minister, Westminster Synagogue, London.*

Asaf Ali-Asghar Fyzee. *Vice-Chancellor, University of Jammu and Kashmir, Srinagar, India, 1957–58. Indian Ambassador to Egypt, 1949–51.*

John G. Gallaher. *Professor of History, Southern Illinois University, Edwardsville.*

The Rev. Maynard Joseph Geiger, O.F.M. *Former Historian of the Franciscan Fathers of the Pacific Coast and Archivist of Mission, Santa Barbara, Calif.*

The Rev. Joseph Gill, S.J. (d. 1989). *Professor of Byzantine Greek Language and of Byzantine History, Pontifical Oriental Institute, Rome, 1946–67.*

Nahum N. Glatzer (d. 1990). *Professor of Jewish History Brandeis University, Waltham, Mass., 1956–73.*

Judah Goldin. *Professor of Oriental Studies and Post-Biblical Hebrew Literature, University of Pennsylvania, Philadelphia.*

Cyrus H. Gordon. *Emeritus Professor of Hebraic and Near East Studies; Director, Center for Ebla Research; New York University, New York City. Emeritus Professor of Mediterranean Studies, Brandeis University, Waltham, Mass.*

Stephen Gottschalk. *Associate Professor of History, U.S. Naval Postgraduate School, Monterey, Calif., 1972–75. Author of* The Emergence of Christian Science in American Religious Life.

John Grace (d. 1972). *National Chief Secretary, The Salvation Army, New York City, 1961–70.*

Hilda Charlotte Graef. *Author of* The Light and the Rainbow; Mary, A History of Doctrine and Devotion; *and others.*

Ernest (Eugene) Graf (d. 1962). *Monk of Buckfast Abbey, England.*

Robert M. Grant. *Carl Darling Buck Professor Emeritus of Humanities; Emeritus Professor of Early Christian History, Divinity School, University of Chicago.*

John Evelyn Bury Gray. *Reader in Sanskrit, School of Oriental and African Studies, University of London.*

The Rev. Paul Grosjean, S.J. (d. 1964). *Bollandist. Author of* Henrici VI Angliae Regis Miracula Postuma *and others.*

G.E. von Grunebaum (d. 1972). *Professor of History; Director, Near Eastern Center, University of California, Los Angeles, 1957–72.*

The Rev. Pierre Joseph G'sell, O.S.B. (deceased). *Monk at Solesmes Abbey, France.*

Herbert V. Guenther. *Emeritus Professor of Far Eastern Studies, University of Saskatchewan, Saskatoon.*

The Rev. Franco Guerello, S.J. *Professor of Italian Literature, Social Institute, Turin, Italy.*

The Rev. Walter George Gumbley, O.P. (d. 1968). *Occasional Lecturer at Blackfriars, Oxford, 1942–45; 1950–61. Author of* Parish Priests Among the Saints *and others.*

Oliver Robert Gurney. *Emeritus Professor of Assyriology, University of Oxford.*

Oskar Halecki (d. 1973). *Professor of Eastern European History, Graduate School, Fordham University, New York City, 1944–61. Honorary President, Polish Institute of Arts and Science, New York City.*

Edward Elton Young Hales (d. 1986). *Author of* Revolution and Papacy *and others.*

The Rev. François Halkin, S.J. *Bollandist. Author of* Bibliotheca Hagiographica Graeca *and others.*

The Rev. Basil Hall. *Fellow and Dean, St. John's College, University of Cambridge, 1974–79. Professor of Ecclesiastical History, Victoria University of Manchester, 1968–74.*

Bernice Margaret Hamilton. *Associate of St. Edmund's College, University of Cambridge. Former Senior Lecturer in Politics, University of York, Heslington, Eng.*

Robert Theodore Handy. *Henry Sloane Coffin Professor of Church History, Union Theological Seminary, New York City.*

Edward R. Hardy (d. 1981). *Lecturer in Early Church History, University of Cambridge, 1969–75. Professor of Church History, Berkeley Divinity School, New Haven, Conn., 1947–69.*

Ruth Mulvey Harmer. *Professor of English and Modern Languages, California State Polytechnic University, Pomona.*

The Rev. Carl John Hemmer, S.J. *Former Research Assistant of Ecclesiastical History, Colegio de San Estanislao, Salamanca, Spain.*

Carl F.H. Henry. *Theologian. Lecturer-at-Large, World Vision International. Writer and editor on religion.*

The Rev. Ben Mohr Herbster (d. 1984). *President, United Church of Christ, 1961–69.*

Ferdinand Aloys Hermens. *Emeritus Professor of Political Science, University of Cologne.*

The Most Rev. Edward Louis Heston, C.S.C. (d. 1973). *Chairman, Pontifical Social Communications Commission, Vatican City, 1971–73.*

Naofusa Hirai. *Professor of Shinto Studies, Kokugakuin University, Tokyo.*

H.Z. Hirschberg (d. 1976). *Professor of Jewish History in Muslim Countries, Bar-Ilan University, Ramat Gan, Israel.*

The Rev. Ian Hislop, O.P. *Former Provincial of the English Dominican Province.*

John Thayer Hitchcock. *Professor of Anthropology and South Asian Studies, University of Wisconsin, Madison.*

Philip Khuri Hitti (d. 1978). *Professor of Semitic Literature, Princeton University, 1936–54.*

Lauri O. Honko. *Professor of Folkloristics and Comparative Religion, University of Turku, Fin.*

Winthrop S. Hudson. *Adjunct Professor of Religion, University of North Carolina at Chapel Hill. James B. Colgate Professor of the History of Christianity, Colgate Rochester Divinity School, Rochester, N.Y., 1948–77.*

The Rev. Gordon Huelin. *Vicar, St. Margaret Pattens, London. Lecturer in Ecclesiastical History, King's College, University of London.*

William Robert Hutchison. *Charles Warren Professor of the History of Religion in America, Harvard University.*

J. Philip Hyatt (d. 1972). *Professor of Old Testament, Vanderbilt University, Nashville, Tenn., 1944–72.*

S.M. Ikram (d. 1973). *Director, Institute of Islāmic Culture, Lahore, Pak.*

Toshihiko Izutsu. *Professor of Islāmic Studies, McGill University, Montreal, 1969–75.*

Carl T. Jackson. *Professor of History, University of Texas at El Paso.*

Edmond Jacob. *Professor of Old Testament Exegesis, Evangelical Theological Faculty, University of Strasbourg, Fr.*

The Rev. Jerome Vincent Jacobsen, S.J. (d. 1970). *Professor of History, Loyola University, Chicago.*

Thorkild Jacobsen. *Emeritus Professor of Assyriology, Harvard University.*

The Rev. Edwin Oliver James (d. 1972). *Chaplain of All Souls College, University of Oxford. Professor of the History and Philosophy of Religion, University of London.*

The Rev. Daniel T. Jenkins. *Weyerhaeuser Professor of Systematic Theology, Princeton Theological Seminary, N.J., 1981–84.*

Eric John. *Reader in History, Victoria University of Manchester, Eng.*

Sherman Elbridge Johnson. *Dean, Church Divinity School of the Pacific, Berkeley, Calif., 1951–72.*

J. Stillson Judah. *Emeritus Professor of the History of Religions, Pacific School of Religion and Graduate Theological Union, Berkeley, Calif.*

Mark Juergensmeyer. *Associate Professor of Religious Studies, Graduate Theological Union and University of California, Berkeley.*

Max Kaltenmark. *Director of Studies, École Pratique des Hautes Études (Institute for Advanced Research), Paris, 1957–78.*

Arvid S. Kapelrud. *Professor of Old Testament, University of Oslo.*

Firuz Kazemzadeh. *Professor of History, Yale University. Former Chairman, National Spiritual Assembly of the Baha'is of the United States.*

Elie Kedourie. *Professor of Politics, London School of Economics and Political Science, University of London.*

The Rev. John N.D. Kelly. *Principal of St. Edmund Hall, Oxford, 1951–79; Lecturer in Patristic Studies, University of Oxford, 1948–76.*

The Rev. John Arthur Kemp, S.J. (d. 1963). *Professor of Medieval History, Loyola University, Chicago, 1959–63.*

Malcolm H. Kerr (d. 1984). *President, American University of Beirut, 1982–84. Professor of Political Science, University of California, Los Angeles, 1967–82.*

The Rt. Rev. Sylvester Michael Killeen, O. Praem. *Former Chancellor, Saint Norbert College, De Pere, Wis.*

Joseph M. Kitagawa. *Emeritus Professor of the History of Religions and of Far Eastern Languages and Civilizations, University of Chicago.*

George Angus Fulton Knight. *President, Pacific Theological College, Suva, Fiji, 1965–72.*

The Rev. Michael David Knowles, O.S.B. (d. 1974). *Regius Professor of Modern History, University of Cambridge, 1954–63.*

The Most Rev. Franz Cardinal König. *Archbishop of Vienna, 1956–85.*

Gottfried Georg Krodel. *Professor of History and Church History, Valparaiso University, Ind.*

Bruno Kroker. *Free-lance writer on American Protestantism.*

Hans Kühner (d. 1986). *Historian and free-lance writer. Specialist on the history of the Roman Catholic Church and the Papacy. Author of* Encyclopedia of the Papacy *and others.*

Werner Georg Kümmel. *Emeritus Professor of New Testament, Philipps University of Marburgh, Ger.*

Stephan George Kuttner. *Emeritus Professor of Canon Law, University of California, Berkeley. President, Institute of Research and Study in Medieval Canon Law.*

Gerhart B. Ladner. *Emeritus Professor of History, University of California, Los Angeles.*

The Most Rev. Pio Laghi. *Ambassador of the Vatican to the United States.*

Helen B. Lamb (d. 1975). *Author of* Economic Development of India.

The Rev. John William Lamb. *Former Canon of York. Member, National Church Assembly, England. Author of* The Archbishopric of Lichfield *and others.*

Eugene N. Lane. *Professor of Classics, University of Missouri, Columbia.*

Henri Laoust (d. 1983). *Professor of Sociology of Islām, College of France, Paris, 1956–76.*

Harriet Pratt Lattin. *Historian. Author of* The Peasant Boy Who Became Pope.

The Rev. M.-H. Laurent, O.P. (deceased). *Keeper of the Vatican Library.*

Clifford Hugh Lawrence. *Professor of Medieval History, Bedford College, University of London.*

Du-hyon Lee. *Professor, Teacher's College, Seoul National University.*

Sid Z. Leiman. *Professor of Jewish History and Literature; Chairman, Department of Judaic Studies, Brooklyn College, City University of New York.*

The Rev. Augustin Pierre Léonard, O.P. *Professor of Theology, Dominican College of La Sarte, Belg., and University of Notre Dame, Ind.*

The Rev. Joseph Leonard, C.M. (deceased). *Lecturer at St. Mary's College, London. Author of* Saint Vincent de Paul and Mental Prayer.

The Rev. William Paul Le Saint, S.J. *Professor of Theology; President of the Faculty, St. Mary of the Lake Seminary, Mundelein, Ill., 1965–70.*

Sir Shane Leslie (d. 1971). *Author of* Memoir of Cardinal Gasquet *and others.*

Fairy von Lilienfeld. *Professor of the Theology of the Christian East, Friedrich Alexander University of Erlangen-Nürnberg, Ger.*

The Rev. Poul Georg Lindardt. *Professor of Church History, University of Århus, Den., 1942–80.*

Gillian Lindt. *Professor of Religion, Columbia University.*

Franklin Hamlin Littell. *Professor of Religion, Temple University, Philadelphia.*

The Rev. Charles Patrick Loughran, S.J. *Emeritus Professor of European History, Fordham University, New York City.*

Frederick Stanley Lusby. *Professor of Religious Studies, University of Tennessee, Knoxville.*

The Rev. Thomas Timothy McAvoy, C.S.C. (d. 1969). *Archivist and Professor of History, University of Notre Dame, Ind.*

George Englert McCracken. *Emeritus Professor of Classical Languages, Drake University, Des Moines, Iowa.*

The Rev. James Stevenson McEwen. *Professor of Church History, University of Aberdeen, Scot., 1958–77.*

Sister Mary Emmanuel McIver, O.S.U. *Former Professor of Theology, College of New Rochelle, N.Y.*

The Rev. John L. McKenzie, S.J. *Emeritus Professor of Theology, De Paul University, Chicago.*

Joseph Cumming McLelland. *Professor of Philosophy of Religion; Dean, Faculty of Religious Studies, McGill University, Montreal.*

William Hewat McLeod. *Professor of History, University of Otago, Dunedin, New Zealand.*

William Gerald McLoughlin. *Professor of History, Brown University, Providence, R.I. Author of* Modern Revivalism: C.G. Finney to Billy Graham.

John F. McMahon. *General and Commander in Chief, Volunteers of America, New York City, 1958–80.*

The Rev. Francis Gerard McManamin, S.J. *Former Associate Professor of History, Loyola College, Baltimore.*

The Rev. Robert Edward McNally, S.J. (d. 1977). *Professor of Historical Theology, Fordham University, New York City, 1966–77.*

The Very Rev. Joseph McSorley (d. 1963). *Superior General of the Paulist Fathers, 1924–29.*

The Right Rev. Msgr. Richard C. Madden. *Former Pastor, St. John the Beloved, Summerville, S.C.*

William Mahony. *Professor of Religion, Davidson College, N.C.*

George Makdisi. *Professor of Arabic and Islamic Studies; Director, Center of Medieval Studies, University of Pennsylvania, Philadelphia.*

Cyril Alexander Mango. *Bywater and Sotheby Professor of Byzantine and Modern Greek, University of Oxford.*

The Rev. William W. Manross. *Emeritus Professor of Church History, Philadelphia Divinity School, Pa.*

Clyde L. Manschreck. *Chavanne Professor of Religious Studies, Rice University, Houston, Texas. Emeritus Professor of the History of Christianity, Chicago Theological Seminary.*

The Rev. Joseph M.-F. Marique, S.J. (deceased). *Director, Institute of Early Christian Iberian Studies, College of the Holy Cross, Worcester, Mass.*

John S. Marshall (d. 1979). *Professor of Philosophy, University of the South, Sewanee, Tenn., 1946–68.*

Ira Jay Martin III (d. 1983). *Henry Mixter Penniman Professor of Philosophy and Religion, Berea College, Ky., 1966–77.*

Martin E. Marty. *Fairfax M. Cone Distinguished Service Professor, Divinity School, University of Chicago. Senior Editor,* The Christian Century.

Masutani Fumio. *Former Professor of the History of Religion, Taisho University, Tokyo.*

The Rev. Vivian John Manley Matthews. *Priest of the London Oratory, Eng.*

Sengaku Mayeda. *Professor of Indian Philosophy, University of Tokyo.*

Louis Mazoyer. *Former Teacher at the Lycée Condorcet, Paris.*

Sidney Earl Mead. *Professor of History and of Religion, University of Iowa, Iowa City, 1964–72.*

Bernard E. Meland. *Emeritus Professor of Constructive Theology, University of Chicago.*

The Rev. William Moelwyn Merchant. *Professor of English Language and Literature, University of Exeter, Eng., 1961–74. Emeritus Canon of Salisbury Cathedral.*

Reinhold Merkelbach. *Professor of Classics, University of Cologne.*

The Rev. John Meyendorff. *Dean, St. Vladimir's Orthodox Theological Seminary, Tuckahoe, N.Y. Professor of Byzantine and East European History, Fordham University, New York City.*

John Richard Meyer. *Associate Professor of Education, University of Windsor, Ont.*

Rabbi Eugene Mihaly. *Professor of Homiletics and Midrash, Hebrew Union College–Jewish Institute of Religion, Cincinnati, Ohio.*

The Rev. Raymond Joseph Miller, C.SS.R. *Former Pastor, St. Leo's Church, Versailles, Ky.*

Nicholas Byram Millet. *Professor of Near Eastern Studies, University of Toronto.*

Kyong-bae Min. *Professor of Religion, Yonsei University, Seoul.*

Christine Mohrmann. *Former Professor of Early Christian Greek and Latin, and Medieval Latin, Catholic University of Nijmegen, Neth.*

Mary Moriarty. *Benedictine of Stanbrook Abbey, Worcester, Eng. Author of* The Saints in Silhouette; *translator and editor of* A Capuchin Chronicle.

The Rev. Claude Beaufort Moss (d. 1964). *Lecturer at Bishop's College, Cheshunt, Eng.*

David Livingstone Mueller. *Professor of Christian Theology, Southern Baptist Theological Seminary, Louisville, Ky.*

James DeForest Murch (d. 1973). *Member, Board of Administration, 1958–71; Publications Director, 1945–58, National Association of Evangelicals.*

The Rev. Francis Xavier Murphy, C.SS.R. *Emeritus Professor of Patristic Moral Theology, Academia Alfonsiana, Rome. Staff editor for* Patrology, *New Catholic Encyclopedia.*

A. Victor Murray (d. 1967). *President of Cheshunt College, Cambridge, 1945–59. Professor of Education, University of Hull, Eng., 1933–45.*

Tiruppattur Ramaseshayyar Venkatachala Murti. *Emeritus Professor of Philosophy, Banaras Hindu University, Varanasi, India.*

The Rev. Wilfrid Myatt, C.J.M. *Coeditor of* Saint John Eudes: a Spiritual Portrait *and others.*

Seyyed Hossein Nasr. *University Professor of Islamic Studies, George Washington University, Washington, D.C.*

The Rt. Rev. Stephen Charles Neill (d. 1984). *Professor of Philosophy and Religious Studies, University of Nairobi, Kenya, 1969–73.*

James D. Nelson. *Professor of Church History, United Theological Seminary, Dayton, Ohio.*

David Hay Newsome. *Master of Wellington College, Crowthorne, Eng. Fellow of Emmanuel College, University of Cambridge, 1959–70.*

John Thomas Nichol. *Professor of History; Vice President for Academic Affairs, Bentley College, Waltham, Mass.*

The Rev. Richard Patrick Noonan, S.J. *Alumni Director, McQuaid Jesuit High School, Rochester, N.Y.*

John B(oyer) Noss (d. 1980). *Professor of Philosophy, Franklin and Marshall College, Lancaster, Pa. Adjunct Professor of World Religions and the Christian Faith, Lancaster Theological Seminary, Pa.*

Morgan Phelps Noyes (d. 1972). *Associate Professor of Practical Theology, Union Theological Seminary, New York City, 1945–51. Minister, Central Presbyterian Church, Montclair, N.J., 1932–57.*

Geoffrey Fillingham Nuttall. *Lecturer in Church History, New College, University of London, 1945–77.*

The Rev. Austin Oakley (d. 1977). *Secretary, Anglican and Eastern Orthodox Churches Association, London, 1945–53. Vicar of St. Johns, London, 1944–62.*

Sir Dimitri Obolensky. *Emeritus Professor of Russian and Balkan History, University of Oxford.*

The Rev. Elmer O'Brien, S.J. *Writer in Residence, Ignatius College, Guelph, Ont. Research Professor of Theology, Loyola College, Montreal, 1966–73.*

The Rev. Thomas Gerald O'Callaghan, S.J. *Associate Professor of Religious Studies, Fairfield University, Conn.*

Daniel William O'Connor. *Charles A. Dana Professor Emeritus of Religious Studies and of Classical Languages, Saint Lawrence University, Canton, N.Y.*

Tarlach O'Raifeartaigh (deceased). *Chairman, Cultural Relations Committee, Dublin. Editor of* Genealogical Tracts I.

The Rev. William James O'Shea. *Former Professor of Church History and Liturgy, St. Mary's Seminary, Baltimore.*

Eberhard Otto (d. 1974). *Professor of Egyptology, Rupert Charles University of Heidelberg, W.Ger.*

The Rev. Paul F. Palmer, S.J. (d. 1982). *Professor of Theology, Fordham University, New York City.*

Pascal P. Parente (d. 1971). *Professor of Ascetical and Mystical Theology, Catholic University of America, Washington, D.C., 1938–60.*

Herbert William Parke (d. 1986). *Professor of Ancient History, Trinity College, University of Dublin, 1934–73.*

The Rev. Thomas Maynard Parker (d. 1985). *Fellow of University College, Oxford; University Lecturer in Theology, University of Oxford, 1950–73.*

André Parrot (d. 1980). *Archaeologist. Director of the Louvre, Paris, 1968–72.*

Wilhelm Pauck (d. 1981). *Professor of Church History, Union Theological Seminary, New York City, 1953–67.*

The Rev. Ernest Alexander Payne (d. 1980). *President, World Council of Churches, 1968–75.*

Jaroslav Jan Pelikan. *Sterling Professor of History, Yale University.*

Norman Perrin (d. 1976). *Professor of New Testament, University of Chicago, 1969–76.*

Gerald Bernard Phelan (d. 1965). *Professor of Philosophy, St. Michael's College, University of Toronto, and Pontifical Institute of Medieval Studies, Toronto.*

The Rev. Arthur Carl Piepkorn (d. 1973). *Graduate Professor of Systematic Theology, Concordia Seminary, St. Louis, Mo., 1963–73.*

The Rev. Martin Pierce. *Vicar of St. John's Mickleover, Derby, Eng.*

John Richard Thornhill Pollard. *Former Senior Lecturer in Classics, University College of North Wales, University of Wales, Bangor.*

Harry Culverwell Porter. *Lecturer in History, University of Cambridge.*

Eli Daniel Potts. *Associate Professor of History, Monash University, Clayton, Australia. Author of* British Baptist Missionaries in India, 1793–1837.

The Rev. Leon Pouliot, S.J. *Former Teacher of Church History, Collège Sainte-Marie, Montreal.*

James M(atthew) Powell. *Professor of Medieval History, Syracuse University, N.Y.*

Henri-Charles Puech (d. 1986). *Professor of History of Religions, College of France, Paris, 1952–72. Director of Religious Studies, École Pratique des Hautes Études (Institute for Advanced Research), Paris.*

The Rev. William Arthur Purdy. *Secretary for Anglican and Methodist Relations, Secretariat for Promoting Christian Unity, Vatican.*

John Francis Quinn. *Professor of Philosophy, Pontifical Institute of Medieval Studies, Toronto.*

The Very Rev. Msgr. William Joseph Quinn. *Former Executive Secretary, Bishops' Committee for Migrant Workers, Chicago. Former Codirector, Latin American Bureau, National Catholic Welfare Conference, Washington, D.C.*

Gilles Quispel. *Former Professor of Early Church History, State University of Utrecht, Neth.*

Fazlur Rahman (d. 1988). *Professor of Islāmic Philosophy, University of Chicago, 1969–88.*

Helen Louise Redpath (Sister Dominic) (d. 1965). *Bridgettine Nun of Syon Abbey, Devon, Eng.*

Marjorie E. Reeves. *Honorary Fellow and former Vice-Principal, St. Anne's College, Oxford; former Lecturer in Modern History, University of Oxford.*

Ernest Edwin Reynolds (d. 1980). *Author of* Baden-Powell; Three Cardinals; *and others.*

The Rev. James A. Reynolds. *Former Professor of Church History, St. Joseph's Seminary, Yonkers, N.Y.*

The Rev. Joseph Alfred Richard. *Society of Missionaries of Africa, the White Fathers.*

James T. Richardson. *Professor of Sociology and Judicial Studies, University of Nevada, Reno.*

Theodore Henry Robinson (d. 1964). *Professor of Semitic Languages, University College of South Wales and Monmouthshire, Cardiff, 1927–44.*

The Very Rev. Gerard Rooney, C.P. *Former Director, Department of Education, Diocese of Worcester, Mass.*

Herbert Jennings Rose (d. 1961). *Professor of Greek, University of St. Andrews, Scot., 1927–53.*

Henry Rosemont, Jr. *Professor of Philosophy, St. Mary's College of Maryland.*

Erwin I.J. Rosenthal (d. 1991). *Reader in Oriental Studies, University of Cambridge, 1959–71.*

Franz Rosenthal. *Former Sterling Professor of Near Eastern Languages, Yale University.*

Judah M. Rosenthal (d. 1976). *Professor of Biblical Exegesis, College of Jewish Studies, Chicago, 1944–69.*

Anne Ross. *Free-lance writer on Celtic mythology.*

The Rev. Ernest Gordon Rupp (d. 1986). *Dixie Professor of Ecclesiastical History, University of Cambridge, 1968–77.*

The Rev. Edward A. Ryan, S.J. (d. 1964). *Rector, Our Lady of Martyrs Tertianship, Auriesville, N.Y., 1962–64. Professor of Church History, Woodstock College, Md., 1936–62.*

The Rt. Rev. Msgr. J(ohn) Joseph Ryan. *Emeritus Professor of Church History, St. John's Seminary, Brighton, Mass. Emeritus Professor of Medieval History, Pontifical Institute of Medieval Studies, Toronto.*

J. Coert Rylaarsdam. *Emeritus Professor of Old Testament Theology, University of Chicago. Emeritus Professor of Theology, Marquette University, Milwaukee.*

William Merritt Sale III. *Professor of Classics and Comparative Literature, Washington University, St. Louis, Mo.*

Matti Salo. *Former Assistant Professor of Anthropology, Northern Illinois University, DeKalb.*

Ernest R. Sandeen (d. 1982). *Professor of History, Macalester College, St. Paul, Minn., 1973–82.*

Dittakavi Subrahmanya Sarma. *Principal Emeritus of Vivekananda College, Madras.*

Genjun H. Sasaki. *Professor of Buddhism, Otani University, Kyōto, Japan.*

Thomas A. Schafer. *Emeritus Professor of Church History, McCormick Theological Seminary, Chicago.*

Eva Schaper. *Professor of Philosophy, University of Glasgow, Scot.*

Robert P. Scharlemann. *Commonwealth Professor of Religious Studies, University of Virginia, Charlottesville.*

Rivka Schatz-Uffenheimer. *Edmonton Professor of Jewish Mysticism, Hebrew University of Jerusalem.*

Joseph Herman Schauinger. *Professor of History, College of St. Thomas, St. Paul, Minn.*

Annemarie Schimmel. *Professor of Indo-Muslim Culture, Harvard University.*

The Rt. Rev. Alexander Schmemann (d. 1983). *Dean, St. Vladimir's Orthodox Theological Seminary, Crestwood, N.Y.*

Reiner Schürmann. *Professor of Philosophy, Graduate Faculty, New School for Social Research, New York City.*

Amulya Chandra Sen. *Former Editor,* The Indo-Asian Culture. *Author of* Asoka's Edicts *and others.*

Umakant Premanand Shah (d. 1988). *Deputy Director, Oriental Institute, Maharaja Sayajirao University of Baroda, India.*

Roger Sharrock (d. 1991). *Professor of English Language and Literature, King's College, University of London, 1968–81.*

The Rev. Ronald Duncan Mackintosh Shaw (d. 1972). *Missionary Professor, Central Theological College, Rikkyo University, Tokyo, 1922–37.*

The Rt. Rev. Msgr. George William Shea. *Pastor Emeritus, Our Lady of Sorrows Church, South Orange, N.J.*

The Most Rev. Fulton John Sheen (d. 1979). *Bishop of the Diocese of Rochester, N.Y., 1966–69.*

Lancelot Capel Sheppard (d. 1971). *Editor, "Faith and Fact Series,"* Twentieth Century Encyclopaedia of Catholicism.

Franklin Sherman. *Director, Institute for Jewish-Christian Understanding, Muhlenberg College, Allentown, Pa.*

The Rev. Joseph Hsing-san Shih. *Professor of Missions and Sinology, Pontifical Gregorian University, Rome.*

Ailon Shiloh. *Professor and Director of Graduate Studies, Department of Anthropology, University of South Florida, Tampa.*

David Clark Shipley. *Emeritus Professor of Theology, Methodist Theological School, Delaware, Ohio.*

Donald Howard Shively. *Professor of Japanese History and Literature, Harvard University.*

Lou Hackett Silberman. *Hillel Professor Emeritus of Jewish Literature and Thought, Vanderbilt University, Nashville, Tenn.*

Akiba Ernst Simon. *Emeritus Professor of Education, Hebrew University of Jerusalem.*

The Rev. Joachim Frederick Smet, O.Carm. *Editor of Philippe de Mézières's* The Life of St. Peter Thomas.

The Rev. B.T.D. Smith. *Lecturer in Divinity, University of Cambridge, 1915–50.*

Jonathan Z. Smith. *Robert O. Anderson Distinguished Service Professor of the Humanities, University of Chicago.*

The Rev. James Hutchinson Smylie. *Ernest Trice Thompson Professor of Church History, Union Theological Seminary, Richmond, Va.*

The Rev. Norman Henry Snaith (d. 1982). *Principal, 1954–61; Tutor in Old Testament Languages and Literature, 1936–61, Wesley College, Leeds, Eng.*

Ida Sloan Snyder. *Associate and News Director, Bureau of Communications, National Board of the Young Women's Christian Association, New York City.*

The Rev. John Songster, S.J. *Assistant Professor Emeritus of History, Georgetown University, Washington, D.C.*

Jacques Soustelle (d. 1990). *Director of Studies, School of Advanced Studies in the Social Sciences, Paris, 1969–85.*

James C. Spalding. *Professor of Religion, University of Iowa, Iowa City.*

Matthew Spinka (d. 1972). *Professor of Church History, Hartford Seminary Foundation, Conn., 1943–58.*

The Rev. John Stacey. *Secretary, Local Preachers' Office, British Methodist Church, London; Editor, Epworth Press.*

James Stevenson. *Emeritus Fellow of Downing College, Cambridge; formerly University Lecturer in Divinity, University of Cambridge.*

John J. Stoudt. *Professor of Philosophy, Kutztown State College, Pennsylvania, 1965–70. Free-lance writer and researcher.*

Frederick J. Streng. *Professor of the History of Religions, Southern Methodist University, Dallas, Texas.*

The Rev. Dom Anselm Strittmatter, O.S.B. (d. 1978). *Prior, St. Anselm's Abbey, Washington, D.C., 1961–67.*

John Strugnell. *Professor of Christian Origins, Harvard University.*

Herbert P. Sullivan. *Professor of Religion and Dean, Vassar College, Poughkeepsie, N.Y.*

The Very Rev. Norman Sykes (d. 1961). *Dean of Winchester, Eng., 1958–61.*

The Rev. William Telfer (d. 1968). *Canon of Ely. Master of Selwyn College, University of Cambridge, 1947–56.*

Sydney A. Temple, Jr. *Lecturer in Classical Languages, University of Hawaii, Honolulu.*

Mary Frances Thelen. *Professor of Religion, Randolph-Macon Woman's College, Lynchburg, Va. Author of* Man as Sinner in Contemporary American Realistic Theology.

The Rev. Antonine Severin Tibesar, O.F.M. *Emeritus Professor of History, Catholic University of America, Washington, D.C. Former Director, Academy of American Franciscan History, Washington, D.C.*

L.J. Trinterud. *Emeritus Professor of Church History, San Francisco Theological Seminary, San Anselmo, Calif.*

Jacques Truchet. *Professor of French Literature, University of Paris IV.*

Harold Walter Turner. *Director, Study Centre for New Religious Movements in Primal Societies, Selly Oak Colleges, Birmingham, Eng.*

Isadore Twersky. *Littauer Professor of Hebrew Literature and Philosophy, Harvard University.*

Walter Ullmann (d. 1983). *Professor of Medieval History, University of Cambridge, 1972–78; Professor of Ecclesiastical History, 1965–72.*

James Herman Van der Veldt (d. 1977). *Professor of Psychology, Catholic University of America, Washington, D.C., 1945–62. Coauthor of* Psychiatry and Catholicism.

The Rev. Alexander Roper Vidler (d. 1991). *Fellow and Dean of King's College, Cambridge, 1956–66; Lecturer in Divinity, University of Cambridge, 1959–67.*

The Rev. Aubrey Russell Vine (d. 1973). *General Secretary, Free Church Federal Council.*

Arthur Vööbus (d. 1988). *Professor of New Testament and Church History, Lutheran School of Theology at Chicago, 1948–77.*

The Rev. Canon Herbert Montague Waddams (d. 1972). *Residentiary Canon of Canterbury Cathedral, Eng., 1962–72.*

David Waines. *Lecturer in Arabic and Islamic Studies, University of Lancaster, Eng.*

Francis Redding Walton. *Emeritus Director of the Gennadius Library, American School of Classical Studies, Athens.*

The Rt. Rev. and Rt. Hon. John William Charles Wand (d. 1977). *Canon and Treasurer of St. Paul's Cathedral, and Editor,* Church Quarterly Review, *1956–69. Bishop of London, 1944–55.*

James Hamilton Ware, Jr. *Professor of Philosophy and Religion; Chairman, Asian Studies Program, Austin College, Sherman, Texas.*

Edward Ingram Watkin (d. 1981). *Author of* Neglected Saints *and others.*

The Very Rev. Hugh Watt (d. 1968). *Professor of Church History, New College, 1919–50; University of Edinburgh, 1935–50.*

William Montgomery Watt. *Professor of Arabic and Islāmic Studies, University of Edinburgh, 1964–79.*

Rabbi Meyer Waxman (d. 1969). *Professor, Hebrew Theological College, Skokie, Ill.*

The Rev. Gustave Weigel, S.J. (d. 1964). *Professor of Ecclesiology, Woodstock College, Md., 1948–64.*

Egon Joseph Wellesz (d. 1974). *Composer. Reader in Byzantine Music, University of Oxford, 1948–56.*

R.J. Zwi Werblowsky. *Professor of Comparative Religion, Hebrew University of Jerusalem.*

James King West (d. 1984). *Professor of Religion and Philosophy, Catawba College, Salisbury, N.C.*

William J. Whalen. *Associate Professor of Communication, Purdue University, West Lafayette, Ind.; Director of Publications and University Editor; Director, Purdue University Press. Author of* Minority Religions in America *and others.*

The Rev. John Lloyd White, S.M. *Former Provincial Director of Education, Washington Province of the Society of Mary.*

The Very Rev. Henry Charles Whitley (d. 1976). *Minister of St. Giles' Cathedral, Edinburgh, 1954–72.*

Allen Paul Wikgren. *Emeritus Professor of New Testament Language and Literature, University of Chicago.*

Hellmut Wilhelm. *Emeritus Professor of Chinese History and Literature, University of Washington, Seattle.*

Robert L. Wilken. *Professor of the History of Christianity, University of Notre Dame, Ind.*

George Huntston Williams. *Hollis Professor of Divinity, Harvard University.*

J. Paul Williams (d. 1973). *Professor of Religion, Mt. Holyoke College, South Hadley, Mass., 1945–66.*

John Alden Williams. *Professor of Arab Studies, American University in Cairo. Professor of Art and Islamic Studies, University of Texas at Austin.*

Bryan R. Wilson. *Reader in Sociology, University of Oxford.*

Gustaf Wingren. *Emeritus Professor of Systematic Theology, University of Lund, Swed.*

The Rev. Allan Bernard Wolter, O.F.M. *Professor of Philosophy, Catholic University of America, Washington, D.C.*

Douglas Woodruff (d. 1978). *Editor,* The Tablet, London, *1936–67. Author of* Church and State in History *and others.*

Donald Ernest Wilson Wormell (d. 1990). *Professor of Latin, University of Dublin, 1942–78.*

Franklin Woodrow Young. *Amos Ragan Kearns Professor of New Testament and Patristic Studies; Director of Graduate Studies in Religion, Duke University, Durham, N.C.*

Ying-shih Yu. *Charles Seymour Professor of History, Yale University.*

Sa-sun Yun. *Professor, Teacher's College, Seoul National University.*

The Rev. John H. Ziegler, C.S.P. *Former Chaplain to Catholic Students, University of Connecticut, Storrs.*

Larzer Ziff. *Caroline Donovan Professor of English, Johns Hopkins University, Baltimore.*

Part Nine. The History of Mankind

William Wright Abbot. *James Madison Professor of History, University of Virginia, Charlottesville.*

Thomas Perkins Abernethy (d. 1975). *Richmond Alumni Professor of History, University of Virginia, Charlottesville, 1930–61.*

Hélène Ahrweiler. *Chancellor, University of Paris, 1982–89; former Professor of the History of Byzantine Civilization, University of Paris I.*

George Akita. *Professor of History, University of Hawaii at Manoa, Honolulu.*

Victor Alba. *Emeritus Professor of Political Science, Kent State University, Ohio.*

John Richard Alden (d. 1991). *James B. Duke Professor of History, Duke University, Durham, N.C., 1963–75.*

Anthony Dolphin Alderson. *Historian and translator. Director of Transouth Ltd., Fareham, Eng.*

Robert J. Alexander. *Professor of Economics and Political Science, Rutgers University, New Brunswick, N.J.*

Mohammad Ali (deceased). *Professor and Head, Department of History, Kābul University, Afg.*

Frank Raymond Allchin. *Emeritus Reader in Indian Studies, University of Cambridge.*

Mary L. Allison. *Free-lance writer.*

Roberto Almagià (d. 1962). *Professor of Geography, University of Rome, 1915–59.*

Antony Andrewes (d. 1990). *Wykeham Professor of Ancient History, University of Oxford, 1953–77.*

Nikolay Andreyev (d. 1982). *Reader in Russian Studies, University of Cambridge; Fellow of Clare Hall, Cambridge.*

Roy Edgar Appleman. *Lieutenant Colonel, U.S. Army (retired). Historian, National Park Service, U.S. Department of the Interior, Washington, D.C., 1936–70.*

Karl Otmar, Baron von Aretin. *Emeritus Professor of Contemporary History, Technical University of Darmstadt, Ger. Emeritus Head Editor,* Neue Deutsch Biographie.

Hassan Arfa. *Major General, Iranian Army (retired). Author of* Under Five Shahs *and others.*

Daniel Argov. *Former Lecturer in Modern Indian History, Institute of Asian and African Studies, Hebrew University of Jerusalem.*

Maurice Ashley. *Research Fellow, Loughborough University of Technology, Eng., 1967–70. Author of* England in the Seventeenth Century *and others.*

Arthur C.V.D. Aspinall (d. 1972). *Professor of Modern History, University of Reading, Eng., 1947–65.*

Clement Richard Attlee, 1st Earl Attlee (d. 1967). *Prime Minister of Great Britain, 1945–51. Labour Party Leader, 1935–56.*

Jacques, Comte d'Avout (d. 1978). *Historian. Author of* La Querelle des Armagnacs et des Bourguignons *and others.*

The Rev. Tarsicio de Azcona. *Former Professor of Theology, University of Navarre, Pamplona, Spain.*

Michael Graham Balfour. *Emeritus Professor of European History, University of East Anglia, Norwich, Eng.*

Evan Whyte-Melville Balfour-Melville (deceased). *Senior Lecturer in History, University of Edinburgh.*

Manuel Ballesteros Gaibrois. *Professor and Head, Section of American History, University of Madrid.*

Kenneth A. Ballhatchet. *Former Professor of the History of South Asia, School of Oriental and African Studies, University of London.*

John P.V. Dacre Balsdon (d. 1977). *Fellow of Exeter College, University of Oxford, 1928–69.*

Margaret Amelia Banks. *Law Librarian, University of Western Ontario, London.*

Cyril Nelson Barclay (d. 1979). *Brigadier, The Cameronians (Scottish Rifles). Editor,* The Army Quarterly and Defence Journal, *1950–66; coeditor,* Brassey's Annual: The Armed Forces Year Book, *1950–69.*

Thomas Swain Barclay. *Emeritus Professor of Political Science, Stanford University, Calif.*

William Eldon Baringer. *Historical writer. Professor of History, University of Florida, Gainesville, 1977–81.*

John Walton Barker, Jr. *Professor of History, University of Wisconsin, Madison.*

Frank Barlow. *Emeritus Professor of History, University of Exeter, Eng.*

Geoffrey Wallis Steuart Barrow. *Sir William Fraser Professor of Scottish History and Palaeography, University of Edinburgh.*

Dieter Bartels. *Instructor in Social Sciences/Humanities, Yavapai College, Clarkdale, Ariz.*

Michael Bar-Zohar. *Free-lance writer. Member of the Knesset. Lecturer in Political Science, Haifa University, Israel, 1970–73.*

Arthur Llewellyn Basham (d. 1986). *Professor of Asian Civilizations, Australian National University, Canberra.*

Charles R. Bawden. *Emeritus Professor of Mongolian, University of London.*

Douglas C. Baxter. *Associate Professor of History, Ohio University, Athens.*

John Cawte Beaglehole (d. 1971). *Professor of British Commonwealth History, Victoria University of Wellington, N.Z., 1963–66.*

Hubert Irving Beatty. *Professor of History, West Virginia State College, Institute.*

Bernard Winslow Beckingsale. *Former Senior Lecturer in Modern History, University of Newcastle upon Tyne, Eng.*

Samuel Flagg Bemis (d. 1973). *Sterling Professor of Diplomatic History and Inter-American Relations, Yale University, 1945–61.*

D. Mary Benson. *Writer. Author of* Chief Albert Lutuli of South Africa *and others.*

Norman de Mattos Bentwich (d. 1971). *Professor of International Relations, Hebrew University of Jerusalem, 1932–51.*

Marvin David Bernstein. *Emeritus Professor of History, State University of New York at Buffalo.*

Guillaume de Bertier de Sauvigny. *Professor of History, Catholic Institute of Paris, 1949–76.*

Hans H.A. Bielenstein. *Dean Lung Professor of Chinese, Columbia University.*

Wilfred E. Binkley (d. 1965). *Professor of Political Science, Ohio Northern University, Ada.*

T.N. Bisson. *Henry Charles Lea Professor of Medieval History, Harvard University.*

Adrian David Hugh Bivar. *Professor of Iranian Studies, School of Oriental and African Studies, University of London.*

Robert Norman William Blake, Baron Blake. *Provost, Queen's College, University of Oxford, 1968–87.*

Georges Blond (d. 1989) *Novelist and historian. Author of* Pétain, 1856–1951 *and others.*

Martin Blumenson. *Historian, Office of Chief of Military History, Department of the Army, Washington, D.C., 1952–67.*

Sir John Boardman. *Lincoln Professor of Classical Art and Archaeology, University of Oxford.*

Derk Bodde. *Emeritus Professor of Chinese, University of Pennsylvania, Philadelphia.*

Robert Ralph Bolgar. *Fellow and Director of Studies in Modern Languages, King's College, University of Cambridge.*

Hans A. Bornewasser. *Professor at the Theologian Faculty, Catholic University of Tilburg, Neth.*

Alfredo Bosisio. *Former Professor of Medieval History, University of Pavia, Italy.*

Jean Bourdon. *Emeritus Professor of Modern History, University of Nancy, Fr.*

Robert Boutruche (d. 1975). *Professor of Economic History of the Middle Ages, University of Paris, 1958–73.*

William J. Bouwsma. *Sather Professor of History, University of California, Berkeley.*

G.W. Bowersock. *Professor of Ancient History, Institute for Advanced Study, Princeton, N.J.*

Mary Boyce. *Professor of Iranian Studies, School of Oriental and African Studies, University of London.*

Sir (John) Francis Boyd. *Political Correspondent,* The Guardian (*Manchester and London*), *1945–72; Political Editor, 1972–75.*

John Andrew Boyle (d. 1978). *Professor of Persian Studies, Victoria University of Manchester, 1966–78.*

Ernle Bradford (d. 1986). *Author of* The Wind Commands Me: A Life of Sir Francis Drake *and others.*

Harold Whitman Bradley (d. 1990). *Professor of History, Vanderbilt University, Nashville, Tenn., 1954–72. Member, Tennessee House of Representatives, 1964–72.*

Robert J. Braidwood. *Emeritus Professor of Old World Prehistory, Oriental Institute, University of Chicago; Field Director, Oriental Institute Prehistoric Projects.*

Irving Brandt (d. 1976). *Member, Advisory Board, James Madison Papers, University of Chicago. Council Member, Institute of Early American History and Culture, 1959–62.*

Elias Lunn Bredsdorff. *Reader and Head, Department of Scandinavian Studies, University of Cambridge, 1960–79.*

Sidney Reed Brett. *Second Master, King Edward VI School, Nuneaton, Eng., 1921–54. Author of* British History, 1485–1939; John Pym, 1583–1643; *and others.*

Asa Briggs, Baron Briggs. *Provost of Worcester College, University of Oxford.*

Reginald Brill. *Free-lance writer and historian. Author of* Terror of the French: John, Lord Talbot, c. 1388–1453.

Fawn McKay Brodie (d. 1981). *Professor of History, University of California, Los Angeles, 1971–77.*

Adam Bromke. *Professor of Political Science, McMaster University, Hamilton, Ont.*

Thomas Robert Shannon Broughton. *Paddison Professor Emeritus of Classics, University of North Carolina at Chapel Hill.*

B. Katherine Brown. *Historian.*

Delmer M. Brown. *Emeritus Professor of History, University of California, Berkeley.*

Elizabeth A.R. Brown. *Professor of History, Brooklyn College and the Graduate Center, City University of New York.*

Andrew Browning (d. 1972). *Professor of History, University of Glasgow, 1931–57.*

Eleanor Stephens Bruchey. *Seminar Associate, Columbia University.*

Peter Astbury Brunt. *Camden Professor of Ancient History, University of Oxford; Fellow of Brasenose College, Oxford.*

Barbara Buckmaster (The Hon. Mrs. Barbara Miller) (d. 1966). *Writer on Balkan affairs. Member of the Staff, Foreign Research and Press Service, Royal Institute of International Affairs, London.*

Daniel Meredith Bueno de Mesquita (d. 1989). *Lecturer in Modern History, University of Oxford.*

Andrew Robert Burn (d. 1991). *Visiting Professor, A College Year in Athens, Inc., 1969–72. Reader in Ancient History, University of Glasgow, 1965–69.*

Sir Alan Cuthbert Burns (d. 1980). *Permanent Representative of the United Kingdom on the United Nations Trusteeship Council, 1947–56. Governor and Commander in Chief, Gold Coast, 1941–47.*

Alfred Leroy Burt (d. 1971). *Professor of History, University of Minnesota, Minneapolis, 1930–57.*

Ivor F. Burton. *Professor of Social Policy, Bedford College, University of London.*

Claude A. Buss. *Professor of History, U.S. Naval Postgraduate School, Monterey, Calif. Emeritus Professor of History, Stanford University, Calif.*

Sir James Ramsay Montagu Butler (d. 1975). *Regius Professor of Modern History, University of Cambridge, 1947–54. Chief Historian,* Official United Kingdom History of the Second World War *(military series).*

Robert F. Byrnes. *Distinguished Professor of History, Indiana University, Bloomington.*

Theodore John Cadoux. *Former Senior Lecturer in Ancient History, University of Edinburgh.*

Claude Cahen. *Emeritus Professor of Islāmic History, University of Paris.*

James Ford Cairns. *Member, House of Representatives, for the Division of Lalor, Victoria, 1969–77. Lecturer in Economic History, University of Melbourne, 1946–55.*

North Callahan. *Emeritus Professor of History, New York University, New York City.*

Wilfrid Hardy Callcott (d. 1969). *Professor of History, University of South Carolina, Columbia.*

Pedro Calmon (d. 1985). *President, Brazilian Historical and Geographical Institute, Rio de Janeiro.*

George Glenn Cameron (d. 1979). *Professor of Near Eastern Cultures, University of Michigan, Ann Arbor, 1948–75; Chairman, Department of Near Eastern Languages and Literatures, 1948–71.*

Manoel Cardozo (d. 1985). *Professor of History, 1954–78; Curator, Oliveira Lima Library, Catholic University of America, Washington, D.C.*

J.M.S. Careless. *Professor of History, University of Toronto.*

Sten C.O. Carlsson (deceased). *Professor of History, University of Uppsala, Swed.*

André Castelot. *Biographer and historical scriptwriter for radio and television.*

Frank Catania. *Free-lance writer on Southeast Asia.*

John W. Caughey. *Professor of American History, University of California, Los Angeles, 1946–70.*

Raymond Cazelles. *Curator, Condé Museum, Chantilly, Fr.*

David B. Chan. *Professor of History, California State University, Hayward.*

Jean-Léon Charles. *Professor of Military History, Belgian Royal Military Academy, Brussels.*

Jacques Chastenet de Castaing (d. 1978). *Historian and journalist. Author of* Léon Gambetta *and others.*

B.D. Chattopadhyaya. *Associate Professor of History, Jawaharlal Nehru University, New Delhi.*

Jerome Ch'en. *Emeritus Professor of East Asian History, York University, Toronto.*

Jean-Jacques Chevallier. *Emeritus Professor of the History of Political Thought, University of Paris.*

Luciano Chiappini. *Teacher. President, Ferrarese Delegation for the History of Italy. Committeeman, Antonio Frizzi Institute for the History of Ferrara.*

Marquis William Childs (d. 1990). *Staff member,* St. Louis Post-Dispatch, *1926–74; Chief, Washington Bureau, 1962–68.*

Guy Edward Farquhar Chilver (d. 1982). *Professor of Classical Studies, University of Kent at Canterbury, Eng., 1964–76.*

Tse-tsung Chow. *Professor of East Asian Languages, Literature, and History, University of Wisconsin, Madison.*

Ian R. Christie. *Astor Professor Emeritus of British History, University College, University of London.*

Sima M. Ćirković. *Professor of the Medieval History of Yugoslavia, University of Belgrade.*

William Bell Clark (d. 1968). *Naval biographer. Vice President, N.W. Ayer & Son, 1939–50. Editor,* Documentary Naval History of the American Revolution.

Jesse Dunsmore Clarkson (d. 1973). *Professor of History, Brooklyn College, City University of New York, 1945–67.*

Sheldon S. Cohen. *Professor of U.S. and Colonial History, Loyola University, Chicago.*

Henry Jacob Cohn. *Senior Lecturer in History, University of Warwick, Coventry, Eng.*

Hugh Marshall Cole. *Military historian. Author of* The Lorraine Campaign; The Ardennes: Battle of the Bulge.

Douglas Colyer (d. 1978). *Air Marshal. Civil Aviation Representative, Western Europe, Ministry of Transport and Civil Aviation, 1952–60.*

James Richard Connor. *Chancellor and Professor of History, University of Wisconsin, Whitewater.*

F. Hilary Conroy. *Professor of Far Eastern History, University of Pennsylvania, Philadelphia.*

Sarah Gibbard Cook. *Free-lance writer on history and geography.*

W. Mercer Cook (d. 1987). *U.S. Ambassador to Niger, 1961–64; to Senegal and Gambia, 1964–66. Professor and Chairman, Department of Romance Languages, Howard University, Washington, D.C., 1966–70.*

W. Ph. Coolhaas (deceased). *Professor of Colonial History, Utrecht University, Neth.*

J. Terry Copp. *Professor of History, Wilfrid Laurier University, Waterloo, Ont.*

James A(rthur) Corbett. *Emeritus Professor of Medieval History, University of Notre Dame, Ind.*

Cornelius P. Cotter. *Professor of Political Science, University of Wisconsin, Milwaukee.*

Jean Cousin (deceased). *Professor of Latin Language and Literature, University of Besançon, Fr.*

James Coyle. *Free-lance writer on Vietnamese history.*

Peter Craumer. *Consultant and writer on Polish history and affairs.*

Avery Craven (d. 1980). *Professor of American History, University of Chicago, 1927–72.*

Ralph C. Croizier. *Professor of History, University of Victoria, B.C.*

John Anthony Crook. *Professor of Ancient History, University of Cambridge, 1979–84.*

François Marie-Joseph Crouzet. *Professor of the History of Northern Europe, University of Paris IV.*

William Culican (d. 1984). *Reader in History, University of Melbourne, 1972–84.*

Noble E. Cunningham, Jr. *Professor of History, University of Missouri, Columbia.*

Richard N. Current. *University Distinguished Professor Emeritus of History, University of North Carolina, Greensboro.*

Douglas Dakin. *Former Professor and Head, Department of History, Birkbeck College, University of London.*

Stephanie Mary Dalley. *Senior Research Fellow, Somerville College, Oxford; Shillito Fellow in Assyriology, Oriental Institute, University of Oxford.*

Robert V. Daniels. *Emeritus Professor of History, University of Vermont, Burlington.*

Adrien Dansette (d. 1976). *Member of the Academy of Moral and Political Sciences, Paris.*

Cuthbert Collin Davies (d. 1974). *Reader in Indian History, University of Oxford, 1936–63.*

Ernest Albert John Davies. *Publisher, Traffic Engineering and Control; Editor, 1960–76. Member of Parliament for Enfield East, Eng., 1945–59. Chairman, Labour Party Transport Committee, 1945–59.*

William Robert Davies. *Secretary, Liberal Party Organization, 1936–55.*

Warren Royal Dawson (d. 1968). *Hon. Fellow, Imperial College of Science. Hon. Member, Egypt Exploration Society.*

Istvan Deak. *Professor of History, Columbia University.*

Ann Dearden. *Author of* Jordan.

Alexander De Conde. *Professor of History, University of California, Santa Barbara.*

Juliette C. Decreus. *Former Senior Lecturer in French, Queen Mary College, University of London.*

John Coleman de Graft-Johnson (d. 1977). *Editor,* Economic Bulletin of Ghana. *Research Associate Professor of Economics, University of Ghana.*

Herbert Stanley Deighton. *Lecturer in International Politics, Brunel University, Uxbridge, Eng., 1967–73.*

John Duncan Martin Derrett. *Professor of Oriental Laws, University of London.*

Ranjit Ramchandra Desai. *Agriculturist and writer. Author of* Srīmāna Yogī: the Life of Śivajī in Marathi *and others.*

Georges Dethan. *Archivist, French Foreign Ministry Archives, Paris, 1947–88. Chief Editor,* Revue d'Histoire Diplomatique.

Jean Devisse. *Lecturer, University of Paris VIII.*

Harry T. Dickinson. *Professor of History, University of Edinburgh.*

Heide Dienst. *Assistant, Institute of Austrian History Research, University of Vienna.*

Porphyrios Dikaios (d. 1971). *Professor, Archaeological Institute, Rupert Charles University of Heidelberg, W.Ger. Director of Antiquities, Nicosia, Cyprus, 1960–63.*

Dimitrije V. Djordjevic. *Professor of History, University of California, Santa Barbara.*

Mário José Domingues. *Author of* O Marquês de Pombal *and others.*

Jorge I. Domínguez. *Professor of Government; Member, Center for International Affairs, Harvard University.*

David Herbert Donald. *Charles Warren Professor of American History and Professor of American Civilization, Harvard University.*

Gordon Donaldson. *Emeritus Professor of Scottish History and Palaeography, University of Edinburgh.*

Andreas Dorpalen (d. 1982). *Professor of History, Ohio State University, Columbus, 1958–78.*

Clifford Dowdey (d. 1979). *Lecturer in Creative Writing, University of Richmond, Va., 1958–69. Author of* Lee *and others.*

Glanville Downey. *Distinguished Professor Emeritus of History and of Classical Studies, Indiana University, Bloomington.*

Margaret Stefana Drower. *Fellow of University College, London; former Reader in Ancient History, University of London.*

Joaquin Milton Duarte, Jr. *Dom Pedro II Professor of Luso-Brazilian and Hispanic American Studies; Chairman, Department of International Studies, American Graduate School of International Management, Glendale, Ariz.*

Eleanor Shipley Duckett (d. 1976). *Professor of Classical Languages and Literature, Smith College, Northampton, Mass., 1928–49.*

Jack L. Dull. *Associate Professor of History, University of Washington, Seattle.*

Richard S. Dunn. *Professor of History, University of Pennsylvania, Philadelphia.*

Trevor Nevitt Dupuy. *Colonel, U.S. Army (retired). President and Executive Director, Historical Evaluation and Research Organization, McLean, Va.*

Enrique Dussel. *Professor of Ethics, National Autonomous University of Mexico, Mexico City.*

Brainerd Dyer. *Emeritus Professor of History, University of California, Los Angeles.*

Denys G. Dyer. *Former Lecturer in German, University of Oxford.*

Robert Harris Dyson, Jr. *Professor of Anthropology; Curator, Near Eastern Section, University Museum, University of Pennsylvania, Philadelphia.*

David Magarey Earl. *Former Professor of History, Eastern Michigan University, Ypsilanti.*

Robert A. East. *Emeritus Professor of History, Brooklyn College, City University of New York.*

Arimichi Ebisawa. *Former Professor of History, International Christian University, Tokyo.*

W.J. Eccles. *Emeritus Professor of History, University of Toronto.*

Robert Walter Dudley Edwards (d. 1988). *Professor of Modern Irish History, University College, Dublin, National University of Ireland, 1945–79.*

Lajos Elekes. *Former Professor of the Medieval History of Hungary, Eötvös Loránd University, Budapest.*

Nikita Elisséeff. *Professor of Islamic History and Archaeology, University of Lyon II.*

Sir Ivo D'Oyly Elliott (d. 1961). *Indian Civil Service, 1906–32.*

Sir Geoffrey R. Elton. *Regius Professor Emeritus of Modern History, University of Cambridge; Fellow of Clare College, Cambridge.*

Marcel Emerit. *Emeritus Professor of History; Member, Academy of Ethics and Politics, Institute of France.*

William Richard Emerson. *Director, Franklin D. Roosevelt Library, Hyde Park, N.Y.*

Henrik Enander. *Former Lecturer in History, University of Stockholm.*

Jens Engberg. *Professor of History, University of Århus, Den.*

Philippe Erlanger (d. 1987). *Head, Artistic Exchange Department, Ministry of Foreign Affairs, Paris, 1946–68.*

Heinrich Gustav Euler. *Professor of Modern History, University of Würzburg, Ger.*

(Henry) Outram Evennett (d. 1964). *Fellow of Trinity College, Cambridge; Lecturer in History, University of Cambridge, 1930–55.*

John E. Fagg. *Emeritus Professor of History, New York University, New York City.*

Stanley Lawrence Falk. *Deputy Chief Historian, Southeast Asia, U.S. Army Center of Military History, Washington, D.C.*

Cyril Bentham Falls (d. 1971). *Military Correspondent of* The Times *(London), 1939–53. Chichele Professor of the History of War, University of Oxford, 1946–53.*

Raymond Oliver Faulkner (deceased). *Fellow of University College, London; Lecturer in Ancient Egyptian, University College, University of London, 1955–67.*

Lee Nathan Feigon. *Associate Professor of History; Director, East Asian Studies, Colby College, Waterville, Maine. Staff Writer, East Asian Affairs,* Encyclopædia Britannica, *Chicago, 1970–73.*

Isaac M. Fein. *Emeritus Professor of Jewish History, Baltimore Hebrew College.*

John Lister Illingworth Fennell. *Emeritus Professor of Russian, University of Oxford.*

Michael de Ferdinandy. *Emeritus Professor of Humanities, University of Puerto Rico, Río Piedras.*

John Ferguson (d. 1989). *President, Selly Oak Colleges, Birmingham, Eng., 1976–86. Professor, Dean, and Director of Studies in Arts, The Open University, Milton Keynes, Eng., 1969–79.*

William Ferguson. *Reader in Scottish History, University of Edinburgh.*

Sir James Fergusson of Kilkerran, 8th Bart. (d. 1973). *Keeper of the Records of Scotland, 1949–69.*

Ronald Whitaker Ferrier. *Assistant Professor and Head, Department of English, Pahlavi University, Iran, 1963–65.*

Charles Patrick FitzGerald. *Emeritus Professor of Far Eastern History, Australian National University, Canberra.*

Russell H. Fitzgibbon (d. 1979). *Professor of Political Science, University of California, Santa Barbara, 1964–72.*

Geoffrey Bernard Abbott Fletcher. *Professor of Latin, University of Newcastle upon Tyne, Eng., 1963–69. Author of* Annotations on Tacitus.

Michael T. Florinsky (d. 1981). *Professor of Economics, Columbia University, 1956–63.*

David Floyd. *Special correspondent on Communist affairs,* The Daily Telegraph *and* The Sunday Telegraph, *London.*

Philip S. Foner. *Independence Foundation Professor Emeritus of History, Lincoln University, Pennsylvania.*

Michael Richard Daniell Foot. *Professor of History, Victoria University of Manchester, 1967–73.*

William George Forrest. *Fellow of New College, Oxford; Wykeham Professor of Ancient History, University of Oxford.*

Heinrich Fraenkel (d. 1986). *Free-lance writer. Author of* The Other Germany; *coauthor of* Hermann Göring *and many others.*

Enno Franzius. *Historian. Author of* History of the Byzantine Empire *and others.*

Lady Antonia Fraser. *Writer. Author of* Mary, Queen of Scots *and others.*

Greville Stewart Parker Freeman-Grenville. *Honorary Fellow, University of York, Heslington, Eng. Professor of African History, State University of New York College at New Paltz, 1969–74.*

Frank Freidel. *Emeritus Professor of History, Harvard University and University of Washington, Seattle.*

Michael Freund (d. 1973). *Professor of Political Theory and History, Christian Albrecht University of Kiel, W.Ger.*

Jean Claude Froelich (d. 1972). *Director, Center for Advanced Studies on Modern Africa and Asia, University of Paris.*

Richard N. Frye. *Aga Khan Professor of Iranian, Harvard University.*

André Fugier. *Former Professor of Modern History, University of Lyon, Fr.*

Fujimura Michio. *Professor of History, Sophia University, Tokyo.*

Sir Roger Fulford (d. 1983). *Author of* Royal Dukes *and others; coeditor of* The Greville Memoirs.

Edmund Fuller. *Writer and editor. Book Reviewer,* Wall Street Journal. *Coeditor of* Four American Biographies *and others.*

Cyril John Gadd (d. 1969). *Professor of Ancient Semitic Languages and Civilizations, University of London, 1955–60. Keeper, Egyptian and Assyrian Antiquities, British Museum, London, 1948–55.*

Vivian Hunter Galbraith (d. 1976). *Regius Professor of Modern History, University of Oxford, 1947–57.*

Kenneth Garrad. *Professor of Spanish, Flinders University of South Australia, Bedford Park (Adelaide).*

Noel George Garson. *Professor of History, University of the Witwatersrand, Johannesburg.*

Raymond Leonard Garthoff. *U.S. foreign service officer (retired); U.S. Ambassador to Bulgaria, 1977–79.*

Norman Gash. *Emeritus Professor of History, University of St. Andrews, Scot.*

Deno John Geanakoplos. *Professor of History and Religious Studies, Yale University.*

Lucien Genet. *Inspector General of Public Instruction, Paris.*

Sir Hamilton Alexander Rosskeen Gibb (d. 1971). *University Professor and J.R. Jewett Professor of Arabic, Harvard University, 1955–64.*

Frank B. Gibney. *Vice-Chairman, Board of Editors, Encyclopædia Britannica, Inc., Chicago. Vice-Chairman, TBS-Britannica Company Ltd., Tokyo. Author of* The Khrushchev Pattern *and others.*

Frederick Wellington Gibson. *Professor of History, Queen's University at Kingston, Ont.*

Aleksander Gieysztor. *Professor of Medieval History, University of Warsaw.*

Sara D. Gilbert. *Free-lance writer.*

Robert Louis Gilmore. *Emeritus Professor of History, University of Kansas, Lawrence.*

Marija Gimbutas. *Professor of European Archaeology, University of California, Los Angeles.*

Martin Gimm. *Professor of Sinology, University of Cologne.*

Wassil Todorov Gjuzelev. *Professor of Bulgarian Medieval History, University of Sofia.*

Sir John Bagot Glubb (d. 1986). *Lieutenant General; Chief of General Staff, The Arab Legion, Amman, Jordan, 1939–56.*

Jacques Godechot (d. 1989). *Professor of Modern and Contemporary History, 1945–80; Dean, Faculty of Letters, 1961–71, University of Toulouse II, Fr.*

Ludwig von Gogolák. *Author of* Csehszlovákia *and others.*

Alfred Goldberg. *Senior Social Scientist, Rand Corporation, Washington, D.C. Chief, Current History Branch, U.S. Department of the Air Force, 1944–65.*

L. Carrington Goodrich. *Dean Lung Professor Emeritus of Chinese, Columbia University.*

Albert Goodwin. *Emeritus Professor of Modern History, Victoria University of Manchester.*

Cyrus H. Gordon. *Professor of Hebraic Studies; Director, Center for Ebla Research, New York University, New York City. Emeritus Professor of Mediterranean Studies, Brandeis University, Waltham, Mass.*

Walter Otto Julius Görlitz. *Journalist; Editorial Staff,* Die Welt, *Hamburg.*

Norman A. Graebner. *Edward R. Stettinius Professor of History, University of Virginia, Charlottesville.*

William Roger Graham (d. 1988). *Douglas Professor of Canadian History, Queen's University at Kingston, Ont.*

Bruce Grant (d. 1977). *Author of* Isaac Hull: Captain of Old Ironsides *and others.*

Michael Grant. *President and Vice-Chancellor, Queen's University of Belfast, N.Ire., 1959–66.*

Eric William Gray (d. 1990). *Lecturer in Ancient History, University of Oxford; Official Student and Tutor in Roman History, Christ Church, Oxford, 1939–77.*

Richard L. Greaves. *Professor of History, Florida State University, Tallahassee.*

Constance McLaughlin Green (d. 1975). *Director, Washington History Project, American University, Washington, D.C., 1954–60. Pulitzer Prize for History, 1963.*

Fletcher Melvin Green (d. 1978). *Kenan Professor of History, University of North Carolina at Chapel Hill.*

George William Greenaway. *Former Senior Lecturer in History, University of Exeter, Eng.*

Jonas Carl Greenfield. *Professor of Ancient Semitic Languages, Hebrew University of Jerusalem.*

Richard David Greenfield. *Former Director of General Studies, University of Benin, Nigeria.*

Thomas Hoag Greer. *Emeritus Professor of Humanities, Michigan State University, East Lansing.*

John A.S. Grenville. *Professor of Modern History, University of Birmingham, Eng.*

Ian Grey. *Author of* Catherine the Great; The First Fifty Years: Soviet Russia 1917–67; *and others.*

Guy Thompson Griffith (d. 1985). *Laurence Reader in Classics, University of Cambridge, 1951–75; Fellow of Gonville and Caius College, Cambridge.*

Géza Grosschmid. *Professor of Economics, Duquesne University, Pittsburgh; Director, Institute of African Affairs, 1959–70.*

Hans G. Güterbock. *Tiffany and Margaret Blake Distinguished Service Professor Emeritus of Hittitology, Oriental Institute, University of Chicago.*

Denis Rolleston Gwynn (d. 1971). *Research Professor of Modern Irish History, University College, Cork, National University of Ireland, 1946–63.*

Richard Carleton Haines (d. 1977). *Field Architect, 1930–42 and 1949–72; Assistant Professor, 1963–71, Oriental Institute, University of Chicago.*

K.H.D. Haley. *Emeritus Professor of Modern History, University of Sheffield, Eng.*

John Whitney Hall. *Griswold Professor of History, Yale University.*

Theodore S. Hamerow. *Professor of History, University of Wisconsin, Madison.*

Mary Agnes Hamilton (d. 1966). *Editor,* English-Speaking World. *Author of* Sidney and Beatrice Webb *and others.*

The Rev. Raphael Noteware Hamilton, S.J. (d. 1980). *Professor of History, Marquette University, Milwaukee, 1932–64; Archivist, 1960–73.*

Oscar J. Hammen. *Emeritus Professor of History, University of Montana, Missoula.*

Mason Hammond. *Pope Professor Emeritus of Latin Language and Literature; former Professor of Roman History, Harvard University.*

Nicholas G.L. Hammond. *Henry Overton Wills Professor Emeritus of Greek, University of Bristol, Eng.*

Ralph Hammond Innes. *Novelist and writer on history and travel. Author of* The Conquistadors *and many others.*

Eric Walter Handley. *Professor of Greek, University College, University of London.*

Cyril Francis James Hankinson (d. 1984). *Editor,* Debrett's Peerage, *London, 1935–62.*

Willard A. Hanna. *Senior Associate, Universities Field Staff International, Hanover, New Hampshire.*

Sidney Harcave. *Emeritus Professor of History, State University of New York at Binghamton.*

Peter Hardy. *Reader in the History of Islām in South Asia, School of Oriental and African Studies, University of London.*

Claude Harmel. *Editor,* Les Études Sociales et Syndicales, *Paris. Former Secretary, Institute for Social History, Paris.*

John A. Harrison. *Emeritus Professor of History, University of Miami, Coral Gables, Fla. Editor,* The Journal of Asian Studies, *1969–72.*

John Bennett Harrison. *Reader in the History of South Asia, School of Oriental and African Studies, University of London.*

Erich Hugo Hassinger. *Emeritus Professor of Modern History, Albert Ludwig University of Freiburg, Freiburg im Breisgau, Ger.*

Warren W. Hassler, Jr. *Emeritus Professsor of American History, Pennsylvania State University, University Park.*

Ragnhild Marie Hatton. *Emeritus Professor of International History, London School of Economics and Political Science, University of London.*

Alfred F. Havighurst (d. 1991). *Professor of History, Amherst College, Mass, 1954–70.*

Zenos Eric Myhren Hawkinson. *Professor of History, North Park College, Chicago.*

G.R. Hawting. *Senior Lecturer in the History of the Near and Middle East, School of Oriental and African Studies, University of London.*

Shigeru Hayashi (d. 1989). *Professor, Institute of Social Science, University of Tokyo.*

Charles W. Hayford. *Associate, Department of History, Northwestern University, Evanston, Ill., and Center for East Asian Studies, University of Chicago.*

Stephen Heder. *Free-lance writer and consultant on Cambodia.*

Helmut Heiber. *Assistant, Institute for Contemporary History, Munich. Author of* Joseph Goebbels *and others.*

Walter Heinemeyer. *Professor of Medieval History, Philipps University of Marburg, Ger.*

Heinz Heinen. *Professor of Ancient History, University of Trier, Ger.*

Richard Hellie. *Professor of Russian History, University of Chicago.*

Charles Alistair Hennessy. *Professor of History, University of Warwick, Coventry, Eng.*

Stanislaw Herbst (d. 1973). *Professor of Pre-18th Century Polish History, University of Warsaw. President, Polish Historic Society, Warsaw.*

Hans Herzfeld (d. 1982). *Professor of Modern History, Free University of Berlin, 1950–60.*

William B. Hesseltine (d. 1963). *Professor of History, University of Wisconsin, 1940–63.*

Christopher Hibbert. *Historian and biographer. Author of* Benito Mussolini; The Rise and Fall of Il Duce; *and others.*

Agnes H. Hicks. *Member and Honorary Consultant on Scandinavian Affairs, Royal Institute of International Affairs.*

Jay Higginbotham. *Archivist, Mobile Municipal Archives, Ala.*

J.R.L. Highfield. *Emeritus Fellow of Merton College, Oxford; former Lecturer in Modern History, University of Oxford.*

Patrice Louis-René Higonnet. *Goelet Professor of French History, Harvard University.*

John Hugh Hill. *Emeritus Professor of Medieval History, University of Houston, Texas.*

Laurita L. Hill (deceased). *Writer and editor. Instructor in History, University of Texas, Austin, 1963–68.*

Richard Leslie Hill. *Professor of History, Abdullahi Bayero College, Ahmadu Bello University, Kano, Nigeria, 1968–69. Lecturer in Modern Near Eastern History, University of Durham, Eng., 1949–66.*

Thomas Hodgkin (d. 1982). *Writer. Fellow of Balliol College, Oxford; Lecturer in the Government of New States, University of Oxford, 1965–70.*

Fritz L(eo) Hoffmann. *Emeritus Professor of Latin-American History, University of Colorado, Boulder.*

Keigo Hogetsu. *Honorary Professor of Literature, University of Tokyo.*

C. Warren Hollister. *Professor of History, University of California, Santa Barbara.*

Edgar Crawshaw Holt (d. 1975). *Author and journalist. Author of* The Making of Italy, 1815–1870 *and others.*

J.C. Holt. *Emeritus Professor of Medieval History, University of Cambridge.*

Shan-Yüan Hsieh. *Former Assistant Professor of Philosophy, Haverford College, Pa.*

Walther C. Hubatsch. *Professor of Medieval and Modern History, Rhenish Friedrich Wilhelm University of Bonn.*

Jean Hubert. *Emeritus Professor of Medieval Archaeology, École Nationale des Chartes (School of Paleography), Paris.*

Charles O(scar) Hucker. *Emeritus Professor of Chinese and of History, University of Michigan, Ann Arbor.*

Harri Llwyd Hudson-Williams. *Emeritus Professor of Greek, University of Newcastle upon Tyne, Eng.*

Jean-Louis Huot. *Professor of Oriental Archaeology, University of Paris I.*

Joel Hurstfield (d. 1980). *Astor Professor of English History, University College, University of London, 1962–79.*

Mahmud Husain (d. 1975). *Vice-Chancellor, University of Karāchi, Pakistan.*

Joan Mervyn Hussey. *Emeritus Professor of History, Royal Holloway College, University of London.*

Richard Wyatt Hutchinson (d. 1970). *Lecturer in Classical Archaeology, University of Cambridge, 1952–55, and University of Liverpool, 1948–57.*

William Thomas Hutchinson (d. 1976). *Preston and Sterling Morton Professor of American History, University of Chicago, 1955–62.*

Nobutaka Ike. *Emeritus Professor of Political Science, Stanford University, Calif.*

Joseph E. Illick. *Professor of History, San Francisco State University.*

Halil Inalcik. *University Professor Emeritus of History, University of Chicago.*

Denis Liddell Ireland. *Senator, Republic of Ireland, 1948–51. Author of* Patriot Adventure *and others.*

Fahir İz. *Professor of Turkish Literature, Boğaziçi University, Istanbul.*

D. Clayton James. *Biggs Professor of Military History, Virginia Military Institute, Lexington.*

Marius B. Jansen. *Professor of History, Princeton University.*

Wilhelmina Feemster Jashemski. *Emeritus Professor of Ancient History, University of Maryland, College Park.*

Yette Jeandet. *Former Editor,* Literary News, *Bayard-Presse, Paris. Author of* Blanche de Castille, reine de l'unité française *and others.*

Barbara Jelavich. *Distinguished Professor of History, Indiana University, Bloomington.*

Dafydd Jenkins. *Former Reader in Law, University College of Wales, Aberystwyth, University of Wales.*

Robert Thomas Jenkins (d. 1969). *Professor of Welsh History, University College of North Wales, Bangor, University of Wales, 1945–48.*

Rt. Hon. Roy Jenkins. *Member of Parliament. President of the European Commission, 1977–81. Chancellor of the Exchequer, 1967–70.*

John J. Johnson. *Emeritus Professor of History, Stanford University, Calif. Author of* Political Change in Latin America *and others.*

Robert Carl Johnson. *Associate Professor of History, Temple University, Philadelphia.*

Arnold Hugh Martin Jones (d. 1970). *Professor of Ancient History, University of Cambridge, 1951–70.*

Frits de Jong. *Professor of Modern and Contemporary History, University of Amsterdam.*

Adriaan G. Jongkees. *Former Professor of Medieval History, State University of Groningen, Neth.*

Karl H.E. Jordan (d. 1984). *Professor of Medieval and Modern History, Christian Albrecht University of Kiel, W.Ger.*

Albert Jourcin. *Professor agrégé honoraire. Author of* Les Médicis *and others.*

Eino Kaarlo Ilmari Jutikkala. *Professor of Finnish History, University of Helsinki, 1947–50; 1954–74.*

Wadie Jwaideh. *Emeritus Professor of History and Arabic, Indiana University, Bloomington.*

Walter Emil Kaegi, Jr. *Professor of Byzantine and Roman History, University of Chicago.*

Nobuo Kanda. *Professor of East Asian History, Meiji University, Tokyo.*

Robert A. Kann (d. 1981). *Professor of History, Rutgers University, New Brunswick, N.J., 1956–76.*

Enver Ziya Karal. *President, Turkish Historical Society. Former Professor of Contemporary History, University of Ankara.*

Thomas L(indas) Karnes. *Emeritus Professor of History, Arizona State University, Tempe.*

Hugh Francis Kearney. *Former Richard Pares Professor of History, University of Edinburgh.*

Benjamin Keen. *Emeritus Professor of History, Northern Illinois University, De Kalb.*

John L.H. Keep. *Emeritus Professor of Russian History, University of Toronto.*

Harper Kelley (deceased). *Head of Research, National Center for Scientific Research, Paris. Head, Department of Prehistory, Musée de l'Homme, Paris.*

Jerold Kellman. *Free-lance writer.*

Annajane Kennard. *Former Librarian, Straits Times Press, Malaysia.*

John P. Kenyon. *Joyce and Elizabeth Hall Distinguished Professor of Early Modern British History, University of Kansas, Lawrence. Professor of Modern History, University of St. Andrews, Scot., 1981–87.*

Dame Kathleen Mary Kenyon (d. 1978). *Principal, St. Hugh's College, University of Oxford, 1962–73. Director, British School of Archaeology in Jerusalem, 1951–66.*

George Briscoe Kerferd. *Emeritus Professor of Greek, Victoria University of Manchester, Eng.*

Tarif Khalidi. *Professor of History and Archaeology, American University of Beirut.*

Stefan Kieniewicz. *Emeritus Professor of 19th and 20th Century Polish History, University of Warsaw.*

Martin Kilson. *Professor of Government, Harvard University; Research Associate, Harvard Center for International Affairs.*

P.D. King. *Senior Lecturer in History, University of Lancaster, Eng.*

Jay Kinsbruner. *Professor of History, Queens College, City University of New York.*

Russell Amos Kirk. *Author and lecturer. Editor,* The University Bookman.

Donald W. Klein. *Lecturer in Political Science, Tufts University, Medford, Mass.*

Wilfrid F. Knapp. *Fellow and Tutor in Politics, St. Catherine's College, Oxford; Lecturer in Politics, University of Oxford.*

George Harmon Knoles. *Margaret Byrne Professor Emeritus of American History, Stanford University, Calif.*

Bernhard Knollenberg (d. 1973). *Fellow of Saybrook College, Yale University; Yale Librarian, 1938–44. Author of* Origin of the American Revolution *and others.*

Lionel Kochan. *Bearsted Reader in Jewish History, University of Warwick, Eng.*

Helmut Georg Koenigsberger. *Emeritus Professor of History, King's College, University of London.*

Hans Kohn (d. 1971). *Professor of History, City College, City University of New York, 1949–62.*

Frank P. Kolb. *Professor of Ancient History, Eberhard Karl University of Tübingen, Ger.*

E.H. Kossmann. *Emeritus Professor of Modern History, State University of Groningen, Neth.*

E.A. Kracke, Jr. (d. 1976). *Professor of Chinese Literature and Institutions, University of Chicago, 1960–73.*

Carl H(ermann) Kraeling (d. 1966). *Professor of Archaeology, 1950–62; Director, Oriental Institute, 1950–60, University of Chicago.*

Daniel Wilhelmus Kruger. *Former Professor of History, University of the Transkei, Umtata.*

Hyman Kublin. *Emeritus Professor of History, Brooklyn College, City University of New York.*

Harold Kurtz (d. 1972). *Author of* The Trial of Marshal Ney: His Last Years and Death *and others.*

Tadachika Kuwata. *Emeritus Professor of Japanese History, Kokugakuin University, Tokyo.*

Jean Lacouture. *Former Professor, Institute for Political Studies, University of Paris. Adviser, Éditions du Seuil, Paris.*

Jorgen Laessoe. *Professor of Assyriology, University of Copenhagen.*

Robert George Dalrymple Laffan (d. 1972). *University Lecturer, University of Cambridge, 1927–53; Fellow of Queen's College, Cambridge.*

Charles-André Laffargue. *General, French Army (retired). Author of* Foch et la Bataille de 1918 *and others.*

Ursula Schaefer Lamb. *Professor of History, University of Arizona, Tucson.*

Gustave Lanctot (d. 1975). *Dominion Archivist and Deputy Minister of the Canadian Archives, 1937–48.*

Aubrey C(hristian) Land. *Research Professor of History, University of Georgia, Athens.*

Yvonne Lanhers. *Curator, National Archives, Paris.*

Taft Alfred Larson. *Member, House of Representatives, Wyoming State Legislature. William Robertson Coe Distinguished Professor Emeritus of American Studies, University of Wyoming, Laramie.*

Agnes M.C. Latham. *Former Reader in English, Bedford College, University of London.*

Hugh Talmage Lefler. *Kenan Professor Emeritus of History, University of North Carolina at Chapel Hill.*

George Alexander Lensen (d. 1980). *Professor of History, Florida State University, Tallahassee, 1959–80.*

Alexander Marie Norbert Lernet-Holenia (d. 1976). *Novelist and playwright. Author of* Prinz Eugen *and others.*

Jacques Levron. *Honorary Chief Curator, Archives of France, Paris.*

Reuben Levy (d. 1966). *Professor of Persian, University of Cambridge, 1950–58.*

Bernard Lewis. *Cleveland E. Dodge Professor of Near Eastern Studies, Princeton University.*

David Malcolm Lewis. *Professor of Ancient History, University of Oxford.*

Lucjan Ryszard Lewitter. *Professor and Head, Department of Slavonic Studies, University of Cambridge; Fellow of Christ's College, Cambridge.*

K.J. Leyser. *Chichele Professor Emeritus of Medieval History, University of Oxford.*

Alphons Lhotsky (d. 1968). *Professor of Austrian History, University of Vienna, 1951–68.*

Li Chi. *Emeritus Director, Institute of History and Philology, Academia Sinica, Tapei. Director of Excavations at An-yang.*

Heinz Lieberich. *General Director, Bavarian State Archives, Munich.*

Kenneth G. Lieberthal. *Professor of Political Science; Research Associate, Center for Chinese Studies, University of Michigan, Ann Arbor.*

Hans Liebeschütz (d. 1978). *Reader in Medieval History, University of Liverpool, 1955–59.*

Chan Lien. *Professor of Political Science, National Taiwan University, Taipei.*

Adolf Lippold. *Professor of History, University of Regensburg, Ger.*

Donald P. Little. *Professor and Director, Institute of Islāmic Studies, McGill University, Montreal.*

Harold V. Livermore. *Emeritus Professor of Spanish and Portuguese, University of British Columbia, Vancouver.*

Charles Christopher Lloyd (d. 1986). *Professor of History, Royal Naval College, Greenwich, Eng., 1962–66.*

Robert Bruce Lloyd. *Mary Frances Williams Professor of Humanities, Randolph-Macon Woman's College, Lynchburg, Va.*

Jung-pang Lo (d. 1981). *Professor of History, University of California, Davis, 1969–76.*

Henry Cabot Lodge (d. 1985). *Personal Envoy of the President to the Vatican, 1970–77. United States Ambassador to South Vietnam, 1963–64, 1965–67. Representative of the United States to the United Nations, 1953–60.*

Leo Loewenson. *Deputy Librarian and Tutor in Russian History, School of Slavonic Studies, University of London, 1939–56.*

Antonino Lombardo (d. 1989). *Inspector General of National Archives, Rome. Professor of the Study of Archives, University of Rome.*

Stephen Hemsley Longrigg (d. 1979). *Historian and orientalist. Author of* Four Centuries of Modern Iraq *and others.*

Philip Longworth. *Professor of History, McGill University, Montreal.*

Robert Sabatino Lopez (d. 1986). *Professor of History, Yale University, 1955–71.*

Donald William Lucas (d. 1985). *P.M. Laurence Reader in Classics, University of Cambridge, 1952–69.*

Afaf Lutfi al-Sayyid Marsot. *Professor of History, University of California, Los Angeles.*

James G. Lydon. *Professor of History, Duquesne University, Pittsburgh.*

John Lynch. *Emeritus Professor of Latin American History, University of London.*

Carlile Aylmer Macartney (d. 1978). *Research Fellow, All Souls College, University of Oxford, 1936–65. Montagu Burton Professor of International Relations, University of Edinburgh, 1951–57.*

Charles A. McClelland. *Emeritus Professor of International Relations, University of Southern California, Los Angeles.*

Alexander Hugh McDonald (d. 1979). *Lecturer in Ancient History, University of Cambridge, 1952–73.*

Forrest McDonald. *Professor of History, University of Alabama, University.*

Robert Brendan McDowell. *Associate Professor of History, Trinity College, University of Dublin.*

Thomas F. McGann (d. 1982). *Professor of History, University of Texas at Austin.*

Daniel Doyle McGarry. *Professor of Medieval History, St. Louis University, Mo.*

Clarence Fredric McIntosh (d. 1991). *Professor of History, California State University, Chico.*

Denis Mack Smith. *Extraordinary Fellow, Wolfson College, University of Oxford; Senior Research Fellow, All Souls College, Oxford, 1962–87.*

Edward Anthony MacLysaght (d. 1986). *Chairman, Irish Manuscripts Commission, 1956–73. Keeper of Manuscripts, National Library of Ireland, 1949–55.*

Philip Magnus (Sir Philip Magnus-Allcroft) (d. 1988). *Author of* Kitchener *and others.*

Michael Edward Mallett. *Professor of History, University of Warwick, Eng.*

Sir Max Mallowan (d. 1978). *Professor of Western Asiatic Archaeology, University of London, 1947–62. President, British School of Archaeology in Iraq, 1970–78. Archaeologist on staff of the British Museum Expedition to Nineveh, 1931–32; later led many other archaeological expeditions.*

William Manchester. *Adjunct Professor of History; Writer-in-Residence, Wesleyan University, Middletown, Conn.*

Robert Mandrou (d. 1984). *Professor of History, University of Paris X.*

Golo Mann. *Writer. Professor of History and Political Science, Technical University, Stuttgart, W.Ger., 1960–64.*

(Philip) Nicholas Seton Mansergh (d. 1991). *Smuts Professor of the History of the British Commonwealth, University of Cambridge, 1953–70; Master of St. John's College, Cambridge, 1969–79.*

Fosco Maraini. *Writer. Former Lecturer in Japanese, University of Florence.*

Umberto Marcelli. *Lecturer in History, University of Bologna, Italy.*

The Rev. Germain P. Marc'hadour. *Professor of Philology, Catholic University of the West, Angers, Fr.*

John Marlowe. *Free-lance writer. Author of* Anglo-Egyptian Relations, 1800–1953; Cromer in Egypt; *and others.*

Leopold Marquard (deceased). *Publisher. President, South African Institute of Race Relations, 1957–58, 1968. Author of* The Story of South Africa *and others.*

P.J. Marshall. *Rhodes Professor of Imperial History, King's College, University of London.*

Thomas Powderly Martin (d. 1963). *Assistant Chief and Acting Chief, Manuscript Division, Library of Congress, 1928–48.*

J. Alden Mason (d. 1967). *Curator, American Section, University Museum, University of Pennsylvania, 1926–55.*

Paul T. Mason. *Professor of History, Duquesne University, Pittsburgh.*

Philip Mason. *Writer. Director, Institute of Race Relations, London, 1958–69. Indian Civil Service, 1928–47.*

Donald Campbell Charles Masters. *Emeritus Professor of Canadian History, University of Guelph, Ont.*

Gerhard Strassmann Masur (d. 1975). *Professor of History, Sweet Briar College, Lynchburg, Va., 1948–66.*

The Most Rev. David Mathew (d. 1975). *Archbishop of Apamea; Assistant at the Pontifical Throne. Author of* James I.

Therkel Mathiassen (d. 1967). *Curator, Prehistoric Department, National Museum, Copenhagen.*

Neville Maxwell. *Senior Research Officer, Institute of Commonwealth Studies, University of Oxford. South Asia correspondent,* The Times *(London), 1959–67.*

Robert Douthat Meade (d. 1974). *Professor of History, Randolph-Macon Woman's College, Lynchburg, Va., 1939–71.*

Russell Meiggs (d. 1989). *Fellow of Balliol College, Oxford; Lecturer in Ancient History, University of Oxford, 1939–70.*

Julian Louis Meltzer (d. 1977). *Executive Vice-Chairman, Yad Chaim Weizmann National Memorial, and Director, Weizmann Archives, Rehovot, Israel, 1966–75.*

Lucy Shoe Meritt. *Archaeologist. Visiting Scholar, University of Texas at Austin. Editor of Publications, American School of Classical Studies at Athens, 1950–72. Member, Institute for Advanced Study, Princeton, N.J., 1948–73.*

Robert Merle. *Novelist. Author of* Ahmed Ben Bella *and others.*

Barbara G. Mertz. *Historian and writer. Author of* Temples, Tombs and Hieroglyphs *and others.*

John Callan James Metford. *Emeritus Professor of Spanish, University of Bristol, Eng.*

Franz H. Michael. *Emeritus Professor of Far Eastern History and International Affairs, George Washington University, Washington, D.C.*

Earl Schenck Miers (d. 1972). *Historian, editor, and writer. Author of* The American Civil War *and many others.*

Hanns Leo Mikoletzky (d. 1978). *General Director, Austrian State Archives, Vienna. Professor of History, University of Vienna.*

Vladimir F. Minorsky (d. 1966). *Professor of Persian, University of London, 1938–44. Fellow of the British Academy, 1943–66.*

Mairin Mitchell. *Free-lance writer. Author of* The Odyssey of Acurio Who Sailed with Magellan *and others.*

Nancy Mitford (d. 1973). *Writer. Author of* Madame de Pompadour *and others.*

Michel J. Mollat. *Emeritus Professor of History, University of Paris.*

Arnaldo Dante Momigliano (d. 1987). *Alexander White Visiting Professor, University of Chicago, 1975–87. Professor of Ancient History, University College, University of London, 1951–75.*

Nicholas Ivan Momtchiloff (d. 1964). *Economic Adviser, Industrial and Commercial Finance Corporation, London.*

The Rev. Jacques Monet, S.J. *Professor of History, Regis College, Toronto School of Theology, University of Toronto.*

Georges Mongrédien (d. 1980). *Historian. Director of the Municipal Council of Paris and General Council of the Seine, 1947–67.*

Gaston Monnerville. *Member, Constitutional Council of France, 1974–83. President, Senate of France, 1958–68.*

The Rev. Joseph Nestor Moody. *Emeritus Professor of French History, Catholic University of America, Washington, D.C.*

Frank R. Moraes (d. 1974). *Editor in Chief,* The Indian Express, *New Delhi, 1957–72.*

Dale Lowell Morgan (d. 1971). *Historian. Specialist, Bancroft Library, University of California, Berkeley.*

Donald R. Morris. *Publisher, Donald R. Morris Newsletter, Houston, Texas.*

John Robert Morris (d. 1977). *Senior Lecturer in Ancient History, University College, University of London.*

Rudolf Morsey. *Professor of Modern History, Postgraduate School for Administrative Sciences, Speyer, Ger.*

Louis Morton (d. 1976). *Daniel Webster Professor of History, Dartmouth College, Hanover, N.H., 1968–76.*

William Lewis Morton (d. 1980). *Vanier Professor of Canadian History, Trent University, Peterborough, Ont., 1969–75.*

Leonard Mosley. *Author of* Curzon: The End of an Epoch *and others.*

W.E. Mosse. *Emeritus Professor of European History, University of East Anglia, Norwich, Eng.*

Charles Loch Mowat (d. 1970). *Professor of History, University College of North Wales, Bangor, University of Wales, 1958–70.*

Claudius Cornelius Müller. *Head, East Asian Department, Museum of Ethnology, Berlin.*

Stephanie Mullins. *Free-lance writer.*

Joan Margaret Munn-Rankin (d. 1981). *Lecturer in Near Eastern History, University of Cambridge, 1949–81.*

Jean Mary Munro (Jean Dunlop). *Author of* Clan Mackenzie; Clan Gordon; *and others.*

Peter Munz. *Emeritus Professor of History, Victoria University of Wellington, New Zealand.*

James J. Murphy. *Professor of Rhetoric, University of California, Davis.*

Raymond Muse. *Professor and Chairman, Department of History, Washington State University, Pullman, 1956–79.*

Alexander Reginald Myers (d. 1980). *Professor of Medieval History, University of Liverpool, 1967–80.*

Keiji Nagahara. *Professor of History, Hitotsubashi University, Tokyo.*

A.K. Narain. *Professor of History and Indian Studies, University of Wisconsin, Madison.*

Herbert Blair Neatby. *Professor of History, Carleton University, Ottawa.*

Allan Nevins (d. 1971). *Historian. Senior Research Associate, Henry E. Huntington Library and Art Gallery, San Marino, Calif., 1958–69. Dewitt Clinton Professor of History, Columbia University, 1931–58.*

Herbert G. Nicholas. *Rhodes Professor Emeritus of American History and Institutions, University of Oxford.*

Roy Franklin Nichols (d. 1973). *Professor of History; Vice-Provost, 1953–66; and Dean of the Graduate School of Arts and Sciences, 1952–66, University of Pennsylvania, Philadelphia.*

Donald MacGillivray Nicol. *Director, Gennadius Library, American School of Classical Studies at Athens. Koraës Professor Emeritus of Byzantine and Modern Greek History, Language, and Literature, King's College, University of London.*

Louis Nicolas. *Former Professor of Naval History, Naval School, Lanvéoc-Poulmic, Fr.*

Lennart T. Norman. *Archivist and historian.*

John Julius Cooper, 2nd Viscount Norwich. *Writer and broadcaster. Author of* The Normans in the South; The Kingdom in the Sun.

Charles E. Nowell. *Emeritus Professor of History, University of Illinois, Urbana.*

Russel Blaine Nye. *Distinguished Professor of English, Michigan State University, East Lansing, 1965–79.*

Conor Cruise O'Brien. *Pro-Chancellor, University of Dublin. Editor in Chief,* The Observer, *London, 1978–81. Member, Seanad Eireann, Dublin, 1977–79; Dáil Eireann, 1969–77.*

Daniel Patrick O'Connell (d. 1979). *Chichele Professor of International Law, University of Oxford, 1972–79.*

Zoé Oldenbourg-Idalie. *Novelist and free-lance writer. Author of* Catherine the Great *and others.*

Roland Anthony Oliver. *Professor of the History of Africa, School of Oriental and African Studies, University of London, 1963–86.*

Daria Olivier. *Writer, translator, book reviewer, and historian. Author of* Alexandre Ier *and others.*

William J. O'Malley. *Research Fellow on Political and Social Change, Research School of Pacific Studies, Australian National University, Canberra.*

Farouk Omar. *Professor of History, College of Arts, University of Baghdad, Iraq.*

Francis D. Ommanney (d. 1980). *Reader in Marine Biology, University of Hong Kong, 1957–60.*

George Coleman Osborn. *Emeritus Professor of History and Social Sciences, University of Florida, Gainesville.*

John W. Osborne. *Professor of History, Rutgers University, New Brunswick, N.J.*

Andrei Otetea (d. 1977). *Director, Institute of History, Academy of the Socialist Republic of Romania, Bucharest. Professor of Medieval Universal History, University of Bucharest.*

Marcel Pacaut. *Professor of the History of the Middle Ages; Emeritus Director, Institute of Political Studies, University of Lyon.*

Joseph Howard Parks. *Emeritus Professor of History, University of Georgia, Athens.*

V.J. Parry (d. 1974). *Reader in the History of the Near and Middle East, School of Oriental and African Studies, University of London.*

Vladimir T. Pashuto (d. 1983). *Professor, Institute of History of the U.S.S.R., Academy of Sciences of the U.S.S.R., Moscow.*

Hans Patze. *Professor of German History; Director, Institute for Historical Research, Georg August University of Göttingen, Ger.*

George M. Paul. *Professor of Classics, McMaster University, Hamilton, Ont.*

Ante S. Pavelić. *Author of* Dr. Ante Trumbić: Problemi hrvatsko-srpskih odnosa *and others.*

Stanley G. Payne. *Professor of History, University of Wisconsin, Madison.*

H.F. Pearson (deceased). *Author of* A Popular History of Singapore; This Other India: A Biography of Sir Thomas Stamford Raffles.

Howard Henry Peckham. *Director, William L. Clements Library of Americana; Professor of History, University of Michigan, Ann Arbor, 1953–77.*

Roger Pélissier (d. 1972). *Assistant Director, Centre for Far East Documentation, École Pratique des Hautes Études (Institute for Advanced Research), Paris.*

D.H. Pennington. *Former Fellow and Tutor in History, Balliol College, Oxford; Former Lecturer in Modern History, University of Oxford.*

Dame Margery Perham (d. 1982). *Fellow of Nuffield College, Oxford, 1939–63; Reader in Colonial Administration, University of Oxford, 1939–48.*

Luis Pericot García (d. 1978). *Professor of Prehistory, University of Barcelona, Spain.*

Régine Pernoud. *Keeper, Joan of Arc Centre, Orléans, Fr.*

Stewart Henry Perowne (d. 1989). *Orientalist, historian, and lecturer. Author of* The Life and Times of Herod the Great *and others.*

Charles-Edmond Perrin (d. 1974). *Member, Institute of France. Professor of Medieval History, University of Paris, 1937–58.*

Jean Perrot. *Director of the French Archaeological Delegation in Iran.*

Edward Pessen. *Distinguished Professor of History, Baruch College and the Graduate Center, City University of New York.*

Ann Petry. *Novelist. Author of* Harriet Tubman: Conductor on the Underground Railroad *and others.*

Edward Hake Phillips. *Bryan Professor of History, Austin College, Sherman, Texas.*

Robert Pick (d. 1978). *Free-lance writer and editor. Author of* Empress Maria Theresa.

John Whitney Pickersgill. *President, Canadian Transport Commission, Ottawa, 1967–72. Member, House of Commons, Parliament of Canada, 1953–67.*

Dorothy M. Pickles. *Writer, lecturer, and broadcaster. Author of* The Fifth French Republic; The Government and Politics of France; *and others.*

Thomas Jones Pierce (deceased). *Professor of Medieval Welsh History, University College of Wales, Aberystwyth.*

Josephine Ketcham Piercy. *Emeritus Professor of English, Indiana University, Bloomington.*

Francis Stewart Gilderoy Piggott (d. 1966). *Major General, British Army. Author of* Broken Thread; The Elements of Sosho.

Stuart Piggott. *Abercromby Professor of Prehistoric Archaeology, University of Edinburgh, 1946–77.*

Richard E. Pipes. *Frank B. Baird, Jr., Professor of History, Harvard University.*

Richard Pittioni (d. 1985). *Emeritus Professor of Prehistory and Protohistory, University of Vienna.*

Sir John Plumb. *Master of Christ's College, Cambridge, 1978–82; Professor of Modern English History, University of Cambridge, 1966–74.*

Tom Pocock. *Special writer,* The Standard, *London, 1982–88; Defense Correspondent, 1960–73; Travel Editor, 1973–82.*

Jan J. Poelhekke. *Emeritus Professor of Modern History, Catholic University of Nijmegen, Neth.*

Forrest C. Pogue. *Director, Dwight D. Eisenhower Institute for Historical Research, Smithsonian Institution, Washington, D.C., 1974–84.*

Frederik Pohl. *Author of* Tiberius (*under the pseudonym Ernst Mason) and of many works of science fiction.*

Ernesto Pontieri (deceased). *Professor of Medieval and Modern History, University of Naples.*

Gary William Poole. *Associate Editor,* Encyclopædia Britannica, *Chicago, 1970–72.*

The Rev. Stanley Burke-Roche Poole. *Vicar of Littlebourne, Eng., 1948–70. Former Assistant Editor,* Debrett's Peerage.

Ismail K. Poonawala. *Professor of Arabic and Islāmic Studies, University of California, Los Angeles.*

Rollie Edward Poppino. *Professor of History, University of California, Davis.*

George Richard Potter (d. 1981). *Professor of Medieval History, University of Sheffield, Eng.*

Heinrich Potthoff. *Contributor, Commission for the History of Parliamentarism and Political Parties, Bonn.*

Dimitris Pournaras. *Former Publisher and Editor of* Eleutheros (*newspaper*), *Athens. Former Chairman, Greek Broadcasting Corporation.*

Helmut Preidel. *Historian. Author of* Handel und Handwerk im frühgeschichtlichen Mitteleuropa *and others.*

Morgan Philips Price (d. 1973). *Member of Parliament, 1929–31 and 1935–59. Author of* A History of Turkey *and others.*

Thomas Brynmor Pugh. *Reader in History, University of Southampton, Eng.*

Edwin G. Pulleyblank. *Emeritus Professor of Chinese, University of British Columbia, Vancouver.*

Baij Nath Puri. *Emeritus Professor of Ancient Indian History and Archaeology, University of Lucknow, India.*

Sergei Germanovich Pushkarev. *Historian. Author of* The Emergence of Modern Russia, 1801–1917 *and others.*

Robert S. Quimby. *Emeritus Professor of Humanities, Michigan State University, East Lansing.*

Robert Emmett Quirk. *Emeritus Professor of History, Indiana University, Bloomington.*

Horst Rabe. *Professor of History, University of Constance, Ger.*

Hassanein Muhammad Rabie. *Professor of History, University of Cairo.*

Sh. Abdur Rashid. *Adviser, Research Society of Pakistan, Lahore. Director, Historical Research Institute; Head, Department of History, University of the Punjab, Lahore, Pak., 1960–65.*

John Lang Rawlinson. *Professor of History, Hofstra University, Hempstead, N.Y.*

Philip S. Rawson. *Dean, School of Art and Design, Goldsmiths' College, London, 1981–84. Curator, Gulbenkian Museum of Oriental Art and Archaeology, University of Durham, Eng., 1960–79.*

Donald Read. *Professor of Modern English History, University of Kent at Canterbury, Eng.*

Ann Lindsey Reber. *Researcher, Department of History, Duke University, Durham, N.C.*

Thomas C. Reeves. *Professor of History, University of Wisconsin, Parkside.*

Juan Reglá (d. 1973). *Professor of Modern History, University of Valencia, Spain.*

Kurt Reindel. *Professor of History, University of Regensburg, Ger.*

Marcel Reinhard (d. 1973). *Professor of History, University of Paris.*

Robert Vincent Remini. *Professor of History, University of Illinois, Chicago.*

Johannes M. Renger. *Professor of Assyriology, Free University of Berlin, West Berlin.*

Yves Renouard (d. 1965). *Professor of Medieval History, University of Paris.*

Frank E. Reynolds. *Professor of Buddhist Studies and History of Religions, University of Chicago.*

Edward J.M. Rhoads. *Associate Professor of History, University of Texas at Austin.*

Gotthold K.S. Rhode. *Emeritus Professor of East European and Russian History, Johannes Gutenberg University of Mainz, Ger.*

Nicholas V. Riasanovsky. *Sidney Hellman Ehrman Professor of European History, University of California, Berkeley.*

Jean B. Richard. *Honorary Dean, Faculty of Letters and Human Sciences, University of Dijon, Fr.*

Sir Ian Archibald Richmond (d. 1965). *Professor of the Archaeology of the Roman Empire, University of Oxford, 1956–65.*

C.T. Ritchie. *Historian, writer, and artist. Author of* The First Canadian: The Story of Champlain *and others.*

Raymond Ritter (d. 1974). *Attorney. Editor in Chief of the review* Pyrénées. *Author of* Henry IV lui-même.

Helen Anne B. Rivlin. *Emerita Professor of History, State University of New York at Binghamton.*

Nesca A. Robb (d. 1976). *Free-lance writer and lecturer, Author of* William of Orange: A Personal Portrait *and others.*

Michael Roberts. *Professor of Modern History, Queen's University of Belfast, N.Ire., 1954–73.*

Edgar Eugene Robinson (d. 1977). *Margaret Byrne Professor of American History, Stanford University, Calif., 1931–52.*

George Clarence Robinson (d. 1976). *Professor of Political Science, University of Northern Iowa, Cedar Falls.*

George William Robinson. *Professor of History, Eastern Kentucky University, Richmond.*

Michael Roe. *Professor of History, University of Tasmania, Hobart, Australia.*

William R. Roff. *Professor of History, Columbia University.*

Helmuth Rogge. *Chief Archivist, National Records Office, Potsdam, Germany, 1921–45.*

Andrew Frank Rolle. *Robert Glass Cleland Professor of History, Occidental College, Los Angeles.*

Hans Roos (d. 1984). *Professor of East European History, University of the Ruhr, Bochum, W.Ger.*

Eugene Holloway Roseboom, Sr. *Emeritus Professor of History, Ohio State University, Columbus.*

Henry Godfrey Roseveare. *Professor of History, King's College, University of London.*

Ralph J. Roske. *Professor of History, University of Nevada, Las Vegas.*

C.D. Ross (d. 1986). *Professor of Medieval History, University of Bristol, Eng.*

Stanley Robert Ross (d. 1985). *Professor of History, University of Texas at Austin, 1968–85.*

Emanuel Rostworowski. *Professor of Modern History, Historical Institute, Polish Academy of Sciences, Cracow.*

Gordon Oliver Rothney. *Professor of History, University of Manitoba, Winnipeg, 1970–79.*

Jean Pierre Rouch. *Director of Research, National Centre for Scientific Research, Paris.*

John A. Rowe. *Associate Professor of African History, Northwestern University, Evanston, Ill.*

Herbert H. Rowen. *Emeritus Professor of History, Rutgers University, New Brunswick, N.J.*

Nicolai Rubinstein. *Emeritus Professor of History, Westfield College, University of London.*

Peter Edward Russell. *King Alfonso XIII Professor Emeritus of Spanish Studies, University of Oxford; Fellow of Exeter College, Oxford.*

Nils Göran Rystad. *Professor of History, University of Lund, Swed.*

Emilio Sáez (d. 1988). *Professor of Medieval Spanish History, University of Barcelona, Spain, 1959–78. Professor of Medieval History, University of Madrid, 1980–86.*

Leland Livingston Sage (d. 1989). *Emeritus Professor of History, University of Northern Iowa, Cedar Falls, 1932–67.*

Henry W.F. Saggs. *Emeritus Professor of Semitic Languages, University College, Cardiff, University of Wales.*

Robert St. John. *Journalist, lecturer, and foreign affairs radio commentator. Author of* The Boss *and others.*

Edward Togo Salmon (d. 1988). *Messecar Professor of History, McMaster University, Hamilton, Ont., 1954–73.*

Theodore Saloutos (d. 1980). *Professor of History, University of California, Los Angeles, 1956–78.*

Roger M. Savory. *Emeritus Professor of Middle East and Islāmic Studies, University of Toronto.*

Claude Frédéric Armand Schaeffer (d. 1982). *Professor of the Archaeology of Western Asia, College of France, Paris, 1954–69. Director of the French Archaeological Expeditions to Ras Shamra-Ugarit, Syria and Enkomi-Alasia, Cyprus.*

Leonard Bertram Schapiro (d. 1983). *Professor of Political Science (Russian Studies), London School of Economics and Political Science, University of London, 1963–75.*

Theodor Schieffer. *Professor of Medieval and Modern History, University of Cologne, Ger.*

Franz-Josef Schmale. *Professor of Medieval History, University of the Ruhr, Bochum, Ger.*

Karl Michael Schmitt. *Professor of Government, University of Texas at Austin.*

Ronald Milton Schneider. *Professor of Political Science, Queens College, City University of New York.*

Walter V. Scholes (d. 1975). *Professor of History, University of Missouri, Columbia, 1954–75.*

Friedrich Schreyvogl (d. 1976). *Novelist and free-lance writer. Vice-Director, Vienna Burgtheater, 1954–59.*

Alvin J. Schumacher. *Author of* Thunder on Capitol Hill: The Life of Chief Justice Roger B. Taney.

Lee Schwartz. *Free-lance writer and consultant on Polish history.*

Robert L. Scranton. *Emeritus Professor of Classical Art and Archaeology, University of Chicago.*

Howard Hayes Scullard (d. 1983). *Professor of Ancient History, King's College, University of London, 1959–70.*

B. Raphael Sealey. *Professor of History, University of California, Berkeley.*

Jakob Seibert. *Professor of Ancient History, Ludwig Maximilian University of Munich.*

M.V. Seton-Williams. *Former Honorary Research Fellow in Egyptian and Coptic, University College, University of London. Former director of archaeological expeditions in Turkey, Syria, Jordan, Egypt, and Cyprus.*

Charles Seymour (d. 1963). *President, Yale University, 1937–50; Professor of History, 1918–37.*

Irfan Arif Shahîd. *Professor of Arabic, Georgetown University, Washington, D.C.*

David Allen Shannon. *Commonwealth Professor of History, University of Virginia, Charlottesville; Vice President and Provost, 1971–81.*

The Rev. R. Norman Sharp. *Assistant Professor of Old Persian and Pahlavi, Pahlavi University, Shīrāz, Iran, 1962–67.*

Ivan Peter Shaw. *Former Fellow and Secretary, King's College, University of London. Author of* Nationality and the Western Church Before the Reformation.

Hugh Shearman. *Historian and writer on politics and world affairs. Author of* Modern Ireland; Ulster; *and others.*

Eric William Sheppard. *Major, British Army (retired). Author of* A Short History of the British Army *and others.*

George Albert Shepperson. *William Robertson Professor Emeritus of Commonwealth and American History, University of Edinburgh.*

Adrian N. Sherwin-White. *Reader in Ancient History, University of Oxford, 1966–78.*

James Henry Shideler. *Professor of History, University of California, Davis.*

Minoru Shinoda. *Emeritus Professor of History, University of Hawaii at Manoa, Honolulu.*

David C.G. Sibley. *Free-lance writer and artist.*

Winant Sidle. *Brigadier General, U.S. Army.*

Julie Siegel. *Free-lance writer.*

Henry Harrison Simms. *Emeritus Professor of History, Ohio State University, Columbus.*

John Y. Simon. *Professor of History, Southern Illinois University, Carbondale. Executive Director, Ulysses S. Grant Association.*

Eric Norman Simons (d. 1983). *Author of* The Queen and the Rebel: Mary Tudor and Wyatt the Younger *and others.*

John M. Simpson. *Senior Lecturer in Scottish History, University of Edinburgh.*

Roger Henry Simpson. *Historian and lecturer.*

Andrew Annandale Sinclair. *Historian and filmmaker. Author of* Guevara *and others.*

Otis Arnold Singletary. *President, University of Kentucky, Lexington.*

N.K. Sinha (d. 1974). *Professor and Head, Department of History, University of Calcutta, 1955–68.*

Stephan Skalweit. *Emeritus Professor of Modern History, Rhenish Friedrich Wilhelm University of Bonn.*

Fridlev Skrubbeltrang. *Lecturer in Agricultural History, University of Copenhagen, 1956–71.*

Bradford Smith (d. 1964). *Author of* Bradford of Plymouth; Captain John Smith; *and others.*

Lacey Baldwin Smith. *Peter B. Ritzma Professor of Humanities, Northwestern University, Evanston, Ill.*

Robert Ross Smith. *Chief, General History Branch, U.S. Army Center of Military History, Washington, D.C.*

Thomas C. Smith. *Ford Professor of History and Comparative Studies, University of California, Berkeley.*

Kazimierz Maciej Smogorzewski. *London Correspondent,* Kurier Polski (*Warsaw*), *1957–81. Founder and Editor,* Free Europe, *1939–45. Foreign correspondent, 1919–39.*

Albert M. Soboul (d. 1982). *Professor of the History of the French Revolution, University of Paris I.*

Ramón Solís Llorente (d. 1978). *Novelist and historian. Corresponding member, Royal Academy of History, Madrid.*

Albert Somit. *President, Southern Illinois University, Carbondale.*

Dominique Sourdel. *Professor of Muslim Civilization, University of Paris IV.*

Donald Southgate. *Former Reader in Political and Constitutional History, University of Dundee, Scot.*

T.G. Percival Spear (d. 1982). *Fellow of Selwyn College, Cambridge; Lecturer in History, University of Cambridge, 1963–69.*

Arnold Spekke (d. 1972). *Author of* History of Latvia *and others.*

David Spring. *Professor of History, Johns Hopkins University, Baltimore.*

Chester G. Starr. *Bentley Professor of Ancient History, University of Michigan, Ann Arbor.*

Alfred Steinberg. *Writer and historian. Author of* Man from Missouri: The Life and Times of Harry S. Truman *and others.*

S. Henry Steinberg (d. 1969). *Editor,* The Statesman's Year-Book, *1946–69.*

Doris Mary Stenton (d. 1971). *Reader in History, University of Reading, Eng.*

Ruth Stephan (d. 1974). *Writer. Author of* My Crown, My Love *and others.*

George R. Stewart (d. 1980). *Professor of English, University of California, Berkeley, 1942–62.*

Arndt Mathis Stickles (deceased). *Professor of History, Western Kentucky University, Bowling Green.*

Hudson Strode (d. 1976). *Professor of English, University of Alabama, Tuscaloosa, 1924–63.*

David Brian Stronach. *Professor of Near Eastern Studies, University of California, Berkeley.*

Hans Sturmberger. *Former Director, Upper Austrian Provincial Archives, Linz.*

Leo Suryadinata. *Former Research Associate, Centre for Southeast Asian Studies, Kyōto University, Japan.*

N.M. Sutherland. *Emeritus Professor of Early Modern History, Royal Holloway and Bedford New College, University of London.*

Harald Ulrik Sverdrup (d. 1957). *Director, Norwegian Polar Research Institute, Oslo, 1948–57. Director, Scripps Institution of Oceanography, University of California, San Diego, at La Jolla, 1936–48.*

Victor-Lucien Tapié (d. 1974). *Member, Academy of Moral and Political Sciences, Institute of France, Paris, 1963–74. Professor of Modern History, University of Paris IV, 1949–70.*

John Taylor. *Reader in Medieval History, University of Leeds, Eng.*

Robert H. Taylor. *Lecturer in Political Studies, School of Oriental and African Studies, University of London.*

Geoffrey Templeman (d. 1988). *Vice-Chancellor, University of Kent at Canterbury, Eng., 1963–80.*

Henri-Louis-Étienne Terasse (d. 1971). *Curator, Historic Monuments of Morocco, 1935–57. Director, Institute for Advanced Moroccan Studies, Rabat, Mor., 1941–57. Chairman, Department of Islāmic Archaeology, University of Algiers, 1945–57. Director, Casa de Velázquez, Ciudad University, Madrid, 1957–65.*

Romila Thapar. *Professor of Ancient Indian History, Jawaharlal Nehru University, New Delhi.*

David P. Thelen. *Professor of History, Indiana University, Bloomington.*

Alfred Barnaby Thomas. *Emeritus Professor of History, University of Alabama, Tuscaloosa.*

John L. Thomas. *Professor of History, Brown University, Providence, R.I.*

Nicholas de L'Eglise Wolferstan Thomas. *Former Keeper, Department of Archaeology, City Museum, Birmingham, Eng.*

Arthur Frederick Thompson. *Fellow and Tutor of Wadham College, Oxford; Lecturer in Modern History, University of Oxford.*

E.A. Thompson. *Professor of Classics, University of Nottingham, Eng., 1948–79.*

Lewis Thorpe (d. 1977). *Professor of French, University of Nottingham, Eng., 1958–77.*

Roy Gilbert Thurburn. *Brigadier, the Cameronians (Scottish Rifles) (retired). Secretary, Army Museums Ogilby Trust, Ministry of Defence, London, 1957–72.*

Conrad D. Totman. *Professor of History, Northwestern University, Evanston, Ill.*

Hans Louis Trefousse. *Professor of History, Brooklyn College, City University of New York.*

Reginald Francis Treharne (d. 1967). *Professor of History, University College of Wales, Aberystwyth, University of Wales, 1930–67.*

Piero Treves. *Professor of Ancient History, University of Venice, Italy.*

Glenn Tucker (d. 1976). *Free-lance writer and historian. Author of* Tecumseh: Vision of Glory *and others.*

Sir Eric Gardner Turner (d. 1983). *Professor of Papyrology, University College, University of London, 1950–78; Director, Institute of Classical Studies, 1953–63.*

Edward Ullendorff. *Emeritus Professor of Semitic Languages, School of Oriental and African Studies, University of London.*

Esta Ungar. *Research Fellow in Far Eastern History, Research School of Pacific Studies, Australian National University, Canberra.*

Ernesto Valgiglio. *Professor of Greek and Latin Grammar, University of Genoa.*

Glyndon G. Van Deusen (deceased). *Professor of History, University of Rochester, N.Y., 1947–62.*

Frank Everson Vandiver. *President, Texas A&M University, College Station.*

Richard Vaughan. *Former Professor of History, University of Hull, Eng.*

J. Charles Verlinden. *Emeritus Professor of History, State University of Ghent, Belg.*

Jean Vidalenc. *Former Professor of Contemporary History, University of Rouen, Fr.*

Alan John Villiers (d. 1982). *Free-lance writer. President, Society for Nautical Research, London. Author of* Captain James Cook *and many others.*

Marcelle Vioux (deceased). *Free-lance writer. Author of* François I; Henri IV; *and others.*

Hans Volkmann (deceased). *Professor of Ancient History, University of Cologne.*

The Rev. Edward Robert Vollmar, S.J. (d. 1976). *Professor of History and Associate Director of Libraries, St. Louis University, Mo.*

John Waechter. *Former Senior Lecturer in Paleolithic Archaeology, Institute of Archaeology, University of London.*

Peter Busby Waite. *Professor of History, Dalhousie University, Halifax, Nova Scotia.*

Frank W. Walbank. *Rathbone Professor Emeritus of Ancient History and Classical Archaeology, University of Liverpool.*

Paul E. Walker. *Former Associate Professor of Islamic Studies, McGill University, Montreal.*

William Stewart Wallace (d. 1970). *Librarian, University of Toronto. Author of* A History of the Canadian People.

John Michael Wallace-Hadrill (d. 1985). *Chichele Professor of Modern History, University of Oxford, 1974–83; Fellow of All Souls College, Oxford.*

Immanuel Wallerstein. *Distinguished Professor of Sociology, State University of New York at Binghamton.*

Friedrich Walter (d. 1968). *Extraordinary Professor of Modern Austrian History, University of Vienna, 1955–67.*

Yi Chu Wang. *Emeritus Professor of History, Queens College, City University of New York.*

William Reginald Ward. *Professor of Modern History, University of Durham, Eng.*

John Bryan Ward-Perkins (d. 1981). *Director, British School at Rome, 1946–74.*

Brian H. Warmington. *Former Reader in Ancient History, University of Bristol, Eng.*

Oliver Martin Wilson Warner (d. 1976). *Naval historian. Member, Council of the Society of Nautical Research, 1955–60; Council of the Navy Records Society, 1969–70.*

John Steven Watson (d. 1986). *Principal and Vice-Chancellor, University of St. Andrews, Scot., 1966–86.*

William Watson. *Emeritus Professor of Chinese Art and Archaeology; Head, Percival David Foundation of Chinese Art, 1966–83, School of Oriental and African Studies, University of London.*

Bruce Webster. *Senior Lecturer in History, University of Kent at Canterbury, Eng.*

Dame C.V. Wedgwood. *Free-lance writer and historian. Fellow, University College, University of London.*

Saul S. Weinberg. *Emeritus Professor of Classical Archaeology, University of Missouri, Columbia.*

Lynn Weiner. *Free-lance writer.*

Edward Weintal (d. 1973). *Diplomatic Correspondent, Chief European Correspondent, and Contributing Editor,* Newsweek *magazine, 1944–69.*

C. Bradford Welles (d. 1969). *Professor of Ancient History, Yale University, 1940–69.*

Manly Wade Wellman (d. 1986). *Novelist and writer on American history. Author of* Giant in Gray: A Biography of Wade Hampton of South Carolina *and others.*

Edward F. Wente. *Professor of Egyptology, Oriental Institute and Department of Near Eastern Languages and Civilizations, University of Chicago.*

Robert Werner. *Emeritus Professor of Ancient History, Friedrich Alexander University of Erlangen-Nuremberg, Ger.*

Richard Bruce Wernham. *Emeritus Professor of Modern History, University of Oxford; Fellow of Worcester College, Oxford, 1951–72.*

H. van Werveke (d. 1974). *Professor of the History of Belgium, State University of Ghent.*

William C. West. *Consultant on Russian literature and Soviet affairs.*

Gunnar Torvald Westin. *Emeritus Professor of History, University of Stockholm.*

Vera Muriel White. *Former Extramural Lecturer, University of Cambridge.*

Matthew Immanuel Wiencke. *Professor of Classics, Dartmouth College, Hanover, N.H.*

Hermann Wiesflecker. *Professor of Austrian History, University of Graz, Austria.*

Donald N. Wilber. *Free-lance writer and consultant on the Middle East and Southeast Asia. Author of* Iran Past and Present *and others.*

Charles Henry Wilson (d. 1991). *Professor of Modern History, University of Cambridge, 1965–79; Fellow of Jesus College, Cambridge, 1938–91.*

John A. Wilson (d. 1976). *Andrew MacLeish Distinguished Service Professor of Egyptology, University of Chicago, 1953–68.*

Oscar O. Winther (d. 1970). *University Professor of History, Indiana University, Bloomington, 1965–70.*

Donald John Wiseman. *Emeritus Professor of Assyriology, School of Oriental and African Studies, University of London.*

Elizabeth Wiskemann (d. 1971). *Montague Burton Professor of International Relations, University of Edinburgh, 1958–61. Tutor in Modern History, University of Sussex, Eng., 1961–64.*

Gunther Wolf. *Professor of History, University of Stuttgart, Ger.*

James Madison Wood, Jr. *Professor of History, Santa Monica College, Calif.*

Sir Leonard Woolley (d. 1960). *Archaeologist; excavated at Ur, 1922–34, and many other sites. Author of* Digging Up the Past *and others.*

Brian Harvey Goodwin Wormald. *Emeritus Fellow of Peterhouse, Cambridge; Lecturer in History, University of Cambridge, 1948–79.*

Edmund H. Worthy, Jr. *Associate Director, Resident Associate Program, Smithsonian Institution, Washington, D.C.*

Arthur F. Wright (d. 1976). *Charles Seymour Professor of History, Yale University, 1961–76.*

Gordon Wright. *William H. Bonsall Professor Emeritus of History, Stanford University, Calif.*

David K. Wyatt. *Professor of History, Cornell University, Ithaca, N.Y.*

Malcolm Edward Yapp. *Professor of the Modern History of Western Asia, School of Oriental and African Studies, University of London.*

John Howard Young (d. 1978). *W.H. Collins Vickers Foundation Professor of Archaeology, Johns Hopkins University, Baltimore, 1956–78.*

Mary Elizabeth Young. *Professor of History, University of Rochester, N.Y.*

T(heodore) Cuyler Young (d. 1976). *Horatio Whitridge Garrett Professor of Persian Language and History, 1952–69; Chairman, Oriental Studies Department, Princeton University, 1954–69.*

Andrzej Zahorski. *Professor of Modern History, University of Warsaw.*

Ernst Walter Zeeden. *Emeritus Professor of Modern and Medieval History, Eberhard Karl University of Tübingen, Ger.*

Herbert Zeiden. *Free-lance writer in the area of history.*

Nicola Abdo Ziadeh. *Emeritus Professor of Arab History, American University of Beirut.*

E. Zudaire Huarte. *Instructor, Good Counsel Academy, Lecaroz, Spain. Author of* El conde-duque y Cataluña *and others.*

Part Ten. The Branches of Knowledge

Harry Burrows Acton (d. 1974). *Professor of Moral Philosophy, University of Edinburgh, 1964–74.*

Alexander Altmann (d. 1987). *Philip W. Lown Professor of Jewish Philosophy, Brandeis University, Waltham, Mass., 1959–76.*

Mikhail S. Arlazorov. *Staff member, Union of Cinematographers, Moscow.*

A. Hilary Armstrong. *Gladstone Professor Emeritus of Greek, University of Liverpool.*

Richard Paul Aulie. *Former Lecturer in Natural Science, Loyola University, Chicago. Associate Editor, Encyclopædia Britannica, Chicago, 1971–72.*

Edward J. Barbeau. *Professor of Mathematics, University of Toronto.*

George Alfred Barnard. *Emeritus Professor of Mathematics, University of Essex, Eng.*

Glen W. Baxter. *Senior Lecturer on East Asian Studies, Harvard University, 1956–80; Associate Director, Harvard-Yenching Institute, 1964–80.*

Geoffrey H. Beale. *Royal Society Research Professor of Genetics, University of Edinburgh, Scot., 1963–78.*

Yvon Belaval (d. 1988). *Professor of Philosophy, University of Paris I, 1965–79.*

Eric Temple Bell (d. 1960). *Professor of Mathematics, California Institute of Technology, Pasadena, 1926–60.*

Leonard D. Berkovitz. *Professor of Mathematics, Purdue University, West Lafayette, Ind.*

Simeon Berman. *Professor of Mathematics, Courant Institute of Mathematical Sciences, New York University, New York City.*

Michael V. Berry. *Royal Society Research Professor of Physics, University of Bristol, Eng.*

Cyril Bibby. *Principal, Kingston upon Hull College of Education, University of Hull Institute of Education, Eng., 1959–76.*

Peter G. Bietenholz. *Professor of History, University of Saskatchewan, Saskatoon.*

Otto Allen Bird. *Emeritus Professor of Arts and Letters, University of Notre Dame, Ind.*

Haig Bohigian. *Professor of Mathematics and Operations Research, John Jay College of Criminal Justice, City University of New York.*

Otto Friedrich Bollnow. *Emeritus Professor of Philosophy and Education, Eberhard Karl University of Tübingen, Ger.*

Carl B. Boyer (d. 1976). *Professor of Mathematics, Brooklyn College, City University of New York, 1952–76.*

Felix E. Browder. *Vice President for Research; Professor of Mathematics, Rutgers University, New Brunswick, N.J.*

Delwin Brown. *Professor of Religious Studies, Arizona State University, Tempe.*

David L. Buckley. *Free-lance writer on philosophy and music.*

Ulick Peter Burke. *Reader in History, University of Cambridge; Fellow of Emmanuel College, Cambridge.*

Martin D. Burrow. *Professor of Mathematics, Courant Institute of Mathematical Sciences, New York University, New York City.*

Lyman H. Butterfield (d. 1982). *Editor in Chief,* The Adams Papers, *Massachusetts Historical Society, Boston, 1954–75.*

Robert W. Cahn. *Former Professor of Materials Science, University of Sussex, Brighton, Eng.*

Seymour Cain. *Fellow, National Endowment for the Humanities, Washington, D.C., 1979–80. Senior Editor, Religion,* Encyclopædia Britannica, *Chicago, 1967–73.*

A. Robert Caponigri (d. 1983). *Professor of Philosophy, University of Notre Dame, Ind.*

Frederick F. Cartwright. *Emeritus Senior Lecturer in the History of Medicine, King's College Hospital, University of London.*

George Law Cawkwell. *Former Lecturer in Ancient History, University of Oxford; Emeritus Fellow of University College, Oxford.*

Jules-Marie Chaix-Ruy. *Professor of Philosophy, University of Nice, Fr., 1965–67.*

Donald Geoffrey Charlton. *Emeritus Professor of French, University of Warwick, Coventry, Eng.*

Chung-hwan Chen. *Emeritus Professor of Philosophy, University of South Florida, Tampa.*

Alonzo Church. *Professor of Mathematics and Philosophy, University of California, Los Angeles.*

Martin Lowther Clarke. *Former Professor of Latin, University College of North Wales, Bangor, University of Wales.*

Gerald M. Clemence (d. 1974). *Professor of Astronomy, Yale University, 1966–74.*

I. Bernard Cohen. *Victor S. Thomas Professor of the History of Science, Harvard University.*

Frederick Coppotelli. *Free-lance writer on mathematics.*

H.S. MacDonald Coxeter. *Emeritus Professor of Mathematics, University of Toronto.*

Rupert Crawshay-Williams (d. 1977). *Author of* Russell Remembered; Methods and Criteria of Reasoning; *and others.*

The Rev. Theodore Crowley, O.F.M. (d. 1990). *Professor of Scholastic Philosophy, Queen's University of Belfast, N.Ire.*

J.G. Crowther (d. 1983). *Author of* Famous American Men of Science; Science in Modern Society; *and others.*

Glyn Edmund Daniel (d. 1986). *Disney Professor of Archaeology, University of Cambridge, 1974–81; Fellow of St. John's College, Cambridge.*

Joseph Dauben. *Professor of the History of Science, Herbert H. Lehman College, City University of New York, Bronx.*

Charles De Prima. *Emeritus Professor of Mathematics, California Institute of Technology, Pasadena.*

Carlo Diano (d. 1974). *Professor of Greek Literature, University of Padua, Italy.*

Bern Dibner (d. 1988). *Historian of science and technology. Founder and Director, Burndy Library, Norwalk, Conn., 1935–88.*

Paul Dibon. *Former Director, École Pratique des Hautes Études, Paris.*

A. Vibert Douglas (d. 1988). *Professor of Astronomy, Queen's University at Kingston, Ont., 1943–63.*

Seymour Drescher. *University Professor of History, University of Pittsburgh.*

Michael A.E. Dummett. *Wykeham Professor of Logic, University of Oxford; Fellow of New College, Oxford.*

James H. Earle. *Professor and Head, Department of Engineering Design Graphics, Texas A&M University, College Station.*

William R. Eckhardt. *Free-lance writer on mathematics.*

Dorothy Mary Emmet. *Emeritus Professor of Philosophy, Victoria University of Manchester.*

Robert A. Fefferman. *Professor of Mathematics, University of Chicago.*

Louis H. Feldman. *Professor of Classics, Yeshiva University, New York City.*

Raphael Finkel. *Associate Professor of Computer Science, University of Wisconsin, Madison.*

Sir Raymond William Firth. *Emeritus Professor of Anthropology, University of London.*

Ronald Fletcher. *Emeritus Professor of Sociology, University of Reading, Eng.*

Marcel Florkin, M.D. (d. 1979). *Professor of Biochemistry, State University of Liège, Belg.*

Frieda Fordham (deceased). *Training analyst, Society of Analytical Psychology, London.*

Michael S.M. Fordham. *Analytical psychologist. Coeditor of* The Collected Works of C.G. Jung.

Sidney W. Fox. *Distinguished Research Professor of Plant Biology and of Engineering, Southern Illinois University, Carbondale. Former Director, Institute for Molecular and Cellular Evolution; former Research Professor, University of Miami, Coral Gables, Fla.*

Andrew M. Gallant. *Free-lance writer on mathematics.*

W. Horsley Gantt, M.D. (d. 1980). *Associate Professor of Psychiatry, 1932–58; Director, Pavlovian Laboratory, School of Medicine, Johns Hopkins University, Baltimore.*

Elizabeth Belmont Gasking (d. 1973). *Senior Lecturer in the History and Philosophy of Science, University of Melbourne, Australia.*

Frances Carney Gies. *Coauthor of* Leonard of Pisa and the New Mathematics of the Middle Ages *and others.*

Boris Vladimirovich Gnedenko. *Professor of Physics and Mathematics; Head, Faculty of Mathematics, Moscow M.V. Lomonosov State University.*

Kenneth P. Goldberg. *Professor of Mathematics Education, New York University, New York City.*

Arnold Wycombe Gomme (d. 1959). *Professor of Greek, University of Glasgow, 1946–57.*

Samuel L. Greitzer. *Emeritus Professor of Mathematics, Rutgers University, New Brunswick, N.J.*

Ronald Grimsley. *Emeritus Professor of French, University of Bristol, Eng.*

William Keith Chambers Guthrie (d. 1981). *Laurence Professor of Ancient Philosophy, University of Cambridge, 1952–73; Master of Downing College, Cambridge, 1957–72.*

John G. Hargrave (d. 1982). *Author of* The Life and Soul of Paracelsus *and others.*

Melvin Hausner. *Professor of Mathematics, Washington Square College, New York University, New York City.*

Carl G. Hempel. *Stuart Professor Emeritus of Philosophy, Princeton University. University Professor of Philosophy, University of Pittsburgh, Pa.*

Norman V. Henfrey. *Lecturer in English, University of Bristol, Eng.*

Eckhard H. Hess (d. 1986). *Professor of Psychology, University of Chicago, 1959–86.*

Roland John Hill. *Former London Correspondent,* Die Presse *(Vienna) and* Stuttgarter Zeitung, *Stuttgart, W.Ger.*

Peter John Hilton. *Fellow of Battelle Research Center, Seattle, Wash. Distinguished Professor of Mathematics, State University of New York at Binghamton.*

Harry Hochstadt. *Professor and Head, Department of Mathematics, Polytechnic Institute of New York, Brooklyn.*

Banesh Hoffman (d. 1986). *Professor of Mathematics, Queen's College, City University of New York, Flushing.*

Dewey J. Hoitenga, Jr. *Professor of Philosophy, Calvin College, Grand Rapids, Mich.*

Constantin Ludwig Adolph Rudolph Hope. *Vicar, St. Michael's and All Angels, New Marston, Oxford, Eng.*

Michael Anthony Hoskin. *President of Churchill College, University of Cambridge.*

Kung-chuan Hsiao (d. 1981). *Professor of the History of Chinese Thought, University of Washington, Seattle, 1959–68.*

Arthur Hübscher. *Former Director, Schopenhauer Archives, Frankfurt. Senior President, International Schopenhauer Society, Frankfurt.*

Aaron J. Ihde. *Emeritus Professor of Chemistry and History of Science, University of Wisconsin, Madison.*

Yasuke Ikari. *Instructor, Seminar for Indology, Kyōto University.*

Charles Issawi. *Bayard Dodge Professor of Near Eastern Studies, Princeton University.*

Bernard Jaffe (d. 1986). *Free-lance science writer. Chairman, Science Department, James Madison High School, Brooklyn, New York, 1944–58.*

A. Walter James. *Principal, St. Catharine's, Windsor, England, 1974–82. Editor,* The Times *(London)* Educational Supplement, *1952–69.*

Horace M. Kallen (d. 1974). *Professor of Social Philosophy, New School for Social Research, New York City, 1919–52.*

Irving Kaplansky. *Director, Mathematical Sciences Research Institute, Berkeley, Calif.*

Charlotte L. Kellner. *Former Lecturer in Physics, Imperial College of Science and Technology, University of London.*

Joan Kelly-Gadol (d. 1982). *Professor of History, City College, City University of New York, 1972–82.*

Jim Kenevan. *Free-lance writer on mathematics.*

Lester S. King, M.D. *Professorial Lecturer in the History of Medicine, University of Chicago.*

Stephen Cole Kleene. *Emeritus Dean of Letters and Science; Emeritus Professor of Mathematics and Computer Science, University of Wisconsin, Madison.*

David Marcus Knight. *Reader in History of Science, University of Durham, Eng.*

Sir T. Malcolm Knox (d. 1980). *Principal, University of St. Andrews, Scot., 1953–66; Professor of Moral Philosophy, 1936–53.*

Richard Kroner (d. 1974). *Professor of the Philosophy of Religion, Union Theological Seminary, New York City, 1941–55.*

Ludwig M. Landgrebe. *Professor of Philosophy, University of Cologne. Director of the Husserl Archives, Cologne.*

Anneli Lax. *Professor of Mathematics, Washington Square and University College of Arts and Science, New York University, New York City.*

Robert Lekachman (d. 1989). *Distinguished Professor of Economics, Herbert H. Lehman College, City University of New York, 1973–89.*

Casimir Lewy (d. 1991). *Fellow of Trinity College, Cambridge, 1959–91; Reader in Philosophy, University of Cambridge, 1972–82.*

R. Bruce Lindsay (d. 1985). *Hazard Professor of Physics, Brown University, Providence, R.I., 1936–71.*

Antony Charles Lloyd. *Professor of Philosophy, University of Liverpool.*

David Morrice Low (d. 1972). *Classical Lecturer and Subdean, Arts Faculty, King's College, University of London, 1945–57.*

Victor Lowe (d. 1988). *Professor of Philosophy, Johns Hopkins University, Baltimore, 1961–73.*

David Edward Luscombe. *Professor of Medieval History, University of Sheffield, Eng.*

John David Mabbott (d. 1988). *President, St. John's College, University of Oxford, 1963–69. Author of* An Introduction to Ethics *and others.*

Donald Gunn MacRae. *Martin White Professor Emeritus of Sociology, London School of Economics and Political Science, University of London.*

Norman A. Malcolm (d. 1990). *Susan Linn Sage Professor of Philosophy, Cornell University, Ithaca, N.Y., 1964–78.*

Frank J. Malina (d. 1981). *Trustee, International Academy of Astronautics, Paris, 1963–81; President, 1963. Founder-Editor,* Leonardo *(international journal of the contemporary artist).*

Kishore B. Marathe. *Associate Professor of Mathematics, Brooklyn College, City University of New York.*

Herbert S. Matsen. *Associate Professor of Philosophy, University of South Carolina, Columbia, 1972–82.*

Yi Pao Mei. *Henry Luce Professor of Humanities, Tunghai University, T'ai-chung, Taiwan, 1973–77. Professor of Oriental Studies, University of Iowa, Iowa City, 1955–70.*

Philip Merlan (d. 1968). *Professor of German Philosophy and Literature, Scripps College, Claremont, Calif., 1942–68.*

Lorenzo Minio-Paluello (d. 1986). *Reader in Mediaeval Philosophy, University of Oxford, 1956–75. Director of Aristoteles Latinus, 1959–72.*

Arthur Mitzman. *Professor of History, University of Amsterdam.*

M.L. Modica. *Free-lance writer on mathematics.*

Arne D. Naess. *Emeritus Professor of Philosophy, University of Oslo.*

Hajime Nakamura. *Director, Eastern Institute, Inc., Tokyo. Emeritus Professor of Indian and Buddhist Philosophy, University of Tokyo.*

Otto E. Neugebauer. *Emeritus Professor of the History of Mathematics, Brown University, Providence, R.I.*

Robert Maxwell Ogilvie (d. 1981). *Professor of Humanity, University of St. Andrews, Scot.*

Oystein Ore (d. 1968). *Sterling Professor of Mathematics, Yale University, 1931–68.*

James Joseph O'Toole. *University Associates' Professor of Management and Organization, University of Southern California, Los Angeles.*

George A. Pettitt (d. 1976). *Assistant to the President, University of California, Berkeley, 1936–66; Lecturer in Anthropology, 1940–66.*

Henri M. Peyre (d. 1988). *Distinguished Professor of French, Graduate Center, City University of New York, 1969–81. Sterling Professor of French, Yale University, 1938–69.*

Jean Piveteau (d. 1991). *Professor of Palaeontology, University of Paris, 1938–70.*

John P. Plamenatz (d. 1975). *Chichele Professor of Social and Political Theory, University of Oxford, 1967–75; Fellow of All Souls College, Oxford.*

Carl Pomerance. *Research Professor of Mathematics, University of Georgia, Athens.*

Gray Johnson Poole. *Free-lance writer. Coauthor of* Men Who Dig Up History *and others.*

Murray Protter. *Professor of Mathematics, University of California, Berkeley.*

The Rt. Rev. Ian Thomas Ramsey (d. 1972). *Lord Bishop of Durham, Eng., 1966–72. Nolloth Professor of the Philosophy of the Christian Religion, University of Oxford, 1951–66.*

D.D. Raphael. *Emeritus Professor of Philosophy, Imperial College of Science and Technology, University of London.*

The Rev. Charles Earle Raven (d. 1964). *Regius Professor of Divinity, University of Cambridge, 1932–50. Canon of Liverpool, 1924–32.*

Roberto Ridolfi. *Member of Accademia Nazionale dei Lincei. Director of La Bibliofilia, 1944–82. Director of "National Editions of the Works of Savonarola."*

Philip C. Ritterbush. *Historian of science. Program Director, Institute for Cultural Progress, Washington, D.C.*

Alfredo Riva. *Assistant Professor of Industrial Chemistry, University of Bologna, Italy.*

Peter P. Rohde (d. 1978). *Free-lance writer. Author of* Søren Kierkegaard.

Sydney Ross. *Emeritus Professor of Chemistry, Rensselaer Polytechnic Institute, Troy, N.Y.*

Joan Saberhagen. *Free-lance writer on mathematics.*

Sir Edward James Salisbury (d. 1978). *Director, Royal Botanic Gardens, Kew, Eng., 1943–56.*

V.C. Samuel. *Former Dean, Theological College, University of Addis Ababa, Eth.*

Francis Henry Sandbach. *Fellow of Trinity College, Cambridge; Professor of Classics, University of Cambridge, 1967–70.*

Hans Saner. *Free-lance writer. Personal assistant to Professor Karl Jaspers, 1962–69. Author of* Karl Jaspers.

Vera Sanford (deceased). *Professor of Mathematics, State University of New York College at Oneonta, 1943–59.*

Arthur Schlissel. *Professor of Mathematics, John Jay College of Criminal Justice, City University of New York.*

Walter Schulz. *Emeritus Professor of Philosophy, Eberhard Karl University of Tübingen, Ger.*

Jacob T. Schwartz. *Chairman, Department of Computer Science, Courant Institute of Mathematical Sciences, New York University, New York City.*

Joseph Frederick Scott (d. 1971). *Vice-Principal; Principal Lecturer in Mathematics, St. Mary's College, Strawberry Hill, Eng.*

Abraham Seidenberg. *Professor of Mathematics, University of California, Berkeley.*

Jean J. Seznec (d. 1983). *Marshal Foch Professor of French Literature, University of Oxford, 1950–72.*

Robert Shackleton (d. 1986). *Marshal Foch Professor of French Literature, University of Oxford, 1979–86; Bodley's Librarian, 1966–79.*

James Shiel. *Former Reader in the History of Hellenic Thought, University of Sussex, Brighton, Eng.*

Stephen Smale. *Professor of Mathematics, University of California, Berkeley.*

Gertrude Smith (d. 1985). *Professor of Greek, University of Chicago, 1933–72.*

Ian Naismith Sneddon. *Emeritus Professor of Mathematics, University of Glasgow.*

Murray R. Spiegel. *Free-lance writer on mathematics.*

Martin K. Starr. *Professor of Management Science, Columbia University.*

Johannes Steudel (d. 1973). *Professor of the History of Medicine, Rhenish Friedrich Wilhelm University of Bonn.*

Lloyd Grenfell Stevenson, M.D. (deceased). *William H. Welch Professor of the History of Medicine; Director, Institute of the History of Medicine, Johns Hopkins University, Baltimore, 1968–83.*

Ian Nicholas Stewart. *Reader in Mathematics, University of Warwick, Coventry, Eng.*

Brian Vincent Street. *Senior Lecturer in Social Anthropology, University of Sussex, Brighton, Eng.*

Dirk Jan Struik. *Emeritus Professor of Mathematics, Massachusetts Institute of Technology, Cambridge.*

Yoshinori Takeuchi. *Emeritus Professor of Philosophy of Religion, Kyōto University.*

Tang Chun-i. *Former Professor of Philosophy, New Asia College, Chinese University of Hong Kong.*

Brian Tierney. *Bowmar Professor of Humanistic Studies, Cornell University, Ithaca, N.Y.*

Ettore Toffoletto, M.D. *President of the Administration Council, Arts Academy, Bologna, Italy.*

Alan C. Tucker. *Professor of Applied Mathematics and Statistics, State University of New York at Stony Brook.*

Walter Tuvell. *Free-lance writer on mathematics.*

E. Ashworth Underwood, M.D. (d. 1980). *Director, Wellcome Institute of the History of Medicine, London, 1946–64.*

Peter Ungar. *Emeritus Professor of Mathematics, New York University, New York City.*

Arne Unhjem. *Professor of Philosophy, Wagner College, Staten Island, N.Y.*

Rudolf Vierhaus. *Professor and Director, Max Planck Institute for History, Göttingen, Ger.*

Paul D. Vignaux (d. 1987). *President, Section of Religious Sciences, École Pratique des Hautes Études (Institute for Advanced Research), Paris, 1961–72.*

Bartel Leendert van der Waerden. *Emeritus Professor of Mathematics, University of Zürich.*

William Henry Walsh (d. 1986). *Professor of Logic and Metaphysics, University of Edinburgh, 1960–79.*

Yi-T'ung Wang. *Professor of Classical Chinese, University of Pittsburgh.*

Harold W. Wardman. *Emeritus Professor of French Studies, University of Lancaster, Eng.*

Fritz Wehrli. *Professor of Classical Philology, University of Zürich.*

Richard S. Westfall. *Professor of History of Science, Indiana University, Bloomington.*

Gerald James Whitrow. *Emeritus Professor of the History and Applications of Mathematics, Imperial College of Science and Technology, University of London.*

Lothar F.K. Wickert (d. 1989). *Professor of Ancient History, University of Cologne.*

Dallas Willard. *Associate Professor of Philosophy, University of Southern California, Los Angeles.*

Stephen S. Willoughby. *Professor and Chairman, Department of Mathematics Education, New York University, New York City.*

Paul August Wilpert (d. 1967). *Professor of Philosophy and Director of the Thomas Institute, University of Cologne.*

Lien-sheng Yang (d. 1990). *Harvard-Yenching Professor of Chinese History, Harvard University, 1965–80.*

Theodore F. Zelman. *Free-lance writer on mathematics.*

Moses Zucker (d. 1987). *Professor of Biblical Exegesis, Jewish Theological Seminary of America, New York City.*

Geography

Jan Achterstraat. *Director, Sociografisch Bureau, Haarlemmermeer, Neth.*

Evelyn Martha Acomb-Walker. *Emeritus Professor of History, State University of New York College at New Paltz.*

Ebenezer Acquaah-Harrison. *Managing Director and Chairman, Obonoma Press, Ghana.*

André Adam. *Emeritus Professor of Muslim Sociology, University of Paris V.*

Elizabeth S. Adams. *Member, Michigan Historical Commission.*

Frederick Wayne Adrian. *Emeritus Professor of History, University of Nebraska at Omaha.*

Mikhail Mikhaylovich Adrov. *Former Chief Manager, Laboratory of Oceanology, Polar Research Institute of Marine Fisheries and Oceanography, Murmansk, U.S.S.R.*

Dwight Luther Agnew. *Professor of History; Emeritus Dean, School of Liberal Studies, University of Wisconsin-Stout, Menomonie.*

Enayat Ahmad. *Professor and Head, Department of Geography; Dean, Faculty of Arts, University of Ranchi, India.*

Kazi Saied-Uddin Ahmad (d. 1970). *Professor of Geography, University of the Punjab, Lahore, Pak.*

Syed Ahmed (deceased). *Reader and Head of the Department of Geography, Osmania University, Hyderabad, India.*

Frank Oswald Ahnert. *Professor of Physical Geography, Rhenish-Westphalian Technical University, Aachen, Ger. Professor of Geography, University of Maryland, College Park, 1966–74.*

Henrik S. Ahnlund. *Curator of Antiquities of Älvsborg, Swed. Former Director, Archaeological Department, Stockholm Municipal Museum.*

Ayinipalli Aiyappan. *Former Special Officer, Tribal Research and Training Centre, Chevayur, India.*

Hyacinth Iheanyichuku Ajaegbu. *Professor and Head, Department of Geography, University of Jos, Nigeria.*

Robert Edwin Albright (d. 1969). *Professor of Social Studies, State University of New York College at Buffalo.*

William Thomas Alderson. *Director of Museum Studies, University of Delaware, Newark.*

Natalia Vitalyevna Aleksandrovskaya. *Former Associate Professor of Geography, Moscow M.V. Lomonosov State University.*

Lewis M. Alexander. *Professor of Marine Affairs, University of Rhode Island, Kingston.*

John Edmund Allison. *Supervisor, Department of Education, University of Liverpool, 1959–64. Head, Department of Geography, Birkenhead Institute, Eng., 1921–58.*

Roland Allison. *Senior tutor, College of St. Mark and St. John, Plymouth, Eng.*

David Nelson Alloway. *Professor of Sociology, Montclair State College, N.J.*

Ilídio Melo Peres do Amaral. *Professor of Geography, University of Lisbon. Rector, International University, Lisbon.*

Frank Angelo. *Associate Executive Editor, Detroit Free Press, 1971–81.*

Roger M. Anthoine. *Public Information Officer, CERN (European Organization for Nuclear Research), Geneva.*

John Conrad Appel. *Professor of History, East Stroudsburg State College, Pa.*

Rosendo Arguello. *Former President, Academy of the Geography and History of Nicaragua, Managua.*

Donald Ecklund Armagost. *Former Chairman, Department of Anthropology-Sociology, State University of New York College at Potsdam.*

Terence Edward Armstrong. *Emeritus Reader in Arctic Studies, Scott Polar Research Institute, University of Cambridge.*

Ethel Stephens Arnett. *Author of* Greensboro, North Carolina, the County Seat of Guilford; Confederate Guns Were Stacked [at] Greensboro, North Carolina; *and others.*

Nina Yakovlevna Arsenyeva. *Senior Member in Science, Leningrad Department, State Institute of Oceanography.*

Bruce W. Atkinson. *Professor of Geography, Queen Mary College, University of London.*

Jack Nelson Averitt. *Professor of History; Emeritus Dean, Graduate School, Georgia Southern College, Statesboro.*

G.H.P. Aymans. *Professor of Applied Geography, Rhenish Friedrich Wilhelm University of Bonn.*

Paul Bachetta. *Director of Administrative Services, Office of the Mayor, Chambéry, Fr.*

E. Badian. *John Moors Cabot Professor of History, Harvard University.*

Leslie Henry Baines. *Former Clerk of the Peace and Clerk of the County Council, Isle of Wight.*

Albert Wilford Baisler. *Education Consultant, Heald Hobson & Associates, New York City. President, Jamestown Community College, N.Y., 1957–69.*

Frederick Thomas Baker. *Former Director, Lincoln Public Library, City and County Museum, and Usher Gallery, Lincoln, Eng.*

Samuel John Kenneth Baker. *Emeritus Professor of Geography, Makerere University, Kampala, Uganda. Honorary Lecturer in Geography, University of Leicester, Eng., 1968–74.*

Frank Arnold Barnes. *Senior Lecturer in Geography, University of Nottingham, Eng.*

Lucy Goodell Barnes. *Former Research Associate, Massachusetts Institute of Technology, Cambridge.*

Norman Farley James Batchelor. *Former Public Relations Officer, London Borough of Haringey, Eng.*

Merrill D. Beal. *Emeritus Professor of History, Idaho State University, Pocatello.*

Jacqueline Beaujeu-Garnier. *Emeritus Professor of Geography, University of Paris I. President, Society of Geography, Paris.*

J. Murray Beck. *Emeritus Professor of Political Science, Dalhousie University, Halifax, Nova Scotia.*

Virginia Beck. *Emeritus Professor of History, Millersville State College, Pa.*

Alfred M. Beeton. *Director, Great Lakes Environmental Research Laboratory, National Oceanic and Atmospheric Administration, Ann Arbor, Mich. Adjunct Professor of Natural Resources and Atmospheric and Oceanic Science, University of Michigan, Ann Arbor.*

Natalia Maree Belting. *Associate Professor of History, University of Illinois, Urbana.*

Roger William Benedict. *Managing Editor,* Petroleum Intelligence Weekly, *London.*

S. Ann Berich. *Former Instructor in Geography, Youngstown State University, Ohio.*

Simone Bertrand. *Former Director of the Library and of the Tapestry, Bayeux, Fr.*

Jozef Marie Nicolas Beugels. *Senior Official, Kerkrade Municipality, Neth.*

George Athan Billias. *Professor of American History, Clark University, Worcester, Mass.*

Louis Robert Binding. *Committee Clerk, Luanshya Municipal Council, Zambia.*

Claude T. Bissell. *Professor of English, University of Toronto; President, 1958–71.*

Lloyd Deacon Black (d. 1989). *Professor of Geography, Northern Illinois University, De Kalb.*

Vladimir Alekseyevich Blagoobrazov. *Senior Science Editor, Soviet Encyclopaedia Publishing House, Moscow.*

Phyllis Ruth Blakeley. *Associate Archivist, Province of Nova Scotia, Halifax.*

Mary Joyce Boast. *Administration Officer of the Libraries, Southwark, London.*

Ernest Amano Boateng. *Senior consultant and adviser to the Executive Director, United Nations Environment Programme, Nairobi, Kenya. Executive Chairman, Environmental Protection Council of Ghana, Accra, 1973–81.*

Hans Bobek (d. 1990). *Professor of Geography, University of Vienna.*

Eugene Reeves Bock. *Former Editor of the Editorial Page, Anderson (Ind.) Daily Bulletin.*

Norbert Bodenstedt. *Chief Director of Archives, Freising, Ger.*

Hans H. Boesch. *Former Professor of Geography, University of Zürich.*

Victor Morton Bogle. *Chancellor; Professor of History, Indiana University, Kokomo.*

Boris Borisovich Bogoslovsky. *Professor of Physical Geography of the U.S.S.R., Belorussian V.I. Lenin State University, Minsk, U.S.S.R.*

Allan G. Bogue. *Frederick Jackson Turner Professor of History, University of Wisconsin, Madison.*

Janis A. Bokalders. *Former Professor of Economics, University of Latvia, Riga.*

Jan Bollema. *Director, Public Relations and Information Department, Municipality of The Hague.*

Juan M. Bonelli Rubio (d. 1981). *Permanent Secretary, Royal Geographical Society, Madrid.*

Paul Yvan Bonnard. *Municipal Archivist, Aix-en-Provence, Fr.*

James Calvin Bonner. *Professor and Chairman, Department of History and Political Science, Georgia College, Milledgeville, 1944–69.*

Ernst Borchorst. *Town Clerk of Esbjerg, Den.*

Vishnu Vinayak Borkar. *Professor and Head, Department of Economics, Marathwada University, Aurangabad, India.*

Otto Borst. *Emeritus Professor of Regional History, University of Stuttgart, Ger.*

Clara Boscaglia. *Executive Officer, Secretariat of State for Foreign Affairs, San Marino.*

Gérard Boulet. *Schoolteacher, Nîmes, Fr.*

Baruch Boxer. *Professor and Chair, Department of Human Ecology, Cook College, Rutgers University, New Brunswick, N.J.*

Keith Brace. *Literary Editor and Chief Feature Writer,* The Birmingham Post, *Eng.*

John P. van Brakel. *Municipal Works Officer and President, Historical Society, Katwijk, Neth.*

Peter Alexander Brannon (d. 1967). *Director, Alabama Department of Archives and History, Montgomery.*

Moshe Brawer. *Professor of Geography; Dean, Faculty of Humanities, Tel Aviv University, Israel.*

James Shober Brawley. *Telegraph Editor,* Salisbury (*N.C.*) Post.

Edward Joseph Breen. *Lawyer. Editor of* History of Early Fort Dodge and Webster County, Iowa.

John Otis Brew (d. 1988). *Peabody Professor of American Archaeology and Ethnology, Harvard University, 1949–72.*

William Charles Brice. *Emeritus Professor of Geography, Victoria University of Manchester.*

Harold Edward Briggs (deceased). *Professor of History, Southern Illinois University, Carbondale, 1945–65.*

George Mercer Brooke, Jr. *Professor of History, Virginia Military Institute, Lexington, 1958–80.*

Harold Chillingworth Brookfield. *Professor of Human Geography, Australian National University, Canberra.*

Alfred Edward Brown. *Former Director, Enfield Public Library, London Borough of Enfield, Eng.*

Chester Sidney Brown. *Former Director of Parks and Conservation, Department of Natural Resources, Government of Saskatchewan, Regina.*

Richard Holbrook Brown. *Director of Research and Education, Newberry Library, Chicago.*

Robert Eugene Burke. *Professor of History, University of Washington, Seattle. Managing Editor,* Pacific Northwest Quarterly.

Devereux Butcher (d. 1991). *Executive Director, National Parks and Conservation Association, 1942–50. Author of* Exploring Our National Parks and Monuments *and others.*

Gilbert James Butland. *Emeritus Professor of Geography, University of New England, Armidale, Australia.*

Robin Alan Butlin. *Professor of Geography, Loughborough University of Technology, Eng.*

Felix Buttersack. *Editor of* Münchner Merkur (*newspaper*), Munich.

Victor Harrison Cahalane. *President, Defenders of Wildlife, 1962–71. Assistant Director, New York State Museum, Albany, 1955–67. Collaborator, National Park Service, 1955–70.*

George H. Callcott. *Professor of History, University of Maryland, College Park; Vice-Chancellor for Academic Affairs, 1970–76.*

Eila M.J. Campbell. *Emeritus Professor of Geography, Birkbeck College, University of London.*

Erminio Canova. *Schoolmaster and journalist, Guastalla, Italy.*

Gerald M. Capers. *Emeritus Professor of History, Tulane University, New Orleans.*

Albert Sigfrid Carlson (d. 1975). *Professor of Geography, Dartmouth College, Hanover, N.H., 1944–73.*

Juan de M. Carriazo. *Professor of Ancient and Medieval Spanish History, University of Seville, 1927–69.*

Francisco Machado Carrion. *Professor of Geography, Federal University of Rio Grande do Sul, Pôrto Alegre, Braz.*

Carole-Ann Carter. *Tutor in geography.*

Harvey Lewis Carter. *John and Harriet Parker Campbell Professor Emeritus of American History, Colorado College, Colorado Springs; Curator of the Archer B. Hulbert Memorial Collection of Western Americana, 1960–73.*

José Candido de Melo Carvalho. *Professor, National Museum, Rio de Janeiro.*

Theodore J. Cassady. *Former Director, Illinois State Archives, Springfield.*

John Edwards Caswell. *Emeritus Professor of History, California State College, Stanislaus, Turlock, Calif.*

Abdel Kader Chanderli. *Senior Adviser, the Arab Fund, Kuwait. President and General Manager, C.A.M.E.L. Petroleum Company, Algiers, 1969–75. Ambassador of Algeria to the United Nations, 1962.*

Shiba P. Chatterjee (d. 1989). *Professor of Geography, University of Calcutta.*

Jan Christensen. *Assistant Foreign Editor,* Verdens Gang, *Oslo.*

Charles B. Clark. *Professor and Chairman, Department of Political Science and History, Salisbury State College, Md.*

Ira Granville Clark. *Emeritus Professor of History, New Mexico State University, Las Cruces.*

Thomas D. Clark. *Emeritus Professor of History, University of Kentucky. Distinguished Service Professor Emeritus of History, Indiana University, Bloomington.*

Frans de Clercq. *Community Official, Roosendaal en Nispen, Neth.*

Carolyn M. Clewes. *Professor of History, Wheaton College, Norton, Mass., 1954–81.*

Morris Harold Cohen. *Professor of Government, Clark University, Worcester, Mass.*

Saul Bernard Cohen. *President, Queens College, City University of New York, Flushing. Director, Graduate School of Geography, Clark University, 1965–78.*

John Peter Cole. *Professor of Regional Geography, University of Nottingham, Eng.*

John M. Coleman. *Professor of History, Lafayette College, Easton, Pa.*

J(ohn) Winston Coleman, Jr. *Author of* Slavery Times in Kentucky; Lexington During the Civil War; *and others.*

David de Lancey Condon. *Former Assistant Superintendent, Grand Canyon National Park, Arizona.*

Paul Keith Conkin. *Distinguished Professor of History, Vanderbilt University, Nashville, Tenn.*

James Robert Constantine. *Professor of History, Indiana State University, Terre Haute.*

Michael Garnet Cook. *University Archivist; Lecturer in Medieval History, University of Liverpool.*

John Terence Coppock. *Ogilvie Professor of Geography, University of Edinburgh.*

Jean Coppolani. *State Town Planner, Toulouse, Fr.*

Edmund Victor Corbett. *Former Librarian, Wandsworth Public Library, London Borough of Wandsworth, Eng.*

Paul Grant Cornell. *University Archivist; Professor of History, University of Waterloo, Ont.*

William Ainsworth Cornell. *Assistant Executive Secretary, Pennsylvania State Education Association, Harrisburg.*

Robert Cornevin (d. 1988). *Permanent Secretary, Academy of Overseas Sciences, Paris. Head, Centre of Studies and Documentation on Africa and Overseas, Paris.*

E. Merton Coulter (d. 1981). *Professor of History, University of Georgia, Athens, 1923–58.*

John Wesley Coulter (d. 1968). *Professor of Geography, University of Cincinnati, Ohio.*

Joseph Francis Courtney. *Attorney. Lecturer in Public Administration, Northeastern University, Boston.*

Raymond Gibson Cowherd. *Emeritus Professor of History, Lehigh University, Bethlehem, Pa.*

James Stevens Cox. *Editor,* Proceedings of the Dorset Natural History and Archaeological Society, *and others.*

Clark Nixon Crain. *Former Professor of Geography and Regional Development, University of Denver, Colo.*

Albert Charles Crane. *Former Clerk, Border Rural District Council, England.*

Leland Hargrave Creer. *Emeritus Professor of History, University of Utah, Salt Lake City.*

Bernarr Cresap. *Professor of History, University of North Alabama, Florence, 1951–77.*

John Clark Crighton. *Professor of History, Stephens College, Columbia, Mo., 1935–70.*

Virgil Charles Crisafulli. *Emeritus Professor of Economics, Utica College of Syracuse University, N.Y.*

Gerald Roe Crone (d. 1982). *Librarian and Map Curator, Royal Geographical Society, London, 1945–66.*

Jesse Crawford Crowe. *Professor of History, Western Kentucky University, Bowling Green.*

Kenneth Brailey Cumberland. *Former Professor of Geography, University of Auckland, New Zealand.*

Décio Neves da Cunha. *Professor, Centre for General Education, Federal University of Espírito Santo, Vitória, Braz.*

Pedro Cunill. *Professor of Historical Geography, Central University of Venezuela, Caracas.*

Alden (Denzel) Cutshall. *Emeritus Professor of Geography, University of Illinois, Chicago.*

Ernest Rockwell Dalton (d. 1984). *Dean of Instruction, Centenary College for Women, Hackettstown, N.J.*

Arthur Davies. *Reardon-Smith Professor of Geography, University of Exeter, Eng., 1948–71.*

Wayne K.D. Davies. *Professor of Geography, University of Calgary, Alberta.*

James Treadwell Davis. *Emeritus Professor of History, University of Southern Mississippi, Hattiesburg.*

John Armstrong Davison (d. 1966). *Professor of Greek Language and Literature, University of Leeds, Eng., 1951–66.*

Raul d'Eça. *Lecturer on Latin-American affairs. Assistant Career Planning Officer, U.S. Information Agency, 1959–61. Branch Public Affairs Officer, Recife and Belo Horizonte, Braz., Office of International Information and Cultural Affairs, 1947–58.*

John Alvin Decker. *Former Professor of Political Science, Stephens College, Columbia, Mo.*

Gerhard Deissmann. *Former Collaborator and Assistant Director, Bremen Committee for Economic Research, W.Ger.*

Henry Delmont. *Former Curator, J.B. Rames Museum, Aurillac, Fr.*

Abraham Demoz. *Professor of Linguistics, Northwestern University, Evanston, Ill.; Director, Program of African Studies, 1974–80.*

René Julien C. De Roo. *Curator, Royal Museums of Art and History, Brussels. Archivist and Museum Director, Mechelen, Belg., 1949–63.*

Hans Otto Jerphaas de Ruyter de Wildt. *Chief of Educational and Cultural Affairs, Hoorn, Neth.*

P.B. Desai. *Former Professor and Head, Department of Ancient Indian History and Culture, Karnatak University, Dharwar, India.*

Pedro Neiva de Santana. *Governor of Maranhão State. Former Rector, University of Maranhão, São Luis, Braz.*

Jean-Jacques Despois (d. 1978). *Professor of Geography, University of Paris, 1957–69.*

Jack J. Detzler. *Professor of History, Saint Mary's College, Notre Dame, Ind.*

Caio Benjamin Dias. *Former Rector, University of Brasília.*

Samuel Newton Dicken. *Emeritus Professor of Geography, University of Oregon, Eugene.*

Robert Eric Dickinson (d. 1981). *Professor of Geography, University of Arizona, Tucson, 1967–75.*

Kwamina Busumafi Dickson. *Vice-Chancellor, University of Cape Coast, Ghana.*

Alonzo Thomas Dill. *Public Relations Director, Chesapeake Corporation of Virginia, West Point, Va., 1958–80.*

Ernest H.G. Dobby (d. 1981). *Professor of Geography, University of Malaya, Singapore.*

William Mann Dobriner. *Charles A. Dana Professor of Sociology, Lafayette College, Easton, Pa.*

Anatoly Petrovich Domanitsky. *Senior Scientist, Leningrad Hydrological Institute.*

J. Don. *Archivist, Kampen, Neth.*

Desmond Thomas Donovan. *Former Yates-Goldsmid Professor of Geology, University College, University of London.*

Arthur J.M. Doucy. *Professor of Social Economics; former Director, Institute of Sociology, Free University of Brussels.*

Garland Downum. *Emeritus Professor of History, Northern Arizona University, Flagstaff.*

Jean Dresch. *Emeritus Professor of Geography, University of Paris VII.*

Robert Roland Drummond. *Former Professor of Geography, Indiana State University, Terre Haute.*

Raymond Dubé. *Former Editor in Chief,* Le Soleil, *Quebec City.*

George Harry Dury. *Emeritus Professor of Geography and Geology, University of Wisconsin, Madison.*

André Duval. *Former Deputy Mayor, Clichy, Fr.*

Denis John Dwyer. *Professor of Geography, University of Keele, Eng.*

Donald Ray Dyer. *Former Regional Geographic Attaché, U.S. Department of State, Washington, D.C.*

Wilma Dykeman. *Adjunct Professor of English, University of Tennessee, Knoxville. State Historian of Tennessee.*

David Livingstone Dykstra. *Emeritus Professor of History, Hofstra University, Hempstead, N.Y.*

Armand J. Eardley (d. 1972). *Professor of Geology, University of Utah, Salt Lake City, 1965–70; Dean, College of Mines and Mineral Industries, 1954–65.*

The Rev. George Herbert Eastman. *Principal of the London Missionary Society's Training College at Beru, Gilbert and Ellice Islands, 1918–48.*

Herbert Leeson Edlin (d. 1976). *Publications Officer, Forestry Commission of Great Britain, London.*

Kenneth Charles Edwards (d. 1982). *Professor of Geography, University of Nottingham, Eng., 1948–70.*

Emil Egli. *Professor of Geography, Zürich Gymnasium. Lecturer, University of Zürich and Swiss Federal Institute of Technology, Zürich.*

Blake Ehrlich (d. 1974). *Free-lance writer. Author of* Paris on the Seine; London on the Thames; *and many others.*

H.W. Eldermans. *Journalist. Former Editor,* Rotterdamsch Nieuwsblad.

Dorothy M. Ellicott. *Justice of the Peace. Member, City Council of Gibraltar, 1947–55; House of Assembly, 1959–64.*

Robert Neal Elliott. *Associate Professor of History, North Carolina State University, Raleigh.*

Joseph Waldo Ellison (deceased). *Professor of History, Oregon State University, Corvallis.*

Antonia Déa Erdens. *Professor of Geography, Federal University of Bahia, Salvador, Braz.*

Sirri Erinc. *Director, Institute of Marine Sciences and Geography, University of Istanbul.*

Sir Robert Charles Evans. *Principal, University College of North Wales, Bangor, University of Wales. Author of* Kangchenjunga: The Untrodden Peak *and others.*

Russell Charles Ewing (d. 1972). *Professor of History, University of Arizona, Tucson, 1948–72.*

J.D. Eyles. *Lecturer in Geography, Queen Mary College, University of London.*

John Douglas Eyre. *Professor of Geography, University of North Carolina at Chapel Hill.*

John D. Fage. *Emeritus Professor of African History, University of Birmingham, Eng.*

Albert Leonard Farley. *Professor of Geography, University of British Columbia, Vancouver.*

Bertram Hughes Farmer. *Fellow of St. John's College, Cambridge; Reader in South Asian Geography; Director, Centre of South Asian Studies, University of Cambridge.*

Francis Peloubet Farquhar (d. 1975). *Author of* Place Names of the High Sierra *and others.*

Irmgard Feldhaus. *Director, Clemens Sels Museum, Neuss, Ger.*

João Epitácio Fernandes Pimenta (d. 1972). *Judge, First District of Natal, Braz., 1954–57. Member, Electoral Tribunal of Rio Grande do Norte, 1953–57.*

A.M. Ferrar. *Map Curator, University of Hull, Eng.*

Milton Gonçalves Ferreira. *Former Vice Rector and Director of the Faculty of Economics, Federal University of Alagoas, Maceió, Braz.*

George Leonard Fersh. *Associate Director, Joint Council on Economic Education, New York City.*

José Carlos de Figueiredo. *Emeritus Professor of Geography of Brazil, Federal University of Paraná, Curitiba, Braz.*

José de Silva Ribeiro Filho. *Professor of Criminal Law, Federal University of Sergipe, Aracaju, Braz. Secretary, Public Security of the State of Sergipe.*

Ingo Findenegg (d. 1974). *Head, International Biological Program Laboratory, Austrian Academy of Sciences, Klagenfurt.*

George Michael Fitzpatrick. *Emeritus Editor,* New Mexico Magazine.

Betty Lorraine Fladeland. *Professor of History, Southern Illinois University, Carbondale.*

Allen Richard Foley (d. 1978). *Professor of History, Dartmouth College, Hanover, N.H.*

Martin Otto Walter Folkerts. *Assistant Scientist, Institute of Geography and Economic Geography, University of Hamburg.*

Lachlan Maxwell Forbes. *Former Editor,* Polar Record, *Scott Polar Research Institute, University of Cambridge.*

Arthur B. Ford. *Geologist, Branch of Alaskan Geology, Geological Survey, U.S. Department of the Interior, Menlo Park, Calif.*

Enid R.A. Forde. *Professor of Geography, Fourah Bay College, University of Sierra Leone, Freetown.*

Charles Nelson Forward. *Professor of Geography, University of Victoria, B.C.*

Abram John Foster. *Professor of History, Millersville State College, Pa., 1952–79.*

Catharine Osgood Foster. *Teacher of English and American Literature, Bennington College, Vt., 1934–68.*

Lucien Fourez. *Judge, Tribunal of First Instance, Belgium.*

Thomas Walter Freeman (d. 1988). *Professor of Geography, Victoria University of Manchester, 1950–76.*

Marion R. Fremont-Smith. *Attorney, Choate, Hall & Stewart, Boston. Assistant Attorney General, Commonwealth of Massachusetts, 1959–63.*

Richard Antony French. *Senior Lecturer in the Geography of the U.S.S.R., University College and School of Slavonic and East European Studies, University of London.*

Hermann Friedrich. *Former Director, Overseas Museum, Bremen, W.Ger.*

Robert F. Fries. *Emeritus Professor of History, De Paul University, Chicago.*

Grigory Ivanovich Galazy. *Director, Institute of Limnology, Siberian Department, Academy of Sciences of the U.S.S.R., Irkutsk.*

Edward John Gallagher (d. 1978). *Publisher,* Laconia (N.H.) Evening Citizen.

Maureen L. Gallery. *Free-lance writer on Middle Eastern geography.*

Hans Gamma. *Editor. Former Mayor, Altdorf, Switz.*

Vico Garbesi. *Assistant Librarian, Library of Imola, Italy.*

Elizabeth Gard. *Copy Editor,* Hispanic American Historical Review, *Albuquerque, N.M. Editorial Assistant, Geography, Encyclopædia Britannica, Chicago, 1970–71.*

John H. Garland. *Emeritus Professor of Geography, University of Illinois, Urbana.*

Richard Gascon. *Professor of Local History, University of Lyon II.*

Werner Gatz. *Director, Bremen Society for Economic Research, Ger.*

Aleksandr Mikhaylovich Gavrilov. *Senior Scientist, Leningrad Hydrological Institute.*

George Roosevelt Gayler. *Professor of History, Northwest Missouri State University, Maryville.*

Alastair George Geddes. *Former Lecturer in Adult Education, University of Southampton, Eng.*

Clyde Christian Gelbach. *Professor of History, Indiana State University, Pa., 1955–82.*

Susannah C. Gentry. *Associate Editor,* Independence (Mo.) Examiner.

Arch C. Gerlach (d. 1972). *Chief Geographer, Geological Survey, U.S. Department of the Interior, 1967–72. Incumbent, Chair of Geography, Library of Congress.*

Percy Amorey Beaufort Gethin. *Tutor in English and Political Institutions, Lennox Cook School of English, Cambridge, Eng.*

Huricihan Ghaznavi. *Teaching Assistant in Middle Eastern History and Turkish, University of Wisconsin, Madison.*

G.K. Ghori. *Visiting Professor of Geography, University of Benin, Nigeria.*

Arrell Morgan Gibson (d. 1987). *Professor of History, University of Oklahoma, Norman, 1957–87; Curator, Western History Collection, 1959–87.*

Frans Gijzels. *Mayor of Heerlen, Neth.*

Malaquias Gil Arantegui. *Professor of History and Geography, "Pedro Henriquez Urena" National University, Santo Domingo, Dom. Rep.*

Robert Creighton Gilmore. *Associate Professor of History, University of New Hampshire, Durham.*

Marcel Gingras. *Secretary, Public Service Commission of Canada, Ottawa.*

Norton S. Ginsburg. *Director, Environment and Policy Institute, East-West Center, Honolulu. Emeritus Professor of Geography, University of Chicago.*

Francesco Giunta. *Professor of Medieval History, University of Palermo.*

Charles Nelson Glaab. *Professor of History, University of Toledo, Ohio.*

Robert Morton Glendinning. *Emeritus Professor of Geography, University of California, Los Angeles.*

Stephen Goddard. *Deputy Librarian, School of Oriental and African Studies, University of London.*

António Armando Gonçalves Pereira. *Former Professor of Commercial and Maritime Law, Technical University of Lisbon.*

George Goodwin, Jr. *Professor of Politics, University of Massachusetts, Boston.*

Arnold L. Gordon. *Professor of Oceanography, Columbia University.*

Jean Grandmaison. *Keeper of the Archives and Library, Tarascon, Fr.*

Lee Albert Graver. *Emeritus Professor of History and Political Science, Kutztown University, Pa.*

Mabel Green. *Former Lecturer in Geography, College of Education, Hull, Eng.*

Donald Paul Greene. *Former Associate Professor of History and Anthropology, Adams State College, Alamosa, Colo.*

Richard A. Greene. *Columnist and Editorial Writer,* Muncie *(Ind.)* Star.

Gwilym David Gregory. *Principal Assistant, London Borough of Camden Public Libraries, Eng.*

Jack Irving Grenfell. *Justice of the Peace; Town Clerk and Treasurer, City of Ararat, Australia.*

Edward Frederick Greve. *Associate Professor of Library Science, University of Wisconsin, Superior.*

Thomas Melvin Griffiths. *Emeritus Professor of Geography, University of Denver, Colo.*

Theodore Gregory Gronert (d. 1966). *Chairman, Department of History, Wabash College, Crawfordsville, Ind.*

Alberto Passos Guimarães. *Geography Editor,* Enciclopédia Mirador Internacional, *Rio de Janeiro.*

Bernard Victor Gutsell. *Former Professor of Geography, York University, Toronto. Editor,* Cartographica.

LeRoy R. Hafen (deceased). *Professor of History, Brigham Young University, Provo, Utah, 1954–71. State Historian of Colorado, 1924–54.*

Daniel George Edward Hall (d. 1979). *Professor of the History of South-East Asia, University of London, 1949–59.*

J.M. Hall. *Lecturer in Geography, Queen Mary College, University of London.*

Ray Hall. *Lecturer in Geography, Queen Mary College, University of London.*

Robert Burnett Hall (d. 1975). *Colonel, U.S. Army. Professor of Geography, University of Michigan, Ann Arbor; Director, Center for Japanese Studies, 1947–57.*

Louis-Edmond Hamelin. *Geographer, University of Quebec at Trois-Rivières; Rector, 1978–83.*

Edward Hamming. *Professor of Geography, Augustana College, Rock Island, Ill.*

John W. Hanson. *Former Professor of Geography, Michigan State University, East Lansing.*

F. Kenneth Hare. *Chancellor, Trent University, Peterborough, Ont.; University Professor Emeritus of Geography and of Physics, University of Toronto.*

George Dewey Harmon. *Emeritus Professor of American History, Lehigh University, Bethlehem, Pa.*

John Lauren Harr. *Emeritus Professor of History, Northwest Missouri State University, Maryville.*

Ronald James Harrison-Church. *Emeritus Professor of Geography, London School of Economics and Political Science, University of London.*

Mary Harvey. *Lecturer in Geography, Goldsmiths' College, University of London.*

Maria van Hasselt. *Former Curator, History of The Hague Department, Municipal Museum of The Hague.*

Raymond Hastey. *Teacher, Lycée, Cherbourg, Fr.*

Athan(assios) D. Hatzikakidis. *General Director, Institute of Oceanographic and Fisheries Research, Athens.*

Richard Walter Haupt. *Former Director, The Cincinnati Historical Society, Ohio.*

H. Bowman Hawkes. *Emeritus Professor of Geography, University of Utah, Salt Lake City.*

Hubert Howard Hawkins. *Director, Indiana Historical Bureau and Indiana Historical Society, Indianapolis, 1953–76.*

Hermann-Heino Heine. *Taxonomic Botanist, Kew Gardens, London.*

Herbert Lynn Heller. *Emeritus Professor of Education, Baldwin-Wallace College, Berea, Ohio.*

Walter Brookfield Hendrickson. *Emeritus Professor of History, MacMurray College, Jacksonville, Ill.*

Henri Henneguelle. *Mayor of Boulogne, Fr., 1945–47; 1953–77.*

Roger Chatsey Heppell. *Professor of Geography, State University of New York College at Cortland.*

Thomas Herdman (d. 1970). *Senior Lecturer in Geography and Education, Training College, Dudley, Eng.*

Herman Heupers. *Manager, Public Relations Office, Enschede, Neth.*

Sanford Wilson Higginbotham. *Professor of History, Rice University, Houston, Texas. Editor,* Journal of Southern History.

Ernest Gotthold Hildner, Jr. *Professor of History, Illinois College, Jacksonville, 1938–72.*

Marie-Elisabeth Hilger. *Professor of Social and Economic History, Institute for Social and Economic History, University of Hamburg.*

Dorothy Hill. *Research Professor Emeritus of Geology, University of Queensland, St. Lucia, Brisbane, Australia.*

Neal O. Hines. *Former Staff Associate, Laboratory of Radiation Biology, University of Washington, Seattle.*

Mark David Hirsch (d. 1989). *Professor of History, Bronx Community College, City University of New York, 1959–75.*

Edward Henry Hobbs. *Dean of Arts and Sciences, Auburn University, Ala.*

Walter Hoffelner. *Official of the Municipal Council, Steyr, Austria.*

Hans Högn (d. 1980). *Mayor of Hof, W.Ger.*

Stanley Charles Holliday. *Former Chief Librarian, Kensington and Chelsea Public Libraries, London.*

Madhusudan Shriniwas Honrao. *Former Reader and Head, Department of Geography, Karnatak University, Dharwar, India.*

Reginald Horsman. *Distinguished Professor of American History, University of Wisconsin, Milwaukee.*

Jack Luin Hough. *Emeritus Professor of Meteorology and Oceanography and of Geology and Mineralogy, University of Michigan, Ann Arbor.*

James Houston. *Chancellor, Regent College, Vancouver, B.C.*

Henry Forbush Howe, M.D. *Author of* Salt Rivers of the Massachusetts Shore; Massachusetts: There She Is—Behold Her; *and others.*

Lewis Grenfell Huddy. *Former Town Clerk, London Borough of Hackney, Eng.*

Jean Hugli. *Teacher, Technical College, Lausanne, Switz.*

Robert Edward Huke. *Professor of Geography, Dartmouth College, Hanover, N.H.*

Arjuna Hulugalle. *Publishing company director. Coeditor and cotranslator of Reiseführer von Sri Lanka (*"Guide to Ceylon"*).*

Herbert A.J. Hulugalle. *Chairman, Advisory Committee, National and Grindlays Bank, Sri Lanka Branch, Colombo. Ambassador of Ceylon to Italy, 1954–59.*

John Owen Hunt. *Former Clerk, Urban District Council, Matlock, Eng.*

Thomas John Hunt. *Chairman, Somerset Archaeological Society and Somerset Record Society, Eng.*

J.O. Hunwick. *Professor of History, Northwestern University, Evanston, Ill.*

Jacob C. Hurewitz. *Professor of Political Science, Columbia University.*

Georg Illert. *Former Director, State Library, Archives, and Museum, Worms, W.Ger.*

Giuseppe Imbo. *Emeritus Professor of Earth Sciences, University of Naples. Director, Vesuvian Observatory, Naples, 1935–70.*

Robert Henry Irrmann. *Emeritus Professor of History, Beloit College, Wis.; Archivist, 1953–80.*

William Harold Irvine. *Secretary General, Nigerian Tourist Association, Lagos, 1963–68.*

Norman Itzkowitz. *Professor of Near Eastern Studies, Princeton University.*

John David Ives. *Professor and Chairman, Department of Geography, University of California, Davis.*

Phil Rowland Jack. *Professor of History, California State College, Pa.*

Wilbur R. Jacobs. *Professor of History, University of California, Santa Barbara.*

Orville John Jaebker. *Professor and Head, Department of History, University of Evansville, Ind.*

Karel Frederik Otto James. *President, Central Committee of Regional Gasboards, Amerongen. Former Burgomaster, Gouda, Neth.*

Preston E. James (d. 1986). *Maxwell Professor of Geography, Syracuse University, N.Y., 1964–70.*

Neil L. Jamieson, III. *Acting Assistant Professor of Anthropology, Freshman Seminar Program, University of Hawaii at Manoa, Honolulu.*

Brian Michael Jenkins. *Senior Staff Member, The RAND Corporation, Santa Monica, Calif.*

John Leonard Jennewein (d. 1968). *Associate Professor of History, Dakota Wesleyan University, Mitchell, S.D.*

Dorothy O. Johansen. *Emeritus Professor of History, Reed College, Portland, Ore.*

John Edwin Johns. *President, Furman University, Greenville, S.C.*

Bert Willard Johnson. *County Manager, Arlington, Va., 1962–76. City Manager, Evanston, Ill., 1953–62.*

William Stephen Kwesi Johnston (Nana Amoah IV). *Vice-Chairman, Ghana Boy Scouts Association, Central Region. Senior Divisional Chief of Ognaa (Cape Coast) Traditional Area; Local Court Magistrate, Cape Coast, Ghana, 1960–66.*

Clarence F. Jones (d. 1991). *Professor of Geography, Northwestern University, Evanston, Ill., 1945–61.*

Lewis Pinckney Jones. *Kenan Professor of History, Wofford College, Spartanburg, S.C.*

Meirion T. Jones. *Principal Scientific Officer, Marine Information and Advisory Service, Institute of Oceanographic Sciences, Birkenhead, Eng.*

Robert Leslie Jones. *Emeritus Professor of History, Marietta College, Ohio.*

Ronald Jones. *Reader in Geography, Queen Mary College, University of London.*

Stanley Llewellyn Jones. *Professor of History; Vice-Chancellor of Academic Affairs, University of North Carolina at Greensboro.*

Weymouth Tyree Jordan (d. 1968). *Professor, 1949–68, and Head of the Department of History, 1955–68, Florida State University, Tallahassee.*

Derrick Neville Edwin Kain. *Industrial and Business Editor, Natal Witness, Pietermaritzburg, S.Af.*

James Samuel Kaleem. *Former Principal Education Officer, Ministry of Education, Tamale, Ghana.*

Samuel Richey Kamm (deceased). *Professor of History and Social Science, Wheaton College, Ill., 1942–73.*

Otto Kandler. *Professor of Geography, Johannes Gutenberg University of Mainz, Ger.*

Suk Oh Kang. *Former Professor of Geography, Ewha Woman's University, Seoul.*

Helene Juliet Kantor. *Professor of Near Eastern Archaeology, University of Chicago.*

John Haskell Kemble (d. 1990). *Professor of History, Pomona College, Claremont, Calif., 1950–77.*

Peter Alexander Kennedy. *Former County Archivist, Devon County Council, England.*

Joan Margaret Kenworthy. *Principal, St. Mary's College; Honorary Lecturer in Geography, University of Durham, Eng.*

Hendrik Jakob Keuning. *Former Professor of Economics and Social Geography, State University of Groningen, Neth.*

Huỳnh Kim Khánh. *Research Fellow, Institute of Social Studies, The Hague.*

Rudolf Kiepke. *Publisher of Die Warte, Paderborn, Ger.*

Harold Godfrey King. *Librarian and Information Officer, Scott Polar Research Institute, University of Cambridge.*

Spencer Bidwell King, Jr. (d. 1977). *Professor of History, Mercer University, Macon, Ga., 1948–73.*

George Kish (d. 1989). *Professor of Geography, University of Michigan, Ann Arbor.*

Anna Alekseyevna Klyukanova. *Junior Scientist, Institute of Geography, Academy of Sciences of the U.S.S.R., Moscow.*

Anton C.F. Koch. *Former Town archivist and librarian, Deventer, Neth.*

John Kolars. *Professor of Geography, University of Michigan, Ann Arbor.*

Rudolf Koller. *Director of the Municipal Department of Culture and the Arts, Ingolstadt, Ger.*

John G.J. Koreman. *Chief Assistant, Municipal Record Office, Maastricht, Neth.*

Dimiter Konstantinov Kossev. *Editor in Chief, Bulgarian Historical Review. Rector, University of Sofia, 1962–67.*

Hans-Joachim Kramm. *Professor of Economic Geography, College of Education, Potsdam, Ger.*

Walter Kranz. *Former Director, Press and Information Office of the Liechtenstein Government.*

Hermann Kresse. *Editor in Chief, Saarland Edition, Rhein-Saar-Spiegel. Reporter, Saarbrücker Zeitung.*

Werner Kugler (d. 1973). *Burgomaster of Schleswig, W.Ger.*

Werner Th. Kuhn (d. 1973). *Professor of Geography, Staedtisches Gymnasium, Bern. Lecturer, State College, Bern.*

Wiebren Hendrik Kuipers. *Public Relations Officer, Community of Leeuwarden, Neth.*

Eeva-Sinikka Kurikka. *Chief Correspondent, Werner Söderström Osakeyhtiö, Publishers, Helsinki.*

Wilhelm von Kürten. *Professor of Geography, University of Wuppertal, Ger.*

Pieter Th.J. Kuyer. *Keeper of Municipal Records, 's Hertogenbosch, Neth.*

Nikolay Timofeyevich Kuznetsov. *Chief Research Associate, Laboratory of Mountain Geosystems, Institute of Geography, Academy of Sciences of the U.S.S.R., Moscow.*

Alexander Atta Yaw Kyeremamaten. *Director, Ghana National Cultural Centre, Kumasi.*

Howard Lackman. *Professor of History, University of Texas at Arlington.*

Ernest McPherson Lander, Jr. *Alumni Professor of History, Clemson University, S.C.*

Elfrieda Wilhelmina Henrietta Lang. *Curator of Manuscripts, Lilly Library, Indiana University, Bloomington, 1965–74.*

Robert Millard Langdon (d. 1967). *Associate Professor of History, Civilian Faculty, U.S. Naval Academy.*

Richard W. Lariviere. *Assistant Professor of Sanskrit, University of Texas at Austin.*

Helge Larsen. *Minister of Education, Danish Government, 1968–71.*

François Lasserre. *Emeritus Professor of Classical Greek, University of Lausanne, Switz.*

Geoffrey Charles Last. *Adviser, Imperial Ethiopian Ministry of Education and Fine Arts, Addis Ababa.*

Louis-Noël Latour. *Curator, Museum of the Hôtel-Dieu, Beaune, Fr.*

Keith Eric Lauder. *Former Town Clerk, London Borough of Barking, Eng.*

Heinz Lauenroth. *Chief City Official and Director, Cultural and Sport Department, Hanover, Ger.*

Joseph J. Lauer. *Africana Librarian, University of California, Los Angeles.*

J.H.G. Lebon (d. 1969). *Reader in Geography, School of Oriental and African Studies, University of London, 1966–69.*

Enoch Lawrence Lee. *Emeritus Professor of History, The Citadel, Charleston, S.C.*

Roger Kendrick Lee. *Lecturer in Geography, Queen Mary College, University of London.*

Aureliano Leite (d. 1976). *President of the São Paulo Historical and Geographical Institute. Member of the São Paulo Academy of Letters. Member of the Brazilian Historical and Geographical Institute.*

Celso de Paiva Leite. *Professor, Centre of Applied Social Sciences, Federal University of Paraíba, João Pessoa, Braz.*

Robert Lemaire. *Librarian of the Municipal Library, Beauvais, Fr.*

Walter John Lemke (d. 1968). *Professor of Journalism, University of Arkansas, Fayetteville.*

John Herbert Le Patourel (d. 1981). *Research Professor of Medieval History, University of Leeds, Eng., 1970–74.*

Edith Veronica Lewis. *Reference Librarian, Finsbury Library, London Borough of Islington, Eng.*

George Knowlton Lewis. *Emeritus Professor of Geography, Boston University.*

Reginald George Lickfold. *Former Town Clerk, Weston-super-Mare, Eng.*

George Lighton. *Principal of Stevenage College of Further Education, Stevenage, Eng. Former Senior Geography Master, Queen's College, Georgetown, British Guiana.*

José Lourenço de Lima. *Professor of Romance Languages, Federal University of Pernambuco, and Catholic University of Pernambuco, Recife, Braz.*

Miguel Alves de Lima. *Professor of Physical Geography, State University of Rio de Janeiro; former Director, Earth Sciences Institute.*

Steffen Linvald. *Director of Copenhagen City Museum, 1952–79.*

Aleksandr Petrovich Lisitsin. *Head, Laboratory of Physical Methods of Research, Institute of Oceanology, Academy of Sciences of the U.S.S.R., Moscow.*

Georges Livet. *Professor of Modern History, University of Strasbourg II, Fr.*

Donald Lloyd. *Former Deputy Clerk, Urban District Council of Winsford, Eng.*

Seton H.F. Lloyd. *Emeritus Professor of Western Asiatic Archaeology, University of London.*

W. Duane Lockard. *Professor of Political Science, Princeton University.*

M. John Loeffler. *Emeritus Professor of Geography, University of Colorado, Boulder.*

Julius Loennechen. *British Vice-Consul, Kristiansund, Nor.*

Rayford Whittingham Logan (d. 1982). *Professor of History, Howard University, Washington, D.C., 1938–72.*

Richard F. Logan. *Emeritus Professor of Geography, University of California, Los Angeles.*

Alan R. Longhurst. *Director-General, Atlantic Ocean Science and Surveys, Bedford Institute of Oceanography, Dartmouth, Nova Scotia.*

Richard Lowitt. *Former Professor of History, University of Kentucky, Lexington.*

Myron Harper Luke. *Emeritus Professor of History, C.W. Post College, Long Island University, Greenvale, N.Y.*

Gustav Johannes Luntowski. *Town Archivist, Dortmund, Ger. Former Town Archivist and Chief Librarian, Lüneburg, W.Ger.*

Anthony Thornton Luttrell. *Former Assistant Director, British School at Rome.*

Vasily Yosifovich Lymarev. *Professor of Geography, Kaliningrad State University, U.S.S.R.*

Charles Maas. *Director, Cultural Office, Villach, Austria.*

John Morris McClelland, Jr. *Former Editor and Publisher,* Longview (*Wash.*) Daily News.

Margaret McDerby. *Librarian in Charge, Reference and Museum Services, London Borough of Barnet, Eng.*

William Duff Mackay. *Town Clerk and Treasurer, Richmond, S.Af. Town Clerk, Ladysmith, S.Af., 1946–61.*

Henry Miller Madden. *Adjunct Professor of Bibliography, California State University, Fresno; Librarian, 1949–79.*

Desiderio Maggioni. *Former Member for Milano-Pavia, Chamber of Deputies, Italy.*

William Richard Maidment. *Former Borough Librarian, London Borough of Camden, Eng.*

Vasile Malinschi. *Governor, National Bank of the Socialist Republic of Romania, 1963–77. Member, Section of Economics and Sociological Research, Academy of the Socialist Republic of Romania, Bucharest.*

Ulrich W. Mammey. *Research Associate, Federal Institute for Population Research, Wiesbaden, Ger. Associate of the Geographical Institute, Johann Wolfgang Goethe University of Frankfurt.*

Gordon Manley (d. 1980). *Professor of Environmental Sciences, University of Lancaster, Eng., 1964–68.*

Luis Marden. *Former Chief, Foreign Editorial Staff,* National Geographic Magazine, *Washington, D.C.*

Aleksandr Mefodyevich Marinich. *Director, Department of Geography, C.I. Subotin Institute of Geophysics, Ukrainian S.S.R. Academy of Sciences, Kiev.*

Albert John Marino. *Assistant City Editor,* New Britain (*Conn.*) Herald.

Nemesio Marqués. *General Secretary to the Bishop of Urgel, Coprince of Andorra.*

Hendrik Michiel Martens. *Burgomaster, Ermelo, Neth., 1938–62.*

Jean Martin-Demézil. *Archivist, Département of Loir-et-Cher, France, 1941–78.*

Marion E. Marts. *Emeritus Professor of Geography, University of Washington, Seattle.*

Kenneth Mason (d. 1976). *Lieutenant Colonel, Royal Engineers. Professor of Geography, University of Oxford, 1932–53.*

Philip Parker Mason. *Professor of History, Wayne State University, Detroit.*

Matsui Taketoshi. *Former Professor of Human Geography, Nagoya University, Japan.*

Eberhard Matthes. *Former Town Archivist, Eisenach, E.Ger.*

John E. Mawby. *Associate Professor of Geology, California State University, Fresno.*

William Richard Mead. *Emeritus Professor of Geography, University College, University of London.*

Howard Brett Melendy. *Professor of History, San Jose State University, Calif.*

Ralph Robertson Mellon, M.D. (deceased). *Director, Institute of Pathology, Western Pennsylvania Hospital, Pittsburgh, 1927–53.*

Roy E.H. Mellor. *Emeritus Professor of Geography, University of Aberdeen, Scot.*

Alberto Mennella. *Archivist and Departmental Head, Municipality of Torre del Greco, Italy.*

Jean Michel Mercadier. *Director, Honoré de Balzac College of Secondary Education, Albi, Fr.*

(Ethel) Doris Mercer. *Head Archivist, Greater London Council.*

Horst Messerschmidt. *Burgomaster of Bernburg, Ger.*

Patricia Meyer. *Reference Librarian, Borough of Wandsworth, Eng.*

Dorothy Middleton. *Assistant Editor, Geographical Journal, 1953–71. Author of* Baker of the Nile *and others.*

R.E. Millard. *Former Clerk of the Peace and Clerk of the County Council, Buckinghamshire, Eng.*

Maynard Malcolm Miller. *Professor of Geology; Emeritus Dean, College of Mines and Earth Resources; Director, Glaciological and Arctic Sciences Institute, University of Idaho, Moscow.*

Paul Eugene Million, Jr. *Associate Professor of History, Purdue University, West Lafayette, Ind.*

Norah Mitchell. *Teacher at the Kodai School, Madurai District, Tamil Nadu, India.*

Mario Modiano. *Athens Correspondent,* The Times *(London).*

Maurice P. Moffatt. *Former Professor and Chairman, Department of Social Studies, Montclair State College, N.J.*

Jay Monaghan (d. 1981). *Consultant, Wyles Collection of Lincolniana and Western Americana, University of California, Santa Barbara. State Historian of Illinois, 1946–51.*

Robert Scott Monahan. *Former Forester and Manager of Outing Properties, Dartmouth College, Hanover, N.H.*

Annie Monginoux. *Librarian, Saint-Étienne Municipal Library, Fr.*

Francis John Monkhouse (d. 1975). *Professor of Geography, University of Southampton, Eng., 1954–66.*

Powell A. Moore (d. 1967). *Professor of History, Indiana University, Bloomington.*

Amélia A. Norgueira Moreira (deceased). *Professor of Geography, Federal University of Ceará, Fortaleza, Braz.*

Gladys Margery Morris. *Former Clerk, Ashburton Urban District Council, Eng.*

James Davidson Morrison. *Emeritus Professor of History, Southeastern State College, Durant, Okla.*

Ralph Ernest Morrow. *Professor of History, Washington University, St. Louis, Mo.*

Richard Lee Morton (d. 1974). *Professor of History, College of William and Mary, Williamsburg, Va., 1921–59.*

Heinz Motel. *Chief of Tourist Office, Göttingen, Ger.*

Malcolm Herbert Moule. *Professor of English History, University of the Pacific, Stockton, Calif.*

Alan Bertram Mountjoy. *Reader in Geography, Bedford College, University of London.*

Pieter Mourik. *Municipal Economic Adviser, Haarlem, Neth.*

Ottheinz Münch. *City Archivist, Kaiserslautern, Ger.*

John A. Munroe. *H. Rodney Sharp Professor Emeritus of History, University of Delaware, Newark.*

Aleksey Mikhaylovich Muromtsev. *Head, Space Research Laboratory, Marine Fisheries and Oceanography Institute, Moscow.*

Keith A. Murray. *Emeritus Professor of History, Western Washington University, Bellingham.*

Maurice Murzeau. *Director, Information Bureau, Angers, Fr.*

Alice F.A. Mutton (d. 1979). *Reader in Geography, Queen Mary College, University of London.*

Geoffrey Myers. *Former United Nations Correspondent,* The London Daily Telegraph.

Merle Wentworth Myers. *Emeritus Professor of Geology and Geography, Mississippi State University, Starkville.*

Sarah K. Myers. *Editor,* The Geographical Review, *1973–78.*

Dnyandeo Giraji Narkhede. *Lecturer in Geography, Nagpur Mahavidyalaya, Nagpur University, India.*

Maria Teresa Anzidei Natali. *Teacher of Literature, Scuola Media Statale Petrocchi, Rome.*

Philippus Rudolph Nell. *Town Clerk, Boksburg, S.Af.*

Werner Neugebauer. *Former Director, Office for Prehistory and Early History, Office of the Mayor of Lübeck, W.Ger.*

Edward J. Nichols. *Emeritus Professor of English Composition, Pennsylvania State University, University Park.*

Joan Nicklin. *Free-lance writer on geography.*

Henri Nicolaï. *Professor and Head, Department of Human Geography, Free University of Brussels.*

Willem Petrus van Niekerk. *Town Clerk and Treasurer, Jagersfontein, S.Af.*

Ursula Niemann. *Curator of Bielefeld Town Archives, Ger.*

Yevgeny Gurevich Nikiforov. *Senior Scientist, Arctic and Antarctic Scientific Research Institute, Leningrad.*

Nancy Paine Norton. *Professor of History, Wheaton College, Norton, Mass.*

Boniface Ihewunwa Obichere. *Professor of History, University of California, Los Angeles.*

John Gerard O'Connor. *Former Instructor of Art, University of New Mexico. Director, Gallup Museum of Indian Arts and Crafts, N.M., 1956–60.*

Andrew Charles O'Dell (d. 1966). *Professor of Geography, University of Aberdeen, 1951–66.*

Herman Martinus Oldenhof. *Burgomaster of Ede, Neth., 1952–62.*

Kjeld Olsen. *Municipal Official of Randers, Den.*

Frederick Irving Olson. *Professor of History, University of Wisconsin, Milwaukee.*

Simeon Hongo Ominde. *Professor of Geography; Director, Population Studies and Research Institute, University of Nairobi, Kenya.*

Gordon Oosterman. *Principal, Middletown Christian School, Pa. Former Professor of Geography, Calvin College, Grand Rapids, Mich.*

Leonard Edwin Ortzen. *Normandy Correspondent, French Radio's English-Language Service, 1949–64. Author of* The Gallic Land *and others.*

George Augustus Osborn (d. 1972). *Editor,* Sault Ste. Marie (*Mich.*) Evening News.

David Oteiza. *Professor of Geography of the Western Hemisphere, National University of La Plata, Arg.*

Fred Mallery Packard (d. 1981). *International Specialist, National Park Service, U.S. Department of the Interior, 1963–78. Secretary, International Commission on National Parks, International Union for Conservation of Nature and Natural Resources, 1958–69; 1975–78.*

Reinhard E. Paesler. *Lecturer, Institute for Economic Geography, Ludwig Maximilian University of Munich.*

Elwin Lawrence Page (deceased). *Lawyer. Author of* Judicial Beginnings in New Hampshire, 1640–1700 *and others.*

S. Pandey. *Head, Cartography Division, National Bureau of Soil Survey and Land Use Planning, Indian Agricultural Research Institute, New Delhi.*

Clifton W. Pannell. *Professor of Geography, University of Georgia, Athens.*

William Henry Parker. *Lecturer in Geography of the U.S.S.R., University of Oxford, 1964–79. Author of* Canada: A Travel Guide *and others.*

Edward Caffrey Parr. *Former Town Clerk and Chief Executive Officer, Teesside County Borough Council, Eng.*

James Jerome Parsons. *Emeritus Professor of Geography, University of California, Berkeley.*

John Harris Paterson. *Former Professor of Geography, University of Leicester, Eng.*

Ntsomo Payanzo. *Former Assistant Professor of Sociology, National University of Zaire, Lubumbashi.*

Dick N. Pazen. *Research Analyst, Wisconsin Legislative Reference Bureau, Madison.*

Anne Merriman Peck. *Writer, illustrator, and painter. Former Instructor of Creative Writing, Extension Department, University of Arizona, Tucson.*

Mary Tunstall Pedoe (d. 1965). *Lecturer, University of Sudan, Khartoum.*

George Pendle (d. 1977). *Managing Director, Pendle & Rivett Ltd., London. Author of* Pelican History of Latin America *and others.*

Pietro Perin. *Assistant Secretary, Commune of Pordenone (Udine), Italy.*

Maurice Perret (deceased). *Chief Editor,* Académie International du Tourisme: Revue. *Director, Syndicat d'Initiative de Grenoble, Fr., 1945–56.*

Eugene Thor Petersen. *Superintendent, Mackinac Island State Park Commission, Mich.*

Harry St. John Bridger Philby (d. 1960). *Explorer in Arabia. Author of* The Heart of Arabia *and others.*

Walter Fernando Piazza. *Professor of History, Federal University of Santa Catarina, Florianópolis, Braz.*

David Joshua Pittman. *Professor and Chairman, Department of Sociology, Washington University, St. Louis.*

Forrest Pitts. *Professor of Geography, University of Hawaii at Manoa.*

Cyril Ernest Charles Reginald Platten. *Former Town Clerk, London Borough of Enfield, Eng.*

Henri Polge. *Town Archivist, Gers, Fr.*

Philip Wayland Porter. *Professor of Geography, University of Minnesota, Minneapolis.*

Bernard A. Pothier. *Research Editor,* Dictionary of Canadian Biography, *1967–69.*

Merritt Bloodworth Pound (d. 1970). *Professor of Political Science, University of Georgia, Athens, 1941–64.*

William Stevens Powell. *Boshamer Professor Emeritus of History, University of North Carolina at Chapel Hill.*

Charles Aloysius Paul Prangers. *Information Officer, City of The Hague, Neth.*

Pierre du Prey. *Novelist and journalist. Technical Adviser to the Minister of State, Abidjan, Ivory Coast.*

Dalias Adolph Price. *Emeritus Professor of Geography, Eastern Illinois University, Charleston.*

Colette Prieur. *Keeper, Jean de la Fontaine Museum; Keeper, Library and Archives, Château Thierry, Fr.*

Joseph Prinz. *Former Director of City Archives, Münster, W.Ger.*

Ralph Mansell Prothero. *Professor of Geography, University of Liverpool.*

Merle C. Prunty, Jr. (d. 1982). *Alumni Foundation Distinguished Professor of Geography, University of Georgia, Athens, 1969–82.*

Friedrich (Johann Diedrich) Prüser. *Director, Bremen State Archives, Bremen, W.Ger., 1937–57.*

Zain ol-Abedin Rahnema. *Secretary General of the P.E.N. Club of Iran, Teherān. Former Member of the Parliament of Iran.*

Giuseppe Raimondi. *Official in the Press Office, City House, Rapallo, Italy.*

William Francis Raney (d. 1962). *Professor of European History, Lawrence College, Appleton, Wis.*

R.V.R. Chandrasekhara Rao. *Professor and Head, Department of Political Science; Dean, School of Social Sciences, University of Hyderabad, India.*

Wilhelm Felix Rausch. *City Archivist, Linz, Austria.*

Charles Wyatt Raymond. *Director, Maritime Resource Management Service, Amherst, Nova Scotia.*

Leo Franklyn Redfern. *President, Keene State College, N.H., 1969–79.*

John Rice. *Professor of Geography, University of Minnesota, Minneapolis.*

Robert William Richmond. *Assistant Executive Director and Treasurer, Kansas State Historical Society, Topeka.*

Dorothy Lois Riker. *Editor, Indiana Historical Bureau, Indianapolis, 1946–71.*

Brian Birley Roberts (d. 1978). *Research Associate, Scott Polar Research Institute, University of Cambridge, 1960–78.*

Blackwell Pierce Robinson (d. 1991). *Associate Professor of History, University of North Carolina at Greensboro.*

J. Lewis Robinson. *Emeritus Professor of Geography, University of British Columbia, Vancouver.*

Öivind Rödevand. *Lecturer in Geography Teaching, University of Oslo.*

Rolland C. Rogers. *Emeritus Professor of History, San Jose State University, Calif.*

Irmentraud Rohrmayr. *Town Archivist, Straubing, Ger.*

Guido Rotthoff. *Director of Municipal Archives, Krefeld, Ger.*

Joseph S. Roucek. *Professor of Social Science, Queensborough Community College, City University of New York, Bayside, 1967–72.*

Jean-Maurice Rouquette. *Curator of the Museum, Arles, Fr.*

B.B. Roy. *Former Professor of Agricultural Chemistry, University of Calcutta.*

Erich Ruckgaber. *Editor,* Fellbacher Zeitung, *Ger.*

William Willis Ruff. *Former Clerk of the Surrey County Council, Eng.*

Karl Ruppert. *Professor and Head, Institute for Economic Geography, Ludwig Maximilian University of Munich.*

A. Bower Sageser. *Professor of American History, Kansas State University, Manhattan, 1941–73.*

Henry de Surirey de Saint-Remy. *Chief Librarian, Historical Library of the City of Paris, 1953–74.*

Leslie Arthur Sallnow. *Former Public Relations and Information Officer, Waltham Forest, Eng.*

Carl Fredrik Sandelin. *Novelist. Former General Manager and Editor in Chief, Finnish News Agency, Helsinki.*

Irwin Taylor Sanders. *Emeritus Professor of Sociology, Boston University.*

Jonathan Sanger. *Former Associate Editor,* Américas *magazine.*

Paul Jean Sanlaville. *Research Associate, National Centre for Scientific Research, Lyon.*

Ann Margaret Savours. *Assistant Keeper, National Maritime Museum, London.*

Michael Schattenhofer. *Former Director, Munich State Archives.*

James Ralston Scobie (d. 1981). *Professor of History, University of California, San Diego, 1977–81.*

Thomas Morris Hornby Scott. *Former Town Clerk, London Borough of Sutton, Eng.*

Se-Il Sonn. *Senior editorial writer,* Dong-A Ilbo *newspaper, Seoul.*

Tsepon W.D. Shakabpa (d. 1989). *Historian. Minister of Finance, Tibet, 1939–51. Chief Representative of the Dalai Lama to the Government of India, 1959–66.*

Abd el Aziz Torayah Sharaf. *Professor of Geography, Islamic University of Imam Muhammad Ibn Saud, Riyadh, Saudi Arabia.*

Abdu Aly Shata. *Director, Desert Research Institute, Cairo.*

Donald Henry Sheehan (d. 1974). *President and Professor of History, Whitman College, Walla Walla, Wash., 1968–74.*

Arseny Vladimirovich Shnitnikov (d. 1983). *Senior Scientist, Lake Studies Institute, Academy of Sciences of the U.S.S.R., Leningrad.*

Hugh de Sausmarez Shortt. *Former Curator, Salisbury and South Wiltshire Museum, Eng.*

Alfred Osipovich Shpaykher (d. 1978). *Senior Scientist, Arctic and Antarctic Scientific Research Institute, Leningrad.*

Phillip Raymond Shriver. *Emeritus President; Professor of History, Miami University, Oxford, Ohio.*

Francis Butler Simkins (d. 1966). *Professor of History, Longwood College, Farmville, Va.*

David Stanley Simonett. *Director, Land Evaluation and Land Use Studies, Earth Satellite Corporation, Washington, D.C.*

Edward Smethurst Simpson. *Professor of Geography, University of Newcastle upon Tyne, Eng.*

Frederick Bernard Singleton (d. 1988). *Reader and Chairman, Postgraduate School of Yugoslav Studies, University of Bradford, Eng.*

Karl A. Sinnhuber. *Emeritus Professor of Economic Geography, Vienna University of Commerce.*

Raleigh Ashlin Skelton (d. 1970). *Superintendent, Map Room, British Museum, 1950–67.*

Vladimir Ilich Slavin. *Professor, Moscow M.V. Lomonosov State University.*

Axel Mose Sløk. *Managing Director and Editor, Confederation of Danish Agricultural Employers' Associations, Copenhagen.*

Arthur Eltringham Smailes (d. 1984). *Professor of Geography, Queen Mary College, University of London, 1955–73.*

Gerald Wayne Smith. *Academic Dean; Professor of History, Waynesburg College, Pa.*

Helen L. Smith. *Associate Professor of Geography, Middle Tennessee State University, Murfreesboro, 1970–74.*

Walter Charles Dudley Smith. *Town Engineer, Boksburg, S.Af.*

Felix Eugene Snider. *Former Librarian and former Director, Department of Library Science, Southeast Missouri State College, Cape Girardeau.*

Aleksey Aleksandrovich Sokolov. *Director, Leningrad Hydrological Institute, 1968–81.*

Jacob Spelt. *Professor of Geography, University of Toronto.*

Joseph E. Spencer (d. 1984). *Professor of Geography, University of California, Los Angeles.*

Karl R. Stadler (d. 1987). *Former Professor and Head, Institute of Modern and Contemporary History, Johannes Kepler University of Linz, Austria.*

Sir Laurence Dudley Stamp (d. 1966). *Professor of Social Geography, University of London, 1948–58.*

Dan Stanislawski. *Research Associate in Geography, University of California, Berkeley.*

William Richard Stanley. *Professor of Geography, University of South Carolina, Columbia.*

Martin Purefoy Statham. *Former County Archivist, West Suffolk, Eng.*

Robert Walter Steel. *Principal, University College of Swansea, 1974–82; Vice-Chancellor, University of Wales, 1979–81.*

Harriet Grace Steers. *Lecturer in Geography, University of Cambridge, 1936–66.*

Hugo Steneberg. *Municipal Official, Witten, Ger.*

Cj Stevens. *Professor and Chairman, Department of Speech and Theatre, Herbert H. Lehman College, City University of New York.*

David Stick. *Author of* Outer Banks of North Carolina; The Cape Hatteras Seashore; *and others.*

Joseph Stocker. *Author of* Arizona: A Guide to Easier Living.

Henry Gordon Stokes. *Author of* English Place-Names *and others.*

James Herbert Stone. *Emeritus Professor of Humanities, San Francisco State University.*

Goffe Struiksma. *Municipal Official, Heerenveen, Neth.*

Alfred Donald Sumberg. *Associate General Secretary, American Association of University Professors. Professor of Social Studies, East Stroudsburg State College, Pa., 1956–67.*

Charles Grayson Summersell. *Emeritus Professor of History, University of Alabama, University.*

Tatyana Yosifovna Supranovich. *Senior Scientist and Head, Division of Sea Dynamics, Far Eastern Hydrometeorological Research Institute, Vladivostok, U.S.S.R.*

Robert M. Sutton. *Professor of History; Director of the Illinois Historical Survey, University of Illinois, Urbana.*

Arthur Ronald Taffs. *Former Public Relations Officer, London Borough of Lewisham, Eng.*

Tamotsu Takahashi. *Senior Researcher, Institute of Developing Economies, Tokyo.*

Charles Antoine Peter Takes. *Former Director, International Institute for Land Reclamation and Improvement, Wageningen, Neth.*

Mohamed Talbi. *Emeritus Professor, Faculty of Letters and Human Sciences, University of Tunis.*

Ken-Chi Tanabe. *Professor of Geography, University of Tokyo.*

Charlton W. Tebeau. *Emeritus Professor of History, University of Miami, Coral Gables, Fla.*

Tenzing Norgay (d. 1986). *Field Director of Training, Himalayan Mountaineering Institute, Darjeeling, India. The first man (with Edmund Hillary) to reach the summit of Mount Everest.*

Johannes Theodoor Thijsse. *Professor of Hydraulics, Technological University of Delft, Neth., 1938–63.*

John Thompson. *Professor of Geography, University of Illinois at Urbana-Champaign.*

Robert Ribblesdale Thornton. *Former Town Clerk, Leicester, Eng.*

Harry Thorpe (d. 1977). *Professor and Head, Department of Geography, University of Birmingham, Eng.*

Robert H. Thorsbro. *Chief of Production, Danish Tourist Board, Copenhagen.*

Arthur E. Tiedemann. *Professor of History, City College, City University of New York.*

James L. Tigner. *Professor of History, University of Nevada, Reno.*

Robert Tinthoin. *Chief Archivist, Deux-Sèvres, Fr., 1959–63. Chief Archivist, Department of Oran, 1938–56, and Director of Museum of Oran, Alg., 1941–56.*

Hong Djin Tjia. *Professor of Geology, National University of Malaysia, Bangi.*

Augusto Torre (d. 1977). *Professor and Chairman, Department of Modern and Contemporary History, University of Bologna, Italy, 1956–60.*

Pietro Torrione. *Director of Biella Library and Museum, Italy.*

J. Allen Tower (d. 1961). *Professor of Geography, Birmingham-Southern College, Birmingham, Ala.*

Mary Curry Tresidder. *Honorary Chairman of the Board, Yosemite Park & Curry Company, Yosemite National Park, Calif.*

Jean-Léon-François Tricart. *Professor and Director, Centre of Applied Geography, University of Strasbourg I, Fr.*

Hsu-pai Tseng. *Chairman of the Board, Central News Agency, Taipei. Professor of Journalism, National Chengchi University, Taipei. Dean, Sun Yat-sen Memorial Research Institute, College of Chinese Culture, Taipei.*

The Rt. Rev. Cyril James Tucker. *Former Anglican Bishop of the Falkland Islands and in Argentina.*

Erol Tümertekin. *Former Professor of Geography, University of Istanbul.*

Necdet Tunçdilek. *Associate Professor of Geography, University of Istanbul.*

David Turnock. *Reader in Geography, University of Leicester, Eng.*

Denis C. Twitchett. *Gordon Wu Professor of Chinese Studies, Princeton University.*

Roger Henry Van Bolt. *Director, Sloan Museum, Flint, Mich., 1965–81.*

Burke G. Vanderhill. *University Service Professor of Geography, Florida State University, Tallahassee.*

Albert Edward Van Dusen. *Professor of History, University of Connecticut, Storrs. State Historian.*

Milton I. Vanger. *Emeritus Professor of History, Brandeis University, Waltham, Mass.; Chairman of Latin American Studies, 1971–81.*

R. Suzanne Van Meter. *Professor of History, Clarion State College, Pa.*

Milorad Vasović. *Professor of Regional Geography, University of Belgrade.*

Gustave Vaucher. *State Archivist, Geneva, Switz., 1940–66.*

Christiaan van Veen. *President, Federation of Netherlands Industry. Minister of Education and Science, Government of the Netherlands, 1971–73.*

Anna Johanna Versprille. *Keeper of the Public Records, Leiden, Neth.*

Hermann Wahl. *Town Archivist, Pforzheim, Ger.*

Frank Walker. *Former Senior Lecturer in Geography, University of Bristol, Eng.*

Peter Franklin Walker. *Professor of History, University of North Carolina at Chapel Hill.*

Bernard J. Wall (d. 1974). *Free-lance writer. Author of* Report on the Vatican; A City and a World; *and many others.*

Joseph Frazier Wall. *Rosenfield Professor of History, Grinnell College, Iowa.*

Ernest Wallace. *Horn Professor Emeritus of History, Texas Tech University, Lubbock.*

Helen Margaret Wallis. *Former Map Librarian, British Library, London.*

Mildred Marie Walmsley. *Associate Professor of Geography, Case Western Reserve University, Cleveland.*

Peter Walne. *County Archivist, Hertfordshire County Council, England.*

Clyde C. Walton. *Director of Libraries, University of Colorado, Boulder.*

Judson Clements Ward, Jr. *Executive Vice President, Emory University, Atlanta, Ga., 1970–79; Dean of the Faculties, 1957–79.*

William Stanley Alphonsus Warren. *Town Clerk, Blantyre, Malawi.*

Burton DeWitt Watson. *Free-lance translator. Professor of Chinese, Columbia University, 1967–73.*

Richard John Waygood. *Former Municipal Committee Clerk, Romsey, Eng.*

Glenn Weaver. *Professor of History, Trinity College, Hartford, Conn.*

Herbert Weaver (d. 1985). *Professor of History, Vanderbilt University, Nashville, Tenn., 1952–74.*

Kempton E. Webb. *Professor of Geography, Columbia University.*

Wilfrid Webster. *Executive Editor,* Atlas of the Marine Environment, *American Geographical Society, New York City.*

Russell Frank Weigley. *Professor of History, Temple University, Philadelphia.*

Ernst Weigt. *Emeritus Professor of Economic Geography, Friedrich Alexander University of Erlangen-Nuremberg, Ger.*

John H. Wellington. *Emeritus Professor of Geography, University of the Witwatersrand, Johannesburg.*

Merle William Wells. *Historian and Archivist, Idaho State Historical Society, Boise.*

Geoffrey Edleston Wheeler (d. 1990). *Lieutenant Colonel, Indian Army. Director, Central Asian Research Centre, London, 1953–68.*

Paul Frank Wheeler. *Professor of Sociology, State University of New York at Albany.*

Nathan Laselle Whetten (d. 1984). *Professor of Sociology, University of Connecticut, Storrs, 1938–71; Dean of the Graduate School, 1940–71.*

Edward Stanley White. *Former Town Clerk, Bulawayo, Rhodesia.*

(Charles) Langdon White. *Emeritus Professor of Geography, Stanford University, Calif.*

Maurice Leslie White. *Former Public Relations Officer, London Borough of Hillingdon, Eng.*

Daniel Jay Whitener. *Former Dean, Appalachian State Teachers College, Boone, N.C.; Head, Social Studies Department, 1932–57.*

Vincent Heath Whitney. *Emeritus Professor of Sociology, University of Pennsylvania, Philadelphia; Director, Population Studies Center, 1962–76.*

John Byron Whittow. *Senior Lecturer in Geography, University of Reading, Eng.*

Willard Chester Wichers. *Director, Midwestern Division, Netherlands Information Service; Director, Netherlands Museum, Holland, Mich.*

Johan de Widt. *Burgomaster, Amersfoort, Neth.*

Fritz Wiegand. *Former Director of the Municipal Archives, Erfurt, E.Ger.*

David Willey. *Rome correspondent, British Broadcasting Corporation.*

Eliot Churchill Williams, Jr. *Emeritus Professor of Zoology, Wabash College, Crawfordsville, Ind.*

Frank B. Williams, Jr. *Emeritus Professor of History, East Tennessee State University, Johnson City.*

Richmond Dean Williams. *Director, Eleutherian Mills Historical Library, Greenville, Del.*

George Ernest Willis. *Justice of the Peace, Newbury, Eng. Former Alderman, Newbury Borough Council.*

Harold Fisher Wilson. *Former Professor of History, Glassboro State College, N.J.*

Arthur N.L. Wina. *Member of Parliament, 1962–68 and 1973– ; Minister of Finance, 1963–67; Minister of Education, 1967–68, Government of Northern Rhodesia, renamed Zambia in 1964.*

Conrad L. Wirth. *Former Director, National Park Service, U.S. Department of the Interior, Washington, D.C.*

Malverne Ray Wolfe. *Emeritus Professor of History, California State College, Pa.; Director of Guidance Services, 1957–69.*

Robert Coldwell Wood. *Professor of Political Science, University of Massachusetts, Boston; President, University of Massachusetts, Amherst, 1970–77.*

A. Geoffrey Woodhead. *Fellow of Corpus Christi College, Cambridge; Emeritus Lecturer in Classics, University of Cambridge. Adjunct Professor of Classics, Ohio State University, Columbus.*

Christopher Montague Woodhouse. *Member of Parliament for Oxford, 1959–66, 1970–74.*

L.W. Wright. *Lecturer in Geography, Queen Mary College, University of London.*

Paul Zabel. *Former Public Relations Officer, Gelsenkirchen, W.Ger.*

Clifford Maynard Zierer (deceased). *Professor of Geography, University of California, Los Angeles, 1945–65.*

Joseph Francis Zimmerman. *Professor of Political Science, State University of New York at Albany.*

Friedrich Zollhoefer. *Town Archivist, Kempten, Ger.*

Staff of the Encyclopædia Britannica

Editorial Staff

EDITORS

Donald Duncanson, *Deputy Editor*

Yutorio C. Hori, *Deputy Editor*

Sujata Banerjee

Jane Toomey Baque

Lisa S. Braucher

Robert Curley

Lisa Jacobson

Kathleen Kuiper

George Kenneth Leivers

Erdmut Lerner

Marvin Martin

Paul Mendelson

Michael Nutter

Kenneth R. Pletcher

Amy R. Tao

Deanne Wachel

BIBLIOGRAPHERS

Leah Hotimlanska

Anne-Marie Schroeder

CORRESPONDENCE AND RESEARCH

Helen L. Carlock, *Supervisor*

Lars Mahinske, *Senior Researcher*

Thomas Riggs, *Senior Researcher*

Karen Feldman

ART DEPARTMENT

Cynthia Peterson, *Director*

Marsha Mackenzie, *Operations Manager*

Barbara Epstein, *Senior Picture Editor*

Kay Diffley

John L. Draves

Katharine Hannaford

Patricia A. Henle

Alison Platt Kendall

Margaret Liebezeit

John J. Mahoney

Stephanie Motz

Diana M. Pitstick

Richard A. Roiniotis

CARTOGRAPHY

Barbra A. Vogel, *Manager*

Laurie P. Anderson

Steven Bogdan

Amelia R. Gintautas

Julsun D. Pacheco

Kathryn A. Piffl

LIBRARY

Terry Miller, *Head Librarian*

Shantha Uddin, *Associate Librarian*

David W. Foster, *Curator, Geography*

Robert Lewis, *Assistant Librarian*

Production Staff

Karen M. Barch, *Vice President, Editorial Development*

COPY DEPARTMENT

Anita Wolff, *Manager*

Marilyn Klein, *Copy Supervisor*

Joan Lackowski, *Copy Supervisor*

Patricia Bauer, *Copy Coordinator*

Ann Belaski

Lynette Bertsche

Elizabeth A. Blowers

Linda A. Cifelli

Jennifer Cohen

Madolynn Cronk

Brian Duignan

Laura Gabler

John Gherardini

Anthony Green

Kathy Howard

Glenn Jenne

Lawrence D. Kowalski

Elizabeth Laskey

John Mathews

Deirdre McAllister

Christine Molinari

Kerri O'Hern

Giuseppe Parente

Letricia Riley

Isabella Saccà

Joan E. Sebastian

Dennis Skord

Christine Sullivan

Robert Wells

Judith West

PRODUCTION CONTROL

Mary C. Srodon, *Manager*

Marilyn L. Barton

Stephanie A. Green

Lee Anne Wiggins

COMPOSITION/PAGE MAKEUP

Melvin Stagner, *Manager*

Michael Born, Jr., *Supervisor*

Eram A. Ahmad

Griselda Cháidez

Duangnetra Debhavalya

Christine Ferry

Carol A. Gaines

Vertreasa Hunt

John Krom, Jr.

Thomas J. Mulligan

Maria Ottolino

Arnell Reed

Gwen E. Rosenberg

Yu-chu Wang

Danette Wetterer

INDEX DEPARTMENT

Carmen-Maria Hetrea, *Manager*

Edward Paul Moragne, *Index Supervisor*

Mary L. Reynolds, *Index Supervisor*

Lisa M. Strubin, *Index Supervisor*

Martin L. White, *Index Supervisor*

Mansur G. Abdullah

Philip D. Colvin

Paul K. Cranmer

Craig W. Davis

Simone De Sanctis

Pierina Grano

Manal Salah Issa

Bernard Jablonski

John René Lastré

Elena Mafter

Steven Monti

Stephen S. Seddon

Beverly Sorkin

Joseph Sullivan

Sheila Vasich

Gayl E. Williams

Laura D. Zielinski

Thomas W. Zielonka

Budgets and Control Staff

Elizabeth P. O'Connor, *Director*

Shirley J. Wong

Administrative and Editorial Support Staff

Ana Maria Blanco

Lilia W. Kulas

Velia Palomar

Sophia Preston

Eva M. Rhodes

Ida G. Ritter